Writings and Disputations
Relative to the Lord's Supper

The Parker Society.
Instituted A.D. M.DCCC.XL.

For the Publication of the Works of the Fathers and Early Writers of the Reformed English Church.

WRITINGS AND DISPUTATIONS

OF

THOMAS CRANMER,

ARCHBISHOP OF CANTERBURY,
MARTYR, 1556,

RELATIVE TO THE SACRAMENT OF THE

LORD'S SUPPER.

EDITED FOR
The Parker Society,
BY THE
REV. JOHN EDMUND COX, M.A.,
OF ALL SOULS' COLLEGE, OXFORD, CURATE AND LECTURER OF STEPNEY.

REGENT COLLEGE PUBLISHING
Vancouver, British Columbia

Writings and Disputations Relative to the Lord's Supper

First published 1844 by the Parker Society, Cambridge University Press
This edition reproduced 2001 from the 1844 edition by Regent College Publishing
5800 University Boulevard, Vancouver, B.C. Canada V6T 2E4
www.regentpublishing.com

Views expressed in works published by Regent College Publishing are those of the author and do not necessarily represent the official position of Regent College.

National Library of Canada Cataloguing in Publication Data

Cranmer, Thomas, 1489-1556.
  Writings and Disputations Relative to the Lord's Supper

  Previous ed. has title: Writings and disputations of Thomas Cranmer, Archbishop of Canterbury, martyr, 1556, relative to the sacrament of the Lord's Supper.
  Includes index.
  ISBN 1-55361-026-1 (Canada)
  ISBN 1-57383-214-6 (United States)

  1. Lord's Supper—Church of England. I. Cox, John Edmund, 1812-1890. II. Title. III. Title: Writings and disputations of Thomas Cranmer.
BX5149.C5C7 2001   264'.03036   C2001-910465-0

CONTENTS.

	PAGE
LIFE, State, and Story of Thomas Cranmer	vii
An Answer to a Crafty and Sophistical Cavillation devised by Stephen Gardiner	1
Preface to the Reader	3
BOOK I. Of the Sacrament	9
BOOK III. Of the Presence of Christ	51
BOOK IV. Of the Eating and Drinking	201
BOOK II. Against Transubstantiation	239
BOOK V. Of the Oblation and Sacrifice of Christ	344
Answer to Smith's Preface	368
Matters wherein the Bishop of Winchester varied from other Papists, &c.	380
Disputations at Oxford	389
Index	431
Defensio Veræ et Catholicæ Doctrinæ de Sacramento	1*

The present volume contains the writings of archbishop Cranmer on the Sacrament of the Lord's Supper, together with the disputations held with him at Oxford previously to his condemnation and martyrdom. The writings on the sacrament have been reprinted from the edition of A.D. 1580, and exhibit the latest and most matured corrections of the archbishop, which he is supposed to have made whilst under imprisonment previously to his death. With this later edition, that of 1551,—the original edition of his first work on the sacrament, afterwards embodied by him in his answer to Winchester,— as well as bishop Gardiner's reply to it, have been carefully collated, and care has been taken to note the various readings. The Latin edition of the first work, printed at Emden, A.D. 1557, not previously reprinted, has been added; and this has likewise undergone a careful examination, with the previous edition of the Latin translation, said by Strype to have been made by Sir John Cheke. Wherever the additional references to the works of the Fathers are found in the Emden edition, 1557, they have been noted in the margin of the body of this reprint.

The Disputations held at Oxford are reprinted from the 1583 edition of Foxe's Acts and Monuments, and have been collated with an earlier edition. Thus it is hoped, that the pieces now given will be found to exhibit the last and most accurate thoughts of the archbishop, so far as they exist, arranged in a more complete form than has yet been attempted.

With reference to the succeeding volume, which will contain the rest of the writings of archbishop Cranmer, the Editor has been engaged both at home and on the continent in further researches, especially relating to a correspondence on the sacraments, supposed to exist in some foreign public libraries. But after the most careful personal examination, he is enabled to state, that nothing has been found beyond the letters previously printed by Dr Jenkyns in his valuable edition of the works of the archbishop, except one brief letter written by the archbishop a short time before his martyrdom, and which was discovered at Zurich during the researches made there for the Parker Society. The biographical sketch of the archbishop, and a full account of his remains, will be given with the succeeding volume: but the memoir abridged from Foxe's Acts and Monuments, printed in the edition of A.D. 1580, is here given, to put the reader in possession of a complete copy of that work, printed in the reign of queen Elizabeth, with the exception of a few epistles which will be found in the complete series of letters.

In conclusion, the Editor desires to acknowledge the valuable assistance he has derived from the previous edition of Dr Jenkyns, which has relieved him from many difficulties: nevertheless he has taken nothing from it, but has invariably examined early editions and references for himself, and has stated the result of his own researches.—He has also to acknowledge the kind loan of a copy of the first edition of the archbishop's work on the sacrament from the library of Gloucester Cathedral.

May 10, 1844.

THE LIFE, STATE, AND STORY,

OF THE

REVEREND PASTOR AND PRELATE,

THOMAS CRANMER,

ARCHBISHOP OF CANTERBURY, MARTYR,

BURNED AT OXFORD FOR THE CONFESSION OF CHRIST'S TRUE DOCTRINE.
ANNO 1556. MARCH 21.

FORASMUCH as the life and estate of the most reverend father in God and worthy prelate of godly memory, Thomas Cranmer, late archbishop of Canterbury, together with the original cause and occasion of his preferment to the dignity archiepiscopal, whereunto he was advanced immediately upon the death of bishop Warham, archbishop of the same, beyond all expectation, without support of money or friends, by the only well-liking of the most renowned king of famous memory, Henry the eighth, who with a fatherly care maintained his countenance, and defended his innocent life, undermined sundry times by the manifold attempts of the horrible arch-enemy of Christ and his gospel, Stephen Gardiner, and other his complices; with divers other circumstances of his most commendable conversation, charitable consideration of the poor, constant care in reformation of corrupt religion, his undaunted courage in continual defence of the same, and the perseverance therein to the loss of his life, be already described at large in the book of Acts and Monuments of Martyrs; it may seem needless to make a thorough discourse thereof again at this present. Nevertheless, partly to stop the mouths of slanderous sycophants, and partly for the ease of such as would happily be desirous, upon the view of the title of this book, to be acquainted with the life of the author, being otherwise not able to have recourse to the story at large, as also because his virtuous life and glorious death was such, as can never be commended sufficiently, I have thought it not altogether amiss to renew the remembrance thereof by certain brief notes, referring them that be desirous to know the whole to the story thereof at large.

Thomas Cranmer, archbishop of Canterbury.

Doctor Cranmer made archbishop of Canterbury by king Henry.

Doctor Cranmer always defended by king Henry.

Look for the story at large, in the book of the Acts and Monuments, in the last edition, p. 1752.

It is first therefore to be noted and considered, that the same Thomas Cranmer coming of ancient parentage, from the conquest to be deducted, and continuing sithens in the name and family of a gentleman, was born in a village called Arselacton in Nottinghamshire. Of whose said name and family there remaineth at these days one manor and mansion-house in Lincolnshire, called Cranmer Hall, &c. sometimes of heritage of the said stock and family. Who being from his infancy kept at school, and brought up, not without much good civility, came in process of time unto the university of Cambridge, and there prospering in right good knowledge amongst the better sort of students, was chosen fellow of Jesus college in Cambridge. And so being master of art, and fellow of the same college, it chanced him to marry a gentleman's daughter, by means whereof he lost and gave over his fellowship there, and became the reader in Buckingham college; and for that he would with more diligence apply that his office of reading, placed his said wife in an inn, called the

Thomas Cranmer a gentleman born.

Thomas Cranmer first coming to Cambridge.

Thomas Cranmer fellow of Jesus College.

Dolphin, in Cambridge, the wife of the house being of affinity unto her. By means[1] of whose abode in that inn, and his often repair unto her, arose a certain slanderous report, after he was preferred to be archbishop of Canterbury, bruited abroad by the malicious disdain of certain sycophantical papists, that he was but an hosteler, and altogether devoid of learning; which how falsely was forged upon him, may easily appear hereby, that the masters and fellows of Jesus college, noting the virtuous disposition of the man, and the great travail he took, notwithstanding his marriage, whiles he continued reader in Buckingham college, immediately upon the death of his wife (who not long after their enter marriage was in childbed surprised by death) received him into their fellowship again; where he so behaved himself, that in few years after he became the reader of the divinity lecture in the same college, and in such special estimation and reputation with the whole university, that being doctor of divinity, he was commonly appointed one of the heads (which are two or three of the chiefest learned men) to examine such as yearly profess, in commencement, either bachelors or doctors of divinity, by whose approbation the whole university licenseth them to proceed unto their degree; and again, by whose disallowance the university also rejecteth them for a time to proceed, until they be better furnished with more knowledge.

Thomas Cranmer, after the decease of his wife, chosen again fellow into Jesus College.

Thomas Cranmer made reader and doctor of divinity in Jesus College.

Doctor Cranmer public examiner in Cambridge of them that were to proceed.

Now doctor Cranmer, ever much favouring the knowledge of the scripture, would never admit any to proceed in divinity, unless they were substantially seen in the story of the bible: by means whereof certain friars and other religious persons, who were principally brought up in the study of school-authors, without regard had to the authority of scriptures, were commonly rejected by him; so that he was greatly for that his severe examination of the religious sort much hated and had in great indignation: and yet it came to pass in the end, that divers of them, being thus compelled to study the scriptures, became afterwards very well learned and well affected; insomuch that, when they proceeded doctors of divinity, they could not overmuch extol and commend master doctor Cranmer's goodness towards them, who had for a time put them back to aspire unto better knowledge and perfection. Amongst whom doctor Barret, a white friar, who afterwards dwelt at Norwich, was after that sort handled, giving him no less commendation for his happy rejecting of him for a better amendment. Thus much I repeat, that our apish and popish sort of ignorant priests may well understand that this his exercise, kind of life, and vocation was not altogether hostelerlike.

Friars in hatred with doctor Cranmer.

Doctor Barret.

I omit here how Cardinal Wolsey, after the foundation of his college in Oxford, hearing the fame of his learning, used all means possible to place him in the same; which he refused with great danger of indignation, contenting himself with his former fellowship in Cambridge: until, upon occasion of the plague being in Cambridge, he resorted to Waltham Abbey, and sojourned with one M. Cressey there, whose wife was doctor Cranmer's niece, and two of her children his pupils in Cambridge. During this time the great and weighty cause of king Henry the eighth his divorce with the lady Catharine, dowager of Spain, was in question. Wherein two cardinals, Campeius and Wolsey, were appointed in commission from the pope to hear and determine the controversy between the king and the queen; who by many dilatories, dallying, and delaying, the whole summer, until the month of August, taking occasion to finish their commission, so moved the patience of the king, that in all haste he removed from London to Waltham for a night or twain, whiles the dukes of Norfolk and Suffolk dispatched cardinal Campeius home again to Rome. By means whereof it

Doctor Cranmer, solicited to be fellow of the Cardinal's college in Oxford, refused it.

Question of the king's divorce with Catharine dowager.

[1 By reason, Foxe. Ed. 1583.]

chanced that the king's harbingers lodged, doctor Stephens[2], secretary, and doctor Foxe, almoner, (who were the chief furtherers, preferrers, and defenders of the foresaid cause in the king's behalf,) in the house of the said M. Cressey, where doctor Cranmer was also resident as before. When supper-time came, and all three doctors met together, being of old acquaintance, they entertained each other familiarly: and the said doctor Stephens and doctor Foxe, taking occasion of their happy meeting together, began to confer with doctor Cranmer concerning the king's cause, requesting him to declare his opinion therein.

Whereunto doctor Cranmer answered, that he could say little in the matter, for that he had not studied nor looked for it. Notwithstanding he said to them, that, in his opinion, they made more ado in prosecuting the laws ecclesiastical than needed. "It were better, as I suppose," quoth doctor Cranmer, "that the question, whether a man may marry his brother's wife or no, were decided and discussed by the divines and by the authority of the word of God, whereby the conscience of the prince might be better satisfied and quieted, than thus, from year to year, by frustatory delays to prolong the time, leaving the very truth of the matter unboulted out by the word of God. There is but one truth in it, which the scripture will soon declare, make open and manifest, being by learned men well handled; and that may be as well done in England, in the universities here, as at Rome, or elsewhere in any foreign nation, the authority whereof will compel any judge soon to come to a definitive sentence; and therefore, as I take it, you might this way have made an end of this matter long sithens." When doctor Cranmer had thus ended his tale, the other two well liked of his device, and wished that they had so proceeded aforetime; and thereupon conceived some matter of that device to instruct the king withal, who then was minded to send to Rome again for a new commission.

Now the next day, when the king removed to Greenwich, like as he took himself not well handled by the cardinals in thus deferring his cause, so his mind being unquieted and desirous of an end of his long and tedious suit, he called to him this his two principal doers of his said cause, namely, the said doctor Stephens and doctor Foxe, saying unto them: "What now, my masters," quoth the king, "shall we do in this infinite cause of mine? I see by it there must be a new commission procured from Rome; and when we shall have an end, God knoweth, and not I." When the king had said somewhat his mind herein, the almoner, doctor Foxe, said unto the king again: "We trust that there shall be better ways devised for your majesty, than to make travel so far to Rome[3] any more in your highness' cause, which by chance was put into our heads this other night, being at Waltham:" and so discovered to the king their meeting and conference with doctor Cranmer at M. Cressey's house.

Whereupon doctor Cranmer was sent for in post, being as then removed from Waltham towards his friends in Lincolnshire[4], and so brought to the court to the king. Whom the noble prince benignly accepting, demanded his name, and said unto him: "Were you not at Waltham such a time, in the company of my secretary and my almoner?" Doctor Cranmer affirming the same, the king said again: "Had you not conference with them concerning our matter of divorce now in question after this sort?"—repeating the manner and order thereof. "That is right true, if it please your highness," quoth doctor Cranmer. "Well," said the king, "I well perceive that you have the right scope of this matter. You must understand," quoth the king,

---

[2 i.e. Doctor Stephen Gardiner, sometime bishop of Winchester.]

[3 So far as to Rome, Foxe. Ed. 1583.]
[4 Foxe says "in Nottinghamshire."]

"that I have been long troubled in conscience; and now I perceive that by this means I might have been long ago relieved one way or other from the same, if we had this way proceeded. And therefore, master doctor, I pray you, and nevertheless, because you are a subject, I charge and command you, (all your other business and affairs set apart,) to take some pains to see this my cause to be furthered according to your device, as much as it may lie in you," with many other words in commendation of the queen's majesty.

Doctor Cranmer, much disabling himself to meddle in so weighty a matter, besought the king's highness to commit the trial and examining of this matter, by the word of God, unto the best learned men of both his universities, Cambridge and Oxford. "You say well," said the king, "and I am content therewith. But yet, nevertheless, I will have you specially to write your mind therein." And so, calling the earl of Wiltshire to him, said: "I pray you, my lord, let doctor Cranmer have entertainment in your house at Durham place for a time, to the intent he may be there quiet to accomplish my request, and let him lack neither books nor anything requisite for his study." And thus, after the king's departure, doctor Cranmer went with my lord of Wiltshire unto his house, where he, incontinent, wrote his mind concerning the king's question, adding to the same besides the authorities of scriptures[1], of general councils, and of ancient writers; also his opinion, which was this: that the bishop of Rome had no such authority, as whereby he might dispense with the word of God and the scriptures[2]. When doctor Cranmer had made this book, and committed it to the king, the king said to him: "Will you abide by this, that you have here written, before the bishop of Rome?" "That will I do, by God's grace," quoth doctor Cranmer, "if your majesty do send me thither." "Marry," quoth the king, "I will send you even to him in a sure embassage."

And thus, by means of doctor Cranmer's handling of this matter with the king, not only certain learned men were sent abroad to the most part of the universities in Christendom to dispute the question, but also the same being, by commission, disputed by the divines in both the universities of Cambridge and Oxford, it was there concluded that no such matrimony was by the word of God lawful. Whereupon a solemn embassage was prepared and sent to the bishop of Rome, then being at Bonony, wherein went the earl of Wiltshire, doctor Cranmer, doctor Stokesly, doctor Carne, doctor Benet, and divers other learned men and gentlemen. And when the time came that they should come before the bishop of Rome to declare the cause of their embassage, the bishop, sitting on high in his cloth of estate, and in his rich apparel, with his sandals on his feet, offering, as it were, his foot to be kissed of the ambassadors; the earl of Wiltshire with the rest of the ambassadors, disdaining thereat, stood still, and made no countenance thereunto, and kept themselves from that idolatry. In fine, the pontifical bishop seeing their constancy, without any farther ceremony, gave ear to the ambassadors.

Who entering there before the bishop, offered, on the king's behalf, to be defended, that no man, *jure divino*, could or ought to marry his brother's wife, and that the bishop of Rome by no means ought to dispense to the contrary. Divers promises were made, and sundry days appointed, wherein the question should have been disputed: and when our part was ready to answer, no man there appeared to dispute in that behalf. So in the end, the bishop making to our ambassadors good countenance, and gratifying doctor Cranmer with the office of the penitentiaryship, dismissed them undisputed withal.

[[1] Of the scriptures, Foxe. Ed. 1563.]   [[2] The scripture, ibid.]

Whereupon the earl of Wiltshire and other commissioners, saving doctor Cranmer, returned home again into England. And forthwith doctor Cranmer went to the emperor, being in his journey towards Vienna, in expedition against the Turk, there to answer such learned men of the emperor's council, as would or could say anything to the contrary part. Where amongst the rest, at the same time, was Cornelius Agrippa, an high officer in the emperor's court; who, having private conference with doctor Cranmer in the question, was so fully resolved and satisfied in the matter, that afterwards there was never disputation openly offered to doctor Cranmer in that behalf. For through the persuasion of Agrippa all other learned men there were much discouraged. *Doctor Cranmer ambassador to the emperor.* *Conference between bishop Cranmer and Cornelius Agrippa.*

This matter thus prospering on doctor Cranmer's behalf, as well touching the king's question, as concerning the invalidity of the bishop of Rome's authority, bishop Warham, then archbishop of Canterbury, departed this transitory life; whereby that dignity then being in the king's gift and disposition, was immediately given to doctor Cranmer, as worthy for his travail of such a promotion. Thus much touching the preferment of doctor Cranmer unto his dignity, and by what means he achieved unto the same: not by flattery, nor by bribes, nor by none other unlawful means: which thing I have more at large discoursed, to stop the railing mouths of such, who, being themselves obscure and unlearned, shame not to detract a learned man most ignominiously with the surname of an hosteler, whom, for his godly zeal unto sincere religion, they ought with much humility to have had in regard and reputation. *Doctor Cranmer made archbishop of Canterbury.*

Now as concerning his behaviour and trade of life towards God and the world, being entered[3] into his said dignity. True it is, that he was so throughly furnished with all properties, qualities, and conditions belonging to a true bishop, as that it shall be very hard in these strange days to find many that so nearly resemble that lively exemplar, described by St Paul the apostle in his several epistles to Titus and Timothy: so far he swerved from the common course of common bishops in his time. But because the same is very well deciphered in the story at large[4], it shall not be so needful to discourse all the parts thereof in this place. Yet may not this be forgotten: that, notwithstanding the great charge now committed unto him, the worthy prelate gave himself evermore to continual study, not breaking the order that he used commonly in the university. To wit, by five of the clock in the morning in his study, and so until nine, continuing in prayer and study. From thence, until dinner time, to hear suitors (if the prince's affairs did not call him away), committing his temporal affairs, as well of household as other foreign business, to his officers. For the most part, he would occupy himself in reformation of corrupt religion, and setting forth true and sincere doctrine; wherein he would associate himself always with learned men, for the sifting and boulting out one matter or other, for the commodity and profit of the church of England. After dinner, if any suitors were, he would diligently hear them and dispatch them, in such sort as every man commended his lenity and gentleness. That done, to his ordinary study again until five of the clock, which hour he bestowed in hearing common prayer. After supper he would consume an hour at the least in some godly conference, and then again, until nine of the clock, at one kind of study or other. So that no hour of the day was spent in vain, but was bestowed as tended to God's glory, the service of his prince, or the commodity of the church. *1 Tim. iii. Tit. i.* *The order of doctor Cranmer's study.*

As touching his affability and easiness to be entreated, it was such as that in all honest causes, wherein his letter, counsel, or speech, might gratify either nobleman, *The gentle nature of doctor Cranmer.*

[3 Being now entered, Foxe. Ed. 1583.]   [4 See Foxe. Ed. 1583, p. 1862–1865.]

gentleman, mean man, or poor man, no man could be more tractable, or sooner won to yield. Only in causes appertaining to God and his prince, no man more stout, more constant, or more hard to be won: as in that part his earnest defence in the parliament-house, above three days together, in disputing against the six articles of Gardiner's device, can testify. And though the king would needs have them upon some politic consideration to go forward, yet he so handled himself, as well in the parliament-house, as afterwards by writing so obediently and with such humble behaviour in words towards his prince, protesting the cause not to be his, but Almighty God's who was the author of all truth, that the king did not only well like his defence, willing him to depart out of the parliament-house into the council chamber, whilst the act should pass and be granted, for safeguard of his conscience, which he with humble protestation refused, hoping that his majesty in process of time would revoke them again; but also, after the parliament was finished, the king perceiving the zealous affection that the archbishop bare towards the defence of his cause, which many ways by scriptures and manifold authorities and reasons he had substantially confirmed and defended, sent the lord Cromwell, then vicegerent, with the two dukes of Norfolk and Suffolk, and all the lords of the parliament, to dine with him at Lambeth: where it was declared by the vicegerent and the two dukes, that it was the king's pleasure, that they all should, in his highness' behalf, cherish, comfort, and animate him, as one that for his travail in that parliament had shewed himself both greatly learned, and also discreet and wise, and therefore they willed him not to be discouraged for anything that was passed contrary to his allegations. He most humbly thanked the king's majesty of his great goodness towards him, and them all for their pains, saying: "I hope in God, that hereafter my allegations and authorities shall take place to the glory of God and the commodity of the realm; in the mean time I will satisfy myself with the honourable consent of your honours and the whole parliament."

Doctor Cranmer stout and constant in God's cause.

Doctor Cranmer a stout enemy against the six articles.

Of this coming of the lord Cromwell, and the two dukes to the archbishop.

Here is to be noted, that this man's stout and godly defence of the truth herein so bound the prince's conscience, that he would not permit the truth in that man to be clean overthrown with authority and power; and therefore this way God working in the prince's mind, a plain token was declared hereby, that all things were not so sincerely handled in the confirmation of the said six articles as it ought to have been, for else the prince might have had just cause to have borne his great indignation towards the archbishop. Let us pray that both the like stoutness may be perceived in all ecclesiastical and learned men, where the truth ought to be defended, and also the like relenting and flexibility may take place in princes and noblemen, when they shall have occasion offered them to maintain the same, so that they utterly overwhelm not the truth by self-will, power, and authority. Now in the end this archbishop's constancy was such towards God's cause, that he confirmed all his doings by bitter death in the fire, without respect of any worldly treasure or pleasure. And as touching his stoutness in his prince's cause, the contrary resistance of the duke of Northumberland against him proved right well his good mind that way: which chanced by reason that he would not consent to the dissolving of chanteries until the king came of age, to the intent that they might then better serve to furnish his royal estate, than to have so great treasure consumed in his nonage: which his stoutness, joined with such simplicity, surely was thought to divers of the council a thing incredible, specially in such sort to contend with him who was so accounted in this realm, as few or none would or durst gainstand him.

Example for ecclesiastical pastors.

Archbishop Cranmer in displeasure about the employing of chantry lands.

So dear was to him the cause of God and of his prince, that for the one he would not keep his conscience clogged, nor for the other lurk or hide his head. Otherwise, as it is said, his very enemies might easily entreat him in any cause reasonable: and such things as he granted, he did without any suspicion of rebraiding or meed therefore. So that he was altogether void of the vice of the stubbornness, and rather culpable of overmuch facility and gentleness. Surely if overmuch patience may be a vice, this man may seem peradventure to offend rather on this part than on the contrary. Albeit for all his doings I cannot say: for the most part, such was his mortification that way, that few we shall find in whom the saying of our Saviour Christ so much prevailed as with him, who would not only have a man to forgive his enemies, but also to pray for them: that lesson never went out of his memory. For it was known that he had many cruel enemies, not for his own deserts, but only for his religion's sake: and yet, whatsoever he was that either sought his hindrance, either in goods, estimation, or life, and upon conference would seem never so slenderly anything to relent or excuse himself, he would both forget the offence committed, and also evermore afterwards friendly entertain him, and shew such pleasure to him, as by any means possible he might perform or declare. Insomuch that it came into a common proverb: "Do unto my lord of Canterbury displeasure or a shrewd turn, and then you may be sure to have him your friend whiles he liveth." Of which his gentle disposition in abstaining from revengement, amongst many examples thereof, I will repeat here one. *The singular patience of this archbishop.*

It chanced an ignorant priest and parson in the north parts, the town is not now in remembrance, but he was kinsman of one Chersey a grocer, dwelling within London, (being one of those priests that use more to study at the alehouse than in his chamber or in his study,) to sit on a time with his honest neighbours at the alehouse within his own parish, where was communication ministered in commendation of my lord Cranmer, archbishop of Canterbury. This said parson, envying his name only for religion's sake, said to his neighbours: "What make you of him?" quoth he, "he was but an hosteler, and hath no more learning than the goslings that goeth yonder on the green," with such like slanderous and uncomely words. These honest neighbours of his, not well bearing those his unseemly words, articled against him, and sent their complaint unto the lord Cromwell, then vicegerent in causes ecclesiastical; who sent for the priest and committed him to the Fleet, minding to have had him recant those his slanderous words at Paul's Cross. Howbeit the lord Cromwell, having great affairs of the prince then in hand, forgat his prisoner in the Fleet. So that this Chersey the grocer, understanding that his kinsman was in durance in the Fleet, only for speaking words against my lord of Canterbury, consulted with the priest, and between them devised to make suit rather unto the archbishop for his deliverance, than to the lord Cromwell, before whom he was accused; understanding right well that there was great diversity of natures between those two estates, the one gentle and full of clemency, and the other severe and somewhat intractable, namely against a papist. So that Chersey took upon him first to try my lord of Canterbury's benignity, namely for that his cousin's accusation touched only the offence against him and none other. Whereupon the said Chersey came to one of the archbishop's gentlemen, (whose father bought yearly all his spices and fruit of the said Chersey, and so thereby of familiar acquaintance with the gentleman,) who, opening to him the trouble wherein his kinsman was, requested that he would be a means to my lord his master to hear his suit in the behalf of his kinsman. *A story between the archbishop of Canterbury and a popish priest his enemy.* *The railing of a popish priest against Dr Cranmer.*

The matter was moved. The archbishop, like as he was of nature gentle, and of much clemency, so would he never shew himself strange unto suitors, but incontinently sent for the said Chersey. When he came before him, Chersey declared, "that there was a kinsman of his in the Fleet, a priest of the north country, and as I may tell your grace the truth," quoth Chersey, "a man of small civility and of less learning. And yet he hath a parsonage there, which now (by reason that my lord Cromwell hath *Chersey suing for his kinsman to the archbishop.*

laid him in prison, being in his cure) is unserved; and he hath continued in durance above two months, and is called to no answer, and knoweth not when he shall come to any end, so that this his imprisonment consumeth his substance, will utterly undo him, unless your grace be his good lord." "I know not the man," said the archbishop, "nor what he hath done why he should be thus in trouble."

Said Chersey again: "He only hath offended against your grace, and against no man else, as may well be perceived by the articles objected against him:" the copy whereof the said Chersey then exhibited unto the said archbishop of Canterbury. Who, well perusing the said articles, said: "This is the common talk of all the ignorant papistical priests in England against me. Surely," said he, "I was never made privy unto this accusation, nor of his indurance I never heard before this time. Notwithstanding, if there be nothing else to charge him withal, against the prince or any of the council, I will at your request take order with him, and send him home again to his cure to do his duty:" and so thereupon sent his ring to the warden of the Fleet, willing him to send the prisoner unto him with his keeper at afternoon.

The priest sent for to the archbishop.

When the keeper had brought the prisoner at the hour appointed, and Chersey had well instructed his cousin in any wise to submit himself unto the archbishop, confessing his fault, whereby that way he should most easily have an end and win his favour: thus the parson being brought into the garden at Lambeth, and there sitting under the vine, the archbishop demanded of the parson what was the cause of his indurance, and who committed him to the Fleet? The parson answered and said: "That the lord Cromwell sent him thither, for that certain malicious parishioners of his parish, had wrongfully accused him of words which he never spake nor meant." Chersey, hearing his foolish cousin so far out of the way from his former instruction, said: "Thou dastardly dolt and varlet, is this thy promise that thou madest to me? Is there not a great number of thy honest neighbours' hands against thee to prove thee a liar? Surely, my lord," quoth Chersey, "it is pity to do him good. I am sorry that I have troubled your grace thus far with him."

The archbishop's words unto the parson.

"Well," said the archbishop unto the parson, "if you have not offended me, I can do you no good; for I am entreated to help one out of trouble that hath offended against me. If my lord Cromwell hath committed you to prison wrongfully, that lieth in himself to amend, and not in me. If your offence only touch me, I will be bold to do somewhat for your friend's sake here. If you have not offended against me, then have I nothing to do with you, but that you may go and remain from whence you came." Lord, what ado his kinsman Chersey made with him, calling him all kind of opprobrious names! In the end, my lord of Canterbury seeming to rise and go his ways, the fond priest fell down on his knees, and said: "I beseech your grace to forgive me this offence; assuring your grace that I spake those words, being drunk, and not well advised." "Ah!" said my lord, "this is somewhat, and yet it is no good excuse; for drunkenness evermore uttereth that which lieth hid in the heart of man when he is sober," alleging a text or twain out of the scriptures concerning the vice of drunkenness, which cometh not now to remembrance.

The priest confesseth his fault to the archbishop.

"Now therefore," said the archbishop, "that you acknowledge somewhat your fault, I am content to commune with you, hoping that you are at this present of an indifferent sobriety. Tell me then," quoth he, "did you ever see me, or were you ever acquainted with me before this day?" The priest answered and said, that never in his life he saw his grace. "Why then," said the archbishop, "what occasion had you to call me an hosteler; and that I had not so much learning as the goslings which then went on the green before your face? If I have no learning, you may now try it, and be out of doubt thereof: therefore I pray you appose me, either in grammar or in other liberal

The rash tongues of men slanderously speaking evil by men whom they never knew nor saw before.

sciences; for I have at one time or other tasted partly of them. Or else, if you are a divine, say somewhat that way."

The priest, being amazed at my lord's familiar talk, made answer and said: "I beseech your grace to pardon me. I am altogether unlearned, and understand not the Latin tongue but very simply. My only study hath been to say my service and mass fair and deliberate, which I can do as well as any priest in the country where I dwell, I thank God." "Well," said the other, "if you will not appose me, I will be so bold to appose you, and yet as easily as I can devise, and that only in the story of the bible now in English, in which I suppose that you are daily exercised. Tell me therefore, who was king David's father?" said my lord. The priest stood still pausing a while, and said: "In good faith, my lord, I have forgotten his name." Then said the other again to him: "If you cannot tell that, I pray you tell me then who was Salomon's father?" The fond foolish priest, without all consideration what was demanded of him before, made answer: "Good my lord, bear with me, I am not further seen in the bible, than is daily read in our service in the church." *The priest's answer.* *The mass-priest ignorant in the scripture.*

The archbishop then answering said: "This my question may be found well answered in your service. But I now well perceive, howsoever you have judged heretofore of my learning, sure I am that you have none at all. But this is the common practice of all you, which are ignorant and superstitious priests, to slander, backbite, and hate all such as are learned and well affected towards God's word and sincere religion. Common reason might have taught you, what an unlikely thing it was, and contrary to all manner of reason, that a prince, having two universities within his realm of well learned men, and desirous to be resolved of as doubtful a question as in these many years was not moved the like within Christendom, should be driven to that necessity for the defence of his cause, to send out of his realm an hosteler, being a man of no better knowledge than is a gosling, in an embassage to answer all learned men, both in the court of Rome and in the emperor's court, in so difficult a question as toucheth the king's matrimony, and the divorce thereof. I say, if you were men of any reasonable consideration, you might think it both unseemly and uncomely for a prince so to [do.] But look, where malice reigneth in men, there reason can take no place: and therefore I see by it, that you all are at a point with me, that no reason or authority can persuade you to favour my name, who never meant evil to you, but your both commodity and profit. Howbeit, God amend you all, forgive you, and send you better minds!" *The guise of popish priests, when they favour not the religion of a man, they slander his person.* *Evil-will never said well.*

With these words the priest seemed to weep, and desired his grace to pardon his fault and frailty, so that by his means he might return to his cure again, and he would sure recant those his foolish words before his parishioners so soon as he came home, and would become a new man. "Well," said the archbishop, "so you had need." And giving him a godly admonition to refuse the haunting of the alehouse, and to bestow his time better in the continual reading of the scriptures, he dismissed him from the Fleet. *The archbishop forgiveth and dismisseth the priest.*

How little this prelate we speak of was infected with filthy desire of lucre, and how he was no niggard, all kind of people that knew him, as well learned beyond the seas and on this side, to whom yearly he gave in exhibition no small sums of money, as other, both gentlemen, mean men, and poor men, who had in their necessity that which he could conveniently spare, lend, or make, can well testify. And albeit such was his liberality to all sorts of men, that no man did lack whom he could do for, either in giving or lending; yet nevertheless such was again his circumspection, that when he was apprehended and committed by queen Mary to the tower, he ought no man living a penny that could or would demand any duty of him, but satisfied every man to the uttermost; where else no small sums of money were owing *The liberal doings of this archbishop.*

to him of divers persons, which by breaking their bills and obligations he freely forgave and suppressed before his attainder. Insomuch that when he perceived the fatal end of king Edward should work to him no good success touching his body and goods, he incontinently called his officers, his steward and other, commanding them in any wise to pay, where any penny was owing, which was out of hand dispatched.

The archbishop clearing all his debts before his attainder.

In which archbishop this, moreover, is to be noted, with a memorandum, touching the relief of the poor, impotent, sick, and such as then came from the wars at Bullein[1], and other parts beyond the seas, lame, wounded, and destitute; for whom he provided, besides his mansion-house at Beckisborne in Kent, the parsonage barn well furnished with certain lodgings for the sick and maimed soldiers: to whom were also appointed the almosiner, a physician, and surgeon, to attend upon them, and to dress and cure such as were not able to resort to their countries, having daily from the bishop's kitchen hot broth and meat; for otherwise the common alms of the household was bestowed upon the poor neighbours of the shire. And when any of the impotent did recover, and were able to travel, they had convenient money delivered to bear their charges, according to the number of miles from that place distant. And this good example of mercy and liberal benignity I thought here good not in silence to be suppressed, whereby other may be moved, according to their vocation, to walk in the steps of no less liberality than in him in this behalf appeared.

Amongst all other his virtues, his constancy in Christ's cause, and setting forth the gospel purely and sincerely, was such that he would neither for dread or meed, affection or favour, to swerve at any time or in any point from the truth, as appeared by his sundry trials; wherein neither favour of his prince, nor fear of the indignation of the same, nor any other worldly respect, could alienate or change his purpose, grounded upon that infallible doctrine of the gospel. Notwithstanding, his constant defence of God's truth was ever joined with such meekness toward the king, that he never took occasion of offence against him.

The archbishop Cranmer ever constant in defence of Christ's truth and gospel.

At the setting forth[2] of the six Articles, mention was made before in the story of king Henry's time, how adventurously this archbishop, Thomas Cranmer, did oppose himself, standing, as it were, post alone against the whole parliament, disputing and replying three days together against the said articles; insomuch that the king, when neither he could mislike his reasons, and yet would needs have these articles to pass, required him to absent himself for the time out of the chamber, while the act should pass, as is already declared before. And this was done during yet the state and time of the lord Cromwell's authority. And now that it may appear likewise that after the decay of the lord Cromwell, yet his constancy in Christ's cause did not decay, you shall hear what followed after.

For after the apprehension of the lord Cromwell, when the adversaries of the gospel thought all things sure now on their side, it was so appointed amongst them, that ten or twelve bishops, and other learned men, joined together in commission, came to the said archbishop of Canterbury for the establishing of certain articles of our religion, which the papists then thought to win to their purpose against the said archbishop. For having now the lord Cromwell fast and sure, they thought all had been safe and sure for ever: as indeed to all men's reasonable consideration, that time appeared so dangerous, that there was no manner hope that religion reformed should any one week longer stand, such accompt was then made of the king's untowardness thereunto: insomuch that of all those commissioners, there was not one left to stay on the archbishop's

The archbishop alone standeth in

[1 i.e. Boulogne, which was taken by the English after a siege in the year 1544.]
[2 At the time of setting forth, Foxe. Ed. 1583.]

part, but he alone against them all stood in defence of the truth; and those that he most trusted to, namely, bishop Heath, and bishop Skippe, left him in the plain field: who then so turned against him, that they took upon them to persuade him to their purpose; and having him down from the rest of the commissioners into his garden at Lambeth, there by all manner of effectual persuasions entreated him to leave off his overmuch constancy, and to incline unto the king's intent, who was fully set to have it otherwise than he then had penned, or meant to have set abroad. When those two his familiars, with one or two others his friends, had used all their eloquence and policy, he, little regarding their inconstancy and remissness in God's cause or quarrel, said unto them right notably: "You make much ado to have me come to your purpose, alleging that it is the king's pleasure to have the articles in that sort you have devised them to proceed; and now that you do perceive his highness, by sinister information, to be bent that way, you think it a convenient thing to apply unto his highness's mind. You be my friends both, especially the one of you I did put to his majesty as of trust. Beware, I say, what you do. There is but one truth in our articles to be concluded upon, which if you do hide from his highness by consenting unto a contrary doctrine, and then after in process of time, when the truth cannot be hidden from him, his highness shall perceive how that you have dealt colourably with him, I know his grace's nature so well," quoth the archbishop, "that he will never after trust and credit you, or put any good confidence in you. And as you are both my friends, so therefore I will you to beware thereof in time, and discharge your consciences in maintenance of the truth." But all this would not serve, for they still swerved; and in the end, by discharging of his conscience, and declaring the truth unto the king, God so wrought with the king, that his highness joined with him against the rest; so that the book of articles passing on his side, he won the goal from them all, contrary to all their expectations; when many wagers would have been laid in London, that he should have been laid up with Cromwell at that time in the Tower, for his stiff standing to his tackle. After that day there could neither councillor, bishop, or papist, win him out of the king's favour.

Notwithstanding, not long after that, certain of the council, whose names need not to be repeated, by the enticement and provocation of his ancient enemy, the bishop of Winchester, and other of the same sect, attempted the king against him, declaring plainly, that the realm was so infected with heresies and heretics, that it was dangerous for his highness farther to permit it unreformed, lest peradventure by long suffering such contention should arise and ensue in the realm among his subjects, that thereby might spring horrible commotions and uproars, like as in some parts of Germany it did not long ago; the enormity whereof they could not impute to any so much as to the archbishop of Canterbury, who by his own preaching and his chaplains' had filled the whole realm full of divers pernicious heresies. The king would needs know his accusers. They answered, that forasmuch as he was a councillor, no man durst take upon him to accuse him; but, if it please his highness to commit him to the Tower for a time, there would be accusations and proofs enough against him, for otherwise just testimony and witness against him would not appear; "and therefore your highness," said they, "must needs give us, the council, liberty and leave to commit him to durance."

The king perceiving their importune suit against the archbishop, but yet meaning not to have him wronged and utterly given over unto their hands, granted to them that they should the next day commit him to the Tower for his trial. When night came, the king sent Sir Antony Deny about midnight to Lambeth to the archbishop, willing him forthwith to resort unto him at the court. The message done, the archbishop speedily addressed himself to the court, and coming into the gallery where the

[CRANMER.]

king walked and tarried for him, his highness said: "Ah, my lord of Canterbury, I can tell you news. For divers weighty considerations it is determined by me and the council, that you to-morrow at nine of the clock shall be committed to the Tower, for that you and your chaplains (as information is given us) have taught and preached, and thereby sown within the realm, such a number of execrable heresies, that it is feared, the whole realm being infected with them, no small contentions and commotions will rise thereby amongst my subjects, as of late days the like was in divers parts of Germany; and therefore the council have requested me, for the trial of this matter, to suffer them to commit you to the Tower, or else no man dare come forth as witness in these matters, you being a councillor."

The king's words and advice for the supportation of the archbishop.

When the king had said his mind, the archbishop kneeled down, and said: "I am content, if it please your grace, with all my heart to go thither at your highness's commandment, and I most humbly thank your majesty that I may come to my trial; for there be that have many ways slandered me, and now this way I hope to try myself not worthy of such a report."

The archbishop's answer to the king.

The king, perceiving the man's uprightness joined with such simplicity, said: "Oh Lord, what manner a man be you! what simplicity is in you! I had thought that you would rather have sued to us to have taken the pains to have heard you and your accusers together for your trial without any such endurance. Do not you know what state you be in with the whole world, and how many great enemies you have? Do you not consider, what an easy thing it is to procure three or four false knaves to witness against you? Think you to have better luck that way than your master Christ had? I see it, you will run headlong to your undoing, if I would suffer you. Your enemies shall not so prevail against you, for I have otherwise devised with myself to keep you out of their hands. Yet, notwithstanding, to-morrow when the council shall sit and send for you, resort unto them; and if in charging you with this matter they do commit you to the Tower, require of them, because you are one of them, a councillor, that you may have your accusers brought before them, and that you may answer their accusations before them without any further endurance, and use for yourself as good persuasions that way as you may devise; and if no entreaty or reasonable request will serve, then deliver unto them this my ring, (which then the king delivered unto the archbishop,) and say unto them: 'If there be no remedy, my lords, but that I must needs go to the Tower, then I revoke my cause from you, and appeal to the king's own person by this his token unto you all:' for," said the king then unto the archbishop, "so soon as they shall see this my ring, they know it so well, that they shall understand that I have resumed the whole cause into mine own hands and determination, and that I have discharged them thereof."

The king's favourable care and consideration toward the archbishop of Canterbury.

The king sendeth his signet on the behalf of the archbishop of Canterbury.

The archbishop, perceiving the king's benignity so much to him wards, had much ado to forbear tears. "Well," said the king, "go your ways, my lord, and do as I have bidden you." My lord, humbling himself with thanks, took his leave of the king's highness for that night.

On the morrow, about nine of the clock before noon, the council sent a gentleman usher for the archbishop, who when he came to the council-chamber door, could not be let in, but of purpose, as it seemed, was compelled there to wait among the pages, lackeys, and serving-men all alone. Doctor Butts, the king's physician, resorting that way, and espying how my lord of Canterbury was handled, went to the king's highness and said: "My lord of Canterbury, if it please your grace, is well promoted; for now he is become a lackey or a serving-man, for yonder he standeth this half-hour without the council-chamber door amongst them." "It is not so," quoth the king, "I trow, nor the council hath not so little discretion as to use the metropolitan of the realm in that

The archbishop, being one of the council, made to stand at the council-chamber door waiting. Doctor Butts, the king's physician, a friend of the archbishop.

sort, specially being one of their own number; but let them alone," said the king, "and we shall hear more soon."

Anon the archbishop was called into the council-chamber, to whom was alleged as before is rehearsed. The archbishop answered in like sort as the king had advised him; and in the end when he perceived that no manner of persuasion or entreaty could serve, he delivered to them the king's ring, revoking his cause into the king's hands. The whole council being thereat somewhat amazed, the earl of Bedford with a loud voice, confirming his words with a solemn oath, said: "When you first began this matter, my lords, I told you what would come of it. Do you think that the king will suffer this man's finger to ache? much more, I warrant you, will he defend his life against brabbling varlets. You do but cumber yourselves to hear tales and fables against him." And so incontinently, upon the receipt of the king's token, they all rose and carried to the king his ring, surrendering that matter (as the order and use was) into his own hands. *The archbishop called before the council. The council being set against the archbishop, he sheweth the king's ring, and appealeth from them.*

When they were all come to the king's presence, his highness with a severe countenance said unto them: "Ah, my lords, I thought I had had wiser men of my council than now I find you. What discretion was this in you, thus to make the primate of the realm, and one of you in office, to wait at the council-chamber door amongst serving-men? You might have considered that he was a councillor as well as you, and you had no such commission of me so to handle him. I was content that you should try him as a councillor, and not as a mean subject. But now I well perceive that things be done against him maliciously; and if some of you might have had your minds, you would have tried him to the uttermost. But I do you all to wit, and protest, that if a prince may be beholding unto his subject," (and so solemnly laying his hand upon his breast, said,) "by the faith I owe to God, I take this man here, my lord of Canterbury, to be of all other a most faithful subject unto us, and one to whom we are much beholding," giving him great commendations otherwise. And with that one or two of the chiefest of the council, making their excuse, declared, that in requesting his indurance, it was rather meant for his trial and his purgation against the common fame and slander of the world, than for any malice conceived against him. "Well, well, my lords," quoth the king, "take him and well use him, as he is worthy to be, and make no more ado." And with that every man caught him by the hand, and made fair weather of altogethers, which might easily be done with that man. *The king's words to the council in defence of the archbishop. The lords of the council glad to be friends again with the archbishop.*

And it was much to be marvelled that they would go so far with him, thus to seek his undoing, this well understanding before, that the king most entirely loved him, and always would stand in his defence, whosoever spake against him; as many other times the king's patience was by sinister informations against him tried: insomuch that the lord Cromwell was evermore wont to say unto him: "My lord of Canterbury, you are most happy of all men: for you may do and speak what you list, and, say what all men can against you, the king will never believe one word to your detriment or hindrance." *The king a great supporter of Cranmer. The lord Cromwell's words to the archbishop.*

After the death of king Henry, immediately succeeded his son king Edward, under whose government and protection the state of this archbishop, being his godfather, was nothing appaired, but rather more advanced.

During all this mean time of king Henry aforesaid, until the entering of king Edward, it seemeth that Cranmer was scarcely yet throughly persuaded in the right knowledge of the sacrament, or at least, was not yet fully ripened in the same: wherein shortly after he being more groundly confirmed by conference with bishop Ridley, in process of time did so profit in more riper knowledge, that at last he

b—2

took upon him the defence of that whole doctrine, that is, to refute and throw down first, the corporal presence; secondly, the phantastical transubstantiation; thirdly, the idolatrous adoration; fourthly, the false error of the papists, that wicked men do eat the natural body of Christ; and lastly, the blasphemous sacrifice of the mass. Whereupon in conclusion he wrote five books for the public instruction of the church of England, which instruction yet to this day standeth and is received in this church of England.

The true and godly doctrine of the sacrament, in five books, set forth by the archbishop of Canterbury.

Against these five books of the archbishop, Stephen Gardiner, the arch-enemy to Christ and his gospel, being then in the tower, slubbereth up a certain answer, such as it was, which he in open court exhibited up at Lambeth, being there examined by the archbishop aforesaid, and other the king's commissioners in king Edward's days, which book was entitled, "An Explication and Assertion of the True Catholic Faith, touching the blessed Sacrament of the Altar, with a Confutation of a Book written against the same."

An explication by Stephen Gardiner against Cranmer, archbishop of Canterbury.

Against this explication, or rather a cavilling sophistication of Stephen Gardiner, Doctor of Law, the said archbishop of Canterbury learnedly and copiously replying again, maketh answer, as by the discourse thereof renewed in print is evident to be seen to all such as with indifferent eye will read and peruse the same.

Besides these books above recited of this archbishop, divers other things there were also of his doing, as the Book of Reformation, with the Book of Homilies, whereof part was by him contrived, part by his procurement approved and published. Whereunto also may be adjoined another writing or confutation of his against eighty-eight articles by the convocation devised and propounded, but yet not ratified nor received, in the reign and time of king Henry[1].

And thus much hitherto concerning the doings and travails of this archbishop of Canterbury during the lives both of king Henry and king Edward his son; which two kings so long as they continued, this archbishop lacked no stay of maintenance against all his maligners.

After the death of king Edward, queen Mary coming now to the crown, and being established in the possession of the realm, not long after came to London; and after she had caused first the two dukes of Northumberland and Suffolk, and their two children, the lady Jane and the lord Guilford, both in age tender and innocent of that crime, to be executed; she put the rest of the nobility to their fines, and forgave them, the archbishop of Canterbury only except. Who, though he desired pardon by mean of friends, could obtain none; insomuch that the queen would not once vouchsafe to see him: for as yet the old grudges against the archbishop, for the divorcement of her mother, remained hid in the bottom of her heart. Besides this divorce, she remembered the state of religion changed: all which was reputed to the archbishop, as the chief cause thereof.

Manet alta mente repostum judicium Paridis, spretæque injuria matris. Virg. Æneid. I.

While these things were in doing, a rumour was in all men's mouths, that the archbishop, to curry favour with the queen, had promised to say a *Dirige* mass, after the old custom, for the funeral of king Edward her brother. Neither wanted there some, which reported that he had already said mass at Canterbury; which mass in deed was said by doctor Thornton. This rumour Cranmer thinking speedily to stay, gave forth a writing in his purgation; the tenor whereof being set out at large in the Book of Acts and Monuments, I need not here again to recite.

This doctor Thornton was after the bishop of Dover, a cruel and wicked persecutor.

This bill being thus written, and lying openly a window[2] in his chamber, cometh in by chance Master Scory, bishop then of Rochester, who after he had read and

---

[¹ King Henry eight, Foxe, 1583.]   [² Openly in a window, ibid.]

perused the same, required of the archbishop to have a copy of the bill. The archbishop, when he had granted and permitted the same to Master Scory, by the occasion thereof Master Scory lending it to some friend of his, there were divers copies taken out thereof, and the thing published abroad among the common people: insomuch that every scrivener's shop almost was occupied in writing out the same; and so at length some of those copies coming to the bishops' hands, and so brought to the council, and they sending it to the commissioners, the matter was known, and so he commanded to appear.

Whereupon Dr Cranmer at his day prefixed appeared before the said commissioners, bringing a true inventory, as he was commanded, of all his goods. That done, a bishop of the queen's privy council, being one of the said commissioners, after the inventory was received, bringing in mention of the bill: "My lord," said he, "there is a bill put forth in your name, wherein you seem to be aggrieved with setting up the mass again: we doubt not but you are sorry that it is gone abroad." *[This bishop was doctor Heath, bishop after of York.]*

To whom the archbishop answered again, saying: "As I do not deny myself to be the very author of that bill or letter, so must I confess here unto you, concerning the same bill, that I am sorry the said bill went from me in such sort as it did. For when I had written it, Master Scory got the copy of me, and is now come abroad, and (as I understand) the city is full of it. For which I am sorry, that it so passed my hands: for I had intended otherwise to have made it in a more large and ample manner, and minded to have set it on Paul's Church door, and on the doors of all the churches in London, with mine own seal joined thereto."

At which words, when they saw the constantness of the man, they dismissed him, affirming they had no more at that present to say unto him, but that shortly he should hear further. The said bishop declared afterward to one of Dr Cranmer's friends, that notwithstanding his attainder of treason, the queen's determination at that time was, that Cranmer should only have been deprived of his archbishoprick, and have had a sufficient living assigned him, upon his exhibiting of a true inventory, with commandment to keep his house without meddling with matters of religion. But how that was true, I have not to say. This is certain, that not long after this he was sent unto the tower, and soon after condemned of treason. Notwithstanding, the queen, when she could not honestly deny him his pardon, seeing all the rest were discharged, and specially seeing he last of all other subscribed to king Edward's request, and that against his own will, released to him his action of treason, and accused him only of heresy: which liked the archbishop right well, and came to pass as he wished, because the cause was not now his own, but Christ's; not the queen's, but the church's. Thus stood the cause of Cranmer, till at length it was determined by the queen and the council, that he should be removed from the Tower, where he was prisoner, to Oxford, there to dispute with the doctors and divines. And privily word was sent before to them of Oxford to prepare themselves, and make them ready to dispute. And although the queen and the bishops had concluded before what should become of him, yet it pleased them that the matter should be debated with arguments, that under some honest shew of disputation the murder of the man might be covered. Neither could their hasty speed of revengement abide any long delay: and therefore in all haste he was carried to Oxford. *[Cranmer condemned of treason. Cranmer released of treason, and accused of heresy. Cranmer had to Oxford.]*

What this disputation was, and how it was handled, what were the questions and reasons on both sides, and also touching his condemnation by the university and the prolocutor, because sufficiently it hath been declared in the story at large, we mind now therefore to proceed to his final judgment and order of condemnation, which

xxii THE LIFE, STATE, AND STORY

was the twelfth day of September, anno 1556[1], and seven days before the condemnation of bishop Ridley and Master Latimer.

Of this condemnation, read in the last edition, page 1554.

After the disputations done and finished in Oxford, between the doctors of both universities, and the three worthy bishops, Dr Cranmer, Ridley, and Latimer, sentence condemnatory immediately upon the same was ministered against them by Dr Weston and other of the university: whereby they were judged to be heretics, and so committed to the Mayor and Sheriffs of Oxford, by whom he was carried to Bocardo, their common gaol in Oxford.

In[2] this mean time, while the archbishop was thus remaining in durance, (whom they had kept now in prison almost the space of three years,) the doctors and divines of Oxford busied themselves all that ever they could about Master Cranmer, to have him recant, assaying by all crafty practices and allurements they might devise, how to bring their purpose to pass. And to the intent they might win him easily, they had him to the dean's house of Christ's Church in the said university, where he lacked no delicate fare, played at the bowls, had his pleasure for walking, and all other things that might bring him from Christ. Over and besides all this, secretly and sleightly, they suborned certain men, which, when they could not expunge him by arguments and disputation, should by entreaty and fair promises or any other means allure him to recantation: perceiving otherwise what a great wound they should receive if the archbishop had stood stedfast in his sentence; and again on the other side, how great profit they should get, if he, as the principal standard-bearer, should be overthrown. By reason whereof the wily papists flocked about him with threatning, flattering, entreating, and promising, and all other means: especially, Henry Sydall, and friar John, a Spaniard, de Villa Garcina, to the end to drive him, to the uttermost of their possibility, from his former sentence to recantation: whose force his manly constancy did a great while resist; but at last, when they made no end of calling and crying upon him, the archbishop being overcome, whether through their importunity, or by his own imbecility, or of what mind I cannot tell, at length gave his hand.

The archbishop contented to recant.

It might be supposed that it was done for the hope of life, and better days to come. But as we may since perceive, by a letter of his sent to a lawyer, the most cause why he desired his time to be delayed, was that he would make an end of Marcus Antonius, which he had already begun: but howsoever it was, he recanted, though plain against his conscience.

Causes moving the archbishop to give with the time.

Mary the queen, having now gotten a time to revenge her old grief, received his recantation very gladly; but her purpose to put him to death she would nothing relent. But taking secret counsel how to dispatch Cranmer out of the way, (who as yet knew nothing of her secret hate, and looked for nothing less than death,) appointed doctor Cole, and secretly gave him in commandment, that against the 21st of March he should prepare a funeral sermon for Cranmer's burning, and so instructing him orderly and diligently of her will and pleasure in that behalf, sendeth him away.

The queen's heart set against Cranmer.

The queen conferreth with doctor Cole about Cranmer's burning.

Soon after, the Lord Williams of Thame, and the Lord Shandoys, Sir Thomas Bridges, and Sir John Browne were sent for, with other worshipful men and justices, commanded in the queen's name to be at Oxford at the same day, with their servants and retinue, lest Cranmer's death should raise there any tumult.

Lord Wm. of Thame, Lord Shandoys, Sir Thomas Bridges, Sir John Browne, appointed to be at Cranmer's execution.

Cole, the doctor, having his lesson given him before, and charged by her commandment, returned to Oxford ready to play his part, who, as the day of execution

---

[1 So it is printed in ed. 1580, and in Foxe, ed. 1583, p. 1871.]   [2 See Foxe, ed. 1583, p. 1884.]

drew near, even the day before he came into the prison to Cranmer, to try whether he abode in the catholic faith, wherein before he had left him. To whom when Cranmer had answered, that by God's grace he would daily be more confirmed in the catholic faith; Cole, departing for that time, the next day following repaired to the archbishop again, giving no signification as yet of his death that was prepared; and therefore in the morning, which was the 21st day of March, appointed for Cranmer's execution, the said Cole coming to him asked, if he had any money. To whom when he answered that he had none, he delivered him fifteen crowns to give the poor to whom he would: and so exhorting him so much as he could to constancy in faith, departed thence about his business, as to his sermon appertained.

By this partly, and other like arguments, the archbishop began more and more to surmise what they went about. Then, because the day was not far past, and the lords and knights that were looked for were not yet come, there came to him the Spanish friar, witness of his recantation, bringing a paper with articles, which Cranmer should openly profess in his recantation before the people, earnestly desiring that he would write the said instrument with the articles with his own hand, and sign it with his name: which when he had done, the said friar desired that he would write another copy thereof, which should remain with him; and that he did also. *Cranmer writeth and subscribeth the articles with his own hands.* But yet the archbishop, being not ignorant whereunto their secret devices tended, and thinking that the time was at hand, in which he could no longer dissemble the profession of his faith with Christ's people, he put secretly in his bosom his prayer with his exhortation, written in another paper, which he minded to recite to the people, before he should make the last profession of his faith, fearing lest, if they had heard the confession of his faith first, they would not afterward have suffered him to exhort the people.

Soon after, about nine of the clock, the Lord Williams, Sir Thomas Bridges, Sir John Browne, and the other justices, with certain other noblemen that were sent of the queen's council, came to Oxford with a great train of waiting men. Also of the other multitude on every side (as is wont in such a matter) was made a great concourse and greater expectation.

In this so great frequence and expectation, Cranmer at length cometh from the prison Bocardo unto St Mary's church (because it was a foul and a rainy day), the chief church in the university, in this order. The mayor went before, next him the aldermen in their place and degree; after them was Cranmer brought between two friars, which mumbling to and fro certain psalms in the streets, answered one another, until they came to the church door, and there they began the song of Simeon, *Nunc dimittis;* and entering into the church, the psalm-saying friars brought him to his standing, and there left him. There was a stage set up over against the pulpit, of a mean height from the ground, where Cranmer had his standing, waiting until Cole made him ready to his sermon. *Doctor Cranmer brought to doctor Cole's sermon. Doctor Cranmer set upon a stage.*

The lamentable case and sight of that man gave a sorrowful spectacle to all christian eyes that beheld him. He that late was archbishop, metropolitan and primate of England, and the king's privy councillor, being now in a bare and ragged gown, and ill-favouredly clothed, with an old square cap, exposed to the contempt of all men, did admonish men not only of his own calamity, but also of their state and fortune. For who would not pity his case, and bewail his fortune, and might not fear his own chance, to see such a prelate, so grave a councillor, and of so long continued honour, after so many dignities, in his old years to be deprived of his estate, adjudged to die, and in so painful a death to end his life, and now presently from such fresh ornaments to descend to such vile and ragged apparel?

In this habit, when he had stood a good space upon the stage, turning to a pillar near adjoining thereunto, he lifted up his hands to heaven, and prayed to God once or twice: till at the length Dr Cole coming into the pulpit, and beginning his sermon, entered first into mention of Tobias and Zachary. Whom after that he had praised in the beginning of his sermon, for their perseverance in the true worshipping of God, he then divided his whole sermon into three parts (according to the solemn custom of the schools), intending to speak first of the mercy of God, secondly of his justice to be shewed, and last of all, how the prince's secrets are not to be opened. And proceeding a little from the beginning, he took occasion by and by to turn his tale to Cranmer, and with many hot words reproved him, that once he being endued with the favour and feeling of wholesome and catholic doctrine, fell into the contrary opinion of pernicious error, which he had not only defended by writings, and all his power, but also allured other men to the like[1] with great liberality of gifts, as it were appointing rewards for error; and after he had allured them, by all means did cherish them.

Doctor Cole's sermon divided into three parts.

The sum and effect of doctor Cole's sermon at Oxford.

It were too long to repeat all things, that in long order were then pronounced. The sum of this tripartite declamation was, that he said God's mercy was so tempered with his justice, that he did not altogether require punishment according to the merits of offenders, nor yet sometimes suffered the same altogether to go unpunished, yea, though they had repented: as in David, who when he was bidden choose of three kinds of punishments which he would, and he had chosen pestilence for three days, the Lord forgave him half the time, but did not release all: and that the same thing came to pass in him also, to whom although pardon and reconciliation was due according to the canons, seeing he repented from his errors; yet there were causes why the queen and the council at this time judged him to death; of which, lest he should marvel too much, he should hear some.

If Cole gave this judgment upon Cranmer when he had repented, what judgment is then to be given of Cole which always hath perdured in error, and never yet repented?

First, that being a traitor, he had dissolved the lawful matrimony between the king her father and mother; besides the driving out of the pope's authority, while he was metropolitan.

Secondly, that he had been an heretic, from whom, as from an author and only fountain, all heretical doctrine and schismatical opinions that so many years have prevailed in England, did first rise and spring: of which he had not been a secret favourer only, but also a most earnest defender even to the end of his life, sowing them abroad by writings and arguments, privately and openly, not without great ruin and decay of the catholic church.

If all heretics in England should be burned, where should doctor Cole have been ere now?

And further, it seemed meet, according to the law of equality, that as the death of the Duke of Northumberland of late made even with Thomas More, chancellor, that died for the church, so there should be one that should make even with Fisher of Rochester; and because that Ridley, Hooper, Farrar, were not able to make even with that man, it seemed meet that Cranmer should be joined to them to fill up this part of equality.

Lex non æqualitatis, sed iniquitatis.

Beside these, there were other just and weighty causes, which seemed to the queen and the council, which was not meet at that time to be opened to the common people.

After this, turning his tale to the hearers, he bad all men beware by this man's example, that among men nothing is so high, that can promise itself safety on the earth, and that God's vengeance is equally stretched against all men, and spareth none; therefore they should beware and learn to fear their prince. And seeing the

No state in this earth so high nor so sure, but it may fall.

[¹ To do the like, Foxe, ed. 1583.]

queen's majesty would not spare so notable a man as this, much less in the like cause she would spare other men; that no man should think to make thereby any defence of his error, either in riches or any kind of authority. They had now an example to teach them all, by whose calamity every man might consider his own fortune; who from the top of dignity, none being more honourable than he in the whole realm, and next the king, was fallen into so great misery, as they might now see; being a man of so high degree, some time one of the chiefest prelates in the church, and an archbishop, the chief of the council, the second person in the realm of long time, a man thought in greatest assurance, having a king on his side; notwithstanding all his authority and defence, to be debased from high estate to a low degree; of a councillor to become a caitiff, and to be set in so wretched a state, that the poorest wretch would not change condition with him; briefly, so heaped with misery on all sides, that neither was left in him any hope of better fortune, nor place for worse.

The latter part of his sermon he converted to the archbishop; whom he comforted and encouraged to take his death well, by many places of scripture, as with these and such like: bidding him not mistrust, but he should incontinently receive that the thief did to whom Christ said, *Hodie mecum eris in Paradiso;* that is, "This day thou shalt be with me in Paradise." And out of St Paul he armed him against the terror of the fire, by this: *Dominus fidelis est, non sinet vos tentari ultra quam ferre potestis;* that is, "The Lord is faithful, which will not suffer you to be tempted above your strength:" by the example of the three children, to whom God made the flame to seem like a pleasant dew: adding also the rejoicing of St Andrew in his cross, the patience of St Laurence on the fire; assuring him that God, if he called on him, and to such as die in his faith, either would abate the fury of the flame, or give him strength to abide it. *[marginal: Doctor Cole encourageth the archbishop to take his death patiently.]* *[marginal: 1 Cor. x.]*

He glorified God much in his conversion, because it appeared to be only his work, declaring what travail and conference had been with him to convert him, and all prevailed not, till that it pleased God of his mercy to reclaim him and call him home. In discoursing of which place, he much commended Cranmer, and qualified his former doings, thus tempering his judgment and talk of him, that while the time (said he) he flowed in riches and honour, he was unworthy of his life, and now that he might not live, he was unworthy of death. But lest he should carry with him no comfort, he would diligently labour, he said, and also he did promise in the name of all the priests that were present, immediately after his death there should be diriges, masses, and funerals executed for him in all the churches of Oxford for the succour of his soul. *[marginal: Doctor Cole rejoiceth in the archbishop's conversion, but that rejoicing lasted not long.]* *[marginal: Diriges and masses promised for Cranmer's soul.]*

Cranmer in all this mean time with what great grief of mind he stood hearing this sermon, the outward shews of his body and countenance did better express than any man can declare; one while lifting up his hands and eyes unto heaven, and then again for shame letting them down to the earth. A man might have seen the very image and shape of perfect sorrow lively in him expressed. More than twenty several times the tears gushed out abundantly, dropped down marvellously from his fatherly face. They which were present do testify, that they never saw in any child more tears, than brast out from him at that time, all the sermon while; but specially when he recited his prayer before the people. It is marvellous what commiseration and pity moved all men's hearts, that beheld so heavy a countenance and such abundance of tears in an old man of so reverend dignity. *[marginal: The tears of the archbishop.]*

Cole, after he had ended his sermon, called back the people that were ready to depart, to prayers. "Brethren," said he, "lest any man should doubt of this man's earnest conversion and repentance, you shall hear him speak before you; and therefore I pray you, Master Cranmer, that you will now perform that you promised not long ago, namely, that you would openly express the true and undoubted profession of your faith, that you may take away all suspicion from men, and that all men may understand that you are a catholic in deed." "I will do it" (said the archbishop), "and with a good will;" who by and by rising up, and putting off his cap, began to speak thus unto the people:

Cranmer required to declare his faith.

Cranmer willing to declare his faith.

The words of the archbishop to the people.

"I desire you, well-beloved brethren in the Lord, that you will pray to God for me, to forgive me my sins, which above all men, both in number and greatness, I have committed; but among all the rest, there is one offence, which of all at this time doth vex and trouble me, whereof in process of my talk you shall hear more in his proper place:" and then, putting his hand into his bosom, he drew forth his prayer, which he recited to the people in this sense.

THE PRAYER OF DOCTOR CRANMER, ARCHBISHOP OF CANTERBURY, AT HIS DEATH.

The prayer of the archbishop.

GOOD christian people, my dearly beloved brethren and sisters in Christ, I beseech you most heartily to pray for me to Almighty God, that he will forgive me all my sins and offences, which be many without number, and great above measure. But yet one thing grieveth my conscience more than all the rest, whereof, God willing, I intend to speak more hereafter. But how great and how many soever my sins be, I beseech you to pray God of his mercy to pardon and forgive them all." And here, kneeling down, he said: "O Father of Heaven: O Son of God, Redeemer of the world: O Holy Ghost, three persons and one God, have mercy upon me, most wretched caitiff and miserable sinner. I have offended, both against heaven and earth, more than my tongue can express. Whither then may I go, or whither should I fly? To heaven I may be ashamed to lift up mine eyes, and in earth I find no place of refuge or succour. To thee therefore, O Lord, do I run: to thee do I humble myself, saying: O Lord, my God, my sins be great, but yet have mercy upon me for thy great mercy. The great mystery, that God became man, was not wrought for little or few offences. Thou didst not give thy Son, O heavenly Father, unto death for small sins only, but for all the greatest sins of the world, so that the sinner return to thee with his whole heart, as I do here at this present. Wherefore, have mercy on me, O God, whose property is always to have mercy; have mercy upon me, O Lord, for thy great mercy. I crave nothing, O Lord, for mine own merits, but for thy name's sake, that it may be hallowed thereby, and for thy dear Son Jesus Christ's sake: and now therefore, Our Father of heaven, hallowed be thy name," &c.

And then he rising said:

The last words of exhortation of the archbishop to the people.

"Every man, good people, desireth at that time of their death to give some good exhortation, that other may remember the same before their death, and be the better thereby: so I beseech God grant me grace, that I may speak something at this my departing, whereby God may be glorified, and you edified.

Exhortation to contempt of the world.

"First, it is an heavy case to see that so many folk be so much doted upon the love of this false world, and so careful for it, that of the love of God or the world to come they seem to care very little or nothing. Therefore this shall be my first exhortation, that you set not your minds overmuch upon this glosing world, but upon God and upon the world to come; and to learn to know what this lesson meaneth, which St John teacheth, 'That the love of this world is hatred against God.'

"The second exhortation is, that next, under God, you obey your king and queen willingly and gladly, without murmuring or grudging; not for fear of them only, but much more for the fear of God: knowing that they be God's ministers, appointed by God to rule and govern you; and therefore, whosoever resisteth them, resisteth the ordinance of God. *Exhortation to obedience.*

"The third exhortation is, that you love altogether like brethren and sisters. For, alas! pity it is to see what contention and hatred one christian man beareth to another, not taking each other as brother and sister, but rather as strangers and mortal enemies. But, I pray you, learn and bear well away this one lesson, to do good unto all men, as much as in you lieth, and to hurt no man, no more than you would hurt your own natural loving brother or sister. For this you may be sure of, that whosoever hateth any person, and goeth about maliciously to hinder or hurt him, surely, and without all doubt, God is not with that man, although he think himself never so much in God's favour. *Exhortation to brotherly love.*

"The fourth exhortation shall be to them that have great substance and riches of this world, that they will well consider and weigh three sayings of the scripture. *Exhortation to rich men of this world, moving them to charitable alms.*

"One is of our Saviour Christ himself, who saith: 'It is hard for a rich man to enter into the kingdom of heaven.' A sore saying, and yet spoken of him that knoweth the truth. *Luke xviii.*

"The second is of St John, whose saying is this: 'He that hath the substance of this world, and seeth his brother in necessity, and shutteth up his mercy from him, how can he say that he loveth God?' *1 John iii.*

"The third is of St James, who speaketh to the covetous rich man after this manner: 'Weep you and howl for the misery that shall come upon you: your riches do rot, your clothes be moth-eaten, your gold and silver doth canker and rust, and their rust shall bear witness against you, and consume you like fire: you gather a hoard or treasure of God's indignation against the last day.' Let them that be rich, ponder well these three sentences: for if ever they had occasion to shew their charity, they have it now at this present, the poor people being so many, and victuals so dear. *James v.*

"And now, forasmuch as I am come to the last end of my life, whereupon hangeth all my life past, and all my life to come, either to live with my Master Christ for ever in joy, or else to be in pain for ever with wicked devils in hell, and see before mine eyes presently either heaven ready to receive me, or else hell ready to swallow me up; I shall therefore declare unto you my very faith, how I believe, without any colour or dissimulation: for now is no time to dissemble, whatsoever I have said or written in time past.

"First, I believe in God the Father Almighty, Maker of heaven and earth, &c. And I believe every article of the catholic faith, every word and sentence taught by our Saviour Jesus Christ, his apostles and prophets, in the new and old testament. *The archbishop declareth the true confession of his faith without all colour or dissembling.*

"And now I come to the great thing that so much troubleth my conscience more than any thing that ever I did or said in my whole life, and that is, the setting abroad of a writing contrary to the truth: which now here I renounce and refuse as things written with my hand contrary to the truth which I thought in my heart, and written for fear of death, and to save my life, if it might be; and that is, all such bills and papers which I have written or signed with my hand since my degradation; wherein I have written many things untrue. And forasmuch as my hand offended, writing contrary to my heart, my hand shall first be punished therefore: for, may I come to the fire, it shall be first burned. *The archbishop revoketh his former recantation, and repenteth the same.*

"And as for the pope, I refuse him as Christ's enemy and antichrist, with all his false doctrine.

"And as for the sacrament, I believe as I have taught in my book against the bishop of Winchester; the which my book teacheth so true a doctrine of the sacrament, that it shall stand at the last day before the judgment of God, where the papistical doctrine contrary thereto shall be ashamed to shew her face."

The archbishop refuseth the pope as Christ's enemy, and antichrist. The archbishop standeth to his book written against Winchester. The expectation of the papists deceived.

Here the standers by were all astonied, marvelled, were amazed, did look one upon another, whose expectation he had so notably deceived. Some began to admonish him of his recantation, and to accuse him of falsehood.

Briefly, it was a world to see the doctors beguiled of so great an hope. I think there was never cruelty more notably or better in time deluded and deceived. For it is not to be doubted but they looked for a glorious victory and a perpetual triumph by this man's retractation: who, as soon as they heard these things, began to let down their ears, to rage, fret, and fume; and so much the more, because they could not revenge their grief; for they could now no longer threaten or hurt him. For the most miserable man in the world can die but once: and whereas of necessity he must needs die that day, though the papists had been never so well pleased; now, being never so much offended with him, yet could he not be twice killed of them. And so, when they could do nothing else unto him, yet lest they should say nothing, they ceased not to object unto him his falsehood and dissimulation.

The papists in a great chafe against the archbishop.

Unto which accusation he answered: "Ah, my masters," quoth he, "do not you take it so. Always since I lived hitherto I have been a hater of falsehood, and a lover of simplicity, and never before this time have I dissembled:" and in saying this, all the tears that remained in his body appeared in his eyes. And when he began to speak more of the sacrament and of the papacy, some of them began to cry out, yelp, and bawl; and specially Cole cried out upon him, "Stop the heretic's mouth, and take him away."

Cranmer's answer to the papists.

And then Cranmer being pulled down from the stage, was led to the fire, accompanied with those friars, vexing, troubling, and threatening him most cruelly. "What madness," say they, "hath brought thee again into this error, by which thou wilt draw innumerable souls with thee into hell?" To whom he answered nothing, but directed all his talk to the people, saving that to one troubling him in the way he spake, and exhorted him to get him home to his study, and apply his book diligently, saying, "if he did diligently call upon God, by reading more he should get knowledge." But the other Spanish barker, raging and foaming, was almost out of his wits, always having this in his mouth: *Non fecisti?* "didst thou it not?"

Cranmer pulled down from the stage. Cranmer led to the fire.

But when he came to the place where the holy bishops and martyrs of God, Hugh Latimer and Ridley, were burnt before him for the confession of the truth, kneeling down, he prayed to God; and not long tarrying in prayers, putting off his garments to his shirt, he prepared himself to death. His shirt was made long down to his feet: his feet were bare: likewise his head, when both his caps were off, was so bare, that not one hair could be seen upon it: his beard was long and thick, covering his face with marvellous gravity. Such a countenance of gravity moved the hearts both of his friends and of his enemies.

The archbishop brought to the place of execution.

Then the Spanish friars, John and Richard, of whom mention was made before, began to exhort him and play their parts with him afresh, but with vain and lost labour: Cranmer, with steadfast purpose abiding in the profession of his doctrine, gave his hand to certain old men, and other that stood by, bidding them farewell. And when he had thought to have done so likewise to Ely, the said Ely drew back his hand and refused, saying, "it was not lawful to salute heretics, and specially

M. Ely refuseth to give his hand to the archbishop.

such a one as falsely returned unto the opinions that he had forsworn; and if he had known before that he would have done so, he would never have used his company so familiarly:" and chid those sergeants and citizens, which had not refused to give him their hands. This Ely was a priest lately made, and student in divinity, being then one of the fellows of Brazennose.

Then was an iron chain tied about Cranmer, whom when they perceived to be more steadfast than that he could be moved from his sentence, they commanded the fire to be set unto him. And when the wood was kindled, and the fire began to burn near him, stretching out his arm, he put his right hand into the flame: which he held so steadfast and immoveable, (saving that once with the same hand he wiped his face,) that all men might see his hand burned before his body was touched. His body did so abide the burning of the flame, with such constancy and steadfastness, that standing always in one place without moving of his body, he seemed to move no more than the stake to which he was bound: his eyes were lifted up into heaven, and oftentimes he repeated, his "unworthy right hand," so long as his voice would suffer him: and using often the words of Stephen, "Lord Jesus, receive my spirit," in the greatness of the flame, he gave up the ghost. *The archbishop tied to the stake. Cranmer putteth his right hand, which subscribed, first into the fire. The last words of Cranmer at his death.*

This fortitude of mind, which perchance is rare and not used among the Spaniards, when friar John saw, thinking it came not of fortitude but of desperation, (although such manner examples, which are of the like constancy, have been common here in England,) ran to the lord Williams of Thame, crying that "the archbishop was vexed in mind, and died in great desperation." But he which was not ignorant of the archbishop's constancy, being unknown to the Spaniards, smiled only, and, as it were, by silence rebuked the friar's folly. *The friar's lying report of Cranmer.*

And this was the end of this learned archbishop, whom, lest by evil subscribing he should have perished, by well recanting God preserved; and lest he should have lived longer with shame and reproof, it pleased God rather to take him away, to the glory of his name and profit of his church. So good was the Lord both to his church in fortifying the same with the testimony and blood of such a martyr: and
  so good also to the man, with this cross of tribulation to purge his offences
    in this world, not only of his recantation, but also of his standing
      against John Lambert, and M. Allen, or if there were any other
        with whose burning and blood his hands had been before
          any thing polluted. But especially he had to rejoice that,
            dying in such a cause, he was to be numbered
              amongst Christ's martyrs, much more worthy
                the name St Thomas of Canterbury
                  than he whom the pope
                    falsely before did
                      canonize.

The end of Cranmer's life, Archb. of Cant.

The following is the list of Archbishop Cranmer's writings, extracted from Bishop Tanner's Bibliotheca:

SCRIPSIT *A Preface to the English Translation of the Bible,* Strype in *Vita Cranmer.* App. p. 241. *A catechism of christian doctrine,* MDXLVIII. by Gualter Lynn. Tempore Edw. VI. typis vulgavit in 8vo. *Instruction into the christian religion,* Pr. epist. "It is not unknown unto the hole." Idem hic liber cum *Catechismo,* quia sæpe mentionem facit verborum, "good children." *The ordinances or appointments of the reformed church.* Hic liber fuit, *The Book of Common Prayer,* cum prefat. "There was never any thing." *A book of ordaining ministers.* Idem cum, *The form of ordination, &c.* A. MDL. *A book concerning the Eucharist, with Luther. Ecclesiastical Laws in the time of king Edward.* Hic liber est *Reformatio legum, &c.* a 32 delegatis composita, inter quos Cranmerus erat primarius. *A defence of the catholic doctrine,* Lib. v. Pr. pr. "Our Saviour Christ Jesus, according to the will." London, MDL. 4to. Emdæ MDLVII. 8vo. Latine per Joh. Chekum, cui Archiepiscopus Latinam præfationem addidit ded. regi Edw. VI. pro cura dominici gregis, Lond. MDLIII. Vide hac versione Hospinian. *Histor. Sacram.* par. II. p. 246. a. Transtulit hunc librum etiam Johannes Young, Cantabr. *The doctrine of the Lord's Supper,* Lib. I. *Against the error of transubstantiation,* Lib. I. *How Christ is present in the Lord's Supper,* Lib. I. *Concerning eating the Lord's Supper,* Lib. I. *Concerning the offering up of Christ,* Lib. I. Hæc sunt argumenta quinque librorum *Defensionis Catholicæ Doctrinæ, &c. Responsionem ad sophisticam Gardineri cavillationem contra veram doctrinam de corpore et sanguine Christi in eucharistia,* Lib. v. Anglice. Pr. "I thinke it good, gentle reader," Lond. MDLI. 4to. MDLXXX. fol. Et Latine per Joh. Fox. MS. penes Jo. Strype. Cui libro replicabat Steph. Gardiner sub nomine M. Ant. Constantii, cui etiam libro Cranmer respondere voluit, nisi mors prævenisset. Tres tamen libros responsorios contexuit, quorum duo priores Oxoniæ perierunt. *A book of christian homelies.* Est sc. prima pars homiliarum libri tempore Edw. VI. edit. *A book in answer to the calumnies of Richard Smith.* Pr. "I have now obtained." Lond. MDLI. 4to. MDLXXX. fol. *Confutations of unwritten verities; written against Rich. Smith's book* De Veritatibus non scriptis, qui liber Latine scriptus, sed nunquam, ut mihi quidem videtur, in ea lingua impressus fuit. Pr. translationis, "Ye shal put nothyng to the word." Anglice per E.P. cum prefatione doctissima, Lond. MDLXXXII. 4to. *Twelve books of common places taken out of the doctors, concerning the unlawfulness of marrying the brother's wife,* Lib. II. Hic liber primus esse videtur, quem jussu regis Hen. VIII. conscripsit. In MS. Cotton. Vespas. B. 5. sunt articuli xii., ex quibus demonstratur divortium inter Hen. VIII. et reginam Catharinam necessario esse faciendum. Pr. "Affinitas." *Against the pope's supremacy,* Lib. II. Hæc forte fuit declaratio episcoporum, A. MDXXXVI. contra suprematum papæ, et contra Poli *Ecclesiasticam unionem Against the pope's purgatory,* Lib. II. *Concerning justification,* Lib. II. Hi duo ultimi videntur esse tractatus hujus argumenti ad finem libri, *The institution of a christian man. Pious prayers,* Lib. I. forte orarium sive libellus precationum a rege et clero editus, A. MDXLV. *Against the sacrifice of Mass; and against the adoration of the bread,* Lib. I. Scriptus hic liber in carcere, et videtur esse pars prima *Responsi ad Gardinerum,* sub nomine *Constantii.* XII *Questions about alms, fasting, the mass, &c.* by archb. Cranmer, MS. C. C. C. Cantabr. Misc. B. p. 231. *His declaration concerning the slanderous reports of his setting up mass again,* Ibid. p. 321. et Strype in *Vita Cranmer.* p. 305. Pr. "As the devil." *Disputationes Oxoniæ,* April. 16. MDLIV. Fox. p. 1430, seqq.

Submissiones et recantationes ejus VI. cum oratione ad populum ante mortem. Vis. et exam. per Edm. episc. London. Extant Angl. et Latine London MDLVI. 4to. *Protestationem contra jurisdictionem episcopi Romani.* Extat in *Concil. M. Brit. et Hib.* Vol. III. p. 757. *Mandatum de festo S. Marci evangelistæ celebrando.* Ibid. p. 826. *Aliud de non celebrandis festis diebus in concil. provinc. abrogatis.* Ibid. p. 827. *Literam commissionalem Rich. episcopo Dovor.* Ibid. p. 828. seq. et Strype in *Vita Cranmer. App.* p. 41. *Injunctions given to the diocese of Hereford.* Ibid. p. 843. *Mandatum de nominibus beneficiatorum et beneficiorum.* Ibid. p. 857. *Statutum de numero procuratorum curiæ Cant. confirmatum a T. C.* Ibid. p. 858. seq. *Constitutionem de moderato apparatu escarum.* Ibid. p. 862. *Mandatum pro orationibus pro cessatione pluviæ.* Ibid. p. 868. *Epistolas varias.* 1. M. Bucero post mortem Fagii, MS. C. C. C. Cantabr. Miscell. II. p. 27. *Epistolæ duæ* ad M. Parkerum. Ibid. Miscell. I. 391. quarum una extat Strype in *Vita Parker,* p. 28. *Epistola Lat.* Jo. Vadiano MDXXXVII., super controversia de cœna Domini orta. Strype in *Vita Cranm. App.* n. XXV. etiam edit. per *Colomesium,* Lond. MDCXCIV. 12mo. *Epistolæ* VI. extant ad finem *Responsionis ad Gardinerum,* Lond. MDLXXX. fol. *Epistolæ duæ* ad reginam, et altera ad doct. Martin, et Story ex carcere Oxon. Pr. primæ, "It may please your majesty." .... MDLVI. 8vo. *Epistola* ad Edwardum principem, Fox. 1395. *Epistola* ad consilium sacrum e carcere Oxon. Fox. 1464. *Epistolæ* XVII. Anglicæ et III. Latinæ extant apud Strype in *Vita Cranmer.* in *Append.* et in libro ipso VI. ejus *Epistolæ. Protestationem contra juramentum papæ præstitum,* Strype in *Vita Cranm.* Append. n. v. *Three discourses of faith, justification, and forgiveness of injuries, occasioned upon his review of the king's book, intitl.* The erudition of a christian man. Strype, *Cranm. App.* n. XXXI. Other discourses ; *De consolatione Christianorum contra metum mortis.* Item, *Exhortation to take adversity and sickness patiently.* Ibid. n. XXXII. *Answers to the XV articles of the rebells,* Devon. A. MDXLIX. Ibid. n. XL. *Notes for an homily against the rebellion.* Ibid. n. XLI. *Speech at the coronation of k. Edward,* Strype in *Vita Cranmer.* p. 144. *Articles in the visitation of the diocese of Canterbury,* A. 2. Edw. VI. Pr. "First whether parsons, vicars." Extant in *Collect. canon.* Sparrow Bal. VIII. 90. H. Holland. *Herool.* p. 161.

A fuller account of the writings of Cranmer, with the list of those printed in Dr Jenkyns's edition, will be given with the biographical memoir in the other volume of this collection.

AN ANSWER

UNTO

A CRAFTY AND SOPHISTICAL CAVILLATION,

DEVISED BY

STEPHEN GARDINER,

DOCTOR OF LAW, LATE BISHOP OF WINCHESTER,

AGAINST THE TRUE AND GODLY DOCTRINE OF THE MOST HOLY
SACRAMENT OF THE BODY AND BLOOD OF OUR
SAVIOUR JESUS CHRIST.

BY THE REVEREND FATHER IN GOD

THOMAS CRANMER,

ARCHBISHOP OF CANTERBURY, PRIMATE OF ALL ENGLAND, AND METROPOLITAN.

AN AVNSVVER
BY THE REVEREND FATHER
in God *Thomas* Archbyshop of Canterbury,

Primate of all England and Metropolitane,

Vnto a craftie and Sophisticall cauillation, deuised by

Stephen Gardiner Doctour of Law, late Byshop of Winchester

agaynst the true and godly doctrine of the most holy

Sacrament, of the body and bloud of our

Sauiour *IESV CHRIST.*

Wherein is also, as occasion serueth, aunswered such places of the booke of Doct. Richard Smith, as may seeme any thyng worthy the aunsweryng.

Here is also the true Copy of the booke written, and in open Court deliuered, by D. Stephen Gardiner, not one word added or diminished, but faythfully in all pointes agreeyng with the Originall.

Reuised, and corrected by the sayd Archbyshop at Oxford before his Martyrdome: Wherein hee hath beautified Gardiner's doynges, with asmuch diligence as might be, by applying Notes in the Margent, and markes to the Doctours saying: which before wanted in the first Impression.

Hereunto is prefixed the discourse of the sayd Archbyshops lyfe, and Martyrdome, briefly collected out of his Hystory of the Actes and Monumentes, and in the end is added certaine Notes, wherein Gardiner varied, both from him selfe, and other Papistes, gathered by the sayd Archbyshop.

☞ Read with Iudgement, and conferre with diligence, laying aside all affection on either partie, and thou shalt easely perceaue (good Reader) how slender and weake the allegations and perswasions of the Papistes are, wherewith they goe about to defende their erroneous and false doctrine, and to impugne the truth. Anno. M.D.LI.

AT LONDON
Printed by Iohn Daye, dwellyng ouer Al-

dersgate beneath S. Martines.

Anno. 1 5 8 0.

Cum gratia & Priuilegio,
Regiæ Maiestatis.

A PREFACE TO THE READER.

[Prefixed to the edition of 1551.]

I THINK it good, gentle reader, here in the beginning, to admonish thee of certain words and kinds of speeches, which I do use sometimes in this mine answer to the late bishop of Winchester's book, lest in mistaking thou do as it were stumble at them.

First, this word "sacrament" I do sometimes use (as it is many times taken among writers and holy doctors) for the sacramental bread, water, or wine; as when they say, that *sacramentum est sacræ rei signum*, "a sacrament is the sign of an holy thing." But where I use to speak sometimes (as the old authors do) that Christ is in the sacraments, I mean the same as they did understand the matter; that is to say, not of Christ's carnal presence in the outward sacrament, but sometimes of his sacramental presence. And sometime by this word "sacrament" I mean the whole ministration and receiving of the sacraments, either of baptism, or of the Lord's supper: and so the old writers many times do say, that Christ and the Holy Ghost be present in the sacraments; not meaning by that manner of speech, that Christ and the Holy Ghost be present in the water, bread, or wine, (which be only the outward visible sacraments,) but that in the due ministration of the sacraments according to Christ's ordinance and institution, Christ and his holy Spirit be truly and indeed present by their mighty and sanctifying power, virtue, and grace, in all them that worthily receive the same. [Sacrament.] [*Matt. xxviii.]

Moreover, when I say and repeat many times in my book, that the body of Christ is present in them that worthily receive the sacrament; lest any man should mistake my words, and think that I mean, that although Christ be not corporally in the outward visible signs, yet he is corporally in the persons that duly receive them, this is to advertise the reader, that I mean no such thing; but my meaning is, that the force, the grace, the virtue and benefit of Christ's body that was crucified for us, and of his blood that was shed for us, be really and effectually present with all them that duly receive the sacraments: but all this I understand of his spiritual presence, of the which he saith, "I will be with you until the world's end;" and, "wheresoever two or three be gathered together in my name, there am I in the midst of them;" and, "he that eateth my flesh and drinketh my blood, dwelleth in me, and I in him." Nor no more truly is he corporally or really present in the due ministration of the Lord's supper, than he is in the due ministration of baptism; [that is to say, in both spiritually by grace. And wheresover in the scripture it is said that Christ, God, or the Holy Ghost is in any man, the same is understood spiritually by grace.][1] [Christ's presence in the godly receiver.] [Matt. vi.] [Matt. xviii.] [John vi.]

The third thing to admonish the reader of is this, that when I name Doctor Stephen Gardiner bishop of Winchester[2], I mean not that he is so now; but foras- [The naming of the late bishop of Winchester.]

[N.B.—Wherever the asterisk is placed in the margin, it is to signify that the side-note only occurs in the edition of 1580. The figures in the margin denote the paging of the edition of 1580.]

[1 This passage is only found in the edition of 1580.]

[2 Gardiner had been virtually deprived of his bishoprick Feb. 14, 1550.; (Strype. Memorials of Cranmer, Vol. I. p. 322. Oxford ed. 1840.) but the positive deprivation did not take place till April 18, in the same year.—(Burnet. His. of Reformation, Vol. II. p. 340. Oxford ed. 1829.) The sentence itself is preserved in Foxe's Acts and Monuments, Vol. II. pp. 738, 9, ed. 1631.]

much as he was bishop of Winchester at the time when he wrote his book against me, therefore I answer his book as written by the bishop of Winchester, which else needed greatly none answer for any great learning or substance of matter that is in it.

<small>The real presence of Christ should prove no transubstantiation of the bread and wine.</small>

The last admonition to the reader is this, where the said late bishop thinketh that he hath sufficiently proved transubstantiation, (that is to say, that the substance of bread and wine cannot be in the sacrament, if the body and blood of Christ were there, because two bodies cannot be together in one place,) although the truth be, that in the sacrament of Christ's body there is corporally but the substance of bread only, and in the sacrament of the blood the substance of wine only, yet how far he is deceived, and doth vary from the doctrine of other papists, and also from the principles of philosophy (which he taketh for the foundation of his doctrine in this point), the reader hereby may easily perceive. For if we speak of God's power, the papists affirm, that by God's power two bodies may be together in one place, and then why may not Christ's blood be with the wine in the cup, and his flesh in the same place where the substance of the bread is? And if we consider the cause wherefore two bodies cannot be together in one place by the rules of nature, it shall evidently appear, that the body of Christ may rather be in one place with the substance of the bread, than with the accidents thereof, and so likewise his blood with the wine. For the natural cause wherefore two bodies cannot be together in one place (as the philosophers say) is their accidents, their bigness, and thickness, and not their substances. And then by the very order of nature it repugneth more, that the body of Christ should be present with the accidents of bread, and his blood with the accidents of wine, than with the substances either of bread or wine. This shall suffice for the admonition to the reader, joining thereto the preface in my first book, which is this:

A PREFACE TO THE READER.

[Prefixed to the original edition of the "Defence of the True and Catholick Doctrine of the Sacrament," 1550.]

OUR Saviour Christ Jesus, according to the will of his eternal Father, when the time thereto was fully accomplished, taking our nature upon him, came into this world from the high throne of his Father, to declare unto miserable sinners good news, to heal them that were sick, to make the blind to see, the deaf to hear, and the dumb to speak, to set prisoners at liberty, to shew that the time of grace and mercy was come, to give light to them that were in darkness and in the shadow of death, and to preach and give pardon and full remission of sin to all his elected. And to perform the same he made a sacrifice and oblation of his own body upon the cross, which was a full redemption, satisfaction, and propitiation for the sins of the whole world. And to commend this his sacrifice unto all his faithful people, and to confirm their faith and hope of eternal salvation in the same, he hath ordained a perpetual memory of his said sacrifice, daily to be used in the church to his perpetual laud and praise, and to our singular comfort and consolation; that is to say, the celebration of his holy supper, wherein he doth not cease to give himself, with all his benefits, to all those that duly receive the same supper according to his blessed ordinance. But the Romish antichrist, to deface this great benefit of Christ, hath[1] that his sacrifice upon the cross is not sufficient hereunto, without any other[2] sacrifice devised by him, and made by the priest, or else without indulgences, beads, pardons, pilgrimages, and such other pelfray, to supply Christ's imperfection: and that christian people cannot apply to themselves the benefits of Christ's passion, but that the same is in the distribution of the bishop of Rome; or else that by Christ we have no full remission, but be delivered only from sin, and yet remaineth temporal pain in purgatory due for the same, to be remitted after this life by the Romish antichrist and his ministers, who take upon them to do for us that thing, which Christ either would not or could not do. O heinous blasphemy and most detestable injury against Christ! O wicked abomination in the temple of God! O pride intolerable of antichrist, and most manifest token of the son of perdition, extolling himself above God, and with Lucifer exalting his seat and power above the throne of God! For he that taketh upon him to supply that thing which he pretendeth to be unperfect in Christ, must needs make himself above Christ, and so very antichrist. For what is this else, but to be against Christ, and to bring him in contempt, as one that either for lack of charity would not, or for lack of power he could not, with all his bloodshedding and death, clearly deliver his faithful, and give them full remission of their sins, but that the full perfection thereof must be had at the hands of antichrist of Rome and his ministers? What man of knowledge and zeal to God's honour can with dry eyes see this injury to Christ, and look upon the estate of religion brought in by the papists, perceiving the true sense of God's words subverted by false glosses of man's devising, the true christian religion turned into certain hypo-

*The erroneous doctrine of the papists obscuring the same.

*The state of religion brought in by the papists.

[1 hath taught. Ed. 1551.]   [2 another, 1551.]

critical and superstitious sects, the people praying with their mouths, and hearing with their ears, they wist not what, and so ignorant in God's word, that they could not discern the hypocrisy and superstition from true and sincere religion? This was of late years the face of religion within this realm of England, and yet remaineth in divers realms. But thanks be to Almighty God and to the king's majesty, with his father, a prince of most famous memory! the superstitious sects of monks and friars, that were in this realm, be clean taken away; the scripture is restored unto the proper and true understanding; the people may daily read and hear God's heavenly word, and pray in their own language which they understand, so that their hearts and mouths may go together, and be none of those people whom[1] Christ complained, saying: "These people honour me with their lips, but their hearts be far from me." Thanks be to God! many corrupt weeds be plucked up, which were wont to rot the flock of Christ, and to let the growing of the Lord's harvest.

Matt. xv.

But what availeth it to take away beads, pardons, pilgrimages, and such other like popery, so long as two chief roots remain unpulled up? whereof, so long as they remain, will spring again all former impediments of the Lord's harvest, and corruption of his flock. The rest is but branches and leaves, the cutting away whereof is but like topping and lopping of a tree, or cutting down of weeds, leaving the body standing and the roots in the ground; but the very body of the tree, or rather the roots of the weeds, is the popish doctrine of transubstantiation, of the real presence of Christ's flesh and blood in the sacrament of the altar (as they call it), and of the sacrifice and oblation of Christ made by the priest, for the salvation of the quick and the dead. Which roots if they be suffered to grow in the Lord's vineyard, they will overspread all the ground again with the old errors and superstitions. These injuries to Christ be so intolerable, that no christian heart can willingly bear them. Wherefore, seeing that many have set to their hands, and whetted their tools, to pluck up the weeds, and to cut down the tree of error, I, not knowing otherwise how to excuse myself at the last day, have in this book set to my hand and axe with the rest, to cut down this tree, and to pluck up the weeds and plants by the roots, which our heavenly Father never planted, but were grafted and sown in his vineyard by his adversary the devil, and antichrist his minister. The Lord grant, that this my travail and labour in his vineyard be not in vain, but that it may prosper and bring forth good fruits to his honour and glory! For when I see his vineyard overgrown with thorns, brambles and weeds, I know that everlasting woe apperteineth unto me, if I hold my peace, and put not to my hands and tongue to labour in purging his vineyard. God I take to witness, who seeth the hearts of all men thoroughly unto the bottom, that I take this labour for none other consideration, but for the glory of his name, and the discharge of my duty, and the zeal that I bear toward the flock of Christ. I know in what office God hath placed me, and to what purpose; that is to say, to set forth his word truly unto his people, to the uttermost of my power, without respect of person, or regard of thing in the world, but of him alone. I know what account I shall make to him hereof at the last day, when every man shall answer for his vocation, and receive for the same good or ill, according as he hath done. I know how antichrist hath obscured the glory of God, and the true knowledge of his word, overcasting the same with mists and clouds of error and ignorance through false glosses and interpretations. It pitieth me to see the simple and hungry flock of Christ led into corrupt pastures, to be carried blindfold they know not whither, and to be fed with poison in the stead of wholesome meats. And moved by the duty,

The chief roots of all errors.

What moved the author to write.

[1 of whom, 1551.]

office, and place, whereunto it hath pleased God to call me, I give warning in his [*A warning given by the author. Jer. li. Rev. xiv. xvii. xviii. Matt. xi.] name unto all that profess Christ, that they flee far from Babylon, if they will save their souls, and to beware of that great harlot, that is to say, the pestiferous see of Rome, that she make you not drunk with her pleasant wine. Trust not her sweet promises, nor banquet not with her; for instead of wine she will give you sour dregs, and for meat she will feed you with rank poison. But come to our Redeemer and Saviour Christ, who refresheth all that truly come unto him, be their anguish and heaviness never so great. Give credit unto him, in whose mouth was never found [*Isai. liii. Pet. ii.] guile nor untruth. By him you shall be clearly delivered from all your diseases, of him you shall have full remission *a pœna et a culpa*. He it is that feedeth continually all that belong unto him, with his own flesh that hanged upon the cross, and giveth them drink of the blood flowing out of his own side, and maketh to spring within them water that floweth unto everlasting life. Listen not to the false incantations, sweet whisperings, and crafty juggling[2] of the subtle papists, wherewith they have this many years deluded and bewitched the world; but hearken to Christ, give ear unto his words, which lead[3] you the right way unto everlasting life, there with him to live ever as heirs of his kingdom.
AMEN.

JOHN VI.

It is the spirit that giveth life, the flesh profiteth nothing.

[2 jugglings, 1551.]   [3 shall lead, 1551.]

I. PARKHURSTI.*

Accipe præclarum, Lector studiose, libellum,
  Quem tibi Cranmerus scripserat ante rogos.
Hic docta sanctam tractat ratione synaxin,
  Insistens, Patres quas docuere, viis.
Hic, Gardnere, tuas phaleratas detegit artes,
  Detrahit et larvam, sæve tyranne, tuam:
Atque tuo ipsius jugulum transverberat ense,
  Ut jaceas veluti sensibus absque fera.
Denique rixosis hic obstruit ora Papistis,
  Rixandi posset si tamen esse modus.
Solvitur in cineres corpus, mens scandit ad astra;
  Fama superstes erit tempus in omne memor.

[* These verses are only in the edition of 1580.]

A CRAFTY AND SOPHISTICAL CAVILLATION,

DEVISED BY
M. STEPHEN GARDINER,
DOCTOR OF LAW, LATE BISHOP OF WINCHESTER,

AGAINST THE TRUE AND GODLY DOCTRINE OF THE MOST HOLY SACRAMENT OF THE BODY AND BLOOD OF OUR SAVIOUR CHRIST (CALLED BY HIM "AN EXPLICATION AND ASSERTION THEREOF"), WITH AN ANSWER UNTO THE SAME, MADE BY THE MOST REVEREND FATHER IN GOD, THOMAS ARCHBISHOP OF CANTERBURY, PRIMATE OF ALL ENGLAND AND METROPOLITAN.

THE TITLE OF THE BOOK OF STEPHEN GARDINER,
LATE BISHOP OF WINCHESTER:

AN EXPLICATION AND ASSERTION OF THE TRUE CATHOLIC FAITH, TOUCHING THE MOST BLESSED SACRAMENT OF THE ALTAR, WITH CONFUTATION OF A BOOK WRITTEN AGAINST THE SAME.[1]

THE ANSWER OF THOMAS ARCHBISHOP OF CANTERBURY, &c.

HERE before the beginning of your book you have prefixed a goodly title; but it agreeth with the argument and matter thereof, as water agreeth with the fire. For your book is so far from an explication and assertion of the true catholic faith in the matter of the sacrament, that it is but a crafty cavillation and subtle sophistication, to obscure the truth thereof, and to hide the same, that it should not appear. And in your whole book, the reader (if he mark it well) shall easily perceive, how little learning is shewed therein, and how few authors you have alleged, other than such as I brought forth in my book, and made answer unto: but there is shewed what may be done by fine wit and new devices to deceive the reader, and by false interpretations to avoid the plain words of scripture and of the old authors.

Wherefore, inasmuch as I purpose, God willing, in this defence of my former book, not only to answer you, but by the way also to touch D. Smith,[2] two things I would wish in you both: the one is truth with simplicity; the other is, that either of you both had so much learning as you think you have, or else that you thought of yourself no more than you have in deed. But to answer both your books in few words: the one sheweth nothing else, but what railing without reason or learning, the other what frowardness armed with wit and eloquence, be able to do against the truth. And Smith, because he would be vehement, and shew his heat in the manner of speech, where the matter is cold, hath framed in a manner all his sentences throughout his whole book by interrogations. But if the reader of both your books do no more, but diligently read over my book once again, he shall find the same not so slenderly made, but that I have foreseen all that could be said to the contrary; and that I have fully answered beforehand all that you both have said, or is able to say.

2.

[1 "Made by Stephen, bishop of Winchester,— and exhibited by his own hand for his defence to the King's Majesty's Commissioners at Lambeth." Original edition.]

[2 Dr Smith's book was set forth under this title: "A confutation of the true and Catholic Doctrine, &c."—Strype, Memorials of Cranmer. p. 1089. Oxford edition, 1840. App. lxi. p. 900.]

WINCHESTER.

Forasmuch as among other mine allegations for defence of myself in this matter, moved against me by occasion of my sermon[1] made before the king's most excellent majesty, touching partly the catholic faith of the most precious sacrament of the altar, which I see now impugned by a book set forth under the name of my lord of Canterbury's grace; I have thought expedient for the better opening of the matter, and considering I am by name touched in the said book, the rather to utter partly that I have to say by confutation of that book; wherein I think nevertheless not requisite to direct any speech by special name to the person of him that is entitled author, because it may possibly be that his name is abused, wherewith to set forth the matter, being himself of such dignity and authority in the commonwealth, as for that respect should be inviolable. For which consideration, I shall in my speech of such reproof as the untruth of the matter necessarily requireth, omitting the special title of the author of the book, speak only of the author in general, being a thing to me greatly to be marvelled at, that such matter should now be published out of my lord of Canterbury's pen; but because he is a man, I will not wonder, and because he is such a man, I will reverently use him, and forbearing further to name him, talk only of the author by that general name.

*I would as much as may be do my due to the matter and him also.

CANTERBURY.

The craft of Winchester in the beginning.

The first entry of your book sheweth to them that be wise, what they may look for in the rest of the same, except the beginning vary from all that followeth. Now the beginning is framed with such sleight and subtlety, that it may deceive the reader notably in two things: the one, that he should think you were called into judgment before the king's majesty's commissioners at Lambeth[2] for your catholic faith in the sacrament; the other, that you made your book for your defence therein, which be both utterly untrue. For your book was made or ever ye were called before the said commissioners; and after you were called, then you altered only two lines in the beginning of your book, and made that beginning which it hath now. This am I able to prove, as well otherwise, as by a book which I have of your own hand-writing, wherein appeareth plainly the alteration of the beginning.

And as concerning the cause wherefore ye were called before the commissioners, whereas by your own importune suit and procurement, and as it were enforcing the matter, you were called to justice for your manifest contempt and continual disobedience from time to time, or rather rebellion against the king's majesty, and were justly deprived of your estate for the same, you would turn it now to a matter of the sacrament, that the world should think your trouble rose for your faith in the sacrament; which was no matter nor occasion thereof, nor no such matter was objected against you, wherefore you need to make any such defence. And where you would make that matter the occasion of your worthy deprivation and punishment, (which was no cause thereof,) and cloke your wilful obstinacy and disobedience (which was the only cause thereof), all men of judgment may well perceive, that you could mean no goodness thereby, neither to the king's majesty, nor to his realm.

3.

But as touching the matter now in controversy, I impugn not the true catholic faith which was taught by Christ and his apostles (as you say I do), but I impugn the false papistical faith, invented, devised, and imagined by antichrist and his ministers.

And as for further forbearing of my name, and talking of the author in general (after that you have named me once, and your whole book is directed against my book, openly set out in my name), all men may judge that your doing herein is not for reverence to be used unto me, but that by suppressing of my name, you may the more unreverently and unseemly use your scoffing, taunting, railing, and defaming of the author in general; and yet shall every man understand that your speech is directed to me in especial, as well as if you had appointed me with your finger. And

---

[1] Preached on St Peter's-day, June 29, 1548, which he "chose, because the gospel agreed to his purpose." The causes of accusation against him are set forth in Burnet's Hist. Reform. Vol. II. p. 340. Vol. III. p. 379. Oxford ed. 1829. See Foxe's Acts and Monuments, Vol. II. p. 726, ed. 1631.]

[2 See p. 3, note 2.]

your reverent using of yourself, before the king's highness' commissioners of late, doth plainly declare what reverent respect you have to them that be in dignity and authority in the commonwealth.

WINCHESTER.

This author denieth the real presence of Christ's most precious body and blood in the sacrament. * The sum of the book.

This author denieth transubstantiation.

This author denieth evil men to eat and drink the body and blood of Christ in the sacrament.

These three denials only impugn and tend to destroy that faith, which this author termeth the popish to err in, calling now all popish that believe either of these three articles by him denied, the truth whereof shall hereafter be opened.

Now, because faith affirmeth some certainty: if we ask this author, what is his faith which he calleth true and catholic, it is only this, as we may learn by his book, that in our Lord's supper be consecrate bread and wine, and delivered as tokens only to signify Christ's body and blood: he calleth them holy tokens, but yet noteth that the bread and wine be never the holier: he saith nevertheless they be not bare tokens, and yet concludeth, Christ not to be spiritually present in them, but only as a thing is present in that which signifieth it (which is the nature of a bare token), saying in another place, there is nothing to be worshipped, for there is nothing present but in figure and in a sign: which whosoever saith, calleth the thing in deed absent. And yet the author saith, Christ is in the man that worthily receiveth, spiritually present, who eateth of Christ's flesh and his blood reigning in heaven, whither the good believing man ascendeth by his faith: and as our body is nourished with the bread and wine received in the supper, so the true believing man is fed with the body and blood of Christ. And this is the sum of the doctrine of that faith, which this author calleth the true catholic faith. * Because the author pretendeth a defence of the catholic faith, it were reason to know what it is. *The effect of that this author calleth his faith. *Untrue report.

CANTERBURY.

I desire the reader to judge my faith not by this short, envious, and untrue collection and report, but by mine own book, as it is at length set out in the first part, from the 8th unto the 16th chapter.

And as concerning holiness[a] of bread and wine (whereunto I may add the water in baptism) how can a dumb or an insensible and lifeless creature receive into itself any food, and feed thereupon? No more is it possible that a spiritless creature should receive any spiritual sanctification or holiness. And yet do I not utterly deprive the outward sacraments of the name of holy things, because of the holy use whereunto they serve, and not because of any holiness that lieth hid in the insensible creature. Which although they have no holiness in them, yet they be signs and tokens of the marvellous works and holy effects, which God worketh in us by his omnipotent power. *Bread, wine, and water be not holy, but holy tokens.*

And they be no vain or bare tokens, as you would persuade, (for a bare token is that which betokeneth only and giveth nothing, as a painted fire, which giveth neither light nor heat;) but in the due ministration of the sacraments God is present, working with his word and sacraments. 4. *They be not bare tokens.*

And although (to speak properly) in the bread and wine be nothing in deed to be worshipped, yet in them that duly receive the sacraments is Christ himself inhabiting, and is of all creatures to be worshipped.

And therefore you gather of my sayings unjustly, that Christ is in deed absent; for I say (according to God's word and the doctrine of the old writers) that Christ is present in his sacraments, as they teach also that he is present in his word, when he worketh mightily by the same in the hearts of the hearers. By which manner of speech it is not meant that Christ is corporally present in the voice or sound of the speaker (which sound perisheth as soon as the words be spoken), but this speech meaneth that he worketh with his word, using the voice of the speaker, as his instrument to work by; as he useth also his sacraments, whereby he worketh, and therefore is said to be present in them. *Christ is present in his sacraments.*

[a the holiness, 1551.]

WINCHESTER.

*A catholic faith.
*This author's faith hath no point of a catholic faith.
*Untrue report.
Scripture in letter favoureth not this author's faith.

Now a catholic faith is an universal faith, taught and preached through all, and so received and believed, agreeable and consonant to the scriptures, testified by such as by all ages have in their writings given knowledge thereof, which be the tokens and marks of a true catholic faith, whereof no one can be found in the faith this author calleth catholic.

First, there is no scripture that in letter maintaineth the doctrine of this author's book. For Christ saith not that the bread doth only signify his body absent, nor St Paul saith not so in any place, nor any other canonical scripture declareth Christ's words so. As for the sense and understanding of Christ's words, there hath not been in any age any one approved and known learned man, that hath so declared and expounded Christ's words in his supper, that the bread did only signify Christ's body, and the wine his blood, as things absent.

CANTERBURY.

*My doctrine is catholic by your own description.

The first part of your description of a catholic faith is crafty and full of subtlety; for what you mean by "all" you do not express. The second part is very true, and agreeth fully with my doctrine in every thing, as well in the matter of transubstantiation, of the presence of Christ in the sacrament, and of the eating and drinking of him, as in the sacrifice propitiatory. For as I have taught in these four matters of controversy, so learned I the same of the holy scripture; so is it testified by all old writers and learned men of all ages; so was it universally taught and preached, received and believed, until the see of Rome, the chief adversary unto Christ, corrupted all together, and by hypocrisy and simulation in the stead of Christ erected antichrist; who, being the son of perdition, hath extolled and advanced himself, and sitteth in the temple of God, as he were God himself, loosing and binding at his pleasure, in heaven, hell, and earth; condemning, absolving, canonising, and damning, as to his judgment he thinketh good.

5.

But as concerning your doctrine of transubstantiation, of the real, corporal and natural presence of Christ's body in the bread, and blood in the wine; that ill men do eat his flesh and drink his blood; that Christ is many times offered; there is no scripture that in letter maintaineth any of them (as you require in a catholic faith), but the scripture in the letter doth maintain this my doctrine plainly, that the bread remaineth, *Panis quem frangimus, nonne communicatio corporis Christi est?* "Is not the bread which we break the communion of Christ's body?" And that evil men do not eat Christ's flesh, nor drink his blood; for the scripture saith expressly: "He that eateth my flesh and drinketh my blood, dwelleth in me and I in him," which is not true of ill men. And for the corporal absence of Christ, what can be more plainly said in the letter than he said of himself, "that he forsook the world?" besides other scriptures which I have alleged in my third book, the fourth chapter. And the scripture speaketh plainly in the Epistle to the Hebrews, that Christ was never more offered than once.

1 Cor. x.

John vi.

John xvi.

Heb. vii. ix. x.

Christ is spiritually present.

But here you take such a large scope, that you flee from the four proper matters that be in controversy, unto a new scope devised by you, that I should absolutely deny the presence of Christ, and say, that the bread doth only signify Christ's body absent; which thing I never said nor thought. And as Christ saith not so, nor Paul saith not so, even so likewise I say not so; and my book in divers places saith clean contrary, that Christ is with us spiritually present, is eaten and drunken of us, and dwelleth within us, although corporally he be departed out of this world, and is ascended up into heaven.

WINCHESTER.

An issue.

And to the intent every notable disagreement from the truth may the more evidently appear, I will here in this place (as I will hereafter likewise when the case occurreth) join as it were an issue with this author, that is to say, to make a stay with him in this point triable (as they say) by evidence and soon tried. For in this point the scriptures be already by the author brought forth, the letter whereof proveth not his faith. And albeit he travaileth and bringeth forth the saying of many approved writers, yet is there no one of them that writeth in express words the doctrine of that faith, which this author calleth the faith catholic. And to make the issue plain, and to join it directly, thus I say:

No author known and approved, that is to say, Ignatius, Polycarp, Justin, Irene, Tertullian, Cyprian, Chrysostom, Hilary, Gregory Nazianzen, Basil, Emissen, Ambrose, Cyril, Jerome, Augustine, Damascene, Theophylact, none of these hath this doctrine in plain terms, that the bread only signifieth Christ's body absent; nor this sentence, that the bread and wine be never the holier after consecration, nor that Christ's body is none otherwise present in the sacrament, but in a signification; nor this sentence, that the sacrament is not to be worshipped, because there is nothing present but in a sign. And herein what the truth is, may soon appear, as it shall by their works never appear to have been taught and preached, received and believed universally, and therefore can be called no catholic faith (that is to say) allowed in the whole, through and in outward teaching, preached and believed.

*No writer approved testifieth this author's faith.
*The sum of the issue.

*Outward teaching.

CANTERBURY.

In your issues you make me to say what you list, and take your issue where you list; and then if twelve false varlets pass with you, what wonder is it? But I will join with you this issue, that neither scripture nor ancient author writeth in express words the doctrine of your faith. And to make the issue plain, and to join directly with you therein, thus I say: that no ancient and catholic author hath your doctrine in plain terms. And because I will not take my issue in bye matters (as you do), I will make it in the four principal points, wherein we vary, and whereupon my book resteth.

Your doctrine is not catholic by your own description.

This therefore shall be mine issue: that as no scripture, so no ancient author known and approved, hath in plain terms your transubstantiation: nor that the body and blood of Christ be really, corporally, naturally, and carnally under the forms of bread and wine: nor that evil men do eat the very body and drink the very blood of Christ: nor that Christ is offered every day by the priest a sacrifice propitiatory for sin. Wherefore by your own description and rule of a catholic faith, your doctrine and teaching in these four articles cannot be good and catholic, except you can find it in plain terms in the scripture and old catholic doctors; which when you do, I will hold up my hand at the bar, and say, "guilty": and if you cannot, then it is reason that you do the like, *per legem talionis.*

6.
My issue.

WINCHESTER.

If this author, setting apart the word "catholic", would of his own wit go about to prove, howsoever scripture hath been understood hitherto, yet it should be understood indeed as he now teacheth, he hath herein divers disadvantages and hindrances worthy consideration, which I will particularly note.

First, the prejudice and sentence, given as it were by his own mouth against himself, now in the book called the Catechism in his name set forth.

Secondly, that about seven hundred years ago one Bertram (if the book set forth in his name be his) enterprised secretly the like, as appeareth by the said book, and yet prevailed not.

Thirdly, Berengarius, being indeed but an archdeacon, about five hundred years past, after he had openly attempted to set forth such like doctrine, recanted, and so failed in his purpose.

Fourthly, Wickliff, not much above an hundred years past, enterprised the same, whose teaching God prospered not.

Fifthly, how Luther in his works handled them that would have in our time raised up the same doctrine in Germany, it is manifest by his and their writings; whereby appeareth the enterprise that hath had so many overthrows, so many rebuts, so often reproofs, to be desperate, and such as God hath not prospered and favoured to be received at any time openly as his true teaching.

Herein whether I say true or no, let the stories try me; and it is matter worthy to be noted, because Gamaliel's observation written in the Acts of the Apostles is allowed to mark, how they prosper and go forward in their doctrine, that be authors of any new teaching.

*A notable matter, a man to be condemned by his own former writings.
*Bertram confessed to be of this opinion.

*This author's doctrine often rejected as false.

Acts v.

CANTERBURY.

I have not proved in my book my four assertions by mine own wit, but by the collation of holy scripture, and the sayings of the old holy catholic authors. And as for your five notes, you might have noted them against yourself, who by them have much more disadvantage and hindrance than I have.

My Catechism.

As concerning the Catechism by me set forth, I have answered in my fourth book, the eighth chapter, that ignorant men for lack of judgment and exercise in old authors mistake my said Catechism.

Bertram.

And as for Bertram, he did nothing else but, at the request of king Charles, set out the true doctrine of the holy catholic church, from Christ unto his time, concerning the sacrament. And I never heard nor read any man that condemned Bertram before this time; and therefore I can take no hindrance, but a great advantage at his hands: for all men that hitherto have written of Bertram, have much commended him. And seeing that he wrote of the sacrament at king Charles's request, it is not like that he would write against the received doctrine of the church in those days. And if he had, it is without all doubt that some learned man, either in his time or sithence, would have written against him, or at the least not have commended him so much as they have done.

7.

Berengarius.

Berengarius of himself had a godly judgment in this matter, but by the tyranny of Nicholas the Second he was constrained to make a devilish recantation, as I have declared in my first book, the seventeenth chapter.

Wickliff.

And as for John Wickliff, he was a singular instrument of God in his time to set forth the truth of Christ's gospel; but antichrist, that sitteth in God's temple boasting himself as God, hath by God's sufferance prevailed against many holy men, and sucked the blood of martyrs these late years.

Luther.

And as touching Martin Luther, it seemeth you be sore pressed, that be fain to pray aid of him, whom you have hitherto ever detested. The fox is sore hunted that is fain to take his burrow, and the wolf that is fain to take the lion's den for a shift, or to run for succour unto a beast which he most hateth. And no man condemneth your doctrine of transubstantiation, and of the propitiatory sacrifice of the mass, more severely and earnestly than doth Martin Luther.

The papists have been the cause why the catholic doctrine hath been hindered, and hath not had good success these late years.

But it appeareth by your conclusion, that you have waded so far in rhetorick, that you have forgotten your logic. For this is your argument: Bertram taught this doctrine and prevailed not; Berengarius attempted the same, and failed in his purpose; Wickliff enterprised the same, whose teaching God prospered not; therefore God hath not prospered and favoured it to be received at any time openly as his true teaching. I will make the like reason. The prophet Osea taught in Samaria to the ten tribes the true doctrine of God, to bring them from their abominable superstitions and idolatry: Joel, Amos, and Micheas attempted the same, whose doctrine prevailed not; God prospered not their teaching among those people, but they were condemned with their doctrine; therefore God hath not prospered and favoured it to be received at any time openly as his true teaching.

If you will answer (as you must needs do), that the cause why that among those people the true teaching prevailed not, was by reason of the abundant superstition and idolatry that blinded their eyes, you have fully answered your own argument, and have plainly declared the cause, why the true doctrine in this matter hath not prevailed these five hundred years, the church of Rome (which all that time hath borne the chief swing) being overflown and drowned in all kind of superstition and idolatry, and therefore might not abide to hear of the truth. And the true doctrine of the sacrament (which I have set out plainly in my book) was never condemned by no council, nor your false papistical doctrine allowed, until the devil caused antichrist his son and heir, Pope Nicholas the Second, with his monks and friars, to condemn the truth and confirm these your heresies.

And where of Gamaliel's words you make an argument of prosperous success in this matter, the scripture testifieth how antichrist shall prosper and prevail against saints no short while, and persecute the truth. And yet the counsel of Gamaliel was very discreet and wise. For he perceived that God went about the reformation of religion grown in those days to idolatry, hypocrisy and superstition, through traditions of Pharisees; and therefore he moved the rest of the council to beware, that they did not rashly and unadvisedly condemn that doctrine and religion which was approved by God, lest in so doing they should not only resist the apostles, but God himself. Which counsel if you had marked and followed, you would not have done so unsoberly in many things as you have done.

And as for the prosperity of them that have professed Christ and his true doctrine, they prospered with the papists as St John Baptist prospered with Herod, and our Saviour Christ with Pilate, Annas, and Caiphas. Now which of these prospered best, say you? Was the doctrine of Christ and St John any whit the worse, because the cruel tyrants and Jews put them to death for the same?

8.

WINCHESTER.

But all this set apart, and putting aside all testimonies of the old church, and resorting only to the letter of the scripture, there to search out an understanding, and in doing thereof to forget what hath been taught hitherto: how shall this author establish upon scripture that he would have believed? What other text is there in scripture that encountereth with these words of scripture, "This is my body," whereby to alter the signification of them? There is no scripture saith, Christ did not give his body, but the figure of his body; nor the giving of Christ's body in his supper, verily and really so understood, doth not necessarily impugn and contrary any other speech or doing of Christ, expressed in scripture. For the great power and omnipotency of God excludeth that repugnance which man's reason would deem, of Christ's departing from this world, and placing his humanity in the glory of his Father.

*These words, "This is my body," agree in sense with the rest of the scripture.
*Untrue report.
*This author hath no words of scripture for the ground of his faith.

CANTERBURY.

The scripture is plain, and you confess also that it was bread that Christ spake of when he said, "This is my body." And what need we any other scripture to encounter with these words, seeing that all men know that bread is not Christ's body, the one having sense and reason, the other none at all? Wherefore in that speech must needs be sought another sense and meaning, than the words of themselves do give, which is (as all old writers do teach, and the circumstances of the text declare) that the bread is a figure and sacrament of Christ's body. And yet, as he giveth the bread to be eaten with our mouths, so giveth he his very body to be eaten with our faith. And therefore I say, that Christ giveth himself truly to be eaten, chewed, and digested; but all is spiritually with faith, not with mouth. And yet you would bear me in hand, that I say that thing which I say not; that is to say, that Christ did not give his body, but the figure of his body. And because you be not able to confute that I say, you would make me to say that you can confute.

"This is my body," is no proper speech.

As for the great power and omnipotency of God, it is no place here to dispute what God can do, but what he doth. I know that he can do what he will, both in heaven and in earth, and no man is able to resist his will. But the question here is of his will, not of his power. And yet if you can join together these two, that one nature singular shall be here and not here, both at one time, and that it shall be gone hence when it is here, you have some strong syment[1], and be a cunning geometrician; but yet you shall never be good logician, that would set together two contradictories: for that, the schoolmen say, God cannot do.

God's omnipotency.
Psal. cxv.
Rom. ix.

WINCHESTER.

If this author without force of necessity would induce it, by the like speeches, as when Christ said, "I am the door," "I am the vine," "he is Helias," and such other; and because it is a figurative speech in them, it may be so here, which maketh no kind of proof that it is so here; but yet, if by way of reasoning I would yield to him therein, and call it a figurative speech, as he doth; what other point of faith is there then in the matter, but to believe the story, that Christ did institute such a supper, wherein he gave bread and wine for a token of his body and blood, which is now after this understanding no secret mystery at

9.
*An answer to the like speeches in appearance.
*The faith of this author is but to believe a story.
*The Lord's supper hath no miracle in

[¹ Cement.]

all, or any ordinance above reason? For commonly men use to ordain in sensible things remembrances of themselves when they die or depart the country. So as in the ordinance of this supper, after this understanding, Christ shewed not his omnipotency, but only benevolence, that he loved us, and would be remembered of us. For Christ did not say, Whosoever eateth this token eateth my body, or eateth my flesh, or shall have any profit of it in special, but, "Do this in remembrance of me."

it by this author's understanding.
*No promise made to a token in the supper, or in John vi.

CANTERBURY.

I make no such vain inductions, as you imagine me to do, but such as be established by scripture and the consent of all the old writers. And yet both you and Smith use such fond inductions for your proof of transubstantiation, when you say, God can do this thing, and he can make that thing; whereof ye would conclude, that he doth clearly take away the substance of bread and wine, and putteth his flesh and blood in their places, and that Christ maketh his body to be corporally in many places at one time; of which doctrine[1] you have not one iota in all the whole scripture.

And as concerning your argument made upon the history of the institution of Christ's supper, like fond reasoning might ungodly men make of the sacrament of baptism, and so scoff out both these high mysteries of Christ. For when Christ said these words after his resurrection, "Go into the whole world, and preach unto all people, baptizing them in the name of the Father, the Son, and the Holy Ghost:" here might wicked blasphemers say, What point of faith is in these words, but to believe the story, that Christ did institute such a sacrament, wherein he commanded to give water for a token? which is now, after this understanding, no secret mystery at all, or any ordinance above reason: so as in the ordinance of this sacrament, after this understanding, Christ shewed not his omnipotence. For he said not then, Whosoever receiveth this token of water, shall receive remission of sin, or the Holy Ghost, or shall have any profit of it in especial, but, "Do this."

Injury to baptism.

Matt. ult. Mark ult.

WINCHESTER.

And albeit this author would not have them bare tokens, yet and[2] they be only tokens, they have no warrant signed by scripture for any apparel at all. For the sixth of John speaketh not of any promise made to the eating of a token of Christ's flesh, but to the eating of Christ's very flesh, whereof the bread (as this author would have it) is but a figure in Christ's words, when he said, "This is my body." And if it be but a figure in Christ's words, it is but a figure in St Paul's words, when he said, "The bread which we break, is it not the communication of Christ's body?" that is to say, a figure of the communication of Christ's body (if this author's doctrine be true), and not the communication indeed. Wherefore, if the very body of Christ be not in the supper delivered in deed, the eating there hath no special promise, but only commandment to do it in remembrance. After which doctrine why should it be noted absolutely for a sacrament and special mystery, that hath nothing hidden in it, but a plain open ordinance of a token for a remembrance; to the eating of which token is annexed no promise expressly, nor any holiness to be accompted to be in the bread or wine (as this author teacheth), but to be called holy, because they be deputed to an holy use? If I ask the use, he declareth to signify. If I should ask what to signify? There must be a sort of good words framed without scripture. For scripture expresseth no matter of signification of special effect.

*Tokens be but tokens, howsoever they be garnished with gay words without scripture.

*Untrue report.

*Every special sacrament hath promise annexed and hath a secret hidden truth.

10.

CANTERBURY.

If I granted for your pleasure that the bare bread (having no further respect) were but only a bare figure of Christ's body, or a bare token (because that term liketh you better, as it may be thought for this consideration, that men should think that I take the bread in the holy mystery to be but as it were a token of 'I recommend me unto you'), but if I grant, I say, that the bare bread is but a bare token of Christ's body, what have you gained thereby? Is therefore the whole use of the bread in the whole action and ministration of the Lord's holy supper but a naked or nude and bare token? Is not one loaf being broken and distributed among faithful people in the Lord's supper, taken and eaten of them, a token that the body of Christ

Bread is not a vain and bare token.

[¹ doctrines, 1551.]   [² i. e. if.]

was broken and crucified for them; and is to them spiritually and effectually given, and of them spiritually and fruitfully taken and eaten, to their spiritual and heavenly comfort, sustentation and nourishment of their souls, as the bread is of their bodies? And what would you require more? Can there be any greater comfort to a christian man than this? Is here nothing else but bare tokens?

But yet importune adversaries, and such as be wilful and obstinate, will never be satisfied, but quarrel farther, saying, What of all this? Here be a great many of gay words framed together, but to what purpose? For all be but signs and tokens as concerning the bread. But how can he be taken for a good christian man, that thinketh that Christ did ordain his sacramental signs and tokens in vain, without effectual grace and operation? For so might we as well say, that the water in baptism is a bare token, and hath no warrant signed by scripture for any apparel at all: for the scripture speaketh not of any promise made to the receiving of a token or figure only. And so may be concluded, after your manner of reasoning, that in baptism is no spiritual operation in deed, because that washing in water in itself is but a token.

But to express the true effect of the sacraments: As the washing outwardly in water is not a vain token, but teacheth such a washing as God worketh inwardly, in them that duly receive the same; so likewise is not the bread a vain token, but sheweth and preacheth to the godly receiver, what God worketh in him by his almighty power secretly and invisibly. And therefore as the bread is outwardly eaten indeed in the Lord's supper, so is the very body of Christ inwardly by faith eaten indeed of all them that come thereto in such sort as they ought to do, which eating nourisheth them into everlasting life.

And this eating hath a warrant signed by Christ himself in the sixth of John, where Christ saith: "He that eateth my flesh and drinketh my blood, hath life everlasting." But they that to the outward eating of the bread, join not thereto an inward eating of Christ by faith, they have no warrant by scripture at all, but the bread and wine to them be vain, nude, and bare tokens. *A warrant. John vi.*

And where you say that scripture expresseth no matter of signification [of] special effect in the sacraments of bread and wine, if your eyes were not blinded with popish errors, frowardness, and self-love, ye might see in the twenty-second of Luke, where Christ himself expresseth a matter of signification, saying: *Hoc facite in mei commemorationem:* "Do this in remembrance of me." And St Paul likewise, 1 Cor. xi. hath the very same thing; which is a plain and direct answer to that same your last question, whereupon you triumph at your pleasure, as though the victory were all yours. For ye say, when this question is demanded of me, What to signify? "Here must be a sort of good words framed without scripture." But here St Paul answereth your question in express words, that it is the Lord's death that shall be signified, represented, and preached in these holy mysteries, until his coming again. And this remembrance, representation and preaching of Christ's death, cannot be without special effect, except you will say that Christ worketh not effectually with his word and sacraments. And St Paul expresseth the effect, when he saith: "The bread which we break is the communion of Christ's body." But by this place and such like in your book, ye disclose yourself to all men of judgment, either how wilful in your opinion, or how slender in knowledge of the scriptures you be. *11. Luke xxii. 1 Cor. xi. 1 Cor. xi. 1 Cor. x.*

WINCHESTER.

And therefore like as the teaching is new, to say it is an only figure, or only signifieth; so the matter of signification must be newly devised, and new wine have new bottles, and be thoroughly new, after fifteen hundred and fifty years, in the very year of jubilee (as they were wont to call it) to be newly erected and builded in Englishmen's hearts.

* A new teaching of only figure. How can a faith be called catholic that beginneth to be published now.

CANTERBURY.

It seemeth that you be very desirous to abuse the people's ears with this term, "new," and with the "year of jubilee," as though the true doctrine of the sacrament by me taught should be but a new doctrine, and yours old (as the Jews slandered *Mark i.*

the doctrine of Christ by the name of newness); or else that in this year of jubilee, you would put the people in remembrance of the full remission of sin, which they were wont to have at Rome this year, that they might long to return to Rome for pardons again, as the children of Israel longed to return to Egypt for the flesh that they were wont to have there.

But all men of learning and judgment know well enough that this your doctrine is no older than the bishop of Rome's usurped supremacy, which though it be of good age by number of years, yet is it new to Christ and his word. If there were such darkness in the world now, as hath been in that world which you note for old, the people might drink new wine of the whore of Babylon's cup, until they were as drunk with hypocrisy and superstition, as they might well stand upon their legs, and no man once say, black is their eye. But now, (thanks be to God!) the light of his word so shineth in the world, that your drunkenness in this year of jubilee is espied, so that you cannot erect and build your popish kingdom any longer in Englishmen's hearts, without your own scorn, shame and confusion. The old popish bottles must needs burst, when the new wine of God's holy word is poured into them.

WINCHESTER.

12.

* Tokens how to discern truth from falsehood.

* 1 Kings iii.

A lesson of Solomon's judgment.

* Truth needeth no aid of lies.

* Truth loveth simplicity and plainness.

Which new teaching, whether it proceedeth from the spirit of truth or no, shall more plainly appear by such matter as this author uttereth wherewith to impugn the true faith taught hitherto. For among many other proofs, whereby truth after much travail in contention at the last prevaileth and hath victory, there is none more notable, than when the very adversaries of truth (who pretend, nevertheless, to be truth's friends) do by some evident untruth bewray themselves. According whereunto, when the two women contended before king Solomon for the child yet alive, Solomon discerned the true natural mother from the other, by their speeches and sayings; which in the very[1] mother were ever conformable unto nature, and in the other, at the last evidently against nature. The very true mother spake always like herself, and never disagreed from the truth of nature, but rather than the child should be killed (as Solomon threatened when he called for a sword) required[2] it to be given whole alive to the other woman. The other woman that was not the true mother cared more for victory than for the child, and therefore spake that was in nature an evidence that she lied calling herself mother, and saying, "Let it be divided," which no[3] natural mother could say of her own child. Whereupon proceedeth Solomon's most wise judgment, which hath this lesson in it,—ever where contention is, on that part to be the truth, where all sayings and doings appear uniformly consonant to the truth pretended; and on what side a notable lie appeareth, the rest may be judged to be after the same sort. For truth needeth no aid of lies, craft, or sleight, wherewith to be supported or[4] maintained. So as in the entreating of the truth of this high and ineffable mystery of the sacrament, on what part thou, reader, seest craft, sleight, shift, obliquity, or in any one point an open manifest lie, there thou mayest consider, whatsoever pretence be made of truth, yet the victory of truth not to be there intended, which loveth simplicity, plainness, direct speech, without admixtion of shift or colour.

CANTERBURY.

The church of Rome is not the true mother of the catholic faith.

* Absurda et falsa.

If either division or confusion may try the true mother, the wicked church of Rome (not in speech only, but in all other practices) hath long gone about to oppress, confound and divide the true and lively faith of Christ, shewing herself not to be the true mother, but a most cruel stepmother, dividing, confounding and counterfeiting all things at her pleasure, not contrary to nature only, but chiefly against the plain words of scripture.

For here in this one matter of controversy between you, Smith, and me, you divide against nature the accidents of bread and wine from their substances, and the substance of Christ from his accidents; and contrary to the scripture you divide our eternal life, attributing unto the sacrifice of Christ upon the cross only the beginning thereof, and the continuance thereof you ascribe unto the sacrifice of popish priests.

[1 In the very true mother, 1551.]
[2 Required rather, 1551.]
[3 No true natural mother, 1551.]
[4 Supported and maintained, 1551.]

And in the sacraments you separate Christ's body from his spirit, affirming that in baptism we receive but his spirit, and in the communion but his flesh: and that Christ's spirit reneweth our life, but increaseth it not; and that his flesh increaseth our life, but giveth it not. And against all nature, reason, and truth, you confound the substance of bread and wine with the substance of Christ's body and blood, in such wise as you make but one nature and person of them all. And against scripture and all conformity of nature, you confound and jumble so together the natural members of Christ's body in the sacrament, that you leave no distinction, proportion, nor fashion of man's body at all.

And can your church be taken for the true natural mother of the true doctrine of Christ, that thus unnaturally speaketh, divideth, and confoundeth Christ's body? *The speaking of the true mother.*

If Solomon were alive, he would surely give judgment that Christ should be taken from that woman, that speaketh so unnaturally, and so unlike his mother, and be given to the true church of the faithful, that never digressed from the truth of God's word, nor from the true speech of Christ's natural body, but speak according to the same, that Christ's body, although it be inseparable, annexed unto his Godhead, yet it hath all the natural conditions and properties of a very man's body, occupying one place, and being of a certain height and measure, having all members distinct and set in good order and proportion. And yet the same body joined unto his divinity, is not only the beginning, but also the continuance and consummation of our eternal and celestial life. By him we be regenerated, by him we be fed and nourished from time to time, as he hath taught us most certainly to believe by his holy word and sacraments, which remain in their former substance and nature, as Christ doth in his, without mixtion or confusion. This is the true and natural speaking in this matter, like a true natural mother, and like a true and right believing christian man. *13.*

Marry, of that doctrine which you teach, I cannot deny but the church of Rome is the mother thereof, which in scripture is called Babylon, because of commixtion or confusion: which in all her doings and teachings so doth mix and confound error with truth, superstition with religion, godliness with hypocrisy, scripture with traditions, that she sheweth herself alway uniform and consonant, to confound all the doctrine of Christ, yea, Christ himself, shewing herself to be Christ's stepmother, and the true natural mother of antichrist. *Rome is the mother of the papistical faith.*

And for the conclusion of your matter here, I doubt not but the indifferent reader shall easily perceive what spirit moved you to write your book. For seeing that your book is so full of crafts, sleights, shifts, obliquities, and manifest untruths, it may be easily judged, that whatsoever pretence be made of truth, yet nothing is less intended, than that truth should either have victory, or appear and be seen at all.

WINCHESTER.

And that thou, reader, mightest by these marks judge of that is here entreated by the author against the most blessed sacrament, I shall note certain evident and manifest untruths, which this author is not afraid to utter, (a matter wonderful, considering his dignity, if he that is named be the author indeed,) which should be a great stay of contradiction, if anything were to be regarded against the truth. * The name of the author great, wherewith to put men to silence.

First, I will note unto the reader, how this author termeth the faith of the real and substantial presence of Christ's body and blood in the sacrament to be the faith of the papists: which saying, what foundation it hath, thou mayest consider of that followeth. * An impudent untruth.

Luther, that professed openly to abhor all that might be noted popish, defended stoutly the presence of Christ's body in the sacrament, and to be present really and substantially, even with the same words and terms.

Bucer, that is here in England, in a solemn work that he writeth upon the Gospels, professeth the same faith of the real and substantial presence of Christ's body in the sacrament, which he affirmeth to have been believed of all the church of Christ from the beginning hitherto.

Justus Jonas hath translated a catechism out of Dutch into Latin, taught in the city of Nuremberg in Germany, where Hosiander is chief preacher, in which catechism they be accounted for no true christian men, that deny the presence of Christ's body in the sacrament. The words * The faith of the sacrament in the catechism imp proveth this author's doctrine now.

"really" and "substantially" be not expressed as they be in Bucer, but the word "truly" is there, and, as Bucer saith, that is, substantially. Which catechism was translated into English in this author's name about two years past.

14.

Philip Melancthon, no papist nor priest, writeth a very wise epistle in this matter to Œcolampadius, and signifying soberly his belief of the presence of Christ's very body in the sacrament; and to prove the same to have been the faith of the old church from the beginning, allegeth the sayings of Irene, Cyprian, Chrysostom, Hilary, Cyril, Ambrose, Theophylact, which authors he esteemeth both worthy credit, and to affirm the presence of Christ's body in the sacrament plainly without ambiguity. He answereth to certain places of St Augustine, and saith all Œcolampadius' enterprise to depend upon conjectures, and arguments applausible to idle wits, with much more wise matter, as that epistle doth purport, which is set out in a book of a good volume among the other epistles of Œcolampadius, so as no man may suspect anything counterfeit in the matter.

One Hippinus, or Œpinus, of Hamburgh, greatly esteemed among the Lutherans, hath written a book to the king's majesty that now is, published abroad in print, wherein much inveighing against the church of Rome, doth in the matter of the sacrament write as followeth: "Eucharistia is called by itself a sacrifice, because it is a remembrance of the true sacrifice offered upon the cross, and that in it is dispensed the true body and true blood of Christ, which is plainly the same in essence, that is to say substance, and the same blood in essence signifying, though the manner of presence be spiritual, yet the substance of that is present, is the same with that in heaven."

* Erasmus commendeth to the world the work of Algerus upon the sacrament.

* The body of Christ hidden under the signs.

* Erasmus would all to repent, that follow Berengarius' error.

Erasmus, noted a man that durst and did speak of all abuses in the church liberally, taken for no papist, and among us so much esteemed, as his paraphrases of the gospel is ordered to be had in every church of this realm, declareth in divers of his works most manifestly his faith of the presence of Christ's body in the sacrament, and by his epistles recommendeth to the world the work of Algerus in that matter of the sacrament, whom he noteth well exercised in the scriptures, and the old doctors, Cyprian, Hilary, Ambrose, Jerome, Augustine, Basil, Chrysostom. And for Erasmus' own judgment, he saith we have an inviolable foundation of Christ's own words, "This is my body," rehearsed again by St Paul: he saith further, the body of Christ is hidden under those signs; and sheweth also upon what occasions men have erred in reading the old fathers, and wisheth that they which have followed Berengarius in error would also follow him in repentance. I will not, reader, encumber thee with more words of Erasmus.

* Peter Martyr doth with lies impugn the faith of the sacrament.

An issue.

* This author would with the envious words of papists oppress the truth.

Peter Martyr, of Oxford, taken for no papist, in a treatise he made of late of the sacrament, which is now translated into English, sheweth how as touching the real presence of Christ's body, it is not only the sentence of the papists, but of other also; whom the said Peter nevertheless doth with as many shifts and lies as he may impugn for that point, as well as he doth the papists for transubstantiation, but yet he doth not, as this author doth, impute that faith of the real presence of Christ's body and blood to the only papists. Whereupon, reader, here I join with the author an issue, that the faith of the real and substantial presence of Christ's body and blood in the sacrament is not the device of papists, or their faith only, as this author doth considerately slander it to be, and desire therefore that according to Solomon's judgment this may serve for a note and mark, to give sentence[1] for the true mother of the child. For what should this mean, so without shame openly and untruly to call this faith popish, but only with the envious word of papist to overmatch the truth?

CANTERBURY.

This explication of the true catholic faith noteth to the reader certain evident and manifest untruths uttered by me (as he saith), which I also pray thee, good reader, to note for this intent, that thou mayest take the rest of my sayings for true, which he noteth not for false, and doubtless they should not have escaped noting as well as the other, if they had been untrue, as he saith the other be. And if I can prove these things also true, which he noteth for manifest and evident untruths, then me thinketh[2] it is reason that all my sayings should be allowed for true, if those be proved true which only be rejected as untrue. But this untruth is to be noted in him generally, that he either ignorantly mistaketh, or willingly misreporteth almost all that I say. But now note, good reader, the evident and manifest untruths which I

15.

[¹ For to give sentence, 1551.]   [² Me think, 1551.]

utter, as he saith. The first is, that the faith of the real presence is the faith of ^{Four manifest untruths.} the papists. Another is, that these words, "My flesh is verily meat," I do translate thus[3]: "My flesh is very meat." Another is, that I handle not sincerely the words of St Augustine, speaking of the eating of Christ's body. The fourth is, that by these words, "This is my body," Christ intendeth not to make the bread his body, but to signify that such as receive that worthily be members of Christ's body. These be the heinous and manifest errors which I have uttered.

As touching the first, that the faith of the real and substantial presence of Christ's body and blood in the sacrament is the faith of the papists, this is no untruth, but a most certain truth. For you confess yourself, and defend in this book, that it is your faith: and so do likewise all the papists. And here I will make an issue with you, that the papists believe the real, corporal, and natural presence of Christ's body and blood in the sacrament. Answer me directly without colour, whether it be so or not. If they believe not so, then they believe as I do, for I believe not so: and then let them openly confess that my belief is true. And if they believe so, then say I true when I say that it is the papists' faith. And then is my saying no manifest untruth, but a mere truth; and so the verdict in the issue passeth upon my side by your own confession.

The first untruth, that the faith of the real presence is the faith of the papists. Mine issue.

And here the reader may note well, that once again you be fain to fly[4] for succour unto M.[5] Luther, Bucer, Jonas, Melancthon, and Œpinus, whose names[6] were wont to be so hateful unto you, that you could never with patience abide the hearing of them: and yet their sayings help you nothing at all. For although these men in this and many other things have in times past, and yet peradventure some do (the veil of old darkness not clearly in every point removed from their eyes), agree with the papists in part of this matter, yet they agree not in the whole: and therefore it is true nevertheless, that this faith which you teach is the papists' faith. For if you would conclude, that this is not the papists' faith, because[7] Luther, Bucer, and other, believe in many things as the papists do, then by the same reason you may conclude that the papists believe not that Christ was born, crucified, died, rose again, and ascended into heaven, which things Luther, Bucer and the other, constantly both taught and believed: and yet the faith of the real presence may be called rather the faith of the papists than of the other, not only because the papists do so believe, but specially for that[8] the papists were the first authors and inventors of that faith, and have been the chief spreaders abroad of it, and were the cause that other were blinded with the same error.

Luther. Bucer. Jonas. Melancthon. Œpinus.

But here may the reader note one thing by the way, that it is a foul clout that you would refuse to wipe your nose withal, when you take such men to prove your matter, whom you have hitherto accounted most vile and filthy heretics. And yet now you be glad to fly[4] to them for succour, whom you take for God's enemies, and to whom you have ever had a singular hatred. You pretend that you stay yourself upon ancient writers: and why run you now to such men for aid, as be not only new, but also as you think, be evil and corrupt in judgment; and to such as think you, by your writings and doings, as rank a papist as is any at Rome?

And yet not one of these new men (whom you allege) do thoroughly agree with your doctrine, either in transubstantiation, or in carnal eating and drinking of Christ's flesh and blood, or in the sacrifice of Christ in the mass, nor yet thoroughly in the real presence. For they affirm not such a gross presence of Christ's body, as expelleth the substance of bread, and is made by conversion thereof into the substance of Christ's body, and is eaten with the mouth. And yet if they did, the ancient authors that were next unto Christ's time (whom I have alleged) may not give place unto these new men in this matter, although they were men of excellent learning and judgment, howsoever it liketh you to accept them.

16.

But I may conclude that your faith in the sacrament is popish, until such time as you can prove that your doctrine of transubstantiation and of the real presence was

---

[3 I translate thus, 1551.]
[4 Flee, 1551.]
[5 Martin Luther, 1551.]
[6 Whose names before were wont, 1551.]
[7 Because that Luther, 1551.]
[8 But for that specially, that the papists, 1551.]

universally received and believed, before the bishops of Rome defined and determined the same. And when you have proved that, then will I grant that in your first note you have convinced me of an evident and manifest untruth, and that I untruly charge you with the envious name of a papistical faith.

But in your issue you term the words at your pleasure, and report me otherwise than I do say: for I do not say that the doctrine of the real presence is the papists' faith only, but that it was the papists' faith, for it was their device. And herein will I join with you an issue: that the papistical church is the mother of transubstantiation, and of all the four principal errors which I impugn in my book.

* Mine issue.

WINCHESTER.

It shall be now to purpose to consider the scriptures touching the matter of the sacrament, which the author pretending to bring forth faithfully as the majesty thereof requireth, in the rehearsal of the words of Christ out of the gospel of St John, he beginneth a little too low, and passeth over that pertaineth to the matter, and therefore should have begun a little higher at this clause: "*And the bread which I shall give you is my flesh, which I will give for the life of the world. The Jews therefore strived between themselves, saying, How can this man give his flesh to be eaten? Jesus therefore said unto them, Verily, verily I say unto you, Except ye eat the flesh of the Son of man, and drink his blood, ye have no life in you. Whoso eateth my flesh, and drinketh my blood, hath eternal life, and I will raise him up at the last day. For my flesh is very meat, and my blood very drink. He that eateth my flesh, and drinketh my blood, dwelleth in me, and I in him. As the living Father hath sent me, and I live by the Father: even so he that eateth me shall live by me. This is the bread which came down from heaven. Not as your fathers did eat manna and are dead. He that eateth this bread shall live for ever.*"

[John vi.]

Here is also a fault in the translation of the text, which should be thus in one place: "*For my flesh is verily meat, and my blood is verily drink.*" *In which speech the verb that coupleth the words "flesh" and "meat" together, knitteth them together in their proper signification, so as the flesh of Christ is verily meat, and not figuratively meat*[1], *as the author would persuade. And in these words of Christ may appear plainly, how Christ taught the mystery of the food of his humanity, which he promised to give for food, even the same flesh that he said he would give for the life of the world; and so expresseth the first sentence of this scripture here by me wholly brought forth, that is to say,* "*and the bread which I shall give you is my flesh, which I shall give for the life of the world;*" *and so is it*[2] *plain that Christ spake of flesh in the same sense that St John speaketh in, saying,* "*The word was made flesh,*" *signifying by flesh the whole humanity. And so did Cyril agree to Nestorius, when he upon these texts reasoned how this eating is to be understanded of Christ's humanity, to which nature in Christ's person is properly attribute to be eaten as meat spiritually to nourish man, dispensed and given in the sacrament. And between Nestorius and Cyril was this diversity in understanding the mystery, that Nestorius esteeming of each nature in Christ a several person, as it was objected to him, and so dissolving the ineffable unity, did so repute the body of Christ to be eaten as the body of a man separate. Cyril maintained the body of Christ to be eaten as a body inseparable, united to the Godhead, and for the ineffable mystery of that union the same to be a flesh that giveth life. And then as Christ saith,* "*If we eat not the flesh of the Son of man, we have not life in us,*" *because Christ hath ordered the sacrament of his most precious body and blood, to nourish such as be by his holy Spirit regenerate. And as in baptism we receive the Spirit of Christ, for the renewing of our life, so do we in this sacrament of Christ's most precious body and blood receive Christ's very flesh, and drink his very blood, to continue and preserve, increase and augment, the life received.*

* Cyril and Nestorius.

17.

* In baptism we receive Christ's spirit to give life, in the Lord's supper we receive his flesh and blood to continue life.

And therefore in the same form of words Christ spake to Nicodemus of baptism, that he speaketh here of the eating of his body and drinking of his blood, and in both sacraments giveth, dispenseth, and exhibiteth indeed, those celestial gifts in sensible elements, as Chrysostom saith. And because the true, faithful, believing men do only by faith know the Son of man to be in unity of person the Son of God, so as for the unity of the two natures in Christ, in one person, the flesh of the Son of man is the proper flesh of the Son of God.

Saint Augustine said well when he noted these words of Christ, "*Verily, verily, unless ye eat the flesh of the Son of man,*" *&c., to be a figurative speech, because after the bare letter it seemeth unprofitable, considering that flesh profiteth nothing in itself, esteemed in the own nature*

[1 These words, "and not figuratively meat," are not found in the 1551. ed. of Winchester's book.]   [2 And so it is, 1551.]

alone; but as the same flesh in Christ is united to the divine nature, so is it, as Christ said, (after Cyril's exposition,) spirit and life, not changed into the divine nature of the spirit, but for the ineffable union in the person of Christ thereunto. It is vivificatrix, *as Cyril said, and as the holy Ephesine council decreed: "A flesh giving life," according to Christ's words: "Who eateth my flesh, and drinketh my blood, hath eternal life, and I will raise him up at the latter day." And then to declare unto us, how in giving this life to us Christ useth the instrument of his very human body, it followeth: "For my flesh is verily meat, and my blood is verily drink[3]." So like as Christ sanctifieth by his godly Spirit, so doth he sanctify us by his godly flesh, and therefore repeateth again, to inculcate the celestial thing of this mystery, and saith: "He that eateth my flesh, and drinketh my blood, dwelleth in me and I in him," which is the natural and corporal union between us and Christ. Whereupon followeth, that as Christ is naturally in his Father, and his Father in him, so he that eateth verily the flesh of Christ, he is by nature in Christ, and Christ is naturally in him, and the worthy receiver hath life increased, augmented, and confirmed by the participation of the flesh of Christ.*

And because of the ineffable union of the two natures, Christ said, "This is the food that came down from heaven," because God (whose proper flesh it is) came down from heaven, and hath another virtue than manna had, because this giveth life to them that worthily receive it: which manna (being but a figure thereof) did not, but being in this food Christ's very flesh, inseparably united to the Godhead, the same is of such efficacy, as he that worthily eateth of it shall live for ever. And thus I have declared the sense of Christ's words, brought forth out of the gospel of St John. Whereby appeareth, how evidently they set forth the doctrine of the mystery of the eating of Christ's flesh, and drinking his blood in the sacrament, which must needs be understanded of a corporal eating, as Christ did after order in the institution of the said sacrament, according to his promise and doctrine here declared.

CANTERBURY.

Here before you enter into my second untruth (as you call it), you find fault by the way, that in the rehearsal of the words of Christ, out of the Gospel of St John, I begin a little too low. But if the reader consider the matter for the which I allege St John, he shall well perceive that I began at the right place where I ought to begin. For I do not bring forth St John for the matter of the real presence of Christ in the sacrament, whereof is no mention made in that chapter; and as it would not have served me for that purpose, no more doth it serve you, although you cited the whole gospel. But I bring St John for the matter of eating Christ's flesh and drinking his blood, wherein I passed over nothing that pertaineth to the matter, but rehearse the whole fully and faithfully. And because the reader may the better understand the matter, and judge between us both, I shall rehearse the words of my former book, which be these.

18.

*THE supper of the Lord, otherwise called the holy communion or sacrament of the body and blood of our Saviour Christ, hath been of many men, and by sundry ways very much abused, but specially within these four or five hundred years. Of some it hath been used as a sacrifice propitiatory for sin, and otherwise superstitiously, far from the intent that Christ did first ordain the same at the beginning, doing therein great wrong and injury to his death and passion. And of other some it hath been very lightly esteemed, or rather contemned and despised as a thing of small or of none effect. And thus between both the parties hath been much variance and contention in divers parts[4] of christendom. Therefore to the intent that this holy sacrament or Lord's supper may hereafter neither of the one party be contemned or lightly esteemed, nor of the other party be abused to any other purpose than Christ himself did first appoint and ordain the same, and that so the contention on both parties may be quieted and ended, the most sure and plain way is to cleave unto

[Book I.] Chap. I. The abuse of the Lord's supper.

[3 My blood verily drink, 1551.]

* The title of this book runs thus in the original edition: "The first book is of the true and Catholic doctrine and use of the Sacrament of the Body and Blood of our Saviour Christ."]

[4 Places, 1551.]

holy scripture: wherein whatsoever is found, must be taken for a most sure ground, and an infallible truth; and whatsoever cannot be grounded upon the same, touching our faith, is man's device, changeable and uncertain. And therefore here are set forth the very words that Christ himself and his apostle St Paul spake, both of the eating and drinking of Christ's body and blood, and also of the eating and drinking of the sacrament of the same. First, as concerning the eating of the body and drinking of the blood of our Saviour Christ, he speaketh himself in the sixth chapter of St John in this wise:

<small>Chap. II.
The eating of the body of Christ.
John vi.</small>

"Verily, verily, I say unto you, except ye eat the flesh of the Son of man, and drink his blood, you have no life in you. *Whoso eateth my flesh and drinketh my blood, hath eternal life,* and I will raise him up at the last day. For my flesh is very meat, and my blood is very drink. He that eateth my flesh, and drinketh my blood, *dwelleth in me and I in him.* As the living Father hath sent me, and I live by the Father, even so *he that eateth me, shall live by me.* This is the bread which came down from heaven. Not as your fathers did eat manna, and are dead. *He that eateth this bread shall live for ever.*"

Here have I rehearsed the words of Christ faithfully and fully, so much as pertaineth to the eating of Christ's flesh, and drinking of his blood. And I have begun neither too high nor too low, but taking only so much as served for the matter.

<small>19.
The second untruth, for "verily meat," translating "very meat."</small>

But here have I committed a fault (say you) in the translation, for "verily meat" translating "very meat." And this is another of the evident and manifest untruths by me uttered, as you esteem it. Wherein a man may see, how hard it is to escape the reproaches of Momus. For what an horrible crime (trow you) is committed here, to call "very meat" that which is "verily meat"! As who should say, that "very meat" is not "verily meat," or that which is "verily meat" were not "very meat." The old authors say "very meat," ἀληθὴς βρῶσις, *verus cibus,* in a hundred places.

<small>* Origenes in Levit. Hom. VII. Propterea ergo et caro ejus verus est cibus, et sanguis ejus verus est potus. Et in Matt. Hom. XII. Caro mea vera est esca, et sanguis meus verus est potus. Hieron. in Eccl. cap. iii. Caro enim verus est cibus, et sanguis ejus verus est potus. August. in Psal. xxxiii. Caro mea vera est esca, et sanguis meus vere potus est. Damas. lib. iv. cap. 14. Caro mea verus est cibus, et sanguis meus verus est potus. Euthymius in Jo. cap. ix. Caro mea verus est cibus, et sanguis meus verus est potus.
The nature of a cuttle.
*Plin. lib. ix. cap. 29.
* Eccl. xxxvii.
Christ is verily and truly given in the sacrament, but yet spiritually.</small>

And what skilleth it for the diversity of the words, where no diversity is in the sense? and whether we say, "very meat," or "verily meat," it is a figurative speech in this place, and the sense is all one. And if you will look upon the New Testament lately set forth in Greek by Robert Stevens, you shall see that he had three Greek copies, which in the said sixth chapter of John have ἀληθής and not ἀληθῶς. So that I may be bold to say, that you find fault here where none is.

And here in this place you shew forth your old condition (which you use much in this book) in following the nature of a cuttle[1]. "The property of the cuttle," saith Pliny, "is to cast out a black ink or colour, whensoever she spieth herself in danger to be taken, that the water being troubled and darkened therewith, she may hide herself and so escape untaken." After like manner do you throughout this whole book; for when you see no other way to fly and escape, then you cast out your black colours, and mask yourself so in clouds and darkness, that men should not discern where you be come, which is a manifest argument of untrue meaning: for he that meaneth plainly, speaketh plainly; *et qui sophistice loquitur, odibilis est,* saith the wise man. For he that speaketh obscurely and darkly, it is a token that he goeth about to cast mists before men's eyes that they should not see, rather than to open their eyes that they may clearly see the truth.

And therefore to answer you plainly, the same flesh that was given in Christ's last supper was given also upon the cross, and is given daily in the ministration of the sacrament. But although it be one thing, yet it was diversely given. For upon the cross Christ was carnally given to suffer and to die; at his last supper he was spiritually given in a promise of his death; and in the sacrament he is daily given in remembrance of his death. And yet it is all but one Christ that was promised to die, that died indeed, and whose death is remembered; that is to say, the very same Christ, the eternal Word that was made flesh. And the same flesh was also given to be spiritually eaten, and was eaten in deed, before his supper, yea, and before his incarnation also.

[1 Of the cuttle, 1551.]

Of which eating, and not of sacramental eating, he spake in the sixth of John: "My flesh is very meat, and my blood is very drink. He that eateth my flesh, and drinketh my blood, dwelleth in me, and I in him." *John vi.*

And Cyril, I grant, agreed to Nestorius in the substance of the thing that was eaten, (which is Christ's very flesh,) but in the manner of eating they varied. For Nestorius imagined a carnal eating (as the papists do) with mouth, and tearing with teeth. But Cyril in the same place saith, that Christ is eaten only by a pure faith, and not that he is eaten corporally with our mouths, as other meats be, nor that he is eaten in the sacrament only. *Cyril. anathematismo. 11.*

And it seemeth you understand not the matter of Nestorius, who did not esteem Christ to be made of two several natures and several persons, (as you report of him;) but his error was, that Christ had in him naturally but one nature and one person, affirming that he was a pure man, and not God by nature, but that the Godhead by grace inhabited, as he doth in other men. *20. Nestorius.*

And where you say that in baptism we receive the spirit of Christ, and in the sacrament of his body and blood we receive his very flesh and blood; this your saying is no small derogation to baptism, wherein we receive not only the spirit of Christ, but also Christ himself, whole body and soul, manhood and Godhead, unto everlasting life, as well as in the holy communion. For St Paul saith, *Quicunque in Christo baptizati estis, Christum induistis*: "As many as be baptized in Christ, put Christ upon them:" nevertheless, this is done in divers respects; for in baptism it is done in respect of regeneration, and in the holy communion in respect of nourishment and augmentation. *Injury to baptism. Gal. iii.*

But your understanding of the sixth chapter of John is such as never was uttered of any man before your time, and as declareth you to be utterly ignorant of God's mysteries. For who ever said or taught before this time, that the sacrament was the cause why Christ said, "If we eat not the flesh of the Son of man, we have not life in us?" The spiritual eating of his flesh, and drinking of his blood by faith, by digesting his death in our minds, as our only price, ransom, and redemption from eternal damnation, is the cause wherefore Christ said: "That if we eat not his flesh, and drink not his blood, we have not life in us; and if we eat his flesh, and drink his blood, we have everlasting life." And if Christ had never ordained the sacrament, yet should we have eaten his flesh, and drunken his blood, and have had thereby everlasting life; as all the faithful did before the sacrament was ordained, and do daily when they receive not the sacrament. And so did the holy men that wandered in the wilderness, and in all their life-time very seldom received the sacrament; and many holy martyrs, either exiled, or kept in prison, did daily feed of the food of Christ's body, and drank daily the blood that sprang out of his side, or else they could not have had everlasting life, as Christ himself said in the gospel of St John, and yet they were not suffered with other christian people to have the use of the sacrament. And therefore your argument in this place is but a *fallax a non causa, ut causa*, which is another trick of the devil's sophistry. *In the sixth chapter of John, Christ spake not of corporal eating. John vi.*

And that in the sixth of John Christ spake neither of corporal nor sacramental eating of his flesh, the time manifestly sheweth. For Christ spake of the same present time that was then, saying: "The bread which I will give is my flesh," and, "He that eateth my flesh, and drinketh my blood, dwelleth in me, and I in him, and hath everlasting life:" at which time the sacramental bread was not yet Christ's flesh. For the sacrament was not then yet ordained; and yet at that time all that believed in Christ, did eat his flesh, and drink his blood, or else they could not have dwelled in Christ, nor Christ in them. *John vi.*

Moreover, you say yourself, that in the sixth of St John's gospel, when Christ said, "The bread is my flesh," by the word "flesh" he meant his whole humanity, (as is meant in this sentence, "The word was made flesh,") which he meant not in the word "body," when he said of bread, "This is my body;" whereby he meant not his whole humanity, but his flesh only, and neither his blood nor his soul. And in the sixth of John Christ made not bread his flesh, when he said, "The bread is my flesh:" but he expounded in those words, what bread it was that he meant of, when *John vi. John i. 21.*

he promised them bread that should give them eternal life. He declared in those words, that himself was the bread that should give life, because they should not have their fantasies of any bread made of corn. And so the eating of that heavenly bread could not be understood of the sacrament, nor of corporal eating with the mouth; but of spiritual eating by faith, as all the old authors do most clearly expound and declare. And seeing that there is no corporal eating, but chewing with the teeth or swallowing (as all men do know), if we eat Christ corporally, then you must confess that we either swallow up Christ's flesh, or chew and tear it with our teeth, (as pope Nicholas constrained Berengarius to confess,) which St Augustine saith is a wicked and heinous thing. But in few words to answer to this second evident and manifest untruth (as you object against me), I would wish you as truly to understand these words of the sixth chapter of John, as I have truly translated them.

WINCHESTER.

Now, where the author, to exclude the mystery of corporal manducation, bringeth forth of St Augustine such words as entreat of the effect and operation of the worthy receiving of the sacrament; the handling is not so sincere as this matter requireth. For, as hereafter shall be entreated, that is not worthily and well done, may (because the principal intent faileth) be called not done, and so St Augustine saith: "Let him not think to eat the body of Christ, that dwelleth not in Christ;" not because the body of Christ is not received, which by St Augustine's mind evil men do to their condemnation, but because the effect of life faileth. And so the author by sleight, to exclude the corporal manducation of Christ's most precious body, uttereth such words, as might sound Christ to have taught the dwelling in Christ to be an eating: which dwelling may be without this corporal manducation in him that cannot attain the use of it, and dwelling in Christ is an effect of the worthy manducation, and not the manducation itself, which Christ doth order to be practised in the most precious sacrament institute in his supper. Here thou, reader, mayest see how this doctrine of Christ (as I have declared it) openeth the corporal manducation of his most holy flesh, and drinking of his most precious blood, which he gave in his supper under the form of bread and wine.

CANTERBURY.

The third untruth, of the handling the words of S. Augustine. Mine issue.

This is the third evident and manifest untruth, whereof you note me. And because you say that in citing of St Augustine in this place, I handle not the matter so sincerely as it requireth, let here be an issue between you and me, which of us both doth handle this matter more sincerely; and I will bring such manifest evidence for me, that you shall not be able to open your mouth against it. For I allege St Augustine justly as he speaketh, adding nothing of myself. The words in my book be these.

August. in Joan. Tractat. xxvi.

"Of these words of Christ it is plain and manifest, that the eating of Christ's body[1], and drinking of his blood, is not like the eating and drinking of other meats and drinks. For although without meat and drink man cannot live, yet it followeth not that he that eateth and drinketh shall live for ever. But as touching this meat and drink of the body and blood of Christ it is true, both he that eateth and drinketh them hath everlasting life; and also he that eateth and drinketh them not, hath not everlasting life. For to eat that meat, and drink that drink, is to dwell in Christ, and to have Christ dwelling in him; and therefore no man can say or think that he eateth the body of Christ or drinketh his blood, except he dwelleth in Christ, and have Christ dwelling in him. Thus have you heard of the eating and drinking of the very flesh and blood of our Saviour Christ."

22.

Eodem Tract. Aug. de Civit. lib. 21. cap. 25.

Thus allege I St Augustine truly, without adding any thing of mine own head, or taking any thing away. And what sleight I used is easy to judge: for I cite di-

---

[1 Flesh, 1551.]

rectly the places, that every man may see whether I say true or no. And if it be not true, quarrel not with me, but with St Augustine, whose words I only rehearse. And that which St Augustine saith, spake before him St Cyprian, and Christ himself also plainly enough; upon whose words I thought I might be as bold to build a true doctrine for the setting forth of God's glory, as you may be to pervert both the words of Cyprian, and of Christ himself, to stablish a false doctrine to the high dishonour of God, and the corruption of his most true word. For you add this word "worthily," whereby you gather such an unworthy meaning of St Augustine's words as you list yourself. And the same you do to the very words of Christ himself, who speaketh absolutely and plainly, without adding of any such word as you put thereto. What sophistry this is, you know well enough. Now if this be permitted unto you, to add what you list, and to expound how you list, then you may say what you list without controlment of any man, which it seemeth you look for. Worthily.

And not of like sort, but of like evilness do you handle (in reprehending of my second untruth, as you call it) another place of St Augustine in his book *de doctrina Christiana*, where he saith, that the eating and drinking of Christ's flesh and blood is a figurative speech: which place you expound so far from St Augustine's meaning, that whosoever looketh upon his words, may by and by discern that you do not, or will not, understand him. But it is most like (the words of him being so plain and easy) that purposely you will not understand him, nor nothing else that is against your will, rather than you will go from any part of your will and received opinion. For it is plain and clear that St Augustine in that place speaketh not one word of the separation of the two natures in Christ; and although Christ's flesh be never so surely and inseparably united unto his Godhead (without which union it could profit nothing), yet being so joined, it is a very man's flesh, the eating whereof (after the proper speech of eating) is horrible and abominable. Wherefore the eating of Christ's flesh must needs be otherwise understood, than after the proper and common eating of other meats with the mouth, which eating after such sort could avail nothing. And therefore St Augustine in that place declareth the eating of Christ's flesh to be only a figurative speech. And he openeth the figure so as the eating must be meant with the mind, not with the mouth, that is to say, by chewing and digesting in our minds, to our great consolation and profit, that Christ[2] died for us. Thus doth St Augustine open the figure and meaning of Christ, when he spake of the eating of his flesh and drinking of his blood. And his flesh being thus eaten, it must also be joined unto his divinity, or else it could not give everlasting life, as Cyril and the council Ephesine truly decreed. But St Augustine declared the figurative speech of Christ to be in the eating, not in the union. And whereas, to shift off the plain words of Christ, spoken in the sixth of John, "He that eateth my flesh, and drinketh my blood, dwelleth in me, and I in him," you say that dwelling in Christ is not the manducation; you say herein directly against St Cyprian, who saith, *Quod mansio nostra in ipso sit manducatio*, "That our dwelling in him is the eating:" and also against St Augustine, whose words be these: *Hoc est ergo manducare escam illam, et illum bibere potum, in Christo manere, et illum manentem in se habere:* "This is to eat that meat, and drink that drink, to dwell in Christ, and to have Christ dwelling in him." And although the eating and drinking of Christ be here defined by the effect, (for the very eating is the believing,) yet wheresoever the eating is, the effect must be also, if the definition of St Augustine be truly given. And therefore, although good and bad eat carnally with their teeth bread, being the sacrament of Christ's body; yet no man eateth his very flesh, which is spiritually eaten, but he that dwelleth in Christ, and Christ in him.

August. de doctrina Christiana, lib. iii. cap. 13. How Christ's flesh is eaten.

23.

John vi.

Cyprian. in sermone de cœna Domini. Aug. in Joan. Tract. xxvi.

And where in the end you refer the reader to the declaration of Christ's words, it is an evil sequel: you declare Christ's words thus, ergo, they be so meant. For by like reason might Nestorius have prevailed against Cyril, Arius against Alexander, and the Pope against Christ. For they all prove their errors by the doctrine

---

[² Was crucified and died, 1551.]

of Christ after their own declarations, as you do here in your corporal manducation. But of the manducation of Christ's flesh, I have spoken more fully in my fourth book, the second, third, and fourth chapters.

Now before I answer to the fourth untruth which I am appeached of, I will rehearse what I have said in the matter, and what fault you have found. My book hath thus.

[Book I.] Chap. III.

The eating of the sacrament of his body. Matt. xxvi.

"Now as touching the sacraments of the same, our Saviour Christ did institute them in bread and wine at his last supper which he had with his apostles, the night before his death, at which time, as Matthew saith, 'When they were eating, Jesus took bread, and when he had given thanks, he brake it, and gave it to his disciples, and said, Take, eat: this is my body. And he took the cup, and when he had given thanks he gave it to them, saying, Drink ye all of this, for this is my blood of the new testament, that is shed for many for the remission of sins. But I say unto you, I will not drink henceforth of this fruit of the vine, until that day when I shall drink it new with you in my Father's kingdom.'"

This thing is rehearsed also of St Mark in these words.

Mark xiv.

"As they did eat, Jesus took bread, and when he had blessed, he brake it, and gave it to them, and said, Take, eat: this is my body. And taking the cup, when he had given thanks, he gave it to them, and they all drank of it, and he said to them, This is my blood of the new testament, which is shed for many. Verily I say unto you, I will drink no more of the fruit of the vine, until that day that I drink it new in the kingdom of God."

The evangelist St Luke uttereth this matter on this wise.

Luke xxii.

24.

"When the hour was come, he sat down, and the twelve apostles with him. And he said unto them, I have greatly desired to eat this *Pascha* with you before I suffer: for I say unto you, henceforth I will not eat of it any more, until it be fulfilled in the kingdom of God. And he took the cup, and gave thanks, and said, Take this, and divide it among you: for I say unto you, I will not drink of the fruit of the vine, until the kingdom of God come. And he took bread, and when he had given thanks, he brake it, and gave it unto them, saying, This is my body, which is given for you: this do in remembrance of me. Likewise also when he had supped, he took the cup, saying, This cup is the new testament in my blood, which is shed for you."

Hitherto you have heard all that the evangelists declare, that Christ spake or did at his last supper, concerning the institution of the communion and sacrament of his body and blood. Now you shall hear what St Paul saith concerning the same, in the tenth chapter of the first to the Corinthians, where he writeth thus:

1 Cor. x.

"Is not the cup of blessing, which we bless, a communion of the blood of Christ? Is not the bread, which we break, a communion of the body of Christ? We being many, are one bread, and one body: for we all are partakers of one bread, and one cup."

And in the eleventh he speaketh on this manner.

1 Cor. xi.

"That which I delivered unto you I received of the Lord. For the Lord Jesus the same night in the which he was betrayed took bread, and when he had given thanks, he brake it, and said, Take, eat; this is my body, which is broken for you: do this in remembrance of me. Likewise also he took the cup, when supper was done, saying, This cup is the new testament in my blood. Do this, as often as ye drink it, in remembrance of me: for as oft as you shall eat this bread, and drink this cup, you shew forth the Lord's death till he come. Wherefore whosoever shall eat of this bread, or drink of this cup unworthily, shall be guilty of the body and blood of the Lord. But let a man examine himself, and so eat of the bread, and drink of the cup. For he that eateth and drinketh unworthily, eateth and drinketh his own damnation, because he maketh no difference of the Lord's body. For this cause many are weak and sick among you, and many do sleep."

By these words of Christ rehearsed of the evangelists, and by the doctrine also of St Paul, which he confesseth that he received of Christ, two things specially are to be noted.

First, that our Saviour Christ called the material bread which he brake, his body; and the wine, which was the fruit of the vine, his blood. And yet he spake not this to the intent that men should think that the material bread is his very body, or that his very body is material bread; neither that wine made of grapes is his very blood, or that his very blood is wine made of grapes: but to signify unto us, as St Paul saith, that the cup is a communion of Christ's blood that was shed for us, and the bread is a communion of his flesh that was crucified for us. So that although in the truth of his human nature, Christ be in heaven, and sitteth on the right hand of God the Father, yet whosoever eateth of the bread in the supper of the Lord, according to Christ's institution and ordinance, is assured of Christ's own promise and testament, that he is a member of his body, and receiveth the benefits of his passion which he suffered for us upon the cross. And likewise he that drinketh of that holy cup in the supper of the Lord, according to Christ's institution, is certified by Christ's legacy and testament, that he is made partaker of the blood of Christ which was shed for us. And this meant St Paul, when he saith, "Is not the cup of blessing which we bless a communion of the blood of Christ? Is not the bread which we break a communion of the body of Christ?" so that no man can contemn or lightly esteem this holy communion, except he contemn also Christ's body and blood, and pass not whether he have any fellowship with him or no. And of those men St Paul saith, "that they eat and drink their own damnation, because they esteem not the body of Christ."

Chap. IV.
Christ called the material bread his body.
1 Cor. x.
Mark ult.
25.
1 Cor. xi.

The second thing which may be learned of the foresaid words of Christ and St Paul is this: that although none eateth the body of Christ and drinketh his blood, but they have eternal life, (as appeareth by the words before recited of St John,) yet both the good and the bad do eat and drink the bread and wine, which be the sacraments of the same. But beside the sacraments, the good eat[1] everlasting life, the evil everlasting death. Therefore St Paul saith: "Whosoever shall eat of the bread, or drink of the cup of the Lord unworthily, he shall be guilty of the body and blood of the Lord." Here St Paul saith not, that he that eateth the bread, or drinketh the cup of the Lord unworthily, eateth and drinketh the body and blood of the Lord; but, is guilty of the body and blood of the Lord. But what he eateth and drinketh St Paul declareth, saying: "He that eateth and drinketh unworthily, eateth and drinketh his own damnation." Thus is declared the sum of all that scripture speaketh of the eating and drinking both of the body and blood of Christ, and also of the sacrament of the same.

Chap. v.
Evil men do eat the sacrament, but not the body of Christ.
1 Cor. xi.

And as these things be most certainly true, because they be spoken by

Chap. VI.

[1 Eateth, 1551.]

Christ himself, the author of all truth, and by his holy apostle St Paul, as he received them of Christ; so all doctrines contrary to the same be most certainly false and untrue, and of all christian men to be eschewed, because they be contrary to God's word. And all doctrine concerning this matter, that is more than this, which is not grounded upon God's word, is of no necessity, neither ought the people's heads to be busied, or their consciences troubled with the same. So that things spoken and done by Christ, and written by the holy evangelists and St Paul, ought to suffice the faith of Christian people, as touching the doctrine of the Lord's supper, and holy communion or sacrament of his body and blood.

These things suffice for a christian man's faith concerning this sacrament.

Which thing being well considered and weighed, shall be a just occasion to pacify and agree both parties, as well them that hitherto have contemned or lightly esteemed it, as also them which have hitherto for lack of knowledge or otherwise ungodly abused it.

Chap. VII.

Christ ordained the sacrament to move and stir all men to friendship, love, and concord, and to put away all hatred, variance, and discord, and to testify a brotherly and unfeigned love between all them that be the members of Christ: but the devil, the enemy of Christ and of all his members, hath so craftily juggled herein, that of nothing riseth so much contention as of this holy sacrament.

The sacrament which was ordained to make love and concord is turned into the occasion of variance and discord.

God grant that, all contention set aside, both the parties may come to this holy communion with such a lively faith in Christ, and such an unfeigned love to all Christ's members, that as they carnally eat with their mouths this sacramental bread, and drink the wine, so spiritually they may eat and drink the very flesh and blood of Christ which is in heaven, and sitteth on the right hand of his Father; and that finally by his means they may enjoy with him the glory and kingdom of heaven! Amen.

WINCHESTER.

26. *Now let us consider the texts of the evangelists, and St Paul, which be brought in by the author as followeth.*

Matt. xxvi. *"When they were eating, Jesus took bread, and when he had given thanks, he brake it, giving it to his disciples, and said, Take, eat; this is my body. And he took the cup, and when he had given thanks, he gave it to them, saying, Drink ye all of this; for this is my blood of the new testament, that is shed for many for the remission of sins. But I say unto you, I will not drink henceforth of this fruit of the vine, until that day when I shall drink it new with you in my Father's kingdom."*

Mark xiv. *"As they did eat, Jesus took bread, and when he had blessed, he brake it, and gave it to them, and said, Take, eat; this is my body. And taking the cup, when he had given thanks, he gave it to them: and they all drank of it. And he said unto them, This is my blood of the new testament, which is shed for many. Verily I say unto you, I will drink no more of the fruit of the vine, until that day that I drink it new in the kingdom of God."*

Luke xxii. *"When the hour was come, he sat down, and the twelve apostles with him; and he said unto them, I have greatly desired to eat this Pascha with you, before I suffer: for I say unto you, henceforth I will not eat of it any more, until it be fulfilled in the kingdom of God. And he took the cup, and gave thanks, and said, Take this, and divide it among you: for I say unto you, I will not drink of the fruit of the vine, until the kingdom of God come. And he took bread, and when he had given thanks, he brake it, and gave it unto them, saying, This is my body which is given for you: this do in remembrance of me. Likewise also when he had supped, he took the cup, saying, This cup is the new testament in my blood, which is shed for you."*

1 Cor. x. *"Is not the cup of blessing which we bless a communion of the blood of Christ? Is not the bread which we break a communion of the body of Christ? We, being many, are one bread, and one body; for we are all partakers of one bread, and of one cup."*

1 Cor. xi. *"That which I delivered unto you, I received of the Lord. For the Lord Jesus, the same night in the which he was betrayed, took bread, and when he had given thanks, he brake it, and*

said, Take, eat; this is my body, which is broken for you: do this in remembrance of me. Likewise also he took the cup when supper was done, saying, This cup is the new testament in my blood: do this, as often as ye drink it, in remembrance of me. For as often as you shall eat this bread, and drink this cup, ye shew forth the Lord's death till he come. Wherefore whosoever shall eat of this bread, or drink of this cup unworthily, shall be guilty of the body and blood of the Lord. But let a man examine himself, and so eat of the bread, and drink of the cup. For he that eateth and drinketh unworthily, eateth and drinketh his own damnation; because he maketh no difference of the Lord's body. For this cause many are weak and sick among you, and many do sleep."

After these texts brought in, the author doth in the fourth chapter begin to traverse Christ's intent, that he intended not by these words, "This is my body," to make the bread his body, but to signify that such as receive that worthily be members of Christ's body. The catholic church, acknowledging Christ to be very God and very man, hath from the beginning of these texts of scripture confessed truly Christ's intent, and effectual miraculous work to make the bread his body, and the wine his blood, to be verily meat and verily drink, using therein his humanity wherewith to feed us, as he used the same wherewith to redeem us; and as he doth sanctify us by his holy Spirit, so to sanctify us by his holy divine flesh and blood; and as life is renewed in us by the gift of Christ's holy Spirit, so life to be increased in us by the gift of his holy flesh. So he that believeth in Christ, and receiveth the sacrament of belief, which is baptism, receiveth really Christ's Spirit: and likewise[1] he that, having Christ's Spirit, receiveth also the sacrament of Christ's body and blood, doth really receive in the same, and also effectually, Christ's very body and blood. And therefore Christ in the institution of this sacrament said, delivering that he consecrated: "This is my body," &c. And likewise of the cup: "This is my blood," &c. And although to man's reason it seemeth strange that Christ, standing or sitting at the table, should deliver them his body to be eaten: yet when we remember Christ to be very God, we must grant him omnipotent, and by reason thereof, repress in our thoughts all imaginations how it might be, and consider Christ's intent by his will, preached unto us by scriptures, and believed universally in his church. But if it may now be thought seemly for us to be so bold, in so high a mystery, to begin to discuss Christ's intent: what should move us to think that Christ would use so many words, without effectual and real signification, as he rehearsed touching the mystery of this sacrament?

* The fourth untruth, that by these words, *Hoc est corpus meum*, Christ meant not to make the bread his body.

27.

First, in the sixth of John, when Christ had taught of the eating of him[2], being the bread descended from heaven, and declaring that eating to signify believing, whereat was no murmuring, that then he should enter to speak of giving of his flesh to be eaten, and his blood to be drunken, and to say that[3] he would give a bread, that is, his flesh, which he would give for the life of the world. In which words Christ maketh mention of two gifts; and therefore as he is truth, must needs intend to fulfil them both. And therefore[4] as we believe the gift of his flesh to the Jews to be crucified; so we must believe the gift of his flesh to be eaten, and of that gift, livery[5] and seisme[6], as we say, to be made of him, that is in his promises faithful (as Christ is) to be made in both. And therefore when he said in his supper, "Take, eat, this is my body," he must needs intend plainly as his words of promise required. And these words in his supper purport to give as really then his body to be eaten of us, as he gave his body indeed to be crucified for us; aptly nevertheless, and conveniently for each effect, and therefore in manner of giving diversely, but in the substance of the same[7] given, to be as his words bear witness, the same, and therefore said, "This is my body that shall be betrayed for you;" expressing also the use, when he said, "Take, eat:" which words, in delivering of material bread, had been superfluous; for what should men do with bread when they take it, but eat it, specially when it is broken?

But as Cyril saith: "Christ opened there unto them the practice of that doctrine he spake of in the sixth of St John, and because he said he would give his flesh for food, which he would give for the life of the world, he for fulfilling of his promise said: "Take, eat, this is my body," which words have been taught and believed to be of effect, and operatory, and Christ under the form of bread to have been[8] his very body. According whereunto St Paul noteth the receiver to be guilty, when he doth not esteem it our Lord's body, wherewith it pleaseth Christ to feed such as be in him regenerate, to the intent that as man was redeemed

---

[1 "So he;" original ed. of Winchester's book.]
[2 Himself, 1551.]
[3 To say he would give, 1551.]
[4 Wherefore, 1551.]
[5 Livery: i.e. the act of giving.]
[6 Seisme: i.e. seizin, the act of taking.]
[7 The same body given, 1551.]
[8 Given, 1551.]

by Christ, suffering in the nature of his humanity, so to purchase for man the kingdom of heaven, lost by Adam's fall. Even likewise in the nature of the same humanity, giving it to be eaten, he ordained it[1] to nourish man, and make him strong to walk, and continue his journey, to enjoy that kingdom. And therefore to set forth lively unto us the communication of the substance of Christ's most precious body in the sacrament, and the same to be indeed delivered, Christ used plain words, testified by the evangelists. St Paul also rehearsed the same words in the same plain terms in the eleventh to the Corinthians; and in the tenth, giving (as it were) an exposition of the effect, useth the same proper words, declaring the effect to be the communication of Christ's body and blood. And one thing is notable touching the scripture, that in such notable speeches uttered by Christ, as might have an ambiguity, the evangelists by some circumstance declared it, or sometime opened it by plain interpretation: as when Christ said "he would dissolve the temple, and within three days build it again;" the evangelist by and by addeth for interpretation: "This he said of the temple of his body." And when Christ said, "He is Elias," and "I am the true vine," the circumstance of the text openeth the ambiguity.

* Neither St Paul, nor the Evangelists, add any words whereby to take away the signification of bread and wine.

But to shew that Christ should not mean of his very body when he so spake[2], neither St Paul after, nor the evangelists in the place, add any words or circumstances, whereby to take away the proper signification of the words "body" and "blood," so as the same might seem not in deed given (as the catholic faith teacheth), but in signification, as the author would have it. For, as for the words of Christ, "The Spirit giveth life, the flesh profiteth nothing," be to declare the two natures in Christ, each in their property apart considered, but not as they be in Christ's person united the mystery of which union such as believed not Christ to be God could not consider, and yet to insinuate that unto them, Christ made mention of his descension from heaven, and after of his ascension thither again, whereby they might understand him very God, whose flesh taken in the virgin's womb, and so given spiritually to be eaten of us, is (as I have before opened) vivifick, and giveth life.

And this shall suffice here to shew how Christ's intent was to give verily (as he did in deed) his precious body and blood to be eaten and drunken, according as he taught them to be verily meat and drink; and yet gave and giveth them so under form of visible creatures to us, as we may conveniently and without horror of our nature receive them, Christ therein condescending to our infirmity. As for such other wrangling as is made in understanding[3] of the words of Christ, shall after be spoken of by further occasion.

CANTERBURY.

* The fourth untruth, that Christ intended not by these words, "This is my body," to make the bread his body. The variance between you and Smith.

Against Smith.

Now we be come to the very pith of the matter, and the chief point whereupon the whole controversy hangeth, whether in these words, "This is my body," Christ called bread his body: wherein you and Smith agree like a man and woman that dwelled in Lincolnshire, as I have heard reported, that what pleased the one misliked the other, saving that they both agreed in wilfulness. So do Smith and you agree both in this point, that Christ made bread his body, but that it was bread which he called his body, when he said, "This is my body," this you grant, but Smith denieth it. And because all Smith's buildings clearly fall down, if this his chief foundation be overthrown, therefore must I first prove against Smith, that Christ called the material bread his body, and the wine which was the fruit of the vine his blood. "For why did you not prove this, my Lord?" saith Smith: "would you that men should take you for a prophet, or for one that could not err in his sayings?"

Christ called bread his body.

First I allege against Smith's negation your affirmation, which, as it is more true in this point than his negation, so for your estimation it is able[4] to countervail his saying, if there were nothing else: and yet, if Smith had well pondered what I have written in the second chapter of my second book, and in the seventh and eighth chapters of my third book, he should have found this matter so fully proved, that he neither is, nor never shall be able to answer thereto. For I have alleged the scripture, I have alleged the consent of the old writers, holy fathers, and martyrs, to prove that Christ called bread his body, and wine his blood. For the evangelists,

Matt. xxvi.
Mark xiv.
Luke xxii.

speaking of the Lord's supper, say, that "he took bread, blessed it, brake it, and gave it to his disciples, saying, This is my body. And of the wine he said, Take this,

---

[[1] To be eaten, ordained to nourish, 1551.]
[[2] He so spake these words in his supper, 1551.]
[[3] In the understanding, 1551.]
[[4] Is it able, 1551.]

divide it among you, and drink it: this is my blood." I have alleged Irene[5], saying *Ireneus.*
that "Christ confessed bread to be his body, and the cup to be his blood." I have
cited Tertullian, who saith in many places that "Christ called bread his body." I *Tertullianus.*
have brought in for the same purpose Cyprian, who saith that "Christ called such *Cyprianus.*
bread as is made of many corns joined together, his body: and such wine he named
his blood, as is pressed out of many grapes." I have written the words of Epipha- *Epiphanius.*
nius, which be these, that "Christ speaking of a loaf which is round in fashion, and
can neither see, hear, nor feel, said of it, 'This is my body.'" And St Jerome, writing *Hierony-*
ad Hedibiam, saith that "Christ called the bread which he brake his body." And *mus.*
St Augustine saith, that "Jesus called meat his body, and drink his blood." And *Augustinus.*
Cyril saith more plainly, that "Christ called the pieces of bread his body." And *Cyrillus.*
last of all I brought forth Theodorete, whose saying is this, that "when Christ gave *Theodoretus.*
the holy mysteries, he called bread his body, and the cup mixed with wine and
water he called his blood." All these authors I alleged, to prove that Christ called 29.
bread his body, and wine his blood.

Which because they speak the thing so plainly as nothing can be more, and
Smith seeth that he can devise nothing to answer these authors, like a wily fox, he
stealeth away by them softly, as he had a flea in his ear, saying nothing to all
these authors, but that they prove not my purpose. If this be a sufficient answer,
let the reader be judge; for in such sort I could[6] make a short answer to Smith's
whole book in this one sentence, that nothing that he saith proveth his purpose.
And as for proofs of his saying, Smith hath utterly none but only this fond reason:
that if Christ had called bread his body, then should bread have been crucified for
us, because Christ added these words: "This is my body, which shall be given to
death for you." If such wise reason shall take place, a man may not take a loaf
in his hand made of wheat that came out of Dantzic, and say this is wheat that
grew in Dantzic, but it must follow, that the loaf grew in Dantzic. And if the
wife shall say, This is butter of my own cow, Smith shall prove by this speech
that her maid milked butter. But to this fantastical or rather frantic reason, I have
spoken more in mine answer to Smith's preface.

Howbeit, you have taken a wiser way than this, granting that Christ called
bread his body, and wine his blood: but adding thereto, that Christ's calling was
making. Yet here may they that be wise learn by the way, how evil-favouredly
you and Smith agree[7] among yourselves.

And forasmuch as Smith hath not made answer unto the authors by me alleged
in this part, I may justly require that for lack of answer in time and place where
he ought to have answered, he may be condemned as one that standeth mute. And
being condemned in this his chief demur, he hath after nothing to answer at all:
for this foundation being overthrown, all the rest falleth down withal.

Wherefore now will I return to answer you in this matter, which is the last of
the evident and manifest untruths, whereof you appeach me.

I perceive here how untoward you be to learn the truth, being brought up all
your life in papistical errors. If you could forget your law, which hath been your
chief profession and study from your youth, and specially the canon law which
purposely corrupteth the truth of God's word, you should be much more apt to
understand and receive the secrets of holy scripture. But before those scales fall
from your Saulish eyes, you neither can nor will perceive the true doctrine of this
holy sacrament of Christ's body and blood. But yet I shall do as much as lieth
in me, to teach and instruct you, as occasion shall serve; so that the fault shall be
either in your evil bringing up altogether in popery, or in your dulness, or frowardness, if you attain not true[8] understanding of this matter.

[5 These references are given and verified in the reprint of the "Defence of the Sacrament," which is inserted in the body of this book (Book III. cap. 8.), and will be found in the "Confutation of the second book against transubstantiation."]

[6 could I, 1551.]

[7 do agree, 1551.]

[8 the true understanding, 1551.]

God's miraculous works in the sacrament.

Where you speak of the miraculous working of Christ, to make bread his body, you must first learn that the bread is not made really Christ's body, nor the wine his blood, but sacramentally. And the miraculous working is not in the bread, but in them that duly eat the bread, and drink that drink. For the marvellous work of God is in the feeding; and it is christian people that be fed, and not the bread.

30. Injury to baptism.

And so the true confession and belief of the universal church, from the beginning, is not such as you many times affirmed, but never can prove: for the catholic church acknowledgeth no such division between Christ's holy flesh and his Spirit, that life is renewed in us by his holy Spirit, and increased by his holy flesh; but the true faith confesseth that both be done by his holy Spirit and flesh jointly together, as well the renovation, as the increase of our life. Wherefore you diminish here the effect of baptism, wherein is not given only Christ's Spirit, but whole Christ. And

Mine issue.

herein I will join an issue with you. And you shall find, that although you think I lack law wherewith to follow my plea, yet I doubt not but I shall have help of God's word enough, to make all men perceive that you be but a simple divine, so that for lack of your proofs, I doubt not but the sentence shall be given upon my side by all learned and indifferent judges, that understand the matter which is in controversy between us.

God's omnipotency.

And where you say that we must repress our thoughts and imaginations, and by reason of Christ's omnipotency judge his intent by his will, it is a most certain truth that God's absolute and determinate will is the chief governor of all things, and the rule whereby all things must be ordered, and thereto obey. But where (I pray you) have you any such will of Christ, that he is really, carnally, corporally, and naturally, under the forms of bread and wine? There is no such will of Christ set forth in the scripture, as you pretend by a false understanding of these words, "This is my body." Why take you then so boldly upon you to say, that this is Christ's will and intent, when you have no warrant in scripture to bear you?

Matt. xxvi.

Gen. i.

It is not a sufficient proof in scripture, to say, God doth it, because he can do it. For he can do many things which he neither doth, nor will do. He could have sent more than twelve legions of angels to deliver Christ from the wicked Jews, and yet he would not do it. He could have created the world and all things therein in one moment of time, and yet his pleasure was to do it in six days.

In all matters of our christian faith, written in holy scripture, for our instruction and doctrine, how far soever they seem discrepant from reason, we must repress our imaginations, and consider God's pleasure and will, and yield thereto, believing him to be omnipotent; and that by his omnipotent power, such things are verily so as holy scripture teacheth. Like as we believe that Christ was born of the blessed virgin Mary, without company of man: that our Saviour Christ the third day rose again from death: that he in his humanity ascended into heaven: that our bodies at the day of judgment shall rise again; and many other such like things, which we all that be true christian men, do believe firmly, because we find these things written in scripture. And therefore we (knowing God's omnipotency) do believe that he hath brought some of the said things to pass already, and those things that are yet to come, he will by the same omnipotency without doubt likewise bring to pass.

31.

Now if you can prove that your transubstantiation, your fleshly presence of Christ's body and blood, your carnal eating and drinking of the same, your propitiatory sacrifice of the mass, are taught us as plainly in the scripture, as the said articles of our faith be, then I will believe that it is so in deed. Otherwise, neither I nor any man that is in his right wits, will believe your said articles, because God is omnipotent, and can make it so. For you might so, under pretence of God's omnipotency, make as many articles of our faith as you list, if such arguments might take place, that God by his omnipotent power can convert the substance of bread and wine into the substance of his flesh and blood: ergo he doth so indeed.

And although Christ be not corporally in the bread and wine, yet Christ used not so many words, in the mystery of his holy supper, without effectual signification. For he is effectually present, and effectually worketh not in the bread and wine, but in the godly receivers of them, to whom he giveth his own flesh spiritually to feed upon, and his own blood to quench their great inward thirst.

And here I would wish you to mark very well one true sentence which you have uttered by the way, which is, that Christ declared that eating of him signified believing, and start not from it another time. And mark the same, I pray thee, gentle reader. For this one sentence assoileth almost all the arguments that be brought by this lawyer, in his whole book against the truth. *Eating signifieth believing.*

And yet to the said true saying you have joined another untruth, and have yoked them both together in one sentence. For when Christ had taught of the eating of him, being the bread descended from heaven, there was no murmuring thereat, say you. Which your saying I cannot but wonder at, to see you so far deceived in a matter so plain and manifest. And if I had spoken such an evident and manifest untruth, I doubt not but it should have been spoken of to Rome gates. For the text saith there plainly, *Murmurabant Judæi de illo, quod dixisset, Ego sum panis vivus, qui de cœlo descendi:* "The Jews murmured at him because he said, 'I am the bread of life that came from heaven.'" But when you wrote this, it seemeth you looked a little too low, and should have looked higher. *Three untruths uttered by you in this one place. The first. John vi.*

[1]And here by this one place the reader may gather of your own words your intent and meaning in this your book, if that be true which you said before, that ever where contention is, on what part the reader seeth in any one point an open manifest lie, there he may consider (whatsoever excuse be made of truth) yet the victory of truth not to be there intended.

Another untruth also followeth incontinently, that when Christ said, "The bread which I will give you is my flesh, which I will give for the life of the world;" in these words, say you, Christ maketh mention of two gifts. But what be those two gifts, I pray you? and by what words is the diversity of those two gifts expressed? If the giving, as Smith saith, be giving to death, then those two gifts declare that Christ died for us twice. And if one of Christ's gifts have livery and seisin, why hath not the other likewise? And when was then that livery and seisin given? And if eating of Christ be believing, as you said even now, then livery and seisin is given when we first believe, whether it be in baptism, or at any other time. *The second. John vi.*

But what you mean by these words, that Christ gave in his supper his body as really to be eaten of us, as he did to be crucified for us, I understand not, except you would have Christ so really eaten of his apostles at his supper with their teeth, as he was after crucified, whipped, and thrust to the heart with a spear. But was he not then so really and corporally crucified, that his body was rent and torn in pieces? And was not he so crucified then, that he never was crucified after? Was he not so slain then, that he never died any more[2]? And if he were so eaten at his supper, then did his apostles tear his flesh at the supper, as the Jews did the day following? And then how could he now be eaten again? or how could he be crucified the day following, if the night before he were after that sort eaten all up? But "aptly," say you, "and conveniently." Marry, Sir, I thank you; but what is that "aptly and conveniently," but spiritually and by faith, as you said before, not grossly with the teeth, as he was crucified? And so the manner was diverse, I grant, and the substance all one. *32.*

But when Christ said, "The bread which I will give is my flesh, which I will give for the life of the world," if he had fulfilled this promise at his supper, as you say he did, then what needed he after to die that we might live, if he fulfilled his promise of life at his supper? Why said the prophets, that he should be wounded for our iniquities, and that by his wounds we should be healed, if we had life, and were healed before he was wounded? Why doth the catholic faith teach us to believe that we be redeemed by his blood-shedding, if he gave us life (which is our redemption) the night before he shed his blood? And why saith St Paul that there is no remission without blood-shedding? Yea, why did he say[3], *Absit mihi gloriari, nisi in cruce?* "God forbid *The third. That Christ fulfilled not his promise to give us life at his supper. John vi. Isai. liii. Rom. iii. Heb. ix. Gal. vi.*

[1 The edition of 1551 omits this paragraph altogether: it seems to have been an addition made by Cranmer in the revision of the work.]

[2 no more, 1551.]

[3 did St Paul say, 1551.]

that I should rejoice, but in the cross only." Why did he not rather say, *Absit mihi gloriari, nisi in cœna Domini*[1]? "God forbid that I should rejoice, but in the Lord's supper:" whereat, as you say, the promise of life was fulfilled. This is godly doctrine for such men to make, as being ignorant in God's word, wander in fantasies of their own devices, and *putantes se esse sapientes, stulti facti sunt*. But the true faithful believing man professeth, that Christ by his death overcame him that was the author of death, and hath reconciled us to his Father, making us his children, and heirs of his kingdom; that as many as believe in him should not perish, but have life everlasting. Thus saith the true christian man, putting his hope of life and eternal salvation neither in Christ's supper, (although the same be to him a great confirmation of his faith,) nor in any thing else, but with St Paul saith[2], *Mihi absit gloriari, nisi in cruce Domini nostri Jesu Christi:* "God save me that I rejoice in nothing, but in the cross of our Lord Jesu Christ."

And when this true believing man cometh to the Lord's supper, and (according to Christ's commandment) receiveth the bread broken, in remembrance that Christ's body was broken for him upon the cross, and drinketh the wine in remembrance of the effusion of Christ's blood for his sins, and unfeignedly believeth the same, to him the words of our Saviour Christ be effectuous and operatory: "Take, eat; this is my body, which is given for thee: and drink of this, for this is my blood which is shed for thee, to the remission of thy sins." And as St Paul saith, "the bread unto him is the communion of Christ's body, and the wine the communion of his blood." For the effect of his godly eating (as you truly herein gather of St Paul's words) is the communication of Christ's body and blood, but to the faithful receiver, and not to the dumb creatures of bread and wine, under whose forms the catholic faith teacheth not the body and blood of Christ invisibly to be hidden. And as to the godly eater (who duly esteemeth Christ's body, and hath it in such price and estimation as he ought to have) the effect is the communication of Christ's body; so to the wicked eater, the effect is damnation and everlasting woe.

33. *A warrant for apparel.*

And now I am glad that here yourself have found out a warrant for the apparel of bread and wine, that they shall not go altogether naked, and be nude and bare tokens, but have promises of effectual signification, which now you have spied[3] out both in the words of Christ and St Paul.

Christ's ambiguous speeches were not always opened by the evangelists.

Now for the ambiguity of Christ's speeches, it is not always true, that such speeches of Christ as might have ambiguity, the evangelists either plainly or by circumstances open them. For Christ speaking so many things in parables, similes, allegories, metaphors, and other tropes and figures, although sometime Christ himself, and sometime the evangelists open the meaning, yet for the most part the meaning is left to the judgment of the hearers, without any declaration. As when Christ said: "Gird your loins, and take light candles in your hands." And when he said: "No man that setteth his hand to the plough, and looketh behind him, is meet for the kingdom of God." And when he said: "Except the grain of wheat falling upon the ground, die, it remaineth sole." And as St Matthew saith: "Christ spake not to the people without parables, that the scriptures might be fulfilled, which prophesied of Christ, that he should open his mouth in parables."

And although some of his parables Christ opened to the people, some to his apostles only, yet some he opened to neither of both, as can appear, but left them to be considered by the discretion of the hearers. And when Christ called Herod a fox, Judas a devil, himself a door, a way, a vine, a well; neither he nor the evangelists expounded these words, nor gave warning to the hearers that he spake in figures: for every man that had any manner of sense or reason, might well perceive that these sentences could not be true in plain form of words, as they were spoken. For who is so ignorant, but he knoweth that a man is not a fox, a devil, a door, a way, a vine, a well?

"This is my body", is no proper speech.

And so likewise when Christ brake the bread, and commanded his disciples to

---

[1 *Nisi cœna dominica*, 1551.]
[2 but saith with St Paul, 1551.]
[3 espied, 1551.]

eat it, and said, "This is my body;" and of the wine he said, "Divide it among you, drink it, this is my blood:" no man that was there present was so fond, but he knew well that the bread was not Christ's body, nor the wine his blood. And therefore they might well know that Christ called the bread his body, and the wine his blood for some figure, similitude, and property of the bread and wine unto his flesh and blood: for as bread and wine be foods to nourish our bodies, so is the flesh and blood of our Saviour Christ, (being annexed unto his deity,) the everlasting food of our souls.

And although the evangelists in that place do not fully express the words in this sense, yet adjoining the sixth chapter of John (speaking of the spiritual manducation of Christ) to the circumstances of the text in the three evangelists, reciting Christ's last supper, the whole matter is fully gathered, as old authors of the church have declared. For do not the circumstances of the text, both before and after the eating and drinking, declare that there is very bread and wine? Is not that which is broken and eaten bread? and that which is divided, drunken? And the fruit of the vine, is it not very wine? And doth not the nature of sacraments require that the sensible elements should remain in their proper nature, to signify an higher mystery and secret working of God inwardly, as the sensible elements be ministered outwardly? And is not the visible and corporal feeding upon bread and wine a convenient and apt figure and similitude to put us in remembrance, and to admonish us how we be fed invisibly and spiritually by the flesh and blood of Christ, God and man? And is not the sacrament taken away, when the element is taken away? Or can the accidents of the element be the sacrament of substantial feeding? Or did ever any old author say, that the accidents were the sacramental signs without the substances?

But for the conclusion of your matter, here I would wish that you would once truly understand me. For I do not say that Christ's body and blood be given to us in signification, and not in deed. But I do as plainly speak as I can, that Christ's body and blood be given to us in deed, yet not corporally and carnally, but spiritually and effectually, as you confess yourself within twelve lines after.

WINCHESTER.

The author uttereth a great many words, from the eighth to the seventeenth chapter of the first book, declaring spiritual hunger and thirst, and the relieving of the same by spiritual feeding in Christ, and of Christ, as we constantly believe in him, to the confirmation of which belief, the author would have the sacraments of baptism, and of the body and blood of Christ, to be adminicles[4] as it were, and that we by them be preached unto, as in water, bread, and wine, and by them all our sins[5], as it were, spoken unto, or properly touched; which matter in the gross, although there be some words by the way not tolerable, yet if those words set apart, the same were in the sum granted, to be good teaching and wholesome exhortation, it containeth so no more but good matter not well applied. For the catholic church that professeth the truth of the presence of Christ's body in the sacrament, would therewith use that declaration of hunger of Christ, and that spiritual refreshing in Christ, with the effect of Christ's passion and death, and the same to be the only mean of man's regeneration and feeding also, with the differences of that feeding from bodily feeding, for continuing this earthly life. But this toucheth not the principal point that should be entreated: whether Christ so ordered to feed such as be regenerate in him, to give to them in the sacrament the same his body, that he gave to be crucified for us. The good man is fed by faith, and by merits of Christ's passion, being the mean of the gift of that faith, and other gifts also, and by the suffering of the body of Christ, and shedding of his most precious blood on the altar of the cross: which work and passion of Christ is preached unto us by words and sacraments, and the same doctrine received of us by faith, and the effect of it also. And thus far goeth the doctrine of this author.

But the catholic teaching by the scriptures goeth further, confessing Christ to feed such as be regenerate in him, not only by his body and blood, but also with his body and blood, delivered in this sacrament by him in deed to us, which the faithful, by his institution and commandment,

---

[4 adminicles; i. e. helps, supports.]   [5 senses, 1551.]

receive with their faith and with their mouth also, and with those special dainties be fed specially at Christ's table. And so God doth not only preach in his sacraments, but also worketh in them, and with them, and in sensible things giveth celestial gifts, after the doctrine of each sacrament, as in baptism the Spirit of Christ, and in the sacrament of the altar the very body and blood of Christ, according to the plain sense of his words which he spake: "This is my body," &c. And this is the catholic faith, against which, how the author will fortify that he would have called catholic, and confute that he improveth, I intend hereafter more particularly to touch in discussion of that is said.

CANTERBURY.

35.   I mistrust not the indifferency of the reader so much, but he can well perceive how simple and slender a rehearsal you have made here of my eight annotations, and how little matter you have here to say against them, and how little your sayings require any answer.

And because this may the more evidently appear to the reader, I shall rehearse my words here again.

[Book i.]
Chap. viii.

Although in this treaty of the sacrament of the body and blood of our Saviour Christ, I have already sufficiently declared the institution and meaning of the same, according to the very words of the gospel and of St Paul; yet it shall not be in vain somewhat more at large to declare the same, according to the mind, as well of holy scripture, as of old ancient authors, and that so sincerely and plainly, without doubts, ambiguities, or vain questions, that the very simple and unlearned people may easily understand the same, and be edified thereby.

And this by God's grace is mine only intent and desire, that the flock of Christ dispersed in this realm (among whom I am appointed a special pastor) may no longer lack the commodity and fruit, which springeth of this heavenly knowledge. For the more clearly it is understood[1], the more sweetness, fruit, comfort, and edification it bringeth to the godly receivers thereof. And to the clear understanding of this sacrament, divers things must be considered.

Chap. ix.
The spiritual hunger and thirstiness of the soul.

First, that as all men of themselves be sinners, and through sin be in God's wrath, banished far away from him, condemned to hell and everlasting damnation, and none is clearly innocent, but Christ alone: so every soul inspired by God is desirous to be delivered from sin and hell, and to obtain at God's hands mercy, favour, righteousness, and everlasting salvation.

Eph. ii.
Rom. iii.

And this earnest and great desire is called in scripture, "the hunger and thirst of the soul:" with which kind of hunger David was taken, when he said:

Psal. xlii.
Psal. lxiii.

"As an hart longeth for springs of water, so doth my soul long for thee, O God." "My soul thirsteth[2] after God, who is the well of life. My soul thirsteth for thee, my flesh wisheth for thee."

Rom. iv.
Rom. vii.

And this hunger the silly poor sinful soul is driven unto by means of the law, which sheweth unto her the horribleness of sin, the terror of God's indignation, and the horror of death and everlasting damnation.

Rom. viii.

And when she seeth nothing but damnation for her offences by justice and accusation of the law, and this damnation is ever before her eyes, then in this great distress the soul being pressed with heaviness and sorrow, seeketh for some comfort, and desireth some remedy for her miserable and sorrowful estate. And this feeling of her damnable condition, and greedy desire of refreshing, is the spiritual hunger of the soul.

And whosoever hath this godly hunger is blessed of God, and shall have

---

[1 understand, 1551.]   [2 hath thirsted, 1551.]

meat and drink enough, as Christ himself said: "Blessed be they that hunger _{Matt. v.} and thirst for righteousness, for they shall be filled full." And on the other side, they that see not their own sinful and damnable estate, but think themselves holy enough, and in good case and condition enough, as they have no spiritual hunger, so shall they not be fed of God with any spiritual food. For as Almighty God feedeth them that be hungry, so doth he send away empty _{Luke i.} all that be not hungry.

But this hunger and thirst is not easily perceived of the carnal man. For when he heareth the Holy Ghost speak of meat and drink, his mind is by and by in the kitchen and buttery, and he thinketh upon his dishes and pots, his mouth and his belly.

36.

But the scripture in sundry places useth special words, whereby to draw our gross minds from the phantasying of our teeth and belly, and from this carnal and fleshly imagination. For the apostles and disciples of Christ, when they were yet carnal, knew not what was meant by this kind of hunger and meat; and therefore when they desired him to eat, (to withdraw their minds from carnal meat) he said unto them: "I have other meat to eat which you know not." And why knew they it not? Forsooth, because their minds were _{John iv.} gross as yet, and had not received the fulness of the Spirit. And therefore our Saviour Christ, minding to draw them from this grossness, told them of another kind of meat than they phantasied, (as it were) rebuking them, for that they perceived not that there was any other kind of eating and drinking, besides that eating and drinking which is with the mouth and throat.[3]

Likewise when he said to the woman of Samaria, "Whosoever shall drink _{John iv.} of that water that I shall give him, shall never be thirsty again;" they that heard him speak those words, might well perceive that he went about to make them well acquainted with another kind of drinking, than is the drinking with the mouth and throat. For there is no such kind of drink, that with once drinking can quench the thirst of a man's body for ever. Wherefore, in saying he shall never be thirsty again, he did draw their minds from drinking with the mouth unto another kind of drinking, whereof they knew not, and unto another kind of thirsting, wherewith as yet they were not acquainted. And[4] also, when our Saviour Christ said, "He that cometh to me shall not hunger, _{John vi.} and he that believeth on me shall never be thirsty;" he gave them a plain watchword, that there was another kind of meat and drink than that wherewith he fed them at the other side of the water, and another kind of hungering and thirsting than was the hungering and thirsting of the body. By these words therefore he drove the people to understand another kind of eating and drinking, of hungering and thirsting, than that which belongeth only for the preservation of temporal life.

Now then as the thing that comforteth the body is called meat and drink, of a like sort the scripture calleth the same thing that comforteth the soul meat and drink.

Wherefore as here before in the first note is declared the hunger and _{Chap. x.} drought of the soul, so is it now secondly to be noted, what is the meat, drink, and food of the soul.

The spiritual food of the soul.

The meat, drink, food, and refreshing of the soul is our Saviour Christ, as he said himself: "Come unto me all you that travail and be laden, and _{Matt. xi.} I will refresh you." And, "If any man be dry," saith he, "let him come to _{John vii.} me and drink. He that believeth in me, floods of water of life shall flow out

---

[3 and the throat, 1551.]   [4 Also when, 1551.]

<small>John vi.</small> of his belly." And, "I am the bread of life," saith Christ; "he that cometh to me, shall not be hungry: and he that believeth in me, shall never be dry." For as meat and drink do comfort the hungry body, so doth the death of Christ's body and the shedding of his blood comfort the soul, when she is after her sort hungry. What thing is it that comforteth and nourisheth the body? Forsooth, meat and drink. By what names then shall we call the body and blood of our Saviour Christ (which do comfort and nourish the hungry soul) but by the names of meat and drink? And this similitude caused our Saviour to say: "My flesh is very meat, and my blood is very drink." For there is no kind of meat that is comfortable to the soul, but only the death of Christ's blessed body; nor no kind of drink that can quench her thirst, but only the blood-shedding of our Saviour Christ, which was shed for her offences. For as there is a carnal generation, and a carnal feeding and nourishment; so is there also a spiritual generation, and a spiritual feeding.

<small>37.
[John vi.
1551.]</small>

And as every man by carnal generation of father and mother, is carnally begotten and born unto this mortal life: so is every good Christian spiritually born by Christ unto eternal life.

And as every man is carnally fed and nourished in his body by meat and drink, even so is every good christian man spiritually fed and nourished in his soul by the flesh and blood of our Saviour Christ.

[And as the body liveth by meat and drink, and thereby increaseth and groweth from a young babe unto a perfect man, (which thing experience teacheth us;) so the soul liveth by Christ himself, by pure faith eating his flesh and drinking his blood[1].]

<small>John vi.</small> And this Christ himself teacheth us in this sixth[2] of John, saying: "Verily, verily I say unto you, Except ye eat the flesh of the son of man, and drink his blood, you have no life in you. Whoso eateth my flesh, and drinketh my blood, hath eternal life, and I will raise him up at the last day. For my flesh is very meat, and my blood is very drink. He that eateth my flesh, and drinketh my blood, dwelleth in me, and I in him. As the living Father hath sent me, and I live by the Father; even so he that eateth me, shall live by me."

<small>Gal. ii.</small> And this St Paul confessed[3] himself, saying: "That I have life, I have it by faith in the Son of God. And now it is not I that live, but Christ liveth in me."

<small>Chap. xi.</small> The third thing to be noted is this, that although our Saviour Christ resembleth his flesh and blood to meat and drink, yet he far passeth and excelleth all corporal meats and drinks. For although corporal meats and drinks do nourish and continue our life here in this world, yet they begin not our life. For the beginning of our life we have of our fathers and mothers: and the meat, after we be begotten, doth feed and nourish us, and so preserveth us for a time. But our Saviour Christ is both the first beginner of our spiritual life, (who first begetteth us unto God his Father,) and also afterward he is our lively food and nourishment.

<small>Christ far excelleth all corporal food.</small>

Moreover meat and drink do feed[4] and nourish only our bodies, but Christ is the true and perfect nourishment both of body and soul. And besides that, bodily food preserveth the life but for a time, but Christ is such a spiritual and perfect food, that he preserveth both body and soul for ever; as he said

---

[1 This passage is omitted in both the 1551 and 1580 editions, as well as in ed. Embd. 1557. It is here inserted from the original edition of the "Defence."]

[2 in the sixth of John, 1551.]
[3 confessed of himself, 1551.]
[4 doth, 1551.]

unto Martha: "I am a resurrection[5] and life. He that believeth in me, although he die, yet shall he live. And he that liveth and believeth in me, shall not die for ever." John xi.

Fourthly it is to be noted, that the true knowledge of these things is the true knowledge of Christ, and to teach these things is to teach Christ. And the believing and feeling of these things is the believing and feeling of Christ in our hearts. And the more clearly we see, understand, and believe these things, the more clearly we see and understand Christ, and have more fully our faith and comfort in him. Chap. xii. The sacraments were ordained to confirm our faith.

And although our carnal generation and our carnal nourishment be known to all men by daily experience, and by our common senses; yet this our spiritual generation and our spiritual nutrition be so obscure and hid unto us, that we cannot attain to the true and perfect knowledge and feeling of them, but only by faith, which must be grounded upon God's most holy word and sacraments.

And for this consideration our Saviour Christ hath not only set forth these things most plainly in his holy word, that we may hear them with our ears, but he hath also ordained one visible sacrament of spiritual regeneration in water, and another visible sacrament of spiritual nourishment in bread and wine, to the intent, that as much as is possible for man, we may see Christ with our eyes, smell him at our nose, taste him with our mouths, grope him with our hands, and perceive him with all our senses. For as the word of God preached putteth Christ into our ears, so likewise these elements of water, bread, and wine, joined to God's word, do after a sacramental manner put Christ into our eyes, mouths, hands, and all our senses. 38.

And for this cause Christ ordained baptism in water, that as surely as we see, feel, and touch water with our bodies, and be washed with water, so assuredly ought we to believe, when we be baptized, that Christ is verily present with us, and that by him we be newly born again spiritually, and washed from our sins, and grafted in the stock of Christ's own body, and be apparelled, clothed, and harnessed with him, in such wise, that as the devil hath no power against Christ, so hath he none against us, so long as we remain grafted in that stock, and be clothed with that apparel, and harnessed with that armour. So that the washing in water of baptism is, as it were, shewing of Christ before our eyes, and a sensible touching, feeling, and groping of him, to the confirmation of the inward faith, which we have in him.

And in like manner Christ ordained the sacrament of his body and blood in bread and wine, to preach unto us, that as our bodies be fed, nourished, and preserved with meat and drink, so as touching our spiritual life towards God we be fed, nourished, and preserved by the body and blood of our Saviour Christ; and also that he is such a preservation unto us, that neither the devils of hell, nor eternal death, nor sin, can be able to prevail against us, so long as by true and constant faith we be fed and nourished with that meat and drink.

And for this cause Christ ordained this sacrament in bread and wine (which we eat and drink, and be chief nutriments of our body), to the intent that as surely as we see the bread and wine with our eyes, smell them with our noses, touch them with our hands, and taste them with our mouths, so assuredly ought we to believe that Christ is a spiritual[6] life and sustenance of our souls, like as the said bread and wine is the food and sustenance of our bodies. And no less ought we to doubt, that our souls be fed and live by Christ, than Hugo de S. Vict. de Sacramentis, Tractat. vi. cap. 3.
[Rabanus de instit. clericorum, Lib. i. cap. 31. Bernardus de cœna Domini. Ed. Emb. 1577.]

---

[5] I am resurrection, 1551.]   [6] is our spiritual life, 1551.]

that our bodies be fed and live by meat and drink. Thus our Saviour Christ, knowing us to be in this world, as it were, but babes and weaklings in faith, hath ordained sensible signs and tokens whereby to allure and to draw us to more strength and more constant faith in him. So that the eating and drinking of this sacramental bread and wine is, as it were, shewing[1] of Christ before our eyes, a smelling of him with our noses, feeling[2] and groping of him with our hands, and an eating, chewing, digesting, and feeding upon him to our spiritual strength and perfection.

Chap. XIII. Wherefore this sacrament was ordained in bread and wine.

Fifthly, it is to be noted, that although there be many kinds of meats and drinks which feed the body, yet our Saviour Christ (as many ancient authors write) ordained this sacrament of our spiritual feeding in bread and wine, rather than in other meats and drinks, because that bread and wine do most lively represent unto us the spiritual union and knot of all faithful people, as well unto Christ, as also among themselves. For like as bread is made of a great number of grains of corn, ground, baken, and so joined together, that thereof is made one loaf; and an infinite number of grapes be pressed together in one vessel, and thereof is made wine; likewise is the whole multitude of true christian people spiritually joined, first to Christ, and then among themselves together in one faith, one baptism, one Holy Spirit, one knot and bond of love.

39. Hugo de S. Vict. de Sacramentis, Tractat. vi. cap. 3.

Chap. XIV. The unity of Christ's mystical body.

Sixthly, it is to be noted, that as the bread and wine which we do eat be turned into our flesh and blood, and be made our very flesh and very blood, and so be[3] joined and mixed with our flesh and blood, that they be made one whole body together; even so be all faithful Christians spiritually turned into the body of Christ, and so be[3] joined unto Christ, and also together among themselves, that they do make but one mystical body of Christ, as St Paul saith: "We be one bread and one body, as many as be partakers of one bread and one cup." And as one loaf is given among many men, so that every one is partaker of the same loaf; and likewise one cup of wine is distributed unto many persons, whereof every one is partaker; even so our Saviour Christ (whose flesh and blood be represented by the mystical bread and wine in the Lord's supper) doth give himself unto all his true members, spiritually to feed them, nourish them, and to give them continual life by him. And as the branches of a tree, or member of a body, if they be dead, or cut off, they neither live, nor receive any nourishment or sustenance of the body or tree; so likewise ungodly and wicked people, which be cut off from Christ's mystical body, or be dead members of the same, do not spiritually feed upon Christ's body and blood, nor have any life, strength, or sustentation thereby.

1 Cor. x.

Dionysius, *Eccl. Hier. cap. 3.

Chap. XV. This sacrament moveth all men to love and friendship.

Seventhly, it is to be noted, that whereas nothing in this life is more acceptable before God, or more pleasant unto man, than christian people to live together quietly in love and peace, unity and concord, this sacrament doth most aptly and effectuously move us thereunto. For when we be made all partakers of this one table, what ought we to think, but that we be all members of one spiritual body, whereof Christ is the head; that we be joined together in one Christ, as a great number of grains of corn be joined together in one loaf? Surely, they have very hard and stony hearts, which with these things be not moved: and more cruel and unreasonable be they than brute beasts, that cannot be persuaded to be good to their christian brethren and neighbours, for whom Christ suffered death, when in this sacra-

---

[[1] a shewing, 1551.]   [[2] a feeling, 1551.]   [[3] be so, 1551.]

ment they be put in remembrance that the Son of God bestowed his life for his enemies. For we see by daily experience, that eating and drinking together maketh friends, and continueth friendship: much more then ought the table of Christ to move us so to do. Wild beasts and birds be made gentle by giving them meat and drink: why then should not christian men wax meek and gentle with this heavenly meat of Christ? Hereunto we be stirred and moved, as well by the bread and wine in this holy supper, as by the words of holy scripture recited in the same. Wherefore, whose heart soever this holy sacrament, communion, and supper of Christ will not kindle with love unto his neighbours, and cause him to put out of his heart all envy, hatred, and malice, and to grave in the same all amity, friendship, and concord, he deceiveth himself, if he think that he hath the Spirit of Christ dwelling within him.

But all these foresaid godly admonitions, exhortations, and comforts, do the papists (as much as lieth in them) take away from all christian people by their transubstantiation.

For if we receive no bread nor wine in the holy communion, then all these lessons and comforts be gone, which we should learn and receive by eating of the bread, and drinking of the wine: and that fantastical imagination giveth an occasion utterly to subvert our whole faith in Christ. For seeing that this sacrament was ordained in bread and wine (which be foods for the body) to signify and declare unto us our spiritual food by Christ; then if our corporal feeding upon the bread and wine be but fantastical, (so that there is no bread nor wine[4] there indeed to feed upon, although they appear there to be,) then it doth us to understand, that our spiritual feeding in Christ is also fantastical, and that indeed we feed not of him: which sophistry is so devilish and wicked, and so much injurious to Christ, that it could not come from any other person, but only from the devil himself, and from his special minister antichrist.

40. The doctrine of transubstantiation doth clean subvert our faith in Christ.

The eighth thing that is to be noted is, that this spiritual meat of Christ's body and blood is not received in the mouth, and digested in the stomach, (as corporal meats and drinks commonly be,) but it is received with a pure heart and a sincere faith. And the true eating and drinking of the said body and blood of Christ is, with a constant and lively faith to believe, that Christ gave his body, and shed his blood upon the cross for us, and that he doth so join and incorporate himself to us, that he is our head, and we his members, and flesh of his flesh, and bone of his bones, having him dwelling in us, and we in him. And herein standeth the whole effect and strength of this sacrament. And this faith God worketh inwardly in our hearts by his holy Spirit, and confirmeth the same outwardly to our ears by hearing of his word, and to our other senses by eating and drinking of the sacramental bread and wine in his holy supper.

Chap. xvi. The spiritual eating is with the heart, not with the teeth.

What thing then can be more comfortable to us, than to eat this meat, and drink this drink? whereby Christ certifieth us, that we be spiritually, and truly, fed and nourished by him, and that we dwell in him, and he in us. Can this be shewed unto us more plainly, than when he saith himself, "He that eateth me shall live by me?"

John vi.

Wherefore, whosoever doth not contemn the everlasting life, how can he but highly esteem this sacrament? How can he but embrace it as a sure pledge of his salvation? And when he seeth godly people devoutly receive

---

[4 bread and wine, 1551.]

the same, how can he but be desirous oftentimes to receive it with them? Surely no man that well understandeth, and diligently weigheth these things, can be without a great desire to come to this holy supper.

All men desire to have God's favour, and when they know the contrary, that they be in his indignation, and cast out of his favour, what thing can comfort them? How be their minds vexed! What trouble is in their consciences! All God's creatures seem to be against them, and do make them afraid, as things being ministers of God's wrath and indignation towards them, and rest or comfort can they find none, neither within them, nor without them. And in this case they do hate as well God, as the devil; God, as an unmerciful and extreme judge, and the devil as a most malicious and cruel tormentor.

And in this sorrowful heaviness, holy scripture teacheth them, that our heavenly Father can by no means be pleased with them again, but by the sacrifice and death of his only-begotten Son, whereby God hath made a perpetual amity and peace with us, doth pardon the sins of them that believe in him, maketh them his children, and giveth them to his first-begotten Son Christ, to be incorporate into him, to be saved by him, and to be made heirs of heaven with him. And in the receiving of the holy supper of our Lord, we be put in remembrance of this his death, and of the whole mystery of our redemption. In the which supper is made mention of his testament, and of the aforesaid communion of us with Christ, and of the remission of our sins by his sacrifice upon the cross.

41.

Wherefore in this sacrament, (if it be rightly received with a true faith,) we be assured that our sins be forgiven, and the league of peace and the testament of God is confirmed between him and us, so that whosoever by a true faith doth eat Christ's flesh, and drink his blood, hath everlasting life by him. Which thing when we feel in our hearts at the receiving of the Lord's supper, what thing can be more joyful, more pleasant, or more comfortable unto us?

Luke xxii.
1 Cor. xi.
*Matt. xxvi.
Luke xxii.
*Mark xiv.

All this to be true is most certain by the words of Christ himself, when he did first institute his holy supper, the night before his death, as it appeareth as well by the words of the evangelists, as of St Paul. "Do this," saith Christ, "as often as you drink it, in remembrance of me." And St Paul saith: "As often as you eat this bread, and drink this cup, you shall shew the Lord's death until he come." And again Christ said: "This cup is a new testament in mine own blood, which shall be shed for the remission of sins."

This doctrine here recited may suffice for all that be humble and godly, and seek nothing that is superfluous, but that is necessary and profitable: and therefore, unto such persons may be made here an end of this book. But unto them that be contentious papists and idolaters, nothing is enough. And yet, because they shall not glory in their subtle inventions and deceivable doctrine (as though no man were able to answer them), I shall desire the readers of patience to suffer me a little while, to spend some time in vain, to confute their most vain vanities. And yet the time shall not be altogether spent in vain, for thereby shall more clearly appear the light from the darkness, the truth from false sophistical subtleties, and the certain word of God from men's dreams and fantastical inventions.

Although I need make no further answer, but the rehearsal of my words, yet thus much will I answer, that where you say, that I speak some words by the way not tolerable, if there had been any such they should not have failed to be expressed and named to their reproach, as other have been. Wherefore the reader may take a day with you before he believe you, when you reprove me for using some intolerable words, and in conclusion name not one of them.

And as for your catholic confession, that Christ doth indeed feed such as be regenerated in him, not only by his body and blood, but also with his body and blood at his holy table, this I confess also: but that he feedeth Jews, Turks, and infidels, if they receive the sacrament, or that he corporally feedeth our mouths with his flesh and blood, this neither I confess, nor any scripture or ancient writer ever taught; but they teach that he is eaten spiritually in our hearts and by faith, not with mouth and teeth, except our hearts be in our mouths, and our faith in our teeth.

Thus you have laboured sore in this matter, and spun a fair thread, and brought this your first book to a goodly conclusion. For you conclude your book with blasphemous words against both the sacrament of baptism and the Lord's supper, niggardly pinching God's gifts, and diminishing his liberal promises made unto us in them. For where Christ hath promised in both the sacraments to be assistant with us whole both in body and Spirit (in the one to be our spiritual regeneration and apparel, and in the other to be our spiritual meat and drink), you clip his liberal benefits in such sort, that in the one you make him to give but only his Spirit, and in the other but only his body. And yet you call your book an explication and assertion of the true catholic faith.

Injury to both sacraments.

42.

Here you make an end of your first book, leaving unanswered the rest of my book. And yet, forasmuch as Smith busieth himself in this place with the answer thereof, he may not pass unanswered again, where the matter requireth. The words of my book be these.

D. Smith.

But these things cannot manifestly appear to the reader, except the principal points be first set out, wherein the papists vary from the truth of God's word, which be chiefly four.

[Book i.] Chap. xvii. Four principal errors of the papists.

First, the papists say, that in the supper of the Lord, after the words of consecration, (as they call it,) there is none other substance remaining, but the substance of Christ's flesh and blood, so that there remaineth neither bread to be eaten, nor wine to be drunken. And although there be the colour of bread and wine, the savour, the smell, the bigness, the fashion, and all other (as they call them) accidents, or qualities and quantities of bread and wine, yet, say they, there is no very bread nor wine, but they be turned into the flesh and blood of Christ. And this conversion they call "transubstantiation," that is to say, "turning of one substance into another substance." And although all the accidents, both of the bread and wine, remain still, yet, say they, the same accidents be in no manner of thing, but hang alone in the air, without anything to stay them upon. For in the body and blood of Christ, say they, these accidents cannot be, nor yet in the air; for the body and blood of Christ, and the air, be neither of that bigness, fashion, smell, nor colour, that the bread and wine be. Nor in the bread and wine, say they, these accidents cannot be; for the substance of bread and wine, as they affirm, be clean gone. And so there remaineth whiteness, but nothing is white: there remaineth colours, but nothing is coloured therewith: there remaineth roundness, but nothing is round: and there is bigness, and yet nothing is big: there is sweetness, without any sweet thing; softness, without any soft thing; breaking, without any thing broken; division, without anything divided: and so other qualities and quantities, without anything to receive them. And this doctrine they teach as a necessary article of our faith.

The first is of[1] the presence of Christ.

But it is not the doctrine of Christ, but the subtle invention of antichrist, first decreed by Innocent the third, and after more at large set forth by school authors, whose study was ever to defend and set abroad to the world all

* Innocen III.

[1 The first is of transubstantiation, 1551.]

such matters as the bishop of Rome had once decreed. And the devil, by his minister antichrist, had so dazzled the eyes of a great multitude of christian people in these latter days, that they sought not for their faith at the clear light of God's word, but at the Romish antichrist, believing whatsoever he prescribed unto them, yea, though it were against all reason, all senses, and God's most holy word also. For else he could not have been very antichrist indeed, except he had been so repugnant unto Christ, whose doctrine is clean contrary to this doctrine of antichrist. For Christ teacheth that we receive very bread and wine in the most blessed supper of the Lord, as sacraments to admonish us, that as we be fed with bread and wine bodily, so we be fed with the body and blood of our Saviour Christ spiritually: as in our baptism we receive very water, to signify unto us, that as water is an element to wash the body outwardly, so be our souls washed by the Holy Ghost inwardly.

De summa Trin. et fide catholica. [* Firmiter, paragrapho una.]

43.

The second principal thing, wherein the papists vary from the truth of God's word, is this: They say, that the very natural flesh and blood of Christ, which suffered for us upon the cross, and sitteth at the right hand of the Father in heaven, is also really, substantially, corporally, and naturally, in or under the accidents of the sacramental bread and wine, which they call the forms of bread and wine. And yet here they vary not a little among themselves, for some say, that the very natural body of Christ is there, but not naturally, nor sensibly. And other say, that it is there naturally and sensibly, and of the same bigness and fashion that it is in heaven, and as the same was born of the blessed virgin Mary, and that it is there broken and torn in pieces with our teeth. And this appeareth partly by the school authors, and partly by the confession of Berengarius[1], which Nicholas the second constrained him to make, which was this: That of the sacraments of the Lord's table the said Berengarius should promise to hold that faith which the said pope Nicholas and his council held, which was, that not only the sacraments of bread and wine, but also the very flesh and blood of our Lord Jesus Christ are sensibly handled of the priest in the altar, broken and torn with the teeth of the faithful people. But the true catholic faith, grounded upon God's most infallible word, teacheth us, that our Saviour Christ (as concerning his man's nature and bodily presence) is gone up unto heaven, and sitteth at the right hand of his Father, and there shall he tarry until the world's end, at what time he shall come again to judge both the quick and the dead, as he saith himself in many scriptures: "I forsake the world," saith he, "and go to my Father." And in another place he saith: "You shall ever have poor men among you, but me shall not you[2] ever have." And again he

The second is of the presence of Christ in the sacrament.

De consecra. dist. 1. Ego Bereng. * Lege Roffen. contra Œcol. in procœmio. lib. 3. corroborat. 5.

* Christ is not corporally in earth.

John xvi.
Matt. xxvi.

[1 Ego Berengarius indignus sancti Mauritii Andegavensis ecclesiæ Diaconus cognoscens veram, catholicam, et apostolicam fidem, anathematizo omnem hæresim, præcipue eam, de qua hactenus infamatus sum: quæ astruere conatur panem et vinum, quæ in altari ponuntur, post consecrationem solummodo sacramentum, et non verum corpus et sanguinem Domini nostri Jesu Christi esse, nec posse sensualiter, nisi in solo sacramento, manibus sacerdotum tractari, vel frangi, aut fidelium dentibus atteri. Consentio autem sanctæ Romanæ et apostolicæ Sedi: et ore et corde profiteor de sacramentis Dominicæ mensæ eandem fidem me tenere, quam dominus et venerabilis Papa Nicolaus et hæc sancta Synodus auctoritate evangelica et apostolica tenendam tradidit, mihique firmavit: scilicet panem et vinum, quæ in altari ponuntur, post consecrationem non solum sacramentum, sed etiam verum corpus et sanguinem Domini nostri Jesu Christi esse, et sensualiter, non solum sacramento, sed in veritate manibus sacerdotum tractari, frangi, et fidelium dentibus atteri: jurans per sanctam et homousion Trinitatem, per hæc sacrosancta Christi evangelia. Eos vero, qui contra hanc fidem venerint, cum dogmatibus et sectatoribus suis æterno anathemate dignos esse pronuntio. Quod si ego ipse aliquando contra hæc aliquid sentire aut prædicare præsumpsero, subjaceam canonum severitati. Lecto et perlecto sponte subscripsi.—Corpus Juris Canonici. Gratiani Decreti tertia pars. "*De Consecrat.*" Dist. II. c. xlii. cols. 1932, 3. Ed. Lugd. 1618.]

[2 you shall not, 1551.]

saith: "Many hereafter shall come and say, look here is Christ, or look there he is, but believe them not." And St Peter saith in the Acts, that "heaven must receive Christ until the time that all things shall be restored." And St Paul, writing to the Colossians, agreeth hereto, saying: "Seek for things that be above, where Christ is sitting at the right hand of the Father." And St Paul, speaking of the very sacrament, saith: "As often as you shall eat this bread, and drink this cup, shew forth the Lord's death until he come." "Till he come," saith St Paul, signifying that he is not there corporally present. For what speech were this, or who useth of him that is already present to say, "until he come?" For, "until he come[3]," signifieth that he is not yet present. This is the catholic faith, which we learn from our youth in our common creed, and which Christ taught, the apostles followed, and the martyrs confirmed with their blood.

Matt. xxiv.
Acts iii.
Col. iii.
1 Cor. xi.

And although Christ in his human nature, substantially, really, corporally, naturally, and sensibly, be present with his Father in heaven, yet sacramentally and spiritually he is here present[4]. For in water, bread, and wine, he is present, as in signs and sacraments; but he is indeed spiritually in those faithful, christian people, which according to Christ's ordinance be baptized, or receive the holy communion, or unfeignedly believe in him. Thus have you heard the second principal article, wherein the papists vary from the truth of God's word and from the catholic faith.

Now the third thing, wherein they vary, is this.

The papists say, that evil and ungodly men receive in this sacrament the very body and blood of Christ, and eat and drink the selfsame thing that the good and godly men do. But the truth of God's word is contrary, that all those that be godly members of Christ, as they corporally eat the bread and drink the wine, so spiritually they eat and drink Christ's very flesh and blood. And as for the wicked members of the devil, they eat the sacramental bread, and drink the sacramental wine, but they do not spiritually eat Christ's flesh, nor drink his blood, but they eat and drink their own damnation.

44. The third is, that evil men eat and drink the very body and blood of Christ.

The fourth thing, wherein the popish priests dissent from the manifest word of God, is this. They say that they offer Christ every day for remission of sin, and distribute by their masses the merits of Christ's passion. But the prophets, apostles, and evangelists, do say that Christ himself in his own person made a sacrifice for our sins upon the cross, by whose wounds all our diseases were healed, and our sins pardoned; and so did never no priest, man, nor creature, but he, nor he did the same never more than once. And the benefit hereof is in no man's power to give unto any other, but every man must receive it at Christ's hands himself, by his own faith and belief, as the prophet saith.

The fourth is of the daily sacrifice of Christ.
Abacuk ii.

Here Smith findeth himself much grieved at two false reports, wherewith he saith that I untruly charge the papists. One, when I write that some say, that the very natural body of Christ is in the sacrament naturally and sensibly; which thing Smith utterly denieth any of them to say, and that I falsely lay this unto their charge. And moreover it is[5] very false, saith he, that you lay unto our charges, that we say, that Christ's body is in the sacrament as it was born of the virgin, and that it is broken and torn in pieces with our teeth. This also Smith saith[6] is a false report of me.

* D. Smith. Some say that Christ is naturally in the sacrament.

But whether I have made any untrue report or no, let the books be judges. As

---

[3 until I come, 1551.]
[4 He is here present in water, bread, and wine, as in signs and sacraments, but he is indeed spiritually in the faithful christian people, 1551.]
[5 it is also very false, 1551.]
[6 saith Smith, 1551.]

touching the first, the bishop writeth thus in his book of the Devil's Sophistry, the fourteenth leaf: "Good men were never offended with breaking of the host, which they daily saw, being also persuaded Christ's body to be present in the sacrament naturally and really." And in the eighteenth leaf he saith these words: "Christ, God and man, is naturally present in the sacrament." And in ten or twelve places of this, his last book, he saith, "that Christ is present in the sacrament 'naturally,' 'corporally,' 'sensibly,' and 'carnally,' as shall appear evidently in the reading thereof." So that I make no false report herein, who report no otherwise[1] than the papists have written and published openly in their books.

A manifest falsehood in the printing of the bishop's book.

And it is not to be passed over, but worthy to be noted, how manifest falsehood is used in the printing of this bishop's book, in the one hundred and thirty-sixth leaf. For where the bishop wrote (as I have two copies to shew, one of his own hand, and another exhibited by him in open court before the king's commissioners), that Christ's body in the sacrament is truly present, and therefore really present, corporally also, and naturally; the printed book now set abroad hath changed this word "naturally," and in the stead thereof hath put these words, "but yet supernaturally," corrupting and manifestly falsifying the bishop's book[2].

45.

Who was the author of this untrue act, I cannot certainly define; but if conjectures may have place, I think the bishop himself would not command to alter the book in the printing, and then set it forth with this title, that it was the same book that was exhibited by his own hand, for his defence, to the king's majesty's commissioners at Lambeth.

And I think the printer, being a Frenchman, would not have enterprised so false a deed of his own head, for the which he should have no thanks at all, but be accused of the author as a falsifier of his book.

Now forasmuch as it is not like, that either the bishop or the printer would play any such pranks, it must then be some other, that was of counsel in the printing of the book; which being printed in France (whither you be now fled from your own native country), what person is more like to have done such a noble act than you? who being so full of craft and untruth in your own country, shew yourself to be no changeling, wheresoever you be come. And the rather it seemeth to me to be you than any other person, because that the book is altered in this word "naturally," upon which word standeth the reproof of your saying. For he saith that Christ is in the sacrament "naturally," and you deny that any man so saith, but that Christ is there "supernaturally." Who is more like therefore to change in his book "naturally" into "supernaturally" than you, whom the matter toucheth, and no man else? But whether my conjectures be good in this matter I will not determine, but refer it to the judgment of the indifferent reader.

Some say that Christ is rent and torn with teeth in the sacrament.

Now as concerning the second untrue report, which I should make of the papists, I have alleged the words of Berengarius' recantation, appointed by pope Nicholas the second, and written *De consecrat. dist.* 2, which be these, "that not only the sacraments of bread and wine, but also the very flesh and blood of our Lord Jesu Christ, are sensibly handled of the priest in the altar, broken, and torn with the teeth of the faithful people."

Thus the reader may see that I misreport not the papists, nor charge them with any other words than they do write; that is to say, "that the body of Christ is naturally and sensibly in the sacrament, and broken and torn in pieces with our teeth."

"But," saith Smith, "the meaning of Berengarius in his recantation was otherwise, that the forms of bread[3] and wine are broken and torn with our teeth, but Christ is received wholly, without breaking of his body, or tearing with our teeth." Well, whatsoever the meaning of Berengarius was, his words be as I report; so that I make

[1 none otherwise, 1551.]

[2 In the 1551 edition of Winchester's Explication, p. 136, the passage is thus given: "It is truly present, and therefore really present, corporally also, and but yet supernaturally, with relation to the truth of the body present, and not to the manner of presence, which is spiritual." The reader, however, is directed in the "certain faults escaped in the printing," appended to the beginning of the book, to read "naturally" for "supernaturally." Cranmer's version of these renderings, it is evident, is the only one which can make the sense clear and distinct.]

[3 the forms only of bread, 1551.]

no false report of the papists, nor untruly charge them with that they say not. But how should men know what the papists mean, when they say one thing, and mean another? For Berengarius said, "that not only the sacraments be broken and torn with our teeth," and you say he meant contrary, "that only the sacraments be broken and torn with our teeth." Berengarius said, "that also the very flesh and blood of Christ be broken and torn," and you say he meant clean contrary, "that the flesh and blood of Christ be not broken and torn." Well, then would I fain learn, how it may be known what the papists mean, if they mean yea, when they say nay, and mean nay, when they say yea.

And as for St John Chrysostom, and other old authors, by whom you would excuse this manner of speech, they help you herein nothing[4] at all. For not one of them speak after this sort that Berengarius doth. For although they say sometimes that we see Christ, touch him, and break him, (understanding that speech not of Christ himself, but of the sacraments which represent him,) yet they use no such form of speech as was prescribed to Berengarius, that we see, feel, and break, not only the sacraments, but also Christ himself.

46.

And likewise of Loth[5], Abraham, Jacob, Joshua, Mary Magdalene, and the apostles, whom you bring forth in this matter, there is no such speech in the scripture as Berengarius useth. So that all these things be brought out in vain, having no colour to serve for your purpose, saving that something you must say to make out your book.

And as for all the rest that you say in this process, concerning the presence of Christ visible and invisible, needeth no answer at all, because you prove nothing of all that you say in that matter, which may easily therefore[6] be denied by as good authority as you affirm the same. And yet all the old writers that speak of the diversity of Christ's substantial presence and absence, declare this diversity to be in the diversity of his two natures, (that in the nature of his humanity he is gone hence, and present in the nature of his divinity,) and not that in divers respects and qualities of one nature he is both present and absent; which I have proved in my third book, the fifth chapter.

And forasmuch as you have not brought one author for the proof of your saying, but your own bare words, nor have answered to the authorities alleged by me in the foresaid place of my third book, reason would that my proofs should stand and have place, until such time as you have proved your sayings, or brought some evident matter to improve mine. And this, I trust, shall suffice to any indifferent reader, for the defence of my first book.

WINCHESTER.

Wherein I will keep this order. First, to consider the third book, that speaketh against the faith of the real presence of Christ's most precious body and blood in the sacrament: then against the fourth, and so return to the second, speaking of transubstantiation, whereof to talk, the real presence not being discussed, were clearly superfluous. And finally, I will somewhat say of the fifth book also.

CANTERBURY.

But now to return to the conclusion of the bishop's book. As it began with a marvellous sleight and subtlety, so doth he conclude the same with a like notable subtlety, changing the order of my books, not answering them in such order as I wrote them, nor as the nature of the things requireth. For seeing that, by all men's confessions, there is bread and wine before the consecration; the first thing to be discussed in this matter is, whether the same bread and wine remain still after the consecration, as sacraments of Christ's most precious body and blood. And next, by order of nature and reason, is to be discussed, whether the body and blood of Christ,

Why the order of my book was changed by the bishop.

[4 nothing herein, 1551.]
[5 i. e. Lot.]
[6 which may therefore easily, 1551.]

represented by those sacraments, be present also with the said sacraments: and what manner of presence Christ hath, both in the sacraments, and in them that receive the sacraments.

47. But for what intent the bishop changed this order, it is easy to perceive. For he saw the matter of transubstantiation so flat and plain against him, that it was hard for him to devise an answer in that matter, that should have any appearance of truth, but all the world should evidently see him clearly overthrown at the first onset. Wherefore he thought, that although the matter of the real presence hath no truth in it at all, yet forasmuch as it seemed to him to have some more appearance of truth than the matter of transubstantiation hath, he thought best to begin with that first, trusting so to juggle in the matter, and to dazzle the eyes of them that be simple and ignorant, and specially of such as were already persuaded in the matter, that they should not well see nor perceive his legerdemain. And when he had won credit with them in that matter, by making them to wonder at his crafty juggling, then thought he, it should be a fit and meet time for him to bring in the matter of transubstantiation. For when men be amazed, they do wonder rather than judge: and when they be muffled and blindfolded, they cannot find the right way, though they seek it never so fast, nor yet follow it, if it chance them to find it; but give up clearly their own judgment, and follow whomsoever they take to be their guide. And so shall they lightly follow me in this matter of transubstantiation, (thought the bishop,) if I can first persuade them and get their good wills in the real presence. This sleight and subtlety thou mayest judge certainly, good reader, to be the cause, and none other, wherefore the order of my book is changed without ground or reason.

The end of the first book.

THE CONFUTATION OF THE THIRD BOOK.

[WINCHESTER.]

IN the beginning of the third book, the author hath thought good to note certain differences, which I will also particularly consider. It followeth in him thus.

"They teach that Christ is in the bread and wine: but we say, according to the truth, that he is in them that worthily eat and drink the bread and wine."

Note here, reader, even in the entry of the comparison of these differences, how untruly the true faith of the church is reported, which doth not teach that Christ is in the bread and wine (which was the doctrine of Luther); but the true faith is, that Christ's most precious body and blood is, by the might of his word and determination of his will, which he declareth by his word, in his holy supper present under form of bread and wine. The substance of which natures of bread and wine is converted into his most precious body and blood, as it is truly believed and taught in the catholic church, of which teaching this author cannot be ignorant. So as the author of this book reporteth an untruth wittingly against his conscience, to say they teach (calling them papists) that Christ is in the bread and wine, but they agree in form of teaching with that the church of England teacheth at this day, in the distribution of the holy communion, in that it is there said, the body and blood of Christ to be under the form of bread and wine. And thus much serveth for declaration of the wrong and untrue report of the faith of the catholic church, made of this author in the setting forth of this difference on that part, which it pleaseth him to name papists.

And now to speak of the other part of the difference on the author's side, when he would tell what he and his say, he conveyeth a sense craftily in words to serve for a difference, such as no catholic man would deny. For every catholic teacher granteth, that no man can receive worthily Christ's body[1] and blood in the sacrament, unless he hath by faith and charity Christ dwelling in him. For otherwise, such one as hath not Christ in him, receiveth Christ's body in the sacrament unworthily, to his condemnation. Christ cannot be received worthily, but into his own temple, which be ye, Saint Paul saith; and yet, he that hath not Christ's Spirit in him, is not his. As for calling it bread and wine, a catholic man forbeareth not that name, signifying what those creatures were before the consecration in substance. Wherefore appeareth, how the author of this book, in the lieu and place of a difference, which he pretendeth he would shew, bringeth in that under a "but", which every catholic man must needs confess, that Christ is in them who worthily eat and drink the sacrament of his body and blood, or the bread and wine, as this author speaketh.

But as[2] this author would have spoken plainly, and compared truly the difference of the two teachings, he should in the second part have said somewhat contrary to that the catholic church teacheth, which he doth not; and therefore as he sheweth untruth in the first report, so he sheweth a sleight and shift in the declaration of the second part, to say that repugneth not to the first matter, and that no catholic man will deny, considering the said two teachings be not of one matter, nor shoot not, (as one might say,) to one mark. For the first part is of the substance of the sacrament to be received, where it is truth, Christ to be present, God and man. The second part is of Christ's spiritual presence in the man that receiveth, which indeed must be in him before he receive the sacrament, or he cannot receive the sacrament worthily, as before[3] is said, which two parts may stand well without any repugnancy; and so both the differences thus taught make but one catholic doctrine. Let us see what the author saith further.

48.
[The author, Orig. Ed. 1551.]

[The answer, Ib. 1551.]
*Untrue report.

*The teaching hitherto even at this day of the church of England agreeth with that this author calleth papists'.

*Crafty conveyance of speech by this author.

*Worthy receiving of Christ's precious body and blood.

1 Cor. vi.

*A difference should be of contraries

CANTERBURY.

Now the crafts, wiles, and untruths of the first book being partly detected, after I have also answered to this book, I shall leave to the indifferent reader to judge whether it be of the same sort or no. But before I make further answer, I shall

---

[¹ Christ's precious body, 1551.] [² But and this author, 1551.] [³ Afore, 1551.]

rehearse the words of mine own third book, which you attempt next, out of order, to impugn. My words be these:

[Book iii.[1] Chap. I. The presence of Christ in the sacrament.]

Now this matter of transubstantiation being, as I trust, sufficiently resolved, (which is the first part before rehearsed, wherein the papistical doctrine varieth from the catholic truth,) order requireth next to entreat of the second part, which is of the manner of the presence of the body and blood of our Saviour Christ in the sacrament thereof; wherein is no less contention than in the first part.

For a plain explication whereof, it is not unknown to all true faithful christian people, that our Saviour Christ, (being perfect God, and in all things equal and coeternal with his Father,) for our sakes became also a perfect man, taking flesh and blood of his blessed mother and virgin Mary, and, saving sin, being in all things like unto us, adjoining unto his divinity a most perfect soul [and a most perfect body: his soul being endued with life, sense, will, reason, wisdom, memory, and all other things required to the perfect soul[2]] of man: and his body being made of very flesh and bones, not only having all members of a perfect man's body, in due order and proportion, but also being subject to hunger, thirst, labour, sweat, weariness, cold, heat, and all other like infirmities and passions of a man, and unto death also, and that the most vile and painful upon the cross; and after his death he rose again, with the selfsame visible and palpable body, and appeared therewith, and shewed the same unto his apostles, and especially to Thomas, making him to put his hands into his side, and to feel his wounds. And with the selfsame body he forsook this world, and ascended into heaven, (the apostles seeing and beholding his body when it ascended,) and now sitteth at the right hand of his Father, and there shall remain until the last day, when he shall come to judge the quick and dead.

Christ corporally is ascended into heaven. Acts iii.

This is the true catholic faith, which the scripture teacheth, and the universal church of Christ hath ever believed from the beginning, until within these four or five hundred years last passed, that the bishop of Rome, with the assistance of his papists, hath set up a new faith and belief of their own devising, that the same body, really, corporally, naturally, and sensibly, is in this world still, and that in an hundred thousand places at one time, being inclosed in every pix, and bread consecrated.

Chap. II.

And although we do affirm (according to God's word), that Christ is in all persons that truly believe in him, in such sort, that with his flesh and blood he doth spiritually nourish[3] and feed them, and giveth them everlasting life, and doth assure them thereof, as well by the promise of his word, as by the sacramental bread and wine in his holy supper, which he did institute for the same purpose; yet we do not a little vary from the heinous errors of the papists. For they teach, that Christ is in the bread and wine; but we say (according to the truth), that he is in them that worthily eat and drink the bread and wine.

The difference between the true and papistical doctrine concerning the presence of Christ's body.

Here it pleaseth you to pass over all the rest of my sayings, and to answer only to the difference between the papists and the true catholic faith. Where in the first[4] ye find fault that I have untruly reported the papistical faith, (which you call[5] the faith of the church,) which teacheth not, say you[6], that Christ is in the bread and wine, but under the forms of bread and wine. But to answer you[7], I say, that the

The first comparison.

[1 In the original edition this is the heading of the third book: "The third book teacheth the manner how Christ is present in his supper."]

[2 This passage appears only in the edition, 1551, being entirely omitted in that of 1580.]

[3 Nourish them, and, 1551.]
[4 Wherein first ye find, 1551.]
[5 He calleth, 1551.]
[6 Saith he, 1551.]
[7 To answer him, 1551.]

papists do teach, that Christ is in the visible signs, and whether they list to call them bread and wine, or the forms of bread and wine, all is one to me; for the truth is, that he is neither corporally in the bread and wine, nor in or under the forms and figures of them, but is corporally in heaven, and spiritually in his lively members, which be his temples where he inhabiteth. And what untrue report is this, when I speak of bread and wine to the papists, to speak of them in the same sense that the papists mean, taking bread and wine for the forms and accidents of bread and wine?

50. Misreport of bread and wine for the forms and figures of them.

And yourself also do teach, to understand by the bread and wine, not their substances, but accidents. And what have I offended then, in speaking to you after your own manner of speech, which yourself doth approve and allow by and by after, saying these words? "As for calling it bread and wine, a catholic man forbeareth not that name." If a catholic man forbeareth not that name, and catholic men be true men, then true men forbear not that name. And why then charge you me with an untruth, for using that name, which you use yourself, and affirm catholic men to use; but that you be given altogether to find faults rather in other, than to amend your own, and to reprehend that in me, which you allow in yourself and other, and purposely will not understand my meaning, because ye would seek occasion to carp and controul?

For else what man is so simple that readeth my book, but he may know well, that I mean not to charge you for affirming of Christ to be in the very bread and wine? For I know that you say, there is neither bread nor wine, (although you say untruly therein;) but yet forasmuch as the accidents of bread and wine you call bread and wine, and say that in them is Christ, therefore I report of you, that you say Christ is in the bread and wine, meaning, as you take bread and wine, the accidents thereof.

Yet D. Smith was a more indifferent reader of my book than you in this place, who understood my words as I meant and as the papists use, and therefore would not purposely calumniate and reprehend that was well spoken. But there is no man so dull as he that will not understand. For men know that your wit is of as good capacity as D. Smith's is, if your will agreed to the same.

Smyth.

But as for any untrue report made by me herein willingly against my conscience (as you untruly report of me), by that time[8] I have joined with you throughout your book, you shall right well perceive, I trust, that I have said nothing wittingly, but that my conscience shall be able to defend at the great day, in the sight of the everliving God, and that I am able before any learned and indifferent judges to justify by holy scriptures, and the ancient doctors of Christ's church, as I will appeal the consciences of all godly men, that be any thing indifferent, and ready to yield to the truth, when they read and consider my book.

And as concerning the form of doctrine used in this church of England in the holy communion, that the body and blood of Christ be under the forms of bread and wine, when you shall shew the place where this form of words is expressed, then shall you purge yourself of that, which in the meantime I take to be a plain untruth.

The book of common prayer.

Now for the second part of the difference, you grant that our doctrine is true, that Christ is in them that worthily eat and drink the bread and wine; and if it differ not from yours, then let it pass as a thing agreed upon by both parties. And yet if I would captiously gather of your words, I could as well prove by this second part, that very bread and wine be eaten[9] and drunken after consecration, as you could prove by the first, that Christ is in the very bread and wine. And if a catholic man call that bread and wine[10], (as you say in the second part of the difference,) what meant you then in the first part of this difference, to charge me with so heinous a crime (with a note to the reader), as though I had sinned against the Holy Ghost, because I said, "that the papists do teach that Christ is in the bread and wine?" Do not you affirm here yourself the same that I report? that the papists (which you call the catholics), do not forbear to call the sacrament, (wherein they put the real and

The second part.

51.

[8 By that time that I have, 1551.] [9 Ed. 1551, omits the words "eaten and".]
[10 Called bread and wine, 1551.]

corporal presence,) bread and wine? Let the reader now judge, whether you be caught in your own snare or no. But such is the success of them that study to wrangle in words, without any respect of opening the truth.

But letting that matter pass, yet we vary from you in this difference. For we say not, as you do, that the body of Christ is corporally, naturally, and carnally, either in the bread and wine, or forms of bread and wine, or in them that eat and drink thereof. But we say, that he is corporally in heaven only, and spiritually in them that worthily eat and drink the bread and wine. But you make an article of the faith, which the old church never believed nor heard of.

And where you note in this second part of the difference a sleight and craft, as you note an untruth in the first; even as much craft is in the one as untruth in the other, being neither sleight nor untruth in either of both. But this sleight, say you, I use, putting that for a difference, wherein is no difference at all, but every catholic man must needs confess. Yet once again, there is no man so deaf as he that will not hear, nor so blind as he that will not see, nor so dull as he that will not understand. But if you had indifferent ears, indifferent eyes, and indifferent judgment, you might well gather of my words a plain and manifest difference, although it be not in such terms as contenteth your mind. But because you shall see that I mean no sleight nor craft, but go plainly to work, I shall set out the difference truly as I meant, and in such your own terms as I trust shall content[1] you, if it be possible. Let this therefore be the difference.

* The difference.

They say that Christ is corporally under, or in the forms of bread and wine: we say, that Christ is not there, neither corporally, nor spiritually; but in them that worthily eat and drink the bread and wine, he is spiritually, and corporally in heaven[2].

Here, I trust, I have satisfied, as well the untrue report wittingly made, as you say, in the first part of the difference against my conscience, as the craft and sleight used in the second part. But what be you eased now by this? We say as the scripture teacheth, that Christ is corporally ascended into heaven, and nevertheless he is so[3] in them that worthily eat the bread and drink the wine, given and distributed at his holy supper, that he[4] feedeth and nourisheth them with his flesh and blood unto eternal life. But we say not (as you do, clearly without ground of scripture), that he is corporally under the forms of bread and wine, where his presence should be without any profit or commodity, either to us, or to the bread and wine.

Repugnances.

52.

And here in this difference, it seemeth that you have either clearly forgotten, or negligently overshot yourself, uttering that thing unawares which is contrary to your whole book. For the first part (which is of the being of Christ in the sacramental bread and wine,) is of the substance of the sacrament to be received, say you, where it is true, Christ to be present God and man. The second part, say you, which is of the being of Christ in them that worthily eat and drink the bread and wine, is of Christ's spiritual presence. Of your which words[5] I see nothing to be gathered, but that as concerning his substantial presence, Christ is received into the sacramental bread and wine; and as for them that worthily receive the sacrament, he is in them none otherwise than after a spiritual presence: for else why should ye say, that the second part is of Christ's spiritual presence, if it be as well of his corporal, as of his[6] spiritual presence? Wherefore, by your own words, this difference should be understanded of two different beings of Christ, that in the sacrament he is by his substance, and in the worthy receivers spiritually, and not by his substance; for else the differences repugn not, as you object against me. Wherefore either you write one thing and mean another, or else, as you write of other, God so blindeth the adversaries of the truth, that in one place or other they confess the truth unawares.

Now follow my words in the second comparison.

[1 I trust to content you, 1551.]
[2 He is spiritually, but not corporally, 1551.]
[3 Ed. 1551, entirely omits the words, "corporally ascended into heaven, and nevertheless he is so."]
[4 Ed. 1551, omits the words "that he", and adds, "in whom he is not in vain but,".]
[5 Of which your words, 1551.]
[6 Ed. 1551, omits "of his."]

They say, that when any man eateth the bread, and drinketh the cup, Christ goeth into his mouth or stomach with the bread and wine, and no further. But we say, that Christ is in the whole man, both in body and soul of him that worthily eateth the bread, and drinketh the cup, and not in his mouth or stomach only.

The second comparison.

WINCHESTER.

In this comparison, the author termeth the true catholic teaching at his pleasure, to bring it in contempt: which doing in rude speech would be called otherwise than I will term it. Truth it is, as St Augustine saith, we receive in the sacrament the body of Christ with our mouth; and such speech other use, as a book set forth in the archbishop of Canterbury's name, called a Catechism, willeth children to be taught that they receive with their bodily mouth the body and blood of Christ: which I allege, because it shall appear it is a teaching set forth among us of late, as hath been also, and is by the book of common prayer, being the most true catholic doctrine of the substance of the sacrament, in that it is there so catholicly spoken of: which book this author doth after specially allow, howsoever all the sum of his teaching doth improve it in that point. So much is he contrary to himself in this work, and here in this place, not caring what he saith, reporteth such a teaching in the first part of this difference, as I have not heard of before. There was never man of learning that I have read termed the matter so, that Christ goeth into the stomach of the man that received[7], and no further. For that is written contra Stercoranistas, *is nothing to this teaching; nor the speech of any gloss, if there be any such, were herein to be regarded. The catholic doctrine is, that by the holy communion in the sacrament we be joined to Christ really, because we receive in the holy supper the most precious substance of his glorious body, which is a flesh giving life. And that is not digested into our flesh, but worketh in us and attempereth by heavenly nurture our body and soul, being partakers of his passion, to be conformable to his will, and by such spiritual food to be made more spiritual. In the receiving of which food in the most blessed sacrament, our body and soul, in them that duly communicate, work together in due order, without other discussion of the mystery than God hath appointed; that is to say, the soul to believe as it is taught, and the body to do as God hath ordered, knowing that glorious flesh by our eating cannot be consumed or suffer, but to be most profitable unto such as do accustome worthily to receive the same. But to say that the church teacheth how we receive Christ at our mouth, and he goeth into our stomach and no further, is a report which by the just judgment of God is suffered to come out of the mouth of them that fight against the truth in this most high mystery.*

*A sect reproved that were called Stercoranists.

Now where this author in the second part, by an adversative with a "but" to make the comparison, telleth what he and his say, he telleth in effect that which every catholic man must needs and doth confess. For such as receive Christ's most precious body and blood in the sacrament worthily, they have Christ dwelling in them, who comforteth both body and soul; which the church hath ever taught most plainly. So as this comparison of difference in his two parties is made of one open untruth, and a truth disguised, as though it were now first opened by this author and his; which manner of handling declareth what sleight and shift is used in the matter.

53.

CANTERBURY.

In the first part of this comparison I go not about to term the true catholic faith, for the first part in all the comparisons is the papistical faith, which I have termed none otherwise than I learned of their own terming; and therefore if my terming please you not (as indeed it ought to please no man), yet lay the blame in them that were the authors and inventors of that terming, and not in me, that against them do use their own terms, terming the matter as they do themselves, because they should not find fault with me, as you do, that I term their teaching at my pleasure.

And as for receiving of the body of Christ with our mouths, truth it is, that St Augustine, Ambrose, Chrysostom, and other use such speeches, that we receive the body of Christ with our mouths, see him with our eyes, feel him with our hands, break him and tear him with our teeth, eat him and digest him, (which speech I have

---

[[7] Receiveth, 1551.]

also used in my catechism;) but yet these speeches must be understand figuratively, (as I have declared in my fourth book, the eighth chapter, and shall more fully declare hereafter,) for we do not these things to the very body of Christ, but to the bread whereby his body is represented.

The book of common prayer.

And yet the book of common prayer neither useth any such speech nor giveth any such doctrine, nor I in no point improve that godly book, nor vary from it. But yet glad am I to hear that the said book liketh you so well, as no man can mislike it, that hath any godliness in him joined with knowledge.

That the papists say, that Christ goeth no further than the mouth or stomach.

But now to come to the very matter of this article: it is marvel that you never read, that Christ goeth into the mouth or stomach of that man that receiveth, and no further, being a lawyer, and seeing that it is written in the gloss of the law, *De consecrat. dist.* 2. *Tribus gradibus*, in these words: " It is certain that as soon as the forms be torn with the teeth, so soon the body of Christ is gone up into heaven[1]." And in the chapter, *Non iste*[2], is another gloss to the same purpose. And if you had

Thomas Bonaventura.
Read Smith, folio 64.

read Thomas de Aquino and Bonaventure, great clerks and holy saints of the pope's own making, and other school-authors, then should you have known what the papists do say in this matter. For some say, that the body of Christ remaineth so long as the form and fashion of bread remaineth, although it be in a dog, mouse, or in the jakes. And some say, it is not in the mouse nor jakes, but remaineth only in the person that eateth it, until it be digested in the stomach, and the form of bread be gone. Some say, it remaineth no longer than the sacrament is in the eating, and may be felt, seen, and tasted in the mouth.

Hugo. Innocentius III.
Lib. cap. 15.
54.

And this, besides Hugo, saith pope Innocentius himself, who was the best learned and the chief doer in this matter of all the other popes. Read you never none of these authors, and yet take upon you the full knowledge of this matter? Will you take upon you to defend the papists, and know not what they say? Or do you know it, and now be ashamed of it, and for shame will deny it?

And seeing that you teach, that "we receive the body of Christ with our mouths," I pray you, tell whether it go any further than the mouth or no? and how far it goeth?— that I may know your judgment herein: and so shall you be charged no further than with your own saying, and the reader shall perceive what excellent knowledge you have in this matter.

And where you say, "that to teach that we receive Christ at our mouth, and he goeth into our stomach, and no further, cometh out of the mouth of them that fight against the truth in this most high mystery:" here, like unto Caiphas, you prophesy the truth unawares. For this doctrine cometh out of the mouth of none, but of the papists, which fight against the holy catholic truth of the ancient fathers, saying, that Christ tarrieth no longer than the proper forms of bread and wine remain, which cannot remain after perfect digestion in the stomach.

And I say not that the church teacheth so, as you feign me to say, but that the papists say so. Wherefore I should[3] wish you to report my words as I say, and not as you imagine me to say, lest you hear again (as you have heard heretofore), of your wonderful learning and practice in the devil's sophistry.

The second part.

Now as concerning the second part of this comparison, here you grant that my saying therein is true, and that every catholic man must needs, and doth confess the same. By which your saying, you must also condemn almost all the school-authors

Innocentius III.

and lawyers, that have written of this matter, with Innocent the third also, as men not catholic, because they teach that Christ goeth no further, nor tarrieth no longer, than the forms of bread and wine go, and remain in their proper kind.

[1 " Certum est, quod species quam cito dentibus teruntur, tam cito in cœlum rapitur corpus Christi." —Corpus Juris Canonici : Decreti tertia pars : " *de consecrat.*" Dist. II. " *Tribus gradibus*," col. 1922. Lugduni, 1618.]

[2 " Hug. species tamen bene vadunt in corpus. Sed nunquid ibi est sacramentum? Non, quia desinit ibi esse corpus Christi: et tandiu est ibi sacramentum, quandiu est corpus Christi. Sed quandiu hoc sit, id est, usque ad quem locum procedat per gulam, nescio. Sed licet non sit sacramentum, cum est in corpore, si tamen evomerit illud, cum veneratione est servandum, quia sacramentum fuit."—Ib. Dist. II. " *Non iste panis*," col. 1942. Ib.]

[3 Would, 1551.]

And yet now your doctrine, as far as I can gather of your obscure words, is this: that Christ is received at the mouth, with the forms of bread and wine, and goeth with them into the stomach. And although they go no further in their proper kinds, yet there Christ leaveth them, and goeth himself further into every part of the man's body, and into his soul also: which your saying seemeth to me to be very strange. For I have many times heard, that a soul hath gone into a body, but I never heard that a body went into a soul. But I ween, of all the papists you shall be alone in this matter, and find never a fellow to say as you do.

And of these things which I have here spoken, I may conclude, that this comparison of difference is not made of an open untruth and a truth disguised, except you will confess the papistical doctrine to be an open untruth.

Now the words of my third comparison be these.

They say, that Christ is received in the mouth, and entereth in with the bread and wine. We say that he is received in the heart, and entereth in by faith.

WINCHESTER.

Here is a pretty sleight in this comparison, where both parts of the comparison may be understood on both sides, and therefore here is by the author in this comparison no issue joined. For the worthy receiving of Christ's body and blood in the sacrament is both with mouth and heart; both in fact and faith. After which sort, St Peter in the last supper received Christ's body, whereas in the same[4] *Judas received it with mouth and in fact only; whereof St Augustine speaketh in this wise:* Non dicunt ista, nisi qui de mensa Domini vitam sumunt, sicut Petrus, non judicium, sicut Judas, et tamen ipsa utrique fuit una, sed non utrique valuit ad unum, quia ipsi non erant unum[5]. *Which words be thus much to say:* "*That they say not so, (as was before entreated), but such as receive life of our Lord's table, as Peter did, not judgment, as Judas, and yet the table was all one to them both; but it was not to all one effect in them both, because they were not one.*" *Here St Augustine noteth the difference in the receiver, not in the sacrament received, which being received with the mouth only, and Christ entering in mystery only, doth not sanctify us, but is the stone of stumbling, and our judgment and condemnation; but if he be received with mouth and body, with heart and faith, to such he bringeth life and nourishment. Wherefore in this comparison, the author hath made no difference, but with divers terms the catholic teaching is divided into two members, with a* "*but,*" *fashioned nevertheless in another phrase of speech than the church hath used, which is so common in this author, that I will not hereafter note it any more for a fault. But let us go further*[6].

55. August. contra lit. Petil. lib. 2. cap. 47.

CANTERBURY.

There is nothing in this comparison worthy to be answered; for if you can find no difference therein, yet every indifferent reader can. For when I report the papists' teaching, that they say Christ is received in the mouth, and entereth in with the bread and wine, and for an adversative thereto I say, that we, (which follow the scriptures and ancient writers), say that he is received in the heart, and entereth in by faith, every indifferent reader understandeth this adversative upon our side, that we say Christ is not received in the mouth, but in the heart, specially seeing that in my fourth book, the second and third chapters, I make purposely a process thereof, to prove that Christ is not eaten with mouths and teeth. And yet to eschew all such occasions of sleight as you impute unto me in this comparison, to make the comparison more full and plain, let this be the comparison.

Whether Christ be received in the mouth.

They say that Christ is received with the mouth, and entereth in with the bread and wine: we say that he is not received with the mouth, but with heart, and entereth in by faith. And now, I trust, there is no sleight in this comparison, nor both the parts may not be understand on both sides, as you say they might before.

*The difference.

And as for St Augustine, serveth nothing for your purpose, to prove that Christ's body is eaten with the mouth. For he speaketh not one word in the place by you

August. contra lit. Petil. lib. 2. cap. 47.

[4 In the same supper, 1551.]   [5 August. Opera, Tom. VIII. p. 107. Ed. Paris. 1535.]
[6 Let us go further, 1551.]

alleged, neither of our mouths, nor of Christ's body. But it seemeth you have so fervent desire[1] to be doing in this matter, that you be like to certain men, which have such a fond delight in shooting, that so they be doing, they pass not how far they shoot from the mark. For in this place of St Augustine against the Donatists, he shooteth not at this butt[2], whether Christ's very natural body be received with our mouths, but whether the sacraments in general be received both of good and evil. And there he declareth, that it is all one water, whether Simon Peter, or Simon Magus be christened in it; all one table of the Lord, and one cup, whether Peter sup thereat, or Judas; all one oil, whether David or Saul were anointed therewith. Wherefore he concludeth thus: *Memento ergo sacramentis Dei nihil obesse mores malorum hominum, quo illa vel omnino non sint, vel minus sancta sint, sed ipsis malis hominibus, ut hæc habeant ad testimonium damnationis, non ad adjutorium sanitatis*[3]. "Remember, therefore," saith St Augustine, "that the manners of evil men hinder not the sacraments of God, that either they utterly be not, or be less holy; but they hinder the evil men themselves, so that they have the sacraments to witness of their damnation, not to help of their salvation." And all the process spoken there by St Augustine is spoken chiefly of baptism, against the Donatists, which said, that the baptism was naught, if either the minister or the receiver were naught. Against whom St Augustine concludeth, that the sacraments of themselves be holy, and be all one, whether the minister or receiver be good or bad. But this place of St Augustine proveth as well your purpose, that Christ's body is received by the mouth, as it proveth that Paul's steeple is higher than the cross in Cheap[4]. For he speaketh not one word of any of[5] them all. And therefore in this place where you pretend to shoot at the butt, you shoot quite at rovers[6], and clean from the mark.

August. contra lit. Petil. lib. 2. cap. 47.

56.

And yet if Judas received Christ with the bread, as you say, and the devil entered with the bread, as St John saith, then was the devil and Christ in Judas both at once. And then how they agreed I marvel: for St Paul saith, that Christ and Belial cannot agree. O! what a wit had he need to have, that will wittingly maintain an open error, directly against God and his word, and all holy ancient writers!

John xiii.

1 Cor. x.

Now followeth the fourth comparison in my book.

The fourth comparison.

They say, that Christ is really in the sacramental bread, being reserved a whole year, or so long as the form of bread remaineth: but after the receiving thereof he flieth up, say they, from the receiver unto heaven, as soon as the bread is chewed in the mouth, or changed in the stomach: but we say, that Christ remaineth in the man that worthily receiveth it, so long as the man remaineth a member of Christ.

WINCHESTER.

This comparison is like the other before, whereof the first part is garnished and embossed with untruth; and the second part is that the church hath ever taught most truly, and that all must believe: and therefore that piece hath no untruth in the matter, but in the manner only, being spoken as though it differed from the continual open teaching of the church, which is not so. Wherefore in the manner of it in utterance signifieth an untruth, which in the matter itself is nevertheless most true. For undoubtedly Christ remaineth in the man that worthily receiveth the sacrament, so long as the man remaineth a member of Christ. In this first part there is a fault in the matter of the speech; for explication whereof I will examine it particularly. This author saith, "they say, that Christ is really in the sacramental bread, being reserved an whole year, &c." The church giving faith to Christ's word, when he said, "This is my body," &c., teacheth the body of Christ to be present in the sacrament under the form of bread; unto which words when we put the word "really," it serveth only to express that truth in open words, which was before[7] to be understood in sense. For in Christ, who was the body of all the shadows and figures of the law, and who did exhibit and give in his sacraments of the

*Pugnat cum aliis papistis.

*Christ is the body of all the figures.

[1 Fervent a desire, 1551.]
[2 Butt: i. e. a mark.]
[3 August. Opera, Tom. VII. p. 107. Ed. Paris. 1535.]
[4 In the Cheap, 1551.]
[5 Of none of, 1551.]
[6 At rovers: i. e. at random.]
[7 Afore, 1551.]

new law the things promised in his sacraments of the old law, we must understand his words in the institution of his sacraments without figure, in the substance of the celestial thing of them: and therefore when he ordered his most precious body and blood to be eaten and drunken of us, under the forms of bread and wine; we profess and believe, that truly he gave us his most precious body in the sacrament for a celestial food, to comfort and strengthen us in this miserable life. And for certainty of the truth of his work therein, we profess he giveth us his body really, that is to say, in deed his body, the thing itself, which is the heavenly part of the sacrament, called Eucharistia; *having the visible form of bread and wine, and containing invisibly the very body and blood of our Saviour Christ, which was not wont to be reserved otherwise, but to be ready for such as in danger of death call for it, and the same, so long as it may be used, is still the same sacrament, which only time altereth not. Whereof Cyril wrote to this sense many hundred years past, and Hesychius also, and what ought to be done when by negligence of the minister it were reserved overlong. Marry, where it liketh the author of these differences, to say the church teacheth, Christ to flee up from the receiver unto heaven, so soon as the bread is chewed in the mouth, or changed in the stomach, this manner of speech implieth as though Christ left the seat of his majesty in heaven, to be present in the sacrament, which is most untrue. The church acknowledgeth, believeth, and teacheth truly, that Christ sitteth on the right hand of his Father in glory, from whence he shall come to judge the world; and also teacheth Christ's very body and blood, and Christ himself God and man, to be present in the sacrament, not by shifting of place, but by the determination of his will, declared in scriptures, and believed of the catholic church; which articles be to reason impossible, but possible to God omnipotent: so as being taught of his will, we should humbly submit all our senses and reason to the faith of his will and work declared in his scriptures.*

In the belief of which mysteries is great benefit and consolation, and in the unreverent search and curious discussion of them, presumptuous boldness and wicked temerity. I know by faith Christ to be present, but the particularity how he is present, more than I am assured he is truly present, and therefore in substance present, I cannot tell; but present he is, and truly is, and verily is, and so in deed, that is to say, really is, and unfeignedly is, and therefore in substance is, and, as we term it, substantially is present. For all these adverbs, really, substantially, with the rest, be contained in the one word "is," spoken out of his mouth, that speaketh as he meaneth, truly and certainly, as Christ did, saying: "This is my body that shall be betrayed for you;" who then carried himself in his hands after a certain manner, as St Augustine saith, which never man besides him could do, who in that his last supper gave himself to be eaten without consuming. The ways and means whereof no man can tell, but humble spirits, as they be taught, must constantly believe it, without thinking or talking of flying, of stying[8] of Christ again unto heaven, where Christ is in the glory of his Father continually, and is nevertheless, because he will so be, present in the sacrament, whole God and man, and dwelleth corporally in him that receiveth him worthily.

Wherefore, reader, when thou shalt again well consider this comparison, thou shalt find true, how the first part is disguised with untrue report of the common teaching of the church, howsoever some gloss or some private teacher might speak of it; and the second part, such as hath been ever so taught. One thing I think good to admonish the reader, that whatsoever I affirm, or precisely deny, I mean within the compass of my knowledge; which I speak not because I am in any suspicion or doubt of that I affirm, or deny, but to avoid the temerity of denying as "never," or affirming as "ever," which be extremities. And I mean also of public doctrine by consent received, so taught, and believed, and not that any one man might blindly write, as uttering his fancy, as this author doth for his pleasure. There followeth in the author thus.

*Marginal notes: *Really, that is, in deed. 57. Cyrillus ad Cœlosyrium episcopum. Hesychius, in Levit. lib. 3. cap. 3. *Christ being present in the sacrament, is at the same time present in heaven. *Truly. *Really. *Substantially. Augustin. Psal. xxxiii. *What is found in a blind gloss, may not be taken for the teaching of the church, and yet I never read of flying. *It is in man dangerous to affirm, or deny, extremities, although they be true, for it maketh him suspect of presumption.*

CANTERBURY.

Because this comparison, as you say, is like the other, therefore it is fully answered before in the other comparisons. And here yet again it is to be noted, that in all these four comparisons you approve and allow for truth the second part of the comparison which we say. And where you say that Christ undoubtedly remaineth in the man that worthily receiveth the sacrament, so long as that man remaineth a member of Christ: how agreeth this with the common saying of all the papists, that Christ is contained under the forms of bread and wine, and remaineth there no longer

Marginal note: How long Christ tarrieth with the receiver of the sacrament.

[8 Stying: i.e. soaring, ascending.]

than the forms of bread and wine remain? Wherefore in this point all the whole rout of the papists will condemn for untruth that which you so constantly affirm to be undoubtedly true.

58.

Metonymia.

And when the papists teach, that the body of Christ is really in the sacrament under the form of bread, they speak not this, giving faith to Christ his words, as you say they do, for Christ never spake any such words; and as for this saying of Christ, "This is my body," it is a figurative speech, called *metonymia*, when one thing is called by the name of another which it signifieth, and it hath no such sense as you pretend; for there is a great diversity between these two sayings, "This is my body," and "the body of Christ is really in the sacrament under the form of bread." But the papists have set Christ's words upon the tenters[1], and stretched them out so far, that they make his words to signify as pleaseth them, not as he meant.

The fathers in the old law received the same things in their sacraments that we do in ours.

And this is a marvellous doctrine of you, to say that Christ was the body of all the shadows and figures of the law, and did exhibit and give in his sacraments of the new law the things promised in the sacraments of the old law. For he is the body of all the figures, as well of the new law as of the old; and did exhibit and give his promises in the sacraments of the old law, as he doth now in the sacraments of the new law. And we must understand the words spoken in the institution of the sacraments in both the laws, figuratively, as concerning the sacraments, and without figure, as concerning the things by them promised, signified, and exhibited: as in circumcision was given the same thing to them that is given to us in baptism, and the same by manna that we have at the Lord's table. Only this difference was between them and us, that our redemption by Christ's death and passion was then only promised, and now it is performed and past. And as their sacraments were figures of his death to come, so be our[2] figures of the same now past and gone. And yet it was all but one Christ to them and us[3]; who gave life, comfort, and strength to them by his death to come, and giveth the same to us by his death passed.

And he was in their sacraments spiritually and effectually present, and for so much truly and really present, that is to say, in deed, before he was born, no less than he is now in our sacraments present after his death and ascension into heaven. But as for carnal presence, he was to them not yet come: and to us he is come, and gone again unto his Father, from whom he came.

Reservation. Cyril. Hesychius.

And as for the reservation of the sacrament, neither Cyril nor Hesychius speak any word what ought to be done with the sacrament, when by negligence of the minister it were reserved over long. But Hesychius sheweth plainly, that nothing ought to be reserved, but to be burned whatsoever remained.

De consecrat. d. 2. "Tribus gradibus."

And as for the "flying of Christ up into heaven, so soon as the bread is chewed in the mouth, or changed in the stomach," I say not that the church teacheth so, but that papists say so; which forasmuch as you say that it liketh me to report this most untruly, read what the gloss saith upon the chapter, *Tribus gradibus, de Consecrat. dist.* 2, and there you shall find these words: *Certum est, quod species quam cito dentibus teruntur, tam cito in cœlum rapitur corpus Christi*[4]. And if this gloss be false and erroneous, why was it published and set out by the authority of the papists? Why hath it been written and printed in so many countries, and so many years without reproof, or any fault found therein by any man?

59.

But here may wise men learn to beware of your doctrine. For you reprove those papists which have written of this matter four or five hundred years past, and do invent a new device of your own. And therefore wise men, when they see you teach one doctrine, and the papists that were before your time teach another, they will believe none of you all.

The benefit and comfort in this sacrament.

And where you say, that in the belief of this mystery is great benefit and consolation: what benefit, I beseech you, is it to us, if Christ be really and corporally in the forms of bread and wine a month or two, or a year or two? And if we receive him really and corporally with the bread and wine into our mouths or stomachs,

---

[1 Upon the tenters; i. e. upon the stretch.]
[2 Ours, 1551.]
[3 And to us, 1551.]
[4 Vide supra, p. 56.]

and no further, and there he tarrieth not in that sort, but departeth away from us by and by again, what great benefit or comfort, I pray you, is such a corporal presence unto us? And yet this is the teaching of all the papists, although you seem to vary from them in this last point, of Christ's sudden departure. But when the matter shall be throughly answered, I ween you will agree with the rest of the papists, that as concerning his carnal presence, Christ departeth from us, at the least when the forms of bread and wine be altered in the stomach. And then, I pray you, declare what comfort and benefit we have by this carnal presence, which by and by is absent, and tarrieth not with us? Such comfort have weak and sick consciences at the papists' hands, to tell them that Christ was with them, and now he is gone[5] from them. Nevertheless, in the belief of this mystery, (if it be understanded according to God's word,) is great benefit and consolation; but to believe your addition unto God's word, is neither benefit nor wisdom.

And I pray you, shew in what place the scripture saith, "that under the forms of bread and wine is the body of Christ, really, corporally, and naturally;" or else acknowledge them to be your own addition, beside[6] God's word, and your stout assertion herein to be but presumptuous boldness and wicked temerity, affirming so arrogantly that thing, for the which you have no[7] authority of God's word.

And where you seem to be offended with the discussion of this matter, what hurt, I pray you, can gold catch in the fire, or truth with discussing? Lies only fear discussing. The devil hateth the light, because he hath been a liar from the beginning, and is loth that his lies should come to light and trial. And all hypocrites and papists be of a like sort afraid, that their doctrine should come to discussing, whereby it may evidently appear that they be endued with the spirit of error and lying. If the papists had not feared that their doctrines should have been espied, and their opinions have come to discussing, the scriptures of God had been in the vulgar and English tongue many years ago. But, God be praised! at the length your doctrine is come to discussing, so that you cannot so craftily walk in a cloud, but the light of God's word will always shew where you be. Our Saviour Christ, in the fifth of John, willeth us to search the scriptures, and to try out the truth by them. And shall not we then with humble reverence search the truth in Christ's sacraments? John v.

And if we cannot[8] tell how Christ is present, why do you then say, "that he is substantially present, corporally present, naturally and carnally present?" The manner of presence.

And how sure be you, that Christ is in substance present, because he is truly present? Are you assured that this your doctrine agreeth with God's word? Doth not God's word teach a true presence of Christ in spirit, where he is not present in his corporal substance? As when he saith: "Where two or three be gathered together in my name, there am I in the midst of them." And also when he saith: "I shall be with you till[9] the end of the world." Was it not a true presence that Christ in these places promised? And yet can you not of this true presence gather such a corporal presence of the substance of Christ's manhood, as you unlearnedly, contrary to the scriptures, go about to prove in the sacrament. For when Christ said, "This is my body," it was bread, which is called[10] his body in a figurative speech, as all old authors[11] teach, and as I have proved in my third book, the eighth and eleventh chapters. And the manner how Christ carried himself in his own hands, St Augustine declareth it to be figuratively. 60.
Matt. xviii.
Matt. xxviii.

And because you can find no repugnance between the two parts of this comparison, to make them more plain, I shall fill them up with more words, as I did the other comparisons before. This, therefore, shall be the comparison.

They say, that Christ is really and corporally in the sacramental bread being reserved, so long as the form of bread remaineth, although it be an whole year and more: but after the receiving thereof, he flieth up from the receiver into heaven, as soon as the bread is chewed in the mouth or digested in the stomach. But we say, The comparison.

[5 And now is gone, 1551.]
[6 Besides, 1551.]
[7 None, 1551.]
[8 And if you cannot, 1551.]

[9 Until, 1551.]
[10 Which he called, 1551.]
[11 As all the old authors, 1551.]

that after what manner Christ is received of us, in the same wise he remaineth in us, so long as we remain the members of Christ.

And where in the end you admonish the reader, that whatsoever you affirm or precisely deny, you mean within the compass of your knowledge, and of public doctrine, and of doctrine by consent received: what do you here else, but devise certain sleights, and prepare for yourself privy holes to start out at, whensoever you should be taken with a manifest lie? So that you should not be compelled to abide by any word that you say. For by these crafty sleights and shifts, of the compass of your knowledge, and of public doctrine, and of doctrine by common consent received, you mean to say ever what you list. And though never so manifest a lie or untruth be laid to your charge, yet shall no man never be able to prove it so manifestly against you, but you shall have one of these three shifts to flee out at for your defence.

Now followeth in my book the fifth comparison.

The fifth comparison.

They say, that in the sacrament the corporal members of Christ be not distant in place one from another, but that wheresoever the head is, there be the feet; and wheresoever the arms be, there be the legs: so that in every part of the bread and wine is altogether whole head, whole feet, whole flesh, whole blood, whole heart, whole lungs, whole breast, whole back, and altogether whole, confused and mixed without distinction or diversity. O what a foolish and an abominable invention is this, to make of the most pure and perfect body of Christ such a confuse and monstrous body! And yet can the papists imagine nothing so foolish, but all christian people must receive the same as an oracle of God, and as a most certain article of their faith, without whispering to the contrary.

WINCHESTER.

61. *This is a marvellous rhetoric, and such as the author hath overseen himself in the utterance of it, and confesseth himself prettily abused, to the latter end of his years to have believed that he now calleth so foolish. But to the purpose. In the book of common prayer, now at this time set forth in this realm, "It is ordered to teach the people, that in each part of the bread consecrate, broken, is the whole body of our Saviour Christ, which is agreeable to the catholic doctrine." Upon occasion hereof, it liketh this author to multiply language by enumeration of parts; and because reason without faith directeth the bodily eye to so little a visible quantity in the host, this author beareth in hand the catholic church to say and teach all that fond reason deviseth; whereas the church in the doctrine of this mystery, denieth all that reason without faith deviseth: and therefore when we acknowledge by faith Christ's body present, although we say it is present truly, really, substantially, yet we say, our senses be not privy to that presence, or[1] the manner of it, but by instruction of faith; and therefore we say Christ's body to be not locally present, not by manner of quantity, but invisible[2], and in no sensible manner, but marvellously in a sacrament and mystery truly, and in such a spiritual manner as we cannot define and determine, and yet by faith we know his body present, the parts of which be in themselves distinct one from another, in their own substance, but not by circumscription of several places to be comprehended of our capacity; which parts we can by no demonstration[3] place, nor by imagination displace, diminish, alter, or confound, as this author for his pleasure reporteth, who writeth monstrously in so high a mystery, and impudently beareth in hand the catholic church to teach that he listeth to bear in hand, may by wanton reason be deduced of the teaching[4]; whereas all true christian men believe simply Christ's words, and trouble not their heads with such consequences as seem to strive with reason. This is in the author no whispering, but plainly railing, wherein if he had remembered himself well, he would not have spoken of all christian men in the receipt of that he intendeth to disprove. And if he would say he spake it by an irony or scorn, yet it implieth that all had received that he thus mocketh, which, after the sort he writeth, was never*

* Pugnat cum aliis papistis.

[¹ Nor, 1551.]
[² Invisibly, 1551.]
[³ We cannot by demonstration, 1551.]

[⁴ The original copy of Winchester's book reads, "of their teaching."]

devised by papist or other to be so taught, otherwise than as this author might read it, as an idle argument, to shew absurdity in reason. For in God's works, as the sacraments be, we must think all seemliness in deed without deformity, even as we believe all God's judgments just and true, although reason conclude in them evident iniquity. Man's reason, when it seemeth most gallant, is full of spots and folly. God's works be all seemliness, without confusion, monster, or any such absurdity, as this author supposeth. Although I cannot in the sacrament with the eye of my reason locally distinct Christ's head from his foot, his legs from his arm. And where in the book of common prayer it is truly said, in each part of the bread consecrate broken to be Christ's whole body, if one of curiosity would question with me, and I of folly would answer him, first, where is Christ's head? I should say, here, pointing with my finger, he would think it first, a little head. Then he would ask, where is his foot? and I should say there, and point in the same place again, for there is none other left. If he replied, that I pointed before the same for the head, might not the third, a catholic man, that stood by, trow you, wisely call us both mad, to go about to discuss that we must grant we see not; and when by faith we know only the being present of Christ's most precious body, then by blind reason to discuss the manner of being in the situation of such parts as we do not see? Now if there came among us a fourth man as a mediator, and would do as king Alexander did, when he could not open the knot of Gordius, he did cut it with his sword, if this man should say, I will relieve this matter. You believe Christ's body is present indeed, really and substantially. Leave out "really and substantially," and say his body is present in signification, and then it may be easily conceived, by reason, that Christ's body, being never so great, may be as well signified by a little piece of bread, as by a great piece of bread: even as a man may write a great man's name, as well in small letters short, as in great letters at length. And to commend further his device unto us, would percase[5] tell how many absurdities, as he thinketh, and inconveniences might be avoided by it. This fourth man I speak of, making himself a mediator, but in deed unmeet therefore, because he hath no participation with faith; yet if our religion and faith were man's invention, as that of Numa Pompilius was, he should not utter this his conceit all idly. For he speaketh of a jolly easy way, without any mystery or marvel at all. But our faith is of hearing, as hath been preached continually from the beginning, grounded upon the most sure truth of the word of God, and therefore cannot be attempered as man would devise it, to exclude travail in carnal reason. For then the Sabellians were to be hearkened unto, who by their heresy took away all the hard and difficile[6] questions in the mystery of the Trinity.

The Arians also relieved much man's reason in consideration of Christ's death, denying him to be of the same substance with his Father, which was a pestilent heresy. Now in the sacrament to say, Christ's body is present only by signification, as it relieveth in some men's judgments the absurdities in reason, which ought not to be relieved, so it condemneth all the true public faith, testified in the church from the beginning hitherto, and sheweth the learned holy men to have wondered in their writings at that which hath no wonder at all, to ordain one thing to be the signification of another, which is practised daily among men. But from the beginning the mystery of the sacrament hath been with wonder marvelled at, how Christ made bread his body, and wine his blood, and under the figure of those visible creatures gave invisibly his precious body and blood presently there. And as he gave, saith St Bernard[7], his life for us, so he gave his flesh to us, in that mystery to redeem us, in this to feed us. Which doings of Christ we must understand to have been perfected, not in an imagination of a figure and signification, but really in very deed, truly and unfeignedly; not because we believe it so, but because he wrought it so; whose works we must believe to be most perfectly true, according to the truth of the letter, where no absurdity in scripture driveth us from it, howsoever it seem repugnant to our reason, be we never so wise and witty; which man's reason now-a-days inflamed with fury of language, is the only adversary against the most blessed sacrament, as it may appear by these comparisons of differences throughly[8] considered.

*What is received of all christian men hath therein a manifest token in truth.

*It is a folly to answer a curious demander.

Quintus Curtius *maketh mention of this faith of Alexander. Faith of God and his work cannot, by man's device, have any qualification.

62.

Sabellians.

Arians.

Bernard super Cant. ser. 31.

CANTERBURY.

Did not you believe, I pray you, many years together, that the bishop of Rome was Christ's vicar, and the head of his church?

[5 Percase: i.e. perchance, perhaps.]
[6 Difficile: i.e. difficult.]
[7 "Animam pro illis, carnem illis. Illam in pretium, istam in cibum. Res mira: ipse pastor, ipse pascua est, ipse redemptio."—Bernardus, super Cant. Serm. xxxi. col. 664. Lutet. Paris. 1640.]
[8 Thoroughly, 1551.]

It is good at all times to convert from error to truth.

If you did not, you wittingly and willingly defended a false error in the open parliament. But sithens that time, you have called that belief, as it is indeed, very foolish. And if you confessed your ignorance in that matter, be no more abashed to confess it in this, if you have respect more unto God's truth, than to your own estimation. It is lawful and commendable for a man to learn from time to time, and to go from his ignorance, that he may receive and embrace the truth. And as for me, I am not, I grant, of that nature that the papists for the most part be, who study to devise all shameful shifts, rather than they will forsake any error wherewith they were infected in youth. I am glad to acknowledge my former ignorance (as St Paul, St Cyprian, St Augustine, and many other holy men did, who now be with Christ), to bring other to the knowledge of the truth, of whose ignorance I have much ruth[1] and pity. I am content to give place to God's word, that the victory may be Christ's. What a member had the church of God lost, if Paul would have been as froward as some papists be, that will stick to their error tooth and nail, though the scripture and ancient writers be never so plain and flat against them! Although St Paul erred, yet because his error was not wilful, but of ignorance, so that he gave place to the truth when it was opened unto him, he became of a most cruel persecutor a most fervent setter forth of the truth, and apostle of Christ.

1 Tim. i.

63.

And would God I were as sure that you be changed indeed in those matters of religion, wherein with the alteration of this realm you pretend a change, as I am glad even from the bottom of my heart, that it hath pleased Almighty God, in this latter end of my years, to give me knowledge of my former error, and a will to embrace the truth, setting apart all manner of worldly respects, which be special hinderances, that hold back many from the free profession of Christ and his word.

The book of common prayer.

And as for the book of common prayer, although it say, that in each part of the bread broken is received the whole body of Christ, yet it saith not so of the parts unbroken, nor yet of the parts or whole reserved, as the papists teach. But as in baptism we receive the Holy Ghost, and put Christ upon us, as well if we be christened in one dish full of water taken out of the font, as if we were christened in the whole font or river; so we be as truly fed, refreshed, and comforted by Christ, receiving a piece of bread at the Lord's holy table, as if we did eat an whole loaf. For as in every part of the water in baptism is whole Christ and the Holy Spirit, sacramentally, so be they in every part of the bread broken, but not corporally and naturally, as the papists teach.

The papists say, that whole Christ is in every part of the consecrated bread.

And I bear not the catholic church in hand, as you report of me, that it saith and teacheth that whole Christ is in every part of the bread consecrated, but I say that the papists so teach. And because you deny it, read the chief pillars of the papists,—Duns, and Thomas de Aquino, which the papists call St Thomas; who say, that Christ is whole under every part of the forms of bread and wine, not only when the host is broken, but when it is whole also. "And there is no distance," saith he, "of parts one from another, as of one eye from another, or of the eye from the ear, or the head from the feet." These be Thomas's words: *Christus totus est sub qualibet parte specierum panis et vini, non solum cum frangitur hostia, sed etiam cum integra manet. Nec est distantia partium ab invicem, ut oculi ab oculo, aut oculi ab aure, aut capitis a pedibus, sicut est in aliis corporibus organicis. Talis enim distantia est in ipso corpore Christi vero, sed non prout est in hoc sacramento*[2]. And not only the papists do thus write and teach, but the pope himself, Innocentius the

Thomas, 3. part. sum. q. 76. art. 3.

Innocentius III. *lib. 4. cap. 8.

[1 Ruth: i. e. sorrow.]

[2 Conclusio.—Cum corpus Christi sit in hoc sacramento eo modo quo substantia est sub dimensionibus, manifestum est, totum Christum sub qualibet parte specierum panis aut vini contineri, sive frangatur hostia, sive integra remaneat.—Et ideo manifestum est, quod totus Christus est sub qualibet parte specierum panis, etiam hostia integra manente, et non solum cum frangitur.—Et ideo quia conversio substantiæ panis directe terminatur ad substantiam corporis Christi, secundum cujus modum proprie et directe est in hoc sacramento corpus Christi, talis distantia partium est quidem in ipso corpore Christi vero: sed non secundum hanc distantiam comparatur ad hoc sacramentum, sed secundum modum suæ substantiæ. Thos. Aquinas, Tertia pars. Quæst. lxxvi. Art. iii. p. 190. Ed. Antwerp. 1624.]

third. And so bear I in hand, or report of the papists nothing but that which they say indeed.

And yet you say, the church saith not so; which I affirm also: and then it must needs follow, that the doctrine of the papists is not the doctrine of the church. Which papists, not by reason without faith, but against as well reason as faith, would direct our minds to seek in every little crumb of bread, whole Christ, and to find him in so many places there, as be small crumbs in the bread.

And where you traverse the matter of the judgment of our senses herein, it is quite and clean from the matter, and but a crafty shift, to convey the matter to another thing that is not in question; like unto crafty malefactors, which perceiving themselves to be sore pursued with a hound, make a new train to draw the hound to another fresh suit. For I speak not of the judgment of our senses in this matter, whether they perceive any distinction of parts and members or no; but whether indeed there be any such distinction in the sacrament or no, which the papists do deny. And therefore I say not untruly of them, that in the sacrament they say, "There is no distance of parts, one from another."

And if the parts in their substance be distinct one from another, as you say, and be not so distinct in the sacrament, as Thomas saith, then must it follow that the parts in their own substance be not in the sacrament. And if this distinction of parts be in the true body of Christ, and not in the sacrament, as Thomas saith, then followeth it again, that the true body of Christ is not in the sacrament.

And forasmuch as I speak not one word of the comprehension of our senses, to what purpose do you bring this in, if it be not to draw us to a new matter, to avoid that which is in controversy? You do herein as if James should buy of John a parcel of land, and by his attorney take state and possession therein; and after, John should traverse the matter, and say that there was never no state delivered, and thereupon join their issue; and when James should bring forth his witnesses for the state and possession, then should John run to a new matter, and say that James saw the[3] possession delivered: what were this allegation of John to the purpose of the thing that was in issue, whether the possession were delivered indeed or no? Were this any other thing than to avoid the issue craftily by bringing in a new matter[4]? And yet this shift is a common practice of you in this book, and this is another point of the devil's sophistry, wherein it is pity that ever such a wit as you have should be occupied. *A subtil sleight.*

Again you say, that impudently I bear the catholic church in hand, to teach that I list to bear in hand may by wanton reason be deduced of their teaching, whereas all true christian men believe simply Christ's words, and trouble not their heads with such consequences. "This is in the author no whispering, but plain railing," say you. This is your barking eloquence, wherewith your book is well furnished: for as dogs bark at the moon without any cause, so do you in this place. For I do no more but truly report what the papists themselves do write, and no[5] otherwise; not bearing the catholic church in hand that it so teacheth, but charging the papists that they so teach; not bearing the papists in hand what I list, or what by wanton reason may be deduced of their teaching, but reporting only what their own words and sayings be. *Wanton reason.*

And if they be no true christian men that trouble their heads with such matters, as you affirm they be not, then was Innocent the third, the chief author of your doctrine both of transubstantiation and of the real presence, no true christian man, as I believe well enough: then was your St Thomas no true christian man: then Gabriel, Duns, Durand, and the great rabblement of the school-authors, which taught your doctrine of transubstantiation and of the real presence, were not true christian men. And in few words to comprehend the whole, then were almost[6] none that taught that doctrine true christian men, but yourself alone. For almost all with one consent do teach, that whole Christ is really in every part of the host. *True christian men.*

[³ Saw not, 1551.] [⁵ None otherwise, 1551.]
[⁴ Of a new matter, 1551.] [⁶ Then was almost, 1551.]

But your terms here of railing, mocking, and scorning, I would have taken patiently at your hand, if your tongue and pen had not overshot themselves in bragging so far, that the truth by you should be defaced. But now I shall be so bold as to send those terms thither, from whence they came. And for the matter itself, I am ready to join an issue with you, notwithstanding all your stout and boasting words.

"But in God's works," say you, "as the sacraments be, we must think all seemliness indeed without deformity." But what seemliness is this in a man's body, that the head is where the feet be, and the arms where the legs be? which the papists do teach, and yourself seem to confess, when you say, that the parts of Christ's body be distinct in themselves, one from another in their own substance, but not by circumscription of several places. And yet you seem again to deny the same in your wise dialogue, or quadrilogue, between the curious questioner, the foolish answerer, your wise catholic man standing by, and the mediator.

A dialogue. In which dialogue you bring in your wise catholic man to condemn of madness all such as say, that Christ's head is there where his feet be; and so you condemn of madness not only all the scholastical doctors, which say that Christ is whole in every part of the consecrated bread, but also your own former saying, where you deny the distinction of the parts of Christ's body in several places. Wherefore the mediator seemeth wiser than you all, who, loosing this knot of Gordius, saith, that "Christ's body, (how big soever it be,) may be as well signified by a little piece of bread as by a great:" and so, as concerning the reason of a sacrament, all is one, whether it be an whole bread, or a piece of it, as it skilleth not whether a man be christened in the whole font, or in a part of the water taken out thereof. For the respect and consideration of the sacrament is all one in the less and more[1].

But this fourth man, say you, hath no participation with faith, condemning all the true public faith testified in the church from the beginning hitherto, which hath ever with wonder marvelled at the mystery of the sacrament, which is no wonder at all, if bread be but a signification of Christ's body. This is a wonderful saying of you, as of one that understood nothing utterly what a sacrament meaneth, and what is to be wondered at in the sacrament. For the wonder is, not how God worketh in the outward visible sacrament, but his marvellous work is in the worthy receivers of the sacraments. The wonderful work of God is not in the water, which only washeth the body; but God by his omnipotent power worketh wonderfully in the receivers thereof, scouring, washing, and making them clean inwardly, and, as it were, new men and celestial creatures. This have all old authors wondered at; this wonder passeth the capacities of all men's wits, how damnation is turned into salvation, and of the son of the devil condemned into hell is made the son of God and inheritor of heaven. This wonderful work of God all men may marvel and wonder at, but no creature is able sufficiently to comprehend it. And as this is wondered at in the sacrament of baptism, how he that was subject unto death receiveth life by Christ and his holy Spirit: so is this wondered at in the sacrament of Christ's holy table, how the same life is continued and endureth for ever by continual feeding upon Christ's flesh and his blood. And these wonderful works of God towards us we be taught by God's holy word, and his sacraments of bread, wine, and water; and yet be not these wonderful works of God in the sacraments, but in us.

And although many authors use this manner of speech, that Christ maketh bread his body, and wine his blood, and wonder thereat; yet those authors mean not of the bread and wine in themselves, but of the bread and wine eaten and drunken of faithful people. For when Christ called bread his body, and wine his blood, he spake not those words to the bread and wine, but to the eaters and drinkers of them, saying, "Eat, this is my body; drink, this is my blood:" signifying to them that worthily do eat that bread and drink that cup, that they be inwardly and invisibly fed with Christ's flesh and blood, as they outwardly and visibly receive the sacraments of them.

To be short, here in this process you use plenty of words at your pleasure, to make the reader believe that I should suppose confusion, monstrousness, absurdity,

[1 The less and the more, 1551.]

and unseemliness to be in God's holy sacraments, where as I do no more but tell what monstrous absurdities and errors the papists do teach in the sacraments. But if the reader take good heed to your talk, he shall find that you, lacking good matter to answer this comparison, do fall unto railing, and enforce your pen to invent such stuff as might bring me into hatred undeserved; which kind of rhetoric is called *Canina facundia*, and is used only of them that hunt for their own praise by the dispraise of their adversary, which is yet another trick of the devil's sophistry.

And because you would bring me into more extreme hatred, you couple me with Sabellius and Arrius, whose doctrines, as you say, were facile and easy, as here you confess mine for to be. But if all such expositions as make the scriptures plain should by and by be slanderously compared to the doctrines of Arrius and Sabellius, then should all the expositions of the doctors be brought in danger, because that by their pains they have made hard questions facile and easy. And yet, whether the doctrine which I set forth be easy to understand or not, I cannot define, but it seemeth so hard that you cannot understand it; except you will put all the fault in your own wilfulness, that you can, and will not understand it.

<small>Sabellius. Arrius.</small>

Now followeth the sixth comparison.

Furthermore, the papists say, that a dog or a cat eateth[2] the body of Christ, if they by chance do eat the sacramental bread. We say, that no earthly creature can eat the body of Christ, nor drink his blood, but only man.

WINCHESTER.

I have read that some[3] entreat these chances of dogs and cats, but I never heard any of that opinion[4], to say or write so, as a doctrine, that a dog or a cat eateth the body of Christ, and set it forth for a teaching, as this author most impudently supposeth; and I marvel much that such a word, and such a report, can come out of a christian man's mouth, and therefore this is by the author a marvellous surmise, whereupon to take occasion to bring the adversative "but" for the author's part, being such a saying on that side as all christendom hath ever taught, that no creature can eat the body and drink the blood[5] of Christ, but only man. But this abominable surmised untruth in the former part of his[6] comparison, may be taken for a proof, whether such beastly asseverations proceed from the spirit of truth or no; and whether truth be there intended, where such blasphemy is surmised. But let us see the rest.

<small>*The contrary hereof is noted for a doctrine.</small>

<small>*Pugnat cum aliis papistis.</small>

CANTERBURY.

Yet still in these comparisons you grant that part of the difference to be true which I affirm; but you say that I report untruly of the papists, impudently bearing them in hand, to say such abominable and beastly asseverations as you never heard. Whereby appeareth your impudent arrogancy in denial of that thing which either you know the papists do say, or you are in doubt whether they say or say not, having not read what it is that they say. For why do they reject the Master of the Sentences in this point, that he said, "a mouse or brute beast receiveth[7] not the body of Christ, although they seem to receive it?" Wherein if you say, as the Master did, that the mouse receiveth not the body of Christ, look for no favour at the papists' hands, but to be rejected as the Master was, unless they forbear you upon favour, and because that in other matters you have been so good a captain for them, they will pardon you this one fault. And so is this first part of the difference no untrue surmise of me, but a determination of the papists, condemning whosoever would say the contrary. And this is a common proposition among the school divines, that the body of Christ remaineth so long as the form of the bread is remaining, wheresoever it be, whereof

<small>Whether a bird or beast eat the body of Christ.</small>

<small>*Lib. 4. distinct. 13. In erroribus, fol 134. b.</small>
<small>*Vide Marcum Constantium.</small>
<small>fol. 72. object. 94.</small>

[² Eat, 1551, and Orig. Ed.]
[³ Some that, 1551.]
[⁴ Of that abominable opinion, Orig. Ed. Winchester, 1551.]
[⁵ Can eat the body and blood, 1551.]
[⁶ Of this comparison, Orig. Ed. Winchester, 1551.]
[⁷ Receive, 1551.]

THE THIRD BOOK.

<small>Thomas. part. sum. q. 80. art. iii.</small> your St Thomas writeth thus: *Quidam vero dixerunt, quod quam primum sacramentum sumitur a mure vel cane, desinit ibi esse corpus Christi. Sed hoc derogat veritati hujus sacramenti. Substantia enim panis sumpta a peccatore tamdiu manet, dum per calorem naturalem est in digestione: igitur tamdiu manet corpus Christi sub speciebus sacra-* <small>Peryn.</small> *mentalibus*[1]. And Peryn[2], in his book printed and set abroad in this matter for all men to read, saith: "That although the mouse, or any other beast, do eat the sacrament, yet nevertheless the same is the very and real body of Christ." And he asketh, "what inconvenience it is against the verity of Christ's real body in the sacrament, though the impassible body lie in the mouth or maw of the beast? Is it not therefore the body of Christ? Yes, undoubtedly," saith he. So that now these abominable opinions and beastly asseverations, (as you truly term them, meaning thereby to bite me, as appeareth,) be fit terms, and meet for the papists, whose asseverations they be.

Now followeth the seventh comparison.

They say, that every man, good and evil, eateth the body of Christ. We say, that both do eat the sacramental bread, and drink the wine; but none do eat the very body of Christ, and drink his blood, but only they that be lively members of his body.

WINCHESTER.

In this comparison the former part, speaking of such men as be by baptism received into Christ's church, is very true, confirmed by St Paul, and ever since affirmed in the <small>*A demur upon this issue.</small> *church; in the proof whereof here in this book I will not travel, but make it a demur as it were in law, whereupon to try the truth of the whole matter. If that doctrine, called by this author the doctrine of the papists, and is indeed the catholic doctrine, be not in this point true, let all be so judged for me. If it be true, as it is most true, let that be a mark whereby to judge the rest of this author's untrue asseverations. For undoubtedly St Augustine saith:* <small>August. contra Literas Petil. lib. 20.</small> *"We may not of men's matters esteem the sacraments: they be made by him whose they be; but worthily used they bring reward, unworthily handled they bring judgment. He that dispenseth the sacrament worthily, and he that useth it unworthily, be not one; but that thing is one, whether it be handled worthily or unworthily, so as it is neither better ne worse, but* <small>*Marcus Constantius dicit quod ethnici idem fortasse sumunt quod bruti in sacramentum tantum.</small> *life or death of them that use it." Thus saith St Augustine, and therefore be the receivers*[3] *worthy or unworthy, good or evil, the substance of Christ's sacrament is all one, as being God's work, who worketh uniformly, and yet is not in all that receive of like effect, not of*[4] *any alteration or diminution in it, but for the diversity of him that receiveth. So as the report made here of the doctrine of the catholic church under the name of papists is a very true report, and for want of grace reproved by the author as though it were no true doctrine. And the second part of the comparison on the author's side, contained under "we say" by them that in hypocrisy pretend to be truth's friends, containeth an untruth to the simple* <small>*The word "very" may make wrangling.</small> *reader, and yet hath a matter of wrangling to the learned reader, because of the word "very," which, referred to the effect of eating the body of Christ, whereby to receive life, may be so spoken, that none receive the body of Christ with the very effect of life, but such as eat the sacrament spiritually, that is to say, with true faith worthily. And yet evil men, as*

[1 Cranmer here, as above, p. 64, quotes the substance of Thomas Aquinas, rather than his exact words, which run thus: "Quidam antiqui erraverunt, dicentes, quod corpus Christi nec etiam sacramentaliter a peccatoribus sumitur, sed quam cito labiis peccatoris contingitur, tam cito sub speciebus sacramentalibus desinit esse corpus Christi. Sed hoc est erroneum: derogat enim veritati hujus sacramenti, ad quam—pertinet quod manentibus speciebus corpus Christi sub eis esse non desinat. Species autem manent, quamdiu substantia panis maneret, sibi ibi adesset. Manifestum est autem quod substantia panis assumpta a peccatore, non statim esse desinit, sed manet quandiu per calorem naturalem digeratur. Unde tamdiu corpus Christi sub speciebus sacramentalibus manet a peccatoribus sumptis."—Tertia pars, p. 204. Art. iii. q. 80. Antverp. 1624.]

[2 Dr Peryn was master of the Black-friars in Smithfield. He submitted to voluntary exile during the reign of Henry VIII.; and after twenty years returned home in the reign of Mary, and opposed the reformed religion. He preached and published four sermons on the Eucharist. Vid. Strype's Eccl. Mem. Vol. III. Part 2. p. 116. Ed. Oxford, 1822.]

[3 Receiver, 1551.]

[4 For any alteration, 1551.]

Judas, receive the same very body, touching the truth of the presence thereof, that St Peter did. For in the substance of the sacrament, which is God's work, is no variety, who ordaineth all (as afore) uniformly; but in man is the variety, amongst whom he that receiveth worthily Christ's body, receiveth life, and he that receiveth unworthily, receiveth condemnation. There followeth further.

CANTERBURY.

I thank you for this demur, for I myself could have chosen no better for my purpose. And I am content that the trial of the whole matter be judged hereby, as you desire. You say, that "all that be baptized, good and evil, eat the body of Christ;" and I say, only the good, and not the evil. *A demur. Whether evil men eat the body of Christ.*

Now must neither I nor you be judges in our own causes: therefore let Christ be judge between us both, whose judgment it is not reason that you refuse. Christ saith: "Whosoever eateth my flesh, and drinketh my blood, dwelleth in me, and I in him. As the living Father hath sent me, and I live by the Father, even so he that eateth me shall live by me. This is the bread which came down from heaven: not as your fathers did eat manna, and are dead: he that eateth this bread shall live for ever." Now I ask you this question, Whether evil men shall live for ever? Whether they live by Christ? Whether they dwell in Christ? and have Christ dwelling in them? If you say nay, (as you must needs if you will say the truth,) then have I proved my negative (wherein stood the demur), that ill men eat not Christ's body nor drink his blood; for if they did, then by Christ's own words they should live for ever, and dwell in Christ, and have Christ dwelling in them. And what proofs will you require more upon my part in this demur? For if Christ be with me, who can be able to stand against me? *John vi.*

But you allege for you St Paul, who speaketh for you nothing at all. For the messenger will not speak against him that sent him. I know that St Paul in the eleventh to the Corinthians, speaketh expressly of the unworthy eating of the bread, but in no place of the unworthy eating of the body of Christ. And if he do, shew the place, or else the demur passeth against you, and the whole matter tried with me, by your own pact and covenant. And yet for further proof of this demur, I refer me to the 1st, 2nd, 3rd, 4th, and 5th chapters of my fourth book. *1 Cor. xi.*

And where you bring St Augustine to be witness, his witness in that place helpeth nothing your cause. For he speaketh there generally of the using of the sacraments well or ill, as the diversity of men be, rehearsing by name the sacrament of circumcision, of the paschal lamb, and of baptism. Wherefore if you will prove any real and corporal presence of Christ by that place, you may as well prove that he was corporally present in circumcision, in eating of the paschal lamb, and in baptism, as in the Lord's supper. *August. contra Lit. Petil. lib. 2. cap. 37.*

And here ye use such a subtilty to deceive the simple reader, that he hath good cause to suspect your proceedings, and to take good heed of you in all your writings, who do nothing else but go about to deceive him. For you conclude the matter of the substance of the sacrament, that the reader might think that place to speak only of the sacrament of Christ's body and blood, and to speak of the substance thereof, where St Augustine neither hath that word "substance," nor speaketh not one word specially of that sacrament; but all his process goeth chiefly of baptism, which is all one, (saith St Augustine against the Donatists, which reproved baptism for the vice of the minister,) whether the minister be good or ill, and whether he minister it to good or to ill. For the sacrament is all one, although the effect be diverse, to good and to evil.

And as for them whom ye say that in hypocrisy pretend to be truth's friends, all that be learned and have any judgment, know that it is the papists, which no few years past, by hypocrisy and feigned religion, have uttered and sold their lies and fables instead of God's eternal truth, and in the place of Christ have set up idols and antichrist. *Truth's feigned friends.*

And for the conclusion of this comparison, in this word "very" you make such a wrangling, (where none occasion is given,) as never was had before this time of any *Very.*

learned man. For who heard ever before this time that an adjective was referred to a verb, and not to his proper substantive, of any man that had any learning at all?

<small>August. in Joan. Tra. 59.</small>

And as for the matter of Judas is answered before. For he received not the bread that was the Lord, as St Augustine saith, but the bread of the Lord. Nor no man can receive the body of Christ unworthily, although he may receive unworthily the sacrament thereof.

<small>Smith.</small>

And hitherto D. Smith hath found no fault at all in my comparisons, whereby the reader may see how nature passeth art, seeing here much more captiousness in a subtil sophistical wit, than in him that hath but learned the sophistical art.

Now followeth the eighth comparison.

<small>The eighth comparison.</small>

They say, that good men eat the body of Christ and drink his blood, only at that time when they receive the sacrament. We say, that they eat, drink, and feed of Christ continually, so long as they be members of his body.

WINCHESTER.

What forehead, I pray you, is so hardened, that can utter this among them that know any thing of the learning of Christ's church? In which it is a most common distinction, that there is three manner of eatings of Christ's body and blood: one spiritual only, which is <small>*Three manner of eatings.</small> *here affirmed in the second part of "we say," wherein the author and his say as the church saith: another eating is both sacramentally and spiritually, which is when men worthily communicate in the supper: the third is sacramentally only, which is by men unworthy,* <small>*Cause of error.</small> *who eat and drink in the holy supper to their condemnation only. And the learned men in Christ's church say, that the ignorance and want of observation of these three manner of eatings causeth the error in the understanding of the scriptures and such fathers' sayings, as have written of the sacrament. And when the church speaketh of these three manner of eatings, what an impudency is it to say, that the church teacheth good men only to eat the body of Christ and drink his blood, when they receive the sacrament, being the truth otherwise; and yet a diversity there is of eating spiritually only, and eating spiritually and sacramentally, because in the supper they receive his very flesh and*[1] *blood indeed, with the effects of all graces and gifts to such as receive it spiritually and worthily; whereas out of the supper, when we eat only spiritually by faith, God that worketh without his sacraments, as seemeth to him, doth relieve those that believe and trust in him, and suffereth them not to be destitute of that is necessary for them, whereof we may not presume contemning the sacrament,* <small>*God's promises annexed to his sacraments.</small> *but ordinarily seek God, where he hath ordered himself to be sought, and there to assure ourself of his covenants and promises, which be most certainly annexed to his sacraments,* <small>*We must, in teaching, exalt the sacraments after their dignity.</small> *whereunto we ought to give most certain trust and confidence: wherefore to teach the spiritual manducation to be equal with the spiritual manducation and sacramental also, that is to diminish the effect of the institution of the sacrament, which no christian man ought to do.*

CANTERBURY.

<small>70.</small>

Who is so ignorant that hath read any thing at all, but he knoweth that distinction of three eatings? But no man that is of learning and judgment, understandeth the <small>Three manner of eatings.</small> three diverse eatings in such sort as you do, but after this manner: that some eat only the sacrament of Christ's body, but not the very body itself; some eat his body and not the sacrament; and some eat the sacrament and body both together. The sacrament (that is to say, the bread) is corporally eaten and chewed with the teeth in the mouth: the very body is eaten and chewed with faith in the spirit. Ungodly men, when they receive the sacrament, they chew in their mouths, like unto Judas, the sacramental bread, but they eat not the celestial bread, which is Christ. Faithful christian people, such as be Christ's true disciples, continually from time to time record in their minds the beneficial death of our Saviour Christ, chewing it by faith in the cud of their spirit, and digesting it in their hearts, feeding and com-

---

[[1] Very flesh and very blood, 1551.]

forting themselves with that heavenly meat, although they daily receive not the sacrament thereof; and so they eat Christ's body spiritually, although not the sacrament thereof. But when such men for their more comfort and confirmation of eternal life, given unto them by Christ's death, come unto the Lord's holy table; then, as before they fed spiritually upon Christ, so now they feed corporally also upon the sacramental bread: by which sacramental feeding in Christ's promises, their former spiritual feeding is increased, and they grow and wax continually more strong in Christ, until at the last they shall come to the full measure and perfection in Christ. This is the teaching of the true catholic church, as it is taught by God's word. And therefore St Paul, speaking of them that unworthily eat, saith, that they eat the bread, but not that they eat the body of Christ, but their own damnation. *True sacramental eating.* 1 Cor. xi.

And where you set out with your accustomed rhetorical colours a great impudency in me, that would report of the papists that good men eat the body of Christ and drink his blood only when they receive the sacrament, seeing that I know that the papists make a distinction of three manner of eatings of Christ's body, whereof one is without the sacrament: I am not ignorant indeed, that the papists grant a spiritual eating of Christ's body without the sacrament; but I mean of such an eating of his body, as his presence is in the sacrament, and as you say he is there eaten, that is to say, corporally. Therefore to express my mind more plainly to you, that list not understand, let this be the comparison. *Whether Christ be really eaten without the sacrament.*

They say that after such a sort as Christ is in the sacrament, and there eaten, so good men eat his body and blood only when they receive the sacrament. [We say, that as they eat and drink Christ in the sacrament,]² so do they eat, drink, and feed upon him continually, so long as they be members of his body. *The comparison.*

Now the papists say, that Christ is corporally present in the sacrament, and is so eaten only when men receive the sacrament. But we say, that the presence of Christ in his holy supper is a spiritual presence: and as he is spiritually present, so is he spiritually eaten of all faithful christian men, not only when they receive the sacrament, but continually so long as they be members spiritual of Christ's mystical body. And yet this is "really" also, (as you have expounded the word,) that is to say, in deed and effectually. And as the Holy Ghost doth not only come to us in baptism, and Christ doth there clothe us, but they do the same to us continually so long as we dwell in Christ; so likewise doth Christ feed us so long as we dwell in him and he in us, and not only when we receive the sacrament. So that as touching Christ himself, the presence is all one, the clothing all one, and the feeding all one, although the one for the more comfort and consolation have the sacrament added to it, and the other be without the sacrament. 71. *Really.*

The rest that is here spoken is contentious wrangling to no purpose.

But now cometh in Smith with his five eggs, saying that I have made here five lies in these comparisons. "The first lie is," saith he, "that the papists do say, that good men do eat and drink Christ's body and blood only when they receive the sacrament:" which thing Smith saith the papists do not say, but that they then only do eat Christ's body and drink his blood corporally, which sufficeth for my purpose. For I mean no³ other thing, but that the papists teach such a corporal eating of Christ's body as endureth not, but vanisheth away, and ceaseth at the furthest within few hours after the sacrament is⁴ received. But forasmuch as Smith agreeth here with you, the answer made before to you will serve for him also. And yet Smith here shall serve me in good stead against you, who have imputed unto me so many impudent lies, made against the papists in the comparisons before rehearsed: and Smith saith that this is the first lie, which is in the eighth comparison. And so shall Smith, (being mine adversary and your friend,) be such a witness for me, as you cannot except against, to prove that those things which before you said were impudent lies, be no lies at all. For this "is the first lie," saith Smith; and then my sayings before must be all true, and not impudent lies. *Smith.*

[² The 1580 Ed. omits this sentence.] [⁴ Sacrament be received, 1551.]
[³ None other, 1551.]

Now to the ninth comparison.

They say, that the body of Christ that is in the sacrament, hath his own proper form and quantity. We say, that Christ is there sacramentally and spiritually, without form or quantity.

WINCHESTER.

[The answer. Orig. Ed. Winch. 1551.]
*Christ's body is understanded of his humanity.
*The unity of Christ's manhood and Godhead.

In this comparison is both sleight and craft: in the first part of it, which is that "they say," there is mention of the body of Christ, which is proper of the humanity of Christ. In the second part, which is of "we say," there is no mention of Christ's body, but of Christ, who in his divine nature is understanded present without a body. Now the sacrament is institute of Christ's body and blood; and because the divine nature in Christ continueth the unity with the body of Christ, we must needs confess where the body of Christ is there is whole Christ, God and man. And when we speak of Christ's body, we must understand a true body, which hath both form and quantity; and therefore such as confess the true catholic faith, they affirm of Christ's body all truth of a natural body, which although it hath all those truths of form and quantity, yet they say, Christ's body is not present after the manner of quantity, nor in a visible form, as it was conversant in this present life: but that there is truly in the sacrament the very true body of Christ, which good men believe upon the credit of Christ that said so, and knowledge therewith the manner of that presence to be an high mystery, and the manner so spiritual, as the carnal man cannot by discourse of reason reach it, but in his discourse shall (as this author doth) think it a vanity and foolishness: which foolishness nevertheless overcometh the wisdom of the world. And thus have I opened what they say on the catholic part.

*A marvellous saying of this author without scripture.
*Christ in the institution of the sacrament, spake of his humanity, saying, "This is my body." Phil. ii.

Now for the other part, whereof this author is, and with his faith "we say," the words seem to imply, that Christ's human body is not in the sacrament, in that it is said, "Christ to be there sacramentally and spiritually, without form or quantity," which saying hath no scripture for it. For the scripture speaketh of Christ's body which was betrayed for us, to be given us to be eaten. Where also Christ's divinity is present, as accompanying his humanity, which humanity is specially spoken of, the presence of which humanity when it is denied, then is there no text to prove the presence of Christ's divinity specially, that is to say, otherwise than it is by his omnipotency present every where. And to conclude this piece of comparison, this manner of speech was never, I think, read, that Christ is present in the sacrament without form or quantity. And St Paul speaketh of a form in the Godhead, Qui quum in forma Dei esset, "Who when he was in the form of God." So as if Christ be present in the sacrament without all form, then is he there neither as God nor man; which is a stranger teaching than yet hath been heard or read of: but into such absurdities indeed do they fall, who entreat irreverently and untruly this high mystery. This is here worthy a special note, how by the manner of the speech in the latter part of this difference the teaching seemeth to be, that Christ is spiritually present in the sacrament, because of the word "there," which thou, reader, mayest compare how it agreeth with the rest of this author's doctrine. Let us go to the next.

*There.
*Note this contrariety in the author.

CANTERBURY.

Such is the nature of many, that they can find many knots in a plain rush, and doubts where no doubts ought to be found. So find you "sleight and craft," where I meant all things simply and plainly. And to avoid such sleight and craft as you gather of my words, I shall express them plainly thus.

*The comparison.

The papists say, that the body of Christ that is in the sacrament, hath his own proper form and quantity. We say, that the body of Christ hath not his proper form and quantity, neither in the sacrament, nor in them that receive the sacrament; but is in the sacrament sacramentally, and in the worthy receivers spiritually, without the proper form and quantity of his body. This was my meaning at the first, and no man that had looked of this place indifferently, would have taken the second part of this comparison to be understanded of Christ's divine nature: for the bread and wine be sacraments of his body and blood, and not of his divinity, as Theodoretus saith; and therefore his divine nature is not sacramentally in the sacrament, but his human nature only. And what manner of speech had this been, to say of Christ's divine nature, that it is in the sacrament without quantity, which hath in it no manner

Theodoret. Dialog. 1.

of quantity wheresoever it be? And where I set forth these comparisons to shew wherein we vary from the papists, what variance had been in this comparison, if I had understood the first part of Christ's humanity, and the second of his divinity?

The reader by this one place, among many other, may easily discern, how captious you be to reprehend whatsoever I say, and to pervert every thing into a wrong sense: so that in respect of you, Smith is a very indifferent taker of my words, although indeed he far passeth the bounds of honesty. D. Smith.

But to come directly to the matter, if it be true that you say, that in the sacrament Christ's body hath all the forms and quantities of a natural body, why say you then that his body is not there present after the manner of quantity? Declare what difference is between form and quantity, and the manner of quantity. And if Christ's body in the sacrament have the same quantity, that is to say, the same length, breadth, and thickness, and the same form, that is to say, the same due order and proportion; of the members and parts of his body, that he had when he was crucified, and hath now in heaven, (as he hath by your saying here in this place,) then I pray you declare further, how the length, breadth, and thickness of a man, should be contained in quantity within the compass of a piece of bread, no longer nor broader than one or two inches, nor much thicker than one leaf of paper: how an inch may be as long as an ell, and an ell as short as an inch: how length and roundness shall agree in one proportion; and a thick and thin thing be both of one thickness: which you must warrant to be brought to pass, if the form and quantity of Christ's body be contained under the form and quantity of such bread and wine as we now use. Whether, in the sacrament, Christ's body hath his proper form and quantity.

But as Smith in the last comparison did me good service against you, so shall you in this comparison do me good service against him. For among the five lies wherewith he charges me in these comparisons, he accounteth this for one, that I report of the papists, that Christ's body in the sacrament hath his proper form and quantity, which you say is a truth. And therefore, if I make a lie herein, as Smith saith I do, yet I lie not alone, but have you to bear me company. And yet once again more may the reader here note, how the papists vary among themselves. D. Smith.

And it is untrue that you say, that good men believe upon the credit of Christ, that there is truly in the sacrament the very true body of Christ. For Christ called bread his body, and wine his blood, (which, as the old authors say, must needs be understanded figuratively;) but he never said that his true body is truly in the sacrament, as you here report of him.

And the manner of his presence you call so high a mystery, that the carnal man cannot reach it. And indeed, as you feign the matter, it is so high a mystery, that never man could reach it but yourself alone. For you make the manner of Christ being in the sacrament so spiritual, that you say his flesh, blood, and bones be there really and carnally; and yet you confess in your book, that you never read in any old author that so said. And this manner of handling of so pure a mystery is neither godly foolishness nor wordly, but rather a mere frenzy and madness.

And although the scripture speak of Christ's body to be eaten of us, yet that is understanded of spiritual and not of corporal eating, and of spiritual not of corporal presence. The scripture saith, that Christ hath forsaken[1] the world, and is ascended into heaven. Upon which words St Augustine, Vigilius, and other ancient authors do prove, that as concerning the nature of his manhood, Christ is gone hence, and is not here, as I declared in my third book, the 3rd, 4th, 5th, and 6th chapters. John xvi. Mark xvi. Luke xxiv Acts i.

And where you think that this matter of speech was never read, that Christ is present in the sacrament without form or quantity, I am sure that it was never read in any approved author, that Christ hath his proper form and quantity in the sacrament. And Duns saith, "that his quantity is in heaven, and not in the sacrament." Scotus, 4. Sent. Dist. 10. q. 1.

And when I say that Christ is in the sacrament sacramentally, and without form and quantity, who would think any man so captious, so ignorant, or so full

---

[¹ Ed. 1551 reads "forsaken;"—Ed. 1580 reads "forespoken,"—which is evidently a misprint.]

of sophistry, to draw my words to the form of Christ's divinity, which I speak most plainly of the form and quantity of his body and humanity? as I have before declared. And although some other might be so far overseen, yet specially you ought not so to take my words; forasmuch as you said not past sixteen lines before, that my words seem to imply, that I meant of Christ's human body.

74. All.

And because it may appear how truly and faithfully you report my words, you add this word "all," which is more than I speak, and marreth all the whole matter. And you gather thereof such absurdities as I never spake, but as you sophistically do gather, to make a great matter of nothing.

There.

And where of this word "there" you would conclude repugnance in my doctrine, that where in other places I have written that Christ is spiritually present in them that receive the sacrament, and not in the sacraments of bread and wine, and now it should seem that I teach contrary, that Christ is spiritually present in the very bread and wine; if you pleased to understand my words rightly, there is no repugnance in my words at all. For by this word "there," I mean not in the sacraments of bread and wine, but in the ministration of the sacrament, as the old authors for the most part, when they speak of the presence of Christ in the sacrament, they mean in the ministration of the sacrament. Which my saying varieth from no doctrine that I have taught in any part of my book.

Now followeth the tenth comparison.

They say, that the fathers and prophets of the old testament did not eat the body, nor drink the blood of Christ. We say, that they did eat his body and drink his blood, although he was not yet born nor incarnated.

WINCHESTER.

*A riddle may contain truth of nay and yea, being in appearance two contraries.

This comparison of difference is clerkly conveyed, as it were of a riddle, wherein nay and yea, when they be opened, agree and consent. The fathers did eat Christ's body and drink his blood in the¹ truth of promise, which was effectual to them of redemption to be wrought, not in truth of presence (as we do) for confirmation of redemption already wrought. They had a certain promise, and we a certain present payment: they did eat Christ spiritually, believing in him that was to come, but they did not eat Christ's body present in the sacrament, sacramentally and spiritually, as we do. Their sacraments were figures of the things, but ours contain the very things. And therefore albeit in a sense to the learned men it may be verified, that the fathers did eat the body of Christ, and drink his blood; yet there is no such form of words in scripture, and it is more agreeable to the simplicity of scripture, to say the fathers before Christ's nativity did not eat the body and blood of Christ, which body and blood Christ himself truly took of the body of the virgin Mary. For although St Paul, in the tenth to the Corinthians, be so understanded of some, as the fathers should eat the same spiritual meat, and drink the same spiritual drink that we do, to which understanding all do not agree, yet following that understanding, we may not

*Augustinus. *A special difference in St Augustine.

so press the words, as there should be no difference at all; and this one² difference St Augustine noteth, how their sacraments contained the promise of that, which in our sacrament is given. Thus he saith: "And this is evident of itself, how to us in the holy supper Christ saith, 'This is my body that shall be betrayed for you; take, eat:' which was never said to the fathers, although their faith in substance agreed with ours, having all one Christ and Mediator, which they looked for to come, and we acknowledge to be already come." 'Come,' and 'to come,' as St Augustine saith, differeth. But Christ is one, by whom all was created³, and man's fall repaired, from whom is all feeding, corporal and spiritual, and in whom all is restored in heaven and in earth. In this faith of Christ, the fathers were fed with heavenly spiritual food, which was the same with ours in respect of the restitution by Christ, and redemption by them hoped, which is achieved by the mystery of the body and blood of Christ; by reason whereof I deny not, but it may be said in a good sense, how they did eat the body and blood of Christ, before he was incarnate: but, as I said before, scripture speaketh not so, and it is no wholesome fashion of speech

*Joan of Kent's obstinacy.

at this time, which furthereth in sound to the ears of the rude the pestilent heresy wherein Joan of

75.

[¹ In truth of promise, 1551.]   [² This one special difference, 1551.]   [³ Create, 1551.]

Kent obstinately died, that is to say, that Christ took nothing of the virgin, but brought his body with him from above; being a thing worthy to be noted, how the old heresy, denying the true taking of the flesh of Christ in the virgin's womb, at the same time to revive, when the true deliverance of Christ's flesh in the holy supper, to be of us eaten, is also denied. For as it is a mere truth without figure, and yet an high mystery, God's work in the incarnation of Christ, wherein our flesh was of Christ truly taken of the virgin's substance: so is it a mere truth, without figure, in the substance of the celestial thing, and yet an high mystery and God's work, in the giving of the same true flesh, truly to be in the supper eaten. When I exclude figure in the sacrament, I mean not of the visible part, which is called a figure of the celestial invisible part, which is truly there without figure, so as by that figure is not impaired the truth of that presence; which I add to avoid cavillation. And to[4] make an end of this comparison, this I say, that this article declareth wantonness, to make a difference in words, where none is in the sense rightly taken, with a novelty of speech not necessary to be uttered now. *Novelty of speech.

CANTERBURY.

Note well here, reader, how the cuttle cometh in with his dark colours.

Where I speak of the substance of the thing that is eaten, you turn it to the manner and circumstances thereof, to blind the simple reader, and that you may make thereof a riddle of yea and nay, as you be wont to make black white, and white black; or one thing yea and nay, black and white at your pleasure.

But to put away your dark colours, and to make the matter plain, this I say, that the fathers and prophets did eat Christ's body and drink his blood in promise of redemption to be wrought, and we eat and drink the same flesh and blood in confirmation of our faith in the redemption already wrought. *The fathers did eat Christ's flesh and drink his blood.*

But as the fathers did eat and drink, so did also the apostles at Christ's supper, in promise of redemption to be wrought, not in confirmation of redemption already wrought. So that if wrought and to be wrought make the diversity of presence and not presence, then the apostles did not eat and drink the flesh and blood of Christ really present, because the redemption was not then already wrought, but promised the next day to be wrought.

And although before the crucifying of his flesh and effusion of his blood our redemption was not actually wrought by Christ, yet was he spiritually and sacramentally present, and spiritually and sacramentally eaten and drunken, not only of the apostles at his last supper before he suffered his passion, but also of the holy patriarchs and fathers before his incarnation, as well as he is now of us after his ascension.

And although in the manner of signifying there be great difference between their sacraments and ours, yet, as St Augustine saith, both we and they receive one thing in the diversity of sacraments[5]. And our sacraments contain presently the very things signified, no more than theirs did. For in their sacraments they were by Christ presently regenerated and fed, as we be in ours; although their sacraments were figures of the death of Christ to come, and ours be figures of his death now past. And as it is all one Christ that was to be born and to die for us, and afterward was born indeed and died indeed, whose birth and death be now past; so was the same Christ, and the same flesh and blood eaten and drunken of the faithful fathers before he was born or dead, and of his apostles after he was born and before he was dead, and of faithful christian people is now daily eaten and drunken after that both his nativity and death be past. And all is but one Christ, one flesh, and one blood, as concerning the substance, yet that which to the fathers was to come, is to us past. And nevertheless the eating and drinking is all one; for neither the fathers did, nor we do eat carnally and corporally with our mouths, but both the fathers did, and we do eat spiritually by true and lively faith. The body *The diversity of the sacraments of the new and old testament. August. in Joan. Tract. 26.*

[4 So ed. 1551. In that of 1580 *to* is omitted.]
[5 "Sacramenta illa fuerunt: in signis diversa sunt, sed in re quæ significatur paria sunt."— August. in Joannem, Tract. XXVI. Pars IX. Ed. Basil. ap. Amerbach. 1506.]

The fathers did eat Christ's body and drink his blood before he was born.

of Christ was and is all one to the fathers and to us, but corporally and locally he was not[1] yet born unto them, and from us he is gone, and ascended up into heaven. So that to neither he was nor is carnally, substantially, and corporally present, but to them he was, and to us he is spiritually present, and sacramentally also; and of both sacramentally, spiritually, and effectually eaten and drunken, to eternal salvation and everlasting life.

And this is plainly enough declared in the scripture to them that have willing minds to understand the truth. For it is written in the old testament, Ecclus. xxiv. in the person of Christ thus: "They that eat me, shall yet hunger, and they that drink me shall yet be thirsty."

1 Cor. x.

And St Paul writeth to the Corinthians, saying: "Our fathers did all eat the same spiritual meat, and did all drink the same spiritual drink; and they drank of that spiritual rock that followed them, which rock was Christ." These words St Augustine expounding, saith: "What is to eat the same meat, but that they did eat the same which we do? Whosoever in manna understood Christ, did eat the same spiritual meat that we do, that is to say, that meat which was received with faith, and not with bodies. Therefore to them that understood and believed, it was the same meat and the same drink. So that to such as understood not, the meat was only manna, and the drink only water; but to such as understood, it was the same that is now. For then was Christ to come, who is now come. To come and is come, be divers words, but it is the same Christ." These be St Augustine's sayings[2].

August. de Util. Pœniten.

And because you say, "that it is more agreeable to the scripture to say, that the fathers before Christ's nativity did not eat the body and drink the blood of Christ"; I pray you, shew me one scripture that so saith. And shew me also one approved author that disallowed St Augustine's mind by me here alleged, because you say, "that all do not agree to his understanding." And in the seventy-seventh Psalm, St Augustine saith also: "The stone was Christ." Therefore the same was the meat and drink of the fathers in the mystery, which is ours; but in signification the same, not in outward form. For it is one Christ himself, that to them was figured in the stone, and to us manifestly appeared in flesh. And St Augustine saith plainly, "that both manna and our sacrament signifieth Christ, and that although the sacraments were divers, yet in the thing by them meant and understand they were both like." And so after the mind of St Augustine it is clear, that the same things were given to the faithful receivers in the sacraments of the old testament that be given in the new: the same to them was circumcision, that to us is baptism; and to them by manna was given the same thing, that now is given to us in the sacramental bread.

August. in Psal. lxxvii.

August. in Joan. Tract. 26.

77.

And if I would grant for your pleasure, that in their sacraments Christ was promised, and that in ours he is really given; doth it not then follow as well that Christ is given in the sacrament of baptism, as that he is given in the sacrament of his flesh and blood? And St Augustine, *contra Faustum*, esteemeth them mad, that think diversity between the things signified in the old and new testament, because the signs be diverse[3]; and expressing the matter plainly, saith, "that the flesh and blood of our sacrifice before Christ's coming was promised by sacrifices of similitudes, in his passion was given indeed, and after his ascension is solemnly put in our memory by the sacrament[4]."

August. contra Faustum, lib. 19. cap. 16. et 20. cap. 21.

[1 Here again it is necessary to follow ed. 1551. The 1580 ed. omits *not*.]

[2 "Eundem, inquit, cibum spiritalem manducaverunt. Quid est 'eundem,' nisi quia eum quem etiam nos?—Quicunque in manna Christum intellexerunt, eundem quem nos cibum spiritalem manducaverunt: id est, qui fide capiebatur, non qui corpore hauriebatur.—Et eundem ergo cibum, eundem potum, sed intelligentibus et credentibus. Non intelligentibus autem, illud solum manna, illa sola aqua: credenti autem idem qui nunc. Tunc enim Christus venturus, modo Christus venit. Venturus et venit, diversa verba sunt, sed idem Christus."—August. de Utilitate Pœnitentiæ, Lib. I. Pars x.]

[3 "Quanto errore delirent, qui putant signis sacramentisque mutatis, etiam res ipsas esse diversas." August. contra Faustum, Lib. XIX. cap. xvi. Pars iv.]

[4 "Hujus sacrificii caro et sanguis ante adventum Christi per victimas similitudinum promittebatur: in passione Christi per ipsam veritatem reddebatur: post ascensum Christi per sacramentum memoriæ celebratur."—Ibid. Lib. XX. cap. xxi.]

And the thing which you say St Augustine[5] noteth to be given in the sacraments of the new testament, and to be promised in the sacraments of the old, St Augustine expresseth the thing which he meant, that is to say, salvation and eternal life by Christ. And yet in this mortal life we have not eternal life in possession, but in promise, as the prophets had. But St Augustine saith, that we have the promise, because we have Christ already come, which by the prophets was promised before that he should come; and therefore St John the baptist was called more than a prophet, because he said: "Here is the Lamb of God already present, which the prophets taught us to look for until he came." August. in Psal. lxxiii.

John i.

The effect therefore of St Augustine's words plainly to be expressed, was this, that the prophets in the old testament promised a Saviour to come and redeem the world, which the sacraments of that time testified until his coming: but now he is already come, and hath by his death performed that was promised, which our sacraments testify unto us, as St Augustine declareth more plainly in his book, *De fide ad Petrum*, the 19th chapter[6]. So that St Augustine speaketh of the giving of Christ to death, (which the sacraments of the old testament testified to come, and ours testify to be done,) and not of the giving of him in the sacraments. August. de Fide ad Pet. cap. 19.

And forasmuch as St Augustine spake generally of all the sacraments, therefore if you will by his words prove, that Christ is corporally in the sacrament of the holy communion, you may as well prove, that he is corporally in baptism; for St Augustine speaketh no more of the one than of the other. But where St Augustine speaketh generally of all the sacraments, you restrain the matter particularly to the sacrament of the Lord's supper only, that the ignorant reader should think, that St Augustine spake of the corporal presence of Christ in the sacraments, and that only in the sacraments of bread and wine; whereas St Augustine himself speaketh only of our salvation by Christ, and of the sacraments in general.

And nevertheless, as the fathers had the same Christ and Mediator that we have, (as you here confess,) so did they spiritually eat his flesh and drink his blood as we do, and spiritually feed of him, and by faith he was present with them, as he is with us, although carnally and corporally he was yet to come unto them, and from us is gone up to his Father into heaven.

This, besides St Augustine, is plainly set out by Bertram above six hundred years past, whose judgment in this matter of the sacrament although you allow not (because it utterly condemneth your doctrine therein,) yet forasmuch as hitherto his teaching was never reproved by none, but by you alone, and that he is commended of other as an excellent learned man in holy scripture, and a notable famous man, as well in living as learning, and that among his excellent works this one is specially praised, which he wrote of the matter of the sacrament of the body and blood of our Lord, therefore I shall rehearse his teaching in this point, how the holy fathers and prophets, before the coming of Christ, did eat Christ's flesh and drink his blood: so that, although Bertram's saying be not esteemed with you, yet the indifferent reader may see what was written in this matter, before your doctrine was in- Bertram.

78.

[5 "Sacramenta non eadem, quia alia sunt sacramenta dantia salutem, alia promittentia Salvatorem. Sacramenta novi testamenti dant salutem, sacramenta veteris testamenti promiserunt Salvatorem. Cum ergo jam teneas promissa, quid quæris promittentia? Salvatorem habens jam in hoc teneas promissa, non quod jam acceperimus vitam æternam, sed quia jam venerit Christus, qui per prophetas prænunciabatur."—August. in Psal. lxxiii. Tom. VIII. p. 327. Ed. Paris. 1635.]

[6 "Firmissime tene, et nullatenus dubites, ipsum unigenitum Deum, Verbum carnem factum, se pro nobis obtulisse sacrificium et hostiam Deo in odorem suavitatis: cui cum Patre et Spiritu sancto a patriarchis, prophetis, et sacerdotibus tempore veteris testamenti animalia sacrificabantur; et cui nunc, id est, tempore novi testamenti, cum Patre et Spiritu sancto, cum quibus illi est una divinitas, sacrificium panis et vini in fide et caritate sancta ecclesia catholica per universum orbem terræ offerre non cessat. In illis enim carnalibus victimis figuratio fuit carnis Christi, quam pro peccatis nostris ipse sine peccato fuerat oblaturus, et sanguinis quem erat effusurus in remissionem peccatorum nostrorum. In isto autem sacrificio gratiarum actio atque commemoratio est carnis Christi, quam pro nobis obtulit, et sanguinis quem pro nobis idem Deus effudit."—August. de fide ad Petrum diaconum, Cap. xix. Pars x. Basil. ap. Amerbach. 1506. In Ed. Paris. 1635. Tom. III. p. 391, 2. This treatise is censured by Erasmus as spurious; and the author is said to be Fulgentius.—Vid. Riveti Critica Sacra, p. 389. Genev. 1626. "Coci censura Patrum," pp. 341, 2. Helm. 1683.]

Smith.

vented. And although his authority be not received of you, yet his words may serve against Smith, who herein more learnedly, and with more judgment than you, approveth this author. This is Bertram's doctrine[1]. "St Paul saith, that all the old fathers did eat the same spiritual meat, and drink the same spiritual drink. But peradventure thou wilt ask, which the same? Even the very same that christian people do daily eat and drink in the church. For we may not understand divers things, when it is one and the self-same Christ, which in times past did feed with his flesh, and made to drink of his blood, the people that were baptized in the cloud and sea, in the wilderness, and which doth now in the church feed christian people with the bread of his body, and giveth them to drink the flood of his blood. When he had not yet taken man's nature upon him, when he had not yet tasted death for the salvation of the world, not redeemed us with his blood, nevertheless even then our forefathers, by spiritual meat and invisible drink, did eat his body in the wilderness and drink his blood, as the apostle beareth witness, saying: 'The same spiritual meat, the same spiritual drink.' For he that now in the church, by his omnipotent power, doth spiritually convert bread and wine into the flesh of his body, and into the flood of his own blood, he did then invisibly so work, that manna which came from heaven was his body, and the water his blood." Now by the things here by me alleged it evidently appeareth, that this is no novelty of speech to say, that the holy fathers and prophets did eat Christ's flesh, and drink his blood. For both the scripture and old authors use so to speak, how much soever the speech mislike them that like no fashion but their own[2].

Joan of Kent.

And what doth this further the pestilent heresy of Joan of Kent? Is this a good argument? The fathers did eat Christ's flesh and drink his blood spiritually before he was born; ergo after he was not corporally born of his mother? Or because he was corporally born, is he not therefore daily eaten spiritually of his faithful people? Because he dwelt in the world corporally from his incarnation unto his ascension, did he not therefore spiritually dwell in his holy members before that time, and hath so done ever sithens, and will do to the world's end? Or if he be eaten in a figure, can you induce thereof that he was not born without a figure? Do not such kind of arguments favour the error of Joan of Kent? Yea, do they not manifestly approve her pestiferous heresy, if they were to be allowed? What man that meaneth the truth, would bring in such manner of reasoning to deface the truth? And yet it is not to be denied, but that Christ is truly eaten, as he was truly born; but the one corporally and without figure, and the other spiritually and with a figure.

Now followeth my eleventh comparison.

The eleventh comparison.

They say, that the body of Christ is every day many times made, as often as there be masses said, and that then and there he is made of bread and wine. We say, that Christ's body was never but once made, and then not of the nature and substance of bread and wine, but of the substance of his blessed mother.

[1 " Cum cibus vel potus ille futuri corporis Christi sanguinisque mysterium quod celebrat ecclesia præmonstraret, eandem tamen escam spiritualem manducasse, et eundem potum spiritualem bibisse patres nostros sanctus Paulus asseverat. Quæris fortasse, quam eandem? nimirum ipsam quam hodie populus credentium in ecclesia manducat et bibit. Non enim licet diversa intelligi, quoniam unus idemque Christus est, qui et populum in deserto, in nube et in mari baptizatum sua carne pavit, suo sanguine tunc potavit, et in ecclesia nunc credentium populum sui corporis pane, sui sanguinis unda pascit ac potat. Mirum certe, quoniam incomprehensibile et inæstimabile: nondum hominem assumpserat, nondum pro salute mundi mortem degustaverat, nondum sanguine suo nos redemerat; et jam nostri patres in deserto per escam spiritualem potumque invisibilem ejus corpus manducabant, et ejus sanguinem bibebant, velut testis existit apostolus, clamans: ' eandem escam spiritualem manducasse, eundem potum spiritualem bibisse patres nostros.' Ipse namque qui nunc in ecclesia omnipotenti virtute panem et vinum in sui corporis carnem et proprii cruoris undam spiritualiter convertit, ipse tunc quoque manna de cœlo datum corpus suum, et aquam de petra profusam proprium sanguinem invisibiliter operatus est." Bertram. Lib. de Corp. et Sang. Dom. Cap. xxii. xxiii. xxv. pp. 12—14.—Ed. Oxford, 1838.]

[2 That like no fashion of speech but their own, 1551.]

WINCHESTER.

The body of Christ is by God's omnipotency, who so worketh in his word, made present unto us at such time, as the church pray[3] it may please him so to do, which prayer is ordered to be made in the book of common prayer now set forth[4]. Wherein we require of God, the creatures of bread and wine to be sanctified, and to be to us the body and blood of Christ, which they cannot be, unless God worketh it, and make them so to be: in which mystery it was never taught, as this author willingly misreporteth, that Christ's most precious body is made of the matter of bread, but in that order exhibited and made present unto us, by conversion of the substance of bread into his precious body; not a new body made of a new matter of bread and wine, but a new presence of the body, that is never old, made present there, where the substance of bread and wine was before. So as this comparison of difference is mere wrangling, and so evident as it needeth no further answer but a note. Lo, how they be not ashamed to trifle in so great a matter, and without cause by wrong terms to bring the truth in slander, if it were possible. May not this be accounted as a part of God's punishment, for men of knowledge to write to the people such matter seriously, as were not tolerable to be by a scoffer devised in a play, to supply when his fellow had forgotten his part?

<small>*The book of common prayer in this realm.</small>

<small>*Christ's body in the sacrament is not made of the matter of bread.</small>

CANTERBURY.

Christ is present whensoever the church prayeth unto him, and is gathered together in his name. And the bread and wine be made unto us the body and blood of Christ, (as it is in the book of common prayer,) but not by changing the substance of bread and wine into the substance of Christ's natural body and blood, but that in the godly using of them they be unto the receivers Christ's body and blood: as of some the scripture saith, that their riches is their redemption, and to some it is their damnation; and as God's word to some is life, to some it is death and a snare, as the prophet saith. And Christ himself to some is a stone to stumble at, to some is a raising from death, not by conversion of substances, but by good or evil use: that thing which to the godly is salvation, to the ungodly is damnation. So is the water in baptism, and the bread and wine in the Lord's supper, to the worthy receivers Christ himself and eternal life, and to the unworthy receivers everlasting death and damnation, not by conversion of one substance into another, but by godly or ungodly use thereof. And therefore, in the book of the holy communion, we do not pray absolutely that the bread and wine may be made the body and blood of Christ, but that unto us in that holy mystery they may be so; that is to say, that we may so worthily receive the same, that we may be partakers of Christ's body and blood, and that therewith in spirit and in truth we may be spiritually nourished. And a like prayer of old time were all the people wont to make at the communion of all such offerings as at that time all the people used to offer, praying that their offerings might be unto them the body and blood of Christ.

<small>The book of common prayer.</small>

<small>Prov. xiii. Rom. i. 1 Cor. i. 2 Cor. ii. James i. Isai. viii. Matt. xxii. 1 Pet. ii. John xi.</small>

<small>*Domin. 3. post Trin. Secret. Munera tibi, Domine, quibus oblata sanctifica, ut tui nobis unigeniti corpus et sanguis fiant ad medelam.</small>

And where you say, "it was never taught as I say, that Christ's body is made of the matter of bread," you knowingly and willingly misreport me. For I say not of the matter of bread, but of bread; which when you deny that the papists so say, it seemeth you be now ashamed of the doctrine, which the papists have taught this four or five hundred years. For is it not plainly written of all the papists, both lawyers and school-authors, that the body of Christ in the sacrament is made of bread, and his blood of wine? And they say not that his body is made present of bread and wine, but is made of bread and wine. Be not their books in print ready to be shewed? Do they not say, that the substance of the bread neither remaineth still, nor is turned into nothing, but into the body of Christ? And do not

<small>Whether the body of Christ be made of bread.</small>

[3 Prayeth, 1551.]

[4 Winchester here refers to these words in the first Service Book of Edward VI., in the prayer of consecration: "With thy holy Spirit and word vouchsafe to bless and sanctify these thy gifts and creatures of bread and wine, that they may be unto us the body and blood of thy most dearly beloved Son Jesus Christ." In the second Service Book of Edward VI. the passage was changed, as it now stands.]

yourself also say here in this place, that the substance of bread is converted into Christ's precious body? And what is that else but the body of Christ to be made of bread, and to be made of a new matter[1]? For if the bread do not vanish away into nothing, but be turned into Christ's body, then is Christ's body made of it; and then it must needs follow that Christ's body is made of new[2], and of another substance than it was made of in his mother's womb: for there it was made of her flesh and blood, and here it is made of bread and wine. And the papists say not (as you now would shift off the matter) that Christ's body is made present of bread, but they say plainly without addition, that it is made of bread. Can you deny that this is the plain doctrine of the papists, *Ex pane fit Corpus Christi*, "Of bread is made the body of Christ," and that the substance of bread is turned into the substance thereof? And what reason, sentence, or English, could be in this saying, "Christ's body is made present of bread?" Marry, to be present in bread might be some sentence, but that speech will you in nowise admit.

Pugnat cum aliis papistis.

And this your saying here, if the reader mark it well, turneth over quite and clean all the whole papistical doctrine in this matter of the sacrament, as well touching transubstantiation, as also the carnal presence. For their doctrine with one whole consent and agreement is this: That the substance of bread remaineth not, but is turned into the substance of Christ's body, and so the body of Christ is made of it. But this is false, say you, and "not tolerable to be by a scoffer devised in a place[3], to supply when his fellow had forgotten his part." And so the whole doctrine of the papists, which they have taught these four or five hundred years, do you condemn with condign reproaches, as a teaching intolerable, not to be devised by a scoffer in a play. Why do you then take upon you to defend the papistical doctrine, if it be so intolerable? Why do you not forsake those scoffers and players, which have juggled with the world so long, and embrace the most certain truth, that Christ's body is not made of bread? And seeing that you embrace it here in this one place, why stand you not constantly therein, but go from it again in all the rest of your book, defending the papistical doctrine, clean contrary to yours in this point, in that they teach that Christ's body is made of bread?

Making by conversion.

*Gen. ii.
*John ii.

And you vary so much from yourself herein, that although you deny the papists' sayings[4] in words, that Christ's body is made of bread, yet in effect you grant and maintain the same, which you say is intolerable, and not to be devised by a scoffer in a play. For you say, that Christ calleth bread his body, and that his calling is making: and then if he make bread his body, it must needs follow that he maketh his body of the bread. Moreover, you say, that Christ's body is made present by conversion, or turning of the substance of bread into the substance of his precious body; whereof must follow[5], that his body is made of bread. For whensoever one substance is turned into another[6], then the second is made of the first: as, because earth was turned into the body of Adam, we say that Adam was made of earth; and that Eve was made of Adam's rib, and the wine in Galilee made of water, because the water was turned into wine, and the rib of Adam's side into the body of Eve. If the water had been put out of the pots, and wine put in for the water, we might have said that the wine had been made present there, where the water was before. But then we might not have said that the wine had been made of the water, because the water was emptied out, and not turned into wine. But when Christ turned the water into the wine, then by reason of that turning we say that the wine was made of the water. So likewise if the bread be turned into the substance of Christ's body, we must not only say that the body of Christ is present where the bread was before, but also that it is made of the bread, because that the substance of the bread is converted and turned into the substance of his body. Which thing the papists saw must needs follow, and therefore they plainly confessed that the body of Christ

---

[1 And to be made anew of a new matter, 1551.]
[2 Is made new, 1551.]
[3 Play, 1551. Evidently the correct reading.

See Winchester in the preceding page.]
[4 Saying, 1551.]
[5 Must also follow, 1551.]
[6 Into another substance, 1551.]

was made of bread; which doctrine, as you truly say in this place, is intolerable, and not to be devised by a scoffer in a play, when his fellow had forgotten his part. And yet you so far forget yourself in this book, that throughout the same, whatsoever you say here, you defend the same intolerable doctrine, not to be devised by a scoffer.

And where Smith accounteth here my fourth lie, that I say, that the papists say, that Christ's body is made of bread and wine; here Smith and you agree both together in one lie. For it is truth and no lie, that the papists so say and teach; as Smith in other parts of his book saith, that Christ's body is made of bread, and that priests do make Christ's body. _{D. Smith.}

[7] My twelfth comparison is this.

They say, that the mass is a sacrifice satisfactory for sin, by the devotion of the priest that offereth, and not by the thing that is offered. But we say, that their saying is a most heinous[8], yea, and detestable error against the glory of Christ: for the satisfaction for our sins is not the devotion nor offering of the priest, but the only host and satisfaction for all the sins of the world is the death of Christ, and the oblation of his body upon the cross, that is to say, the oblation that Christ himself offered once upon the cross, and never but once, nor never any but he[9]. And therefore that oblation which the priests make daily in their papistical masses, cannot be a satisfaction for other men's sins by the priest's devotion: but it is a mere illusion, and subtle craft of the devil, whereby antichrist hath many years blinded and deceived the world.

WINCHESTER.

This comparison is out of the matter of the presence of Christ's most precious body in the sacrament, which presence this author, in the first part of his comparison, seemeth by implication to grant, when he findeth fault that the priest's devotion should be a sacrifice satisfactory, and not the thing that is offered; which manner of doctrine I never read, and I think myself it ought to be improved[10], if any such there be to make the devotion of the priest a satisfaction. For undoubtedly Christ is our satisfaction wholly and fully, who hath paid our whole debt to God the Father, for the appeasing of his just wrath against us, and hath cancelled the bill obligatory, as St Paul saith, that was against us. For further opening whereof, if it be asked how he satisfied; we answer as we be taught by the scriptures: By the accomplishment of the will of his Father, in his innocent, willing, and obedient suffering[11] the miseries of this world without sin, and the violent persecution of the world, even to the death of the cross, and shedding of his most precious blood. Wherein was perfected the willing sacrifice that he made of himself to God the Father for us, of whom it was written in the beginning of the book, that he should be the body and perfect accomplishment of all sacrifices, as of whom all other sacrifices before were shadows and figures.

And here is to be considered, how the obedient will in Christ's sacrifice is specially to be noted, who suffered because he would: which St Paul setteth forth in declaration of Christ's humility. And although that willing obedience was ended and perfected on the cross, to the which it continued from the beginning, by reason whereof the oblation is in St Paul's speech attributed thereunto: yet as in the sacrifice of Abraham, when he offered Isaac, the earnest will of offering was accounted for the offering indeed, whereupon it is said in scripture that Abraham offered Isaac, and the declaration of the will of Abraham is called the offering; so the declaration of Christ's will in his last supper was an offering of him to God the Father, assuring there his apostles of his will and determination, and by them all the world, that his body should be betrayed for them and us, and his precious blood shed for remission of sin, which his word he confirmed then with the gift of his precious body to be eaten, and his precious blood to be drunken. In which mystery he declared his body and blood to be

[The answer. Orig. Ed. Winchester.]

* Christ is our satisfaction.

* How Christ satisfied.

* Christ's will.

[7 Now my twelfth comparison, 1551.]

[8 A most heinous lie, and detestable error, Orig. ed.]

[9 Nor never none but he, 1551, and Orig. ed.]

[10 I think it myself it ought to be improved, 1551, and Orig. ed. Winchester.]

[11 In his innocent suffering, his willing and obedient suffering, 1551, and Orig. ed. Winch.]

the very sacrifice of the world, by him offered to God the Father, by the same will that he said his body should be betrayed for us; and thereby ascertained us that to be in him[1] willing, that the Jews on the cross seemed to execute by violence and force against his will. And therefore as Christ offered himself on the cross, in the execution of the work of his will; so he offered himself in his supper, in declaration of his will, whereby we might be the more assured of the effect of his death, which he suffered willingly and determinately for the redemption of the world, with a most perfect oblation and satisfaction for the sins of the world, exhibited and offered by him to God the Father, for the reconciliation of man's nature to God's favour and grace.

*Christ's once offering.

And this I write, because this author speaketh so precisely how Christ offered himself never but once. Whereby if he mean by once offering the whole action of our redemption, which was consummate and perfected upon the cross, all must confess the substance of that work of redemption by the oblation of Christ on the cross[2] to have been absolutely finished, and so once offered for all. But there is no scripture whereupon we might conclude, that Christ did in this mortal life, but in one particular moment of time, offer himself to his Father.

Phil. ii.

For St Paul describeth it to the Philippians, under the word of humiliation, to have continued the whole time of Christ's conversation here, even to the death, the death of the cross. And that this obedience to God in humility is called offering, appeareth by St Paul, when he

Rom. xii.

exhorted[3] us to offer our bodies, which meaneth a continual obedience in the observation of God's will, and he calleth oblationem gentium, to bring them to the faith[4]. And Abraham's willing obedience, ready at God's commandment to offer Isaac, is called the offering of Isaac, and is in very deed a true offering. And every man[5] offereth himself to God when he yieldeth to God's calling, and presenteth himself ready to do God's will and commandment, who then may be said to offer his service, that is to say, to place his service in sight, and before him, before whom it should be done.

And because our Saviour Christ, by the decree of the whole Trinity, took man's nature upon him, to suffer death for our redemption; which death, in his last supper, he declared plainly he would suffer: we read in St Cyprian how Christ offered himself in his supper, fulfilling the figure of Melchisedech, who by the offering of bread and wine signified that high mystery of Christ's supper, in which Christ, under the form of bread and wine, gave his very body and blood to be eaten and drunken, and in the giving thereof declared the determination of his glorious passion, and the fruit and effect thereof. Which doing was a sweet and pleasant oblation to God the Father, containing a most perfect obedience to God's will and pleasure. And in the mystery of this supper was written, made, and sealed, a most perfect testimony for an effectual memory of Christ's offering of himself to his Father, and of his death and passion, with the fruit thereof. And therefore Christ ordained this supper to be observed and continued for a memory of his coming[6]: so as we that saw not with our bodily eyes Christ's death and passion, may, in the celebration of the supper, be most surely ascertained of the truth out of Christ's own mouth, who still speaketh in the person of the minister of the church, "This is my body that is betrayed for you; this is my blood that is shed for you in remission of sin:" and therewith maketh his very body and his precious blood truly present[7], to be taken of us, eaten, and drunken. Whereby we be assured, that Christ is the same to us that he was to them, and useth us as familiarly as he did them; offereth himself to his Father for us as well as for them; declareth his will in the fruit of his death to pertain as well to us as to them. Of which death we be assured by his own mouth, that he suffered the same to the effect he spake of; and by[8] the continual feeding in this high mystery of the same very body that suffered, and feeding of it without consumption, being continually exhibited unto us a living body and a lively blood, not only our soul is specially and spiritually comforted, and our body thereby reduced to more conformable obedience to the soul, but also we, by the participation of this most precious body and blood, be ascertained of the resurrection and regeneration of our bodies and flesh, to be by God's power made incorruptible and immortal, to live, and have fruition in God, with our souls[9] for ever.

Wherefore having this mystery of Christ's supper, so many truths in it, the church hath

---

[1 Ascertained us to be in him, Orig. ed. Winchester.]
[2 Of Christ's body on the cross, 1551.]
[3 Exhorteth, Orig. ed. Winch.]
[4 To faith. Ibid.]
[5 And each man, 1551.]

[6 A memory to his coming, 1551.]
[7 His very body truly present, and his precious blood truly present, 1551.]
[8 By supplied from Orig. ed. Winch. It is wanting in both editions of Cranmer.]
[9 With our soul, 1551.]

OF THE PRESENCE OF CHRIST.

celebrate them all, and knowledged them all of one certainty in truth, not as figures, but really and in deed[10]; that is to say, as our bodies[11] shall be in the general resurrection regenerate in deed, so we believe we feed here of Christ's body in deed. And as it is true that Christ's body in deed is betrayed for us, so it is true that he giveth us to eat his very body in deed. And as it is true that Christ was in earth, and did celebrate this supper: so it is true that he commanded it to be celebrated by us till he come. And as it is true that Christ was very God omnipotent, and very man: so it is true that he could do that he affirmed by his word himself to do. And as he is most sincere truth: so may we be truly assured that he would, and did, as he said. And as it is true that he is most just: so it is true that he assisteth the doing of his commandment in the celebration of the holy supper. And therefore, as he is author of this most holy sacrament of his precious body and blood: so is he the maker of it, and is the invisible priest, who, as Emissene saith, by his secret power, with his word, changeth the visible creatures into the substance of his body and blood. Wherein man, the visible priest and invisible minister, by order of the church, is only a dispenser of the mystery, doing and saying as the Holy Ghost hath taught the church to do and say[12]. *Truths linked together.

*Emissenus. *Christ is the invisible priest. 1 Cor. iv.

Finally, as we be taught by faith all these to be true: so when wanton reason (faith being asleep) goeth about by curiosity to impair any one of these truths, the chain is broken, the links sparkle abroad, and all is brought in danger to be scattered and scambled at. Truths have been abused, but yet they be true, as they were before; for no man can make that is true false: and abuse is man's fault, not the thing's[13]. Scripture in speech giveth to man as God's minister the name of that action which God specially worketh in that mystery. So it pleaseth God to honour the ministry of man in his church, by whom it also pleaseth him to work effectually. And Christ said, "They that believe in me, shall do the works that I do, and greater." When all this honour is given to man, as spiritually to regenerate, when the minister saith "I baptize thee," and to remit sin to such as fall after, to be also a minister in consecration of Christ's most precious body, with the ministration of other sacraments, benediction[14], and prayer: if man should then wax proud, and glory as of himself, and extol his own devotion in these ministries; such men should beway their own naughty hypocrisy, and yet thereby impair not the very dignity of the ministry, ne the very true fruit and effect thereof. And therefore when the church by the minister, and with the minister[15], prayeth that the creatures of bread and wine, set on the altar (as the book of common prayer in this realm hath ordered), may be unto us the body and blood of our Saviour Christ; we require then the celebration of the same supper, which Christ made to his apostles, for to be the continual memory of his death, with all fruit and effect, such as the same had in the first institution. *Errors.

Wherefore when the minister pronounceth Christ's words, as spoken of his mouth, it is to be believed, that Christ doth now, as he did then. And it is to be noted, that although in the sacrament of baptism the minister saith, "I baptize thee," yet in the celebration of his supper[16] the words be spoken in Christ's person, as saying himself, "This is my body that is broken for you," which is to us not only a memory, but an effectual memory, with the very presence of Christ's body and blood, our very sacrifice: who doing now, as he did then, offereth himself to his Father as he did then, not to renew that offering, as though it were imperfect, but continually to refresh us, that daily fall and decay. And as St John saith, "Christ is our advocate and entreateth for us," or pleadeth for us, not to supply any want on God's behalf, but to relieve our wants in edification, wherein the ministry of the church travaileth to bring man to perfection in Christ, which Christ himself doth assist, and absolutely perform in his church, his mystical body. Now when we have Christ's body thus present in the celebration of the holy supper, and by Christ's mouth present unto us, saying, "This is my body which is betrayed for you," then have we Christ's body recommended unto us as our sacrifice, and a sacrifice propitiatory for all the sins of the world, being the only sacrifice of Christ's church, the pure and clean sacrifice whereof the prophet Malachi spake, and whereof the fathers in Christ's church have since the beginning continually written; the very true presence whereof, most constantly believed, hath increased from time to time such ceremonies as have been used in the celebration of that supper, in which by Christ's own mouth we be ascertained of his most glorious death and passion, and the self same body that suffered, delivered unto us in mystery, to be eaten of us, and therefore so to be worshipped and acknowledged of us as *One offering of Christ, not many. 1 John ii.

Mal. i.

[10 But really in deed, 1551.]
[11 As our body, 1551.]
[12 To be done and said, 1551.]
[13 Man's fault, and not the things, 1551.]

[14 Benedictions, Orig. ed. Winch.]
[15 Orig. ed. Winch. omits the words, 'and with the minister.']
[16 Of this supper, Orig. ed. Winch.]

our very only sacrifice, in whom, by whom, and for whom, our other private gifts and sacrifices be acceptable, and no otherwise[1].

*Errors.

*The whole church by the minister, the priest, offereth Christ present as a sacrifice propitiatory, wherein is shewed our Lord's death.

And therefore, as Christ declareth in the supper himself an offering, and sacrifice for our sin, offering himself to his Father as our mediator, and so therewith recommendeth to his Father the church, his body, for which he suffereth: so the church at the same supper in their offering of lauds and thanks, with such other gifts as they have received from God, join themselves with their head Christ, presenting and offering him, as one by whom, for whom, and in whom, all that by God's grace man can do well, is available and acceptable, and without whom nothing by us done can be pleasant in the sight of God. Whereupon this persuasion hath been duly conceived, which is also in the book of common prayer in the celebration of the holy supper retained, that it is very profitable at that time, when the memory of Christ's death is solemnized, to remember with prayer all estates of the church, and to recommend them to God, which St Paul to Timothy seemeth to require. At which time, as Christ signifieth unto us by the certainty of his death, and giveth us to be eaten, as it were in pledge, the same his precious body that suffered: so we, for declaration of our confidence in the death and sacrifice, do kindly remember with thanks his special gifts, and charitably remember the rest of the members of Christ's church with prayer, and, as we are able, should with our bodily goods remember at that time specially to relieve such as have need by poverty.

And again, as Christ putteth us in remembrance of his great benefit, so we should throughly remember him for our part, with the true confession of this mystery, wherein is recapitulate a memorial of all gifts and mysteries that God in Christ hath wrought for us. In the consideration and estimation whereof, as there hath been a fault in the security of such as, so their names were remembered in this holy time of memory, they cared not how much they forgat themselves: so there may be a fault in such as, neglecting it, care not whether they be remembered there at all, and therefore would have it nothing but a plain eating and drinking. How much the remembrance in prayer may avail, no man can prescribe; but that it availeth, every christian man must confess. Man may nothing arrogate to his devotion. But St James

James v.

said truly, Multum valet oratio justi assidua. It is to be abhorred to have hypocrites that counterfeit devotion, but true devotion is to be wished of God and prayed for, which is God's gift, not to obscure his glory, but to set it forth; not that we should then trust in men's merits and prayers, but laud and glorify God in them; qui talem potestatem dedit hominibus, *one to be judged able to relieve another with his prayer, referring all to proceed from God, by the mediation of our Saviour and Redeemer, Jesus Christ.*

I have tarried long in this matter, to declare that, for the effect of all celestial or worldly gifts to be obtained of God in the celebration of Christ's holy supper, when we call it the communion, is now prayed for to be present, and is present, and with God's favour shall be obtained, if we devoutly, reverently, charitably, and quietly use and frequent the same, without other innovations than the order of the book prescribeth. Now to the last difference.

CANTERBURY.

85.

How is "this comparison out of the matter of the presence of Christ's most precious body in the sacrament," when the papists say that the mass is not a sacrifice propitiatory, but because the presence of Christ's most precious body being presently there? And yet if this comparison be out of the matter (as you say it is), why do you then wrestle and wrangle with it so much? And do I "seem to grant the presence of Christ's body in the first part of my comparison," when I do nothing there but rehearse what the papists do say? But because all this process (which you bring in here out of tune and time) belongeth to the last book, I will pass it over unto the proper place, only by the way touching shortly some notable words.

Whether the mass be satisfactory by the devotion of the priest. Thom. part. 3. q. 79. art. 5[3].

Although you "never read that the oblation of the priest is satisfactory by devotion of the priest," yet nevertheless the papists do so teach, and you may find it in their St Thomas, both in his Sum, and upon the fourth of the sentences; whose words[2] have been read in the universities almost these three hundred years, and never until this day reproved by any of the papists in this point. He saith: *Quod sacrificium*

[1 And none otherwise, 1551.]
[2 Works, 1551.]
[3 Hoc sacramentum simul est sacrificium et sacramentum.—In quantum vero est sacrificium habet vim satisfactivam, &c. Thomas Aquinas, Pars III. Quæst. lxxix. Art. 5. p. 202. Antverp. 1624.]

sacerdotis habet vim satisfacticam, sed in satisfactione magis attenditur affectus offerentis, quam quantitas oblationis. Ideo satisfactoria est illis pro quibus offertur, vel etiam offerentibus, secundum quantitatem suæ devotionis, et non pro tota pœna.

But here the reader may see in you, that the adversaries of the truth sometime be enforced to say the truth, although sometime they do it unawares; as Caiaphas prophesied the truth, and as you do here confess, that Christ is our satisfaction wholly and fully. Joh. xi.

And yet the reader may note your inconstancy. For afterward, in the last book, you give Christ such a nip, that of that whole satisfaction you pinch half away from him, and ascribe it to the sacrifice of the priest, as I shall more fully declare in my answer to the last book. For you say there, "that the sacrifice of Christ giveth us life, and that the sacrifice of the priest continueth our life."

And here, good reader, thou art to be warned, that this writer in this place goeth about craftily to draw thee from the very work of our full redemption, wrought by our Saviour Christ upon the cross, unto a sacrifice (as they say) made by him the night before at his last supper. And forasmuch as every priest (as the papists say) maketh the same sacrifice in his mass, therefore, consequently, it followeth by this writer, that we must seek our redemption at the priest's sacrifice. And so Christ's blessed passion (which he most obediently and willingly suffered for our salvation upon the cross,) was not the only and sufficient sacrifice for remission of our sins.

The only will, I grant, both in good things and evil, is accepted[4] or rejected before God, and sometime hath the name of the fact[5], as the will of Abraham to offer his son is called the oblation of his son; and Christ called him an adulterer in his heart, that desireth another man's wife, although there be no fact committed in deed. The declaration of Christ's will to die, was not a sacrifice propitiatory for sin. Heb. xi. Matt. v.

And yet Abraham's will alone was not called the oblation of his son, but his will declared by many facts and circumstances: for he carried his son three days' journey to the place where God had appointed him to slay and offer his son Isaac, whom he most entirely loved. He cut wood to make the fire for that purpose, he laid the wood upon his son's back, and made him carry the same wood wherewith he should be brent[6]. And Abraham himself (commanding his servants to tarry at the foot of the hill) carried the fire and sword, wherewith he intended (as God had commanded) to kill his own son,[7] whom he so deeply loved. And by the way as they went, his son said unto his father: "Father, see, here is fire and wood, but where is the sacrifice that must be killed?" How these words of the son pierced the father's heart, every loving father may judge by the affection which he beareth to his own children. For what man would not have been abashed and stayed at these words? thinking thus within himself: "Alas! sweet son, thou dost ask me where the sacrifice is, thyself art the same sacrifice that must be slain, and thou (poor innocent) carriest thine own death upon thy back, and the wood wherewith thyself must be brent. Thou art he whom I must slay, which art most innocent, and never offended." Such thoughts, you may be sure, pierced through Abraham's heart, no less than the very death of his son should have done: as David lamentably bewailed his son lying in the pangs of death, but after he was dead he took his death quietly and comfortably enough. But nothing could alter Abraham's heart, or move him to disobey God; but forth on he goeth with his son to the place which God had appointed, and there he made an altar, and laid the wood upon it, and bound his son, and laid him upon the heap of the wood in the altar, and took the sword in his hand, and lifted up his arm to strike and kill his son, and would have done so in deed if the angel of God had not letted[8] him, commanding him in the stead of his son to take a ram that was fast by the horns in the briars. This obedience of Abraham unto God's commandment in offering of his son, declared by so many acts and circumstances, is called in the scripture the offering of his son, and not the will only. Gen. xxii. 2 Kings xii. [2 Sam.]

[4 Be accepted, 1551.]
[5 Have the names of the fact, 1551.]
[6 Brent, i. e. burnt.]
[7 To kill his son, 1551.]
[8 Letted, i. e. hindered, prevented.]

Nor the scripture calleth not the declaration of Christ's will in his last supper to suffer death by the name of a sacrifice satisfactory for sin, nor saith not that he was there offered in deed. For the will of a thing is not in deed the thing. And if the declaration of his will to die had been an oblation and sacrifice propitiatory for sin, then had Christ been offered not only in his supper, but as often as he declared his will to die. As when he said, long before his supper many times, that he should be betrayed, scourged, spit upon, and crucified, and that the third day he should rise again: and when he bade them destroy the temple of his body, and he would build it up again within three days: and when he said that he would give his flesh for the life of the world, and his life for his sheep.

Matt. xx.
Mark x.
Luke xviii.
John ii.
John vi.
John x.

And if these were sacrifices propitiatory or satisfactory for remission of sin, what needed he then after to die, if he had made the propitiatory sacrifice for sin already? For either the other was not vailable thereto, or else his death was in vain, as St Paul reasoneth of the priests of the old law, and of Christ. And it is not read in any scripture, that Christ's will, declared at his supper, was effectuous and sufficient for our redemption, but that his most willing death and passion was the oblation sufficient to endure for ever and ever, world without end.

Heb. viii.

87. But what sleights and shifts this writer doth use to wind the reader into his error, it is wonder to see, by devising to make two sacrifices of one will; the one by declaration, the other[1] by execution; a device such as was never imagined before of no man, and meet to come out of a fantastical head. But I say precisely, that Christ offered himself never but once, because the scripture so precisely and so many times saith so; and having the same for my warrant, it maketh me the bolder to stand against you, that deny that thing which is so often times repeated in scripture. And where you say, that "there is no scripture whereupon we might conclude that Christ did in this mortal life, but in one particular moment of time, offer himself to the Father:" to what purpose you bring forth this moment of time I cannot tell, for I made no mention thereof, but of the day of his death; and the scripture saith plainly, that as it is ordained for every man to die but once, so Christ was offered but once; and saith further, that sin is not forgiven but by effusion of blood, and therefore if Christ had been offered many times, he should have died many times. And of any other offering of Christ's body for sin, the scripture speaketh not. For although St Paul to the Philippians speaketh of the humiliation of Christ by his incarnation, and so to worldly miseries and afflictions, even unto death upon the cross; yet he calleth not every humiliation of Christ a sacrifice and oblation for remission of sin, but only his oblation upon Good Friday, which as it was our perfect redemption, so was it our perfect reconciliation, propitiation, and satisfaction for sin. And to what purpose you make here a long process of our sacrifices of obedience unto God's commandments, I cannot devise. For I declare in my last book, that all our whole obedience unto God's will and commandments is a sacrifice acceptable to God, but not a sacrifice propitiatory: for that sacrifice Christ only made, and by that his sacrifice all our sacrifices be acceptable to God, and without that none is acceptable to him. And by those sacrifices all christian people offer themselves to God, but they offer not Christ again for sin; for that did never creature but Christ himself alone, nor he never but upon Good Friday. For although he did institute the night before a remembrance of his death[2], under the sacraments of bread and wine, yet he made not at that time the sacrifice of our redemption and satisfaction for our sins, but the next day following. And the declaration of Christ at his last supper, that he would suffer death, was not the cause wherefore Cyprian said that Christ offered himself in his supper. For I read not in any place of Cyprian, to my remembrance, any such words that Christ offered himself in his supper; but he saith, that Christ offered the same thing which Melchisedech offered[3]. And if Cyprian say in any place

*Rom. vi.
*Heb. vii. ix. x.
*1 Pet. iii.

Heb. ix.
*Ibidem.

Phil. ii.

Cyprianus,
lib. 2. epist. 3.

[1 And the other, 1551.]
[2 A sacrament of his death, 1551.]
[3 Nam quis magis sacerdos Dei summi, quam Dominus noster Jesus Christus? qui sacrificium Deo patri obtulit, et obtulit hoc idem quod Melchisedech obtulerat, id est, panem et vinum, suum scilicet corpus et sanguinem.—Cyprian. ad Cæcilium, Epist. lxiii. p. 143. Paris. 1574.]

that Christ offered himself in his supper, yet he said not that Christ did so for this cause, that in his supper he declared his death. And therefore here you make a deceitful *fallax* in sophistry, pretending to shew that thing to be a cause, which is not the true cause indeed. For the cause why Cyprian, and other old authors, say that Christ made an oblation and offering of himself in his last supper, was not that he declared there that he would suffer death, (for that he had declared many times before;) but the cause was, that there he ordained a perpetual memory of his death, which he would all faithful christian people to observe from time to time, remembering his death, with thanks for his benefits, until his coming again. And therefore the memorial of the true sacrifice made upon the cross, as St Augustine saith, is called by the name of a sacrifice, as a thing that signifieth another thing is called by the name of the thing which it signifieth, although in very deed it be not the same[4]. *August. ad Bonifacium, epist. 23.*

And the long discourse that you make of Christ's true presence, and of the true eating of him, and of his true assisting us in our doing of his commandment, all these be true. For Christ's flesh and blood be in the sacrament truly present, but spiritually and sacramentally, not carnally and corporally. And as he is truly present, so is he truly eaten and drunken, and assisteth us. And he is the same to us that he was to them that saw him with their bodily eyes. But where you say, that he is as familiar with us as he was with them, here I may say the French term which they use for reverence sake, *Save vostre grace*. And he offered not himself then for them upon the cross, and now offereth himself for us daily in the mass; but upon the cross he offered himself both for us and for them. For that his one sacrifice of his body, then only offered, is now unto us by faith as available as it was then for them. "For with one sacrifice," as St Paul saith, "he hath made perfect for ever them that be sanctified." *Heb. x.*

88.

And where you speak of the participation of Christ's flesh and blood, if you mean of the sacramental participation only, that thereby we be ascertained of the regeneration[5] of our bodies, that they shall live, and have the fruition of God with our souls for ever, you be in an horrible error. And if you mean a spiritual participation of Christ's body and blood, then all this your process is in vain, and serveth nothing for your purpose to prove that Christ's flesh and blood be corporally in the sacrament, under the forms of bread and wine, and participated of them that be evil, as you teach; which be no whit thereby the more certain of their salvation, but of their damnation, as St Paul saith. *1 Cor. xi.*

And although the holy supper of the Lord be not a vain or fantastical supper, wherein things should be promised, which be not performed, to them that worthily come thereunto, but Christ's flesh and blood be there truly eaten and drunken in deed; yet that mystical supper cannot be without mysteries and figures. And although we feed in deed of Christ's body, and drink in deed his blood, yet not corporally, quantitatively, and palpably, as we shall be regenerated at the resurrection, and as he was betrayed, walked here in earth, and was very man. And therefore, although the things by you rehearsed be all truly done, yet all be not done after one sort and fashion; but some corporally and visibly, some spiritually and invisibly. And therefore to all your comparisons or similitudes here by you rehearsed, if there be given to every one his true understanding, they may be so granted all to be true. But if you will link all these together in one sort and fashion, and make a chain thereof, you shall far pass the bonds of wanton reason, making a chain of gold and copper together, confounding and mixing together corporal and spiritual, heavenly and earthly things, and bring all to very madness and impiety, or plain and manifest heresy.

And because one single error pleaseth you not, shortly after you link a number of errors almost together[6] in one sentence, as it were to make an whole chain of errors, saying not only that Christ's body is verily present in the celebration of the holy supper, meaning of corporal presence, but that it is also our very sacrifice, and sacrifice propitiatory for all the sins of the world, and that it is the only sacrifice of the *A chain of errors.*

[4 See the passage which is quoted at length below, p. 124.]

[5 Of our regeneration of our bodies, 1551.]

[6 Together almost, 1551.]

church, and that it is the pure and clean sacrifice, whereof Malachi spake, and that Christ doth now in the celebration of this supper as he did when he gave the same to his apostles, and that he offereth himself now as he did then, and that the same offering is not now renewed again. This is your chain of errors, wherein is not one link of pure gold, but all be copper[1], feigned, and counterfeit: for neither is Christ's body verily and corporally present in the celebration of his holy supper, but spiritually; nor his body is not the very sacrifice, but the thing whereof the sacrifice was made; and the very sacrifice was the crucifying of his body, and the effusion of his blood unto death. Wherefore of his body was not made a sacrifice propitiatory for all the sins of the world at his supper, but the next day after upon the cross. Therefore saith the prophet, that we were made whole by his wounds: *Livore ejus sanati sumus*.

Nor that sacrifice of Christ in the celebration of the supper is not the only sacrifice of the church, but all the works that christian people do to the glory of God be sacrifices of the church, smelling sweetly before God. And they be also the pure and clean sacrifice whereof the prophet Malachi did speak. For the prophet Malachi spake of no such sacrifices as only priests make, but of such sacrifice as all christian people make both day and night, at all times and in all places.

Nor Christ doth not now as he did at his last supper, which he had with his apostles; for then, as you say, he declared his will, that he would die for us: and if he do now as he did then, then doth he now declare that he will die for us again.

But as for offering himself now as he did then, this speech may have a true sense, being like to that which sometime was used at the admission of unlearned friars and monks unto their degrees in the universities: where the doctor that presented them deposed that they were meet for the said degrees, as well in learning as in virtue. And yet that deposition in one sense was true, when indeed they were meet neither in the one nor in the other. So likewise, in that sense Christ offereth himself now as well as he did in his supper; for indeed he offered himself a sacrifice propitiatory for remission of sin in neither of both, but only upon the cross, making there a sacrifice full and perfect for our redemption, and yet by that sufficient offering made only at that time he is a daily intercessor for us to his Father for ever. Finally, it is not true that the offering in the celebration of the supper is not renewed again. For the same offering that is made in one supper is daily renewed and made again in every supper, and is called the daily sacrifice of the church.

Thus have I broken your chain, and scattered your links, which may be called the very chain of Beelzebub, able to draw into hell as many as come within the compass thereof. And how would you require that men should give you credit, who within so few lines knit together so many manifest lies? It is another untruth also which you say after, that Christ declared in the supper himself an offering and sacrifice for sin; for he declared in his supper, not that he was then a sacrifice, but that a sacrifice should be made of his body, which was done the next day after, by the voluntary effusion of his blood: and of any other sacrificing of Christ for sin the scripture speaketh not. For although the scripture saith that our Saviour Christ is a continual intercessor[2] for us unto his Father, yet no scripture calleth that intercession a sacrifice for sin, but only the effusion of his blood, which it seemeth you make him to do still, when you say that he suffereth; and so by your imagination he should now still be crucified, if he now suffer, as you say he doth. But it seemeth you pass not greatly what you say, so that you may multiply many gallant words to the admiration of the hearers. But forasmuch as you say that Christ offereth himself in the celebration of the supper, and also that the church offereth him, here I would have you declare how the church offereth Christ, and how he offereth himself, and wherein those offerings stand, in words, deeds, or thoughts, that we may know what you mean by your daily offerings of Christ. Of offering ourselves unto God in all our acts and deeds, with lauds and thanksgiving, the scripture maketh

---

[1 One link true gold, but all copper be, 1551.]   [2 Is now a continual intercessor, 1551.]

mention in many places: but that Christ himself in the holy communion, or that the priests make any other oblation than all christian people do, because these be papistical inventions without scripture, I require nothing but reason of you, that you should so plainly set out these devised offerings, that men might plainly understand what they be, and wherein they rest. Now in this comparison, truth it is, as you say, that you have spent many words, but utterly in vain, not to declare, but to darken the matter. But if you would have followed the plain words of scripture, you needed not[3] to have tarried so long, and yet should you have made the matter more clear a great deal.

Now followeth my last comparison.

They say, that Christ is corporally in many places at one time, affirming that his body is corporally and really present in as many places as there be hosts consecrated. We say, that as the sun corporally is ever in heaven, and no where else, and yet by his operation and virtue the sun is here in earth, by whose influence and virtue all things in the world be corporally regenerated, increased, and grow to their perfect state; so likewise our Saviour Christ bodily and corporally is in heaven, sitting at the right hand of his Father, although spiritually he hath promised to be present with us upon earth unto the world's end. And whensoever two or three be gathered together in his name, he is there in the midst among them, by whose supernal[4] grace all godly men be first by him spiritually regenerated, and after increase and grow to their spiritual perfection in God, spiritually by faith eating his flesh, and drinking his blood, although the same corporally be in heaven, far distant from our sight.

The thirteenth comparison.

WINCHESTER.

The true teaching is, that Christ's very body is present under the form of bread, in as many hosts as be consecrate, in how many places soever the hosts be consecrate, and is there really and substantially, which words "really and substantially" be implied, when we say, truly present. The word "corporally" may have an ambiguity and doubleness in respect and relation: one is to the truth of the body present, and so it may be said, Christ is corporally present in sacrament; if the word[5] corporally be referred to the manner of the presence, then we should say, Christ's body were present after a corporal manner, which we say not, but in a spiritual manner; and therefore not locally nor by manner of quantity, but in such manner as God only knoweth, and yet doth us to understand by faith the truth of the very presence, exceeding our capacity to comprehend the manner "how." This is the very true teaching to affirm the truth of the presence of Christ's very body in the sacrament, even of the same body that suffered, in plain, simple, evident terms and words, such as cannot by cavillation be mistaken and construed, so near as possibly man's infirmity permitteth and suffereth. Now let us consider in what sort the author and his company, which he calleth "we say," do understand the sacrament, who go about to express the same by a similitude of the creature of the sun, "which sun," this author saith, "is ever corporally in heaven, and no where else, and yet by operation and virtue is here in earth: so Christ is corporally in heaven, &c." In this matter of similitudes, it is to be taken for a truth undoubted, that there is no creature by similitude, ne any language of man able to express God and his mysteries. For and things that be seen or heard might throughly express God's invisible mysteries, the nature whereof is that they cannot throughly be expressed, they were no mysteries: and yet it is true, that of things visible, wherein God worketh wonderfully, there may be great resemblances[6], some shadows, and as it were inductions, to make a man astonied in consideration of things invisible, when he seeth things visible so wonderfully wrought, and to have so marvellous effects. And divers good catholic devout men have by divers natural things gone about to open unto us the mystery of the Trinity, partly by the sun, as the author[7] doth in the sacrament, partly by fire, partly by the soul of man, by the musician's

[The answer. Orig. Ed. Winchester.]

Really, substantially, truly, corporally.

Manner of presence.

The true simple doctrine of the presence of Christ's body in the sacraments.

91.

God's mysteries cannot be thoroughly opened by similitudes.

[3 You needed not indeed, 1551.]
[4 Supernal, i. e. heavenly.]
[5 Present in the sacrament, but if the word,

&c., 1551.]
[6 Some resemblances, 1551.]
[7 As this author, 1551.]

science, the art, the touch with the player's fingers, and the sound of the chord, wherein wit[1] hath all travailed the matter, yet remaineth dark, ne cannot be throughly set forth by any similitude. But to the purpose of this similitude of the sun, which sun, this author saith, "is only corporally in heaven, and no where else," and in the earth the operation and virtue of the sun: so as by this author's supposal, the substance of the sun should not be in earth, but only by operation and virtue: wherein if this author erreth, he doth the reader to understand, that if he err in consideration of natural things, it is no marvel though he err in heavenly things. For, because I will not of myself begin the contention with this author of the natural work of the sun, I will bring forth the saying of Martin Bucer, now resident at Cambridge, who vehemently, and for so much truly, affirmeth the true real presence of Christ's body in the sacrament: for he saith, Christ said not, this is my spirit, this is my virtue, but, "this is my body:" wherefore, he saith, we must believe Christ's body to be there, the same that did hang upon the cross, our Lord himself, which in some part to declare, he useth the similitude of the sun for his purpose, to prove Christ's body present really and substantially in the sacrament, where this author useth the same similitude to prove the body of Christ really absent. I will write in here as Bucer speaketh it in Latin, expounding the twenty-sixth chapter of St Matthew, and then I will put the same in English. Bucer's words be these:

Bucerus.

Bucerus in Matt. cap. xxvi.

Ut sol vere uno in loco cœli visibilis circumscriptus est, radiis tamen suis præsens vere et substantialiter exhibetur ubilibet orbis: ita Dominus etiamsi circumscribatur uno loco cœli arcani et divini, id est gloriæ Patris, verbo tamen suo et sacris symbolis vere et totus ipse Deus et homo præsens exhibetur in sacra cœna, eoque substantialiter; quam præsentiam non minus certo agnoscit mens credens verbis his Domini et symbolis, quam oculi vident et habent solem præsentem demonstratum et exhibitum sua corporali luce. Res ista arcana est, et novi Testamenti, res fidei: non sunt igitur huc admittendæ cogitationes de præsentatione corporis, quæ constat ratione hujus vitæ etiamnum patibilis et fluxæ. Verbo Domini simpliciter inhærendum est, et debet fides sensuum defectui præbere supplementum. Which is thus much in English: "As the sun is truly placed determinately in one place of the visible heaven, and yet is truly and substantially present by means of his beams elsewhere in the world abroad: so our Lord, although he be comprehended in one place of the secret and divine heaven, that is to say, the glory of his Father, yet nevertheless by his word and holy tokens he is exhibit present truly whole God and man, and therefore in substance in his holy supper; which presence man's mind, giving credit to his words and tokens, with no less certainty acknowledgeth, than our eyes see, and have the sun present, exhibited, and shewed with his corporal light. This is a deep secret matter, and of the new testament, and a matter of faith; and therefore herein thoughts be not to be received of such a presentation of the body as consisteth in the manner of this life transitory, and subject to suffer. We must simply cleave to the word of Christ, and faith must relieve the default of our senses."

92.

Thus hath Bucer expressed his mind, whereunto, because the similitude of the sun doth not answer in all parts, he noteth wisely in the end, how this is a matter of faith, and therefore upon the foundation of faith we must speak of it, thereby to supply where our senses fail. For the presence of Christ, and whole Christ, God and man, is true, although we cannot think of the manner "how." The chief cause why I bring in Bucer is this, to shew how, in his judgment, we have not only in earth the operation and virtue of the sun, but also the substance of the sun, by mean of the sun-beams, which be of the same substance with the sun, and cannot be divided in substance from it; and therefore we have in earth the substantial presence of the sun, not only the operation and virtue. And howsoever the sun above in the distance appeareth unto us of another sort, yet the beams that touch the earth be of the same substance with it, as clerks say, or at the least as Bucer saith, whom I never heard accompted papist; and yet for the real and substantial presence of Christ's very body in the sacrament, writeth pithily and plainly, and here encountereth this author with his similitude of the sun directly; whereby may appear, how much soever Bucer is esteemed otherwise, he is not with this author regarded in the truth of the sacrament, which is one of the high mysteries in our religion. And this may suffice for that point of the similitude, where this author would have Christ none otherwise present in the sacrament, than he promised to be in the assembly of such as be gathered together in his name: it is a plain abolition of the mystery of the sacrament, in the words whereof Christ's human body is exhibit and made

---

[[1] Wherein when wit, 1551.]

present with his very flesh to feed us, and to that singular and special effect[2] *the other presence of Christ in the assembly made in his name is not spoken of; and it hath no appearance of learning in scriptures, to conclude under one consideration a specialty and a generality. And therefore it was well answered of him that said, "If I could tell reason, there were no faith:" if I could shew the like, it were not singular. Which both be notable in this sacrament, where condemning all reason, good men both constantly believe that Christ sitteth on the right hand of his Father, very God and man, and also without change of place doth nevertheless make himself by his power present, both God and man, under the form of bread and wine, at the prayer of the church and by the ministry of the same, to give life to such as with faith do according to his institution in his holy supper worthily receive him, and to the condemnation of such as do unworthily presume to receive him there. For the worthy receiving of whom we must come endued with Christ, and clothed with him seemly in that garment, to receive his most precious body and blood, Christ whole God and man, whereby he then dwelleth in us more abundantly, confirming in us the effects of his passion, and establishing our hope of resurrection, then to enjoy the regeneration of our body, with a full redemption of body and soul, to live with God in glory for ever.*

August. serm. de tempore. 159.

CANTERBURY.

In this comparison I am glad that at the last we be come so near together; for you be almost right heartily welcome home, and I pray you let us shake hands together[3]. For we be agreed, as me seemeth, that Christ's body is present, and the same body that suffered: and we be agreed also of the manner of his presence. For you say that the body of Christ is not present but after a spiritual manner, and so say I also. And if there be any difference between us two, it is but a little and in this point only: that I say that Christ is but spiritually in the ministration of the sacrament, and you say that he is but after a spiritual manner in the sacrament. And yet you say that he is corporally in the sacrament, as who should say that there were a difference between spiritually, and a spiritual manner; and that it were not all one, to say that Christ is there only after a spiritual manner, and not only spiritually.

A concord in the spiritual presence.

But if the substance of the sun be here corporally present with us upon earth, then I grant that Christ's body is so likewise: so that he of us two that erreth in the one, let him be taken for a vain man, and to err also in the other. Therefore I am content that the reader judge indifferently between you and me, in the corporal presence of the sun; and he that is found to err, and to be a fool therein, let him be judged to err also in the corporal presence of Christ's body.

The presence of the sun.

93.

But now, master Bucer, help this man at need: for he that hath ever hitherto cried out against you, now being at a pinch driven to his shifts, crieth for help upon you: and although he was never your friend, yet extend your charity to help him in his necessity. But master Bucer saith not so much as you do: and yet if you both said that the beams of the sun be of the same substance with the sun, who would believe either of you both? Is the light of the candle the substance of the candle? or the light of the fire the substance of the fire? Or is the beams of the sun any thing but the clear light of the sun? Now, as you said even now of me, if you err so far from the true judgment of natural things, that all men may perceive your error, what marvel is it if you err in heavenly things?

M. Bucer.

And why should you be offended with this my saying, that Christ is spiritually present in the assembly of such as be gathered together in his name? And how can you conclude hereof, that this is a plain abolition of the mystery of the sacrament, because that in the celebration of the sacrament I say that Christ is spiritually present? Have not you confessed yourself that Christ is in the sacrament but after a spiritual manner? And after that manner he is also among them that be assembled together in his name. And if they that say so do abolish the mystery of the sacrament, then do you abolish it yourself, by saying that Christ is but after a spiritual

---

[² Special effect, which in the other, 1551.]   [³ *Together* omitted, 1551.]

manner in the sacrament, after which manner you say also that he is in them that be gathered together in his name, as well as I do, that say he is spiritually in both. But he that is disposed to pick quarrels, and to calumniate all things, what can be spoken so plainly, or meant so sincerely, but he will wrest it unto a wrong sense? I say that Christ is spiritually and by grace in his supper, as he is when two or three be gathered together in his name, meaning that with both he is spiritually, and with neither corporally; and yet I say not that there is no difference. For this difference there is, that with the one he is sacramentally, and with the other not sacramentally, except they be gathered together in his name to receive the sacrament. Nevertheless the selfsame Christ is present in both, nourisheth and feedeth both, if the sacrament be rightly received. But that is only spiritually, as I say, and only after a spiritual manner, as you say.

And you say further, that before we receive the sacrament, we must come endued with Christ, and seemly clothed with him. But whosoever is endued and clothed with Christ hath Christ present with him after a spiritual manner, and hath received Christ whole both God and man, or else he could not have everlasting life. And therefore is Christ present as well in baptism as in the Lord's supper. For in baptism be we endued with Christ, and seemly clothed with him, as well as in his holy supper we eat and drink him.

Gal. iii.

WINCHESTER.

94. *Thus I have perused these differences, which, well considered, methink sufficient to take away and appease all such differences as might be moved against the sacrament, the faith whereof hath ever prevailed against such as have impugned it. And I have not read of any that hath written against it, but somewhat hath against his enterprise in his writings appeared, whereby to confirm it, or so evident untruths affirmed, as whereby those that be as indifferent to the truth as Salomon was in the judgment of the living child, may discern the very true mother from the other, that is to say, who plainly intend the true child to continue alive, and who could be content to have it be destroyed by division. God of his infinite mercy have pity on us, and grant the true faith of this holy mystery uniformly to be conceived in our understandings, and in one form of words to be uttered and preached, which in the book of common prayer is well termed, not distant from the catholic faith in my judgment.*

CANTERBURY.

Three parts made of two.

You have so perused these differences, that you have made more difference than ever was before: for where before there were no more but two parts, the true catholic doctrine, and the papistical doctrine, now come you in with your new fantastical inventions, agreeing with neither part, but to make a song of three parts, you have devised a new voluntary descant, so far out of tune, that it agreeth neither with the tenor nor mean, but maketh such a shameful jar, that godly ears abhor to hear it. For you have taught such a doctrine as never was written before this time, and uttered therein so many untruths and so many strange sayings, that every indifferent reader may easily discern that the true christian faith in this matter is not to be sought at your hands. And yet in your own "writings appeareth something to confirm the truth, quite against your own enterprise," which maketh me have some hope, that after my answer heard, we shall in the principal matter no more strive for the child, seeing that yourself have confessed that Christ is but after a spiritual manner present with us. And there is good hope that God shall prosper this child to live many years, seeing that now I trust you will help to foster and nourish it up as well as I.

The true mother of the child.

And yet if division may shew a step-mother, then be not you the true mother of the child, which in the sacrament make so many divisions. For you divide the substances of bread and wine from their proper accidences, the substances also of Christ's flesh and blood from their accidences, and Christ's very flesh sacramentally from his very blood, although you join them again *per concomitantiam*; and you divide the sacrament so that the priest receiveth both the sacrament of Christ's body and of his blood, and the lay people (as you call them) receive no more but the sacrament of his body, as though the sacrament of his blood and of our redemption pertained only to the priests. And the cause of our eternal life and salvation you divide in such sort between Christ and the priest, that you attribute the beginning thereof to the sacrifice of Christ upon the cross, and the continuance thereof you attribute to the sacrifice of the priest in the mass, as you do write plainly in your last book. Oh! wicked step-mothers, that so divide Christ, his sacraments, and his people!

After the differences followeth the third, fourth, fifth, and sixth chapters of my book, which you bind as it were altogether in one fardel[1], and cast them quite away, by the figure which you call "rejection," not answering one word to any scripture or old writer, which I have there alleged for the defence of the truth. But because the reader may see the matter plainly before his eyes, I shall here rehearse my words again, and join thereto your answer. My words be these.

95.

Now to return to the principal matter, lest it might be thought a new device of us, that Christ, as concerning his body and his human nature, is in heaven, and not in earth; therefore by God's grace it shall be evidently proved, that this is no new devised matter, but that it was ever the old faith of the catholic church, until the papists invented a new faith, that Christ really, corporally, naturally, and sensibly is here still with us in earth, shut up in a box, or within the compass of bread and wine.

[Book iii.] Chap. III. *Christ corporally is in heaven, and not in earth.

This needeth no better nor stronger proof than that which the old authors bring for the same, that is to say, the general profession of all christian people in the common creed, wherein, as concerning Christ's humanity, they be taught to believe after this sort: That he was conceived by the Holy Ghost, born of the virgin Mary: that he suffered under Pontius Pilate: was crucified, dead and buried: that he descended into hell, and rose again the third day, that he ascended into heaven, and sitteth at the right hand of his almighty Father, and from thence shall come to judge the quick and dead.

The proof thereof by our profession in our common creed.

This hath been ever the catholic faith of christian people, that Christ (as concerning his body and his manhood) is in heaven, and shall there continue until he come down at the last judgment.

And forasmuch as the creed maketh so express mention of the article of his ascension, and departing hence from us, if it had been another article of our faith, that his body tarrieth also here with us in earth, surely in this place of the creed was so urgent an occasion given to make some mention thereof, that doubtless it would not have been passed over in our creed with silence. For if Christ (as concerning his humanity) be both here, and gone hence, and both these two be articles of our faith, when mention was made of the one in the creed, it was necessary to make mention of the other, lest by professing the one we should be dissuaded from believing the other, being so contrary the one to the other.

To this article of our creed accordeth holy scripture, and all the old ancient doctors of Christ's church. For Christ himself said, "I leave the world, and go to my Father." And also he said, "You shall ever have poor folks with you, but you shall not ever have me with you." And he gave warning of this error beforehand, saying that the time would come when many deceivers should be in the world, and say, "Here is Christ, and there is Christ, but believe them not," said Christ. And St Mark writeth in the last chapter of his gospel, that the Lord Jesus was taken up into heaven, and sitteth at the right hand of his Father. And St Paul exhorteth all men to seek for things that be above in heaven, "where Christ," saith he, "sitteth at the right hand of God" his Father. Also he saith, that "we have such a bishop, that sitteth in heaven at the right hand of the throne of God's majesty;" and that he, "having offered

Chap. IV.
The proof hereof by the scripture.
John xvi.
Matt. xxvi.

Matt. xxiv.

Mark xvi.

Col. iii.

Heb. viii.

Heb. x.

[1 Fardel, i.e. a bundle.]

one sacrifice for sins, sitteth continually at the right hand of God, until his enemies be put under his feet as a footstool." And hereunto consent all the old doctors of the church.

Chap. v.
96.
The proof thereof by ancient authors.
Origen. in Matt. Hom. 33.

First Origen upon Matthew[1] reasoneth this matter, how Christ may be called a stranger that is departed into another country, seeing that he is with us alway unto the world's end, and is among all them that be gathered together in his name, and also in the midst of them that know him not; and thus he reasoneth: If he be here among us still, how can he be gone hence as a stranger departed into another country? whereunto he answereth, that Christ is both God and man, having in him two natures. And as a man he is not with us unto the world's end, nor is present with all his faithful that be gathered together in his name: but his divine power and spirit is ever with us. Paul, saith he, was absent from the Corinthes in his body, when he was present with them in his spirit: so is Christ, saith he, gone hence, and absent in his humanity, which in his divine nature is every where. And in this saying, saith Origen, we divide not his humanity, (for St John [1 John iv.] writeth, that "no spirit that divideth Jesus can be of God,") but we reserve to both his natures their own properties.

In these words Origen hath plainly declared his mind, that Christ's body is not both present here with us, and also gone hence and estranged from us. For that were to make two natures of one body, and to divide the body of Jesus, forasmuch as one nature cannot at one time be both with us, and absent from us. And therefore saith Origen, that the presence must be understanded of his divinity, and the absence of his humanity.

August. ad Dardan. epist. 57.

And according hereunto St Augustine writeth thus in an Epistle *Ad Dardanum*: "Doubt not but Jesus Christ as concerning the nature of his manhood is now there, from whence he shall come. And remember well and believe the profession of a christian man, that he rose from death, ascended into heaven, sitteth at the right hand of his Father, and from that place, and none other, shall he come to judge the quick and the dead. And he shall come, as the angels said, as he was seen go into heaven, that is to say, in the same form and substance, unto the which he gave immortality, but changed not nature. After this form, (saith he, meaning his man's nature,) we may not think that he is every where. For we must beware, that we do not so stablish his divinity, that we take away the verity of his body[2]." These be St Augustine's plain words. And by and by after he addeth these words: "The Lord Jesus as God is every where, and as man is in heaven[3]." And finally he concludeth this matter in these few words: "Doubt not but our Lord Jesus Christ is every where as God, and as a dweller he is in man that is the temple of God, and he is in a certain place in heaven, because of the measure of a very body[4]."

[Hunc locum citat Leo, epistola ultima, ad probandum in Christo veram formam humanam. Et in tota epistola, forma accipitur pro substantia. Ed. Embd. 1557.]

[1 Secundum hanc divinitatis suæ naturam non peregrinatur, sed peregrinatur secundum dispensationem corporis quod suscepit.—Hæc autem dicentes non solvimus suscepti corporis hominem, cum sit scriptum apud Johannem, "Omnis spiritus qui solvit Jesum, non est ex Deo:" sed unicuique substantiæ proprietatem servamus.—Origen. in Matt. cap. xxv. Tract. 33. Ed. Bened. Tom. III. p. 883.]

[2 Noli itaque dubitare ibi nunc esse hominem Christum Jesum, unde venturus est, memoriterque recole et fideliter tene Christianam confessionem, quoniam resurrexit a mortuis, ascendit in cœlum, sedet ad dexteram Patris, nec aliunde quam inde venturus est ad vivos mortuosque judicandos. Et sic venturus est, illa angelica voce testante, quemadmodum ire visus est in cœlum, id est, in eadem carnis forma atque substantia, cui profecto immortalitatem dedit, naturam non abstulit. Secundum hanc formam non est putandus ubique diffusus. Cavendum est enim, ne ita divinitatem astruamus hominis, ut veritatem corporis auferamus.—August. de Præsentia Dei, ad Dardanum, (Epist. lvii.) Lib. I. cap. iii. Pars VIII. Basil. ap. Amerbach. 1506.]

[3 Una enim persona Deus et homo est, et utrumque est unus Christus Jesus, ubique per id quod Deus est, in cœlo autem per id quod homo. —Ibid. cap. iv.]

[4 Et ubique totum præsentem esse (i. e. Chris-

And again St Augustine writeth upon the gospel of St John: "Our Saviour Jesus Christ," saith St Augustine, "is above, but yet his truth is here. His body wherein he arose is in one place, but his truth is spread every where[5]." In Johan. Tract. 30.

And in another place of the same book St Augustine expounding these words of Christ, "You shall ever have poor men with you, but me you shall not ever have," saith, that "Christ spake these words of the presence of his body[6]. For," saith he, "as concerning his divine majesty, as concerning his providence, as concerning his infallible and invisible grace, these words be fulfilled which he spake, 'I am with you unto the world's end.' But as concerning the flesh which he took in his carnation[7], as concerning that which was born of the virgin, as concerning that which was apprehended by the Jews, and crucified upon a tree, and taken down from the cross, lapped in linen clothes and buried, and rose again, and appeared after his resurrection; as concerning that[8] flesh, he said, 'You shall not ever have me with you.' Wherefore seeing that as concerning his flesh he was conversant with his disciples forty days, and they accompanying, seeing, and not following him[9], he went up into heaven, both he is not here (for he sitteth at the right hand of his Father), and yet he is here, for he departed not hence as concerning the presence of his divine majesty. As concerning the presence of his majesty, we have Christ ever with us; but as concerning the presence of his flesh, he said truly to his disciples, 'Ye shall not ever have me with you.' For as concerning the presence of his flesh, the church had Christ but a few days; yet now it holdeth him fast by faith, though it see him not with eyes." All these be St Augustine's words. Tract. 50.

97.

Also in another book[10], entitled to St Augustine, is written thus: "We must believe and confess that the Son of God (as concerning his divinity) is invisible, without a body, immortal, and incircumscriptible: but as concerning his humanity, we ought to believe and confess that he is visible, hath a body, and is contained in a certain place, and hath truly all the members of a man." De Essentia Divinitatis.

Of these words of St Augustine it is most clear, that the profession of the catholic faith is, that Christ (as concerning his bodily substance and nature of man) is in heaven, and not present here with us in earth. For the nature and property of a very body is to be in one place, and to occupy one place, and not to be everywhere, or in many places at one time. And though the

---

tum Jesum) non dubites tanquam Deum, et in eodem templo Dei esse tanquam inhabitantem Deum, et in loco aliquo cœli propter veri corporis modum.—Ibid. cap. xx.]

[5 Sursum est Dominus, sed etiam hic est veritas Dominus. Corpus enim Domini, in quo resurrexit, uno loco esse potest: veritas ejus ubique diffusa est.—August. in Evangelium Joannis, Tract. xxx. Pars ix.]

[6 Loquebatur enim de præsentia corporis sui. Nam secundum majestatem suam, secundum providentiam, secundum ineffabilem et invisibilem gratiam impletur quod ab eo dictum est, Ecce ego vobiscum sum omnibus diebus usque ad consummationem sæculi. Secundum carnem vero quam verbum assumpsit, secundum id quod de virgine natus est, secundum id quod a Judæis comprehensus est, quod ligno confixus, quod de cruce depositus, quod linteis involutus, quod in sepulchro conditus, quod in resurrectione manifestatus, non semper habebitis me vobiscum. Quare? Quoniam conversatus est secundum corporis præsentiam quadraginta diebus cum discipulis suis, et eis deducentibus videndo, non sequendo, ascendit in cœlum, et non est hic. Ibi enim sedet ad dexteram Patris: et hic est. Non enim recessit præsentia majestatis. Aliter. Secundum præsentiam majestatis semper habemus Christum: secundum præsentiam carnis recte dictum est discipulis, Me autem non semper habebitis. Habuit enim illum ecclesia secundum præsentiam carnis paucis diebus: modo fide tenet, oculis non videt.—Ibid. Tract. l. Pars ix.]

[7 Incarnation, 1551.]

[8 The, 1551.]

[9 And following him, 1551. This is evidently a misprint in that edition, which Cranmer appears to have corrected as it was printed in the 1580 edition, since the words of Augustine are, "videndo, non sequendo." See note 6.]

[10 Et idcirco eundem Dei filium secundum substantiam divinitatis suæ invisibilem et incorporeum et immortalem et incircumscriptum nos credere et confiteri oportet. Juxta humanitatem vero visibilem, corporeum, localem, atque omnia membra humana veraciter habentem credere convenit et confiteri.—August. de Essentia Divinitatis, Pars x. Ibid. This treatise is censured as spurious. Vid. "James' Corruptions of Scripture, Councils, and Fathers." p. 53. Lond. 1843. Riveti Crit. Sacr. p. 395. Geneva. 1626.]

body of Christ after his resurrection and ascension was made immortal, yet this nature was not taken away, for then, as St Augustine saith, it were no very body. And further St Augustine sheweth both the manner and form how Christ is here present with us in earth, and how he is absent, saying that he is present by his divine nature and majesty, by his providence, and by grace; but by his human nature and very body he is absent from this world, and present in heaven.

Cyrillus in Johan. lib. vi. cap. 14.

Cyrillus likewise, upon the gospel of St John[1], agreeth fully with St Augustine, saying: "Although Christ took away from hence the presence of his body, yet in majesty[2] of his Godhead he is ever here, as he promised to his disciples at his departing, saying, 'I am with you ever unto the world's end.'"

Lib. ix. cap. 21.

And in another place of the same book St Cyril saith thus: "Christian people must believe, that although Christ be absent from us as concerning his body, yet by his power he governeth us and all things, and is present with all them that love him. Therefore he said: 'Truly, truly I say unto you, wheresoever there be two or three gathered together in my name, there am I in the midst of them.' For like as when he was conversant here in earth as a man, yet then he filled heaven, and did not leave the company of angels; even so being now in heaven with his flesh, yet he filleth the earth, and is in them that love him. And it is to be marked, that although Christ should go away only as concerning his flesh, (for he is ever present in the power of his divinity,) yet for a little time he said he would be with his disciples[3]." These be the words of St Cyril.

Ambrosius in Lucam, lib. x. cap. 24.

St Ambrose also saith, that "we must not seek Christ upon earth, nor in earth, but in heaven, where he sitteth at the right hand of his Father[4]."

Gregorius in Hom. Paschatis. [Vid. Embd. Ed. in fine tomi hujus.]

And likewise St Gregory writeth thus: "Christ," saith he, "is not here by the presence of his flesh, and yet he is absent no where by the presence of his majesty[5]."

What subtlety, thinkest thou, good reader, can the papists now imagine to defend their pernicious error, that Christ his human nature[6] is bodily here in earth, in the consecrated bread and wine; seeing that all the old church of Christ believed the contrary, and all the old authors wrote the contrary?

98.

For they all affirmed and believed, that Christ, being but one person, hath nevertheless in him two natures or substances, that is to say, the nature of his Godhead, and the nature of his manhood. They say further-

---

[1 Οὕτω διακεισόμεθα φρονοῦντες ὀρθῶς, ὅτι κἂν ἐκ τοῦ κόσμου γένηται διὰ τὴν σάρκα, παρέσται πάλιν οὐδὲν ἧττον τοῖς ἐν αὐτῷ, καὶ ἐπιστατήσει τοῖς ὅλοις ἡ θεία τε καὶ ἄρρητος αὐτοῦ φύσις.— Cyril. Alex. in Evangelium Joannis. Lib. VI. Tom. IV. p. 600. Ed. Aubert. Paris. 1638.—But Cranmer's quotation is evidently made from the Latin edition, which reads as follows : Sed diligenter hic animadvertendum, quod etsi corporis sui præsentiam hinc subduxerit, majestate tamen divinitatis semper adest : sicut ipse a discipulis abiturus pollicetur : Ecce ego vobiscum sum omnibus diebus usque ad consummationem sæculi.—Tom. I. col. 323. Basil. 1566.]

[2 In his majesty, 1551.]

[3 Διακεῖσθαι δὲ δεῖν ἀναγκαῖον εἶναι φημὶ τοὺς οἵ γε φρονοῦσιν ὀρθῶς, καὶ ἱδρυμένην ἔχουσι τὴν πίστιν, ὡς εἰ καὶ ἄπεστιν ἡμῶν τῇ σαρκί, τὴν πρὸς Θεὸν καὶ πατέρα στειλάμενος ἀποδημίαν, ἀλλ᾽ οὖν τῇ θείᾳ δυνάμει περιέπει τὰ σύμπαντα, καὶ συμπάρεστι τοῖς ἀγαπῶσιν αὐτόν. Διὰ γάρ τοι τοῦτο καὶ ἔφασκεν· Ἀμὴν, ἀμὴν, λέγω ὑμῖν, ὅπου ἐὰν συναχθέντες ὦσι δύο ἢ τρεῖς εἰς τὸ ἐμὸν ὄνομα, ἐκεῖ εἰμι ἐν μέσῳ αὐτῶν. Ὥσπερ γὰρ ἀνθρώποις ἔτι συνδιαιτώμενος, καὶ ἐπὶ γῆς ὑπάρχων μετὰ σαρκὸς, ἐπλήρου μὲν οὐρανοὺς, συνὴν δὲ τότε τοῖς ἁγίοις ἀγγέλοις, οὐκ ἀπελείπετό τε τῶν ἄνω χωρῶν· οὕτω καὶ νῦν ὑπάρχων ἐν οὐρανοῖς μετὰ τῆς ἰδίας σαρκὸς, πληροῖ μὲν τὴν γῆν, σύνεστι δὲ τοῖς ἑαυτοῦ γνωρίμοις. ἐπιτηρεῖ δὲ ὅπως, καίτοι κατὰ μόνην τὴν σάρκα χωρίζεσθαι προσδοκῶν, (σύνεστι γὰρ ἡμῖν τῇ δυνάμει τῆς Θεότητος διὰ παντός,) ἔτι μικρὸν χρόνον μεθ᾽ ἡμῶν ἔσεσθαι φησί.—Ibid. Lib. IX. cap. xxi. Tom. IV. p. 747.]

[4 Ergo non supra terram, nec in terra, nec secundum carnem te quærere debemus, si volumus invenire. *Nunc enim secundum carnem jam non novimus Christum*. Denique Stephanus non supra terram quæsivit, qui stantem te ad dexteram Dei vidit.—Ambros. in Lucam, Lib. X. cap. xxiv. Tom. III. p. 109. Colon. Agrip. 1616.]

[5 Non est hic, dicitur, per præsentiam carnis, qui tamen nusquam deerat per præsentiam majestatis.—Gregorii Papæ Op. Homil. XXI. Tom. II. p. 123. J. Antv. 1672.]

[6 That Christ in his human nature, 1551.]

more, that Christ is both gone hence from us unto heaven, and is also here with us in earth, but not in his human nature, (as the papists would have us to believe,) but the old authors say that he is in heaven, as concerning his manhood, and nevertheless both here and there, and every where, as concerning his Godhead. For although his divinity be such, that it is infinite, without measure, compass, or place, so that as concerning that nature he is circumscribed with no place, but is every where, and filleth all the world: yet as concerning his human nature, he hath measure, compass, and place, so that when he was here upon earth, he was not at the same time in heaven; and now that he has ascended into heaven, as concerning that nature he hath now forsaken the earth, and is only in heaven. For one nature that is circumscribed, compassed, and measured, cannot be in divers places at one time. That is the faith[7] of the old catholic church, as appeareth as well by the authors before rehearsed, as by these that hereafter followeth. Chap. VI. One body cannot be in divers places at one time.

St Augustine, speaking that a body must needs be in some place, saith, that if it be not within the compass of a place, it is nowhere; and if it be nowhere, then it is not[8]. And St Cyril, considering the proper nature of a very body, said, that if the nature of the Godhead were a body, it must needs be in a place, and have quantity, greatness, and circumscription[9]. Ad Dardanum. Cyrillus de Trin. Lib. ii.

If then the nature of the Godhead must needs be circumscribed, if it were a body, much more must the nature of Christ's manhood be circumscribed, and contained within the compass of a certain place.

Didymus also, in his book *de Spiritu Sancto*, which St Jerome did translate, proveth, that the Holy Ghost is very God, because he is in many places at one time, which no creature can be. For, saith he, all creatures, visible and invisible, be circumscribed and environed either within one place, (as corporal and visible things be,) or within the propriety of their own substance, (as angels and invisible creatures be;) so that no angel, saith he, can be at one time in two places. And forasmuch as the Holy Ghost is in many men at one time, therefore, saith he, the Holy Ghost must needs be God[10]. Didymus de Spiritu Sancto, Lib. i. c. 1.

The same affirmeth St Basil, that the angel which was with Cornelius, was not at the same time with Philip; nor the angel which spake to Zachary in the altar, was not the same time in his proper place in heaven. But the Holy Ghost was at one time in Habakkuk, and in Daniel in Babylon, and with Jeremy in prison, and with Ezekiel in Chober; whereby he proveth that the Holy Ghost is God[11]. Basilius de Spiritu Sancto, cap. 22.

Wherefore the papists, (which say, that the body of Christ is in an infinite number of places at one time,) do make his body to be God, and so confound the

---

[7 This is the faith, 1551, and Orig. ed.]

[8 Nam spatia locorum tolle corporibus, nusquam erunt; et quia nusquam erunt, nec erunt. Tolle ipsa corpora qualitatibus corporum, non erit ubi sint, et ideo necesse est ut non sint.—August. ad Dardanum, cap. viii. Pars VIII. Basil. ap. Amerbach. 1506.]

[9 Εἰ γὰρ ὅλως τομῆς τε καὶ μερισμοῦ, καὶ ὧν ἐκεῖνοι φασίν, ἡ θεία φύσις ἀνέχεται, νοείσθω καὶ σῶμα· εἰ δὲ τοῦτο, καὶ ἐν τόπῳ πάντως που, καὶ ἐν μεγέθει, καὶ ποσῷ.—Cyril. cum Hermia Dialogus de Trinitate, Lib. II. (corpora non sunt sine loco et circumscriptione). Tom. V. Pars I. p. 447. Ed. Aubert. Paris. 1638.]

[10 Ipse Spiritus sanctus, si unus de creaturis esset, saltem circumscriptam haberet substantiam, sicut universa quæ facta sunt. Nam etsi non circumscribantur loco et finibus invisibiles creaturæ, tamen proprietate substantiæ finiuntur. Spiritus autem sanctus, cum in pluribus sit, non habet substantiam circumscriptam.—Didymus de Spiritu Sancto, Lib. I. cap. i. ad calcem Hieron. Ed. Villars. Tom. II. p. 105.]

[11 Ὁ γὰρ τῷ Κορνηλίῳ ἐπιστὰς ἄγγελος οὐκ ἦν ἐν ταὐτῷ καὶ παρὰ τῷ Φιλίππῳ· οὐδὲ ὁ ἀπὸ τοῦ θυσιαστηρίου τῷ Ζαχαρίᾳ διαλεγόμενος κατὰ τὸν αὐτὸν καιρὸν καὶ ἐν οὐρανῷ τὴν οἰκείαν στάσιν ἐπλήρου. τὸ μέν τοι πνεῦμα ὁμοῦ τε καὶ ἐν Ἀββακοὺμ ἐνεργεῖν, καὶ ἐν Δανιὴλ ἐπὶ τῆς Βαβυλωνίας πεπίστευται· καὶ ἐν τῷ καταρράκτῃ [εἴρηται] εἶναι μετὰ Ἱερεμίου, καὶ μετὰ Ἰεζεκιὴλ ἐπὶ τοῦ Χοβάρ. πνεῦμα γὰρ Κυρίου πεπλήρωκε τὴν οἰκουμένην. Basil. de Spiritu Sancto, cap. xxii. Tom. II. p. 342. Paris. 1637.]

two natures of Christ, attributing to his human nature that thing which belongeth only to his divinity; which is a most heinous and detestable heresy.

Against whom writeth Fulgentius in this wise, speaking of the distinction and diversity of the two natures in Christ:

<small>Fulgentius ad Trasimundum Regem, Lib. ii.</small>

"One and the self-same Christ," saith he, "of mankind was made a man, compassed in a place, who of his Father is God, without measure or place. One and the self-same person, as concerning his man's substance, was not in heaven, when he was in earth, and forsook the earth when he ascended into heaven: but as concerning his godly substance, which is above all measure, he neither left heaven when he came from heaven, nor he left not the earth, when he ascended into heaven: which may be known by the most certain word of Christ himself, who, to shew the placing of his humanity, said to his disciples, 'I ascend up to my Father and your Father, to my God and your God.' Also when he had said of Lazarus that he was dead, he added, saying: 'I am glad for your sakes, that you may believe, for I was not there.' But to shew the unmeasurable compass of his divinity, he said to his disciples, 'Behold, I am with you always unto the world's end.' Now how did he go up into heaven, but because he is a very man, contained within a place? Or how is he present with faithful people, but because he is very God, being without measure[1]?"

Of these words of Fulgentius it is declared most certainly, that Christ is not here with us in earth but by his Godhead, and that his humanity is in heaven only, and absent from us.

<small>Vigilius contra Eutychen, Lib. i.</small>

Yet the same is more plainly shewed, if more plainly can be spoken, by Vigilius, a bishop and an holy martyr. He writeth thus against the heretic Eutyches, which denied the humanity of Christ, holding opinion that he was only God, and not man: whose error Vigilius confuting, proveth that Christ had in him two natures joined together in one person, the nature of his Godhead, and the nature of his manhood. Thus he writeth[2]:

<small>John xiv.</small>
<small>John xvi.</small>

"Christ said to his disciples, 'If you loved me you would be glad, for I go unto my Father.' And again he said, 'It is expedient for you that I go, for if I go not, the Comforter shall not come unto you.' And yet surely the eternal Word of God, the virtue of God, the wisdom of God, was ever with his Father,

---

[1 Unus idemque secundum carnem de matre temporaliter natus, qui secundum divinitatem de Patre permanet sempiternus: unus idemque homo localis ex homine, qui est Deus immensus ex Patre: unus idemque secundum humanam substantiam absens cœlo, cum esset in terra, et derelinquens terram, cum ascendisset in cœlum; secundum divinam vero immensamque substantiam, nec cœlum dimittens, cum de cœlo descendit, nec terram deserens, cum ad cœlum ascendit. Quod ipsius Domini certissimo potest cognosci sermone; qui ut localem ostenderet humanitatem suam, dicit discipulis suis, "Ascendo ad Patrem meum et ad Patrem vestrum, Deum meum et Deum vestrum." De Lazaro quoque cum dixisset, "Lazarus mortuus est," adjunxit dicens: "Et gaudeo propter vos, ut credatis, quoniam non eram ibi." Immensitatem vero suæ divinitatis ostendens discipulis dicit: "Ecce ego vobiscum sum omnibus diebus, usque ad consummationem sæculi." Quomodo autem ascendit in cœlum, nisi quia localis et verus est homo? aut quomodo adest fidelibus suis, nisi quia idem immensus et verus est Deus?—Fulgent. ad Trasimundum Regem. Lib. II. cap. xiii. p. 107. Paris. 1684.]

[2 Ait discipulis suis, "Si diligeretis me, gauderetis, quia vado ad Patrem, quia Pater major me est." Et iterum: "Expedit vobis ut ego eam; si enim ego non abiero, Paracletus ad vos non veniet." Et certe verbum Dei, virtus Dei, sapientia Dei, semper apud Patrem et in Patre fuit, etiam quando in nobis nobiscum fuit. Neque enim cum terrena misericorditer incoluit, de cœlesti habitatione recessit. Cum Patre enim ubique est totus pari divinitate, quem nullus continet locus. Plena sunt quippe omnia Filio, nec est aliquis locus divinitatis ejus præsentia vacuus. Unde ergo et quo se iturum dicit, aut quomodo se ad Patrem perrecturum adserit, a quo sine dubio nunquam recessit? Sed hoc erat ire ad Patrem et recedere a nobis, auferre de hoc mundo naturam quam susceperat ex nobis. Vides ergo eidem naturæ proprium fuisse, ut auferretur et abiret a nobis, quæ in fine temporum reddenda est nobis, secundum attestantium vocem angelorum, "Hic Jesus, qui receptus est a vobis, sic veniet, quemadmodum vidistis eum euntem in cœlum." Nam vide miraculum, vide utriusque proprietatis mysterium: Dei Filius, qui secundum humanitatem suam recessit a nobis, secundum divinitatem suam ait nobis, "Ecce ego vobiscum sum omnibus diebus usque ad consummationem sæculi."—Vigilius Afer Adversus Eutychen, Lib. I. Tom. V. p. 712. Colon. Agrip. 1618.]

and in his Father, yea, even at the same time when he was with us, and in us. For when he did mercifully dwell in this world, he left not his habitation in heaven: for he is every where whole with his Father, equal in divinity, whom no place can contain; for the Son filleth all things, and there is no place that lacketh the presence of his divinity. From whence then, and whither did he say he would go? Or how did he say, that he went to his Father, from whom doubtless he never departed; but that to go to his Father, and from us, was to take from this world that nature which he received of us? Thou seest therefore that it was the property of that nature to be taken away and go from us, which in the end of the world shall be rendered again to us, as the angels witnessed, saying: 'This Jesus which is taken from you, shall come again like as you saw him going up into heaven.' For look upon the miracle, look upon the mystery of both the natures: the Son of God, as concerning his humanity, went from us; as concerning his divinity, he said unto us: 'Behold, I am with you all the days unto the world's end.'" Acts i. Matt. ult.

Thus far have I rehearsed the words of Vigilius, and by and by he concludeth thus[3]: "He is with us, and not with us. For those whom he left, and went from them, as concerning his humanity, those he left not, nor forsook them not, as touching his divinity. For as touching the form of a servant, which he took away from us into heaven, he is absent from us; but by the form of God, which goeth not from us, he is present with us in earth, and nevertheless, both present and absent, he is all one Christ."

Hitherto you have heard Vigilius speak, that Christ, as concerning his bodily presence and the nature of his manhood, "is gone from us, taken from us, is gone up into heaven, is not with us, hath left us, hath forsaken us." But as concerning the other nature of his deity, "he is still with us," so that he is both "with us, and not with us, with us in the nature of his deity, and not with us in the nature of his humanity." And yet more clearly doth the same Vigilius declare the same thing in another place, saying[4]: 100. Contra Euty-chen, Lib. iv.

"If the word and flesh were both of one nature, seeing that the word is every where, why is not the flesh then every where? For when it was in earth, then verily it was not in heaven: and now when it is in heaven, it is not surely in earth. And it is so sure that it is not in earth, that as concerning it we look for him to come from heaven, whom as concerning his eternal word we believe to be with us in earth. Therefore by your doctrine," saith Vigilius unto Eutyches, who defended that the divinity and humanity in Christ was but one nature, "either the word is contained in a place with his flesh, or else the flesh is every where

---

[3 Sed et nobiscum est, et non est nobiscum. Quia quos reliquit, et a quibus discessit humanitate sua, non reliquit nec deseruit divinitate sua. Per formam enim servi, quam abstulit a nobis in cœlum, absens est nobis: per formam Dei, quæ non recedit a nobis, in terris præsens est nobis; tamen et præsens et absens ipse unus idemque est nobis.—Ibid.]

[4 Si verbi et carnis una natura est, quomodo, cum verbum ubique sit, non ubique inveniatur et caro? Namque quando in terra fuit, non erat utique in cœlo: et nunc, quia in cœlo est, non est utique in terra, et in tantum non est, ut secundum ipsam Christum spectemus venturum de cœlo, quem secundum verbum nobiscum esse credimus in terra. Igitur secundum vos, aut verbum cum carne sua loco continetur, aut caro cum verbo ubique est, quando una natura contrarium quid et diversum non recipit in se ipsa. Diversum est autem et longe dissimile circumscribi loco, et ubique esse; et quia verbum ubique est, caro autem ejus ubique non est, apparet unum eundemque Christum utriusque esse naturæ; et esse quidem ubique secundum naturam divinitatis suæ, et loco contineri secundum naturam humanitatis suæ: creatum esse, et initium non habere: morti subjacere, et mori non posse: quod unum illi est ex natura verbi, qua Deus est, aliud ex natura carnis, qua idem Deus homo est. Igitur unus Dei Filius, idemque hominis factus Filius; habet initium ex natura carnis suæ, et non habet initium ex natura divinitatis suæ: creatus est per naturam carnis suæ, et non est creatus per naturam divinitatis suæ: circumscribitur loco per naturam carnis suæ et loco non capitur per naturam divinitatis suæ: minor est etiam angelis per naturam carnis suæ, et æqualis est Patri secundum naturam divinitatis suæ: mortuus est natura carnis suæ, et non est mortuus natura divinitatis suæ.—Ibid. Lib. iv. p. 722.]

with the word. For one nature cannot receive in itself two diverse and contrary things. But these two things be diverse and far unlike, that is to say, to be contained in a place, and to be every where. Therefore inasmuch as the word is every where, and the flesh is not every where, it appeareth plainly, that one Christ himself hath in him two natures; and that by his divine nature he is every where, and by his human nature he is contained in a place; that he is created, and hath no beginning; that he is subject to death, and cannot die: whereof one he hath by the nature of his word, whereby he is God, and the other he hath by the nature of his flesh, whereby the same God is man also. Therefore one Son of God, the self-same was made the son of man; and he hath a beginning by the nature of his flesh, and no beginning by the nature of his Godhead. He is created by the nature of his flesh, and not created by the nature of his Godhead. He is comprehended in a place by the nature of his flesh, and not comprehended in a place by the nature of his Godhead. He is inferior to angels in the nature of his flesh, and is equal to his Father in the nature of his Godhead. He died by the nature of his flesh, and died not by the nature of his Godhead. This is the faith and catholic confession, which the apostles taught, the martyrs did corroborate, and faithful people keep unto this day."

All these be the sayings of Vigilius, who according to all the other authors before rehearsed, and to the faith and catholic confession of the apostles, martyrs, and all faithful people unto his time, saith, that as concerning Christ's humanity, when he was here on earth, he was not in heaven, and now when he is in heaven, he is not in earth; for one nature cannot be both contained in a place in heaven, and be also here in earth at one time. And forasmuch as Christ is here with us in earth, and also is contained in a place in heaven, he proveth thereby, that Christ hath two natures in him, the nature of a man, whereby he is gone from us, and ascended into heaven, and the nature of his Godhead, whereby he is here with us in earth. So that it is not one nature that is here with us, and that is gone from us, that is ascended into heaven and there contained, and that is permanent here with us in earth. Wherefore the papists (which now of late years have made a new faith, that Christ's natural body is really and naturally present both with us both here in earth[1], and sitteth at the right hand of his Father in heaven,) do err in two very horrible heresies:

The one, that they confound his two natures, his Godhead and his manhood, attributing unto his humanity that thing which appertaineth only to his divinity, that is to say, to be in heaven, earth[2], and in many places at one time. The other is, that they divide and separate his human nature or his body, making of one body of Christ two bodies and two natures, one which is in heaven, visible and palpable, having all members and proportions of a most perfect natural man; and another which they say is in earth here with us, in every bread and wine that is consecrated, having no distinction, form, nor proportion of members: which contrarieties and diversities, as this holy martyr Vigilius saith, cannot be together in one nature.

WINCHESTER.

These differences end in the forty-eighth leaf, in the second column. I intend now to touch the further matter of the book with the manner of handling of it[3], and where an evident untruth is, there to join an issue, and where sleight and craft is, there to note it in the whole.

The matter of the book, from thence unto the fifty-sixth leaf, touching the being of Christ in

---

[1 Both with us here in earth, 1551, and Orig. ed.]   [2 In heaven and earth, 1551, Orig. ed.]
[3 Of the handling of it, 1551.]

heaven and not in earth, is out of purpose superfluous. The article of our creed that Christ ascended to heaven, and sitteth on the right hand of his Father, hath been and is most constantly believed of true christian men, which the true faith of Christ's real presence in the sacrament doth not touch or impair. Nor Christ being whole God and man in the sacrament, is thereby either out of heaven, or to be said conversant in earth, because the conversation is not earthly, but spiritual and godly, being the ascension of Christ, the end of his conversation in earth; and therefore all that reasoning of the author is clearly void, to travail to prove that is not denied, only for a sleight to make it seem as though it were denied.

*Christ's ascension the end of his conversation in earth.

*Sleight.

CANTERBURY.

Here is such a sleight used by you, as is worthy to be noted of all men. For I go not only about to prove in this place only that Christ, as concerning his human nature, is in heaven, (which I know you deny not,) but I prove also that he is so in heaven, that he is not in earth, which you utterly deny, and it is the chief point in contention between us. But by this craft of appeaching me of sleight, that I go about to prove that thing which you deny not, (which is untrue,) you have used such a sleight, that you pass over eight leaves of my book together, wherein I prove that Christ, as concerning his corporal presence, is not here in earth, and you answer not one word to any of my arguments. And I pray thee note, good reader, what a strange manner of sleight this is, to pass over eight leaves together clearly unanswered, and that in the chief point that is in variance between us, under pretence that I use sleight, where in deed I use none, but prove plainly that Christ is not bodily in heaven and in earth, both at one time. If he had but touched mine arguments glancing by them, it had been somewhat: but utterly to fly away[4], and not once to touch them, I think thou wilt judge no small sleight and craft therein. And methink in good reason, the matter ought to be judged against him for default of answer, who being present answereth nothing at all to the matter whereof he is accused; seeing that the law saith: *Qui tacet, consentire videtur.*

A sleight to avoid answering.

Yet Smith is to be commended in respect of you, who attempteth at the least to see what shifts he could make to avoid my proofs, and busieth himself rather than he would stand mute, to say something to them. And yet in deed it had been as good for him to have said nothing at all, as to say that which is nothing to the purpose.

Smith.

First to the scriptures by me alleged particularly, he utterly answereth nothing. To Origen and St Augustine by name, and to all the other authors by me alleged, he maketh this brief answer in general, that whatsoever those authors say, they mean no more, but that Christ is not here in earth visibly, naturally, and by circumscription, and yet nevertheless he is in the sacrament above nature, invisibly, and without circumscription. This subtle distinction hath Smith devised, (or rather followeth other papists therein,) to answer the authors which I have alleged. And yet of Smith's own distinction it followeth, that Christ is not in the sacrament carnally and corporally. For if Christ be in the sacrament but supernaturally, invisibly, and without circumscription, then he is not there carnally and corporally, as St Augustine reasoneth *ad Dardanum*[5]. But yet Smith only saith that the authors so meant, and proveth not one word of his saying, supposing that the old holy writers be like to the papists, which write one thing, and when they list not, or cannot defend it, they say they mean another.

Origen. Augustine. 102.

Smith's vain distinction.

For those authors make no such distinction as Smith speaketh of, affirming divers and contrary things to be in one nature of Christ in divers respects; but their distinction is of the two natures in Christ, that is to say, the nature of his Godhead, and the nature of his manhood. And they affirm plainly, that the diversity whereof they spake cannot be in one nature, as you say it is, but must needs argue and prove diversity of natures. And therefore by that diversity and instinction[6] in Christ they prove against the heretics that Christ hath two natures in him; which were utterly

---

[[4] To flee away, 1551.]   [[5] See note 8, p. 97.]   [[6] Distinction, 1551.]

no proof at all, if one nature in divers respects might have that diversity: for the heretics should have had a ready answer at hand, that such diversity proveth not that Christ had two natures, for one nature may have such diversity, if it be true that Smith saith. And so Smith, with other papists which saith as he doth, putteth a sword in the heretics' hands to fight against the catholic faith. This, good reader, thou shalt easily perceive, if thou do no more but read the authors which I have in this place alleged.

<small>How both these sayings may be true, that Christ is with us, and also gone from us. The sum of the old authors writing in this matter.</small>

And yet, for thy more ready instruction, I shall make a brief rehearsal of the chief effect of them, as concerning this matter. To answer this question, how it can be said that Christ is a stranger, and gone hence into heaven, and yet is also here with us in earth, Smith and other papists resolve this matter by divers respects in one nature of Christ; but the old catholic writers which I alleged, resolve the matter by two natures in Christ, affirming most certainly that such two diverse things cannot have place both in one nature. And therefore say they, that Christ is gone hence and is absent in his humanity, who in his deity is still here with us. They say also that as concerning his man's nature, the catholic profession in our creed teacheth us to believe that he hath made it immortal, but not changed the nature of a very man's body; for his body is in heaven, and in one certain place of heaven, because that so requireth the measure and compass of a very man's body.

It is also, say they, visible, and hath all the members of a perfect man's body. And further they say, that if Christ's body were not contained within the compass of a place, it were no body, insomuch that if the Godhead were a body, it must needs be in a place, and have quantity, bigness, and circumscription. For all creatures, say they, visible and invisible, be circumscribed and contained within a certain compass, either locally within one place, as corporal and visible things be, or else within the property of their own substance, as angels and invisible creatures be. And this is one strong argument whereby they prove that the Holy Ghost is God, because he is in many places at one time, which no creature can be, as they teach. And yet they say moreover, that Christ did not ascend into heaven but by his humanity, nor is not here in earth but by his divinity, which hath no compass nor measure. And finally they say, that to go to his Father from us, was to take from us that nature which he received of us: and therefore when his body was in earth, then surely it was not in heaven; and now when it is in heaven, surely it is not in earth. For one nature cannot have in itself two sundry and contrary things.

All things[1] here rehearsed be written by the old ancient authors which I have alleged, and they conclude the whole matter in this wise, that this is the faith and catholic confession, which the apostles taught, the martyrs did corroborate, and faithful people keep unto this day. Whereby it appeareth evidently, that the doctrine of Smith and the papists at that day was not yet sprung, nor had taken no root.

Wherefore diligently ponder and weigh, I beseech thee, gentle reader, the sayings of these authors, and see whether they say, that one nature in Christ may be both in heaven and in earth, both here with us and absent from us at one time; and whether they resolve this matter of Christ's being in heaven and in earth, as Smith doth, to be understand of his manhood in diversity of these respects visible and invisible. And when thou hast well considered the authors' sayings, then give credit to Smith as thou shalt see cause.

But this allegation of these authors hath made the matter so hot, that the bishop of Winchester durst not once touch it, and Smith, as soon as he had touched it, felt it so scalding hot, that he durst not abide it, but shrank away by and by for fear of burning his fingers. Now hear what followeth further in my book.

<small>Chap. VII. An answer to the papists, alleging for them these words: "This is my body."</small>

But now, seeing that it is so evident a matter, both by the express words of scripture, and also by all the old authors of the same, that our Saviour Christ (as concerning his bodily presence) is ascended into heaven, and is not here in earth; and seeing that this hath been the true confession of

[1 All these things, 1551.]

the catholic faith ever since Christ's ascension; it is now to be considered what moved the papists to make a new and contrary faith, and what scriptures have they[2] for their purpose. What moved them I know not, but their own iniquity, or the nature and condition of the see of Rome, which is of all other most contrary to Christ, and therefore most worthy to be called the see of antichrist. And as for scripture, they allege none but only one, and that not truly understood, but to serve their purpose wrested out of tune, whereby they make it to jar and sound contrary to all other scriptures pertaining to the matter.

"Christ took bread," say they, "blessed, and brake it, and gave it to his disciples, saying, This is my body." These words they ever still repeat and beat upon, that Christ said, "This is my body." And this saying they make their sheet-anchor, to prove thereby as well the real and natural presence of Christ's body in the sacrament, as their imagined transubstantiation. For these words of Christ, say they, be most plain and most true. Then forasmuch as he said, "This is my body," it must needs be true that that thing which the priest holdeth in his hands is Christ's body. And if it be Christ's body, then can it not be bread. Whereof they gather by their reasoning, that there is Christ's body really present, and no bread. *The argument of the papists.* *104.*

Now forasmuch as all their proof hangeth only upon these words, "This is my body:" the true sense and meaning of these words must be examined. But, say they, what need they any examination? what words can be more plain, than to say, "This is my body?" *The answer.*

Truth it is indeed, that the words be as plain as may be spoken; but that the sense is not so plain, it is manifest to every man that weigheth substantially the circumstances of the place. For when Christ gave bread to his disciples, and said, "This is my body," there is no man of any discretion, that understandeth the English tongue, but he may well know by the order of the speech that Christ spake those words of the bread, calling it his body: as all the old authors also do affirm, although some of the papists deny the same. Wherefore this sentence cannot mean as the words seem and purport, but there must needs be some figure or mystery in this speech, more than appeareth in the plain words. For by this manner of speech plainly understand without any figure, as the words lie, can be gathered none other sense, but that bread is Christ's body, and that Christ's body is bread; which all christian ears do abhor to hear. Wherefore in these words must needs be sought out another sense and meaning than the words of themselves do bear. *The interpretation of these words: "This is my body."*

And although the true sense and understanding of these words be sufficiently declared before, when I spake of transubstantiation, yet to make the matter so plain that no scruple or doubt shall remain, here is occasion given more fully to entreat thereof: in which process shall be shewed, that these sentences of Christ, "This is my body," "This is my blood," be figurative speeches. And although it be manifest enough by the plain words of the gospel, and proved before in the process of transubstantiation, that Christ spake of bread, when he said, "This is my body;" likewise that it was very wine which he called his blood; yet lest the papists should say, that we suck this out of our own fingers, the same shall be proved by testimony of the old authors, to be the true and old faith of the catholic church: whereas the school authors and papists shall not be able to shew so much as one word of any ancient author to the contrary. *Chap. VIII. Christ called bread his body, and wine his blood.*

[[2] They have, 1551, and Orig. ed.]

Iren. contra Valent. Lib. IV. capp. 32. 34. 57.

First, Irenæus, writing against the Valentinians, in his fourth book saith, that "Christ confessed bread (which is a creature) to be his body, and the cup to be his blood." And in the same book he writeth thus also: "The bread wherein the thanks be given is the body of the Lord." And yet again in the same book he saith, that Christ taking "bread of the same sort that our bread is of, confessed that it was his body; and that that thing which was tempered in the chalice was his blood." And in the fifth book he writeth further, "that of the chalice (which is his blood) a man is nourished, and doth grow by the bread," which is his body[1].

Lib. v.

These words of Irenæus be most plain, that Christ taking very material bread, a creature of God, and of such sort as other bread is which we do use, called that his body, when he said, "This is my body;" and the wine also which doth feed and nourish us, "he called his blood."

Tertul. adversus Judæos. 105.

Tertullian likewise, in his book written against the Jews, saith that "Christ called bread his body[2]." And in his book against Marcion he oftentimes repeateth the self-same words.

Cyprian. ad Magnum. Lib. i. Epist. 6.

And St Cyprian, in the first book of his epistles, saith the same thing, that "Christ called such bread as is made of many corns joined together his body, and such wine he called his blood, as is pressed out of many grapes, and made into wine[3]." And in his second book he saith these words: "Water is not the blood of Christ, but wine[4]." And again in the same epistle he saith, that "it was wine which Christ called his blood; and that if wine be not in the chalice, then we drink not of the fruit of the vine[5]." And in the same epistle he saith, that "meal alone, or water alone, is not the body of Christ, except they be both joined together, to make thereof bread[6]."

Lib. ii. Epist. 3.

Epiphan. in Ancorat.

Epiphanius also saith that Christ, speaking of a "loaf which is round in fashion, and cannot see, hear, nor feel, said of it: 'This is my body'[7]."

Hier. ad Hedibiam.

And St Jerome, writing *ad Hedibiam*, saith these words: "Let us mark that the bread which the Lord brake, and gave to his disciples, was the body of our Saviour Christ, as he said unto them: 'Take and eat; this is my body[8].'"

[1 Sed et suis discipulis dans consilium, primitias Deo offerre de suis creaturis, non quasi indigenti, sed ut ipsi nec infructuosi nec ingrati sint, eum qui ex creatura est panis accepit, et gratias egit, dicens: "Hoc est corpus meum." Et calicem similiter, qui est ex ea creatura, quæ est secundum nos, suum sanguinem confessus est, et novi Testamenti novam docuit oblationem.—Irenæus, contr. Valent. Lib. IV. cap. 32, p. 323. Quomodo autem constabit eis, eum panem in quo gratiæ actæ sint, corpus esse Domini sui—Quemadmodum enim qui est a terra panis, percipiens invocationem Dei, jam non communis panis est, sed eucharistia, ex duabus rebus constans, terrena et cœlesti. Cap. 34. pp. 326, 7. Quando ergo et mixtus calix et factus panis percipit verbum Dei, et fit eucharistia sanguinis et corporis Christi, ex quibus augetur et consistit carnis nostræ substantia. Lib. v. cap. ii. p. 397. ed. Oxon. 1702.]

[2 Sic enim Christus revelavit, panem corpus suum appellans. Tertullian. adversus Judæos, p. 196, et adversus Marcionem, Lib. IV. p. 458. Lutetiæ Paris. 1664.]

[3 Nam quando Dominus corpus suum panem vocat de multorum granorum adunatione congestum; et quando sanguinem suum vinum appellat, de botris atque acinis plurimis expressum atque in unum coactum. (Editio Erasmica in vinum).—Cyprian. ad Magnum. Lib. I. Epist. vi. p. 208. Paris. 1574.]

[4 Sanguis Christi non aqua est utique, sed vinum.—Id. ad Cæcilium. Lib. II. Epist. iii. p. 143.]

[5 Vinum fuisse, quod sanguinem suum dixit. Quomodo autem de creatura vitis novum vinum cum Christo in regno patris bibemus, si in sacrificio Dei patris et Christi vinum non offerimus nec calicem Domini dominica traditione miscemus?—Ib. p. 145.]

[6 Quomodo nec corpus Domini potest esse farina sola, aut aqua sola, nisi utrumque adunatum fuerit et copulatum, et panis unius compage solidatum.—Ib. 146.]

[7 Ἀνέστη ἐν τῷ δείπνῳ, καὶ ἔλαβε τάδε· καὶ εὐχαριστήσας εἶπε, τοῦτο μου ἐστὶ τόδε· καὶ ὁρῶμεν ὅτι οὐκ ἴσόν ἐστιν, οὐδὲ ὅμοιον, οὐ τῇ ἐνσάρκῳ εἰκόνι, οὐ τῇ ἀοράτῳ θεότητι, οὐ τοῖς χαρακτῆρσι τῶν μελῶν· τὸ μὲν γάρ ἐστι στρογγυλοειδὲς καὶ ἀναίσθητον, ὡς πρὸς τὴν δύναμιν· καὶ ἠθέλησεν χάριτι εἰπεῖν, τοῦτό μου ἐστὶ τόδε.—Epiphanius, in Ancorato, Cap. lvii. Tom. II. p. 60. Ed. Patav. Paris. 1622.]

[8 Nos autem audiamus panem, quem fregit Dominus, deditque discipulis suis, esse corpus Domini Salvatoris, ipso dicente ad eos: "Accipite et comedite, hoc est corpus meum."—Hieron. Hedibiæ. Quæst. ii. Tom. III. p. 95. Francof. 1684.]

And St Augustine also saith, "that although we may set forth Christ by mouth, by writing, and by the sacrament of his body and blood, yet we call neither our tongue, nor words, nor ink, letters, nor paper, the body and blood of Christ; but that we call the body and blood of Christ, which is taken of the fruit of the earth, and consecrated by mystical prayer." And also he saith: "Jesus called meat his body, and drink his blood[9]." ^{Aug. de Trin Lib. iii. cap. 4.} ^{De Verbis Apostol. Serm. 2.}

Moreover Cyril upon St John saith, that "Christ gave to his disciples pieces of bread, saying: 'Take, eat; this is my body[10].'" ^{Cyrill. in Joan. Lib. iv. cap. 14.}

Likewise Theodoretus saith: "When Christ gave the holy mysteries, he called bread his body, and the cup mixed with wine and water, he called his blood[11]." ^{Theodoretus in Dialog. 1.}

By all these foresaid authors and places, with many more, it is plainly proved, that when our Saviour Christ gave bread unto his disciples, saying, "Take and eat; this is my body;" and likewise when he gave them the cup, saying, "Divide this among you, and drink you all of this, for this is my blood;" he called then the very material bread his body, and the very wine his blood.

That bread, I say, that is one of the creatures here in earth among us, and that groweth out of the earth, and is made of many grains of corn beaten into flour, and mixed with water, and so baken and made into bread, of such sort as other our bread is, that hath neither sense nor reason, and finally that feedeth and nourisheth our bodies; such bread Christ called his body, when he said, "This is my body:" and such wine as is made of grapes pressed together, and thereof is made drink, which nourish[12] the body, such wine he called his blood.

This is the true doctrine, confirmed as well by the holy scripture, as by all ancient authors of Christ's church, both Greeks and Latins; that is to say, that when our Saviour Christ gave bread and wine to his disciples, and spake these words, "This is my body, this is my blood," it is very bread and wine which he called his body and blood.

Now let the papists shew some authority for their opinion, either of scripture, or of some ancient author. And let them not constrain all men to follow their fond devices, only because they say it is so, without any other ground or authority, but their own bare words. For in such wise credit is to be given to God's word only, and not to the word of man. As many of them as I have read (the bishop of Winchester only excepted) do say, that Christ called not bread his body, nor wine his blood, when he said, "This is my body, this is my blood." And yet in expounding these words they vary among themselves; which is a token that they be uncertain of their own doctrine.

For some of them say, that by this pronoun demonstrative "this" Christ understood not the bread and wine, but his body and blood.

And other some say, that by the pronoun "this" he meant neither the bread nor wine, nor his body nor blood; but that he meant a particular thing un-

---

[9 Potuit tamen significando prædicare Dominum Jesum Christum, aliter per linguam suam, aliter per epistolam, aliter per sacramentum corporis et sanguinis ejus. Nec linguam quippe ejus, nec membranas, nec atramentum, nec significantes sonos lingua editos, nec signa literarum conscripta pelliculis, corpus Christi et sanguinem dicimus, sed illud tantum quod ex fructibus terræ acceptum et prece mystica consecratum.—Augustin. de Trinitate. Lib. III. cap. 4. Pars v. Basil. ap. Amerbach. 1506.]

[10 Τοῖς γὰρ ἤδη πεπιστευκόσι διακλάσας τὸν ἄρτον ἐδίδου, λέγων· Λάβετε, φάγετε· τοῦτό ἐστι τὸ σῶμά μου.—Cyrill. in Joannem. Lib. IV. cap. 14. Tom. IV. p. 360. Ed. Aubert. Paris. 1638. In the Latin version, *fragmenta panis dedit.*]

[11 Ἐν δέ γε τῇ τῶν μυστηρίων παραδόσει σῶμα τὸν ἄρτον ἐκάλεσε, καὶ αἷμα τὸ κρᾶμα.—Theodoretus in Dialogo 1. Tom. IV. p. 26. Halæ 1769-94.]

[12 Nourisheth, 1551, and Orig ed.]

certain, which they call *individuum vagum*, or *individuum in genere*; I trow some mathematical quiddity, they cannot tell what[1].

But let all these papists together shew any one authority, either of scripture or of ancient author, either Greek or Latin, that saith as they say, that Christ called not bread and wine his body and blood, but *individuum vagum*; and for my part I shall give them place and confess that they say true.

And if they can shew nothing for them of antiquity, but only their own bare words, then it is reason that they give place to the truth confirmed by so many authorities, both of scripture and of ancient writers, which is, that Christ called very material bread his body, and very wine made of grapes his blood.

WINCHESTER.

After this the author occupieth a great number of leaves, that is to say, from the fifty-seventh leaf unto the seventy-fourth, to prove Christ's words, "This is my body," to be a figurative speech. Sleight and shift is used in the matter, without any effectual consecution, to him that is learned.

First, the author saith, Christ called "bread" his body, confessed[2] "bread" his body. To this is answered, Christ's calling is a making, as St Paul saith: Vocat ea quæ non sunt, tanquam ea quæ sint; *"He calleth that be not as they were." And so his calling (as Chrysostom[3] and the Greek commentaries say) is a making; which also the catechism teacheth, translated by Justus Jonas in Germany, and after by this author in English. Tertullian saith: "Christ made bread his body;" and it is all one speech in Christ being God, declaring his ordinances, whether he use the word "call," or "make;" for in his mouth to call is to make*[4].

Cyprian saith[5] *according hereunto, how bread is by God's omnipotency made flesh: whereupon also this speech, 'Bread is flesh,' is as much to say as 'made flesh;' not that bread being bread is flesh, but that was bread is flesh by God's omnipotency; and so this author, entreating this matter as he doth, hath partly opened the faith of transubstantiation. For indeed bread being bread is not Christ's body, but that was bread is now Christ's body, because bread is made Christ's body, and because Christ called bread his body, which was in Christ to make bread his body. When Christ made water wine, the speech is very proper to say, water is made wine. For after like manner of speech we say, Christ justifieth a wicked man, Christ saveth sinners, and the physician hath made the sick man whole, and such diet will make an whole man sick. All these speeches be proper and plain, so as the construction*[6] *be not made captious and sophistical, to join that was to that now is, forgetting the mean work.*

When Christ said, "This is my body," there is no[7] *necessity that the demonstration "this" should be referred to the outward visible matter, but may be referred to the invisible substance. As in the speech of God the Father upon Christ in baptism: "This is my Son."*

And here, when this author taketh his recreation to speak of the feigning of the papists, I shall join this issue in this place, that he understandeth not what he saith, and if his knowledge be no better than is uttered here in the pen, to be in this point clearly condemned of ignorance.

CANTERBURY.

Here is another sleight, such as the like hath not lightly been seen. For where I wrote that when Christ said, "This is my body," it was bread that he called his body, you turn the matter to make a descant upon these two words, "calling" and

---

[1 The various opinions may be found collected by bishop Jewell in his Reply to Harding, Article 24. on *Individuum vagum*, p. 462, &c.]

[2 Christ confessed bread, 1551.]

[3 διὰ τοῦτο οὐδὲ εἶπε, καὶ παράγοντος τὰ οὐκ ὄντα, ἀλλὰ καλοῦντος, τὴν πλείονα εὐκολίαν δηλῶν. ὥσπερ γὰρ, κ. τ. ἑ.—Chrysost. in Epist. ad Rom. Hom. viii. Tom. IX. p. 504. Ed. Bened.]

[4 Acceptum panem, et distributum discipulis, corpus illum suum fecit, hoc est corpus meum dicendo, id est, figura corporis mei.—Tertullian. adversus Marcionem. Lib. IV. pp. 457, 8. Lutetiæ Paris. 1664.]

[5 Panis iste quem Dominus discipulis porrigebat, non effigie sed natura mutatus, omnipotentia verbi factus est caro.—Cyprian. (Arnoldi) De Cœna Domini. p. 468. Paris. 1574.]

[6 So as construction, but not made captious, Orig. ed. Winch.]

[7 *no* inserted from edit. 1551.]

"making," that the minds of the readers should be so occupied with the discussion of these two words, that in the meantime they should forget what thing it was that was called and made. Like unto men that dare larks[8], which hold up an hoby, that the larks' eyes being ever upon the hoby, should not see the net that is laid on their heads.

And yet finally you grant that which Smith denieth, that it was bread which Christ called his body, when he said, "This is my body." And so that which was not his body in deed he called his body, who calleth things that be not, as they were the things in deed. And if his calling be making, then his calling bread his body is making bread his body: and so is not only Christ's body made present, but also the bread is made his body, because it is called his body; and so must bread be the thing whereof Christ's body is made: which before you denied in the eleventh comparison, calling that saying so foolish, that it were "not tolerable to be devised by a scoffer in a play to supply when his fellow had forgotten his part." And thus should you conclude yourself, if Christ's calling were making, which in deed is not true: for then should Christ have made himself a vine, when he called himself a vine; and have made St John the blessed virgin Mary's son, when he called him her son; and should have made his apostles vine-branches, when he called them so; and should have made Peter a devil, when he called him devil.

Rom. iv. Whether Christ's calling be making.

John xv. John xix. John xv. Matt. xvi.

After, when you come to make answer unto the authors cited by me in this place, first you skip over Irene, the eldest author of them all, because, I think, he is too hard meat for you well to digest, and therefore you will not once taste of him. Irenæus.

In Tertullian and Cyprian you agree again, that when Christ said, "This is my body," it was bread that he called his body. And so when he said "this" he meant the bread, making demonstration upon it: as before you have said more at large in your book, which you named, "The Detection of the Devil's Sophistry[9]." And herein you say more truly than the other papists do, (which deny that the demonstration was made upon the bread,) although you say not true in the other part that Christ's calling was making. Tertullian. Cyprian. Whether bread be called Christ's body.

And if his calling be changing of the bread and making it the body of Christ, yet then it is not true to speak of the bread, and to say that it is the body of Christ. For when one thing is changed into another, the first still remaining, it may be said both that it is made the other thing, and that it is the other thing, (as when cloth is made a gown, we may say this cloth is made a gown, and also this cloth is a gown;) but when the former matter or state remaineth not, it may be said that it is made the other thing, but not that it is the other thing: as when Christ had turned water into wine[10]. And likewise, although we say, a wicked man is made just, a sick man is made whole, or an whole man sick, yet it is no true speech to say a wicked man is just, a sick man is whole, or an whole man is sick; because the former state remaineth not. And therefore, although it might in speech be allowed that the bread is made Christ's body, when the bread is gone, yet can it not be proper and approved speech to say, it is his body, except the bread remain still. For of that thing which is not, it cannot be said that it is Christ's body. For if it be his body, it must needs be by the rule of logic, *a tertio adjacente ad secundum adjacens*. Conversion two manner of ways. *John ii. 108.

And I marvel how you have overshot yourself in this place, when you teach how and after what manner bread is made Christ's body. "Not that bread (say you) being bread is his body, but that which was bread is now made his body:" whereof it followeth necessarily that his body is made of bread. For as the wine in the Cana of Galilee was made of water, when the substance of water was turned into the substance of wine; so if in the sacrament the substance of bread be turned into the substance of Christ's body, then is his body in the sacrament made of bread: which Christ's body made of bread. John ii.

[8 To dare larks, i. e. to frighten in order to catch them. An hoby, i. e. a species of hawk.]

[9 Gardiner's "Detection of the Devil's Sophistrie, wherwith he robbeth the unlearned people of the true byleef in the most blessed Sacrament of the aulter," was first published in 1546, and was replied to by Hooper and others before the publication of Cranmer's first book on the Sacrament.]

[10 In Ed. 1551, after "as when Christ had turned water into wine," follow these words, "It was true to say water is made wine, but not to say water is wine."]

in[1] the eleventh comparison you affirmed to be so foolish a saying, as were "not tolerable to be devised by a scoffer in a play to supply when his fellow had forgotten his part."

Therefore I have not here "partly opened the faith of transubstantiation," as you say of me; but you have here manifestly opened the wisdom of the papistical doctrine, which is more foolish than were to be devised by a scoffer in a play.

Whether Christ called bread his body.

But what need I much to contend with you in this place, seeing that you grant the thing for the which I cited all these authors, that is to say, that Christ called bread his body when he said, "This is my body?"

And in your "Detection of the Devil's Sophistry," as you call it, you say that Christ spake plainly, "This is my body," making demonstration of the bread when he said, "This is my body." But it seemeth you be sorry that you have granted so much, and that you spake those words unadvisedly, before you knew what the papists had written in this matter[2]; and now, when you perceive how far you vary from them, you would fain call your words back again, and prepare a way for the same, saying thus: "When Christ said, 'This is my body,' there is no necessity that the demonstration 'this' should be referred to the outward visible matter, but may be referred to the invisible substance." In these your words it seemeth you begin to doubt in that thing which before you certainly affirm without all doubt.

And when you have confessed the whole matter that I do here prove, which is only this, that Christ called bread his body, and wine his blood, when he said, "This is my body, this is my blood:" yet you conclude your answer with an issue of mine ignorance, that it is so great that I "understand not what I say, if my knowledge be no better than is uttered here in my pen." And yet my words be so plain, that the least child, as they say, in the town may understand them. For all my study is to speak plain, that the truth may be known, and not with dark speeches, as you do, to hide the truth. But when I had made a plain issue against all the papists in general, it had been your part to have joined in the said issue, and not to devise new issues.

Smith.

109.

*Mine issue.

But because neither you nor Smith dare join with me in mine issue, I shall repeat mine issue again, and take it for confessed of you both, because neither of you dare say the contrary, and join an issue with me therein. My issue is this: "Let all the papists together shew any one authority, either of scripture or of ancient author, either Greek or Latin, that saith as they say, that Christ called not bread and wine his body and blood, but *individuum vagum;* and for my part I shall give them place and confess that they say true. And if they can shew nothing for them of antiquity, but only their own bare words, then it is reason that they give place to the truth confirmed by so many authorities, both of scripture and of ancient writers, which is, that Christ called very material bread his body, and very wine made of grapes his blood."

Smith.

Now it shall not be much amiss to examine here the wise device of M. Smith, what he can say to this matter, that the opinion of divers doctors may be known, as well of Doctor Smith, as of Doctor Gardiner. "It is very false," saith Smith to me, "that you do say, that as these words 'This is my body' do lie, there can be gathered of them none other sense, but that bread is Christ's body, and that Christ's body is bread. For there can no such thing be gathered of those words, but only that Christ gave his disciples his very body to eat, into which he had turned the bread, when he spake those words." First, Smith useth here a great and manifest falsehood in reciting of my sentence, leaving out those words, which should declare the truth of my saying. For I say, that by this manner of speech plainly understand without any figure, there can be gathered none other sense, but that bread is Christ's body. In which my sentence he leaveth out these words, "by this manner of speech plainly understand without any figure;" which words be so material, that in them resteth the pith and trial of the whole sentence.

Matt. xiv.

When Christ took the five loaves and two fishes, and looking up into heaven

---

[1 *Is in*, edit. 1580. by a manifest error.]   [2 In that matter, 1551.]

blessed them, and brake them, and gave them unto his disciples, that they should distribute them unto the people, if he had then said, Eat; this is meat, which shall satisfy your hunger: by this manner of speech, plainly understand without any figure, could any other sense have been gathered, but that the bread and fishes which he gave them was meat? And if at the same time he had blessed wine, and commanding them to drink thereof, had said, "This is drink which shall quench your thirst:" what could have been gathered of those words, plainly understand without any figure, but that he called wine drink? So likewise when he blessed bread and wine, and gave them to his disciples, saying, "Eat, this is my body;" "Drink, this is my blood:" what can be gathered of this manner of speech, plainly understand without any figure, but that he called the bread his body, and wine his blood? For Christ spake not one word there of any changing or turning of the substance of the bread, no more than he did when he gave the loaves and fishes. And therefore the manner of speech is all one, and the changing of the substances can no more be proved by the phrase and fashion of speech, to be in the one than in the other, whatsoever you papists dream of your own heads without scripture, that the substance of the bread is turned into the substance of Christ's body.

<small>Mark vi.
Luke ix.
John vi.</small>

But Smith bringeth here news, using such strange and novelty of speech, as other papists use not; which he doth either of ignorance of his grammar, or else that he dissenteth far from other papists in judgment. For he saith, that Christ had turned the bread when he spake these words, "This is my body." And if Smith remember his accidence, the preterpluperfect tense signifieth the time that is more than perfectly past; so that if Christ had turned the bread when he spake those words, then was the turning done before and already past, when he spake those words, which the other papists say was done after, or in the pronunciation of the words. And therefore they use to speak after this sort, that when he had spoken the words, the bread was turned, and not that he had turned the bread when he spake the words.

<small>Smith.

110.</small>

Another novelty of speech Smith useth in the same place, saying, that Christ called his body bread, because he turned bread into it; it seemeth and appeareth still to be it, it hath the quality and quantity of bread, and because it is the food of the soul, as corporal meat is of the body. These be Smith's words, which if he understand of the outward form of bread, it is a novelty to say, that it is the food of the soul; and if he mean of the very body of Christ, it is a more strange novelty to say, that it hath the quantity and quality of bread. For there was never man, I trow, that used that manner of speech, to say that the body of Christ hath the quantity and quality of bread, although the papists use this speech, that the body of Christ is contained under the form, that is to say, under the quantities and qualities of bread.

Now when Smith should come to make a direct answer unto the authorities of the old writers, which I have brought forth to prove that Christ called bread his body, when he said, "This is my body;" Smith answereth no more but this: "The doctors which you, my lord, allege here for you, prove not your purpose." Forsooth, a substantial answer, and well proved, that the doctors by me alleged prove not my purpose; for Smith saith so. I looked here, that Smith should have brought forth a great number of authors to approve his saying, and to reprove mine, specially seeing that I offered fair play to him, and to all the papists joined with him in one troop.

For after that I had alleged for the proof of my purpose a great many places of old authors, both Greeks and Latins, I provoked the papists to say what they could to the contrary. "Let all the papists together," said I, "shew any one authority for them, either of scripture or ancient author, either Greek or Latin, and for my part I shall give them place. And if they can shew nothing for them of antiquity, then is it reason that they give place to the truth, confirmed by so many authorities, both of scripture and of ancient writers, which is, that Christ called very material bread his body, and very wine made of grapes his blood."

Now I refer to thy judgment, indifferent reader, whether I offered the papists reason or no; and whether they ought not, if they had any thing to shew, to have brought it forth here: and forasmuch as they have brought nothing, (being thus provoked with all their counsel,) whether thou oughtest not to judge, that they have nothing in deed to shew, which if they had, without doubt we should have heard of it in this place. But we hear nothing at all, but these their bare words, "Not one of all these doctors saith as ye do, my Lord." Which I put in thy discretion, indifferent reader, to view the doctor's words by me alleged, and so to judge.

111.

But they say not that there is only bread in the sacrament, saith Smith, and not Christ's body: what then? What is that to purpose here in this place, I pray you? For I go not about in this place to prove that only bread is in the sacrament, and not Christ's body: but in this place I prove only, that it was very bread, which Christ called his body, and very wine which he called his blood, when he said, "This is my body, this is my blood:" which Smith with all his rablement[1] of the papists deny, and yet all the old authors affirm it with doctor Stephen Gardiner, late bishop of Winchester also, who saith, "that Christ made demonstration upon the bread, when he said, 'This is my body'." And as all the old authors be able to countervail the papists, so is the late bishop able to match Smith in this matter; so that we have, at the least, a Rowland for an Oliver. But shortly to comprehend the answer of Smith: where I have proved my sayings, a dozen leaves together, by the authority of scripture and old catholic writers, is this a sufficient answer, only to say without any proof, that all my travail is lost? and that all that I have alleged is nothing to the purpose? Judge indifferently, gentle reader, whether I might not, by the same reason, cast away all Smith's whole book, and reject it quite and clean with one word, saying, "All his labour is lost, and to no purpose." Thus Smith and Gardiner being answered, I will return again to my book, where it followeth thus.

Chap. ix.
"Bread is my body,"
"wine is my blood," be figurative speeches.

Now this being fully proved, it must needs follow consequently, that this manner of speaking is a figurative speech. For in plain and proper speech, it is not true to say that bread is Christ's body, or wine his blood. For Christ's body hath a soul, life, sense, and reason: but bread hath neither soul, life, sense, nor reason.

Likewise in plain speech it is not true, that we eat Christ's body, and drink his blood. For eating and drinking, in their proper and usual signification, is with the tongue, teeth, and lips, to swallow, divide, and chaw in pieces: which thing to do to the flesh and blood of Christ, is horrible to be heard of any Christian.

Chap. x.
"To eat Christ's flesh" and "drink his blood," be figurative speeches.

So that these speeches, "To eat Christ's body and drink his blood," "to call bread his body, and wine his blood[2]," be speeches not taken in the proper signification of every word, but by translation of these words, "eating" and "drinking," from the signification of a corporal thing to signify a spiritual thing; and by calling a thing that signifieth by the name of the thing which is signified thereby. Which is no rare nor strange thing, but an usual manner and phrase in common speech. And yet, lest this fault should be imputed unto us, that we do feign things of our own heads without authority, (as the papists be accustomed to do,) here shall be cited sufficient authority, as well of scriptures[3] as of old ancient authors, to approve the same.

John vi.
[Ed. 1551.]

First, when our Saviour Christ, in the sixth of John, said, that he was the bread of life, which whosoever did eat, should not die, but live for ever; and that the bread which he would give us, was his flesh; and therefore whosoever should eat his flesh, and drink his blood, should have everlasting

---

[1 With all the rablement, 1551.]
[2 Ed. 1551, and also the Orig. ed., omit these words, "to call bread his body, and wine his blood."]
[3 As well of scripture, 1551, and Orig. ed.]

life; and they that should not eat his flesh, and drink his blood, should not have everlasting life: when Christ had spoken these words, with many more, of the eating of his flesh, and drinking of his blood, both the Jews, and many also of his disciples, were offended with his words, and said: "This is an hard saying. For how can he give us his flesh to be eaten?" Christ, perceiving their murmuring hearts, (because they knew none other eating of his flesh, but by chawing and swallowing,) to declare that they should not eat his body after that sort, nor that he meant of any such carnal eating, he said thus unto them: "What if you see the Son of man ascend up where he was before? It is the spirit that giveth life, the flesh availeth nothing: the words which I spake unto you be spirit and life."

These words our Saviour Christ spake, to lift up their minds from earth to heaven, and from carnal to spiritual eating, that they should not phantasy that they should with their teeth eat him present here in earth: for his flesh so eaten, saith he, should nothing profit them. And yet so they should not eat him, for he would take his body away from them, and ascend with it into heaven; and there by faith, and not with teeth, they should spiritually eat him, sitting at the right hand of his Father. And therefore, saith he, "The words which I do speak be spirit and life:" that is to say, are not to be understand, that we shall eat Christ with our teeth, grossly and carnally, but that we shall spiritually and ghostly with our faith eat him, being carnally absent from us in heaven; and in such wise as Abraham and other holy fathers did eat him, many years before he was incarnated and born, as St Paul saith: "That all they did eat the same spiritual meat that we do, and drink[4] the same spiritual drink; that is to say, Christ." For they spiritually by their faith were fed and nourished with Christ's body and blood, and had eternal life by him, before he was born, as we have now, that come after his ascension. 1 Cor. x.

Thus have you heard the declaration of Christ himself, and of St Paul, that the eating and drinking of Christ's flesh and blood is not taken in the common signification, with mouth and teeth to eat and chaw a thing, being present, but by a lively faith in heart and mind to chaw and digest a thing, being absent, either ascended hence into heaven, or else not yet born upon earth.

WINCHESTER.

In the sixtieth leaf the author entreateth, whether it be a plain speech of Christ to say, "Eat and drink," speaking of his body and blood. I answer, the speech of itself is proper, commanding them present to eat and drink that is proposed for them: and yet it is not requisite that the nature of man should with like common effect work, in eating and drinking that heavenly meat and drink, as it doth in earthly and carnal meats. In this mystery man doth as Christ ordained, that is to say, receive with his mouth that is ordered to be received with his mouth, granting it nevertheless of that dignity and estimation, that Christ's words affirm: and whether he so doth or no, Christ's ordinance is as it is in the substance of itself alone, whereof no good man judgeth carnally or grossly, ne discusseth the unfaithful question "how," which he cannot conceive, but leaveth the deepness thereof, and doth as he is bidden. This mystery receiveth no man's thoughts. Christ's institution hath a property in it, which cannot be discussed by man's sensual reason. Christ's words be spirit and life, which this author wresteth with his own gloss, to exclude the truth of the eating of Christ's flesh in his supper. And yet for a shift, if a man would join issue with him, putteth to his speech the words "grossly" and "carnally," which words in such a rude understanding be terms meeter to express how dogs devour paunches, than to be inculked in speaking of this high mystery. Wherein

[Terms meet to express how dogs devour paunches. Orig. ed.]

[4 Drank, 1551, and Orig. ed.]

[An issue. Ed. 1551.]

I will make the issue with this author, that no catholic teaching is so framed[1] *with such terms, as though we should eat Christ's most precious body grossly, carnally, joining those words so together. For else "carnally" alone may have a good signification, as Hilary useth it: but contrariwise speaking in the catholic teaching of the manner of Christ's presence, they call it a spiritual manner of presence, and yet there is present by God's power the very true natural body and blood of Christ, whole God and man, without leaving his place in heaven: and in the holy supper men use their mouths and teeth, following Christ's commandment in the receiving of that holy sacrament, being in faith sufficiently instruct, that they cannot, ne do not tear, consume, or violate that most precious body and blood, but unworthily receiving it, are cause of their own judgment and condemnation.*

CANTERBURY.

The eating of Christ's body is not with teeth.

Eating and drinking with the mouth being so plain a matter, that young babes learn it, and know it before they can speak, yet the cuttle here with his black colours and dark speeches goeth about so to cover and hide the matter, that neither young nor old, learned nor unlearned, should understand what he meaneth. But for all his masking, who is so ignorant but he knoweth, that eating in the proper and usual signification is to bite and chaw in sunder with the teeth? And who knoweth not also, that Christ is not so eaten? Who can then be ignorant that here you speak a manifest untruth, when you say that Christ's body to be eaten is of itself a proper speech, and not figurative? Which is by and by confessed by yourself, when you say that we do not eat that heavenly meat as we do other carnal meats, which is by chawing and dividing with the mouth and teeth. And yet we receive with the mouth that is ordained to be received with the mouth, that is to say, the sacramental bread and wine, esteeming them nevertheless unto us, when we duly receive them, according unto Christ's words and ordinance.

But where you say, that of the substance of Christ's body no good man judgeth carnally, ne discusseth the unfaithful question "how": you charge yourself very sore in so saying, and seem to make demonstration upon yourself, of whom may be said,

*Luke xix.

Ex ore tuo te judico. For you both judge carnally in affirming a carnal presence, and a carnal eating; and also you discuss this question "how," when you say that Christ's body is in the sacrament really, substantially, corporally, carnally, sensibly, and naturally, as he was born of the virgin Mary, and suffered on the cross.

John vi.

And as concerning these words of Christ, "The words which I do speak be spirit and life;" I have not wrested them with mine own gloss, as you misreport, but I have cited for me the interpretation of the catholic doctors and holy fathers of the church, as I refer to the judgment of the reader.

But you teach such a carnal and gross eating and drinking of Christ's flesh and blood, as is "more meet to express how dogs devour paunches, than to set forth the high mystery" of Christ's holy supper. For you say that Christ's body is present really, substantially, corporally, and carnally, and so is eaten; and that we eat Christ's body as eating is taken in common speech: but in common speech it is taken for chawing and gnawing, as dogs do paunches: wherefore of your saying it followeth,

114.

that we do so eat Christ's body, as dogs eat paunches; which all christian ears abhor for to hear.

But why should I join with you here an issue in that matter which I never spake? For I never read, nor heard no man that said, saving you alone, that we do eat Christ grossly, or carnally, or as eating is taken in common speech without any figure; but all that ever I have heard or read say quite clean contrary. But you, who affirm that we eat Christ carnally, and as eating is taken in common speech, (which is carnally and grossly to chew with the teeth,) must needs consequently grant, that we eat him grossly and carnally, as dogs eat paunches. And this is a strange thing to hear, that where before you said, that Christ is present but after a spiritual manner, now you say that he is eaten carnally.

[¹ So formed, Orig. ed. Winch.]

And where you say, that in the holy supper men use their mouth and teeth, truth it is that they so do, but to chaw the sacrament, not the body of Christ. And if they do not tear that most precious body and blood, why say you then that they eat the body of Christ, as eating is taken in common speech? And wherefore doth that false papistical faith of pope Nicholas, (which you wrongfully call catholic,) teach that Christ's body is torn with the teeth of the faithful? *De Consecr. dist.* 2. *Ego*[2]. Nicholas the second. De Consecr. dist. 2. Ego.

Now follow the particular authorities which I have alleged for the interpretation of Christ's words, which if you had well considered, you would not have said, as you do, that I wrested Christ's words with mine own gloss. For[3] I begin with Origen, saying:

And Origen, declaring the said eating of Christ's flesh and drinking of his blood not to be understand as the words do sound, but figuratively, writeth thus upon these words of Christ: "Except you eat my flesh, and drink my blood, you shall not have life in you." "Consider," saith Origen[4], "that these things written in God's books are figures, and therefore examine and understand them as spiritual, and not as carnal men. For if you understand them as carnal men, they hurt you, and feed you not. For even in the gospels is there found letter that killeth. And not only in the old testament, but also in the new is there found letter that slayeth him, that doth not spiritually understand that which is spoken. For if thou follow the letter or words of this that Christ said, 'Except you eat my flesh, and drink my blood,' this letter killeth." Origen. in Levit. Ho. 7.
John vi.

Who can more plainly express in any words, that the eating and drinking of Christ's flesh and blood are not to be taken in common signification, as the words pretend and sound, than Origen doth in this place?

WINCHESTER.

Now I will touch shortly what may be said to the particular authorities brought in by this author. Origen is noted (among other writers of the church) to draw the text to allegories, who doth not thereby mean to destroy the truth of the letter, and therefore when he speaketh of a figure, saith not there is only a figure[5], *which exclusive "only" being away, (as it is not found by any author catholic taught that the speech of Christ of the eating of his flesh to be only a figure,) this author hath nothing avanced his purpose. As for spiritual understanding meaneth not any destruction of the letter where the same may stand with the rules of our faith*[6]. *All Christ's words be life and spirit, containing in the letter many times that is above our capacity, as specially in this place of the eating of his flesh, to discuss the particularities of "how;" and yet we must believe to be true that Christ saith, (although we cannot tell how:) for when we go about to discuss of God's mystery "how," then we fall from faith, and wax carnal men, and would have God's ways like ours.* Origenes.

115.

CANTERBURY.

Here may every man that readeth the words of Origen plainly see, that you seek in this weighty matter nothing but shifts and cavillations. For you have nothing answered

---

[2 Ego Berengarius.....anathematizo omnem hæresin,....quæ astruere conatur panem et vinum, quæ in altari ponuntur, post consecrationem solummodo sacramentum, et non verum corpus et sanguinem Domini nostri Jesu Christi esse, et non posse sensualiter, nisi in solo sacramento, manibus sacerdotum tractari vel frangi, aut fidelium dentibus atteri. Decret. Gratian. Pars III. De Consecr. Dist. 2. col. 2021. Antv. 1573.]

[3 First, 1551.]

[4 Agnoscite quia figuræ sunt, quæ in divinis voluminibus scripta sunt, et ideo tanquam spiritales et non tanquam carnales examinate et intelligite quæ dicuntur. Si enim quasi carnales ista suscipitis, lædunt vos, et non alunt. Est enim et in evangeliis litera quæ occidit: non solum in veteri Testamento occidens litera deprehenditur. Est et in novo Testamento litera, quæ occidat eum, qui non spiritaliter quæ dicuntur adverterit. Si enim secundum literam sequaris hoc ipsum quod dictum est, "Nisi manducaveritis carnem meam, et biberitis sanguinem meum," occidit hæc litera. Origen. in Levit. Hom. VII. Tom. II. p. 225. ed. Bened.]

[5 There is a only figure, 1551.]

[6 The rule of our faith, Orig. ed. Winch.]

directly to Origen, although he directly writeth against your doctrine. For you say that the eating of Christ's flesh is taken in the proper signification without a figure. Origen saith there is a figure. And Origen saith further, that it is only a figurative speech, although not adding this word "only," yet adding other words of the same effect. For he saith, that we may not understand the words as the letter soundeth: and saith further, that if we understand the words of Christ in this place as the letter soundeth, the letter killeth. Now who knoweth not, that to say these words, "not as the letter soundeth," and "the letter killeth," be as much to say, as only spiritually, and only otherwise than the letter soundeth? Wherefore you must spit upon your hands and take better hold, or else you cannot be able to pluck Origen so shortly from me. And I marvel that you be not ashamed thus to trifle with the ancient authors in so serious a matter, and such places, where the reader only looking upon the author's words may see your dealing.

The next is Chrysostom, whom I cite thus.

<small>Chrysostom in Johannem Hom. 46.</small>

And St John Chrysostom[1] affirmeth the same, saying, that "if any man understand the words of Christ carnally, he shall surely profit nothing thereby. For what mean these words, 'the flesh availeth nothing'? He meant not of flesh[2], (God forbid!) but he meant of them that fleshly and carnally understood those things that Christ spake. But what is carnal understanding? To understand the words simply as they be spoken, and nothing else. For we ought not so to understand the things which we see, but all mysteries must be considered with inward eyes, and that is spiritually to understand them."

In these words St John Chrysostom sheweth plainly that the words of Christ concerning the eating of his flesh and drinking of his blood, are not to be understand simply, as they be spoken, but spiritually and figuratively.

WINCHESTER.

<small>Chrysostom</small>

St Chrysostom declareth himself, how mysteries must be considered with inward eyes, which is a spiritual understanding, whereby the truth of the mystery is not (as it were by a figurative speech) impaired, but with an humility of understanding in a certain faith of the truth marvelled at. And here the author of this book[3] useth a sleight to join figuratively to spiritually, as though they were always all one, which is not so.

CANTERBURY.

As you have handled Origen before, even so do you handle Chrysostom. Wherefore I only refer the reader to look upon the words of Chrysostom recited in my book, who saith, that to understand the words of eating of Christ's flesh, simply as they be spoken, is a carnal understanding. And then can it be no proper speech, (as you say it is,) because it cannot be understand as the words be spoken, but must have another understanding spiritually.

Then followeth next St Augustine, of whom I write thus:

<small>Augustinus de doctrina Christ. lib. 3. 116.</small>

And yet most plainly of all other St Augustine doth declare this matter in his book *De doctrina Christiana*, in which book he instructeth christian people how they should understand those places of scripture which seem hard and obscure.

"Seldom," saith he, "is any difficulty in proper words, but either the circumstance of the place, or the conferring of divers translations, or else the original

---

[1 Ἐὰν γὰρ αὐτὸ σαρκικῶς τὶς ἐκλάβοι, οὐδὲν ἀπώνατο. τί οὖν, οὐκ ἔστι ἡ σὰρξ αὐτοῦ σάρξ; καὶ σφόδρα μὲν οὖν. καὶ πῶς εἶπεν, ἡ σὰρξ οὐκ ὠφελεῖ οὐδέν; οὐ περὶ τῆς ἑαυτοῦ σαρκὸς λέγων· μὴ γένοιτο· ἀλλὰ περὶ τῶν σαρκικῶς ἐκλαμβανόντων τὰ λεγόμενα. τί δέ ἐστι τὸ σαρκικῶς νοῆσαι; τὸ ἁπλῶς εἰς τὰ προκείμενα ὁρᾶν, καὶ μὴ πλέον τι φαντάζεσθαι. τοῦτο γάρ ἐστι σαρκικῶς. χρὴ δὲ μὴ οὕτω κρίνειν τοῖς ὁρωμένοις, ἀλλὰ πάντα τὰ μυστήρια τοῖς ἔνδον ὀφθαλμοῖς κατοπτεύειν. τοῦτο γάρ ἐστι πνευματικῶς.—Chrysost. in Joannem. Hom. xlvii. (al. 46.) Tom. VIII. p. 278. Ed. Bened.]

[2 Of his flesh, 1551, and Orig. ed.]

[3 Of the book, Orig. ed. Winch.]

tongue wherein it was written, will make the sense plain. But in words that be altered from their proper signification, there is great diligence and heed to be taken. And specially we must beware, that we take not literally any thing that is spoken figuratively: nor contrariwise, we must not take for a figure any thing that is spoken properly." "Therefore must be declared," saith St Augustine, "the manner how to discern a proper speech from a figurative. Wherein," saith he, "must be observed this rule, that if the thing which is spoken be to the furtherance of charity, then it is a proper speech, and no figure. So that if it be a commandment that forbiddeth any evil or wicked act, or commandeth any good or beneficial thing, then it is no figure. But if it command any ill or wicked thing, or forbiddeth[4] anything that is good and beneficial, then it is a figurative speech. Now, this saying of Christ, 'Except ye eat the flesh of the Son of man, and drink his blood, you shall have no life in you,' seemeth to command an heinous and wicked thing: therefore it is a figure, commanding us to be partakers of Christ's passion, keeping in our minds, to our great comfort and profit, that his flesh was crucified and wounded for us[5]." This is briefly the sentence of St Augustine in his book *De doctrina Christiana*.

And the like he writeth in his book *De catechisandis rudibus*[6], and in his book *Contra adversarium legis et prophetarum*[7], and in divers other places, which for tediousness I pass over. For if I should rehearse all the authorities of St Augustine and others, which make mention of this matter, it would weary the reader too much.

_{De catech. rudi. cap. 26. Contra adversar. legis et Prophet. lib. ii. cap. 9.}

Wherefore to all them that by any reasonable means will be satisfied, these things before rehearsed are sufficient to prove, that the eating of Christ's flesh and drinking of his blood is not to be understand simply and plainly (as the words do properly signify), that we do eat and drink him with our mouths: but it is a

---

[4 forbid, 1551, and Orig. ed.]

[5 Rarissime igitur et difficillime inveniri potest ambiguitas in propriis verbis, quantum ad libros divinarum scripturarum spectat, quam non aut circumstantia ipsa sermonis qua cognoscitur scriptorum intentio, aut interpretum collatio, aut præcedentis linguæ solvat inspectio. Sed verborum translatorum ambiguitates, de quibus deinceps loquendum est, non mediocrem curam industriamque desiderant. Nam in principio cavendum est, ne figuratam locutionem ad literam accipias.—Neque illud quod proprio verbo significatur, referat ad aliam significationem.—Augustin. de Doctrina Christiana, Lib. III. Cap. iv. v. Pars IV. Basil. ap Amerbach. 1506. Demonstrandus est igitur prius modus inveniendæ locutionis, proprianne an figurata sit. Ib. Cap. x. Servabitur ergo in locutionibus figuratis regula hujusmodi, ut tam diu versetur diligenti consideratione quod legitur, donec ad regnum charitatis interpretatio perducatur. Si autem hoc jam proprie sonat, nulla putetur figurata locutio. Si præceptiva locutio est, aut flagitium aut facinus vetans, aut utilitatem aut beneficentiam jubens; non est figurata: si autem flagitium aut facinus videtur jubere, aut utilitatem aut beneficentiam vetare, figurata est. 'Nisi manducaveritis,' inquit, 'carnem Filii hominis et sanguinem biberitis, non habebitis vitam in vobis:' facinus vel flagitium videtur jubere. Figura est ergo, præcipiens passioni Domini esse communicandum, et suaviter atque utiliter recondendum in memoria, quod pro nobis caro ejus crucifixa et vulnerata sit. Ib. Cap. xv. xvi.]

[6 De sacramento sane quod accepit, cum ei bene commendatum fuerit, signacula quidem rerum divinarum esse visibilia, sed res ipsas invisibiles in eis honorari: nec sic habendam esse illam speciem benedictione sanctificatam, quemadmodum habetur in usu quolibet. Dicendum etiam quid significet et sermo ille quem audivit, quid in illo condiat [condatur], cujus illa res similitudinem gerit. Deinde monendus est ex hâc occasione, ut si quid etiam in scripturis audiat quod carnaliter sonet, etiam si non intelligit, credat tamen spiritale aliquid significari, quod ad sanctos mores futuramque vitam pertineat. Hoc autem ita breviter discet, ut quicquid audierit ex libris canonicis, quod ad dilectionem æternitatis et veritatis et sanctitatis et ad dilectionem proximi referre non possit, figurate dictum vel gestum esse credat; atque ita conetur intelligere ut ad illam geminam referat dilectionem.—Augustin. de Catechizandis rudibus, Cap. xxvi. Pars IV.]

[7 Sicut mediatorem Dei et hominum, hominem Christum Jesum, carnem suam nobis manducandam bibendumque sanguinem dantem, fideli corde atque ore suscipimus: quamvis horribilius videatur humanam carnem manducare, quam perimere, et humanum sanguinem potare quam fundere: atque in omnibus sanctis scripturis, secundum sanæ fidei regulam figurate dictum vel factum si quid exponitur, de quibuslibet rebus et verbis quæ sacris paginis continentur, expositio illa ducatur, non aspernanter sed sapienter audiamus.—Augustin. contra adversarium legis et Prophetarum, Lib. II. Cap. ix. Pars VIII.]

figurative speech spiritually to be understand, that we must deeply print and fruitfully believe in our hearts, that his flesh was crucified and his blood shed for our redemption. And this our belief in him is to eat his flesh and drink his blood, although they be not present here with us, but be ascended into heaven: as our forefathers before Christ's time did likewise eat his flesh and drink his blood, which was so far from them, that he was not yet then born.

WINCHESTER.

Augustinus.

St Augustine, according to his rules of a figurative and proper speech, taketh this speech, "Except ye eat," &c., for a figurative speech; because it seemeth to command in the letter carnally understood an heinous and wicked thing to eat the flesh of a man, as man's carnal imagination conceiveth it: as appeared by the Capharnaites, who murmured at it. And therefore because only faithful men can by faith understand this mystery of the eating of Christ's flesh in the sacrament, in which we eat not the carnal flesh of a common man, as the letter soundeth, but the very spiritual flesh of Christ, God and man, as faith teacheth; it is in that respect well noted for a figurative speech, for that it hath such a sense in the letter as is hidden from the unfaithful: so as the same letter being to faithful men spirit and life (who in humility of faith understandeth the same), is to the faithful[1] a figure, as containing such a mystery as by the outward bark of the letter they understand not: upon which consideration it seemeth probable that the other fathers, also signifying a great secrecy in this mystery of the sacrament, wherein is a work of God ineffable, such as the ethnick ears could not abide, they termed it a figure, not thereby to diminish the truth of the mystery, as the proper and special name of a figure doth, but by the name of a figure reverently to cover so great a secrecy, apt only to be understanded of men believing: and therefore the said fathers, in some part of their works, in plain words express and declare the truth of the mystery, and the plain doctrine thereof according to the catholic faith, and in the other part pass it over with the name of a figure, which consideration in St Augustine's writings may be evidently gathered: for in some place no man more plainly openeth the substance of the sacrament than he doth, speaking expressly of the very body and blood of Christ contained in it; and yet therewith in other places noteth in those words a figure, not thereby to contrary his other plain sayings and doctrine, but meaning by the word "figure" to signify a secret deep mystery hidden from carnal understanding. For avoiding and expelling of which carnality he giveth this doctrine here of this text: "Except ye eat," &c., which, as I said before, in the bare literal sense implieth to carnal judgment other carnal circumstances to attain the same flesh to be eaten, which in that carnal sense cannot be but by wickedness. But what is this to the obeying of Christ's commandment in the institution of his supper, when he himself[2] delivereth his body and blood in these mysteries, and biddeth "eat and drink?" There can be no offence to do as Christ biddeth, and therefore St Augustine's rule

*Contrary.

pertaineth not to Christ's supper, wherein when Christ willeth us to use our mouth, we ought to dare do as he biddeth; for that is spiritual understanding, to do as is commanded without carnal thought or murmuring in our sensual device how it can be so. And St Augustine in the same place, speaking de communicando passionibus Christi, *declareth plainly he meaneth of the sacrament.*

CANTERBURY.

If thou takest not very good heed, reader, thou shalt not perceive where the cuttle becometh. He wrappeth himself so about in darkness, and he cometh not near the net by a mile, for fear he should be taken. But I will draw my net nearer to him that he shall not escape. I say that the words which Christ spake of the eating of his flesh and drinking of his blood were spoken by a figure, and he would avoid the matter by saying, that "those words have a spiritual mystery in them;" which is most true, and nothing contrary to my saying, but confirmeth the same. For the words of eating and drinking be figurative speeches, because they have a secret and hid spiritual mystery in them, and cannot be taken otherwise than in that spiritual mystery, which is a

---

[¹ Unfaithful, 1551. See p. 118, at the beginning.]   [² When himself delivereth, 1551.]

figure. And, moreover, you plainly here confess, that to eat Christ's flesh and to drink his blood be figurative speeches. But you traverse the cause, wherefore they be figurative speeches; which is not material in this place, where my process is only to prove that they be figurative speeches. And forasmuch as you grant here all that I take upon me to prove, which is that they be figurative speeches, what needeth all this superfluous multiplication of words, when we agree in the matter which is here in question?

And as for the cause of the figure, you declare it far otherwise than St Augustine doth, as the words of St Augustine do plainly shew to every indifferent reader. For the cause, say you, is this, that "in the sacrament we eat not the carnal flesh of a common man, as the letter soundeth, but the very spiritual flesh of Christ, God and man, and in that respect it is well noted for a figurative speech."

In which one sentence be three notable errors or untruths. The first is, that you say "the letter soundeth that we eat the carnal flesh of a common man;" which your saying the plain words of the gospel do manifestly reprove. For Christ, separating himself in that speech from all other men, spake only of himself, saying, "My flesh is very meat, and my blood is very drink: he that eateth my flesh and drinketh my blood, dwelleth in me and I in him." The second is, that you call the flesh of Christ a "spiritual flesh," as before you said that he is spiritually eaten. And so by your doctrine his flesh is spiritual, and is spiritually eaten, and all is spiritual: which hath need of a favourable interpretation, if it should be counted a sound and catholic teaching. And if all be spiritual and done spiritually, what meaneth it then that in other places you make so often mention that he is present and eaten carnally, corporally, and naturally? [John vi.]

The third is, that you say "the speech of Christ is noted figurative in respect of the eating of the flesh of a common man," which is utterly untrue. For the authors note not the figurative speech in that respect; but as Christ spake of his own flesh joined unto his divinity, whereby it giveth life, even so do the authors note a figurative speech in respect of Christ's own flesh, and say thereof that the letter cannot be true without a figure. For although Christ be both God and man, yet his flesh is a very man's flesh, and his blood is truly man's blood, (as is the flesh and blood of his blessed mother,) and therefore cannot be eaten and drunken properly, but by a figure. For he is not meat and drink of the body, to be eaten corporally with mouth and teeth, and to be digested in the stomach: but he is the meat of the soul, to be received spiritually in our hearts and minds, and to be chawed and digested by faith.

And it is untrue that you here say, that "the proper and special name of a figure diminisheth the truth of the mystery." For then Christ in vain did ordain the figures, if they diminish the mysteries.

And the authors term it here a figure, not thereby to "cover the mystery," but to open the mystery, which was indeed in Christ's words by figurative speeches understand. And with the figurative speech were the ethnick and carnal ears offended, not with the mystery, which they understood not. And not to the ethnick and carnal, but to the faithful and spiritual ears, the words of Christ be figurative, and to them the truth of the figures be plainly opened and declared by the fathers: wherein the fathers be worthy much commendation, because they travailed to open plainly unto us the obscure and figurative speeches of Christ. And yet in their said declarations they taught us, that these words of Christ, concerning the eating of his flesh and drinking of his blood, are not to be understanded plainly, as the words properly signify, but by a figurative speech.

Nor St Augustine never wrote in all his long works, as you do, that Christ is in the sacrament corporally, carnally, or naturally, or that he is so eaten, nor, I dare boldly say, he never thought it. For if he had, he would not have written so plainly, as he doth in the places by me alleged, that we must "beware that we take not literally any thing that is spoken figuratively." And specially he would not have expressed by name the words of "eating Christ's flesh and drinking his blood," and have said that they be figurative speeches. But St Augustine doth not only tell how we may not take those words, but also he declareth how we ought to take and understand the eating of Christ's flesh and drinking of his blood, which, as he saith, is this: "To keep in our minds, to our great comfort and profit, that Christ was crucified and shed his blood for us, and so to be partakers of his passion. This," saith St Augustine, "is to eat his flesh and to drink his blood."

And St Augustine saith not as you do, that Christ's words be "figurative to the unfaithful;" for they be figurative rather to the faithful than to the unfaithful. For the unfaithful take them for no figure or mystery at all, but rather carnally, as the Capernaites did. And there is indeed no mystery nor figure in eating with the mouth (as you say Christ's flesh is eaten), but in eating with the soul and spirit is the figure and mystery. For the eating and drinking with the mouth is all one to the faithful and unfaithful, to the carnal and spiritual, and both understand in like what is eating and drinking with the mouth. And therefore in no place do the doctors declare, that there is a figure or mystery in eating and drinking of Christ's body with our mouths, or that there is any truth in that mystery; but they say clean contrary, that he is not eaten and drunken with our mouths. And if in any place any old author write, that there is a figure or mystery in eating and drinking of Christ with our mouths, shew the place if you will have any credit. St Augustine specially (whom you do here allege for your purpose) saith directly against you: *Nolite parare fauces sed cor*, "Prepare not your mouth or jaws, but your heart." And in another place he saith, *Quid paras ventrem et dentem? Crede et manducasti:* "Why dost thou prepare thy belly and teeth? Believe, and thou hast eaten."

August. de verbis Domini. Serm. 33. In Io. Tract. 25.

But to avoid the saying of St Augustine by me alleged, you say that St Augustine's rule pertaineth not to Christ's supper: which your saying is so strange, that you be the first that ever excluded the words of Christ from his supper. And St Augustine meant as well at the supper as at all other times, that the eating of Christ's flesh is not to be understanded carnally with our teeth (as the letter signifieth), but spiritually with our minds, as he in the same place declareth. And how can it be that St Augustine's rule pertaineth not to Christ's supper, when by the rule[1] he expoundeth Christ's words in the sixth of John, which you say Christ spake of his supper? Did Christ speak of his supper, and St Augustine's words expounding the same pertain not to the supper? You make St Augustine an expositor like yourself, that commonly use to expound both doctors and scriptures clean from the purpose, either for that by lack of exercise in the scriptures and doctors you understand them not, or else that for very frowardness you will not understand[2] any thing that misliketh you. And where you say that we must do as Christ commanded us, without carnal thought or sensual device, is not this a carnal thought and sensual device which you teach, that we eat Christ corporally with our teeth; and contrary to that which you said before, that Christ's body in the sacrament is a spiritual body, and eaten only spiritually? Now how the teeth can eat a thing spiritually, I pray you tell me.

Now thou seest, good reader, what avail all those glosses of "carnal flesh and spiritual flesh," of "the flesh of Christ, and the flesh of a common man," of "a figure to the unfaithful, and not to the faithful," that "the fathers termed it a figure, because else the
120. ethnick ears could not abide it," and "because they would reverently cover the mystery." And when none of these shifts will serve, he runneth to his sheet-anchor, that St Augustine's rule pertaineth nothing to Christ's supper. Thus mayest thou see, with what sincerity he handleth the old writers. And yet he might right well have spared all his long talk in this matter, seeing that he agreeth fully with me in the state of the whole cause, that to eat Christ's flesh and to drink his blood be figurative speeches. For he that declareth the cause why they be figurative speeches agreeth in the matter that they be figurative speeches. And so have I my full purpose in this article.

Now hear what followeth in my book.

Chap. XI. This is my body, this is my blood, be figurative speeches.

The same authors did say also, that when Christ called the bread his body, and the wine his blood, it was no proper speech that he then used; but as all sacraments be figures of other things, and ye have the very names

---

[1 By that rule, 1551.] [2 You will understand, 1551.]

of the things which they do signify; so Christ instituting the sacrament of his most precious body and blood, did use figurative speeches, calling the bread by the name of his body, and the wine he called his blood, because it represented his blood.

The bread representeth Christ's body and the wine his blood.

Tertullian herein writing against Marcion[3], saith these words: "Christ did not reprove bread, whereby he did represent his very body." And in the same book he saith, that Jesus "taking bread and distributing it amongst his disciples made it his body, saying, 'This is my body;' that is to say," saith Tertullian, "a figure of my body." And therefore, saith Tertullian, "that Christ called bread his body, and wine his blood," because that in the old testament bread and wine were figures of his body and blood.

Tertullianus contra Marcionem. Lib. 1.

WINCHESTER.

Tertullian speaking of the representation of Christ's very body, in which place he termeth "the same body," speaketh catholicly in such phrase as St Jerome speaketh: and then Tertullian saith afterward, as this author therein truly bringeth him forth, that Christ made the bread his body, which bread was in the mouth of the prophet a figure of his body. Wherefore it followeth by Tertullian's confession, when Christ made the bread his body, that Christ ended the figure, and made it the truth, making now his body that was before the figure of his body. For if Christ did no more but make it a figure still, then did he not make it his body, as Tertullian himself saith he did. And Tertullian therefore, being read thus, as appeareth to me most probable, that "that is to say" in Tertullian should be only referred to the explication of the first "this;" as when Tertullian had alleged Christ's words, saying "this is my body," and putteth to of his own, "that is to say, the figure of my body," these words, "that is to say," should serve to declare the demonstration "this" in this wise, "that is to say, this," which the prophet called the figure of the body, is now my body. And so Tertullian said before that Christ had made bread his body, which bread was a figure of his body with the prophet, and now endeth in the very truth, being made his body by conversion (as Cyprian sheweth) of the nature of bread into his body. Tertullian reasoned against the Marcionists; and because a figure in the prophet signifieth a certain unfeigned truth of that is signified, seeing Christ's body was figured by bread in the prophet Jeremy, it appeareth Christ had a true body; and that the bread was of Christ approved for a figure, he made now his very body[4]. And this may be said evidently to Tertullian, who reasoning against heretics useth the commodity of arguing, and giveth no doctrine of the sacrament to further this author's purpose. And what advantage should the heretics have of Tertullian, if he should mean that these words, "This is my body," had only this sense, 'this is the figure of my body,' having himself said before that Christ made bread his body? If so plain speech, to make bread his body, containeth no more certainty in understanding but the figure of a body, why should not they say, that a body in Christ should ever be spoken of a body in a figure, and so no certainty of any true body in Christ by Tertullian's words? This place of Tertullian is no secret point of learning, and hath been of Œcolampadius and other alleged, and by other catholic men answered unto it; whereof this author may not think now as upon a wrangling argument to satisfy a conjecture devised, thereby to confirm a new teaching. Finally, Tertullian termeth it not an only figure, which this author must prove, or else he doth nothing.

Tertullianus. * The author had left out "the same."

121.

[³ Sed ille quidem usque nunc nec aquam reprobavit.—nec panem, quo ipsum corpus suum repræsentat. Tertullianus, Adversus Marcionem. Lib. i. p. 372. Acceptum panem et distributum discipulis, corpus illum suum fecit, 'Hoc est corpus meum' dicendo, id est, figura corporis mei. Figura autem non fuisset, nisi veritatis esset corpus. Ceterum vacua res, quod est phantasma, figuram capere non posset. Aut si propterea panem corpus sibi finxit, quia corporis carebat veritate: ergo panem debuit tradere pro nobis. Faciebat ad unitatem Marcionis, ut panis crucifigeretur. Cur autem panem corpus suum appellat, et non magis peponem, quem Marcion cordis loco habuit? Non intelligens veterem fuisse istam figuram corporis Christi, dicentis per Hieremiam, "adversus me cogitaverunt cogitatum dicentes, Venite, conjiciamus lignum in panem ejus;" scilicet crucem in corpus ejus. Itaque illuminator antiquitatum quid tunc voluerit significasse panem satis declaravit, corpus suum vocans panem. Ibid. Lib. iv. pp. 457, 8. Paris. 1664.]

[⁴ he made it now his very body, 1551.]

CANTERBURY.

Tertullian saith not "an only figure." Oh what a wrangling and wresting is here made! what crooks be cast! what leaping about is here, to avoid a foil! And yet I refer to any indifferent man that shall read the place of Tertullian, to judge whether you have truly expounded him, or in the wrestling with him be quite overthrown, and have a flat fall upon your back. For Tertullian saith not, that the bread was a figure of Christ's body only in the prophet, as you expound Tertullian, but saith, "that bread and wine were figures in the old testament, and so taken in the prophets, and now be figures again in the new testament, and so used of Christ himself in his last supper."

And where Tertullian saith, that Christ made bread his body, he expoundeth himself how Christ made bread his body, adding by and by these words, "that is to say, a figure of his body." But if thou canst forbear, good reader, (when thou readest the fond handling of Tertullian by this ignorant and subtle lawyer,) I pray thee laugh not; for it is no matter to be laughed at, but to be sorrowed, that the most ancient authors of Christ's church should thus be eluded in so weighty causes. O Lord, what shall these men answer to thee at the last day, when no cavillations shall have place?

These be Tertullian's words: "Jesus taking bread, and distributing it among his disciples, made it his body, saying, 'This is my body,' that is to say, a figure of my body." Here Tertullian expoundeth not the saying of the prophet, but the saying of Christ, "This is my body." And where Tertullian hath but once the word "this," you say "the first this." And so you make a wise speech to say "the first," where is but one. And Tertullian speaketh of "this" in Christ's words, when he said, "This is my body;" and you refer them to the prophet's words, which be not there, but be spoken of long after. And if you had not forgotten your grammar and all kind of speech, or else hurled away all together purposely to serve your own wilful device, you would have referred the demonstration[1] of his antecedent before, and not to a thing that in order cometh long after. And "bread" in the prophet was but a figurative speech, but in Christ's words was not only a figurative speech, but also a figurative thing; that is to say, very material bread, which by a figurative speech Christ ordained to be a figure and a sacrament of his body. For as the prophet by this word "bread" figured Christ's body, so did Christ himself institute very material bread to be a figure of his body in the sacrament. But you refer "this" to the bread in the prophet, which Christ spake, as Tertullian saith, of the bread in the gospel. And Christ's words must needs be understood of the bread which he gave to his apostles, in the time of the gospel, after he had ended the supper of the law. And if Christ made the bread in the prophet his very body, which was no material bread, but this word "bread," then did Christ make this word bread his body, and converted this word bread into the substance of his body. This is the conclusion of your subtle sophistication of Tertullian's words.

Now, as concerning St Cyprian, whom you here allege, he spake of a sacramental, and not of a corporal and carnal conversion, as shall be plainly declared, when I come to the place of Cyprian, and partly I have declared already in mine other book.

And Tertullian proved not in that place the verity of Christ's body by the figure of the prophet, but by the figure which Christ ordained of his body in his last supper. For he went not about to prove that Christ should have a body, but that he had then a true body, because he ordained a figure thereof, which could have had no figure, as Tertullian saith, if it had been but a fantastical body, and no true body in deed.

Wherefore this which you say, in answering to the plain words of Tertullian, may be said of them that care not what they say; but it cannot be "said evidently," that is spoken so sophistically.

But "if so plain speech" of Tertullian, say you, that Christ "made bread his body, contain no more certainty in understanding but the figure of a body, why should not the body of Christ ever be taken for a figure, and so no certainty of any true body to

---

[1 The demonstrative, 1551.]

be in Christ?" This reason had been more fit to be made by a man that had lost both his wit and reason. For in this place Tertullian must needs be so understand, that by the body of Christ is understand the figure of his body, because Tertullian so expoundeth it himself. And must it be always so, because it is here so? Must ever Christ's body be taken for a figure, because it is here taken for a figure, as Tertullian saith? Have you so forgotten your logic, that you will make a good argument, *a particulari ad universale?* By your own manner of argumentation, because you make a naughty argument here in this place, shall I conclude that you never make none good? Surely this place of Tertullian, as you have handled it, is neither secret nor manifest point either of learning, wit, or reason, but a mere sophistication, if it be no worse.

What other papists have answered to this place of Tertullian, I am not ignorant, nor I am sure you be not so ignorant but you know that never none answered as you do. But your answer varieth as much from all other papists', as yours and theirs also do vary from the truth.

Here the reader may note by the way, how many foul shifts you make to avoid the saying of Tertullian. First you say, that "bread was a figure in the prophet's mouth, but not in Christ's words." Second, that the thing which the prophet spake of was not that which Christ spake of. Third, that other have answered this place of Tertullian before. Fourth, that you call this matter but "a wrangling argument." Fifth, that if Tertullian call bread a figure, yet he "termeth it not only figure[2]." These be your shifts. Now let the reader look upon Tertullian's plain words, which I have rehearsed in my book, and then let him judge whether you mean to declare Tertullian's mind truly, or no.

And it is not requisite for my purpose to prove that bread is only a figure, for I take upon me there to prove no more but that the bread is a figure representing Christ's body, and the wine his blood. And if bread be a figure, and not only a figure, then must you make bread both the figure and the truth of the figure.

Now hear what other authors I do here allege.

And St Cyprian the holy martyr saith of this matter, that "Christ's blood is shewed in the wine, and the people in the water that is mixed with the wine; so that the mixture of the water to the wine signifieth the spiritual commixtion and joining of us unto Christ[3]." Cyprianus, Lib. ii. Epist. 3.

By which similitude Cyprian meant not that the blood of Christ is wine, or the people water, but as the water doth signify and represent the people, so doth the wine signify and represent Christ's blood; and the uniting of the water and wine together signifieth the uniting of Christian people unto Christ himself.

And the same St Cyprian in another place, writing hereof, saith, that "Christ in his last supper gave to his apostles with his own hands bread and wine, which he called his flesh and blood; but in the cross he gave his very body to be wounded with the hands of the soldiers, that the apostles might declare to the world, how and in what manner bread and wine may be the flesh and blood of Christ." And the manner he straightways declareth thus, that "those things which do signify, and those things which be signified by them, may be both called by one name[4]." De unctione Chrismatis.

[2 He termeth it not an only figure, 1551.]

[3 Videmus in aqua populum intelligi, in vino vero ostendi sanguinem Christi. Quando autem in calice vino aqua miscetur, Christo populus adunatur, et credentium plebs ei, in quem credidit, copulatur et conjungitur.—Cyprian. Epist. lxiii. Cæcilio fratri. (Lib. ii. Epist. iii.) p. 146. Par. 1574.]

[4 Dedit itaque Dominus noster in mensa, in qua ultimum cum Apostolis participavit convivium, propriis manibus panem et vinum : in cruce vero manibus militum corpus tradidit vulnerandum; ut in Apostolis secretius impressa sincera veritas, et vera sinceritas, exponeret gentibus, quomodo vinum et panis caro esset et sanguis, et quibus rationibus causæ effectibus convenirent, et diversa nomina vel species ad unam reducerentur essentiam, et significantia et significata eisdem vocabulis censerentur. Cyprian. De unctione Chrismatis, p. 477. This

Here it is certain, by St Cyprian's mind, wherefore and in what wise bread is called Christ's flesh, and wine his blood; that is to say, because that every thing that representeth and signifieth another thing, may be called by the name of the thing which it signifieth.

Chrys. in Ps. xxii.

And therefore St John Chrysostom saith, that "Christ ordained the table of his holy supper for this purpose, that in that sacrament he should daily shew unto us bread and wine for a similitude of his body and blood[1]."

Jero. in Matt. xxvi.

St Jerome likewise saith upon the gospel of Matthew, that "Christ took bread, which comforteth man's heart, that he might represent thereby his very body and blood[2]."

Ambros. de his qui mysteriis initiantur, cap. ult.

Also St Ambrose, if the book be his that is entitled *De his qui mysteriis initiantur*, saith, that "before the consecration another kind is named, but after the consecration the body of Christ is signified. Christ said his blood: before the consecration it is called another thing, but after the consecration is signified the blood of Christ[3]."

De Sacramentis, Lib. vi. cap. 1.

And in his book *De Sacramentis*, if that be also his, he writeth thus: "Thou dost receive the sacrament for a similitude of the flesh and blood of Christ, but thou dost obtain the grace and virtue of his true nature[4]." "And receiving the bread, in that food thou art partaker of his godly substance."

Lib. iv. cap. 4.

And in the same book he saith: "As thou hast in baptism received the similitude of death, so likewise dost thou in the sacrament drink the similitude of Christ's precious blood[5]." And again he saith in the said book:

Lib. iv. cap. 5. [Ut nullus horror cruoris sit: et pretium tamen operetur redemptionis. Emb. Ed. 1557.] 1 Cor. xi.

"The priest saith, 'Make unto us this oblation to be acceptable,' which is the figure of the body and blood of our Lord Jesu Christ[6]."

And upon the epistle of St Paul to the Corinthians he saith, "that in eating and drinking the bread and wine, we do signify the flesh and blood, which were offered for us. And the old testament," he saith, "was instituted in blood, because that blood was a witness of God's benefit; in signification and figure whereof we take the mystical cup of his blood, to the tuition of our body and soul[7]."

124.

Of these places of St Chrysostom, St Jerome, and St Ambrose, it is clear, that in the sacramental bread and wine is not really and corporally the very

---

Treatise is spurious.—Vid. James' Corruptions of Scripture, &c. p. 19. Lond. 1843.]

[1 The passage is not in the Greek of Chrysostom. It stands as follows in the Homily, "incerto auctore," printed in the Latin edition of Chrysostom, Paris. 1570. Tom. I. col. 720. Et quia istam mensam præparavit servis et ancillis in conspectu eorum, ut quotidie in similitudinem corporis et sanguinis Christi panem et vinum secundum ordinem Melchisedech nobis ostenderet in sacramento, ita dicit, *Parasti in conspectu meo mensam adversus eos qui tribulant me*.]

[2 *Cœnantibus autem eis, accepit Jesus panem, &c.* Postquam typicum pascha fuerat impletum, et agni carnes cum apostolis comederat, assumit panem, qui confortat cor hominis, et ad verum paschæ transgreditur sacramentum; ut quomodo in præfiguratione ejus Melchisedec, summi Dei sacerdos, panem et vinum offerens fecerat, ipse quoque veritatem sui corporis et sanguinis repræsentaret.—Hieronymus, Commentarii in Matt. Lib. iv. cap. 26. Tom. IX. p. 64. Francof. 1684.]

[3 *Ipse clamat Dominus Jesus; Hoc est corpus meum.* Ante benedictionem verborum cœlestium species nominatur, post consecrationem corpus Christi significatur. Ipse dicit sanguinem suum. Ante consecrationem aliud dicitur, post consecrationem sanguis nuncupatur. Ambros. de Initiandis. Tom. IV. p. 166. Ed. Colon. Agrip. 1616.]

[4 Ideo in similitudine quidem accipis sacramentum, sed vere naturæ gratiam virtutemque consequeris: tu, qui accipis carnem, divinæ ejus substantiæ in illo participaris alimento. De Sacram. Lib. vi. cap. i. Tom. IV. p. 176.]

[5 Sicut enim mortis similitudinem sumpsisti, ita etiam similitudinem pretiosi sanguinis bibis.—Lib. iv. cap. iv. Tom. IV. p. 173.]

[6 Dicit sacerdos: Fac nobis, inquit, hanc oblationem adscriptam, rationabilem, acceptabilem: quod sit in figuram corporis et sanguinis Domini nostri Jesu Christi.—Ib. Lib. iv. cap. v. Tom. IV. p. 173.]

[7 Quia enim morte Domini liberati sumus, hujus rei memores, in edendo et potando carnem et sanguinem, quæ pro nobis oblata sunt, significamus.—Testamentum ergo sanguine constitutum est, quia beneficii divini sanguis testis est. In cujus typum nos calicem mysticum sanguinis ad tuitionem corporis et animæ nostræ percipimus.—Id. in 1 Corinth. xi. Tom. III. p. 184. But these commentaries are considered to be spurious.]

natural substance of the flesh and blood of Christ, but that the bread and wine be similitudes, mysteries and representations, significations, sacraments, figures, and signs of his body and blood: and therefore be called, and have the name of his very body[8], flesh, and blood.

Signs and figures have the names of the things which they signify.

WINCHESTER.

Cyprian shall be touched after, when we speak of him again.

Cyprianus.

Chrysostom shall open himself hereafter plainly.

Chrysostom.

St Jerome speaketh here very pithily, using the word "represent," which signifieth a true real exhibition: for St Jerome speaketh of the representation of the truth of Christ's body, which truth excludeth an only figure. For howsoever the visible matter of the sacrament be a figure, the invisible part is a truth: which St Jerome saith is here represented, that is to say, made present, which only signification doth not.

Hieronym.

St Ambrose shall after declare himself: and it is not denied, but the authors in speaking of the sacrament used these words, "sign," "figure," "similitude," "token;" but those speeches exclude not the verity and truth of the body and blood of Christ, for no approved author hath this exclusion[9], to say an only sign, an only token, an only similitude, or an only signification, which is the issue with this author.

Ambrosius.

*No author saith an only figure.

CANTERBURY.

Here you shift off St Cyprian and Chrysostom with fair promise to make answer to them hereafter, who approve plainly my saying, that the bread representeth Christ's body, and the wine his blood; and so you answer here only to St Jerome. In answering to whom you were loth, I see well, to leave behind any thing that might have any colour to make for you, that expound this word "represent" in St Jerome to signify real exhibition. Here appeareth that ye can, when you list, change the signification of words, that can make *vocare* to signify *facere*, and *facere* to signify *sacrificare*, as you do in your last book. And why should you not then in other words (when it will serve for like purposes) have the like liberty to change the signification of words when you list? And if this word "represent" in St Jerome's words signify real exhibition, then did Melchisedech really exhibit Christ's flesh and blood, who, as the same St Jerome saith, did represent his flesh and blood by offering bread and wine.

Hieronymus.

Represent.

And yet in the Lord's supper, rightly used, is Christ's body exhibited indeed spiritually, and so really, if you take really to signify only a spiritual and not a corporal and carnal exhibition. But this real and spiritual exhibition is to the receivers of the sacrament, and not to the bread and wine.

Really.

And mine issue in this place is no more, but to prove that these sayings of Christ, "This is my body, this is my blood," be figurative speeches, signifying that the bread representeth Christ's body, and the wine his blood; which forasmuch as you confess, there needed no great contention in this point, but that you would seem in words to vary, where we agree in the substance of the matter, and so take occasion to make a long book, where a short would have served.

And as for the exclusion[10] "only," many of the authors, as I proved before, have the same exclusive, or other words equivalent thereto. And as for the sacramental signs, they be only figures. And of the presence of Christ's body yourself hath this exclusive, that Christ is but after a spiritual manner present, and I say he is but spiritually present.

125.

Now followeth St Augustine.

And yet St Augustine sheweth this matter more clearly and fully than any of the rest, specially in an epistle which he wrote *ad Bonifacium*, where he

Augustinus ad Bonifacium. Epist. 23.

[8 The Original ed., and that of 1551, omit the word "body" in this sentence.]

[9 This exclusive, 1551.]

[10 The exclusive, 1551.]

saith: "That a day or two before Good Friday, we use in common speech to say thus, 'To-morrow, or this day two days, Christ suffered his passion;' where in very deed he never suffered his passion but once, and that was many years past. Likewise upon Easter-day we say, 'This day Christ rose from death;' where in very deed it is many hundred years sithens he rose from death. Why then do not men reprove us as liars, when we speak in this sort, but because we call these days so, by a similitude of those days wherein these things were done in deed? And so it is called that day, which is not that day in deed, but by the course of the year it is a like day. And such things be said to be done that day for the solemn celebration of the sacrament, which things in deed were not done that day, but long before. Was Christ offered any more but once? And he offered himself: and yet in a sacrament or representation, not only every solemn feast of Easter, but every day he is offered to the people; so that he doth not lie that saith, 'He is every day offered.' For if sacraments had not some similitude or likeness of those things whereof they be sacraments, they could in no wise be sacraments. And for their similitude and likeness, commonly they have the name of the things, whereof they be sacraments. Therefore, as after a certain manner of speech the sacrament of Christ's body is Christ's body, the sacrament of Christ's blood is Christ's blood; so likewise the sacrament of faith is faith. And to believe is nothing else but to have faith; and therefore when we answer for young children in their baptism, that they believe, which have not yet the mind to believe, we answer that they have faith, because they have the sacrament of faith. And we say also that they turn unto God, because of the sacrament of conversion unto God; for that answer pertaineth to the celebration of the sacrament. And likewise speaketh the apostle of baptism, saying, that 'by baptism we be buried with him into death:' he saith not that we signify burial, but he saith plainly, that we be buried. So that the sacrament of so great a thing is not called but by the name of the thing itself[1]."

Hitherto I have rehearsed the answer of St Augustine unto Boniface, a learned bishop, who asked of him, how the parents and friends could answer for a young babe in baptism, and say in his person that he believeth and converteth unto God, when the child can neither do nor think any such things.

Whereunto the answer of St Augustine is this: that forasmuch as baptism is the sacrament of the profession of our faith, and of our conversion unto

[1 Nempe sæpe ita loquimur, ut pascha propinquante dicamus, crastinam vel perendinam Domini passionem, cum ille ante tam multos annos passus sit, nec omnino nisi semel illa passio facta sit. Nempe ipso die Dominico dicimus, 'Hodie Dominus resurrexit,' cum ex quo resurrexit tot anni transierunt. Cur nemo tam ineptus est, ut nos ita loquentes arguat esse mentitos, nisi quia istos dies secundum illorum quibus hæc gesta sunt similitudinem nuncupamus, ut dicatur ipse dies qui non est ipse, sed revolutione temporis similis ejus; et dicatur illo die fieri, propter sacramenti celebrationem, quod non illo die, sed jam olim factum est? Nonne semel immolatus est Christus in se ipso? et tamen in sacramento non solum per omnes paschæ solemnitates, sed omni die populis immolatur, nec utique mentitur qui interrogatus eum responderit immolari. Si enim sacramenta quandam similitudinem earum rerum quarum sacramenta sunt non haberent, omnino sacramenta non essent. Ex hac autem similitudine plerumque etiam ipsarum rerum nomina accipiunt. Sicut ergo secundum quendam modum sacramentum corporis Christi corpus Christi est, sacramentum sanguinis Christi sanguis Christi est, ita sacramentum fidei fides est. Nihil est autem aliud credere quam fidem habere. Ac per hoc cum respondetur parvulus credere, qui fidei nondum habet affectum, respondetur fidem habere propter fidei sacramentum, et convertere se ad Deum propter conversionis sacramentum, quia et ipsa responsio ad celebrationem pertinet sacramenti. Sicut de ipso baptismo Apostolus, 'Consepulti,' inquit, 'sumus Christo per baptismum in mortem.' Non ait, sepulturam significavimus: sed prorsus ait, 'Consepulti sumus.' Sacramentum ergo tantæ rei non nisi ejusdem rei vocabulo nuncupavit. Augustin. ad Bonifacium de Bapt. parvul. Epist. xxiii. Tom. II. p. 36. Paris. 1637.]

God, it becometh us so to answer for young children coming thereunto, as to the² sacrament apperteineth, although the children in deed have no knowledge of such things.

And yet in our said answers we ought not to be reprehended as vain men or liars, forasmuch as in common speech we use daily to call sacraments and figures by the names of the things that be signified by them, although they be not the same thing indeed. As every Good Friday, as often as it returneth from year to year, we call it the day of Christ's passion: and every Easter-day we call the day of his resurrection: and every day in the year, we say that Christ is offered: and the sacrament of his body, we call it his body: and the sacrament of his blood, we call it his blood: and our baptism St Paul calleth our burial with Christ. And yet in very deed Christ never suffered but once, never arose but once, never was offered but once, nor in very deed in baptism we be not buried, nor the sacrament of Christ's body is not his body, nor the sacrament of his blood is not his blood. But so they be called, because they be figures, sacraments, and representations of the things themselves, which they signify, and whereof they bear the names. Thus doth St Augustine most plainly open this matter in his epistle to Bonifacius.

Of this manner of speech, (wherein a sign is called by the name of the thing which it signifieth,) speaketh St Augustine also right largely in his questions *super Leviticum, et contra Adamantium*, declaring how blood in scripture is called the soul. "A thing which signifieth," saith he, "is wont to be called by the name of the thing which it signifieth, as it is written in the scripture: 'The seven ears be seven years.' The scripture saith not, 'signifieth seven years.' 'And seven kine be seven years,' and many other like. And so said St Paul, 'that the stone was Christ,' and not that it signified Christ, but even as it had been he indeed, which nevertheless was not Christ by substance, but by signification. Even so," saith St Augustine, "because the blood signifieth and representeth the soul, therefore in a sacrament or signification it is called the soul³." And *contra Adamantium* he writeth much like, saying: "In such wise is blood the soul, as the stone was Christ; and yet the apostle saith not that the stone signified Christ, but saith it was Christ. And this sentence, 'blood is the soul,' may be understand to be spoken in a sign or figure; for Christ did not stick to say, 'This is my body,' when he gave the sign of his body⁴."

Here St Augustine, rehearsing divers sentences, which were spoken figuratively, that is to say, when one thing was called by the name of another, and yet was not the other in substance, but in signification, as "the blood is the soul;" "seven kine be seven years;" "seven ears be seven years;" "the stone was Christ;" among such manner of speeches, he rehearseth those

---

[² That, Orig. ed. and 1551.]

[³ Solet autem res quæ significat, ejus rei nomine quam significat nuncupari, sicut scriptum est, 'Septem spicæ septem anni sunt.' Non enim dixit, septem annos significant. 'Et septem boves septem anni sunt:' et multa hujusmodi. Hinc est quod dictum est: 'Petra erat Christus.' Non enim dixit, petra significat Christum, sed tanquam hoc esset, quod utique per substantiam non hoc erat, sed per significationem. Sic et sanguis, quoniam propter vitalem quandam corpulentiam animam significat, in sacramentis anima dictus est.—Augustin. super Levit. Lib. III. Quæst. lvii. Tom. IV. p. 95.]

[⁴ Sic est enim sanguis anima, quomodo petra erat Christus:—de quibus [loquebatur] Apostolus cum hæc diceret, nec tamen ait, 'petra significabat Christum,' sed ait, 'petra erat Christus.' Quæ rursus ne carnaliter acciperetur, spiritalem ille vocat: id est, eam spiritaliter intelligi docet.

Possum etiam interpretari præceptum illud in signo esse positum. Non enim Dominus dubitavit dicere, 'Hoc est corpus meum,' cum signum daret corporis sui.—Ibid. contra Adamantium, cap. 12. pars iii. Basil. ap. Amerbach. 1506.

The position of these quotations is reversed by Cranmer.]

<small>Matt. xxvi.</small> words which Christ spake at his last supper, "This is my body." Which declareth plainly St Augustine's mind, that Christ spake those words figuratively, not meaning that the bread was his body by substance, but by signification.

<small>Contra Maximinum, Lib. iii. cap. 22.</small> And therefore St Augustine saith, *contra Maximinum*, that "in the sacraments we must not consider what they be, but what they signify; for they be signs of things, being one thing and signifying another[1]." Which he <small>In Lib. Sententiarum Prosperi de Consecrat. Dist. 2. "Hoc est."</small> doth shew specially of this sacrament, saying: "The heavenly bread, which is Christ's flesh, by some manner of speech is called Christ's body, when in very deed it is the sacrament of his body. And that offering of the flesh, which is done by the priest's hands, is called Christ's passion, death, and crucifying, not in very deed, but in a mystical signification[2]."

WINCHESTER.

As for St Augustine ad Bonifacium, the author shall perceive his fault at Martin Bucer's hand, who in his epistle dedicatory of his enarrations of the gospels, rehearseth his mind of <small>Bucerus.</small> *St Augustine in this wise.* Est (scribit divus Augustinus) secundum quendam modum sacramentum corporis Christi corpus Christi; sacramentum sanguinis Christi sanguis Christi. At secundum quem modum? Ut significet tantum corpus et sanguinem Domini absentia? Absit: honorari enim et percipi in symbolis visibilibus corpus et sanguinem Domini, idem passim scribit. *These words of Bucer may be thus Englished: "St Augustine writeth: 'The sacrament of the body of Christ is after a certain manner the body of Christ, the sacrament of the blood of Christ, the blood of Christ.' But after what manner? that it should signify only the body and blood absent? Absit, in no wise; for the same St Augustine writeth in many places, the body and blood of Christ to be honoured, and to be received in those visible tokens." Thus saith Bucer, who understandeth not St Augustine to say the sacrament of Christ's body, to be Christ's body after a certain manner of speech, as this author doth: nor St Augustine hath no such words, but only,* secundum quendam modum, *after a certain manner, whereunto to put "of speech" is an addition more than truth required of necessity. In these words of Bucer may appear his whole judgment concerning St Augustine, who affirmeth the very true presence of the thing signified in the sacrament; which truth established in the matter, the calling it a sign, or a token, a figure, a similitude, or a shewing, maketh no matter when we understand the thing really present that is signified. Which and it were not indeed in the sacrament, why should it, after Bucer's true understanding of St Augustine, be honoured there? Arguing upon men's speeches may be without end; and the authors[3] upon diverse respects speak of one thing diversely.* <small>*Authors for doctrine should be read where they expound the matter without contention.</small> *Therefore we should resort to the pith and knot of the matter, and see what they say in expounding the special place, without contention, and not what they utter in the heat of their disputation, ne to search their dark and ambiguous places, wherewith to confound that they speak openly and plainly.*

CANTERBURY.

<small>M. Bucer.</small> What need you to bring Martin Bucer to make me answer, if you could answer yourself? But because you be ashamed of the matter, you would thrust Martin Bucer in your place, to receive rebuke[4] for you. But in this place he easeth you nothing at all; for he saith no more but that the body and blood of Christ be exhibited unto the worthy receivers of the sacrament, which is true, but yet spiritually, not corporally.

[1 Hæc enim sacramenta sunt, in quibus non quid sit, sed quid ostendant semper attenditur: quoniam signa sunt rerum, aliud existentia, aliud significantia.—Ibid. contra Maximinum, Lib. III. cap. 22. pars XI. Basil. ap. Amerbach. 1506.]

[2 Sicut ergo cœlestis panis, qui vere Christus caro est, suo modo vocatur corpus Christi, cum revera sit sacramentum corporis Christi, illius videlicet, quod visibile, palpabile, mortale in cruce est suspensum; vocaturque ipsa immolatio carnis, quæ sacerdotis manibus fit, Christi passio, mors, crucifixio, non rei veritate, sed significante mysterio. Corpus Juris Canonici. Gratiani Decreti. tert. pars. De consecrat. Dist. ii. "Hoc est." cap. xlviii. Tom. I. col. 1937. Lugd. 1618.—Cranmer quoted this passage from the Corpus Juris Canonici, and not from Augustine.]

[3 Thauctour, 1551.]

[4 To receive the rebuke for you, 1551.]

And I never said that Christ is utterly absent, but I ever affirmed that he is truly *The true presence of Christ.* and spiritually present, and truly and spiritually exhibited unto the godly receivers: but corporally is he neither in the receivers, nor in or under the forms of bread or wine, as you do teach clearly without the consent of master Bucer, who writeth no such thing.

And where I allege of St Augustine, that the sacrament of Christ's body is called Christ's body, after a certain manner of speech, and you deny that St Augustine meant of a certain manner of speech, but saith only after a certain manner: read the place of St Augustine who will, and he shall find that he speaketh of the manner of speech, and that of such a manner of speech, as calleth one thing by the name of another, where it is not the very thing in deed. For of the manner of speech is all the process there, as appeareth by these his words: "A day or two before Good Friday, we use in common speech to say, To-morrow, or this day two days, Christ suffered, &c. Likewise upon Easter-day we say, This day Christ rose. And why do no men reprove us as liars, when we speak in this sort? And we call those days so by a similitude, &c. And so it is called that day, which is not that day in deed. And sacraments commonly have the name of the things whereof they be sacraments. Therefore as after a certain manner the sacrament of Christ's body is Christ's body; so likewise the sacrament of faith is faith. And likewise saith St Paul, that in baptism we be buried, he saith not that we signify burial, but he saith plainly that we be buried: so that the sacrament of so great a thing is called by the name of the thing." 128. All these be St Augustine's words, shewing how in the common use of speech one thing may have the name of another. Wherefore when Doctor Gardiner saith that St Augustine spake not of the manner of speech, thou mayest believe him hereafter as thou shalt see cause, but if thou trust his words too much, thou shalt soon be deceived.

As for the real presence of Christ in the sacrament, I grant that he is really present after such sort as you expound really in this place, that is to say, in deed, and *Really.* yet but spiritually. For you say yourself, that he is but after a spiritual manner there, and so is he spiritually honoured, as St Augustine saith.

But as concerning heat of disputation, mark well the words of St Augustine, good reader, cited in my book, and thou shalt see clearly that all this multiplication of words is rather a juggling than a direct answer. For St Augustine writeth not in heat of disputation, but temperately and gravely, to a learned bishop, his dear friend, who demanded a question of him. And if St Augustine had answered in heat of disputation, or for any other respect otherwise than the truth, he had not done the part of a friend, nor of a learned and godly bishop. And whosoever judgeth so of St Augustine, hath small estimation of him, and sheweth himself to have little knowledge of St Augustine.

But in this your answer to St Augustine, you utter where you learned a good part of your divinity, that is, of Albertus Pighius, who is the father of this shift, and *Albertus Pighius.* with this sleight eludeth St Augustine when he could no[5] otherwise answer: as you do now shake off the same St Augustine, resembling as it were in that point the lively countenance of your father Pighius.

Next in my book followeth Theodoret.

And to this purpose it is both pleasant, comfortable, and profitable to read *Theodoretus in dialogis.* Theodoretus in his dialogues, where he disputeth and sheweth at length how the names of things be changed in scripture, and yet things remain still. And for example he proveth that the flesh of Christ is in the scripture sometime called a vail or covering, sometime a cloth, sometime a vestment, and sometime a stole: and the blood of the grape is called Christ's blood, and the names of bread and wine, and of his flesh and blood, Christ doth so change, that sometime he calleth his body corn or bread, and sometime

---

[5 none, 1551.]

contrary he calleth bread his body. And likewise his blood sometime he calleth wine, and sometime contrary he calleth wine his blood.

For the more plain understanding whereof it shall not be amiss to recite his own sayings in his foresaid dialogues, touching this matter of the holy sacrament of Christ's flesh and blood. The speakers in these dialogues be Orthodoxus, the right believer, and Eranistes, his companion, but not understanding the right faith.

In the first dialogue.

Orthodoxus saith to his companion: [1]Dost thou not know that God calleth bread his flesh? ERAN. I know that.

ORTH. And in another place he calleth his body corn.

John xii.

ERAN. I know that also, for I have heard him say: "The hour is come that the Son of man shall be glorified," &c. "Except the grain of corn that falleth in the ground die, it remaineth sole; but if it die, then it bringeth forth much fruit."

129.
Matt. xxvi.
Mark xiv.
Luke xxii.

ORTH. When he gave the mysteries or sacraments, he called bread his body, and that which was mixt in the cup he called his blood.

ERAN. So he called them.

ORTH. But that also which was his natural body may well be called his body, and his very blood also may be called his blood.

ERAN. It is plain.

ORTH. But our Saviour without doubt changed the names, and gave to the body the name of the sign or token, and to the token he gave the name of the body. And so when he called himself a vine, he called blood that which was the token of blood.

John xv.

ERAN. Surely thou hast spoken the truth. But I would know the cause wherefore the names were changed.

ORTH. The cause is manifest to them that be expert in true religion. For he would that they which be partakers of the godly sacraments, should not set their minds upon the nature of the things which they see, but by the changing of the names should believe the things which be wrought in them by grace. For he that called that, which is his natural body, corn and bread, and also called himself a vine, he did honour the visible tokens and signs with the names of his body and blood, not changing the nature, but adding grace to nature.

John xii.
Matt. xxvi.
John xv.

ERAN. Sacraments be spoken of sacramentally, and also by them be manifestly declared things which all men know not.

Gen. xlvi.

ORTH. Seeing then that it is certain that the patriarch called the Lord's body a vestment and apparel, and that now we be entered to speak of godly sacraments, tell me truly of what thing thinkest thou this holy meat to be a token and figure; of Christ's divinity, or of his body and blood?

ERAN. It is clear that it is the figure of those things whereof it beareth the name.

ORTH. Meanest thou of his body and blood?

ERAN. Even so I mean.

ORTH. Thou hast spoken as one that loveth the truth: for the Lord when he took the token or sign, he said not, This is my divinity; but "This is my body," and "This is my blood." And in another place: "The bread which I will give is my flesh, which I will give for the life of the world."

John vi.

[ORTH. Porro si sunt vera, corpus

ERAN. These things be true, for they be God's words.

[[1] Theodoretus, in Dialogo i. Tom. IV. pp. 25-27. Halæ. 1769-94.]

All these writeth Theodoretus in his first dialogue.

And in the second he writeth the same in effect, and yet in some thing[2] more plainly, against such heretics as affirmed, that after Christ's resurrection and ascension his humanity was changed from the very nature of man[3] and turned into his divinity. Against whom thus he writeth[4]:

ORTH. Corruption, health, sickness, and death, be accidents, for they go and come.

ERAN. It is meet they be so called.

ORTH. Men's bodies after their resurrection be delivered from corruption, death, and mortality, and yet they lose not their proper nature.

ERAN. Truth it is.

ORTH. The body of Christ therefore did rise quite clean from all corruption and death, and is impassible, immortal, glorified with the glory of God, and is honoured of the powers of heaven, and it is[5] a body, and hath the same bigness that it had[6] before.

ERAN. Thy saying[7] seem true and according to reason; but after he was ascended up into heaven, I think thou wilt not say, that his body was not turned[8] into the nature of his Godhead[9].

ORTH. I would not so say for the persuasion of man's reason: nor I am not so arrogant and presumptuous to affirm any thing which scripture passeth over in silence. But I have heard St Paul cry, "that God hath ordained a day when he will judge all the world in justice by that man which he appointed before, performing his promise to all men, and raising him from death." I have learned also of the holy angels, that he will come after that fashion, as his disciples saw him go to heaven. But they saw a nature of a certain bigness, not a nature which had no bigness. I heard furthermore the Lord say: "You shall see the Son of man come in the clouds of heaven." And I know that every thing that men see hath a certain bigness: for that nature that hath no bigness cannot be seen. Moreover to sit in the throne of glory, and to set the lambs upon his right hand, and the goats upon his left hand, signifieth a thing that hath quantity and bigness.

Hitherto have I rehearsed Theodoretus' words, and shortly after Eranistes saith[10]:

ERAN. We must turn every stone, as the proverb saith, to seek out the truth, but specially when godly matters be propounded.

ORTH. Tell me then the sacramental signs which be offered to God by his priests, whereof be they signs, sayest thou?

ERAN. Of the Lord's body and blood.

ORTH. Of a very body? or not of a very body?

ERAN. Of a very body.

ORTH. Very well, for an image must be made after a true pattern: for painters follow nature, and paint the images of such things as we see with our eyes.

ERAN. Truth it is.

ORTH. If therefore the godly sacraments represent a true body, then is the Lord's body yet still a body, not converted into the nature of his Godhead, but replenished with God's glory.

[2 Things, 1551, and Orig. ed.]
[3 Of a man, 1551, and Orig. ed.]
[4 Id. in Dialogo ii. Tom. IV. pp. 122, 3.]
[5 And yet it is, 1551, and Orig. ed.]
[6 Hath, 1551. The Orig. ed. reads with that of 1580.]
[7 Sayings, 1551, and Orig. ed.]
[8 Was turned, 1551, and Orig. ed.]
[9 Of the Godhead, 1551, and Orig. ed.]
[10 Theodoret. ubi supra, pp. 122, 3.]

Side notes: utique habebat Dominus. ERAN. Et ego incorporeum illum esse dico. ORTH. Sed fateris illum habuisse corpus. Ed. Emb. 1551.] Dialogue 2.

*Christ's body glorified hath his form, bigness, and quantity.

Acts xvii. Acts i. Matt. xxiv.

ERAN. It cometh in good time that thou makest mention of God's sacraments; for by the same I shall prove that Christ's body is turned into another nature. Answer therefore unto my questions.

ORTH. I shall answer.

ERAN. What callest thou that which is offered before the invocation of the priest?

ORTH. We must not speak plainly; for it is like that some be present which have not professed Christ.

ERAN. Answer covertly.

ORTH. It is a nourishment made of seeds that be like.

ERAN. Then how call we the other sign?

ORTH. It is also a common name that signifieth a kind of drink.

ERAN. But how dost thou call them after the sanctification?

ORTH. The body of Christ, and the blood of Christ.

ERAN. And dost thou believe that thou art made partaker of Christ's body and blood?

ORTH. I believe so.

ERAN. Therefore as the tokens of God's body and blood be other things before the priest's invocation, but after the invocation they be changed, and be other things; so also the body of Christ after his assumption is changed into his divine substance.

ORTH. Thou art taken with thine own net. For the sacramental signs go not from their own nature after the sanctification, but continue in their former substance, form, and figure, and may be seen and touched as well as before: yet in our minds we do consider what they be made, and do repute and esteem them and have them in reverence, according to the same things that they be taken for. Therefore compare their images to the pattern, and thou shalt see them like. For figure[1] must be like to the thing itself. For Christ's body hath his former fashion, figure, and bigness, and, to speak at one word, the same substance of his body: but after his resurrection it was made immortal, and of such power, that no corruption nor death could come unto it; and it was exalted unto that dignity, that it was set at the right hand of the Father, and honoured of all creatures, as the body of him that is the Lord of nature.

ERAN. But the sacramental token changeth his former name; for it is no more called as it was before, but is called Christ's body. Therefore must his body after his ascension be called God, and not a body.

ORTH. Thou seemest to me ignorant: for it is not called his body only, but also the bread of life, as the Lord called it. So the body of Christ we call a godly body, a body that giveth life, God's body, the Lord's body, our master's body; meaning[2] that it is not a common body, as other men's bodies be, but that it is the body of our Lord Jesu Christ, both God and man.

[Jesus enim Christus heri et hodie ille ipse, et in æternum. Embd. Ed. 1557.]

This have I rehearsed of the great clerk and holy bishop Theodoretus, whom some of the papists perceiving to make so plainly against them, have defamed, saying that he was infected with the error of Nestorius.

Here the papists shew their old accustomed nature and condition, which is even in a manifest matter rather to lie without shame, than to give place unto the truth, and confess their own error. And although his adversaries

---

[[1] a figure, 1551.]   [[2] So the Orig. edit. and 1551; that of 1580 has *name ning*.]

falsely bruited such a fame against him, when he was yet alive, nevertheless he was purged thereof by the whole council of Chalcedon, about eleven hundred years ago. [Quem Leo primus episto. 61. charissimum fratrem appellat. Fmbd. Ed. 1537.]

And furthermore in his book which he wrote against heresies, he specially condemneth Nestorius by name. And also all his three books of his dialogues before rehearsed he wrote chiefly against Nestorius, and was never herein noted of error this thousand year, but hath ever been reputed and taken for an holy bishop, a great learned man, and a grave author, until now at this present time, when the papists have nothing to answer unto him, they begin in excusing of themselves to defame him.

Thus much have I spoken for Theodoretus, which I pray thee be not weary to read, good reader, but often and with delectation, deliberation, and good advertisement to read. For it containeth plainly and briefly the true instruction of a christian man, concerning the matter, which in this book we treat upon.

First, that our Saviour Christ in his last supper, when he gave bread and wine to his apostles, saying, "This is my body; this is my blood;" it was bread which he called his body, and wine mixed in the cup which he called his blood: so that he changed the names of the bread and wine, which were the mysteries, sacraments, signs, figures, and tokens of Christ's flesh and blood, and called them by the names of the things which they did represent and signify; that is to say, the bread he called by the name of his very flesh, and the wine by the name of his blood. [Five principal things to be noted in Theodoret. Ed. 1551.]

Second, that although the names of bread and wine were changed after sanctification, yet, nevertheless, the things themselves remained the selfsame that they were before the sanctification, that is to say, the same bread and wine in nature, substance, form, and fashion.

The third, seeing that the substance of the bread and wine be not changed, why be then their names changed, and the bread called Christ's flesh, and the wine his blood? Theodoretus sheweth that the cause thereof was this, that we should not have so much respect to the bread and wine (which we see with our eyes, and taste with our mouths) as we should have to Christ himself, in whom we believe with our hearts, and feel and taste him by our faith, and with whose flesh and blood (by his grace) we believe that we be spiritually fed and nourished. These things we ought to remember and revolve in our minds, and to lift up our hearts from the bread and wine unto Christ that sitteth above. And because we should so do, therefore after the consecration they be no more called bread and wine, but the body and blood of Christ.

The fourth, it is in these sacraments of bread and wine, as it is in the very body of Christ. For as the body of Christ before his resurrection and after is all one in nature, substance, bigness, form, and fashion; and yet it is not called as another common body, but with addition, for the dignity of his exaltation, it is called a heavenly, a godly, an immortal, and the Lord's body: so likewise the bread and wine before the consecration and after is all one in nature, substance, bigness, form, and fashion; and yet it is not called as other common bread, but for the dignity whereunto it is taken, it is called with addition, heavenly bread, the bread of life, and the bread of thanksgiving.

The fifth, that no man ought to be so arrogant and presumptuous to affirm for a certain truth in religion any thing which is not spoken of in holy scripture. And this is spoken to the great and utter condemnation of the papists, which make and unmake new articles of our faith from time to time at their pleasure, without any scripture at all, yea, quite and clean contrary to scripture. And yet will they have all men bound to believe whatsoever they invent, upon peril of damnation and everlasting fire. And yet will they constrain[1] with fire and fagot all men to consent (contrary to the manifest words of God) to these their errors in this matter of the holy sacrament of Christ's body and blood:

First, that there remaineth no bread nor wine after the consecration, but that Christ's flesh and blood is made of them.

Second, that Christ's body is really, corporally, substantially, sensibly, and naturally in the bread and wine.

Thirdly, that wicked persons do eat and drink Christ's very body and blood.

Fourthly, that priests offer Christ every day, and make of him a new sacrifice propitiatory for sin.

Thus for shortness of time I do make an end of Theodoretus, with other old ancient writers, which do most clearly affirm that to eat Christ's body and to drink his blood be figurative speeches. And so be these sentences likewise which Christ spake at his supper: "This is my body;" "this is my blood."

WINCHESTER.

Theodoretus.   *The author bringeth in Theodoret, a Greek, whom to discuss particularly were long and tedious: one notable place there is in him which toucheth the point of the matter, which place Peter Martyr allegeth in Greek, and then translateth it into Latin, not exactly as other have done to the truth; but as he hath done, I will write here[2]. And then will I write the same, translated into English by one that hath translated Peter Martyr's book; and then will I add the translation of this author, and finally, the very truth of the Latin, as I will abide by, and join an issue with this author in it, whereby thou, reader, shalt perceive with what sincerity things be handled.*

P. Martyr.   *Peter Martyr hath of Theodoret this in Latin, which the same Theodoret, in a disputation with an heretic, maketh the catholic man to say:* Captus es iis quæ tetenderas retibus. Neque enim post sanctificationem mystica symbola illa propria sua natura egrediuntur; manent enim in priori sua substantia, et figura, et specie, adeoque et videntur, et palpantur, quemadmodum et antea. Intelliguntur autem quæ facta sunt, et creduntur, et adorantur tanquam ea existentia, quæ creduntur. *He that translateth Peter Martyr in English, doth express these words thus:* "Lo, thou art now caught in the same net which thou hadst set to catch me in. For those same mystical signs do not depart away out of their own proper nature after the hallowing of them. For they remain still in their former substance, and their former shape, and their former kind, and are even[3] as well seen and felt as they were afore. But the things that are done are understanded, and are believed, and are worshipped, even as though they were in very deed the things that are believed." *This is the common translation into English of Peter Martyr's book translated, which this author doth translate after his fashion thus:* "Thou art taken with thine own net; for the sacramental signs go not from their own nature after the sanctification, but continue in their former substance, form, and figure, and be seen and touched as well as before. Yet in our minds we do consider what they be made, and do repute and esteem them and have them in reverence according to the same things that they be taken for." *Thus is the translation of this author. Mine English of this Latin is thus:*

"Thou art taken with the same nets thou didst lay forth. For the mystical tokens after the sanctification go not away out of their proper nature. For they abide in their former substance, shape, and form, and so far forth, that they may be seen and felt as they might before. But they be understanded that they be made, and are believed, and are worshipped, as being the same things which be believed." *This is my translation, who in the first sentence*

[1 And they would constrain, 1551, and Orig. ed.]
[2 I will write in here, 1551.]
[3 Ever, 1551. Orig. ed. Winch. reads with ed. 1580.]

mean not to vary from the other translations touching the remain of substance, shape, form, or figure: I will use all those names. But in the second part, where Theodoret speaketh of our belief what the tokens be made, and where he saith those tokens be worshipped, as being the same things which be believed, thou mayest see, reader, how this author flieth the words "believe" and "worship," which the common translation in English doth plainly and truly express, howsoever the translator[4] swerved by colour of the word tanquam, which there, after the Greek, signifieth the truth, and not the similitude only; like as St Paul, Vocat ea quæ non sunt, tanquam sint, *which is to make to be in deed, not as though they were. And the Greek is there* ὡς ὄντα, *as it is here* ὥσπερ ἐκεῖνα ὄντα[5]. *And it were an absurdity to believe things otherwise than they be, as though they were, and very idolatry to worship wittingly[6] that is not, as though it were in deed. And therefore in these two words, that they believed[7] that they be made and be worshipped, is declared by Theodoret his faith of the very true real presence of Christ's glorious flesh, whereunto the Deity is united, which flesh St Augustine, consonantly to this Theodoret, said must be worshipped before it be received. The word "worshipping" put here in English is to express the word* adorantur, *put by Peter in Latin, signifying adoring, being the verb in Greek of such signification, as is used to express godly worship with bowing of the knee. Now, reader, what should I say by this author, that conveyeth these two words of believing and worshipping, and instead of them cometh in with reverence, taking, reputing, and esteeming? whereof thou mayest esteem how this place of Theodoret pinched this author, who could not but see that adoring of the sacrament signifieth the presence of the body of Christ to be adored, which else were an absurdity; and therefore the author took pain to ease it with other words of calling, believing, reputing, and esteeming, and for adoration, reverence. Consider what praise this author giveth Theodoret, which praise condemneth this author sore. For Theodoret, in his doctrine, would have us believe the mystery, and adore the sacrament, where this author after in his doctrine professeth there is nothing to be worshipped at all. If one should now say to me, "Yea, sir, but this Theodoret seemeth to condemn transubstantiation, because he speaketh so of the bread:" thereunto shall be answered when I speak of transubstantiation, which shall be after the third and fourth book discussed[8]. For before the truth of the presence of the substance of Christ's body may appear, what should we talk of transubstantiation? I will travail no more in Theodoret, but leave it to thy judgment, reader, what credit this author ought to have, that handleth the matter after this sort.*

* Adoration of the sacrament.

CANTERBURY.

This bladder is so puffed up with wind, that it is marvel it brasteth not. But be patient awhile, good reader, and suffer until the blast of wind be past, and thou shalt see a great calm, the bladder broken, and nothing in it but all vanity.

There is no difference between your translation and mine, saving that mine is more plain, and giveth less occasion of error; and yours, as all your doings be, is dark and obscure, and containeth in it no little provocation to idolatry. For the words of Theodoret, after your interpretation, contain both a plain untruth and also manifest idolatry: for the signs and tokens which he speaketh of, be the very forms and substances of bread and wine. For the nominative case to the verb of adoring, in Theodoret, is not the body and blood of Christ, but the mystical tokens, by your own translation: which mystical tokens if you will have to be the very body and blood of Christ, what can be spoken more untrue or more foolish? And if you will have them to be worshipped with godly worship, what can be greater idolatry? Wherefore I, to eschew such occasions of error, have translated the words of Theodoretus faithfully and truly as his mind was, and yet have avoided all occasions of evil: for *tanquam,* or ὥσπερ ἐκεῖνα ὄντα, signifieth not the truth, as you say, but is an adverb of similitude, as it is likewise in this place of St Paul: *Vocat ea quæ non sunt, tanquam sint.* For St

---

[4 that translator, 1551.]

[5 The original of Theodoret is as follows: ΟΡΘ. Ἑάλως αἷς ὕφηνες ἄρκυσιν. οὐδὲ γὰρ μετὰ τὸν ἁγιασμὸν τὰ μυστικὰ σύμβολα τῆς οἰκείας ἐξίσταται φύσεως. μένει γὰρ ἐπὶ τῆς προτέρας οὐσίας, καὶ τοῦ σχήματος, καὶ τοῦ εἴδους, καὶ ὁρατά ἐστι, καὶ ἁπτά, οἷα καὶ πρότερον ἦν· νοεῖται δὲ ἅπερ ἐγένετο, καὶ πιστεύεται, καὶ προσκυνεῖται, ὡς ἐκεῖνα ὄντα ἅπερ πιστεύεται. Theodoret. ubi supra, p. 126.]

[6 Orig. ed. Winch. omits the word "wittingly."]

[7 they be believed, 1551.]

[8 Orig. ed. Winch. instead of, "which shall be after the third and fourth book discussed," reads, "which shall be the last."]

Paul saith, "as though they were;" which indeed were not, as he said the next word before, *non sunt,* "they be not." And nevertheless unto God all things be present; and those things which in their nature be not yet present, unto God were ever present, in whom be not these successions of time, before and after: for Christ the Lamb in his present was slain before the world began; and a thousand year to his eyes be but as it were yesterday; and one day before him is as it were a thousand year, and a thousand year as one day.

<small>Rev. xiii.
Psal. lxxxiii.
2 Pet. iii.</small>

<small>August. de Doct. Christ. Lib. iii. cap. 9.</small>

And if you had read and considered a saying of St Augustine, *De doctrina Christiana,* Lib. III. cap. 9, you might have understand this place of Theodoret better than you do. "He serveth under a sign," saith St Augustine, "who worketh or worshippeth any sign, not knowing what it signifieth. But he that worketh or worshippeth a profitable sign ordained of God, the strength and signification whereof he understandeth, he worshippeth not that which is seen and is transitory, but rather that thing whereto all such signs ought to be referred." And anon after he saith further: "At this time when our Lord Jesus Christ is risen, we have a most manifest argument of our freedom, and be not burdened with the heavy yoke of signs which we understand not; but the Lord and the teaching of his apostles hath given to us a few signs for many, and those most easy to be done, most excellent in understanding, and in performing most pure; as the sacrament of baptism, and the celebration of the body and blood of our Lord, which every man when he receiveth knoweth whereunto they be referred, being taught that he worship not them with a carnal bondage, but rather with a spiritual freedom. And as it is a vile bondage to follow the letter, and to take the signs for the things signified by them; so to interpret the signs to no profit, is an error that shrewdly spreadeth abroad[1]." These words of St Augustine, being conferred with the words of Theodoret, may declare plainly what Theodoret's meaning was. For where he saith that we may not worship with a carnal bondage the visible signs, (meaning of water in baptism, and of bread and wine in the holy communion,) when we receive the same, but rather ought to worship the things whereunto they be referred, he meant that although those signs or sacraments of water, bread, and wine ought highly to be esteemed, and not to be taken as other common water, baker's bread, or wine in the tavern, but as signs dedicated, consecrated, and referred to an holy use; and by those earthly things to represent things celestial; yet the very true honour and worship ought to be given to the celestial things, which by the visible signs be understand, and not to the visible signs themselves. And nevertheless, both St Augustine and Theodoret count it a certain kind of worshipping the signs, the reverent esteeming of them above other common and profane things, and yet the same principally to be referred to the celestial things represented by the signs; and therefore saith St Augustine *potius,* "rather." And this worship is as well in the sacrament of baptism, as in the sacrament of Christ's body and blood. And therefore, although whosoever is baptized unto Christ, or eateth his flesh and drinketh his blood in his holy supper, do first honour him; yet is he corporally and carnally neither in the supper, nor in baptism, but spiritually and effectually.

Now where you leave the judgment of Theodoret to the reader, even so do I also, not doubting but the indifferent reader shall soon espy, how little cause you have so to boast, and blow out your vain-glorious words as you do. But hear now what followeth next in my book.

[1 Sub signo enim servit qui operatur aut veneratur aliquam rem significantem, nesciens quid significet: qui vero aut operatur, aut veneratur utile signum divinitus institutum, cujus vim significationemque intelligit, non hoc veneratur quod videtur et transit, sed illud potius quo talia cuncta referenda sunt.—Hoc vero tempore posteaquam resurrectione Domini nostri manifestissimum indicium nostræ libertatis illuxit, nec eorum quidem signorum, quæ jam intelligimus, operatione gravi onerati sumus; sed quædam pauca pro multis, eademque factu facillima, et intellectu augustissima, et observatione castissima ipse Dominus et apostolica tradidit disciplina: sicuti est baptismi sacramentum, et celebratio corporis et sanguinis Domini. Quæ unusquisque cum percipit, quo referantur imbutus agnoscit, ut ea non carnali servitute, sed spiritali potius libertate veneretur. Ut autem literam sequi, et signa pro rebus quæ iis significantur accipere, servilis infirmitatis est; ita inutiliter signa interpretari, male vagantis erroris est. Augustin. De doctrina Christiana, Lib. III. cap. 9. Pars IV. Basil. ap. Amerbach. 1506.]

And marvel not, good reader, that Christ at that time spake in figures, when he did institute that sacrament, seeing that it is the nature of all sacraments to be figures. And although the scripture be full of schemes, tropes, and figures, yet specially it useth them when it speaketh of sacraments. *Chap. xii. Figurative speeches be not strange.*

When the ark, which represented God's majesty, was come into the army of the Israelites, the Philistines said that God was come into the army. And God himself said by his prophet Nathan, that from the time that he had brought the children of Israel out of Egypt, he dwelled not in houses, but that he was carried about in tents and tabernacles. And yet was not God himself so carried about, or went in tents or tabernacles: but because the ark, which was a figure of God, was so removed from place to place, he spake of himself that thing, which was to be understand of the ark. *1 Sam. iv. 2 Sam. vii. 136.*

And Christ himself oftentimes spake in similitudes, parables, and figures; as when he said: "The field is the world, the enemy is the devil, the seed is the word of God;" "John is Elias;" "I am a vine, and you be the branches;" "I am bread of life;" "my Father is an husbandman, and he hath his fan in his hand, and will make clean his floor, and gather the wheat into his barn, but the chaff he will cast into everlasting fire;" "I have a meat to eat which you know not;" "work not meat that perisheth, but that endureth unto everlasting life;" "I am a good shepherd;" "the Son of man will set the sheep at his right hand, and the goats at his left hand;" "I am a door, one of you is the devil;" "whosoever doeth my Father's will, he is my brother, sister, and mother:" and when he said to his mother and to John, "This is thy son," "this is thy mother." *Christ himself used figurative speeches. Matt. xiii. Matt. xi. & xvii. John xv. John vi. Matt. iii. John iv. *Ego cibum habeo manducare quem vos nescitis. John vi. John x. Matt. xxv. John x. John vi. Matt. xii. John xix.*

These, with an infinite number of like sentences, Christ spake in parables, metaphors, tropes, and figures. But chiefly when he spake of the sacraments, he used figurative speeches.

As when in baptism he said, "that we must be baptized with the Holy Ghost," meaning of spiritual baptism. And like speech used St John the Baptist, saying of Christ, "that he should baptize with the Holy Ghost and fire." And Christ said, "that we must be born again, or else we cannot see the kingdom of God." And said also: "Whosoever shall drink of that water which I shall give him, he shall never be dry again. But the water which I shall give him, shall be made within him a well, which shall spring into everlasting life." And St Paul saith, "that in baptism we clothe us with Christ, and be buried with him." This baptism and washing by the fire and the Holy Ghost, this new birth, this water that springeth in a man and floweth into everlasting life, and this clothing and burial, cannot be understand of any material baptism², material washing, material birth, clothing, and burial; but by translation of things visible into things invisible, they must be understand spiritually and figuratively. *Acts i. Matt. iii. John iii. John iv. *Qui biberit ex aqua quam ego dabo, &c. Ibidem. Rom. vi. Gal. iii.*

After the same sort the mystery of our redemption, and the passion of our Saviour Christ upon the cross, as well in the new as in the old testament, is expressed and declared by many figures and figurative speeches.

As the pure paschal lamb without spot signified Christ, the effusion of the lamb's blood signified the effusion of Christ's blood; and the salvation of the children of Israel from temporal death by the lamb's blood signified our salvation from eternal death by Christ's blood. *The Paschal Lamb.*

And as Almighty God, passing through Egypt, killed all the Egyptians' heirs in every house, and left not one alive, and nevertheless he passed by

---

[² *Of any baptism,* 1551.]

the children of Israel's houses, where he saw the lamb's blood upon the doors, and hurted none of them, but saved them all by the means of the lamb's blood; so likewise at the last judgment of the whole world, none shall be passed over and saved but that shall be found marked with the blood of the most pure and immaculate Lamb, Jesus Christ. And forasmuch as the shedding of that lamb's blood was a token and figure of the shedding of Christ's blood then to come; and forasmuch also as all the sacraments and figures of the old testament ceased and had an end in Christ; lest by our great unkindness we should peradventure be forgetful of the great benefit of Christ, therefore at his last supper, (when he took his leave of his apostles to depart out of the world,) he did make a new will and testament, wherein he bequeathed unto us clean remission of all our sins, and the everlasting inheritance of heaven. And the same he confirmed the next day with his own blood and death.

The Lord's Supper.

137.

And lest we should forget the same, he ordained not a yearly memory, (as the paschal lamb was eaten but once every year,) but a daily remembrance he ordained thereof in bread and wine, sanctified and dedicated to that purpose, saying: "This is my body; this cup is my blood, which is shed for the remission of sins: do this in remembrance of me:"—admonishing us by these words, spoken at the making of his last will and testament, and at his departing out of the world, (because they should be the better remembered,) that whensoever we do eat the bread in his holy supper, and drink of that cup, we should remember how much Christ hath done for us, and how he died for our sakes. Therefore saith St Paul: "As often as ye shall eat this bread, and drink the cup, you shall shew forth the Lord's death until he come."

Matt xxvi.

1 Cor. xi.

And forasmuch as this holy bread broken, and the wine divided, do represent unto us the death of Christ now past, as the killing of the paschal lamb did represent the same yet to come; therefore our Saviour Christ used the same manner of speech of bread and wine, as God before used the paschal lamb[1].

For as in the old testament God said, "This is the Lord's pass-by, or passover"; even so saith Christ in the new testament, "This is my body; this is my blood." But in the old mystery and sacrament the lamb was not the Lord's very passover or passing by, but it was a figure which represented his passing by: so likewise in the new testament the bread and wine be not Christ's very body and blood, but they be figures, which by Christ's institution be unto the godly receivers thereof sacraments, tokens, significations, and representations of his very flesh and blood; instructing their faith, that as the bread and wine feed them corporally and continue this temporal life, so the very flesh and blood of Christ feedeth them spiritually, and giveth everlasting life.

Exod. xii.

Matt. xxvi.

And why should any man think it strange to admit a figure in these speeches, "This is my body," "this is my blood;" seeing that the communication the same night, by the papists' own confessions, was so full of figurative speeches? For the apostles spake figuratively when they asked Christ, "where he would eat his passover or pass-by:" and Christ himself used the same figure, when he said: "I have much desired to eat this passover with you."

What figurative speeches were used at Christ's last supper.

Matt. xxvi.

Mark xiv.
Luke xxii.

Also, to eat Christ's body and to drink his blood, I am sure they will not say that it is taken properly, to eat and drink, as we do eat other meats and drinks.

And when Christ said, "This cup is a new testament in my blood," here in one sentence be two figures: one in this word, "cup," which is not taken for the cup itself, but for the thing contained in the cup: another is in this word,

---

[1 Of the Paschal Lamb, 1551.]

"testament;" for neither the cup, nor the wine contained in the cup, is Christ's testament, but is a token, sign, and figure, whereby is represented unto us his testament, confirmed by his blood.

And if the papists will say, as they say indeed, that by this cup is neither meant the cup, nor the wine contained in the cup, but that thereby is meant Christ's blood contained in the cup, yet must they needs grant that there is a figure. For Christ's blood is not in proper speech the new testament, but it is the thing that confirmed the new testament. And yet by this strange interpretation the papists make a very strange speech, more strange than any figurative speech is. For this they make the sentence: "This blood is a new testament in my blood." Which saying is so fond and so far from all reason, that the foolishness thereof is evident to every man.

138.

WINCHESTER.

As for the use of figurative speeches to be accustomed in scripture is not denied. But Philip Melancthon in an epistle to Œcolampadius of the sacrament, giveth one good note of observation in difference between the speeches in God's ordinances and commandments, and otherwise[2]. *For if in the understanding*[3] *of God's ordinances and commandments figures may be often received; truth shall by allegories be shortly subverted, and all our religion reduced to significations. There is no speech so plain and simple but it hath some piece of a figurative speech, but such as expresseth the common plain understanding; and then the common use of the figure causeth it to be taken as a common proper speech. As these speeches, "drink up this cup," or "eat this dish*[4]*," is indeed a figurative speech, but by custom made so common that it is reputed the plain speech, because it hath but one only understanding commonly received. And when Christ said, "This cup is the new testament," the proper speech thereof in letter hath an absurdity in reason, and faith also. But when Christ said, "This is my body," although the truth of the literal sense hath an absurdity in carnal reason, yet hath it no absurdity in humility of faith, nor repugneth not to any other truth of scripture. And seeing it is a singular miracle of Christ whereby to exercise us in the faith, understood as the plain words signify in their proper sense, there can no reasoning be made of other figurative speeches to make this to be their fellow and like unto them. No man denieth the use of figurative speeches in Christ's supper, but such as be equal with plain proper speech, or be expounded by other evangelists in plain speech.*

Melancthon.
*The speech in scripture, where God commandeth or ordereth, is spiritually to be considered.
*Figurative speech by custom made proper.

CANTERBURY.

I see well you would take a dung-fork to fight with, rather than you would lack a weapon. For how highly you have esteemed Melancthon in times past, it is not unknown. But whatsoever Melancthon saith, or howsoever you understand Melancthon, where is so convenient a place to use figurative speeches as when figures and sacraments be instituted? And St Augustine giveth a plain rule how we may know when God's commandments be given in figurative speeches[5], and yet shall neither the truth be subverted, nor our religion reduced to significations. And how can it be but that in the understanding of God's ordinances and commandments figures must needs be often received, (contrary to Melancthon's saying,) if it be true that you say, "that there is no speech so plain and simple, but it hath some piece of a figurative speech?" But now be all speeches figurative, when it pleaseth you. What need I then to travail any more to prove that Christ in his supper used figurative speeches, seeing that all that he spake was spoken in figures by your saying?

And these words "This is my body," spoken of the bread, and "This is my blood,"

[² The epistle referred to appears to be that inserted in Œcolampadii Dialogus, Quid de Eucharistia veteres tum Græci tum Latini senserint, Basil. 1590. "Nullam enim firmam rationem invenio, quæ conscientiæ discedenti a proprietate verborum satisfaciat......Cum proprietas verborum cum nullo articulo fidei pugnet, nulla satis magna causa est cur eam deseramus." pp. 14, 15. The letter is dated Spires, an. 1529.]

[³ For if theunderstanding, 1551. Evidently an error of the press.]

[⁴ Eat up this dish, 1551. Orig. ed. reads as ed. 1580.]

[⁵ See before, p. 115, note 5.]

spoken of the cup, express no plain common understanding, whereby the common use of these figures should be equal with plain proper speeches, or cause them to be taken as common proper speeches: for you say yourself, "that these speeches in letter have an absurdity in reason." And as they have absurdity in reason, so have they "absurdity in faith." For neither is there any reason, faith, miracle, nor truth, to say that material bread is Christ's body. For then it must be true that his body is material bread, a *conversa ad convertentem;* for of the material bread spake Christ those words, by your confession[1]. And why have not these words of Christ, "This is my body," an absurdity both in faith and reason, as well as these words, "This cup is the new testament," seeing that these words were spoken by Christ as well as the other, and the credit of him is all one whatsoever he saith?

139.

But if you will needs understand these words of Christ, "This is my body," as the plain words signify in their proper sense, (as in the end you seem to do, repugning therein to your own former saying,) you shall see how far you go, not only from reason, but also from the true confession of the christian faith.

Christ spake of bread, say you, "This is my body;" appointing by this word "this" the bread: whereof followeth, as I said before, if bread be his body, that his body is bread: and if his body be bread, it is a creature without sense and reason, having neither life nor soul; which is horrible of any christian man to be heard or spoken.

Hear now what followeth further in my book.

Chap. XIII. Answer to the authorities and arguments of the papists.

Now forasmuch as it is plainly declared and manifestly proved, that Christ called bread his body, and wine his blood, and that these sentences be figurative speeches; and that Christ, as concerning his humanity and bodily presence, is ascended into heaven with his whole flesh and blood, and is not here upon earth; and that the substance of bread and wine do remain still, and be received in the sacrament, and that although they remain, yet they have changed their names, so that the bread is called Christ's body, and the wine his blood; and that the cause why their names be changed is this, that we should lift up our hearts and minds from the things which we see unto the things which we believe and be above in heaven; whereof the bread and wine have the names, although they be not the very same things in deed: these things well considered and weighed, all the authorities and arguments, which the papists feign to serve for their purpose, be clean wiped away.

Chap. XIV. One brief answer to all.

For whether the authors, which they allege, say that we do eat Christ's flesh and drink his blood; or that the bread and wine is converted into the substance of his flesh and blood; or that we be turned into his flesh; or that in the Lord's supper we do receive his very flesh and blood; or that in the bread and wine is received that which did hang upon the cross; or that Christ hath left his flesh with us; or that Christ is in us and we in him; or that he is whole here and whole in heaven; or that the same thing is in the chalice, which flowed out of his side; or that the same thing is received with our mouth, which is believed with our faith; or that the bread and wine after the consecration be the body and blood of Christ; or that we be nourished with the body and blood of Christ; or that Christ is both gone hence and is still here; or that Christ at his last supper bare himself in his own hands: these and all other like sentences may not[2] be understood of Christ's humanity literally and carnally, as the words in common speech do properly signify; for so doth no man eat Christ's flesh, nor drink his blood, nor so is not the bread and wine[3] after the consecration his flesh and blood, nor so is not his flesh and blood whole here in earth eaten with our mouths, nor so did not Christ take himself in his own hands.

[1 By your own confession, 1551.]
[2 *Not* omitted in edit. 1580.]
[3 The Orig. ed. and ed. 1551, add the following words, "turned into his flesh and blood, nor we into him; nor so is the bread and wine," and the passage then runs on as above, "after the consecration," &c.]

But these and all other like sentences, which declare Christ to be here in earth, and to be eaten and drunken of christian people, are to be understanded either of his divine nature, (whereby he is everywhere,) or else they must be understanded figuratively, or spiritually. For figuratively he is in the bread and wine, and spiritually he is in them that worthily eat and drink the bread and wine; but really, carnally, and corporally, he is only in heaven, from whence he shall come to judge the quick and dead.

This brief answer will suffice for all that the papists can bring for their purpose, if it be aptly applied. And for the more evidence hereof, I shall apply the same to some such places, as the papists think do make most for them, that by the answer to those places the rest may be the more easily answered unto.

140.

WINCHESTER.

In the seventy-fourth leaf this author goeth about to give a general solution to all that may be said of Christ's being in earth, in heaven, or in the sacrament; and giveth instructions how these words of Christ's divine nature, figuratively, spiritually, really, carnally, corporally, may be placed: and thus he saith: "Christ in his divine nature may be said to be in the earth, figuratively in the sacrament, spiritually in the man that receiveth, but really, carnally, corporally, only in heaven." Let us consider the placing of these terms. When we say Christ is in his divine nature everywhere, is he not really also everywhere, according to the true essence of his Godhead? in deed everywhere? That is to say, not in fantasy, nor imagination, but verily, truly, and therefore really, as we believe, so in deed every where? And when Christ is spiritually in good men by grace, is not Christ in them really by grace? but in fantasy and imagination? And therefore whatsoever this author saith, the word "really" may not have such restraint to be referred only to heaven, unless the author would deny that substance of the Godhead, which as it comprehendeth all, being incomprehensible, and is everywhere without limitation of place, so as it is, truly it is, in deed is, and therefore really is; and therefore of Christ must be said, wheresoever he is in his divine nature by power or grace, he is there really, whether we speak of heaven or earth.

*Really.

As for the terms "carnally" and "corporally," as this author seemeth to use them in other places of this book to express the manner of presence of the human nature in Christ, I marvel by what scripture he shall[4] prove that Christ's body is so carnally and corporally in heaven. We be assured by faith, grounded upon the scriptures, of the truth of the being of Christ's flesh and body there, and the same to be a true flesh and a true body; but yet in such sense as this author useth the terms carnal and corporal against the sacrament to imply a grossness, he cannot so attribute those terms to Christ's body in heaven. St Augustine after the gross sense of carnally, saith: "Christ reigneth not carnally in heaven." And Gregory Nazianzen saith: "Although Christ shall come in the last day to judge, so as he shall be seen; yet there is in him no grossness," he saith, and referreth the manner of his being to his knowledge only. "And our resurrection," St Augustine saith, "although it shall be of our true flesh, yet it shall not be carnally." And when this author had[5] defamed as it were the terms "carnally" and "corporally," as terms of grossness, to whom he used always to put as an adversative the term "spiritually," as though carnally and spiritually might not agree in one; now for all that he would place them both in heaven, where is no carnality, but all the manner of being spiritual, where is no grossness at all, the secrecy of the manner of which life is hidden from us, and such as eye hath not seen, or ear heard, or ascended into the heart and thought of man.

*Carnally.
*Corporally.

August. de Civitat. Dei
Gregor. Nazianzen. de Baptismo.

I know these terms carnally and corporally may have a good understanding out of the mouth of him that had not defamed them with grossness, or made them adversaries to spiritual; and a man may say Christ is corporally in heaven because the truth of his body is there, and carnally in heaven because his flesh is truly there: but in this understanding both the words carnally and corporally may be coupled with the word spiritually, which is against this author's teaching, who appointeth the word spiritually to be spoken of Christ's presence in the man that received the sacrament worthily, which speech I do not disallow; but as Christ is spiritually in the man that doth receive the sacrament worthily, so is he in him spiritually before he receive, or else he cannot receive worthily, as I have before said. And by this appeareth how this author, to

*How Christ may be said to be corporally and carnally in heaven.

141.

[⁴ Will, 1551.]   [⁵ Hath, 1551.]

*Christ is present in the sacrament as he is in heaven.

frame his general solution, hath used neither of the terms "really," "carnally," and "corporally[1]," or "spiritually," in a convenient order, but hath in his distribution misused them notably. For Christ in his divine nature is really everywhere, and in his human nature is carnally and corporally, as these words signify substance of the flesh and body, continually in heaven to the day of judgment, and nevertheless after that signification present in the sacrament also. And in those terms in that signification the fathers have spoken of the[2] effect of the eating of Christ in the sacrament, as in the particular solutions to the authors hereafter shall appear. Marry as touching the use of the word "figuratively," to say that Christ is figuratively in the bread and wine, is a saying which this author hath not proved at all, but is a doctrine before this divers times reproved, and now by this author in England renewed.

CANTERBURY.

Although my chief study be to speak so plainly that all men[3] may understand every thing what I say, yet nothing is plain to him that will find knots in a rush. For when I say that all sentences which declare Christ to be here in earth, and to be eaten and drunken of christian people, are to be understood either of his divine nature, (whereby he is everywhere,) or else they must be understood figuratively or spiritually; (for figuratively he is in the bread and wine, and spiritually he is in them that worthily eat and drink the bread and wine; but really, carnally and corporally, he is only in heaven;) you have termed these my words as it liketh you, but far otherwise than I either wrote or meant, or than any indifferent reader would have imagined.

For what indifferent reader would have gathered of my words, that Christ in his divine nature is not really in heaven? For I make a disjunctive, wherein I declare a plain distinction between his divine nature and his human nature. And of his divine nature I say in the first member of my division, which is in the beginning of my aforesaid words, that by that nature he is everywhere. And all the rest that followeth is spoken of his human nature, whereby he is carnally and corporally only in heaven.

Really.

And as for this word "really," in such a sense as you expound it, (that is to say, not in fantasy nor imagination, but verily and truly,) so I grant that Christ is really, not only in them that duly receive the sacrament of the Lord's supper, but also in them that duly receive the sacrament of baptism, and in all other true christian people at other times when they receive no sacrament. For all they be the members of Christ's body, and temples in whom he truly inhabiteth, although corporally and really (as the papists take that word "really") he be only in heaven, and not in the sacrament. And although in them that duly receive the sacrament he is truly and in deed, and not by fancy and imagination, and so really, (as you understand "really,") yet is he not in them corporally, but "spiritually," as I say, and "only after a spiritual manner," as you say.

Carnally and corporally.

And as for these words, "carnally" and "corporally," I defame them not; for I mean by carnally and corporally none otherwise than after the form and fashion of a man's body, as we shall be after our resurrection, that is to say, visible, palpable, and circumscribed, having a very quantity with due proportion and distinction of members, in place and order, one from another. And if you will deny Christ so to be in heaven, I have so plain and manifest scriptures against you, that I will take you for no christian man, except that you revoke that error. For sure I am that Christ's natural body hath such a grossness, or stature and quantity, if you will so call it, because the word grossness, grossly taken, as you understand it, soundeth not well in an incorruptible and immortal body.

142.

Grossly.

Marry, as for any other grossness, as of eating, drinking, and gross avoiding of the same, with such other like corruptible grossness, it is for gross heads to imagine or think either of Christ, or of any body glorified.

Augustinus.

And although St Augustine may say, that Christ reigneth not carnally in heaven, yet he saith plainly, that his body is of such sort that it is circumscribed and contained in one place.

[1 Carnally, corporally, or spiritually, 1551.]
[2 Of the sacrament, Orig. ed. Winch. omitting the intermediate words.]
[3 So that all men, 1551.]

And Gregory Nazianzen meant that Christ should not come at the last judgment in a corruptible and mortal flesh, as he had before his resurrection, and as we have in this mortal life, (for such grossness is not to be attributed to bodies glorified;) but yet shall he come with such a body as he hath since his resurrection, absolute and perfect in all parts and members of a man's body, having hands, feet, head, mouth, side and wounds, and all other parts of a man visible and sensible, like as we shall all appear before him at the same last day, with this same flesh in substance that we now have, and with these same eyes shall we see God our Saviour. Marry to what fineness and pureness our bodies shall be then changed, no man knoweth in the peregrination of this world, saving that St Paul saith, "that he shall change this vile body, that he may make it like unto his glorious body." But that we shall have diversity of all members, and a due proportion of men's natural bodies, the scripture manifestly declareth, whatsover you can by a sinister gloss gather of Nazianzen to the contrary, that glorified bodies have no flesh nor grossness. *Nazianzenus.* *Phil. iii.*

But see you not how much this saying of St Augustine (that our resurrection shall not be carnally) maketh against yourself? For if we shall not rise carnally, then is not Christ risen carnally, nor is not in heaven carnally. And if he be not in heaven carnally, how can he be in the sacrament carnally, and eaten and drunken carnally with our mouths, as you say he is? And therefore, as for the terms "carnally and corporally," it is you that defame them by your gross taking of them, and not I, that speak of none other grossness, but of distinction of the natural and substantial parts, without the which no man's body can be perfect.

And whereas here, in this process, you attribute unto Christ none other presence in heaven but spiritual, without all manner of grossness or carnality, so that all manner of being is spiritual, and none otherwise than he is in the sacrament, here I join an issue with you for a joint, and for the price of a fagot. I wondered all this while that you were so ready to grant, that Christ is but after a spiritual manner in the sacrament; and now I wonder no more at that, seeing that you say he is but after a spiritual manner in heaven. And by this means we may say that he hath but a spiritual manhood, as you say that he hath in the sacrament but a spiritual body. And yet some carnal thing and grossness he hath in him, for he hath flesh and bones, which spirits lack; except that to all this impiety you will add, that his flesh and bones also be spiritual things, and not carnal. And it is not without some strange prognostication, that you be now waxed altogether so spiritual. *Whether Christ be in heaven but after a spiritual manner. An issue.* *143.*

Now as concerning the word "figuratively," what need this any proof, that Christ is in the sacraments figuratively? which is no more to say but sacramentally. And you grant yourself that Christ, under the figure of visible creatures, gave invisibly his precious body. And you say that Christ said, "This is my body," using the outward signs of the visible creatures. And this doctrine was never reproved of any catholic man, but hath at all times and of all men been allowed without contradiction, saving now of you alone. Now followeth my answer to the authors particularly. *Figuratively.*

And first, to St Clement. My words be these.

They allege St Clement, whose words be these, as they report: "The sacraments of God's secrets are committed to three degrees: to a priest, a deacon, and a minister: which with fear and trembling ought to keep the leavings of the broken pieces of the Lord's body, that no corruption be found in the holy place, lest by negligence great injury be done to the portion of the Lord's body." And by and by followeth: "So many hosts must be offered in the altar as will suffice for the people. And if any remain, they must not be kept until the morning, but be spent and consumed of the clerks with fear and trembling. And they that consume the residue of the Lord's body may not by and by take other common meats, lest they should mix that holy portion with the meat, which is digested by the belly, and avoided by the fundament. Therefore if the Lord's portion be eaten in the morning, *Chap. xv. The answer to Clemens, Epist. 2.*

the ministers that consume it must fast unto six of the clock; and if they do take it at three or four of the clock, the minister must fast until the evening."

Thus much writeth Clement of this matter: if the epistle which they allege were Clement's, (as in deed it is not, but they have feigned many things in other men's names, thereby to stablish their feigned purposes,) nevertheless whosesoever the epistle was, if it be thoroughly considered, it maketh much more against the papists than for their purpose. For by the same epistle appeareth evidently three special things against the errors of the papists.

The first is, that the bread in the sacrament is called the Lord's body, and the pieces of the broken bread be called the pieces and fragments of the Lord's body, which cannot be understand but figuratively.

The second is, that the bread ought not to be reserved and hanged up, as the papists everywhere do use.

The third is, that the priests ought not to receive the sacrament alone, (as the papists commonly do, making a sale thereof unto the people,) but they ought to communicate with the people.

And here is diligently to be noted, that we ought not unreverently and unadvisedly to approach unto this meat[1] of the Lord's table, as we do to other common meats and drinks, but with great fear and dread, lest we should come to that holy table unworthily, wherein is not only represented, but also spiritually given unto us, very Christ himself.

And therefore we ought to come to that board of the Lord with all reverence, faith, love, and charity, fear, and dread, according to the same.

WINCHESTER.

144.

Let us now consider what particular answers this author deviseth to make to the fathers of the church; and first what he saith to St Clement's Epistle, his handling whereof is worthy to be noted.

Clement.

First, he saith the epistle is not Clement's, but feigned, as he saith many other things be for their purpose, he saith, which solution is short and may be soon learned of naughty men, and naughtily applied further as they list. But this I may say, if this epistle were feigned of the papists, then do they shew themselves fools that could feign no better, but so as this author might of their feigned epistle gather three notes against them. This author's notes be these: first, "that the bread in the sacrament is called the Lord's body, and that the broken bread be called the pieces and fragments of the Lord's body." Mark well, reader, this note that speaketh so much of bread, where the words of the epistle in the part here alleged name no bread at all. If this author hath read so much mention of bread in another[2] part of the epistle, why bringeth he not that forth to fortify his note? I have read after the same[3] epistle, panes sanctuarii, but they would not help this author's note; and yet for the other matter joined with them, they would slander another way. And therefore seeing this author hath left them out, I will go no further than is here alleged.

The calling of bread by enunciation for a name is not material, because it signifieth that was, but in that is here alleged is no mention of bread to prove the note; and to faithful men the words of the epistle reverently express the remain of the mysteries, in which when many hosts be offered in the altar, according to the multitude that should communicate, those many hosts after consecration be not many bodies of Christ, but of many breads one body of Christ. And yet, as we teach in England now in the book of common prayer, in every part of that is broken is the whole body of our Saviour Christ. Man's words cannot suffice to express God's mysteries, nor can[4] utter them so, as froward reason shall not find matter to wrangle. And yet to stay reason may suffice, that as in one loaf of bread broken every piece broken is a piece of that bread, and every piece of the bread broken is in itself a whole piece of bread, and so whole bread, for every piece hath an whole substance of bread in it: so we truly speak of the host consecrated, to avoid

---

[1 The meat, 1551, and Orig. ed.]
[2 Any other, 1551.]
[3 In the same, 1551.]
[4 Cannot, Orig. ed. Winch.]

the *fantasy of multiplication of Christ's body, which in all the hosts, and all the parts of the hosts, is but one, not broken nor distribute by pieces, and yet in a speech, to tell and signify that is broken, called in name the leaving "pieces of the body," "portion of the body," "residue of the body;" in which nevertheless each one piece is Christ's whole body.*

So as this speech having a figure, hath it of necessity to avoid the absurdity, whereby to signify a multitude of bodies, which is not so, and the sound of the speech christian ears do abhor. But this I ask, where is the matter of this author's note, that bread is called Christ's body? where there is no word of bread in the words alleged; and if there were, as there is not, it were worthy no note at all. For that name is not abhorred, and the catholic faith teacheth that the fraction is in the outward sign, and not in the body of Christ, invisibly present, and signified so to be present by that visible sign. The second note of this author is touching reserving, which Clement might seem to deny, because he ordered the remain to be received of the clerks, thinking so best; not declaring expressly that nothing might be reserved to the use of them that be absent. The contrary whereof appeareth by Justin the Martyr[5], Justin. Apol. 2. *who testifieth a reservation to be sent to them that were sick, who and they dwell far from the church, as they do in some places, it may by chance in the way, or trouble in the sick man, tarry till the morning or it be received. And Cyril[6] writeth expressly, that in case it so doth,* Cyrillus ad Calosyrium. *the mystical benediction, by which terms he calleth the sacrament, remaineth still in force. When this author findeth fault at hanging up of the sacrament, he blameth only his own country and the isles hereabout; which fault Linehood[7], after he had travelled other countries* *Linehood wrote a comment of the constitutions provincial of England. *found here, being the manner of custody in reservation otherwise used than in other parts. But one thing this author should have noted of Clement's words when he speaketh of fearing and trembling, which and the bread were never the holier, as this author teacheth, and but only a signification, why should any man fear or tremble more in their presence than he*

145.

doth when he heareth of Christ's supper, the gospel read, or himself or any other saying his creed, which in words signify as much as the bread doth, if it be but a signification? And Peter Martyr saith, that words signify more clearly than these signs do, and saith further Peter Martyr. *A marvellous speech of Peter Martyr, unless he be a sacramentary, and then he speaketh like himself. *in his disputation with Chedsay, that we receive the body of Christ, no less by words than by the sacramental signs; which teaching if it were true, why should this sacrament be trembled at? But because this author noteth the epistle of Clement to be feigned, I will not make with him any foundation of it, but note to the reader the third note, gathered by this author of Clement's words, which is, "that priests ought not to receive alone," which the words of the epistle prove not. It sheweth indeed what was done, and how the feast is indeed prepared for the people as well as the priest.*

And I never read any thing of order in law or ceremony forbidding the people to communicate with the priest, but all the old prayers and ceremonies sounded as the people did communicate with the priest. And when the people is prepared for, and then come not, but fearing and trembling forbear to come, that then the priest might not receive his part alone, the words of this epistle shew not. And Clement, in that he speaketh so of leavings, seemeth to think of that case of disappointment of the people that should come, providing in that case the clerks to receive the residue; whereby should appear, if there were no store of clerks, but only one clerk, as some poor churches have no more, then a man might rather make a note of Clement's mind, that in that case one priest might receive all alone[8], and so upon a chance keep the feast alone. But whatsoever we may gather, that note of this author remaineth unproved, that the priest ought not to receive alone.

And here I dare therefore join an issue with this author, that none of his three feigned notes An issue. *is grounded of any words of this that he noteth a feigned epistle, taking only words[9] that he allegeth here. This author upon occasion of this epistle, which he calleth feigned, speaketh more reverently of the sacrament than he doth in other places, which methink worthy to be noted of me. Here he saith that very Christ himself is not only represented, but also spiritually given unto us*

[5 Καὶ ἡ διάδοσις καὶ ἡ μετάληψις ἀπὸ τῶν εὐχαριστηθέντων ἑκάστῳ γίνεται, καὶ τοῖς οὐ παροῦσι διὰ τῶν διακόνων πέμπεται. Just. Op. Par. 1742. Apol. I. (al. II.) 67. p. 83.]

[6 Ἀκούω δὲ ὅτι εἰς ἁγιασμὸν ἀπρακτεῖν φασὶν τὴν μυστικὴν εὐλογίαν, εἰ ἀπομένοι λείψανον αὐτῆς, εἰς ἑτέραν ἡμέραν. μαίνονται δὲ ταῦτα λέγοντες. οὐ γὰρ ἀλλοιοῦται Χριστός, οὐδὲ τὸ ἅγιον αὐτοῦ σῶμα μεταβληθήσεται, ἀλλ' ἡ τῆς εὐλογίας δύνα-μις, καὶ ἡ ζωοποιὸς χάρις διηνεκής ἐστιν ἐν αὐτῷ.— Cyrillus, ad Calosyrium. Ed. Aubert. Tom. VI. p. 365. Ed. Par. 1638.]

[7 Linehood or Lindwood compiled the Provincial Constitutions in the time of king Henry VI. and is referred to by Beal, clerk of the Council, as an authority, in Strype, Whitgift, II. p. 138.]

[8 Receive alone, Orig. ed. Winch.]

[9 The only words, 1551.]

in this table; for so I understand the word "wherein." And then if very Christ himself be represented and given in the table, the author meaneth not the material table, but by the word "table" the meat upon the table; as the word mensa, *"a table," doth signify in the 16th of the Acts, and the 10th of the Corinthians*[1]. *Now if very Christ himself be given in the meat, then is he present in the meat to be given. So as by this teaching very Christ himself is not only figuratively in the table, that is to say, the meat of the table, which this author now calleth representing, but is also spiritually given in the table, as these words sound to me. But whether this author will say very Christ himself is given spiritually in the meat, or by the meat, or with the meat, what scripture hath he to prove that he saith, if the words of Christ be only a figurative speech, and the bread only signify Christ's body? For if the words of the institution be but in figure, man cannot add of his device any other substance or effect than the words of Christ purport: and so this supper, after this author's teaching in other places of his book, where he would have it but a signification, shall be a bare memory of Christ's death, and signify only such communication of Christ, as we have otherwise by faith in that benefit of his passion, without any special communication of the substance of his flesh in this sacrament, being the same only a figure, if it were true that this author would persuade in the conclusion of this book, although by the way he saith otherwise, for fear percase and trembling, that he conceiveth even of an epistle which he himself saith is feigned.*

Acts xvi.
1 Cor. x.

CANTERBURY.

It is no marvel, though this epistle feigned by the papists many years passed do vary from the papists in these latter days. For the papistical church at the beginning was not so corrupt as it was after, but from time to time increased in errors and corruption more and more, and still doth, according to St Paul's saying: "Evil men and deceivers wax ever worse, both leading other into error, and erring themselves." For at the first beginning they had no private masses, no pardons in purgatory, no reservation of the bread; they knew no masses of *Scala Cœli*, no lady psalters, no transubstantiation; but of later days all these, and an infinite number of errors besides, were invented and devised without any authority of God's word. As yourself have newly invented[2] a great sort of new devices contrary to the papists before your time, as that Christ is in the sacrament carnally and naturally; that the demonstration was made upon the bread when Christ said, "This is my body;" that the word "satisfactory" signifieth no more but the priest to do his duty; with many other things, which here for shortness of time I will omit at this present, purposing to speak of them more hereafter. And the epistles of Clement were feigned before the papists had run so far in errors as they be now. For yet at that time was not invented, as I said, the error of transubstantiation, nor the reservation of the sacrament, nor the priests did not communicate alone without the people. But that the said epistle of Clement was feigned, be many most certain arguments. For there be five epistles of Clement so knit together, and referring one to another, that if one be feigned, all must needs be feigned.

2 Tim. iii. 146.

Clement's epistles feigned.

Now neither Eusebius in *Ecclesiastica Historia*, nor St Jerome, nor Gennadius, nor any other old writer, maketh any mention of those epistles; which authors, in rehearsing what works Clement wrote, (not leaving out so much as one epistle of his,) would surely have made some mention of the five epistles, which the papists long before our time feigned in his name, if there had been any such in their time.

Moreover those epistles make mention, that Clement at James's request wrote unto him the manner of Peter's death: but how could that be, seeing that James was dead seven years before Peter? For James died the seventh year, and Peter the fourteenth year, of Nero the emperor.

Thirdly, it is contained in the same epistles, that Peter made Clement his successor, which could not be true, forasmuch as next to Peter succeeded Linus, as all the histories tell.

Fourthly, the author of those epistles saith, that he made the book called *Itinerarium*

[1 To the Corinth. 1551.]   [2 As yourself newly invented, 1551.]

Clementis, which was but feigned in Clement's name, as it is declared, Dist. xv., *Sancta*[3]. And then it followeth likewise of the other epistles.

Fifthly, the author of those epistles taketh upon him to instruct St James in the sacraments, and in all manner fashion[4] how he should use himself in his vocation, as he[5] should say, that James, who learned of Christ himself, knew not how to use himself in the necessary points of Christ's religion, except Clement must teach him.

Sixthly, there be few things in those epistles that either be observed at this day, or were at any time observed sithens Christ's religion first began.

Seventhly, a great number of scriptures in those epistles be so far wrested from the true sense thereof, that they have an evil opinion of Clement that think that he would do such injury to God's word.

Eighthly, those epistles spake of palls, and archdeacons, and other inferior orders, which is not like that those things began so soon, but (as the histories[6]) were invented many years after Peter's time.

And finally, in one of those epistles is contained a most pernicious heresy, that all things ought to be common, and wives also, which could not be the doctrine of Clement, being the most pestilent error of the Nicolaites, whom the Holy Ghost doth hate, as he testifieth in the Apocalypse. Rev. ii.

Now, all these things considered, who, having either wit or good opinion of the apostles and their disciples, can think that they should write any such epistles?

But the epistle of St Clement, say you, speaketh not of bread. What was it then, Clement spake of bread. I pray you, that he meant, when he spake of the broken pieces in the Lord's supper? If it were not bread, it must be some other thing which Christ did eat at that supper. Peradventure you will say, as some stick not to say now-a-days, that Christ had some other meat at that supper than bread, as, if he fared daintily, (which we never read,) you might imagine he had capon, partridge, or pheasant; or, if he fared hardly, at the least you would say he had cheese to eat with his bread, because you will defend that he did not eat dry bread alone. Such vain phantasies men may have, that will speak without God's word, which maketh mention in that holy supper of nothing but of bread and wine. But let it be that Christ had as many dishes as you can devise, yet I trust you will not say, that he called all those his body, but only the bread. And so St Clement, speaking of the broken pieces of the Lord's body, of the residue and fragments of the Lord's body, of the portion and leaving of the Lord's body, must needs speak all this of bread. And thus is it manifest false that you say, that the epistle of Clement speaketh nothing of bread.

And then, forasmuch as he calleth the leavings of the same the broken pieces of the Lord's body, and the fragments and portion thereof he calleth the fragments and portion of the Lord's body, he sheweth that the bread remaineth, and that the calling thereof the Lord's body is a figurative speech. The body of Christ hath no fragments nor broken pieces, and therefore the calling here is so material, that it proveth fully Calling of bread is material. the matter, that to call bread Christ's body is a figurative speech. And although to avoid the matter you devise subtle cavillations, saying that calling is not material, because it signifieth that was; yet they that have understanding, may soon discern what a vain shift this is, imagined only to blind the ignorant reader's eyes. But if that which is bread before the consecration be after no bread, and if it be against the christian faith to think that it is still bread, what occasion of error should this be, to call it still bread after consecration? Is not this a great occasion of error to call it bread still, if it be not bread still?

And yet in this place of Clement the calling can in no wise signify that was before consecration, but must needs signify that is after consecration. For this place speaketh of fragments, broken pieces, and leavings, which can have no true understanding before consecration, at what time there be yet no broken pieces, fragments, nor leavings, but be all done after consecration.

[3 Item Itinerarium nomine Petri Apostoli, quod appellatur sancti Clementis, Lib. VIII. apocryphum.—Corpus Juris Canonici. Gratian. Decreti Prima pars. Dist. xv. cap. 3. "Sancta Romana Ecclesia." Tom. I. col. 57. Lugd. 1618.]

[4 In all manner and fashion, 1551.]

[5 As who should say, 1551.]

[6 As the histories tell, 1551.]

But you wrangle so much in this matter to avoid absurdities, that you snarl yourself into so many and heinous absurdities, as you shall never be able to wind yourself out. For you say that Christ's body, (which in all the hosts and in all the parts of the hosts is but one, not broken, nor distributed,) is called the leaving pieces of the body, portion of the body, residue of the body, and yet every piece is Christ's whole body; which things to be spoken of Christ's body christian ears abhor for to hear. And if you will say that your book is false, that you meant all these leaving pieces, portion, and residue, to be understand of the hosts, and not of Christ's body, then you confess the hosts, which be broken, to be called by name the leavings or pieces of Christ's body, the portion of his body, the residue of his body, by a figurative speech, which is as much as I speak in my first note. And so appeareth how vainly you have travailed for the confutation of my first note.

Of reservation.

Now as touching the second note: Clement declareth expressly, that nothing might be reserved. For where he saith, that "if any thing remain, it must not be kept until the morning, but be spent and consumed of the clerks;" how could he declare more plainly that nothing might be reserved, than by those words?

And as for Justin, he speaketh not one word of sick persons, as you report of him.

And concerning Cyril *ad Calosyrium*[1], would to God that work of Cyril might come abroad! for I doubt not but it would clearly discuss this matter; but I fear that some papists will suppress it, that it shall never come to light. And where you say, that Linehood found fault with his own country of England, and blamed this realm because they hanged up the sacrament, contrary to the use of other countries; you have well excused me that I am not the first finder of this fault, but many years ago that fault was found, and that it was not the use of other countries to hang it up. And yet the use of other countries was fond enough, even as they had charge and commandment from Innocentius III. and Honorius III.[2]

Receiving with fear and trembling.

And as for the receiving of the sacrament with fear and trembling, ought not they that be baptized in their old age, or in years of discretion, come to the water of baptism with fear and trembling, as well as to the Lord's supper? Think you that Simon Magus was not in as great damnation for the unworthy receiving of baptism, as Judas was for the unworthy receiving of the Lord's supper? And yet you will not say that Christ is really and corporally in the water, but that the washing in the water is an outward signification and figure, declaring what God worketh inwardly in them that truly be baptized. And likewise speaketh this epistle of the holy communion. For every good christian man ought to come to Christ's sacraments with great fear, humility, faith, love, and charity.

Aug. 50, homiliarum Hom. 26.

And St Augustine saith that the gospel is to be received or heard with no less fear and reverence than the body of Christ. Whose words be these: *Interrogo vos, fratres et sorores, dicite mihi: Quid? vobis plus esse videtur verbum Dei an corpus Christi? Si vere vultis respondere, hoc utique dicere debetis, quod non sit minus verbum Dei quam corpus Christi. Et ideo quanta solicitudine observamus, quando nobis corpus Christi ministratur, ut nihil ex ipso de nostris manibus in terram cadat, tanta solicitudine observemus, ne verbum Dei quod nobis erogatur, dum aliquid aut cogitamus aut loquimur, de corde nostro pereat: quia non minus reus erit qui verbum Dei negligenter audierit, quam ille qui corpus Christi in terram cadere sua negligentia permiserit.* "I ask this question of you, brethren and sistern," saith St Augustine, "answer me, Whether you think greater, the word of God, or the body of Christ? If you will answer the truth, verily, you ought to say thus: That the word of God is no less than the body of Christ. And therefore with what carefulness we take heed, when the body of Christ is ministered unto us, that no part thereof fall out of our hands on the earth, with as great carefulness let us take heed, that the word of God which is ministered unto us, when we think or speak of vain matters, perish not out of our hearts. For he that heareth the word of God negligently shall be guilty of no less fault than he that suffereth the body of Christ to fall upon the ground through his

---

[1 This Treatise was published in 1605, with a translation in Latin by Bonavent. Vulcanius.—Vid. Io. Geo. Walch. Biblioth. Patrist. p. 446.]

[2 Decretal. Greg. Lugd. 1618. Lib. III. Tit. xliv. cap. i. and Tit. xli. cap. x.]

negligence." This is the mind of St Augustine. And as much we have in scripture for the reverent hearing and reading of God's holy word, or the neglecting thereof, as we have for the sacraments.

But it seemeth by your pen and utterance of this matter, that you understand not the ground and cause, whereupon should arise the great fear and trembling in their hearts, that come to receive the sacraments; for you shew another consideration thereof than the scripture doth. For you seem to drive all the cause of fear to the dignity of the body of Christ, there corporally present and received; but the scripture declareth the fear to rise of the indignity and unworthiness of the receivers. "He that eateth and drinketh unworthily," threateneth God's word, "eateth and drinketh his own damnation." The causes of fear and trembling.

And *Centurio*, considering his own unworthiness, was abashed to receive Christ into his house, saying: "Lord, I am not worthy that thou shouldest come under the covering of my house." And the same thing made Peter afraid to be near unto Christ, and to say: "Go from me, O Lord, for I am a sinner." And all christian men ought not to fear and tremble only, when they receive the sacraments, but whensoever they hear God's word, and threatenings pronounced against sinners. Matt. viii. Luke v.

Now as concerning the third note, thou shalt see plainly, good reader, that here[3] is nothing here answered directly, but mere cavillations sought, and shift to avoid. For if all the old prayers and ceremonies sound, as the people did communicate with the priest, (as you say they do, and so they do indeed, and that as well in the communion of drinking as eating,) then either the people did communicate with them in deed, and received the sacrament under both the kinds, or else the prayers had been false, and the ceremonies frustrate and in vain. And is it like, that the priests in that time would have used unto God such untrue prayers, as should declare that the people did communicate with them, if in deed none did communicate with them? as it should have been by your imagined chances and cases. The people received with the priests.

But it appeareth by the words of the epistle, that the whole multitude of the people that was present did communicate at those days, so that the priest could not communicate alone, except he would communicate when no man was in the church. But by the answer of this sophister here in this place, thou mayest see an experience, good reader, whether he be as ready to see those things that make against him, as he is painful and studious to draw (as it were) by force all things to his purpose, to make them, at the least, to seem to make for him, although they be never so much against him. As appeareth by all these his suppositions, that all the people which were prepared for should in those days withdraw themselves from the communion, and not one of them come unto it; that the clerks should receive all that was provided for the people; that one clerk should receive that which many clerks ought to have received. And so in conclusion by only his feigned suppositions he would persuade, that the priest should receive all alone. 150.

By such pretty cases, of the people disappointing the priests, and of lack of store of clerks, you might daily find[4] cavillations with all godly ordinances. For whereas God ordained the paschal lamb to be eaten up clean in every house; and where there were not enough in one house to eat up the lamb, they should call of their neighbours so many as should suffice to eat up the whole lamb, so that nothing should remain: here you might bring in your "upon a chance," that they that lacked company to eat up a whole lamb, dwelt alone far from other houses, and could not come together; or could not get any such lamb as was appointed for the feast, or if their neighbours lacked company also. And what if they had no spit to roast the lamb? And whereas it was commanded, that they should be shoed, what if perchance they had no shoes? And if perchance a man's wife were not at home, and all his servants falled sick of the sweat or plague, and no man durst come to his house, then must he turn the spit himself, and eat the lamb all alone. Such chances you purposely devise, to establish your private mass, that the priest may eat all alone. But by such a like reason as you make here, a man might prove, that the priest should preach or say matins to himself alone, in case, as you say, that the people, which should come, would disappoint him. For what *The paschal lamb.

[3 That there is nothing, 1551.]   [4 Dayly, and find, 1551.]

if the people disappoint the priest, say you, and come not to the communion? What if the people disappoint the priest, say I, and come not to matins nor sermon? shall he therefore say matins and preach, when no man is present but himself alone? But your imagined case hath such an absurdity in it, as is not tolerable to be thought to have been in christian people in that time, when Clement's epistles were written, that when all the people should receive the communion with the priest, yet not one would come, but all would disappoint him. And yet in that case I doubt not but the priest would have abstained from ministration unto more opportunity, and more access of christian people, as he would have done likewise in saying of matins and preaching. Wherefore in your case I might well answer you, as St Jerome answered the argument made in the name of the heretic Jovinian, which might be brought against the commendation of virginity, "What if all men would live virgins, and no man marry? how should then the world be maintained?" "What if heaven fall," said St Jerome? What if no man will come to the church? is your argument; for all that came in those days received the communion. What if heaven fall? say I. For I have not so evil opinion of the holy church in those days, to think that any such thing could chance among them, that no one would come, when all ought to have come.

<small>Hieron. adversus Jovinianum. Lib. i.</small>

<small>151.
*Mine issue.</small>

Now when you come to your issue, you make your case too strait for me to join an issue with you, binding me to the bare and only words of Clement, and refusing utterly his mind. But take the words and the mind together, and I dare adventure an issue to pass by any indifferent readers, that I have proved all my three notes.

And where you say, that upon occasion of this epistle I speak more reverently of the sacrament than I do in other places: if you were not given altogether to calumniate and deprave my words, you should perceive in all my book through, even from the beginning to the end thereof, a constant and perpetual reverence given unto the sacraments of Christ, such as of duty all christian men ought to give.

Nevertheless you interpret this word "wherein" far from my meaning. For I mean not that Christ is spiritually either in the table, or in the bread and wine that be set upon the table; but I mean that he is present in the ministration and receiving of that holy supper, according to his own institution and ordinance: like as in baptism, Christ and the Holy Ghost be not in the water, or font, but be given in the ministration, or to them that be truly baptized in the water.

<small>Bare significations.</small>

And although the sacramental tokens be only significations and figures, yet doth Almighty God effectually work, in them that duly receive his sacraments, those divine and celestial operations which he hath promised, and by the sacraments be signified. For else they were vain and unfruitful sacraments, as well to the godly as to the ungodly. And therefore I never said of the whole supper, that it is but a signification or a bare memory of Christ's death; but I teach that it is a spiritual refreshing, wherein our souls be fed and nourished with Christ's very flesh and blood to eternal life. And therefore bring you forth some place in my book, where I say that the Lord's supper is but a bare signification without any effect or operation of God in the same; or else eat your words again, and knowledge that you untruly report me.

But hear what followeth further in my book.

<small>Ignatius in episto. ad Ephesianos.
Irenæus Lib. v. contra Valentin.</small>

Here I pass over Ignatius and Irenæus, which make nothing for the papists' opinions, but stand in the commendation of the holy communion, and in exhortation of all men to the often and godly receiving thereof. And yet neither they, nor no man else, can extol and commend the same sufficiently, according to the dignity thereof, if it be godly used as it ought to be.

WINCHESTER.

<small>Ignatius.
Irenæus.</small>

This author saith he passeth over Ignatius and Irenæus; and why? Because they make nothing, he saith, for the papists' purpose. With the word "papist" the author playeth at his pleasure. But it shall be evident that Irene doth plainly confound this author's purpose, in the denial of the true presence of Christ's very flesh in the sacrament; who, although he use not the words "real and substantial," yet he doth effectually comprehend in his speech of the sacrament the virtue and strength of those words. And for the truth of the sacrament is

OF THE PRESENCE OF CHRIST.

Irenæus specially alleged, insomuch as Melancthon, when he writeth to Œcolampadius, that   Philip. Melanct.
he will allege none but such as speak plainly[1], *he allegeth Irenæus for one, as appeareth by his said epistle to Œcolampadius. And Œcolampadius himself is not troubled so much with answering any other to shape any manner of evasion, as to answer Irenæus, in whom he notably stumbleth. And Peter Martyr, in his work, granteth Irenee to be specially alleged, to*   152.
whom when he goeth about to answer, a man may evidently see how he masketh himself. And this author bringeth in Clement's epistle, of which no great count is made, although it be not contemned, and passeth over Irenæus, that speaketh evidently in the matter, and was as old as Clement, or not much younger. And because Ignatius was of that age, and is alleged by Theodoret to have written in his epistle ad Smyrnenses, *whereof may appear his faith of the mystery of the sacrament, it shall serve to good purpose to write in the words of the same Ignatius here upon the credit of the said Theodoret*[2], *whom this author so much*   Theodoret. Dialogo. 3.
commendeth: the words of Ignatius be these: Eucharistias et oblationes non admittunt, quod non confiteantur eucharistiam esse carnem servatoris nostri Jesu Christi, quæ pro peccatis nostris passa est, quam Pater sua benignitate suscitavit. *Which words be thus much in English;* "They do not admit eucharistias *and* 'oblations,' *because they do not confess* eucharistiam *to be the flesh of our Saviour Jesu Christ: which flesh suffered for our sins, which flesh the Father by his benignity hath stirred up." These be Ignatius' words, which I have not throughly Englished, because the word* eucharistia *cannot be well Englished, being a word of mystery, and signifieth (as Irenæus openeth) both the parts of the sacrament, heavenly and earthly, visible and invisible. But in that Ignatius openeth his faith thus, he taketh*[3] eucharistia *to be the flesh of our Saviour Christ that suffered for us, he declareth the sense of Christ's words,* "This is my body," *not to be figurative only, but to express the truth of the very flesh there given; and therefore (Ignatius saith)* eucharistia *is the flesh of our Saviour Christ, the same that suffered and the same that rose again. Which words of Ignatius so pithily open the matter, as they declare therewith the faith*[4] *also of Theodoret that doth allege him, so as if the*[5] *author would make so absolute a work as to peruse all the fathers' sayings, he should not thus leap over Ignatius, nor Irene neither, as I have before declared. But this is a colour of rhetoric called "rejection" of that is hard to answer, and is here a pretty shift or sleight,*   *Sleight.
whereby thou, reader, mayest consider how this matter is handled.

CANTERBURY.

It shall not need to make any further answer to you here as concerning Irenæus, but only to note one thing, that if any place of Irenæus had served for your purpose, you would not have failed here to allege it. But because you have nothing that maketh for you in deed, therefore you allege nothing in especial, (lest in the answer it should evidently appear to be nothing,) and so slide you from the matter, as though all men should believe you, because you say it is so.

And as for the place of Irenee alleged by Melancthon in an epistle, Œcolampadius[6]   Irenee.
(without any such troubling of himself as you imagine) maketh a plain and easy answer thereto; although Melancthon wrote not his said epistle to Œcolampadius, (as you, negligently looking upon their works, be deceived,) but to Fridericus Myconius. And

---

[[1] Nonnulli sine delectu maximum numerum testimoniorum congesserunt, in quibus pleraque sunt ambigua et obscura: nos tantum ea recitavimus, quæ videbantur esse quam maxime perspicua. Melancth. Epist. Frid. Myconio. This Epistle is inserted in Œcolampadius's Dialogue referred to above, p. 137. The above quotation will be found in p. 33 of the edition there described.]

[[2] Εὐχαριστίας καὶ προσφορὰς οὐκ ἀποδέχονται*, διὰ τὸ μὴ ὁμολογεῖν τὴν εὐχαριστίαν σάρκα εἶναι τοῦ Σωτῆρος ἡμῶν Ἰησοῦ Χριστοῦ, τὴν ὑπὲρ τῶν ἁμαρτιῶν ἡμῶν παθοῦσαν, ἣν τῇ χρηστότητι ὁ Πατὴρ ἤγειρεν. Theodoretus. Dialog. iii. Tom. IV. p. 231. Halæ. 1769-94.]

[[3] Thus as he taketh, 1551.]
[[4] Therewith that faith, Orig. ed. Winch.]
[[5] So as if this author, 1551.]
[[6] The passages of Irenæus quoted by Melancthon are from the 4th and 5th books contra Valentinum: Irenæus dicit, Calicem eucharistiæ communicationem sanguinis Domini, et panem quem frangimus communicationem corporis ejus. Item dicit: Calicem, qui est creatura, suum corpus confirmavit, ex quo auget corpora nostra. Quando ergo et mistus calix et factus panis percipit verbum Dei, fit eucharistia sanguinis et corporis Christi, ex quibus augetur et subsistit carnis nostræ substantia. …Idem et alio loco dicit: Quomodo dicunt carnem in corruptionem devenire, et non percipere vitam, quæ a corpore Domini et sanguine alitur? The "plain and easy answer" of Œcolampadius begins thus: At si ego essem Valentinus vel Manichæus, nihil terrerer, si sic argueres: Panis est corpus Christi, vel, Christi corpus edimus carnaliter; igitur resurrecturi sumus. Inutilis enim esset consequentia. Œcolampad. Dialog. pp. 51, 52, 188, seqq.]

* Ed. Patrum Apostol. Opera Tubingæ, 1842. (Hefele.) Ignatii Epist. ad Smyrnæos, p. 172, for προσφορὰς οὐκ ἀποδέχονται, reads προσευχῆς ἀπέχονται.

the words of Irenee alleged by Melancthon mean in effect no more, but to prove that our bodies shall rise again, and be joined unto our souls, and reign with them in the eternal life to come. For he wrote against Valentine, Marcion, and other heretics, which denied the resurrection of our bodies, from whom it seemeth you do not much dissent, when you say that our bodies shall rise spiritually[1], if you mean that they shall rise without the form and fashion of men's bodies, without distinction and proportion of members. For those shall be marvellous bodies, that shall have no shape nor fashion of bodies, as you say Christ's body is in the sacrament, to whose body ours shall be like after the resurrection.

<small>153. Why bread is called Christ's body and wine his blood.</small>

But to return to answer Irenee clearly and at large, his meaning was this, that as the water in baptism is called *aqua regenerans*, "the water that doth regenerate," and yet it doth not regenerate in deed, but is the sacrament of regeneration wrought by the Holy Ghost, and called so to make it to be esteemed above other common waters: so Christ confessed the creatures of bread and wine, joined unto his words in his holy supper, and there truly ministered, to be his body and blood; meaning thereby, that they ought not to be taken as common bread, or as bakers' bread, and

<small>Smyth.</small>

wine drunken in the tavern, (as Smith untruly jesteth of me throughout his book;) but that they ought to be taken for bread and wine wherein we give thanks to God, and therefore be called *eucharistia corporis et sanguinis Domini*, "the thanking of Christ's body and blood," as Irenee termeth them; or *mysteria corporis et sanguinis Domini*, "the mysteries of Christ's[2] flesh and blood," as Dionysius calleth them; or *sacramenta corporis et sanguinis Domini*, "the sacraments of Christ's flesh and blood," as divers other authors use to call them. And when Christ called bread and wine his body and blood, why do the old authors change, in many places, that speech of Christ, and call them *eucharistia, mysteria, et sacramenta corporis et sanguinis Domini*, "the thanksgiving, the mysteries, and the sacraments of his flesh and blood," but because they would clearly expound the meaning of Christ's speech, that when he called the bread and wine his flesh and blood, he meant to ordain them to be the sacraments of his flesh and blood?—according to such a speech as St Augustine expresseth, how the sacraments of Christ's flesh and blood be called his flesh and blood, and yet in deed they be not his flesh and blood, but the sacraments thereof, signifying unto the godly receivers, that as they corporally feed of the bread and wine, (which comfort[3] their hearts and continue this corruptible life for a season,) so spiritually they feed of Christ's very flesh, and drink his very blood. And we be in such sort united unto him, that his flesh is made our flesh, his holy Spirit uniting him and

<small>Eph. v. Eph. i. iv. Col. i.</small>

us so together, that we be flesh of his flesh, and bone of his bones, and make all one mystical body, whereof he is the head, and we the members. And as feeding, nourishing, and life, cometh from the head, and runneth into all parts of the body; so doth eternal nourishment and life come from Christ unto us completely and fully, as well into our bodies as souls. And therefore if Christ our head be risen again, then shall we that be the members of his body surely rise also; forasmuch as the

<small>1 Cor. xv.</small>

members cannot be separated from the head, but seeing that as he is our head and eternal food, we must needs by him live with him for ever. This is the argument of Irenee against those heretics which denied the resurrection of our bodies. And these things the sacraments of bread and wine declare unto us: but neither the carnal presence, nor the carnal eating of Christ's flesh, maketh the things so to be, nor Irenee meant no such thing. For then should all manner of persons that receive the sacraments, have everlasting life, and none but they.

Thus have I answered to Irenee plainly and shortly, and Œcolampadius needed not to trouble himself greatly with answering this matter. For by the corporal eating and drinking of Christ's flesh and blood, Irenee could never have proved the resurrection of our bodies to eternal life.

<small>Peter Martyr.</small>

And Peter Martyr[4] maketh the matter so plain, that he concludeth Irenæus' words to make directly against the doctrine of the papists.

[1 Spiritual, 1551.]
[2 His, 1551.]

[3 Comforteth their hearts, and continueth, 1551.]
[4 Irenæus adversus hæreticos Valentinianos,

The answer also is easily made to the place which you allege out of Ignatius, where he calleth *eucharistia* the flesh of our Saviour Jesus Christ. For he meaneth no more but that it is the sacrament of his flesh, or the mystery of his flesh, or, as Irenee said, *eucharistia* of his flesh, as even now I declared in mine answer to Irenee. And your long process here may have a short answer gathered of your own words. This word *eucharistia*, say you, "cannot be well Englished:" but the body of Christ is good and plain English; and then if *eucharistia* be such a thing as cannot be well Englished, it cannot be called the body of Christ, but by a figurative speech. And how can you then conclude of Ignatius' words, that "This is my body," is no figurative speech? It seemeth rather that the clean contrary may be concluded. For if these two speeches be like and of one sense, ("*eucharistia* is Christ's body," and "This is my body,") and the first be a declaration of the second, is this a good argument, The first is a figure, ergo, the second is none? Is it not rather to be gathered upon the other side thus, The first is a declaration of the second, and yet the first is a figure, ergo, the second is also a figure? And that rather than the first; because the declaration should be a more plain speech than that which is declared by it.

And as for your "colour of rhetoric," which you call "rejection," it is so familiar with yourself, that you use it commonly in your book, when I allege any author, or speak any thing that you cannot answer unto.

And yet one thing is necessary to admonish the reader, that Ignatius in this epistle entreateth not of the manner of the presence of Christ in the sacrament, but of the manner of his very body, as he was born of his mother, crucified, and rose again, appeared unto his apostles, and ascended into heaven: which things divers heretics said were not done verily in deed, but apparently to men's sights, and that in deed he had no such carnal and corporal body, as he appeared to have. And against such errors speaketh that epistle, and not of the real and corporal presence of Christ in the sacrament; although *eucharistia*, or the sacrament, be ordained for a remembrance of that very body, and so hath the name of it, as the sacraments[5] have the names of the things which they signify. But by this so manifest writhing[6] of the mind of Ignatius from that true sense[7] and purpose that was meant, to another sense and purpose that was not meant, may appear the truth of the papists, who wrast and misconstrue all old ancient writers and holy doctors to their wicked and ungodly purposes.

Next in my book followeth mine answer to Dionysius.

Dionysius also, whom they allege to praise and extol this sacrament, (as indeed it is most worthy, being a sacrament of most high dignity and perfection, representing unto us our most perfect spiritual conjunction unto Christ, and our continual nourishing, feeding, comfort, and spiritual life in him,) yet he never said that the flesh and blood of Christ was in the bread and wine, really, corporally, sensibly and naturally, (as the papists would bear us in hand;) but he calleth ever the bread and wine signs, pledges, and tokens, declaring unto the faithful receivers of the same, that they receive Christ spiritually, and that they spiritually eat his flesh and drink his blood. And although the bread and wine be figures, signs, and tokens of Christ's flesh and blood, (as S. Dionyse calleth them, both before the consecration and after,) yet the Greek annotations upon the same Dionyse do say, that the very things themselves be above in heaven.

And as the same Dionyse maketh nothing for the papists' opinions in this point

---

'Panis terrenus,' inquit, 'accepta vocatione à verbo Dei, non amplius est communis panis, sed efficitur eucharistia, quæ constat ex duabus rebus, nimirum terrena et cœlesti.' In primis non negat eucharistiam panem esse, nisi illum communem feceris. Postea dicit, ex duabus rebus constare, quarum una terrestris est, ut panis, altera cœlestis, ut corpus Christi. Atque ut ex una parte retinetur veritas, scilicet quoad corpus Domini, ita in altera est conservanda, videlicet quoad panem. Et addit per similitudinem, ita corpora nostra illam sumentia, non sunt amplius corruptibilia.—Peter Martyr. De sacramento Eucharistiæ, p. 94, 5. Tiguri. 1552.]

[5 As sacraments, 1551.]
[6 Writing, 1551.]
[7 From the true sense, 1551.]
[8 This treatise is spurious; for proof of which see "James' Corruptions of Scripture," &c. p. 7, Ed. London. 1843.]

of Christ's real and corporal presence, so in divers other things he maketh quite and clean against them, and that specially in three points; in transubstantiation, in reservation of the sacrament, and in the receiving of the same by the priest alone.

WINCHESTER.

Dionysius.

As touching Dionysius, a wise reader may, without any note of mine, see how this author is troubled in him, and calleth for aid the help of him that made the Greek commentaries upon Dionysius, and pleadeth therewith the form of the words "really," "corporally," "sensibly," and "naturally," whereof two, that is to say, "really" and "sensibly," the old authors in syllables used not, for so much as I have read, but "corporally" and "naturally" they used speaking of this sacrament. This Dionyse spake of this mystery after the dignity of it, not contending with any other for the truth of it as we do now, but extolling it as a marvellous high mystery, which, if the bread be never the holier, and were only a signification, (as this author teacheth,) were no high mystery at all. As for the things of the sacrament to be in heaven, the church teacheth so, and yet the same things be in deed present in the sacrament also, which is a mystery so deep and dark from man's natural capacity, as is only to be believed supernaturally, without asking of the question "how," whereof St Chrysostom maketh an exclamation in this wise:

Chrysostom. de Sacerdot. Lib. iii.

"O great benevolence of God towards us! He that sitteth above with the Father, at the same hour is holden here with the hands of all men, and giveth himself to them that will clasp and embrace him[1]." Thus saith Chrysostom, confessing to be above and here the same things at once, and not only[2] in men's breasts but hands also, to declare the inward work of God, in the substance of the visible sacrament, whereby Christ is present in the midst of our senses, and so may be called sensibly present, although man's senses cannot comprehend and feel, or taste of him in their proper nature. But as for this Dionyse, he doth[3], without argument, declare his faith in the adoration he maketh of this sacrament, which is openly testified in his works, so as we need not to doubt[4] what his faith was. As for this author's notes, they be[5] descant voluntary[6], without the tenor part, being belike ashamed to allege the text itself, lest his three notes might seem feigned without ground, as before in St Clement's epistle, and therefore I will not trouble the reader with them.

CANTERBURY.

I ask no more of the reader, but to read my book, and then to judge how much I am troubled with this author. And why may I not cite the Greek commentaries for testimony of the truth? Is this to be termed a "calling for aid?" Why is not then the allegation of all authors a calling for aid? Is not your doing rather a calling for aid, when you be fain to fly for succour to Martin Luther, Bucer, Melancthon, Epinus, Jonas, Peter Martyr, and such other, whom all the world knoweth you never favoured, but ever abhorred their names? May not this be termed a "calling for aid," when you be driven to such a strait and need, that you be glad to cry to such men for help, whom ever you have hindered and defamed as much as lay in you to do?

And as for pleading of those words, "really," "corporally," "sensibly," and "naturally," they be your own terms, and the terms wherein resteth the whole contention between you and me: and should you be offended because I speak of those

156.

terms? It appeareth now that you be loth to hear of those words, and would very gladly have them put in silence, and so should the variance between you and me be clearly ended. For if you will confess, that the body of Christ is not in the sacrament really, corporally, sensibly, and naturally, then you and I shall shake hands, and be both earnest friends of the truth.

"Really" and "sensibly" be not found in any old author.

And yet one thing you do here confess, (which is worthy to be noted and had in memory,) that you read not in any old author, that the body of Christ is really and sensibly in the sacrament. And hereunto I add, that none of them say, that

---

[1] Ὢ τῆς Θεοῦ φιλανθρωπίας· ὁ μετὰ τοῦ πατρὸς ἄνω καθήμενος, κατὰ τὴν ὥραν ἐκείνην τῶν ἁπάντων κατέχεται χερσί, καὶ δίδωσιν αὐτὸν τοῖς βουλομένοις περιπτύξασθαι καὶ περιλαβεῖν.—Chrysostom. de Sacerdotio. Lib. III. Tom. I. p. 382. Ed. Bened.]

[2] At once, not only, &c. 1551.]

[3] For this, Dionyse doth, 1551.]

[4] We need not doubt, 1551.]

[5] Notes be descant, 1551.]

[6] Descant voluntary: i. e. a song or tune composed in parts, played at will without any settled rule or rhythm.]

he is in the bread and wine corporally nor naturally. No, never no papist said, that Christ's body is in the sacrament naturally nor carnally, but you alone, (who be the first author of this gross error, which Smith himself condemneth, and denieth that ever[7] Christian man so taught,) although some say that it is there "really," some "substantially," and some "sensibly." {Smith.}

Now as concerning the high mystery which St Denys speaketh of, he declareth the same to be in the marvellous and secret working of God in his reasonable creatures, (being made after his image, and being his lively temples, and Christ's mystical body,) and not in the unreasonable and unsensible and unlively creatures of bread and wine, wherein you say the deep and dark mystery standeth. But notwithstanding any holiness or godliness wrought in the receivers of them, yet they be not the more holy or godly in themselves, but be only tokens, significations, and sacraments of that holiness, *which Almighty God by his omnipotent power worketh in us. And for their holy significations they have the name of holiness*[8], as the water in baptism is called *aqua sanctificans, unda regenerans,* "hallowing or regenerating water," because it is the sacrament of regeneration and sanctification. {Holiness in the sacraments.}

Now as concerning Chrysostom's saying, that Christ is in our hands, Chrysostom saith, (as I have rehearsed in my book,) not only that he is in our hands, but also that we see him with our eyes, touch him, feel him, and grope him, fix our teeth in his flesh, taste it, break it, eat it, and digest it, make red our tongues, and dye them with his blood, &c.; which things cannot be understand of the body and blood of Christ but by a figurative speech, as I have more at large declared in my fourth book, the eighth chapter. And therefore St Augustine, *De Verbis Domini sermone* xxxiii. saith clean contrary to Chrysostom, that we touch not Christ with our hands: "*Non tangimus Dominum,*" saith he. This speech therefore of Chrysostom declareth not the inward work of God in the substance of the visible sacrament, but signifieth what God worketh inwardly in true believers. {Christ in our hands.} {Augustin. de verbis Domini sermone 33.}

And whereas you say, that my notes "be descant voluntary without the tenor part," I have named both the book and chapter where St Dionyse telleth, how the priest, when he cometh to the receiving of the sacraments, he divideth the bread in pieces, and distributeth the same to all that be present; which one sentence containeth sufficiently all my three notes. So that if you be disposed to call my notes descant, there you may find the plain song or tenor part of them. And it is no marvel that you cannot judge well of my descant, when you see not, or will not see, the plain song, whereupon the descant was made.

Now followeth Tertullian, of whom I write thus: 157.

Furthermore they do allege Tertullian[9], that he constantly affirmeth that in the sacrament of the altar we do eat the body and drink the blood of our Saviour Christ. To whom we grant, that our flesh eateth and drinketh the bread and wine, which be called the body and blood of Christ, because, as Tertullian saith, they do represent his body and blood, although they be not really the same in very deed. And we grant also, that our souls by faith do eat his very body and blood[10], but that is spiritually, sucking out of the same everlasting life. But we deny that unto this spiritual feeding is requiring[11] any real and corporal presence. {The answer to Tertullianus de Resurrectione carnis.}

And therefore this Tertullian speaketh nothing against the truth of our

---

[7 Ever any, 1551.]

[8 The words between asterisks are printed twice over by mistake in edit. 1580.]

[9 Denique, cum anima Deo allegitur, ipsa est quæ efficit, ut anima allegi possit. Scilicet caro abluitur, ut anima emaculetur. Caro ungitur, ut anima consecretur. Caro signatur, ut et anima muniatur. Caro manus impositione adumbratur, ut et anima spiritu illuminetur. Caro corpore et sanguine Christi vescitur, ut et anima de Deo saginetur. Non possunt ergo seperari in mercede, quas opera conjungit.—Tertullian. De Resurrectione carnis, cap. 8, p. 330. Lutetiæ Paris. 1664. Acceptum panem et distributum discipulis, corpus suum illum fecit, 'Hoc est corpus meum' dicendo, id est, figura corporis mei......Cur autem panem corpus suum appellat, et non magis peponem, quem Marcion cordis loco habuit, non intelligens veterem fuisse istam figuram corporis Christi. Adv. Marcion. Lib. iv. cap. 40.]

[10 And drink his blood, 1551, and Orig. ed.]

[11 Required, 1551, and Orig. ed.]

catholic doctrine, but he speaketh many things most plainly for us, and against the papists, and specially in three points:

First, in that he saith that Christ called bread his body.

The second, that Christ called it so, because it representeth his body.

The third, in that he saith, that by these words of Christ, "This is my body," is meant, "This is a figure of my body."

WINCHESTER.

Tertullianus. *Of Tertullian I have spoken before, and so hath this author also [1]forgotten here one notable thing in Tertullian, where Tertullian saith, that "Christ made the bread his body," not only called it so, as appear[2] by Tertullian's words, reported by this author before. This note that I make now of Tertullian maketh against this author's purpose, but yet it maketh with the truth, which this author should not impugn. The second note gathered of Tertullian, by this author, is not true; for Christ called it his body, and made it his body, as Tertullian saith. And the third note of this author is in controversy of reading, and must be so understood, as may agree with the rest of Tertullian's sayings, which, after my reading, doth evidently prove, and at the least doth not improve, the catholic doctrine of Christ's church universally received, although it improveth that which this author calleth here our catholic doctrine, most imprudently[3] and untruly reporting the same.*

CANTERBURY.

I desire no more but that the reader will look upon the place of Tertullian before mentioned, and see what you speak there, and what is mine answer thereto, and so confer them together and judge.

And that the reader will note also, that here covertly you have granted my first note, that Christ called bread his body, but so slyly, that the reader should not by your will perceive it. And where you deny my second note upon Tertullian, that Christ called it his body, because it represented his body, the words of Tertullian be these: "That Christ reproveth not bread, wherein he representeth his own body[4]." As for my third note, yet once again, reader, I beseech thee turn back and look upon the place, how this lawyer hath expounded Tertullian, if thou canst with patience abide to hear of so foolish a gloss.

And where he saith that this author Tertullian "must be so understand as may agree with the rest of his sayings," would to God you would so do not only in Tertullian, but also in all other authors! for then our controversy should be soon at a point. And it is a most shameless impudency of you, to affirm that the catholic church universally teacheth that Christ is really, sensibly, corporally, naturally, carnally, and substantially, present in the visible forms of bread and wine, seeing that you cannot prove any one of these your sayings, either by scripture, or by the consent of the catholic church, but only by the papistical church, which now many years hath borne the whole swing.

158.

Now followeth Origen, to whom I answer thus.

The answer to Origen. Numer. Hom. 7.

Moreover they allege for them Origen, (because they would seem to have many ancient authors favourers of their erroneous doctrine,) which Origen is most clearly against them. For although he do say, as they allege, that those things which before were signified by obscure figures, be now truly, in deed, and in their very nature and kind, accomplished and fulfilled; and for the declaration thereof he bringeth forth three examples, one of the stone that floweth water, another of the sea and cloud, and the third of manna, which in the old testament did signify Christ to come, who is now come in deed, and is manifested and exhibited unto us, as it were face to face and sensibly, in his word, in the sacrament of regeneration, and the sacraments of bread and wine:

[1 Also, and forgotten here, 1551.]
[2 May appear, 1551.]
[3 Impudently, 1551.]
[4 Sed ille quidem usque nunc nec aquam reprobavit Creatoris,....nec panem, quo ipsum corpus suum repræsentat, etiam in sacramentis propriis egens mendicitatibus Creatoris. Adv. Marcion. Lib. I. cap. 14.]

yet Origen meant not that Christ is corporally either in his word, or in the water of baptism, or in the bread and wine; nor that we carnally and corporally be regenerated and born again, or eat Christ's flesh and blood. For our regeneration in Christ is spiritual, and our eating and drinking is a spiritual feeding; which kind of regeneration and feeding requireth no real and corporal presence of Christ, but only his presence in spirit, grace, and effectual operation.

And that Origen thus meant that Christ's flesh is a spiritual meat, and his blood a spiritual drink, and that the eating and drinking of his flesh and blood may not be understand literally, but spiritually, it is manifested by Origen's own words, in his seventh homily upon the book called Leviticus; where he sheweth that those words must be understand figuratively, and whosoever understandeth them otherwise, they be deceived, and take harm by their own gross understanding. _{In Levit. Hom. 7.}

WINCHESTER.

Origen's words be very plain, and meaning also, which speak of manifestation and exhi- _{Origenes.} *bition, which be two things to be verified three ways in our religion, that is to say, in the word, and regeneration, and the sacrament of bread and wine, as this author termeth it: which Origen saith not so, but thus, "the flesh of the word of God," not meaning in every of these after one sort, but after the truth of the scripture in each of them. Christ in his word is manifested and exhibited unto us, and by faith, that is, of hearing, dwelleth in us spiritually; for so we have his Spirit. Of baptism St Paul saith, "as many as be baptized be clad in Christ." Now, in the sacrament of bread and wine, by Origen's rule, Christ should be manifested and exhibited unto us after the scriptures, so as the sacrament of bread and wine should not only signify Christ, that is to say, preach him, but also exhibit him sensibly, as Origen's words be reported here to be. So as Christ's words, "This is my body," should be words not of figure or shewing, but of exhibiting Christ's body unto us, and sensibly, as this author allegeth him, which should signify, to be received with our mouth, as Christ commanded, when he said, "Take, eat, &c." diversely from the other two ways, in which by Christ's Spirit we be made participant of the benefit of his passion wrought in his manhood. But in this sacrament we be made participant of his Godhead, by his humanity exhibit unto us for food: and so, in this mystery, we receive him man and God; and in the other, by mean of his Godhead, be participant of the effect of his passion suffered in his manhood.* _{*Origen hath "facie ad faciem," but I take this author as he allegeth Origen. *Errors. When I say "by his manhood," I mean corporally, as Cyril speaketh.}

In this sacrament Christ's manhood is represented and truly present, whereunto the Godhead is most certainly united, whereby we receive a pledge of the regeneration of our flesh, to be in the general resurrection spiritual with our soul, as we have been in baptism made spiritual by regeneration of the soul: which in the full redemption of our bodies shall be made perfect. And therefore this author may not compare baptism with the sacrament throughly; in which baptism Christ's manhood is not really present, although the virtue and effect of his most precious blood be there: but the truth of the mystery of this sacrament is to have Christ's body, his flesh and blood, exhibited, whereunto eating and drinking is, by Christ in his supper, appropriate. In which supper Christ said, "This is my body," which Bucer noteth; and that Christ said not, "This is my spirit," "This is my virtue." Wherefore, after Origen's teaching, if Christ be not only manifested, but also exhibited "sensibly" in the sacrament, then is he in the sacrament in deed, that is to say, "really;" and then is he there "substantially," because the substance of the body is there; and is there "corporally" also, because the very body is there; and "naturally," because the natural body is there; not understanding corporally and naturally in the manner of presence, nor sensibly neither. For then were the manner of presence within man's capacity, and that is false: and therefore the catholic teaching is, that the manner of Christ's presence in the sacrament is spiritual and supernatural, not corporal, not carnal, not natural, not sensible, not perceptible, but only spiritual, the "how" and manner whereof God knoweth; and we, assured by his word, know only the truth to be so, that it is there in deed, and therefore really to be also received with our hands and mouths; and so sensibly there, the body that suffered, and therefore his natural body there, the body of very flesh, and therefore his carnal body, the body truly, and therefore his corporal body there. But as for the manner of presence, that is only spiritual, as I said before, and here in the inculcation of these words. I am tedious to a learned reader, but yet this author enforceth me thereunto, who with these words, "carnally," "corporally," "grossly," _{159. *Sensibly. *Really. *Substantially. *Corporally. *Naturally.}

"sensibly," "naturally," applying them to the manner of presence, doth maliciously[1] and craftily carry away the reader from the simplicity of his faith; and by such absurdities, as these words grossly understood import, astonisheth the simple reader in consideration of the matter, and useth these words, as dust afore their eyes, which to wipe away, I am enforced to repeat the understanding of these words oftener than elsewhere necessary. These things well considered, no man doth more plainly confound this author than this saying of Origen, as he allegeth it, whatsoever other sentences he would pick out of Origen, when he useth liberty of allegories to make him seem to say otherwise. And as I have declared afore, to understand Christ's words spiritually, is to understand them as the Spirit of God hath taught the church, and to esteem God's mysteries most true in the substance of the thing so to be, although the manner exceedeth our capacities, which is a spiritual understanding of the same. And here also this author putteth in for "figuratively," "spiritually[2]," to deceive the reader.

CANTERBURY.

You observe my words here concerning Origen so captiously, as though I had gone about scrupulously to translate his sayings word by word, which I did not; but because they were very long, I went about only to rehearse the effect of his mind briefly and plainly, which I have done faithfully and truly, although you captiously carp and reprehend the same.

160.

And whereas, craftily to alter the sayings of Origen, you go about to put a diversity of the exhibition of Christ in these three things, in his word, in baptism, and in his holy supper, as though in his word and in baptism he were exhibited spiritually, and in his holy supper sensibly to be eaten with our mouths: this distinction you have dreamed in your sleep, or imagined of purpose. For Christ after one sort is exhibited in all these three, in his word, in baptism, and in the Lord's supper; that is to say, spiritually, and for so much in one sort, as before you have confessed yourself. And Origen putteth no such diversity as you here imagine, but declareth one manner of giving of Christ unto us in his word, in baptism, and in the Lord's supper; that is to say, in all these three *secundum speciem*; that as unto the Jews Christ was given in figures, so to us he is given *in specie*, that is to say, *in rei veritate*, in his very nature: meaning nothing else but that unto the Jews he was promised in figures, and to us, after his incarnation, he is married and joined in his proper kind, and in his words and sacraments as it were sensibly given.

As it were.

But howsoever I report Origen, you captiously and very untruly do report me. For whereas I say, that in God's word, and in the sacraments of baptism and of the Lord's supper, Christ is manifested and exhibited unto us, as it were face to face and sensibly, you, leaving out these words, "as it were," make a quarrel to this word "sensibly;" or rather, you make that word "sensibly" the foundation of all your weak building, as though there were no difference between "sensibly," and "as it were sensibly;" and as it were all one thing a man to lie sleeping, and as he were sleeping; or dead, and as he were dead. Do not I write thus in my first book, "that the washing in the water of baptism is as it were a shewing of Christ before our eyes, and a sensible touching, feeling, and groping of him?" And do these words import that we see him and grope him in deed? And further I say, "that the eating and drinking of the sacramental bread and wine is as it were a shewing of Christ before our eyes, a smelling of him with our noses, and a feeling and groping of him with our hands." And do we therefore see him in deed with our corporal eyes, smell him with our noses, and put our hands in his side and feel his wounds? If it were so in deed, I would not add these words, "as it were." For what speech were this, of a thing that is in deed to say, "as it were?" For these words, "as it were," signify that it is not so in deed. So now likewise in this place of Origen, where it is said, "that Christ in his words and sacraments is manifested and exhibited unto us, as it were face to face and sensibly," it is not meant that Christ is so exhibited in deed face to face and sensibly, but the sense is clean contrary, that he is

---

[1 Orig. ed. Winch. omits the words "maliciously and."]

[2 For "spiritually," "figuratively," Orig. ed. Winch.]

not there given sensibly, nor face to face. Thus it appeareth how uprightly you handle this matter, and how truly you report my words. But the further you proceed in your answer, the more you shew crafty juggling, legerdemain, pass a God's name to blind men's eyes, strange speeches, new inventions, not without much impiety as the words sound, but what the meaning is no man can tell but the maker himself. But as the words be placed, it seemeth you mean, that in the Lord's supper we be not "made by Christ's Spirit participant of the benefit of his passion;" nor by baptism or God's word we be not "made participant of his Godhead by his humanity:" and furthermore by this distinction, (which you feign without any ground of Origen,) we receive not "man and God" in baptism; nor in the Lord's supper we be not "by means of his Godhead made participant of the effect of his passion." In baptism also, by your distinction, we receive not "a pledge of the resurrection of our flesh," but in the Lord's supper; nor Christ is not truly present in baptism. Which your said differences do not only derogate and diminish the effect and dignity of Christ's sacraments, but be also blasphemous against the ineffable unity of Christ's person, separating his divinity from his humanity. Here may all men of judgment see by experience, how divinity is handled when it cometh to the discussion of ignorant lawyers.

161.

And in all these your sayings (if you mean as the words be), I make an issue with you for the price of a fagot. And where you say, that "our flesh in the general resurrection shall be spiritual," here I offer a like issue, except you understand a spiritual body to be a sensible and palpable body, that hath all perfect members distinct; which thing in sundry places of your book you seem utterly to deny. And where you make this difference between baptism and this sacrament, that in baptism Christ is not really present, expounding "really present" to signify no more but to be in deed present, yet after a spiritual manner, if you deny that presence to be in baptism; yet the third fagot I will adventure with you, for your strange and ungodly doctrine within twenty lines together; who may in equality of error contend with the Valentines, Arians, or Anabaptists.

*Three issue for my part.

An issue.

*The third issue.

But when you come here to your "lies" (declaring the words, "sensibly," "really," "substantially," "corporally," and "naturally"), you speak so fondly, unlearnedly, and ignorantly, as they that know you not might think that you understood neither grammar, English, nor reason. For who is so ignorant but he knoweth that adverbs that end in "ly" be adverbs of quality, and being added to the verb they express the manner, form, and fashion how a thing is, and not the substance of it? As speaking wisely, learnedly, and plainly, is to speak after such a form and manner as wise men, learned, and plain men, do speak: and to do wisely and godly is to do in such sort and fashion as wise and godly men do. And sometime the adverb "ly" signifieth the manner of a thing that is in deed, and sometime the manner of a thing that is not. As when a man speaketh wisely, that is wise indeed: and yet sometimes we say, "fools speak wisely;" which although they be not wise, yet they utter some speeches in such sort as though they were wise. The king, we say, useth himself princely in all his doings, (who is a prince in deed,) but we say also of an arrogant, wilful, and proud man, that he useth himself princely and imperiously, although he be neither prince nor emperor: and yet we use so to speak of him, because of the manner, form, and fashion of using himself. And if you answer foolishly and unlearnedly, be you therefore a fool and unlearned? Nay, but then your answers be made in such wise, manner, sort, and fashion, as you were neither learned nor wise. Or if you send to Rome or receive private letters from thence, be you therefore a papist? God is judge thereof; but yet do you popishly, that is to say, use such manner and fashion as the papists do. But where the form and manner lacketh, there the adverbs of quality in "ly" have no place, although the thing be there in deed. As when a wise man speaketh not in such a sort, in such a fashion and wise, as a wise man should speak, notwithstanding that he is wise in deed, yet we say not that he speaketh wisely, but foolishly. And the godly king David did ungodly when he took Bersabe, and slew Urie her husband, because that manner of doing was not godly. So do all Englishmen understand by these words, "sensibly," "substantially," "corporally," "naturally," "carnally," "spiritually," and such like, the manner and form of being, and not the thing itself

[*Adverb in] "ly."

2 Sam. xi.

162.

without the said forms and manners. For when Christ was born, and rose from death, and wrought miracles, we say not that he did these things naturally, because the mean and manner was not after a natural sort, although it was the selfsame Christ in nature. But we say that he did eat, drink, sleep, labour, and sweat, talk, and speak naturally, not because only of his nature, but because the manner and fashion of doing was such as we use to do. Likewise when Jesus passed through the people, and they saw him not, he was not then sensibly and visibly among them; their eyes being letted in such sort that they could not see and perceive him. And so in all the rest of your adverbs, the speech admitteth not to say that Christ is there substantially, corporally, carnally, and sensibly, where he is not after a substantial, corporal, carnal, and sensual form and manner. This the husbandman at his plough, and his wife at her rock[1], is able to judge, and to condemn you in this point, and so can the boys in the grammar-school, that you speak neither according to the English tongue, grammar, nor reason, when you say that these words and adverbs, "sensibly," "corporally," and "naturally," do not signify a corporal, sensible, and natural manner. I have been here somewhat long and tedious, but the reader must pardon me; for this subtile and evil device of your own brain, without ground or authority, containeth such absurdities, and may cast such mists before men's eyes to blind them that they should not see, that I am constrained to speak thus much in this matter, and yet more shall do, if this suffice not. But this one thing I wonder much at, that you being so much used and accustomed to lie, do not yet know what "ly" meaneth.

Luke iv.

But at length in this matter, (when you see none other shift,) you be fain to fly to the church for your shot-anchor[2]. And yet it is but the Romish church. For the old and first church of Christ is clearly against you. And Origen saith not as you do, that "to understand the said words of Christ spiritually is to understand them as the Spirit of God hath taught the church;" but to understand them spiritually is to understand them otherwise than the words sound: "for he that understandeth them after the letter," saith Origen, "understandeth them carnally, and that understanding hurteth and destroyeth. For in plain understanding of eating and drinking without trope or figure, Christ's flesh cannot be eaten, nor his blood drunken."

Next followeth in order St Cyprian, of whom I write thus:

The answer to Cyprian, Lib. ii. Epist. 3.

And likewise meant Cyprian, in those places which the adversaries of the truth allege of him, concerning the true eating of Christ's very flesh and drinking of his blood. For Cyprian spake of no gross and carnal eating with the mouth, but of an inward spiritual and pure eating with heart and mind: which is to believe in our hearts that his flesh was rent and torn for us upon the cross, and his blood shed for our redemption; and that the same flesh and blood now sitteth at the right hand of the Father, making continual intercession for us: and to imprint and digest this in our minds, putting our whole affiance and trust in him, as touching our salvation, and offering ourselves clearly unto him, to love and serve him all the days of our life; this is truly, sincerely, and spiritually to eat his flesh, and to drink his blood.

163.

Gen. ix.

Gen. xiv.

And this sacrifice of Christ upon the cross was that oblation, which Cyprian saith was figured and signified before it was done, by the wine which Noe drank, and by the bread and wine which Melchisedech gave to Abraham, and by many other figures which St Cyprian there rehearseth. And now when Christ is come, and hath accomplished that sacrifice, the same is figured, signified, and represented unto us by that bread and wine, which faithful people receive daily in the holy communion. Wherein like as with their mouths carnally they eat the bread and drink the wine, so by their faith

---

[1 Rock: i.e. a distaff, or staff, held in the hand, from which, in spinning, the wool was spun by twirling a spindle below.]

[2 Shot-anchor, the same as sheet-anchor.]

spiritually they eat Christ's very flesh and drink his very blood. And hereby it appeareth, that St Cyprian clearly affirmeth the most true doctrine, and is wholly upon our side.

And against the papists he teacheth most plainly, that the communion ought to be received of all men under both kinds: and that Christ called bread his body, and wine his blood: and that there is not transubstantiation, but that bread remaineth there as a figure to represent Christ's body, and wine to represent his blood, and that those which be not the lively members of Christ do eat the bread and drink the wine, and be not nourished[3] by them; but the very flesh and blood of Christ they neither eat nor drink.

Thus have you declared the mind of St Cyprian.

WINCHESTER.

As touching Cyprian, this author maketh an exposition of his own device, which he would Cyprianus. *have taken for an answer unto him. Whereas Cyprian of all other, like as he is ancient within two hundred and fifty years of Christ, so did he write very openly in the matter; and therefore Melancthon, in his epistle to Œcolampadius, did choose him for one whose words* Melancthon. *in the affirmation of Christ's true presence in the sacrament had no ambiguity. And like judgment doth Hippinus, in his book before alleged, give of Cyprianus' faith in the sacra-* Hippinus *ment: which two I allege to countervail the judgment of this author, who speaketh of his own head as it liketh him, playing with the words "gross" and "carnal," and using the word "represent," as though it expressed a figure only. Hippinus, in the said book, allegeth Cyprian to say, (Lib. iii. ad Quirinum[4]) "that the body of our Lord is our sacrifice in flesh," meaning,* Cyprian. Lib. *as Hippinus saith, "eucharistiam," wherein St Augustine, (as Hippinus saith further,) in the* iii. ad Quirinum. *prayer for his mother, speaking of the bread and wine of eucharistia, saith, "that in it is dispensed the holy host and sacrifice, whereby was cancelled the bill obligatory that was against us." And further, Hippinus saith, that "the old men called the bread and wine of our Lord's supper a sacrifice, an host, and oblation, for that specially, because they believed and taught the true body of Christ and his true blood to be distribute in the bread and wine of eucharistia;" and, as St Augustin saith, ad Januarium, "to enter in, and be received with the* Augustinus. *mouth of them that eat." These be Hippinus' very words, who, because he is, I think, in this author's opinion, taken for no papist, I rather speak in his words than in mine own, whom in another part of this work this author doth, as it were for charity, by name slander to be a papist. Wherefore the said Hippinus' words shall be, as I think, more weighty to oppress this author's talk than mine be; and therefore, howsoever this author handleth before the words of St Cyprian (de Unctione Chrismatis), and the word "shewing" out of his epistles, yet the same Cyprian's faith appeareth so certain otherwise, as those places shall need no further answer of me here, having brought forth the judgment of Hippinus and Melancthon how they understand St Cyprian's faith, which thou, reader, oughtest to regard more than the assertion of this author, specially when thou hast read how he hath handled Hilary, Cyril, Theophylact, and Damascene, as I shall hereafter touch.*

CANTERBURY.

Whether I "make an exposition of Cyprian by mine own device," I leave to the judgment of the indifferent reader. And if I so do, why do not you prove the same substantially against me? For your own bare words, without any proof, I trust the indifferent reader will not allow, having such experience of you as he hath. And if Cyprian of all other had writ[5] most plainly against me, as you say without proof, Melancthon. who thinketh that you would have omitted here Cyprian's words, and have fled to Epinus. Melancthon and Epinus for succour?

164.

[3 And be nourished, 1551, and Orig. ed.]

[4 *Cum timore et honore Eucharistiam accipiendam.* In Levitico : Anima autem quæcunque manducaverit ex carne sacrificii salutaris, quod est Domini, et immunditia ipsius super ipsum est, peribit anima illa de populo suo. Item ad Corinthios prima : Quicunque ederit panem, aut biberit calicem Domini indigne, reus erit corporis et sanguinis Domini.—Cyprian. "ad Quirinum," Lib. III. cap. 94. p. 390. Paris. 1574.]

[5 Had written, 1551.]

And why do you allege their authority for you, which in no wise you admit when they be brought against you? But it seemeth that you be faint-hearted in this matter, and begin to shrink; and like one that refuseth the combat, and findeth the shift to put another in his place, even so it seemeth you would draw back yourself from the danger, and set me to fight with other men, that in the mean time you might be an idle looker on. And if you as grand captain take them but as mean soldiers to fight in your quarrel, you shall have little aid at their hands; for their writings declare openly that they be against you more than me, although in this place you bring them for your part, and report them to say more and otherwise than they say indeed.

And as for Cyprian and St Augustine, here by you alleged, they serve nothing for your purpose, nor speak nothing against me, by Epinus' own judgment. For Epinus saith, "That *eucharistia* is called a sacrifice, because it is a remembrance of the true sacrifice which was offered upon the cross, and that in it is dispensed the very body and blood, yea, the very death of Christ, (as he allegeth of St Augustine in that place,) the holy sacrifice whereby he blotted out and cancelled the obligation of death, which was against us, nailing it upon the cross, and in his own person won the victory, and triumphed against the princes and powers of darkness." This passion, death, and victory of Christ is dispensed and distributed in the Lord's holy supper, and daily among Christ's holy people. And yet all this requireth no corporal presence of Christ in the sacrament, nor the words of Cyprian *ad Quirinum* neither. For if they did, then was Christ's flesh corporally present in the sacrifice of the old testament fifteen hundred years before he was born; for of those sacrifices speaketh that text alleged by Cyprian *ad Quirinum*, whereof Epinus and you gather these words, "that the body of our Lord is our sacrifice in flesh." And howsoever you wrest Melancthon or Epinus, they condemn clearly your doctrine, that "Christ's body is corporally contained under the forms or accidents of bread and wine."

Cyprian ad Quirinum. cap. 94.

Next in my book is Hilarius.

But Hilarius, think they, is plainest for them in this matter, whose words they translate thus[1]:

The answer to Hilarius. 8. de Trinitate.

"If the word were made very flesh[2], and we verily receive the word being flesh, in our Lord's meat, how shall not Christ be thought to dwell naturally in us? who being born man, hath taken unto him the nature of our flesh, that cannot be severed, and hath put together the nature of his flesh to the nature of his eternity under the sacrament of the communion of his flesh unto us. For so we be all one, because the Father is in Christ, and Christ in us. Wherefore whosoever will deny the Father to be naturally in Christ, he must deny first either himself to be naturally in Christ, or Christ to be naturally in him. For the being of the Father in Christ, and the being of Christ in us, maketh us to be one in them. And therefore if Christ have taken verily the flesh of our body, and the man that was verily born of the virgin Mary is Christ, and also we receive under the true mystery the flesh of his body, by means whereof we shall be one, (for the Father is in Christ, and Christ in us,) how shall that be called the unity of will, when the natural property, brought to pass by the sacrament, is the sacrament of unity?"

165.

[1 Si enim vere Verbum caro factum est, et nos vere Verbum carnem cibo dominico sumimus, quomodo non naturaliter manere in nobis existimandus est, qui et naturam carnis nostræ jam inseparabilem sibi homo natus assumpsit, et naturam carnis suæ ad naturam æternitatis sub sacramento nobis communicandæ carnis admiscuit? Ita enim omnes unum sumus, quia et in Christo Pater est, et Christus in nobis est. Quisquis ergo naturaliter Patrem in Christo negabit, neget prius non naturaliter vel se in Christo, vel Christum sibi inesse; quia in Christo Pater, et Christus in nobis, unum in his esse nos faciunt. Si vere igitur carnem corporis nostri Christus assumpsit, et vere homo ille, qui ex Maria natus fuit, Christus est, nosque vere sub mysterio carnem corporis sui sumimus, et per hoc unum erimus, quia Pater in eo est, et ille in nobis, quomodo voluntatis unitas aperitur, cum naturalis per sacramentum proprietas perfectæ sacramentum sit unitatis? Hilarius De Trinitate. Lib. VIII. pp. 133, 134. Ed. Basil. 1535.]

[2 If the word was made verily flesh, 155 , and Orig. ed.]

Thus doth the papists, (the adversaries of God's word and of his truth,) allege the authority of Hilarius, either perversely and purposely, as it seemeth, untruly reciting[3] him and wresting his words to their purpose, or else not truly understanding him.

For although he saith that Christ is naturally in us, yet he saith also that we be naturally in him. And nevertheless, in so saying he meant not of the natural and corporal presence of the substance of Christ's body and of ours, (for as our bodies be not after that sort within his body, so is not his body after that sort within our bodies;) but he meant, that Christ in his incarnation received of us a mortal nature, and united the same unto his divinity, and so be we naturally in him.

And the sacraments of baptism and of his holy supper, (if we rightly use the same,) do most assuredly certify us, that we be partakers of his godly nature, having given unto us by him immortality and life everlasting; and so is Christ naturally in us. And so be we one with Christ, and Christ with us, not only in will and mind, but also in very natural properties.

And so concludeth Hilarius against Arius, that Christ is one with his Father, not in purpose and will only, but also in very nature.

And as the union between Christ and us in baptism is spiritual, and requireth no real and corporal presence; so likewise our union with Christ in his holy supper is spiritual, and therefore requireth no real and corporal presence.

And therefore Hilarius, speaking there of both the sacraments, maketh no difference between our union with Christ in baptism, and our union with him in his holy supper: and saith further, that as Christ is in us, so be we in him; which the papists cannot understand corporally and really, except they will say, that all our bodies be corporally within Christ's body. Thus is Hilarius answered unto, both plainly and shortly.

WINCHESTER.

This answer to Hilary, in the seventy-eighth leaf[4], *requireth a plain, precise issue, worthy to be tried*[5] *apparent at hand. The allegation of Hilary toucheth specially me, who do say and maintain that I cited Hilary truly (as the copy did serve), and*[6] *translate him truly in English after the same words in Latin. This is one issue which I qualify with the*[7] *copy,* An issue. *because I have Hilary now better correct, which better correction setteth forth more lively the truth than the other did, and therefore that I did translate was not so much to the advantage of that I alleged Hilary for, as is that in the book that I have now better correct. Hilary's words in the book newly corrected be these:* Si enim vere Verbum caro factum est, et nos Hilarius. vere Verbum carnem cibo dominico sumimus, quomodo non naturaliter manere in nobis existimandus est: qui et naturam carnis nostræ jam inseparabilem sibi homo natus assumpserit[8], et naturam carnis suæ ad naturam æternitatis sub sacramento nobis communicandæ carnis admiscuit? Ita enim omnes unum sumus, quia et in Christo pater est, et Christus in nobis est. Quisquis ergo naturaliter Patrem in Christo negabit, neget prius non naturaliter vel se in Christo vel Christum sibi inesse, quia in Christo Pater et Christus in nobis unum in iis[9] esse nos faciunt. Si vere igitur carnem corporis nostri Christus sumpsit[10], et vere homo ille qui ex Maria natus fuit Christus est, nosque vere sub mys- 166. terio carnem corporis sui sumimus, et per hoc unum erimus, quia Pater in eo est et ille in nobis, quomodo voluntatis unitas asseritur, cum naturalis per sacramentum proprietas perfectæ[11] sacramentum sit unitatis? *My translation is this:* "*If the word was made verily flesh, and we verily receive the word, being flesh, in our Lord's meat, how shall not Christ be thought to dwell naturally in us, who, being born man, hath taken unto him the nature of*

[3 Citing, 1551, and Orig. ed.]
[4 i. e. of the original edition.]
[5 and apparent, 1551.]
[6 Did, 1551.]
[7 A copy, 1551.]

[8 In Hilary, and in Orig. ed. Winch. "assumpsit."]
[9 In Hilary, "his."]
[10 "Assumpsit," 1551, as in Hilary.]
[11 In Hilary, "perfecta."]

our flesh that cannot be severed, and hath put together the nature of his flesh to the nature of his eternity, under the sacrament of the communion of his flesh unto us? for so we be all one, because the Father is in Christ, and Christ in us. Wherefore, whosoever will deny the Father to be naturally in Christ, must deny, first, either himself to be naturally in Christ, or Christ not to be naturally in him; for the being of the Father in Christ, and the being of Christ in us, maketh us to be one in them. And therefore, if Christ hath taken verily the flesh of our body, and the man that was born of the virgin Mary is verily Christ, and also we verily receive under a mystery the flesh of his body, by means whereof we shall be one, for the Father is in Christ, and Christ in us; how shall that be called the unity of will, when the natural propriety brought to pass by the sacrament is the sacrament of perfect unity?"

This translation differeth from mine other, whereat this author findeth fault; but wherein? The word vero was in the other copy an adjective, and I joined it with mysterio, and therefore said "the true mystery:" which word "mystery" needed no such adjective "true," for every mystery is true of itself. But to say, as Hilary truly correct saith, "that we receive under the mystery, truly, the flesh of Christ's body," that word "truly," so placed, setteth forth lively the real presence and substantial presence of that is received, and repeateth again the same that was before said, to the more vehemency of it. So as this correction is better than my first copy, and according to this correction is Hilarius alleged by Melancthon to Œcolampadius for the same purpose I allege him. Another alteration in the translation thou seest, reader, in the word perfectæ, which in my copy was perfecta, and so was joined to proprietas, which now in the genitive case, joined to unitatis, giveth an excellent sense to the dignity of the sacrament, how the natural propriety by the sacrament is a sacrament of perfect unity, so as the perfect unity of us with Christ is to have his flesh in us, and to have Christ bodily and naturally dwelling in us by his manhood, as he dwelleth in us spiritually by his Godhead: and now I speak in such phrase as Hilary and Cyril speak, and use the words [as they use them,][1] whatsoever this author saith, as I will justify by their plain words.

An issue.

And so I join now with this author an issue, that I have not perversely used the allegation of Hilary, but alleged him as one that speaketh most clearly of this matter; which Hilary, in his eighth book de Trinitate, entreateth how many divers ways we be one in Christ, among which he accompteth faith for one: then he cometh to the unity in baptism, where he handleth the matter above some capacities; and because there is but one baptism, and all that be baptized be so regenerate in one dispensation, and do the same thing, and be one in one, they that be one by the same thing be, as he saith, in nature one. From that unity in baptism he cometh to declare our unity with Christ in flesh, which he calleth the sacrament of perfect unity, declaring how it is when Christ, who took truly our flesh mortal in the virgin's womb, delivereth us the same flesh glorified truly to be communicate with our flesh, whereby as we be naturally in Christ, so Christ is naturally in us: and when this is brought to pass, then the unity between Christ and us is perfected. For as Christ is naturally in the Father of the same essence by the divine nature, [and God the Father naturally in Christ his Son, very God of the same essence in the divine nature:][2] so we be naturally in Christ by our natural flesh which he took in the virgin's womb, and he naturally in us by the same flesh in him glorified, and given to us, and received of us in the sacrament. For Hilary saith in plain words, how Christ's very flesh and Christ's very blood, received and drunken (accepta et hausta), bring this to pass. And it is notable, how Hilary compareth together the "truly" in Christ's taking of our flesh in the virgin's womb, with the "truly" of our taking of his flesh (in cibo dominico) in our Lord's meat: by which words he expresseth the sacrament, and after reproveth those that said, we were only united by obedience and will of religion to Christ, and by him so to the Father, as though by the sacrament of flesh and blood no propriety of natural communion were given unto us: whereas both by the honour given unto us we be the sons of God, and by the Son dwelling carnally in us, and we being corporally and inseparably unite in him, the mystery of true and natural unity is to be preached. These be Hilary's words. For this latter part, where thou hearest, reader, the Son of God to dwell carnally in us, not after man's gross imagination, for we may not so think of godly mysteries, but "carnally" is referred to the truth of Christ's flesh, given to us in this sacrament; and so is "naturally" to be understood, that we receive Christ's natural flesh for the truth of it, as Christ received our natural flesh of the virgin, although we receive Christ's flesh glorified incorruptible, very spiritual, and in a spiritual manner delivered unto us. Here is mention made of the word "corporal;" but I shall speak of that

*Unity in faith.
*Unity in baptism.

*Unity in flesh.

Hilarius.

167.

*Carnally.
*Naturally.

[¹ These words are omitted in the 1580. ed.] [² This clause is found only in the Orig. ed. Winch.]

in the discussion of Cyril. This Hilary was before St Augustine, and was known both of him and St Jerome, who called him Tubam Latini eloquii *against the Arians. Never man found fault at this notable place of Hilary. Now let us consider how the author of this book forgetteth himself, to call Christ in us naturally by his Godhead, which were then to make us all gods by nature, which is over-great an absurdity, and Christ in his divine nature dwelleth only in his Father naturally, and in us by grace. But as we receive him in the sacrament of his flesh and blood, if we receive him worthily, so dwelleth he in us naturally, for the natural[3] communication of our nature and his. And therefore, where this author reporteth Hilary to make no difference between our union to Christ in baptism, and in the supper, let him trust in[4] him no more that told him so: or if this author will take upon him as of his own knowledge, then I must[5] say, and (if he were another) would say, an answer in French, that I will not express. And hereupon will I join in[6] the issue, that in* An issue. *Hilary the matter is so plain otherwise than this author rehearseth, as it hath no colour of defence to the contrary. And what Hilary speaketh of baptism and our unity therein, I have before touched; and this unity in flesh is after treated apart.*

What shall I say to this so manifest untruth, but that it confirmeth that I have in other observed, how there was never one of them that I have read writing against the sacrament, but hath in his writings said somewhat so evidently in the matter, or out of the matter, discrepant from truth, as might be a certain mark to judge the quality of his spirit?

CANTERBURY.

Here you confess that you cited Hilary untruly, but you impute the fault to your copy. What copy you had I know not, but as well the citation of Melancthon, as all the printed books that ever I saw, have otherwise than you have written; and therefore it seemeth that you never read any printed book of Hilarius. Marry it might be that you had from Smith a false copy written, who informed me that you had of Smith. him all the authorities that be in your book: and having all the authorities that he had with great travail gathered, by and by you made your book, and stole from him all his thank and glory, like unto Esop's chough, which plumed himself with other birds' feathers. But wheresoever you had your copy, all the books set forth by public faith have otherwise than you have cited. And although the false allegation of Hilary toucheth you somewhat, yet chiefly it toucheth Smith, who hath erred much worse in his translation than you have done, albeit neither of you both handle the matter sincerely and faithfully, nor agree the one with the other.

But I trow it be your chance to light upon false books. For whereas in this sentence, *Quisquis ergo naturaliter Patrem in Christo negabit, neget prius naturaliter vel se in Christo, vel Christum sibi inesse*, one false print for *naturaliter* hath *non natu-* Non natura-*raliter;* it seemeth that you chanced upon that false print. For if you have found liter. Hilary truly corrected, as you say you have, your fault is the more, that out of a 168. true copy would pick out an untrue translation. And if you have so done, then by putting in a little pretty "not," where none ought to be, with that little pretty trip you have clean overthrown yourself. For if it be an error to deny that Christ is not naturally in us, (as it is rehearsed[7] for an error,) then must it be an error to affirm "that Christ is naturally in us." For it is all one thing to deny[8] that he is not, and to affirm that "he is naturally in us." And so by your own translation you overthrow yourself quite and clean, in that you say in many places of your book, that "Christ is naturally in us," and ground your saying upon Hilary: whereas now, by your own translation, Hilary rejecteth that clearly as an heinous error.

And as concerning this word "truly," it setteth not lively forth a real and sub- Truly. stantial presence, as you say it doth; for Christ is truly in all his faithful people, and they[9] truly eat his flesh and drink his blood, and yet not by a real and corporal, but by a spiritual and effectual presence.

And as concerning the word *perfecta* or *perfectæ*[10], in the print which I have of your Perfecta.

[3 Mutual, Orig. ed. Winch.]
[4 Trust him, 1551.]
[5 I would say, (if he were another,) an answer in French, Orig. ed. Winch.]
[6 Join the issue, 1551.]

[7 As it is here rehearsed, 1551.]
[8 *To deny*, omitted in ed. 1580.]
[9 There, 1580.]
[10 *Perfecta* or perfect, ed. 1551.]

book, is neither of both, but be left quite out. Nevertheless that fault I impute to no untruth in you, but rather to the negligence either of your pen or of the printer.

But for the perfectness of the unity between Christ and us, you declare here the[1] perfect unity to be that which is but the one half of it. For the perfect unity of us with Christ is, not only to have Christ corporally and naturally dwelling in us, but likewise we to dwell corporally and naturally in him. And Hilary declareth the second part to pertain to our unity with Christ, as well as the first; which of sleight and policy you leave out purposely, because it declareth the meaning of the first part, which is not that Christ is in them that receive the sacrament, and when they receive the sacrament only, but that he naturally tarrieth and dwelleth in all them that pertain to him, whether they receive the sacrament or no. And as he dwelleth naturally in them, so do they in him.

*Mine issue.

And although you have excused your perversity by your false copy, yet here I will join an issue with you, that you did neither allege Hilary's words before truly, nor yet now do truly declare them. As for the first part, you have confessed yourself that you were deceived by a false copy: and therefore, in this part, I plead that you be guilty by your own confession. And as concerning the second part, Hilary speaketh not of the unity of Christ with the sacrament, nor of the unity of Christ with us only when we receive the sacrament, nor of the unity of us with Christ only, but also with his Father; by which unity we dwell in Christ and Christ in us, and also we dwell in the Father and the Father in us. For as Christ being in his Father, and his Father in him, hath life of his Father, so he being in us, and we in him, giveth unto us the nature of his eternity, which he received of his Father; that is to say, immortality and life everlasting, which is the nature of his Godhead. And so have we the Father and the Son dwelling in us naturally, and we in them, forasmuch as he giveth to us the nature of his eternity which he had of his Father, and honoureth us with that honour which he had of his Father. But Christ giveth not this nature of eternity to the sacrament, except you will say that the sacrament shall have everlasting life; as you must needs say, if Christ dwell naturally in it, after Hilary's manner of reasoning. For by the saying of Hilary, where Christ dwelleth, there dwelleth his Father, and giveth eternal life by his Son.

John xiv.
John v.
John vi.

Naturally.

169.

And so be you a goodly saviour, that can bring to everlasting life both bread and drink, which never had life. But as this nature of eternity is not given to the sacrament, so is it not given to them that unworthily receive the sacrament, which eat and drink their own damnation. Nor it is not given to the lively members of Christ only when they receive the sacrament, but so long as they spiritually feed upon Christ, eating his flesh and drinking his blood, either in this life or in the life to come: for so long have they Christ naturally dwelling in them, and they in him. And as the Father naturally dwelleth in Christ, so by Christ doth he naturally dwell in us.

And this is Hilary's mind, to tell how Christ and his Father dwell naturally in his faithful members, and what unity we have with them, (that is to say, an unity of nature, and not of will only), and not to tell how Christ dwelleth in the sacrament, or in them that unworthily receive[2] it, that he dwelleth in them at that time only, when they receive the sacrament. And yet he saith that this unity of faithful people unto God is by faith taught by the sacrament of baptism and of the Lord's table, but wrought by Christ by the sacrament and mystery of his incarnation and redemption, whereby he humbled himself unto the lowliness of our feeble nature, that he might exalt us to the dignity of his godly nature, and join us unto his Father in the nature of his eternity.

Thus is plainly declared Hilary's mind, who meant nothing less than, as you say, to entreat how many divers ways we be one in Christ, but only to entreat and prove that we be naturally in Christ, and Christ in us. And this one thing he proveth by our faith, and by the sacrament of baptism, and of the Lord's supper, and still he saith as well that we be naturally and corporally in him, as that he is naturally in us.

And where you speak of the unity in baptism, and say that Hilary "handleth that matter above some capacities;" howsoever Hilary handleth the matter, you handle it

[1 Here to be the, edit. 1580.]
[2 Receive the sacrament: or if they worthily receive it, that he dwelleth, &c., 1551.]

in such sort as I think passeth all men's capacities, unless yourself make a large commentary thereto. For what these your words mean, "Because there is but one baptism, and all that be baptized be so regenerate in one dispensation, and do the same thing, and be one in one, they that be one by the same thing be, as he saith, in nature one;" and what that one thing is which they do that be baptized; I think no man can tell, except you read the riddle yourself.

And now to your issue. If you can shew of the words of Hilary in this place, that Christ is naturally in the sacraments of bread and wine, or in wicked persons, or in godly persons only when they receive the sacrament, then will I confess the issue to pass upon your side, that you have declared this author truly, and that he maketh most clearly for you against me. And if you cannot shew this by Hilary's words, then must you hold up your hand and say, "Guilty!"

And yet furthermore, when Hilary saith that we be naturally in Christ, he meaneth not that our bodies be contained within the compass of his body, but that we receive his natural eternity. And so likewise, when he saith that Christ dwelleth naturally and carnally in us, he meaneth not that his body is contained corporally within the compass of our mouths or bodies, (which you must prove by his plain words, if you will justify your issue, that he speaketh most clearly for you,) but he meaneth that Christ communicateth and giveth unto us the nature of his eternity or everlasting life. And he dwelleth in us by his incarnation, as St John saith: *Verbum caro factum est, et habitavit in nobis*, "The word was made flesh, and dwelled in us." And as he may be said to dwell in us by receiving of our mortal nature, so may we be said to dwell in him by receiving the nature of his immortality. And "never man found fault," as you truly say, "at this notable place of Hilary;" nor, again, never learned man hitherto expounded him as you do.

And when I said that Christ is in us naturally by his Godhead, I forgat not what I said, as you say of me; for I plainly expounded what I meant by naturally, that is to say, not by natural substance to make us gods, but by natural condition giving unto us immortality and everlasting life which he had of his Father, and so making us partakers of his godly nature, and uniting us to his Father. And if we attain to the unity of his Father, why not unto the unity of the Godhead, not by natural substance, but by natural propriety? As Cyril saith that we be made the children of God and heavenly men by participation of the divine nature, as St Peter also teacheth. And so be we one in the Father, in the Son, and in the Holy Ghost.

And where you say that we "receive Christ in the sacrament of his flesh and blood, if we receive him worthily;" here you have given good evidence against yourself, that we receive him not, and that he dwelleth not in us naturally, except we receive him worthily. And therefore where you say that there is "none that writeth against the truth in the sacrament, but he hath in his writings somewhat discrepant from truth, that might be a certain mark to judge his spirit;" this is so true, that yourself differ not only from the truth in a number of places, but also from your own sayings.

And where you bid me "trust him no more that told me that Hilary maketh no difference between our union in Christ in baptism, and in his holy supper," it was very Hilary himself of whom I learned it, who saith that in both the sacraments the union is natural, and not in will only. And if you will say the contrary, I must tell you the "French answer" that you would tell me. And herein I will not refuse your issue. *Mine issue.

Now come we to Cyril, of whom I write as followeth.

And this answer to[3] Hilarius will serve also unto Cyril, whom they allege to speak after the same sort that Hilarius doth, that Christ is naturally in us. The words which they recite be these[4]: "We deny not," saith Cyril against the

Marginal notes: 170. John i. 2 Pet. i. The answer to Cyrillus. Lib. x. cap. 13.

[3 Of, 1551, and Orig. ed.]

[4 "Ὅτι μὲν γὰρ διαθέσει τῇ νοουμένῃ κατὰ τὴν τελείαν ἀγάπην, ὀρθῇ τε καὶ ἀδιαστρόφῳ πίστει, φιλαρέτῳ τε καὶ εἰλικρινεῖ λογισμῷ συνενούμεθα πνευματικῶς τῷ Χριστῷ, οὐδαμῶς ἐξαρνήσεται τῶν παρ' ἡμῖν δογμάτων ὁ λόγος· συνερούμεν γὰρ ὅτι δὴ μάλα τοῦτό φασιν ὀρθῶς· τὸ δέ γε καταθαρσῆσαι λέγειν, ὡς οὐδεὶς ἡμῖν συναφείας τῆς κατὰ σάρκα πρὸς αὐτὸν ὁ λόγος, ὁλοκλήρως ἀπᾷδον ταῖς θεοπνεύστοις γραφαῖς ἐπιδείξομεν. πῶς γὰρ ἂν ἀμφίλογον, ἢ τίς ἂν ὅλως ἐνδοιάσαι ποτὲ τῶν εὖ φρονεῖν εἰωθότων, ὡς ἄμπελος μέν ἐστι κατὰ τοῦτο Χριστός· ἡμεῖς γὰρ κλημάτων ἀποτελοῦντες σχῆμα τὴν ἐξ αὐτοῦ καὶ παρ' αὐτοῦ ζωὴν εἰς αὐτοὺς κομιζόμεθα·

heretic, "but we be spiritually joined to Christ by faith and sincere charity; but that we should have no manner of conjunction in our flesh with Christ, that we utterly deny, and think it utterly discrepant from God's holy scriptures. For who doubteth but Christ is so the vine-tree, and we so the branches, as we get thence our life? Hear what St Paul saith: 'We be all one body with Christ, for though we be many, we be one in him: all we participate in one food.' Thinketh this heretic that we know not the strength and virtue of the mystical benediction? which when it is made in us, doth it not make Christ by communication of his flesh to dwell corporally in us? Why be the members of faithful men's bodies called the members of Christ? 'Know you not,' saith St Paul, 'that your members be the members of Christ? And shall I make the members of Christ parts of the whore's body? God forbid.' And our Saviour also saith: 'He that eateth my flesh and drinketh my blood, dwelleth in me and I in him.'"

Although in these words Cyril doth say, that Christ doth dwell corporally in us when we receive the mystical benediction, yet he neither saith that Christ dwelleth corporally in the bread, nor that he dwelleth in us corporally only at such times as we receive the sacrament, nor that he dwelleth in us and not we in him; but he saith as well, that we dwell in him, as that he dwelleth in us. Which dwelling is neither corporal nor local, but an heavenly, spiritual, and supernatural dwelling, whereby so long as we dwell in him and he in us, we have by him everlasting life. And therefore Cyril saith in the same place, that Christ is the vine, and we the branches, because that by him we have life. For as the branches receive life and nourishment of the body of the vine, so receive we by him the natural property of his body, which is life and immortality, and by that means we, being his members, do live and are spiritually nourished.

And this meant Cyril by this word "corporally," when he saith that Christ dwelleth corporally in us. And the same meant also St Hilarius by this word "naturally," when he said that Christ dwelleth naturally in us. And as St Paul, when he said that in Christ dwelleth the full divinity "corporally," by this word "corporally" he meant not that the divinity is a body, and so by that body dwelleth bodily in Christ. But by this word "corporally" he meant, that the divinity is not in Christ accidentally, lightly, and slenderly, but substantially and perfectly, with all his might and power: so that Christ was not only a mortal man to suffer for us, but also he was immortal God able to redeem us.

So St Cyril, when he said that Christ is in us "corporally," he meant that we have him in us, not lightly and to small effect and purpose, but that we have him in us substantially, pithily, and effectually, in such wise that we have by him redemption and everlasting life.

And this I suck not out of mine own fingers, but have it of Cyril's own express words, where he saith[1]: "A little benediction draweth the whole man to

καίτοι τοῦ Παύλου λέγοντος, Οἱ γὰρ πάντες ἓν σῶμά ἐσμεν ἐν Χριστῷ, ὅτι εἷς ἄρτος οἱ πολλοὶ ἐσμέν· οἱ γὰρ πάντες ἐκ τοῦ ἑνὸς ἄρτου μετέχομεν. λεγέτω γάρ τις ἡμῖν τὴν αἰτίαν, καὶ διδασκέτω παρελθὼν τῆς μυστικῆς εὐλογίας τὴν δύναμιν. γίνεται γὰρ ἐν ἡμῖν διὰ τί; ἆρ' οὐχὶ καὶ σωματικῶς ἡμῖν ἐνοικίζουσα τὸν Χριστὸν τῇ μεθέξει καὶ κοινωνίᾳ τῆς ἁγίας αὐτοῦ σαρκός; ἀλλ' οἶμαι λέγειν ὀρθῶς· γράφει γὰρ ὁ Παῦλος γεγενῆσθαι τὰ ἔθνη σύσσωμα καὶ συμμέτοχα καὶ συγκληρονόμα Χριστοῦ. σύσσωμα τοιγαροῦν κατὰ ποῖον ἀπεφάνθη τρόπον; ἀξιωθέντα γὰρ μετασχεῖν τῆς εὐλογίας τῆς μυστικῆς, ἓν πρὸς αὐτὸν γέγονε σῶμα, καθάπερ ἀμέλει καὶ τῶν ἁγίων ἕκαστος ἀποστόλων. ἐπεὶ διὰ ποίαν αἰτίαν μέλη τοῦ Χριστοῦ τὰ οἰκεῖα, μᾶλλον δὲ τὰ πάντων, ὡς αὐτοῦ κατωνόμασε μέλη; γράφει γὰρ οὕτως· οὐκ οἴδατε ὅτι τὰ μέλη ὑμῶν μέλη Χριστοῦ ἐστιν; ἄρας οὖν τὰ μέλη τοῦ Χριστοῦ, ποιήσω πόρνης μέλη; μὴ γένοιτο· ἀλλὰ καὶ αὐτὸς ὁ σωτὴρ, ὁ τρώγων μου τὴν σάρκα, φησὶ, καὶ πίνων μου τὸ αἷμα, ἐν ἐμοὶ μένει, κἀγὼ ἐν αὐτῷ.—Cyrill. In Joannem. Lib. x. cap. 13. Tom. IV. pp. 862,3.—Ed. Aubert. Paris. 1638.]

[1 Οὕτως ὀλιγίστη πάλιν εὐλογία σύμπαν ἡμῶν εἰς ἑαυτὴν ἀναφύρει τὸ σῶμα, καὶ τῆς ἰδίας ἐνεργείας ἀναπληροῖ, οὕτω τε ἐν ἡμῖν γίνεται Χριστὸς, καὶ ἡμεῖς αὖ πάλιν ἐν αὐτῷ.—Cyril. in Joannem. Lib. IV. cap. 17. 1b. p. 365.]

God, and filleth him with his[2] grace, and after this manner Christ dwelleth in us, and we in Christ."

But as for corporal eating and drinking with our mouths, and digesting with our bodies, Cyril never meant that Christ doth so dwell in us, as he plainly declareth. "Our sacrament," saith he, "doth not affirm the eating of a man, drawing wickedly christian people to have gross imaginations and carnal fantasies of such things as be fine and pure, and received only with a sincere faith[3]." "But as two waxes, that be molten and put together, they close so in one, that every part of the one is joined to every part of the other, even so," saith Cyril, "he that receiveth the flesh and blood of the Lord, must needs be so joined with Christ, that Christ must be in him, and he in Christ[4]." *Anathematismo xi. In Johan. Lib. iv. cap. 17.* *172.*

By these words of Cyril appeareth his mind plainly, that we may not grossly and rudely think of the eating of Christ with our mouths, but with our faith, by which eating, (although he be absent hence bodily, and be in the eternal life and glory with his Father,) yet we be made partakers of his nature, to be immortal, and have eternal life and glory with him.

And thus is declared the mind as well of Cyril as of Hilarius.

WINCHESTER.

The author saith, such answer as he made to Hilary will serve for Cyril; and indeed, to say truth, it is made after the same sort, and hath even such an error as the other had, saving it may be excused by ignorance. For where the author travaileth here to expound the word "corporally," which is a sore word in Cyril against this author, and therefore taketh labour to temper it with the word corporaliter *in St Paul, applied to the dwelling of the divinity in Christ; and yet not content therewith, maketh further search, and would gladly have somewhat to confirm his fancy out of Cyril himself, and seeketh in Cyril where it is not to be found, and seeketh not where it is to be found: (for Cyril telleth himself plainly, what he meaneth by the word "corporally," which place and this author had found, he might have spared a great many of words uttered by divination; but then the truth of that place hindereth and quaileth in manner all the book:) I will at my peril bring forth Cyril's own words truly upon the 17th chapter of St John.* *Cyril.*

Corporaliter Filius per benedictionem mysticam nobis ut homo unitur, spiritualiter autem ut Deus[5]. Which be in English thus much to say: "The Son is unite as man corporally to us by the mystical benediction, spiritually as God." These be Cyril's words, who nameth the sacrament of the body and blood of Christ the mystical benediction, and sheweth in this sentence, how himself understandeth the words "corporally" and "spiritually;" that is to say, when Christ uniteth himself to us as man, which he doth giving his body in this sacrament to such as worthily receive it, then he dwelleth in them corporally, which Christ was before in them spiritually, or else they could not worthily receive him to the effect of that unity corporal and corporal dwelling; by which word "corporal" is understood no grossness at all, which the nature of a mystery excludeth, and yet keepeth truth still, being the understanding only attained by faith. But where the author of the book allegeth Cyril **Lege Cyrillum in Joh. Lib. ix. cap. 47. [Cyrillus in Joan. cap. 17. Orig. ed. Winch.]*

[2 With grace, 1551, and Orig. ed.]

[3 Ἆρ' οὖν, ὡς ἕτερόν τινα υἱὸν, καὶ Χριστὸν παρὰ τὸν ἐκ Θεοῦ λόγον, τὸν φαινόμενον εἶναι διαβεβαιούμενος· ᾧ καὶ μόνῳ τὸ τῆς ἀποστολῆς προσενεμήκε χρῆμα, οὐκ ἀνθρωποφαγίαν ἡμῶν ἀποφαίνει τὸ μυστήριον, παριστὰς ἀνοσίως εἰς ἐξιτήλους ἐννοίας τῶν πιστευσάντων τὸν νοῦν· καὶ λογισμοῖς ἀνθρωπίνοις ὑποφέρειν ἐπιχειρῶν, ἃ μόνως καὶ ἀζητήτῳ πίστει προσλαμβάνεται;—Ib. Apologet. adv. Orient. Anath. xi. Def. Cyril. Tom. VI. p. 193.]

[4 Ὥσπερ γὰρ εἴτις κηρὸν ἑτέρῳ συνάψειε κηρῷ, πάντως δήπου καὶ ἕτερον ἐν ἑτέρῳ γεγονότα κατόψεται· τὸν αὐτὸν, οἶμαι, τρόπον καὶ ὁ τὴν σάρκα δεχόμενος τοῦ σωτῆρος ἡμῶν Χριστοῦ, καὶ πίνων αὐτοῦ τὸ τίμιον αἷμα, καθά φησιν αὐτὸς, ἓν ὡς πρὸς αὐτὸν εὑρίσκεται συνανακιρνάμενος ὥσπερ καὶ ἀναμιγνύμενος αὐτῷ διὰ τῆς μεταλήψεως, ὡς ἐν Χριστῷ μὲν αὐτὸν εὑρίσκεσθαι, Χριστὸν δὲ αὖ πάλιν ἐν αὐτῷ.—Id. in Joannem. Lib. iv. cap. ii. Tom. IV. pp. 364, 5.]

[5 Γίνεται μὲν γὰρ ἐν ἡμῖν ὁ υἱὸς, σωματικῶς μὲν ὡς ἄνθρωπος, συνανακιρνάμενός τε καὶ συνενούμενος δι' εὐλογίας τῆς μυστικῆς· πνευματικῶς δὲ αὖ πάλιν ὡς Θεός, τῇ τοῦ ἰδίου πνεύματος ἐνεργείᾳ, καὶ χάριτι τὸ ἐν ἡμῖν ἀνακτίζων πνεῦμα πρὸς καινότητα ζωῆς, καὶ τῆς θείας αὐτοῦ φύσεως κοινωνοὺς καθιστάς. σύνδεσμος οὖν ἄρα τῆς ἑνότητος ἡμῶν τῆς πρὸς Θεὸν καὶ πατέρα διαφαίνεται Χριστὸς, ἑαυτοῦ μὲν ἡμᾶς ἐξαρτήσας ὡς ἄνθρωπος, Θεῷ δὲ ὡς Θεὸς ἐνυπάρχων φυσικῶς τῷ ἰδίῳ γεννήτορι.—Id. in Joannem. Lib. ix. cap. xlvii. Ib. pp. 1001, 2.]

in words to deny the eating of a man, and to affirm the receiving in this sacrament to be only by faith; it shall appear, I doubt not, upon further discussion, that Cyril saith not so, and the translations of Cyril into Latin after the print of Basil, in a book called "Antidotum," and of whole Cyril's works printed at Cologne, have not in that place such sentence: so as following the testimony of those books set forth by public faith in two sundry places, I should call the allegation of Cyril made by this author in this point untrue, as it is indeed in the matter untrue. And yet because the original error proceedeth from Œcolampadius, it shall serve to good purpose to direct the original fault to him; as he well deserveth to be, as he is noted guilty of it, whose reputation deceived many in the matter of the sacrament; and being well noted how the same Œcolampadius corrupteth Cyril, it may percase somewhat work with this author, to consider how he hath in this place been deceived by him. I will write here the very words of Cyril in Greek, as they be of Œcolampadius brought forth and published in his name; whereby the reader that understandeth the Greek, as many do at this time, may judge of Œcolampadius' conscience in handling this matter. The words of Cyril be alleged of Œcolampadius to be these in Greek: Ἆρ᾽ οὖν ὡς ἕτερόν τινα υἱὸν καὶ Χριστὸν παρὰ τὸν ἐκ θεοῦ θεὸν λόγον τὸν φαινόμενον εἶναι διαβεβαιοῦνται, ᾧ καὶ τὸ τῆς ἀποστολῆς προσνενέμηται χρῆμα, οὐκ ἀνθρωποφαγίαν ἡμῶν ἀποφαίνει τὸ μυστήριον, παριστῶν ἀνοσίως εἰς ἐξιτήλους ἐννοίας τῶν πιστευόντων νοῦν, καὶ λογισμοῖς ἀνθρωπίνοις ἐπιχειρῶν, ἃ μόνῃ καὶ ψιλῇ καὶ ἀζητήτῳ πίστει λαμβάνεται.

173. *These words be by Œcolampadius translated in this wise:* Nonne igitur eum qui videtur filium et Christum, alium a Deo verbo, qui ex Deo esse affirmant, cui apostolatus functio tributa sit? Non enim sacramentum nostrum hominis manducationem asserit, mentes credentium ad crassas cogitationes irreligiose introtrudens, et humanis cogitationibus subjicere enitens ea quæ sola, et pura, et inexquisita fide capiuntur. *This is Œcolampadius' translation of the Greek, as the same is by Œcolampadius alleged. Which, compared with the Greek, and the congruity and phrase of the Greek tongue considered, doth plainly open a corruption in the Greek text. First, in the word* διαβεβαιοῦνται, *which should be a participle in the singular number* διαβεβαιῶν, *as* παριστῶν, *and* ἐπιχειρῶν, *all which participles depend of the third person reproved of Cyril, and nominative case to the verb* ἀποφαίνει, *which hath the noun* μυστήριον *his accusative case; for congruity will not suffer* μυστήριον *to be the nominative case, as Œcolampadius maketh it, because* παριστῶν *and* ἐπιχειρῶν *should then depend on it, which be the masculine gender, and* μυστήριον *the neuter: and besides that, the sense hath so no good reason to attribute assertion to the mystery by the way of declaration: the mystery of nature secret hath need of declaration, and maketh none, but hideth rather; and the mystery cannot declare properly that should lead or subdue men to vain imagination. But Cyril, intending to reprove the conclusion of him that attributeth to that is seen in Christ the nature*[1] *(meaning the person of his humanity,) the office of the apostle, and so thereby seemeth to make in Christ two several persons, esteeming that is seen another son from the second person, sheweth how that man so concluding** *doth affirm an absurdity, that is to say, declareth†that mystery of our* humanam commixtionem, *for so hath the public translation, and not* ἀνθρωποφαγίαν, *which should signify eating of a man, as Œcolampadius would have it, and cannot with this construction to make* μυστήριον *the accusative case have any sense; and then that man so concluding may be said therewith leading‡ the mind of them that believe into slender and dark imaginations or thoughts, and so‖ going about to bring under man's reasonings such things as be taken§ or understood by an only simple, bare, and no curious faith. And this is uttered by Cyril by interrogation,* Ἆρ᾽ οὖν, *which continueth unto the last word of all that is here written in Greek, ending in the word* λαμβάνεται. *But Œcolampadius, to frame these words to his purpose, corrupteth the participle* διαβεβαιῶν, *and maketh it* διαβεβαιοῦνται, *whereby he might cut off the interrogative; and then is he yet fain to add evidently that is not in the Greek, a copulative causal* enim; *and then when* μυστήριον *is, by the cutting off the interrogation and the addition of* enim, *made the nominative case, then cannot* παριστῶν *and* ἐπιχειρῶν *depend of it, because of the gender, and* τὸ μυστήριον, *because of the article, determineth the principal mystery in Christ's person; and after*[3] *public translation, it should seem the Greek word was not* ἀνθρωποφαγίαν, *but* ἀνθρωπομιγίαν, *which in the public translation is expressed with these two words,* humanam commixtionem. *This one place, and*[4] *there were no more like, may shew*

* διαβεβαι-
ῶν.
† ἀποφαίνει
τὸ μυστή-
ριον ἡμῶν.

‡ παρισ-
τῶν.
‖ ἐπιχει-
ρῶν.
§ [λαμβά-
νεται².]

[¹ "The nature of his humanity," omitting the intermediate words, Orig. ed. Winch.]

[² λαμβάνεται at the side is only found in the Orig. ed. Winch.]

[³ After the public, 1551.]

[⁴ And : here and elsewhere for *if*.]

with what conscience Œcolampadius handled the matter of the sacrament, who was learned in the Greek tongue, much exercised in translations, and had once written a grammar of the Greek; and yet in this place abuseth himself and the reader in perverting Cyril against all congruities of the speech, against the proper significations of the words, against the convenient connection of the matter, with depravation of the phrase and corruption of certain words, all against the common and public translation; and when he hath done all this, concludeth in the end that he hath translated the Greek faithfully, when there is by him used no good faith at all, but credit and estimation of learning by him abused to deceive well-meaning simplicity, and serveth for some defence to such as be bold to use and follow his authority in this matter: as the author of the book seemeth to have followed him herein, for else the public authentic translations which be abroad, as I said, of the prints of Basil and Cologne, have no such matter; and therefore the fault of the author is to leave public truth and search matter whispered in corners. But thus much must be granted, though in the principal matter, that in the mystery of the sacrament we must exclude all grossness, and yet for the truth of God's secret work in the sacrament grant also, that[5] in such as receive the sacrament worthily, Christ dwelleth in them corporally, as Cyril saith, and naturally and carnally, as Hilary saith. And with this true understanding, after the simplicity of a Christian faith, which was in these fathers, Hilary and Cyril, the contention of these three envious words, in gross capacities grossly taken, "natural," "carnal," and "corporal," which carnality hath engendered, might soon be much assuaged: and this author also, considering with himself how much he hath been overseen in the understanding of them, and the speciality in this place of himself and Œcolampadius, might take occasion to repent and call home himself, who wonderfully wandereth in this matter of the sacrament, and having lost his right way, breaketh up hedges, and leapeth over ditches, with a wonderous travail to go whither he would not, being not yet (as appeareth) determined where he would rest, by the variety of his own doctrine, as may appear in sundry places, if they be compared together.

174.

CANTERBURY.

I said very truly when I said, that such answer as I made to Hilary will serve for Cyril; for so will it do indeed, although you wrangle and strive therein never so much: for Cyril and Hilary entreat both of one matter, that we be united together and with Christ, not only in will, but also in nature, and be made one, not only in consent of godly religion, but also that Christ, taking our corporal nature upon him, hath made us partakers of his godly nature, knitting us together with him unto his Father and to his holy Spirit. Now let the indifferent reader judge whether you or I be in error, and whether of us both hath most need to excuse himself of ignorance. Would God you were as ready humbly to yield in those manifest errors which be proved against you, as you be stout to take upon you a knowledge in those things, wherein ye be most ignorant! But $\phi\iota\lambda\alpha\upsilon\tau\iota\alpha$[6] is a perilous witch.

Now whereas I have truly expounded this word "corporally" in Cyril, when he saith that Christ dwelleth corporally in us, and have declared how that word "corporally," as Cyril understandeth it, maketh nothing for your purpose, that Christ's flesh should be corporally contained (as you understand the matter) under the form of bread, (for he neither saith that Christ dwelleth corporally in the bread, nor that he dwelleth in them corporally that be not lively members of his body, nor that he dwelleth in his lively members at such time only as they receive the sacrament, nor that he dwelleth in us corporally, and not we in him; but he saith as well that we dwell in him, as that he dwelleth in us;) and when I have also declared that Cyril's meaning was this, that as the vine and branches be both of one nature, so the Son of God, taking unto him our human nature, and making us partakers of his divine nature, giving unto us immortality and everlasting life, doth so dwell naturally and corporally in us, and maketh us to dwell naturally and corporally in him; and where, as I have proved this by Cyril's own words, as well in that place in his tenth book upon St John's Gospel, the thirteenth chapter, as in his fourth book, the seventeenth chapter; you answer no more to all this, but say that I "seek in Cyril where it is not to be found, and seek not where it is to be found." A substantial answer, be you sure, and a learned. For you do here like a keeper which I knew once, required to

Corporally.

[5 Orig. ed. Winch. omits the words, "grant also that."]   [6 Self-love.]

follow a suit with his hound, after one that had stolen a deer; and when his hound was in his right suit, and had his game fresh before him, and came near to the house and place where the deer was indeed, after he had a little inkling that it was a special friend of his that killed the deer, and then being loth to find the suit, he plucked back his hound, being in the right way, and appointed him to hunt in another place where the game was not, and so deceived all them that followed him, as you would here do to as many as will follow you. For you promise to bring the reader to a place where he shall find the meaning of this word "corporally;" and when he cometh to the place where you appoint, the word is spoken of there, but the meaning thereof is not declared, neither by you nor by Cyril in that place: and so the reader, by your fair promise, is brought from the place where the game is truly indeed, and brought to another place where he is utterly disappointed of that he sought for.

For where you send the reader to this place of Cyril, "The Son is united as man corporally unto us by the mystical benediction, spiritually as God": here indeed in this sentence Cyril nameth this word "corporally," but he telleth not the meaning thereof, which you promised the reader that he should find here.

Nevertheless Cyril meaneth no more by these words, but that Christ is united unto us two manner of ways, by his body and by his Spirit. And he is also a band and knot to bind and join us to his Father, being knit in nature unto both; to us as a natural man, and to his Father as natural God, and himself knitting us and God his Father together.

*Cyril. in Johan. Lib. ix. cap. 5. ult. Ita ego naturaliter præsum quia ex ipso natus, vos autem ex me, et ego in vobis etiam naturaliter, ea ratione qua homo factus sum. 1 Tim. iii. Ephes. iii.

And although Cyril say that Christ is united unto us corporally by the mystical benediction, yet in that place the material[1] benediction may well be understand of his incarnation, which as Cyril and Hilary both call "an high mystery," so was it to us a marvellous "benediction," that he that was immortal God would become for us a mortal man; which mystery St Paul saith was "without controversy great," and was hid from the world, and at the last opened, that gentiles should be made partakers of the promises in Christ, which by his flesh came down unto us.

But to give you all the advantage that may be, I will grant for your pleasure, that by "the mystical benediction" Cyril understood the sacrament of Christ's flesh and blood, as you say, and that Christ is thereby united corporally unto us. Yet saith not Cyril, that this unity is only when we receive the sacrament, nor extendeth to all that receive the sacrament, but unto them that, being renewed to a new life, be made partakers of the divine nature, which nature Cyril himself upon the sixth chapter of John declareth to be life. But he speaketh not one word of the corporal presence of Christ in the forms of bread and wine, nor no more doth Hilary. And therefore I may well approve that I said, that the answer made unto Hilary will very well also serve for Cyril. And yet neither of them both hath one word that serveth for your purpose, that Christ's flesh and blood should be in the sacrament under the forms of bread and wine.

And where you say that Christ uniteth himself to us as man, when he giveth his body in the sacrament to such as worthily receive it, if you will speak as Cyril and other old authors used to do, Christ did unite himself to us as man at his incarnation. And here again you give evidence against your own issue, affirming our unity unto Christ no further than we receive the sacrament worthily. And then they that receive it unworthily be not united corporally unto Christ, nor eat his flesh, nor drink his blood; which is the plain mind both of Hilary and also of Cyril, and directly with the state of my fourth book, and against your answer to the same.

And here you, pretending to declare again what is meant by this word "corporal," do tell the negative, that there is "no grossness meant thereby," but the affirmative, what is meant thereby, you declare not as you promised. But if you mean plainly, speak plainly, whether Christ's body, being in the sacrament under the forms of bread and wine, have head, feet, arms, legs, back and belly, eyes, ears and mouth, distinct and in due order and proportion? Which if he lack, the simplest man or woman knoweth that it cannot be a perfect corporal man's body, but rather an imaginative

---

[1 Mystical, 1551.]

or phantastical body, as Marcion and Valentine taught it to be. Express here fully and plainly what manner of body you call this corporal body of Christ.

And where you say that I "allege Cyril to deny in words the eating of a man, and to affirm the receiving in this sacrament to be only by faith," and yet it shall appear by further discussing[2], say you, that Cyril saith not so: if you had not rubbed shame out of your forehead, you would not have said that he saith not so, and be taken with so manifest an untruth. For although you, like a grammarian, ruffle in your cases, genders, numbers, and persons, and in matters of no learning trouble the reader to shew yourself learned, corrupting the Greek, Latin, and English, to draw them to your purpose; yet shall you never prove that Cyril speaketh of any other eating of Christ, but by faith.

And to make the matter plain, which it seemeth you yet understand not, I shall shortly rehearse, as well the argument of Nestorius as the answer of Cyril. Nestorius, the heretic, said that Christ was but a pure man, and not God, and that he had but a common body such as other men have, whereunto the Godhead was only assistant, as it is to other men. And to prove the same, he alleged Christ's own words, when he said: "He that eateth my flesh, &c." and "He that eateth me," and "As the living Father sent me." And forasmuch as Christ said, that he had flesh, and was eaten and sent, and God cannot be eaten nor sent, said Nestorius, therefore concluded he, that Christ was not God, but man, whose flesh might be eaten and sent: whose gross argumentation Cyril confuting saith, "that by his rude reasoning of eating, he draweth men's minds wickedly to fancy of the eating of man's flesh, (meaning of the eating thereof with tooth and mouth,) and so to imagine carnally and grossly such things of Christ as be understand to be done with an only and pure faith." And as Nestorius made his argument of the eating of man's flesh, even so did Cyril make his answer of the eating of the same, and not of the commixtion thereof. For unto what purpose should commixtion serve in that place, and whereunto should Christ's body be commixted? Or why should Cyril charge Nestorius with commixtion in Christ, seeing that he was charged with the clean contrary, as you say, that he separated the natures in Christ, and did not confound and commixt them? And furthermore, if Nestorius had made his argument of the eating, and Cyril had made his answer of the commixtion, they had foughten *Andabatarum more*, as the proverb saith, "like two blind men, that when one striketh in one place, the other holdeth up his buckler to defend in another place." Therefore may all men judge, that have any judgment at all, how unjustly you judge and condemn that godly and excellent learned man, Œcolampadius, for this word ἀνθρωποφαγίαν, which you say would be ἀνθρωπομιγίαν, which word in Greek I think was never read, nor hath in that place neither sense nor reason. And what an heady and intolerable arrogancy is this of you, of your own vain conjecturing to alter the Greek text without any Greek copy to ground yourself upon, altering ἀνθρωποφαγίαν into ἀνθρωπομιγίαν, and διαβεβαιοῦνται into διαβεβαιῶν, contrary to the translations of Œcolampadius and Musculus, not "whispered in corners," as you with your railing words would defame the matter, but published abroad to the world. And at the end you conclude altogether with interrogation, contrary to the two translations which yourself do allege, being printed, the one at Basil and the other at Cologne. And you, using such a licence to alter and change all things at your pleasure, are offended with Œcolampadius for changing of any case, gender, number, verb or participle, yea, for one tittle or prick of interrogation, which liberty hath ever been suffered in all interpreters, so they went not from the true sense. But you can spy a little mote in another man's eye, that cannot see a great block in your own.

Nevertheless, if I should divine without the book, as you do, I would rather think that διαβεβαιοῦνται should be διαβεβαιοῦνται, (for such small errors in one letter be easily committed in the printing,) and then concluding with an interrogation, as you would have it, the sense of the Greek should be this in English: "Doth not Nestorius affirm, that he who was seen and sent is another Son and Christ beside the Word, which is God of God? Doth not he say, that our sacrament is the eating of a man, unreverently leading faithful minds unto vain and gross imaginations, and going about

---

[² Discussion, 1551.]

to compass with man's phantasy those things which be received only with a pure and simple faith?" Where Cyril in these words reproveth Nestorius, in that he said that our sacrament is the eating of a man. Doth not he himself affirm the contrary, that our sacrament is not the eating of a man, as I said in my book? For else why should he reprehend Nestorius for saying the contrary? And doth not Cyril say also, that this sacrament "is received only with a pure and simple faith?" And yet you find fault with me, because I say that Cyril affirmeth the receiving in this sacrament to be only by faith; which your saying being so manifest contrary to Cyril's words, I refer me to the judgment of all indifferent readers, what trust is to be given to you in this matter. And as for Œcolampadius, if the printer in the stead of πάριστον made παριστῶν, and for ἐπίχειρον printed ἐπιχειρῶν, which may soon chance in printing, then may μυστήριον be the nominative case, notwithstanding all your vehement inveighing and vain babbling against Œcolampadius.

Yet after your scurrility and railing against Œcolampadius, you temper yourself somewhat, saying that "in such as receive the sacrament worthily, Christ dwelleth corporally, as Cyril saith; and naturally and carnally, as Hilary saith." This is the third evidence which you give against yourself, signifying that Christ is not corporally in them that receive not the sacrament worthily.

_{178.} And here you begin to smack of some true understanding, when you say that Christ dwelleth in them that worthily receive the sacrament, so that you would add thereto, that he dwelleth not only in them when they receive the sacrament, but whensoever by a lively faith they spiritually eat his flesh and drink his blood.

And where you say, that "by the variety of my doctrine it appeareth that I am not yet determined whither to go," you keep still your old conditions, and shew yourself to be always one man, in this point to charge other men with your own faults. For whereas my doctrine is throughly uniform and constant, yours is so variable and uncertain, that you agree with no man, nor with yourself neither, as I intend by God's grace particularly to set out in the end of my book.

And in these two authors, Hilary and Cyril, you vary three times from your answer unto my fourth book. For here you say no more, but that Christ is corporally in them that receive the sacrament worthily: and in the answer to my fourth book you say, that he is corporally in all them that receive the sacrament, whether it be worthily or unworthily.

Now followeth thus in my book.

<small>Basilius, Nyssenus, and Nazianzenus.</small> And here may be well enough passed over Basilius, Gregorius Nyssenus, and Gregorius Nazianzenus, partly because they speak little of this matter, and partly because they may be easily answered unto, by that which is before declared and often repeated; which is, that a figure hath the name of the thing whereof it is the figure, and therefore of the figure may be spoken the same thing that may be spoken of the thing itself. And as concerning the eating of Christ's flesh and drinking of his blood, they spake of the spiritual eating and drinking thereof by faith, and not of corporal eating and drinking with the mouth and teeth.

WINCHESTER.

<small>Basilius, Grego. Nissenus. Grego. Nazianzenus. [Berengarius. Bertrame. Orig. ed. Winch.] Messaliani heretici. Anthropomorphitæ. Nestoriani.</small> As for Basil, Gregory Nyssen, and Gregory Nazianzen, this author saith they speak little of this matter, and indeed they spake[1] not so much as other do; but that they speak is not discrepant, nor contrarieth not that other afore them had written. For in the old church the truth of this mystery was never impugned openly and directly that we read of, before Berengarius, five hundred years past, and secretly by one Bertram before that, but only by the Messalians, who said the corporal eating did neither good nor hurt. The Anthropomorphites also, who said the virtue of the mystical benediction endured not to the next day, of whom Cyril speaketh, and the Nestorians by consecution of their learning, that divided Christ's flesh from the deity. And where this author would have taken for a true supposal, that Basil, Gregory Nazianzen, and Nyssen, should take the sacrament to be

<small>*Only.</small> figurative only, that is to be denied. And likewise it is not true that this author teacheth,

---

[¹ Speak, Orig. ed. Winch.]

that of the figure may be spoken the same thing that may be spoken of the thing itself. And that I will declare thus. Of the thing itself, that is, Christ's very body being present in deed, it may be said, "Adore it, worship it there," which may not be said of the figure. It may be said of the very thing being present there, that "it is a high miracle to be there," "it is above nature to be there," "it is an high secret mystery to be there." But none of these speeches can be conveniently said of the only figure, that it is such a miracle, so above nature, so high a mystery to be a figure. And therefore it is no true doctrine to teach, that we may say the same of the figure, that may be said of the thing itself. And where this author speaketh of the spiritual eating, and corporal eating, he remaineth in his ignorance what the word "corporal" meaneth, which I have opened in discussing of his answer to Cyril. Faith is required in him that shall eat spiritually, and the corporal eating institute in Christ's supper requireth the reverent use of man's mouth, to receive our Lord's meat and drink, his own very flesh and blood, by his omnipotency prepared in that supper, which not spiritually, that is to say, not innocently[2] (as St Augustine[3] in one place expoundeth "spiritually") received, bringeth judgment and condemnation, according to St Paul's words.

*179. *Of corporal manducation, lege Roffeum adv. Œcolampadium, Lib. iii. cap. 13.[4] August. in Joan. tract. xxvi.*

CANTERBURY.

Where you say that "in the old church the truth of this mystery was never impugned openly," you say herein very truly; for the truth which I have set forth, was openly received and taught of all that were catholic without contradiction, until the papists devised a contrary doctrine. And I say further, that the untruth which you teach, was not at that time improved of no man, neither openly nor privily. For how could your doctrine be impugned in the old church, which was then neither taught nor known?

And as concerning Bertram, he did not write secretly; for he was required by king Charles to write in this matter, and wrote therein as the doctrine of the church was at that time, or else some man would have reprehended him, which never none did before you, but make mention of his works unto his great praise and commendation. And the Massalians were not reproved for saying, that "corporal eating doth neither good nor hurt," neither of Epiphanius, nor of St Augustine, nor Theodoret, nor of any other ancient author that I have read. Marry, that the sacraments do neither good nor hurt, and namely baptism, is laid unto the Massalians' charge; and yet the corporal receiving without the spiritual availeth nothing, but rather hurteth very much, as appeared in Judas and Simon Magus. And as for the three heresies of the Massalians, Anthropomorphites, and Nestorians[5], I allow none of them, although you report them otherwise than either Epiphanius or St Augustine doth.

Bertram.

*Messaliani, *De iis habetur in Hist. Trip. Lib. vii. cap. 11. et in Theodoreto, Lib. iv. cap. 11.

And where you say that I "would have taken for a supposal, that Basil, Nazianzen, and Nyssene should take the sacrament to be figurative only," still you charge me untruly with that I neither say nor think. For I knowledge, as all good christian men do, that Almighty God worketh effectually with his sacraments.

And where you report me to say another untruth, "that of a figure may be spoken the same thing, that may be spoken of the thing itself," that I say true therein witnesseth plainly St Augustine and Cyprian. And yet I speak not universally, nor these examples that you bring make anything against my sayings. For the first example may be said of the figure, if Dr Smith say true. And because you two write both against my book, and agree so evil one with another, as it is hard for untrue sayers to agree in one tale; therefore in this point I commit you together, to see which of you is most valiant champion. And as for your other three examples, it is not true of the thing itself, that Christ's body is present in the sacrament "by miracle or above nature," although by miracle and above nature he is in the ministration of his holy supper among them that godly be fed thereat. And thus be your frivolous cavillations answered.

*Smith.

And where you say that I am ignorant what this word, "corporal," meaneth, *Corporal.*

[2 Innocently, Orig. ed, Winch.]

[3 Videte ergo, fratres, panem cœlestem spiritaliter manducare, innocentiam ad altare apportare. Augustin. in Joan. Tractat. xxvi.]

[4 i. e. Fisher's (bishop of Rochester) book against Œcolampadius, De Veritate Corporis, &c. Colon. 1527. The title of this 13th chapter is: *Ex esu victimarum veteris legis docemur Christi carnem corporaliter edendam esse.*]

[5 An account of the Messalians, or Euchites, may be found in Mosheim, Eccles. Hist. Cent. iv. Chap. V. § 24; of the Anthropomorphites, ibid. Cent. x. Chap. V. § 4; of the Nestorians, ibid. Cent. v. Chap. V. § 12.]

surely then I have a very gross wit, that am ignorant in that thing, which every ploughman knoweth. But you make so fine a construction of this word "corporal," that neither you can tell what you mean yourself, nor no man can understand you, as I have opened before in the discussing of Cyril's mind.

And as for "the reverent use of man's mouth" in the Lord's holy supper, the bread and wine outwardly must be reverently received with the mouth, because of the things thereby represented, which by faith be received inwardly in our hearts and minds, and not eaten with our mouths, as you untruly allege St Paul to say, whose words be of the eating of the sacramental bread, and not of the body of Christ.

Now followeth next mine answer to Eusebius Emissenus, who is as it were your chief trust and sheet-anchor.

The answer to Emissenus.

Likewise Eusebius Emissenus is shortly answered unto: for he speaketh not of any real and corporal conversion of bread and wine into Christ's body and blood, nor of any corporal and real eating and drinking of the same; but he speaketh of a sacramental conversion of bread and wine, and of a spiritual eating and drinking of the body and blood. After which sort Christ is as well present in baptism, as the same Eusebius plainly there declareth, as he is in the Lord's table: which is not carnally and corporally, but by faith and spiritually. But of this author is spoken before more at large in the matter of transubstantiation.

WINCHESTER.

Emissen.

This author saith that Emissen is shortly answered unto, and so is he, if a man care not what he saith, as Hilary was answered and Cyril. But else, there can no short or long answer confound the true plain testimony of Emissen, for the common true faith of the church in the sacrament. Which Emissen hath this sentence, "That the invisible priest, (by the secret power with his word,) turneth the visible creatures into the substance of his body and blood, saying thus: 'This is my body'; and again repeating the same sanctification, 'This is my blood.' Wherefore as at the beck of him commanding the heights of heavens, the deepness of the floods, and largeness of lands were founded of nothing: by like power in spiritual sacraments, where virtue commandeth, the effect of the truth serveth." These be Emissen's words[1]*, declaring his faith plainly of the sacrament, in such terms as cannot be wrested or writhed, who speaketh of a turning and conversion of the visible creatures into the substance of Christ's body and blood: he saith not into the sacrament of Christ's body and blood, nor figure of Christ's body and blood, whereby he should mean a only sacramental conversion, as this author would have it; but he saith, "into the substance of Christ's body and blood [declaring the truth of Christ's body and blood*[2]*] to be in the sacrament." For the words "substance" and "truth" be of one strength, and shew a difference from a figure, wherein the truth is not in deed present, but signified to be absent. And because it is a work supernatural, and a great miracle, this Emissen represseth man's carnal reason, and succoureth the weak faith with remembrance of like power of God in the creation of this world*[3]*, which were brought forth out of time by Emissen, if Christ's body were not in substance present, as Emissen's words be, but in figure only, as this author teacheth.*

*Only.

And where this author coupleth together the two sacraments, of baptism and of the body and blood of Christ, as though there were no difference in the presence of Christ in either, he putteth himself in danger to be reproved of malice or ignorance. For although these mysteries be both great, and man's regeneration in baptism is also a mystery and the secret work of God, and hath a great marvel in that effect; yet it differeth from the mystery of the sacrament, touching the manner of Christ's presence, and the working of the effect also. For in baptism our union with Christ is wrought without the real presence of Christ's humanity, only in the virtue and effect of Christ's blood, the whole Trinity there working as author, in whose name the sacrament is expressly ministered, where our soul is regenerate and made spiritual, but not our body in deed, but in hope only that for the Spirit of Christ dwelling in us our mortal bodies shall be resuscitate, and as we have in baptism been buried with Christ, so we be assured to be partakers of his resurrection. And so in this sacrament we be unite to Christ's manhood by this divinity. But in the sacrament of Christ's body and blood we be in nature united to Christ as man, and by his glorified flesh made partakers also of his divinity; which mystical

---

[1 Emissen's sayings, Orig. ed. Winch.]   [3 Of the world, 1551.]
[2 Orig. ed. Winch. inserts this passage.]

union representeth unto us the high estate of our glorification, wherein body and soul shall in the general resurrection, by a marvellous regeneration of the body, be made both spiritual, the special pledge whereof we receive in this sacrament, and therefore it is the sacrament (as Hilary saith) of perfect unity. And albeit the soul of man be more precious than the body, and the nature of the Godhead in Christ more excellent than the nature of man in him glorified, and in baptism man's soul is regenerate in the virtue and effect of Christ's passion and blood, Christ's Godhead present there without the real presence of his humanity; although for these respects the excellency of baptism is great; yet because the mystery of the sacrament of the altar, where Christ is present both man and God, in the effectual unity that is wrought between our bodies, our souls and Christ's, in the use of this sacrament, signifieth the perfect redemption of our bodies in the general resurrection, which shall be the end and consummation of all our felicity. This sacrament of perfect unity is the mystery of our perfect estate, when body and soul shall be all spiritual; and hath so a degree of excellency, for the dignity that is esteemed in every end and perfection: wherefore the word "spiritual" is a necessary word *Spiritual. *in this sacrament, to call it a spiritual food, as it is indeed, for it is to work in our bodies a spiritual effect, not only in our souls: and Christ's body and flesh is a spiritual body and flesh*[4], *and yet a true body and flesh. And it is present in this sacrament after a spiritual* *Spiritual manner. *manner, granted and taught of all true teachers, which we should receive also spiritually, which* *Spiritually. *is by having Christ before spiritually in us to receive it so worthily. Wherefore, like as in the invisible substance of the sacrament there is nothing carnal but all spiritual, taking the word "carnal" as it signifieth "grossly" in man's carnal judgment: so where the receivers of that food bring carnal lusts or desires, carnal fancies or imaginations with them, they receive the same precious food unworthily to their judgment and condemnation. For they judge not truly, after the simplicity of a true Christian faith, of the very presence of Christ's body. And this sufficeth to wipe out that this author hath spoken of Emissen against the truth.*

CANTERBURY.

I have so plainly answered unto Emissen in my former book, partly in this place, and partly in the second part of my book, that he that readeth over those two places, shall see most clearly that you have spent a great many of words here in vain, and need no further answer at all. And I had then such a care what I said, that I said nothing but according to Emissenus' own mind, and which I proved by his own words. But if you find but one word that in speech soundeth to your purpose, you stick to that word tooth and nail, caring nothing what the author's meaning is.

And here is one great token of sleight and untruth to be noted in you, that you *A sleight. write diligently every word so long as they seem to make with you. And when you come to the very place where Emissen declareth the meaning of his words, there you leave all the rest out of your book, which cannot be without a great untruth and fraud, to deceive the simple reader. For when you have recited these words of Emissen, 182. "that the invisible priest by the secret power with his word turneth the visible creatures into the substance of his body and blood," and so further as serveth to your affection, when you come even to the very place where Emissen declareth these words, there you leave and cut off your writing.

But because the reader may know what you have cut off, and thereby know Emissen's meaning, I shall here rehearse Emissen's words which you have left out. "If thou wilt know," saith Emissen[5], "how it ought not to seem to thee a thing new and

---

[4 Orig. ed. Winch. omits the words "is a spiritual body and flesh."]

[5 Item *Eusebius Emisenus*, 6.——Recedat ergo omne infidelitatis ambiguum: quandoquidem qui auctor est muneris, ipse etiam testis est veritatis. Nam invisibilis Sacerdos visibiles creaturas in substantiam corporis et sanguinis sui verbo suo secreta potestate convertit, ita dicens, *Accipite, et comedite: hoc est enim corpus meum:* et sanctificatione repetita, *Accipite, et bibite: hic est sanguis meus.* Ergo sicut ad nutum præcipientis Domini repente ex nihilo substiterunt excelsa cœlorum, profunda fluctuum, vasta terrarum: ita pari potestate in spiritualibus sacramentis ubi præcipit virtus, servit effectus. Quanta itaque et quam celebranda beneficia vis divinæ benedictionis operetur, attende: et ut tibi novum et impossibile videri non debeat, quod in Christi substantiam terrena et mortalia convertuntur, teipsum, qui jam in Christo es regeneratus, interroga: Dudum alienus a vita, peregrinus a misericordia, a salutis via intrinsecus mortuus exulabas: subito initiatus Christi legibus, et salutaribus mysteriis innovatus, in corpus ecclesiæ non videndo sed credendo transiluisti, et de filio perditionis adoptivus Dei filius fieri occulta puritate meruisti: in mensura visibili permanens, major factus es teipso invisibiliter, sine quantitatis augmento: cum ipse atque idem esses, multo alter fidei

impossible, that earthly and incorruptible things be turned into the substance of Christ, look upon thyself which art made new in baptism. When thou wast far from life, and banished as a stranger from mercy and from the way of salvation, and inwardly wast dead, yet suddenly thou begannest another new life in Christ, and wast made new by wholesome mysteries, and wast turned into the body of the church, not by seeing, but by believing; and of the child of damnation, by a secret pureness thou wast made the son of God. Thou visibly didst remain in the same measure that thou hadst before, but invisibly thou wast made greater, without any increase of thy body. Thou wast the self same person, and yet by increase of faith thou wast made another man. Outwardly nothing was added, but all the change was inwardly. And so was man made the son of Christ, and Christ formed in the mind of man. Therefore as thou, putting away thy former vileness, didst receive a new dignity, not feeling any change in thy body; and as the curing of thy disease, the putting away thine infection, the wiping away of thy filthiness, be not seen with thine eyes, but believed in thy mind; so likewise when thou dost go up to the reverend altar to feed upon the spiritual meat, in thy faith look upon the body and blood of him that is thy God, honour him, touch him with thy mind, take him in the hand of thy heart, and chiefly drink him with the draught of thy inward man." These be Emissen's own words. Upon which words I gather his meaning in his former words by you alleged. For where you bring in these words, "That Christ by his secret power with his word turneth the visible creatures into the substance of his body and blood," straightways in these words by me now rehearsed he sheweth, what manner of turning that is, and after what manner the earthly and corruptible things be turned into the substance of Christ: "even so," saith he, "as it is in baptism," wherein is no transubstantiation. So that I gather his meaning of his own plain words, and you gather his meaning by your own imagination, devising such phantastical things as neither Emissen saith, nor yet be catholic.

Truth. And this word "truth" you have put unto the words of Emissen, of your own head, which is no true dealing. For so you may prove what you list, if you may add to the authors what words you please. And yet if Emissen had used both the words, "substance" and "truth," what should that help you? For Christ is in substance and truth present in baptism, as well as he is in the Lord's supper; and yet is he not there carnally, corporally, and naturally.

Only. I will pass over here, to aggravate the matter, how untruly you add to my words this word "only," in an hundred places, where I say not so: what true and sincere dealing this is, let all men judge.

183. Now as concerning my coupling together of the two sacraments of baptism and of the body and blood of Christ, Emissen himself coupleth them both together in this place, and saith that the one is like the other, without putting any difference, even as I truly recited him. So that there appeareth neither "malice nor ignorance" in me; but in you, adding at your pleasure such things as Emissen saith not, to deceive the simple reader, and adding such your own inventions, as be neither true nor catholic, appeareth much shift and craft joined with untruth and infidelity.

Errors. For what christian man would say, as you do, that Christ is not indeed, (which you call "really,") in baptism? Or that we be not regenerated, both body and soul, as well in baptism as in the sacrament of the body and blood of Christ? Or that in baptism we be not united to Christ's divinity by his manhood? Or that baptism representeth not to us the high state of our glorification, and the perfect redemption of our bodies in the general resurrection? In which things you make difference between baptism and the sacrament (as you call it) of the altar. Or what man that were

---

processibus extitisti: in exteriori nihil additum est, et totum in interiori mutatum est: ac sic homo Christi filius effectus, et Christus in hominis mente formatus est. Sicut ergo sine corporali sensu, præterita utilitate deposita, subito novam indutus es dignitatem: et sicut hoc, quod in te Deus læsa curavit, infecta diluit, immaculata detersit, non sunt oculis nec sensibus tuis credita: ita cum reverendum altare cœlestibus cibis satiandus ascendis, sacrum Dei tui corpus et sanguinem fide respice, honora, mirare, mente continge, cordis manu suscipe, et maxime haustu interiore assume.—Corpus Juris Canonici, Tom. I. Decreti tertia pars. "De Consecrat." Dist. I. cap. 35. "Quia corpus." col. 1926-28. Lugduni. 1618.]

learned in God's word would affirm, that in the general resurrection our bodies and souls shall be all spiritual? I know that St Paul saith that in the resurrection our bodies shall be spiritual, meaning in the respect of such vileness, filthiness, sin, and corruption, as we be subject unto in this miserable world: yet he aith not that our bodies shall be all spiritual. For notwithstanding such spiritualness as St Paul speaketh of, we shall have all such substantial parts and members as pertain to a very natural man's body. So that in this part our bodies shall be carnal, corporal, real, and natural bodies, lacking nothing that belongeth to perfect men's bodies. And in that[1] respect is the body of Christ also carnal, and not spiritual. And yet we bring none other carnal imaginations of Christ's body, nor mean none other, but that Christ's body is carnal in this respect, that it hath the same flesh and natural substance which was born of the virgin Mary, and wherein he suffered and rose again, and now sitteth at the right hand of his Father in glory; and that the same his natural body now glorified hath all the natural parts of a man's body in order, proportion, and place distinct, as our bodies shall be in these respects carnal after our resurrection. Which manner of carnalness and diversity of parts and members if you take away now from Christ in heaven, and from us after our resurrection, you make Christ now to have no true man's body, but a fantastical body, as Marcion and Valentine did: and as concerning our bodies, you run into the error of Origen, which fancied and imagined, that at the resurrection all things should be so spiritual, that women should be turned into men, and bodies into souls.

Spiritual.

And yet it is to be noted by the way, that in your answer here to Emissene, you make "spiritually" and a "spiritual manner" all one.

Now followeth mine answer to St Ambrose in this wise.

And now I will come to the saying of St Ambrose, which is always in their mouths. "Before the consecration," saith he[2], as they allege, "it is bread, but after the words of the[3] consecration it is the body of Christ."

The answer to Ambrosius de Sacramentis, Lib. iv. cap. 4.

For answer hereunto, it must be first known what consecration is.

Consecration is the separation of any thing from a profane and worldly use unto a spiritual and godly use.

Consecration. 184.

And therefore when usual and common water is taken from other uses, and put to the use of baptism in the name of the Father, and of the Son, and of the Holy Ghost, then it may rightly be called consecrated water, that is to say, water put to an holy use.

*In iis Roffeum. ii. cap. 25.

Even so, when common bread and wine be taken and severed from other bread and wine to the use of the holy communion, that portion of bread and wine, although it be of the same substance that the other is from the which it is severed, yet it is now called consecrated, or holy bread and holy wine.

Not that the bread and wine have or can have any holiness in them, but that they be used to an holy work, and represent holy and godly things. And therefore St Dionyse[4] called the bread holy bread, and the cup an holy cup, as soon as they be set upon the altar to the use of the holy communion.

De Eccl. Hierar. cap. 3.

But specially they may be called holy and consecrated, when they be separated to that holy use by Christ's own words[5], which he spake for that purpose, saying of the bread, "This is my body," and of the wine, "This is my blood."

Matt. xxvi. Mark xiv. Luke xxii.

So that commonly the authors, before those words be spoken, do take the bread and wine but as other common bread and wine; but after those words be pronounced over them, then they take them for consecrated and holy bread and wine.

Not that the bread and wine can be partakers of any holiness or godliness,

---

[1 So ed. 1551. In 1580, the.]
[2 Sed panis iste panis est ante verba sacramentorum; ubi accesserit consecratio, de pane fit caro Christi. Ambros. de Sacramentis, Lib. iv. cap. iv.
Tom. IV. p. 173. Colon. Agrip. 1616.]
[3 Words of consecration, 1551, and Orig. ed.]
[4 Vid. supra, p. 151.]
[5 Of Christ's own words, 1551, and Orig. ed.]

or can be the body and blood of Christ, but that they represent the very body and blood of Christ, and the holy food and nourishment which we have by him. And so they be called by the names of the body and blood of Christ, as the sign, token, and figure is called by the name of the very thing which it sheweth and signifieth.

And therefore as St Ambrose, in the words before cited by the adversaries, saith, that "before the consecration it is bread, and after the consecration it is Christ's body," so in other places he doth more plainly set forth his meaning, saying these words: "Before the benediction of the heavenly words, it is called another kind of thing; but after the consecration, is signified the body of Christ. Likewise before the consecration it is called another thing; but after the consecration it is named the blood of Christ[1]." And again he saith: "When I treated of the sacraments, I told you that that thing which is offered before the words of Christ, is called bread; but when the words of Christ be pronounced, then it is not called bread, but it is called by the name of Christ's body[2]."

<small>De his qui mysteriis initiantur, cap. ult.</small>

<small>De sacramentis, Lib. v. cap. 4.</small>

By which words of St Ambrose it appeareth plainly, that the bread is called by the name of Christ's body after the consecration; and although it be still bread, yet after consecration it is dignified by the name of the thing which it representeth: as at length is declared before in the process of transubstantiation, and specially in the words of Theodoretus.

And as the bread is a corporal meat, and corporally eaten, so, saith St Ambrose[3], "is the body of Christ a spiritual meat, and spiritually eaten," and that requireth no corporal presence.

<small>De sacramentis, Lib. vi. cap. 1.</small>

WINCHESTER.

<small>Ambrosius.</small>

As touching St Ambrose, this author taketh a great enterprise to wrestle with him, whose plain and evident words must needs be a rule to try his other words by, if any might be writhed. What can be more plainly spoken than St Ambrose speaketh, when he saith these words? "It is bread before consecration, but after it is Christ's body[4]." By the word "consecration" is signified, as it is here placed, God's omnipotent work. Wherefore in this place it comprehendeth as much as Emissene said in these words, "he converteth by the secret power of his word." God is the worker, and so consecration signifieth the whole action of his omnipotency in working the substance of this high mystery; and therefore the definition of the word "consecration," as it is generally taken, cannot be a rule to the understanding of it in this high mystery, where it is used to express a singular work, as the circumstance of St Ambrose writing doth declare. For as Philip Melancthon writeth to Œcolampadius, "St Ambrose would never have travailed to accumulate so many miracles as he doth," speaking of this matter to declare God's omnipotency, "and he had not thought the nature of bread to be changed in this mystery[5]." These be Melancthon's very words. Now to answer the question, as it were, at the word "change," this author shall come with a "sacramental change," which is a device in terms to blind the rude reader. St Ambrose doth express plainly what the change is when he writeth the words before rehearsed.

<small>*Consecration.
185.</small>

<small>Melancthon.</small>

<small>*Sacramental change.</small>

"It is bread before the consecration, but after it is the body of Christ." Can a change be more plainly declared? The near[6] way for this author had been to have joined Ambrose with Clement, and called him feigned by the papists, rather than after the effect of consecration so opened by St Ambrose himself to travail to prove what it may signify, if it were in another matter; and then to admonish the reader how the bread and wine have no holiness, which

---

[1 Ante benedictionem verborum cœlestium species nominatur, post consecrationem corpus Christi significatur.—Ante consecrationem aliud dicitur, post consecrationem sanguis nuncupatur. Ambros. de Initiandis, cap. ult. Tom. IV. p. 166.]

[2 Memini sermonis mei cum de sacramentis tractarem. Dixi vobis quod ante verba Christi quod offertur panis dicatur; ubi Christi verba deprompta fuerint, jam non panis dicitur, sed Christi corpus appellatur. Quare ergo in oratione Dominica quæ postea sequitur, ait, Panem nostrum? Panem quidem dixit, sed ἐπιούσιον, hoc est supersubstantialem. Id. de Sacramentis, Lib. v. cap. iv. Tom. IV. p. 175.]

[3 Id. Lib. vi. cap. i. Tom. IV. p. 176.]

[4 The body of Christ. Orig. ed. Winch.]

[5 Hæc tam longa recitatio exemplorum clare ostendit auctorem [h.e. Ambrosium] sensisse, panem non esse tantum signum, sed naturam panis mutari.—The quotation (as before observed, p. 149), is from Melancthon's Letter to Myconius, p. 55. of Œcolampadius's Dialogue.]

[6 Nearer, Orig. ed. Winch.]

OF THE PRESENCE OF CHRIST.

form of speech not understood of the people engendereth some scruple that needeth not, being no sound form of doctrine: for St Paul speaketh and teacheth thus, that the creatures be sanctified by the word of God and prayer; and St Augustine writeth of sanctified bread to be given to them that be catechised before they be baptized: and this author himself expoundeth St Cyprian in the thirty-fifth leaf[7] *of this book, how the divinity is poured into the bread sacramentally, which is a strange phrase; not expressing there Cyprian's mind, and far discrepant from the doctrine here.*

1 Tim. iv.
De peccat. merit. et remiss. Lib. ii. cap. 26.
[Cyprian de cœna Domini. Orig. ed. Winch.]

And in another place this author saith, that as hot and burning iron is iron still, and yet hath the force of fire; so the bread and wine be turned into the virtue of Christ's flesh and blood. By which similitude bread may conceive virtue, as iron conceiveth fire; and then as we call iron burning and fiery, so we may call bread virtuous and holy, unless the author would again resemble bread to a whetstone, that may make sharp and have no sharpness in it at all. Which matter I declare thus to shew, that as this author dissenteth from truth in other, so he dissenteth from that he uttereth for truth himself, and walketh in a maze, impugning the very truth in this sacrament, and would have that taken for a catholic doctrine that is not one, and the same doctrine through this whole book, so far off is it from the whole of christian teaching. But now let us consider what speeches of St Ambrose this author bringeth forth, wherewith to alter the truth of the very plain proper speech of St Ambrose, saying: "It is bread before the consecration; and after it is Christ's body [8]*."*

St Ambrose, as this author saith in another place, saith thus: "Before the benediction of the heavenly words it is called another kind of thing; but after the consecration is signified the body and blood of Christ." And another speech thus: "Before the consecration it is called another thing; but after the consecration it is named the blood of Christ." And yet a third speech, where the word "call" is used before and after both, as thou, reader, mayest see in this author's book, in the eighty-third leaf[9]*. Now, good reader, was there ever man so overseen as this author is, who seeth not St Ambrose in these three latter speeches to speak as plainly as in the first? For in the last speech St Ambrose saith, it is called bread before the consecration, and called the body of Christ after the consecration. And I would demand of this author, doth not this word "call" signify the truth that is bread in deed before the consecration? which if it be so, why shall not the same word "call" signify also the very truth added to the words of the body of Christ after the consecration? And likewise when he saith, speaking of the body of Christ, the word "signified" or "named," which is as much as "call." The body of Christ is signified there, for Christ said "This is my body," &c., using the outward signs of the visible creatures to signify the body and blood present, and not absent. Was not Christ the true Son of God, because the angel said, "He shall be called the Son of God?" But in these places of St Ambrose, to express plainly what he meant by "calling," he putteth that word "call" to the bread before the consecration, as well as to the body of Christ after the consecration; thereby to declare how in his understanding the word*[10] *"call" signifieth as much truth in the thing whereunto it is added after consecration as before; and therefore as it is by St Ambrose called bread before consecration, signifying it was so indeed, so it is "called," "signified" or "named", (which three thus placed be all one in effect,) the body of Christ after the consecration, and is so in deed, agreeable to the plain speech of St Ambrose, where he saith: "It is bread before consecration, and it is the body of Christ after consecration." As touching the spirituality of the meat of Christ's body I have spoken before; but where this author addeth, "it requireth no corporal presence," he speaketh in his dream, being oppressed with sleep of ignorance, and cannot tell what "corporal" meaneth, as I have opened before by the authority of Cyril. Now let us see what this author saith to Chrysostom.*

*Luke i. 186.

CANTERBURY.

It is not I that wrestle with St Ambrose, but you, who take great pain to wrest his words clean contrary to his intent and meaning. But where you ask this question, What can be more plain than these words of St Ambrose, "It is bread before consecration, and after, it is Christ's body?" these words of St Ambrose be not fully so plain as you pretend, but clean contrary. For what can be spoken either more unplain or untrue, than to say of bread after consecration, that it is the body of Christ, unless the same be understand in a figurative speech? For although Christ's body, as you say, be there after consecration, yet the bread is not his body, nor his body is not made of it, by your confession. And therefore the saying of St Ambrose, that it is Christ's body, cannot be true in plain speech. And therefore St Ambrose in the

Whether bread be Christ's body.

[7 See below, Book II. chap. 11.]
[8 But after, it is the body of Christ. Orig. ed. Winch.]
[9 Vide supra, p. 178.]
[10 This word, Orig. ed. Winch.]

same place, where he calleth it the body and blood of Christ, he saith, it is a figure of his body and blood. For these be his words: *Quod est figura corporis et sanguinis Domini nostri Jesu Christi.*

And as for the word "consecration," I have declared the signification thereof according to the mind of the old authors, as I will justify.

And for the writing of Melancthon to Œcolampadius, you remain still in your old error, taking Myconius for Œcolampadius. And yet the change of bread and wine in this sacrament, which Melancthon speaketh of, is a sacramental change, as the nature of a sacrament requireth, signifying how wonderfully Almighty God by his omnipotency worketh in us his lively members, and not in the dead creatures of bread and wine.

<small>A sacramental change.</small>

And the change is in the use, and not in the elements kept and reserved, wherein is not the perfection of a sacrament. Therefore, as water in the font or vessel hath not the reason and nature of a sacrament, but when it is put to the use of christening, and then it is changed into the proper nature and kind of a sacrament, to signify the wonderful change which Almighty God by his omnipotency worketh really in them that be baptized therewith; such is the change of the bread and wine in the Lord's supper. And therefore, the bread is called Christ's body after consecration, as St Ambrose saith, and yet it is not so really, but sacramentally. For it is neither Christ's mystical body, (for that is the congregation of the faithful dispersed abroad in the world,) nor his natural body, (for that is in heaven,) but it is the sacrament both of his true natural body, and also of his mystical body, and for that consideration hath the name of his body, as a sacrament or sign may bear the name of the very thing that is signified and represented thereby.

<small>187.</small>

And as for the foresaid books entitled to St Ambrose, if I joined Ambrose with Clement, and should say that the said books entitled in the name of St Ambrose, *de sacramentis, et de mysteriis initiandis*, were none of his, I should say but as I think, and as they do think that be men of most excellent learning and judgment, as I declared in my second book, which speaketh of transubstantiation. And so doth judge not only Erasmus, but also Melancthon (whom you allege for authority when he maketh for your purpose), suspecteth the same. And yet I plainly deny not these books to be his, (for your pleasure to give you as much advantage as you can ask,) and yet it availeth you nothing at all.

<small>Holy bread.</small>

But here I cannot pass over, that you be offended, because I say, that bread and wine be called holy, when they be put to an holy use, not that they have any holiness in them, or be partakers of any holiness or godliness. I would feign learn of Smith and you, when the bread and wine be holy. For before they be hallowed or consecrated, they be not holy by your teaching, but be common baker's bread and wine of the tavern; and after the consecration, there is neither bread or wine, as you teach: at what time then should the bread and wine be holy? But the creatures of bread and wine be much bound unto you, and can no less do than take you for their saviour. For if you can make them holy and godly, then shall you glorify them, and so bring them to eternal bliss. And then you may as well save the true labouring bullocks, and innocent sheep and lambs, and so understand the prophet, *Homines et jumenta salvabis, Domine.*

<small>Psal. xxxv.</small>

But "to admonish the reader," say you, "how the bread and wine have no holiness, this fortune[1] of speech, not understand of the people, engendereth some scruple that needeth not." By which your saying I cannot tell what the people may understand, but that you have a great scruple that you have lost your holy bread. And yet St Paul speaketh not of your holy bread, as you imagine, being utterly ignorant, as appeareth, in the scripture; but he speaketh generally of all manner of meats, which christian people receive with thanksgiving unto God, whether it be bread, wine, or water, fish, flesh, white meat, herbs, or what manner of meat and drink so ever it be.

And the sanctified bread, which St Augustine writeth, to be given to them that be catechised, was not holy in itself, but was called holy for the use and signification.

<small>August. de peccatorum meritis et remiss. Lib. ii. cap. 26. Cyprianus.</small>

And I express St Cyprian's mind truly, and not a whit discrepant from my doctrine here, when I say, that the divinity may be said to be poured, or put sacramen-

---

[1 Form, 1551.]

tally into the bread; as the Spirit of God is said to be in the water of baptism, when it is truly ministered, or in his word when it is sincerely preached, with the Holy Spirit working mightily in the hearts of the hearers. And yet the water in itself is but a visible element, nor the preacher's word of itself is but a sound in the air, which as soon as it is heard, vanisheth away, and hath in itself no holiness at all, although for the use and ministry thereof it may be called holy. And so likewise may be said of the sacraments, which, as St Augustine saith, "be as it were God's visible word."

188. Holy bread.

And whereas you rehearse out of my words in another place, that "as hot and burning iron is iron still, and yet hath the force of fire, so the bread and wine be turned into the virtue of Christ's flesh and blood:" you neither report my words truly, nor understand them truly. For I declare, in my book, virtue to be in them that godly receive bread and wine, and not in the bread and wine. And I take virtue there to signify might and strength, or force, as I name it, (which in the Greek is called δύναμις, after which sense we say, that there is virtue in herbs, in words, and in stones,) and not to signify virtue in holiness, (which in Greek is called ἀρετή), whereof a person is called virtuous, whose faith and conversation is godly. But you sophistically and fraudulently do of purpose abuse the word "virtue" to another signification than I meant, to approve by my words your own vain error, that bread should be virtuous and holy, making in your argument a fallax or craft, called equivocation. For where my meaning is, that the death of Christ, and the effusion of his blood, have effect and strength in them that truly receive the sacrament of his flesh and blood, you turn the matter quite, as though I should say, that the bread were godly and virtuous; which is a very frantic and ungodly opinion, and nothing pertaining to mine application of the similitude of iron. But this is the mother of many errors, both in interpretation of scriptures, and also in understanding of old ancient writers, when the mind and intent of him that maketh a similitude is not considered, but the similitude is applied unto other matters than the meaning was. Which fault may be justly noted in you here, when you reason by the similitude of hot burning iron, that bread may conceive such virtue as it may be called virtuous and holy. For my only purpose was by that similitude to teach, that iron, remaining in his proper nature and substance, by conceiving of fire may work another thing than is the nature of iron. And so likewise bread, remaining in his proper nature and substance, in the ministration of the sacrament, hath another use than to feed the body. For it is a memorial of Christ's death, that by exercise of our faith our souls may receive the more heavenly food. But this is a strange manner of speech, (which neither scripture, nor approved author ever used before you,) to call the sacramental bread virtuous, as you do. But into such absurdities men do commonly fall, when they will of purpose impugn the evident truth.

But "was there ever any man so overseen," say you, "as this author is? Who seeth not St Ambrose in these three latter speeches to speak as plainly as in the first?" Was there ever any man so destitute of reason, say I, but that he understandeth this, that when bread is called bread, it is called by the proper name, as it is in deed; and when bread is called the body of Christ, it taketh the name of a thing, which it is not in deed, but is so called by a figurative speech? And calling, say you, in the words of Christ signifieth making, which if it signifieth when bread is called bread, then were calling of bread a making of bread. And thus is answered your demand, why this word "call" in the one signifieth the truth, and in the other not: because that the one is a plain speech, and the other a figurative. For else by your[2] reasoning out of reason, when the cup which Christ used in his last supper was called a cup, and when it was called Christ's blood, all was one calling, and was of like truth without figure: so that the cup was Christ's blood in deed.

Bread is bread, is a plain speech. Bread is Christ's body, is a figurative speech.

189.

And likewise when[3] the stone that flowed out water was called a stone, and when it was called Christ; and the ark also when it was called the ark, and when it was called God; all these must be one speech and of like truth, if it be true which you here say. But as the ark was an ark, the stone a stone, and bread very bread, and the cup a cup, plainly without figurative speech; so when they be called God, Christ,

Numb. xx.
1 Cor. x.
1 Sam. iv.

[2 Our, 1580.]   [3 When, omitted in 1580.]

the body and blood of Christ, this cannot be a like calling, but must needs be understand by a figurative speech. For as Christ in the scripture is called a lamb for his innocency and meekness, a lion for his might and power, a door and way, whereby we enter into his Father's house, wheat and corn for the property of dying before they rise up and bring increase; so is he called bread, and bread is called his body, and wine his blood, for the property[1] of feeding and nourishing. So that these and all like speeches, (where as one substance is called by the name of another substance diverse and distinct in nature,) must needs be understand figuratively by some similitude or propriety of one substance unto another, and can in no wise be understand properly and plainly without a figure. And therefore, when Christ is called the Son of God, or bread is called bread, it is a most plain and proper speech; but when Christ is called bread, or bread is called Christ, these can in no wise be formal and proper speeches, (the substances and natures of them being so diverse,) but must needs have an understanding in figure, signification or similitude, (as the very nature of all sacraments require,) as all the old writers do plainly teach. And therefore the bread after consecration is not called Christ's body, because it is so in deed; for then it were no figurative speech, as all the old authors say it is.

Corporal.

And as for this word "corporal," you openly confessed your own ignorance in the open audience of all the people at Lambeth: when I asked you, what corporal body Christ hath in the sacrament, and whether he had distinction of members or no, your answer was in effect that you could not tell. And yet was that a wiser saying than you spake before in Cyril, where you said, that Christ hath only a spiritual body and a spiritual presence, and now you say, he hath a corporal presence. And so you confound corporal and spiritual, as if you knew not what either of them meant, or wist not, or cared not what you said. But now I will return to my book, and rehearse mine answer unto St John Chrysostom, which is this.

The answer to Chrysostomus.

Now let us examine St John Chrysostom, who in sound of words maketh most for the adversaries of the truth; but they that be familiar and acquainted with Chrysostom's manner of speaking, (how in all his writings he is full of allusions, schemes, tropes, and figures,) shall soon perceive that he helpeth nothing their purposes, as it shall well appear by the discussing of those places which the papists do allege of him, which be specially two. One is *In Sermone de Eucharistia in Encæniis,* and the other is *De proditione Judæ.*

And as touching the first, no man can speak more plainly against them than St John Chrysostom speaketh in that sermon. Wherefore it is to be wondered why they should allege him for their party, unless they be so blind in their opinion that they can see nothing, nor discern what maketh for them, nor what against them. For there he hath these words: "When you come to these mysteries," speaking of the Lord's board and holy communion, "do not think that you receive by a man the body of God[2]," meaning of Christ. These be St John Chrysostom's own words in that place.

190. In Sermone de eucharistia in Encæniis.

Then if we receive not the body of Christ at the hands of a man, ergo, the body of Christ is not really, corporally, and naturally in the sacrament, and so given to us by the priest. And then it followeth that all the papists be liars, because they feign and teach the contrary.

But in[3] this place of St Chrysostom is touched before more at length in answering to the papists' transubstantiation.

Wherefore now shall be answered the other place which they allege of Chrysostom in these words[4]: "Here he is present in the sacrament and doth

De Proditione Judæ.

[1 Propriety, 1551.]

[2 Διὸ καὶ προσερχόμενοι μὴ ὡς ἐξ ἀνθρώπου νομίσητε μεταλαμβάνειν τοῦ θείου σώματος. Chrysost. In sermone de eucharistia in Encæniis. (Ed. Bened. de Pœnitentia.) Hom. ix. Tom. II. p. 356.]

[3 But this place, 1551, and Orig. ed.]

[4 Πάρεστιν ὁ Χριστὸς, καὶ νῦν ἐκεῖνος ὁ τὴν τράπεζαν διακοσμήσας ἐκείνην, οὗτος καὶ ταύτην διακοσμεῖ νῦν. οὐδὲ γὰρ ἄνθρωπός ἐστιν ὁ ποιῶν τὰ προκείμενα γενέσθαι σῶμα καὶ αἷμα Χριστοῦ· ἀλλ' αὐτὸς ὁ σταυρωθεὶς ὑπὲρ ἡμῶν Χριστός. σχῆμα πληρῶν ἕστηκεν ὁ ἱερεύς, τὰ ῥήματα φθεγγόμενος ἐκεῖνα· ἡ δὲ δύναμις καὶ ἡ χάρις τοῦ θεοῦ ἐστι. τοῦτό μού ἐστι τὸ σῶμα, φησί. τοῦτο τὸ

consecrate, which garnished the table at the maundy or last supper. For it is not man which maketh of the bread and wine, being set forth to be consecrated, the body and blood of Christ; but it is Christ himself, which for us is crucified, that maketh himself to be there present. The words are uttered and pronounced by the mouth of the priest, but the consecration is by the virtue, might, and grace of God himself. And as this saying of God, 'Increase, be multiplied, and fill the earth,' once spoken by God, took always effect toward generation; even so the saying of Christ, 'This is my body,' being but once spoken, doth throughout all churches to this present, and shall to his last coming, give force and strength to this sacrifice." Gen. i.
Matt. xxvi.
Mark xiv.
Luke xxii.

Thus far they rehearse of Chrysostom's words. Which words, although they sound much for the purpose[5], yet if they be throughly considered and conferred with other places of the same author, it shall well appear that he meant nothing less than that Christ's body should be corporally and naturally present in the bread and wine, but that in such sort he is in heaven only; and in our minds by faith we ascend up into heaven, to eat him there, although sacramentally, as in a sign and figure, he be in the bread and wine, (and so is he also in the water of baptism;) and in them that rightly receive the bread and wine he is in a much more perfection than corporally, (which should avail them nothing,) but in them he is spiritually with his divine power, giving them eternal life.

And as in the first creation of the world all living creatures had their first life by God's only word, (for God only spake his word, and all things were created by and by accordingly,) and after their creation he spake these words, "Increase and multiply;" and by the virtue of those words all things have gendered and increased ever since that time; even so after that Christ said, "Eat, this is my body;" and "Drink, this is my blood: do this hereafter in remembrance of me;" by virtue of these words, and not by virtue of any man, the bread and wine be so consecrated, that whosoever with a lively faith doth eat that bread and drink that wine, doth spiritually eat, drink, and feed upon Christ sitting in heaven with his Father. And this is the whole meaning of St Chrysostom. Gen. i.
Matt. xxvi.
Mark xiv.
Luke xxii.

And therefore doth he so often say that we receive Christ in baptism. And when he hath spoken of the receiving of him in the holy communion, by and by he speaketh of the receiving of him in baptism, without declaring any diversity of his presence in the one from his presence in the other.

He saith also in many places, that "We ascend into heaven, and do eat Christ sitting there above." And where St Chrysostom and other authors do speak of the wonderful operation of God in his sacraments, passing all man's wit, senses, and reason, they mean not of the working of God in the water, bread, and wine, but of the marvellous working of God in the hearts of them that receive the sacraments; secretly, inwardly, and spiritually transforming them, renewing, feeding, comforting, and nourishing them with his flesh and blood, through his most holy Spirit, the same flesh and blood still remaining in heaven. Ad Populum Antiochenum. Hom. 61. et in Johannem. Hom. 45. 191.

Thus is this place of Chrysostom sufficiently answered unto. And if any man require any more, then let him look what is recited of the same author before, in the matter of transubstantiation.

ῥῆμα μεταρρυθμίζει τὰ προκείμενα. καὶ καθάπερ ἡ φωνὴ ἐκείνη ἡ λέγουσα, Αὐξάνεσθε, καὶ πληθύνεσθε, καὶ πληρώσατε τὴν γῆν, ἐρρέθη μὲν ἅπαξ, διὰ παντὸς δὲ τοῦ χρόνου γίνεται ἔργῳ ἐνδυναμοῦσα τὴν φύσιν τὴν ἡμετέραν πρὸς παιδοποιΐαν· οὕτω καὶ ἡ φωνὴ αὕτη ἅπαξ λεχθεῖσα καθ' ἑκάστην τράπεζαν ἐν ταῖς ἐκκλησίαις, ἐξ ἐκείνου μέχρι σήμερον, καὶ μέχρι τῆς αὐτοῦ παρουσίας, τὴν θυσίαν ἀπηρτισμένην ἐργάζεται. — Chrysostom. de Proditione Judæ, Hom. i. Tom. II. p. 384. Ed. Bened.]

[5 For their purpose, 1551, and Orig. ed.]

WINCHESTER.

Chrysostom.

This author noteth in Chrysostom two places, and bringeth them forth: and in handling the first place, declareth himself to trifle in so great a matter, evidently to his own reproof. For where, in the second book of his work, entreating transubstantiation, he would the same words of Chrysostom, by this form of speech in the negative, should not deny precisely; and when Chrysostom saith, "Do not think that you by man receive the body of God, but that we should not consider man in the receiving of it;" here this author doth allege these words, and reasoneth of them as though they were terms of mere denial. But I would ask of this author this question: If Chrysostom's faith had been, that we receive not the body of God in the sacrament verily, why should he use words idly to entreat of whom we received the body of God, which after this author's doctrine we receive not at all, but in figure; and no body at all, which is of Christ's humanity, being Christ, as this author teacheth, spiritually, that is, by his divine nature in him only that worthily receiveth, and in the very sacrament, as he concludeth in this book, only figuratively. Turn back, reader, to the thirty-sixth leaf in the author's book, and read it with this, and so consider upon what principle here is made an ergo. I will answer that place when I speak of transubstantiation, which shall be after answered to the third and fourth book, as the natural order of the matter requireth.

Chrysost. de Sacer. Lib. iii.

The second place of Chrysostom that this author bringeth forth, he granteth it soundeth much against him, and favoureth his adversaries, but with conferring and considering he trusteth to alter it from the true understanding. And not to expound, but confound the matter, he joineth in speech the sacrament of baptism with this sacrament, (which shift this author used untruly in Hilary,) and would now bear in hand, that the presence of Christ were none otherwise in this sacrament than in baptism, which is not so; for in this sacrament Christ's humanity and Godhead is really present, and in baptism his Godhead with the effectual virtue of his blood, in which we be washed, not requiring by scripture any real presence thereof for dispensation of that mystery, as I have before touched discussing the answer to Emissene[1]; whereas Chrysostom speaking of this sacrament, whereof I have before spoken, and Melancthon alleging it to Œcolampadius, saith thus: "The great miracle and great benevolence of Christ is, that he sitteth above with his Father, and is the same hour in our hands here to be embraced of us." And therefore, where this author would note the wonder of God's work in the sacrament to be wonderful for the work and effect in man, this is one piece of truth; but in the sacrament of the body and blood of Christ, the old fathers wonder at the work in the sacrament, how bread is changed into the body of Christ, how Christ sitting in heaven, God and man, is also man and God in the sacrament, and being worthily received, dwelleth in such carnally and naturally, as Hilary saith, and corporally, as Cyril saith. How this can be no man can tell, no faithful man should ask; and yet it is the true catholic faith to be truly so wrought. For, as Emissene saith: "he that is the author of it, he is the witness of it." And therefore I will make it an issue with this author, that the old fathers, speaking of the wonderful operation of God in this sacrament, refer it not only to the virtue and effect of this sacrament, nor to the virtue specially, but chiefly to the operation of God in the substance of this sacrament, and the sacrament self; for such a difference St Augustine maketh, saying: Aliud est sacramentum, aliud virtus sacramenti, "The sacrament is one, the virtue of the sacrament is another." Finally, in answering to Chrysostom, this author doth nothing but spend words in vain, to the more plain declaration of his own ignorance, or worse.

An issue.

In Joan. Tractat. 26. 192.

CANTERBURY.

As concerning Chrysostom, you have spent so many taunting and scornful words in waste, without cause, that I need to waste no words here at all to make you answer: but refer the reader to my book, the twenty-fifth leaf and thirty-sixth leaf, and to the thirty-second, thirty-third, and thirty-fourth leaf, where the reader shall find all that is here spoken fully answered unto[2].

Christ is verily and truly present and received.

But always you be like yourself, proceeding in amplification of an argument against me, which you have forged yourself, and charge me therewith untruly. For I use not this speech, that we receive not the body of God at all, that we receive it but in a figure. For it is my constant faith and belief, that we receive Christ in the sacra-

---

[1 Of Emissene, Orig. ed. Winch.]

[2 All these references are to passages in the second book "Of the Error of Transubstantiation," as well as those alluded to above by Winchester.]

ment verily and truly; and this is plainly taught and set forth in my book. But that "verily" as I with Chrysostom and all the old authors take it, is not of such a sort as you would have it. For your understanding of "verily" is so Capernaical, so gross, and so dull in the perceiving of this mystery, that you think a man cannot receive the body of Christ verily, unless he take him corporally in his corporal mouth, flesh, blood, and bones, as he was born of the virgin Mary. But it is certain, that Chrysostom meant not, that we receive Christ's body verily after such a sort, when he saith, "Do not think that you receive by a man the body of God." And yet, because I deny only this gross understanding, you misreport my doctrine, that I should say, we "receive not Christ at all, but in a figure, and no body at all:" wherein you untruly and slanderously report me, as my whole book and doctrine can witness against you. For my doctrine is, that the very body of Christ, which was born of the virgin Mary, and suffered for our sins, giving us life by his death, the same Jesus, as concerning his corporal presence, is taken from us, and sitteth at the right hand of his Father; and yet is he by faith spiritually present with us, and is our spiritual food and nourishment, and sitteth in the midst of all them that be gathered together in his name. And this feeding is a spiritual feeding, and an heavenly feeding, far passing all corporal and carnal feeding; and therefore there is a true presence and a true feeding in deed, and not "in a figure only, or not at all," as you most untruly report my saying to be. This is the true understanding of the true presence, receiving and feeding upon the body and blood of our Saviour Christ, and not, as you deprave the meaning and true sense thereof, that the receiving of Christ truly and verily is the receiving corporally with the mouth corporal[3], or that the spiritual receiving is to receive Christ only by his divine nature, which thing I never said nor meant. Turn, I pray thee, gentle reader, to the thirty-sixth leaf of my book, and note these words there, which I allege out of Chrysostom. "Do not think," saith he, "that you receive by a man the body of God." Then turn over the leaf, and in the twentieth line, note again my saying that, "in the holy communion Christ himself is spiritually eaten and drunken, and nourisheth the right believers." Then compare those sayings with this place of this ignorant lawyer, and thou shalt evidently perceive, that either he will not, or cannot, or at the least he doth not understand what is meant in the book of common prayer, and in my book also, by the receiving and feeding upon Christ spiritually.

But it is no marvel, that Nicodemus and the Capernaites understand not Christ, before they be born anew, and forsaking their papistical leaven, have learned another lesson of the Spirit of God, than flesh and blood can teach them. Much talk the papists make about this belief, that we must believe and have a stedfast faith, that Christ's body is corporally there, where the visible forms of bread and wine be: of which belief is no mention made in the whole scripture, which teacheth us to believe and profess, that Christ (as concerning his bodily presence) hath forsaken the world, and is ascended into heaven, and shall not come again until the restitution of all things that be spoken of by prophets. But whereas, in the feeding upon Christ's body and drinking of his blood, there is no mouth and teeth can serve, but only the inward and spiritual mouth of faith, there the papists keep silence like monks, and speak very little. And the cause why, is flesh and blood, which so blindeth all the Nicodemes and Capernaites, that they cannot understand what is spiritual nativity, spiritual circumcision, spiritual hunger and thirst, and spiritual eating and drinking of the flesh and blood of our Saviour Christ: but they hang all together so in the letter, that they cannot enter into the kingdom of the spirit; which knowledge if that you had, you should soon perceive upon what principle my *ergo* were made. And where you pervert the order of the books, setting the cart before the horse, that is to say, the third and fourth book before the second, saying that the natural order of the matter so requireth, here the reader may note an evident mark of all subtle papists, which is under the pretence and colour of order to break that order, whereby the falsehead of their doctrine should best be detected, and the truth brought to light. For when they perceive a window open, whereby the light may shine in, and the

---

[3 Corporal mouth, 1551.]

truth appear, then they busily go about to shut that window, and to draw the reader from that place to some mystical and obscure matter where more darkness is, and less light can be seen. And when, besides the darkness of the matter, they have by their subtle sophistry cast such a mist over the reader's eyes, that he is become blind, then dare they make him judge, be the matter never so untrue. And no marvel, for he is now become so blindfold and subject unto them, that he must say whatsoever they bid him, be it never so much repugnant to the evident truth. In such sort it is in the matter of the sacrament. For the papists perceiving that their error should easily be espied, if the matter of transubstantiation were first determined, the plain words of the scripture, the consent of ancient writers, the articles of our faith, the nature of a sacrament, reason, and all senses making so evidently against it, therefore none of the subtle papists will be glad to talk of transubstantiation, but they will always bear men in hand, that other matters must first be examined, as the late bishop doth here in this place.

194.

Now, in the second place of Chrysostom, where you say, that "in this sacrament Christ's humanity and Godhead is really present, and in baptism his Godhead with the effectual virtue of his blood, in which we be washed, not requiring by scripture any real presence thereof for the dispensation of that mystery," in this matter I have joined an issue with you before in the answer unto Origen, which shall suffice for answer here also.

Chrysosto-mus.

And where St John Chrysostom speaketh of "the great miracle of Christ, that he sitteth above with his Father, and is the same hour here with us in our hands," truth it is, that Christ sitteth above with his Father in his natural body, triumphant in glory, and yet is the same hour in our hands sacramentally, and present in our hearts by grace and spiritual nourishment. But that we should not think, that he is corporally here with us, St Augustine[1] giveth a rule in his epistle *ad Dardanum*, saying: *Cavendum est ne ita divinitatem astruamus hominis, ut veritatem corporis auferamus:* "We must foresee that we do not so affirm the divinity of him that is man, that we should thereby take away the truth of his body." And forasmuch as it is against the nature and truth of a natural body to be in two places at one time, therefore you seem to speak against the truth of Christ's natural body, when you teach that his body is in heaven naturally, and also naturally in the sacrament. For whosoever affirmeth that Christ's body is in sundry places as his Godhead is, seemeth to deify Christ's body by St Augustine's rule. But like as it is not to be thought, that *Quicquid est in Deo, est putandum ubique ut Deus*, "that whatsoever is in God, is every where as God is;" so must we not think that his body may be at one time every where, where his Godhead is. But Christ is, saith Augustine, *Ubique per id quod est Deus, in cœlo autem per id quod est homo;* "Every where in that he is God, but in heaven in that he is man." Wherefore his presence here of his body must be a sacramental presence; and the presence of his divinity, of his grace, of his truth, of his majesty and power, is real and effectual in many places, according to his word.

August. ad Dard.

August. ad Dard.

Wherein is the miracle.

Now, as concerning your issue, I refuse it not, but say, that the great miracle whereat the Jews wondered, and which our Saviour Christ meant, and the old fathers speak of, is of the eating of Christ's flesh and drinking of his blood, and how by flesh and blood we have everlasting life. Now, if you can bring good testimony for you, that the sacrament eateth Christ's flesh and drinketh his blood, and that it shall live for ever, which never had life, and that God's operation and work is more in dumb creatures than in man, then I must needs and will confess the issue to pass with you. And when I hear your testimonies, I shall make answer; but before I hear them, I should do nothing else but spend words in vain, and beat the wind to no purpose.

Now hear what I have answered to Theophilus Alexandrinus.

The answer to Theophilus in Mar. xiv.

Yet furthermore, they bring for them Theophilus Alexandrinus, who, as they allege, saith thus[2]: "Christ giving thanks, did break, which also we do,

---

[1 August. ad Dardanum. Pars VIII. cap. iii. iv. Basil. ap. Amerbach. 1506.]

[2 Εὐλογήσας δὲ, ἀντὶ τοῦ εὐχαριστήσας, ἔκλασε τὸν ἄρτον. ὅπερ καὶ ἡμεῖς ποιοῦμεν, εὐχὰς ἐπιλέγοντες. τοῦτό ἐστι τὸ σῶμά μου, τοῦτο δὲ νῦν λαμβάνετε. οὐ γὰρ ἀντίτυπος τοῦ κυριακοῦ

adding thereto prayer. And he gave unto them, saying, 'Take, this is my body;' this that I do now give, and that which ye now do take. For the bread is not a figure only of Christ's body, but it is changed into the very body of Christ. For Christ saith: 'The bread which I will give you is my flesh.' Nevertheless the flesh of Christ is not seen for our weakness, but bread and wine are familiar unto us. And surely if we should visibly see flesh and blood, we could not abide it. And therefore our Lord, bearing with our weakness, doth retain and keep the form and appearance of bread and wine, but he doth turn the very bread and wine into the very flesh and blood of Christ."

John vi.

These be the words which the papists do cite out of Theophilus upon the gospel of St Mark. But by this one place it appeareth evidently, either how negligent the papists be in searching out and examining the sayings of the authors, which they allege for their purpose, or else how false and deceitful they be, which willingly and wittingly have made in this one place, and as it were with one breath, two loud and shameful lies.

195.

The first is, that because they would give the more authority to the words by them alleged, they (like false apothecaries that sell *quid pro quo*) falsify the author's name, fathering such sayings upon Theophilus Alexandrinus[3], an old and ancient author, which were indeed none of his words, but were the words of Theophylactus, who was many years after Theophilus Alexandrinus. But such hath ever been the papistical subtilties, to set forth their own inventions, dreams, and lies, under the name of antiquity and ancient authors.

The second lie or falsehood is, that they falsify the author's words and meaning, subverting the truth of his doctrine. For where Theophylactus, (according to the catholic doctrine of ancient authors,) saith, that "almighty God, condescending to our infirmity, reserveth the kind of bread and wine, and yet turneth them into the virtue of Christ's flesh and blood;" they say, that "he reserveth the forms and appearances of bread and wine, and turneth them into the verity of his flesh and blood;" so turning and altering kinds into forms and appearances, and virtue into verity, that of the virtue of the flesh and blood they make the verity of his flesh and blood. And thus they have falsified as well the name as the words of Theophylactus, turning verity into plain and flat falsity.

But to set forth plainly the meaning of Theophylactus in this matter. As hot and burning iron is iron still, and yet hath the force of fire; and as the flesh of Christ still remaining flesh giveth life as the flesh of him that is God; so the sacramental bread and wine remain still in their proper kinds, and yet to them that worthily eat and drink them they be turned not into the corporal presence, but into the virtue of Christ's flesh and blood.

And although Theophylactus spake of the eating of the very body of Christ, and the drinking of his very blood, (and not only[4] of the figures of them,) and of the conversion of the bread and wine into the body and blood of Christ; yet he meaneth not of a gross, carnal, corporal and sensible conversion of the bread

---

σώματός ἐστιν ὁ ἄρτος· ἀλλ' εἰς αὐτὸ ἐκεῖνο μεταβάλλεται τὸ σῶμα τοῦ Χριστοῦ. καὶ ὁ Κύριος γὰρ λέγει· ὁ ἄρτος ὃν ἐγὼ δώσω, ἡ σάρξ μου ἐστίν. οὐκ εἶπεν, ἀντίτυπός ἐστι τῆς σαρκός μου, ἀλλ' ἡ σάρξ μου ἐστί——καὶ πῶς φησὶν, οὐ γὰρ σὰρξ καθορᾶται; διὰ τὴν ἡμετέραν, ὦ ἄνθρωπε, ἀσθένειαν. ἐπειδὴ γὰρ ὁ μὲν ἄρτος καὶ ὁ οἶνος συνήθη ἡμῖν, αἷμα δὲ προκείμενον καὶ σάρκα ὁρῶντες, οὐκ ἂν ἠνέγκαμεν, ἀλλ' ἀπενάρκησαμεν, διὰ τοῦτο συγκαταβαίνων ἡμῖν ὁ φιλάνθρωπος τὸ μὲν εἶδος ἄρτου καὶ οἴνου φυλάττει, εἰς δύναμιν δὲ σαρκὸς καὶ αἵματος μεταστοιχειοῖ.—Theoph. in Marcum, cap. xiv. Tom. I. p. 249. Ed. Venet. 1754.]

[3 Theophilus was Patriarch of Alexandria, A.D. 385. Theophylact was Archbishop of Bulgaria, A.D. 1071. His Commentaries on the Gospels were generally supposed to be compiled from Chrysostom and other of the fathers. Vid. Cave Hist. Lit. &c.]

[4 One, 1551; Orig. ed. reads with ed. 1580.]

and wine, nor of a like eating and drinking of his flesh and blood, (for so not only our stomachs would yearn, and our hearts abhor to eat his flesh and to drink his blood, but also such eating and drinking could nothing profit or avail us;) but he spake of the celestial and spiritual eating of Christ, and of a sacramental conversion of the bread, calling the bread not only a figure, but also the body of Christ, giving us by these words[1] to understand, that in the sacrament we do not only eat corporally the bread, (which is a sacrament and figure of Christ's body,) but spiritually we eat also his very body, and drink his very blood. And this doctrine of Theophylactus is both true, godly and comfortable.

WINCHESTER.

196. Theophylact. Now followeth, as it is entitled, Theophylact, being the words in deed not of Theophylact, as he writeth upon Mark, and therefore they were not alleged as his words, but as the words of Theophilus Alexandrinus, wherein this author traverseth a falsehood on the alleger's part to wrong name the author. In which allegation, I say, if there be a fault, as I know none, it is no lie, but a probable error for a man to believe another better learned than himself; and as I found it alleged I reported it again, so as having mine author learned whom I followed, I am discharged of malice, being the author such whom I followed, as might possibly have had such a work of Theophilus, containing those words as they be alleged, the negative whereof how this author should prove I cannot tell, because of the common saying, Bernardus non vidit omnia; and therefore, there may be a Theophilus Alexandrinus having these words alleged in their form, for any demonstration this author can make to the contrary. Whether there be or no any such to be shewed, it is not material, being so many testimonies besides. As for Theophylact's words, I grant they be not, for he wrote his mind more plainly in another place of his works, as I shall hereafter shew, and by the way make **An issue.** an issue with this author, that no catholic writer among the Greeks hath more plainly set forth the truth of the presence of Christ's body in the sacrament, than Theophylact hath; as shall appear by and by, after I have noted to the reader this, how Œcolampadius of Germany, ***Theophylact translated by Œcolampadius.*** about a two year before he impugned the truth of Christ's presence in the sacrament, he translated out of Greek into Latin the works of the said Theophylact, and gave the Latin church thereby some weapon wherewith to destroy his wicked folly afterward, not unlike the chance in this author, translating into English, two years by-past, the catechism of Germany: and as Œcolampadius hath since his folly or madness against the sacrament confessed, (as appeareth,) that he did translate Theophylact, so as we need not doubt of it; so this author hath now in this work confessed the translation of the catechism, which one in communication would needs have made me believe had been his man's doing, and not his. Hear now, reader, how plainly Theophylact speaketh upon the Gospel of St John, expounding the sixth chapter[2]:

Theophylact's words. "Take heed that the bread which is eaten of us in the mysteries, is not only a certain figuration of the flesh of our Lord, but the flesh itself of our Lord; for he said not, The bread which I shall give is the figure of my flesh, but it is my flesh. For that bread, by the mystical benediction, is transformed by the mystical words and presence of the Holy Ghost into the flesh of our Lord. And it should trouble no man, that the bread is to be believed flesh: for whilst our Lord walked in flesh and received nourishment of bread, that bread he did eat was changed into his body, and was made like to his holy flesh; and as it is customably in man's feeding served to the sustentation and increase of it, therefore the

---

[¹ Giving us those words, Orig. ed. Giving us by those words, 1551.]

[² Πρόσχες δὲ ὅτι ὁ ἄρτος ὁ ἐν τοῖς μυστηρίοις ὑφ' ἡμῶν ἐσθιόμενος οὐκ ἀντίτυπόν ἐστι τῆς τοῦ Κυρίου σαρκὸς, ἀλλ' αὐτὴ ἡ τοῦ Κυρίου σάρξ. οὐ γὰρ εἶπεν, ὅτι ὁ ἄρτος ὃν ἐγὼ δώσω, ἀντίτυπόν ἐστι τῆς σαρκός μου, ἀλλ' ἡ σάρξ μου ἐστί. μεταποιεῖται γὰρ ἀπορρήτοις λόγοις ὁ ἄρτος οὗτος διὰ τῆς μυστικῆς εὐλογίας, καὶ ἐπιφοιτήσεως τοῦ ἁγίου πνεύματος, εἰς σάρκα τοῦ Κυρίου. Καὶ μή τινα θροείτω τὸ τὸν ἄρτον σάρκα πιστεύεσθαι, καὶ γάρ τοι καὶ ἐν σαρκὶ περιπατοῦντος τοῦ Κυρίου, καὶ τὴν ἐξ ἄρτου τροφὴν προσιεμένου, ὁ ἄρτος ἐκεῖνος ὁ ἐσθιόμενος εἰς σῶμα αὐτοῦ μετεβάλλετο, καὶ συνεξωμοιοῦτο τῇ ἁγίᾳ αὐτοῦ σαρκί, καὶ εἰς αὔξησιν καὶ σύστασιν συνεβάλλετο κατὰ τὸ ἀνθρώπινον· καὶ νῦν οὖν ὁ ἄρτος εἰς σάρκα τοῦ Κυρίου μεταβάλλεται. καὶ πῶς φησιν, οὐχὶ καὶ σὰρξ φαίνεται ἡμῖν, ἀλλ' ἄρτος; διὰ τὸ μὴ ἡμᾶς ἀηδίζεσθαι πρὸς τὴν βρῶσιν. εἰ μὲν γὰρ σὰρξ ἐφαίνετο, ἀηδῶς ἂν διεκείμεθα πρὸς τὴν μετάληψιν, νῦν δὲ τῇ ἡμετέρᾳ ἀσθενείᾳ συγκαταβαίνοντος τοῦ Κυρίου τοιαύτη φαίνεται ἡμῖν ἡ μυστικὴ βρῶσις, οἷα ἔστιν ἡ συνήθης ἡμῖν.—Theoph. in Joannem. cap. vi. Tom. I. p. 594. Ed. Venet. 1754.]

bread now also is changed into the flesh of our Lord. And how is it then that it appeareth not flesh but bread? That we should not loathe the eating of it; for if flesh did appear, we should be unpleasantly disposed to the communion of it. Now our Lord condescending to our infirmity, the mystical meat appeareth such to us, as those we have been accustomed unto." Hitherto I have faithfully expressed Theophylact's words out of Latin of Œcolampadius' translation, without terming the substantial points otherwise than the words purport in Latin. By which may appear what was Theophylact's meaning, what doctrine he giveth of the sacrament, and how his own words upon St Mark be to be understood, when he saith, Speciem quidem panis et vini servat, in virtutem autem carnis et sanguinis [Theophylact. Orig. ed. Winch.] transelementat: in corrupting of which words this author maketh a great matter, when they were not alleged for his; but as they be his, servare speciem may be well translate "form and appearance," because upon St John, before alleged, he saith of the bread, "it appeareth." And as for these words, "the virtue of Christ's flesh and blood," must be understood to agree with the plain place of Theophylact upon St John, and upon St Mark also, to signify not only virtue, but verity of the flesh and blood of Christ. For if Theophylact by that speech meant "the virtue of the body of Christ," and not the "verity of the very body," as this author saith he did, why should Theophylact, both upon St Mark, and also upon St John, ask this question, "Why doth not the flesh appear?" if himself by those words should teach there were only present the virtue of the flesh; who, and he had meant so, would not have asked the question; 198. or if he had, would have answered it thus accordingly, "There is no flesh in deed, but the virtue of the flesh," and that had been a plain answer and such as he would have made. This author will ask then, Why doth Theophylact use this phrase to say, "changed into the virtue of the body of Christ?" Hereunto I answer, that this word "virtue" in phrase of speech many times only filleth the speech, and is comprehended in the signification of his genitive following; and therefore, as Luke in the twenty-second chapter saith, a dextris virtutis Dei, so in the Acts in the same sentence³ is spoken a dextris Dei, both out of one pen; and a dextris virtutis Dei is no more to say than a dextris Dei; and so is virtutem carnis et sanguinis no more to say but in carnem et sanguinem, which sentence the same Theophylact hath upon St John before alleged, in this saying, "The bread is changed into flesh;" and in Mark in this phrase, "into the virtue of flesh," being like these speeches, a dextris Dei, and a dextris virtutis Dei. Which and it had liked this author to have considered, he should have taken Theophylact's speech as Theophylact understandeth himself, and said the words alleged in the name of Theophilus Alexandrinus were not Theophylact's words, and then he had said for so much true, (which would do well among,) and the words be not indeed Theophylact's words, nor were not alleged for his. Now when this author saith, "they were not Theophilus Alexandrinus's words;" that is a large negative, and will be hardly proved otherwise than by addition of the author's knowledge for any thing that he can find, and so there shall be no absurdity to grant it. And thus I return to mine issue with this author, that Theophylact himself hath no such meaning expressed in words as this author attributed⁴ unto him, but an evident contrary meaning, saving herein I will agree with this author, that Theophylact meant not "grossly," "sensibly," and "carnally," as these words sound in carnal men's judgments. For we may not so think of God's mysteries, the work whereof is not carnal nor corporal, for the manner of it; but the manner spiritual, and yet in the sacrament of the body and blood of Christ, because Christ is in his very true flesh present, he may be said so carnally present, and naturally, after Hilary, and corporally, after Cyril; *Carnally, naturally, corporally. understanding the words of the truth of that is present, Christ's very body and flesh, and *Manner, only spiritually. not of the manner of the presence, which is only spiritual, supernatural, and above man's capacity: and therefore a high mystery, a great miracle, a wonderful work, which it is wholesome to believe simply with a sincere faith, and dangerous to search and examine with a curious imagination, such as idleness and arrogancy would tempt a man unto, and by devising of a figure or metaphor bring it within the compass of our busy reason.

CANTERBURY.

This is a pretty sleight of you to pass over the author's name, saying that you found it so alleged in an author, and tell not in what author. There is surely some hid mystery in this matter, that you would not have his name known. For if you had found any approved author who had fathered these words upon Theophilus Alexandrinus,

---

[³ In the Acts the same sentence, Orig. ed. Winch.]   [⁴ Attributeth, Orig. ed. Winch.]

I doubt not but I should have heard him here named, it should have served so much for your purpose. For to what purpose should you conceal his name, if you had any such author? But shall I open the mystery of this matter? Shall I by conjectures tell the author which you followed, as you by conjecture gathered of him the name of Theophilus? Thomas de Aquino, in his *Catena Aurea,* citeth the words by you alleged in these letters, "Theoph."; which letters be indifferent, as well to Theophilus as to Theophylact's, so that you might have christened the child whether you would by the name of Theophilus or of Theophylactus. And because Theophilus was a more ancient author, and of more learning and estimation than was Theophylact, therefore the name pleased you better, to give more credit to your sayings, and so of "Theoph." you made the whole name "Theophilus." And because one Theophilus was a bishop of Alexandria, you added as it were his surname, calling him "Theophilus Alexandrinus." And if Thomas was not the author which you followed in this matter, peradventure it might be doctor Fisher, sometime bishop of Rochester, who, writing in the same matter that you do, was, or would be deceived as you be. But what author soever you followed, you shall not honestly shake off this matter, except you tell his name. For else I will say that you be fain to bring in for you feigned authors, whispered in corners. And yet, that Theophilus wrote not the words alleged upon Mark, this is no small proof,—that Theophylact hath the same sentences, word by word, and that neither St Hierome, Gennadius, Eusebius, Trithemius, nor any other that ever wrote hitherto, made ever any mention that Theophilus wrote upon the gospel of St Mark.

And as concerning your issue, thus much I grant without issue, that no catholic writer among the Greeks hath more plainly spoken for you than Theophylact hath; and yet when that shall be well examined, it is nothing at all, as I have plainly declared, shewing your untruth as well in allegation of the author's words, as in falsifying his name.

And as for "the catechism of Germany" by me translated into English, to this I have answered before; and truth it is, that either you understand not the phrase of the old authors of the church, or else of purpose you will not understand me. But hereunto you shall have a more full answer when I come to the proper place thereof, in the fourth part of my book.

And as concerning the words of Theophylact upon the gospel of John, he speaketh to one effect, and useth much like terms upon the gospels of Matthew, Mark, and John, whereunto I have sufficiently answered in my former book. And because the answer may be the more present, I shall rehearse some of my words here again. "Although," said I, "Theophylactus spake of the eating of the very body of Christ, and the drinking of his very blood, and not only of the figures of them, and of the conversion of the bread and wine into the body and blood of Christ, yet he meaneth not of a gross, carnal, corporal, and sensible conversion of the bread and wine, nor of a like eating and drinking of his flesh and blood, (for so not only our stomachs would yearn, and our hearts abhor to eat his flesh and to drink his blood, but also such eating and drinking could nothing profit and avail us;) but he spake of the celestial and spiritual eating of Christ, and of a sacramental conversion of the bread, calling the bread not only a figure, but also the body of Christ; giving us by those words to understand, that in the sacrament we do not only eat corporally the bread, (which is a sacrament and figure of Christ's body,) but spiritually we eat also his very body, and drink his very blood. And this doctrine of Theophylactus is both true, godly, and comfortable." This I wrote in my former book, which is sufficient to answer unto all that you have here spoken.

And as concerning the bread that Christ did eat and feed upon, it was naturally eaten, as other men eat, naturally changed, and caused a natural nourishment, and yet the very matter of the bread remained, although in another form; but in them that duly receive and eat the Lord's holy supper all is spiritual, as well the eating as the change and nourishment, which is none impediment to the nature of bread, but that it may still remain.

And where you come to the translation of this word *species*, to signify "appearance," this is a wonderful kind of translation, to translate *specie* in "appearance," because *apparet* is truly translated "appeareth:" with like reason *aurum* might be translated "meat," because *edere* signifieth "to eat."

And your other translation is no less wonderful, where you turn the "virtue" of Christ's body into the "verity." And yet to cloak your folly therein, and to cast a mist before the reader's eyes, that he should not see your untruth therein, you say that by "virtue" in that place must be understood "verity." First, whatsoever be understand by the word "virtue," your faith in translation is broken. For the sense being ambiguous, you ought in translation to have kept the word as it is, leaving the sense to be expended by the indifferent reader, and not by altering the word to make such a sense as please you; which is so foul a fault in a translator, that if Œcolampadius had so done, he should have been called a man faulty and guilty, a corrupter, a deceiver, an abuser of other men, a perverter, a depraver, and a man without faith: as he might be called that would translate *verbum caro factum est*, "the second person became man;" which although it be true in meaning, yet it is not true in translation, nor declareth the faith of the translator.

Verity for virtue.

But now as your translation is untrue, so is the meaning also untrue and unexcusable. For what man is so far destitute of all his senses, that he knoweth not a difference between the verity of Christ's body and the virtue thereof? Who can pretend ignorance in so manifest a thing? Doth not all men know, that of every thing the virtue is one, and the substance another?—except in God only, who is of that simplicity without multiplication of anything in him, or diversity, that his virtue, his power, his wisdom, his justice, and all that is said to be in him, be neither qualities nor accidents, but all one thing with his very substance. And neither the right hand of God, nor the virtue of God, (which you bring for an example, and serveth to no purpose, but to blind the ignorant reader,) be any thing else but the very substance of God, (although in diversity of respects and considerations they have diversity of names,) except you will divide the most single substance of God into corporal parts and members, following the error of the Anthropomorphites. But the like is not in the body of Christ, which hath distinction of integral parts, and the virtue also, and qualities distinct from the substance.

And yet, if the example were like, he should be an evil translator, or rather a corrupter, that for *a dextris virtutis Dei* would translate *a dextris Dei*, or contrariwise. And therefore all translators in those places follow the words as they be, and be not so arrogant to alter one title in them, thereby to make them one in words, although the thing in substance be one. For words had not their signification of the substances, or of things only, but of the qualities, manners, respects, and considerations. And so may one word signify divers things, and one thing be signified by divers words. And therefore he that should for one word take another, because they be both referred to one substance, as you have done in this place, should make a goodly piece of work of it; not much unlike to him that should burn his house, and say he made it, because the making and burning was both in one matter and substance.

A dextris Dei. A dextris virtutis Dei.

200.

It is much pity that you have not bestowed your time in translation of good authors, that can skill so well of translation, to make *speciem* to signify appearance, and that take virtue sometime for verity, and sometime for nothing; and *a dextris virtutis Dei* to signify no more but *a dextris Dei*, and *virtutem carnis* to signify no more but *carnem*, and *virtutem sanguinis*, *sanguinem*. And why not? seeing that such words signify *ad placitum*, that is to say, as please you to translate them.

And it seemeth to be a strange thing, that you have so quick an eye to espy other men's faults, and cannot see in Theophylact his plain answer, but to take upon you to teach him to answer. For when he asketh the question, "Why doth not the flesh appear?" he should have answered, say you, "that the flesh is not there in deed, but the virtue of the flesh:" I pray you, doth not he answer plainly the same in effect? Is not his answer to that question this, as you confess yourself, "that the forms of bread and wine be changed into the virtue of the body of Christ?" And what would you require more? Is not this as much to say, as the virtue of the flesh is there, but not the substance corporally and carnally?

And yet another third error is committed in the same sentence, because one sentence should not be without three errors at the least in your translation. For whereas Theophylact hath but one accusative case, you put thereto other two more of your own head. And as you once taught Barnes[1], so now you would make Theophylact your scholar, to say what you would have him. But that the truth may appear, what Theophylact said, I shall rehearse his own words in Greek: συγκαταβαίνων ἡμῖν ὁ φιλάνθρωπος τὸ μὲν εἶδος ἄρτου καὶ οἴνου φυλάττει, εἰς δύναμιν δὲ σαρκὸς καὶ αἵματος μεταστοιχειοῖ; which words translated into Latin be these: *Condescendens nobis benignus Deus speciem quidem panis et vini servat, in potestatem autem carnis et sanguinis transelementat.* And in English they be thus much to say: "The merciful God, condescending to our infirmity, conserveth still the kind of bread and wine, but turneth them into the virtue of his flesh and blood." To this sentence you do add of your own authority these words "the bread and wine," which words Theophylact hath not, which is an untrue part of him that pretendeth to be a true interpreter. And by adding those words, you alter clearly the author's meaning. For where the author's meaning was, that we should abhor to eat Christ's flesh and drink his blood in their proper form and kind, yet Almighty God hath ordained that in his holy supper we should receive the forms and kinds of bread and wine, and that those kinds should be turned (unto them that worthily receive the same) into the virtue and effect of Christ's very flesh and blood, although they remain still in the same kind and form of bread and wine. And so by him the nature and kind of bread and wine remain; and yet the same be turned into the virtue of flesh and blood. So that the word "forms" is the accusative case, as well to the verb turneth, as to the verb conserveth: but you, to make Theophylact serve your purpose, add of your own head two other accusative cases, that is to say, "bread and wine," besides Theophylact's words; wherein all men may consider how little you regard the truth, that to maintain your untrue doctrine once devised by yourselves, care not what untruth you use besides to corrupt all doctors, making so many faults in translation of one sentence.

201.

And if the words alleged upon Mark were not Theophylact's words, but the words of Theophilus Alexandrinus, as you say, at the least Theophylact must borrow them of Theophilus, because the words be all one, sixteen lines together, saving this word "verity," which Theophylact turneth into "virtue." And then it is to be thought that he would not alter that word, (wherein all the contention standeth,) without some consideration. And specially when Theophilus speaketh of the verity of Christ's body, as you say, if Theophylact had thought the body had been there, would he have refused the word, and changed verity into virtue, bringing his own faith into suspicion, and giving occasion of error unto other?

And where, to excuse your error in translation, you say that the words by you alleged in the name of Theophilus Alexandrinus be not Theophylact's words, and I deny that they be Theophilus' words; so then be they nobody's words, which is no detriment to my cause at all, because I took him for none of my witness; but it is in a manner a clear overthrow of your cause, which take him for your chief and principal witness, saying "that no catholic writer among the Greeks hath more plainly set forth the truth of the presence of Christ's body in the sacrament than Theophylactus hath," and hereupon you make your issue.

And yet have I a good cause to call them Theophylact's words, forasmuch as I find them in his works printed abroad, saving one word which you have untruly corrupted, because that word pleaseth you not. And yet am I not bound to admit that your witness is named Theophilus, except you have better proofs thereof than this, that one saith he hath him in a corner, and so allegeth him. It is your part to prove your own witness, and not my part that stand herein only at defence. And yet to every indifferent man I have shewed sufficient matter to reject him.

Hear now my answer to St Hierome.

The answer to Hieronymus super epistol. ad Titum.

Besides this, our adversaries do allege St Hierome[2] upon the epistle *ad Titum*,

---

[1 Vide Burnet's Hist. of the Reformation, Vol. I. p. 592. Oxford, 1829, and Foxe's Acts and Monuments, Vol. II. p. 525. Lond. 1631.]

[2 Tantum interest inter propositionis panes et corpus Christi, quantum inter umbram et corpora, inter imaginem et veritatem, inter exemplaria futurorum, et ea ipsa quæ per exemplaria præfigurabantur. Jerom. Comment. in Epist. ad Titum, cap. i. 8, 9. Tom. IX. p. 199. Ed. Francof. 1684.]

that there is as great difference between the loaves called *panes propositionis*, and the body of Christ, as there is between the shadow[3] of a body and the body itself; and as there is between an image and the thing itself, and between an example of things to come and the things that be prefigured by them.

These words of St Hierome, truly understand, serve nothing for the intent of the papists. For he meant that the shew-bread of the law was but a dark shadow of Christ to come; but the sacrament of Christ's body is a clear testimony that Christ is already come, and that he hath performed that which was promised, and doth presently comfort and feed us spiritually with his precious body and blood, notwithstanding that corporally he is ascended into heaven.

202.

WINCHESTER.

This author travaileth to answer St Hierome, and to make him the easier for him to deal with, he cutteth off that followeth in the same St Hierome, which should make the matter open and manifest, how effectually St Hierome speaketh of the sacrament of Christ's body and blood. "There is," saith St Hierome, "as great difference between the loaves called panes propositionis, *and the body of Christ, as there is between the shadow of a body and the body itself; and as there is between an image and the true thing itself, and between an example of things to come and the things that be prefigured by them. Therefore as meekness, patience, sobriety, moderation, abstinence of gain, hospitality also, and liberality should be chiefly in a bishop, and among all laymen an excellency in them; so there should be in him a special chastity, and as I should say, chastity that is priestly, that he should not only abstain from unclean[4] work, but also from the cast of his eye, and his mind free from error of thought, that should make the body of Christ[5]." These be St Hierome's words in this place. By the latter part whereof appeareth plainly how St Hierome meaneth of Christ's body in the sacrament, of which the loaves that were* panes propositionis *were a shadow, as St Hierome saith; that bread being "the image, and this the truth," that "the example, and this that was prefigured." So as if Christ's body in the sacrament should be there but figuratively, as this author teacheth, then were the bread of proposition figure of a figure, and shadow of a shadow, which is over great an absurdity in our religion. Therefore there cannot be a more plain proof to shew, that by St Hierome's mind Christ's body is verily in the sacrament and not figuratively only, than when he noteth* panes propositionis *to be the figure and the shadow of Christ's body in the sacrament. For, as Tertullian[6] saith,* figura non esset, nisi veritatis esset corpus: *"The other were not to be called a figure, if that[7] answered unto it, were not of truth," which is the sense of Tertullian's words. And therefore St Hierome could with no other words have expressed his mind so certainly and plainly, as with these, to confess the truth of Christ's body in the sacrament. And therefore regard not, reader, what this author saith: for St Hierome affirmeth plainly Christ's true body to be in the sacrament, the consecration whereof although St Hierome attributeth to the minister, yet we must understand him, that he taketh God for the author and worker, notwithstanding by reason of the ministry in the church the doing is ascribed to man as minister, because Christ said,* Hoc facite, *after which speech salvation, remission of sin, and the work in other sacraments is attribute to the minister, being nevertheless the same the proper and special works of God.*

And this I add, because some be unjustly offended to hear that man should make the body of Christ. And this author findeth fault before at the word "making," which religiously heard and reverently spoken should offend no man; for man is but a minister, wherein he should not glory. And Christ maketh not himself of the matter of bread, nor maketh himself so oft of bread a new body; but sitting in heaven doth, as our invisible priest, work in the ministry of the visible priesthood of his church, and maketh present by his omnipotency his glorified body and blood in this high mystery, by conversion of the visible creatures of bread and wine, as Emissene saith, into the same. This author of this book, as thou, reader, mayest

Hieronym.

*Tertullianus adversus Marcionem, Lib. iv.

[3 A shadow, 1551, and Orig. ed.]

[4 An unclean work, Orig. ed. Winch.]

[5 Quomodo itaque mansuetudo, patientia, sobrietas, moderatio, abstinentia lucri, hospitalitas quoque, et benignitas, præcipue esse debent in episcopo, et inter cunctos laicos continentia : sic et castitas propria, et (ut ita dixerim) pudicitia sacerdotalis, ut non solum ab opere se immundo abstineat, sed etiam a jactu oculi, et cogitationis errore, mens Christi corpus confectura sit libera. Ib. p. 199.]

[6 Figura autem non fuisset, nisi veritatis esset corpus. Tertul. adversus Marcionem. Lib. IV. p. 458. Ed. Lutet. Paris. 1644.]

[7 If that, that answered, &c. 1551.]

perceive, applieth the figure of the breads, called panes propositionis, *to the body of Christ to come, whereas St Hierome calleth them the figure of Christ's body in the sacrament, and therefore doth fashion his argument in this sense. If those breads, that were but a figure, required so much cleanness in them that should eat them, that they might not eat of them, which a day or two before had lien with their wives; what cleanness is required in him that should make the body of Christ! Whereby thou mayest see how*[1] *this author hath reserved this notable place of St Hierome to the latter end, that thou shouldest in the end, as well as in the midst, see him evidently snarled, for thy better remembrance.*

CANTERBURY.

203. To these words of St Hierome I have sufficiently answered in my former book. And now to add something thereto, I say that he meaneth not that *panes propositionis* be figures of the sacrament, but of Christ's very body. And yet the same body is not only in the sacrament figuratively, but it is also in the true ministration thereof spiritually present and spiritually eaten, as in my book I have plainly declared. But how is it possible that Caius Ulpian, or Scevola, Batholus, Baldus or Curtius, should have knowledge what is meant by the spiritual presence of Christ in the sacrament, and of the spiritual eating of his flesh and blood, if they be void of a lively faith, feeding and comforting their souls with their own works, and not with the breaking of the body and shedding of the blood of our Saviour Christ?

The meat that the papists live by is indulgences and pardons, and such other remission of sins as cometh all from the pope, which giveth no life, but infecteth and poisoneth: but the meat that the true christian man liveth by, is Christ himself, who is eaten only by faith, and so eaten is life and spirit, giving that life that endureth and continueth for ever. God grant that we may learn this heavenly knowledge of the spiritual presence, that we may spiritually taste and feed of this heavenly food!

Now, where you say "that there cannot be a more plain proof to shew that Christ's body is verily in the sacrament, and not figuratively only," than when St Hierome noteth *panes propositionis* to be the figure and shadow of Christ's body in the sacrament. "For," as Tertullian saith, "the other were not to be called a figure, if that which answereth to it were not of truth." Here your "for" is a plain *fallax a non causa ut causa*[2], and a wondrous subtlety is used therein. For where Tertullian proveth that Christ had here in earth a very body, which Marcion denied, because that bread was instituted to be a figure thereof, and there can be no figure of a thing that is not, you allege Tertullian's words, as though he should say, that Christ's body is in the sacrament under the form of bread; whereof neither Tertullian entreated in that place, nor it is not required, that the body should be corporally where the figure is, but rather it should be in vain to have a figure when the thing itself is present. And therefore you untruly report both of St Hierome and Tertullian: for neither of them both do say, as you would gather of their words, that Christ's body is in the sacrament really and corporally.

Whether the body of Christ be made of the matter of bread.

And where you say, "that Christ maketh not himself of the matter of bread," either you be very ignorant in the doctrine of the sacrament, as it hath been taught these five hundred years, or else you dissemble the matter. Hath not this been the teaching of the school divines, yea, of Innocent himself, that the matter of this sacrament is bread of wheat, and wine of grapes? Do they not say, that the substance of bread is turned into the substance of Christ's flesh, and that his flesh is made of bread? And who worketh this, but Christ himself? And have you not confessed all this in your book of the "Devil's Sophistry?" Why do you then deny here that which you taught before, and which hath been the common approved doctrine of the

204. papists so many years? And because it should have the more authority, was not this put into the mass-books, and read every year, *Dogma datur Christianis, quod in carnem transit panis, et vinum in sanguinem?* Now, seeing that you have taught so many years, that the matter and substance of bread is not consumed to nothing,

---

[1 Here, Orig. ed. Winch.]   [2 Ad causam, 1551.]

but is changed and turned into the body of Christ, so that the body of Christ is made of it, what mean you now to deny that Christ is made of the matter of bread? When water was turned into wine, was not the wine made of the water? And when the rod was turned into a serpent, and water into blood, the earth into a man, and his rib into a woman, were not the woman, man, blood, and serpent, made of the matter of the rib, the earth, the water, and the rod? And is not every thing made of that which is turned into it? As bread is made of corn; wine of grapes; beer of water, hops, and malt; and so of all things like? And when you have confessed yourselves, so many years past, that Christ is made of bread in the sacrament, what moveth you now to say, that Christ maketh not himself of the matter of bread, except that either you will say, that the priest doth it and not Christ, which were an intolerable blasphemy; or that the truth is of such a nature that even the very adversaries thereof, sometime unwares, acknowledge it; or else that force of arguments constraineth you to confess the truth against your will, when you see none other shift to escape? But if you take upon you to defend the received doctrine of the papists, you must affirm that doctrine which they affirm, and say that bread in the sacrament is the matter whereof Christ's body is made; whereof must then needs follow, *ex consequenti*, that he hath from time to time a new body, made of new bread, besides the body which was incarnated, and never but once made, nor of none other substance but of his mother. So that it is but a vain cavillation, only to elude simple people, or to shift off the matter, to say, as you do, "that Christ is not made of the bread, but is made to be present there." For then should he have said, "There is my body," and not, "This is my body." And to be present requireth no new making: but to be present by conversion requireth a new making: as the wine that was bought at the marriage in the Cane of Galilee, if there were any such, was present without conversion, and so without new making; but the wine that was made of water, was present by conversion, which could not be without new making. And so must Christ's body be newly made, if it be present by corporal conversion of the substance of bread into the substance of it. And now I refer to every indifferent reader, to judge between us both, which of us is most snarled.

Now let us examine the other authors following in my book.

And the same is to be answered unto all that the adversaries bring of St Augustine, Sedulius, Leo, Fulgentius, Cassiodorus, Gregorius, and other, concerning the eating of Christ in the sacrament.

Augustinus, Sedulius, Leo, Fulgentius, Cassiodorus, Gregorius.

John ii. Exod. vii. Gen. ii.

Which thing cannot be understood plainly as the words sound, but figuratively and spiritually, as before is sufficiently proved, and hereafter shall be more fully declared in the fourth part of this book.

WINCHESTER.

Because this author, who hitherto hath answered none substantially, would nevertheless be seen to answer all, he windeth up six of them in one fardell, St Augustine, Sedulius, Leo, Fulgentius, Cassiodorus, and Gregorius, and dispatcheth them all with an ut supra: and among them I think he would have knit up all the rest of the learned men of all ages, amongst whom I know none that write as this author doth of the sacrament, or impugneth the catholic faith as this author doth by the envious name of papists. Since Christ's time there is no memory more than of six, that have[3] affirmed that doctrine, which this author would have called now the catholic doctrine, and yet not written by them of one sort, neither received in belief in public profession; but secretly, when it happened, begun by conspiration, and in the end ever hitherto extinct and quenched. First was Bertram, then Berengarius, then Wicliff, and in our time, Œcolampadius, Zuinglius, and Joachimus Vadianus. I will not reckon Peter Martyr, because such as know him saith he is not learned; nor this author, because he doth but as it were translate Peter Martyr, saving he roveth at solutions, as liketh his phantasy, as I have before declared. Which matter being thus, it is a strange title of this book, to call it the true catholic doctrine.

205.

Augustinus, Sedulius, Leo, Fulgentius, Cassiodorus, Gregorius.

*Peter Martyr.

[³ Hath, 1551.]

CANTERBURY.

All that you have these many years gathered together for your purpose, or that can be gathered, may be well trussed up in a very small fardell, and very easily borne and carried away, for any weight that is therein. For your doings be like to him, that would fain seem to have something, and having nothing else, filleth a great mail full of straw, that men should think he carried something, where indeed a little budget had been sufficient for so much in value.

And as for your own doctrine, it is so strange, that neither it agreeth with the scripture, nor with the old catholic church, nor yet with the later[1] church or congregation of the papists: but you stand post alone, after the fall of the papistical doctrine, as sometime an old post standeth when the building is overthrown.

And where you say, "that since Christ's time there is no more but six that have affirmed the doctrine that I have taught;" all that have been learned, and have read the old authors of the catholic church, may evidently see the contrary, that sithens Christ's time the doctrine of my book was ever the catholic and public received faith of the church, until Nicholas the second's time, who compelled Berengarius to make such a devilish recantation, that the papists themselves be now ashamed of it. And since that time, have many thousands been cruelly persecuted only for the profession of the true faith. For no man might speak one word against the bishop of Rome's determination herein, but he was taken for an heretic, and so condemned, as Wicliff, Huss, and an infinite number more.

Nicholas the second. Berengarius.

Bertram.

And as for Bertram, he was never before this time detected of any error that ever I read, but only now by you. For all other that have written of him, have spoken much to his commendation and praise. But I know what the matter is: he hath written against your mind, which is a fault and error great enough.

As for Dr Peter Martyr, he is of age to answer for himself: but concerning him, that told you that he was not learned, I would wish you to leave this old rooted fault in you, to be light of credit. For I suppose, that if his learning that told you that lie, and yours also, were set both together, you should be far behind Master Peter Martyr. Marry, in words I think that you alone would overlay two Peter Martyrs; he is so sober a man, and delighteth not in wasting of words in vain. And none do say that he is not learned, but such as know him not, or be not learned themselves, or else be so malicious or envious, that they wittingly speak against their own conscience. And, no doubt, that man bringeth himself out of the estimation of a learned man, which hath heard him reason and read, and saith that he is not learned. And whosoever misreporteth him, and hath never heard him, may not be called so well *momus* as *sycophanta*, whose property is to misreport them whom they neither see nor know.

206.

Peter Martyr.

Now resteth only Damascene, of whom I write thus.

But here John Damascene may in no wise be passed over, whom for his authority the adversaries of Christ's true natural body do reckon as a stout champion, sufficient to defend all the whole matter alone. But neither is the authority of Damascene so great that they may oppress us thereby, nor his words so plain for them, as they boast and untruly pretend. For he is but a young new author in the respect of those, which we have brought in for our party. And in divers points he varieth from the most ancient authors, (if he mean as they expound him;) as when he saith, that "the bread and wine be not figures," which all the old authors call figures; and that "the bread and wine consume not, nor be avoided downward," which Origen and St Augustine affirm; or that "they be not called the examples of Christ's body after the consecration," which shall manifestly appear false by the liturgy ascribed unto St Basil.

The answer to Damascenus de fide Orth. Lib. iv. cap. 14. [Quem fortissimum et acerrimum propugnatorem naturalis et corporalis præsentiæ adversarii inducunt. Embd. Edit.]

And moreover the said Damascene was one of the bishop of Rome's chief

---

[1 Latter, 1551.]

proctors against the emperors, and as it were his right hand, to set abroad all idolatry by his own hand-writing. And therefore, if he lost his hand[2], as they say he did, he lost it by God's most righteous judgment, whatsoever they feign and fable of the miraculous restitution of the same. And yet whatsoever the said Damascene writeth in other matters, surely in this place, which the adversaries do allege, he writeth spiritually and godly, although the papists either of ignorance mistake him, or else willingly wrest him and writhe him to their purpose, clean contrary to his meaning.

The sum of Damascene his doctrine in this matter is this[3]: That as Christ, being both God and man, hath in him two natures; so hath he two nativities, one eternal, and the other temporal. And so likewise we, being as it were double men, or having every one of us two men in us, the new man and the old man, the spiritual man and the carnal man, have a double nativity; one of our first carnal father Adam, (by whom, as by ancient inheritance, cometh unto us malediction and everlasting damnation,) and the other of our heavenly Adam, that is to say, of Christ, by whom we be made heirs of celestial benediction and everlasting glory and immortality.

And because this Adam is spiritual, therefore our generation by him must

---

[[2] For the account of this restoration of Damascene's hand, vide Winchester's "Detection of the Devil's Sophistry," f. 35.]

[[3] Ἐπειδὴ διπλοῖ τινές ἐσμεν καὶ σύνθετοι, δεῖ καὶ τὴν γέννησιν διπλῆν εἶναι, ὁμοίως καὶ τὴν βρῶσιν σύνθετον· ἡ μὲν οὖν γέννησις ἡμῖν δι' ὕδατος καὶ πνεύματος δέδοται, φημὶ δὲ τοῦ ἁγίου βαπτίσματος· ἡ δὲ βρῶσις, αὐτὸς ὁ ἄρτος τῆς ζωῆς, ὁ κύριος ἡμῶν Ἰησοῦς Χριστὸς, ὁ ἐκ τοῦ οὐρανοῦ καταβάς.—Damascenus, de Fide Orth. Lib. IV. cap. 14. Ed. Basil. 1559. Tom. I. p. 315.

Ἄρτος δὲ καὶ οἶνος παραλαμβάνεται· οἶδε γὰρ ὁ Θεὸς τὴν ἀνθρωπίνην ἀσθένειαν, ὡς τὰ πολλὰ τὰ μὴ κατὰ τὴν συνήθειαν τετριμμένα ἀποστρέφεται δυσχεραίνουσα· τῇ οὖν συνήθει συγκαταβάσει κεχρημένος, διὰ τῶν συνηθῶν τῆς φύσεως ποιεῖ τὰ ὑπὲρ φύσιν· καὶ ὥσπερ ἐπὶ τοῦ βαπτίσματος, ἐπειδὴ ἔθος ἀνθρώποις ὕδατι λούεσθαι, καὶ ἐλαίῳ χρίεσθαι, συνέζευξε τῷ ἐλαίῳ καὶ ὕδατι τὴν χάριν τοῦ πνεύματος, καὶ ἐποίησεν αὐτῷ λουτρὸν ἀναγεννήσεως, οὕτως ἐπειδὴ ἔθος τοῖς ἀνθρώποις ἄρτον ἐσθίειν, ὕδωρ τε καὶ οἶνον πίνειν, συνέζευξεν αὐτοῖς τὴν αὐτοῦ θεότητα, καὶ πεποίηκεν αὐτὰ σῶμα καὶ αἷμα αὐτοῦ, ἵνα διὰ τῶν συνήθων καὶ κατὰ φύσιν ἐν τοῖς ὑπὲρ φύσιν γενώμεθα. Σῶμά ἐστιν ἀληθῶς ἡνωμένον θεότητι, τὸ ἐκ τῆς ἁγίας παρθένου σῶμα, οὐχ ὅτι τὸ ἀναληφθὲν σῶμα ἐξ οὐρανοῦ κατέρχεται, ἀλλ' ὅτι αὐτὸς ὁ ἄρτος καὶ οἶνος μεταποιοῦνται εἰς σῶμα καὶ αἷμα Θεοῦ. εἰ δὲ τὸν τρόπον ἐπιζητεῖς πῶς γίνεται, ἀρκεῖ σοι ἀκοῦσαι, ὅτι διὰ πνεύματος ἁγίου, ὥσπερ καὶ ἐκ τῆς ἁγίας θεοτόκου διὰ πνεύματος ἁγίου ἑαυτῷ καὶ ἐν ἑαυτῷ ὁ κύριος σάρκα ὑπεστήσατο· καὶ πλέον οὐδὲν γινώσκομεν, ἀλλ' ὅτι ὁ λόγος τοῦ Θεοῦ ἀληθής ἐστι καὶ ἐνεργὴς καὶ παντοδύναμος, ὁ δὲ τρόπος ἀνεξερεύνητος· οὐ χεῖρον δὲ καὶ τοῦτο εἰπεῖν, ὅτι ὥσπερ φυσικῶς διὰ τῆς βρώσεως ὁ ἄρτος, καὶ ὁ οἶνος καὶ τὸ ὕδωρ διὰ τῆς πόσεως, εἰς σῶμα καὶ αἷμα τοῦ ἐσθίοντος καὶ πίνοντος μεταβάλλονται, καὶ οὐ γίνονται ἕτερον σῶμα παρὰ τὸ πρότερον αὐτοῦ σῶμα· οὕτως ὁ τῆς προθέσεως ἄρτος οἶνος τε καὶ ὕδωρ διὰ τῆς ἐπικλήσεως καὶ ἐπιφοιτήσεως τοῦ ἁγίου πνεύματος ὑπερφυῶς μεταποιοῦνται εἰς τὸ σῶμα τοῦ Χριστοῦ καὶ τὸ αἷμα, καὶ οὐκ εἰσὶ δύο, ἀλλ' ἓν καὶ τὸ αὐτό.——Οὐκ ἔστι τύπος ὁ ἄρτος καὶ ὁ οἶνος τοῦ σώματος καὶ αἵματος τοῦ Χριστοῦ· μὴ γένοιτο· ἀλλ' αὐτὸ τὸ σῶμα τοῦ κυρίου τεθεωμένον, αὐτοῦ τοῦ κυρίου εἰπόντος, Τοῦτό μου ἐστί, οὐ τύπος τοῦ σώματος, ἀλλὰ τὸ σῶμα· καὶ οὐ τύπος τοῦ αἵματος, ἀλλὰ τὸ αἷμα.——τιμήσωμεν αὐτὸ πάσῃ καθαρότητι ψυχικῇ τε καὶ σωματικῇ· διπλοῦν γάρ ἐστι.——ἄνθρακα εἶδεν Ἡσαΐας· ἄνθραξ δὲ ξύλον λιτὸν οὐκ ἔστι, ἀλλ' ἡνωμένον πυρί· οὕτως καὶ ὁ ἄρτος τῆς κοινωνίας οὐκ ἄρτος λιτός ἐστιν, ἀλλ' ἡνωμένος θεότητι· σῶμα δὲ ἡνωμένον θεότητι οὐ μία φύσις ἐστίν, ἀλλὰ μία μὲν τοῦ σώματος, τῆς δὲ ἡνωμένης αὐτῷ θεότητος ἑτέρα· ὥστε τὸ συναμφότερον οὐ μία φύσις, ἀλλὰ δύο.——Σῶμά ἐστι καὶ αἷμα Χριστοῦ, εἰς σύστασιν τῆς ἡμετέρας ψυχῆς τε καὶ σώματος χωροῦν, οὐ δαπανώμενον, οὐ φθειρόμενον, οὐκ εἰς ἀφεδρῶνα χωροῦν, μὴ γένοιτο· ἀλλ' εἰς τὴν ἡμῶν οὐσίαν καὶ συντήρησιν, βλάβης παντοδαπῆς ἀμυντήριον, ῥύπου παντὸς καθαρτήριον. —— Οὗτος ὁ ἄρτος ἐστὶν ἡ ἀπαρχὴ τοῦ μέλλοντος ἄρτου, ὅς ἐστιν ὁ ἐπιούσιος· τὸ γὰρ ἐπιούσιον δηλοῖ, ἢ τὸν μέλλοντα, τουτέστι τὸν τοῦ μέλλοντος αἰῶνος, ἢ τὸν πρὸς συντήρησιν τῆς οὐσίας ἡμῶν λαμβανόμενον· εἴτε οὖν οὕτως, εἴτε οὕτως τὸ τοῦ κυρίου σῶμα προσφυῶς λεχθήσεται· πνεῦμα γὰρ ζωοποιοῦν ἐστιν ἡ σὰρξ τοῦ κυρίου. διότι ἐκ τοῦ ζωοποιοῦ πνεύματος συνελήφθη· τὸ γὰρ γεγεννημένον ἐκ τοῦ πνεύματος πνεῦμά ἐστι· τοῦτο δὲ λέγω οὐκ ἀναιρῶν τὴν τοῦ σώματος φύσιν, ἀλλὰ τὸ ζωοποιὸν καὶ θεῖον τούτου δηλῶσαι βουλόμενος. Εἰ δὲ καὶ τινὲς ἀντίτυπα τοῦ σώματος καὶ αἵματος τοῦ κυρίου τὸν ἄρτον καὶ τὸν οἶνον ἐκάλεσαν, ὡς ὁ θεοφόρος ἔφη Βασίλειος, οὐ μετὰ τὸ ἁγιασθῆναι εἶπον, ἀλλὰ πρὶν ἁγιασθῆναι, αὐτὴν τὴν προσφορὰν οὕτω καλέσαντες. Μετάληψις δὲ λέγεται· δι' αὐτῆς γὰρ τῆς Ἰησοῦ θεότητος μεταλαμβάνομεν. κοινωνία δὲ λέγεταί τε καὶ ἔστιν ἀληθῶς διὰ τὸ κοινωνεῖν ἡμᾶς δι' αὐτῆς τῷ Χριστῷ, καὶ μετέχειν αὐτοῦ τῆς σαρκός τε καὶ τῆς θεότητος· κοινωνεῖν δὲ καὶ ἑνοῦσθαι ἀλλήλοις δι' αὐτῆς. ἐπεὶ γὰρ ἐξ ἑνὸς ἄρτου μεταλαμβάνομεν οἱ πάντες ἓν σῶμα Χριστοῦ καὶ ἓν αἷμα, καὶ ἀλλήλων μέλη γινόμεθα, σύσσωμοι Χριστοῦ χρηματίζοντες.—Ib. pp. 317, 18, 19.]

be spiritual, and our feeding must be likewise spiritual. And our spiritual generation by him is plainly set forth in baptism; and our spiritual meat and food is set forth in the holy communion and supper of the Lord. And because our sights be so feeble that we cannot see the spiritual water wherewith we be washed in baptism, nor the spiritual meat wherewith we be fed at the Lord's table; therefore to help our infirmities, and to make us the better to see the same with a pure faith, our Saviour Christ hath set forth the same, as it were before our eyes, by sensible signs and tokens, which we be daily used and accustomed unto.

And because the common custom of men is to wash in water, therefore our spiritual regeneration in Christ, or spiritual washing in his blood, is declared unto us in baptism by water. Likewise our spiritual nourishment and feeding in Christ is set before our eyes by bread and wine, because they be meats and drinks which chiefly and usually we be fed withal; that as they feed the body, so doth Christ with his flesh and blood spiritually feed the soul.

And therefore the bread and wine be called examples of Christ's flesh and blood; and also they be called his very flesh and blood, to signify unto us, that as they feed us carnally, so do they admonish us, that Christ with his flesh and blood doth feed us spiritually, and most truly, unto everlasting life.

And as Almighty God by his most mighty word and his holy Spirit and infinite power brought forth all creatures in the beginning, and ever sithens hath preserved them; even so by the same word and power he worketh in us, from time to time, this marvellous spiritual generation and wonderful spiritual nourishment and feeding, which is wrought only by God, and is comprehended and received of us by faith.

And as bread and drink by natural nourishment be changed into a man's body, and yet the body is not changed, but is the same[1] that it was before: so, although the bread and wine be sacramentally changed into Christ's body, yet his body is the same, and in the same place that it was before; that is to say, in heaven, without any alteration of the same.

And the bread and wine be not so changed into the flesh and blood of Christ that they be made one nature, but they remain still distinct in nature; so that the bread in itself is not his flesh, and the wine his blood, but unto them that worthily eat and drink the bread and wine, to them the bread and wine be his flesh and blood; that is to say, by things natural, and which they be accustomed unto, they be exalted unto things above nature. For the sacramental bread and wine be not bare and naked figures, but so pithy and effectuous, that whosoever worthily eateth them, eateth spiritually Christ's flesh and blood, and hath by them everlasting life.

Wherefore, whosoever cometh to the Lord's table, must come with all humility, fear, reverence, and purity of life, as to receive not only bread and wine, but also our Saviour Christ, both God and man, with all his benefits, to the relief and sustentation both of their bodies and souls.

This is briefly the sum and true meaning of Damascene concerning this matter.

Wherefore, they that gather of him either the natural presence of Christ's body in the sacraments of bread and wine, or the adoration of the outward and visible sacrament; or that after the consecration there remaineth no bread, nor wine, nor other substance, but only the substance of the body and blood of Christ; either they understand not Damascene, or else of wilful frowardness

---

[¹ But the same, 1551, and Orig. ed.]

they will not understand him: which rather seemeth to be true by such collections as they have unjustly gathered and noted out of him.

For although he say that Christ is the spiritual meat; yet as in baptism the Holy Ghost is not in the water, but in him that is unfeignedly baptized; so Damascene meant not, that Christ is in the bread, but in him that worthily eateth the bread.

208.

And though he say that the bread is Christ's body, and the wine his blood, yet he meant not that the bread, considered in itself, or the wine in itself, being not received, is his flesh and blood: but to such as by unfeigned faith worthily receive the bread and wine, to such the bread and wine are called by Damascene the body and blood of Christ, because that such persons, through the working of the Holy Ghost, be so knit and united spiritually to Christ's flesh and blood, and to his divinity also, that they be fed with them unto everlasting life.

Furthermore, Damascene saith not that the sacrament should be worshipped and adored, as the papists term it, which is plain idolatry; but that we must worship Christ, God and man. And yet we may not worship him in bread and wine, but sitting in heaven with his Father, and being spiritually within ourselves.

Nor he saith not, that there remaineth no bread nor wine, nor none other substance, but only the substance of the body and blood of Christ; but he saith plainly, "that as a burning coal is not wood only, but fire and wood joined together; so the bread of the communion is not bread only, but bread joined to the divinity." But those that say, that there is none other substance but the substance of the body and blood of Christ, do not only deny that there is bread and wine, but by force they must deny also, that there is either Christ's divinity or his soul. For if the flesh and blood, the soul and divinity, of Christ be four substances, and in the sacrament be but two of them, that is to say, his flesh and blood, then where is his soul and divinity? And thus these men divide Jesus, separating his divinity from his humanity: of whom St John saith: "Whosoever divideth Jesus, is not of God, but he is antichrist."

1 John iv.

And moreover, these men do separate Christ's body from his members in the sacrament, that they leave him no man's body at all. For as Damascene saith, that the distinction of members pertain so much to the nature of man's[2] body, that where there is no such distinction, there is no perfect man's body: but by these papists' doctrine, there is no such distinction of members in the sacrament; for either there is no head, feet, hands, arms, legs, mouth, eyes, and nose at all; or else all is head, all feet, all hands, all arms, all legs, all mouth, all eyes, and all nose. And so they make of Christ's body no man's body at all.

In libro de duabus in Christo voluntatibus.

Thus being confuted the papists' errors, as well concerning transubstantiation, as the real, corporal, and natural presence of Christ in the sacrament, which were two principal points purposed in the beginning of this work; now it is time something to speak of the third error of the papists, which is concerning the eating of Christ's very body, and drinking of his blood.

[*Thus endeth the third Book*[3].]

[[2] Of a man's body, 1551, and Orig. Ed.]   [[3] Orig. Ed.]

WINCHESTER.

Damascene.

Last of all, the author busieth himself with Damascene, and goeth about to answer him by making of a sum; which sum is so wrong accompted, that every man that readeth Damascene may be auditor to control it. And this will I say, Damascene writeth so evidently in the matter, that Peter Martyr, for a shift, is fain to find fault in his judgment and age; and yet he is eight hundred years old at the least, and I say at the least, because he is reckoned of some half as old again. And whatsoever his judgment were, he writeth (as Melancthon saith) his testimony of the faith of the sacrament as it was in his time. I would write in here Damascene's words, to compare them with the sum[1] collected by this author, whereby to disprove his particulars plainly; but the words of Damascene be to be read, translated already abroad.

Concomitance.

As for the "four substances" which this author by accompt numbereth of Christ, might have been left unreckoned by tale, because among them that be faithful, and understand truly, wheresoever the substance of Christ's very body is, there is also understood by concomitance to be present the substance of his soul, as very man, and also of the Godhead as very God. And in the matter of the sacrament therefore, contending with him that would have the substance of bread there, it may be said there is in the sacrament the only substance of Christ's body, because the word "only" thus placed excludeth other strange substances, and not the substances which without contention be known and confessed unite with Christ's body. And so a man may be said to be alone in his house when he hath no strangers, although he hath a number of his own men. And Erasmus noteth how the evangelist writeth Christ to have prayed alone, and yet certain of his disciples were there. And if in a contention raised, whether the father and son were both killed in such a field or no, I defended the father to have been only killed there, and thereupon a wager laid, should I lose, if by proof it appeared, that not only the father, but also three or four of the father's servants were slain, but the son escaped? And as in this speech the word "only" served to exclude that was in contention, and not to reduce the number to one; no more is it in the speech that this author would reprove, and therefore needed not to have occupied himself in the matter, wherein I heard him once say in a good audience, himself was satisfied. In which mind I would he had continued; and having so slender stuff as this is, and the truth so evident against him, not to have resuscitate this so often reproved untruth, wherein never hitherto any one could prevail.

CANTERBURY.

As for Damascene needeth no further answer than I have made in my former book. But I pray the reader, that he will diligently examine the place, and so to be an indifferent auditor betwixt us two.

Now when you be called to accompt for the number of substances in the sacrament, I perceive by your wrangling, that you be somewhat moved with this audit, for because you be called to accompt. And I cannot blame you, though it somewhat grieve you; for it toucheth the very quick. And although I myself can right well understand your numbers, that when you name but one, you mean four; yet you should have considered beforehand, to whom your book was written. You wrote to plain simple people in the English tongue, which understand no further but one to be one, and four to be four. And therefore when you say there is but one, and mean four, you attemper not your speech to the capacities of them to whom you write.

Now have I answered to all your frivolous cavillations against my third book, and
   fortified it so strongly, that you have spent all your shot and powder in
      vain. And I trust I have either broken your pieces, or pegged
         them, that you shall be able to shoot no more: or if you
           shoot, the shot shall be so faint that it shall not
             be able to pierce through a paper leaf.
             And the like I trust to do to all
                the munition and ordi-
                  nance laid against
                     my fourth
                      book.

[1 The same, Orig. ed. Winch.]

THE CONFUTATION OF THE FOURTH BOOK.

[WINCHESTER.]

THUS having perused the effect of the third book, I will likewise peruse the fourth, and then shall follow in direct course to speak of the matter of transubstantiation. In this fourth book the author entreateth eating and drinking of Christ's body and blood: and in the first part thereof travaileth to confirm his purpose, and in the second part answereth as he can to his adversaries, and so taketh occasion to speak of adoration.

His chief purpose is to prove that evil men receive not the body and blood of Christ in the sacrament, which after this author's doctrine is a very superfluous matter. For if the sacrament be only a figure, and the body and blood of Christ be there only figuratively, whereto should this author dispute of evil men's eating, when good men cannot eat Christ in the sacrament, because he is not there? For by the effect of this author's doctrine the sacrament is but a visible preaching by the tokens and signs of bread and wine; that in believing and remembering Christ's benefits, with revolving them in our mind, we should in faith feed upon Christ spiritually, believing that, as the bread and wine feedeth and nourisheth our bodies, so Christ feedeth and nourisheth our souls: which be good words, but such as the words in Christ's supper do not learn us, and yet may[2] be well gathered, not to limit the mystery of the supper, but to be spoken and taught touching the believing and remembering Christ's benefits, with the revolving of them in our mind, thereby to learn us how to feed upon Christ continually without the use of the visible sacrament; being called[3] of St Augustine "the invisible sacrament[4]," wherein by faith we be nourished with the word of God and the virtue of Christ's body and blood, which the true teaching of the church calleth spiritual manducation only, without which no man is to be accompted a true member of the mystical body of Christ. And therefore whoso feedeth upon Christ thus spiritually, must needs be a good man, for only good men be true members of Christ's mystical body: which spiritual eating is so good a fruit as it declareth the tree necessarily to be good; and therefore it must be and is a certain conclusion, that only good men do eat and drink the body and blood of Christ spiritually, that is to say, effectually to life. So as this author shall have of me no adversary therein. And if this author had proved that to be the true doctrine, that Christ's very body and blood is not present in the visible sacrament, then might he have left this fourth book unwritten. For after his doctrine, as I said before, good men do not eat Christ's body in the sacrament under the visible signs, for because it is not there, and then much less should evil men reach it.

In the catholic teaching, all the doctrine of eating of Christ is concluded in two manner of eatings; one in the visible sacrament sacramental, another spiritual without the sacrament. And because in the eating of the visible sacrament St Paul speaketh of unworthy, the same true teaching, to open the matter more clearly according to scripture, noteth unto us three manner of eatings, one spiritual only, which only good men do, feeding in faith without the visible sacrament. Another is both spiritual and sacramental, which also good men only do, receiving the visible sacrament with a true sincere charitable faith. The third manner of eating is sacramental only, which (after St Paul) evil men do unworthily, and therefore have judgment and condemnation, and be guilty of our Lord's body, not esteeming our Lord's body there. And here ariseth the knot of contention with this author, who saith, "evil men eat but the sacramental bread:" whereunto I reply, No more do good men neither, if this author's doctrine of the sacrament be true, seeing he will have it but a figure: if this author will say

August. in Sermone Domini in Monte. Lib. iii.

[² And may be, Orig. ed. Winch.]
[³ Being that called, 1551.]
[⁴ Si quis autem etiam illa quæ de victu corporis necessario, vel sacramento Dominici corporis istam sententiam vult accipere, oportet ut conjuncte accipiantur omnia tria, ut scilicet quotidianum panem simul petamus et necessarium corpori, et sacramentum visibile, et invisibile verbi Dei. August. De Sermone Domini in Monte, Lib. ii. cap. 7. Pars iii. Basil. ap. Amerbach. 1506.]

the effect is other in good men than in evil men, I will not strive therein. But to discuss this matter, evidently we must rightly open the truth, and then must consider the visible sacraments as they be of God's ordinance, who directeth us where to seek for his gifts, and how: whose working albeit it be not restrained by his sacraments, and therefore God may and doth invisibly sanctify and salve as it pleaseth him; yet he teacheth us of his ordinary working, in the visible sacraments, and ordereth us to seek his gifts of health and life there; whereupon St Augustine noteth how baptism, among the christian men of Africa, was very well called health, and the sacrament of Christ's body called life, as in which God giveth health and life, if we worthily use them[1]. The ordinance of these sacraments is God's work, the very author of them, who as he is in himself uniform, as St James saith, "without alteration," so, as David saith, "his works be true," which is as much as uniform; for "truth" and "uniform" answereth together. As God is all goodness, so all his works be good. So as considering the substance of God's works and ordinances as they be in themselves[2], they be always uniform, certain, and true in their substance as God ordered them. Among men, for whom they be wrought and ordered, there is variety; good men, evil men, worthy, unworthy; but as St Paul saith, there is but "one Lord, one faith, one baptism." And the parable of the sower, which Christ declared himself, sheweth a diversity of the grounds where the seed did fall; but the seed was all one that did fall in the good ground, and that did fall in the naughty ground, but it fructified only in the good ground, which seed Christ calleth his word; and in the sixth of St John saith, "his word is spirit and life;" so as by the teaching of Christ spirit and life may fall upon naughty men, although for their malice it tarrieth not, nor fructifieth not in them. And St Augustine[3], according hereunto, noteth how Christ's words be spirit and life, "although thou dost carnally understand them, and hast no fruit of them; yet so they be spirit and life, but not to thee:" whereby appeareth the substance of God's ordinance to be one, though we in the using of it vary. The promises of God cannot be disappointed by man's infidelity, as St Paul saith; which place Luther allegeth to shew the unity in the substance of baptism, whether it be ministered to good or evil. But St Paul to the Corinthians declareth it notably in these words: "We be the good savour of Christ in them that be saved, and them that perish." Here St Paul noteth the savour good and one to divers men; but, after the diversity in men, of divers effects in them, that is to say, the savour of life, and the savour of death: which saying of St Paul the Greek scholies, gathered by Œcumenius, open and declare with similitudes in nature very aptly. The dove, they say, and the beetle shall feed both upon one ointment, and the beetle die of it, and the dove strengthened by it; the diversity in the effect following of the diversity of them that eat, and not of that is eaten, which is alway one. According hereunto St Augustine, against the Donatists, giveth for a rule the sacraments to be one in all, although they be not one that receive and use them. And therefore to knit up this matter for the purpose, I intend and write it; for we must consider the substance of the visible sacrament of Christ's body and blood to be always as of itself it is, by Christ's ordinance: in the understanding whereof this author maketh variance, and would have it by Christ's ordinance but a figure, which he hath not proved; but and he had proved it, then is it in substance but a figure, and but a figure to good men. For it must be in substance one to good and bad; and so neither to good nor bad this sacrament is otherwise dispensed than it is truly taught to be by preaching.

Wherefore if it be more than a figure, as it is in deed, and if by Christ's ordinance it hath present, under the form of those visible signs of bread and wine, the very body and blood of Christ, as hath been truly taught hitherto, then is the substance of the sacrament one always, as the ointment was, whether doves eat of it or beetles. And this issue I join with this author, that he shall not be able by any learning to make any diversity in the substance of this sacrament, whatsoever diversity follow in the effect. For the diversity of the effect is occasioned in them that receive, as before is proved. And then, to answer this author, I say that only good men eat and drink the body and blood of Christ spiritually, as I have declared, but all, good and evil, receive the visible sacrament of that substance God hath ordained it, which in it hath no variance, but is all one to good and evil.

[1 Optime Punici Christiani baptismum ipsum nihil aliud quàm salutem, et sacramentum corporis Christi nihil aliud quàm vitam vocant. August. De Peccatorum Meritis et Remissione. Lib. I. cap. 24. Pars vi.]

[2 As they be themselves, Orig. ed. Winch.]

[3 Quid est, spiritus et vita sunt? spiritaliter intelligenda sunt. Intellexisti spiritaliter? spiritus et vita sunt. Intellexisti carnaliter? etiam sic illa spiritus et vita sunt, sed tibi non sunt.—August. in Evangelium Joannis. Tractat. xxvii. de cap. vi. Pars ix.]

CANTERBURY.

In this book, because you agree with me almost in the whole, I shall not need much to travail in the answer; but leaving all your pretty taunts against me, and glorious boasting of yourself, which neither beseemeth our persons, nor hindereth the truth, nor furthereth your part, but by pompous words to win a vain glory and fame of them that be unlearned, and have more regard to words than judgment of the matter, I shall only touch here and there such things as we vary in, or that be necessary for the defence of the truth.

212.

First, after the sum of my fourth book, collected as pleaseth you, at the first dash you begin with an untrue report, joined to a subtle deceit or fallax, saying that my chief purpose is to prove that evil men receive not the body and blood of Christ in the sacrament. And hereupon you conclude that my fourth book is superfluous. But of a false antecedent, all that be learned do know that nothing can be rightly concluded. Now mine intent and purpose in the fourth book is not to prove that evil men receive not the body and blood of Christ in the sacrament, (although that be true,) but my chief purpose is to prove, that evil men eat not Christ's flesh nor drink not his blood, neither in the sacrament nor out of the sacrament; as on the other side good men eat and drink them, both in the sacrament and out of the sacrament.

And in the word "sacrament," which is of your addition, is a subtle fallax, called double understanding. For when the sacrament is called only a figure, as you rehearse, wherein the body and blood of Christ be only figuratively, there the word "sacrament" is taken for the outward signs of bread and wine. And after, when you rehearse that the sacrament is a visible preaching by the tokens and signs of bread and wine, in believing and remembering Christ's benefits, there the word "sacrament" is taken for the whole ceremony and ministration of the sacrament. And so when you go about by equivocation of the word to deceive other men, you fall into your own snare, and be deceived yourself, in that you think you convey the matter so craftily that no man can espy you.

The word "sacrament."

But to utter the matter plainly without fallax or cavillation, I teach that no man can eat Christ's flesh and drink his blood but spiritually; which forasmuch as evil men do not, although they eat the sacramental bread until their bellies be full, and drink the wine until they be drunken, yet eat they neither Christ's flesh, nor drink his blood, neither in the sacrament nor without the sacrament, because they cannot be eaten and drunken but by spirit and faith, whereof ungodly men be destitute, being nothing but world and flesh.

This therefore is the sum of my teaching in this fourth book, that in the true ministration of the sacrament Christ is present spiritually, and so spiritually eaten of them that be godly and spiritual. And as for the ungodly and carnal, they may eat the bread and drink the wine, but with Christ himself they have no communion or company; and therefore they neither eat his flesh nor drink his blood, which whosoever eateth hath (as Christ saith himself) life by him, as Christ hath life by his Father. "And to eat Christ's body or drink his blood," saith St Augustine, "is to have life[4]." For whether Christ be in the sacrament corporally, as you say, or spiritually in them that rightly believe in him, and duly receive the sacrament, as I say, yet certain it is, that there he is not eaten corporally, but spiritually. For corporal eating with the mouth is to chaw and tear in pieces with the teeth, after which manner Christ's body is of no man eaten; although Nicholas the Second made such an article of the faith, and compelled Berengarius so to profess[5]. And therefore, although Christ were corporally in the sacrament, yet seeing that he cannot be corporally eaten, this book cometh in good

1 Cor. vi.
John vi.
213.
August. in Jo. Tract. 26, et de verbis Apost. Sermon. ii.

Nicolaus secundus.

[4 Qui manducat ejus carnem, et bibit ejus sanguinem, habet vitam eternam.—August. In Evangelium Joannis. Tract. xxvi. de cap. vi. Pars ix.

Illud manducare refici est:...illud bibere quid est, nisi vivere? Manduca vitam, bibe vitam: habebis vitam, et integra est vita. Tunc autem hoc erit, id est, vita unicuique erit corpus et sanguis Christi, si quod in sacramento visibiliter sumitur, in ipsa veritate spiritaliter manducetur, spiritaliter bibatur.—August. de verbis Apostoli. Serm. ii. cap. i.]

[5 See p. 113, note 4.]

place, and is very necessary to know that Christ's body cannot be eaten but spiritually, by believing and remembering Christ's benefits, and revolving them in our mind, believing that as the bread and wine feed and nourish our bodies, so Christ feedeth and nourisheth our souls.

And ought this to come out of a christian man's mouth, "That these be good words, but such as the words of Christ's supper do not learn us?" Do not the words of Christ's supper learn us to eat the bread and drink the wine in the remembrance of his death? Is not the breaking and eating of the bread, after such sort as Christ ordained, a communication of Christ's body unto us? Is not the cup likewise a communication of his blood unto us? Should not then christian people, according hereunto, in faith feed upon Christ spiritually, believing that as the bread and wine feed and nourish their bodies, so doth Christ their souls with his own flesh and blood? And shall any christian man now say that "these be good words, but such as the words in Christ's supper do not learn us?"

Luke xxii. 1 Cor. xi. 1 Cor. x.

And yet these said words limit not the mystery of the supper: forasmuch as that mystery of eating Christ's flesh and drinking his blood extendeth further than the supper, and continueth so long as we be lively members of Christ's body. For none feed nor be nourished by him, but that be lively members of his body; and so long and no longer feed they of him than they be his true members, and receive life from him. For feeding of him is to receive life.

But this is not that "invisible sacrament" which you say St Augustine speaketh of *in sermone Domini in monte*[1], the third book. For he calleth there the daily bread, which we continually pray for, either corporal bread and meat, which is our daily sustenance for the body, or else the visible sacrament of bread and wine, or the invisible sacrament of God's word and commandments; of the which sacraments God's word is daily heard, and the other is daily seen. And if by the invisible sacrament of God's word St Augustine meant our nourishment by Christ's flesh and blood, then be we nourished with them, as well by God's word as by the sacrament of the Lord's supper.

August. in Sermone Domini in Monte. Lib. ii.

But yet whosoever told you that St Augustine wrote this in the third book *de sermone Domini in monte*, trust him not much hereafter, for he did utterly deceive you. For St Augustine wrote no more but two books *de sermone Domini in monte;* and if you can make three of two, as you do here, and one of four, as you did before in the substances of Christ, you be a marvellous auditor, and then had all men need to beware of your accompts, lest you deceive them. And you cannot lay the fault here in the printer; for I have seen it written so both by your own hand, and by the hand of your secretary.

Now when you have wrangled in this matter as much as you can, at length you confess the truth, that "whoso feedeth upon Christ spiritually must needs be a good man, (for only good men be members of Christ's mystical body,) which spiritual eating is so good a fruit, as it declareth the tree necessarily to be good: and therefore it must be and is a certain conclusion, that only good men do eat and drink the body and blood of Christ spiritually, that is to say, effectually to life." This you write in conclusion, and this is the very doctrine that I teach, and in the same terms: marry, I add thereto, that the eating of Christ's body is a spiritual eating, and the drinking of his blood is a spiritual drinking; and therefore no evil man can eat his flesh nor drink his blood, as this my fourth book teacheth, and is necessary to be written. For although neither good nor evil men eat Christ's body in the sacrament under the visible signs, in the which he is not but sacramentally; yet the good feed of him spiritually, being[2] inhabiting spiritually within them, although corporally he be absent

---

[1 Panis quotidianus aut pro his omnibus dictus est, quæ hujus vitæ necessitatem sustentant, de quo cum præcipit ait, 'Nolite cogitare de crastino:' ut ideo sit additum 'da nobis hodie:' aut pro sacramento corporis Christi, quod quotidie accipimus: aut pro spiritali cibo, de quo idem Dominus dicit, 'Operamini escam quæ non corrumpitur;' et illud, 'Ego sum panis vitæ, qui de cœlo descendi.'— August. De Sermone Domini in monte. Lib. II. Cap. vii. Pars iii.]

[2 Being and, 1551.]

and in heaven; but the evil men neither feed upon him corporally nor spiritually, (from whom he is both the said ways absent,) although corporally they eat and drink with their mouths the sacraments of his body and blood.

Now where you note here three manner of eatings, and yet but two manner of eatings of Christ, this your noting is very true, if it be truly understand. For there be indeed three manner of eatings, one spiritual only, another spiritual and sacramental both together, and the third sacramental only: and yet Christ himself is eaten but in the first two manner of ways, as you truly teach. And for to set out this distinction somewhat more plainly, that plain men may understand it, it may thus be termed: that there is a spiritual eating only, when Christ by a true faith is eaten without the sacrament; also there is another eating both spiritual and sacramental, when the visible sacrament is eaten with the mouth, and Christ himself is eaten with a true faith; the third eating is sacramentally only, when the sacrament is eaten, and not Christ himself. So that in the first is Christ eaten without the sacrament; in the second he is eaten with the sacrament; and in the third the sacrament is eaten without him; and therefore it is called sacramental eating only, because only the sacrament is eaten, and not Christ himself. After the two first manner of ways godly men do eat, who feed and live by Christ: the third manner of ways the wicked do eat; and therefore, as St Augustine[3] saith, "they neither eat Christ's flesh nor drink his blood, although every day they eat the sacrament thereof, to the condemnation of their presumption." And for this cause also St Paul saith not, " He that eateth Christ's body and drinketh his blood unworthily, shall have condemnation, and be guilty of the Lord's body:" but he saith, " He that eateth this bread, and drinketh the cup of the Lord unworthily, shall be guilty of the Lord's body, and eateth and drinketh his own damnation, because he esteemeth[4] not the Lord's body."

Three manner of eatings.

August. in Joh. Tract. 26.

1 Cor. xi.

And here you commit two foul faults. One is, that you declare St Paul to speak of the body and blood of Christ, when he spake of the bread and wine. The other fault is, that you add to St Paul's words this word " there," and so build your work upon a foundation made by your own self.

215.

And where you say, that if my doctrine be true, "neither good men nor evil eat but the sacramental bread;" it can be none other but very frowardness and mere wilfulness, that you will not understand that thing which I have spoken so plainly, and repeated so many times. For I say, that good men eat the Lord's body spiritually to their eternal nourishment, whereas evil men eat but the bread carnally to their eternal punishment. And as you note of St Augustine[5], that "baptism is very well called health, and the sacrament of Christ's body called life, as in which God giveth health and life if we worthily use them;" so is the sacramental bread very well called Christ's body, and the wine his blood, as in the ministration whereof Christ giveth us his flesh and blood, if we worthily receive them.

August. de peccatorum meritis et remiss. Lib. i. cap. 24.

And where you teach how "the works of God in themselves be alway true and uniform in all men, without diversity in good and evil, in worthy and unworthy," you bring in this mystical matter here clearly without purpose or reason, far passing the capacity of simple readers, only to blind their eyes withal. By which kind of teaching it is all one work of God, to save and to damn, to kill and to give life, to hate and to love, to elect and to reject; and to be short, by this kind of doctrine God and all his works be one, without diversity either of one work from another, or of his works from his substance. And by this means it is all one work of God in baptism and in the Lord's supper. But all this is spoken quite besides the matter, and serveth for nothing but to cast a mist before men's eyes, as it seemeth you seek nothing else through your whole book.

The works of God uniform.

And this your doctrine hath a very evil smack, that "spirit and life should fall

---

[3 Ac per hoc qui non manet in Christo, et in quo non manet Christus, proculdubio nec manducat spiritaliter carnem ejus, nec bibit ejus sanguinem, licet carnaliter et visibiliter premat dentibus sacramentum corporis et sanguinis Christi: sed magis tantæ rei sacramentum ad judicium sibi manducat et bibit.—August. in Joannem. Tract. xxvi. de cap. vi. Pars ix.]

[4 Esteemed, 1551.]

[5 See before, p. 202.]

upon naughty men, although for their malice it tarry not." For by this doctrine you join together in one man Christ and Belial, the Spirit of God and the spirit of the devil, life and death, and all at one time; which doctrine I will not name what it is, for all faithful men know the name right well, and detest the same. And what ignorance can be shewed more in him that accompteth himself learned, than to gather of Christ's words, where he saith, "his words be spirit and life," that spirit and life should be in evil men because they hear his words? For the words which you recite by and by of St Augustine shew how vain your argument is, when he saith: "The words be spirit and life, but not to thee that dost carnally understand them[1]." What estimation of learning or of truth would you have men to conceive of you, that bring such unlearned arguments, whereof the invalidity appeareth within six lines after? Which must needs declare in you either much untruth and unsincere proceeding, or much ignorance, or at the least an exceeding forgetfulness, to say any thing reproved again within six lines after. And if the promises of God, as you say, be not disappointed by our infidelity, then if evil men eat the very body of Christ and drink his blood, they must needs dwell in Christ, and have Christ dwelling in them, and by him have everlasting life, because of these promises of Christ, *Qui manducat meam carnem, et bibit meum sanguinem, in me manet et ego in eo. Et qui manducat meam carnem et bibit meum sanguinem, habet vitam æternam:* "He that eateth my flesh and drinketh my blood, hath everlasting life. And he that eateth my flesh and drinketh my blood, dwelleth in me and I in him." And yet the third promise, *Qui manducat me, et ipse vivet propter me:* "He that eateth me, he shall also live by me." These be three promises of God, which if they cannot be disappointed by our infidelity, then if evil men eat the very body of Christ and drink his blood, as you say they do in the sacrament, then must it needs follow that they shall have everlasting life, and that they dwell in Christ and Christ in them, because our infidelity, say you, cannot disappoint God's promises.

And how agreeth this your saying with that doctrine which you were wont earnestly to teach both by mouth and pen, "that all the promises of God to us be made under condition," if our infidelity cannot disappoint God's promises? For then the promises of God must needs have place, whether we observe the condition or not.

But here you have fetched a great compass and circuit utterly in vain, to reprove that thing which I never denied, but ever affirmed, which is: "That the substance of the visible sacrament of the body and blood of Christ, (which I say is bread and wine in the[2] sacrament, as water is in baptism,) is all one substance to good and to bad, and to both a figure." But that under the form of bread and wine is corporally present by Christ's ordinance his very body and blood, either to good or to ill, that you neither have nor can prove; and yet thereupon would you bring in your conclusion here, wherein you commit that folly in reasoning, which is called *petitio principii*.

What need you to make herein any issue, when we agree in the matter? For in the substance I make no diversity, but I say that the substance of Christ's body and blood is corporally present neither in the good eater, nor in the evil. And as for the substance of bread and wine, I say they be all one, whether the good or evil eat and drink them: as the water of baptism is all one, whether Simon Peter or Simon Magus be christened therein; and it is one word that to the evil is a savour of death, and to the good is a savour of life; and as it is one sun that shineth upon the good and the bad, that melteth butter, and maketh the earth hard; one flower whereof the bee sucketh honey, and the spider poison, and one ointment (as Œcumenius saith) that killeth the beetle, and strengtheneth the dove. Nevertheless as all that be washed in the water be not washed with the Holy Spirit, so all that eat the sacramental bread, eat not the very body of Christ. And thus you see that your issue is to no purpose, except you would fight with your own shadow.

Now forasmuch as after all this vain and frivolous consuming of words, you begin to make answer unto my proofs, I shall here rehearse my proofs and arguments, to

---

[1 See before, p. 202.]   [2 In that sacrament, 1551.]

the intent that the reader, seeing both my proofs and your confutations before his eyes, may the better consider and give his judgment therein.

My fourth book beginneth thus[3].

The gross error of the papists is, of the carnal eating and drinking of Christ's flesh and blood with our mouths.

Chap. I. Whether evil men do eat and drink Christ. 217.

For they say, that "whosoever eat and drink the sacraments of bread and wine, do eat and drink also with their mouths Christ's very flesh and blood, be they never so ungodly and wicked persons." But Christ himself taught clean contrary in the sixth of John, that we eat not him carnally with our mouths, but spiritually with our faith, saying: "Verily, verily, I say unto you, he that believeth in me hath everlasting life. I am the bread of life. Your fathers did eat manna in the wilderness, and died. This is the bread that came from heaven, that whosoever shall eat thereof shall not die. I am the lively bread that came from heaven. If any man eat of this bread, he shall live for ever. And the bread which I will give is my flesh, which I will give for the life of the world."

John vi.

The godly only eat Christ.

This is the most true doctrine of our Saviour Christ, that whosoever eateth him shall have everlasting life. And by and by it followeth in the same place of St John more clearly: "Verily, verily I say unto you, except you eat the flesh of the Son of man, and drink his blood, you shall not have life in you. He that eateth my flesh and drinketh my blood hath life everlasting, and I will raise him again at the last day: for my flesh is very meat, and my blood is very drink. He that eateth my flesh, and drinketh my blood, dwelleth in me and I in him. As the living Father hath sent me, and I live by the Father, even so he that eateth me shall live by me. This is the bread which came down from heaven: not as your fathers did eat manna, and are dead: he that eateth this bread shall live for ever."

John vi.

This taught our Saviour Christ as well his disciples as the Jews at Capernaum, that the eating of his flesh and drinking of his blood was not like to the eating of manna. For both good and bad did eat manna; but none do eat his flesh and drink his blood, but they have everlasting life. For as his Father dwelleth in him, and he in his Father, and so hath life by his Father; so he that eateth Christ's flesh and drinketh his blood, dwelleth in Christ, and Christ in him, and by Christ he hath eternal life.

What need we any other witness, when Christ himself doth testify the matter so plainly, that whosoever eateth his flesh and drinketh his blood hath everlasting life; and that to eat his flesh and to drink his blood is to believe in him; and whosoever believeth in him hath everlasting life? Whereof it followeth necessarily, that ungodly persons, (being limbs of the devil,) do not eat Christ's flesh nor drink his blood, except the papists would say that such have everlasting life.

But as the devil is the food of the wicked, which he nourisheth in all iniquity, and bringeth up into everlasting damnation; so is Christ the very food of all them that be the lively members of his body, and them he nourisheth, feedeth, bringeth up, and cherisheth unto everlasting life.

And every good and faithful christian man feeleth in himself how he feedeth of Christ, eating his flesh and drinking of his blood. For he putteth the whole hope and trust of his redemption and salvation in that only sacrifice, which Christ made upon the cross, having his body there broken, and

Chap. II. What is the eating of Christ's flesh and drinking of his blood.

[3 The title of the fourth book runs thus in the Orig. ed.: "The fourth Book is of the eating and drinking of the body and blood of our Saviour Christ."]

his blood there shed for the remission of his sins. And this great benefit of Christ the faithful man earnestly considereth in his mind, chaweth and digesteth it with the stomach of his heart, spiritually receiving Christ wholly into him, and giving again himself wholly unto Christ.

And this is the eating of Christ's flesh and drinking of his blood, the feeling whereof is to every man the feeling how he eateth and drinketh Christ, which none evil man nor member of the devil can do.

218.

Chap. III. Christ is not eaten with teeth, but with faith. Cyprian de Cœna Domini.

For as Christ is a spiritual meat, so is he spiritually eaten and digested with the spiritual part of us, and giveth us spiritual and eternal life, and is not eaten, swallowed, and digested with our teeth, tongues, throats, and bellies.

Therefore saith St Cyprian: "He that drinketh of the holy cup, remembering this benefit of God, is more thirsty than he was before; and lifting up his heart unto the living God, is taken with such a singular hunger and appetite, that he abhorreth all gally and bitter drinks of sin, and all savour of carnal pleasure is to him as it were sharp and sour vinegar. And the sinner being converted, receiving the holy mysteries of the Lord's supper, giveth thanks unto God, and boweth down his head, knowing that his sins be forgiven, and that he is made clean and perfect, and his soul (which God hath sanctified) he rendereth to God again as a faithful pledge, and then he glorieth with Paul, and rejoiceth saying: 'Now it is not I that live, but it is Christ that liveth within me.' These things be practised and used among faithful people, and to pure minds the eating of his flesh is no horror but honour, and the spirit delighteth in the drinking of the holy and sanctifying blood. And doing this, we whet not our teeth to bite, but with pure faith we break the holy bread[1]." These be the words of Cyprian.

August. de Verbis Domini Sermo. xxxiii. In Joan. Tractat. xxv.

And according unto the same, St Augustine saith: "Prepare not thy jaws, but thy heart[2]." And in another place he saith: "Why dost thou prepare thy belly and thy teeth? Believe, and thou hast eaten[3]." But of this matter is sufficiently spoken before, where it is proved, that to eat Christ's flesh and drink his blood be figurative speeches.

Chap. IV. The good only eat Christ.

And now to return to our purpose, that only the lively members of Christ do eat his flesh and drink his blood, I shall bring forth many other places of ancient authors before not mentioned.

Origenes in Matt. cap. xv.

First, Origen writeth plainly after this manner: "The Word was made flesh and very meat, which whoso eateth shall surely live for ever, which no evil man can eat. For if it could be, that he that continueth evil might eat the Word made flesh, seeing he is the Word and bread of life, it should not have been written: 'Whosoever eateth this bread, shall live for ever[4].'" These

---

[¹ Hanc Dei gratiam recolens, qui de sacro calice bibit, amplius sitit: et ad Deum vivum erigens desiderium, ita singulari fame illo uno appetitu tenetur, ut deinceps fellea peccatorum horreat pocula, et omnis sapor delectamentorum carnalium sit ei quasi rancidum radensque palatum acutæ mordacitatis acetum. Ad hæc inter sacra mysteria ad gratiarum actiones convertitur, et inclinato capite, munditia cordis adepta, se intelligens consummatum, restitutus peccator sanctificatam Deo animam quasi depositum custoditum fideliter reddit, et deinceps cum Paulo gloriatur et lætatur dicens: *Galat. ii.* "Vivo jam non ego, vivit vero in me Christus." Hæc in Christi commemoratione retractantur a fidelibus, et defæcatis animis carnis ejus edulium non est horrori, sed honori, potuque sancti et sanctificantis sanguinis spiritus delectatur. Hæc quotiens agimus, non dentes ad mordendum acuimus, sed fide sincera panem sanctum frangimus et partimur. Cyprian. (i. e. Arnold. ap. Cyprian.) De Cœna Domini. p. 471. Ed. Paris. 1574.]

[² Noli parare fauces, sed cor. August. de Verbis Domini. Sermo. xxxiii. cap. v. Tom. X. p. 49. Ed. Paris. 1635.]

[³ Ut quid paras dentes et ventrem? Crede, et manducasti. Id. In Joannem, de cap. vi. Tract. xxv. Pars ix. Basil. ap. Amerbach. 1506.]

[⁴ Πολλὰ δ' ἂν καὶ περὶ αὐτοῦ λέγοιτο τοῦ λόγου, ὃς γέγονε σὰρξ καὶ ἀληθινὴ βρῶσις, ἥν τινα ὁ φαγὼν πάντως ζήσεται εἰς τὸν αἰῶνα, οὐδενὸς δυναμένου φαύλου ἐσθίειν αὐτήν· εἰ γὰρ οἷόν τε ἦν ἔτι φαῦλον μένοντα ἐσθίειν τὸν γενόμενον σάρκα, λόγον ὄντα, καὶ ἄρτον ζῶντα, οὐκ ἂν ἐγέγραπτο, ὅτι πᾶς ὁ φαγὼν τὸν ἄρτον τοῦτον ζήσεται εἰς τὸν αἰῶνα. Origen. in Matt. xv. Tom. III. p. 499. Ed. Bened.]

words be so plain, that I need say nothing for the more clear declaration of them. Wherefore you shall hear how Cyprian agreeth with him.

Cyprian in his sermon, ascribed unto him, of the Lord's supper, saith: "The author of this tradition said, that except we eat his flesh and drink his blood, we should have no life in us; instructing us with a spiritual lesson, and opening to us a way to understand so privy a thing, that we should know, that the eating is our dwelling in him, and our drinking is as it were an incorporation in him, being subject unto him in obedience, joined unto him in our wills, and united in our affections. The eating therefore of this flesh is a certain hunger and desire to dwell in him." Cyprianus in Serm. de Cœna Domini.

Thus writeth Cyprian of the eating and drinking of Christ. And a little after he saith, that "none do eat of this Lamb, but such as be true Israelites, that is to say, pure christian men, without colour or dissimulation[5]."

And Athanasius, speaking of the eating of Christ's flesh and drinking of his blood, saith, that "for this cause he made mention of his ascension into heaven, to pluck them from corporal phantasy, that they might learn hereafter that his flesh was called the celestial meat that came from above, and a spiritual food, which he would give. 'For those things that I speak to you,' saith he, 'be spirit and life.' Which is as much to say, as that thing which you see, shall be slain and given for the nourishment of the world, that it may be distributed to every body spiritually, and be to all men a conservation unto the resurrection of eternal life[6]." Athanasius de Peccato in Spiritum Sanctum.

In these words Athanasius declareth the cause why Christ made mention of his ascension into heaven, when he spake of the eating and drinking of his flesh and blood. The cause after Athanasius' mind was this: that his hearers should not think of any carnal eating of his body with their mouths, (for as concerning the presence of his body, he should be taken from them, and ascend into heaven,) but that they should understand him to be a spiritual meat, and spiritually to be eaten, and by that refreshing to give eternal life, which he doth to none but to such as be his lively members.

And of this eating speaketh also Basilius, that "we eat Christ's flesh and drink his blood, being made by his incarnation and sensible life partakers of his word and wisdom. For his flesh and blood he calleth all his mystical conversation here in his flesh and his doctrine, consisting of his whole life, pertaining both to his humanity and divinity; whereby the soul is nourished and brought to the contemplation of things eternal[7]." Basilius, Epistol. 141.

[5 Dixerat sane hujus traditionis magister, quod nisi manducaremus ejus carnem, et biberemus ejus sanguinem, non haberemus vitam in nobis: spiritali nos instruens documento, et aperiens ad rem adeo abditam intellectum, ut sciremus quod mansio nostra in ipso sit manducatio, et potus quasi quædam incorporatio, subjectis obsequiis, voluntatibus junctis, affectibus unitis. Esus igitur carnis hujus quædam aviditas est, et quoddam desiderium manendi in ipso....Una est domus ecclesiæ, in qua agnus editur: nullus ei communicat, quem Israelitici nominis generositas non commendat.—Cyprian. de Cœna Domini, pp. 469-470. Ed. Paris. 1574.]

[6 Διὰ τοῦτο τῆς εἰς οὐρανοὺς ἀναβάσεως ἐμνημόνευσε τοῦ υἱοῦ τοῦ ἀνθρώπου, ἵνα τῆς σωματικῆς ἐννοίας αὐτοὺς ἀφελκύσῃ, καὶ λοιπὸν τὴν εἰρημένην σάρκα βρῶσιν ἄνωθεν οὐράνιον, καὶ πνευματικὴν τροφὴν παρ' αὐτοῦ διδομένην μάθωσιν. Ἃ γὰρ λελάληκα, φησίν, ὑμῖν, πνεῦμά ἐστι καὶ ζωή· ἴσον τῷ εἰπεῖν, τὸ μὲν δεικνύμενον καὶ διδόμενον ὑπὲρ τῆς τοῦ κόσμου σωτηρίας ἐστὶν ἡ σὰρξ ἣν ἐγὼ φορῶ· ἀλλ' αὕτη ὑμῖν καὶ τὸ ταύτης αἷμα παρ' ἐμοῦ πνευματικῶς δοθήσεται τροφή, ὥστε πνευματικῶς ἐν ἑκάστῳ ταύτην ἀναδίδοσθαι, καὶ γίνεσθαι πᾶσιν φυλακτήριον εἰς ἀνάστασιν ζωῆς αἰωνίου.—Athanasius, Epist. IV. Ad Serapium, de Peccato in Spiritum Sanctum. Tom. I. Pars ii. p. 710. Ed. Bened. Paris. 1698.]

[7 Τρώγομεν γὰρ αὐτοῦ τὴν σάρκα, καὶ πίνομεν αὐτοῦ τὸ αἷμα, κοινωνοὶ γινόμενοι διὰ τῆς ἐνανθρωπήσεως, καὶ τῆς αἰσθητῆς ζωῆς, τοῦ λόγου καὶ τῆς σοφίας. σάρκα γὰρ καὶ αἷμα πᾶσαν αὐτοῦ τὴν μυστικὴν ἐπιδημίαν ὠνόμασε, καὶ τὴν ἐκ πρακτικῆς καὶ φυσικῆς καὶ θεολογικῆς συνεστῶσαν διδασκαλίαν ἐδήλωσε, δι' ἧς τρέφεται ψυχή, καὶ πρὸς τὴν τῶν ὄντων τέως θεωρίαν παρασκευάζεται.—Basil. Epistola cxli. Tom. III. p. 167. Ed. Paris. 1638.]

Thus teacheth Basilius how we eat Christ's flesh and drink his blood, which pertaineth only to the true and faithful members of Christ.

Hieronymus in Esaiam. cap. 66. St Hierome also saith: "All that love pleasure more than God, eat not the flesh of Jesu, nor drink his blood; of the which himself saith: 'He that eateth my flesh and drinketh my blood, hath everlasting life[1].'"

In Hieremiam. And in another place St Hierome saith, that "heretics do not eat and drink the body and blood of the Lord[2]."

In Oseam, cap. 8. And moreover he saith, that "heretics eat not the flesh of Jesu, whose flesh is the meat of faithful men[3]."

Thus agreeth St Hierome with the other before rehearsed, that heretics and such as follow worldly pleasures eat not Christ's flesh nor drink his blood, because that Christ said, "He that eateth my flesh, and drinketh my blood, hath everlasting life."

Ambrosius de benedictione patriarcharum, cap. 9. De his, qui mysteriis initiantur. De Sacramentis, Lib. iv. cap. 5. And St Ambrose saith, that "Jesus is the bread which is the meat of saints, and that he that taketh this bread, dieth not a sinner's death: for this bread is the remission of sins[4]." And in another book to him intituled, he writeth thus: "This bread of life which came down[5] from heaven, doth minister everlasting life; and whosoever eateth this bread, shall not die for ever, and is the body of Christ[6]." And yet in another book, set forth in his name, he saith on this wise:

Lib. v. cap. 3. "He that did eat manna died; but he that eateth this body, shall have remission of his sins, and shall not die for ever[7]." And again he saith: "As often as thou drinkest thou hast remission of thy sins[8]."

These sentences of St Ambrose be so plain in this matter, that there needeth no more, but only the rehearsal of them.

Augustinus in sententiis ex Prospero decerptis, cap. 341. But St Augustine in many places, plainly discussing this matter, saith: "He that agreeth not with Christ, doth neither eat his body nor drink his blood, although, to the condemnation of his presumption, he receive every day the sacrament of so high a matter[9]."

De Civitate Dei, Lib. xxi. cap. 25. 220. And moreover, St Augustine most plainly resolveth this matter in his book *De civitate Dei*, disputing against two kinds of heretics: whereof the one said[10],

---

[1 Omnes voluptatis magis amatores, quam amatores Dei, nec comedunt carnem Jesu, neque bibunt sanguinem ejus, de quo ipse loquitur: "Qui comedit carnem meam et bibit sanguinem meum, habet vitam æternam."—Hieron. Comment. in Esaiam. cap. lxvi. 17. Tom. V. p. 215. Ed. Francof. 1684.]

[2 Non comedent et non bibent, (i. e. hæretici,) subauditur corpus et sanguinem Salvatoris.—Hieron. Comment. in Hieremiam. cap. xxii. 15. Tom. V. p. 264.]

[3 Isti (i. e. hæretici,) multas immolant hostias, et comedunt carnes earum, unam Christi hostiam deserentes, nec comedentes ejus carnem, cujus caro cibus credentium est.—Hieron. Comment. in Osee. cap. viii. 13. Tom. VI. p. 26.]

[4 Hic ergo panis factus est esca sanctorum.— Qui autem accipit, non moritur peccatoris morte, quia panis hic remissio peccatorum est. Ambros. De benedictionibus Patriarcharum.—cap. ix. Tom. I. p. 198. Ed. Colon. Agripp. 1616.]

[5 Which came from heaven, 1551, and Orig. ed.]

[6 Ista autem esca quam accipitis, iste panis vivus qui descendit de cœlo, vitæ æternæ substantiam subministrat: et quicumque hunc panem manducaverit, non morietur in æternum; et est corpus Christi.—Id. De Initiandis. cap. viii. Tom. IV. p. 165.]

[7 Deinde manna qui manducavit, mortuus est. Qui manducaverit hoc corpus, fiet ei remissio peccatorum, et non morietur in æternum.—Id. De Sacramentis, Lib. IV. cap. v. Tom. IV. p. 174.]

[8 Quotiescumque enim bibis, remissionem accipis peccatorum.—Id. ib. Lib. v. cap. iii. Tom. IV. p. 175. The Benedictine editors maintain that the "De initiandis" is a genuine Treatise of St Ambrose, and they have also placed the "De sacramentis" amongst his works, but they have not decided upon its authenticity. There is little question that both are spurious Treatises. Vide Coci Censura Patrum, p. 266. Helms. 1683. Riveti Critica Sacra. p. 294. Genev. 1626. Jo. Geo. Walchii. Bibl. Patrist. p. 409. Jenæ. 1834.]

[9 Nam qui discordat a Christo, nec carnem ejus manducat, nec sanguinem bibit; etiam si tantæ rei sacramentum ad judicium suæ præsumptionis quotidie indifferenter accipiat.—August. Lib. Sentent. Prosp. 341. Tom. III. p. 435. Ed. Paris. 1635.]

[10 Sed jam respondeamus etiam illis, qui non solum diabolo et angelis ejus, sicut nec isti, sed ne ipsis quidem omnibus hominibus liberationem ab æterno igne promittunt; verum eis tantum qui Christi baptismate abluti, et corporis ejus et sanguinis participes facti sunt, quomodo libet vixerint in quacumque hæresi vel impietate fuerint....Quamobrem quod ait Dominus Jesus, "Hic est panis, qui de cœlo descendit: si quis ex ipso manduca-

that "as many as were christened, and received the sacrament of Christ's body and blood, should be saved, howsoever they lived or believed, because that Christ said, 'This is the bread that came from heaven, that whosoever shall eat thereof shall not die.' 'I am the bread of life, which came from heaven, whosoever shall eat of this bread, shall live for ever.' Therefore," said these heretics, "all such men must needs be delivered from eternal death, and at length be brought to eternal life." The other said, that "heretics and schismatics might eat the sacrament of Christ's body, but not his very body, because they be no members of his body." And therefore they promised not everlasting life to all that received Christ's baptism and the sacrament of his body, but "to[11] all such as professed a true faith, although they lived never so ungodly. For such," said they, "do eat the body of Christ, not only in a sacrament, but also in deed, because they be members of Christ's body."

But St Augustine, answering to both these heresies, saith: "That neither heretics, nor such as profess a true faith in their mouths, and in their living shew the contrary, have either a true faith, (which worketh by charity, and doth none evil,) or are to be counted among the members of Christ. For they cannot be both members of Christ and members of the devil. Therefore," saith he, "it may not be said that any of them eat the body of Christ. For when Christ saith, 'He that eateth my flesh, and drinketh my blood, dwelleth in me, and I in him;' he sheweth what it is, (not sacramentally, but in deed,) to eat his body and drink his blood: which is, when a man dwelleth so in Christ, that Christ dwelleth in him. For Christ spake those words as if he should say, he that dwelleth not in me, and in whom I dwell not, let him not say or think that he eateth my body, or drinketh my blood." [Vide Emb. ed. in fine tomi hujus.]

These be the plain words of St Augustine, that such as live ungodly, although they may seem to eat Christ's body, (because they eat the sacrament of his body,) yet in deed they neither be members of his body, nor do eat his body.

Also upon the gospel of St John he saith, that "he that doth not eat his flesh and drink his blood, hath not in him everlasting life: and he that eateth his flesh, and drinketh his blood, hath everlasting life. But it is not so in those meats, which we take to sustain our bodies: for although without them we cannot live, yet it is not necessary, that whosoever receiveth them shall live; for they may die by age[12], sickness, or other chances. But in this meat and drink of the body and blood of our Lord, it is otherwise. For both they that In Joan. Tractat. 26.

[Vide Emb. ed. in fine tomi hujus.]

---

verit non morietur: ego sum panis vivus, qui de cœlo descendi: si quis manducaverit ex hoc pane, vivet in æternum," quomodo sit accipiendum, merito quæritur. Et ab istis quidem quibus nunc respondemus, hunc intellectum auferunt illi, quibus deinde respondendum est: hi sunt autem qui hanc liberationem, nec omnibus habentibus sacramentum baptismatis et corporis Christi, sed solis catholicis, quamvis male viventibus, pollicentur; qui non solum sacramento (inquiunt) sacramento, sed re ipsa manducaverunt corpus Christi, in ipso scilicet ejus corpore constituti. ...Ac per hoc quicunque agunt talia, nisi in sempiterno supplicio non erunt, quia in Dei regno esse non poterunt. In his enim perseverando usque in hujus vitæ finem, non utique dicendi sunt in Christo perseverasse usque in finem, quia in Christo perseverare est in ejus fide perseverare. Quæ fides, ut eam definit idem Apostolus, "per dilectionem operatur. Dilectio autem," sicut idem alibi dicit, "malum non operatur." Nec isti duo ergo dicendi sunt manducare corpus Christi, quoniam nec in membris computandi sunt Christi. Ut enim alia taceam, "non possunt simul esse et membra Christi et membra meretricis." Denique ipse dicens, "Qui manducat carnem meam, et bibit sanguinem meum, in me manet, et ego in eo," ostendit quid sit non sacramento tenus, sed revera corpus Christi manducare, et ejus sanguinem bibere: hoc est enim in Christo manere, ut in illo maneat et Christus. Sic enim hoc dixit, tanquam diceret: qui non in me manet, et in quo ego non maneo, non se dicat aut existimet manducare corpus meum, aut bibere sanguinem meum.—August. de Civitate Dei. Lib. xxi. cap. xxv. Pars vii. Ed. Basil. ap. Amerbach. 1506.]

[11 But all such, 1551, and Orig. ed.]
[12 For age, 1551, and Orig. ed.]

eat and drink them not, have not everlasting life: and contrariwise, whosoever eat and drink them, have everlasting life."

Note and ponder well these words of St Augustine; "That the bread and wine and other meats and drinks, which nourish the body, a man may eat, and nevertheless die: but the very body and blood of Christ no man eateth, but that hath everlasting life." So that wicked men cannot eat nor drink them, for then they must needs have by them everlasting life.

And in the same place St Augustine saith further: "The sacrament of the unity of Christ's body and blood is taken in the Lord's table, of some men to life, and of some men to death; but the thing itself, (whereof it is a sacrament,) is taken of all men to life, and of no man to death." And moreover he saith: "This is to eat that meat, and drink that drink, to dwell in Christ, and to have Christ dwelling in him. And for that cause, he that dwelleth not in Christ, and in whom Christ dwelleth not, without doubt he eateth not spiritually his flesh nor drinketh his blood, although carnally and visibly with his teeth he bite the sacrament of his body and blood[1]."

221.
[Sed magis tantæ rei sacramentum ad judicium manducat. Emb. ed.]

Thus writeth St Augustine in the twenty-sixth Homily of St John. And in the next Homily following, he saith thus: "This day our sermon is of the body of the Lord, which he said he would give to eat for eternal life. And he declared the manner of his gift and distribution, how he would give his flesh to eat, saying: 'He that eateth my flesh and drinketh my blood, dwelleth in me and I in him.' This therefore is a token or knowledge, that a man hath eaten and drunken; that is to say, if he dwell in Christ, and have Christ dwelling in him; if he cleave so to Christ, that he is not severed from him. This therefore Christ taught and admonished by these mystical or figurative words, that we should be in his body under him our head among his members, eating his flesh, nor[2] forsaking his unity[3]."

In Joh. Tractat. 27.

And in his book, *De Doctrina Christiana*, St Augustine saith, as before is at length declared, "that to eat Christ's flesh, and to drink his blood, is a figurative speech signifying the participation of his passion, and the delectable remembrance to our benefit and profit, that his flesh was crucified and wounded for us[4]."

De Doctrina Christiana, Lib. iii. cap. 16.

And in another sermon also, *De Verbis Apostoli*, he expoundeth what is the eating of Christ's body and the drinking of his blood, saying: "The eating is to

De Verbis Apostoli, Sermo ii.

[1 Qui ergo non manducat ejus carnem, nec bibit ejus sanguinem, non habet in se vitam : et qui manducat ejus carnem, et bibit ejus sanguinem, habet vitam æternam. Ad utrumque autem respondit quod dixit, æternam. Non ita est in hac esca, quam sustentandæ hujus corporalis vitæ causa sumimus: nam qui eam non sumpserit, non vivet; nec tamen qui eam sumpserit vivet. Fieri enim potest, ut senio, vel morbo, vel aliquo casu, plurimi et qui eam sumpserint, moriantur. In hoc vero cibo et potu, id est, corpore et sanguine Domini, non ita est: nam et qui eam non sumit, non habet vitam; et qui eam sumit habet vitam, et hanc utique æternam..... Hujus rei sacramentum, id est, unitatis corporis et sanguinis Christi alicubi quotidie, alicubi certis intervallis dierum in dominica mensa præparatur, et de mensa dominica sumitur, quibusdam ad vitam, quibusdam ad exitium. Res vero ipsa, cujus et sacramentum est, omni homini ad vitam, nulli ad exitium, quicunque ejus particeps fuerit.... Hoc est ergo manducare illam escam, et illum bibere potum, in Christo manere, et illum manentem in se habere. Ac per hoc qui non manet in Christo, et in quo non manet Christus, proculdubio nec manducat spiritaliter carnem ejus, nec bibit ejus sanguinem, licet carnaliter et visibiliter premat dentibus sacramentum corporis et sanguinis Christi; sed magis tantæ rei sacramentum ad judicium sibi manducat et bibit.—August. In Joannem. Tract. xxvi. De cap. vi. Pars ix. Ed. Basil. ap. Amerbach. 1506.]

[2 Not, 1551, and Orig. ed.]

[3 Est enim (i. e. sermo), de corpore Domini, quod dicebat se dare ad manducandum propter æternam vitam. Exposuit autem modum attributionis hujus et doni sui, quomodo daret carnem suam manducare, dicens : "Qui manducat carnem meam, et bibit sanguinem meum, in me manet, et ego in illo." Signum quia manducavit et bibit, hoc est : si manet et manetur, si habitat et inhabitatur, si hæret ut non deseratur. Hoc ergo nos docuit et admonuit mysticis verbis, ut simus in ejus corpore sub ipso capite in membris ejus, edentes carnem ejus, non relinquentes unitatem ejus.—August. in Joannem. Tract. xxvii. De cap. vi. Pars ix.]

[4 See p. 115.]

be refreshed, and the drinking what is it but to live? Eat life, drink life. And that shall be, when that which is taken visibly in the sacrament, is in very deed eaten spiritually and drunken spiritually[5]."

By all these sentences of St Augustine it is evident and manifest, that all men, good and evil, may with their mouths visibly and sensibly eat the sacrament of Christ's body and blood; but the very body and blood themselves be not eaten but spiritually, and that of the spiritual members of Christ, which dwell in Christ, and have Christ dwelling in them, by whom they be refreshed and have everlasting life.

And therefore saith St Augustine, that "when the other apostles did eat bread that was the Lord, yet Judas did eat but the bread of the Lord, and not the bread that was the Lord[6]." So that the other apostles with the sacramental bread did eat also Christ himself, whom Judas did not eat. And a great number of places more hath St Augustine for this purpose, which for eschewing of tediousness, I let pass for this time, and will speak something of St Cyril. *In Joh. Tract. 59.* [Vide Emb. ed. in fine tomi hujus.]

Cyril, upon St John in his gospel, saith, that "those which eat manna died, because they received thereby no strength to live ever, (for it gave no life, but only put away bodily hunger); but they that receive the bread of life, shall be made immortal, and shall eschew all the evils that pertain to death, living with Christ for ever[7]." And in another place he saith: "Forasmuch as the flesh of Christ doth naturally give life, therefore it maketh them to live that be partakers of it. For it putteth death away from them, and utterly driveth destruction out of them[8]." *Cyrillus, in Joh. Lib. iv. cap. 10.* *Cap. 12.*

And he concludeth the matter shortly in another place in few words, saying, that "when we eat the flesh of our Saviour, then have we life in us. For if things that were corrupt, were restored by only touching of his clothes, how can it be that we shall not live that eat his flesh?" And further he saith, "That as two waxes be molten together, do run every part into other; so he that receiveth Christ's flesh and blood, must needs be joined so with him, that Christ must be in him, and he in Christ[9]." *Cap. 14.* *Cap. 17.*

Here St Cyril declareth the dignity of Christ's flesh being inseparably annexed unto his divinity, saying, that it is of such force and power, that it giveth everlasting life. And whatsoever occasion of death it findeth, or let of eternal life, it putteth out and driveth clean away all the same, from them that eat that meat and receive that medicine. Other medicines or plaisters sometime heal, and sometime heal not; but this medicine is of that effect and strength, that

---

[5 Illud manducare refici est.—Illud bibere quid est, nisi vivere? Manduca vitam, bibe vitam: habebis vitam, et integra est vita. Tunc autem hoc erit, id est, vita unicuique erit corpus et sanguis Christi, si quod in sacramento visibiliter sumitur, in ipsa veritate spiritaliter manducetur, spiritaliter bibatur.—August. de Verbis Apostoli, Sermo ii. Tom. X. p. 94. Paris. 1635.]

[6 Illi manducabant panem Dominum, ille (i. e. Judas,) panem Domini contra Dominum: illi vitam, ille pœnam.—August. in Joannem, Tract. LIX. De cap. xiii. Pars IX. Basil. ap. Amerbach.]

[7 Οὐκοῦν οἱ μὲν φαγόντες τὸ μάννα, φησί, τετελευτήκασιν, ὡς οὐδεμιᾶς δηλονότι ζωῆς μετουσίαν παρ' αὐτοῦ δεξάμενοι· οὐ γὰρ ἦν ὄντως ζωοποιόν, λιμοῦ δὲ μᾶλλον ἐπίκουρον σαρκικοῦ, καὶ ὡς ἐν τύπῳ τοῦ ἀληθεστέρου παραληφθέν. οἱ δὲ τὸν ἄρτον ἐν ἑαυτοῖς εἰσκομίζοντες τῆς ζωῆς γέρας ἕξουσι τὴν ἀθανασίαν, φθορᾶς τε καὶ τῶν ἐκ ταύτης κακῶν παντελῶς ἀλογήσαντες, πρὸς ἀμήρυτόν τε καὶ ἀτελεύτητον βίον τοῦ κατὰ Χριστὸν ἀναβήσονται μῆκος.—Cyril. in Joannem, Lib. IV. cap. x. Tom. IV. p. 351. ed. Aubert. Paris. 1638.]

[8 Διὰ τοῦτο ζωοποιεῖ τοὺς μετέχοντας αὐτοῦ τὸ σῶμα Χριστοῦ. ἐξελαύνει γὰρ τὸν θάνατον, ὅταν ἐν τοῖς ἀποθνήσκουσι γένηται, καὶ ἐξίστησι φθοράν.—Id. Lib. IV. cap. xii. Tom. IV. p. 354.]

[9 Καὶ εἰ διὰ μόνης ἁφῆς τῆς ἁγίας σαρκὸς ζωοποιεῖται τὸ ἐφθαρμένον, πῶς οὐχὶ πλουσιωτέραν ἀποκερδανοῦμεν τὴν ζωοποιὸν εὐλογίαν, ὅταν αὐτῆς καὶ ἀπογευσώμεθα;—Ὥσπερ γὰρ εἴτις κηρῷ ἕτερῳ συνάψειε κηρόν, πάντως δήπου καὶ ἕτερον ἐν ἑτέρῳ γεγονότα κατόψεται· τὸν αὐτόν, οἶμαι, τρόπον καὶ ὁ τὴν σάρκα δεχόμενος τοῦ σωτῆρος ἡμῶν Χριστοῦ, καὶ πίνων αὐτοῦ τὸ τίμιον αἷμα, καθά φησιν αὐτός, ἕν, ὡς πρὸς αὐτὸν εὑρίσκεται συνανακιρνάμενος ὥσπερ καὶ ἀναμιγνύμενος αὐτῷ διὰ τῆς μεταλήψεως, ὡς ἐν Χριστῷ μὲν αὐτὸν εὑρίσκεσθαι, Χριστὸν δὲ αὖ πάλιν ἐν αὐτῷ.—Id. Lib. IV. capp. xiv. xvii. Tom. IV. pp. 361, 4, 5.]

it eateth away all rotten and dead flesh, and perfectly healeth all wounds and sores that it is laid unto.

This is the dignity and excellency of Christ's flesh and blood, joined to his divinity; of the which dignity Christ's adversaries, the papists, deprive and rob him, when they affirm, that such men do eat his flesh and receive this plaister, as remain still sick and sore, and be not holpen thereby.

Thus hast thou heard, gentle reader, the grounds and proofs, which moved me to write the matter of this fourth book, that good men only eat Christ's flesh and drink his blood. Now shalt thou hear the late bishop's confutation of the same.

WINCHESTER.

And as for the scriptures and doctors which this author allegeth to prove that only good men receive the body and blood of Christ, I grant it without contention, speaking of spiritual manducation and with lively faith without the sacrament. But in the visible sacrament evil men receive the same that good men do, for the substance of the sacrament is by God's ordinance all one. And if this author would use for a proof, that in the sacrament Christ's very body is not present, because evil men receive it, that shall be no argument; for the good seed when it was sown did fall in the evil ground, and although Christ dwelleth not in the evil man, yet he may be received of the evil man to his condemnation, because he receiveth him not to glorify him as God, as St Paul saith, non dijudicans corpus domini, *"not esteeming our Lord's body." And to all that ever this author bringeth to prove, that evil men eat not the body of Christ, may be said shortly, that spiritually they eat it not, besides the sacrament, and in the sacrament they eat it not effectually to life, but condemnation. And that is and may be called a not eating; as they be said not to hear the word of God, that hear it not profitably. And because the body of Christ of itself is ordained to be eaten for life, those that unworthily eat to condemnation*[1]*, although they eat in deed, may be said not to eat, because they eat unworthily; as a thing not well done may be in speech called not done, in respect of the good effect wherefore it was chiefly ordered to be done. And by this rule thou, reader, mayest discuss all that this author bringeth forth for this purpose*[2]*, either out of scriptures or doctors. For evil men eat not the body of Christ to have any fruit by it, as evil men be said not to hear God's word to have any fruit by it; and yet as they hear the words of spirit and life, and nevertheless perish, so evil men eat in the visible sacrament the body of Christ, and yet perish. And as I said, this answereth*[3] *the scripture with the particular sayings of Cyprian, Athanase, Basil, Hierome, and Ambrose.*

As for St Augustine, which this author allegeth, de civitate Dei, *the same St Augustine doth plainly say there in this place*[4] *alleged, how the good and evil receive the same sacrament, and addeth, "but not with like profit," which words this author suppresseth, and therefore dealeth not sincerely. As for St Augustine shall be hereafter more plainly declared. Finally, he that receiveth worthily the body and blood of Christ, hath everlasting life, dwelleth in Christ and Christ in him: he that receiveth unworthily, which can be only in the sacrament, receiveth not life, but condemnation.*

CANTERBURY.

223. If you "grant without contention" that which I do prove, then you must grant absolutely and frankly without any addition, that only good men eat and drink the body and blood of Christ. For so say all the scriptures and authors plainly, which I have alleged, without your addition of spiritual manducation: and not one of them all say as you do, that "in the visible sacrament evil men receive the same that good men do."

But I make no such vain proofs as you feign in my name, that "in the sacrament Christ's very body is not present, because evil men receive it." But this argument were good, although I make no such: Evil men eat and drink the sacrament, and yet they

---

[1 Eat condemnation, Orig. ed. Winch.]
[2 For his purpose, 1551.]
[3 Thus answereth, 1551.]
[4 In the place, 1551.]

eat and drink not Christ's flesh and blood: ergo, his flesh and blood be not really and corporally in the sacrament.

And when you say that Christ "may be received of the evil man to his condemnation," is this the glory that you give unto Christ, that his whole presence in a man, both with flesh, blood, soul, and spirit, shall make him never the better? and that Christ shall be in him, that is a member of the devil? And if an evil man have Christ in him for a time, why may he not then have him still dwelling in him? For if he may be in him a quarter of an hour, he may be also an whole hour, and so a whole day, and an whole year, and so shall God and the devil dwell together in one house. And this is the crop that groweth of your sowing, if Christ fall in evil men, as good seed falleth in evil ground.

And where you say, that "all that ever I bring to prove that evil men eat not the body of Christ, may be shortly answered," truth it is, as you said in one place of me, that all that I have brought may be shortly answered, if a man care not what he answer; as it seemeth you pass not much what you answer, so that you may lay on load of words. For whereas I have fully proved, as well by authority of scripture as by the testimony of many old writers, that although evil men eat the sacramental bread, and drink the wine, which have the names of his flesh and blood, yet they eat not Christ's very flesh nor drink his blood[5]: your short and whole answer is this, that evil men may be said not to eat Christ's flesh and drink his blood, because they do it not fruitfully, as they ought to do; "and that may be called a not eating, as they may be said not to hear God's word, that hear it not profitably; and a thing not well done, may be in speech called not done, in the respect of the good effect." I grant such speeches be sometime used, but very rarely; and when the very truth cometh in discussion, then such paradoxes are not to be used. As if it come in question whether a house be builded, that is not well builded, then the definition of the matter must not be[6], that it is not builded[7] although the carpenters and other workmen have failed in their covenant and bargain, and not builded the house in such sort as they ought to have done. So our Saviour Christ teacheth that all heard the word, whether the seed fell in the highway, or upon the stones, or among the thorns, or in the good ground. Wherefore when this matter cometh in discussion among the old writers, whether evil men eat Christ's body or no, if the truth had been that evil men eat it, the old writers would not so precisely have defined the contrary, that they eat not, but would have said they eat it, but not effectually, not fruitfully, not profitably. But now the authors which I have alleged, define plainly and absolutely, that evil men eat not Christ's body, without any other addition. But after this sort that you do use, it shall be an easy matter for every man to say what liketh him, and to defend it well enough, if he may add to the scriptures and doctors' words at his pleasure, and make the sense after his own phantasy. The scriptures and doctors which I allege do say in plain words, as I do say, "that evil men do not eat the body of Christ nor drink his blood, but only they that have life thereby."

Now come you in with your addition and gloss, made of your own head, putting thereto this word "effectually." If I should say that Christ was never conceived nor born, could not I avoid all the scriptures that you can bring to the contrary, by adding this word "apparently," and defend my saying stoutly? And might not the Valentinians, Marcionists and other, that said that Christ died not for us, defend their error with addition, as they did, of this word "putative" to all the scriptures that were brought against them? And what heresy can be reproved, if the heretics may have that liberty that you do use, to add of their own heads to the words of scripture? —contrary unto God's word directly, who commandeth us to add nothing to his word, nor to take anything away.

That may be said not done, that is not well done.

Luke viii.

224.

Deut. xii.

And yet moreover, the authorities, which I have brought to approve my doctrine, do clearly cast away your addition, adding the cause why evil men cannot eat Christ's flesh nor drink his blood. And you have taught almost in the beginning of your

---

[5 Nor drink blood, 1551.]
[6 Of the matter must be, 1551.]
[7 After the words, "is not builded," the 1551 edition adds, "but that it is builded."]

book, "that Christ's body is but a spiritual body, and after a spiritual manner eaten by faith." And now you have confessed, "that whoso feedeth upon Christ spiritually, must needs be a good man." How can you then defend now, that evil men eat the body of Christ; except you will now deny that which you granted in the beginning, and now have forgotten it, "that Christ's body cannot be eaten but after a spiritual manner by faith?" Wherein it is marvel, that you, having so good a memory, should forget the common proverb, *Mendacem memorem esse oportet*.

And it had been more convenient for you to have answered fully to Cyprian, Athanasius, Basil, Hierome, and Ambrose, than when you cannot answer, to wipe your hands of them with this slender answer, saying, that you have answered. And whether you have or no, I refer to the judgment of the reader.

<small>August. de Civit. Dei, Lib. xxi. cap. 25.</small>

And as concerning St Augustine, *De civitate Dei*, he saith: "That evil men receive the sacrament of Christ's body, although it availeth them not." But yet he saith in plain words, "that we ought not to say, that any man eateth the body of Christ, that is not in the body[1]." And if the reader ever saw any mere cavillation in all his life-time, let him read the chapter of St Augustine, and compare it to your answer, and I dare say he never saw the like.

225.

And as for the other places of St Augustine by me alleged, with Origen and Cyril, for the more ease you pass them over with silence, and dare eat no such meat, it is so hard for you to digest. And thus have you with post haste run over all my scriptures and doctors, as it were playing at the post, with still passing and giving over every game. And yet shall you never be able for your part to bring any scripture that serveth for your purpose, except you may be suffered to add thereto such words as you please.

Then come you to my questions, wherein I write thus.

<small>Chap. v.</small>

And now, for corroboration of Cyril's saying, I would thus reason with the papists, and demand of them: When an unrepentant sinner receiveth the sacrament, whether he have Christ's body within him or no?

If they say "no," then have I my purpose, that evil men, although they receive the sacrament of Christ's body, yet receive they not his very body. If they say "yea," then I would ask them further, Whether they have Christ's Spirit within them or no?

If they say "nay," then do they separate Christ's body from his Spirit, and his humanity from his divinity, and be condemned by the scripture as very antichrists, that divide Christ.

<small>Rom. viii.</small>

And if they say "yea," that a wicked man hath Christ's Spirit in him, then the scripture also condemneth them, saying, that as "he which hath not the Spirit of Christ is none of his; so he that hath Christ in him liveth, because he is justified: and if his Spirit that raised up Jesus from death dwell in you, he that raised Jesus from death, shall give life to your mortal bodies, for his Spirit's sake, which dwelleth in you."

Thus on every side the scripture condemneth the adversaries of God's word.

And this wickedness of the papists is to be wondered at, that they affirm Christ's flesh, blood, soul, holy Spirit, and his deity, to be in a man that is subject to sin, and a limb of the devil. They be wonderful jugglers and conjurers, that with certain words can make God and the devil to dwell together in one man, and make him both the temple of God, and the temple of the devil. It appeareth that they be so blind that they cannot see the light from darkness, Belial from Christ, nor the table of the Lord from the table of devils. Thus

---

[1 Ac per hoc hæretici et schismatici ab hujus unitate corporis separati possunt idem percipere sacramentum, sed non sibi utile, imo vero etiam noxium.... Sed rursus etiam isti qui recte intelligunt non dicendum esse eum manducare corpus Christi, qui in corpore non est Christi, non recte, &c.—August. De Civitate Dei. Lib. xxi. cap. xxv. Pars vii. Ed. Basil. ap. Amerbach. 1506.]

is confuted this third intolerable error and heresy of the papists: "That they which be the limbs of the devil, do eat the very body of Christ, and drink his blood;" manifestly and directly contrary to the words of Christ himself, who saith: "Whosoever eateth my flesh, and drinketh my blood, hath everlasting life."

WINCHESTER.

But to encounter directly with this author where he opposeth by interrogation, and would be answered, "whether an unrepentant sinner, that receiveth the sacrament, hath Christ's body within him or no?" Mark, reader, this question, which declareth that this author talketh of the sacrament, not as himself teacheth, but as the true teaching is, although he mean otherwise: for else how can an unrepentant sinner receive Christ's body, but only in the sacrament unworthily? and how could he receive it unworthily, and it were not there[2]? But to answer to this question[3], I answer "no;" for it followeth not, he received him, ergo, he hath him in him; for the vessel being not meet, he departed from him, because he was a sinner, in whom he dwelleth not. And where this author, now become a questionist, maketh two questions, of Christ's body, and his Spirit, as though Christ's body might be divided from his Spirit; he supposeth other to be as ignorant as himself. For the learned man will answer, that an evil man by force of God's ordinance, in the substance of the sacrament, received in deed Christ's very body there present, whole Christ, God and man; but he tarried not, nor dwelled not, nor fructified not in him, nor Christ's Spirit entered not into that man's soul, because of the malice and unworthiness of him that received. For Christ will not dwell with Belial nor abide with sinners. And what hath this author won now by his forked question? wherein he seemeth to glory as though he had embraced an absurdity that he hunted for; wherein he sheweth only his ignorance, who putteth no difference between the entering of Christ into an evil man by God's ordinance in the sacrament, and the dwelling of Christ's Spirit in an evil man, which by scripture cannot be, ne is by any catholic man affirmed. For St Paul saith: "In him that receiveth unworthily, remaineth judgment and condemnation." And yet St Paul's words plainly import, that those did eat the very body of Christ, which did eat unworthily, and therefore were guilty of the body and blood of Christ. Now, reader, consider what is before written, and thou shalt easily see what a fond conclusion this author gathereth in the ninety-seventh leaf, as though the teaching were, that the same man should be both the temple of God, and the temple of the devil; with other terms, wherewith it liketh this author to refresh himself, and feigneth an adversary such as he would have, but hath none, for no catholic man teacheth so, nor it is not all one to receive Christ and to have Christ dwelling in him. And a figure thereof was in Christ's conversation upon earth, who tarrieth[4] not with all that received him in outward appearance; and there is noted a difference that some believed in Christ, and yet Christ committed not himself to them. And the gospel praiseth them that hear the word of God and keep it, signifying many to have the word of God and not to keep it; as they that receive Christ by his ordinance in the sacrament, and yet because they receive him not according to the intent of his ordinance worthily, they are so much the worse thereby through their own malice. And therefore to conclude this place with the author, "whosoever eateth Christ's flesh and drinketh his blood, hath everlasting life," with St Paul's exposition, if he doth it worthily; or else by the same St Paul, he hath condemnation.

226.

[2 Cor. vi. Orig. ed. Winch.]

[1 Cor. xi. ibid.]

[John iii. ibid.]
[Luke xi. ibid.]

[1 Cor. xi. ibid.]

CANTERBURY.

Here the reader shall evidently see your accustomed manner, that when you be destitute of answer, and have none other shift, then fall you to scoffing and scolding out the matter, as sophisters sometimes do at their problems. But as ignorant as I am, you shall not so escape me. First you bid the reader mark, that I "talk of the sacrament, not as I teach myself." But I would have the reader here mark, that you report my words as you list yourself, not as I speak them. For you report my question as I should say, that "an unrepentant sinner should receive Christ's body," whereas I speak of the receiving of the sacrament of the body, and not of the very body itself.

Moreover, I make my question of the being of Christ's body in an unpenitent sinner, and you turn "being" into "abiding," because "being" biteth you so sore.

[2 And he were not there, Orig. ed. Winch.]   [3 To the question, Ibid.]   [4 Tarried, Ibid.]

<small>Whether a sinner have Christ within him.</small>

First you confess that an unrepentant sinner, receiving the sacrament, hath not Christ's body within him; and then may I say that he eateth not Christ's body, except he eat it without him. And although "it followeth not, he received Christ, ergo, he hath him in him;" yet it followeth necessarily, he receiveth him, ergo, he hath him within him for the time of the receipt; as a bottomless vessel, although it keep no liquor, yet for the time of the receiving it hath the liquor in it. And how can Christ "depart from an unpenitent sinner," as you say he doth, if he have him not at all? And because of mine ignorance, I would fain learn of you, that take upon you to be a man of knowledge, how an evil man receiving Christ's very body, and whole Christ, God and man, as you say an evil man doth; and Christ's body being such as it cannot be divided from his Spirit, as you say also; how this evil man, receiving Christ's Spirit, should be an evil man for the time that he hath Christ's Spirit within him? Or how can he receive Christ's body and Spirit, according to your saying, and have them not in him for the time he receiveth them? Or how can Christ enter into an evil man, as you confess, and be not in him, into whom he entereth, at that present time? These be matters of your knowledge, as you pretend, which if you can teach me, I must confess mine ignorance: and if you cannot, forsomuch as you have spoken them, you must confess the ignorance to be upon your own part.

<small>1 Cor. xi.</small>

And St Paul saith not, as you untruly recite him, that "in him that receiveth unworthily remaineth judgment and condemnation," but that he eateth and drinketh condemnation. And where you say, that "St Paul's words plainly import, that those did eat the very body of Christ, which did eat unworthily," ever still you take for a supposition the thing which you should prove. For St Paul speaketh plainly of the eating of the bread and drinking of the cup, and not one word of eating of the body and drinking of the blood of Christ. And let any indifferent reader look upon my questions, and he shall see that there is not one word answered here directly unto them, except mocking and scorning be taken for answer.

And where you deny, that of your doctrine it should follow, that "one man should be both the temple of God and the temple of the devil," you cannot deny but that your own teaching is, that Christ entereth into evil men, when they receive the sacrament. And if they be his temple into whom he entereth, then must evil men be his temple, for the time they receive the sacrament, although he tarry not long with them. And for the same time they be evil men, as you say, and so must needs be the temple of the devil. And so it followeth of your doctrine and teaching, that at one time a man shall be the temple of God and the temple of the devil. And in your figure of Christ upon earth, although he tarried not long with every man that received him, yet for a time he tarried with them. And the word of God tarrieth for the time with many, which after forget it, and keep it not. And then so must it be by these examples in evil men receiving the sacrament, that for a time Christ must tarry in them, although that time be very short. And yet for that time, by your doctrine, those evil men must be both the temples of God and of Belial.

<small>2 Cor. vi.</small>

And where you pretend to conclude this matter by the authority of St Paul, it is no small contumely and injury to St Paul, to ascribe your feigned and untrue gloss unto him that taught nothing but the truth, as he learned the same of Christ. For he maketh mention of the eating and drinking of the bread and cup, but not one word of the eating and drinking of Christ's body and blood.

<small>1 Cor. xi.</small>

Now followeth in my book my answer to the papists in this wise:

<small>Chap. vi. The answer to the papists. 1 Cor. xi.</small>

But lest they should seem to have nothing to say for themselves, they allege St Paul in the eleventh to the Corinthians, where he saith: "He that eateth and drinketh unworthily, eateth and drinketh his own damnation, not discerning the Lord's body."

But St Paul in that place speaketh of the eating of the bread and drinking of the wine, and not of the corporal eating of Christ's flesh and blood, as it is manifest to every man that will read the text. For these be the words of

St Paul: "Let a man examine himself, and so eat of the bread and drink of the cup; for he that eateth and drinketh unworthily, eateth and drinketh his own damnation, not discerning the Lord's body."

In these words St Paul's mind is, that forasmuch as the bread and wine in the Lord's supper do represent unto us the very body and blood of our Saviour Christ, by his own institution and ordinance, therefore, although he sit in heaven at his Father's right hand, yet should we come to this mystical bread and wine with faith, reverence, purity, and fear, as we would do if we should come to see and receive Christ himself sensibly present. For unto the faithful Christ is at his own holy table present, with his mighty Spirit and grace, and is of them more fruitfully received, than if corporally they should receive him bodily present: and therefore they that shall worthily come to this God's board, must after due trial of themselves consider first, who ordained this table; also what meat and drink they shall have that come thereto, and how they ought to behave themselves thereat. He that prepared the table is Christ himself: the meat and drink wherewith he feedeth them that come thereto as they ought to do, is his own body, flesh, and blood. They that come thereto, must occupy their minds in considering how his body was broken for them, and his blood shed for their redemption; and so ought they to approach to this heavenly table with all humbleness of heart and godliness of mind, as to the table wherein Christ himself is given. And they that come otherwise to this holy table, they come unworthily, and do not eat and drink Christ's flesh and blood, but eat and drink their own damnation; because they do not duly consider Christ's very flesh and blood, which be offered there spiritually to be eaten and drunken, but despising Christ's most holy supper, do come thereto as it were to other common meats[1] and drinks, without regard of the Lord's body, which is the spiritual meat of that table.

WINCHESTER.

In the ninety-seventh leaf and the second column, the author beginneth to traverse the words of St Paul to the Corinthians, and would distinct unworthy eating in the substance of the sacrament received, which cannot be. For our unworthiness cannot alter the substance of God's sacrament, that is evermore all one, howsoever we swerve from worthiness to unworthiness. And this I would ask of this author, why should it be a fault in the unworthy not to esteem the Lord's body, when he is taught, if this author's doctrine be true, that it is not there at all? If the bread[2] after this author's teaching be but a figure of Christ's body, it is then but as manna was, the eating whereof unworthily and unfaithfully was no guilt[3] of Christ's body. Erasmus noteth these words of St Paul, "to be guilty of our Lord's body," to prove the presence of Christ's body there, who compareth such an offender to the Jews, that did shed Christ's blood maliciously, as those do profane it unprofitably; in which sense the Greek commentaries do also expound it. And where this author bringeth in the words of St Paul as it were to point out the matter: "Let a man examine himself, and so eat of the bread and drink of the cup, for he that eateth unworthily, &c." these words of examining and so eating declare the thing to be one ordered to be eaten, and all the care to be used on our side, to eat worthily, or else St Paul had not said, "and so eat." And when St Paul saith, "eat judgment," and this author well remember himself, he must call judgment the effect of that is eaten, and not the thing eaten; for judgment is neither spiritual meat nor corporal, but the effect of the eating of Christ in evil men, who is salvation to good, and judgment to evil. And therefore, as good men eating Christ have salvation, so evil men eating Christ have condemnation; and so for the diversity of the eaters of Christ's body, followeth, as they be worthy or unworthy, the effect of condemnation or life; Christ's sacrament and his work also, in the substance of that sacrament, being always one. And whatsoever this author talketh otherwise in this matter, is mere trifles.

[Erasmus, Orig. ed. Winch.]
*In his epistle dedicatory of Alger.
[1 Cor. xi. Orig. ed. Winch.]
*To eat.

229.

[1 To other meats, 1551, and Orig. ed.]
[2 If this bread, Orig. ed. Winch.]
[3 So ed. 1551. In 1580 it is printed *gift*, by mistake.]

CANTERBURY.

As touching mine answer here to the words of St Paul, you would fain have them hid with darkness of speech, that no man should see what I mean. For, as Christ said, *Qui male agit, odit lucem;* and therefore, that which 'I have spoken in plain speech, you darken so with your obscure terms, that my meaning can not be understand. For I speak in such plain terms, as all men understand, that when St Paul said, "He that eateth and drinketh unworthily, eateth and drinketh his own damnation;" in that place he spake of the eating of the bread and drinking of the cup, and not of the corporal eating and drinking of Christ's flesh and blood. These my plain words you do wrap up in these dark terms, that I "would distinct the unworthy eating in the substance of the sacrament received." Which your words vary so far from mine, that no man can understand by them my meaning, except you put a large comment thereto. For I distinct the unworthy eating none otherwise, than that I say, that when St Paul speaketh of unworthy eating, he maketh mention of the unworthy eating of the bread, and not of the body of Christ.

And where you ask me this question, "Why it should be a fault in the unworthy, not to esteem the Lord's body, when it is not there at all?" there is in my book a full and plain answer unto your question already made, as there is also to your whole book. So that in making of my book, I did foresee all things that you could object against it: insomuch that here is not one thing in all your book, but I can shew you a sufficient answer thereto, in one place or other of my former book. And in this your question here moved, I refer the reader to the words of my book in the same place.

And where you say, "That if the bread be but a figure, it is like manna:" as concerning the material bread, truly it is like manna; but as concerning Christ himself, he said of himself: "Not as your fathers did eat manna and are dead; he that eateth this bread shall live for ever." And as concerning Erasmus and the Greek commentaries, neither of them saith upon the place of St Paul, as you allege them to say. And whatsoever it pleaseth you to gather of these words, "examining and so eating," yet St Paul's words be very plain, that he spake not of the eating of the very body of Christ, but of the eating of the material bread in the sacrament, which is all one, whether the good or evil eat of it; and all the care is on our side, to take heed that we eat not that bread unworthily. For as the eating of the bread unworthily, not of Christ himself, (who can not be eaten unworthily,) hath the effect of judgment and damnation; so eating of the same bread worthily hath the effect of Christ's death and salvation. And as he that eateth the bread worthily may be well said to eat Christ and life; so he that eateth it unworthily may be said to eat the devil and death, as Judas did, into whom with the bread entered Satan. For unto such it may be called *Mensa dæmoniorum, non mensa Domini;* "not God's board, but the devil's." And so in the eaters of the bread worthily or unworthily, followeth the effect of everlasting life or everlasting death. But in the eating of Christ himself is no diversity, but whosoever eateth him hath everlasting life; forasmuch as the eating of him can be to none damnation but salvation, because he is life itself. And whatsoever you babble to the contrary, is but mere fables, devised without God's word, or any sufficient ground.

Now followeth mine answer unto such authors as the papists wrest to their purpose.

Chap. VII.
The answer to the papists' authors.

But here may not be passed over the answer unto certain places of ancient authors, which at the first shew seem to make for the papists' purpose, that evil men do eat and drink the very flesh and blood of Christ. But if those places be truly and throughly weighed, it shall appear, that not one of them maketh for their error, that evil men do eat Christ's very body.

The first place is of St Augustine, *contra Cresconium Grammaticum,* where he saith: "That although Christ himself say, 'He that eateth not my flesh, and drinketh not my blood, shall not have life in him,' yet doth not his apostles teach, that the same is pernicious to them which use it not well? For he saith: 'Whosoever eateth the bread, and drinketh the cup of the Lord unworthily, shall be guilty of the body and blood of the Lord[1].'"

In which words St Augustine seemeth to conclude, that as well the evil as the good do eat the body and blood of Christ, although the evil have no benefit, but hurt thereby.

But consider the place of St Augustine diligently, and then it shall evidently appear, that he meant not of the eating of Christ's body, but of the sacrament thereof. For the intent of St Augustine there is to prove that good things avail not to such persons as do evil use them; and that many things which of themselves be good, and be good to some, yet to other some they be not good. As that light is good for whole eyes, and hurteth sore eyes: that meat which is good for some, is evil for other some: one medicine healeth some, and maketh other sick: one harness doth harm one, and cumbereth another: one coat is meet for one, and too strait for another. And after other examples, at the last St Augustine sheweth the same to be true in the sacraments, both of baptism and the Lord's body, which he saith do profit only them that receive the same worthily.

And the words of St Paul, which St Augustine citeth, do speak of the sacramental bread and cup, and not of the body and blood. And yet St Augustine called[2] the bread and the cup the flesh and blood, not that they be so indeed, but that they signify, as he saith in another place, *contra Maximinum*.

"In sacraments," saith he, "is to be considered, not what they be, but what they shew. For they be signs of other things, being one thing and signifying another[3]." Contra Maximinum, Lib. iii. cap. 22.

Therefore, as in baptism those that come feignedly, and those that come unfeignedly, both be washed with the sacramental water, but both be not washed with the Holy Ghost, and clothed with Christ: so in the Lord's supper both eat and drink the sacramental bread and wine, but both eat not Christ himself, and be fed with his flesh and blood, but those only which worthily receive the sacrament.

And this answer will serve to another place of St Augustine, against the Donatists, where he saith, that "Judas received the body and blood of the Lord[4]." For as St Augustine in that place speaketh of the sacrament of baptism, so doth he speak of the sacrament of the body and blood, which nevertheless he calleth the body and blood, because they signify and represent unto us the very body, flesh, and blood. 231. De Bap. contra Donatist. Lib. v. cap. 8.

[1 Quamvis ipse Dominus dicat, "Nisi quis manducaverit carnem meam, et biberit sanguinem meum, non habebit in se vitam"; nonne idem Apostolus docet etiam hoc perniciosum male utentibus fieri? Ait enim: "Quicunque manducaverit panem, et biberit calicem Domini indigne, reus erit corporis et sanguinis Domini."—August. contra Cresconium Grammaticum, Lib. I. cap. XXV. Pars VI. Basil. ap. Amerbach. 1506.]

[2 Calleth, Orig. ed.]

[3 Hæc enim sacramenta sunt in quibus non quid sint, sed quid ostendant semper attenditur: quoniam signa sunt rerum, aliud existentia, et aliud significantia.—August. contra Maximin. Lib. III. cap. XXII. Pars XI.]

[4 Sicut enim Judas, cui buccellam tradidit Dominus, non malum accipiendo, sed male accipiendo locum in se diabolo præbuit: sic indigne quisque sumens Dominicum sacramentum non efficit, ut quia ipse malus est malum sit, aut quia non ad salutem accipit, nihil acceperit. Corpus enim Domini et sanguis Domini nihilominus erat etiam illis quibus dicebat Apostolus, "Qui manducat indigne, judicium sibi manducat et bibit."—August. De baptismo contra Donatistas. Lib. v. cap. viii. Pars v.]

WINCHESTER.

And yet he goeth about, because he will make all things clear, to answer such authors "as the papists," he saith, "bring for their purpose." And first he beginneth with St Augustine, who writeth as plainly against this author's mind as I would have devised it, if I had no conscience of truth more than I see some have, and might with a secret wish have altered St Augustine as I had list. And therefore here I make a plain issue with this author, that in the searching of St Augustine he hath trusted his man or his friend over-negligently in so great a matter, or he hath willingly gone about to deceive the reader. For in the place of St Augustine against the Donatists, alleged here by this author, which he would with the rest assail, St Augustine hath these formal words in Latin: Corpus Domini et sanguis Domini nihilominus erat etiam illis quibus dicebat Apostolus, "Qui manducat indigne, judicium sibi manducat et bibit;" *which words be thus much in English: "It was nevertheless the body of our Lord and the blood of our Lord also unto them to whom the apostle said, 'He that eateth unworthily, eateth and drinketh judgment to himself.'" These be St Augustine's words, who writeth notably and evidently, that it was nevertheless the body and blood of Christ to them that received unworthily, declaring that their unworthiness doth not alter the substance of that sacrament, and doth us to understand therewith the substance of the sacrament to be the body and blood of Christ; and nevertheless so, though the receivers be unworthy: wherein this author is so overseen, as I think there was never learned man before that durst in a commonwealth, where learned men be, publish such an untruth as this is, to be answered in a tongue that all men knew*[1]. *Yet Peter Martyr wrote in Latin, and rejoiceth not, I think, to have his lies in English. I will bring in here another place of St Augustine to this purpose:* Illud etiam, quod ait, 'Qui manducat carnem meam, et bibit sanguinem meum, in me manet et ego in illo,' quomodo intellecturi sumus? Nunquid etiam illos sic[2] poterimus accipere, de quibus dixit[2] Apostolus, quod 'judicium sibi manducent et bibant,' quum ipsam carnem manducent, et ipsum sanguinem bibant? Nunquid et Judas Magistri venditor et traditor impius, quamvis primum ipsum manibus ejus confectum sacramentum carnis et sanguinis ejus cum ceteris discipulis, sicut apertius Lucas Evangelista declarat, manducaret et biberet, mansit in Christo, aut Christus in eo? Multi denique, qui vel corde ficto carnem illam manducant, et sanguinem bibunt, vel quum manducaverint et biberint, apostatæ fiunt, nunquid manent in Christo, aut Christus in eis? Sed profecto est quidam modus manducandi illam carnem, et bibendi illum sanguinem: quomodo qui manducaverit et biberit, in Christo manet et Christus in eo. Non ergo quocunque modo quisquam manducaverit carnem Christi, et biberit sanguinem Christi, manet in Christo, et in illo Christus; sed certo quodam modo, quem modum utique ipse videbat, quando ista dicebat[3]. *The English of these words is this: "That same that he also saith, 'Who eateth my flesh and drinketh my blood, dwelleth in me and I in him;' how shall we understand it? May we understand also of them of whom the apostle speak*[4], *that they did eat to themselves, and drink, judgment, when they did eat the same flesh and drink the same blood, the flesh itself, the blood itself? Did not Judas, the wicked seller and betrayer of his master, when he did eat and drink (as Lucas the Evangelist declareth) the first sacrament of the flesh and blood of Christ made with his own hands, dwell in Christ, and Christ in him? Finally, many that with a feigned heart eat that flesh and drink the blood, or when they have eaten and drunken become apostates, do not they dwell in Christ, or Christ in them? But undoubtedly there is a certain manner of eating that flesh and drinking that blood; after which manner whosoever eateth and drinketh, dwelleth in Christ, and Christ in him. Therefore, not in whatsoever manner any man eateth the flesh of Christ, and drinketh the blood of Christ, he dwelleth in Christ, and Christ in him, but after a certain manner, which manner he saw when he said these words." This is the sense of St Augustine's saying in Latin, whereby appeareth the faith of St Augustine to be, in the sacrament to be eaten and drunken the very body and blood of Christ, which for the substance of the sacrament evil men receive as good men do; that is to say, as St Augustine doth point it out by his words, the same flesh and the same blood of Christ, with such an expression of speech*[5], *as he would exclude all difference that device of figure might imagine, and therefore saith,* Ipsam carnem, ipsum sanguinem; *which signify*[6] *the self-same in deed, not by name only, as the*

[1 Know, 1551.]
[2 "Hic," and "dicit," in the above edition of Op. August.]
[3 August. de verbis Domini, in Evang. secundum Matth. Sermo. xi. cap. xi. Tom. X. p. 18. Paris. 1635.]
[4 Spake, Orig. ed. Winch.]
[5 An express speech, Orig. ed. Winch.]
[6 Signifieth, 1551.]

author of the book would have St Augustine understood; and when that appeareth, as it is most manifest, that Judas received the same, being wicked, that good men do, how the same is before the receipt by God's omnipotency present in the visible sacrament, and so not received by the only instrument of faith, which in evil men is not lively; but by the instrument of the mouth, wherein it entereth with the visible element; and yet, as St Augustine saith, dwelleth not in him that so unworthily receiveth; because the effect of dwelling of Christ is not in him that receiveth by such a manner of eating as wicked men use. Whereby St Augustine teacheth the diverse effect to ensue of the diversity of the eating, and not of any diversity of that which is eaten, whether the good man or evil man receive the sacrament. If I would here encumber the reader, I could bring forth many more places of St Augustine to the confusion and reproof of this author's purpose; and yet, notwithstanding, to take away that he might say of me, that I weigh not St Augustine, I think good to allege and bring forth the judgment of Martin Bucer   *Bucerus.
touching St Augustine, who understandeth St Augustine clear contrary to this author, as may plainly appear by that the said Bucer writeth in few words in his epistle dedicatory of the great work he sent abroad of his enarrations of the gospels, where his judgment of St Augustine in this point he uttereth thus: Quoties scribit etiam Judam ipsum corpus et sanguinem Domini Bucerus *sumsisse! Nemo itaque auctoritate S. patrum dicet Christum in sacra cœna absentem esse. The sense in English is this:* "How often writeth he," *speaking of St Augustine,* "Judas also to have received the self body and blood of our Lord! No man therefore, by the authority of the fathers, can say Christ to be absent in the holy supper." *Thus saith Bucer, who understandeth St Augustine, as I have before alleged him, and gathereth thereof a conclusion, that no man can by the fathers' sayings prove Christ to be absent in the holy supper. And therefore, by Bucer's judgment, the doctrine of this author can be in no wise catholic, as dissenting from that hath been before taught and believed. Whether Bucer will still continue in that he hath so solemnly published to the world, and by me here alleged, I cannot tell; and whether he do or no, it maketh no matter: but thus he hath taught in his latter judgment with a great protestation, that he speaketh without respect other than to the truth, wherein, because he seemed to dissent from his friends, he saith:* φίλος μὲν Σωκράτης, ἀλλὰ φιλτάτη ἡ ἀλήθεια, τιμιωτάτη ἡ ἐκκλησία: *which words have an imitation of an elder saying, and be thus much to say;* "Socrates is my friend, truth is my best beloved, and the church most regarded." *And with this Bucer closeth his doctrine of the sacrament, after he knew all that Zuinglius and Œcolampadius could say in the matter. And here I will leave to speak of Bucer, and bring forth Theodoretus*[7]*, a man most*[8] *extolled by this author, who saith plainly in his commentaries upon* Theodoretus in epist. i. Cor. xi. *St Paul, how Christ delivered to Judas his precious body and blood; and declareth further therewith in that sacrament to be the truth. So as this author can have no foundation upon either to maintain his figurative speech, or the matter of this fourth book, which his words plainly impugn. St Hierome in his commentaries upon the prophet Malachi hath first this* Hieronymus. *sentence:* Polluimus panem, id est corpus Christi, quando indigne accedimus ad altare, et sordidi mundum sanguinem bibimus[9]: "We defile the bread, that is to say, the body of Christ, when we come unworthy[10] to the altar, and being filthy drink the clean blood." *Thus saith St Hierome, who saith,* "Men filthy drink the clean blood;" *and in another place after, the same St Hierome saith:* Polluit [enim] Christi mysteria indigne accipiens corpus ejus et sanguinem; "He that unworthily receiveth the body and blood of Christ, defileth the mysteries." *Can any words be more manifest and evident to declare St Hierome's mind, how in the visible sacrament men receive unworthily, which be evil men, the body and blood of Christ?*

CANTERBURY.

In this point I will join a plain issue with you, that I neither willingly go about to deceive the reader in the searching of St Augustine, (as you use to do in every place,) nor I have not trusted my "man or friend" herein, (as it seemeth you have done overmuch,) but I have diligently expended and weighed the matter myself. For although in such weighty matters of scripture and ancient authors you must needs trust your 233. An issue.

[7 Ἀνέμνησεν αὐτοὺς τῆς ἱερᾶς ἐκείνης καὶ παναγίας νυκτός, ἐν ᾗ καὶ τῷ τυπικῷ πάσχα τὸ τέλος ἐπέθηκε, καὶ τοῦ τύπου τὸ ἀρχέτυπον ἔδειξε, καὶ τοῦ σωτηρίου μυστηρίου τὰς θύρας ἀνέῳξε, καὶ οὐ μόνον τοῖς ἕνδεκα ἀποστόλοις, ἀλλὰ καὶ τῷ προδότῃ, τοῦ τιμίου μετέδωκε σώματός τε καὶ αἵματος. Theodoretus, in Epist. i. Cor. xi. Tom. III. pp. 237, 8. Ed. Halæ, 1769-94.]

[8 Much, Orig. ed. Winch.]

[9 Hieronymi Opera. Comment. in Malachiam. capp. i. iii. Tom. VI. pp. 233, 237. Ed. Francof. 1684.]

[10 Unworthily, Orig. ed. Winch.]

men, (without whom I know you can do very little, being brought up from your tender age in other kinds of study,) yet I, having exercised myself in the study of scripture and divinity from my youth, (whereof I give most hearty lauds and thanks to God,) have learned now to go alone, and do examine, judge, and write all such weighty matters myself; although, I thank God, I am neither so arrogant nor so wilful, that I will refuse the good advice, counsel, and admonition of any man, be he man or master, friend or foe.

Augustin. de Bapt. cont. Donat. Lib. v. cap. 8.

But as concerning the place alleged by you out of St Augustine, let the reader diligently expend mine whole answer to St Augustine, and he shall, I trust, be fully satisfied. For St Augustine in his book, *De baptismo contra Donatistas*, (as I have declared in my book[1],) speaketh of the morsel of bread and sacrament which Judas also did eat, as St Augustine saith. And in this speech he considered (as he writeth *contra Maximinum*), not what it is, but what it signifieth; and therefore he expresseth the matter by Judas more plainly in another place, saying, that "he did eat the bread of the Lord, not the bread being the Lord," (as the other apostles did,) signifying thereby that the evil eat the bread, but not the Lord himself: as St Paul saith that they eat and drink *panem et calicem Domini*, "the bread and the cup of the Lord," and not that they eat the Lord himself. And St Augustine saith not, as you feign of him, that the substance of this sacrament is the body and blood of Christ, but the substance of this sacrament is bread and wine, (as water is in the sacrament of baptism,) and the same be all one, not altered by the unworthiness of the receivers. And although St Augustine, in the words by you recited, call the sacrament of Christ's body and blood his body and blood, yet is the sacrament no more but the sacrament thereof, and yet is it called the body and blood of Christ, as "sacraments have the names of the things whereof they be sacraments;" as the same St Augustine teacheth most plainly *ad Bonifacium*.

August. In Johan. tract. 59.

And I have not so far overshot myself or been overseen, that I would have attempted to publish this matter, if I had not before-hand excussed the whole truth therein from the bottom. But because I myself am certain of the truth, (which hath been hid these many years, and persecuted by the papists with fire and fagot, and should be so yet still if you might have your own will,) and because also I am desirous that all my countrymen of England, (unto whom I have no small cure and charge to tell the truth,) should no longer be kept from the same truth; therefore have I published the truth which I know in the English tongue, to the intent that I may edify all by that tongue, which all do perfectly know and understand. Which my doing, it seemeth, you take in very evil part, and be not a little grieved thereat, because you would rather have the light of truth hid still under the bushel, than openly to be set abroad that all men may see it. And I think that it so little grieveth M. Peter Martyr, that his book is in English, that he would wish it to be translated likewise into all other languages.

234.
[Matt. v.]
Ed. 1551.

August. de Verbis Domini, Ser. xi. The self-same flesh that was crucified and is sensible, is eaten of Christ's people.

Now, where you gather of the words of St Augustine, *De verbis Domini*[2], that both the evil and good eat one body of Christ, the self-same in substance, "excluding all difference that device of figure might imagine;" to this I answer, that although you express the body of Christ with what terms you can devise, calling it, as you do in deed, the flesh that was born of the virgin Mary, the same flesh, the flesh itself, yet I confess that it is eaten in the sacrament. And to express it yet more plainly than peradventure you would have me, I say, that the same visible and palpable flesh, that was for us crucified, and appeared after his resurrection, and was seen, felt, and groped, and ascended into heaven, and there sitteth at his Father's right hand, and at the last day shall come to judge the quick and the dead; that self-same body, having all the parts of a man's body, in good order and proportion, and being visible and tangible, I say, is eaten of christian people at his holy supper: what will you now require more of me concerning the truth of the body? I suppose you be sorry that I grant you so much, and yet what doth this help you? For the diversity is not in the body, but in the eating thereof, no man eating it carnally; but the good eating it both sacramentally and spiritually, and the evil only sacramentally, that is to say,

[[1] Vide p. 221.]   [[2] Vide p. 222.]

figuratively. And therefore hath St Augustine these words, *certo quodam modo*, "after a certain manner," because that the evil eat the sacrament, which after a certain manner is called the very body of Christ; which manner St Augustine himself declareth most truly and plainly in an epistle *ad Bonifacium*, saying: "If sacraments had not some similitude or likeness of those things whereof they be sacraments, they could in no wise be sacraments. And for their similitude and likeness, they have commonly the name of the things whereof they be sacraments. Therefore after a certain manner the sacrament of Christ's body is Christ's body, the sacrament of Christ's blood is Christ's blood[3]." This epistle is set out in my book, the sixty-fourth leaf[4], which I pray the reader to look upon for a more full answer unto this place. And after that manner Judas and such like did eat the morsel of the Lord's bread, but not the bread that is the Lord, but a sacrament thereof which is called the Lord, as St Augustine saith. So that with the bread entered not Christ with his Spirit into Judas, (as you say he doth into the wicked,) but Satan entered into him, as the gospel testifieth. And if Christ entered then into Judas with the bread, as you write, then the devil and Christ entered into Judas both at once. *August. ad Bonifacium episto. 23.* *John xiii.*

As concerning M. Bucer, what mean you to use his authority, whose authority you never esteemed heretofore? And yet Bucer varieth much from your error: for he denieth utterly that Christ is really and substantially present in the bread, either by conversion or inclusion, but in the ministration he affirmeth Christ to be present: and so do I also, but not to be eaten and drunken of them that be wicked and members of the devil, whom Christ neither feedeth nor hath any communion with them. And to conclude in few words the doctrine of M. Bucer in the place by you alleged, he dissenteth in nothing from Œcolampadius and Zuinglius. Wherefore it seemeth to me somewhat strange, that you should allege him for the confirmation of your untrue doctrine, being so clearly repugnant unto his doctrine. *Master Bucer.* *235.*

The words of Theodoretus, if they were his, be so far from your report, that you be ashamed to rehearse his words as they be written, which when you shall do, you shall be answered. But in his dialogues he declareth in plain terms not only the figurative speech of Christ in this matter, but also wherefore Christ used those figurative speeches, as the reader may find in my book, the sixty-seventh, sixty-eighth, sixty-ninth, and seventieth leaves[5]. By which manner of speech it may be said, that Christ delivered to Judas his body and blood, when he delivered it him in a figure thereof. *Theodoretus.*

And as concerning St Hierome, he calleth the mysteries or mystical bread and wine Christ's flesh and blood, as Christ called them himself, and the eating of them he calleth the eating of Christ's flesh and blood, because they be sacraments and figures, which represent unto us his very flesh and blood. And all that do eat the said sacraments be said to eat the body of Christ, because they eat the thing which is a representation thereof. But St Hierome meant not, that evil men do indeed eat the very body of Christ; for then he would not have written upon Esay, Jeremy, and Osee the contrary, saying, that heretics and evil men neither eat his flesh nor drink his blood, which whosoever eateth and drinketh hath everlasting life. *Non comedunt carnem Jesu*, saith he upon Esay, *neque bibunt sanguinem ejus, de quo ipse loquitur:* "*Qui comedit carnem meam et bibit meum sanguinem, habet vitam æternam*[6]." And yet he that cometh defiled unto the visible sacraments, defileth not only the sacraments, but the contumely thereof pertaineth also unto Christ himself, who is the author of the sacraments; and as the same St Hierome saith: *Dum sacramenta violantur, ipse, cujus sunt sacramenta, violatur*[7]: "When the sacraments, saith he, be violated, then is he violated also to whom the sacraments appertain." *Hieronymus.* *Hieron. in Esaiam, cap. 66.* *Hieron. in Malachiam, cap. 1.*

Now hear what followeth in the order of my book.

And, as before is at length declared, a figure hath the name of the thing that is signified thereby. As a man's image is called a man, a lion's image a lion, a bird's image a bird, and an image of a tree and herb is called a tree or *Chap. VIII.* *Figures be called by the names of the things which they signify.*

[3 Vide p. 124, note 1.]
[4 Vide pp. 123, 4.] [5 Vide pp. 128—130.]
[6 Hieron. Comment. in Esaiam, cap. lxvi.

Tom. V. p. 215. Francof. 1684.]
[7 Id. Comment. in Malachiam, cap. i. Tom. VI. p. 233.]

herb; so were we wont to say, "Our lady of Walsingham," "our lady of Ipswich," "our lady of grace," "our lady of pity," "St Peter of Milan," "St John of Amias¹," and such like; not meaning the things themselves, but calling their images by the name of the things by them represented. And likewise we were wont to say, "Great St Christopher of York or Lincoln;" "our lady smileth, or rocketh her child;" "let us go in pilgrimage to St Peter at Rome, and St James in Compostella;" and a thousand like speeches, which were not understand of the very things, but only of the images of them.

So doth St John Chrysostom say, that we see Christ with our eyes, touch him, feel him, and grope him with our hands, fix our teeth in his flesh, taste it, break it, eat it, and digest it, make red our tongues and die them with his blood, and swallow it, and drink it².

236. And in a catechism by me translated and set forth, I used like manner of speech, saying, that with our bodily mouths we receive the body and blood of Christ. Which my saying divers ignorant persons, not used to read old ancient authors, nor acquainted with their phrase and manner of speech, did carp and reprehend for lack of good understanding³.

For this speech, and other before rehearsed of Chrysostom, and all other like, be not understand of the very flesh and blood of our Saviour Christ, (which in very deed we neither feel nor see,) but that which we do to the bread and wine, by a figurative speech is spoken to be done to the flesh and blood, because they be the very signs, figures, and tokens instituted of Christ, to represent unto us his very flesh and blood.

And yet as with our corporal eyes, corporal hands, and mouths, we do corporally see, feel, taste, and eat the bread, and drink the wine, (being the sign and sacraments of Christ's body,) even so with our spiritual eyes, hands, and mouths, we do spiritually see, feel, taste, and eat his very flesh, and drink his very blood.

Eusebius Emissenus in Serm. de Eucharistia.

As Eusebius Emissenus saith: "When thou comest to the reverend altar to be filled with spiritual meats, with thy faith look upon the body and blood of him that is thy God; honour him, touch him with thy mind, take him with the hand of thy heart, and drink him with the draught of thine inward man⁴." And these spiritual things require no corporal presence of Christ himself, who sitteth continually in heaven at the right hand of his Father.

And as this is most true, so is it full and sufficient to answer all things that the papists can bring in this matter, that hath any appearance for their party.

WINCHESTER.

[This author, Orig. ed. Winch.]

And yet these plain places of authority dissembled of purpose, or by ignorance passed over, this author, as though all things were by him clearly discussed to his intent, would by many conceits furnish and further his matters, and therefore playeth with our lady's smiling, rocking her child, and many good mowes⁵, so unseemly for his person, as it maketh⁶ me almost forget him and myself also. But with such matter he filleth his leaves, and forgetting himself⁷, maketh

---

[¹ Amiens, where John the Baptist's skull, as it is called, is still preserved.]

[² Οὐκ ἰδεῖν αὐτὸν μόνον παρέσχε τοῖς ἐπιθυμοῦσιν, ἀλλὰ καὶ ἅψασθαι, καὶ φαγεῖν, καὶ ἐμπῆξαι τοὺς ὀδόντας τῇ σαρκί, καὶ συμπλακῆναι, καὶ τὸν πόθον ἐμπλῆσαι πάντα.—Chrysost. in Joann. Hom. xlvi. Tom. VIII. p. 272, Ed. Bened. Paris. 1728.]

[³ This paragraph is entirely omitted in the Emb. edition, 1557.—The catechism referred to is that set forth in the year 1548, translated from the Latin of Justus Jonas, who had translated it from its German original.]

[⁴ Ita cum reverendum altare cœlestibus cibis satiandus ascendis, sacrum Dei tui corpus, et sanguinem fide respice, honora, mirare, mente continge, cordis manu suscipe, et maxime haustu interiore assume.—Corpus Juris Canonici. Gratiani decret. tertia pars. De consecrat. Dist. i. cap. xxxv. "Quia corpus." Tom. col. 1928. Ed. Lugd. 1618.]

[⁵ Mowes, i. e. wry-mouths, distorted faces, grimaces.]

[⁶ That it maketh, Orig. ed. Winch.]

[⁷ His leaves forgetting, Orig. ed. Winch.]

mention of the catechism by him translate, the original whereof confuteth these two parts of this book in few words, being printed in Germany, wherein, besides the matter written, is set forth in picture the manner of the ministering of this sacrament; where is the altar with candle light set forth, the priest apparelled after the old sort, and the man to receive kneeling, bare-head, and holding up his hands, whiles the priest ministereth the host to his mouth, a matter as clear contrary to the matter of this book, as is light and darkness, which now this author would colour with speeches of authors in a book written to instruct rude children; which is as slender an excuse as ever was heard, and none at all, when the original is looked on.

Emissen, to stir up men's devotion coming to receive this sacrament, requireth the root and foundation thereof in the mind of man as it ought to be, and therefore exhorteth men to take the sacrament with the hand of the heart, and drink with the draught of the inward man, which men must needs do that will worthily repair to this feast. And as Emissen speaketh these devout words of the inward office of the receiver, so doth he in declaration of the mystery shew how the invisible priest with his secret power by his word doth convert the visible creatures into the substance of his body and blood, whereof I have before entreated. The author upon these words devoutly spoken by Emissen saith: "There is required no corporal presence of Christ's precious body in the sacrament;" continuing in his ignorance what the word "corporal" meaneth. But to speak of Emissen, if by his faith the very body and blood of Christ were not present upon the altar, why doth he call it a reverend altar? Why to be fed there with spiritual meat[8]? and why should faith be required to look upon the body and blood of Christ that is not there on the altar, but, as this author teacheth, only in heaven? And why should he that cometh to be fed, honour these mysteries[9] there? And why should Emissen allude to the hand of the heart, and draught of the inward man, if the hand of the body and draught of the outward man had none office there? All this were vain eloquence, and a mere abuse and illusion, if the sacramental tokens were only a figure. And if there were no presence but in figure, why should not Emissen rather have followed the plain speech of the angel to the women that sought Christ, Jesum quæritis, non est hic; "Ye seek Jesus, he is not here;" and say as this author doth, This is only a figure, do no worship here, go up to heaven; and down with the altar, for fear of illusion?—which Emissen did not, but called it a reverend altar, and inviteth him that should receive to honour that food with such good words as before, so far discrepant from this author's teaching as may be; and yet from him he taketh occasion to speak against adoration.

Emissenus.

237.

CANTERBURY.

Here for lack of good matter to answer, you fall again to your accustomed manner, trifling away the matter with mocking and mowing. But if you thought your doctrine good, and mine erroneous, and had a zeal to the truth and to quiet men's consciences, you should have made a substantial and learned answer unto my words. For dallying and playing, scolding and mowing, make no quietness in men's consciences. And all men that know your conditions, know right well, that if you had good matter to answer, you would not have hid it, and passed over the matter with such trifles as you use in this place. And St John Chrysostom you skip over, either as you saw him not, or as you cared not how slenderly you left the matter.

And as concerning the Catechism, I have sufficiently answered in my former book. But in this place may appear to them that have any judgment, what pithy arguments you make, and what dexterity you have in gathering of authors' minds, that would gather my mind and make an argument here of a picture, neither put in my book, nor by me devised, but invented by some fond painter or carver, which paint and grave whatsoever their idle heads can fancy. You should rather have gathered your argument upon the other side, that I mislike the matter, because I left out of my book the picture that was in the original before. And I marvel you be not ashamed to allege so vain a matter against me, which indeed is not in my book, and if it were, yet were it nothing to the purpose. And in that Catechism I teach not, as you do, that the body and blood of Christ is contained in the sacrament, being reserved, but that in the ministration thereof we receive the body and blood of Christ; whereunto if it may please you to add or understand this word "spiritually," then is the doctrine of my Catechism sound and good in all men's ears, which know the true doctrine of the sacraments.

The Catechism.

[8 Meats, Orig. ed. Winch.]   [9 Those mysteries, ibid.]

Emissen.

As for Emissen, you agree here with me, that he speaketh not of any receiving of Christ's body and blood with our mouths, but only with our hearts. And where you say, that you have entreated before, "how the invisible priest with his secret power doth convert the visible creatures into the substance of his body and blood," I have in that same place made answer to those words of Emissen, but most plainly of all in my former book, the twenty-fifth leaf[1]. And Emissen saith not that Christ is corporally present in the sacrament, and thereof you be not ignorant, although you do pretend the contrary, which is somewhat worse than ignorance.

Corporal. 238.

And what this word "corporal" meaneth, I am not ignorant. Marry, what you mean by "corporal" I know not, and the opening thereof shall discuss the whole matter. Tell therefore plainly without dissimulation or coloured words, what manner of body it is that Christ hath in the sacrament? Whether it be a very and perfect man's body, with all the members thereof, distinct one from another, or no? For that understand I to be a man's corporal body, that hath all such parts, without which may be a body, but no perfect man's body: so that the lack of a finger maketh a lack in the perfection of a man's body. Marry, if you will make Christ such a body as bread and cheese is, (wherein every part is bread and cheese, without form and distinction of one part from another,) I confess mine ignorance, that I know no such body to be a man's body. Now have I shewed mine ignorance: declare now your wit and learning. For sure I am that Christ hath all those parts in heaven; and if he lack them in the sacrament, then lacketh he not a little of his perfection. And then it cannot be one body that hath parts and hath no parts.

Reverend altar.

And as concerning the words of Emissen, calling the altar a "reverend altar," those words prove no more the real presence of Christ in the altar, than the calling of the font of baptism a "reverend font," or the calling of marriage "reverend matrimony," should conclude that Christ were corporally present in the water of baptism, or in the celebration of matrimony. And yet is not Christ clearly absent in the godly administration of his holy supper, nor present only in a figure, (as ever you untruly report me to say;) but by his omnipotent power he is effectually present by spiritual nourishment and feeding, as in baptism he is likewise present by spiritual renewing and regenerating. Therefore where you would prove the corporal presence of Christ by the reverence that is to be used at the altar, as Emissen teacheth, with no less reverence ought he that is baptized to come to the font, than he that receiveth the communion cometh to the altar: and yet is that no proof that Christ is corporally in the font. And whatsoever you have here said of the coming to the altar, the like may be said of coming to the font. For although Christ be not corporally there, yet, as St Hierome saith[2], if the sacraments be violated, then is he violated whose sacraments they be.

*Hieronymus in Malachiam, cap. 1.

Now followeth after in my book the manner of adoration in the sacrament.

Chap. ix.

The adoration in the sacrament. *De adoratione lege Roffen. et Œcol. Lib. iii. cap. 4, 5[4].

Now it is requisite to speak something of the manner and form of worshipping of Christ[3] by them that receive this sacrament, lest that in the stead of Christ himself be worshipped the sacrament. For as his humanity, joined to his divinity, and exalted to the right hand of his Father, is to be worshipped of all creatures in heaven, earth, and under the earth; even so if in the stead thereof we worship the signs and sacraments, we commit as great idolatry as ever was, or shall be to the world's end.

The simple people be deceived.

And yet have the very antichrists (the subtlest enemies that Christ hath) by their fine inventions and crafty scholastical divinity deluded many simple souls, and brought them to this horrible idolatry, to worship things visible, and made with their own hands, persuading them that creatures were their Creator, their God, and their Maker.

[1 This occurs in the second book, against the Error of Transubstantiation. See below, p. 268.]

[2 Hieron. in Malachiam, cap. i. Tom. VI. p. 233. Ed. Francof. 1638.]

[3 Christ himself, 1551. Orig. ed. reads with 1580.]

[4 See note, p. 173.]

For else what made the people to run from their seats to the altar, and from altar to altar, and from sacring[5] (as they called it) to sacring, peeping, tooting, and gazing at that thing which the priest held up in his hands, if they thought not to honour that thing which they saw? What moved the priests to lift up the sacrament so high over their heads; or the people to cry to the priest, "Hold up! hold up!" and one man to say to another, "Stoop down before;" or to say, "This day have I seen my Maker;" and, "I cannot be quiet, except I see my Maker once a-day?" What was the cause of all these, and that as well the priest as the people so devoutly did knock and kneel at every sight of the sacrament, but that they worshipped that visible thing which they saw with their eyes, and took it for very God? For if they worshipped in spirit only Christ, sitting in heaven with his Father, what needed they to remove out of their seats to toot and gaze, as the apostles did after Christ, when he was gone up into heaven? If they worshipped nothing that they saw, why did they rise up to see? Doubtless, many of the simple people worshipped that thing which they saw with their eyes.

And although the subtle papists do colour and cloke the matter never so finely, saying that they worship not the sacraments which they see with their eyes, but that thing which they believe with their faith to be really and corporally in the sacraments; yet why do they then run from place to place, to gaze at the things which they see, if they worship them not, giving thereby occasion to them that be ignorant to worship that which they see? Why do they not rather quietly sit still in their seats, and move the people to do the like, worshipping God in heart and in spirit, than to gad about from place to place to see that thing, which they confess themselves is not to be worshipped?

And yet, to eschew one inconvenience, (that is to say, the worshipping of the sacrament,) they fall into another as evil, and worship nothing there at all. For they worship that thing (as they say) which is really and corporally, and yet invisibly present under the kinds of bread and wine, which (as before is expressed and proved) is utterly nothing. And so they give unto the ignorant occasion to worship bread and wine, and they themselves worship nothing there at all.

WINCHESTER.

As touching the adoration of Christ's flesh in the sacrament, which adoration is a true confession of the whole man, soul[6] and body, if there be opportunity of the truth of God in his work, is in my judgment well set forth in the book of common prayer, where the priest is ordered to kneel and make a prayer in his own, and the name of all that shall communicate, confessing therein that is prepared there; at which time nevertheless that is not adored that the bodily eye seeth, but that which faith knoweth to be there invisibly present, which and there be nothing, as this author now teacheth, it were not well. I will not answer this author's eloquence, but his matter, where it might hurt.

*Adoration.
*What true adoration is.

CANTERBURY.

Whereas I have shewed what idolatry was committed by means of the papistical doctrine concerning adoration of the sacrament, because that answer to my reasons you cannot, and confess the truth you will not, therefore you run to your usual shift, passing it over with a toy and scoff, saying, that you "will not answer mine eloquence, but the matter;" and yet indeed you answer neither of both, but under pretence of mine eloquence you shift off the matter also. And yet other eloquence I used not, but the accustomed speech of the homely people, as such a matter requireth.

[5 Sacring, i.e. consecrating. But technically it is applied to the lifting up of the consecrated bread for the people to worship.]

[6 Whole man's soul, Orig. ed. Winch.]

And where you say, that "it were not well" to worship Christ in the sacrament, "if nothing be there," (as you say I teach,) if you mean that Christ cannot be worshipped but where he is corporally present, (as you must needs mean, if your reason should be to purpose,) then it followeth of your saying, that we may not worship Christ in baptism, in the fields, in private houses, nor in no place else where Christ is not corporally and naturally present. But the true teaching of the holy catholic church is, that although Christ, as concerning his corporal presence, be continually resident in heaven, yet he is to be worshipped not only there, but here in earth also, of all faithful people, at all times, in all places, and in all their works.

Hear now what followeth further in my book.

<small>August. in Psal. xcviii.</small>

But the papists, for their own commodity to keep the people still in idolatry, do often allege a certain place of St Augustine upon the Psalms, where he saith, that "no man doth eat the flesh of Christ, except he first worship it," and that "we do not offend in worshipping thereof, but we should offend if we should not worship it[1]."

That is true which St Augustine saith in this place. For who is he that professeth Christ, and is spiritually fed and nourished with his flesh and blood, but he will honour and worship him, sitting at the right hand of his Father, and render unto him from the bottom of his heart all laud, praise, and thanks, for his merciful redemption?

And as this is most true, which St Augustine saith, so is that most false, which the papists would persuade upon St Augustine's words, that the sacramental bread and wine, or any visible thing, is to be worshipped in the sacrament. For St Augustine's mind was so far from any such thought, that he forbiddeth utterly to worship Christ's own flesh and blood alone, but in consideration and as they be annexed and joined to his divinity. How much less then could he think or allow that we should worship the sacramental bread and wine, or any outward or visible sacrament, which be shadows, figures, and representations of Christ's flesh[2] and blood!

And St Augustine was afraid, lest in worshipping of Christ's very body we should offend; and therefore he biddeth us, when we worship Christ, that we should not tarry and fix our minds upon his flesh, which of itself availeth nothing, but that we should lift up our minds from the flesh to the spirit, which giveth life: and yet the papists be not afraid by crafty means to induce us to worship those things which be signs and sacraments of Christ's body.

But what will not the shameless papists allege for their purpose, when they be not ashamed to maintain the adoration of the sacrament by these words of St Augustine? Wherein he speaketh not one word of the adoration of the sacrament, but only of Christ himself.

And although he say, that Christ gave his flesh to be eaten of us, yet he meant not that his flesh is here corporally present, and corporally eaten, but only spiritually. As his words declare plainly, which follow in the same place, where St Augustine, as it were in the person of Christ, speaketh these words:

"It is the spirit that giveth life, but the flesh profiteth nothing. The words which I have spoken unto you be spirit and life. That which I have spoken, understand you spiritually. You shall not eat this body which you see, and drink that blood which they shall shed that shall crucify me. I have commended unto you a sacrament: understand it spiritually, and it shall give

---

[1] Nemo autem illam carnem manducat, nisi prius adoraverit: inventum est quemadmodum adoretur tale scabellum pedum Domini, et non solum non peccemus adorando, sed peccemus non adorando. August. in Psalm. xcviii. Tom. VIII. p. 452. Ed. Paris. 1635.]

[2] Christ's very flesh, 1551, and Orig. ed. Winch.]

you life. And although it must be visibly ministered, yet it must be invisibly understand³."

These words of St Augustine, with the other before recited, do express his mind plainly, that Christ is not otherwise to be eaten than spiritually, (which spiritual eating requireth no corporal presence,) and that he intended not to teach here any adoration, either of the visible sacraments or of any thing that is corporally in them. For indeed there is nothing really and corporally in the bread to be worshipped, although the papists say that Christ is in every consecrated bread.

WINCHESTER.

As in the wrong report of St Augustine, who speaking of the adoration of Christ's flesh, Augustinus. *given to be eaten, doth so fashion his speech, as it cannot with any violence be drawn to such an understanding, as though St Augustine should mean of the adoring of Christ's flesh in heaven, as this author would have it. St Augustine speaketh of the giving of Christ's flesh to us to eat, and declareth after that he meaneth in the visible sacrament; which must be invisibly understanded and spiritually, not as the Capernaites did understand Christ's words, carnally to eat that body cut in pieces; and therefore there may be no such imaginations to eat Christ's body after the manner he walked here, nor drink his blood as it was shed upon the cross; but it is a mystery and sacrament that is godly of God's work, supernatural above man's understanding, and therefore spiritually understanded shall give life, which life carnal understanding must needs exclude. And by these my words I think I declare truly St Augustine's meaning of the truth of this sacrament, wherein Christ giveth truly his flesh to be eaten, the flesh he spake of before taken of the virgin. For the spiritual understanding that St Augustine speaketh of, is not to exclude the truth of God's work in the sacrament, but to exclude carnal imagination from musing of the manner of the work, which is in mystery such as a carnal man cannot comprehend. In which matter if St Augustine had had such a faith of the visible sacrament, as the author⁴ saith himself hath now of late, and calleth it catholic; St Augustine would have uttered it, as an expositor, plainly in this place, and said, there is but a figure of Christ's body: Christ's body and flesh is in heaven, and not in this visible sacrament: Christ's speech that was esteemed so hard, was but a figurative speech: and where Christ said, "This is my body," he meant only of the figure of his body: which manner of saying St Augustine useth not in this place; and yet he could speak plainly, and so doth he, declaring us first the truth of the flesh that Christ giveth to be eaten, that is to say, the same flesh that he took of the virgin. And yet because Christ giveth it not in a visible manner, nor such a manner as the Capernaites thought on, nor such a manner as any carnal man can conceive; being also the flesh⁵ in the sacrament, given not a common flesh, but a lively, godly, and spiritual flesh; therefore St Augustine useth words and speech whereby he denieth the gift of that body of Christ which we did see, and of the blood that was shed, so as by affirmation and denial so near together of the same to be given, and the same not to be given, the mystery should be thus far opened, that for the truth of the thing given it is the same, and touching the manner of the giving and the quality of the flesh given it is not the same. And because it is the same, St Augustine saith before we must worship it; and yet because it is now an hidden godly mystery, we may not have carnal imaginations of the same, but godly, spiritually, and invisibly understand it.*

CANTERBURY.

As concerning the words of St Augustine, which you say I do wrong report, let every indifferent reader judge, who maketh a wrong report of St Augustine, you or I: 242. for I have reported his words as they be, and so have not you. For St Augustine August. in saith not, that Christ's body is eaten in the visible sacrament, as you report, but that "Christ hath given us a sacrament of the eating of his body," which must be

---

[³ "Spiritus est qui vivificat, caro autem nihil prodest. Verba quæ locutus sum vobis, spiritus est et vita." Spiritaliter intelligite quod locutus sum. Non hoc corpus quod videtis manducaturi estis, et bibituri illum sanguinem quem fusuri sunt qui me crucifigent. Sacramentum aliquod vobis commendavi: spiritaliter intellectum vivificabit vos. Etsi necesse est illud visibiliter celebrari, oportet tamen invisibiliter intelligi. Ib.]

[⁴ This author, 1551.]

[⁵ The flesh given in the sacrament, Orig. ed. Winch.]

understand invisibly and spiritually, as you say truly in that point. But to the spiritual eating is not required any local or corporal presence in the sacrament, nor St Augustine saith not so, as you in that point unjustly report him: and although the work of God in his sacraments be effectual and true, yet the working of God in the sacraments is not his working by grace in the water, bread, and wine, but in them that duly receive the same, which work is such as no carnal man can comprehend.

And where you say, that "if St Augustine had meant as I do, he would in this place have declared a figure, and have said, that here is but a figure, and we eat only a figure, but Christ himself is gone up into heaven and is not here," it is too much arrogancy of you to appoint St Augustine's words, what he should say in this place, as you would lead an hound in a line where you list, or draw a bear to the stake. And here still you cease not untruly to report me. For I say not, that in the Lord's supper is but a figure, or that Christ is eaten only figuratively; but I say, "that there is a figure, and figurative eating." And doth not St Augustine sufficiently declare a figure in Christ's words, when he saith, "that they must be understand spiritually?" And what man can devise to express more plainly, both that in Christ's speech is a figure, and that his body is not corporally present, and corporally eaten, than St Augustine doth in a thousand places, but specially in his epistle *ad Bonifacium, ad Dardanum, ad Januarium, de Doctrina Christiana, de Catechisandis rudibus, in Quest. super Levit. de Civitate Dei, contra Adimantum, contra Adversarium legis et prophetarum, in Epistolam et Evangelium Johannis, in Sermone ad infantes, et de Verbis apostoli*? The flesh of Christ is a true flesh, and was born of a woman, died, rose again, ascended into heaven, and sitteth at the right hand of his Father; but yet is he eaten of us spiritually, and in the manner of the eating, there is the mystery and secret, and yet the true work of God.

And where you understand the invisible mystery, which St Augustine speaketh of, to be in the diversity of the body of Christ, seen or not seen, you be far deceived. For St Augustine speaketh of the mystery that is in the eating of the body, and not in the diversity of the body, which in substance is ever one without diversity. The meaning therefore of St Augustine was this, that when Christ said, "Except you eat the flesh of the Son of man, you shall not have life in you," he meant of spiritual and not carnal eating of his body. For if he had intended to have described the diversity of the manner of Christ's body visible and invisible, he would not have said, "This body which you see," but this body in such manner as you see it, or in such like terms, you shall not eat. But to eat Christ's flesh, saith St Augustine, is fruitfully to remember that the same flesh was crucified for us. And this is spiritually to eat his flesh and drink his blood.

John vi.

*August. de Doct. Christiana, Lib. iii. cap. 4.

WINCHESTER.

243.

Hieron. ad Ephesios.

And because St Hierome, who was of St Augustine's time, writeth in his commentaries upon St Paul, ad Ephesios, that may serve for the better opening hereof, I will write it in here. The words be these: "The blood and flesh of Christ is two ways understanded, either the spiritual and godly, of which himself said, 'My flesh is verily meat, and my blood is verily drink; and unless ye eat my flesh and drink my blood, ye shall not have everlasting life:' or the flesh which was crucified and the blood which was shed by the spear. According to this division, the diversity of flesh and blood is taken in Christ's saints, that there is one flesh that shall see the salvation of God, another flesh and blood that cannot possess the kingdom of heaven[1].*" These be St Hierome's words. In which thou, reader, seest a denial of that flesh of Christ to be given, to be eaten, that was crucified, but the flesh given to be eaten to be a godly and spiritual flesh; and a distinction made between them, as is in our flesh; of which it may be said, that the flesh we walk in here shall not see God, that is to say, as it is corruptible, according to the text*

[1 Dupliciter vero sanguis Christi et caro intelligitur, vel spiritualis illa atque divina, de qua ipse dixit, "Caro mea vere est cibus, et sanguis meus vere est potus;" et, "nisi manducaveritis carnem meam, et sanguinem meum biberitis, non habebitis vitam æternam:" vel caro et sanguis quæ crucifixa est, et qui militis effusus est lancea. Juxta hanc divisionem et in sanctis ejus diversitas sanguinis et carnis accipitur, ut alia sit caro quæ visura est salutare Dei, alia caro et sanguis quæ regnum Dei non queant possidere. Hieron. in Ephesios, cap. i. v. 7. Tom. IX. p. 163. Ed. Francof. 1684.]

of St Paul, "Flesh and blood shall not possess heaven," and yet[2] we must believe and hope with 1 Cor. xv.
Job truly, "that the same our flesh shall see God in heaven:" after which division likewise we receive not in the sacrament Christ's flesh that was crucified, being so a visible and mortal flesh, but Christ's flesh glorified, incorruptible, and impassible, a godly and spiritual flesh. And so that is but one in substance, and always so that same one is nevertheless for the alteration in the manner of the being of it divided, and so called not the same; wherein St Hierome and St Augustine used both one manner of speaking: and St Hierome, resembling the division that he rehearseth of Christ's flesh to the division of our flesh in the resurrection, doth more plainly open how the same may be called not the same, because we believe certainly the resurrection of the same flesh we walk in, and yet it shall be by the garment of incorruptibility not the same in quality; and so be verified the scriptures "that flesh shall not possess heaven," and, "I shall see God in my flesh." And here I will note to the reader, by the way, St Hierome writeth this distinction of Christ's flesh as a matter agreed on, and then in catholic doctrine received, not of his invention, but in the catholic faith as a principle established; which declareth the belief to have been of that very godly and spiritual flesh given really in the sacrament: for else to eat only in faith is specially[3] to remember Christ's flesh as it was visibly crucified, wherein was accomplished the oblation for our sin[4]; and St Paul willeth us in the supper to shew forth and profess the death of Christ, for so Christ would have his death continually expressed till his coming: and if St Hierome with other should have meant of the eating of Christ as he sitteth in heaven reigning, this distinction of Christ's flesh were an idle matter and out of purpose, to compare the distinction in it to be like the distinction of our flesh to enter into heaven, and not to enter into heaven, the same and not the same. And thus I say that this place of St Hierome sheweth so evidently both his and St Augustine's faith, that wrote at the same time, as there cannot be desired a more evident matter.

CANTERBURY.

To what purpose you should bring in here this place of St Hierome, (making much against you and nothing for you,) I cannot conceive. For he declareth no more in this place, but that as all men in this world have passible bodies, subject to much filthiness, corruption, and death, and yet after our resurrection we shall be delivered from corruption, vileness, weakness, and death, and be made incorruptible, glorious, mighty, and spiritual: so Christ's body in earth was subject unto our infirmities, his flesh being crucified, and his blood being shed with a spear, which now, as you truly say, is "glorified, impassible, incorruptible, and a spiritual" body; but yet not so spiritual that his humanity is turned into his divinity, and his body into his soul, as some heretics fantasy, nor that the diversity of his members be taken away, and so left without arms and legs, head and feet, eyes and ears, and turned into the form and fashion of a bowl, as the papists imagine. The sun and the moon, the fire and the air, be bodies, but no man's bodies, because they lack heart and lungs, head and feet, flesh and blood, veins and sinews to knit them together. When Christ was transfigured, his face shined like the sun, and with his mouth he spake to Moyses and Helias. And after his resurrection we read of his flesh and bones, his hands and feet, his side and wounds, visible and palpable, and with mouth, tongue, and teeth, he did eat and speak; and so like a man he was in all proportions and members of man, that Mary Magdalene could not discern him from a gardener. And take away flesh and skin, sinews and bones, blood and veins, and then remaineth no man's body. For take away distinction and diversity of parts and members, how shall Peter be Peter, and Paul be Paul? How shall a man be a man, and a woman a woman? And how shall we see with our eyes, and hear with our ears, grope with our hands, and go with our feet? For either we shall do no such things at all, or see with every part of our bodies, and likewise hear, speak, and go, if there be no diversity of members. This I have spoken for this purpose, to declare that St Hierome, speaking of Christ's divine and spiritual flesh, excludeth not thereby any corporal member that pertaineth to the substance of a man's natural body, but that now being glorified, it is the same in all parts that it was before. And that same flesh, being first born mortal of the virgin Mary, and now being glorified

Spiritual body.

244.

Matt. xvii.

Luke xxiv.
John xx.

John xx.

[[2] And yet notwithstanding, Orig. ed. Winch.]
[[3] Is spiritually, Ibid.]

[[4] For our sins, Ibid.]

and immortal, as well the holy fathers did eat before he was born, and his apostles and disciples whiles he lived with us here in earth, as we do now when he is glorified. But what availeth all this to your purpose, except you could prove, that to a spiritual eating is required a corporal presence?

And where you say, that "St Hierome and St Augustine use both one manner of speaking," that is not true. For St Hierome speaketh of the diversity of the body of Christ, and St Augustine of the diversity of eating thereof. And yet here is to be noted by the way, that you say, we receive not in the sacrament Christ's flesh that was crucified: which your words seem to agree evil with Christ's words, who the night before he was crucified declared to his disciples, that he gave them the same body that should suffer death for them. And the apostles received the body of Christ, yet passible and mortal, which the next day was crucified; and if we receive not in the sacrament the body that was crucified, then receive we not the same body that the apostles did. And here in your idle talk you draw by force St Hierome's words to the sacrament, when St Hierome speaketh not one word of the sacrament in that place: let the reader judge.

And here, for the conclusion of the matter, you fantasy and imagine such novelties, and wrap them up in such dark speeches, that we had need to have Joseph or Daniel to expound your dreams. But to make a clear answer to your dark reason, the body of Christ is glorified and reigneth in heaven; and yet we remember with thankful minds, that the same was crucified and emptied of blood for our redemption: and by faith to chaw and digest this in our hearts is to eat his flesh and to drink his blood. But your brain rolleth so in fantasies, that you wot not where to get out, and one of your sayings impugneth another. For first you say, that "we receive not in the sacrament the flesh that was crucified," and now you say that "we receive him not as he sitteth in heaven and is glorified," and so must you needs grant that we receive him not at all.

WINCHESTER.

But to return to St Augustine touching adoration: if the very flesh of Christ were not in the sacrament truly present, which is as much to say, as in substance present; if it were not in deed present, that is to say really present; if it were not corporally present, that is to say, the very body of Christ there present, God and man; if these truths consenting in one were not there, St Augustine would never have spoken of adoration there. No more he doth, saith this author, there, but in heaven: let St Augustine's words, quoth I, be judge, which be these: "No man eateth that flesh but he first worshippeth it. It is found out how such a footstool of the Lord's foot should be worshipped, and not only that we do not sin in worshipping, but we do sin in not worshipping it." These be St Augustine's words, which, I said before, cannot be drawn to an understanding of the worshipping of Christ's flesh in heaven, where it remaineth continually glorified, and is of all men christened continually worshipped. For as St Paul saith: "Christ is so exalted that every tongue should confess, that our Saviour Christ is in the glory of his Father." So as the worshipping of Christ there, in the estate of his glory where he reigneth, hath neither "afore" ne "after," but an "ever" continual worshipping in glory. Wherefore St Augustine, speaking of a "before," must be understanded of the worshipping of Christ's flesh present in the sacrament, as in the dispensation of his humility, which Christ ceaseth not to do reigning in glory: for although he hath finished his humble patible conversation, yet he continueth his humble dispensation in the perfection of his mystical body; and as he is our invisible priest for ever, and our advocate with his Father, and so for us to him a mediator, to whom he is equal; so doth he vouchsafe in his supper which he continueth to make an effectual remembrance of his offering for us, of the new testament confirmed in his blood, and by his power maketh himself present in this visible sacrament, to be therein of us truly eaten, and his blood truly drunken, not only in faith, but with the truth and ministry of our bodily mouth, as God hath willed and commanded us to do: which presence of Christ in this humility of dispensation to relieve us and feed us spiritually, we must adore, as St Augustine saith, before we eat; and "we do not sin in adoring, but we sin in not adoring," remembering the divine nature unite unto Christ's flesh, and therefore of flesh not severed from the Godhead. Which admonishment of St Augustine declareth he meant not of the worshipping of Christ's flesh in heaven, where can be no danger of such a thought, where all tongues confess Christ to be in the

OF THE EATING AND DRINKING.

glory of his Father; of which Christ, as he is there in glory continually to be worshipped, it were a cold saying of St Augustine to say, "We do not sin in worshipping Christ in heaven, but sin in not worshipping him[1]*," as though any could have doubted whether Christ should be worshipped in his humanity in heaven, being inseparably unite to the divinity. And when I say, in his humanity, I speak not properly as that mystery requireth; for as Christ's person is but one of two perfect natures, so the adoration is but one, as Cyril declareth it, and therefore abhorreth the addition of a syllable to speak of co-adoration. And will this author attribute to St Augustine such a grossness to have written and given for a lesson, that no man sinneth to worship Christ's flesh in heaven reigning in glory? Wherefore taking this to be so far from all probability, I said before, these words of St Augustine cannot be drawn with any tenters to stretch so far as to reach to heaven, where every christian man knoweth and professeth the worshipping of Christ in glory, as they be taught also to worship him in his dispensation*[2] *of his humility, when he maketh present himself in this sacrament, whom we should not receive into our mouth before we adore him. And by St Augustine's rule, we not only not sin in adoring, but also sin in not adoring him.*

CANTERBURY.

Where you speak of the adoration of Christ in the sacrament, saying, "that if he were not there present, substantially, really, and corporally, St Augustine would never have spoken of adoration there;" in this word "there," you use a great doubleness and fallax, for it may be referred indifferently either to the adoration, or to the presence. If it be referred to the presence, then it is neither true, nor St Augustine saith no such thing, that Christ is really, substantially, and corporally present there. If it be referred to the worshipping, then it is true, according to St Augustine's mind, that there in the receiving of the sacrament in spirit and truth, we glorify and honour Christ sitting in heaven at his Father's right hand. But to this adoration is required no real, substantial, and corporal presence, as before I have declared: for so did Jacob worship Christ before he was born, and all faithful christian people do worship him in all places wheresoever they be, although he carnally and corporally be far distant from them; as they daily honour the Father and pray unto him, and yet say, *Qui es in cœlis*, confessing him to be in heaven. And therefore, to avoid all the ambiguity and fallax of your speech, I say, that we being here do worship here Christ, being not corporally here, but with his Father in heaven.

246. There. Gen. xxviii. Matt. vi.

And although all christian men ought of duty continually to worship Christ being in heaven, yet because we be negligent to do our duties therein, his word and sacraments be ordained to provoke us thereunto: so that, although otherwise we forgat our duties, yet when we come to any of his sacraments, we should be put in remembrance thereof. And therefore said Christ, as St Paul writeth, "As often as you shall eat this bread and drink this cup, shew forth the Lord's death until he come." And, "Do this," said Christ, "in remembrance of me." And the worshipping of Christ in his glory should be ever continual, without either "before" or "after." Nevertheless, forasmuch as by reason of our infirmity, ingratitude, malice, and wickedness, we go far from our offices and duties herein, the sacraments call us home again, to do that thing which before we did omit, that at the least we may do at some time that which we should do at all times.

1 Cor. xi. Luke xxii.

And where you speak of the humiliation of Christ in the sacrament, you speak without the book. For the scripture termeth not the matter in that sort, but calleth his humiliation only his incarnation and conversation with us here in earth, being obedient even unto death, and for that humiliation he is now from that time forward exalted for ever in glory: and you would pluck him down from his glory to humiliation again. And thus is Christ entreated, when he cometh to the handling of ignorant lawyers, blind sophisters, and popish divines; but the true worshippers of Christ worship him in spirit, sitting in his high glory and majesty, and pluck him not down from thence, corporally to eat him with their teeth, but "spiritually in heart ascend up," as St Chrysostom saith, "and feed upon him where he sitteth in his high throne of glory with his Father." To which spiritual feeding is required no bodily

Humiliation. Phil. ii.

[1 Worshipping, as though, Orig. ed. Winch.]   [2 In this dispensation, Ibid.]

presence, nor also mouth nor teeth; and yet they that receive any sacrament, must adore Christ, both before and after, sitting in heaven in the glory of his Father. And this is neither, as you say it is, a cold nor gross teaching of St Augustine in this place, to worship the flesh and humanity of Christ in heaven: nor your teaching is not so far from all doubts, but that you seem so afraid yourself to stand to it, that when you have said, that Christ is "to be worshipped in his humanity," as it were to excuse the matter again, you say you "speak not properly."

247.

St Augustine's doctrine is necessary. Psal. xcviii.

And this doctrine of St Augustine was very necessary for two considerations. One is for the exposition of the psalm, which he took in hand to declare, where in one verse is commanded to worship the earth, being God's footstool; and this he saith may be understand in the flesh of Christ, which flesh being earth, and the food of faithful christian people, is to be worshipped of all that feed and live by him. For notwithstanding that his flesh is earth of earth, and a creature, and that nothing ought to be worshipped but God alone; yet is found out in Christ the explication of this great doubt and mystery, how flesh, earth, and a creature, both may and ought to be worshipped: that is to say, when earth and flesh being united to the Godhead in one person, is one perfect Jesu Christ, both God and man. And this is neither a cold nor gross saying of St Augustine, but an explication of the divine and high mystery of his incarnation.

The other cause, why it is necessary both to teach and to exhort men to honour Christ's flesh in heaven, is this, that some know it not, and some do it not. For some heretics have taught, that Christ was but a man, and so not to be honoured. And some have said, that although he be both God and man, yet his divinity is to be honoured, and not his humanity. For extirpation of which errors, it is no gross nor cold saying, that Christ's flesh in heaven is to be honoured. And some know right well, that whole Christ, God and man, ought to be honoured with one entire and godly honour, and yet forgetting themself in their facts, do not according to their knowledge; but treading the Son of God under their feet, and despising the blood, whereby they were sanctified, crucify again the Son of God, and make him a mockingstock to all the wicked. And many professing Christ, yet having vain cogitations and fantasies in their heads, do worship and serve antichrist, and thinking themselves wise, become very fools indeed. And count you it then a cold and a gross saying, that Christ in heaven is to be honoured; wherein so many old authors have travailed and written so many books, and wherein all godly teachers travail from time to time? And yet bring you here nothing to prove, that St Augustine spake of the real presence of Christ's flesh in the sacrament, and not of Christ being in heaven, but this your "cold and gross" reason.

Heb. x.
Heb. vi.

And this will serve to answer also the place here following of St Ambrose, who spake not of the worshipping of Christ only at the receiving of the sacrament, but at all times and of all reasonable creatures, both men and angels.

WINCHESTER.

And for the more manifest confirmation that St Augustine ought thus to be understood, I shall bring in St Ambrose's saying, of whom it is probable St Augustine to have learned that he writeth in this matter.

Ambrosius de Spiritu sancto, Lib. iii. cap. 12.

St Ambrose's words, in his book De Spiritu Sancto, Lib. iii. cap. 12., *be these:* Non mediocris igitur quæstio, et ideo diligentius consideremus quid sit scabellum. Legimus enim alibi: "Cœlum mihi thronus, terra autem scabellum pedum meorum." Sed nec terra adoranda nobis, quia creatura est Dei. Videamus tamen ne terram illam dicat adorandam propheta, quam Dominus Jesus in carnis assumptione suscepit. Itaque per scabellum terra intelligitur, per terram autem caro Christi, quam hodie quoque in mysteriis adoramus, et quam apostoli in Domino Jesu, ut supra diximus, adorarunt. Neque enim divisus Christus, sed unus[1]. *Which words may be Englished thus:* "It is therefore no mean question, and therefore we should more diligently consider, what is the footstool. For we read in another

248.

[[1] Ambros. de Spiritu Sancto, Lib. iii. cap. 12. Tom. IV. p. 123. Ed. Col. Agrip. 1616. The Orig. ed. Winch. omits the words "be these."]

place, 'Heaven is my throne, and the earth the footstool of my feet.' But yet the earth is not to be worshipped of us, because it is a creature of God. And yet let us see though lest the prophet mean that earth to be worshipped, which our Lord Jesus took in the taking of flesh. So then by the footstool let the earth be understood, and then by the earth the flesh of Christ, which we do now worship also in the mysteries, and which the apostles, as we have before said, worshipped in our Lord Jesu; for Christ is not divided, but one." Hitherto St Ambrose, whereby may appear how St Ambrose and St Augustine took occasion to open their faith and doctrine touching adoration, upon discussion of the self-same words of the prophet David. And St Ambrose expressly noteth our adoration in the mysteries where we worship Christ's flesh invisibly present, as the apostles did, when Christ was visibly present with them. And thus with these so plain words of St Ambrose consonant to those of St Augustine, and the opening of St Augustine's words as before, I trust I have made manifest, how this author travaileth against the stream, and laboureth in vain to writhe St Augustine to his purpose in this matter. The best is in this author, that he handleth St Augustine no worse than the rest, but all after one sort, because they be all of like sort against his new catholic faith, and confirm the old true catholic faith, or do not improve it. For of this high mystery the authors write some more obscurely and darkly than other, and use diversities of speeches and words, wherewith the true doctrine hath been of a very few impugned, but ever in vain, as I trust in God this shall be most in vain[2], having this author uttered such untruths with so much blind ignorance, as this work well weighed and considered, (that is to say, who made it, when he made it, and of like how many were, or might have been and should have been, of counsel in so great a matter, who, if they were any[3], be all reproved in this one work,) all such circumstances considered, this book may do as much good to relieve such perplexity, as alteration hath engendered, and so do as good service in the truth[4], as was meant thereby to hinder and impair it. And this shall suffice for an answer to this fourth book.

CANTERBURY.

Here appeareth your sincerity in proceeding in this matter. For you leave out those words of St Ambrose, which maketh his meaning plain, that the prophet spake of the mystery of Christ's incarnation: *Si negant quia in Christo etiam incarnationis adoranda mysteria sunt, &c.*: "If they deny," saith he, "that the mysteries of the incarnation in Christ be to be honoured, &c." And a little after: *Qua ratione ad incarnationis dominicæ sacramentum spectare videatur, quod ait propheta, Adorate scabellum pedum ejus, consideremus*: "Let us consider by what means this saying of the prophet, 'Worship his footstool,' may be seen to pertain to the sacrament of Christ's incarnation." And after the words by you rehearsed, followeth by and by: *Cum igitur incarnationis adorandum sit sacramentum, &c.*: "Seeing then that the sacrament of the incarnation is to be honoured." In these words sheweth St Ambrose plainly, that the worshipping of Christ's flesh is understand of the mystery of his incarnation. So that St Ambrose meant, not only that men should worship Christ when they receive the sacrament, but that all creatures, at all times, should worship him. And therefore, he expresseth there by name, how the angels did worship him, and also Mary Magdalene and the apostles after his resurrection, when they received not the sacrament. And so did also the shepherds and the wise men worship him, yet being in his infancy: and the prophet, after the mind of St Augustine and St Ambrose, commanded to honour him before his incarnation; and we likewise honour him sitting now in heaven after his ascension. For so far is faith able to reach, without either tentering or stretching.

Matt. xxviii.
Luke ii.
Matt. ii.

249.

Thus have I answered to all that you have brought against my fourth book, not obscurely, as you like a cuttle have done, hiding yourself in your dark colours, but plainly to the capacity of all men as much as I can. And this have I done with some pain of writing, but little or no study for the matter, being a very easy thing for defence of the truth to answer by God's word, and ancient authors, to an ignorant lawyer, being well exercised in neither of both, but making such divinity as he can dream in his sleep, or devise of his own brain, or hath sucked out of the papistical laws and decrees, and, for lack of arguments, furnishing up his book with pretty toys, with glorious boasting, and scornful taunting; and with picking out of my book such

---

[² In God shall be most in vain, Orig. ed. Winch.]

[³ If there were any, Ibid.]
[⁴ To the truth, 1551.]

sentences, as he persuadeth himself, that he can make some colour of apparent answer, to deceive the reader. And such places as he seeth his rhetoric will not serve, he passeth them away slightly, because he is afraid to file his hands therewith. Wherefore, I may now right well and justly conclude here mine answer to his confutation, with the words of my fourth book, which be these:

<small>Matt. xxiv.</small>

But our Saviour Christ himself hath given us warning beforehand, that such false Christians and false teachers should come, and hath bid us to beware of them, saying: "If any man tell you that Christ is here, or Christ is there, believe him not. For there shall rise false Christs, and false prophets, and shall shew many signs and wonders, so that if it were possible, the very elect should be brought into error. Take heed, I have told you beforehand."

Thus our Saviour Christ, like a most loving Pastor and Saviour of our souls, hath given us warning beforehand of the perils and dangers that were to come, and to be wise and ware, that we should not give credit unto such teachers as would persuade us to worship a piece of bread, to kneel to it, to knock to it, to creep to it, to follow it in procession, to lift up our hands to it, to offer to it, to light candles to it, to shut it up in a chest or box, to do all other honour unto it, more than we do unto God; having alway this pretence or excuse for our idolatry, "Behold, here is Christ." But our Saviour Christ calleth them false prophets, and saith: "Take heed, I tell you before; believe them not. If they say to you, Behold, Christ is abroad, or in the wilderness, go not out: and if they say, that he is kept in close places, believe them not."

<small>Matt. xxiv.</small>

<small>Chap. x. They be the papists that have deceived the people.</small>

And if you will ask me the question, Who be these false prophets and seducers of the people? the answer is soon made: The Romish antichrists and their adherents; the authors of all error, ignorance, blindness, superstition, hypocrisy, and idolatry.

<small>Innocentius tertius.</small>

<small>Honorius tertius.</small>

For Innocentius the third, one of the most wicked men that ever was in the see of Rome, did ordain and decree, that the host should be diligently kept under lock and key[1]. And Honorius the third not only confirmed the same, but commanded also, that the "priests would[2] diligently teach the people from time to time, that when they lifted up the bread, called the host, the people should then reverently bow down; and that likewise they should do when the priest carrieth the host unto sick folks[3]." These be the statutes and ordinances of Rome, under pretence of holiness, to lead the people unto all error and idolatry; not bringing them by bread unto Christ, but from Christ unto bread.

<small>250.</small>

<small>Chap. xi. An exhortation to the true honouring of Christ in the sacrament.</small>

But all that love and believe Christ himself, let them not think that Christ is corporally in the bread; but let them lift up their hearts unto heaven, and worship[4] him, sitting there at the right hand of his Father. Let them worship him in themselves, whose temples they be, in whom he dwelleth and liveth spiritually: but in no wise let them worship him, as being corporally in the bread. For he is not in it, neither spiritually, as he is in man, nor corporally, as he is in heaven, but only sacramentally, as a thing may be said to be in the figure, whereby it is signified. Thus is sufficiently reproved the third principal error of the papists concerning the Lord's supper, which is, "That wicked members of the devil do eat Christ's very body, and drink his blood."

Thus endeth the Fourth Book.

[1 Statuimus ut in cunctis ecclesiis chrisma et eucharistia sub fideli custodia clavibus adhibitis conserventur. Decret. Concil. Lateran. iv. cap. xx. anno 1215. Labbei Conc. Tom. XXII. p. 1007.]

[2 Should, 1551, and Orig. ed.]

[3 Sacerdos vero frequenter doceat plebem suam, ut cum in celebratione missarum elevatur hostia salutaris, se reverenter inclinet, idem faciens cum eam defert presbyter ad infirmum. Decretal. Lib. III. Tit. xli.]

[4 Worshipping, edit. 1580.]

THE CONFUTATION OF THE SECOND BOOK.

[WINCHESTER.]

HAVING declared how much against all truth this author would bear in hand, that the real presence, the corporal presence, and substantial presence of Christ's most precious body and blood in the sacrament is not the true catholic doctrine, but a device of the papists, which is a term wherewith this author doth uncharitably charge the king's true subjects, among whom he knoweth a great many to be of that faith he calleth now papish: but setting words apart and to come to the matter, as I have shewed this author to err partly by wilfulness, partly by ignorance in the understanding of the old authors concerning the true real presence of Christ's body and blood in the sacrament; so I trust to shew this author overseen in the article of transubstantiation. For entry whereunto, first I say this, that albeit the word transubstantiation was first spoken of by public authority in that assembly of learned men of Christendom in a general council[5], where the bishop of Rome was present[6], yet the true matter signified by that word was older and believed before upon the true understanding of Christ's words, and was in that council confessed, not for the authority of the bishop of Rome, but for the authority of truth, being the article such as toucheth not the authority of the bishop of Rome, but the true doctrine of Christ's mystery, and therefore in this realm, the authority of Rome ceasing, was also confessed for a truth by all the clergy of this realm in an open council[7], specially discussed; and though the hardness of the law that by parliament was established of that and other articles hath been repelled, yet that doctrine was never hitherto by any public council, or any thing set forth by authority, impaired, that I have heard: wherefore methinketh this author should not improve it by the name of the bishop of Rome, seeing we read how truth was uttered by Balaam and Caiaphas also: and St Paul teacheth the Philippians, that whether it be by contention or envy, so Christ be preached, the person should not impair the opening of truth, if it be truth, which Luther indeed would not allow for truth, impugning the article of transubstantiation, not meaning thereby, as this author doth, to impair the truth of the very presence of Christ's most precious body in the sacrament of the altar, as is aforesaid, in the discussion of which truth of transubstantiation I for my part should be special defended by two means, wherewith to avoid the envious name of papist. One is, that Zuinglius himself, who was no papist, as is well known, nor good christian man, as some said, neither, saith plainly, writing to Luther in the matter of the sacrament: "It must needs be true, that if the body of Christ be really in the sacrament, there is of necessity transubstantiation also." Wherefore seeing by Luther's travail, who favoured not the bishop of Rome neither, and also by evidence of the truth, most certain and manifest, it appeareth that according to the true catholic faith Christ is really present in the sacrament, it is now by Zuinglius' judgment a necessary consequence of that truth to say there is transubstantiation also; which shall be one mean of purgation, that I defend not transubstantiation as depending of the bishop of Rome's determination, which was not his absolutely, but of a necessity of the truth, howsoever it liketh Duns or Gabriel[8] to write in it, whose sayings this author useth for his pleasure. Another defence is, that this author himself saith "that it is over great an absurdity to say, that bread insensible," with many other terms that he addeth, "should be the body of Christ;" and therefore I think, that the "is," that is to say, the inward nature and essence of that Christ delivered in his supper to be eaten and drunken, was of his body and blood, and not of the bread and wine, and therefore can well agree with this author, that the bread of wheat is not the body of Christ, nor the body of Christ made of it as of a matter; which considerations will enforce him that believeth the truth of the presence of the substance of Christ's body, as the true catholic faith teacheth, to assent to transubstantiation, not as determined by the church of Rome, but as a consequent of truth believed in the mystery of the sacrament: which transubstantiation how this author would impugn, I will without quarrel of envious words consider, and, with true opening of his handling the matter, doubt not to make the reader to see that he fighteth against the truth.

I will pass over the unreverent handling of Christ's words, "This is my body," which words

[Num. xxi. John xi. Orig. ed. Winch.]

Zuinglius.

251.

[5 The fourth General Council of Lateran, A.D. 1215.]

[6 Innocentius III.]

[7 This was held in 1539, at which Cranmer vehemently opposed the passing of the Six Articles.]

[8 Duns Scotus or Gabriel Biel.]

I heard this author (if he be the same that is named) once rehearse more seriously in a solemn and open audience[1]*, to the conviction and condemnation, as followed, of one that erroneously maintained against the sacrament the same that this author calleth now the catholic faith.*

CANTERBURY.

In this book, which answereth to my second book rather with taunting words than with matter, I will answer the chief points of your intent, and not contend with you in scolding, but will give you place therein.

Papists were the authors of transubstantiation.

First, I charge none with the name of papists, but that be well worthy thereof. For I charge not the hearers, but the teachers, not the learners, but the inventors of the untrue doctrine of transubstantiation; not the king's faithful subjects, but the pope's darlings, whose faith and belief hangeth of his only mouth. And I call it their doctrine, not only because they teach it, but because they made it, and were the first finders of it.

And as in the third book, concerning the real presence of Christ's body and blood in the sacrament, you have not shewed my ignorance or wilfulness, but your own; so do you now much more in the matter of transubstantiation: "which word," say you, "albeit the same was first spoken of in the general council, where the bishop of Rome was present, yet the true matter signified by that word was older." Here at the first brunt you confess, that the name of "transubstantiation" was given at the council: so that either the matter was not before, (as it was not in deed,) or at the least it was before a nameless child, as you do grant, until the holy father Innocent the third, which begat it, assembled a company of his friends as godfathers to name the child. And by what authority the council defined the matter of "transubstantiation," it may easily appear. For authority of scripture have they none, nor none they do allege. And what the authority of the pope was there, all men may see, being present in the same no less than eight hundred abbots and priors, who were all the pope's own children, of him created and begotten.

252. The council in England.

And as for the "confession of all the clergy of this realm in an open council, the authority of Rome ceasing," you speak here a manifest untruth wittingly against your conscience. For you know very well, (and if you will deny it, there be enough yet alive can testify,) that divers of the clergy, being of most godly living, learning, and judgment, never consented to the articles which you speak of. And what marvel was it, that those articles (notwithstanding divers learned men repugning,) passed by the most voices of the parliament? seeing that although the authority of Rome was then newly ceased, yet the darkness and blindness of errors and ignorance that came from Rome still remained, and overshadowed so this realm, that a great number of the parliament had not yet their eyes opened to see the truth. And yet how that matter was enforced by some persons, they know right well that were then present. But after, when it pleased almighty God more clearly to shine unto us by the light of his word, our eyes by his goodness were opened, darkness discussed, and that which was done in ignorance and darkness, was by knowledge and light in public council reversed and taken away, as well concerning the doctrine as the hardness of the law. For if the doctrine had been true and godly, there is no christian-hearted man, but he would have desired the establishment and continuance thereof. But the doctrine being false, and such as came only from Rome, they be not worthy to be likened to those truths which came from God, and were uttered by Balaam and Caiaphas, but to be numbered among those lies which came from his vicar, who,

John viii. when he speaketh lies, *ex propriis loquitur*, "he speaketh properly of himself."

And the bishop of Rome was not clean gone out of England, as soon as the laws were made against his authority, but remained still by his corrupt doctrine, as I fear me he doth yet in some men's hearts, who were the chief procurers and setters forthward of the foresaid law. But yet is all together to be imputed to the bishop of Rome, forasmuch as from thence came all the foresaid errors, ignorance, and corruption, into these parties.

Now where you take upon you here to purge yourself of papistry by me and

---

[1 The allusion of Winchester is here made to the disputation before Henry VIII. A. D. 1538, held by Lambert, in which Cranmer took a part.— Vide Foxe's Acts and Monuments, Vol. II. p. 425. Ed. Lond. 1631, and Examination before Brookes.]

Zuinglius, if you have no better compurgators than us two, you be like to fail in your purgation. For neither of us, I dare say, durst swear for you in this matter, though Zuinglius were alive. Or if your purgation stand to this point, that Christ called not bread made of wheat his body, (although in a formal and proper speech bread is not in deed his body,) you may be as rank a papist as ever was, for any purgation you can make by this way. For Christ called bread made of wheat his body, as the words of the evangelists plainly declare, and all old writers teach; and in your book of the "Devil's Sophistry," you have confessed, saying, that "Christ made demonstration of bread, when he said, 'This is my body.'" And therefore bring some better purgation than this; or else had you been better not to have offered any purgation in a matter that no man charged you withal, than by offering a purgation, and failing therein, to bring yourself into more suspicion.

And whereas in fortification of your matter of transubstantiation, you make your argument thus, that "forasmuch as the body of Christ is really in the sacrament, there is of necessity transubstantiation also;" this your argument hath two great faults in it. The first is, that your antecedent is false, and then you cannot conclude thereof a true consequent. The second fault is, that although the antecedent were granted unto you, "that the body of Christ is really in the sacrament," yet the consequent cannot be inferred thereof, "that there is of necessity transubstantiation." For Christ can make his body to be present in the sacrament, as well with the substance of the bread as without it, and rather with the substance of bread than with the accidents; forasmuch as neither Christ's body there occupieth any place, as you say yourself, nor no more doth the substance of bread by itself, but by means of the accidents, as you say also. *253. Real presence proveth no transubstantiation.*

Now forasmuch as you say, that "you will pass over the unreverent handling of Christ's words, which you heard me once more seriously rehearse in solemn open audience;" I acknowledge that not many years passed I was yet in darkness concerning this matter, being brought up in scholastical and Romish doctrine, whereunto I gave too much credit. And therefore I grant, that you have heard me stand and defend the untruth, which I then took for the truth; and so did I hear you at the same time. But praise be to the everliving God, who hath wiped away those Saulish scales from mine eyes! and I pray unto his divine Majesty with all my heart, that he will likewise do once the same to you. Thy will be fulfilled, O Lord! *I erred once in this matter. Acts ix.*

But forasmuch as you "pass over my handling of Christ's words," (as you use commonly to pass in post when you have no direct answer to make,) I shall here repeat my words again; to the intent that the indifferent reader may presently see how I have handled them, and then judge whether you ought so slenderly to pass them over as you do.

My words be these:

The second book[2].

Thus have you heard declared four things, wherein chiefly the papistical doctrine varieth from the true word of God, and from the old catholic christian faith in this matter of the Lord's supper. *[Book ii.] Chap. i. The confutation of the error of transubstantiation.*

Now, (lest any man should think that I feign any thing of mine own head without any other ground or authority) you shall hear by God's grace as well the errors of the papists confuted, as the catholic truth defended, both by God's most certain word, and also by the most old approved authors and martyrs of Christ's church.

And first, that bread and wine remain after the words of consecration, and be eaten and drunken in the Lord's supper, is most manifest by the plain words of Christ himself, when he ministered the same supper unto his disciples. For, as the evangelists write, "Christ took bread, and brake it, and gave it to his disciples, and said: Take, eat, this is my body." *Chap. ii. The papistical doctrine is contrary to God's word. Matt. xxvi. Mark xiv. Luke xxii.*

[2 The title of this book runs thus in the Orig. ed. "The second Book is against the error of Transubstantiation."]

Here the papists triumph of these words, when Christ said: "This is my body:" which they call the words of consecration. For, say they, as soon as these words be fully ended, there is no bread left, nor none other substance, but only Christ's body. When Christ said "this," the bread, say they, remained. And when he said "is," yet the bread remained. Also, when he added "my," the bread remained still. And when he said "bo," yet the bread was there still. But when he had finished the whole sentence, "This is my body," then, say they, the bread was gone, and there remained no substance but Christ's body; as though the bread could not remain when it is made a sacrament. But this negative, that there is no bread, they make of their own brains, by their unwritten verities, which they most highly esteem[1].

Oh, good Lord! how would they have bragged, if Christ had said, "This is no bread!" But Christ spake not that negative, "This is no bread;" but said affirmingly, "This is my body;" not denying the bread, but affirming that his body was eaten, meaning spiritually, as the bread was eaten corporally.

And that this was the meaning of Christ, appeareth plainly by St Paul, in the tenth chapter to the Corinthians, the first epistle, where he, speaking of the same matter, saith: "Is not the bread which we break the communion of the body of Christ?" Who understood the mind of Christ better than St Paul, to whom Christ shewed his most secret counsels? And St Paul is not afraid, for our better understanding of Christ's words, somewhat to alter the same, lest we might stand stiffly in the letters and syllables, and err in mistaking the sense and meaning[2]. For whereas our Saviour Christ brake the bread, and said, "This is my body;" St Paul saith, "that the bread which we break is the communion of Christ's body." Christ said, "his body;" and St Paul said, "the communion of his body:" meaning, nevertheless, both one thing, "that they which eat the bread worthily, do eat spiritually Christ's very body." And so Christ calleth the bread his body, as the old authors report, because it representeth his body, and signifieth unto them which eat that bread according to Christ's ordinance, that they do spiritually eat his body, and be spiritually fed and nourished by him, and yet the bread remaineth still there as a sacrament to signify the same. But of these words of consecration shall be spoken hereafter more at large.

Therefore, to return to the purpose: that the bread remaineth, and is eaten in this sacrament, appeareth by the words of Christ, which he spake before the consecration[3]. For that Christ "took bread, and brake it, and gave it to his disciples, and said, Take, eat;" all this was done and spoken before the words of consecration. Wherefore they must needs be understood of the very bread, that Christ took bread, brake bread, gave bread to his disciples, commanding them to take bread and eat bread. But the same is more plain and evident of the wine, that it remaineth, and is drunken at the Lord's supper, as well by the words that go before, as by the words that follow after the consecration. For, before the words of consecration, Christ took the cup of wine, and gave it unto his disciples, and said, "Drink ye all of this:" and after the words of consecration followeth, "They drank all of it."

Now I ask all the papists, what thing it was that Christ commanded his disciples to drink, when he said, "Drink ye all of this?" The blood of Christ was not yet there by their own confession; for these words were spoken[4]

[1 The Orig. ed. omits the words, "which they most highly esteem." The 1551 ed. for "most," reads "must."]

[2 And err in mistaking of Christ's words, Or. ed.]

[3 By the words which go before the consecration, Orig. ed.]

[4 For it was spoken, Orig. ed.]

before the consecration: therefore it could be nothing else but wine that he commanded them to drink.

Then I ask the papists once again, whether the disciples drank wine or not? If they say, "yea," then let them recant their error, that there was no wine remaining after the consecration. If they say, "nay," then they condemn the apostles of disobedience to Christ's commandment, which drank not wine as he commanded them. Or rather they reprove Christ as a juggler, which commanded his apostles to drink wine; and when they came to the drinking thereof, he himself had conveyed it away. Moreover, before Christ delivered the cup of wine to his disciples, he said unto them: "Divide this among you." *Luke xxii.*

Here I would ask the papists another question, what thing it was that Christ commanded his disciples to divide among them? I am sure they will not say it was the cup, except they be disposed to make men laugh at them. Nor I think they will not say it was the blood of Christ, as well because the words were spoken before the consecration, as because the blood of Christ is not divided, but spiritually given whole in the sacrament. Then could it be understand of nothing else but of wine, which they should divide among them, and drink all together.

Also when the communion was ended, Christ said unto his apostles: "Verily, I say unto you, that I will drink no more henceforth of this fruit of the vine, *Matt. xxvi. Mark xiv.* until that day that I shall drink it new with you in my Father's kingdom." By these words it is clear, that it was very wine that the apostles drank at that godly supper. For the blood of Christ is not the fruit of the vine, nor the accidents of wine, nor none other thing is the fruit of the vine, but the very wine only[5].

How could Christ have expressed more plainly, that bread and wine remain, than by taking the bread in his hands, and breaking it himself, and giving it unto his disciples[6], commanding them to eat it; and by taking the cup of wine in his hands, and delivering it unto them, commanding them to divide it among them, and to drink it; and calling it "the fruit of the vine?" These words of Christ be so plain, that if an angel of heaven would tell us the contrary, he ought not to be believed. And then much less may we believe the subtle lying papists[7].

If Christ would have had us to believe, as a necessary article of our faith, that there remaineth neither bread nor wine, would he have spoken after this sort, using all such terms and circumstances as should make us believe that still there remaineth bread and wine?

What manner of teacher make they of Christ, that say he meant one thing, when his words be clean contrary? What christian heart can patiently suffer this contumely of Christ?

But what crafty teachers be these papists, who devise phantasies of their own heads directly contrary to Christ's teaching, and then set the same abroad to christian people, to be most assuredly believed as God's own most holy word! St Paul did not so, but followed herein the manner of Christ's speaking, in calling of "bread" "bread," and "wine" "wine," and never altering Christ's words herein. "The bread which we break," saith he, "is it not the communion of Christ's body?" *1 Cor. x.*

Now I ask again of the papists, whether he spake this of the bread consecrated or not consecrated? They cannot say that he spake it of the bread

---

[5 But very wine only, Orig. ed.]
[6 And giving unto his disciples, 1551, and Orig. ed.]
[7 Subtle lying of the papists, 1551, and Orig. ed.]

unconsecrated, for that is not the communion of Christ's body by their own doctrine. And if St Paul spake it of bread consecrated, then they must needs confess that after consecration such bread remaineth, as is broken bread, which can be none other than very true material bread. And straightways after, St Paul saith in the same place, that "we be partakers of one bread and one cup." And in the next chapter, speaking more fully of the same matter, four times he nameth the bread and the cup, never making mention of any transubstantiation, or remaining of accidents without any substance; which things he would have made some mention of, if it had been a necessary article of our faith, to believe that there remaineth no bread nor wine. Thus it is evident and plain, by the words of scripture, that after consecration remaineth bread and wine, and that the papistical doctrine of transubstantiation is directly contrary to God's word.

WINCHESTER.

But to the purpose, the simplicity of faith in a christian man's breast doth not so precisely mark and stay at the syllables of Christ's words, as this author pretendeth; and knowing by faith the truth of Christ's words, that as he said he wrought, doth not measure God's secret working after the prolation of our syllables, whose work is in one instant, howsoever speech in us require a successive utterance: and the manner of handling this author useth to bring the mystical words in contempt, were meeter in an ethnick's mouth to jest out all, than to pass the lips of such an author, to play with the syllables after this sort. For although he may read in some blind gloss, that in the instant of the last syllable God's work is to be accompted wrought, being a good lesson to admonish the minister to pronounce all; yet it is so but a private opinion, and reverently uttered, not to put the virtue in the last syllable, nor to scorn the catholic faith: after which manner, taking example of this author, an ethnick should jest of fiat lux, *at* fi *was nothing, and then at* at *was yet nothing, at* lu *was nothing but a little little paring, put an* x *to it, and it was suddenly* lux, *and then the light*[1]. *What christian man would handle either place thus? And therefore, reader, let this entry of the matter serve for an argument, with what spirit this matter is handled: but to answer that this author noteth with an exclamation, "O, good Lord! how would they have bragged if Christ had said, This is no bread!" here I would question with this author, whether Christ said so or no, and reason thus: Christ's body is no material bread: Christ said, "This is my body;" ergo, he said, "This is no bread*[2].*" And the first part of this reason this author affirmeth in the fifty-ninth leaf*[3]. *And the second part is Christ's words; and therefore to avoid this conclusion the only way is to say that Christ's speech was but a figure, which the catholic doctrine saith is false; and therefore, by the catholic doctrine, Christ saying, "This is my body," saith in effect, "This is no bread;" whereat this author saith, "They would brag if Christ had said so." In speech is to be considered that every "yea" containeth a "nay" in it naturally; so as whosoever saith, "This is bread," saith "it is no wine:" whosoever saith, "This is wine," saith, "it is no beer." If a lapidary saith, "This is a diamond," he saith "it is no glass;" he saith "it is no crystal;" he saith "it is no white sapphire." So Christ saying, "This is my body," saith "it is no bread." Which plainness of speech caused Zuinglius to say plainly: "If there be present the substance of the body of Christ, there is transubstantiation;" that is to say, not the substance of bread; and therefore who will plainly deny transubstantiation, must deny the true presence of the substance of Christ's body, as this author doth; wherein I have first convinced him, and therefore use that victory for his overthrow in transubstantiation. I have shewed before how Christ's words were not figurative when he said, "This is my body;" and yet I will touch here such testimony as this author bringeth out of one Hilary*[4], *for the purpose of transubstantiation, in the twenty-fifth leaf of this book*[5], *in these words: "There is a figure," saith Hilary, "for bread and wine be outwardly seen; and there is also a truth of that figure, for the body and blood of Christ be of a truth inwardly believed." These be Hilary's words, as this author allegeth them, who was, he saith, within three hundred and fifty years of Christ. Now I call to thy judgment, good reader, could any man devise more pithy words for the proof of the real presence of Christ's body and blood, and the condemnation of this author, that would have an only figure? Here in Hilary's words is a figure compared to truth, and sight outwardly*

[1 And then light, 1551.]
[2 Is not bread, Orig. ed. Winch.]
[3 Vid. p. 105.]
[4 Out of Hilary, Orig. ed. Winch.]
[5 Vid. p. 272.]

to belief inwardly. Now our belief is grounded upon God's word, which is this: "This is my body;" in which words Hilary testifieth that is inwardly believed is a truth; and the figure is in that is seen outwardly. I take Hilary here as this author allegeth him, whereby I ask the reader, is not this author overthrown, that Christ's speech is not figurative, but true and proper, being inwardly true that we believe? Ye will say unto me, "What is this to transubstantiation, to the reproof whereof it was brought in? because he saith bread and wine is seen[6]." First, I say that it overthroweth this author for truth of the presence of Christ's body, and every overthrow therein overthroweth this author in transubstantiation, not by authority of the church of Rome, but by consequence in truth, as Zuinglius saith, who shall serve me to avoid papistry. If one ask me, "What say ye then to Hilary, that bread and wine is seen[6]?" I say they be indeed seen, for they appear so, and therefore be called so; as Isaac said of Jacob, it was his voice, and yet by his sense of feeling denied him Esau, which was not Esau, but was Jacob, as the voice from within did declare him. If ye will ask me, how can there, according to Hilary's words, be in the outward visible creatures any figure, unless the same be in deed as they appear, bread and wine, I will answer: "Even as well as this outward object of the sensible hairyness of Jacob, resembling Esau, was a figure of Christ's humanity, and of the very humanity in deed." Thus may Hilary be answered, to avoid his authority from contrarying transubstantiation. But this author shall never avoid that himself hath brought out of Hilary, which overthroweth him in his figurative speech, and consequently in his denial of transubstantiation also, as shall appear in the further handling of this matter. Where this author in the eighteenth leaf[7] compareth these St Paul's words, "The bread that we break, is it not the communion of the body of Christ?" to the expounding of Christ's words, "This is my body," I deny that: for Christ's words declared the substance of the sacrament when he said, "This my body;" and St Paul declareth the worthy use of it according to Christ's institution; and by the words, "The bread that we break," doth signify the whole use of the supper, wherein is breaking, blessing, thanksgiving, dispensing, receiving, and eating: so as only breaking is not the communion, and yet by that part in a figure of speech St Paul meaneth all, being the same as appeareth by the scripture, a term in speech, "to go break bread," although it be not always so taken, whereby to signify "to go celebrate our Lord's supper;" and therefore bread in that place may signify the common bread, as it is adhibited to be consecrated; which by the secret power of God turned into the body of Christ, and so distributed and received, is the communion of the body of Christ, as the cup is likewise of the blood of Christ after the benediction, which benediction was not spoken of in the bread, but yet must be understood. As for calling of Christ's bread his body, is to make it his body, who as St Paul saith calleth that is not, as it were, and so maketh it to be.

[Gen. xxvii. Orig. ed. Winch.]

[Primo. Orig. ed. Winch.]

The arguments this author useth in the nineteenth and twentieth leaf[8], of the order of Christ's speeches as the evangelists rehearse them, be captious devices of this author, in case he knoweth what St Augustine writeth; or else ignorance, if he hath not read St Augustine de Doctrina Christiana[9], where he giveth a rule of recapitulation, as he calleth it, when that is told after, that was done afore; and therefore we may not argue so firmly upon the order of the telling in the speech. St Augustine bringeth an example that by order of telling "Adam was in paradise or any tree was brought forth for feeding," with divers other, wherewith I will not encumber the reader. The evangelist rehearseth what Christ said and did simply and truly, which story we must so place in understanding, as we trifle not with the mystery, at staying and stopping of letters and syllables. And therefore though the word "take, eat," go before the words, "This is my body," we may not argue that they took it and eat it afore Christ had told them what he gave them; and all these often rehearsals of bread, with "he took bread," and "brake bread," and "blessed bread," and if ye will add "held bread," all this induce no consequence that he therefore gave bread. For he gave that he had consecrate, and gave that he made of bread. If Christ, when he was tempted to make stones bread, had taken the stones and blessed them and delivered them, saying, "This is bread," had he then delivered stones, or rather that he made of stones bread? Such manner of reasoning useth Peter Martyr, as this author doth, whose folly I may well say he saw not to eschew it, but (as appeareth) rather to follow it. And yet, not content to use this fond reasoning, this author calleth papists to witness that they might laugh at it, because the evangelist telleth the story so as Christ said, "drink," and then told after what it was, this author fancieth that the apostles should be so hasty to drink ere Christ had told them what he gave; which and they had, I think he would have stayed the cup with his hand, or bid them tarry, whiles he had told them more. I will no further

Augustine, Lib. iii. cap. 36.

[6 Are seen, Orig. ed. Winch.]
[7 Vid. p. 242.]
[8 Vid. pp. 242, 243.]

[9 Augustin. De Doctrina Christiana. Lib. III. cap. 36. Pars iv. Ed. Basil. ap. Amberbach.]

travail with this reasoning, which it is pity to hear in such a matter of gravity, of such consequence as it is both in body and soul. We may not trifle with Christ's words after this sort. When St Paul saith, " We be partakers of one bread;" he speaketh not of material bread, but of Christ's body, our heavenly bread, which to all is one, and cannot be consumed, but able to feed all the world: and if this author giveth credit to Theodoretus, whom he calleth an holy man, then shall he never find the sacrament called bread after the sanctification, but the bread of life; the like whereof should be in an epistle of Chrysostom[1], as Peter Martyr allegeth, not yet printed, by whose authority[2] if they have any, as in their place this author maketh much of them, all these arguments be all trifles, for all the naming of bread by Christ, and St Paul, and all other, must be understood before the sanctification and not after. And if thou, reader, lookest after upon Theodoretus and that epistle, thou shalt find true that I say, whereby all this questioning with the papists is only a dallying for this author's pleasure, against his own authors, and all learning.

CANTERBURY.

Where you say, that "the simplicity of faith in a christian man's breast doth not so precisely mark and stay at the syllables of Christ's words, as I pretend," here may the world see what simplicity is in the papists. For I do nothing else but rehearse what the papists say, that "until these words be fully ended, *hoc est corpus meum*, there is bread, and after those words be fully ended, there is no more bread, but only Christ himself." And the same simplicity do you declare by and by to be in yourself, when you say, that "God's work is in one instant, howsoever speech require in us a successive utterance." Then if God change the bread into Christ's body in one instant, tell me, I pray you, in which instant? For seeing that our pronunciation is by succession of time, I think you will not say, that the work of God is done before the last syllable be pronounced, (for then Christ's body should be there before the words of consecration were fully finished,) nor I think you will not deny, but whensoever the words of consecration be fully pronounced, then is Christ's body there. Wherefore by your own judgment you vary not in this matter from the other papists, but must needs say, that God's secret work herein is measured after the prolation of our syllables, and so it is none other person that teacheth to play with syllables in this high mystery, but the papists only. And yourself do teach in this same place, that it is a good lesson to say, that in the instant of the last syllable God's work is to be accounted wrought. And I find it not in blind glosses, but in the chief authors of the papists, that the conversion is not wrought before the whole sentence is finished, *hoc est corpus meum*.

The creation of the world.

And it is no direct answer, but a mere cavillation and illusion, to bring in here the creation of the world, when God said, *fiat lux*, to be a like matter unto transubstantiation. For God's speech requireth no succession of time, as the speech of the priest doth. Therefore this is but a playing, to shew your subtle wit and crafty rhetoric, whereby your spirit may be judged, whether you go about clearly to set forth the truth, or by dark colours and unlike examples to hide and cover it.

259.

This is no bread.

John xix.

And where you question with me, going about by a subtle sophistical argument, to prove that Christ said, "This is no bread," I shall make another argument of the same form, which shall shew how strong your argument is. St John is not the son of the virgin Mary. Christ said to her, "This is thy son;" ergo, he said, "This is not John." The first part I am sure you will affirm in effect. The second part is Christ's words; and as the second part in my argument is a figurative speech, so is it in yours, so that in every point the arguments be like. And therefore as mine argument is naught, so is yours also, and all that you bring in to follow thereof. And if I list to dally, as you do, in such a matter, I could conclude directly against you, that in the sacrament is not Christ's body, thus: "Christ's body is not material bread:" St Paul said, "it is bread:" ergo, he said it is not Christ's body. The first part you affirm, the second part St Paul affirmeth. And therefore to avoid this conclusion, the only way is, to say that Christ's speech was a figurative speech, when he said, "This is my body." For else by the catholic doctrine St Paul, saying that it is bread, saith in effect it is not the body of Christ. Thus may you see what availeth your sophistication, when I am constrained *sophisticari cum sophista, ut ars deludatur arte*.

1 Cor. x. & xi.

[[1] Ad Cæsarium Monachum. Vid. p. 274.]   [[2] Authorities, 1551.]

And of like effect is your argument of "yea" and "nay," when you say, "every yea containeth a nay in it naturally." Therefore Christ, saying it is his body, saith it is no bread. If this form of argument were infallible, then I may turn the same to you again, and overthrow you with your own weapon thus. St Paul said, "it is bread," ergo, it is not Christ's body: if the affirmation of the one be a negation of the other. And by such sophistication you may turn up all the truth quite and clean, and say that Christ was neither God nor man, because he said he was a vine and bread. "And every yea," say you, "containeth a nay in it naturally." Yea and nay.

And where you boast, that you have "convinced me in the matter of the real presence of Christ's body," I trust the indifferent reader will say, that you triumph before the victory, saying that you have won the field, when in deed you have lost it, and when Goliath's head is smitten off with his own sword. But the old English proverb is here true, "that it is good beating of a proud man: for when he is all-to beaten back and bone, yet will he boast of his victory, and brag what a valiant man he is." 1 Sam. xvii.

And it is another vain brag also that you make, when you say, that you "have shewed before, that Christ's words were not figurative, when he said, 'This is my body.'" For you have neither proved that you say, nor have answered to my proofs to the contrary, as I refer to the judgment of all indifferent readers, but you have confessed that Christ called bread his body, and made demonstration upon the bread, when he said, "This is my body." How can then this speech be true, but by a figure, that bread is Christ's body? seeing that in proper speech, as you say, "every yea containeth a nay, and the affirmation of one thing is the denial of another."

And where you allege, as it were against me, the words of Hilary, "that there is both a figure and a truth of that figure;" for answer hereunto the truth is, that your matter here is gathered of an untruth, that I would have only a figure, whereas I say plainly, as Hilary saith, "that in the true ministration of the sacrament is both a figure and a truth: the figure outwardly, and the truth inwardly." For bread and wine be sensible signs and sacraments, to teach us outwardly, what feedeth us inwardly. Outwardly we see and feel bread and wine with our outward senses, but inwardly by faith we see and feed upon Christ's true body and blood. But this is a spiritual feeding by faith, which requireth no corporal presence. And here I ask you two questions. One is this, whether Hilary say that the body of Christ is under the forms of bread and wine, and that corporally? If he say not so, as the reader shall soon judge, looking upon his words, then stand I upright without any fall or foil: for Hilary saith not as you do. The other question is, whether Hilary do not say that there is a figure: let the reader judge also, and see whether you be not quite overthrown with your own crook, in saying that Christ's speech is not figurative. And yet the third question I may add also, why St Hilary should say, that bread and wine be figures, if there be no bread nor wine there at all, but be taken clean away by transubstantiation? And whereas for answer hereto you take the example of Jacob, who for his hairiness resembled Esau, and was, as you say, a figure of Christ's very humanity; you do like an unskilful mariner, that to avoid a little tempest, runneth himself upon a rock. For where you make Jacob, who resembled Esau, and was not he in deed, to be a figure of Christ's humanity, you make by this example, that as Jacob by his hairiness resembled Esau, and was not he in deed, so Christ by outward appearance resembled a man, and yet he was no man in deed. Hilary.
260.

And where you deny that these words of St Paul, "Is not the bread which we break the communion of the body of Christ?" declare the meaning of Christ's words, "This is my body," because Christ's words, say you, "declare the substance, and St Paul's words declare the use:" I deny that Christ's body is the substance of the visible sacrament. For the substance of the sacrament is bread and wine, and the thing thereby signified is Christ's body and blood. 1 Cor. x.

And this is notable which you say, "that these words, 'the bread which we break,' do signify the whole use of the supper, not only breaking, but also blessing, thanksgiving, dispensing, receiving and eating, and that 'bread' in this place signifieth common bread, taken to be consecrated." In which saying it is a world to see the phantasies of men's devices, how uncertain they be in matters pertaining to God. How agreeth this your saying with your doctrine of transubstantiation? For if St Paul, when he said, "the Breaking signifieth the whole use of the supper.

bread which we break, is it not the communion of Christ's body?" meant by "bread," "common bread," and by "breaking," meant also the "blessing, thanksgiving, receiving, and eating," then is common bread "broken, blessed, received, and eaten." And then where becometh your transubstantiation, if common bread be eaten in the sacrament? And when is the bread turned into the body of Christ, if it remain common bread until it be eaten? Yet now you seem to begin something to savour of the truth, that the bread remaineth still in his proper nature, enduring the whole use of the supper.

<small>Rom. iv.</small>

And as touching this place of St Paul, that "God calleth things that be not, as they were," if it pertain unto the sacrament, where Christ called "bread his body," what could you have alleged more against yourself? For if in this place "Christ call that which is not, as it were," then Christ called bread as it were his body, and yet it is not his body in deed.

<small>261.</small>

<small>Whether all the evangelists told the history of the supper out of order.</small>

But in this your answer to the arguments brought in by me out of the very words of the evangelists, is such a shameless arrogancy and boldness shewed, as abhorreth all christian ears for to hear; which is, that "three evangelists, telling the manner of Christ's holy supper, not one of them all do tell the tale in right order, but subvert the order of Christ's doings and sayings, and that in such a necessary matter of our religion, that the definition of the whole truth standeth in the order." "The evangelists," say you, "rehearse what Christ said and did, simply and truly." But is this a simple and true rehearsal of Christ's words and deeds, to tell them out of order, otherwise than Christ did and said them? And St Paul also, if it be as you say, speaking of that same matter, committeth the like error. And yet never no ancient author, expounding the evangelists or St Paul, could spy out this fault, and in their commentaries give us warning thereof. And I am not so ignorant, but I have many times read St Augustine, *De doctrina Christiana*, where he saith: "That sometimes in scripture a thing is told after, that was done before[1]." But St Augustine saith not that it is so in this matter: nor I am not so presumptuous to say that all the three evangelists, with St Paul also, disordered the truth of the story in a matter wherein the truth cannot be known but by the order. St Augustine, *De consensu Evangelistarum*, saith, that "that which Luke rehearseth of the chalice, before the giving of the bread, was spoken by Christ after the distribution of the bread, as the other two evangelists report the same[2]." And if these words, *Hoc est corpus meum*, had been put out of the right place in all the three evangelists, and also in St Paul, would not St Augustine have given warning thereof, as well as of the other? And would all other authors expounding that place have passed over the matter in silence, and have spoken not one word thereof; specially being a matter of such weight, that the catholic faith and our salvation, as you say, hangeth thereof? Do not all the proofs you have, hang of these words, *Hoc est corpus meum*? "This is my body?" And shall you say now, that they be put out of their place? And then you must needs confess, that you have nothing to defend yourself, but only one sentence, and that put out of order, and from his right place, as you say yourself; where in deed the evangelists and apostles, being true rehearsers of the story in this matter, did put those words in the right place. But you, having none other shift to defend your error, do remove the words, both out of the right place and the right sense. And can any man that loveth the truth, give his ears to hear you, that turn upside down both the order and sense of Christ's words, contrary to the true narration of the evangelists, contrary to the interpretation of all the old authors, and the approved faith of Christ's church, even from the beginning, only to maintain your wilful assertions and papistical opinions? So long as the scripture was in the interpretation of learned divines, it had the right sense; but when it came to the handling of ignorant lawyers and sophistical papists, such godly men as were well exercised in holy scripture, and old catholic writers, might declare and defend the truth at their perils: but the papistical sophisters and lawyers would ever define and determine all matters as pleased them.

<small>August. de Consensu Evangelistarum. Lib. iii.</small>

<small>Luke xxii.
Matt. xxvi.
Mark xiv.</small>

<small>262.</small>

[1 Vid. p. 245.]

[2 Hæc et Marcus Lucasque commemorant. Quod enim Lucas de calice bis commemoravit, prius antequam panem daret, deinde posteaquam panem dedit; illud quod superius dixit præoccupavit ut solet: illud vero quod ordine suo posuit, non commemoravera superius.—August. De Consensu Evangelistarum. Lib. III. cap. i. Tom. IV. p. 202. Ed. Paris. 1635.]

But all truths agree to the truth, and falsehood agreeth not with itself: so it is a plain declaration of untruth, that the papists vary so among themselves. For some say that Christ consecrated by his own secret power without sign or words: some say that his benediction was his consecration: some say that he did consecrate with these words, *Hoc est corpus meum;* and yet those vary among themselves: for some say that he spake these words twice, once immediately after benediction, at what time they say he consecrated, and again after when he commanded them to eat it, appointing then to his apostles the form of consecration. And lately came new papists with their five eggs, and say that the consecration is made only with these five words, *Hoc est enim corpus meum.* And last of all come you and Smith with yet your newer devices, saying that Christ spake those words before he gave the bread and immediately after the breaking, manifestly contrary to the order of the text, as all the evangelists report, and contrary to all old authors of the catholic church, which all with one consent say, that Christ gave bread to his apostles, and contrary to the book of common prayer by you allowed, which rehearseth the words of the evangelists thus: "That Christ took bread, and when he had blessed and given thanks, he brake it and gave it to his disciples;" where all the relation is made to the bread. Is this your faithful handling of God's word, for your pleasure to turn the words as you list? Is it not a thing much to be lamented, that such as should be the true setters forth of Christ's gospel, do trifle with Christ's words after this sort, to alter the order of the gospel after their own phantasy? Can there be any trifling with Christ's words, if this be not? And shall any christian man give credit to such corrupters of holy scripture? Have you put upon you harlots' faces, that you be past all shame, thus to abuse God's word to your own vanity?

The variance of the papists in consecration.

Smith.

And be you not ashamed likewise so manifestly to bely me, that I "fancy that the apostles should be so hasty to drink, or Christ had told them what he gave?" whereas by my words appeareth clean contrary, that they drank not before all Christ's words were spoken.

And where you say, "that Christ gave that he had consecrated, and that he made of bread;" here you grant that Christ's body, which he gave to his disciples at his last supper, was made of bread. And then it must follow, that either Christ had two bodies, the one made of the flesh of the virgin Mary, the other of bread, or else that the self-same body was made of two divers matters, and at divers and sundry times. Now what doctrine this is, let them judge that be learned. And it is worthy a note, how inconstant they be that will take upon them to defend an untruth; and how good memories they had need to have, if they should not be taken with a lie. For here you say that Christ's body in the sacrament is made of bread; and in the eleventh comparison you said, that "this saying is so fond, as were not tolerable to be by a scoffer devised in a play, to supply when his fellow had forgotten his part."

Christ's body made of bread.

And where you say that St Paul speaketh not of material bread, but of Christ's body, when he saith, "that we be partakers of one bread," the words of the text be plain against you. For he speaketh of the bread that is broken, whereof every man taketh part, which is not Christ's body; except you will say that we eat Christ's body divided in pieces, as the gross Capernaites imagined. And St Augustine with other old authors do write, that "St Paul spake of such bread as is made of a great multitude of grains of corn gathered together, and united into one material loaf, as the multitude of the spiritual members of Christ be joined together into one mystical body of Christ."

1 Cor. x.

263.

And as concerning Theodoret and Chrysostom, they say as plainly as can be spoken, that the bread remaineth after consecration, although we call it by a more excellent name of dignity, that is to say, by the name of Christ's body. But what estimation of wisdom or learning soever you have of yourself, surely there appeareth neither in you in this place, where upon the alteration of the name of bread you would gather the alteration of the substance, or transubstantiation. Be not kings and emperors very men, although they be ever called by the names of their royal and imperial dignities? Or are they therefore gods, because the prophet calleth them so? And who ever called you a man, sithens you were a bishop? and yet that dignity took not from you the

Chrysostom. Theodoret.

Alteration of names unto dignity.

Psal. lxxxii.

nature of a man. And the pope is a man, although he be called *Julius*, or *Pater sanctissimus*, or *Hypocrita impiissimus*. So is bread still bread, although it represent the body of Christ, and be called in that respect, as a figure, the very body of Christ.

<small>Bread after the sanctification.</small>

And where you say, that "the naming of bread by Christ and St Paul and all other must be understood before the sanctification and not after," St Paul's own words reprove this your saying most manifestly. For he calleth it bread when it is the communion of Christ's body, and when it is eaten, saying: "The bread which we break, is it not the communion of Christ's body?" and, "As often as you eat this bread and drink this cup:" and, "Whosoever eateth the bread and drinketh the cup of the Lord unworthily:" and, "Let a man try himself, and so eat of that bread and drink of the cup:" and, "He that eateth and drinketh unworthily," &c. Now these sayings cannot be understood before the sanctification, except you will grant that the bread was Christ's body, and that it was eaten, before it was sanctified. Wherefore, let every reader that knoweth any thing, judge whether you seek any truth in this matter, or whether you study to search out vain cavillations, and yet the same being clean contrary to the manifest words of holy scripture, and to all approved writers. Wherefore, gentle reader, weigh St Paul's words, whether he call it bread after the sanctification, or only before; and as thou findest St Paul make with this man's saying, that trifleth away the truth, so thou mayest believe him in all other things. Hitherto is discussed how the doctrine of transubstantiation is against God's word: now followeth in my book how the same is against nature, whereof I write thus:

<small>1 Cor. x.</small>

<small>1 Cor. xi.</small>

<small>Chap. III. The papistical doctrine is against reason.</small>

Let us now consider also, how the same is against natural reason and natural operation, which although they prevail not against God's word, yet when they be joined with God's word, they be of great moment to confirm any truth. Natural reason abhorreth *vacuum*, that is to say, that there should be any empty place, wherein no substance should be. But if there remain no bread nor wine, the place were they were before, and where their accidents be, is filled with no substance, but remaineth *vacuum*, clean contrary to the order of nature.

<small>264.</small>

We see also that the wine, though it be consecrated, yet will it turn to vinegar, and the bread will mould; which then be nothing else but sour wine and mouldy bread, which could not wax sour nor mouldy, if there were no bread nor wine there at all.

And if the sacraments were now brent, as in the old church they burned all that remained uneaten, let the papists tell what is brent. They must needs say, that it is either bread or the body of Christ. But bread, say they, is none there; then must they needs burn the body of Christ, and be called Christ-burners, (as heretofore they have burned many of his members,) except they will say, that accidents burn alone without any substance, contrary to all the course of nature.

The sacramental bread and wine also will nourish, which nourishment naturally cometh of the substance of the meats and drinks, and not of the accidents.

The wine also will poison, as divers bishops of Rome have had experiences, both in poisoning of other, and being poisoned themselves; which poisoning they cannot ascribe to the most wholesome blood of our Saviour Christ, but only to the poisoned wine.

And most of all, it is against the nature of accidents to be in nothing. For the definition of accidents is to be in some substance, so that if they be, they must needs be in something; and if they be in nothing, then they be not. And a thousand things more of like foolishness do the papists affirm by their transubstantiation, contrary to all nature and reason: as that two bodies be in one place, and one body in many places at one time; and that substances be gendered of accidents only, and accidents converted into substances; and a body to be in a place and occupy no room; and generation to be without corruption, and corruption without generation; and that substances be made of nothing, and turned into nothing[1], with many such like things, against all order and principles of nature and reason.

WINCHESTER.

In the third chapter written in the twenty-first leaf[2], it troubleth this author that the doctrine of transubstantiation is, in his judgment, against natural reason and natural operation: in the entry of which matter he granteth wisely that they should not prevail against God's word, and yet, he saith, when they be joined with God's words[3], they be of great moment to confirm any truth; wherein if he meaneth to confirm God's word by reason, or God's mysteries by natural operation, mine understanding cannot reach that doctrine, and is more strange to me, than this author maketh transubstantiation to be to him. As for the reason of vacuum declareth a vacuum, that nature abhorreth not. And if we speak after the rules of nature, quantity filleth the place rather than substance. And shortly to answer this author, it is not said in the doctrine of transubstantiation, that there remaineth nothing; for in the visible form of bread remaineth the proper object of every sense truly: that is seen with the bodily eye is truly seen, that is felt is truly felt, that is savoured is truly savoured; and those things corrupt, putrify, nourish, and consume after the truth of the former nature, God so ordering it that create all, using singularly that creature of bread, not to unite it unto him as he did man's nature, to be in bread impanate and breaded, as he was in flesh incarnate. And as for reason in place of service as being inferior to faith, will agree with the faith of transubstantiation well enough. For if our faith of the true presence of Christ's very body be true, as it is most true, grounded upon these words[4] of Christ, "This is my body;" then reason yielding to[5] that truth, will not strive with transubstantiation, but plainly affirm that by his judgment[6], if it be the body of Christ, it is not bread. For in the rule of common reason, the grant of one substance is the denial of another; and therefore reason hath these conclusions throughly, whatsoever is bread is no wine, whatsoever is wine is no milk, and so forth.

265.

*Conclusions of reason.

And therefore being once believed this to be the body of Christ, reason saith by and by, it is not bread by the rule aforesaid, whereby appeareth how reason doth not strive with transubstantiation, being once conquered with faith of the true presence of Christ's body, which is most evident, and no whit darkened by any thing this author hath brought. As for natural operation, is not in all men's judgments as this author taketh it, who seemeth to repute it for an inconvenience, to say that the accidents of wine do sour and wax vinegar. But Ulpian, a man of notable learning, is not afraid to write in the law, In venditionibus, de contrahenda emptione, in the Pandects, that of wine and vinegar there is (prope eadem οὐσία) in manner one substance: wherein he sheweth himself far against this author's skill, which I put for an example to shew that natural operations have had in natural men's judgments divers considerations, one sometime repugnant to another, and yet the authors of both opinions called philosophers all. Among which some thought, for example, they spake wisely, that esteemed all things to alter as swiftly as the water runneth in the stream, and thought therefore no man could utter a word, being the same man in the end of the word that he was when he began to speak, and used a similitude: Like as a man standing in one place cannot touch the same one water twice in a running stream, no more can a man be touched the same man twice, but he altereth as swiftly as doth the stream. These were laughed to scorn, yet they thought themselves wise in natural speculation. Aristotle, that is much esteemed and worthily, fancied a first matter in all things to be one; in which consideration he seemeth to be as extreme in a stay, as the other fond philosophers were in moving. By which two extremities I condemn not natural speculation, wherewith, I think, God pleased for man to marvel in contemplation of his inferior works, and to tame his rash wit in the inexplicable variety of it; but to use it so, as to make it an open adversary to religion, it is meseemeth without all purpose. The doctrine of transubstantiation doth not teach no earthly thing to remain in the sacrament, but contrariwise, that the visible form of bread and wine is there as the visible figure[7] of the sacrament, and to be the same in greatness, in thickness, in weight, in savour, in taste, in propriety also to corrupt, putrify, and nourish as it did before; and yet the substance of those visible creatures to be converted

*Read Smith, fol. 64.

[1 Orig. ed. omits the words, "and that substances be made of nothing and turned into nothing."]
[2 Vid. p. 250.]
[3 Word, 1551.]

[4 Upon the words, Orig. ed. Winch.]
[5 Yielding in. Ibid.]
[6 By her judgment. Ibid.]
[7 Sign. Ibid.]

into the substance, as Emissen saith, of the body of Christ. And here will reason do service to faith, to say if there be a conversion indeed, as faith teacheth, and none of the accidents be converted, then the substance is converted: for in every thing, all is substance and accidents; but the accidents be not changed, and yet a change there is; it must needs be then that substance is changed. Which deduction reason will make, and so agree with transubstantiation in convenient due service. And thus I have gotten reason's good will, whatsoever this author saith, and from the ground of faith have by reason deduced such a conclusion to prove transubstantiation, as unless he destroy the true faith of the presence of Christ's very body, which he cannot, must needs be allowed. And as for natural operation of putrifying, engendering worms, burning, and such experiences, which being the substance of bread absent, this author thinketh cannot be so, when he hath thought thoroughly, he can of his thought conclude it only to be a marvel, and it be so as against the common rules of philosophy, wherein as meseemeth it were a nearer way, as we be admonished to leave searching of "how" of the work of God in the mystery of Christ's presence, being that the celestial part of the sacrament, so not to search "how" in the experience of the operation of nature, of the visible earthly part of the sacrament. When God sent manna in [the] desert, the people saw many marvels in it, besides the common operation of nature, and yet they never troubled themselves with "hows." And as one very well writeth, it is consonant, that as there is a great miracle in the work of God to make there present the substance of the body of Christ, so likewise to knowledge the miracle in the absence of the substance of bread, and both the heavenly and earthly part of the sacrament to be miraculous, and so many miracles to be joined together in one, agreeth with the excellency of the sacrament. As for the objections this author maketh in this matter, be such as he findeth in those scholastical writers that discuss as they may, or labour thereabout wherewith to satisfy idle imaginations, and to make learned men prompt and ready to say somewhat to these trifles, whose arguments this author taketh for his principal foundation. For plain resolution and avoiding whereof, if I would now, for my part, bring forth their solutions and answers, there were a part of school theology, so brought into English, to no great praise of either of our learnings, but our vain labour, to set abroad other men's travails, to trouble rude wits with matter not necessary, and by such unreverent disputing and alteration to hinder the truth. Finally, all that this author rehearseth of absurdity, repugneth in his estimation only to the conclusion of philosophy, which should nothing move the humble simplicity of faith in a christian man, who marvelleth at God's works and reputeth them true, although he cannot comprehend the ways and means of them.

CANTERBURY.

Here in the beginning of this chapter, it is a strange thing to me that you should think strangeness in my saying, that natural reason and operation joined to God's word should be of great moment to confirm any truth: not that they add any authority to God's word, but that they help our infirmity; as the sacraments do to God's promises, which promises in themselves be most certain and true. For did not the eating and drinking of Christ, his labouring and sweating, his agony and pangs of death, confirm the true faith of his incarnation? And did not his eating with the apostles confirm and stablish their faith of his resurrection? Did not the sight of Christ and feeling of his wounds induce Thomas to believe that Christ was risen, when neither the report of the devout woman, nor yet of the apostles which did see him, could cause him to believe Christ's resurrection? And when they took our Saviour Christ for a spirit, did not he cause them by their sight and feeling of his flesh and bones to believe that he was very man, and no spirit, as they phantasied? Which sensible proofs were so far from derogation of faith, that they were a sure establishment thereof. Wherefore if your understanding cannot reach this doctrine, it is indeed very slender in godly things.

And as for my reason of *vacuum*, you have not yet answered thereto, for nature suffereth not any place to be without some substance, which by means of his quantity filleth the place. And quantity without substance to fill any place, is so far from the rules of nature, that by order of nature quantity without substance hath neither filling nor being. And although I do not say, that by the doctrine of transubstantiation there remaineth nothing, (so that all that you speak to answer that matter is to no purpose, but *res vacua*,) yet by the doctrine of transubstantiation joined unto nature, there should remain utterly nothing indeed: for substance remaineth none by your doctrine of transubstantiation, and without substance can be no accidents by the rules of nature. Therefore comparing your doctrine and nature together, either you must recant your doctrine of transubstantiation, or confess that nothing remaineth, or at the least grant that your teaching repugneth to the order of nature; which sufficeth for me in this place, where my purpose is only to shew how the doctrine of transubstantiation is against nature and reason.

Now where you so often speak of the visible form of bread remaining, by this word "form" you sweetly deceive yourself, thinking that it doth much advance your faith of transubstantiation, understanding by that word the accidences, similitudes, and likeness without substance remaining, misunderstanding both holy scripture and the ancient doctors. St Paul, speaking of Christ's incarnation, saith, that "he being in form of God, did humble himself, taking upon him the form of man." By which words St Paul meant not that Christ was like unto God, and not God in deed, nor yet that he was like unto man, and not very man in deed, but that he was and is very God and very man, having two substances, one of his Godhead, and the other of his manhood, united together in one person. And the ancient doctors writing of this sacrament, when they speak of the forms of bread and wine, do use this vocable "form," as St Paul useth it, to signify very bread and very wine, or the substances of bread and wine, and not the similitude or likeness of bread and wine without the substances, as you fantasy and imagine.

267. The word form. Phil. ii.

And you, after this sort wrasting holy scriptures and doctors for maintenance of your error of transubstantiation, do lead yourself craftily into another heinous error, (if this your proposition be true, that the grant of one substance is a denial of any other,) which is, to deny Christ either to be very God or man. For by your sentence, if he in substance be God, then can he not have the substance of man: for the grant of one substance is a denial of any other, as ye say.

And like as ye do err in misunderstanding of the scripture and doctors, so do you err in reason and judgment of things; your own eyes, nose, mouth, and fingers, bearing witness against you of your wilful error and folly. For what man is living, which hath his right wits, that can believe as you teach, that the proper object of every sense remaineth, that is to say, colour, taste, savour, &c., and yet the former substance of bread and wine is gone? And here, to further your belief of transubstantiation, you do exaggerate your accustomed absurdity of impanation of Christ's body; as if every man that believeth not your error of transubstantiation must of necessity fall into the error of impanation, or as if I defended the said impanation. But whether I defended any such fond opinion or no, or whether I have herein sufficiently answered the papists, I refer to the judgment of all wise and learned men, that be any thing indifferent, which have read my book.

Impanation.

And as concerning natural reason, where you say it will agree with the doctrine of transubstantiation well enough, if the faith of the true presence of Christ's very body be true: for answer hereto I say, that if your phantastical belief of the real presence of Christ's natural body in the sacrament were as true as the gospel, (as none opinion can be more erroneous and fond,) yet would both faith and reason judge that there were still bread: faith, because holy scripture manifestly saith so; reason, because it is so, not only to all our senses, but also in all the effects and operations of bread. And reason cannot discern but that Christ's body may be as well present with the substance of bread, as with the accidents, and that rather also, forasmuch as you confess yourself, that after the rules of nature quantity filleth the place rather than substance. And so may reason judge the body of Christ to be the body of Christ, and yet the bread to be the bread still, and wine to be wine and no bread, nor none other confusion of natures to be there against reason.

268.

And as touching natural operation, in the handling thereof you shew your ignorance in natural philosophy, which teacheth that in mutation from one quality to another is required one substance to receive both the qualities. For white of itself cannot be made black, nor cold hot; but one substance may be now hot, now cold;

now black, now white: as cold water may be made hot, although cold in itself cannot be hot. Therefore you cannot blame me, to think in this a great inconvenience and absurdity in nature, that sweetness of itself should change into sourness, when the substance of wine is gone, and no substance remaining to receive this mutation, this matter being so clean contrary to the precepts and rules of natural philosophy.

<small>Ulpian.</small>

And I marvel that you cannot see how much Ulpian, whom you allege, maketh against yourself, and with my saying, that both in wine and vinegar remaineth substance, which is changed from sweet to sour; so that the sweet of itself is not made sour, but that substance which before was sweet is after sour. And therefore what great skill you have in citing of Ulpian, to prove that the accidents of wine without substance do sour and wax vinegar, let the wise reader judge.

But Ulpian seemeth to me to have another sense than all men can perceive: but I will not discuss the mind of Ulpian, because I am no lawyer, lest you should cast the proverb in my teeth, *Ne sutor ultra crepidam*.

But to what purpose you should bring in the diversity of judgments in natural operations, and the extreme fondness of philosophers, some in moving, some in staying, I cannot devise, except it be the permission of God, that as some of the philosophers by their fond opinions in nature made themselves laughing-stocks to all men, of reason so should ye papists do. And yet so much more is the papistical opinion of transubstantiation to be laughed to scorn of all men, as it passeth the fondness of all the philosophers, and that so far, that the fondest of the philosophers would have laughed at it, and have clapped it out of their schools with one consent, as an opinion more meet for frantic and mad men than for men of natural reason. And as fond opinions as some philosophers had, yet was there none that so far erred in reason to say, that accidences might stand without any substance; but all with one uniform consent agreed, that accidences had none other being or remaining but in their substances. And yet if the faith of our religion taught us the contrary, then reason must yield to faith. But your doctrine of transubstantiation is as directly contrary to the plain words of scripture as it is against the order of natural reason.

And where you say that the doctrine of transubstantiation doth not teach, that no earthly thing remaineth, but that "the visible form of bread and wine remaineth the same in greatness, in thickness, in weight, in savour, in taste, in property also to corrupt, putrify, and nourish, as it did before," tell plainly, I pray you, what thing it is which you call the visible form of bread and wine, whether it be an accidence or a substance; and if it be an accidence, shew whether it be a quantity or quality, or what other accidence it is, that all men may understand what thing it is which, as you say, is the same greatness, thickness, weight, savour, and other properties.

<small>269.</small>

<small>Emissen.</small>

And where you allege Emissen for the conversion of the substance of bread and wine, this conversion, as Emissen saith, and as I have declared before, is like to our conversion in baptism, where outwardly is no alteration of substance, (for no sacramental alteration maketh alteration of the substance,) but the marvellous and secret alteration is inwardly in our souls. And as the water in baptism is not changed, but sacramentally, (that is to say, made a sacrament of spiritual regeneration, which before was none,) so in the Lord's supper neither the substance nor accidences of bread and wine be changed, but sacramentally; but the alteration is inwardly in the souls of them that spiritually be refreshed and nourished with Christ's flesh and blood. And this our faith teacheth us, and natural reason doth good service to faith herein against your imagined transubstantiation. So that you have not gotten reasons, goodwill, nor consent to your vain doctrine of transubstantiation, although you had proved your real presence; which hitherto you have not done, but have taken great pain to shoot away all your bolts in vain, missing quite and clean both the prick and the whole butt.

And yet in the end you take a good ready way for your own advantage, like unto a man that had shot all his shafts clean wide from the butt, and yet would bear all men in hand that he had hit the prick. And when other should go about to measure how far his shafts were wide from the butt, he would take up the matter himself, and command them to leave measuring, and believe his own saying, that his arrows stuck all fast in the mark, and that this was the nearest way to finish the contention: even so do you in this matter, willing all men to leave searching of "how" in the mystery of Christ's presence in the sacrament, saying that to be the nearest way. And it were a much nearer way for you indeed, if all men would leave searching of "how," and without ground or reason believe as well your transubstantiation as your corporal presence of Christ's body, only because you do say it is so. But St Peter requireth every christian man to be ready to render a reason of his 1 Pet. iii. faith to every one that asketh; and St Paul requireth in a christian bishop, that he Tit. i. should be "able to exhort by wholesome doctrine, and to convince the gainsayers," and not to require other men to give faith unto him without asking of "how," or "why," only because he saith so himself. The old catholic authors tell, wherefore Christ called bread his body, and how christian people fed of his body. And the blessed virgin Luke i. Mary asked how she should conceive a child, never having company with man. And you tell yourself how Christ is in heaven, how in us, and how in the sacrament, declaring all to be but after a spiritual manner. And what manner of men be you, that we may not ask you "how," to render a reason of your transubstantiation, being a matter by you only devised, clearly without God's word.

But at length, when you have sweat well-favouredly in answering to mine arguments of natural reason and natural operation, you be fain to confess a great part to be true, and to turn altogether into miracles, and that into such kind of miracles, as the old catholic writers never knowledged nor touched in none of their works. For besides the chief miracle, which you say is in the conversion of the substance of bread into the substance of Chirst's body, and of the wine into his blood, there be other miracles, when the forms of wine turn into vinegar, and when bread mouldeth, or a man doth vomit it, or the mouse eateth it, or the fire burneth it, or worms breed in it, and in all like chances, God still worketh miracles, yea, even in poisoning with the consecrated wine. And the multitude of such miracles, as you do judge, pertaineth to the excellency of the sacrament; whereas among the school-authors this is a common received proposition, *non esse ponenda miracula sine necessitate*. [Miracles. 270.]

And where you say, that I make my principal foundation upon the arguments of the scholastical writers, although mine arguments deduced out of the scholastical authors be unto you insoluble, and therefore you pass them over unanswered, yet I make no foundation at all upon them, but my very foundation is only upon God's word, which foundation is so sure, that it will never fail. And mine arguments in this place I bring in only to this end, to shew how far your imagined transubstantiation is, not only from God's word, but also from the order and precepts of nature, and how many and portentous absurdities you fall into by means of the same. Which it seemeth you do confess by holding your peace, without making answer thereto.

But now let us consider what is next in my book.

The papistical doctrine is also against all our outward senses, called our five wits. For our eyes say, they see there bread and wine: our noses smell bread and wine: our mouths taste, and our hands feel bread and wine. And although the articles of our faith be above all our outward senses, so that we believe things which we can neither see, feel, hear, smell, nor taste; yet they be not contrary to our senses, at the least so contrary, that in such things which we from time to time do see, smell, feel, hear, and taste, we shall not trust our senses, but believe clean contrary. Christ never made no such article of our faith. Our faith teacheth us to believe things that we see not, but it doth not bid us, that we shall not believe that we see daily with our eyes, and hear with our ears, and grope with our hands. For although our senses cannot reach so far as our faith doth, yet so far as the compass of our senses doth usually reach, our faith is not contrary to the same, but rather our senses do confirm our faith. Or else what availed it to St Thomas, for the con- [Chap. IV. The papistical doctrine is also against all our senses. John xx.]

firmation of Christ's resurrection, that he did put his hand into Christ's side, and felt his wounds, if he might not trust his senses, nor give no credit thereto?

[Lege Aug. in Psal. xxix. Præfat. Enarrationis 2, et Hilarium De Trin. Lib. iii. et contra Constantium. Embd. ed.]

And what a wide door is here opened to Valentinianus, Marcion, and other heretics, which said, "that Christ was not crucified, but that Simon Cyrenæus was crucified for him, although to the sight of the people it seemed that Christ was crucified?" or to such heretics as said, that "Christ was no man, although to men's sights he appeared in the form of man, and seemed to be hungry, dry, weary, to weep, sleep, eat, drink, yea, and to die like as other men do. For if we once admit this doctrine, that no credit is to be given to our senses, we open a large field, and give a great occasion unto an innumerable rabblement of most heinous heresies.

271. And if there be no trust to be given to our senses in this matter of the sacrament, why then do the papists so stoutly affirm, that the accidents remain after the consecration, which cannot be judged but by the senses? For the scripture speaketh no word of the accidents of bread and wine, but of the bread and wine themselves. And it is against the nature and definition of accidents, to be alone without any substance. Wherefore, if we may not trust our senses in this matter of the sacrament, then if the substance of the bread and wine be gone, why may we not then say, that the accidents be gone also? And if we must needs believe our senses as concerning the accidents of bread and wine, why may we not do the like of the substance, and that rather than of the accidents: forasmuch as after the consecration, the scripture saith in no place that there is no substance of bread nor of wine, but calleth them still by such names as signify the substances, and not the accidents?

And finally, if our senses be daily deceived in this matter, then is the sensible sacrament nothing else but an illusion of our senses. And so we make much for their purpose that said, that "Christ was a crafty juggler, that made things appear to men's sights, that in deed were no such things, but forms only, figures, and appearances of them."

But to conclude in few words this process of our senses, let all the papists lay their heads together, and they shall never be able to shew one article of our faith so directly contrary to our senses, that all our senses by daily experience shall affirm a thing to be, and yet our faith shall teach us the contrary thereunto.

WINCHESTER.

As in answering to the third chapter, I have shewed how reason received into faith's service doth not strive with transubstantiation, but agreeth well with it; so I trust to shew how

*Contrarium habetur in libro vocato, The Devil's Sophistry, fol. 6, 10, 11, 12, 15, 21.

man's senses, which this author calleth "the five wits," be no such direct adversaries to transubstantiation, as a matter whereof they can no skill. And therefore to a question this author asketh in the end of the second column in the twenty-second leaf[1], which is this. "If we believe our senses in the accidents, why may we not do the like of the substance?" I answer thus, that the senses can no skill of substance, as learned men speak of substance, nor this author neither, if a man should judge him by this question. For and a sensual man, one that followeth his rude senses, would say, "Come hither, master scholar, I hear much talking in this world of substance and accidence," and if he were of a merry nature would say, his little boy had learned his accidence, but himself woteth not perfectly what substance meaneth, as clerks term it, and bringing forth a piece of bread, another of cheese, and a pot of ale, would desire the scholar to learn him the substance of them, and shew it with his finger, and shew him also what difference between the substance of bread, cheese, and the ale[2]; I think the scholar, with the advice of all at Cambridge and Oxford also, could not do it; and the

---

[[1] Vid. supra.]   [[2] And ale, Orig. ed. Winch.]

more the scholar should travail with such a rude man so sensual in the matter, I think he should be the further off, unless the sensual man would set apart his rude wits and learn of the scholar some reasonable understanding, which is, that the substance is the inward nature, wherein those that be accidents do naturally stay the quantity immediately, and the rest by mean of quantity, in which the rest may be said to stay; which words were new divinity to this man, who, touching the bread, would ask the scholar roundly, "Callest thou not this substance, this good thick[3] piece that I handle?" The scholar would answer, "Sir, as I shall answer you, you will say I play the sophister; for I must speak learning to you, that you can no skill of. And be not angry though I tell you so; for and ye were learned, ye would not ask me this question; for substance, as it is properly understood to be of this or that thing, is properly neither seen by itself nor felt, and yet by reason comprehended truly to be in that we feel or see: nevertheless in common speech, and in the speech of such as for the purpose speak after the common capacity, the word "substance" is used to signify that is seen or felt, and so ye may say, ye see the substance or feel the substance of bread, and yet ye do in deed see but the colour, and by it the largeness, and feel the heat or coldness, moisture or dryness, weight or lightness, hardness or softness, thickness and thinness. If ye will learn what substance is, ye must leave your outward senses, and consider in your understanding how in every thing that is there is a stay, which we call a substance, being the principal part of every thing, which failing, we say that special thing not to be: as where the substance of bread is not, there that special thing bread is not, because bread is, as every other natural visible thing is, of two parts, substance and accidents. Now if the one part, that is to say substance, be not there, which can be but by miracle, then is no bread properly there, because the one and chief part is not there: and yet I say not nothing is there, for the other part remaining hath a being as God's visible creature, and may be called the visible part of bread[4], and therefore the outward kind and form of bread, and the appearance of bread and a true sensible part of bread, and therefore be called also by the name of bread; not that it is so properly, but after the common speech and capacity of men, and may be called the nature of bread, signifying the property, and the matter of bread, signifying the grossness." The rude man, I think, would hereat say, "Here is sophistry in deed, for here is substance, and no substance: matter of bread, and no bread; appearance of bread, and no bread; called bread, and no bread; this is plain juggling where it happeneth." Wherein this rude man, for want of true understanding of the words, and perfect consideration of the matter, speaketh thus fondly; who, if he should thereupon require the scholar to shew him some difference of the very substance between bread, cheese, and ale, what could the learned scholar answer here, but even frankly declare his ignorance, and say, "I know none?" which is as much to say as, "I know there is a difference, but I wot not what it is." Whereunto I trow the rude man would say to the scholar: "Then art thou with all thy learning as very a fool as I, to speak of a difference, and cannot tell what it is." Now, if the scholar should utter even the extremity of his learning in proper terms, and say, "I know bread is no cheese, and cheese is no ale, and of their accidental parts I can indeed shew differences, but of the very substance none;" the rude man, if his nature were not over dull, would laugh roundly, to hear a scholar utter for a point of learning that bread is no cheese, and cheese is no ale, which whoso knoweth not is a very fool; and merely to knit up the matter would keep the accidents of his bread, cheese, and ale for himself, and give the substance to the scholar, if he can divide it, as a reward for his cunning to his better nurture. And this I write after this gross sort, to shew that this matter of substance is not commonly understood as senses exercised in learning perceive it, and how man's outward senses cannot, as this author would have it, be judges of the inward nature of substance, which reason persuadeth to be, using the service of the senses for induction of the knowledge [of it][5], in which judgment upon their report happeneth many times much deceit. Titus Livius speaketh of a great number of divers dishes of meat made in a solemn supper, whereat the guests wondered to see such a variety at that time of the year; and when they demanded of it, answer was made, the substance was but one, all hog's flesh, so as the alteration in the accidents deceived their judgments. That stone, which among many, thought to have some skill, hath been taken for a precious diamond, hath after by cunning lapidaries been judged to be but a white sapphire, and contrariwise: so easily may our judgment upon the report of our senses fall in error; not that the senses be properly deceived, but rather the man that is grossly sensual, and judgeth fondly by them. For the very substance is not the proper object of any of the five wits, but of their report considered in reason denied,

*Cœna Chalcidensis Hospitis. Livius in 5. de Bello Macedonico.

[3 Good round thick. Orig. ed. Winch.] [4 Of the bread. Ibid.] [5 1551, and Orig. ed. Winch.]

and sometime guessed at, whereof ensueth great error and quid pro quo among the poticaries and learned also in things strange, whereof they have but accidental marks. Wherefore upon consideration of the premises it may easily appear how the question of this author, why the senses be not believed in knowledge of substance as in knowledge of accidents, may be reasonably answered. And then if the judgment of reason in the estimation of God's natural works and denying this or that substance, when by accidents it should seem otherwise, reason doth stay sensuality, and when men of experience, knowledge, and credit, have determined such a certain stone to be a very true diamond, other ignorant will be ashamed to say the contrary; and if a man fearing himself deceived to have bought one kind of drugs for another, and yet mistrusting wisely his own judgment, having caused it to be viewed by men of knowledge, good faith, and honesty, if they affirm it to be the very thing, this man will then condemn his own imagination, and upon credit call it so, and take it so to be: wherefore if in these things, I say, reason doth in a man stay sensuality, and if knowledge with honesty ruleth the judgment of rude understanding[1], and finally, if credit among men be so much regarded, how much more convenient is it that faith in God's word (wherein can be no deceit as there is in men) should alter and change man's judgment in reason, and bring it into the obedience of faith! Of that is bread after the judgment of our reason, after the report of our senses, Christ determineth unto us the substance of that to be his body, saying, "This is my body:" why shall not now a true christian man answer ever according to his faith, to say and profess the same to be the substance of Christ's body upon credit of Christ's words, as well as the carnal man will upon report of his senses conclude in reason there to be the substance of bread? whereby is not taken away the credit of our senses, as this author supposeth, which have their objects still true as they had before: for the colour, greatness, savour, and taste, all remain truly with the experiences of them as before: upon whose report reason nevertheless, now reduced to the obsequy of faith, forbeareth reverently to conclude against the truth of faith, but according to faith confesseth the substance to be the very substance of Christ's body, and the accidents to remain in their very true nature, because faith teacheth not the contrary, and that it agreeth with the rule of faith so to be, and therefore remaineth a very true greatness, thickness, and weight, which may be called in common speech "substance," signifying the outward nature. And in that sense Theodoret, reasoning with an heretic, seemeth to call it, because, having spoken of substance remaining, he declareth what he meaneth by it, adding, "it may be seen and felt as before;" which is not the nature of substance properly, but by like common speech that remaineth may be called "matter," as Origen called it; wherein also remain the true savour and taste, with true propriety to corrupt, or putrify, and also nourish; God so ordering the use of the creature of bread and likewise wine in this mystery, as the inward nature of them, which indeed is the substance, but only comprehended in reason and understanding, is converted into the most precious substance of Christ's body and blood, which is indeed a substance there present by God's omnipotency, only to be comprehended by faith, so far as may be understood of man's weakness and imbecility. And where this author putteth a danger, if senses be not trusted, there is a gap open to the Valentinians and Marcionists, and therefore bringeth in the feeling of St Thomas: hereunto I say, that the truth of that feeling dependeth upon a true belief, according to the scriptures, that Christ was very man; for else the body glorified of Christ, as St Gregory noteth[2], was not of the own glorified nature, then either visible or palpable; but therein Christ condescended to man's infirmity, and as he was truth itself, left that a true testimony to such as humbly were disposed by grace to receive it, not to convince heretics, who can devise wayward answers to the external acts of Christ, as now-a-days they delude the miraculous entering of Christ to his disciples, the doors being shut. Our faith of the true manhood in Christ is truly believed by true preaching thereof, and by the scriptures; not by the outward senses of men, which altogether, we must confess, could be no certain, inevitable proof thereof. And therefore Christ appearing to his disciples going into Emmaus opened the scriptures to them for the proof of his death, that he suffered as very man; and yet he used also in some part to preach to their senses, with sensible exhibition of himself unto them. And so all Christ's doings, which were most true, do bear testimony to the truth; but in their degree of testimony, and the feeling of St Thomas, being (as St Gregory saith) miraculous, serveth for proof of another thing, that God's work in miracle doth not impair the truth of the thing wrought; and so St Thomas touched then Christ as truly by miracle, after his resurrection, in his body glorified, as if he had touched his body before glorification. Finally, in Christ's acts or his ordinances be no illusions: all is truth and perfect truth, and our senses in the visible

---

[1 Rude of understanding. Orig. ed. Winch.]   [2 Homil. Pasc. xxvi.]

forms of bread and wine be not illuded, but have their proper objects in those accidents; and reason in carnal understanding, brought and subdued in obsequy to faith, doth in the estimation of the host consecrate yield to faith, according whereunto we confess truly the same to be the body of Christ.

Where this author would all the papists to lay all their heads together, &c., I know no such papists: but this I say without farther counsel, which this author with all his counsel shall not avoid, we believe most certainly the resurrection of our flesh, and be persuaded by catholic teaching that the same flesh by participation of Christ's godly flesh in the sacrament shall be made incorruptible; and yet after[3] the judgment of our senses and conclusions gathered of them, considering the manner of the continual [wasting of the said bodies, appear the utter][4] consumption, whereof some philosophers have at length after their reason declared their mind, whom christian men contemn with all the experience of senses, which they allege being vehement in that matter. We read in scripture of the feeding of angels, when Lot received them.

[Joan. vi. Orig. ed. Winch.]

[Gen. xviii. Ib.]

CANTERBURY.

As in your answer to the third chapter of my book you have done nothing but dallied and trifled, even so do you likewise in the fourth chapter, and yet far more unseemly than in the third. For doth it become a christian bishop of a matter of religion and a principal article of our faith to make a matter of bread and cheese; and of the holy supper of the Lord to make a resemblance of a dinner of hog's flesh? And yet for persuasion of your purpose you make, as it were, a play in a dialogue between a rude man and a learned scholar, wherein the matter is so learnedly handled that the simple rude man sheweth himself to have more knowledge than both you and your learned scholar. And why you should bring in this matter, I know not, except it be to shew your ignorance to be as great in logic and philosophy as it is in divinity. For what an ignorance is this, to say that a man can know no difference between one substance and another, and that substances be not judged by any senses; and that all natural things be of these two parts, of substances and accidents; and that their[5] accidents be part of their substances, and be called their substances, their natures, and matters! Was there ever any such learning uttered before this time? May not all men now evidently perceive into what a strait your error hath driven you, that you have none other defence but to fly to such absurdities as be against the judgment of the whole world? Would you make men believe that they know not the substance of the bread from drink, nor of chalk from cheese? Would you lead the world into this error, that Christ was never in deed seen, heard, nor felt, when he walked here with his apostles? Did he not prove the truth of his very flesh and bones by sight, saying, "A spirit hath not flesh and bones, as you see me have?" And although substances be not seen and known to our senses but by their accidents, yet be they indeed known, and properly known, and truly known by their accidents, and more properly seen than their accidents be. For the accidents be rather the means to know the substance by, than the things that be known. Is not wine known from beer by the taste? and mustard from sugar? Is not one man known by his voice from another? and a shalm[6] from a drum? And is not a man discerned[7] from a beast, and one[8] from another by sight? But when you turn up all speeches, all reason, and all manner of knowledge, it is less to be marvelled that you turn up divinity also, wherein you can less skill than in the rest.

The rude man and learned scholar.

Absurdities.

Luke ult.

And where you say, that "the senses can no skill of substances, because they may be deceived therein," so may they also be in the accidents. For do not the sun and moon sometime look red by means of the vapours between us and them? And doth not spectacles make all things look of the same colour that they be of? And if you hold up your finger directly between your eyes and a candle, looking full at the candle, your finger shall seem two; and if you look full at your finger, the candle shall seem two. And an ague maketh sweet things seem bitter, and that is sweet to one is bitter to another. And if a man having very hot hands, and another very cold,

---

[3 And yet not after. Orig. ed. Winch.]
[4 The Orig. ed. Winch. omits the words within brackets: they are found, however, in ed. 1551.]
[5 The accidences, ed. 1551.]
[6 A shalm: i. e. a kind of musical pipe.]
[7 Differed, ed. 1551.] [8 One man, Ib.]

if they handle both one thing, the one shall think it hot, and the other cold So that the senses may err as well in the accidents as in the substances, and cannot err in the substances, except they err also in the accidents.

<small>Substance.</small>

But in speaking of "substance," you declare such a substance as never was nor never shall be, phantasying substance by your imagination to be a thing in itself, separated from all accidents; and so confounding the substances of all things, and mixting heaven and earth together, you make all substances but one substance, without any difference.

<small>1 Cor. xv.</small>

And where Almighty God hath taught by his word that there be heavenly bodies and earthly bodies, and that every seed hath his own proper body, and that all flesh is not one flesh, but the flesh of men, of beasts, of fish, and of fowl, be divers; you teach by your words that all flesh is one flesh, and all substances one substance, and so confound you all flesh with hog's flesh, making an hotch-potch, like unto him that made a great variety of dishes all of hog's flesh. For take away the accidents, and I pray you what difference is between the bodily substance of the sun and the moon, of a man and a beast, of fish and flesh, between the body of one beast and another, one herb and another, one tree and another, between a man and a woman? yea, between our body and Christ's? and generally between any one corporal thing and another? For is not the distinction of all bodily substances known by their accidents? without the which a man's body cannot be known to be a man's body. And as substances cannot be substances without accidents, so the nature of accidents cannot be without substances, whose being and definition is to be in substances.

But as you speak of substances and accidents against scripture, sense, reason, experience, and all learning, so do you also speak manifestly against yourself. For you say, that "every thing that is must have a substance wherein it is stayed, and that every natural visible thing is of two parts, of substance and accidents;" and yet by your transubstantiation you leave no substance at all, to stay the accidents of the bread and wine.

<small>Accidents.</small>

And, moreover, this is a marvellous teaching of you, to say that the accidents of bread be one part of bread, and be called "the outward kind of bread, the sensible part of bread, the nature and matter of bread, and very bread." Was there ever any such learning taught before this day, that accidents should be called parts of substances, the nature of substances, and the matter of substances, and the very substances themselves?

<small>276.</small>

If ever any man so wrote, tell who it is, or else knowledge the truth, that all these matters be invented by your own imagination, whereof the rude man may right well say, Here is sophistry indeed, and plain juggling. But you convey not your juggling so craftily but that you be taken (as the Greeks term it) ἐπαυτοφώρῳ, even with the manner.

<small>A lapidary.</small>

Now, as concerning your expert lapidary, if his senses be deceived, how shall he judge a true stone from a counterfeit? Doth he not diligently look upon it with his sight, to discern truly of it? For tell me, I pray you, how a man without senses shall judge a true diamond?

Put out his eyes, and is not a white sapphire, a diamond, and a glass, all one in his judgment? Marry, if he be a man of clear sight, of true knowledge and experience in the judgment of stones, and be therewithal a man of good faith and honesty, as you tell the tale, they that be ignorant will be ashamed to control his judgment. But if he be blind, or be a man neither of faith nor honesty, but his experience hath been ever exercised to deceive all that trust him, and to sell them white sapphires for diamonds, then no man that wise is will take a glass or sapphire at his hands of trust, although he say it be a true diamond. Even so likewise the papists, (being so accustomed with these[1] merchandises of glistering glasses and counterfeit drugs[2] to deceive the world), what wise men will trust them with their feigned transubstantiation, being so manifestly against the plain words of scripture, against all reason, sense[3], and ancient writers? And although you have taken never so great labour and pains in this place to answer mine arguments, (wherein you do nothing else but shew your ignorance in philosophy and logic,) yet all is in vain, except you could prove tran-

---

[[1] Their, 1551.]   [[2] Dredges, 1551.]   [[3] Senses, 1551.]

substantiation to be a matter of our faith; which being not proved, all that you have spoken here serveth to no purpose, nor concludeth nothing. For you are not so ignorant in sophistry but you know well enough, that of a false antecedent can no consequent directly follow.

And as concerning these words of Christ, "This is my body," by your own teaching in these words he called bread his body, which can be no formal and proper speech, but spoken by a figure, as the order of the text plainly declareth, and all the old authors do testify.

And where you say, that "although the substance of bread and wine be gone, yet the senses have their proper object still remaining," as they had before, that is to say, the colours, greatness, thickness, weight, savour, and taste; express then, I pray you, plainly, what thing it is that is coloured, great, thin or thick, heavy or light, savoury or tasted. For seeing you confess that these do remain, you must confess also that there remaineth bread: for that greatness, thickness, thinness, colours, and weight, be not in the body of Christ, nor in the air, which cannot be weighed; and in something they must needs be: for by your own saying, "every thing hath a substance to stay it;" therefore they must needs be in the substance of bread and wine. And to say that the accidents of bread be the natures, matters, and substances thereof, is nothing else but to declare to the world that you make words to signify at your pleasure.

But other shift have you none to defend your transubstantiation, but to devise such monstrous kinds of speeches as were never heard of before. For you say, that "the nature, matter, and substance of bread and wine remain not, but be changed into the body and blood of Christ:" the old writers say directly contrary, that the nature, matter, and substance remain. "Christ," saith Theodoret, "called bread and wine his body and blood, and yet changed not their natures." And again he saith: "The bread and wine after the consecration lose not their proper nature, but keep their former substance, form, and figure, which they had before[4]." And Origen saith, that "the matter of bread availeth nothing, but as concerning the material part thereof it goeth down into the belly, and is avoided downward[5]." And Gelasius saith, that "the nature and substance of bread and wine cease not to be[6]." Now seeing that your doctrine (who teach that the nature, matter, and substance of bread and wine be changed and remain not) is as clean contrary to these old writers, with many other, as black is contrary to white, and light to darkness, you have no remedy to defend your error and wilful opinion, but to imagine such portentous and wonderful kinds of speeches to be spoken by these authors, as never were uttered before by no man, that is to say, that the outward appearance and accidents of any thing should be called the nature, matter, and substance thereof. But such monsters had you rather bring forth, than you would in one jot relent in your error once by you uttered, and undertaken by you[7] defended. And yet bring you nothing for the proof of your saying, but that if the author's words should be understand as they be spoken, this should follow thereof, that bread and wine should be seen and felt; which as no man doubteth of, but all men take it for a most certain truth, so you take it for a great inconvenience and absurdity. So far be you forced in this matter to vary in speech and judgment from the sentence and opinion of all men.

And as touching the belief of St Thomas, although he believed certainly that Christ was a man, yet he believed not that Christ was risen and appeared to the apostles, but thought rather that the apostles were deceived by some vision or spirit, which appeared to them in likeness of Christ, which he thought was not he in deed. And so thought the apostles themselves until Christ said: *Videte manus meas et pedes, quia ego ipse sum: palpate et videte, quia spiritus carnem et ossa non habent, sicut me videtis habere.* "See my hands and my feet, for I am he: grope and see, for a spirit hath no flesh and bones, as you see that I have." And so thought also St Thomas, until such time as he put his hands into Christ's side and felt his wounds,

[4 See above, p. 133.] [5 See below, p. 266.]
[6 Et tamen esse non desinit substantia vel natura panis et vini.—Gelasii adv. Eutych. et Nest. Sect. v. Pars iii. p. 671, in Biblioth. Patrum, Colon. 1518.]
[7 Undertaken to be by you, 1551.]

and by his sense of feeling perceived that it was Christ's very body, and no spirit nor phantasy, as before he believed. And so in St Thomas the truth of feeling depended not upon the true belief of Christ's resurrection, but the feeling of his senses brought him from misbelief unto the right and true faith of that matter. And as for St Gregory, he speaketh no such thing as you report, that "the glorified body of Christ was of the own nature neither visible nor palpable," but he saith clean contrary, that "Christ shewed his glorified body to St Thomas palpable, to declare that it was of the same nature that it was of before his resurrection:" whereby it is plain, after St Gregory's mind, that if it were not palpable, it were not of the same nature. And St Gregory saith further in the same homily: *Egit miro modo superna clementia, ut discipulus ille dubitans, dum in magistro suo vulnera palparet carnis, in nobis vulnera sanaret infidelitatis. Plus enim nobis Thomæ infidelitas ad fidem, quam fides credentium discipulorum profuit: quia dum ille ad fidem palpando reducitur, nostra mens omni dubitatione postposita in fide solidatur.* "The supernal clemency wrought marvellously, that the disciple which doubted, by groping the wounds of flesh in his master, should heal in us the wounds of infidelity. For the lack of faith in Thomas profited more to our faith than did the faith of the disciples that believed. For when he is brought to faith by groping, our mind is stablished in faith without all doubting." And why should St Gregory write thus, if our senses availed nothing unto our faith, nor could nothing judge of substances? And do not all the old catholic authors prove the true humanity of Christ by his visible conversation with us here in earth; that he was heard preach, seen eating and drinking, labouring and sweating? Do they not also prove his resurrection by seeing, hearing, and groping of him? which if it were no proof, those arguments were made in vain against such heretics that denied his true incarnation. And shall you now take away the strength of their arguments, to the maintenance of those old condemned heresies, by your subtile sophistications? The touching and feeling of Christ's hands, feet, and wounds was a proof of his resurrection, not, as you say, to them that believed, but, as St Gregory saith, to them that doubted.

And if all things that Christ did and spake to our outward senses prove not that he was a natural man, as you say with Marcion, Menander, Valentinus, Apollinaris, with other like sort, then I would know how you should confute the said heresies? Marry, will you say peradventure, by the scripture, which saith plainly, *Verbum caro factum est.* But if they would say again, that he was called a man and flesh because he took upon him the form of a man and flesh, and would say that St Paul so declareth it, saying, *Formam servi accipiens*, and would then say further, that form is the accidence of a thing, and yet hath the name of "substance," but is not the substance in deed, what would you then say unto them? If you deny that the forms and accidences be called "substances," then go you from your own saying. And if you grant it, then will they avoid all the scriptures that you can bring to prove Christ a man, by this cavillation, that the appearances, forms, and accidences of a man may be called a man, as well as you say that the forms and accidences of bread be called bread. And so prepare you certain propositions and grounds for heretics to build their errors upon, which after, when you would, you shall never be able to overthrow.

And where you say that Thomas touched truly Christ's body glorified, how could that be, when touching, as you say, is not of the substance but of the accidents only? and also Christ's body glorified, as you say, is neither visible nor palpable. And whereas indeed you make Christ's acts illusions, and yet in words you pretend the contrary; call you not this illusion of ourselves, when a thing appeareth to our senses which is not the same thing in deed? When Jupiter and Mercury, as the comedy telleth, appeared to Alcumena in the similitude of Amphitryo and Sosia, was not Alcumena deceived thereby? And poticaries that sell juniper-berries for pepper, being no pepper indeed, deceive they not the buyers by illusion of their senses? Why then is not in the ministration of the holy communion an illusion of our senses, if our senses take for bread and wine that which is not so indeed?

Finally, whereas I required earnestly all the papists to lay their heads together, and to shew one article of our faith so directly contrary to our senses, that all our senses by daily experience shall affirm a thing to be, and yet our faith shall teach us the contrary thereunto; where, I say, I required this so earnestly of you, and with such circumstances, and you have yet shewed none, I may boldly conclude that you can shew none. For sure I am if you could, being so earnestly provoked thereunto, you would not have failed to shew it in this place. As for the article of our resurrection, and of the feeding of angels, serve nothing for this purpose. For my saying is of the daily experience of our senses, and when they affirm a thing to be; but the resurrection of our flesh, and the feeding of angels, be neither in daily experience of our senses, nor our senses affirm them not so to be. Now after the matter of our senses followeth in my book the authorities of ancient writers in this wise.

Now forasmuch as it is declared how this papistical opinion of transubstantiation is against the word of God, against nature, against reason, and against all our senses, we shall shew furthermore, that it is against the faith and doctrine of the old authors of Christ's church, beginning at those authors which were nearest unto Christ's time, and therefore might best know the truth herein.

*Chap. v. The papistical doctrine is contrary to the faith of the old authors of Christ's church. [Vid. Embd. ed. in fine tomi hujus.] *Justinus Martyr.*

First, Justinus, a great learned man, and an holy martyr, the oldest author that this day is known to write any treaty upon the sacraments, and wrote not much after one hundred years after Christ's ascension.

He writeth in his second Apology, that "the bread, water, and wine in this sacrament are not to be taken as other common meats and drinks be, but they be meats ordained purposely to give thanks to God, and therefore be called *Eucharistia*, and be called also the body and blood of Christ; and that it is lawful for none to eat or drink of them but that profess Christ, and live according to the same. And yet the same meat and drink," saith he, " is changed into our flesh and blood, and nourisheth our bodies[1]."

By which saying it is evident, that Justinus thought that the bread and wine remained still; for else it could not have been turned into our flesh and blood to nourish our bodies.

WINCHESTER.

I will spend no more words herein, but having avoided this author's reasoning against transubstantiation, now let us examine his authorities. First he beginneth with Justin the Martyr, whose words be not truly by this author here reported, which be these truly translate out of the Greek: "When the priest hath ended his thanksgiving and prayers, and all the people hath said ' Amen,' they whom we call deacons give to every one then present a part of the bread and of the wine and water consecrated, and carry part to those that be absent; and this is that food which is among us called Eucharistia, *whereof it is lawful for no man to be partaker, except he be persuaded those things to be true that be taught us, and be baptized in the water of regeneration in remission of sins, and ordereth his life after the manner which Christ hath taught. For we do not take these for common bread or drink; but like as Jesus Christ our Saviour, incarnate by the word of God, had flesh and blood for our salvation, even so we be taught the food, wherewith our flesh and blood be nourished by alteration, when it is consecrate by the prayer of his word, to be the flesh and blood of the same Jesus incarnate. For the apostles in those their works, which be called gospels, teach that Jesus did so command them, and after he had taken the bread, and ended his thanksgiving, said, "Do this in my remembrance, This is my body;" and likewise taking the cup after he had given thanks, said, " This is my blood," and did give them to his apostles only. And here I make an issue with this author, that he*

Justinus.

280.

An issue.

[1] Καὶ ἡ τροφὴ αὕτη καλεῖται παρ' ἡμῖν εὐχαριστία, ἧς οὐδενὶ ἄλλῳ μετασχεῖν ἐξόν ἐστιν, ἢ τῷ πιστεύοντι ἀληθῆ εἶναι τὰ δεδιδαγμένα ὑφ' ἡμῶν, καὶ λουσαμένῳ τὸ ὑπὲρ ἀφέσεως ἁμαρτιῶν καὶ εἰς ἀναγέννησιν λουτρόν, καὶ οὕτως βιοῦντι ὡς ὁ Χριστὸς παρέδωκεν· οὐ γὰρ ὡς κοινὸν ἄρτον οὐδὲ κοινὸν πόμα ταῦτα λαμβάνομεν, ἀλλ' ὃν τρόπον διὰ λόγου Θεοῦ σαρκοποιηθεὶς Ἰησοῦς Χριστὸς ὁ σωτὴρ ἡμῶν, καὶ σάρκα καὶ αἷμα ὑπὲρ σωτηρίας ἡμῶν ἔσχεν, οὕτως καὶ τὴν δι' εὐχῆς λόγου τοῦ παρ' αὐτοῦ εὐχαριστηθεῖσαν τροφήν, ἐξ ἧς αἷμα καὶ σάρκες κατὰ μεταβολὴν τρέφονται ἡμῶν, ἐκείνου τοῦ σαρκοποιηθέντος Ἰησοῦ καὶ σάρκα καὶ αἷμα ἐδιδάχθημεν εἶναι.—Justin. Martyr. Apologia II. (Ed. Bened. i.) p. 162. Ed. Paris. 1551.]

wittingly corrupteth Justin in the allegation of him, who writeth not in such form of words as this author allegeth out of his second Apology, nor hath any such speech: "The bread, water, and wine in this sacrament are meats ordained purposely to give thanks to God, and therefore be called **Eucharistia**;" nor hath not these words, "They be called the body and blood of Christ;" but hath in plain words, "That we be taught this food consecrate by God's word to be the flesh and blood of Christ, as Christ in his incarnation took flesh and blood;" nor hath not this form of words placed to have that understanding, how the same meat and drink is changed into our flesh and blood. For the words in Justin speaking of alteration of the food, have an understanding of the food as it is before the consecration, shewing how Christ used those creatures in this mystery, which by alteration nourish our flesh and blood.

For the body of Christ, which is the very celestial substance of the host consecrate, is not changed, but without all alteration spiritually nourisheth the bodies and souls of them that worthily receive the same to immortality: whereby appeareth this author's conclusion, that bread and wine remain still, which is turned into our flesh and blood, is not deduced upon Justin's words truly understood, but is a gloss invented by this author, and a perverting of Justin's words, and their true meaning[1]. Whereupon I may say and conclude, even as this author erreth in his reasoning of mother wit against transubstantiation, even so erreth he in the first allegation of his authorities by plain misreporting; let it be further named or thought on as the thing deserveth.

CANTERBURY.

In this holy martyr Justinus I do not go about to be a translator of him, nor I bind not myself precisely to follow the form of his words, which no translator is bound unto, but I set forth only his sense and meaning. For where Justin hath a good long process in this matter, I take no more but that is directly to the purpose of transubstantiation, which is the matter being here in question. And the long words of Justin I knit up together in as few words as I can, rendering the sense truly, and not varying far from the words. And this have I done, not willingly to corrupt Justin, as you *Mine issue. maliciously deprave, (and thereupon will I join with you in your issue,) but I do it to recite to the reader Justin's mind shortly and plainly; whereas you, professing to observe scrupulously the words, observe indeed neither the words nor the sentence of Justin. But this is your fashion when you lack good matter to answer, then, to find something to fill up your book, you turn the matter into trifling and cavillation in words.

You say that Justin hath not this speech, "the bread, water, and wine in this sacrament are meats ordained purposely to give thanks to God;" and yet by your own translation he hath the same thing in effect: and yet indeed the words be neither as you nor as I say; and as they be in Greek, they cannot be expressed in English but by a paraphrasis. The words be these in Greek, τοῦ εὐχαριστηθέντος ἄρτου καὶ οἴνου καὶ ὕδατος, and in our tongue, as near as may be Englished, signify thus: "The bread and wine and water of thanksgiving," or, as Irenæus saith, "in which thanks be 281. given." And neither hath Justin this word "sacrament," as I say, nor this word "consecrated," as you say. May not all men therefore evidently see that your chief study is to make cavillations and dallying in words? And all the rest of my sayings which you deny to be in Justin, be there very plainly in sense, as I will be judged by the indifferent reader.

And what need I willingly to corrupt Justin, when his words, after your allegation, serve more for my purpose against your feigned transubstantiation, than as I allege them myself? For if the deacons give to every one present a part of the bread, wine, and water consecrated, and send part to them that be absent, as you report Justin's words, do not then bread, wine, and water, remain after consecration, seeing that they be distributed to divers men in parts? For I think you will not say that the body of Christ is divided into parts, so that one man receiveth an hand, and another a leg. And Justin saith further, that the same food of bread, wine, and water, called *Eucharistia*, nourisheth our flesh and blood by alteration, which they could not do if no bread, wine, nor water, were there at all.

[1 Meanings, Orig. ed. Winch.]

But here is not to be passed over one exceeding great craft and untruth in your translation, that to cast a mist before the reader's eyes you alter the order of Justin's words in that place, where the pith of the matter standeth. For where Justin saith of the food of bread, wine, and water, after the consecration, that they nourish our flesh and blood by alteration, the "nourishment" which Justin putteth after "consecration," you untruly put it before the "consecration," and so wilfully and craftily alter the order of Justin's words, to deceive the reader; and in this point will I join an issue with you. *Mine issue. Is such craft and untruth to be used of bishops, and that in matters of faith and religion, whereof they pretend and ought to be true professors? But I marvel not so much at your sleights in this place, seeing that in the whole book throughout you seek nothing less than the truth. And yet all your sleights will not serve you; for how can the food, called *Eucharistia*, nourish before the consecration, seeing it is not eaten until after the consecration?

The next author in my book is Irene, whom I allege thus.

Next him was Irenæus, above one hundred and fifty years after Christ, who, as it is supposed, could not be deceived in the necessary points of our faith, for he was a disciple of Polycarpus, which was disciple to St John the Evangelist. *Irenæus contra Valentinum, Lib. iv. cap. 34.*

This Irenæus followeth the sense of Justinus wholly in this matter, and almost also his words, saying, that "the bread wherein we give thanks unto God, although it be of the earth, yet when the name of God is called upon it, it is not then common bread, but the bread of thanksgiving, having two things in it, one earthly, and the other heavenly[2]." What meant he by the heavenly thing, but the sanctification which cometh by the invocation of the name of God? And what by the earthly thing, but the very bread which, as he said before, is of the earth; and which also, he saith, doth nourish our bodies, as other bread doth which we do use?

WINCHESTER.

Next Justin is Irene, in the allegation of whom this author maketh also an untrue report, who hath not this form of words in the fourth book contra Valentinum, *that "the bread wherein we give thanks unto God, although it be of the earth, yet when the name of God is called upon, it is not then common bread, but the bread of thanksgiving, having two things in it, one earthly, and the other heavenly." This is Irene, alleged by this author, who, I say, writeth not in such form of words. For his words be these: "Like as the bread which is of the earth, receiving the calling of God, is now no common bread, but* eucharistia, *consisting of two things, earthly and heavenly, so our bodies, receiving* eucharistia, *be no more corruptible." These be Irene's words, where Irene doth not call the bread, "receiving the calling of God," the bread of thanksgiving, but* eucharistia; *and in this* eucharistia *he sheweth how that, that he calleth the heavenly things[3], is the body and blood of Christ, and therefore saith in his fifth book: "When the chalice mixt, and the bread broken, receive the word of God, it is made* eucharistia, *of the body and blood of Christ, of which the substance of our flesh is stayed and increased. And how say they that our flesh is not able to receive God's gift, who is eternal life, which flesh is nourished with the body and blood of Christ?" These be also Irene's words, whereby appeareth, what he meant by the heavenly thing in* eucharistia, *which is the very presence of Christ's body and blood. And for the plain testimony of this faith, this Irene hath been commonly alleged, and specially of Melancthon and Œcolampadius, as one most ancient and most plainly testifying the same. So as his very words, truly alleged, overthrow this author in the impugnation of Christ's real presence in the sacrament, and therefore can nothing help this author's purpose against transubstantiation. Is not this a goodly and godly entry of this author, in the first two authorities that he bringeth in to corrupt them both?*

282.

[² Ὡς γὰρ ἀπὸ γῆς ἄρτος, προσλαμβανόμενος τὴν ἔκκλησιν τοῦ Θεοῦ, οὐκέτι κοινὸς ἄρτος ἐστὶν, ἀλλ' εὐχαριστία, ἐκ δύο πραγμάτων συνεστηκυῖα, ἐπιγείου τε καὶ οὐρανίου.—Irenæus adversus Hæreses Valent. Lib. IV. cap. 34. p. 327. Ed. Oxon. 1702.]

[³ Thing, 1551.]

CANTERBURY.

Who seeth not, that as you did before in Justin, so again in Irene, you seek nothing else but mere cavillations and wrangling in words? Is not *eucharistia* called in English, "thanksgiving?" If it be not, tell you what it is called in English. And doth not Irene say, *Panes in quo gratiæ actæ sunt?* that is to say, "bread wherein thanks be given?" What have I offended then in Englishing *eucharistiam*, "thanksgiving?" Do not I write to Englishmen, which understand not what this Greek word, *eucharistia*, meaneth? What great offence is it then in me to put it into English, that Englishmen may understand what is said? Should I do as you do, put Greek for English, and write so obscurely that the Englishmen should not know the author's meaning?

And do you not see how much the words of Ireneus, by you alleged, make against yourself? These be his words after your citation: "When the chalice mixt, and the bread broken, receive the word of God, it is made *eucharistia* of the body and blood of Christ, of which the substance of our flesh is stayed and increased." Doth not Irene say here plainly, that "the chalice mixt, and the bread broken, after the word of God, which you call the words of consecration, is made *eucharistia* of the body and blood of Christ," and not the body and blood of Christ? And saith he not further, that "they stay and increase the substance of our bodies?" But how can those things stay and increase our bodies, which be transubstantiated and gone before we receive them? And have you forgotten now in Irene, what you said in the next leaf before in Justin, that "the alteration and nourishment by the food of bread and wine was understand before the consecration?" which you confess now to be after the consecration. And when you thus obscure the author's words, perverting and corrupting both the words and sentences, yet shall you conclude your untrue dealing with these words concerning me: "Is not this a goodly and godly entry of this author, in the first two authorities that he bringeth in to corrupt them both?"

Now followeth Origen next in my book.

283.
Origenes in Matth. Cap. xv.
[Vid. Emb. ed. in fine hujus tomi.]

Shortly after Irenæus was Origen, about two hundred years after Christ's ascension; who also affirmeth that the material bread remaineth, saying that "the matter of the bread availeth nothing, but goeth down into the belly, and is avoided downward; but the word of God spoken upon the bread is it that availeth[1]."

WINCHESTER.

Origen.

As for Origen in his own words saith, "the matter of the bread remaineth;" which, as I have before opened, it may be granted, but yet he termeth it not as this author doth, to call it material bread. When God formed Adam of clay, the matter of the clay remained in Adam, and yet the material clay remained not; for it was altered into another substance: which I speak not to compare equally the forming of Adam to the sacrament, but to shew it not to be all one to say the material bread and the matter of bread. For the accidents of bread may be called the matter of bread, but not the material bread, as I have somewhat spoken thereof before; but such shifts be used in this matter, notwithstanding the importance of it.

[Gen. i. Orig. ed. Winch.]

CANTERBURY.

What should I tarry much in Origen, seeing that you confess that he saith, "the matter of bread remaineth;" and Origen saith, that "the meat which is sanctified, *juxta id quod habet materiale in ventrem abit*," that is to say, "as concerning the material

---

[1] Τὸ ἁγιαζόμενον βρῶμα διὰ λόγου Θεοῦ καὶ ἐντεύξεως, κατ' αὐτὸ μὲν τὸ ὑλικὸν εἰς τὴν κοιλίαν χωρεῖ, καὶ εἰς ἀφεδρῶνα ἐκβάλλεται· κατὰ δὲ τὴν ἐπιγενομένην αὐτῷ εὐχὴν, κατὰ τὴν ἀναλογίαν τῆς πίστεως, ὠφέλιμον γίνεται, καὶ τῆς τοῦ νοῦ αἴτιον διαβλέψεως, ὁρῶντος ἐπὶ τὸ ὠφελοῦν· καὶ οὐχ ἡ ὕλη τοῦ ἄρτου, ἀλλ' ὁ ἐπ' αὐτῷ εἰρημένος λόγος ἐστὶν ὁ ὠφελῶν τὸν μὴ ἀναξίως τοῦ Κυρίου ἐσθίοντα αὐτόν.—Origenes, Comment. in Matt. xv. Tom. III. p. 499. Ed. Bened. Paris. 1733-59.]

part thereof goeth into the belly?" So that by Origen's teaching both the bread and the material part of bread remain. So that your example of clay relieveth you nothing in this your answer unto Origen.

But when you see that this shift will not serve, then you fly to another, and say, "that the accidents of bread be called the matter of bread;" which is so shameful a shift, as all that have any manner of knowledge may plainly see your manifest impudency. But many "such shifts you use in this matter, notwithstanding the importance of it."

Now let us come to Cyprian, of whom I write in this manner.

After Origen came Cyprian the holy martyr, about the year of our Lord 250, who writeth against them that ministered this sacrament with water only, and without wine. "Forasmuch," saith he, "as Christ said, 'I am a true vine,' therefore the blood of Christ is not water, but wine; nor it can not be thought that his blood, whereby we be redeemed and have life, is in the cup, when wine is not in the cup, whereby the blood of Christ is shewed[2]." *Cyprian ad Cæcilium lib. ii. epist. 3. [Vid. Emb. ed. in fine tomi hujus.]*

What words could Cyprian have spoken more plainly, to shew that the wine doth remain, than to say thus: "If there be no wine, there is no blood of Christ?"

And yet he speaketh shortly after as plainly in the same epistle. "Christ," saith he, "taking the cup, blessed it, and gave it to his disciples, saying, 'Drink ye all of this: for this is the blood of the new testament, which shall be shed for many for the remission of sins. I say unto you, that from henceforth I will not drink of this creature of the vine, until I shall drink with you new wine in the kingdom of my Father.' By these words of Christ," saith St Cyprian, "we perceive that the cup which the Lord offered was not only water, but also wine, and that it was wine that Christ called his blood; whereby it is clear that Christ's blood is not offered, if there be no wine in the chalice[3]." And after it followeth: "How shall we drink with Christ new wine of the creature of the vine, if in the sacrifice of God the Father and of Christ we do not offer wine[4]?" *Matt. xxvi.*

284.

In these words of St Cyprian appeareth most manifestly, that in this sacrament is not only offered very wine that is made of grapes that come of the vine, but also that we drink the same. And yet the same giveth us to understand, that if we drink that wine worthily, we drink also spiritually the very blood of Christ, which was shed for our sins.

WINCHESTER.

St Cyprian's words do not impugn transubstantiation, for they tend only to shew that wine is the creature appointed to the celebration of this mystery, and therefore water only is no due matter according to Christ's institution. And as the name wine must be used before the consecration to shew the truth of it then, so it may also be used for a name of it after to shew what it was; which is often used. And in one place of Cyprian by this author here alleged it appeareth, St Cyprian by the word wine signifieth the heavenly wine of the vineyard of the Lord of Sabaoth, calling it new wine, and alluding therein to David. And *Cyprian.*

[2 Nam cum dicat Christus, "Ego sum vitis vera;" sanguis Christi non aqua est utique, sed vinum. Nec potest videri sanguis ejus, quo redempti et vivificati sumus, esse in calice, quando vinum desit calici, quo Christi sanguis ostenditur.—Cyprian. ad Cæcilium de Sacramento Dominici Calicis. Epist. LXIII. (Lib. ii. Epist. 3.) p. 143. Ed. Paris. 1574.]

[3 Calicem etenim sub die passionis accipiens, benedixit, et dedit discipulis suis, dicens: "Bibite ex hoc omnes: hic est enim sanguis novi testamenti, qui pro multis effundetur in remissionem peccatorum. Dico vobis, non bibam a modo ex ista creatura vitis, usque in diem illum, quo vobiscum bibam novum vinum in regno patris mei." Qua in parte invenimus calicem mixtum fuisse quem Dominus obtulit, et vinum fuisse quod sanguinem suum dixit. Unde apparet sanguinem Christi non offerri, si desit vinum calici.—Ib. p. 145.]

[4 Quomodo autem de creatura vitis novum vinum cum Christo in regno Patris bibemus, si in sacrificio Dei Patris et Christi vinum non offerimus, nec calicem Domini dominica traditione miscemus?—Ib. p. 145.]

this doth Cyprian shew in these words: "How shall we drink with Christ new wine of the creature of the vine, if, in the sacrifice to God the Father and Christ, we do not offer wine?" Is not here mention of new wine of the creature of the vine? What new wine can be but the blood of Christ, the very wine consecrate by God's omnipotency, of the creature of the vine offered? And therefore this one place may give us a lesson in Cyprian, that as he useth the word "wine" to signify the heavenly drink of the blood of Christ, made by consecration of the creature of wine, so when he nameth the bread "consecrate bread," he meaneth the heavenly bread Christ, who is the bread of life. And so Cyprian can make nothing by those words against transubstantiation, who writeth plainly of the change of the bread by God's omnipotency into the flesh of Christ, as shall after appear, where this author goeth about to answer to him.

CANTERBURY.

Cyprian's words tend not only to shew that wine is the creature appointed to the celebration of the mystery, but that it is also there present, and drunken in the mystery. For these be his words: "It cannot be thought that Christ's blood is in the cup, when wine is not in the cup, whereby the blood of Christ is shewed." And again he saith: "It was wine that Christ called his blood;" and that "it is clear, that Christ's blood is not offered, if there be no wine in the chalice." And further he saith: "How shall we drink with Christ new wine of the creature of the vine, if in the sacrifice of God the Father and of Christ, we do not offer wine?" In these words Cyprian saith not, that Christ is the wine which we drink, but that with Christ we drink wine, that cometh of the vine-tree; and that Christ's blood is not there, when wine is not there. And where is now your transubstantiation, that taketh away the wine? For take away the wine, and take away by Cyprian's mind the blood of Christ also.

But, lest any man should stumble at Cyprian's words, where he seemeth to say that the blood of Christ should be really in the cup, he saith nor meaneth no such thing, but that it is there sacramentally or figuratively. And his meaning needeth none other gathering, but of his own words that follow next after in the same sentence, that "by the wine the blood of Christ is shewed." And shortly after he saith, that "the cup which the Lord offered was wine," and that "it was wine that Christ called his blood."

Now come we to Emissene, your principal stay, in whom is your chief glory. Of him thus I write.

285.
Eusebius Emissenus.

Eusebius Emissenus, a man of singular fame and learning, about three hundred years after Christ's ascension, did in few words set out this matter so plainly, (both how the bread and wine be converted into the body and blood of Christ, and yet remain still in their nature; and also how, besides the outward receiving of bread and wine, Christ is inwardly by faith received in our hearts,) all this, I say, he doth so plainly set out, that more plainness cannot be reasonably desired in this matter. For he saith, that "the conversion of the visible creatures of bread and wine into the body and blood of Christ is like unto our conversion in baptism, where outwardly nothing is changed, but remaineth the same that was before; but all the alteration is inwardly and spiritually."

*De consecr. Distinction. ii. *Quia.*

"If thou wilt know," saith he[1], "how it ought not to seem to thee a new

---

[1 Et ut tibi novum et impossibile videri non debeat, quod in Christi substantiam terrena et mortalia convertuntur, teipsum, qui jam in Christo es regeneratus, interroga. Dudum alienus a vita, peregrinus a misericordia, a salutis via intrinsecus mortuus exulabas: subito initiatus Christi legibus, et salutaribus mysteriis innovatus, in corpus ecclesiæ non videndo, sed credendo transiluisti, et de filio perditionis adoptivus Dei filius fieri occulta puritate meruisti: in mensura visibili permanens, major factus es teipso invisibiliter, sine quantitatis augmento, cum ipse atque idem esses, multo alter fidei processibus extitisti: in exteriori nihil additum est, et totum in interiori mutatum est: ac sic homo Christi filius effectus, et Christus in hominis mente formatus est. Sicut ergo sine corporali sensu, præterita vilitate deposita, subito novam indutus es dignitatem: et sicut hoc, quod in te Deus læsa curavit, infecta diluit, immaculata detersit, non sunt oculis nec sensibus tuis credita: ita cum reverendum altare cœlestibus cibis satiandus ascendis, sacrum Dei tui corpus et sanguinem fide respice, honora, mirare, mente continge, cordis manu suscipe, et maxime haustu interiore as-

thing and impossible, that earthly and corruptible things be turned into the substance of Christ, look upon thyself, which art made new in baptism: when thou wast far from life, and banished as a stranger from mercy and from the way of salvation, and inwardly wast dead, yet suddenly thou begannest another life in Christ, and wast made new by wholesome mysteries, and wast turned into the body of the church, not by seeing, but by believing: and of the child of damnation, by a secret pureness, thou wast made the chosen son of God. Thou visibly didst remain in the same measure that thou hadst before, but invisibly thou wast made greater, without any increase of thy body. Thou wast the self-same person, and yet by the increase of faith thou wast made another man. Outwardly nothing was added, but all the change was inwardly. And so was man made the son of Christ, and Christ formed in the mind of man. Therefore as thou, putting away thy former vileness, didst receive a new dignity, not feeling any change in thy body; and as the curing of thy disease, the putting away of thine infection, the wiping away of thy filthiness, be not seen with thine eyes, but are believed in thy mind: so likewise when thou dost go up to the reverend altar, to feed upon spiritual meat, in thy faith look upon the body and blood of him that is thy God; honour him, touch him with thy mind, take him in the hand of thy heart, and chiefly drink him with the draught of thy inward man."

Hitherto have I rehearsed the sayings of Eusebius, which be so plain that no man can wish more plainly to be declared, that this mutation of the bread and wine into the body and blood of Christ is a sacramental mutation, and that outwardly nothing is changed. But as outwardly we eat the bread, and drink the wine with our mouths, so inwardly by faith we spiritually eat the very flesh, and drink the very blood of Christ.

WINCHESTER.

As touching Emissene, by whose words is expressly testified the truth of the real presence Emissene. *of Christ in the sacrament, and also the sense of the doctrine of transubstantiation, this author maketh himself bold over him, and so bold that he dare corrupt him; which Emissene writeth not, "that man is turned into the body of the church." And here I make an issue with* An issue. *this author, that Emissene hath not that word of "turning" in that place, and man to be turned into the body of the church is no convenient speech, to signify a change in him that is regenerate by baptism. He indeed that is thrust out of the chancel for his misdemeanour in servicetime may be said turned into the body of the church. But Emissene speaketh not so here; but because the same Emissene, declaring the mystery of the sacrament, saith, "the visible creatures be turned into the substance of the body of Christ," this author thought it would sound gaily well, to the confusion of that true doctrine of turning, to speak in baptism of the turning of a man into the body of the church. And it may be commonly observed in* 286. *this author, when he allegeth any authority of others, he bringeth forth the same in such form of words as he would have them, and not as they be, for the most part or very often; and once of purpose were over often in so high a matter as this is. And yet in this Emissene's authority, after all the pain taken to reforge him, Emissene's doctrine plainly confoundeth this author's teaching. This author maketh a note, that there is in man, baptized, nothing changed outwardly, and therefore in the sacrament neither; and it must be granted: for the doctrine of transubstantiation teacheth not in the sacrament any outward change. For the substance of the bread and wine is an inward nature, and so is substance of one defined. And to speak of the thing changed then, as in man the change is in the soul, which is the substance of man; so, for the thing changed in the visible creatures, should be also*

---

sume.—Eusebius Emissenus. (Corpus Juris Canonici. De Consecrat. Dist. II. Cap. xxxv. "Quia corpus." Tom. I. col. 1927, 8. Ed. Lugd. 1618.) Many of the writings ascribed to Eusebius Emissenus are thought to be spurious, and have been condemned as such. Vid. James' Corruption of Scripture, &c. Lond. 1843. p. 72. Cave's His. Lit. Coci Censura Patrum. pp. 227-232. Ed. Helmst. 1683. Riveti Critica Sacra. pp. 228-231. Genev. 1626.]

changed, and is changed, the substance of the bread and wine to answer therein to the other. And we must consider how this comparison of the two changes is made as it were by proportion, wherein each change hath his special end and term, "whereunto," and therefore, according to the term and end, hath his work of change, special and several, both by God's work. Thus I mean: the visible creatures hath their end and term "whereunto" the change is made, the very body and blood of Christ, which body being a true body, we must say, is a corporal substance. The soul of man hath his end and term, a spiritual alteration, incorporal, to be regenerate the son of God. And then the doctrine of this Emissene is plain this, that each change is of like truth; and then it followeth, that if the change of man's soul in baptism be true and not in a figure, the change likewise in the sacrament is also true and not in a figure. And if man's soul by the change in baptism be in deed, that is to say, really, made the son of God, then is the substance of the bread, which is as it were the soul of the bread, (I am bold here in speech to use the word soul, to express proportion of the comparison,) but even so is the inward nature of the bread, which is substance, turned and changed into the body of Christ, being the term and end of that change. And here I say "so," not to declare the manner, but the truth of the end, that is to say, as really and in deed the change is in the substance of bread as in the soul of man: both these changes be marvellous, and both be in the truth of their change, whereunto they be changed, of like truth and reality to be done indeed: they resemble one another in the secrecy of the mystery and the ignorance of our senses, for in neither is any outward change at all; and therefore there was never man tripped himself more handsomely to take a fall, than this author doth in this place, not only in corrupting evidently and notably the words of Emissene without purpose, whereby nevertheless he shewed his good-will, but also by setting forth such matter, as overturneth all his teaching at once.

For now the author must say the change in man's soul by baptism, to be there made the son of God, is but in figure and signification, not true and real in deed; or else grant the true catholic doctrine of the turn of the visible creatures into the body and blood of Christ, to be likewise not in figure and signification, but truly, really, and in deed: and for the thing changed, as the soul of man, man's[1] inward nature, is changed; so the inward nature of the bread is changed.

And then is that evasion taken away, which this author useth in another place, of sacramental change, which should be in the outward part of the visible creatures to the use of signification. This author noteth the age of Emissene, and I note withal, how plainly he writeth for confirmation of the catholic teaching, who indeed, because of his ancient and plain writing for declaration of the matter in form of teaching without contention, is one whose authority the church hath much in allegation used to the conviction of such as have impugned the sacrament, either in the truth of the presence of Christ's very body, or transubstantiation; for the speaking of the inward change doth point as it were the change of the substance of bread, with resembling thereunto the soul of man changed in baptism. This one author, not being of any reproved, and of so many approved, and by this in the allegation after this manner corrupt, might suffice for to conclude all brabbling against the sacrament.

CANTERBURY.

287. Turning.

Where I have corrupted Emissene, let the reader be judge. But when Emissene speaketh godly of the alteration, change, and turning of a man from the congregation of the wicked unto the congregation of Christ, which he calleth "the body of the church," and from the child of death unto the child of God, this must be made a matter of scoffing, to "turn light fellows out of the chancel into the body of the church." Such trifling now-a-days becometh "gaily well" godly bishops. What if in the stead of "turning" I had said "skipt over," as the word *transiluisti* signifieth, which, although peradventure the books be false and should be *transisti*, I have translated "turning?" should I have so escaped a mock, trow you? You would then have said, he that so doth, goeth not out of the chancel door into the body of the church, but skippeth over the stalls. But that Emissene meant of turning is clear, as well by the words that go before, as those which go after; which I refer to the judgment of the indifferent reader.

[1 The soul of man in man's, &c. Orig. ed. Winch.]

But forasmuch as you would persuade men, that this author maketh so much for your purpose, I shall set forth his mind plainly, that it may appear how much you be deceived. Emissene's mind is this, that although our Saviour Christ hath taken his body hence from our bodily sight, yet we see him by faith, and by grace he is here present with us; so that by him we be made new creatures, regenerated by him, and fed and nourished by him, which generation and nutrition in us is spiritual, without any mutation appearing outwardly, but wrought within us invisibly by the omnipotent power of God. And this alteration in us is so wonderful, that we be made new creatures in Christ, grafted into his body, and of the same receive our nourishment and increasing. And yet visibly with our bodily eyes we see not these things, but they be manifest unto our faith by God's word and sacraments. And Emissene declareth none other real presence of Christ in the sacrament of his body and blood, than in the sacrament of baptism, but spiritually by faith to be present in both. *Emissenus' mind.

And where Emissene speaketh of the conversion of earthly creatures into the substance of Christ, he speaketh that as well of baptism as of the Lord's supper, as his own words plainly declare. "If thou wilt know," saith he, "how it ought not to seem to thee a new thing and impossible, that earthly and corruptible things be turned into the substance of Christ, look upon thyself, which art made new in baptism." And yet he meant not, that the water of baptism in itself is really turned into the substance of Christ, nor likewise bread and wine in the Lord's supper; but that in the action water, wine, and bread, as sacraments, be sacramentally converted, unto him that duly receiveth them, into the very substance of Christ. So that the sacramental conversion is in the sacraments, and the real conversion is in him that receiveth the sacraments; which real conversion is inward, invisible, and spiritual. For the outward corporal substances, as well of the name as of the water, remain the same that they were before. And therefore saith Emissene: "Thou visibly didst remain in the same measure that thou hadst before, but invisibly thou wast made greater without any increase of thy body; thou wast the self-same person, and yet by the increase of faith thou wast made another man. Outwardly nothing was added, but all the change was inwardly." In these words hath Emissene plainly declared, that the conversion in the sacraments, whereof he spake when he said, that earthly and corruptible things be turned into the substance of Christ, is to be understand in the receivers by their faith, and that in the said conversion the outward substance remaineth the self-same that was before. And that Emissene meant this, as well in the sacrament of the Lord's supper, as in the sacrament of baptism, his own words plainly declare. So that the substance of Christ, as well in baptism as the Lord's supper, is seen, not with our eyes, but with our faith; and touched not with our bodies, but with our minds; and received not with our hands, but with our hearts; eaten and drunken not with our outward mouths, but with our inward man. *Conversion.

289.

And where Emissene saith, that Christ hath taken his body from our sight into heaven, and yet in the sacrament of his holy supper he is present with his grace through faith, he doth us to understand, that he is not present in the forms of bread and wine out of the ministration, (except you will say, that faith and grace be in the bread when it is kept and hanged up,) but when the bread and wine be eaten and drunken according to Christ's institution, then, to them that so eat and drink, the bread and wine is the body and blood of Christ, according to Christ's words: *Edite, hoc est corpus meum. Bibite, hic est calix sanguinis mei.* And therefore[2] in the book of the holy communion, we do not pray that the creatures of bread and wine may be the body and blood of Christ; but that they may be to us the body and blood of Christ; that is to say, that we may so eat them, and drink them, that we may be partakers of his body crucified, and of his blood shed for our redemption. The Book of Common Prayer.

Thus have I declared the truth of Emissene's mind, which is agreeable to God's word and the old catholic church. But now what illusions and dreams you fantasy of Emissene's words, it is a wonder to hear. First, that the substance of bread and wine is "an inward nature," and that in baptism the whole man is not regenerated, Absurdities.

[2 Vid. p. 79.]

but "the soul" only; and that the soul of man is "the substance" of man, and made the son of God. And now, when it serveth for your purpose, the body of Christ is a corporal substance, which in all your book before was but a spiritual body, and the substance of bread and wine be visible creatures, which were wont with you to be inward and invisible natures: and now is the inward nature of the bread the substance of the bread, whereas in other places the outward forms be the substance: so little substance is in your doctrine, that from time to time you thus alter your sayings. This is no tripping, but so shameful a fall, and in so foul and stinking a place, that you shall never be able to sponge the filthiness out of your clothes, and to make yourself sweet again.

289. And you appoint at your pleasure both *terminum a quo*, *terminum ad quem*, and the changes, and the things that be changed, altogether otherwise than Emissene doth. For in Emissene the changes be regeneration, and nourishing or augmentation; the thing that is changed is the man, both in regeneration, and in nutrition or augmentation; and in regeneration *terminus a quo* is the son of perdition; and *terminus ad quem* is the son of God. And in nutrition *terminus a quo* is the hunger and thirst of the man; and *terminus ad quem* is the feeding and satisfying of his hunger and thirst. But you appoint the changes to be transubstantiation and regeneration, and the things that be changed in transubstantiation you say is the substance of bread and wine, and the same to be *terminum a quo*, and the flesh and blood of Christ, say you, is *terminus ad quem*. And in regeneration you assign *terminum a quo*, to be the soul of man only; and *terminum ad quem*, to be regenerated the son of God. And so being eight things in these two mutations, in each of them the change, the thing that is changed, the thing from whence it is changed, and the thing whereunto it is changed, you have missed the butt clearly in all, saving two, that is to say, regeneration and the thing whereunto regeneration is made, and in all other six you missed the cushion quite. And yet if the change were in the substance of bread and wine proportionably to the change of the soul, being the substance of man, as you say; if you should make the proportions agree, then as the soul, being the man's substance, remaineth without transubstantiation, so must the bread and wine remain without transubstantiation. And if the substance of the bread and wine be not the visible sign in the Lord's supper, because "substance", as you say, "is a thing invisible," then is not the substance of water the visible sign in baptism, being no more visible the substance of the one, than the substance of the other.

Now of Hilary I write thus.

Hilarius.

Hilarius also in few words saith the same. "There is a figure," saith he, "for bread and wine be outwardly seen. And there is also a truth of that figure, for the body and blood of Christ be of a truth inwardly believed[1]." And this Hilarius was within less than three hundred and fifty years after Christ.

WINCHESTER.

Hilarius.

But I will examine more particularities. I have before answered to Hilary, to whom nevertheless I would aptly have said somewhat now, to note how he distincteth outwardly and inwardly by belief and corporal sight. For outwardly, as Emissene saith, we see no change, and therefore we see after consecration, as before, which we may therefore call bread; but we believe that inwardly is, which, as Emissene saith, is the substance of the body of Christ, whereunto the change is made of the inward nature of bread, as by the comparison of Emissene doth appear.

CANTERBURY.

Your distinction made here of "outwardly" and "inwardly," is a plain confusion of Hilarius' mind, and contrary to that which you wrote before in Emissene. For there

---

[1 Corpus Christi, quod sumitur de altari, figura est, dum panis et vinum extra videtur: veritas autem, dum corpus et sanguis Christi in veritate interius creditur.—Corpus Juris Canonici. De Consecrat. Dist. II. cap. lxxix. "Corpus Christi." Tom. II. col. 1956. Ed. Lugduni. 1618. By a note at this place in the "Corpus Jur. Canon." it appears that this passage is not to be found in Hilary.]

you said, that "the visible creatures be changed," meaning by the visible creatures the substances of bread and wine; and now, when Hilary saith that "bread and wine be seen," you say that "their substances be not seen, but the outward forms only," which, you say, "be called bread and wine." But here appeareth into how narrow a strait you be driven, that be fain for a shift to say, "that the accidents of bread without the substance be called bread."

Epiphanius is next in my book.

And Epiphanius, shortly after the same time, saith, that "the bread is meat, but the virtue that is in it is it that giveth life[2]." But if there were no bread at all, how could it be meat?

290. Epiphanius contra Hæreses. Lib. iii. Tom. ii. et in Anacephaleosi.

WINCHESTER.

These words of Epiphanius do plainly overturn this author's doctrine of a figurative speech; for a figure cannot give life, only God giveth life: and the speech of this Epiphanius of the sacrament doth necessarily imply the very true presence of Christ's body, author of life. And then, as often as the author is overthrown in the truth of the presence, so often is he, by Zuinglius' rule, overthrown in transubstantiation. As for the name of bread is granted because it was so, and transubstantiation doth not take away, but it is meat because of the visible matter remaining.

These[3] sayings be sought out by this author only to wrangle, not taken out where the mystery is declared and preached to be taught as a doctrine thereof, but only signified by the way, and spoken of upon occasion, the sense whereof faithful men know otherwise than appeareth at the first readings to the carnal man: but by such like speeches the Arians impugned the divinity of Christ.

[Epiphanius. Orig. ed. Winch.]

CANTERBURY.

Epiphanius, speaking of the bread in the Lord's supper, and the water in baptism, saith, that they "have no power nor strength of themselves, but by Christ:" so that the bread feedeth, and the water washeth the body; but neither the bread nor water give life, nor purge to salvation, but only the might and power of Christ that is in them: and yet not in them reserved, but in the action and ministration, as it is manifest of his words. And therefore, as in baptism is neither the real and corporal presence of Christ's body, nor transubstantiation of the water; no more is in the Lord's supper either Christ's flesh and blood really and corporally present, or the bread and wine transubstantiated. And therefore Epiphanius calleth not bread by that name because it was so, but because it is so in deed, and nourished[4] the body. As Hilary said, "there is a figure, for bread and wine be openly seen:" he saith not, there was a figure, for bread and wine were openly seen. And the figure giveth not life, nor washeth not inwardly, but Christ that is in the figure, *tanquam signatum in signo*. And where you be fain to say, that "accidents be meat without substance," all the world may judge how shameful a shift this is, and how contrary to this principle of philosophy, *Ex eisdem sunt et nutriuntur omnia*. Oh, what absurdities you be driven unto for the defence of your papistical inventions!

Now cometh St John Chrysostom, of whom in my book is thus written.

About the same time, or shortly after, about the year of our Lord 400, St John Chrysostom writeth thus against them that used only water in

Chrysost. in Matt. cap. xxvi. Hom. 83.

[² Ἐνταῦθα ἐν Χριστῷ τῷ ἰσχυροποιουμένῳ τῆς δυνάμεως τοῦ ἄρτου καὶ τῆς τοῦ ὕδατος ἰσχύος· ἵνα οὐκ ἄρτος ἡμῖν γένηται δύναμις, ἀλλὰ δύναμις ἄρτου· καὶ βρῶσις μὲν ὁ ἄρτος, ἡ δὲ δύναμις ἐν αὐτῷ εἰς ζωογόνησιν.—Epiphanius, adversus Hæreses. Lib. III. Tom. I. p. 1098. ed. Patav. Paris. 1622.]

[³ This, 1551.]   [⁴ Nourisheth, 1551.]

the sacrament. "Christ," saith he, "minding to pluck up that heresy by the roots, used wine as well before his resurrection, when he gave the mysteries, as after at his table without mysteries. For he saith, 'Of the fruit of the vine;' which surely bringeth forth no water, but wine[1]."

These words of Chrysostom declare plainly, that Christ in his holy table both drank wine and gave wine to drink, which had not been true if no wine had remained after the consecration, as the papists feign. And yet more plainly St Chrysostom declareth this matter in another place, saying: "The bread before it be sanctified is called bread, but when it is sanctified by the means of the priest, it is delivered from the name of bread, and is exalted to the name of the Lord's body, although the nature of bread doth still remain[2]."

Ad Cæsarium Monachum.

291.

"The nature of bread," saith he, "doth still remain," to the utter and manifest confutation of the papists, which say, "that the accidents of bread do remain, but not the nature and substance."

WINCHESTER.

Chrysostom.

Chrysostom speaketh in this place of wine, as, Cyprian did before, against those that offer no wine, but water. Chrysostom saith thus: "Christ used wine;" and I grant he did so. For he did consecrate that creature, and, as Emissene saith, "turned it in the celebration and dispensation of these mysteries." But this saying toucheth nothing the doctrine of transubstantiation. The second saying of Chrysostom, which I never read but in Peter Martyr's book, who saith it is not printed, toucheth this author's doctrine much, if the bread by consecration be "delivered from the name of bread, and exalted to the name of our Lord's body." Now consider, reader: if this manner of speech by Chrysostom here meaneth an effectual naming, to make the substance of the body of Christ present, (as Chrysostom in his public approved works is understanded of all to teach,) then is the deliverance from the name of bread of like effect, to take away the reason of the name of bread, which is the change in substance thereof. Or if the author will say that by the name of bread Chrysostom understandeth the bare name, how can that stand without reproof of St Paul, who, after this author's mind, calleth it bread after consecration? and so do many other by this author alleged. Here percase may be said, "What should I reason what he meant, when he saith plainly the nature of bread still remaineth?" To this I say, that as Chrysostom, in this place of an epistle not published by credit, saith "that the nature of bread remaineth:" so Cyprian, that was older than he, saith, "the nature of bread is changed," which Chrysostom in his other works, by public credit set abroad, seemeth not to deny. Now the word "nature" signifieth both the substance and also propriety of the nature. The substance therefore, after Cyprian, by the word of God is changed, but yet the proper effect is not changed, but in the accidences remain without illusion; by which divers signification and acception of the word "nature," both the sayings of St Cyprian and St Chrysostom (if this be his saying) may be accorded, and, notwithstanding the contrariety in letter, agree nevertheless in sense between themselves, and agree with the true doctrine of transubstantiation. Add to this, how the words of Chrysostom next following this sentence, alleged by this author, and as it seemeth of purpose left here out, do both confound this author's enterprise, and confirm the true doctrine: which words be these, "And is not called two bodies, but one body of the Son of God." Of Chrysostom I shall speak again hereafter.

*The word "nature," hath two significations.

[1 Τίνος ἕνεκεν οὐχ ὕδωρ ἔπιεν ἀναστάς, ἀλλ' οἶνον; ἄλλην αἵρεσιν πονηρὰν πρόῤῥιζον ἀνασπῶν. ἐπειδὴ γάρ εἰσίν τινες ἐν τοῖς μυστηρίοις ὕδατι κεχρημένοι, δεικνὺς ὅτι ἡνίκα τὰ μυστήρια παρέδωκεν, οἶνον παρέδωκε, καὶ ἡνίκα ἀναστὰς χωρὶς μυστηρίων ψιλὴν τράπεζαν παρετίθετο, οἴνῳ ἐκέχρητο ἐκ τοῦ γεννήματός, φησι, τῆς ἀμπέλου. ἡ ἄμπελος δὲ οἶνον, οὐχ ὕδωρ γεννᾷ.—Chrysostom. In Matt. cap. xxvi. Hom. LXXXII. (al. 83.) Tom. VII. p. 784. ed. Bened.]

[2 Sicut enim antequam sanctificetur panis, panem nominamus; divina autem illum sanctificante gratia, mediante sacerdote, liberatus est quidem ab appellatione panis, dignus autem habitus Dominici Corporis appellatione, etiamsi natura panis in ipso permansit—Id. Ad Cæsarium Monachum. Tom. III. p. 743. The authenticity of this book, which was brought by P. Martyr to England and given to Cranmer, is much disputed; a Latin version only being extant, with the exception of a few passages in Greek. Vid. Chrysost. Op. ed. Bened. Tom. III. p. 736. Jo. Geo. Walchius. Bibl. Patrist. pp. 194, 295. Ed. Jenæ 1834. Burnet's Hist. of the Reformation, Tom. III. p. 736. Ed. Oxford, 1829. Dupin. Eccl. Writers, Cent. V.]

CANTERBURY.

The first place of Chrysostom by me alleged, you say, "toucheth not the doctrine of transubstantiation." But you rehearse but a piece of Chrysostom's words. For he saith not only that Christ used wine, but also drank wine in the mysteries, and the very wine of the grape. And how could then the wine be transubstantiate, except it were transubstantiate after it was drunken?

Now as touching the second part of Chrysostom, where he saith, that "the bread, when it is consecrated, is delivered from the name of bread and is exalted to the name of the Lord's body, and yet the nature of bread doth still remain," he meaneth that the bread is delivered from the bare name of bread, to represent unto us the body of Christ, according to his institution, which was crucified for us; not that he is present or crucified in the bread, but was crucified upon the cross. And the bread is not so clearly delivered from the name of bread, that it is no bread at all, (for he saith, "the nature of bread doth still remain,") nor that it may not be called by the name of bread; but it is so delivered, that commonly it is called by the higher name of the Lord's body, which to us it representeth. As you and I were delivered from our surnames, when we were consecrated bishops, sithens which time we have so commonly been used of all men to be called bishops, you of Winchester, and I of Canterbury, that the most part of the people know not that your name is Gardiner, and mine Cranmer. And I pray God that we, being called to the name of lords, have not forgotten our own baser estates, that once we were simple squires. And yet should he have done neither of us wrong, that should have called us by our right names, no more than St Paul doth any injury to the bread in the sacrament, calling it bread, although it have also an higher name of dignity, to be called the body of Christ. And as the bread, being a figure of Christ's body, hath the name thereof, and yet is not so in deed; so I pray God, that we have not rather been figures of bishops, bearing the name and title of pastors and bishops before men, than that we have in deed diligently fed the little flock of Christ with the sweet and wholesome pasture of his true and lively word.

292. Changing of names.

And where you allege Cyprian, to avoid thereby the saying of Chrysostom in the epistle by me cited, you take Cyprian clearly amiss, as I have plainly opened hereafter in the eleventh chapter of this book[3], whereunto for to avoid the tediousness of repeating, I refer the indifferent reader; unto which mine answer there, helpeth much that you grant here, that the word "nature" signifieth both the substance and also the propriety. For in Cyprian it is not taken for the substance, as you would fain have it, but for the property. For the substance of bread still remaining in them that duly receive the same, the property of carnal nourishment is changed into a spiritual nourishment, as more largely in mine answer to you in that place shall be declared.

Cyprian.

The word "nature."

And where you would somewhat relieve yourself by certain words of Chrysostom, which immediately follow the sentence by me alleged, which words be these, "that the bread after consecration is not called two bodies, but one body of the Son of God," upon which words you would gather your transubstantiation; how effectual your argument is in this matter, may appear by another like. Stephen Gardiner, after he was consecrated, was called the bishop of Winchester, and not two bishops but one bishop: ergo Stephen Gardiner was transubstantiate. And a counter laid by an auditor for a thousand pounds, is not then called a counter but a thousand pounds: ergo, it is transubstantiated. And the man and wife after marriage be called but one body: ergo, there is transubstantiation. This must be the form of your argument, if you will prove transubstantiation by these words of Chrysostom.

Now come we to St Ambrose.

At the same time was St Ambrose, who declared the alteration of bread and wine into the body and blood of Christ, not to be such, that the nature and

Ambrosius.

[3 See p. 308, &c.]

substance of bread and wine be gone, but that through grace there is a spiritual mutation by the mighty power of God, so that he that worthily eateth of that bread, doth spiritually eat Christ, and dwelleth in Christ, and Christ in him.

293.
De iis qui mysteriis initiantur, cap. ult. et de Sacramentis, Lib. iv. cap. 4.

"For," saith St Ambrose[1], speaking of this change of bread into the body of Christ, "if the word of God be of that force that it can make things of nought, and those things to be which never were before, much more it can make things that were before, still to be, and also to be changed into other things."

And he bringeth for example hereof the change of us in baptism, wherein a man is so changed, as is before declared in the words of Eusebius, that he is made a new creature, and yet his substance remaineth the same that was before.

WINCHESTER.

Ambrosius.

St Ambrose doth not, as this author would have it, impugn transubstantiation, but confirmeth it most plainly, because he teacheth the true presence of Christ's body in the sacrament, which, he saith, is by change, and things still remaining, and that may be verified in the outward visible matter, that is to say, the accidents remaining with their proper effects, which therefore may worthily be called things. And here I would ask this author, if his teaching, as he pretendeth, were the catholic faith, and the bread only signified Christ's body, what should need this force of God's word that St Ambrose speaketh of, to bring in the creation of the world, whereby to induce man's faith in this mystery to the belief of it? As for the example of baptism to shew the change in man's soul, whereof I have spoken, declaring Emissene, serveth for an induction not to lean[2] to our outward senses, ne to mistrust the great miracle of God in either, because we see none outward experience of it; but else it is not necessary that the resemblance shall answer in equality, otherwise than as I said afore, each part answering his convenient proportion, and as for their comparison of resemblance, baptism with the sacrament, this author in his doctrine specially reproveth, in that he cannot, I think, deny, but man by regeneration of his soul in baptism is the partaker of holiness; but as for the bread, he specially admonisheth, that it is not partaker of holiness by this consecration: but howsoever this author in his own doctrine snarleth himself, the doctrine of St Ambrose is plain, that before the consecration it is bread, and after the consecration the body of Christ; which is an undoubted affirmation then to be no bread, howsoever the accidents of bread do remain.

CANTERBURY.

St Ambrose teacheth not the real and corporal presence of Christ's body in the sacrament, as I have proved sufficiently in my former book, the sixty-fourth, eighty-first, and eighty-second leaves[3], and in mine answer unto you in this book. But against transubstantiation he teacheth plainly, that after consecration not only things remain, but also that the things changed still remain. And what is this but a flat condemnation of your imagined transubstantiation? For if the things changed in the sacrament do still remain, and the substances of bread and wine be changed, then it followeth that their substances remain, and be not transubstantiated; so that your untrue and crafty shift will not relieve your matter any whit, when you say, that the accidence of bread is bread, wherein all the world knoweth how much you err from the truth. And better it had been for you to have kept such sayings secret unto yourself, which no man can speak without blushing, except he be past all shame, than to shew your shameful shifts open unto the world, that all men may see them: and specially when the shewing thereof only discovereth your shame, and easeth you

---

[1 Quod si tantum valuit humana benedictio, ut naturam converteret; quid dicimus de ipsa consecratione divina, ubi verba ipsa Domini salvatoris operantur?—Sermo ergo Christi qui potuit ex nihilo facere quod non erat, non potest ea quæ sunt, in id mutare quod non erant? Non enim minus est novas rebus dare quam mutare naturas.—Ambros. De initiandis, cap. ix. Tom. IV. p. 166. Colon. Agrip 1616.—Vides ergo quam operatorius sit sermo Christi. Si ergo tanta vis est in sermone Domini Jesu, ut inciperent esse quæ non erant: quanto magis operatorius est, ut quæ erant, in aliud commutentur. Id. De Sacramentis, Lib. iv. cap. iv. Ib. See p. 210.]

[2 To leave, Orig. ed. Winch.]

[3 See pp. 122, 177, 8.]

nothing at all. For the accidences be not changed, as you say yourself, but the substances. And then if the things that be changed remain, the substance must remain, and not be transubstantiated. And St Ambrose bringeth forth to good purpose the creation of the world, to shew the wonderful work of God, as well in the spiritual regeneration, and spiritual feeding and nourishing of the lively members of Christ's body, as in the creation and conservation of the world. And therefore David calleth the spiritual renovation of man by the name of creation, saying: *Cor mundum crea in me Deus*, "O God, create in me a new heart." And as for any further answer here unto Ambrose needeth not, but because you refer you here to Emissene, they which be indifferent may read what I have answered unto Emissene a little before, and so judge.

294.

Psal. l.

Now let us examine St Augustine.

And St Augustine about the same time wrote thus: "That which you see in the altar is the bread and the cup, which also your eyes do shew you. But faith sheweth further, that bread is the body of Christ, and the cup his blood[4]." [Here he declareth two things: that in the sacrament remaineth bread and wine which we may discern with our eyes; and that the bread and wine be called the body and blood of Christ.]

Augustinus in Sermone ad Infantes.

[Vid. Embd. ed. in fine tomi hujus.]

And the same thing he declareth also as plainly in another place, saying: "The sacrifice of the church consisteth of two things, of the visible kind of the element, and of the invisible flesh and blood of our Lord Jesu Christ, both of the sacrament and of the thing signified by the sacrament: even as the person of Christ consisteth of God and man, forasmuch as he is very God and very man. For every thing containeth in it the very nature of those things whereof it consisteth. Now the sacrifice of the church consisteth of two things, of the sacrament, and of the thing thereby signified, that is to say, the body of Christ. Therefore there is both the sacrament, and the thing of the sacrament, which is Christ's body[5]."

In Lib. Sententiarum Prosperi.

[Vid. Embd. ed.]

What can be devised to be spoken more plainly against the error of the papists, which say that no bread nor wine remaineth in the sacrament? For as the person of Christ consisteth of two natures, that is to say, of his manhood and of his Godhead, and therefore both those natures remain in Christ; even so, saith St Augustine, the sacrament consisteth of two natures, of the elements of bread and wine, and of the body and blood of Christ, and therefore both these natures must needs remain in the sacrament.

For the more plain understanding thereof, it is to be noted, that there were certain heretics, as Simon, Menander, Marcion, Valentinus, Basilides, Cerdon, Manes, Eutyches, Manichæus, Apollinaris, and divers other of like sorts, which said, that Christ was very God, but not a very man, although in eating, drinking, sleeping, and all other operations of man, to men's judgments he appeared like unto a man.

[4 Quod videtis, panis est et calix, quod vobis etiam oculi vestri renuntiant: quod autem fides vestra postulat instruenda, panis est corpus Christi, calix sanguis Christi. Augustin. Ad Infantes, Serm. cclxxii. Tom. V. p. 1103. ed. Bened. Instead of the passage within brackets, the Orig. ed. reads thus: "Here he declareth four things to be in the sacrament: two that we see, which be bread and wine; and other two, which we see not, but by faith only, which be the body and blood of Christ."]

[5 Sacrificium scilicet ecclesiæ duobus confici, duobus constare, visibili elementorum specie, et invisibili Domini nostri Jesu Christi carne et sanguine, sacramento, et re sacramenti id est, corpore Christi; sicut Christi persona constat et conficitur Deo et homine, cum ipse Christus verus sit Deus, et verus homo: quia omnis res illarum rerum naturam et veritatem in se continet, ex quibus conficitur. Conficitur autem sacrificium ecclesiæ sacramento et re sacramenti, id est, corpore Christi. Est igitur sacramentum, et res sacramenti, id est, corpus Christi. August. in Lib. sent. Prosperi. (Corpus Juris Canonici. De consecrat. Dist. ii. cap. 48. Hoc est. Col. 1936, 37. Lugd. 1618.) Cranmer quoted this passage from the Master of the Sentences: it is not found in the Appendix either of the Benedictine or Louvain editions of the works of St Augustine.]

Other there were, as Artemon, Theodorus, Sabellius, Paulus Samasatenus, Marcellus, Photinus, Nestorius, and many other of the same sects, which said, that he was a very natural man, but not very God, although in giving the blind their sight, the dumb their speech, the deaf their hearing, in healing suddenly with his word all diseases, in raising to life them that were dead, and in all other works of God, he shewed himself as he had been God.

Yet other there were, which seeing the scripture so plain in those two matters, confessed that he was both God and man, but not both at one time. For before his incarnation, said they, he was God only, and not man, and after his incarnation he ceased from the Godhead[1], and became a man only, and not God until his resurrection or ascension; and then, say they, he left his manhood and was only God again, as he was before his incarnation. So that when he was man, he was not God; and when he was God, he was not man.

But against these vain heresies the catholic faith, by the express word of God, holdeth and believeth, that Christ after his incarnation left not his divine nature, but remained still God, as he was before, being together at one time, as he is still, both perfect God and perfect man.

And for a plain declaration hereof, the old ancient authors give two examples. One is of man, which is made of two parts, of a soul and of a body, and each of these two parts remain in man at one time: so that when the soul by the almighty power of God is put into the body, neither the body nor soul perisheth thereby, but thereof is made a perfect man, having a perfect soul and a perfect body, remaining in him both at one time. The other example, which the old authors bring in for this purpose, is of the holy supper of our Lord, which consisteth, say they, of two parts, of the sacrament or visible element of bread and wine, and of the body and blood of Christ. And as in them that duly receive the sacrament, the very natures of bread and wine cease not to be there, but remain there still, and be eaten and drunken corporally, as the body and blood of Christ be eaten and drunken spiritually; so likewise doth the divine nature of Christ remain still with his humanity.

Let now the papists avaunt themselves of their transubstantiation, that there remaineth no bread nor wine in the ministration of the sacrament, if they will defend the wicked heresies before rehearsed, that Christ is not God and man both together. But to prove that this was the mind of the old authors, beside the saying of St Augustine here recited, I shall also rehearse divers other.

WINCHESTER.

Augustinus. *In the twenty-sixth leaf[2] this author bringeth forth two sayings of St Augustine, which when this author wrote, it is like he neither thought of the third or first book of this work. For these two sayings declare most evidently the real presence of Christ's body and blood in the sacrament, affirming the same to be the sacrifice of the church, whereby appeareth it is no figure only. In the first saying of St Augustine is written thus: "how faith sheweth me that bread is the body of Christ." Now whatsoever faith sheweth is a truth, and then it followeth that of a truth it is the body of Christ: which speech, "bread is the body of Christ," is as much to say as it is made the body of Christ, and made not as of a matter, but, as Emissene wrote, by conversion of the visible creature into the substance of the body of Christ; and, as St Augustine in the same sentence writeth, "it is bread before the consecration, and after the flesh of Christ." As for the second saying of St Augustine, how could it with more plain words be written, than to say that "there is both the sacrament and the thing of the sacrament," which is Christ's body, calling the same the sacrifice of the church? Now if Christ's body be there, it is truly there, and in deed there, which is really there: as for there in a figure, were as much to say as not there[3] in truth and in deed, but only signified to be*

[1 His Godhead, 1551, and Orig. ed.]   [2 Vid. p. 277.]   [3 Were to say not there, Orig. ed. Winch.]

absent, which is the nature of a figure in his proper and special speech. But St Augustine saith, even as the author bringeth him forth, and yet he gave[4] his privy nip by the way thus: "It is said of St Augustine there be two things in the sacrifice, which be contained in it, whereof it consisteth, so as the body of Christ is contained in this sacrifice by St Augustine's mind." According whereunto, St Augustine is alleged to say in the same book, from whence this author took this saying, also these words following: "Under the kinds of bread and wine which we see, we honour things invisible, that is to say, the flesh and blood of Christ; nor we do not likewise esteem these two kinds as we did before the consecration, for we must faithfully confess before the consecration to be bread and wine that nature formed, and after consecration, the flesh and blood of Christ, which the benediction hath consecrate." Thus saith St Augustine, as he is alleged out of that book[5], which in deed I have not, but he hath the like sense in other places; and for honouring of the invisible heavenly things there, which declare the true and real presence, St Augustine hath the like in his book, De Catechisandis Rudibus, and in the ninety-eighth psalm, where he speaketh of adoration. This may be notable to the reader, how this author concludeth himself in the faith of the real presence[6] of Christ's body, by his own collection of St Augustine's mind, which is as he confesseth in his own words, noting St Augustine, that "as the person of Christ consisteth of two natures, so the sacrament consisteth of two natures, of the elements of bread and wine, and of the body and blood of Christ, and therefore both these natures do remain in the sacrament." These be this author's own words, who, travailing to confound transubstantiation, confoundeth evidently himself by his own words touching the real presence. For he saith the nature of the body and blood of Christ must remain in the sacrament, and as truly as the natures of the manhood and Godhead were in Christ, for thereupon he argueth. And now let this author choose whether he will say any of the natures, the manhood or the Godhead, were but figuratively in Christ; which and he do, then may he the better say for the agreement of his doctrine, the nature of the body and blood of Christ is but figuratively in the sacrament. And if he say, as he must needs say, that the two natures be in Christ's person really, naturally, substantially, then must he grant by his own collection the truth of the being of the nature of the body and blood of Christ to be likewise in the sacrament, and thereby call back all that he hath written against the real presence of Christ's body in the sacrament, and abandon his device of a presence by signification, which is in truth a plain absence as himself also speaketh openly, which open speech cannot stand, and is improved by this open speech of his own.

296.
*Out of the Master of the Sentences and Decrees.

*The book of St Augustine De Sent. Prosperi is not commonly had.

Likewise where he saith "the nature of the body and blood of Christ remain in the sacrament," the word "remain" being of such signification, as it betokeneth not only to be there, but to tarry there, and so there is declared the sacrifice of the church, which mystery of sacrifice is perfected before the perception; and so it must be evident how the body of Christ is there, that is to say, on the altar before we receive it, to which altar, St Augustine saith, we come to receive it. There was never man overturned his own assertions more evidently, than this author doth here in this place; the like whereof I have observed in other that have written against this sacrament, who have by the way said somewhat for it, or they have brought their treatise to an end.

It will be said here, Howsoever this author doth overthrow himself in the real presence of Christ's very body, yet he hath pulled down transubstantiation, and done[7] as crafty wrestlers do, falling themselves on their back, to throw their fellow over them. But it is not like; for as long as the true faith of the real presence standeth, so long transubstantiation standeth[8], not by authority of determination, but by a necessary consequence of the truth, as I said before, and as Zuinglius defendeth plainly: and as for these places of St Augustine may be answered unto, for they speak of the visible nature and element, which remain truly in the propriety of their nature, for so much as remaineth, so as there is true real and bodily matter of the accidents of bread and wine, not in fantasy or imagination, whereby there should be illusion in the senses, but so in deed as the experience doth shew, and the change of substance of the creatures into a better substance should not impair the truth of that remaineth, but that remaineth doth in deed remain, with the same natural effects by miracle that it had when the substance was there; which is one marvel in this mystery, as there were diverse more in manna, the figure of it. And then

---

[4 He have, Ibid.]
[5 Magister Sententiarum, Lib. iv. Dist. x. fol. 351. ed. Col. 1576.]
[6 In the real presence, Ibid.]
[7 And do as, Ibid.]
[8 So long standeth transubstantiation, 1551.]

a miracle in God's working doth not impair the truth of the work. And therefore I noted before, how St Thomas did touch Christ after his resurrection truly, and yet it was by miracle, as St Gregory writeth. And further we may say, touching the comparison, that when a resemblance is made of the sacrament to Christ's person, or contrariwise of Christ's person to declare the sacrament, we may not press all parts of the resemblance, with a thorough equality in consideration of each part by itself, but only have respect to the end wherefore the resemblance is made. In the person of Christ be joined two whole perfect natures inseparably unite, (which faith the Nestorians impugned,) and yet unite without confusion of them, (which confusion the Eutychians in consequence of their error affirmed,) and so arguments be brought of the sacrament, wherewith to convince both, as I shall shew, answering to Gelasius. But in this place St Augustine useth the truth most certain of the two natures in Christ's person, whereby to declare his belief in the sacrament; which belief, as Hilary before is by this author alleged to say, is of that is inwardly. For that is outwardly of the visible creature, "we see," he saith, "with our bodily eye," and therefore therein is no point of faith that should need such a declaration, as St Augustine maketh. And yet making the comparison, he rehearseth both the truths on both sides, saying: "As the person of Christ consisteth of God and man, so the sacrifice of the church consisteth of two things, the visible kind of the element, and the invisible flesh and blood," finishing the conclusion of the similitude, that therefore there is in the sacrifice of the church both the sacrament and the thing of the sacrament, Christ's body, that which is invisible, and therefore required declaration, that is by St Augustine opened in the comparison; that is to say, the body of Christ to be there truly, and therewith, that needed no declaration, that is to say, the visible kind of the element is spoken of also as being true, but not as a thing which was intended to be proved, for it needed not any proof as the other part did. And therefore it is not necessary to press both parts of the resemblance so, as because in the nature of Christ's humanity there was no substance converted in Christ, which had been contrary to the order of that mystery, which was to join the whole nature of man to the Godhead in the person of Christ, that therefore in this mystery of the sacrament, in which by the rules[1] of our faith Christ's body is not impanate, the conversion of the substance of the visible elements should not therefore be. If truth answereth to truth for proportion of the truth in the mystery, that is sufficient. For else the natures be not so unite in one hypostasy in the mystery of the sacrament, as there be[2] in Christ's person, and the flesh of man in Christ by union of the divinity is a divine spiritual flesh, and is called and is a lively flesh; and yet the author of this book is not afraid to teach the bread in the sacrament to have no participation of holiness, wherein I agree not with him, but reason against him with his own doctrine; and much I could say more, but this shall suffice. The words of St Augustine for the real presence of Christ's body be such as no man can wrest or writhe to another sense, and with their force have made this author to overthrow[3] himself in his own words. But that St Augustine saith, touching the nature of bread and the visible element of the sacrament, without wresting or writhing, may be agreed in convenient understanding with the doctrine of transubstantiation, and therefore is an authority familiar with those writers that affirm transubstantiation by express words, out of whose quiver this author hath pulled out his bolt[4], and as it is out of his bow sent, turneth back and hitteth himself on the forehead; and yet after his fashion, by wrong and untrue translation, he sharpened it somewhat, not without some punishment of God, evidently by the way by his own words to overthrow himself.

* The Master of the Sentences hath these words of St Augustine.

In the second column of the twenty-seventh leaf, and the first of the twenty-eighth leaf[5], this author maketh a process in declaration of heresies in the person of Christ, for conviction whereof, this author saith, the old fathers used arguments of two examples, in either of which examples were two natures together, the one not perishing ne confounding the other. One example is in the body and soul of man: another example of the sacrament, in which be two natures, an inward heavenly, and an outward earthly, as in man there is a body and a soul.

I leave out this author's own judgment in that place, and of thee, O reader, require thine, whether those fathers that did use both these examples to the confutation of heretics, did not believe, as appeareth by the process of their reasoning in this point, did they not, I say, believe, that even as really and as truly, as the soul of man is present in the body, so really and so truly is the body of Christ, which in the sacrament is the inward invisible thing, as the soul is in the body, present in the sacrament? For else, and the body of Christ were not as truly and

---

[[1] In the which by the rule, Orig. ed. Winch.]
[[2] As they be, 1551.]
[[3] This author overthrow, Orig. ed. Winch.]
[[4] This bolt, Ibid.] [[5] Vid. pp. 277, 8.]

really present in the sacrament, as the soul is in man's body, that argument of the sacrament 298.
*had not two things present, so as the argument of the body and soul had, whereby to shew how
two things may be together without confusion of either, each remaining in his nature: for if the
teaching of this author in other parts of this book were true, then were the sacrament like a
body lying in a trance, whose soul for the while were in heaven, and had no two things, but
one bare thing, that is to say, bread, and bread never the holier with signification of another
thing so far absent, as is heaven from earth; and therefore, to say as I probably think, this
part of this second book against transubstantiation was a collection of this author when he
minded to maintain Luther's opinion against transubstantiation only, and to strive for bread
only, which notwithstanding the new enterprise of this author to deny the real presence, is so
fierce and vehement, as it overthroweth his new purpose ere he cometh in his order in his book to
entreat of it. For there can no demonstration be made more evident for the catholic faith of the
real presence of Christ's body in the sacrament, than that the truth of it was so certainly believed,
as they took Christ's very body as verily in the sacrament, even as the soul is present in the body
of man.*

CANTERBURY.

When you wrote this, it is like that you had not considered my third book, wherein is a plain and direct answer to all that you have brought in this place, or elsewhere, concerning the real presence of Christ's body and blood in the sacrament. And how slender proofs you make in this place, to prove the real presence because of the sacrifice, every man may judge, being neither your argument good, nor your antecedent true. For St Augustine saith not, that the body and blood of Christ is the sacrifice of the church; and if he had so said, it inferreth not this conclusion, that the body of Christ should be really in the bread, and his blood in the wine.

And although St Augustine saith, that "bread is Christ's body," yet if you had well marked the sixty-fourth, sixty-fifth, and sixty-sixth leaves of my book[6], you should there have perceived how St Augustine declareth at length, in what manner of speech that is to be understand, that is to say figuratively, in which speech the thing that signifieth and the thing that is signified have both one name, as St Cyprian manifestly teacheth[7]. For in plain speech, without figure, bread is not the body of Christ by your own confession, who do say, that the affirmation of one substance is the negation of another. And if the bread were made the body of Christ, as you say it is, then must you needs confess, that the body of Christ is made of bread, which before you said "was so foolish a saying, as were not tolerable by a scoffer to be devised in a play, to supply when his fellow had forgotten his part." And seeing that the bread is not annihilate and consumed into nothing, as the school authors teach, then must it needs follow, that the body of Christ is made of the matter of bread; for that it is made of the form of bread, I suppose you will not grant.

How bread is Christ's body.

Cyprianus de Unctione Chrismatis.

And as touching the second place of St Augustine, he saith not that the body and blood of Christ be really in the sacrament, but that in the sacrifice of the church, that is to say, in the holy administration of the Lord's supper, is both a sacrament and the thing signified by the sacrament, the sacrament being the bread and wine, and the thing signified and exhibited being the body and blood of Christ. But St Augustine saith not, that the thing signified is in the bread and wine, to whom it is not exhibited, nor is not in it, but as in a figure; but that it is there in the true ministration of the sacrament, present to the spirit and faith of the true believing man, and exhibited truly and in deed, and yet spiritually, not corporally.

299.

And what need any more evident proofs of St Augustine's mind in this matter, how bread is called Christ's body, than St Augustine's own words cited in the same place, where the other is *de Consecratione*, Dist. ii, "*Hoc est quod dicimus?*" These be St Augustine's words there cited: *Sicut cœlestis panis, qui Christi caro est, suo modo vocatur corpus Christi, cum revera sit sacramentum corporis Christi, illius videlicet, quod visibile, quod palpabile, mortale, in cruce positum est, vocaturque ipsa immolatio carnis, quæ sacerdotis manibus fit, Christi passio, mors, crucifixio, non rei*

De Consecrat. Dist. 2. "Hoc est."

[6 Vid. pp. 123—127.]   [7 Vid. p. 121.]

veritate, sed significanti mysterio: sic sacramentum fidei, quod baptismus intelligitur, fides est[1]. "As the heavenly bread, which is Christ's flesh, after a manner is called the body of Christ, where in very deed it is a sacrament of Christ's body, that is to say, of that body which being visible, palpable, mortal, was put upon the cross; and as that offering of the flesh which is done by the priest's hands, is called the passion, the death, the crucifying of Christ, not in truth of the thing, but in a signifying mystery; so is the sacrament of faith, which is baptism, faith." These words be so plain and manifest, that the expositor, being a very papist, yet could not avoid the matter, but wrote thus upon the said words: *Immolatio, quæ fit a presbytero, improprie appellatur Christi passio, vel mors, vel crucifixio: non quod sit illa, sed quia illam significat*[2]. And after he saith: *Cœleste sacramentum, quod vere repræsentat Christi carnem, dicitur corpus Christi, sed improprie. Unde dicitur, suo modo, sed non rei veritate, sed significanti mysterio; ut sit sensus, vocatur Christi corpus, id est, significat*[3]. "The offering which the priest maketh, is called improperly the passion, death, or crucifying of Christ, not that it is that, but that it signifieth it." And "the heavenly sacrament, which truly representeth Christ's flesh, is called Christ's body, but improperly. And therefore is said, after a manner, but not in the truth of the thing, but in the signifying mystery: so that the sense is this, it is called the body of Christ, that is to say, signifieth." Now the words of St Augustine being so plain, that none can be more, and following the other words within ten lines, so that you can allege no ignorance, but you must needs see them, it can be none other but a wilful blindness, that you will not see, and also a wilful concealing and hiding of the truth from other men, that they should not see neither.

And this one place is sufficient at full to answer whatsoever you can bring of the presence of Christ in the sacrament of bread and wine. For after consecration the body and blood of Christ be in them but as in figures, although in the godly receivers he is really present by his omnipotent power, which is as great a miracle in our daily nourishing, as is wrought before in our regeneration. And therefore is Christ no less to be honoured of them that feed of him in his holy supper, than of them that be grafted in him by regeneration.

300.

And whereas I said upon St Augustine's words, that "the sacrament consisteth of two natures," in that place I collected more of St Augustine's words in your favour, than indeed St Augustine saith, because you should not say that I nipped him. For St Augustine saith not, that the sacrament consisteth of two natures, and therefore both these natures must needs remain in the sacrament; but he saith that the sacrifice consisteth of two things, which he calleth also natures, and thereof it followeth, that those two things must be in the sacrifice, which is to be understand, in the ministration, not in the bread and wine reserved.

And very true it is, as St Augustine saith, that "the sacrifice of the church consisteth of two things, of the sacrament, and of the thing thereby signified, which is Christ's body, as the person of Christ consisteth of God and man." But yet this resemblance is not altogether like, as you say truly for so much; for the person of Christ consisteth so of his Godhead and manhood, they they be both in him in real presence and unity of person. But in the sacrifice it is otherwise, where neither is any such union between the sacrament and the truth of the sacrament, nor any such presence of the body of Christ. For in the bread and wine Christ is but figuratively, as I said before, and in the godly receivers spiritually, in whom also he tarrieth and remaineth so long as they remain the members of his body.

Similitudes may not be pressed in all points, but in the

But if Christ's similitudes should be so narrowly pressed, as you press here the similitude of the two natures of Christ in the sacrament, collecting that because the body and blood of Christ be truly present in the due administration of the sacra-

---

[1 Corpus Juris Canonici. De Consecrat. Dist. ii. cap. 48. "Hoc est." col. 1937. Ed. Lugd. 1618.]

[2 Gloss. in Corpus Juris Canonici. De Consecrat. Dist. ii. col. 1936. Lugd. 1618.]

[3 Ib. col. 1937.]

ment, therefore they must be there naturally present, as the two natures of the humanity and divinity be in Christ; many wicked errors should be established by them: as if the similitude of the wicked steward were strained as you strain and force this similitude, men might gather, that it is lawful for christian men to beguile their lords and masters whiles they be in office, to help themselves when they be out of office, because the Lord praised the wicked steward; yet you know that the similitude was not taught of our Saviour Christ for that purpose, for God is no favourer of falsehood and untruth. So you do wrong both to the holy doctors and to me, to gather of our similitude any other doctrine than we mean by the said similitude. Nor any reasonable man can say, that I am forced by confessing two natures in Christ's person really, naturally, and substantially, to confess also the nature of the body and blood of Christ to be likewise in the sacrament, except he could prove that the holy doctors, and I following their doctrine, do teach and affirm, that the natures of bread and wine are joined in the sacrament with the natural body and blood of Christ in unity of person, as the natures of God and man be joined in our Saviour Christ: which we do not teach, because we find no such doctrine taught by Christ, by his apostles, nor evangelists.

purpose wherefore they be brought. Luke xvi.

Therefore take your own collection to yourself, and make yourself answer to such absurdities and inconvenience as you do infer, by abusing and forcing of the doctors' similitude to another end than they did use it.

And it is not necessary for our eternal salvation, nor yet profitable for our comfort in this life, to believe that the natural body and blood of Christ is really, substantially, and naturally present in the sacrament. For if it were necessary or comfortable for us, it is without doubt, that our Saviour Christ, his apostles, and evangelists, would not have omitted to teach this doctrine distinctly and plainly. Yea, our Saviour would not have said, *Spiritus est qui vivificat, caro non prodest quicquam;* "The Spirit giveth life, the flesh availeth nothing."

The faith of the real presence in the forms is unprofitable and uncomfortable.

301.

John vi.

But this doctrine, which the holy doctors do teach, is agreeable to holy scripture, necessary for all Christian persons to believe for their everlasting salvation, and profitable for their spiritual comfort in this present life; that is to say, that the sacrament of Christ's body and blood in the natures and substances of bread and wine is distributed unto all men, both good and evil which receive it, and yet that only faithful persons do receive spiritually by faith the very body and blood of our Saviour Christ. So that Christ's natural body is not in the sacrament really, substantially, and corporally, but only by representation and signification, and in his lively members by spiritual and effectual operation.

The profit and comfort of the true doctrine.

But it appeareth that you be foul deceived in judgment of the doctrine set out in my book. And if you were not either utterly ignorant in holy scriptures and doctors, or not obstinately bent to pervert the true doctrine of this holy sacrament, you would never have uttered this sentence: "That there never was man overturned his own assertions more evidently than this author doth." For I am well assured that my doctrine is sound, and therefore do trust that I shall be able to stand by mine assertions before all men that are learned, and be any thing indifferent, and not bent obstinately to maintain errors, as you be, when you, tumbling and tossing yourself in your filthy fantasies of transubstantiation, and of the real and carnal presence of Christ's body, shall be ashamed of your assertions. But I marvel not much of your stout bragging here, because it is a common thing with you, to dash me in the teeth with your own faults.

And it is untrue that you say, that "the sacrifice is perfected before the perception." For if the sacrifice be perfected before the perception, it is perfected also before the consecration. For between the consecration and perception was no sacrifice made by Christ, as appeareth in the evangelists, but the one followed immediately of the other. And although Christ being in heaven be one of the parts whereof the sacrifice consisteth, and be present in the sacrifice, yet he is not naturally there present, but sacramentally in the sacrament, and spiritually in the receivers.

And by this which I have now answered, I have wrestled with you so in the matter of Christ's presence, that I have not "fallen upon my back myself to pull you over me," but I standing upright myself, have given you such a fall, that you shall never be able to recover. And now that I have brought you to the ground, although it be but a small piece of manhood to strike a man when he is down, yet for the truth's sake, unto whom you have ever been so great an adversary, I shall beat you with your transubstantiation, as they say, both back and bone. How say you, sir? is whiteness or other colours the nature of bread and wine, (for the colours be only visible by your doctrine;) or be they elements? or be accidents the bodily matter? Lie still, ye shall be better beaten yet for your wilfulness. Be the accidents of bread substances, as you said not long before? and if they be substances, what manner of substances be they, corporal or spiritual? If they be spiritual, then be they souls, devils, or angels? And if they be corporal substances, either they have life or no life. I trust you will say at the least, that bread hath life, because you said but even now almost, that "the substance of bread is the soul of it." Such absurdities they fall into that maintain errors.

302.

But at length when the similitude of the two natures in Christ, remaining both in their proper kinds, must needs be answered unto, then cometh in again the cuttle with his colours to hide himself, that he should not be seen, because he perceiveth what danger he is in to be taken: and when he cometh to the very net, he so stoutly striveth, wrangleth, and wrestleth, as he would break the net, or else by some craft wind himself out of it; but the net is so strong, and he so surely masted therein, that he shall never be able to get out.

Two examples of the two natures in Christ, one in a man, the other in the sacrament.

For the old catholic authors, to declare that two natures remain in Christ together, that is to say, his humanity and his divinity, without corruption or wasting of any of the said two natures, do give two examples thereof: one is of the body and soul, which both be in a man together, and the presence of the one putteth not away the other. The other example is of the Lord's supper, or ministration of the sacrament, where is also together the substance and nature of bread and wine with the body and blood of Christ; and the presence of the one putteth not away the other, no more than the presence of Christ's humanity putteth away his divinity. And as the presence of the soul driveth not away the body, nor the presence of the flesh and blood of Christ driveth not away the bread and wine; so doth not the presence of Christ's humanity expel his divinity, but his divinity remaineth still with his humanity, as the soul doth with the body, and the body of Christ with the bread. And then if there remain not the nature and substance of bread, it must follow also, that there remaineth not the divine nature of Christ with his humanity, or else the similitude is clearly dissolved.

But yet say you, "we may not press all parts of the resemblance with a thorough equality, but only have respect to the end, wherefore the resemblance is made." And do you not see, how this your saying taketh away your own argument of the real presence in the sacrament; and nevertheless setteth you no whit more at liberty concerning transubstantiation, but masteth you faster in the net, and maketh it more stronger to hold you? For the old authors make this resemblance only to declare the remaining of two natures, not the manner and form of remaining, which is far diverse in the person of Christ from the union in the sacrament. For the two natures of Christ be joined together in unity of person, which unity is not between the sacrament and the body of Christ. But in that point wherein the resemblance is made, there must needs be an equality by your own saying. And forasmuch as the resemblance was made only for the remaining of two natures; therefore as the perfect natures of Christ's manhood and Godhead do both remain, and the perfect nature of the soul and the body both also remain, so must the perfect nature of Christ's body and blood, and of bread and wine, also remain. But forasmuch as the similitude was not made for the manner of remaining, nor for the place, therefore the resemblance requireth not, that the body and blood of Christ should be united to the bread and wine in person or in place, but only that the natures should remain every one in his kind. And so be you clean overthrown with your transubstantiation, except you will join yourself with those heretics, which denied Christ's humanity and divinity to remain both together.

303.

And it seemeth that your doctrine varieth very little from Valentine and Marcion, (if it vary any thing at all,) when you say that Christ's flesh was a spiritual flesh. For when St Paul, speaking of Christ's body, said "we be members of his body, of his flesh and of his bones," he meant not of a spiritual body, as Ireneus saith[1], (for a spirit hath no flesh nor bones,) but of a very man's body, that is made of flesh, sinews, and bones. And so with striving to get out of the net, you roll yourself faster into it.

Spiritual flesh.

Irenæus contra Valentin. Lib. v.

And as for the words of St Augustine, make nothing for the real presence, as I have before declared. So that therein I neither have foil nor trip; but for all your brags, hooks, and crooks, you have such a fall, as you shall never be able to stand upright again in this matter. And my shafts be shot so straight against you, and with such a force, that they pierce through shield and habergeon in such sort, that all the harness you have is not able to withstand them, or to make one arrow to start back, although to avoid the stroke you shift your place, seeking some mean to fly the fight. For when I make mine argument of transubstantiation, you turn the matter to the real presence, like unto a surgeon that hath no knowledge, but when the head is wounded or sore, he layeth a plaister to the heel; or, as the proverb saith: *Interrogatus de alliis, respondet de cœpis:* "when you be asked of garlic, you answer of onions."

And this is one pretty sleight of sophistry, or of a subtle warrior, when he seeth himself overmatched and not able to resist, then by some policy quite to put off, or at the least to delay the conflict; and so do you commonly in this book of transubstantiation. For when you be sore pressed therein, then you turn the matter to the real presence. But I shall so straitly pursue you, that you shall not so escape. For where you say, that "the fathers which used the examples of the sacrament, and of the body and blood of Christ, to shew the unity of two natures in Christ, did believe that as really and as truly the soul of man is present in the body, so really and so truly is the body of Christ present in the sacrament:" the fathers neither said nor believed as you here report, but they taught that both the sacrament and the thing thereby represented, which is Christ's body, remain in their proper substance and nature, the sign being here and the thing signified being in heaven; and yet of these two consisteth the sacrifice of the church.

A sleight.

But it is not required that the thing signified should be really and corporally present in the sign and figure, as the soul is in the body, because there is no such union of person; nor it is not required in the soul and body that they should be ever together, for Christ's body and soul remained both, without either corruption or transubstantiation, when the soul was gone down into hell, and the body rested in the sepulchre. And yet was he then a perfect man, although his soul was not then really present with the body. And it is not so great a marvel that his body should be in heaven and the sacrament of it here, as it is that his body should be here and his soul in hell.

304.

And if the sacrament were a man, and the body of Christ the soul of it, (as you dream in your trance,) then were the sacrament not in a trance, but dead for the time, whilst it were here, and the soul in heaven. And like scoffing you might make of the sacrament of baptism as you do in the sacrament of Christ's body, that it lieth here in a trance, when Christ, being the life thereof, is in heaven.

And where you think that "my second book against transubstantiation was a collection of me, when I minded to maintain Luther's opinion against transubstantiation only," you have no probation of your thought, but still you remain in your dreams, trances, and vain fantasies, which you have used throughout your book; so that whatsoever is in the bread and wine, there is in you no transubstantiation, no alteration in this thing at all.

[[1] Καθὼς ὁ μακάριος Παῦλός φησιν ἐν τῇ πρὸς Ἐφεσίους ἐπιστολῇ· ὅτι μέλη ἐσμὲν τοῦ σώματος, ἐκ τῆς σαρκὸς αὐτοῦ, καὶ ἐκ τῶν ὀστέων αὐτοῦ· οὐ περὶ πνευματικοῦ τινος καὶ ἀοράτου ἀνθρώπου λέγων ταῦτα· τὸ γὰρ πνεῦμα οὔτε ὀστέα οὔτε σάρκα ἔχει· ἀλλὰ περὶ τῆς κατὰ τὸν ἀληθινὸν ἄνθρωπον οἰκονομίας, τῆς ἐκ σαρκὸς καὶ νεύρων καὶ ὀστέων συνεστώσης.—Irenæus, adversus Hæreses Valent. Lib. v. Cap. ii. pp. 398, 9. Ed. Oxon. 1702.]

And what availeth it you so often to affirm this untruth, "that the body of Christ is present in the sacrament, as the soul of man is present in the body," except you be like to them that tell a lie so often, that with often repeating they think men believe it, and sometime by often telling they believe it themselves? But the authors bring not this similitude of the body and soul of man, to prove thereby the presence of Christ's body in the sacrament, but to prove the two natures of the Godhead and the manhood in the person of Christ.

Let us now discuss the mind of Chrysostom in this matter, whom I bring thus in my book.

Chrysostom. ad Cæsarium Monachum.

St John Chrysostom writeth against the pestilent error of Apollinaris, which affirmed that the Godhead and manhood in Christ were so mixed and confounded together, that they both made but one nature. Against whom St John Chrysostom writeth thus:

"When thou speakest of God, thou must consider a thing that in nature is single, without composition, without conversion that is invisible, immortal, incircumscriptible, incomprehensible, with such like. And when thou speakest of man, thou meanest a nature that is weak, subject to hunger, thirst, weeping, fear, sweating, and such like passions, which cannot be in the divine nature. And when thou speakest of Christ, thou joinest two natures together in one person, who is both passible and impassible: passible as concerning his flesh, and impassible in his deity[1]."

And after he concludeth, saying: "Wherefore Christ is both God and man: God by his impassible nature, and man because he suffered. He himself being one person, one Son, one Lord, hath the dominion and power of two natures joined together, which be not of one substance, but each of them hath his properties distinct from the other. And therefore remaineth there two natures, distinct, and not confounded. For as before the consecration of the bread, we call it bread, but when God's grace hath sanctified it by the priest, it is delivered from the name of bread, and is exalted to the name of the body of the Lord, although the nature of bread remain still in it, and it is not called two bodies, but one body of God's Son; so likewise here, the divine nature resteth in the body of Christ, and these two make one Son, and one person[2]."

305.

These words of Chrysostom declare, and that not in obscure terms, but in plain words, that after the consecration the nature of bread remaineth still, although it have an higher name, and be called the body of Christ, to signify unto the godly eaters of that bread, that they spiritually eat the supernatural bread of the body of Christ, who spiritually is there present, and dwelleth in them, and they in him, although corporally he sitteth in heaven at the right hand of his Father.

[1 Deum ergo quando dicis, dilectissime, agnovisti id quod simplex est naturæ, quod incompositum, quod inconvertibile, quod invisibile, quod immortale, quod incircumscriptibile, quod incomprehensibile, et istis similia. Hominem autem dicens, significasti quod naturæ est infirmum, esuritionem, sitim, super Lazarum lacrymas, metum, sudoris ejectionem, et his similia, quibus id quod divinum est extra est. Christum autem quando dicis, conjunxisti utrumque: unde et passibilis dicatur idem ipse et impassibilis: passibilis quidem carne; impassibilis autem deitate.—Chrysost. ad Cæsarium Monachum. Tom. III. p. 743. Ed. Bened. Paris. 1721. Vid. p. 274, note 2.]

[2 Et Deus et homo Christus: Deus propter impassibilitatem, homo propter passionem. Unus Filius, unus Dominus, idemi pse procul dubio unitarum naturarum unam dominationem, unam potestatem possidens, etiamsi non consubstantiales exsistunt, et unaquæque incommixtam proprietatis conservat agnitionem, propter hoc quod inconfusa sunt duo. Sicut enim antequam sanctificetur panis, panem nominamus; divina autem illum sanctificante gratia, mediante sacerdote, liberatus est quidem ab appellatione panis, dignus autem habitus Dominici corporis appellatione, etiamsi natura panis in ipso permansit, et non duo corpora, sed unum corpus Filii prædicamus; sic et hic divina ἐνιδρυσάσης, id est, insidente corpori natura, unum Filium, unam personam utraque hæc fecerunt.—Ib.]

WINCHESTER.

St Chrysostom's words in deed, if this author had had them either truly translated unto him, or had taken the pains to have truly translated them himself, which (as Peter Martyr saith) be not in print, but were found in Florence, a copy whereof remaineth in the archdeacon or archbishop of Canterbury's hands; or else, if this author had reported the words as they be translated into English out of Peter Martyr's book, where in some point the translator in English seemeth to have attained by guess the sense more perfectly than Peter Martyr uttereth it himself; if either of this had been done, the matter should have seemed for so much the more plain. But what is this, to make foundation of an argument upon a secret copy of an epistle uttered at one time in divers senses? I shall touch one special point: Peter Martyr saith in Latin, whom the translator in English therein followeth, "that the bread is reputed worthy the name of the Lord's body." This author, Englishing the same place, termeth it "exalted to the name of the Lord's body," which words of exalting come nearer to the purpose of this author to have the bread but a figure, and therewith never the holier of itself. But a figure can never be accounted worthy that name of our Lord's body, the very thing of the sacrament, unless there were the thing in deed, as there is by conversion, as the church truly teacheth. Is not here, reader, a marvellous diversity in report, and the same so set forth, as thou that canst but read English must evidently see it?—God ordering it so as such varieties and contradictions should so manifestly appear, where the truth is impugned. Again, this author maketh Chrysostom to speak strangely in the end of this authority, that the divine nature resteth in the body of Christ, as though the nature of man were the stay to the divine nature; whereas in that union the rest is an ineffable mystery, the two natures in Christ to have one substance called and termed an hypostasy, and therefore he that hath translated Peter Martyr into English doth translate it thus: "The divine constitution, the nature of the body adjoined, these two both together make one Son and one person."

Thou, reader, mayest compare the books that be abroad of Peter Martyr in Latin, of Peter Martyr in English, and this author's book, with that I write, and so deem whether I say true or no. But to the purpose of St Chrysostom's words, if they be his words: he directeth his argument to shew by the mystery of the sacrament, that as in it there is no confusion of natures, but each remaineth in his property, so likewise in Christ the nature of his Godhead doth not confound the nature of his manhood. If the visible creatures were in the sacrament by the presence of Christ's body there truly present, invisible[3] also as that body is, impalpable also as that body is[4], incorruptible also as that is[4], then were the visible nature altered, and as it were confounded, which Chrysostom saith is not so; for the nature of the bread remaineth, by which word of "nature" is conveniently signified the property of nature. For proof whereof, to shew remaining of the property without alteration, Chrysostom maketh only the resemblance; and before I have shewed how nature signifieth the property of nature, and may signify the outward part of nature, that is to say, the accidents, being substance in his proper signification the inward nature of the thing, of the conversion whereof is specially understand[5] transubstantiation.

CANTERBURY.

Where you like not my translation of Chrysostom's words, I trow you would have me to learn of you to translate, you use such sincerity and plainness in your translation. Let the learned reader be judge. I did translate the words myself out of the copy of Florence, more truly than it seemeth you would have done. But when you see the words of Chrysostom so manifest and clear against your feigned transubstantiation, (for he saith, "that the nature of bread remaineth still,") you craftily for a shift fall to the carping of the translation, because you cannot answer to the matter. And yet the words of Chrysostom cited by master Peter Martyr in Latin out of Florence copy, and my translation, and the translation of master Peter's book in English, do agree fully here in sense, although the words be not all one, which neither is required nor lightly found in any two translators; so that all your wrangling in the diversity of the translations is but a sleight and common practice of you, when you cannot answer the matter, to seek faults in the translation where none is.

And for the special point, wherein you do note "a marvellous diversity in report,"

[3 Being invisible, Orig. ed. Winch.]   [4 Also as that is, Ibid.]   [5 Understanded, 1551.]

and would gather thereof no truth to be where such diversity is, let the reader be judge what a wonderful diversity it is. The Latin is this, *Panis dignus habitus est Dominici corporis appellatione.* The translator of M. Peter Martyr's book saith: "The bread is reputed worthy the name of the Lord's body." My translation hath, "The bread is exalted to the name of the body of the Lord." When a man is made a lord or knight, if one say of him, that he is reputed worthy the name of a lord or knight, and another say, that he is exalted to the name of a lord or knight, what difference is between these two sayings? Is not this a wonderful diversity? I pray thee, judge indifferently, good reader.

A figure requireth not the presence of the thing that is signified.

But, say you, "a figure can never be counted worthy the name of the thing, unless the thing were there in deed." Wrangle then with St John Chrysostom himself, and not with me, who saith, that the bread is exalted to the name of the Lord's body, or is reputed worthy the name of the Lord's body, after the sanctification, and yet the nature of the bread remaineth still; which cannot be as you say, if the body of Christ were there present.

And who heard ever such a doctrine as you here make, that the thing must be really and corporally present where the figure is? For so must every man be corporally buried in deed when he is baptized, which is a figure of our burial. And when we receive the sacrament of Christ's body, then is accomplished the resurrection of our bodies, for that sacrament you affirm to be the figure thereof. But your doctrine herein is clean contrary to the judgment of Lactantius, and other old writers, who teach that figures be in vain and serve to no purpose, when the things by them signified be present[1].

Rom. vi.

Lactantius Instit. Lib. II. cap. i.

And where you think it strange to say, that the divine nature is, or resteth in the body of Christ, it is nothing else but to declare your ignorance in God's word and ancient authors, in reading of whom forasmuch as you have not been much exercised, it is no marvel though their speech seem strange unto you. The Greek word of Chrysostom is ἐνιδρυσάσης, which I pray you English, and then we shall see what a strange speech you will make. Did you never hear tell at the least, that the Word was incarnated? or, *Verbum caro factum est?* And what signifieth this word "incarnate," but God to be made man, and his divine nature to be in flesh? Doth not St John bid us beware, that "we believe not every spirit; for there be many false prophets, and every spirit," saith he, "that confesseth not Jesus Christ to have come in flesh, is not of God, but is the spirit of antichrist?" Is this then a strange speech to you, that the divine nature resteth in the flesh, that is to say, in the body of Christ? which if you deny, you know whose spirit you have. But your trust is altogether in obscure speeches, wherewith you trust so to darken the matter, that no man shall understand it; lest that if they understand it, they must needs perceive your ignorance and error.

John i.

307.

1 John iv.

But when you promise to come to the purpose, (as, to say the truth, all that you said before is clearly without purpose, but when you promise, I say, now at length to come to the purpose,) your answer is nothing to the purpose of St Chrysostom's mind: for he made not his resemblance, as you say he did, only to shew the remaining of the accidents, which you call the properties, but to shew the remaining of the substances, with all the natural properties thereof: that as Christ had here in earth his divinity and humanity, remaining every of them with his natural properties; the substance of his Godhead being "a nature single without composition, without conversion, invisible, immortal, incircumscriptible, incomprehensible, and such like," (for these be Chrysostom's own words;) and the substance of his humanity being "a feeble nature, subject to hunger, thirst, weeping, fear, sweating, and such passions," so is it in the bread and Christ's body, that the bread after sanctification or consecration, as you call it, remaineth in his substance that it had before; and likewise doth the body of Christ remain still in heaven in his very true substance, whereof the bread is a sacrament and figure. For else, if the substance of the bread remained not, how could

---

[1 Sed tamen postquam Deus ille præsto esse cœpit, jam simulacro ejus opus non est. Lactant. Instit. Lib. II. De Origine erroris. cap. ii.]

Chrysostom bring it for a resemblance to prove that the substance of Christ's humanity remaineth with his divinity? Marry, this that you say had been a gay lesson for the Manichees, to say that there appeareth bread by all the accidents thereof, and yet is none in deed; that then by this similitude they might say likewise, that Christ appeared a man by all the accidents and properties of a man, and yet he was none in deed. And to make an end of this author, your vain comment will not serve you, to call the accidents of bread the nature of bread, except you will allow the same in the Manichees, that the nature of Christ's body is nothing else but the accidents thereof.

Now followeth Gelasius of the same matter.

Hereunto accordeth also Gelasius, writing against Eutyches and Nestorius, of whom the one said, that "Christ was a perfect man, but not God;" and the other affirmed clean contrary, that "he was very God, but not man." But against these two heinous heresies, Gelasius proveth by most manifest scriptures, that Christ is both God and man, and that after his incarnation remaineth[2] in him [as well] the nature of his Godhead, [as the nature of his manhood,][3] so that he hath in him two natures with their natural properties, and yet is he but one Christ.

Gelasius contra Eutychen et Nestorium. [Vid. Embd. ed. in fine tomi hujus.]

And for the more evident declaration hereof he bringeth two examples: the one is of man, who being but one, yet he is made of two parts, and hath in him two natures remaining both together in him, that is to say, the body and the soul, with their natural properties.

The other example is of the sacrament of the body and blood of Christ, "which," saith he, "is a godly thing, and yet the substance or nature of bread and wine do not cease to be there still[4]."

308.

Note well these words against all the papists of our time, that Gelasius, which was bishop of Rome[5] more than a thousand years past, writeth of this sacrament, that the bread and wine cease not to be there still, as Christ ceased not to be God after his incarnation, but remained still perfect God, as he was before.

WINCHESTER.

Now followeth to answer to Gelasius, who abhorring both the heresies of Eutyches and Nestorius, in his treatise against the Eutychians, forgetteth not to compare with their error, in extremity in the one side, the extreme error of the Nestorians on the other side, but yet principally intendeth the confusion of the Eutychians, with whom he was specially troubled. These two heresies were not so gross as the author of this book reporteth them, wherein I will write what Vigilius saith: Inter Nestorii ergo, quondam ecclesiæ Constantinopolitanæ non rectoris, sed dissipatoris, non pastoris, sed prædatoris, sacrilegum dogma et Eutychetis nefariam et detestabilem sectam, ita serpentinæ grassationis sese calliditas temperavit, ut utrumque sine utriusque periculo plerique vitare non possint, dum si quis Nestorii perfidiam damnat, Eutychetis putatur errori succumbere; rursum dum Eutychianæ hæresis impietatem destruit, Nestorii arguitur dogma erigere. *These be Vigilius' words in his first book, which be thus much in English:* "Between the abominable teaching of Nestorius, sometime not ruler but waster, not pastor, but prey-searcher of the church of Constantinople, and the wicked and detestable sect of Eutyches, the craft of the devil's spoiling so fashioned itself, that men could not avoid any of the secrets[6] without danger of the other: so as whiles any man condemneth the falseness of [the] Nestorian, he may be thought fallen to the error of the Eutychian; and whiles he destroyeth the wickedness of the Eutychian's heresy, he may be challenged to relieve the teaching of the Nestorian." *This is the sentence of Vigilius, by which appeareth how these heresies were both subtly conveyed, without so plain contradiction, as this author either by ignorance or of purpose feigneth; as though the Nestorian should say, "that Christ was a perfect man, but not God," and the Eutychian clean contrary,*

Gelasius.

[Vigilius. Dialog. 4. Orig. ed. Winch.]

[2 Remained, 1551, and Orig. ed.]
[3 Orig. ed. omits these words.]
[4 Certe sacramenta, quæ sumimus, corporis et sanguinis Christi divina res est, propter quod et per eadem divinæ efficimur consortes naturæ; et tamen esse non desinit substantia vel natura panis et vini. Gelasii con. Eutych. et Nestor. Sect. v. p. 671. in Biblioth. Patrum. Colon. 1518. An attempt has been unsuccessfully made to shew that this book was not written by Pope Gelasius, but by Gelasius of Cyzicus, or Gelasius of Cæsarea. Vide Cave, Hist. Lit.]
[5 A.D. 492.]
[6 Sects, 1551.]

"very God, but not man." For if the heresies had been such, Vigilius had had no cause to speak of any such ambiguity, as he noteth that a man should hardly speak against the one, but he might be suspected to favour the other. And yet I grant that the Nestorians' saying[1] might imply Christ not to be God, because they would two distinct natures to make also two distinct persons, and so as it were two Christs, the one only man, and the other only God; so as by their teaching, God was neither incarnate, nor (as Gregory Nazianzen saith) "man deitate," for so he is termed to say.

The Eutychians, as St Augustine saith, "reasoning against the Nestorians, became heretics themselves[2];" and because we confess truly by faith but one Christ, the Son of God, very God, the Eutychians say, "although there were in the virgin's womb, before the adunation, two natures, yet after the adunation, in that mystery of Christ's incarnation, there is but one nature, and that to be the nature of God, into which the nature of man was after their fancy transfused, and so confounded:" whereupon, by implication, a man might gather the nature of humanity[3] not to remain in Christ after the adunation in the virgin's womb. Gelasius, detesting both Eutyches and Nestorius, in his process uttereth a catholic meaning against them both; but he directeth special arguments of the two natures in man, and the two natures in the sacrament, chiefly against the Eutychians, to prove the nature of man to continue in Christ after the adunation, being no absurdity for two different natures to constitute one person; the same two natures remaining in their property[4], and the natures to be aliud and aliud, which signifieth different; and yet in that not to be alius and alius in person, which alius and alius in person the Eutychians abhorred, and catholicly for so much against the Nestorians, who by reason of two natures would have two persons; and because those Nestorians fancied the person of Christ patible to suffer all apart, therefore they denied Christ conceived God or born God; for the abolition of which part of their heresy, and to set forth the unity of Christ's person, the blessed virgin was called Θεοτόκος, Deipara, God's mother; which the Nestorians deluded by an exposition, granting she might so be called, because her son, they said, was afterwards God, and so she might be called God's mother, as another woman may be called a bishop's mother, if her son be made a bishop afterward, although he departed no bishop from her.

309.

And hereof I write thus much, because it should appear that Gelasius, by his arguments of the sacrament, and of the two natures in man, went not about to prove that the Godhead remained in Christ after his incarnation, as the author of this book would have it; for the Nestorian said the Godhead was an accession to Christ afterward by merit, and therefore with them there was no talk of remaining, when they esteemed Christ's nature in his conception singular, and only by God's power conceived, but only man. And again the Eutychian so affirmed the continuance of the divine nature in Christ after the adunation, as Gelasius had no cause to prove that was granted, that is to say, the remain of the divine nature, but on the other side to prove the remain of the human nature in Christ, which by the Eutychians was by implication rather denied. Nestorius divided God and man, and granted always both to be in Christ continually, but as two persons; and the person of Christ being God, dwelling within the person of Christ being man, and as Christ man increased, so Christ God dignified him, and so divided one Christ into two persons, because of the two natures so different, which was against the rules of our faith, and destroyed thereby the mystery of our redemption. And the Eutychians, affirming catholicly to be but one person in Christ, did perniciously say there was but one nature in Christ, accounting by implication the human nature transfused into the divine nature, and so confounded. And to shew the narrow passage, Vigilius spake of Cyrillus, a catholic author, because writing of the unity of Christ's person, he expressed his meaning by the word "nature," signifying the whole of any one constitution, which more properly the word "person" doth express. The Eutychians would by that word after gather that he favoured their part, so taking the word at a vantage.

*Nature.
*Person.

* Subsistence.
* Substance.

And because the same Cyrillus used the word "subsistence" to signify "substance," and therefore said "in Christ there were two subsistences," meaning the divine substance and human substance; forasmuch as the word "subsistence" is used to express the person, that is to say, hypostasy: there were that of that word, frowardly understood, would gather he should say,

---

[¹ Sayings, 1551.]

[² Eutychiani ab Eutyche, ... qui cum videretur refutare Nestorium, in Apollinarem Manichæumque transivit, et humanitatis in Christo denegans veritatem, quidquid a verbo nostræ proprietatis receptum est, divinæ tantummodo ascribit essentiæ. Augustin. de V. Hæresibus, Append. See below, p. 293.

[³ Of the humanity, Orig. ed. Winch.]

[⁴ To constitute one, the same remaining two in their property. Ibid.]

"that there were two persons in Christ," which was the Nestorians' heresy that he impugned. Such captiousness was there in words, when arrogant men cared not by what mean to maintain their error. These were both pernicious heresies, and yet subtle; and each had a marvellous pretence of the defence of the glory of God, even as is now pretended against the sacrament. And either part abused many scriptures, and had notable appearances for that they said, so as he that were not well exercised in scriptures, and the rules of our faith, might be easily circumvented. Nestorius was the great archbishop of Constantinople, unto whom Cyril, that condemneth his heresy, writeth, that seeing he slandereth the whole church with his heresy, he must resist him, although he be a father, because Christ saith: "He that loveth his father above me, is not worthy me." But Nestorius, as appeareth, although he used it ill-favouredly, had much learning, and cloked his heresy craftily, denying the gross matter that they imputed to him to teach two Christs, and other specialities laid to his charge; and yet condemning the doctrine of Cyril, and professing his own faith in his own terms, could not hide his heresy so; but it appeareth to be, and contain in effect, that he was charged with, and therefore an admonishing was given by a catholic writer: "Believe not Nestorius, though he say he teach but one Christ." [Matt. x. Orig. ed. Winch.]

If one should here ask, "What is this to the purpose to talk so much of these sects?" I answer: This knowledge shall generally serve to note the manner of them that go about to deceive the world with false doctrine, which is good to learn. Another special service is to declare, how the author of this book either doth not know the state of the matter in these heresies he speaketh of, or else misreporteth them of purpose. And the arguing of Gelasius in this matter well opened, shall give light of the truth of the mystery of the sacrament, who against the Eutychians useth two arguments of examples: one, of the two different natures to remain in one person of man; and yet the Eutychians defamed that conjunction, with remain of two different natures, and called it δυόφυσιν, "double nature;" and Gelasius, to encounter that term, saith, "They will with their μονόφυσις, 'one nature,' reserve not one Christ and whole Christ." And if two different natures, that is to say, soul and body, make but one man, why not so in Christ? For where scripture speaketh of the outward man and inward man, that is to shew (Gelasius saith) two divers qualities in the same man, and not to divide the same[5] into two men; and so intendeth to shew there ought to be no scruple to grant two different natures to remain in their property, for fear that every diverse nature should make a diverse person, and so in Christ divide the unity; concluding that the integrity of Christ cannot be, but both the natures different remaining in their property. Carnal imagination troubled the Eutychians to have one person of two such different natures remaining in their property, which the Nestorians relieved with device of two persons, and the Eutychians by confusion of the human nature. 310.

Then cometh Gelasius to the argument of example from the sacrament of the body and blood of Christ, and noteth the person of Christ to be a principal mystery, and the sacrament an image and similitude of that mystery, which sense his words must needs have, because he calleth Christ the principal mystery; and as in one place he saith "the image and similitude of the body and blood of Christ," so by and by he calleth the sacrament "the image of Christ." And here the words "image" and "similitude" express the manner of presence of the truth of the things represented, to be understanded only by faith as invisibly present. And St Ambrose by this word "image" signifieth the exhibition of truth to man in this life. And to shew the sacrament to be such an image, as containeth the very truth of the thing whereof it is the image, Gelasius declareth in framing his argument in these words: "As bread and wine go into the divine substance, the Holy Ghost bringing it to pass, and yet remain in the property of their nature, so that principal mystery, those natures remaining whereof it is, declare unto us true and whole Christ to continue."

In these words of Gelasius, where he saith "the bread and wine go into the divine substance," is plainly declared the presence of the divine substance; and this divine substance can signify none other substance but of the body and blood of Christ, of which heavenly nature, and earthly nature of the bread and wine, consisteth this sacrament, the image of the principal mystery of Christ's person.

And therefore as in the image be two divers natures and different, remaining in their property, so likewise in the person of Christ, which is the conclusion of Gelasius' argument, should remain two natures. And here were a great danger, if we should say that Christ's body, which is the celestial nature in the sacrament, were there present but in a figure; for it should then imply that in Christ's person, the principal mystery, it were also but in a figure. And therefore as in the mystery of Christ's person ordained to redeem us, being the principal mystery, there is no figure, but truth in consideration of the presence of the two natures, whereof Christ

[5 The same man, Orig. ed. Winch.]

is; so in the sacrament, being a mystery ordered to feed us, and the image of that principal mystery, there is not an only figure but truth of the presence of the natures, earthly and celestial. I speak of the truth of the presence[1], and mean such an integrity of the natures present, as by the rules of our faith is consonant and agreeable to that mystery, that is to say, in the person of Christ, perfect God and perfect man; perfect God to be incarnate, and perfect man to be deitate, as Gregory Nazianzen termeth it.

In the sacrament, the visible matter of the earthly creature in his property of nature for the use of signification is necessarily required, and also, according to the truth of Christ's words, his very body and blood to be invisibly with integrity present, which Gelasius calleth "the divine substance." And I think it worthy to be noted that Gelasius, speaking of the bread and wine, reciteth not precisely the substance to remain, but saith, "the substance or nature," which nature he calleth after the property[2], and the disjunctive may be verified in the last. And it is not necessary the examples to be in all parts equal, as Rusticus Diaconus handleth it very learnedly, contra Acephalos[3]. And Gelasius in opening the mystery of the sacrament speaketh of transition of the bread and wine into the godly substance; which word "transition" is meet to express "transubstantiation;" and therefore St Thomas expressed "transubstantiation" with the same word transire, writing, Dogma datur Christianis, quod in carnem transit panis et vinum in sanguinem. But in the mystery of Christ's person there is no transition of the Deity into the humanity, or humanity into the Deity, but only assumption of the humanity with the adunation of those two perfect natures[4] so different, one person and one Christ, who is God incarnate, and man deitate, as Gregory Nazianzen saith, without mutation, conversion, transition, transelementation, or transubstantiation, which words be proper and special to express how eucharistia is constitute of two different natures, an heavenly and earthly nature; a mystery institute after the example of the principal mystery, wherewith to feed us with the substance of the same glorious body that hath redeemed us. And because in the constitution of this mystery of the sacrament, there is a "transition" of the earthly creature into the divine substance, as Gelasius and St Thomas term it, and "mutation," as Cyprian and Ambrose teach it, which Theophylactus expresseth by the word "transelementation," Emissene by the word "conversion," and all their words reduced into their own proper sense expressed in one word of "transubstantiation:" it cannot be convenient, where the manner of constitution of the two mysteries be so different, there to require a like remaining of the two natures whereof the mysteries be. In the mystery of Christ's person, because there was not of any of the two different natures either mutation, transition, conversion, or transelementation, but only assumption of the humanity, and adunation in the virgin's womb, we cannot say the Godhead to have suffered in that mystery, which were an absurdity, but to have wrought the assumption and adunation of man's nature with it, nor man's nature by that assumption and adunation diminished; and therefore profess truly Christ to be whole God and whole man, and God in that mystery to be made man, and man God; whereas in the sacrament, because of transition, mutation, and conversion of their earthly creatures, wrought by the Holy Ghost, which declareth those earthly creatures to suffer in this conversion, mutation, and transition, we knowledge no assumption of those creatures or adunation with the heavenly nature, and therefore say not, as we do in the principal mystery, that each nature is wholly the other; and as we profess God incarnate, so the body of Christ breaded; and as man is deitate, so the bread is corporate; which we should say, if the rules of our faith could permit the constitution of each mystery to be taught alike, which the truth of God's word doth not suffer. Wherefore, although Gelasius and other argue from the sacrament to declare the mystery of Christ's person, yet we may not press the argument to destroy or confound the property of each mystery, and so violate the rules of our faith; and in the authors not press the words otherwise than they may agree with the catholic teaching, as those did in the words of Cyril, when he spake of "nature" and "subsistence," whereof I made mention before, to be remembered here in Gelasius, that we press not the word "substance" and "nature" in him, but as may agree with the "transition" he speaketh of, by which word other express "transubstantiation." And against the Eutychians, for to improve their confusion, it sufficeth to shew two different natures to be in the sacrament, and to remain in their property, and the divine nature not to confound the earthly nature, nor as it were to swallow it, which was the dream of the Eutychians. And we must forbear to press all parts of the example in the other argument, from the person of man being one of the body[5] and soul, which the church doth profess in

---

[1 Of presence, 1551.]
[2 After property, Orig. ed. Winch.]
[3 See Bibliotheca Patrum, Tom. VI. Pars ii. p. 212. Colon. 1618.]
[4 The adunation of those two natures, and of two perfect natures, 1551.]
[5 Of body, Orig. ed. Winch.]

Symbolo Athanasii, *of all received. For Christ is one person of two perfect natures, whereof the one was before the other in perfection and creation of the other; the one impassible, and the other passible: man is of the soul and body one, two different natures, but such as for their perfection required that unity, whereof none was before other perfect. Of Christ we say, he is consubstantial to his Father by the substance of his Godhead, and consubstantial to man by the substance of his manhood: but we may not say, "man is consubstantial by his soul to angels, and consubstantial in his body to beasts;" because then we should deduce also Christ by mean of us to be consubstantial to beasts. And thus I write to shew, that we may not press the example in every part of it, as the author of this book noteth upon Gelasius, who overturneth his doctrine of the figure.*

312.

CANTERBURY.

I pity you, to see how ye swink[6] and sweat to confound this author Gelasius. And yet his words be so plain against your papistical transubstantiation, that you have clearly lost all your pains, labours, and costs. For these be his words spoken of the sacrament: *Esse non desinit substantia vel natura panis et vini;* "The substance or nature of bread and wine ceaseth not to be." But to avoid and dally away these words that be so clear and plain, must needs be laid on load of words, the wit must be stretched out to the utmost, all fetches must be brought in that can be devised, all colours of rhetoric must be sought out, all the air must be cast over with clouds, all the water darkened with the cuttle's ink; and if it could be, at the least as much as may be, all men's eyes also must be put out, that they should not see. But I would wish that you stood not so much in your own conceit, trusted not so much in your inventions and device of wit, in eloquence, and in craftiness of speech, and multitude of words, looking that no man should dare encounter you, but that all men should think you speak well because you speak much; and that you should be had in great reputation among the multitude of them that be ignorant, and cannot discern perfectly those that follow the right way of truth from other that would lead them out of the way into error and blindness. This standing in your conceit is nothing else but to stand in your own light.

But where you say that these heresies of Nestorius and Eutyches were "not so gross as I report," that the one should say, that "Christ was a perfect man, but not God;" and the other should say clean contrary, that "he was very God, but not man:" of the grossness of these two heresies I will not much contend. For it might be that they were of some misreported, as they were indeed if credit be to be given to divers ancient histories; but this I dare say, that there be divers authors that report of them as I do write, and consequently you grant the same in effect. For you report of the Eutychians, that they did perniciously say, that there was but μονόφυσις, "one nature in Christ:" and of the Nestorians you say, that "they denied Christ to be conceived God or born God, but only man," and then could not he be naturally God, but only man. And therefore neither by ignorance nor of purpose do I report them otherwise than you confess yourself, and than I have learned of other that were before my time. For St Augustine in the place which you do cite of him, hath these words of Nestorius, *Dogmatizare ausus est, Dominum nostrum Jesum Christum hominem tantum;* "he presumed to teach," saith St Augustine, "that our Lord Jesus Christ was but man only." And of Eutyches he saith, *Humanitatis in Christo denegavit veritatem;* "he denied the truth of Christ's manhood[7]." And Gelasius writeth also thus: *Eutychiani dicunt unam esse naturam, id est divinam; ac Nestorius nihilominus memorat singularem:* "The Eutychians say, that there is but one nature in Christ, that is to say, the Godhead: and also Nestorius saith, there is but one nature," meaning the manhood. By which words of St Augustine and Gelasius appeareth, as plainly as can be spoken, the plain contradiction between the Nestorians and the Eutychians, that the one denied the humanity of Christ, and the other his divinity, as I have written in my book; so that neither of ignorance nor of purpose have I feigned any thing: but you, either of malice, or of your accustomed manner to calumniate and find fault with every thing that misliketh you, be it never so well, seek

August. contra Hæreses.

Gelasius adversus Eutychen et Nestorium.

313.

[6 Swink, i. e. labour.]

[7 August. Appendix Trium Hæresium ad lib. de hæresibus. Tom. VI. p. 15. Ed. Paris. 1636. This appendix is considered by the Benedictine editors as spurious. Augustine, they say, died A.D. 430, the Council of Ephesus was held, A.D. 431 to depose Nestorius, and Eutyches was condemned by that of Chalcedon, A.D. 451. Ed. Bened. Tom. VIII. p. 28.]

occasion likewise here to carp and reprehend where no fault is; being like unto Momus, which, when he could find no fault with Venus' person, yet he picked a quarrel to her slipper. And not in this place only, but throughout your whole book, you use this fashion, that when you cannot answer to the principal matter, then you find fault with some bye-matter, whereby it seemeth you intend so to occupy the reader's mind, that he should not see how craftily you convey yourself from direct answering of the chief point of the argument; which when you come unto, you pass it over slenderly, answering either nothing, or very little, and nothing to the purpose.

But yet this bye-matter, which you bring in of the grossness of these two errors, helpeth little your intent, but rather helpeth to fortify my saying against your doctrine of transubstantiation, that your doctrine herein maketh a plain way for the Nestorians and the Eutychians to defend their errors. For if the bread and the body of Christ before the consecration in the sacrament be two natures, and after the consecration in that mystery is but one nature, and that is the body of Christ, into which the nature of bread in your phantasy is transformed and confounded; and if also this mystery be an example of the mystery of Christ's incarnation, as the old authors report, why may not then the Eutychians say, that before the adunation in the virgin's womb the Godhead and manhood were two natures, and yet after the adunation in that mystery of Christ's incarnation there was but one nature, and that to be the nature of God, into which the nature of man was after their phantasy transfused and confounded? And thus have you made by your transubstantiation a goodly pattern and example for the Eutychians to follow in maintenance of their error.

And yet, although the Eutychians said that "the nature of God and of man before their uniting were two," yet I read not that they said, that they were two in the virgin's womb, as you report of them; which is no great matter, but to declare how ignorant you be in the thing whereof you make so great boast, or how little you regard the truth, that wittingly will tell an untruth. But to say my mind frankly, what I think of your declaration of these two heresies, I think a great part thereof you dreamed in your sleep, or imagined, being in some trance, or rapt with some sophistical vision; and part of your dream agreeth neither with approved authors and histories, nor with itself. For first, as touching the Eutychians, where you say that Gelasius "directeth his arguments of the two natures in man, and of the two natures in the sacrament, chiefly against the Eutychians, to prove the nature of man to remain in Christ after the adunation;" whosoever readeth Gelasius shall find otherwise, that he directed his arguments indifferently, as well against Nestorius, as against Eutyches, and no more against the one than against the other. Nor no more did the Eutychians abhor *alius* and *alius*, although some gathered so of their words, than did the Nestorians; which words signify "diversity of person," as *aliud* and *aliud* signify "diversity of nature:" so as the body and soul in one man be *aliud* and *aliud* by reason of diversity of natures, and yet be they not *alius* and *alius*, because that both together make but one person. By means of which difference between *alius* and *aliud*, we say, *Alius Pater, alius Filius, alius Spiritus Sanctus*, and not *aliud Pater, aliud Filius, aliud Spiritus Sanctus*, forasmuch as they be three in persons, and but one in nature and substance. And because Christ is two in nature, that is to say, of his Deity and humanity, and but one in person; therefore we say, *aliud et aliud est divinitas et humanitas*, but not *alius, sed unus est Christus*.

And although Nestorius granted two natures in Christ, yet not, as you say, from his nativity, nor by adunation, but by cohabitation or inhabitation, so that he made but one Christ, (although some otherwise take him,) and not *alium et alium*: after which sort the Godhead is also in other godly men, whom by grace he maketh partakers of his godly nature, although by their natural generation they be but men, without the divine nature united in person, but after obtained by adoption and grace: as, by your example, a man is made bishop, which by natural generation is born but a man.

And that this was Nestorius' opinion, that Christ from his nativity was but man only, and had his Godhead after by adoption or accession, is evident of your own words, when you say, "that the Nestorians denied Christ conceived God, or born God, and that the Godhead was an accession to Christ afterward by merit, and that he was conceived but only man," although shortly after you go from the same, saying, that "both the Godhead and manhood were always in Christ:" such constancy is in your dreamed phantasies.

And where you have written thus much, as you say, because it should appear that Gelasius, by his arguments of the sacrament, and of the two natures of man, went about to prove that the Godhead remained in Christ after his incarnation; you might have bestowed your time better than to have lost so much labour, to impugn the truth. For although neither Nestorius nor Eutyches denied the Godhead of Christ to remain, yet Gelasius went not about only to confute them, but also to set out plainly the true catholic faith, that Christ being incarnated was perfect God and perfect man, and how that might be, both the said natures and substances remaining with all their natural proprieties and conditions, without transubstantiation, abolition, or confusion of any of the two natures. And this he declareth as well by the example of the sacrament, as of the body and soul of man. Wherefore, as true as it is that the body and soul of man, and Godhead and manhood of Christ, remain in their proper substances, natures, and properties, without transubstantiation or perishing of any of them, so must it be in the sacrament.

And in the said heresies, as you say, was some appearance of the truth, every one having scripture, which in sound of words seemed to approve their errors, whereby they deceived many. But as for your feigned doctrine of transubstantiation, it hath no pretence nor appearance of truth by God's word; for you have not one scripture that maketh mention thereof, whereas I have many plain and manifest scriptures, that speaketh in plain terms, that bread is eaten and wine is drunken. And this author Gelasius, with divers other learned men, as well Greeks as Latins, of the old catholic church, affirm in no doubtful words that the bread and wine be not gone, but remain still. From which scriptures and doctors whosoever dissenteth, declareth himself at the least to be ignorant, whereby yet he may excuse himself of a greater blot and infamy.

315.

And this matter being so clear, neither your fine disguising, nor your painted colours, nor your gay rhetoric, nor witty inventions, can so hide and cover the truth that it shall not appear; but the more you labour to strive against the stream, the more faint shall you wax, and at length the truth hath such a violence, that you shall be borne clean down with the stream thereof.

In the end you compare Nestorius and Cyril together, alluding, as it seemeth, to this contention between you and me; which comparison, if it be throughly considered, hath no small resemblance, although there be no little diversity also. Nestorius, say you, was a great archbishop; and so, say I, was Cyril also. Nestorius, say you, as appeareth, "had much learning, but cloked his heresy craftily." But the histories of his time, who should know him best, describe him in this sort, that he was a man of no great learning, but of an excellent natural wit and eloquence, and full of craft and subtilty, by means whereof he was so proud and glorious, that he contemned all men in respect of himself, and disdained the old writers, thinking himself more wise than they all. Now let the indifferent reader judge, whom he thinketh in this your allusion should most resemble the qualities and conditions of Nestorius.

A comparison of Nestorius and Cyril.

And all this that you have brought in here of these two heresies, although it be to no purpose in the principal matter, yet it serveth me to this purpose, that men may conjecture whose nature and wit is most like unto the description of Nestorius, and also how loth you be to come to the matter, and to make a direct answer to Gelasius' words, who saith in plain terms, "that the substance or nature of bread and wine remaineth." Even as glad you be to come to this as a bear is to come to the stake, seeking to run out at this corner or that corner, if it were possible. But all will not help; for you be so fast tied in chains, that, will you, nill you, at length you must come to the stake, although you be never so loth. And Gelasius biteth so sore and hath catched so hard hold of you, that you can never escape, although you attempt all manner of ways, by tooth and by nail, to shake him off.

First, you would shake him off by this pretence, that he useth his two arguments, of the two examples of man and the sacrament, against the Eutychians only. But Gelasius will not so easily leave his hold. For he speaketh indifferently as well against the Nestorians as the Eutychians, declaring by these two examples, how two different natures may remain in Christ, and that the integrity of Christ cannot be, except both the different natures remain in their properties; which condemneth both the foresaid heresies, that affirmed but one nature to be in Christ, the Eutychians his divinity, and the Nestorians his humanity. And yet, if he had used these examples against the Eutychians only, they bite you as sore as if they were used against them both. For if he conclude by these two examples against the Eutychians, as you say he doth, that the integrity of Christ cannot be, but both natures different, that is to say, his manhood and Godhead, must remain in their property, then must it needs be so in the examples also. And then as Christ had in him two natures with their natural properties, neither perishing, but both remaining; and as man hath in him two natures, the soul and the body, both remaining still, so must in the sacrament also the nature of bread and wine remain without transubstantiation, or corruption of any of the natures, according to the said words of Gelasius: *Esse non desinit substantia vel natura panis et vini;* "The substance or nature of bread and wine ceaseth not to be."

316.

And Gelasius bringeth not this image and similitude to that purpose that you would draw it, that is to say, to express the manner of Christ's presence in the sacrament, but to express the manner of two natures in Christ, that they both so remain that neither is corrupted or transubstantiated, no more than the bread and wine be in the sacrament. And by this all men may see, that Gelasius hath fastened his teeth so surely, that you cannot so lightly cast him off with a shake of your chain. And if he meant to express the manner of Christ's presence in the sacrament, as you feign he doth, that the manner is only by faith, whereof he speaketh not one word, yet are you nothing at liberty thereby, but held much more faster than you were before. For Gelasius speaketh of the action of the mystery, and Christ's flesh and blood be present in the action of the mystery only by faith, therefore can they not be present in the bread or wine reserved, which have no faith at all. And presence by faith only requireth no real, material, and corporal presence. For by faith is Christ present in baptism, and by faith Abraham saw him, and the holy fathers did eat his flesh and drink his blood before he was born. And Christ, humbling himself to take upon him our mortal nature, hath exalted us to the nature of his deity, making us to reign with him in his immortal glory, as it were gods. And this, saith Gelasius, God worketh in us by his sacraments, *per quæ divinæ efficimur consortes naturæ, et tamen esse non desinit substantia vel natura panis et vini:* that is to say, "By the sacrament of Christ's body and blood we be associate unto the divine nature, and yet ceaseth not the substance or nature of bread and wine to be." So that the sacrament not being altered in substance, we be altered and go into the divine nature or substance, as Gelasius termeth it, being made partakers of God's eternity.

* Presence by faith requireth no corporal presence.
Gal. iii.
John viii.
1 Cor. x.

And therefore when he speaketh of the going of the sacraments into the divine substance, he meaneth not that the substances of the sacraments go into the substance of God, (which no creature can do,) but that in the action of that mystery, to them that worthily receive the sacraments, to them they be turned into divine substance through the working of the Holy Ghost, who maketh the godly receivers to be the partakers of the divine nature and substance. And that this was the intent and meaning of Gelasius, appeareth by two notable sentences of him, whereof one is this. "Surely," saith he, "the image and similitude of the body and blood of Christ is celebrate in the action of the mystery." The other is, that "by the sacrament we be made partakers of the godly nature." He saith not, that the sacraments be, but that we be made partakers of the nature of Christ's Godhead. And if he should mean, as you have most untruly altered both his words and sense at your pleasure, not that the godly receivers, but that the substance of bread and wine, should go into the divine substance; then were not they changed into his humanity, but into his deity, and so were the bread and wine deified, or at the least made partakers of the divine nature and immortality. But forasmuch as Gelasius saith, that the two natures in Christ remain, in like case as the natures of the sacraments remain, (for he maketh his argument altogether of the remaining of the natures, by the verb *permanere*, and the participle *permanens*,) then, as you say that the integrity of Christ cannot be, except both his natures different remain in their properties, so cannot the integrity of the sacrament be, except the two natures of bread and wine remain in their properties. For else, seeing that the remaining of the natures is in the sacrament as it is in Christ,

317.

as Gelasius saith, then if in the sacraments remain but the accidents and appearance of bread and wine, and not the substances of them, how could Gelasius by the resemblance of the two sacraments of bread and wine, prove the two substances and natures of Christ to remain? Might it not rather be gathered, that only the appearance of Christ's humanity remaineth in accidents, and not the substance of itself, as Marcion saith, and as you say it is in the sacrament; or else, that Christ's humanity is absorbed up by his divinity, and confounded therewith, as the Eutychians say, [and as you say[1]] that the bread and wine is by the body and blood of Christ? But the catholic faith hath taught from the beginning, according to holy scripture, that as the image or sacrament be two diverse natures and different, remaining in their properties, that is to say, bread and wine, so likewise in the person of Christ remain two natures, his divinity and his humanity.

And I pray you, what danger is it to say, that Christ's body is in the sacramental bread, but as in a figure? should that imply, that his body is in his person, but as in a figure? That should be even as good an argument as this: Christ was in the brasen serpent, but in a figure; ergo he is now in heaven but in a figure. For the form of argumentation is all one in the one and the other. And if Christ be in us by virtue and efficacy, although in the sacraments representing the same (as Gelasius saith) he be but sacramentally, figuratively, and significatively, what peril is it to us? And what availeth it us his being in the sacrament, and not in us?

And the two natures in the sacrament, which Gelasius taketh for the image and similitude of the two natures in Christ, be bread and wine, which as they remain, and that truly in their natures and substances, so do the two natures in Christ. And yet be the bread and wine sacraments of the terrestrial nature of Christ, that is to say, of his body and blood, but not of his celestial and divine nature, as you imagine. And they be called sacraments, because they be figures, which, if they were no figures, they were no sacraments. But it is not required, that the thing represented by the figure should be really and corporally present in the figure, when the figure is ordained to represent a thing corporally absent; and the figure were in vain, as Lactantius saith, if the thing were present[2]. *Lactantius, Institut. Lib. ii. cap. 2.*

And at the least wise in this place Gelasius useth the natures and substances of bread and wine, which be sacraments of Christ's flesh and blood, to be images and similitudes in this point, not of his flesh and blood, but of his divine and human nature; that as the bread and wine in the sacrament remain still in their proper kinds, without violation, annihilation, confusion, commixtion, or transubstantiation, so is it in the two natures of Christ's manhood and his Godhead. So that Gelasius useth this similitude for the incarnation of Christ, not for the consecration of the sacrament, as you would pervert his meaning.

318.

And because you would have all your things strange, (as it were one that had come out of a strange country, where he had learned a strange fashion of speech never heard of before, or rather devised it himself,) you call the colours of bread and wine the matter of bread and wine, because colours only be visible, after your teaching. And then must the natural properties of colours be, to signify our feeding spiritual by the body and blood of Christ, that as they feed us spiritually, so do the colours corporally. And then making the argument *ab opposito consequentis ad oppositum antecedentis*, as colours feed not our bodies, so Christ feedeth not our souls. This is the conclusion of your goodly new devised divinity.

And to like effect cometh your other saying in the same sentence, because you were loth to commit but one horrible error in one sentence, that "Gelasius calleth Christ's body and blood his divine substance."

This is a goodly hearing for the Eutychians, who say, that "in Christ is no more natures but his divine substance," which by your interpretation must be true. For if his Godhead be a divine substance, and his body and blood also a divine substance, why should Eutyches be reprehended for denying in Christ to be any other than divine substance? And so shall we bring to pass, that either Christ hath but one substance, or two divine substances, although not of like sort, and so not one human substance. And is it like, that Gelasius, who so long contended against Eutyches for two distinct substances in Christ, human and divine, would in the conclusion

---

[[1] These words are found only in ed. 1551.]   [[2] See p. 288.]

of his disputation so much yield unto the heretic, to grant that Christ's human substance should be a divine substance?

Substance or nature.

And it is worthy to be noted, and double noted, how you wrangle with the words of Gelasius, and wrest them clean out of tune. For where Gelasius saith, that "there remaineth the substance or nature of bread and wine," to declare thereby the remaining of two natures in Christ, you say, that "Gelasius' saying may be verified in the last, and not in the first," that is to say, that the nature of bread and wine remaineth.

Nature for property.

"And nature," say you, "is there taken for the properties, which you call accidents." And so you make Gelasius a goodly teacher, that should so ambiguously speak of two things, when he meaneth but of one. For when he saith, that "the substance or nature remaineth," you say, "he meaneth that only the nature remaineth." And were this tolerable in a learned man, when he meaneth the nature to remain and not the substance, to express it by these terms, The substance or nature remaineth? And if Gelasius mean that the substance of bread and wine remaineth not, but the natures, and then if by nature he understood the accidents, as you untruly surmise of him, and make them the image and similitude to prove Christ's two natures; then they prove no more, but that the accidents of Christ's natures remain, and not the substance: which saying, whether it be a favouring of the Eutychians, Nestorians, Valentinians, Marcionists, Apollinarists, and other of that sort, let the learned be judge.

And although "it be not necessary the examples to be in all parts equal," as you allege of Rusticus Diaconus, yet they must needs be like in the point wherefore they were taken to be examples, for else they were none examples. And therefore, seeing that the bread and wine were of Gelasius brought for examples of Christ's two natures, for this intent, to prove that the two natures of Christ remain in their substance, it must needs be so in the bread and wine, or else they served nothing to that purpose.

319.

And the transition that Gelasius meant of, is in the persons that receive the sacraments, which be transformed into the divine nature, as Gelasius saith, "by efficacy and virtue represented by the sacraments;" but the transition is not in the bread and wine, as you and your Thomas imagine of transition, which remain in the sacrament without substantial mutation, conversion, transition, transelementation, or transubstantiation. For if in the mystery of the sacrament were transition, mutation, conversion, and transelementation of the substance of bread and wine, how could that mystery be an example of the principal mystery of Christ's incarnation, to prove thereby that there is no transition, mutation, conversion, or transelementation of the two substances of Christ in his incarnation? Doth not the remaining of substance in the sacrament prove the remaining of substance in the incarnation? For how can the not remaining of substance be an example, image, and similitude to prove the remaining of the substance? But here appeareth what it is to wrestle against the truth, and to defend an evil cause, and what absurdities wit and eloquence be driven unto, when they strive against God and his word.

And where you think yourself over sore pressed with this argument and similitude of bread and wine to the two natures in Christ, I must needs press the argument and words so far, as pertaineth to the remaining of the natures and substance; for to that end was the image and similitude brought in by Gelasius. And then by argument from the cause, wherefore the resemblance was made, if the substance and nature of the bread and wine remain not in the sacrament, it followeth that the two natures and substance of Christ remain not in his person, which is no sound teaching: wherefore, to make the argument agree with the catholic teaching, we must needs say, that as in the person of Christ remain the two natures and substance of his Godhead and manhood, so in the sacrament remain the natures and substances of bread and wine, that the comparisons may agree with themselves and with the catholic faith. Like as it is also in the other example of the body and soul, which two natures must needs remain in the person of man, without transubstantiation of any nature, if they shall resemble the remaining of the two natures in Christ. And how do the two natures in the sacrament remain in their property, I pray you declare, if the nature of bread and wine be gone? And how doth not the divine nature swallow up the earthly nature, if the nature of bread and wine be so turned into the divine nature, that it remaineth not, but is clearly extinct?

If you may purge yourself in handling of this author by confession of your ignorance, you must obtain it by great favour of them that will so accept it. For else in this one author is affirmed by you many great errors, with wilful depravation of the author's mind, to give weapons to them that be enemies to the truth, and to the subversion of the catholic faith. And no less have you done in Theodoretus next following, because you would handle them both indifferently, and do no more injury to the one than to the other. And as for Cyprian, Ambrose, Theophylact, and Emissene, I have answered to them before. It is time now to hear Theodorete.

Theodoretus also affirmeth the same both in his first and in his second dialogue. In the first he saith thus: "He that called his natural body wheat and bread, and also called himself a vine, the self-same called bread and wine his body and blood, and yet changed not their natures[1]."

Theodoretus in Dialogis.

And in his second dialogue he saith more plainly. "For," saith he, "as the bread and wine after the consecration lose not their proper nature, but keep their former substance, form, and figure which they had before, even so the body of Christ, after his ascension, was changed into the godly substance[2]."

Now let the papists choose which of these two they will grant, (for one of them they must needs grant,) either that the nature and substance of bread and wine remain still in the sacrament after the consecration, and then must they recant their doctrine of transubstantiation, or else that they be of the error of Nestorius and other, which did say, that the nature of the Godhead or of the manhood remained not in Christ after his incarnation or ascension[3]. For all these old authors agree, that it is in the one, as it is in the other.

WINCHESTER.

And if that I have here said be well considered, there may appear the great ignorance of this author in the alleging of Theodorete, the applying of him, and the speaking of Nestorius in the end. For as the Eutychians' reasoning, as St Augustine saith, to confound the Nestorians, fell into an absurdity in the confusion of the two natures in Christ: so Theodoretus, reasoning against the Eutychians, fell in a vehement suspicion to be a Nestorian; like as St Augustine, reasoning against the Manichees for defence of free-will, seemed to speak that the Pelagians would allow; and reasoning against Pelagians, seemed to say that the Manichees would allow: such a danger it is to reduce extremities to the mean, wherein St Augustine was better purged than Theodorete was, although Theodorete was reconciled. But for example of that I have said, this argument of Theodoretus against the Eutychians, to avoid confusion of natures in Christ, sheweth how in the sacrament, where the truth of the mystery of the two natures in Christ may be as it were in similitude learned, the presence of the body of Christ there in the sacrament doth not alter the nature, that is to say, the property of the visible creatures. This saying was that the Nestorians would draw for their purpose to prove distinct persons, against whom Cyril travailed to shew that in the sacrament the flesh of Christ, that was given to be eaten, was given, not as the flesh of a common man, but as the flesh of God; whereby appeared the unity of the Godhead to the manhood in Christ in one person, and yet no confusion, as Theodoretus doth by his argument declare. But whether the printer's negligence, or this author's oversight, hath confounded or confused this matter in the uttering of it, I cannot tell. For the author of this book concludeth solemnly thus by induction of the premises, that "even so the body of Christ was after the ascension changed into the godly substance." I ween the printer left out a "not," and should have said, "not changed into the godly substance;" for so the sense should be, as Peter Martyr reporteth Theodorete.

Theodorete.

[1 Ὁ γὰρ δὴ τὸ φύσει σῶμα σῖτον καὶ ἄρτον προσαγορεύσας, καὶ αὖ πάλιν ἑαυτὸν ἄμπελον ὀνομάσας, οὗτος τὰ ὁρώμενα σύμβολα τῇ τοῦ σώματος καὶ αἵματος προσηγορίᾳ τετίμηκεν, οὐ τὴν φύσιν μεταβαλών, ἀλλὰ τὴν χάριν τῇ φύσει προστεθεικώς. Theod. Dial. i. Tom. IV. p. 26.— Ed. Halæ. 1769—94.]

[2 Οὐδὲ γὰρ μετὰ τὸν ἁγιασμὸν τὰ μυστικὰ σύμβολα τῆς οἰκείας ἐξίσταται φύσεως. μένει γὰρ ἐπὶ τῆς προτέρας οὐσίας, καὶ τοῦ σχήματος, καὶ τοῦ εἴδους, καὶ ὁρατά ἐστι καὶ ἁπτά, οἷα καὶ πρότερον ἦν· νοεῖται δὲ ἅπερ ἐγένετο, καὶ πιστεύεται καὶ προσκυνεῖται, ὡς ἐκεῖνα ὄντα ἅπερ πιστεύεται. παράθες τοίνυν τῷ ἀρχετύπῳ τὴν εἰκόνα, καὶ ὄψει τὴν ὁμοιότητα. χρὴ γὰρ ἐοικέναι τῇ ἀληθείᾳ τὸν τύπον. καὶ γὰρ ἐκεῖνο τὸ σῶμα τὸ μὲν πρότερον εἶδος ἔχει, καὶ σχῆμα, καὶ περιγραφὴν, καὶ ἁπαξαπλῶς εἰπεῖν τὴν τοῦ σώματος οὐσίαν· ἀθάνατον δὲ μετὰ τὴν ἀνάστασιν γέγονε, καὶ κρεῖττον φθορᾶς, καὶ τῆς ἐκ δεξιῶν ἠξιώθη καθέδρας, καὶ παρὰ πάσης προσκυνεῖται τῆς κτίσεως, ἅτε δὴ σῶμα χρηματίζον τοῦ δεσπότου τῆς φύσεως.—Ib. Dial. ii. Tom. IV. p. 126.]

[3 Orig. ed. omits the words, "or ascension."]

And yet the triumph this author maketh against them he calleth for his pleasure papists, with his forked dilemma, maketh me doubt whether he wist what he said or no; because he bringeth in Nestorius so out of purpose, saying the papists must either grant the substance of bread and wine to remain, " or else to be of Nestorius' heresy, that the nature of Godhead remained not."

321. *This author of the book, for the name of Nestorius, should have put Eutyches, and then said for conclusion, the nature of manhood remained not in Christ. And although in Theodorete the substance of bread is spoken of to remain, yet because he doth after expound himself to speak of that is seen and felt, he seemeth to speak of substance after the common capacity, and not as it is truly in learning understanded, an inward, invisible, and not palpable nature, but only perceived by understanding; so as this outward nature that Theodorete speaketh of, may according to his words truly remain, notwithstanding transubstantiation. This author declareth plainly his ignorance, not to perceive whither the argument of Theodorete and Gelasius tendeth, which is properly against the Eutychians rather than the Nestorians. For, and no propriety of bread remain, it proveth not the Godhead in Christ not to remain, but the humanity only to be as it were swallowed up of the divinity, which the Eutychians intended, and specially after Christ's resurrection, against whom the argument by Theodorete is specially brought, howsoever this author confoundeth the Nestorians' and Eutychians' names and taketh one for another, which in so high a matter is no small fault, and yet no great fault among so many other huger and greater, as be in this book committed.*

CANTERBURY.

If that which you have said to Gelasius be well considered and conferred with this in Theodorete, it seemeth by your process in both, that you know not what confusion of natures is. And then your ignorance therein must needs declare that you be utterly ignorant of all their whole discourse, which tendeth only to prove that the two natures in Christ, his divinity and his humanity, be not confounded. And for ignorance of confusion, you confound all together. Gelasius and Theodorete prove, that the two natures in Christ be not confounded, because they remain both in their own substances and properties, so that the remaining declareth no confusion, which should be confounded if they remained not. If a drop of milk be put into a pot of wine, by and by it loseth the first nature and substance, and is confounded with the nature and substance of wine. And if wine and milk be put together in equal quantity, then both be confounded, because neither remaineth, neither perfect wine with his substance and natural proprieties, nor perfect milk with the substance and proprieties of milk; but a confusion, an humble-jumble or hotch-potch, a posset or syllabub is made of them both together, like as in man's body the four elements be confounded to the constitution of the same, not one of the elements remaining in his proper substance, form, and pure natural qualities.

Confusion of natures.

So that if one nature remain not, the same is confounded. And if there be more natures that lose their substance, they be all confounded, except there be an utter consumption or annihilation of the thing that loseth his substance. And therefore the argument, which all the old ecclesiastical authors use, to save the confusion of the two natures in Christ, is to prove, that they both remain. And if we may learn that by the similitude of the sacrament, as Gelasius and Theodorete teach, and you here confess the same, then must needs the substance of bread and wine remain, or else is there none example nor similitude of the remaining of two natures in Christ, but of their confusion; as by your feigned doctrine the substance of bread is confounded with the body of Christ, neither being annihilate, nor remaining, but transubstantiated, confounded, and converted into the substance of Christ's body. And thus with your well understanding of the matter, you confound all together; whereas I with my ignorance, not blaspheming that holy union and mystery of Christ's incarnation, do save all the natures whole, without mixtion, confusion, or transubstantiation, either of the divine and human nature in Christ, or of the soul and body in man, or of the bread and wine in the sacrament; but all the substance and natures be saved and remain clearly with their natural properties and conditions, that the proportion in that point may be like, and one to be the true image and similitude of the other. But surely more gross ignorance or wilful impiety than you have shewed in this matter, hath not lightly been seen or read of.

322.

And where you say, that " I by oversight, or the printer by negligence, have left out a 'not'," if I should have put in that "not" of mine own head, contrary to the Not. original in Greek[1], and to all the translators in Latin, and the translation of master Peter Martyr also, I should have been as far overseen as you be, which as it seemeth of purpose confound and corrupt, you care not whether any author's words, or their meaning.

And as for my "forked dilemma," you shall never be able to answer thereto; but the more you travail therein, the more you shall entangle yourself. For either you must grant, as unwilling as you be, that the nature and substance of bread and wine remain after the consecration, or else that the nature and substance of Christ's humanity and divinity remain not after his incarnation; wherein erred not only Eutyches, whom you say I should have put for Nestorius, but also Marcion, Ebion, Valentinus, Nestorius, and other, as in my book I have declared.

And one thing is principally to be noted in your answer to Theodorete, how you can sophisticate and falsify all men's sayings, be they never so plain. For where between me and the papists the matter here in contention is this, Whether the bread and wine remain in their proper nature and substance or no; I saying that they remain, and the papists saying that they remain not, the issue being in this point, whether they remain, or remain not; I bring for me Chrysostom, who saith, "the nature of bread remaineth[2]:" I bring Gelasius, who saith, that "there ceaseth not the substance or nature of bread and wine[3]:" I bring this Theodorete, whose words be these: "The bread and wine after consecration lose not their proper nature, but keep their former substances, form, and figure[4]." Now how can any man devise to speak the truth in more plain words than these be? For they say the very same words that I say. And yet because the truth is not liked, here must be devised a crafty lawyer's gloss, of them that never sought other but to calumniate the truth, and must be said, against all learning, reason, and speech, that substance is taken for the visible and palpable qualities or accidents. Well, yet then you confess that those old ancient authors agree with me in words, and say as I do, that the bread and wine be not transubstantiated, but remain in their former substance. And then the issue plainly passeth with me by the testimony of these three witnesses, until such time as you can prove that these authors spake one thing, and meant another, and that qualities and accidents be substances. And if you understood whereunto the argument of Theodorete and Gelasius tendeth, you would not say that they spake against the Eutychians, any more than they do against the Nestorians. For if the bread and wine remain not, as you say, but be swallowed up of the body and blood of Christ, then likewise in the principal mystery either the deity must be swallowed up of the humanity, or the humanity of the deity. The contrary whereof is not only against the Eutychians, but also against the Nestorians, Marcionists, and all other that denied any of his two natures to remain perfectly in Christ.

And whereas you, with all the rout of the papists, both privately and openly report me to be unlearned and ignorant, because you would thereby impair my credit in this weighty matter of our faith, my knowledge is not any whit the less, because the papists say it is nothing, nor yours any deal the more, because the papists do say, that you only be learned, whom, for any thing that ever I could perceive in you, I have found more full of words and talk than of learning. And yet the note of ignorance I nothing pass of, if thereby the truth and God's glory should not be hindered.

Now after the reproof of your doctrine of transubstantiation by all the old writers of Christ's church, I write in my book after this manner.

Now forasmuch as it is proved sufficiently, as well by the holy scripture, as by natural operation, by natural reason, by all our senses, and by the most old and best learned authors, and holy martyrs of Christ's church, that the substance of bread and wine do remain, and be received of faithful people in the blessed sacrament, or supper of the Lord; it is a thing worthy to be considered and

Chap. VI. Transubstantiation came from Rome.

[¹ Vid. p. 299. In the original text of the passage here referred to there is no negative. Peter Martyr's translation of the sentence is: Sic et corpus dominicum post assumptionem in divinam est substantiam transmutatum. Loci Communes, Class. IV. cap. 10. Genev. 1623. p. 603.]

[² Vid. p. 274.]   [³ Vid. p. 289.]

[⁴ Vid. p. 299.]

well weighed, what moved the school authors of late years to defend the contrary opinion, not only so far from all experience of our senses, and so far from all reason, but also clean contrary to the old church of Christ and to God's most holy word. Surely nothing moved them thereto so much, as did the vain faith which they had in the church and see of Rome.

<small>Scotus, super 4. Sen. Distinct. xi.</small>

For Joannes Scotus, otherwise called Duns, the subtilest of all the school authors, entreating of this matter of transubstantiation, sheweth plainly the cause thereof. "For," saith he, "the words of the scripture might be expounded more easily and more plainly without transubstantiation, but the church did choose this sense, which is more hard, being moved thereto, as it seemeth, chiefly because that of the sacraments men ought to hold as the holy church of Rome holdeth. But it holdeth, that bread is transubstantiate, or turned into the body, and wine into the blood, as it is shewed, *de Summa Trinitate et Fide Catholica. Firmiter credimus*[1]."

<small>Gabriel, *super Canonem Missæ, Lect. 40.</small>

And Gabriel also, who of all other wrote most largely upon the canon of the mass, saith thus: "It is to be noted, that although it be taught in the scripture, that the body of Christ is truly contained and received of christian people under the kinds of bread and wine, yet how the body of Christ is there, whether by conversion of any thing into it, or without conversion, the body is there with the bread, both the substance and accidents of bread remaining there still, it is not found expressed in the bible. Yet forasmuch as of the sacraments men must hold as the holy church of Rome holdeth, as it is written, *de hæreticis, ad abolendam;* and that church holdeth and hath determined, that the bread is transubstantiated into the body of Christ, and the wine into his blood; therefore is this opinion received of all them that be catholic, that the substance of bread remaineth not, but really and truly is turned, transubstantiated, and changed into the substance of the body of Christ[2]."

<small>324.</small>

<small>Chap. vii.</small>

Thus you have heard the cause, wherefore this opinion of transubstantiation at this present is holden and defended among christian people, that is to say, because the church of Rome hath so determined, although the contrary, by the papists' own confession, appear to be more easy, more true, and more according to the scripture.

<small>[Vid. Embd. ed. in fine tomi hujus.]</small>

But because our English papists, who speak more grossly herein than the pope himself, affirming that the natural body of Christ is naturally in the bread and wine, cannot, nor dare not ground their faith concerning transubstantiation upon the church of Rome; which, although in name it be called most holy, yet indeed it is the most stinking dunghill of all wickedness that is under heaven, and the very synagogue of the devil, which whosoever followeth cannot but stumble, and fall into a pit full of errors: because, I say, the English papists dare not now stablish their faith upon that foundation of Rome, therefore they seek fig-leaves, that is to say, vain reasons, gathered of their own brains and authorities, wrested from the intent and mind of the authors, wherewith to cover and hide their shameful errors. Wherefore I thought it good somewhat to travail herein, to take away those fig-leaves, that their shameful errors may plainly to every man appear.

<small>Chap. viii. The first reason of the papists to prove their transubstantiation.</small>

The greatest reason, and of most importance, and of such strength, as they think, or at the least as they pretend, that all the world cannot answer thereto, is this: "Our Saviour Christ, taking the bread, brake it, and gave it to his

---

[1 Joan. Duns Scot. Op. Lugd. 1639. in Lib. iv. Sentent. Dist. xi. Quæst. 3. Tom. VIII. pp. 616, 18, 19. The original passages of Duns and Gabriel Biel will be found in p. 34 of Cranmer's Latin book at the end of this volume.]

[2 Gabr. Biel. Canon. Missæ Expos. Basil. 1515. Lect. xl. fol. 94. 2.]

disciples, saying, 'This is my body.' Now," say they, "as soon as Christ had spoken these words, the bread was straightway altered and changed, and the substance thereof was converted into the substance of his precious body." Matt. xxvi.
Mark xiv.
Luke xxii.

But what christian ears can patiently hear this doctrine, that Christ is every day made anew, and made of another substance than he was made of in his mother's womb? For whereas at his incarnation he was made of the nature and substance of his blessed mother, now, by these papists' opinion, he is made every day of the nature and substance of bread and wine, which, as they say, "be turned into the substance of his body and blood." O what a marvellous metamorphosis and abominable heresy is this, to say that Christ is daily made anew, and of a new matter! whereof it followeth necessarily, that they make us every day a new Christ, and not the same that was born of the virgin Mary, nor that was crucified upon the cross, [and that it was not the same Christ that was eaten in the supper, which was born and crucified,]³ as it shall be plainly proved by these arguments following. The answer.

First, thus: If Christ's body that was crucified was not made of bread, but the body that was eaten in the supper was made of bread, as the papists say, then Christ's body that was eaten [in the supper]³ was not the same that was crucified. [For if they were all one body, then it must needs follow, that either Christ's body that was eaten was not made of bread, or else that his body that was crucified was made of bread.]⁴

And in like manner it followeth: If the body of Christ in the sacrament be made of the substance of bread and wine, and the same body was conceived in the virgin's womb, then the body of Christ in the virgin's womb was made of bread and wine.

Or else turn the argument thus: The body of Christ in the virgin's womb was not made of bread and wine; but this body of Christ in the sacrament is made of bread and wine: then this body of Christ is not the same that was conceived in the virgin's womb. 325.

Another argument: Christ that was born in the virgin's womb, as concerning his body, was made of none other substance but of the substance of his blessed mother: but Christ in the sacrament is made of another substance; and so it followeth, that he is another Christ.

And so the antichrist of Rome, the chief author of all idolatry, would bring faithful christian people from the true worshipping of Christ that was made and born of the blessed virgin Mary, through the operation of the Holy Ghost, and suffered for us upon the cross, to worship another Christ made of bread and wine through the consecration⁵ of popish priests, which make themselves the makers of God. "For," say they, "the priest by the words of consecration maketh that thing which is eaten and drunken in the Lord's supper, and that," say they, "is Christ himself both God and man;" and so they take upon them to make both God and man.

But let all true worshippers worship one God, one Christ, once corporally made, of one only corporal substance, that is to say, of the blessed virgin Mary; that once died, and rose once again, once ascended into heaven, and there sitteth

---

[³ The Orig. ed. omits the sentences within brackets.]

[⁴ This passage is in the 1551 and 1580 editions only. The Orig. ed. has the following passages, not in either of the above editions:

"And again: If Christ's body that was crucified was not made of bread, and Christ's body that was crucified was the same that was eaten at his last supper, then Christ's body that was eaten was not made of bread.

"And moreover: If Christ's body that was eaten at the last supper was the same that was crucified, and Christ's body that was eaten at the supper was made of bread, as the papists feign, then Christ's body that was crucified was made of bread."]

[⁵ Of a popish priest. And thus the popish priests make themselves, Orig. ed.]

and shall sit at the right hand of his Father evermore; although spiritually he be every day amongst us, and whosoever come together in his name, he is in the midst among them. And he is the spiritual pasture and food of our souls, as meat and drink is of our bodies; which he signifieth unto us by the institution of his most holy supper in the bread and wine[1], declaring that as the bread and wine corporally comfort and feed our bodies, so doth he with his flesh and blood spiritually comfort and feed our souls.

The answer more directly.

And now may be easily answered the papists' argument, whereof they do so much boast: for brag they never so much of their conversion of bread and wine into the body and blood of Christ, yet that conversion is spiritual, and putteth not away the corporal presence of the material bread and wine. But forasmuch as the same is a most holy sacrament of our spiritual nourishment, which we have by the body and blood of our Saviour Christ, there must needs remain the sensible element, that is to say, bread and wine, without the which there can be no sacrament.

As in our spiritual regeneration there can be no sacrament of baptism, if there be no water. For as baptism is no perfect sacrament of spiritual regeneration, without there be as well the element of water, as the Holy Ghost, spiritually regenerating the person that is baptized, which is signified by the said water; even so the supper of the Lord can be no perfect sacrament of spiritual food, except there be as well bread and wine, as the body and blood of our Saviour Christ, spiritually feeding us, which by the said bread and wine is signified.

And howsoever the body and blood of our Saviour Christ be there present, they may as well be present there with the substance of bread and wine, as with the accidents of the same, as the school authors do confess themselves, and it shall be well proved if the adversaries will deny it. Thus you see the strongest argument of the papists answered unto, and the chief foundation whereupon they build their error of transubstantiation utterly subverted and overthrown.

WINCHESTER.

326.

Wherein this author not seeing how little he hath done, concludeth yet as constantly as though he had thrown all down afore him, intending to shew that the doctrine of transubstantiation dependeth only of authority, (which is not so,) using the sayings of Duns and Gabriel, as he reporteth them, for his purpose; because they, as he saith, boast themselves what they could do, if the determination of the council were not: and thus every idle speech may have estimation with this author against the received truth. And from this point of the matter, the author of this book maketh a passage with a little sport at them he fancieth, or liketh to call so, English papists, by the way to enterprise, to answer all such as he supposeth reasons for transubstantiation and authorities also.

* Read Smith, fol. 91, &c.

First, he findeth himself mirth in devising (as he calleth them) the papists to say that Christ is made anew; which fancy, if it were so, is against the real presence as well as transubstantiation. In which words because every wise reader may see how this author playeth, I will say no more but this: Christ is not made anew, nor made of the substance of bread, as of a matter; and that to be the catholic doctrine, this author, if he be right named, knoweth well enough, and yet spendeth two leaves in it.

CANTERBURY.

When I have proved most evidently, as well by the testimony of the scripture, as by the consent of the old authors of Christ's church, both Greeks and Latins, from the beginning continually from time to time, that transubstantiation is against God's most holy word, against the old church of Christ, against all experience of our senses, against all reason, and against the doctrine of all ages, until the bishops of

---

[1 In bread and wine, 1551, and Orig. ed.]

Rome devised the contrary; therefore I conclude that the said doctrine of transubstantiation may justly be called the Romish or papistical doctrine. And where I have shewed further, that the chief pillars of the papistical doctrine, as Duns, Gabriel, Durand, with other do acknowledge, that if it had not been for the determination of the church of Rome, they would have thought otherwise, (which is a most certain argument that this doctrine of transubstantiation came from Rome, and therefore is worthily called a papistical doctrine;) all this must be answered with these words, "as this author reporteth," and "Duns and Gabriel boast what they could do:" whereas neither Duns nor any of the other either brag or boast, but plainly and frankly declare what they think. And if I report them otherwise than they say, reprove me therefore, and tell me wherein. But these be but shifts to shake off the matter that you cannot answer unto. Therefore, until you have made me a more full and direct answer, I am more confirmed in my assertion, to call transubstantiation a papistical doctrine, than I was before.

But here you put me in remembrance of an ignorant reader, whose scholar I was in Cambridge almost forty years passed, who, when he came to any hard chapter which he well understood not, he would find some pretty toy to shift it off, and to skip over unto another chapter, which he could better skill of. The same is a common practice of you throughout your whole book, that when anything in my book presseth you so sore that you cannot answer it, then finely with some merry jest or unseemly taunt you pass it over, and go to some other thing, that you persuade yourself you can better answer; which sleight you use here in two matters together: the one is where I prove the doctrine of transubstantiation to come from Rome; the other is that of your said doctrine of transubstantiation it followeth, that Christ every day is made anew, and of a new matter. In which two matters you craftily slide away from mine arguments, and answer not to one of them. Wherefore I refer to the judgment of the indifferent reader, whether you ought not to be taken for convinced in these two points, until such time as you have made a full answer to my proofs and arguments.

_{327.}

For where you say that "Christ is not made of the substance of bread as of a matter," this is but a slippery evasion. For if Christ be made of bread, either he is made of the matter of bread, or of the form thereof. "But the form," say you, "remaineth, and is not turned into Christ's body." Therefore, if Christ be made of bread, you must needs grant that he is made of the matter of bread.

Now for the answer to the second reason of the papists my book hath thus.

Another reason have they of like strength. If the bread should remain, say they, then should follow many absurdities, and chiefly, that Christ hath taken the nature of bread, as he took the nature of man, and so joined it to his substance. And then, as we have God verily incarnate for our redemption, so should we have him impanate.

Chap. IX. The second argument for transubstantiation.

Thou mayest consider, good reader, that the rest of their reasons be very weak and feeble, when these be the chief and strongest. Truth it is indeed, that Christ should have been impanate, if he had joined the bread unto his substance in unity of person, that is to say, if he had joined the bread unto him in such sort, that he had made the bread one person with himself. But forasmuch as he is joined to the bread but sacramentally, there followeth no impanation thereof, no more than the Holy Ghost is inaquate, that is to say, made water, being sacramentally joined to the water in baptism. Nor he was not made a dove when he took upon him the form of a dove, to signify that he whom St John did baptize was very Christ.

The answer.

*Matt. iii.
Mark i.
Luke iii.*

But rather of the error of the papists themselves, as one error draweth another after it, should follow the great absurdity which they speak upon, that is to say, that Christ should be impanate and invinate. For if Christ do use the bread in such wise, that he doth not adnihilate and make nothing of it, as the papists say, but maketh of it his own body, then is the bread joined to his body in a greater unity than is his humanity to his Godhead. For his Godhead is adjoined unto his humanity in unity of person, and not of nature. But our Saviour Christ, by their saying, adjoineth bread unto his body in unity both of nature and person: so that the bread and the body of Christ be but one thing both in nature and person. And so is there a more entire union between Christ and bread, than between his Godhead and manhood, or between his soul and his body. And thus these arguments of the papists return, like riveted nails, upon their own heads.

WINCHESTER.

The solution to the second reason is almost as fondly handled, alluding from impanation to inaquation, although it was never said in scripture, "This water is the Holy Ghost," but in baptism to be water and the Holy Ghost also. And of the dove is not said, "This is the Holy Ghost," but the Holy Ghost descended as in the resemblance of a dove. The substance of bread is not adnihilate, because God's work is not adnihilation[1], who giveth all being, and adnihilation is a defection of the creature from God; and yet Christ's body is not augmented by the substance of bread, in which body it endeth by conversion, as in the better, without adnihilation, which is a changing by miracle. And when this author knoweth this, or should have known it, or hath forgotten it, he writeth like one that were ignorant, and had read nothing in the matter, as it were to make himself popular, to join himself in ignorance with the rude unlearned people.

CANTERBURY.

As for my solution to the second reason, it is able to stand against your confutation thereof, and to overthrow it quite. For no more is Christ in the bread and wine in the Lord's supper, than the Holy Ghost is in the water of baptism: and therefore if the Holy Ghost be not inaquate, no more is Christ impanate. And when the scripture saith, "Upon whomsoever thou shalt see the Holy Ghost coming down;" and also when St John said, "I saw the Holy Ghost come down like a dove:" did he see any thing but the dove? And yet that which he saw, the scripture there, as well by the voice of God, as by the words of St John, calleth the Holy Ghost. Wherefore the scripture calleth the dove the Holy Ghost. For the speech was as much to say as, "This which I see come down, is the Holy Ghost:" and yet was that the dove, which he saw. And that the dove, which he saw, was the Holy Ghost, was as true a speech, as we, looking upon the bread which we see, do say, "This is the body of Christ." And yet as that speech meaneth not that the Holy Ghost is made a dove, so this speech meaneth not that the body of Christ is impanate; no more than these words of Christ, spoken unto his mother Mary, and to St John, "Lo thy son," and, "Lo thy mother," mean not that John was made Christ, nor that Mary, his mother, was made John's[2] natural mother.

But of your saying it followeth, that the bread is humanate or incarnate. For if these words of Christ, "This is my body," mean as you say, that bread is made Christ's flesh; then, as *Verbum caro factum est*, "The Word was made flesh," concludeth that Christ was incarnate; so *Panis caro factus est*, "the bread is made flesh," concludeth that the bread is incarnate, seeing (as you say) it is not adnihilate.

But of adnihilation you write so strangely, that it seemeth you have written what you dreamed in your sleep, rather than what you learned of any author catholic or infidel. For who ever heard that adnihilation could be wrought but by the only power of God? For the gentile philosophers write according to nature, that *Sicut ex nihilo nihil fit, ita nihil in nihilum redigitur;* "As nothing can be made of nought, so nothing can be turned into nought:" so that as it is the work of God only to make of nought, so it can be but only his work also to turn things into nought. And what man, being never so rude or popular, having any discretion at all, would define adnihilation as you do, that "a defection of a creature from God" should be adnihilation

---

[1 No adnihilation, 1551.]   [2 Was made his natural mother, 1551.]

and turning into nothing? For so should all the angels that fell from God be adnihilate; and so should likewise all apostasy, and all other that by sin relinquish the army of God, and follow his adversary the devil, and all papists, that abandoning Christ (as Judas did) run to antichrist, to whom it were better to be adnihilate, or never to be born, than eternally to remain in God's indignation. Matt. xxvi.

Now followeth the last reason.

Yet a third reason they have, which they gather out of the sixth of John, where Christ saith: "I am lively bread, which came from heaven: if any man eat of this bread, he shall live for ever. And the bread which I will give is my flesh, which I will give for the life of the world." Chap. x. 329. The third reason. John vi.

Then reason they after this fashion. If the bread which Christ gave be his flesh, then it cannot also be material bread; and so it must needs follow, that the material bread is gone, and that none other substance remaineth, but the flesh of Christ only.

To this is soon made answer, that Christ in that place of John spake not of the material and sacramental bread, nor of the sacramental eating, (for that was spoken two or three years before the sacrament was first ordained;) but he spake of spiritual bread, many times repeating, "I am the bread of life, which came from heaven," and of spiritual eating by faith, after which sort he was at the same present time eaten of as many as believed on him, although the sacrament was not at that time made and instituted. And therefore he said: "Your fathers did eat manna in the desert and died, but he that eateth this bread shall live for ever." Therefore this place of St John can in no wise be understand of the sacramental bread, which neither came from heaven, neither giveth life to all that eat[3]. Nor of such bread Christ could have then presently said, "This is my flesh," except they will say, that Christ did then consecrate so many years before the institution of his holy supper. The answer. John vi. John vi.

WINCHESTER.

A third reason this author frameth himself, whereby to take occasion to affirm how the sixth chapter of St John should not appertain to the sacramental manducation; the contrary whereof appeareth as well by the words of Christ in that sixth chapter, saying, "I will give," not "I do give," which promise was fulfilled in the supper, as also by the catholic writers, and specially by Cyril; and therefore I will not further strive with this author in that matter, but see how he can assail the authorities, whereunto he entereth with great confidence.

CANTERBURY.

The third reason I framed not myself, as you say I did, but had it ready framed out of your own shop in your book of the "Devil's Sophistry." And as for the sixth chapter of John, I have sufficiently shewed my mind therein in my answer to Doctor Smith's preface, which shall suffice also for answer to you in this place.

And as for Cyril, is clearly against you, who declareth that when Christ said, "I will give my flesh for the life of the world;" he fulfilled not that promise in his supper, but in the cross. For if Christ had given to us life in his supper, what should he have needed after to die for the same purpose? The words of Cyril be these upon the words of Christ: *Panis quem ego dabo, caro mea est quam ego dabo pro mundi vita. Morior, inquit, pro omnibus, ut per meipsum omnes vivificem, et caro mea omnium redemptio fiat; morietur enim mors morte mea*[4]. Which words mean thus much in English: "I will die for all, that by my death I may give life to all, and that my flesh may be the redemption of all; for death shall die by my death." Thus Cyril. John vi.

[3 Eat it, 1551, and Orig. ed.]

[4 Ἀποθνήσκω, φησίν, ὑπὲρ πάντων, ἵνα πάντας ζωοποιήσω δι' ἐμαυτοῦ, καὶ ἀντίλυτρον τῆς ἁπάντων σαρκὸς τὴν ἐμὴν ἐποιήσαμεν, τεθνήξεται γὰρ ὁ θάνατος ἐν θανάτῳ τῷ ἐμῷ. Cyril. In Joannem, Lib. IV. cap. x. Tom. IV. p. 353. Ed. Aubert. Paris. 1638.]

expoundeth Cyril the words of Christ, that when he said, "I will give," he did not fulfil that promise in his supper, but in the cross, giving us life by his death, not by eating and drinking of him in his supper, as you most ignorantly say. And yet all men may judge how much I bear with you, when I call it but ignorance.

Now followeth mine answer to the authors wrested by the papists.

Chap. XI. Authors wrested by the papists for their transubstantiation.

Now that I have made a full, direct, and plain answer to the vain reasons and cavillations of the papists, order requireth to make likewise answer unto their sophistical allegations and wresting of authors unto their phantastical purposes. There be chiefly three places, which at the first shew seem much to make for their intent; but when they shall be throughly weighed, they make nothing for them at all.

Cyprianus de Cœna Domini.

The first is a place of Cyprian in his sermon of the Lord's supper, where he saith, as is alleged in the "Detection of the Devil's Sophistry:" "This bread, which our Lord gave to his disciples, changed in nature but not in outward form, is by the omnipotency of God's word made flesh[1]."

The answer.

Here the papists stick tooth and nail to these words, "changed in nature:" ergo, say they, the nature of the bread is changed. Here is one chief point of the Devil's sophistry used, who in the allegation of scripture useth ever either to add thereto, or to take away from it, or to alter the sense thereof. And so have they in this author left out those words, which would open plainly all the whole matter. For next the words, which be here before of them recited, do follow these words: "As in the person of Christ the humanity was seen, and the divinity was hid, even so did the divinity ineffably put itself into the visible sacrament." Which words of Cyprian do manifestly shew, that the sacrament doth still remain with the divinity, and that sacramentally the divinity is poured into the bread and wine, the same bread and wine still remaining; like as the same divinity by unity of person was in the humanity of Christ, the same humanity still remaining with the divinity.

[Vide Embd. Ed. in fine tomi hujus.]

And yet "the bread is changed, not in the shape nor substance, but in nature," as Cyprian truly saith; not meaning that the natural substance of bread is clean gone, but that by God's word there is added thereto another higher property, nature and condition, far surpassing[2] the nature and condition of common bread; that is to say, that the bread doth shew unto us, as the same Cyprian saith, that we be partakers of the Spirit of God, and most purely joined unto Christ, and spiritually fed with his flesh and blood, so that now the said mystical bread is both a corporal food for the body, and a spiritual food for the soul.

And likewise is the nature of the water changed in baptism, forasmuch as beside his common nature, which is to wash and make clean the body, it declareth unto us that our souls be also washed and made clean by the Holy Ghost. And thus is answered the chief authority of the doctors, which the papists take for the principal defence of their error. But for further declaration of St Cyprian's mind herein, read the place of him before recited, fol. 24[3].

[Vide Embd. Ed.]

WINCHESTER.

Cyprianus.

First, in Cyprian, who speaketh plainly in the matter, this author findeth a fault, that he is not wholly alleged; whereupon this author brought[4] in the sentence following, not necessary

---

[1 Panis iste quem Dominus discipulis porrigebat, non effigie sed natura mutatus, omnipotentia verbi factus est caro: et sicut in persona Christi humanitas videbatur, et latebat divinitas; ita sacramento visibili ineffabiliter divina se infudit essentia.—Cyprian. de cœna Domini, p. 468. Ed. Paris. 1574. This is a spurious treatise. Vid. James' "Corruption of Scripture," &c. p. 17. Coci Censura Patrum, Helmes. 1683. Riveti Critica Sacra, p. 213. Genev. 1626. Ed. Bened. and Cave's Hist. Lit. It is supposed that it was written by Arnoldus, Abbas Bonæ-Vallis.]

[2 Passing, 1551, and Orig. ed.]

[3 See p. 267.] [4 Bringeth, Orig. ed. Winch.]

to be rehearsed for the matter of transubstantiation, and handsome to be rehearsed for the overthrow of the rest of this author's new catholic faith; and whether that now shall be added was material in the matter of transubstantiation, I require the judgment of thee, O reader.

The first words of Cyprian be these: "This bread which our Lord gave to his disciples, changed in nature, but not in outward form, is by the omnipotency of God's word made flesh." These be Cyprian's words, and then follow these: "As in the person of Christ the humanity was seen and the divinity hidden, even so the divinity ineffably infused itself into the visible sacrament." Thus saith Cyprian, as I can English him, to express the word infudit by Latin English, not liking the English word "shed," because in our English tongue it resembleth spilling and evacuation of the whole; and much less I can agree to use the word "pouring," although infundo in Latin may in the use of earthly things signify so, because pouring noteth[5] a successive working, whereas God's work is in an instant, and for that respect never shedding. But this author had a fancy to use the sound of the word pouring, to serve instead of an argument to improve transubstantiation, meaning the hearer or reader, in the conceiving of the sense of Cyprian thus termed, should fancy the bread in the visible sacrament to be like a sop whereupon liquor were poured; which is a kind of depravation, as thou, reader, by consideration of Cyprian's words and meaning mayest perceive; which Cyprian, having shewed how the bread is made flesh by the omnipotency of God's word, and made by change, then, because this mystery of the sacrament, in consideration of the two natures, celestial and earthly, resembleth the principal mystery of Christ's person, St Cyprian saith in sense, that as in the person of Christ the humanity was seen, and the divinity hidden, so likewise in this sacrament visible is also the divine nature hidden. This is the sense, where for declaration of the work of God, presenting his divine nature, there is used the verb infundit in Latin, by which word the motion of the divine nature is spoken of in scriptures, not because it is a liquid substance to be poured, as the author of this book Englisheth it, signifying a successive operation, but rather as a word (if we should scan it as this author would) signifying the continuance of the term from whence, to the term whereunto, without leaving the one by motion to the other: for there is in the godly nature no local motion, and therefore we say, Christ not leaving his Father descended from heaven, and being in earth was also in heaven; which infusion in some part resembleth, but man's words cannot express God's divine operations.

331.

To the purpose: the first words of Cyprian shew the manner of the constitution of this sacrament to be by mutation of the earthly creatures into the body and blood of Christ: and then, by the words following, sheweth the truth of the substance of the sacrament, to the intent we might use our repair to it and frame our devotion according to the dignity of it, "esteeming," as St Paul saith, "our Lord's body." For the more evident declaration whereof, St Cyprian, by example of the mystery in Christ's person, sheweth Christ's humanity and divinity present in the visible sacrament, of which divinity there is special mention against such, which fancied the flesh of Christ to be given to be eaten, as divided from the divine nature, which was the heresy of the Nestorians, and such other, denying thereby the perfect unity of the two natures in Christ, which the holy synod of Ephesus did specially condemn, as other fathers in their writings did specially prevent with distinct writing against that error. And therefore St Cyprian, not content to shew the presence of Christ's flesh by mutation of the bread, doth after make special mention of Christ's divinity, not concerning[6] that he had said before, but further opening it; and so utterly condemneth the teaching of the author of this book, touching the presence of Christ to be only figuratively. Cyprian saith, that "in the sacrament is the truth, and then there is present the true flesh of Christ, and the Godhead truly, which devotion should knowledge." And as for transubstantiation, according to the first words of St Cyprian, the bread is "changed not in form, but in nature," which is not in the properties of nature, nor in the operation of nature, neither in quantity or quality of nature, and therefore in the inward nature, which is properly substance. This is the plain direct understanding, not by way of addition, as this author of his imagination deviseth, who useth the word "spiritual" as a stop and opposition to the catholic teaching, which is not so, and clearly without learning compareth with this sacrament the water of baptism, of which we read not written that it is changed, as we read of the bread, and therefore the resemblance of water in baptism is used only to blind the rude reader, and serveth for a shift of talk to wind out of that matter that cannot be answered; and as evil debtors shake off their creditors with a bye communication, so this author conveyeth himself away at a back door by water, not doing first as he promised to answer, so as he would avoid Cyprian directly by land.

332.

[⁵ Maketh, 1551. Orig. ed. Winch. reads with Ed. 1580.]   [⁶ Correcting, 1551.]

CANTERBURY.

Where in my former book I found a fault in the allegation of Cyprian, it was indeed no little fault, to allege those words that speak of the change of bread, and to leave out the example most necessary to be rehearsed, which should declare how it was changed; which change is not by transubstantiation, as the example sheweth, but as it is in the person of Christ, whose humanity was not transubstantiate, although it was inseparably annexed unto the deity.

And the words following do not once touch the real and corporal presence of Christ's flesh in the bread; so far it is from the overthrowing of the true catholic faith by me taught. But Cyprian in that place quite and clean overthroweth, as well your real presence, as your imagined transubstantiation, as hereafter by God's grace shall be declared. But first it seemeth to me a strange thing, that such a learned man as you take yourself to be in the tongues, cannot English this verb *infundo*, whereas every grammarian can tell the signification of *fundo*, *effundo*, and *infundo*. But it seemeth you have so dainty a stomach, that you can brook no meat but of your own dressing, though it be never so well dressed of other; yea, you had rather eat it raw, than to take it of another man's dressing. And so much misliketh you all things that other men do, that you be ready to vomit at it.

Infudit.
Smith useth the word "pouring."

No English can please you to this word *infundo* but "Latin English," as you call it; and that is such English as no English man can understand, nor Latin man neither, but only in that sense that I have Englished it. And I pray thee, gentle reader, consider the great weighty cause why no English can please in this place, and thou shalt find it nothing else but ignorance, either of the speech or of God. "Pouring," saith he, "maketh a successive working:" so doth "infusion" say I, and therefore in that respect as unfit a term as "pouring." "But God's work," saith he, "is in an instant." So is his "pouring," say I, and all that he doth, even as well as his "infusion." All man's works be done in succession of time, (for a carpenter cannot build a house in a day,) but God in one moment could make both heaven and earth: so that God worketh without delay of time such things as in us require leisure and time. And yet God hath tempered his speech so to us in holy scripture, that he speaketh of himself in such words as be usual to us, or else could we speak here and learn nothing of God. And therefore whether we say "infusion" or "pouring," all is one thing, and one reason. For in us they be done by little and little, but God worketh the same suddenly in one moment.

Pouring.

333.

And yet if you had well considered the matter, you should not have found the sacraments of God "like sops, wherein liquor is poured," but you should have found "pouring" an apt word to express the abundance of God's working by his grace in the ministration of his holy sacraments. For when there cometh a small rain, then we say it droppeth, or there is a few drops; but when there cometh a great multitude of rain together, for the great abundance of it, we use in common speech to say, it poureth down: so that this word "pouring" is a very apt word to express the multitude of God's mercies and the plentifulness of his grace poured into them whom he loveth, declared and exhibited by his words and sacraments. And howsoever you be disposed by jesting and scoffing to mock out all things, (as your disposition hath been ever given to reprehend things that were well,) yet the indifferent people may judge by this one place, among many other, that you seek rather an occasion to babble without cause, and with idle words to draw your book out at length, than to seek or teach any truth.

Infusion.

And if I should play and scoff in such a matter, as you do, I might dally with the word of "infusion," as you do with the word "pouring." For as you reject my word of pouring, because some fond reader might fancy the bread in the sacrament to be "like a sop wherein liquor were poured," by like reason may I reject your English-Latin of "infuding," because such a reader might fancy thereby the bread to be like water, wherein the divinity is steeped or infuded. As infused rhubarb is called, when it is steeped certain hours in stilled water or wine without seething; and so be roses and violets likewise infused, when they be steeped in warm water to make jalap thereof. But as apothecaries, physicians, surgeons, and alchemists use words of Greek,

Arabic, and other strange languages, purposely thereby to hide their sciences from the knowledge of others, so far as they can; so do you in many parts of your book devise many strange terms, and strange phrases of speech, to obscure and darken thereby the matter of the sacrament, and to make the same meet for the capacities of very few, which Christ ordained to be understanded and exercised of all men.

At the last, as you say, you come to your purpose, not to open the truth, but to hide it as much as you may, and to gather of Cyprian's words your own feigning and not his meaning, who meant nothing less than either of any transubstantiation, or of the corporal presence of Christ in the bread and wine.

And to set out Cyprian's mind in few words, he speaketh of the eating, and not of the keeping of the bread; which, when it is used in the Lord's holy supper, it is not only a corporal meat to nourish the body, but an heavenly meat to nourish the souls of the worthy receivers, the divine majesty invisibly being present, and by a spiritual transition and change uniting us unto Christ, feeding us spiritually with his flesh and blood unto eternal life, as the bread, being converted into the nature of our bodies, feedeth the same in this mortal life. *Cyprian's meaning.*

And that this is the mind of St Cyprian is evident, as well by the words that go before as by the words following the sentence by you alleged. For a little before Cyprian writeth thus: "There is given to us the food of immortal life, differing from common meats, which retaineth the form of corporal substance, and yet proveth God's power to be present by invisible effect[1]." And again after he saith: "This common bread, after it is changed into flesh and blood, procureth life and increase to our bodies. And therefore the weakness of our faith, being holped by the customable effect of things, is taught by a sensible argument that in the invisible sacraments is the effect of everlasting life, and that we be made one by a transition or change, not so much corporal as spiritual. For he is made both bread, flesh, and blood, meat, substance, and life, to his church, which he calleth his body, making it to be partaker of him[2]." Note well these words, good reader, and thou shalt well perceive that Cyprian speaketh not of the bread kept and reserved, but as it is a spiritual nourishment received in the Lord's supper, and as it is fruitfully broken and eaten in the remembrance of Christ's death; and to them that so eat it, Cyprian calleth it "the food of immortal life." And therefore when he saith "that in the invisible sacrament is the effect of everlasting life," he understandeth of them that worthily receive the sacrament: for to the bread and wine pertaineth not eternal life. Nevertheless the visible sacrament teacheth us, that by a spiritual change we be united to Christ's flesh and blood, who is the meat and sustenance of his church, and that we be made partakers of the life everlasting by the power of God, who by his effectual working is present with us, and worketh with his sacraments. *334.*

And here is again to be noted, that Cyprian in this place speaketh of no real presence of Christ's humanity, but of an effectual presence of his divine majesty; and yet "the bread," saith he, "is a food and nourishment of the body." And thus Cyprian proveth nothing against my sayings, neither of the real presence of Christ's flesh and blood, nor of transubstantiation of bread and wine.

And where you be offended with this word "spiritual," it is not my device, but used of St Cyprian himself, not past six or seven lines before the words by you cited, where he declareth the spiritual mutation or transition in the sacraments. And of the change in the sacrament of baptism, as well as in the sacrament of the body and blood of Christ, speaketh not only this author, but also Nazianzen, Emissene, Chrysostom, Ambrose, with all the famous ancient ecclesiastical authors. And this water doth *Spiritual.*

[1 Sed immortalitatis alimonia datur, a communibus cibis differens, corporalis substantiæ retinens speciem, sed virtutis divinæ invisibili efficientia probans adesse præsentiam.—Cyprian. de Cœna Domini. p. 467. Ed. Paris. 1574.]

[2 Panis iste communis, in carnem et sanguinem mutatus, procurat vitam et incrementum corporibus: ideoque ex consueto rerum effectu fidei nostræ adjuta infirmitas, sensibili argumento edocta est visibilibus sacramentis inesse vitæ æternæ effectum, et non tam corporali, quam spiritali transitione Christo nos uniri. Ipse enim et panis, et caro, et sanguis, idem cibus et substantia, et vita factus est ecclesiæ suæ, quam corpus suum appellat, dans ei participationem spiritus.—Ib. pp. 467, 8.]

well to delay your hot wine, whereof you have drunken so much out of the cup of the great whore of Babylon, that the true wine, representing to us our whole redemption by the true blood of Christ, you have clearly transubstantiate and taken away.

Now followeth my answer unto Chrysostom.

Chap. XII. Chrysostomus.

Another authority they have of St John Chrysostom, which they boast also to be invincible. Chrysostom, say they, writeth thus in a certain homily, *De Eucharistia:* "Dost thou see bread? Dost thou see wine? Do they avoid beneath, as other meats do? God forbid! think not so. For as wax, if it be put into the fire, it is made like the fire, no substance remaineth, nothing is left here; so also[1] think thou that the mysteries be consumed by the substance of the body[2]."

At these words of Chrysostom the papists do triumph, as though they had won the field. "Lo," say they, "doth not Chrysostomus the great clerk say most plainly, that we see neither bread nor wine; but that, as wax in the fire, *The answer.* they be consumed to nothing, so that no substance remaineth?" But if they had rehearsed no more, but the very next sentence that followeth in Chrysostom, which craftily and maliciously they leave out, the meaning of St John Chrysostom would easily have appeared, and yet will make them blush, if they be not *335.* utterly past shame. For after the foresaid words of Chrysostom, immediately follow these words:

"Wherefore," saith he, "when ye come to these mysteries, do not think that you receive by a man the body of God, but that with tongues you receive fire by the angels seraphin[3]." And straight after it followeth thus:

"Think that the blood of salvation floweth out of the pure and godly side of Christ, and so coming to it, receive it with pure lips. Wherefore, brethren, I pray you and beseech you, let us not be from the church, nor let us not be occupied there with vain communication; but let us stand fearful and trembling, casting down our eyes, lifting up our minds, mourning privily without speech, and rejoicing in our hearts."

These words of Chrysostom do follow immediately after the other words, which the papists before rehearsed. Therefore if the papists will gather of the words by them recited, that there is neither bread nor wine in the sacrament, I may as well gather of the words that follow, that there is neither priest nor Christ's body.

For as in the former sentence Chrysostom saith, "that we may not think that we see bread and wine;" so in the second sentence he saith, that "we may not think that we receive the body of Christ of the priest's hands." Wherefore, if upon the second sentence, as the papists themselves will say, it cannot be truly gathered, that in the holy communion there is not the body of Christ ministered by the priest; then must they confess also, that it cannot be well and truly gathered upon the first sentence, that there is no bread nor wine.

But there be all these things together in the holy communion, Christ himself spiritually eaten and drunken, and nourishing the right believers; the bread and

---

[1 Nothing is left: so here also, 1551, and Orig. ed.]

[2 Μὴ ὅτι ἄρτος ἐστὶν ἴδῃς, μηδ' ὅτι οἶνός ἐστι νομίσῃς· οὐ γὰρ ὡς αἱ λοιπαὶ βρώσεις εἰς ἀφεδρῶνα χωρεῖ. ἄπαγε, μὴ τοῦτο νόει. ἀλλ' ὥσπερ κηρὸς πυρὶ προσομιλήσας οὐδὲν ἀπουσιάζει, οὐδὲν περισσεύει· οὕτω καὶ ὧδε νόμιζε συναλίσκεσθαι τὰ μυστήρια τῇ τοῦ σώματος οὐσίᾳ.—Chrysostom. De Eucharistia, (al. Hom. ix. de Pœnitentia,) Tom. II. p. 356. Ed. Bened.]

[3 Διὸ καὶ προσερχόμενοι μὴ ὡς ἐξ ἀνθρώπου νομίσητε μεταλαμβάνειν τοῦ θείου σώματος, ἀλλ' ὡς ἐξ αὐτῶν τῶν σεραφὶμ τῇ λαβίδι τοῦ πυρός, ἥνπερ Ἡσαΐας εἶδε, τοῦ θείου σώματος μεταλαμβάνειν νομίζετε, καὶ ὡς τῆς θείας καὶ ἀχράντου πλευρᾶς ἐφαπτόμενα τοῖς χείλεσιν, οὕτω τοῦ σωτηρίου αἵματος μεταλάβωμεν. τοιγαροῦν, ἀδελφοί, τῶν ἐκκλησιῶν μὴ ἀπολειπώμεθα, μήτε πάλιν ἐν αὐταῖς συντυχίαις ἑαυτοὺς ἀσχολῶμεν· στῶμεν ἔμφοβοι καὶ ἔντρομοι, κάτω νεύοντες τὸ ὄμμα, ἄνω δὲ τὴν ψυχήν· στενάζοντες ἀφώνως ἀλαλάζωμεν τῇ καρδίᾳ.—Ibid.]

wine as a sacrament declaring the same; and the priest as a minister thereof. Wherefore St John Chrysostom meant not absolutely to deny that there is bread and wine, or to deny utterly the priest and the body of Christ to be there; but he useth a speech, which is no pure negative, but a negative by comparison.

Negatives by comparison.

Which fashion of speech is commonly used, not only in the scripture, and among all good authors, but also in all manner of languages. For when two things be compared together, in the extolling of the more excellent, or abasing of the more vile, is many times used a negative by comparison, which nevertheless is no pure negative, but only in the respect of the more excellent, or the more base.

As by example. When the people, rejecting the prophet Samuel, desired to have a king, Almighty God said to Samuel: "They have not rejected thee, but me." Not meaning by this negative absolutely, that they had not rejected Samuel, in whose place they desired to have a king, but by that one negative by comparison he understood two affirmatives; that is to say, that they had rejected Samuel, and not him alone, but also that they had chiefly rejected God.

1 Sam. viii.

And when the prophet David said in the person of Christ, "I am a worm, and not a man:" by this negative he denied not utterly that Christ was a man; but the more vehemently to express the great humiliation of Christ, he said, that he was not abased only to the nature of man, but was brought so low, that he might rather be called a worm than a man.

Psal. xxii.

This manner of speech was familiar and usual to St Paul, as when he said: "It is not I that do it, but it is the sin that dwelleth in me." And in another place he saith: "Christ sent me not to baptize, but to preach the gospel." And again he saith: "My speech and preaching was not in words of man's persuasion, but in manifest declaration of the Spirit and power." And he saith also: "Neither he that grafteth, nor he that watereth, is any thing, but God that giveth the increase." And he saith moreover: "It is not I that live, but Christ liveth within me." And, "God forbid that I should rejoice in any thing, but in the cross of our Lord Jesu Christ." And further: "We do not wrestle against flesh and blood, but against the spirits of darkness."

Rom. vii. 336. 1 Cor. i. 1 Cor. ii. 1 Cor. iii. Gal. ii. Gal. vi. Eph. vi.

In all these sentences, and many other like, although they be negatives, nevertheless St Paul meant not clearly to deny that he did that evil whereof he spake, or utterly to say that he was not sent to baptize, who indeed did baptize at certain times, and was sent to do all things that pertained to salvation; or that in his office of setting forth of God's word he used no witty persuasions, which indeed he used most discreetly; or that the grafter and waterer be nothing, which be God's creatures made to his similitude, and without whose work there should be no increase; or to say that he was not alive, who both lived, and ran from country to country to set forth God's glory; or clearly to affirm that he gloried and rejoiced in no other thing than in Christ's cross, who rejoiced with all men that were in joy, and sorrowed with all that were in sorrow; or to deny utterly that we wrestle against flesh and blood, which cease not daily to wrestle and war against our enemies, the world, the flesh, and the devil. In all these sentences, St Paul, as I said, meant not clearly to deny these things, which undoubtedly were all true; but he meant that in comparison of other greater things these smaller were not much to be esteemed, but that the greater things were the chief things to be considered: as that sin committed by his infirmity was rather to be imputed to original sin or corruption of nature, which lay lurking within him, than to his own will and consent: and that although he was sent to baptize, yet he was chiefly sent to preach God's word; and that although he used wise and dis-

1 Cor. i. Rom. xv. 2 Cor. xi.

creet persuasions therein, yet the success thereof came principally of the power of God, and of the working of the Holy Spirit; and that although the grafter and waterer of the garden be some things, and do not a little in their offices, yet it is God chiefly that giveth the increase; and that although he lived in this world, yet his chief life, concerning God, was by Christ, whom he had living within him; and that although he gloried in many other things, yea, in his own infirmities, yet his greatest joy was in the redemption by the cross of Christ; and that although our spirit daily fighteth against our flesh, yet our chief and principal fight is against our ghostly enemies, the subtle and puissant wicked spirits and devils.

<small>2 Cor. xi. & xii.
Gal. v.</small>

The same manner of speech used also St Peter in his first epistle, saying: "That the apparel of women should not be outwardly with braided hair, and setting on of gold, nor in putting on of gorgeous apparel, but that the inward man of the heart should be without corruption."

<small>1 Pet. iii.</small>

In which manner of speech he intended not utterly to forbid all braiding of hair, all gold and costly apparel to all women, (for every one must be apparelled according to their condition, state, and degree;) but he meant hereby clearly to condemn all pride and excess in apparel, and to move all women that they should study to deck their souls inwardly with all virtues, and not to be curious outwardly to deck and adorn their bodies with sumptuous apparel. And our Saviour Christ himself was full of such manner of speeches. "Gather not unto you," saith he, "treasure upon earth," willing thereby rather to set our minds upon heavenly treasure, which ever endureth, than upon earthly treasure, which by many sundry occasions perisheth, and is taken away from us. And yet worldly treasure must needs be had and possessed of some men, as the person, time, and occasion doth serve.

<small>337.
Matt. vi.</small>

Likewise he said: "When you be brought before kings and princes, think not what and how you shall answer." Not willing us by this negative, that we should negligently and unadvisedly answer we care not what; but that we should depend of our heavenly Father, trusting that by his Holy Spirit, he will sufficiently instruct us of answer, rather than to trust of any answer to be devised by our own wit and study.

<small>Matt. x.</small>

And in the same manner he spake, when he said: "It is not you that speak, but it is the Spirit of God that speaketh within you." For the Spirit of God is he that principally putteth godly words into our mouths, and yet nevertheless we do speak according to his moving.

<small>Matt. x.</small>

And to be short, in all these sentences following, that is to say: "Call no man your father upon earth:" "Let no man call you lord or master:" "Fear not them that kill the body:" "I came not to send peace upon earth:" "It is not in me to set you at my right hand or left hand:" "You shall not worship the Father, neither in this mount nor in Jerusalem:" "I take no witness at no man:" "My doctrine is not mine:" "I seek not my glory." In all these negatives, our Saviour Christ spake not precisely and utterly to deny all the foresaid things, but in comparison of them to prefer other things; as to prefer our Father and Lord in heaven above any worldly father, lord, or master in earth, and his fear above the fear of any creature, and his word and gospel above all worldly peace: also to prefer spiritual and inward honouring of God in pure heart and mind, above local, corporal, and outward honour, and that Christ preferred his Father's glory above his own.

<small>Matt. xxiii.
Matt. xxiii.
Matt. x.
Matt. x.
Matt. xx.
John iv.
John v.
John vii.
John viii.</small>

Now forasmuch as I have declared at length the nature and kind of these negative speeches, which be no pure negatives but by comparison, it is easy hereby to make answer to St John Chrysostom, who used this phrase of speech most of any author. For his meaning in his foresaid homily was not, that in the celebration of the Lord's supper is neither bread nor wine, neither priest nor the body of Christ, which the papists themselves must needs confess; but his intent was to draw our minds upward to heaven, that we should not consider so much the bread, wine, and priest, as we should consider his divinity and Holy Spirit given unto us to our eternal salvation.

And therefore in the same place he useth so many times these words, "Think and think not," willing us by these words that we should not fix our thoughts and minds upon the bread, wine, priest, nor Christ's body; but to lift up our hearts higher unto his Spirit and divinity, without the which his body availeth nothing, as he saith himself: "It is the Spirit that giveth life, the flesh availeth nothing." *John vi.*

And as the same Chrysostom in many places moveth us not to consider the water in baptism, but rather to have respect to the Holy Ghost, received in baptism, and represented by the water; even so doth he in this homily of the holy communion move us to lift up our minds from all visible and corporal things to things invisible and spiritual. [Vide Embd. Ed. in fine tomi hujus.]

Insomuch that although Christ was but once crucified, yet would Chrysostom have us to think that we see him daily whipped and scourged before our eyes, and his body hanging upon the cross, and the spear thrust into his side, and the most holy blood to flow out of his side into our mouths. After which manner St Paul wrote to the Galatians, that Christ was painted and crucified before their eyes. *Gal. iii.* 338.

Therefore saith Chrysostom in the same homily a little before the place rehearsed: "What dost thou, O man? didst not thou promise to the priest which said, Lift up your minds and hearts; and thou didst answer, We lift them up unto the Lord? Art not thou ashamed and afraid being at that same hour found a liar? A wonderful thing! The table is set forth, furnished with God's mysteries, the Lamb of God is offered for thee, the priest is careful for thee, spiritual fire cometh out of that heavenly table, the angels seraphin be there present, covering their faces with six wings. All the angelical power with the priest be means and intercessors for thee, a spiritual fire cometh down from heaven, blood in the cup is drunk out of the most pure side unto thy purification. And art not thou ashamed, afraid, and abashed, not endeavouring thyself to purchase God's mercy? O man, doth not thine own conscience condemn thee? There be in the week one hundred and sixty-eight hours, and God asketh but one of them to be given wholly unto him, and thou consumest that in worldly business, in trifling and talking: with what boldness then shalt thou come to these holy mysteries? O corrupt conscience[1]!" *Chrysostomus.*

Hitherto I have rehearsed St John Chrysostom's words, which do shew

---

[¹ Τί ποιεῖς, ἄνθρωπε; οὐχ ὑπέσχου τῷ ἱερεῖ εἰπόντι, ἄνω σχῶμεν ἡμῶν τὸν νοῦν καὶ τὰς καρδίας, καὶ εἶπας, ἔχομεν πρὸς τὸν Κύριον; οὐ φοβῇ, οὐκ ἐρυθριᾷς κατ' αὐτὴν τὴν φοβερὰν ὥραν ψεύστης εὑρισκόμενος; βαβαὶ τοῦ θαύματος. τῆς τραπέζης τῆς μυστικῆς ἐξηρτισμένης, τοῦ ἀμνοῦ τοῦ Θεοῦ ὑπὲρ σοῦ σφαγιαζομένου, τοῦ ἱερέως ὑπὲρ σοῦ ἀγωνιζομένου, πυρὸς πνευματικοῦ ἐκ τῆς ἀχράντου ἀναβλύζοντος τραπέζης, τῶν χερουβὶμ παρισταμένων, καὶ τῶν σεραφὶμ ἱπταμένων, τῶν ἐξαπτερύγων τὰ πρόσωπα κατακαλυπτόντων, πασῶν τῶν ἀσωμάτων δυνάμεων μετὰ τοῦ ἱερέως ὑπὲρ σοῦ πρεσβευουσῶν, τοῦ πυρὸς τοῦ πνευματικοῦ κατερχομένου, τοῦ αἵματος ἐν τῷ κρατῆρι εἰς σὴν κάθαρσιν ἐκ τῆς ἀχράντου πλευρᾶς κενουμένας, οὐ φοβῇ, οὐκ ἐρυθριᾷς καὶ κατὰ ταύτην τὴν φοβερὰν ὥραν ψεύστης εὑρισκόμενος; ἑκατὸν ἑξήκοντα ὀκτὼ ὥρας ἐχούσης τῆς ἑβδομάδος, μίαν καὶ μόνην ὥραν ἀφώρισεν ἑαυτῷ ὁ Θεός· καὶ ταύτην εἰς πράγματα βιωτικὰ καὶ εἰς γελοῖα καὶ εἰς συντυχίας ἀναλίσκεις; μετὰ ποίας λοιπὸν παρρησίας τοῖς μυστηρίοις προσέρχῃ; μετὰ ποίου συνειδότος μεμολυσμένου;—Chrysost. De Eucharistia, ubi supra, p. 349.]

how our minds should be occupied at this holy table of our Lord, that is to say, withdrawn from the consideration of sensible things unto the contemplation of most heavenly and godly things. And thus is answered this place of Chrysostom, which the papists took for an insoluble, and a place that no man was able to answer. But for further[1] declaration of Chysostom's mind in this matter read the place of him before rehearsed, fol. 26 and 28[2].

WINCHESTER.

Chrysostomus.

Answering to Chrysostom, this author complaineth, as he did in Cyprian, of malicious leaving out of that, which when it is brought in, doth nothing impair that went before. Chrysostom would we should consider the secret truth of this mystery, where Christ is the invisible priest, and ministereth in the visible church by his visible minister, the visible priest, whereof Chrysostom would by his words put us in remembrance; not denying thereby the visible ministry, no more than he doth in his other words deny the visible form of bread, and yet would not that we should look only upon that, but whither faith directeth us, that is to say, upon the very body of Christ there invisibly present, which faith knoweth, and knoweth it to be there the very body, and there therefore to be no bread, which bread this true confession of Christ's body present by faith excludeth. But touching the priest, St Chrysostom's words do by no mean teach us that there is no visible priest, but to think that the body of Christ is delivered of Christ's hands, which excludeth not in like sort the minister visible, as faith doth the substance invisible[3] of bread in the sacrament. The one saying in Chrysostom is a godly exhortation according to the truth, the other is a doctrine of faith in the truth: we be not taught that the priest is Christ, but we be taught that the substance of the bread is made Christ's body. And then the question, in the words of Chrysostom, "Seest thou bread?" is as much to say as, Rememberest thy faith; as being one of the faithful that know? which term St Augustine used. And then Chrysostom, to confirm our faith in so high a mystery, declareth how we should think Christ to deliver his body himself, as a thing far exceeding man's power to do it. And with other heavenly words setteth forth the greatness of that mystery, which be words of[4] godly and good meditation, convenient for so high a matter to adorn it accordingly; which because they be wholesome and meet allegories, wherewith to draw and lift up our minds to celestial thoughts, we may not thereby esteem the substance of that mystery to be but in allegory. Here instead of a solution the author filleth three whole leaves with proof of that is not necessary, how a denial by comparison is not utterly a denial, which is indeed true. And as one was answered at Cambridge when he pressed the responsal, "What say ye to mine argument?" which was not indeed of his making[5]: the responsal left his Latin, and told the opponent before all his country friends in plain English: "It is a good argument, sir," quoth he, "but nothing to the purpose." And so is the entreating of this matter of denial by comparison good, but nothing to the purpose here; and it is an observation that requireth good judgment, or else may thereby be induced many absurdities. Chrysostom, as I said before, speaking to the christian man, seemeth to ask whether he useth his faith or no. For if he seeth bread, he seeth not with faith, which seeth the body of Christ there present, and so no bread. If the christian man think of a passage through him of the celestial food, he hath therein no spiritual thought such as faith engendereth, and therefore saith Chrysostom, absit. Here in these words of Chrysostom is no denial with comparison, and therefore this author might have spared his treatise in these three leaves. For in those words, when Chrysostom saith, "Think not thou receivest the body of Christ by a man;" there this author neglecteth[6] his own rule, as in his third book he maketh a solemn argument that by those, St Chrysostom's words, we receive not the body of Christ at all, seeing Chrysostom saith, we may not think we receive it by man. So little substantially is this matter handled, as a man might say, here were many accidental words without a substance or miracle, how strange soever the same seem to this author otherwise.

339.

[1 A further, 1551, and Orig. ed.]
[2 i. e. p. 273 and 286 of this volume.]
[3 A mistake apparently for *visible*.]

[4 With words of, 1551.]
[5 Of his own making, Orig. ed. Winch.]
[6 So neglecteth, Ibid.]

CANTERBURY.

I complained not of your crafty handling of Chrysostom without a just cause; for when you had alleged the words that seemed to make for your purpose, you left out the words that make clearly against you, or which words at the least would open all the whole matter. And yet the words which you leave out, follow immediately the words by you alleged.

And where to discuss this whole matter you say in the beginning, that Chrysostom doth not deny the visible minister, no more than he doth the visible form of bread; here at the first chop you use another policy, not much commendable, altering prettily the words of Chrysostom, making of bread the form of bread. For Chrysostom speaketh of bread and wine, and not of the forms and accidents of them. And if the bread be no more but the visible accidents of bread, then is the minister also no more but the visible accidents of a minister, and so is the priest nothing else but the puppy of a priest. And then the communicants receive no bread of the priest, but a puppy of bread of a puppy of a priest. For Chrysostom speaketh in like form of words of the bread, as he doth of the priest, with these words, "Think not." "Think not that thou seest bread," "think not that thou receivest of a priest." And therefore if this form of speech exclude the substance of bread, it excludeth likewise the substance of the priest. And if the priest remain still, notwithstanding that speech, then may the bread remain also with the same speech. And if your argument be good, there is Christ's body, ergo there is no bread; then may I conclude in the same form of reasoning, there is bread, ergo there is not Christ's body. And so this author maketh nothing for you, but overthroweth your foundation clean, both of transubstantiation and of the real presence.

But to make the mind of Chrysostom somewhat more plain, he teacheth them that come to that holy mystery, with what things their minds should be chiefly occupied, not about earthly and visible things but about things celestial and invisible, and not to consider so much what we see with our eyes, as what we believe in our hearts, not so much what we receive bodily, as what we receive spiritually. And he teacheth not only what we should think we receive, but also of whom we should think to receive it, saying, "When you come to the mysteries, do not think that you receive by a man the body of God, but that you receive fire by the angel seraphin. The thing that we receive," saith he, "is not the body of God, and the person of whom we receive is not a man," like as before immediately he said, that "the thing which we see is not bread." Now if it be not bread in deed that is seen, then it is not the body of Christ in deed that is received, nor he is not a priest in deed of whom we receive it: and on the other side, if it be the very body of Christ that is received, and a very man of whom it is received, then it is very bread in deed that is seen. And where becometh then your transubstantiation?

But to declare briefly and plainly the very truth according to the mind of Chrysostom, as we see with our eyes and eat with our mouths very bread, and see also and drink very wine, so we lift up our hearts unto heaven, and with our faith we see Christ crucified with our spiritual eyes, and eat his flesh thrust through with a spear, and drink his blood springing out of his side with our spiritual mouths of our faith. And as Emissene said, "When we go to the reverend altar to feed upon spiritual meat, with our faith we look upon him that is both God and man, we honour him, we touch him with our minds, we take him with the hands of our hearts, and drink him with the draught of our inward man[7]." So that although we see and eat sensibly very bread and drink very wine, and spiritually eat and drink Christ's very flesh and blood, yet may we not rest there, but lift up our minds to his deity, without the which his flesh availeth nothing, as he saith himself. Further answer needeth not to any thing that you have here spoken. For every learned reader may see at the first shew, that all that you have spoken is nothing else but very trifling in words.

Now followeth St Ambrose.

[7 See p. 269.]

Chap. XIII.
Ambros. de iis, qui Mysteriis initiantur.

Yet there is another place of St Ambrose, which the papists think maketh much for their purpose, but after due examination, it shall plainly appear how much they be deceived. They allege these words of St Ambrose in a book entitled, *De iis, qui initiantur Mysteriis:* "Let us prove that there is not that thing which nature formed, but which benediction did consecrate; and that benediction is of more strength than nature: for by the blessing nature

Exod. iv.

itself is also changed. Moses held a rod, he cast it from him and it was made a serpent. Again he took the serpent by the tail, and it was turned again into the nature of a rod. Wherefore thou seest, that by the grace of the prophet the nature of the serpent and rod was twice changed. The

Exod. vii.

floods of Egypt ran pure water, and suddenly blood began to burst out of the veins of the springs, so that men could not drink of the flood: but at the

341.

prayer of the prophet the blood of the flood went away, and the nature of

Exod. xiv.

water came again. The people of the Hebrews were compassed about, on the one side with the Egyptians, and on the other side with the sea: Moses lifted up his rod, the water divided itself and stood up like a wall, and between

[Josh. iii.]

the waters was left a way for them to pass on foot. And Jordan against nature turned back to the head of his spring. Doth it not appear now, that the nature of the sea-floods, or of the course of fresh water, was changed?

Exod. xvii.

The people was dry, Moses touched a stone, and water came out of the stone. Did not grace here work above nature, to make the stone to bring forth the

Exod. xv.

water, which it had not of nature? Marath was a most bitter flood, so that the people being dry could not drink thereof. Moses put wood into the water, and the nature of the water lost his bitterness, which grace infused did sud-

2 Kings vi.

denly moderate. In the time of Heliseus the prophet, an axe-head fell from one of the prophet's servants into the water: he that lost the iron desired the prophet Heliseus' help, who put the helve into the water, and the iron swam above. Which thing we know was done above nature, for iron is heavier than the liquor of water. Thus we perceive that grace is of more force than nature; and yet hitherto we have rehearsed but the grace of the blessing of the prophets. Now if the blessing of a man be of such value, that it may change nature, what do we say of the consecration of God, wherein is the operation of the words of our Saviour Christ? For this sacrament which thou receivest is done by the word of Christ. Then if the word of Elias was of such power that it could bring fire down from heaven, shall not the word of Christ be of that power, to change the kinds of the elements? Of the making of the

Psal. cxlviii.

whole world thou hast read, that "God spake, and the things were done, he commanded and they were created." The word then of Christ, that could of no things make things that were not, can it not change those things that be

[Vide Embd. Ed. in fine tomi hujus.]

into that thing which before they were not? For it is no less matter to give to things new nature, than to alter natures[1]."

[1 Quantis igitur utimur exemplis, ut probemus non hoc esse quod natura formavit, sed quod benedictio consecravit, majoremque vim esse benedictionis quam naturæ, quia benedictione etiam natura ipsa mutatur? Virgam tenebat Moyses, projecit eam, et facta est serpens. Rursus apprehendit caudam serpentis, et in virgæ naturam revertit. Vides igitur prophetica gratia bis mutatam esse naturam et serpentis et virgæ? Currebant Ægypti flumina puro aquarum meatu, subito de fontium venis sanguis cœpit erumpere. Non erat potus in fluviis. Rursus ad prophetæ preces cruor cessavit fluminum, aquarum natura remeavit. Circumclusus undique erat populus Hebræorum, hinc Ægyptiis vallatus, inde mari clausus: virgam levavit Moyses, separavit se aqua, et in murorum speciem congelavit, atque inter undas via pedestris apparuit. Jordanis retrorsum conversus contra naturam in sui fontis revertitur exordium. Nonne claret naturam vel maritimorum fluctuum vel fluvialis cursus esse mutatam? Sitiebat populus patrum, tetigit Moyses petram, et aqua de petra fluxit. Numquid non præter naturam operata est gratia, ut aquam vomeret petra, quam non habebat natura? Marath fons amarissimus erat, ut sitiens populus bibere non posset. Misit Moyses

Thus far have I rehearsed the words of St Ambrose, (if the said book be his, which they that be of greatest learning and judgment do not think;) by which words the papists would prove, that in the supper of the Lord, after the words of consecration, as they be commonly called, there remaineth neither bread nor wine, because that St Ambrose saith in this place, that "the nature of the bread and wine is changed."

But to satisfy their minds, let us grant for their pleasure, that the foresaid book was St Ambrose' own work: yet the same book maketh nothing for their purpose, but quite against them. For he saith not, that the substance of bread and wine is gone, but he saith, that "their nature is changed;" that is to say, that in the holy communion we ought not to receive the bread and wine as other common meats and drinks, but as things clean changed into a higher estate, nature and condition, to be taken as holy meats and drinks, whereby we receive spiritual feeding and supernatural nourishment from heaven, of the very true body and blood of our Saviour Christ, through the omnipotent power of God, and the wonderful working of the Holy Ghost. Which so well agreeth with the substance of bread and wine still remaining, that if they were gone away, and not there, this our spiritual feeding could not[2] be taught unto us by them.

*The answer.

And therefore in the most part of the examples, which St Ambrose allegeth for the wonderful alteration of natures, the substances did still remain, after the nature and properties were changed. As when the water of Jordan, contrary to his nature, stood still like a wall, or flowed against the stream towards the head and spring, yet the substance of the water remained the same that it was before. Likewise the stone, that above his nature and kind flowed water, was the self-same stone that it was before. And the flood of Marath, that changed his nature of bitterness, changed for all that no part of his substance. No more did that iron, which contrary to his nature swam upon the water, lose thereby any part of the substance thereof. Therefore, as in these alterations of natures the substances nevertheless remained the same that they were before the alterations, even so doth the substance of bread and wine remain in the Lord's supper, and be naturally received and digested into the body, notwithstanding the sacramental mutation of the same into the body and blood of Christ. Which sacramental mutation declareth the supernatural, spiritual, and inexplicable eating and drinking, feeding and digesting, of the body[3] and blood of Christ, in all them that godly, and according to their duty, do receive the sacramental bread[4] and wine.

342.

And that St Ambrose thus meant, that the substance of bread and wine remain still after the consecration, it is most clear by three other examples of the same matter, following in the same chapter. One is of them that be regenerated, in whom, after their regeneration, doth still remain their former

---

lignum in aquam, et amaritudinem suam aquarum natura deposuit, quam infusa subito gratia temperavit. Sub Elisæo propheta uni ex filiis prophetarum excussum est ferrum de securi, et statim mersum est. Rogavit Eliseum qui amiserat ferrum, misit etiam Elisæus lignum in aquam, et ferrum natavit: utique et hoc præter naturam factum esse cognoscimus. Gravior est enim ferri species, quam aquarum liquor. Advertimus igitur majoris esse virtutis gratiam quam naturam? et adhuc tamen propheticæ benedictionis numeramus gratiam. Quod si tantum valuit humana benedictio, ut naturam converteret; quid dicimus de ipsa consecratione divina, ubi verba ipsa Domini salvatoris operantur? Nam sacramentum istud quod accipis, Christi sermone conficitur. Quod si tantum valuit sermo Eliæ, ut ignem de cœlo deponeret; non valebit Christi sermo, ut species mutet elementorum? De totius mundi operibus legisti, "Quia ipse dixit, et facta sunt: ipse mandavit, et creata sunt." Sermo ergo Christi qui potuit ex nihilo facere quod non erat, non potest ea quæ sunt in id mutare quod non erant? Non enim minus est novas rebus dare quam mutare naturas.—Ambros. de Initiandis, cap. ix. Tom. IV. p. 166. Ed. Col. Agrip. 1616. Vide supra, p. 210, note 8.]

[2 Ed. 1580 omits the word *not*.]

[3 Of the same body, Orig. ed.]

[4 The said sacramental bread, Ibid.]

natural substance. Another is of the incarnation of our Saviour Christ, in the which perished no substance, but remained as well the substance of his Godhead, as the substance which he took of the blessed virgin Mary. The third example is of the water in baptism, where the water still remaineth water, although the Holy Ghost come upon the water, or rather upon him that is baptized therein.

Lib. iv. de Sacramentis, cap. 4.

And although the same St Ambrose, in another book entitled *de Sacramentis*, doth say that "the bread is bread before the words of consecration, but when the consecration is done, of bread is made the body of Christ[1]:" yet in the same book and in the same chapter, he telleth in what manner and form the same is done by the words of Christ; not by taking away the substance of the bread, but adding to the bread the grace of Christ's body, and so calling it the body of Christ.

And hereof he bringeth four examples[2]. The first of the regeneration of a man: the second is of the standing of the water of the Red Sea: the third is of the bitter water of Marath: and the fourth is of the iron that swam above the water. In every of the which examples, the former substance remained still, notwithstanding alteration of the natures. And he concludeth the whole matter in these few words: "If there be so much strength in the words of the Lord Jesu, that things had their beginning which never were before, how much more be they able to work, that those things that were before should remain, and also be changed into other things[3]?" Which words do shew manifestly, that notwithstanding this wonderful sacramental and spiritual changing of the bread into the body of Christ, yet the substance of the bread remaineth the same that it was before.

Thus is a sufficient answer made unto three principal authorities, which the papists use to allege, to stablish their error of transubstantiation: the first of Cyprian, the second of St John Chrysostom, and the third of St Ambrose. Other authorities and reasons some of them do bring for the same purpose; but forasmuch as they be of small moment and weight, and easy to be answered unto, I will pass them over at this time, and not trouble the reader with them, but leave them to be weighed by his discretion.

343.

WINCHESTER.

Now let us hear what this author will say to St Ambrose. He rehearseth him of good length, but translateth him for advantage. As among other, in one place where St Ambrose saith, "This sacrament, which thou receivest, is made by the word of Christ;" this author translateth, "Is done by the word of Christ," because making must be understood in the substance of the sacrament chiefly before it is received, and doing may be referred to the effect chiefly: for which purpose it should seem the author of this book cannot away with the word "made," whereat it pleaseth him in another place of this book to be merry, as at an absurdity in the papists, when indeed both St Ambrose here, St Cyprian and St Hierome also in their places use the same word, speaking of this sacrament, and of the wonderful work of God in ordaining the substance of it, by such a conversion as bread is made the body of Christ. But as touching the answer of this author to St Ambrose, it is divers. For first

---

[1 Sed panis iste panis est ante verba sacramentorum: ubi accesserit consecratio, de pane fit caro Christi. Hoc igitur adstruamus. Quomodo potest qui panis est, corpus esse Christi? Consecratione. Consecratio igitur quibus verbis est, et cujus sermonibus? Domini Jesu. Nam reliqua omnia quæ dicuntur, laudem Deo deferunt: oratio præmittitur pro populo, pro regibus, pro ceteris: ubi venitur ut conficiatur venerabile sacramentum, jam non suis sermonibus sacerdos, sed utitur sermonibus Christi.

Ergo sermo Christi hoc conficit sacramentum.—Ambros. de Sacramentis, Lib. iv. cap. iv. Tom. IV. p. 173. Ed. Col. Agrip. 1616. Vide supra, p. 210, note 8.]

[2 Ambros. Ibid. Tom. IV. p. 173.]

[3 Si ergo tanta vis est in sermone Domini Jesu, ut inciperent esse quæ non erant: quanto magis operatorius est, ut quæ erant, in aliud commutentur!—Ib. Lib. iv. cap. iv. Tom. IV. p. 173.]

he doth traverse the authority of the book, which allegation hath been by other heretofore made, and answered unto in such wise, as the book remaineth St Ambrose's still; and Melancthon saith it seemeth not to him unlike his[4], *and therefore allegeth this very place out of him against Œcolampadius. This author will not stick in that allegation, but for answer saith, that "St Ambrose saith not that the substance of the bread and wine is gone:" and that is true, he saith not so in syllables, but he saith so in sense, because he speaketh so plainly of a change in the bread into that it was not; whereunto this author for declaration of change saith: "the bread and wine be changed into an higher estate, nature, and condition," which three words of "estate," "nature," and "condition," be good words to express the change of the bread into the body of Christ, which body is of another nature, another state and condition, than the substance of the bread, without comparison higher.*

But then this author addeth, "to be taken as holy meats and drinks:" wherein if he mean to be taken so, but not to be so, as his teaching in other places of this book is, the bread to be never the holier, but to signify an holy thing; then is the change nothing in deed touching the nature, but only as a coward may be changed in apparel to play Hercules' or Samson's part in a play, himself thereby made never the hardier man at all, but only appointed to signify an hardy man; of which man's change, although his estate and condition might in speech be called "changed" for the time of the play, yet no man would term it thus to say, his nature were changed, whether he meant by the word "nature" the substance of the man's nature or property; for in these two points he were still the same man in Hercules' coat, that he was before the play in his own: so as if there be nothing but a figure in the bread, then for so much this author's other teaching in this book where he saith, "the bread is never the holier," is a doctrine better than this, to teach a change of the bread to a higher nature, when it is only appointed to signify an holy thing. And therefore this author's answer, garnished with these three gay words of "estate," "nature," and "condition," is devised but for a shift, such as agreeth not with other places of this book, nor itself neither. And where St Ambrose marvelleth at God's work in the substance of the sacrament, this author shifteth that also to the effect in him that receiveth, which is also marvellous in deed; but the substance of the sacrament is by St Ambrose specially marvelled at, how bread is made the body of Christ, the visible matter outwardly remaining, and only by an inward change, which is of the inward nature, called properly substance in learning, and a substance in deed, but perceived only by understanding[5], *as the substance present of Christ's most precious body is a very substance in deed of the body invisibly present, but present in deed, and only understanded by most true and certain knowledge of faith. And although this author noteth, how in the examples of mutations brought in by St Ambrose the substances nevertheless remained the same, that skilleth not: for the wonder of those marvels serve for an induction to relieve the weak faith of man in this miracle of the sacrament, and to repress the arrogancy of reason, presuming to search such knowledge in God's secret works, whereof if there might be a reason given, it needeth no faith. And where there is a like, there is no singularity, as this miracle in the sacrament is notably singular, and therefore none other found like unto it. The sacramental mutation, which this author newly so termeth, is a mere shift to avoid, among such as be not learned, the truth of God's miracle in this change, which is in deed such as St Ambrose speaketh of, that of bread is made the body of Christ; which St Ambrose in another place termeth it the grace of the body of Christ: and all is one, for it is a great grace to have the body of Christ for our food present there. And out of Christ's mouth calling the body of Christ is making the body of Christ: which words "calling," "signifying," "naming," used in St Ambrose's writings, do not limit Christ's words, and restrain them to an only calling, an only signifying, or an only naming, but give an understanding agreeable to other of St Ambrose's words, that shew the bread after consecration to be the body of Christ, the calling to be understanded a real calling of the thing that so is made, and likewise a real signifying of the thing in deed present, and a real naming as the thing is in deed; as Christ was named Jesus, because he is the Saviour of his people in deed. And thus perusing this author's answers, I trust I have noted to the reader, with how small substance of matter this author impugneth transubstantiation, and how slenderly he goeth about to answer such authors as by their several writings confirm the same, besides the consent of Christendom universally receiving*

344.

[4 Ego hos libellos video non admodum dissimiles esse aliorum Ambrosii scriptorum. But presently afterwards he adds: Sed ut non sint Ambrosii, (sunt enim sic satis confuse scripti,) apparet tamen circiter illa tempora natos esse. Melancth. in Œcolampadii Dialog. p. 53.]

[5 By inward understanding. Orig. ed. Winch.]

the same; and how, in the mean way, this author hath by his own hands pulled down the same untrue doctrine of the figurative speech, that himself so lately hath devised; or rather, because this matter in his book goeth before, he hath in his second book marred his frame, or ever he cometh to the third book to set it up.

CANTERBURY.

Oh, what a capital crime is here committed, that I have Englished this word, *conficere*, "to do," whose proper signification is, to accomplish, or, make an end of a thing! which being once brought to pass, we use in common speech to say, "I have done:" as, "I have done my house," "I have done my book," "I have done my work," "I have done my day's journey;" that is to say, "I have perfectly done and finished." And is not this fully as much in speech, as to say, "I have made my day's journey," or, "I have made my house, or my book?" But some fault you must find, where none is, partly to keep in use your old custom of calumniation, and partly to satisfy a new toy that you have in your head, that making is in the substance of the sacrament, and doing is in the effect. But whether it be translate "making" or "doing," St Ambrose spake of the wonderful effectual working of God in the use and ministration of the sacraments, and that as well in baptism as in the Lord's supper, and not of his working in the substances of the elements reserved. As for the authority of the book, I stand not in it, so that all your words therein be more than needeth, but to length your book; and yet was the book never allowed amongst men learned and of judgment to be St Ambrose's. And Melancthon, whom you allege for the allowance of it, giveth it two nips, which you have left out of purpose, to serve your affection. For he saith not, as you report, that it seemeth not to him unlike, but that it seemeth not to him far unlike; and yet he confesseth that it is "confusedly written," which is a slender approbation that it should be St Ambrose's.

345.

Changes of things, the substances remaining.

And where you confess that St Ambrose saith not in words, that the substances of bread and wine be gone, and yet saith so in effect, because he speaketh of change, either you know that your argument is naught, and yet bring it in purposely to deceive some simple reader; or your ignorance is more than I would have thought, that of this word "change" would argue change in substance, as though there could be no change but it must be in substance. But if you had well considered the examples of St Ambrose by me alleged, which he bringeth forth for the proofs and similitudes of the change of bread and wine in the sacrament, you should have found that in all the said examples remain the substances, notwithstanding the change: as in the water of Jordan staying to run after the natural course, in the dry stone that contrary to his nature flowed out water, in the bitter water of Marath that was turned into sweetness, in the iron that contrary to nature swam above the water, in the spiritual generation of man above all natural operation, in the sacramental mutation of the water of baptism, and in the incarnation of our Saviour Christ; which all being brought by St Ambrose for example of the change in bread and wine, as in them the substances remained, notwithstanding the changes, so is it in the bread and wine, whereof other were brought for examples.

But in your handling here of St Ambrose, you seem to be utterly ignorant, and not to know difference between sacramental signs, in the use whereof Almighty God inwardly worketh, and other vain signs which be nothing else but outward shews to the eye. For if you understood the matter, would you resemble a knave playing in a prince's coat, in whom nothing is inwardly wrought or altered, unto a man being baptized in water, who hath put upon him outwardly water, but inwardly is apparelled with Christ, and is by the omnipotent working of God spiritually regenerated and changed into a new man? Or would you compare him that banqueteth at a feast to represent an anniversary, or triumph, unto that man that in remembrance of Christ's death eateth and drinketh at his holy supper, giving thanks for his redemption, and comforting himself with the benefit thereof? If you have this opinion and veneration of the sacraments, it is well known what spirit you have, how ignorant you be, and what is to be judged of you. And if you have no such opinion, becometh it you then to dally with such profane examples, tending to the profanation of the sacraments, and deceiving of the readers?

And as for the holiness of bread, I say now as I said before, that neither bread, wine, nor water have any capacity of holiness; but holiness is only in the receivers, and by the bread, water, and wine is sacramentally signified. And therefore the marvellous alteration to an higher estate, nature, and condition, is chiefly and principally in the persons, and in the sacramental signs it is none otherwise but sacramentally and in signification. And whether this be matter of truth, or a thing devised only for a shift, let the reader judge.

Holy bread.

And where you say in your further answer to St Ambrose, that the visible matter of the bread outwardly remaineth, it seemeth you have not well marked the words of St Ambrose, who saith that the words of Christ changeth *species elementorum*. And then if *species*, as you have said before in many places, signify the visible matter, then the visible matter remaineth not, as you say, but is changed, as St Ambrose saith. And so St Ambrose's words, that *species elementorum mutantur*, be clean contrary to your words, that the visible matter remaineth. I will pass over here how you call accidents of bread the matter of bread, against all order of speech, because I have touched that matter sufficiently before.

Visible matter. Forms.

346.

And yet this is not to be passed over, but to be noted by the way, how plainly St Ambrose speaketh against the papists, which say that the body and blood of Christ remain *sub speciebus panis et vini*, "under the forms of bread and wine." And St Ambrose saith, that *species elementorum mutantur*, "the forms of bread and wine be changed."

And where you say, that "in the examples of mutation brought in by St Ambrose, although the substance remain still the same, yet that skilleth not:" your answer here seemeth very strange, to say that that thing skilleth not, which skilleth altogether, and maketh the whole matter. For if in the examples the substances remain, notwithstanding the mutation of the natures by benediction, then do not these examples prove, that the substance of bread and wine remain not. And if this were singular from the examples, as you say it is, then were not the other examples of this. For if the substances remain in them, how can they be brought for examples to prove that the substances of bread and wine remain not? when they be brought for examples, and things that be like, and not that the one should be singular, and unlike from the other. And where you allege this place of St Ambrose for you, nothing can be spoken more directly against you. "For the natures," saith St Ambrose, "of bread and wine be changed." "And the nature," say you, "is the outward visible forms;" and "that that is changed remaineth not," say you also: and so followeth then, that the substances of bread and wine remain, and not the outward visible forms; which is directly against your feigned transubstantiation, and against all that you said hitherto concerning that matter.

And where a "sacramental mutation" is to you a new term, it declareth nothing else but your ignorance in the matter. And although you seem to be ignorant in other authors, yet if you had expended diligently but one chapter of St Ambrose, you should have found three examples of this sacramental mutation, wherein the substances remain entire and whole: one is in the sacrament of Christ's incarnation, another is in a person that is baptized, and the third in the water of baptism; which three examples I alleged in my book, but you thought it better slightly to pass them over, than to trouble your brain with answering to them.

And where you say, that "calling bread the body of Christ is making it in deed the body of Christ, as Christ was called Jesus, because he is the Saviour of all men indeed," here it appeareth, that you consider not the nature of a sacrament. For when sacraments be named or called by the names of the things which they signify, yet they be not the same things indeed, but be so called, as St Augustine saith, "because they have some similitude or likeness to the things which they be called." But Christ was called Jesus our Saviour, as the very true Saviour in deed; not as a sacrament or figure of salvation, as the bread is the sacrament of Christ's flesh, and wine the

Calling. Making.

sacrament of his blood, by which names they be called, and yet be not the very things in deed.

347. Thus have I answered to the chief authors which you allege for transubstantiation, making your own authors not only to overthrow your building, but to dig up your foundation clean from the bottom, and nothing is left you but arrogancy of mind, and boasting of words, as men say that you still fancy with yourself, and brag that you be bishop of Winchester, even as a captain that glorieth in his folly, when he hath lost his castle with ordnance and all that he had.

And at length you be driven to your church, which you call the consent of Christendom universal, when it is no more but the papistical church, that defendeth your transubstantiation.

Now declareth my book the absurdities that follow the error of transubstantiation.

Chap. XIV.
Absurdities that follow of transubstantiation.

And now I will rehearse divers difficulties, absurdities, and inconveniences, which must needs follow upon this error of transubstantiation, whereof not one doth follow of the true and right faith, which is according to God's word.

First, if the papists be demanded, what thing it is that is broken, what is eaten, what is drunken, and what is chawed with the teeth, lips, and mouth in this sacrament, they have nothing to answer, but the accidents. For, as they say, "bread and wine be not the visible elements in this sacrament, but only their accidents." And so they be forced to say, that accidents be broken, eaten, drunken, chawn, and swallowed without any substance at all: which is not only against all reason, but also against the doctrine of all ancient authors.

WINCHESTER.

[The answer. Orig. ed. Winch.]

In the second volume of the forty-third leaf[1], the author goeth about to note six absurdities in the doctrine of transubstantiation, which I intend also to peruse. The first is this.

"First, if the papists be demanded[2]," &c.

Basilius, Hom. i. Hexameron.

This is accompted by this author the first absurdity and inconvenience, which is by him rhetorically set forth with lips, and mouth, and chawing, not substantial terms to the matter, but accidental. For opening of which matter, I will repeat some part again of that I have written before, when I made the scholar answer the rude man in declaration of substance; which is, that albeit that sensible thing which in speech uttered after the capacity of common understanding is called substance, be comprehended of our senses, yet the inward nature of every thing which is in learning properly called substance, is not so distinctly known of us, as we be able to shew it to the senses, or by words of difference to distinct in divers kinds of things one substance from another. And herein, as Basil saith, "If we should go about by separation of all the accidents to discern the substance by itself alone, we should in the experience fail of our purpose, and end in nothing indeed[3]." There is a natural consideration of the abstract, that cannot be practised in experience. And to me if it were asked of common bread, when we break it, whether we break the substance or only the accidents? first I must learnedly say, if the substance be broken, it is by mean of the accident in quantity; and then if it liked me to take my pleasure without learning in philosophy, as this author doth in divinity against the catholic faith, to say in division we break not the substance of bread at all, the heresy in philosophy were not of such absurdity, as this author maintaineth in divinity. For I have some probable matter to say for me, whereas he hath none. For my strange answer I would say, that albeit a natural thing as bread, consisting of matter and essential form with quantity, and thereby other accidents cleaving and annexed, may be well said to be in the whole broken, as we see by experience it is; yet speaking of the substance of it alone, if one should ask whether that be broken, and it should be answered, "Yea," then should the substance appear broken and whole all at one time, seeing in every broken piece of bread is a whole substance of bread,

---

[1 Vide supra.]
[2 The whole passage stands in the Orig. ed. Winch.]
[3 Εἰς οὐδὲν γὰρ καταλήξεις ἑκάστην τῶν ἐνυπαρχουσῶν αὐτῇ ποιοτήτων ὑπεξαιρεῖσθαι τῷ λόγῳ πειρώμενος.—Basil. in Hexameron. Homil. i. Tom. I. p. 9. Ed. Paris. 1721.]

and where the piece of bread broken is so little a crumb, as can no more in deed be divided, we say nevertheless the same to be in substance very bread, and for want of convenient quantity bread invisible: and thus I write to shew that such an answer, to say the accidents be broken, hath no such clear absurdity as this author would have it seem. But leaving of the matter of philosophy to the schools, I will grant that accidents to be without substance is against the common course of natural things, and therefore therein is a special miracle of God. But when the accidents be by miracle without substance, (as they be in the visible part of the sacrament,) then the same accidents to be broken, eaten, and drunken, with all additions this author for his pleasure maketh therein, is no miracle or marvel, and as for absurdity no point at all, for by quantity which remaineth is all division. We ought to confess, and good christian men do profess, the mystery of the sacrament to be supernatural, and above the order of nature; and therefore it is a travail in vain to frame the consideration of it to agree with the terms of philosophy. But where this author saith that nothing can be answered to be broken but the accidents: yes, verily, for in time of contention, as this is, to him that would ask what is broken, I would in other terms answer thus, That thou seest is broken. And then if he would ask further, what that is? I would tell him, The visible matter of the sacrament, under which is present invisibly the substance of the most precious body of Christ. If he will ask yet further, Is that body of Christ broken? I will say, No. For I am learned in faith, that that glorious body now impassible cannot be divided or broken, and therefore it is whole in every part of that is broken, as the substance of bread is in common bread in every part that is broken. According whereunto it is in the book of common prayer set forth, how in each part of that is broken of the consecrate bread is the whole body[4] *of our Saviour Christ*[5]*. If this questioner be further curious, and say, Is not that that is broken bread? I would answer as a believing man by faith, Truly no. For in faith I must call it, because it is truly so, the body of Christ invisibly there, and the breaking to be not in it, but in the visible figure*[6]*. Yea, ye will call it so, saith this questioner, but yet it is bread. Nay, quoth I, my faith is a most certain truth, and believeth things as they verily be; for Christ's word is of strength, not only to shew and declare as other men's words do, but therewith effectual to make it so to be, as it is by him called. And this I write because, howsoever clerks soberly entreat the matter, (such as mind well, I mean, to consider accidents and substance, which terms the rude understand not,) it is not necessary therefore in those terms to make answer to such as be contentiously curious, who labour with questions to dissolve the truth of the mystery; in declaration whereof if we as men stumble and term it otherwise than we should, that is no inconvenience in the mystery, but an imperfection in us that be not able to express it, not having such gifts of God as other have, nor studying to attain learning as other have done. And whatsoever in schools, with a devout mind to answer all captious questions, hath for the exercitation of men's senses been moved soberly and by way of argument objected, that is now picked out by this author, and brought to the common people's ears, in which it might sound evil, they not being able to make answer thereunto, whereby they might be snarled and entangled with vain fancies against that truth, which before without curiosity of questions they truly and constantly believed. Finally, the doctrine of the sacrament is simple and plain, to have the visible forms of bread and wine for signification, the thing whereof is the very body and blood of Christ; which being the truth of the whole, it is no absurdity to confess truly the parts as they be, if occasion require, howsoever it soundeth to the ethnick or carnal man's ears, for whose satisfaction there is no cause why the truth should be altered into a lie, wherewith to make melody to their understandings. For howsoever carnal reason be offended with spiritual truth, it forceth not; but against the whole consent of the ancient doctors no doctrine can be justified, with whose testimony how the faith of the church in the sacrament now agreeth, it is manifest, howsoever it liketh this author to report the contrary.*

348.

*The book of common prayer.

CANTERBURY.

Here may the reader perceive how much you sweat and labour, so that it pitieth me to see what travail you take, babbling many things nothing to the purpose, to answer my first absurdity. And yet at the end you be enforced to affirm all that I

349.

[4 That is broken is the whole body. Orig. ed. Winch.]

[5 "And men must not think less to be received in part than in the whole, but in each of them the whole body of our Saviour Jesu Christ." The Order of the Communion, 1548, p. 10. (Parker Society's edition.)]

[6 Visible sign. Ibid.]

charge you withal, that is to say, that accidents be broken, eaten, drunken, chawed and swallowed, without any substance at all. And more I need not to say here, than before I have answered to your clerkly dialogue between the scholar and the rude man, saving this, that you make all men so wise that they judge accidents in their common understanding to be called substances, and that no man is able to know the difference of one substance from another.

Substances cannot be without accidents.

And here you fall into the same folly that Basil speaketh. For if he that "goeth about to separate accidents from their substance fail of his purpose, and end in nothing in deed," then you separating the accidents of bread from their substance, and the substance of Christ's body from the accidents, by your own saying alleged of Basil, you must fail of your purpose, and in the end bring both the bread and body of Christ to nothing in deed. For the abstraction of accidents from their proper substances, and of substances from their proper accidents, as you truly say in that point, cannot be practised in experience, but is a corruption or adnihilation of both.

And where, to excuse this absurdity, that accidents in the sacramental bread should be broken alone without any substance, you bring in another absurdity, that in common bread the substance is not broken at all; this is no taking away of the first absurdity, but of one absurdity to make two: as once I knew a man, that when he had made a lie, and perceived that he was suspected, by and by he would make two or three much greater lies to excuse the first withal. But if you should say, that we break not the substance of bread at all, it were no more unlearnedly said in philosophy than it is untruly said in divinity.

1 Cor. x. Matt. xxvi. Mark xiv. Luke xxii.

And where you say that you "have probable matter for you, and I have none for me," it is clean contrary. For you have utterly nothing for you, but all the whole world against you, if you say that the substance of common bread is not broken at all. And I have for me the very plain words of Christ, of the apostle, and of the evangelists. "The bread which we break," saith St Paul. "And Christ took bread and brake it," say the three evangelists. But there is no bread, say you, nor no substance of bread is broken. And this "probable matter" have you for yourself, if men will believe yourself alone better than the apostle and the evangelists.

And what should you talk in vain of substance alone, to dazzle the eyes of the ignorant, when there is no such thing, nor never was sithens the world began; and seeing your question in that place is of common bread, where the substance is never alone without accidents? And if the substance of bread might be alone, yet your reason against the breaking of it is so far from all reason, that it should prove as well, that the substance joined to the quantity and accidents cannot be broken, as the substance alone. For in every piece of bread is a whole substance, and then by your argument it cannot be broken.

350.

And where you grant, that "accidents to be without substance is against the common course of natural things, but it is done by a spiritual miracle," this is but a cloud to darken the light. For accidents to be without substances is not only against the common course of natural things, but also against the very nature of accidents, which have none other being but in substances (as they be defined, *accidentis esse est inesse*,) and is also against all philosophy, reason, and working of God sithens the world began. For God never created nor made, with miracle nor without miracle, substances without accidents, nor accidents without substances, as some vainly phantasy *de materia prima*. It is against also the doctrine of the old catholic authors; for never none wrote that accidents were without substances, until the bishop of Rome with his monks and friars defined the contrary.

But note well here, good reader, the end of wit, when it is not stayed by God's word, but shooteth at rovers, or runneth at large, as it were a young colt without a bridle. That nothing is broken but the accidents, this is denied. Then would I fain learn of this great wise man, that so well can dissever substances from accidents, what substance it is that is broken? Not the body of Christ, saith he, for that is whole in every part; nor the bread is not broken, saith he, for our faith teacheth us contrary: then must it be either Christ's divinity or soul that is broken, or else is some other substance there which never man heard of before.

Note also, good reader, how well this author agreeth with himself, which within a little compass denieth so many things, and affirmeth the same again. For first he saith, that to separate substances from the accidents is to bring it to nothing; and yet he separateth from their accidents as well the substances of bread and wine, as of the body of Christ. Before he said, that nothing was broken but the accidents; now he denieth it. Before he saith, the body of Christ is not broken, and shortly after he saith that which is broken is no bread, but the body of Christ. And here it appeareth, how falsehood neither agreeth with truth nor with itself.

And where you allege, that "in the book of common prayer it is set forth, how in each part of that is broken of the consecrated bread is the whole body of our Saviour Christ," what could you have alleged more against yourself? For if the consecrated bread be broken in parts, how can you "answer truly by faith, as a believing man," which answer you make straightways after, that "that which is broken is no bread?" And if you would answer, as you be wont to do, that the accidents of bread be called bread, yet that collusion will not serve you in this place. For seeing that this place speaketh of consecrated bread, answer me to this, whether the substance or accidents be consecrated? And if you say the accidents, then forasmuch as consecration, by your doctrine, is conversion, it must follow that the accidents of bread be converted, and not the substance; and so should you call it transaccidentation, and not transubstantiation: and if you say, that the substance of bread is consecrated, then forasmuch as that which is consecrated is divided into parts, and in every part is the whole body of Christ, you must confess that the substance of bread remaineth with the parts thereof, wherein is received the body of Christ. *The book of common prayer.*

But yet will you say, peradventure, that although this make against transubstantiation, yet it proveth the real presence of Christ's body, seeing that it "is whole in every part of the bread." It is whole indeed in every part of the bread divided, as it is in the whole bread undivided; which is sacramentally, not really, corporally, carnally, and naturally, as you feign and imagine, and would constrain other to believe. And faith denieth not the bread, but teacheth it to remain as a sacrament. And calling of it Christ's body is not making of it to be really so, no more than the calling of the blessed virgin John's mother made not her to be naturally so indeed, nor him to be her son. For although Christ's words effectually spoken be an effectual making, yet his words sacramentally and figuratively spoken declare not the figure or sacrament to be in deed the thing that is signified. *351.*

And if the rude and simple people understand not substance from accidents, as you here affirm, then this thing they may at the leastwise understand, how little they be beholden to you papists, that would bind them to believe, under peril of damnation, such things as they be not able to understand, making articles of their faith to snare them rather than to save them. But what skilleth that to the papists, how many men perish, which seek nothing else but the advancement of their pope, whom they say no man can find fault withal[1]? For though he "neither care for his own soul's health, nor of his christian brother, but draw innumerable people captive with him into hell, yet," say the papists, "no man may reprehend him," nor ask the question why he so doth. *Distin. xl. Si Papa.*

And where you speak of the "soberness" and "devotion" of the school authors, whom before you noted for boasters; what soberness and devotion was in them, being all in manner monks and friars, they that be exercised in them do know, whereof you be none. For the devotion that they had was to their god that created them, which was their pope; by contention, sophistication, and all subtle means they could devise by their wit or learning, to confirm and establish whatsoever oracle came out of their god's mouth. They set up their antichrist directly against Christ, and yet under pretence of Christ made him his vicar-general, giving him power in heaven, earth, and in hell. And is not then the doctrine of transubstantiation, and of the real and sensual presence of Christ in the sacrament, to be believed, trow you, seeing that it came out of such a god's mouth, and was set abroad by so many of his angels? *School authors.*

[1 Corpus Juris Canonici, Distinct. xl. cap. vi. Si Papa. Tom. I. col. 194, 5. Ed. Lugd. 1618.]

Simple and plain doctrine.

And is not this a simple and plain doctrine, I pray you, that visible forms and substances be transubstantiated, and yet accidents remain? A plain doctrine, be you assured, which you confess yourself that the simple and plain people understand not, nor yourself with the help of all the papists is not able to defend it; where the true doctrine of the first catholic christian faith is most plain, clear and comfortable, without any difficulty, scruple or doubt, that is to say, that our Saviour Christ, although he be sitting in heaven in equality with his Father, is our life, strength, food, and sustenance, who by his death delivered us from death, and daily nourisheth and increaseth us to eternal life. And in token hereof he hath prepared bread to be eaten and wine to be drunken of us in his holy supper, to put us in remembrance of his said death, and of the celestial feeding, nourishing, increasing, and of all the benefits which we have thereby; which benefits through faith and the Holy Ghost are exhibited and given unto all that worthily receive the said holy supper. This the husbandman at his plough, the weaver at his loom, and the wife at her rock can remember, and give thanks unto God for the same. This is the very doctrine of the gospel, with the consent wholly of all the old ecclesiastical doctors, howsoever the papists for their pastime put visors upon the said doctors, and disguise them in other coats, making a play and mocking of them.

352.

Now followeth the second absurdity.

Secondly, these transubstantiators do say, contrary to all learning, that the accidents of bread and wine do hang alone in the air, without any substance wherein they may be stayed. And what can be said more foolishly?

WINCHESTER.

[The answer. Sententiarum, distinct. ix. 9, 10. Orig. ed. Winch.]

The Master of the sentences, shewing divers men's sayings in discussion, as they can, of this mystery, telleth what some say, that had rather say somewhat than nothing; which this author rehearseth as a determination of the church, that indeed maketh no doctrine of that point so, but acknowledgeth the mystery to exceed our capacity. And as for the accidents to be stayed, that is to say, to remain without their natural substance, is without difficulty believed of men that have faith, considering the almighty power of Christ, whose divine body is there present. And shall that be accounted for an inconvenience in the mystery, that any one man saith, whose saying is not as a full determination approved? If that man should encounter with this author, if he were alive so to do, I think he would say it were more tolerable in him, of a zeal to agree with the true doctrine, to utter his conceit fondly, than, of a malice to dissent from the true doctrine, this author so fondly to improve his saying. But if he should oppose this author in learning, and ask him how he will understand Fiat lux *in creation of the world, where the light stayed that was then create? But I will proceed to peruse the other differences*[1].

CANTERBURY.

The doctrine that even now was so simple and plain is now again waxed so full of ambiguities and doubts, that learned men in discussing thereof, as they can, be fain to "say rather something than nothing;" and yet were they better to say nothing at all, than to say that is not true, or nothing to purpose. And if the Master of the Sentences' saying in this point vary from the common doctrine of the other papists[2], why is not this his error rejected among other, wherein he is not commonly held? And why do yourself after approve the same saying of the Master, as a thing believed without difficulty, that the accidents be stayed without their natural substance? And then I would know of you wherein they be stayed, seeing they be not stayed in the air, as in their substance, nor in the bread and wine, nor in the body of Christ? For either you must appoint some other stay for them, or else grant, as I say, that they hang alone in the air, without any substance wherein they may be stayed. And either I understand you not in this place, (you speak so diffusely,) or else that thing which the Master spake, and yourself have here affirmed, you call it " a tolerable conceit fondly uttered." And

---

[1 Absurdities. Orig. ed. Winch.]   [2 Of the papists, in 1551.]

whereas to answer the matter of the staying of the accidents, you ask wherein the light was stayed at the creation of the world; this is a very easy opposal, and soon answered unto. For first God created heaven and earth, and after made light, which was stayed in them as it is now, although not divided from the darkness in such sort as it was after.

Now followeth the third absurdity.

Thirdly, that the substance of Christ's body is there really, corporally, and naturally present, without any accidents of the same, And so the papists make accidents to be without substances, and substances to be without accidents.

WINCHESTER.

How Christ's body is in circumstance present, no man can define; but that it is truly present, and therefore really present, corporally also, and naturally[3], with relation to the truth of the body present, and not to the manner of presence, which is spiritual, exceeding our capacity, and therefore therein without drawing away accidents or adding, we believe simply the truth, howsoever it liketh this author without the book to term it at his pleasure, and to speak of substance without accidents and accidents without substance, which perplexity in words cannot jest out the truth of the catholic belief. And this is on the author's part nothing but jesting with a wrong surmise and supposal, as though men had invented and imagined that which by force and truth of the scripture all good men have and must believe, that is to say, the true presence of the substance of the body and blood of Christ in the sacrament, according to the words of Christ, "This is my body;" which exclude the substance of bread, declaring the substance of the body of Christ to be acknowledged and professed in the sacrament by the true faith of a christian man. Compare with this what this author writeth in his ninth difference in the forty-seventh leaf of his book[4], and so consider the truth of this report, and how this author agreeth with himself.

353.
[The answer. Orig. ed. Winch.]
Really, corporally, naturally.

CANTERBURY.

I suspect not the judgment of the indifferent reader so much, but that he can perceive how indirectly you answer to this third absurdity, and be loth, as it seemeth, to answer any thing at all.

But it is no little confirmation of the catholic faith, to see you papists vary so much among yourselves, and you alone to devise so many things contrary to all the rest, and yet you be uncertain yourself what you may say. They say also with one accord, saving only Smith and you, that "in the sacrament be not the qualities and quantities of Christ's body." For he is not there visible and sensible, with his voice to be heard, his colours to be seen, his softness to be felt, his quantities to be extended, and to be local in place, with his other accidents; so that they take away his accidents from the sacrament. Smith saith that he is there, not naturally, as you say, but against nature, with all his qualities and accidents. You dare neither add them nor draw them away, being uncertain whether they be there or no, and being also uncertain whether in the sacrament he have distinction of members or no. But telling the truth is but jesting and railing to you, which for lack of answer be glad to shift off the truth as a matter of jesting.

Smith.

And it is not my "terming without the book and at my pleasure," to speak of substances without accidents, and accidents without substances; for I speak none otherwise therein, than as it hath pleased the papists before to term the same in all their books of that matter, but I termed this matter so upon the papistical books, as they at their pleasure devised or dreamed without all manner of books written before their time. And the force of scripture constraineth no man to the belief of transubstantiation, although the body of Christ were really, corporally, and carnally present, who by his omnipotent power can be present as well with the substances, as with the accidents of bread and wine, as fully is declared before.

[3 And but yet supernaturally. Orig. ed. Winch.]   [4 Vide p. 72.]

354.   And where you allege the disagreeing of me with myself, if you would have taken the pain to read some of the school authors, you should have learned that there is no disagreement in my sayings at all. For they say, that "the body of Christ that is in the sacrament hath his proper forms and quantities," as I said in the forty-seventh leaf[1]. "But yet those accidents," say they, "be in heaven, and not in the sacrament," as I say in this place, not varying one mite from mine other saying. But ignorance in you thinketh a difference where none is at all.

Now followeth the fourth absurdity.

Fourthly, they say, that "the place where the accidents of bread and wine be[2], hath no substance there to fill that place, and so must they needs grant *vacuum*, which nature utterly abhorreth."

WINCHESTER.

[The answer. Orig. ed. Winch.]

This author goeth about to find so many absurdities, that he speaketh he wotteth not what, and where he seeth and feeleth quantity, accompteth the place void for want of substance; as though in consideration of common natural things severally as they be in nature, it were the substance that filled the place, and not rather quantity, although in the natural order of things there is no quantity without substance, and is in this sacrament only by miracle. There wanted a substance in consideration of this absurdity, and was such a vacuum as nature plainly endureth.

CANTERBURY.

All the authors that write what *vacuum* is, account a place that is not filled with a substance which hath quantity in it to be void and empty. So that my saying is not grounded upon ignorance, but upon the mind of all that write in that matter. Whereas your saying, "that quantity alone filleth place, without substance," hath no ground at all but the papists' bare imagination. And if "quantity in the sacrament be without substance by miracle," it is marvel that no[3] ancient writer in no place of their books made any mention of such a miracle. But yourself grant enough for my purpose in this place, "that it is an absurdity in nature, and wrought only by miracle, that quantity occupieth a place alone without substance." Which absurdity followeth not of the true and right faith, but only of your error of transubstantiation.

Now to the fifth absurdity.

Fifthly, they are not ashamed to say, that "substance is made of accidents, when the bread mouldeth or is turned into worms, or when the wine soureth."

WINCHESTER.

[The answer. Orig. ed. Winch.]

True believing men are not ashamed to confess the truth of their faith, whatsoever arguments might be brought of experience in nature to the contrary. For Christ's works we know to be true by a most certain faith: what mouldeth in bread, or soureth in wine, we be not so assured; or whereon worms engender, it is not so fully agreed on among men. The learned lawyer Ulpian writeth, as I have before alleged, that wine and vinegar have in manner one substance, so as when wine soureth and is vinegar, in manner the same substance remaineth; in whom it is thought no absurdity to say by that means that the accidents only sour. And if we agree with the philosophers that there is materia prima, *which in all things is one and altereth not, but as a new form cometh taketh a new name, fancying that as one wave in the water thrusteth away another, so doth one form another; it should seem by this conclusion all alteration to be in accidents, and the corruption of accidents to be the generation of new accidents, the same* materia prima *being as it were* substantia, *that altereth not. And this*

355.   *I write that may be said as it were to make a title to this author's certainty, which is not so sure as he maketh it. Amongst men have been marvellous fancies in consideration of natural things; and it is to me a very great absurdity of that secret, and therefore to our*

[¹ Vide p. 72.]   [² Where the bread and wine be. Orig. ed.]   [³ None, 1551.]

[*knowledge an uncertain work, to deduce an argument, wherewith to impugn our*][4] *certain faith. But to come nearer to the purpose, it is wrong borne in hand, that we affirm worms to be engendered of accidents; but when the worms be engendered, we grant the worms to be, and will rather say, whereof they be we cannot tell, than to say that substance is made of accidents, and that doctrine is not annexed to the faith of transubstantiation, and such as entreat those chances and accidents do not induce that conclusion, but do reasonably avoid it. And yet by the way in moulding and souring it should, meseemeth, be properly said that the accidents mould, and the accidents sour, because we call mould bread bread, sour wine wine; and in wine, as I said before, made vinegar, the former substance hath been in learning accounted in manner to remain: so as this author overshooteth himself, when he matcheth generation of worms with moulding and souring, which differ so far in the speculation. But even as this author's wit is overturned in consideration of the true faith, so doth it appear perverted in consideration of natural things.*

CANTERBURY.

I know not to what purpose you have written all this fond matter, except it be that you would the world should know how ignorant you be in philosophy, which have not learned so much as to know the diversity between the six kinds of movings, generation, corruption, augmentation, diminution, alteration, and moving from place to place: whereof the four last be from accidents to accidents, and the two first from substance to substance. So that all mutation is not in accidents, and the corruption of accidents to be the generation of new accidents, as you unlearnedly imagine, both of that and of *materia prima*, which never was no such thing indeed, but by imagination.

But because you bear me in hand, that I bear the papists wrong in hand, that they affirm worms to be engendered of accidents, I shall rehearse their own words, that the readers may know your ignorance herein, or else how loud a lie you make willingly. *Ex speciebus sacramentalibus*, say they, *generantur vermes, si putrefiant.* "Of the sacramental forms, if they be rotten, be gendered worms." But it is no point of true meaning men now to deny that ever they said any such things, as they have taught in their schools these four or five hundred years, as their own books do plainly testify. And be these papists to be credited, which have taught untruly so many years, and now, when they be pressed withal, go clean from it, and say they never said so, but be "wrong borne in hand?"

And because Smith denieth here the same that you do, that worms be engendered Smith. of the accidents in the sacrament, let him help you to answer this matter. And forasmuch as he saith, that "when the host reserved beginneth to mould and to putrify, and should engender worms, then another substance succeedeth it, of which such things are made," let him tell what substance that is which succeedeth, and whereof that substance is made.

But to return to you again: such philosophy as you make here, learned I never in Aristotle, Plato, nor Pliny; nor I trow none such to be found in any that ever wrote. But as you delight all in singularity, and have made strange divinity, so must you invent as strange philosophy. For who ever heard the *terminus a quo* is changed, or *terminus ad quem*? And whatsoever seemeth to you, (as commonly it seemeth to you that seemeth to no man else,) yet it seemeth to no man else that ever was learned, that accidents be properly changed, but that the substances or subjects be changed from accidents to accidents.

And it is the simplest reason that ever was made, that the accidents mould and sour, because the substance remaineth; so as mould bread is called bread, and sour wine is called wine. For so is hot water and cold water both called water: and yet it is the water that is now hot, now cold, not the accidents. For neither can hot be cold nor cold be hot, nor heat go into coldness, nor coldness into heat; but the subject that receiveth them is now hot, now cold, by alteration, as iron that is now cold is soon made hot; but coldness can never be hotness by no art nor science, forasmuch as they be contrary qualities. And likewise pureness cannot mould, nor

---

[[4] Ed. 1551, and Orig. ed. Winch.]

sweetness cannot be sour; but wine that is sweet may turn into sour wine, and bread that is pure may be changed into mouldy bread. But the more you strive in the matters of philosophy, the more appeareth your ignorance therein, even as it did before in the matters of our faith. And who can condemn your doctrine more clearly than your own Ulpian doth, as you do here allege him? that "in vinegar remaineth in manner the same substance that was in the wine;" whereof it must follow, that when the sacramental wine is turned into vinegar, there must be a substance remaining, which is in manner the same with the substance of the vinegar.

The sixth absurdity.

Sixthly, that substance is nourished without substance, by accidents only, if it chance any cat, mouse, dog, or other thing, to eat the sacramental bread, [or drink the sacramental wine[1].]

These inconveniences and absurdities do follow of the fond papistical transubstantiation, with a number of other errors, as evil or worse than these, whereunto they be never able to answer, as many of them have confessed themselves.

And it is wonder to see, how in many of the foresaid things they vary among themselves: whereas the other doctrine of the scripture and of the old catholic church, but not of the lately corrupted Romish church, is plain and easy, as well to be understood, as to answer to all the aforesaid questions, without any absurdity or inconvenience following thereof; so that every answer shall agree with God's word, with the old church, and also with all reason and true philosophy.

For as touching the first point, what is broken, what is eaten, what drunken, and what chawn in this sacrament, it is easy to answer. The bread and wine, as St Paul saith: "The bread which we break."

[1 Cor. x.]

And as concerning the second and third points, neither is the substance of bread and wine without their proper accidents, nor their accidents hang alone in the air without any substance; but, according to all learning, the substance of the bread and wine reserve their own accidents, and the accidents do rest in their own substances.

And also as concerning the fourth point, there is no point left void after consecration, as the papists dream; but bread and wine fulfil their place, as they did before.

357.

And as touching the fifth point, whereof the worms or moulding is engendered, and whereof the vinegar cometh, the answer is easy to make, according to all learning and experience, that they come according to the course of nature, of the substance of the bread and wine, too long kept, and not of the accidents alone, as the papists do fondly phantasy.

And likewise the substances of bread and wine do feed and nourish the body of them that eat the same, and not only the accidents.

In these answers is no absurdity nor inconvenience, nothing spoken either contrary to holy scripture, or to natural reason, philosophy, or experience, or against any old ancient author, or the primitive or catholic church, but only against the malignant and papistical church of Rome. Whereas on the other side, that cursed synagogue of antichrist hath defined and determined in this matter many things contrary to Christ's words, contrary to the old catholic church, and the holy martyrs and doctors of the same, and contrary to all natural reason, learning, and philosophy.

And the final end of all this antichrist's doctrine is none other, but by subtilty

---

[1. Eds. 1551 and 1580 omit this passage.]

and craft to bring christian people from the true honouring of Christ unto the greatest idolatry that ever was in this world devised; as by God's grace shall be plainly set forth hereafter.

WINCHESTER.

It hath been heard, without fables, of certain men that have lived and been nourished with savours only. And in gold and certain precious stones, that they give a kind of nurture to another substance, without diminution of their substance, experience hath shewed it so, and therefore the principle or maxim that this author gathereth hath no such absurdity in it as he noted, to say that "substance is nourished without substance." But when vermin by chance happen to devour any host, as I am sure they cannot violate Christ's most precious body, so what effect followeth of the rest, what needeth it to be discussed? If it nourisheth, then doth that effect remain, although the substance be not there. If every nurture must needs be of substance, then would those that discuss those chances say the substance to return; but hell gates shall not make me speak against my faith. And if I be asked the question, whether the visible matter of the sacrament nourish; I will answer, Yea. Ergo, saith he, "there is substance:" I deny it. He shall now from the effect to the cause argue by physic; I shall disprove the conclusion by the authority of faith: who is it most meet should yield to other? And if in nature many things be in experience contrary to the general rules, why may not one singular condition be in this visible matter of the sacrament, that, the only substance being changed, all other parts, properties, and effects may remain? Is it an absurdity for a maid to have a child, because it is against the rules of nature? Is it an absurdity the world to be made of nothing, because the philosopher saith, "Of nothing cometh nothing?" The principle of nature is, that whatsoever hath a beginning, hath an end; and yet it is no absurdity to believe our souls to have a beginning without end, and to be immortal. Wherefore, to conclude this matter, it is a great absurdity in this author, to note that for an absurdity in our faith, which repugneth only to the principles of philosophy or reason; when that is only to be accounted for an absurdity, that should repugn to the scripture and God's will, which is the standard to try the rule of our faith. Howsoever reason or philosophy be offended, it forceth not, so God's teaching be embraced and persuaded in faith, which needeth no such plaisters and salves as this author hath devised, to make a sore where none is, and to corrupt that is whole.

[The answer. Orig. ed. Winch.]

CANTERBURY.

Men may here see what feigned fables be sought out to defend your errors and ignorance, which is now so manifest, that it appeareth you never read, or else have forgotten, the very principles and definitions of philosophy: of which this is one, that nutrition is a conversion of substance into substance, that is to say, of the meat into the substance of the thing that is fed. Another is thus: *Ex eisdem sunt et nutriuntur omnia:* "All things be nourished of things like themselves." And so I grant you, that a man made of savours, and a man made of the virtue of gold and precious stones, may be nourished by the same, because he is made of the same. And yet it may be that some certain savour, or the virtue of some precious stone, may increase or continue some humour, whereof a man may be nourished, as we read of some men or certain people that have lived no small time by the savour of apples.

358.

But still in your book you cry "faith, faith," and "catholic faith," when you teach but your own inventions, clean contrary to the true catholic faith and express word of God. And in all your arguments here you commit the greatest vice that can be in reasoning, called *Petitio principii,* taking that thing which is chiefly in controversy to be a principle to induce your conclusion. "Faith, faith," say you, where is no faith, but your bare feigning. I have disproved your faith by God's word, by the universal consent of all Christendom a thousand years together; and you cry out still, "faith, faith," which is not the faith of Christ, but of antichrist. Let christian men now judge, "who should yield to other." If you had proved your doctrine by faith, founded upon God's word, I would condescend unto you, that it is no absurdity that accidents remain when the substance is gone. But God's word is clearly against you, not only in your doctrine of transubstantiation, but also in the doctrine of the real presence, of the eating and drinking, and of the sacrifice of Christ's flesh and blood.

WINCHESTER.

The best plaister and medicine that could now be devised, were to leave apart questions and idle talk, and meekly to submit our capacities to the true faith, and not to overwhelm our understandings with search and inquiry, whereof we shall never find an end, entering the bottomless secrecy of God's mysteries. Let us not seek that is above our reach; but that God hath commanded us let us do. Each man impugneth another's learning with words, none controlleth in others living with better deeds. Let all endeavour themselves to do that God commandeth, and the good occupation thereof shall exclude all such idleness as is cause and occasion of this vain and noisome curiosity. And now to return to this author: whiles he seeth a mote in another man's eye, he feeleth not a beam in his own: who recommendeth unto us specially Theodorete, whom he calleth an holy bishop, and with him doth bring forth a piece of an epistle of St Chrysostom[1]. The doctrine of which two joined with the doctrine of this author, in such sense as this author would have all understood to be called catholic, touching the faith of the sacrament, hath such an absurdity in it as was never heard of in religion. For this author teacheth for his part, that the body of Christ is only really in heaven and not in deed in the sacrament, according whereunto this author teacheth also, the bread to be very bread still; which doctrine if it be true, as this author will needs have it, then join unto it the doctrine of the secret epistle of Chrysostom and Theodorete, whose doctrine is, that after the consecration that is consecrate shall be called no more bread, but the body of Christ. By these two doctrines joined together it shall appear, that we must call that is consecrate by a name that we be learned by this author it is not, and may not by the doctrine of Theodorete call it by the name of the which this author teacheth us in deed it is. And thus[2]: "it is in deed bread," quoth this author; "but call it not so," quoth this Theodorete: "It is not in deed the body of Christ," quoth this author; "but yet in any wise call it so," quoth Theodorete. Here is plain simulation and dissimulation both together. For by forbidding of the name of bread, according to Theodorete's teaching, we dissemble and hide that it is by this author's teaching; and by using the name of our Lord's body, according to Theodorete's teaching, we feign it to be that it is not by this author's teaching, which saith, "there is only a figure:" and by this means, in so high a mystery, we should use untruths on both sides, in simulation and dissimulation, which is a marvellous teaching.

359.

I deny not but things signifying may have the name of that they signify by a figure of speech; but we read not in any doctrine given, that the thing signifying should have the name by figure, and be delivered from the name of that it is in deed. And yet this is now the teaching of this author in defence of his new catholic faith, joined with the teaching of Theodorete, and the secret epistle of St Chrysostom, as this author would have them understood. But those men, Theodorete and Chrysostom, in the sense they meant, as I understand them, taught a true doctrine. For they take the name of the body of Christ in the sacrament to be a real naming of the body of Christ there present in deed, and therefore a true perfect name, which, as St Chrysostom's secret epistle saith, "the thing is worthy to have," declaring by that worthiness the thing named to be there in deed. And likewise I understand the other name of bread worthily done away, because the substance whereupon in reason the name was grounded is changed, according to the true doctrine of transubstantiation: therefore that name of bread in their doctrine is truly laid away, although Theodorete writeth the visible matter of bread and wine to be seen and felt as they were before, and therefore saith "their substance, which there signifieth the outward nature, is seen and felt to remain;" which terms, with convenient understanding, may thus agree with the catholic teaching of transubstantiation, and so in the sacrament on every part, both in the heavenly and earthly part, to be a full, whole, and perfect truth, as the high mystery, being the sacrament of our perfect unity in body and soul with Christ, doth require. Whereby in my judgment, as this author hath against his own determination in this enterprise uttered that confirmeth the truth of the real presence of Christ's most precious body in the sacrament, which he doth in special entreating the words of St Augustine in the twenty-seventh leaf of his book[3], besides that in divers other places he doth the like; so bringing us forth this Theodorete and his secret epistle of St Chrysostom, he hath brought forth that may serve to convince him in transubstantiation. Howbeit as for

---

[[1] Vide pp. 274, 287, 8, 299.]   [[2] As thus, 1551.]   [[3] Vide p. 277.]

transubstantiation, Zuinglius taketh it truly for a necessary consequence of the truth, if there be in the sacrament the real presence of Christ's body, as there is in deed. For as a carnal man, not instruct by faith, as well after consecration as before, as he is of the earth, speaketh and calleth it bread, and asking him what it is will never answer otherwise, and if one asked him whether it were the body of Christ, would think the questioner mocked him; so the faithful spiritual man, answering to that question what it is, would after consecration, according to faith, answer the body of Christ, and think himself mocked if he were asked, is it not bread? unless he had been taught Christ to have said it had been both his body and bread. As for calling it by the name of bread which it was, he would not greatly stick, and one thing may have many names; but one thing is but one substance, whereby to answer to the question what it is, saving only in the person of Christ, wherein we know united the two substances of God and man. And this matter I repeat and summarily touch again, to leave in the reader's breast the principal point of our belief of this mystery to be of the real presence, that is to say, unfeigned substantial presence, and therefore the true presence of Christ's most precious body in the sacrament, which hath been in all ages taught, and been as it is the catholic faith of Christendom, as appeareth by the testimony of the old authors in all ages.

CANTERBURY.

For the conclusion of all these questions, when you see that you can make no answer, but that you be driven to so many absurdities, and that I have answered so plainly unto every one, that there is left neither absurdity nor difficulty at all, then you devise the best way and most easy for yourself, to "lay apart all questions and idle talk;" when all these questions and idle talk needed not, if the papists of their idle brains had not devised their transubstantiation, and thereupon moved this idle talk themselves; which hath been occasion not only of much dissension in all christian realms, but of the effusion also of much innocent blood. _{360.}

But when the papists, like unto Lucifer, have ascended into heaven, and searched by vain and arrogant questions the bowels and secrets of God's majesty and his wisdom; yea, even whether God have made the world so well as he might have done; then they command other to keep silence, and "not to enter into the bottomless secrecy of God's mysteries, nor to seek that is above their reach, but to endeavour themselves to do that God commandeth:" which counsel, as it is most godly and wholesome, so if the papists themselves had observed in the beginning, no man should have needed to have troubled his brains with such frivolous questions and idle talk. But the papists do like boys in the school, that make rods to beat other, and when they should be beaten with the rods which they made themselves, then they wish that all rods were in the fire. So the papists, when they see themselves overthrown in their own questions which they first devised themselves, and to be beaten with their own rods, then they cry, "Peace, hold hands, and question no more."

But to answer the absurdities laid unto the papists' charge, you recompense me again with two great huge absurdities. One is, that "Christ is really but in heaven only:" the other is, that "bread is still bread." Here thou mayest judge, gentle reader, what errors I defend, that am by force driven to such two absurdities, that I am fain to say as I have written in my book, and as the apostles and evangelists said. But beware, I would advise thee, that thou say not as God's word teacheth; for if thou dost, thou mayest be sure to be taken of the papists for an heretic.

Finally, you come to your contradictions of bread and no bread, the body and not the body, simulation and dissimulation; wherein when you have well practised yourself in all your book through, at the last you make as it were a play in a dialogue between Chrysostom, Theodorete, and me. But Chrysostom, Theodorete, and I shall agree well enough; for they tell not what in nowise may be, but what was commonly used; that is to say, not to call the bread by his proper name after consecration, but by the name of the body of Christ. And if you had well considered what I wrote in my book concerning figurative speeches, and negatives by comparison, which you also have allowed, you should have well perceived your labour here spent all in vain. For in all figures and sacraments the signs, remaining in their own proper natures, change nevertheless their names, and be called by the names of the more high and excellent

_{Bread and no bread.}

_{Theodoretus. Chrysostomus.}

_{Why the names of the sacraments be changed.}

things which they signify. And both Chrysostom and Theodorete shew a cause thereof, which is this, that we should not rest in the sight of the sacraments and figures, but lift up our minds to the things that be thereby represented. And yet in the sacraments is neither simulation nor dissimulation, except you will call all figurative speeches simulation, and say that Christ simuled when he said he was a "vine," a "door," a "herdman," "the light of the world," and such like speeches. But it pleaseth you, for refreshing of your wit, (being now so sore travailed with impugning of the truth,) to devise a pretty merry dialogue of "quoth he," and "quoth he." And if I were disposed to dally and trifle, I could make a like dialogue of "simulation" or "dissimulation," of "quoth he" and "quoth you," even between you and Christ.

361.

But, as I have declared before, all things which be exalted to an higher dignity, be called by the names of their dignity, so much that many times their former names be forgotten, and yet nevertheless they be the same things that they were before, although they be not usually so called; as the surnames of kings and emperors, to how many be they known? or how many do call them thereby? but every man calleth them by their royal and imperial dignities. And in like manner is it of figures and sacraments, saving that their exaltation is in a figure, and the dignities royal and imperial be real and in deed. And yet he should not offend, that should call the princes by their original names, so that he did it not in contempt of their estates. And no more should he offend, that did call a figure by the name of the thing that it is indeed, so that he did it not in contempt of the thing that is signified. And therefore Theodorete saith not, that the bread in the sacrament may not be called bread, and that he offendeth that so calleth it; for he calleth it bread himself, but with this addition of dignity, calling it "the bread of life," which it signifieth: as the cap of maintenance is not called barely and simply a cap, but with addition of maintenance. And in like manner we use not in common speech to call bread, wine, and water in the sacraments, simple and common water, bread, and wine: but according to that they represent unto us, we call them "the water of baptism," "the water of life," "sacramental water," "sacramental and celestial bread and wine," "the bread of life," "the drink that quencheth our thirst for ever." And the cause Theodorete sheweth why they be so called, that "we, hearing those names, should lift up our minds unto the things that they be called, and comfort ourselves therewithal." And yet neither in the sacraments, in the cap of maintenance, nor in the imperial or royal majesties, is any simulation or dissimulation; but all be plain speeches in common usage, which every man understandeth.

But there was never man that understood any author further from his meaning, than you do Theodorete and Chrysostom in this place. For they meant not of any real calling by changing of substances, but of a sacramental change of the names remaining the substances. For Theodorete saith in plain words, "that as Christ called bread his body, so he called his body corn, and called himself a vine." Was therefore the substance of his body transubstantiated and turned into corn, or he into a vine? And yet this must needs follow of your saying, if Christ's calling were a putting away of the former substance, according to the doctrine of transubstantiation. But that Theodorete meant not of any such changing of substances, but of changing of names, he declareth so plainly, that no man can doubt of his meaning. These be Theodorete's own words: "Our Saviour without doubt changed the names, and gave to his body the name of the sign, and to the sign the name of his body; and yet," saith he, "they kept their former substance, fashion, and figure." And the cause wherefore Christ doth vouchsafe to call the sacramental bread by the name of his body, and to dignify so earthly a thing by so heavenly a name, Theodorete sheweth to be this, "that the godly receivers of the sacrament, when they hear the heavenly names, should lift up their minds from earth unto heaven, and not to have respect unto the bread outwardly only, but principally to look upon Christ, who with his heavenly grace and omnipotent power feedeth them inwardly."

362.

But there never was such untruth used as you use in this author, to hide the truth and to set forth your untruth. For you alter Theodorete's words, and yet that sufficeth not, but you give such new and strange significations to words as before was never invented. For where Theodorete saith, that "the sacraments remain," you turn that into the visible matter, and then that visible matter, as you take it, must signify accidents. And where Theodorete saith in plain terms, that "the substance remaineth," there must substance also by your saying signify accidents, which you call here "outward nature," contrary to your own doctrine, which have taught hitherto, that "substance is an inward nature, invisible and insensible." And thus your saying here neither agreeth with the truth nor with yourself in other places.

And all these cautels[1] and false interpretations, altering of the words, and corrupting of the sense both of all authors and also of scripture, is nothing else but shameless shifts to deceive simple people, and to draw them from the old catholic faith of Christ's church unto your new Romish errors, devised by antichrist not above four or five hundred years passed.

And where you say, that "in the sacrament, in every part, both in the heavenly and earthly part, is an whole and perfect truth;" how is perfect truth in the earthly part of the sacrament, if there be no bread there at all, but the colour and accidents of bread? For if there be none other truth in the heavenly part of the sacrament, then is not Christ there at all, but only his qualities and accidents.

And as concerning your unjust gathering of mine own words upon St Augustine, I have answered thereunto in the same place.

And where you have set out the answer of the carnal and spiritual man after your own imagination, you have so well devised the matter, that you have made two extremities without any mean. For the true faithful man would answer, not as you have devised, but he would say, according to the old catholic faith and teaching of the apostles, evangelists, martyrs, and confessors of Christ's church, "that in the sacrament or true ministration thereof be two parts, the earthly and the heavenly: the earthly is the bread and wine, the other is Christ himself: the earthly is without us, the heavenly is within us: the earthly is eaten with our mouths, and carnally feedeth our bodies; the heavenly is eaten with our inward man, and spiritually feedeth the same: the earthly feedeth us but for a time, the heavenly feedeth us for ever." Thus would the true faithful man answer, without leaning to any extremity, either to deny the bread or inclosing Christ really in the accidences of bread; but professing and believing Christ really and corporally to be ascended into heaven, and yet spiritually to dwell in his faithful people, and they in him unto the world's end. This is the true catholic faith of Christ, taught from the beginning, and never corrupted but by antichrist and his ministers.

And where you say, that "one thing is but one substance, saving only in the person of Christ," your teaching is untrue, not only in the person of Christ, but also in every man, who is made of two substances, the body and soul. And if you had been learned in philosophy, you would have found your saying false also in every corporal thing, which consisteth of two substances, of the matter, and of the form. And Gelasius sheweth the same likewise in this matter of the sacrament. So untrue it is that you most vainly boast here, that your doctrine hath been taught in all ages, and been the catholic faith; which was never the catholic, but only the papistical faith, as I have evidently proved by holy scripture and the old catholic authors, wherein truly and directly you have not answered to one.

One thing one substance. 363.

WINCHESTER.

In whose particular words although there may be sometime cavillations, yet I will note to the reader four marks and tokens imprinted rather in those old authors' deeds than words, which be certain testimonies to the truth of their faith of the real presence[2] of Christ's most precious body in the sacrament. The first mark is in the process of arguing used by them to the conviction of heretics by the truth of this sacrament, wherein I note not the particular[3] sentences, which sometime be dangerous speeches, but their whole doings. As Irene, who was in the beginning of the church, argueth against the Valentinians that denied the resurrection of our flesh, whom Irene reproveth by the feeding of our souls and bodies with the divine,

---

[1 Cautels, i. e. cautions.]
[2 Of real presence, Orig. ed. Winch.]
[3 Not their particular, ibid.]

glorified flesh of Christ in the sacrament; which flesh, and it be there but in a figure[1], then it should have proved the resurrection of our flesh slenderly, as it were[2] but figuratively. And if the catholic faith had not been then certainly taught, and constantly believed without variance, Christ's very flesh to be in deed eaten in that mystery, it would have been answered of the heretics, it had been but a figure; but that appeareth not, and the other appeareth, which is a testimony to the truth of matter in deed.

[Hilarius. 8 libro de Trin. Orig. ed. Winch.]

Hilary, reasoning of the natural conjunction between us and Christ by mean of this sacrament, expresseth the same to come to pass by the receiving truly the very flesh of our Lord in our Lord's meat, and thereupon argueth against the Arians; which Arians, if it had not been so really in deed, would have answered, But all was spiritually, so as there was no such natural and corporal communion in deed as Hilary supposed, but, as this author teacheth, a figure, and it had been the catholic doctrine; so that argument of Hilary had been of no force. St Chrysostom, Gelasius, and Theodorete, argue of the truth of this mystery to convince the Apollinarists and Eutychians; which were none argument, if Christ's very body were not as really present in the sacrament for the truth of presence, as the Godhead is in the person of Christ; being the effect of the argument this, that as the presence of Christ's body in this mystery doth not alter the property[3] of the visible natures, no more doth the Godhead in the person of Christ extinguish his humanity; which against those heretics served for an argument to exclude confusion of natures in Christ, and had been a dangerous arguing[4] to be embraced of the Nestorians, who would hereby have furthered their heresy, to prove the distinction of natures in Christ without any union; for they would have said: "As the earthly and heavenly natures be so distinct in the sacrament, as the one is not spoken of the other, so be the natures of the humanity and Godhead not united in Christ;" which is false; and in the comparings[5] we may not look that all should answer in equality, but only for the point that it is made[6] for, that is, as in the sacrament the visible element is not extinguished by the presence of Christ's most precious body, no more is Christ's humanity by his Godhead; and yet we may not say, that as in the sacrament be but only accidents of the visible earthly matter, that therefore in the person of Christ be only accidents of the humanity. For that mystery requireth the whole truth of man's nature, and therefore Christ took upon him the whole man, body and soul. The mystery of the sacrament requireth the truth of the accidents only,

864.

being the substance of the visible creatures converted into the body and blood of Christ. And this I write to prevent such cavillations as some would search for. But to return to our matter: all these arguments were vain, if there were not in the sacrament the true presence of Christ's very body, as the celestial part of the sacrament, being the visible forms the earthly thing: which earthly thing remaineth in the former propriety with the very presence of the celestial thing. And this sufficeth concerning the first mark.

CANTERBURY.

As for your four marks and tokens, if you mark them well, you shall perceive most manifestly your ignorance and error, how they note and appoint, as it were with their fingers, your doctrine to be erroneous, as well of transubstantiation as of the real presence.

Irenæus.

And to begin with your first mark: Irenee indeed proved the resurrection of our bodies unto eternal life, because our bodies be nourished with the everlasting food of Christ's body. And therefore as that food is everlasting, so it being joined unto his eternal deity, giveth to our bodies everlasting life. And if the being of Christ's body in any creature should give the same life, then it might peradventure be thought of some fools, that if it were in the bread, it should give life to the bread. But neither reason, learning, nor faith beareth, that Christ's body being only in bread should give life unto a man. So that if it were an article of our faith, to believe that Christ is present in the forms of bread and wine, it were an unprofitable article, seeing that his being in the bread should profit no man.

The meaning of Irenee and other. John vi.

Irenee therefore meaneth not of the being of Christ in the bread and wine, but of the eating of him. And yet he meaneth not of corporal eating, (for so Christ saith himself,

---

[1 But a figure, Orig. ed. Winch.]
[2 And as it were, ibid. and 1551.]
[3 Properties, Orig. ed. Winch.]
[4 Argument, ibid.]
[5 Comparing, ibid.]
[6 The point it is made, ibid.]

that his flesh availeth nothing,) but spiritual eating by faith. Nor he speaketh not of spiritual eating in receiving of the sacrament only, for then our life should not be eternal, nor endure no longer than we be eating of the sacrament; for our spiritual life continueth no longer than our spiritual feeding. And then could none have life but that receive the sacrament, and all should have perished that died before Christ's supper and institution of the sacrament, or that die under age before they receive the sacrament.

But the true meaning of Irenee, Hilary, Cyprian, Cyril, and other that treated of this matter was this, that as Christ was truly made man and crucified for us, and shed his blood upon the cross for our redemption, and now reigneth for ever in heaven; so as many as have a true faith and belief in him, chawing their cuds, and perfectly remembering the same death and passion, which is the spiritual eating of his flesh and drinking of his blood, they shall reign in everlasting life with him. For they spiritually and truly by faith eat his flesh and drink his blood, whether they were before the institution of the sacrament or after. And the being or not being of Christ's body and blood really and corporally in the sacrament under the forms of bread and wine, neither maketh nor marreth, nor is to no purpose in this matter. But for confirmation of this our faith in Christ's death and passion, and for a perpetual memory of the same, hath Christ ordained this holy sacrament, not to be kept, but to be ministered among us to our singular comfort; that as outwardly and corporally we eat the very bread and drink the very wine, and call them "the body and blood of Christ," so inwardly and spiritually we eat and drink the very body and blood of Christ. And yet carnally and corporally he is in heaven, and shall be until the last judgment, when he shall come to judge both the quick and the dead. And in the sacrament, that is to say, in the due ministration of the sacrament, Christ is not only figuratively, but effectually unto everlasting life.

And this teaching impugneth the heresies of the Valentinians, Arians, and other heretics: and so doth not your feigned doctrine of transubstantiation, of the real presence of Christ's flesh and blood in the sacrament, under the forms of bread and wine; and that ungodly and wicked men eat and drink the same, which shall be cast away from the eternal life, and perish for ever. And for further answer to Hilary, I refer the reader to mine other answer made to him before.

And for St Chrysostom, Gelasius, and Theodorete, if there be no bread and wine in the sacrament, their arguments serve for the heretics' purpose, and clean directly against themselves. For their intent against the heretics is to prove, that to the full perfection of Christ is required a perfect soul and a perfect body, and to be perfect God and perfect man; as to the full perfection of the sacrament is required pure and perfect bread and wine, and the perfect body and blood of Christ. So that now turning the argument, if there be no perfect bread and wine, as the papists falsely surmise, then may the heretics conclude against the catholic faith, and convince Chrysostom, Gelasius, and Theodorete with their own weapon, that is to say, with their own similitude, that as in the sacrament lacketh the earthly part, so doth in Christ lack his humanity. And as to all our senses seemeth to be bread and wine, and yet is none indeed; so shall they argue by this similitude, that in Christ seemed to all our senses flesh and blood, and yet was there none in very deed. And thus by your devilish transubstantiation of bread and wine, do you transubstantiate also the body and blood of Christ, not convincing but confirming most heinous heresies. And this is the conclusion of your ungodly feigned doctrine of transubstantiation.

And where you would gather the same conclusion, if Christ's flesh and blood be not really present, it seemeth that you understand not the purpose and intent of these authors. For they bring not this similitude of the sacrament for the real presence, but for the real being: that as the sacrament consisteth in two parts, one earthly and another heavenly, the earthly part being the bread and wine, and the heavenly the body and blood of Christ, and these parts be all truly and really in deed, without colour or simulation, that is to say, very true bread and wine indeed, the very true body and blood of Christ indeed; even likewise in Christ be two natures, his humanity and earthly substance, and his divinity and heavenly substance, and both these be true natures and substances, without colour or dissembling. And thus is this similitude of the sacrament brought in for the truth of the natures, not for the presence of the natures. For Christ was perfect God and perfect man when his soul went down to hell, and his body lay in the grave, because the body and soul were both still united unto his divinity; and yet it was not required that his soul should be present with the body in the sepulture: no more is it now required that his body should be really present in the sacrament; but as the soul was then in hell, so is his body now in heaven. And as it is not required that wheresoever Christ's divinity is, there should be really and corporally his manhood; so it is not required that where the bread and wine be, there should be corporally his flesh and blood.

366.

But as you frame the argument against the heretics, it serveth so little against them, that they may with the same frame and engine overthrow the whole catholic church. For thus you frame the argument: "As the presence of Christ's body in this mystery doth not alter the propriety of the visible natures, no more doth the Godhead in the person of Christ extinguish his humanity." Mark well now, good reader, what followeth hereof. "As the presence of Christ's body in this mystery doth not alter," say you, "the propriety of the visible natures, no more doth the Godhead in the person of Christ extinguish his humanity." "But the presence of Christ's body in this mystery doth so alter the visible natures," as the papists say, "that the substances of bread and wine be extinguished, and there remaineth no substance but of the body of Christ;" ergo, likewise in the mystery of Christ's incarnation the humanity is extinguished by the presence of his Godhead, and so there remaineth no more but the substance of his divinity, as the Eutychians said.

And thus the similitude of Chrysostom, Gelasius, and Theodorete, joined to the saying of the papists, frameth a good argument for the heretics. But those authors framed their argument clean contrary, on this wise: that the bread and wine be not transubstantiate or extinguished, but continue still in their own substances, figures, fashion, and all natural proprieties; and therefore doth the humanity of Christ likewise endure and remain in proper substance with his natural proprieties, without extinction or transubstantiation. For those authors take no bread and wine for the visible proprieties only of bread and wine, but for very true bread and wine, with all their natural qualities and conditions.

And the heretics shall soon find out your cavillation, where, to avoid the matter, you say that "the mystery of the sacrament requireth not the truth of the substance." For why should the authors bring them forth to prove the truth of the substance in Christ, if there were no true substance in them? Thus all your shifts and sophistications be but wind, or colours cast over the truth to blear men's eyes, which colours rubbed off, the truth appeareth clear and plain. And your first mark is not clearly put out, but turned to a mark and spectacle for yourself, wherein you may clearly see your own error, and how foul you have been deceived in this matter, and open your eyes, if God will give you grace to put away your indurate[1] heart, to see the clear truth.

WINCHESTER.

Another certain token is the wondering and great marvelling that the old authors make, how the substance of this sacrament is wrought by God's omnipotency. Baptism is marvelled at, for the wonderful effect that is in man by it, how man is regenerate, not how the water, or the Holy Ghost is there. But the wonder in this sacrament is specially directed to the work of God in the visible creatures, how they be so changed into the body and blood of Christ,

[Cyprian. de Cœna Domini. Orig. ed. Winch.]

367.

which is a work wrought of God before we receive the sacrament. Which work Cyprian saith is ineffable, that is to say, not speakable; which is not so if it be but a figure, for then it may be easily spoken, as this author speaketh it with ease, I think, he speaketh it so often. Of a presence by signification, if it may be so called, every man may speak and tell how; but of the very presence in deed, and therefore the real presence of Christ's body in the sacrament,

---

[¹ Ed. 1580 reads "inducate," which is evidently a misprint.]

no creature can tell how it may be, that Christ ascended into heaven with his human body, and therewith continually reigning there, should make present in the sacrament the same body in deed, which Christ in deed worketh, being nevertheless then at the same hour present in heaven, as St Chrysostom doth with a marvel say. If the marvel were only of God's work in man in the effect of the sacrament, as it is in baptism, it were another matter: but I said before, the wonder is in the work of God, in the substance of the sacrament, before it be received; which declareth the old authors that so wonder to understand the real presence of Christ's very body, and not an only signification, which hath no wonder at all. And therefore seeing St Cyprian wondereth at it, and calleth the work ineffable, St Chrysostom wondereth at it, St Ambrose wondereth at it, Emissene wondereth at it, Cyril wondereth at it: what should we now doubt whether their faith were of a signification only, as this author would have it, which is no wonder at all, or of the real presence, which is indeed a wonderful work? Wherefore where this manifest token and certain mark appeareth in the old fathers, there can no construction[2] of syllables or words dissuade or pervert the truth thus testified.

CANTERBURY.

As touching this your second mark in the ministration of the sacraments, as well of the Lord's holy supper as of baptism, God worketh wonderfully by his omnipotent power in the true receivers, not in the outward visible signs. For it is the person baptized that is so regenerate that he is made a new creature, without any real alteration of the water. And none otherwise it is in the Lord's supper; for the bread and wine remain in their former substance, and neither be fed nor nourished, and yet in the man that worthily receiveth them is such a wonderful nourishment wrought by the mighty power of God, that he hath thereby everlasting life. And this is the "ineffable work of God," whereof Cyprian speaketh.

So that as well in the Lord's supper as in baptism the marvellous working of God, passing the comprehension of all man's wit, is in the spiritual receivers, not in the bread, wine, and water, nor in the carnal and ungodly receivers. For what should it avail the lively members of Christ, that God worketh in his dead and insensible creatures? But in his members he is present, not figuratively, but effectually, and effectually and ineffably worketh in them, nourishing and feeding them so wonderfully, that it passeth all wits and tongues to express.

And nevertheless corporally he is ascended into heaven, and there shall tarry until the world shall have an end. And therefore saith Chrysostom, that Christ is both gone up into heaven, and yet is here received of us, but diversely. For he is gone up to heaven carnally, and is here received of us spiritually. And this wonder is not in the working of God in the substance of the sacrament before it be received, as you feign it to be, nor in them that unworthily receive it carnally, but in them that receive Christ spiritually, being nourished by him spiritually as they be spiritually by him regenerated, that they may be fed of the same thing whereof they be regenerated, and so be throughly *os ex ossibus ejus, et caro ex carne ejus:* "bone of his bones, and flesh of his flesh." Eph. v.

And considering deeply this matter, Cyprian wondereth as much at God's work in baptism, as in the Lord's supper; Chrysostom wondereth as much, Emissene wondereth as much, Cyril wondereth as much; all catholic writers wonder as much, as well how God doth spiritually regenerate us to a new life, as how he doth spiritually feed and nourish us to everlasting life. And although these things be outwardly signified unto us by the sacramental bread, wine, and water, yet they be effectually wrought in us by the omnipotent power of God. Therefore you had need to seek out some other mark or token for your purpose, for this serveth nothing at all: for by his wonderful working Christ is no more declared to be present in the bread and wine, than in the water of baptism.

The wonder in the sacraments.
368.

[[2] There cannot construction, 1551. Orig. ed. Winch. reads with ed. 1580.]

WINCHESTER.

A third token there is by declaration of figures: as for example, St Hierome, when he declareth upon the epistle ad Titum *so advisedly at length, how* panes propositionis *were the figure of the body of Christ in the sacrament; that process declareth the mind of the author to be, that in the sacrament is present the very truth of Christ's body, not in a figure again, to join one shadow to another, but even the very truth to answer the figure; and therefore no particular words in St Hierome can have any understanding contrary to his mind declared in this process.*

CANTERBURY.

To St Hierome I have answered sufficiently before to your confutation of my third book, almost in the end[1], which should be in vain to repeat here again; therefore I will go to your last mark.

WINCHESTER.

Fourthly, another certain mark is, where the old authors write of the adoration of this sacrament, which cannot be but to the things godly, really present. And therefore St Augustine writing in his book De Catechisandis Rudibus, *how the invisible things be honoured in this sacrament, meaning the body and blood of Christ, and in the ninety-eight psalm, speaketh of adoration;* [Theodoretus Dialogo iii. Orig. ed. Winch.] *Theodoretus also speaking specially of adoration of this sacrament: these authors by this mark, that is most certain, take away all such ambiguity as men might by suspicious divination gather sometime of their several words, and declare by this mark of adoration plainly their faith to have been, and also their doctrine understanded as they meant of the real presence of Christ's very body and blood in the sacrament, and Christ himself God and man to be there present, to whose divine nature, and the humanity unite thereunto, adoration may only be directed of us. And so to conclude up this matter, forasmuch as one of these four marks and notes may be found testified and apparent in the ancient writers, with other words and sentences conformable to the same, this should suffice to exclude all arguments of any bye sentences and ambiguous speeches, and to uphold the certainty of the true catholic faith in deed, which this author by a wrong name of the catholic faith impugneth, to the great slander of the truth, and his own reproach.*

CANTERBURY.

Your fourth mark also of adoration proveth no more that Christ is present in the Lord's supper, than he is present in baptism. For no less is Christ to be honoured of him that is baptized, than of him that receiveth the holy communion. And no less ought he that is baptized to believe that in baptism he doth presently in deed and in truth put Christ upon him, and apparel him with Christ, than he that receiveth the holy communion ought to believe that he doth presently feed upon Christ, eating his flesh and drinking his blood: which thing the scripture doth plainly declare, and the old authors in many places do teach. And moreover the form of baptism doth so manifestly declare Christ to be honoured, that it commandeth the devil therein to honour him by these words: *Da honorem Deo: Da gloriam Jesu Christo;* with many other words declaring Christ to be honoured in baptism. And although our Saviour Christ is specially to be adored and honoured, when he by his holy word and sacraments doth assure us of his present grace and benefits; yet not only then, but alway in all our acts and deeds, we should lift up our hearts to heaven, and there glorify Christ with his celestial Father and co-eternal Spirit. So untrue it is that you say, "that adoration cannot be done to Christ, but if he be really present." The papists teach us to have in honour and reverence the forms and accidents of bread and wine, if they

---

[1 Vide supra pp. 192-195.]

AGAINST TRANSUBSTANTIATION.

be vomited up, after the body and blood of Christ be gone away, and say, that they must be had in great reverence, because the body and blood of Christ had been there. "And not only the forms of bread and wine," say they, "must be kept in great reverence, but also the ashes of them (for they command them to be burned into ashes) must be kept with like reverence." And shall you then forbid any man to worship Christ himself, when he doth spiritually and effectually eat his very flesh and drink his very blood, when you will have such honour and reverence done to the ashes, which come not of the body and blood of Christ, but only, as you teach, of the accidents of bread and wine?

Thus have I confuted your confutation of my second book concerning transubstantiation; wherein you be so far from the confutation of my book, as you promised, that you have done nothing else but confounded yourself, studying to seek out such
shifts and cavillations, as before your time were never devised, and yet constrained
to grant such errors and monstrous speeches as to christian ears be intolerable. So that my former book, as well concerning the real presence of
Christ's flesh and blood, as the eating and drinking of the same,
and also transubstantiation, standeth fast and sure, not once
moved or shaken with all your ordinance shot against
it. But it is now much stronger than it was
before, being so mured and bulwarked that
it never need hereafter to fear any as-
sault of the enemies. And now let
us examine your confutation of
the last part of my book,
containing the oblation
and sacrifice of
our Saviour
Christ.

The end of the second Book.

THE CONFUTATION OF THE FIFTH BOOK.

[WINCHESTER.]

AS touching the fifth book, the title whereof is "*Of the oblation and sacrifice of our Saviour Christ*," somewhat is by me spoken before; which although it be sufficient to the matter, yet somewhat more must also be now said, wherewith to encounter the author's imaginations and surmises with the wrong construing of the scriptures and authors, to wrest them besides the truth of the matter and their meaning.

_{*The sacrifice of our Saviour Christ was never taught to be reiterate, but to be often remembered.
370.}

This is agreed and by the scriptures plainly taught, that the oblation and sacrifice of our Saviour Christ was and is a perfect work, once consummate in perfection without necessity of reiteration, as it was never taught to be reiterate, but a mere blasphemy to presuppose it. It is also in the catholic teaching, grounded upon the scripture, agreed, that the same sacrifice once consummate was ordained by Christ's institution in his most holy supper to be in the church often remembered and shewed forth in such sort of shewing, as to the faithful is seen present the most precious body and blood of our Saviour Christ under the forms of bread and wine; which body and blood the faithful church of christian people grant and confess, according to Christ's words, to have been betrayed and shed for the sins of the world, and so in the same supper represented and delivered unto them, to eat and feed of it according to Christ's commandment, as of a most precious and acceptable sacrifice, acknowledging the same precious body and blood to be the sacrifice propitiatory for all the sins of the world, whereunto they only resort, and only accompt that their very perfect[1] oblation and sacrifice of christian people, through which all other sacrifices necessary on our part be accepted[2] and pleasant in the sight of God. And this manner of shewing Christ's death, and keeping the memory of it, is grounded upon the scriptures, written by the evangelists and St Paul, and according thereunto preached, believed, used, and frequented in the church of Christ universally and from the beginning. This author uttering many words at large besides scripture, and against scripture, to deprave the catholic doctrine, doth in a few words, which be in deed good words and true, confound and overthrow all his enterprise; and that issue will I join with him, which shall suffice for the confutation of this book. The few good words of the author, which words I say confound the rest, consist in these two points: one, in that the author alloweth the judgment of *Petrus Lombardus* touching the oblation and sacrifice of the church; another, in that the author confesseth the council of Nice to be holy council[3], as it hath been in deed confessed of all good christian men. Upon these two confessions I will declare the whole enterprise of this fifth book to be overthrown.

_{*The body and blood of Christ is the only sacrifice propitiatory for all the sins of the world. Christ's body is the christian man's sacrifice.}

CANTERBURY.

_{*De sacrificio lege Roffen. et Œcol. Lib. iii. cap. 2. & 3.}

My fifth book hath so fully and so plainly set out this matter of the sacrifice, that for answer to all that you have here brought to the confutation thereof, the reader need to do no more but to look over my book again, and he shall see you fully answered beforehand. Yet will I here and there add some notes, that your ignorance and craft may the better appear.

This far you agree to the truth, that "the sacrifice of Christ was a full and a perfect sacrifice, which needed not to be done no more but once, and yet it is remembered and shewed forth daily." And this is the true doctrine according to God's word. But as concerning the real presence in the accidents of bread and wine, is an untrue doctrine, feigned only by the papists, as I have most plainly declared; and this is one of your errors here uttered.

_{*The sacrifice propitiatory}

Another is, that you call the most "precious body and blood of Christ the sacrifice

---

[1 The very perfect, Orig. ed. Winch.]   [2 Sacrifices necessarily be accepted, ibid.]
[3 To be an holy council, 1551.]

propitiatory for all the sins of the world;" which of itself was not the sacrifice, but the thing whereof the sacrifice was made, and the death of him upon the cross was the true sacrifice propitiatory, that purchased the remission of sin; which sacrifice continued not long, nor was made never but once; whereas his flesh and blood continued ever in substance from his incarnation, as well before the said sacrifice as ever sithens. And that sacrifice propitiatory made by him only upon the cross is of that effect to reconcile us to God's favour, that by it be accepted all our sacrifices of lauds and thanksgiving. *not Christ's very body, but his death in that same body.*

Now before I join with you in your issue, I shall rehearse the words of my book, which when the indifferent reader seeth, he shall be the more able to judge truly between us. My book containeth thus. *371.*

The Fifth Book[4].

The greatest blasphemy and injury that can be against Christ, and yet universally used through the popish kingdom, is this, that the priests make their mass a sacrifice propitiatory, to remit the sins as well of themselves, as of other, both quick and dead, to whom they list to apply the same. Thus under pretence of holiness, the papistical priests have taken upon them to be Christ's successors, and to make such an oblation and sacrifice as never creature made but Christ alone, neither he made the same any more times than once, and that was by his death upon the cross. *Chap. I. The sacrifice of the mass.*

For as St Paul in his epistle to the Hebrews witnesseth, "Although the high priests of the old law offered many times, at the least every year once, yet Christ offered not himself many times; for then he should many times have died. But now he offered himself but once, to take away sin by that offering of himself. And as men must die once, so was Christ offered once, to take away the sins of many." *Chap. II. Heb. ix. The difference between the sacrifice of Christ and of the priests of the old law.*

And furthermore St Paul saith, that "the sacrifices of the old law, although they were continually offered from year to year, yet could they not take away sin, nor make men perfect. For if they could once have quieted men's consciences by taking away sin, they should have ceased, and no more have been offered. But Christ with once offering hath made perfect for ever them that be sanctified, putting their sins clean out of God's remembrance. And where remission of sins is, there is no more offering for sin." *Heb. x.*

And yet further he saith concerning the old testament, that "it was disannulled and taken away, because of the feebleness and unprofitableness thereof, for it brought nothing to perfection. And the priests of that law were many, because they lived not long, and so the priesthood went from one to another: but Christ liveth ever, and hath an everlasting priesthood, that passeth not from him to any man else. Wherefore he is able perfectly to save them that come to God by him, forasmuch as he liveth ever to make intercession for us. For it was meet for us to have such an high priest, that is holy, innocent, without spot, separated from sinners, and exalted up above heaven: who needeth not daily to offer up sacrifice, as Aaron's priests did, first for his own sins, and then for the people: for that he did once, when he offered up himself." Here in his epistle to the Hebrews St Paul hath plainly and fully described unto us the difference between the priesthood and sacrifices of the old testament, and the most high and worthy priesthood of Christ, his most perfect and necessary sacrifice, and the benefit that cometh to us thereby. *Heb. vii.*

[4 The title of this book runs thus in the Orig. ed.: "The fifth book is of the Oblation and Sacrifice of our Saviour Christ."]

For Christ offered not the blood of calves, sheep, and goats, as the priests of the old law have used to do[1], but he offered his own blood upon the cross. And he went not into an holy place made by man's hand, as Aaron did; but he ascended up into heaven, where his eternal Father dwelleth, and before him he maketh continual supplication for the sins of the whole world, presenting his own body, which was torn for us, and his precious blood, which of his most gracious and liberal charity he shed for us upon the cross.

And that sacrifice was of such force, that it was no need to renew it every year, as the bishops did of the old testament, whose sacrifices were many times offered, and yet were of no great effect or profit, because they were sinners themselves that offered them, and offered not their own blood, but the blood of brute beasts; but Christ's sacrifice once offered was sufficient for evermore.

Chap. III. Two kinds of sacrifices.

And that all men may the better understand this sacrifice of Christ, which he made for the great benefit of all men, it is necessary to know the distinction and diversity of sacrifices.

One kind of sacrifice there is, which is called a propitiatory or merciful sacrifice, that is to say, such a sacrifice as pacifieth God's wrath and indignation, and obtaineth mercy and forgiveness for all our sins, and is the ransom for our redemption from everlasting damnation.

The sacrifice of Christ.

And although in the old testament there were certain sacrifices called by that name, yet in very deed there is but one such sacrifice, whereby our sins be pardoned, and God's mercy and favour obtained, which is the death of the Son of God our Lord Jesu Christ; nor never was any other sacrifice propitiatory at any time, nor never shall be.

This is the honour and glory of this our high priest, wherein he admitteth neither partner nor successor. For by his own oblation he satisfied his Father for all men's sins, and reconciled mankind unto his grace and favour. And whosoever deprive him of his honour[2], and go about to take it to themselves, they be very antichrists, and most arrogant blasphemers against God and against his Son Jesus Christ, whom he hath sent.

The sacrifices of the church.

Another kind of sacrifice there is which doth not reconcile us to God, but is made of them that be reconciled by Christ, to testify our duties unto God, and to shew ourselves thankful unto him. And therefore they be called sacrifices of laud, praise, and thanksgiving.

The first kind of sacrifice Christ offered to God for us; the second kind we ourselves offer to God by Christ.

And by the first kind of sacrifice Christ offered also us unto his Father; and by the second we offer ourselves and all that we have unto him and his Father.

And this sacrifice generally is our whole obedience unto God, in keeping his laws and commandments. Of which manner of sacrifice speaketh the prophet David, saying: "A sacrifice to God is a contrite heart." And St Peter saith of all christian people, that they be "an holy priesthood to offer spiritual sacrifices, acceptable to God by Jesu Christ." And St Paul saith, that "alway we offer unto God a sacrifice of laud and praise by Jesus Christ."

Chap. IV. A more plain declaration of the sacrifice of Christ.

But now to speak somewhat more largely of the priesthood and sacrifice of Christ, he was such an high bishop, that he, once offering himself, was sufficient, by once effusion of his blood, to abolish sin unto the world's end. He was so perfect a priest, that by one oblation he purged an infinite heap of

---

[1 Old law used to do, 1551, and Orig. ed.]   [2 Of this honour, 1551, and Orig. ed.]

sins, leaving an easy and a ready remedy for all sinners, that his one sacrifice should suffice for many years unto all men that would not shew themselves unworthy. And he took unto himself not only their sins that many years before were dead, and put their trust in him, but also the sins of those that, until his coming again, should truly believe in his gospel. So that now we may look for none other priest nor sacrifice to take away our sins, but only him and his sacrifice. And as he, dying once, was offered for all, so as much as pertained to him he took all men's sins unto himself: so that now there remaineth no more sacrifices for sin, but extreme judgment at the last day, when he shall appear to us again, not as a man to be punished again, and to be made a sacrifice for our sins, as he was before; but he shall come in his glory without sin, to the great joy and comfort of them which be purified and made clean by his death, and continue in godly and innocent living, and to the great terror and dread of them that be wicked and ungodly. *337. Heb. ix.*

Thus the scripture teacheth, that if Christ had made any oblation for sin more than once, he should have died more than once; forasmuch as there is none oblation and sacrifice for sin but only his death. And now there is no more oblation for sin, seeing that by him our sins be remitted, and our consciences quieted.

And although in the old testament there were certain sacrifices, called sacrifices for sin, yet they were no such sacrifices that could take away our sins in the sight of God, but they were ceremonies ordained to this intent, that they should be, as it were, shadows and figures, to signify beforehand the excellent sacrifice of Christ that was to come, which should be the very true and perfect sacrifice for the sins of the whole world. *Chap. v. The sacrifice of the old law.*

And for this signification they had the name of a sacrifice propitiatory, and were called sacrifices for sins, not because they indeed took away our sins, but because they were images, shadows, and figures, whereby godly men were admonished of the true sacrifice of Christ then to come, which should truly abolish sin and everlasting death.

And that those sacrifices which were made by the priests in the old law could not be able to purchase our pardon, and deserve the remission of our sins, St Paul doth clearly affirm in his said epistle to the Hebrews, where he saith: "It is impossible that our sins should be taken away by the blood of oxen and goats." Wherefore all godly men, although they did use those sacrifices ordained of God, yet they did not take them as things of that value and estimation, that thereby they should be able to obtain remission of their sins before God. *Heb. x.*

But they took them partly for figures and tokens ordained of God, by the which he declared that he would send that Seed, which he promised to be the very true sacrifice for sin, and that he would receive them that trusted in that promise, and remit their sins for the sacrifice after to come.

And partly they used them as certain ceremonies, whereby such persons as had offended against the law of Moses, and were cast out of the congregation, were received again among the people, and declared to be absolved. As for like purposes we use in the church of Christ sacraments by him instituted. And this outward casting out from the people of God, and receiving in again, was according to the law and knowledge of man; but the true reconciliation and forgiveness of sin before God, neither the fathers of the old law had, nor we yet have, but only by the sacrifice of Christ, made in the mount of Calvary. And the sacrifices of the old law were prognostications and figures of the same then to come, as our sacraments be figures and demonstrations of the same now passed.

<small>Chap. VI.
The mass is not a sacrifice propitiatory.
374.</small>

Now by these foresaid things may every man easily perceive, that the offering of the priest in the mass, or the appointing of his ministration at his pleasure, to them that be quick or dead, cannot merit and deserve, neither to himself, nor to them for whom he singeth or saith, the remission of their sins; but that such popish doctrine is contrary to the doctrine of the gospel, and injurious to the sacrifice of Christ. For if only the death of Christ be the oblation, sacrifice, and price wherefore our sins be pardoned, then the act or ministration of the priest cannot have the same office. Wherefore it is an abominable blasphemy to give that office or dignity to a priest, which pertaineth only to Christ; or to affirm that the church hath need of any such sacrifice: as who should say, that Christ's sacrifice were not sufficient for the remission of our sins, or else that his sacrifice should hang upon the sacrifice of a priest.

But all such priests as pretend to be Christ's successors in making a sacrifice of him, they be his most heinous and horrible adversaries. For never no person made a sacrifice of Christ, but he himself only. And therefore St Paul <small>Heb. vii.</small> saith, that "Christ's priesthood cannot pass from him to another." For what needeth any more sacrifices, if Christ's sacrifice be perfect and sufficient? <small>Heb. viii.</small> And as St Paul saith, that if the sacrifices and ministration of Aaron, and other priests of that time, had lacked nothing, but had been perfect and sufficient, then should not the sacrifice of Christ have been required, (for it had been but in vain to add any thing to that which of itself was perfect;) so likewise if Christ's sacrifice, which he made himself, be sufficient, what need we every day to have more and more sacrifices? Wherefore all popish priests that presume to make every day a sacrifice of Christ, either must they needs make Christ's sacrifice vain, unperfect, and unsufficient, or else is their sacrifice in vain which is added to the sacrifice which is already of itself sufficient and perfect.

But it is a wondrous thing to see what shifts and cautels the popish antichrists devise to colour and cloke their wicked errors. And as a chain is so joined together, that one link draweth another after it, so be vices and errors knit together, that every one draweth his fellow with him. And so doth it here in this matter.

<small>Chap. VII.
A confutation of the papists' cavillation.</small>

For the papists, to excuse themselves, do say that they make no new sacrifice, nor none other sacrifice than Christ made (for they be not so blind but they see, that then they should add another sacrifice to Christ's sacrifice, and so make his sacrifice unperfect;) but they say that they make the self-same sacrifice for sin that Christ himself made.

And here they run headlongs into the foulest and most heinous error that ever was imagined. For if they make every day the same oblation and sacrifice for sin that Christ himself made, and the oblation that he made was his death, and the effusion of his most precious blood upon the cross, for our redemption and price of our sins; then followeth it of necessity, that they every day slay Christ, and shed his blood, and so be they worse than the wicked Jews and Pharisees, which slew him and shed his blood but once.

<small>Chap. VIII.
The true sacrifice of all christian people.</small>

Almighty God, the Father of light and truth, banish all such darkness and error out of his church, with the authors and teachers thereof, or else convert their hearts unto him, and give this light of faith to every man, that he may trust to have remission of his sins, and be delivered from eternal death and hell, by the merit only of the death and blood of Christ; and that by his own faith every man may apply the same unto himself, and not take it at the appointment of popish priests, by the merit of sacrifices and oblations!

If we be indeed, as we profess, christian men, we may ascribe this honour and glory to no man, but to Christ alone. Wherefore let us give the whole laud and praise hereof unto him; let us fly only to him for succour; let us hold him fast and hang upon him, and give ourselves wholly to him. And forasmuch as he hath given himself to death for us, to be an oblation and sacrifice to his Father for our sins, let us give ourselves again unto him, making unto him an oblation, not of goats, sheep, kine, and other beasts that have no reason, as was accustomed before Christ's coming, but of a creature that hath reason, that is to say, of ourselves; not killing our own bodies, but mortifying the beastly and unreasonable affections that would gladly rule and reign in us. 375.

So long as the law did reign, God suffered dumb beasts to be offered unto him: but now that we be spiritual, we must offer spiritual oblations in the place of calves, sheep, goats, and doves. We must kill devilish pride, furious anger, insatiable covetousness, filthy lucre, stinking lechery, deadly hatred and malice, foxy wiliness, wolvish ravening and devouring, and all other unreasonable lusts and desires of the flesh. And as many as belong to Christ must crucify and kill these for Christ's sake, as Christ crucified himself for their sakes. Gal. v.

These be the sacrifices of christian men, these hosts and oblations be acceptable to Christ. And as Christ offered himself for us, so is it our duties after this sort to offer ourselves to him again. And so shall we not have the name of christian men in vain; but as we pretend to belong to Christ in word and profession, so shall we indeed be his in life and inward affection; so that within and without we shall be altogether his, clean from all hypocrisy or dissimulation. And if we refuse to offer ourselves after this wise unto him, by crucifying our own wills, and committing us wholly to the will of God, we be most unkind people, superstitious hypocrites, or rather unreasonable beasts, worthy to be excluded utterly from all the benefits of Christ's oblations.

And if we put the oblation of the priest in the stead of the oblation of Christ, refusing to receive the sacrament of his body and blood ourselves, as he ordained, and trusting to have remission of our sins by the sacrifice of the priest in the mass, and thereby also to obtain release of the pains in purgatory, we do not only injury to Christ, but also commit most detestable idolatry. For these be but false doctrines, without shame devised, and feigned by wicked popish priests, idolaters, monks, and friars, which for lucre have altered and corrupted the most holy supper of the Lord, and turned it into manifest idolatry. Wherefore all godly men ought with all their heart to refuse and abhor all such blasphemy against the Son of God. Chap. ix. The popish mass is detestable idolatry, utterly to be banished from all christian congregations.

And forasmuch as in such masses is manifest wickedness and idolatry, wherein the priest alone maketh oblation satisfactory, and applieth the same for the quick and the dead at his will and pleasure, all such popish masses are to be clearly taken away out of christian churches, and the true use of the Lord's supper is to be restored again; wherein godly people assembled together may receive the sacrament every man for himself, to declare that he remembereth what benefit he hath received by the death of Christ, and to testify that he is a member of Christ's body, fed with his flesh, and drinking his blood spiritually.

<small>Chap. x.
Every man ought to receive the sacrament himself, and not one for another.
376.</small>

Christ did not ordain his sacraments to this use, that one should receive them for another, or the priest for all the lay people; but he ordained them for this intent, that every man should receive them for himself, to ratify, confirm, and stablish his own faith and everlasting salvation. Therefore as one man may not be baptized for another, and if he be, it availeth nothing, so ought not one to receive the holy communion for another. For if a man be dry or hungry, he is never a whit eased if another man drink or eat for him; or if a man be all defiled, it helpeth him nothing another man to be washed for him: so availeth it nothing to a man, if another man be baptized for him, or be refreshed for him with the meat and drink at the Lord's table. And

<small>Acts ii.</small>

therefore said St Peter: "Let every man be baptized in the name of Jesu Christ." And our Saviour Christ said to the multitude: "Take, and eat."

<small>Matt. xxvi.</small>

And further he said: "Drink you all of this." Whosoever therefore will be spiritually regenerated in Christ, he must be baptized himself; and he that will live himself by Christ, must by himself eat Christ's flesh and drink his blood.

And briefly to conclude: he that thinketh to come to the kingdom of Christ himself, must also come to his sacraments himself, and keep his commandments himself, and do all things that pertain to a christian man and to his vocation himself; lest, if he refer these things to another man to do them for him, the other may with as good right claim the kingdom of heaven for him.

<small>Chap. xi.
The difference between the priest and the layman.</small>

Therefore Christ made no such difference between the priest and the layman, that the priest should make oblation and sacrifice of Christ for the layman, and eat the Lord's supper from him all alone, and distribute and apply it as him liketh. Christ made no such difference, but the difference that is between the priest and the layman in this matter is only in the ministration; that the priest, as a common minister of the church, doth minister and distribute the Lord's supper unto other, and other receive it at his hands. But the very supper itself was by Christ instituted and given to the whole church, not to be offered and eaten of the priest for other men, but by him to be delivered to all that would duly ask it.

As in a prince's house the officers and ministers prepare the table, and yet other, as well as they, eat the meat and drink the drink; so do the priests and ministers prepare the Lord's supper, read the gospel, and rehearse Christ's words, but all the people say thereto, Amen. All remember Christ's death, all give thanks to God, all repent and offer themselves an oblation to Christ, all take him for their Lord and Saviour, and spiritually feed upon him, and in token thereof they eat the bread and drink the wine in his mystical supper.

<small>[The dignity of priests, Orig. ed.]</small>

And this nothing diminisheth the estimation and dignity of priesthood and other ministers of the church, but advanceth and highly commendeth their ministration. For if they are much to be loved, honoured and esteemed, that be the kings, chancellors, judges, officers, and ministers in temporal matters; how much then are they to be esteemed, that be ministers of Christ's words and sacraments, and have to them committed the keys of heaven, to let in and shut out by the ministration of his word and gospel?

<small>Chap. xii.
The answer to the papists.</small>

Now forasmuch as I trust that I have plainly enough set forth the propitiatory sacrifice of our Saviour Jesu Christ, to the capacity and comfort of all men that have any understanding of Christ; and have declared also the heinous abomination and idolatry of the popish mass, wherein the priests have taken upon them the office of Christ, to make a propitiatory sacrifice for the sins of the people; and I have also[1] told what manner of sacrifice christian people ought to make; it is now necessary to make answer to the subtle persuasions and sophistical cavillations of the papists, whereby they have deceived many a simple man, both learned and unlearned.

377.

The place of St Paul unto the Hebrews, which they do cite for their purpose, maketh quite and clean against them. For where St Paul saith, that "every high priest is ordained to offer gifts and sacrifices for sins," he spake not that of the priests of the new testament, but of the old, which, as he saith, offered calves and goats. And yet they were not such priests that by their offerings and sacrifices they could take away the people's sins; but they were shadows and figures of Christ our everlasting priest, which only by one oblation of himself taketh away the sins of the world. Wherefore the popish priests, that apply this text unto themselves, do directly contrary to the meaning of St Paul, to the great injury and prejudice of Christ, by whom only St Paul saith that the sacrifice and oblation for the sin of the whole world was accomplished and fulfilled.

Heb. v.

And as little serveth for the papists' purpose the text of the prophet Malachi, that "every where should be offered unto God a pure sacrifice and oblation." For the prophet in that place spake no word of the mass, nor of any oblation propitiatory to be made by the priests; but he spake of the oblation of all faithful people, in what place so ever they be, which offer unto God, with pure hearts and minds, sacrifices of laud and praise: prophesying of the vocation of the gentiles, that God would extend his mercy unto them, and not be the God only of the Jews, but of all nations, from east to west, that with pure faith call upon him and glorify his name.

Mal. i.

But the adversaries of Christ gather together a great heap of authors, which, as they say, call the mass or holy communion a sacrifice. But all those authors be answered unto in this one sentence, that they call it not a sacrifice for sin, because that it taketh away our sin, which is taken away only by the death of Christ, but because the holy communion was ordained of Christ to put us in remembrance of the sacrifice made by him upon the cross: for that cause it beareth the name of that sacrifice, as St Augustine declareth plainly in his epistle *ad Bonifacium*, before rehearsed in this book, pp. 123, 124[2]. And in his book *De fide ad Petrum Diaconum*[3], and in his book *De Civitate Dei*, he saith: "That which men call a sacrifice is a sign or representation of the true sacrifice[4]."

Chap. XIII. An answer to the authors.

Augustinus ad Bonifa. De Civita. Lib. x. cap. 5. [Vid. Embd. ed. in fine tomi hujus.]

And the Master of the sentence, of whom all the school-authors take their occasion to write, judged truly in this point, saying: "That which is offered and consecrated of the priest is called a sacrifice and oblation, because it is a memory and representation of the true sacrifice and holy oblation made in the altar of the cross[5]."

Lombardus Lib. iv. Dist. 12. [Vid. Embd. ed.]

And St John Chrysostom, after he had said that Christ is our bishop, which offered that sacrifice that made us clean, and that we offer the same now, lest any man might be deceived by his manner of speaking, he openeth his meaning

Chrysostom. ad Heb. Hom. 17.

[1 And have also, 1551, and Orig. ed.]
[2 Fol. 64. ed. 1551, and Orig. ed. p. 141. ed. 1580, which is a misprint: it should be p. 125.]
[3 Vid. p. 77.]
[4 Sacrificium ergo visibile invisibilis sacrificii sacramentum, id est, sacrum signum est. August. De Civitate Dei. Lib. X. cap. 5. Pars vii. Ed.

Basil. ap. Amerbach. 1506.]
[5 Illud quod offertur et consecratur a sacerdote, vocari sacrificium et oblationem, quia memoria est et repræsentatio veri sacrificii et sanctæ immolationis factæ in ara crucis. Petrus Lombardus, Lib. IV. Dist. 12. p. 745. Colon. 1609.]

more plainly, saying: "That which we do is done for a remembrance of that which was done by Christ; for Christ saith, 'Do this in remembrance of me[1].'" Also Chrysostom, declaring at length that the priests of the old law offered ever new sacrifices, and changed them from time to time, and that christian people do not so, but offer ever one sacrifice of Christ; yet by and by, lest some might be offended with this speech, he maketh as it were a correction of his words, saying, "But rather we make a remembrance of Christ's sacrifice." As though he should say: although in a certain kind of speech we may say that every day we make a sacrifice of Christ, yet in very deed, to speak properly, we make no sacrifice of him, but only a commemoration and remembrance of that sacrifice which he alone made, and never none but he. Nor Christ never gave this honour to any creature, that he should make a sacrifice of him, nor did not ordain the sacrament of his holy supper, to the intent that either the priest or[2] the people should sacrifice Christ again, or that the priests should make a sacrifice of him for the people: but his holy supper was ordained for this purpose, that every man, eating and drinking thereof, should remember that Christ died for him, and so should exercise his faith, and comfort himself by the remembrance of Christ's benefits, and so give unto Christ most hearty thanks, and give himself also clearly unto him.

Wherefore the ordinance of Christ ought to be followed: the priest to minister the sacrament to the people, and they to use it to their consolation. And in this eating, drinking, and using of the Lord's supper, we make not of Christ a new sacrifice propitiatory for remission of sin.

Chap. xiv. The lay persons make a sacrifice as well as the priest.

But the humble confession of all penitent hearts, their acknowledging of Christ's benefits, their thanksgiving for the same, their faith and consolation in Christ, their humble submission and obedience to God's will and commandments, is a sacrifice of laud and praise, accepted and allowed of God no less than the sacrifice of the priest. For Almighty God, without respect of person, accepteth the oblation and sacrifice of priest and lay person, of king and subject, of master and servant, of man and woman, of young and old, yea of English, French, Scot, Greek, Latin, Jew, and Gentile; of every man according to his faithful and obedient heart unto him, and that through the sacrifice propitiatory of Jesu Christ.

Chap. xv. The papistical mass is neither a sacrifice propitiatory, nor of thanksgiving. Luke xvi.

And as for the saying or singing of the mass by the priest, as it was in time passed used, it is neither a sacrifice propitiatory, nor yet a sacrifice of laud and praise, nor in any wise allowed before God, but abominable and detestable; and thereof may well be verified the saying of Christ: "That thing which seemeth an high thing before men is an abomination before God."

They therefore which gather of the doctors, that the mass is a sacrifice for remission of sin, and that it is applied by the priest to them for whom he saith or singeth, they which so gather of the doctors do to them most grievous injury and wrong, most falsely belying them.

Chap. xvi. There was no papistical masses in the primitive church.

For these monstrous things were never seen nor known of the old and primitive church, nor there was not then in one church many masses every day; but upon certain days there was a common table of the Lord's supper, where a number of people did together receive the body and blood of the Lord: but there were then no daily private masses, where every priest received alone, like

---

[[1] Τί οὖν; ἡμεῖς καθ' ἑκάστην ἡμέραν οὐ προσφέρομεν; προσφέρομεν μὲν, ἀλλ' ἀνάμνησιν ποιούμενοι τοῦ θανάτου αὐτοῦ . . . . ἐκείνην προσφέρομεν καὶ νῦν, τὴν τότε τε προσενεχθεῖσαν, τὴν ἀνάλωτον. τοῦτο εἰς ἀνάμνησιν γίνεται τοῦ τότε γενομένου. τοῦτο γὰρ ποιεῖτε, φησιν, εἰς τὴν ἐμὴν ἀνάμνησιν. οὐκ ἄλλην θυσίαν, καθάπερ ὁ ἀρχιερεὺς τότε, ἀλλὰ τὴν αὐτὴν ἀεὶ ποιοῦμεν· μᾶλλον δὲ ἀνάμνησιν ἐργαζόμεθα θυσίας.—Chrysost. in Epist. ad Heb. Hom. xvii. Tom. XII. pp. 168, 9. Ed. Bened.]

[[2] The Orig. ed. omits the words 'the priest or.']

OF THE OBLATION AND SACRIFICE OF CHRIST.

as until this day there is none in the Greek churches, but one common mass in a day. Nor the holy fathers of the old church would not have suffered such ungodly and wicked abuses of the Lord's supper.

But these private masses sprang up of late years, partly through the ignorance and superstition of unlearned monks and friars, which knew not what a sacrifice was, but made of the mass a sacrifice propitiatory, to remit both sin and the pain due for the same; but chiefly they sprang of lucre and gain, when priests found the means to sell masses to the people, which caused masses so much to increase, that every day was said an infinite number, and that no priest would receive the communion at another priest's hand, but every one would receive it alone; neither regarding the godly decree of the most famous and holy council of Nice, which appointed[3] in what order priests should be placed above deacons at the communion[4], nor yet the Canons of the apostles, which command, that when any communion is ministered, all the priests together should receive the same, or else be excommunicate[5]. So much the old fathers misliked that any priest should receive the sacrament alone.

379. Concilium Nicenum, cap. 14. Canones Apostolorum, cap. 8.

Therefore when the old fathers called the mass or supper of the Lord a sacrifice, they meant that it was a sacrifice of lauds and thanksgiving, (and so as well the people as the priest do sacrifice,) or else that it was a remembrance of the very true sacrifice propitiatory of Christ; but they meant in no wise that it is a very true sacrifice for sin, and applicable by the priest to the quick and dead.

For the priest may well minister Christ's words and sacraments to all men, both good and bad; but he can apply the benefit of Christ's passion to no man, being of age and discretion, but only to such as by their own faith do apply the same unto themselves: so that every man of age and discretion taketh to himself the benefits of Christ's passion, or refuseth them himself, by his own faith, quick or dead; that is to say, by his true and lively faith, that worketh by charity, he receiveth them, or else by his ungodliness or feigned faith rejecteth them.

And this doctrine of the scripture clearly condemneth the wicked intentions of the papists in these latter days, which have devised a purgatory to torment souls after this life, and oblations of masses said by the priests to deliver them from the said torments; and a great number of other commodities do they promise to the simple ignorant people by their masses.

Now the nature of man being ever prone to idolatry from the beginning of the world, and the papists being ready by all means and policy to defend and extol the mass for their estimation and profit, and the people being superstitiously enamoured and doted upon the mass, because they take it for a present remedy against all manner of evils, and part of the princes being blinded by papistical doctrine, part loving quietness, and loth to offend their clergy and subjects, and all being captive and subject to the antichrist of Rome, the estate of the world remaining in that case[6], it is no wonder that abuses grew and increased in the church, that superstition with idolatry were taken for godliness and true religion, and that many things were brought in without the authority of Christ: as purgatory, the oblation and sacrificing of Christ by the priest alone,

Chap. XVII. The causes and means how papistical masses entered into the church.

The abuses of the papistical masses.

[3 Appointeth, 1551, and Orig. ed.]

[4 Λαμβανέτωσαν δὲ [οἱ διάκονοι] κατὰ τὴν τάξιν τὴν εὐχαριστίαν μετὰ τοὺς πρεσβυτέρους, ἢ τοῦ ἐπισκόπου διδόντος αὐτοῖς ἢ τοῦ πρεσβυτέρου· ἀλλὰ μηδὲ καθῆσθαι ἐν μέσῳ τῶν πρεσβυτέρων ἐξέστω τοῖς διακόνοις, παρὰ κανόνα γὰρ καὶ παρὰ τάξιν ἐστὶ τὸ γινόμενον. Conc. Nic. Can. xviii. Labb. Tom. II. p. 676.]

[5 Εἴ τις ἐπίσκοπος ἢ πρεσβύτερος ἢ διάκονος ἢ ἐκ τοῦ καταλόγου τοῦ ἱερατικοῦ προσφορᾶς γενομένης μὴ μεταλάβοι, τὴν αἰτίαν εἰπάτω· καὶ ἐὰν εὔλογος ᾖ, συγγνώμης τυγχανέτω· εἰ δὲ μὴ λέγει, ἀφοριζέσθω. Ibid. Tom. I. p. 30.]

[6 In this case, 1551, and Orig. ed.]

the application and appointing of the same to such persons as the priest would sing or say mass for, and to such abuses as they could devise, to deliver some from purgatory, and some from hell, (if they were not there finally by God determined to abide, as they termed the matter,) to make rain or fair weather, to put away the plague and other sicknesses both from man and beast, to hallow and preserve them that went to Jerusalem, to Rome, to St James in Compostella, and other places in pilgrimage, for a preservative against tempest and thunder, against perils and dangers of the sea, for a remedy against murrain of cattle, against pensiveness of the heart, against all manner affliction and tribulations. And finally, they extol their masses far above Christ's passion, promising many things thereby, which were never promised us by Christ's passion: as that if a man hear mass, he shall lack no bodily sustenance that day, nor nothing necessary for him, nor shall be letted in his journey; he shall not lose his sight that day, nor die no sudden death; he shall not wax old in that time that he heareth mass, nor no wicked spirits shall have power of him, be he never so wicked a man, so long as he looketh upon the sacrament. All these foolish and devilish superstitions the papists, of their own idle brain, have devised of late years, which devices were never known in the old church.

380.

Chap. XVIII.
Which church is to be followed.

And yet they cry out against them that profess the gospel, and say that they dissent from the church, and would have them to follow the example of their church. And so would they gladly do, if the papists would follow the first church of the apostles, which was most pure and incorrupt: but the papists have clearly varied from the usage and examples of that church, and have invented new devices of their own brains, and will in no wise consent to follow the primitive church; and yet they would have other to follow their church, utterly varying and dissenting from the first most godly church. But, thanks be to the eternal God! the manner of the holy communion, which is now set forth within this realm, is agreeable with the institution of Christ, with St Paul, and the old primitive and apostolic church, with the right faith of the sacrifice of Christ upon the cross for our redemption, and with the true doctrine of our salvation, justification, and remission of all our sins by that only sacrifice.

A short instruction to the holy communion.

Now resteth nothing, but that all faithful subjects will gladly receive and embrace the same, being sorry for their former ignorance, and every man repenting himself of his offences against God, and amending the same, may yield himself wholly to God, to serve and obey him all the days of his life, and often to come to the holy supper, which our Lord and Saviour Christ hath prepared. And as he there corporally eateth the very bread, and drinketh the very wine; so spiritually he may feed of the very flesh and blood of Jesu Christ his Saviour and Redeemer, remembering his death, thanking him for his benefits, and looking for none other sacrifice at no priest's hands for remission of his sins; but only trusting to his sacrifice, which being both the high priest, and also the Lamb of God, prepared from the beginning to take away the sins of the world, offered up himself once for ever in a sacrifice of sweet smell unto his Father, and by the same paid the ransom for the sins of the whole world: who is before us entered into heaven, and sitteth at the right hand of his Father, as a patron, mediator, and intercessor for us; and there hath prepared places for all them that be lively members of his body, to reign with him for ever, in the glory of his Father; to whom with him, and the Holy Ghost, be glory, honour, and praise for ever and ever. Amen.

Thus having rehearsed the whole words of my last book, I shall return to your issue, and make a joinder or demur with you therein. And if you cannot prove your propitiatory sacrifice of the priests by Petrus Lombardus, and Nicene council, then must you confess by your own issue, that the verdict must justly pass against you, and that you have a fall in your own suit. As for the sacrifice of lauds and thanksgiving, I have set it forth plainly in my book; but the sacrifice propitiatory, devised to be made by the priest in the mass only, is a great abomination before God, how glorious soever it appear before men. And it is set up only by antichrist, and therefore worthy to be abhorred of all that truly profess Christ.

Mine issue.

381.

And first, as concerning Nicene council, because you begin with that first, I will rehearse your words.

Nicene council.

WINCHESTER.

First, to begin with the council of Nice, the same hath opened the mystery of the sacrament of the body and blood of Christ in this wise, "That christian men believe the Lamb that taketh away the sins of the world, to be situate upon God's board, and to be sacrificed of the priests, not after the manner of other sacrifices." This is the doctrine of the council of Nice, and must then be called an holy doctrine, and thereby a true doctrine, consonant to the scriptures, the foundation of all truth. If the author will deny this to have been the teaching of the council of Nice, I shall allege therefore the allegation of the same by Œcolampadius, who, being an adversary to the truth, was yet by God's providence ordered to bear testimony to the truth in this point, and by his mean is published to the world, in Greek, as followeth, which nevertheless may otherwise appear to be true: Ἐπὶ τῆς θείας τραπέζης πάλιν κἀνταῦθα μὴ τῷ προκειμένῳ ἄρτῳ καὶ τῷ ποτηρίῳ ταπεινῶς προσέχωμεν, ἀλλ' ὑψώσαντες τὴν διάνοιαν, πίστει νοήσωμεν κεῖσθαι ἐπὶ τῆς ἱερᾶς ἐκείνης τραπέζης τὸν ἀμνὸν τοῦ Θεοῦ τὸν αἴροντα τὴν ἁμαρτίαν τοῦ κόσμου, ἀθύτως ὑπὸ τῶν ἱερέων θυόμενον, καὶ τὸ τίμιον αὐτοῦ σῶμα καὶ αἷμα ἀληθῶς λαμβάνοντας ἡμᾶς, πιστεύειν ταῦτα εἶναι τὰ τῆς ἡμετέρας ἀναστάσεως σύμβολα. διὰ τοῦτο γὰρ οὔτε πολὺ λαμβάνομεν ἀλλ' ὀλίγον, ἵνα γνῶμεν ὅτι οὐκ εἰς πλησμονήν, ἀλλ' εἰς ἁγιασμόν. Iterum etiam hic in divina mensa, ne humiliter intenti simus ad propositum panem et poculum, sed mente exaltata fide intelligamus, situm esse in sacra illa mensa illum Dei agnum, qui tollit peccata mundi, sacrificatum a sacerdotibus, non victimarum more: et nos pretiosum illius corpus et sanguinem vere sumentes, credere hæc esse resurrectionis nostræ symbola[1]. Ideo enim non multum accipimus, sed parum, ut cognoscanus, quoniam non in satietatem, sed sanctificationem. *These words may be Englished thus: "Again in this godly table, we should not in base and low consideration direct our understanding to the bread and cup set forth; but having our mind exalted, we should understand by faith to be situate in that table the Lamb of God which taketh away the sins of the world, sacrificed of the priests, not after the manner of other sacrifices, and we receiving truly the precious body and blood of the same Lamb, to believe these to be the tokens of our resurrection. And for that we receive not much, but a little, because we should know that not for saturity and filling, but for sanctification[2]."*

This holy council of Nice hath been believed universally in declaration of the mystery of the Trinity, and the sacraments also. And to them that confess that council to be holy, as the author here doth, and to such as profess to believe the determination of that council in the opening of the mystery of the Trinity, with other words than scripture useth, (although they express such sense as in the scriptures[3] is contained,) why should not all such likewise believe the same council in explication of the sacraments, which to do the author hath bound himself, granting that council holy? And then we must believe the very presence of Christ's body and blood on God's board, and that priests do there sacrifice, and be therefore called and named sacrificers[4]. So as those names and terms be to be honoured and religiously spoken of, being in an holy council uttered and confessed, because it was so seen to them and the Holy Ghost, without whose present assistance and suggestion believed to be there the council could not or ought not to be called holy. Now, if we confer with that council of

Priests, sacrificers.

[1 Resurrectionis symbola, Orig. ed. Winch.]

[2 This quotation is made from "The History of the Council of Nice, by Gelasius Cyzicenus," a work of no value or repute. The more authentic histories of the Council do not give the passage.

See Labbé Concilia, Vol. II. pp. 103. 233. Cave's Hist. Lit.]

[3 Scripture, 1551.]

[4 And be therefore called sacrifices, Orig. ed. Winch.]

Nice the testimony of the church beginning at St Dionyse, who was in the time of the apostles, and after him coming to Irenee, who was near the apostles, and then Tertullian, and so St Cyprian, St Chrysostom, St Cyril, St Hierome, St Augustine, and from that age to the time of Petrus Lombardus[1], *all spake of the sacrament to the same effect, and termed it for the word sacrifice and oblation, to be frequented in the church, of the body and blood of Christ, as may be in particularity shewed, whereof I make also an issue with the author.*

* An issue.

CANTERBURY.

382. For answer to Nicene council, it speaketh of a sacrifice of lauds and thanksgiving, which is made by the priest in the name of the whole church, and is the sacrifice as well of the people as of the priest: this sacrifice, I say, the council of Nice speaketh of; but it speaketh not one word of the sacrifice propitiatory, which never none made but only Christ, nor he never made it any more than once, which was by his death. And wheresoever Christ shall be hereafter, in heaven or in earth, he shall never be sacrificed again; but the church continually, in remembrance of that sacrifice, maketh a sacrifice of laud and praise, giving evermore thanks unto him for that propitiatory sacrifice. And in the third chapter of my book here recited, the difference of these two sacrifices is plainly set out.

John i.

And although Nicene council call Christ "the Lamb that taketh away the sins of the world," yet doth it not mean that by the sacrifice of the priest in the mass, but by the sacrifice of himself upon the cross. But here, according to your accustomed manner, you alter some words of the council, and add also some of your own. For the council said not that the Lamb of God is "sacrificed of the priests, not after the manner of other sacrifices;" but that he is sacrificed not after the manner of a sacrifice. And in saying, that Christ is sacrificed of the priest, not like a sacrifice, or after the manner of a sacrifice, the council in these words signified a difference between the 'sacrifice of the priest, and the sacrifice of Christ, which upon the cross offered himself to be sacrificed after the manner of a very sacrifice, that is to say, unto death, for the sins of the world. Christ made the bloody sacrifice, which took away sin: the priest with the church make a commemoration thereof with lauds and thanksgiving, offering also themselves obedient to God unto death. And yet this our sacrifice taketh not away our sins, nor is not accepted but by his sacrifice. The bleeding of him took away our sins, not the eating of him.

* De Conse. Dist. II. cap. 2. "Semel:" et est Prosperi. "Semel immolatus est Christus in semetipso, et tamen quotidie immolatur in sacramento." Glossa ibidem "Id est ejus immolatio repraesentatur, et fit memoria passionis[2]."

And although that council say, that Christ is situate in that table, yet it saith not that he is really and corporally in the bread and wine. For then that council would not have forbid us to direct our minds to the bread and cup, if they had believed that Christ had been really there. But forasmuch as the council commandeth that we shall not direct our minds downward to the bread and cup, but lift them up to Christ by faith, they give us to understand by those words, that Christ is really and corporally ascended up into heaven, unto which place we must lift up our minds, and reach him there by our faith, and not look down to find him in the bread. And yet he is in the bread sacramentally, as the same council saith, that the Holy Ghost is in the water of baptism. And as Christ is in his supper present to feed us, so is he in baptism to clothe and apparel us with his own self, as the same council declareth, whose words be these: "He that is baptized, goeth down into the water, being subject to sin, and held in the bands of corruption; but he riseth up free from bondage and sin, being made by the grace of God his son and heir, and co-inheritor with Christ, and apparelled with Christ himself, as it is written:

Gal. iii.

'As many of you as be baptized unto Christ, you have put Christ upon you[3].'" These

---

[1] That age to Petrus Lombardus, Orig. ed. Winch.]

[2] Decret. Gratian. in Corpus Juris Canonici.—De consecrat. Dist. ii. cap. 52. "Semel." Tom I. col. 1938. Ed. Lugd. 1618.]

[3] Κατέρχεται μὲν οὖν ὁ βαπτιζόμενος ὑπεύθυνος ἁμαρτημάτων, καὶ τῇ τῆς φθορᾶς δουλείᾳ ἐνεχόμενος· ἀνέρχεται δὲ ἐλευθερωθεὶς τῆς τε τοιαύτης δουλείας καὶ τῆς ἁμαρτίας, υἱὸς τοῦ Θεοῦ καὶ κληρονόμος χάριτι αὐτοῦ γεγονώς, συγκληρονόμος δὲ Χριστοῦ, καθὼς γέγραπται· "Ὅσοι εἰς Χριστὸν ἐβαπτίσθητε, Χριστὸν ἐνεδύσασθε. Labb. Concil. Tom. II. col. 888. Florent. 1759.]

OF THE OBLATION AND SACRIFICE OF CHRIST.

words of the council I rehearse only in English, because I will not let nor encumber the reader with the Greek or Latin, as you do, which is nothing else but to rehearse one thing thrice, without need or profit. If I had list, I could have rehearsed all the Greek authors in Greek, and the Latin writers in Latin; but unto Englishmen, unto whom only I write, it were a vain labour or glory, without fruit or profit, or any other cause, except I intended to make my book long for gain of the printer, rather than for profit to the reader.

But to return to the matter: Christ is present in his holy supper, as that holy council saith, even as he is present in baptism, but not really, carnally, corporally, and naturally, as you without ground imagine.

And if he were so present, yet is he not there sacrificed again for sin. For then were his first sacrifice upon the cross in vain, if it sufficed not therefore.

And as for Dionyse, Irenee, Tertullian, with all your other authors, I have answered them in the thirteenth chapter of this my last book. And what need you make an issue in this thing which is not in controversy, and which I affirm in my whole last book? The matter in question is of the "sacrifice propitiatory;" and you make your issue of the sacrifice generally.

Now let us see how you entreat Petrus Lombardus.

WINCHESTER.

For the other point, in that the author approveth the judgment of Petrus Lombardus in the matter, what should I more do, but write in the words of Petrus Lombardus as he hath them? which be these, in the fourth book, the twelfth chapter, alleged by the author: Post hæc quæritur, si quod gerit sacerdos proprie dicatur sacrificium vel immolatio, et si Christus quotidie immoletur[4], vel semel tantum immolatus sit? Ad hoc breviter dici potest, illud quod offertur et consecratur a sacerdote, vocari sacrificium et oblationem, quia memoria est et repræsentatio veri sacrificii et sanctæ immolationis factæ in ara crucis; et semel Christus mortuus in cruce est, ibique immolatus est in semetipso, quotidie autem immolatur in sacramento, quia in sacramento recordatio fit illius, quod factum est semel: unde Augustinus: "Certum habemus, quia Christus resurgens ex mortuis jam non moritur; et tamen, ne obliviscamur quod semel factum est, in memoria nostra omni anno fit, scilicet quando pascha celebratur. Nunquid totiens Christus occiditur? sed tantum anniversaria recordatio repræsentat quod olim factum est, et sic nos facit moveri tanquam videamus Dominum in cruce[5]." Item: "Semel immolatus est Christus in semetipso, et tamen quotidie immolatur in sacramento[6]." Quod sic intelligendum est: quia in manifestatione corporis et distinctione membrorum semel tantum in cruce pependit, offerens se Deo Patri hostiam redemptionis efficacem, eorum scilicet quos prædestinavit. Item Ambrosius: "In Christo semel oblata est hostia ad salutem potens; quid ergo nos? Nonne per singulos dies offerimus? Et si quotidie offeramus, ad recordationem ejus mortis fit; et una est hostia, non multæ: quomodo una et non multæ? quia semel immolatus est Christus. Hoc autem sacrificium exemplum est illius: id ipsum, et semper id ipsum offertur: proinde hoc idem est sacrificium; alioquin dicetur, quoniam in multis locis offertur, multi sunt Christi: non, sed unus ubique est Christus, et hic plenus existens, et illic plenus, sicut quod ubique offertur unum est corpus, ita et unum sacrificium. Christus hostiam obtulit, ipsam offerimus et nunc; sed quod nos agimus recordatio est sacrificii. Nec causa suæ infirmitatis repetitur, quia perficit hominem, sed nostræ, quia quotidie peccamus[7]." Ex his colligitur esse sacrificium et dici quod agitur in altari, et Christum semel oblatum et quotidie offerri, sed aliter tunc, aliter nunc: et etiam quæ sit virtus hujus sacramenti ostenditur: remissio scilicet pecca-

*Immolatur, ut ante.

[4 Quotidie vel immoletur semel, in ed. 1580.]

[5 Et scimus et certum habemus, et fide immobili retinemus, quia "Christus resurgens a mortuis jam non moritur, et mors ei ultra non dominabitur." Verba ista Apostoli sunt: tamen ne obliviscamur quod factum est semel, in memoria nostra semel omni anno fit. Quotiens pascha celebratur, nunquid totiens Christus moritur? Sed tamen anniversaria recordatio quasi repræsentat quod olim factum est, et sic nos facit moneri [al. *moveri*] tanquam videa-

mus in cruce pendentem Dominum.—August. in Psalm. xxi. Præfat. in secundam expositionem. Tom. VIII. p. 43. Ed. Paris. 1635.]

[6 August. Epist. XXIII. Ad Bonifacium. Nonne semel immolatus est Christus in seipso, et tamen in sacramento.... omni die populis immolatur? Tom. II. p. 36.]

[7 In Epist. ad Hebr. x. Tom. III. p. 651. Paris. 1631. But this commentary is entirely omitted by the Benedictine editors, as being certainly spurious.]

torum venialium et perfectio virtutis. *The English whereof is this:* "After this it is asked whether that the priest doth, may be said properly a sacrifice or immolation; and whether Christ be daily immolate or only once? Whereunto it may be shortly answered, That which is offered and consecrate of the priest, is called a sacrifice and oblation, because it is a memory and representation of the true sacrifice and holy immolation done in the altar of the cross. And Christ was once dead on the cross, and there was offered in himself; but he is daily immolate in the sacrament, because in the sacrament there is made a memory of that is once done. Whereupon St Augustine: 'We are assured that Christ rising from death dieth not now,' &c. Yet, lest we should forget that is once done, in our memory every year is done, viz. as often as the pascha is celebrate, is Christ as often killed? only a yearly remembrance representeth that was once done, and so causeth us[1] to be moved as though we saw our Lord on the cross. Also Christ was once offered in himself, and is offered[2] daily in the sacrament. Which is thus to be understood, that in open shewing of his body and distinction of his members he did hang only once upon the cross, offering himself to God the Father an host of redemption effectual for them whom he hath predestinate. Also St Ambrose: 'In Christ the host was once offered being of power to health: what do we then? do we not offer every day? and if we offer every day, it is done to the remembrance of the death of him, and the host is one, not many. How one and not many? because Christ is once offered: this sacrifice is the example of that, the same, and always the same is offered; therefore this is the same sacrifice. Or else it may be said, because offering is[3] in many places, there be many Christs; which is not so, but one Christ is each where, and here full, and there full, so as that which is offered every where is one body, and so also one sacrifice. Christ hath offered the host, we do offer the same also now: but that we do is a remembrance of the sacrifice. Nor there is no cause found of the own invalidity, because it perfecteth the man, but of us, because we daily sin.' Hereof it is gathered that to be a sacrifice and to be so called, that is done in the altar; and Christ to be once offered and daily offered, but otherwise then, and otherwise now: and also it is shewed what is the virtue of this sacrament, that is to say, remission of venial sin and perfection of virtue."

384.

[In Epistola xxiii. Rom. vi. Orig. ed. Winch.]

[The same words hath Chrysostom. Homil. xvii. ad Heb. Orig. ed. Winch.]

[Homil. de Corpore et Sanguine Domini. Orig. ed. Winch.]

Thus writeth Petrus Lombardus, whose judgment because this author alloweth, he must grant that the visible church hath priests in ministery, that offer daily Christ's most precious body and blood in mystery: and then must it be granted, that Christ so offered himself in his supper; for otherwise than he did cannot now be done. And by the judgment of Petrus Lombardus, the same most precious body and blood is offered daily, that once suffered and was once shed. And also by the same Petrus' judgment, which he confirmeth with the saying of other, this daily offering by the priest is daily offered for sin, not for any imperfection in the first offering, but because we daily fall. And by Petrus' judgment appeareth also, how the priest hath a special function to make this offering, by whose mouth God is prayed unto (as Hesychius saith) to make this sacrifice, which Emissene noteth to be wrought by the great power[4] of the invisible priest. By Petrus Lombardus also, if his judgment be true, (as it is in deed, and the author confesseth it so to be,) that is done in the altar is not only called a sacrifice, but also is so, and the same that is offered once and daily to be the same, but otherwise then and[5] otherwise now. But to the purpose: if the author will stand to the judgment of Petrus Lombardus, all his fifth book of this treaty is clearly defaced. And if he will now call back that again, he might more compendiously do the same in the whole treatise, being so far overseen as he is therein.

CANTERBURY.

How is it possible to set out more plainly the diversity of the true sacrifice of Christ made upon the altar of the cross, which was the propitiation of sin, from the sacrifice made in the sacrament, than Lombardus hath done in this place? For the one he calleth the true sacrifice, the other he calleth but a memorial or representation thereof, likening the sacrifice made in the Lord's supper to a year's mind or anniversary, whereat is made a memorial of the death of a person, and yet it is not his death indeed. So in the Lord's supper, according to his commandment, we remem-

---

[1 And causeth us, Orig. ed. Winch.]
[2 And yet is offered, 1551.]
[3 It is offered, Orig. ed. Winch.]
[4 By the power, ibid.]
[5 Then offered and, ibid.]

ber his death, preaching and commending the same until his return again at the last day.

And although it be one Christ that died for us, and whose death we remember, yet it is not one sacrifice that he made of himself upon the cross, and that we make of him upon the altar or table. For his sacrifice was the redemption of the world, ours is not so: his was death, ours is but a remembrance thereof: his was the taking away the sins of the world; ours is a praising and thanking for the same: and therefore his was satisfactory, ours is gratulatory. It is but one Christ that was offered then, and that is offered now; yet the offerings be divers: his was the thing, and ours is the figure; his was the original, and ours is as it were a pattern. Therefore concludeth Lombardus, that Christ was "otherwise offered then and otherwise now." And seeing then that the offerings and sacrifices be divers, if the first was propitiatory and satisfactory, ours cannot be so, except we shall make many sacrifices propitiatory. And then, as St Paul reasoneth, either the first must be insufficient, or the other in vain. And as Christ only made this propitiatory sacrifice, so he made but one, and but once. For the making of any other, or of the same again, should have been (as St Paul reasoneth) a reproving of the first as unperfect and insufficient. And therefore, at his last supper, although Christ made unto his Father sacrifices of lauds and thanksgiving, as these words εὐχαριστήσας and ὑμνήσαντες do declare, yet he made there no sacrifice propitiatory; for then either the sacrifice upon the cross had been void, or the sacrifice at the supper unperfect and unsufficient. And although he had at his supper made sacrifices propitiatory, yet the priests do not so, who do not the same that Christ did at his supper. For he ministered not the sacrament in remembrance of his death, which was not then brought to pass, but he ordained it to be ministered of us in remembrance thereof. And therefore our offering, after Lombardus' judgment, is but a remembrance of that true offering wherein Christ offered himself upon the cross. And so did Christ institute it to be.

385. The diversity of Christ's sacrifice and ours. The sacrifice of Christ.

Heb. vii. viii.

And Lombardus saith not that Christ is daily offered for propitiation of our sins; but because we daily sin, we daily be put in the remembrance of Christ's death, which is the perfect propitiation for sin[6]. And the priest (as Lombardus saith) maketh a memorial of that oblation of Christ, and (as Hesychius saith) he doth it in the name of the people, so that the sacrifice is no more the priest's than the people's. For the priests speak the words, and the people should answer "Amen," as Justinus saith. The priest should declare the death and passion of Christ, and all the people should look upon the cross in the mount of Calvary, and see Christ there hanging, and the blood flowing out of his side into their wounds to heal all their sores; and the priest and people all together should laud and thank instantly the chirurgeon and physician of their souls. And this is the priest's and people's sacrifice, not to be propitiators for sin, but (as Emissene saith) to worship continually in mystery that which was but once offered for the price of sin. And this shortly is the mind of Lombardus, that the thing which is done at God's board is a sacrifice, and so is that also which was made upon the cross, but not after one manner of understanding. For this was the thing indeed, and that is the anniversary or commemoration of the thing.

The sacrifice of the church.

And now have I made it evident, that Petrus Lombardus defaceth in no point my saying of the sacrifice, but confirmeth fully my doctrine, as well of the sacrifice propitiatory made by Christ himself only, as of the sacrifice commemorative and gratulatory made by the priests and people. So that in your issue taken upon Lombard, the verdict cannot but pass with me, by the testimony of Lombard himself. And yet I do not fully allow Lombard's judgment in all matters, who with Gratian his brother, as it is said, were two chief champions of the Romish see, to spread abroad their errors and usurped authority; but I speak of Lombard only to declare that yet in his time they had not erred so far, to make of their mass a sacrifice propitiatory. But in the end of this process Lombard speaketh without the book, when he concludeth this matter thus, that "the virtue of this sacrament is the remission of venial sin and perfection of virtue:" which if Lombard understand of the sacrifice of Christ,

386.

[¹ Proportion for sin, 1580.]

it is too little, to make his sacrifice the remission but of venial sin; and if he understand it of the sacrifice of the priest, it is too much to make the priest's sacrifice either "the perfection of virtue" or "the remission of venial sin," which be the effects only of the sacrifice of Christ.

Now let us consider the rest of your confutation.

WINCHESTER.

The catholic doctrine teacheth not the daily sacrifice of Christ's most precious body and blood to be an iteration of the once perfected sacrifice on the cross, but a sacrifice that representeth that sacrifice, and sheweth it also before the faithful eyes, and refresheth the effectual memory of it; so as in the daily sacrifice, without shedding of blood, we may see with the eye of faith the very body and blood of Christ by God's mighty power, without division, distinctly exhibit, the same body and blood that suffered and was shed for us, which is a lively memorial to stir up our faith, and to consider therein briefly the great charity of God towards us declared in Christ. The catholic doctrine teacheth the daily sacrifice to be the same in essence that was offered on the cross once, assured thereof by Christ's words when he said: "This is my body that shall be betrayed for you." The offering on the cross was and is propitiatory and satisfactory for our redemption and remission of sin, whereby to destroy the tyranny of sin, the effect whereof is given and dispensed in the sacrament of baptism, once likewise ministered and never to be iterate, no more than Christ can be crucified again; and yet by virtue of the same offering such as fall be relieved in the sacrament of penance.

CANTERBURY.

After your wilful wrangling without any cause, at the last of your own swing you come to the truth, purely and sincerely professing and setting forth the same, except in few words here and there cast in, as it were cockle among clean corn. "The offering on the cross," say you, "was and is propitiatory and satisfactory for our redemption and remission of sin, the effect whereof is given and dispensed in the sacrament of baptism, once likewise ministered, and never to be iterate;" but "the catholic doctrine teacheth not that the daily sacrifice is an iteration of the once perfected sacrifice on the cross, but a representation thereof, shewing it before the faithful eyes, and refreshing our memory therewith, so that we may see with the eye of faith the very body and blood of Christ, by God's mighty power exhibit unto us, the same body and blood that suffered and was shed for us." This is a godly and catholic doctrine, but of the cockle, which you cast in by the way, of distinction "without division," I cannot tell what you mean, except you speak out your dreams more plainly. And that it is the same body in substance, that is daily, as it were, offered by remembrance, which was once offered in the cross for sin, we learn not so plainly by these words, "This is my body," *hoc est corpus meum*, as we do by these, *Hic Jesus assumptus est in cœlum*, and, *Qui descendit, ipse est et qui ascendit supra omnes cœlos*: "This Jesus was taken up into heaven," and "he that descended was the same Jesus that ascended above all the heavens."

And where you say, that "by virtue of Christ's sacrifice such as fall be relieved in the sacrament of penance," the truth is, that such as do fall be relieved by Christ, whensoever they return to him unfeignedly with heart and mind. And as for your words concerning the sacrament of penance, may have a popish understanding in it. But at length you return to your former error, and go about to revoke, or at the least evil-favouredly to expound, that which you have before well spoken. Your words be these.

WINCHESTER.

The daily offering is propitiatory also, but not in that degree of propitiation, as for redemption, regeneration, or remission of deadly sin, which was once purchased, and by force thereof is in the sacraments ministered; but for the increase of God's favour, the mitigation

---
387.

Acts i.
Eph. iv.

Penance.

*The mass is a sacrifice propitiatory.

of God's displeasure, provoked by our infirmities, the subduing of temptations, and the perfection of virtue in us. All good works, good thoughts, and good meditations may be called sacrifices, and the same be called sacrifices propitiatory also, for so much as in their degree God accepteth and taketh them through the effect and strength of the very sacrifice of Christ's death, which is the reconciliation between God and man, ministered and dispensed particularly as God hath appointed, in such measure as he knoweth. But St Paul to the Hebrews, exhorting men to charitable deeds, saith: "With such sacrifices God is made favourable," or, "God is propitiate," if we shall make new English. Whereupon it followeth, because the priest in the daily sacrifice doth as Christ hath ordered to be done for shewing forth and remembrance of Christ's death, that act of the priest done according to God's commandment must needs be propitiatory, and provoke God's favour, and ought to be trusted on to have a propitiatory effect with God to the members of Christ's body particularly, being the same done for the whole body, in such wise as God knoweth the dispensation to be meet and convenient; according to which measure God worketh most justly and most mercifully, otherwise than man can by his judgment discuss and determine. To call the daily offering a "sacrifice satisfactory," must have an understanding that signifieth not the action of the priest, but the presence of Christ's most precious body and blood, the very sacrifice of the world once perfectly offered being propitiatory and satisfactory for all the world; or else the word "satisfactory" must have a signification and meaning, as it hath sometime, that declareth the acceptation of the thing done, and not the proper contrevail of the action, after which sort man may satisfy God that is so merciful as he will take in good worth for Christ's sake man's imperfect endeavour, and so the daily offering may be called a sacrifice satisfactory, because God is pleased with it, being a manner of worshipping of Christ's passion according to his institution[1]. But otherwise the daily sacrifice, in respect of the action of the priest, [cannot be][2] called satisfactory, and it is a word indeed that soundeth not well so placed, although it might be saved by a signification, and therefore think that word rather to be well expounded, than by captious understanding brought in slander when it is used, and this speech to be frequented, that the only immolation of Christ in himself upon the altar of the cross is the very satisfactory sacrifice for reconciliation of mankind to the favour of God. And I have not read the daily sacrifice of Christ's most precious body to be called a sacrifice satisfactory, but this speech hath indeed been used, that the priest should sing "satisfactory;" which they understood in the satisfaction of the priest's duty, to attend the prayer he was required to make, and for a distinction thereof they had prayer sometime required without special limitation, and that was called to pray not "satisfactory." Finally in man[3] by any his action to presume to satisfy God by way of countervail, is a very mad and furious blasphemy.*

CANTERBURY.

To defend the papistical error, that the daily offering of the priest in the mass is propitiatory, you extend the word "propitiation" otherwise than the apostles do, speaking of that matter. I speak plainly, according to St Paul and St John, that only Christ is the propitiation for our sins by his death. You speak according to the papists, that the priests in their masses make a sacrifice propitiatory. I call a sacrifice propitiatory, according to the scripture, such a sacrifice as pacifieth God's indignation against us, obtaineth mercy and forgiveness of all our sins, and is our ransom and redemption from everlasting damnation. And on the other side, I call a sacrifice gratificatory, or the sacrifice of the church, such a sacrifice as doth not reconcile us to God, but is made of them that be reconciled to testify their duties, and to shew themselves thankful unto him. And these sacrifices in scripture be not called propitiatory, but sacrifices of justice, of laud, praise, and thanksgiving. But you confound the words, and call one by another's name, calling that propitiatory which the scripture calleth but of justice, laud, and thanking. And all is nothing else but to defend your propitiatory sacrifice of the priests in their masses, whereby they may remit sin, and redeem souls out of purgatory.

And yet all your wiles and shifts will not serve you; for by extending the name

---

[1 Christ's institution, Orig. ed. Winch.]
[2 Ed. 1551, and Orig. ed. Winch.]
[3 Finally man, 1551, and Orig. ed. Winch.]

of a propitiatory sacrifice unto so large a signification as you do, you make all manner of sacrifices propitiatory, leaving no place for any other sacrifice. "For," say you, "all good deeds and good thoughts be sacrifices propitiatory;" and then be the good works of the lay people sacrifices propitiatory, as well as those of the priest. And to what purpose then made you in the beginning of this book a distinction between sacrifices propitiatory and other? Thus for desire you have to defend the papistical errors, you have not fallen only into imaginations contrary to the truth of God's word, but also contrary to yourself.

But let pass away these papistical inventions, and let us humbly profess ourselves, with all our sacrifices, not worthy to approach unto God, nor to have any access unto him, but by that only propitiatory sacrifice which Christ only made upon the cross. And yet let us with all devotion, with whole heart and mind, and with all obedience to God's will, come unto the heavenly supper of Christ, thanking him only for propitiation of our sins. In which holy communion the act of the minister and other be all of one sort, none propitiatory, but all of lauds and thanksgiving. And such sacrifices be pleasant and acceptable to God, as St Paul saith, done of them that be good; but they win not his favour, and put away his indignation from them that be evil. For such reconciliation can no creature make, but Christ alone.

Rom. iii. & v. Acts iv.

And where you say, that "to call the daily offering a sacrifice satisfactory must have an understanding that signifieth not the action of the priest;" here you may see what a business and hard work it is to patch the papists' rags together, and what absurdities you fall into thereby. Even now you said, that the act of the priests must needs be a sacrifice propitiatory; and now, to have an understanding for the same, you be driven to so shameful a shift, that you say either clean contrary, that it is not the action of the priest, but the presence of Christ; or else that the action of the priest is none otherwise satisfactory than all other christian men's works be. For otherwise, say you, the daily sacrifice, in respect of the action of the priest, cannot be called satisfactory. Wherefore at length, knowledging your popish doctrine to sound evil-favouredly, you confess again the true catholic teaching, that "this speech is to be frequented and used, that the only immolation of Christ in himself, upon the altar of the cross, is the very satisfactory sacrifice for reconciliation of mankind to the favour of God."

389.

And where you say, that "you have not read the daily sacrifice of Christ's most precious body to be called a sacrifice satisfactory:" if you have not read of satisfactory masses, it appeareth that you have read but very little of the school-authors. And yet not many years ago you might have heard them preached in every pardon. But because you have not read thereof, read Doctor Smith's book of the sacrifice of the mass, and both your ears and eyes shall be full of it: whose "furious blasphemies" you have, with one sentence, here most truly rejected; wherefore yet remaineth in you some good sparks of the Spirit, that you so much detest such abomination.

Satisfactory masses.

And yet such blasphemies you go about to salve and plaster, as much as you may, by subtle and crafty interpretations. For by such exposition as you make of the satisfactory singing of the priest, in "doing his duty in that he was required to do;" *by this exposition he singeth as well satisfactory in saying of matins as in saying of mass, for in both he doth his duty that he required unto: and*[1] so might it be defended, that the player upon the organs playeth satisfactory, when he doth his duty in playing as he is required. And all the singing men in the church, that have wages thereto, sing satisfactory, as well as the priests, when they sing according to that be hired unto. And then as one singing man or player on the organs, receiving a stipend of many men to play or sing at a certain time, if he do his duty, satisfieth them all at once; so might a priest sing satisfactory for many persons at one time, which the teachers of satisfactory masses utterly condemn. But if you had read Duns, you would have written more clerkly in these matters than you now do.

Now let us hear what you say further.

[1 The passage between asterisks is wanting in ed. 1551.]

WINCHESTER.

Where the author, citing St Paul, Englisheth him thus, that "Christ's priesthood cannot pass from him to another;" these words thus framed be not the simple and sincere expression of the truth of the text, which saith, that "Christ hath a perpetual priesthood:" and the Greek hath a word ἀπαράβατον, which the Greek schools express and expound by the word ἀδιάδοχον, signifying the priesthood of Christ endeth not in him to go to another by succession, as in the tribe of Levi, where was among mortal men succession in the office of priesthood; but Christ liveth ever, and therefore is a perpetual everlasting priest, by whose authority priesthood is now in this visible church, as St Paul ordered to Timothy and Titus, and other places also confirm; which priests, visible ministers to our invisible priest, offer the daily sacrifice in Christ's church; that is to say, with the very presence, by God's omnipotency wrought, of the most precious body and blood of our Saviour Christ, shewing forth Christ's death, and celebrating the memory of his supper and death according to Christ's institution, so with daily oblation and sacrifice of the selfsame sacrifice to kindle in us a thankful remembrance of all Christ's benefits unto us.

[Heb. vii. Orig. ed. Winch.]

[1 Tim. iv. et ad Titum i. Orig. ed. Winch.]

* Priests in the mass offer, that is, shewed forth Christ's death. 390.

CANTERBURY.

Where you find yourself grieved with my citing of St Paul, that "Christ's priesthood cannot pass from him to another," which is not, say you, "the truth of the text, which meaneth that the priesthood of Christ endeth not in him to go to another by succession:" your manner of speech herein is so dark, that it giveth no light at all. For it seemeth to signify, that Christ's priesthood endeth, but not to go to other by succession, but by some other means: which thing if you mean, then you make the endless priesthood of Christ to have an end. And if you mean it not, but that Christ's priesthood is endless, and goeth to no other by succession, nor otherwise; then, I pray you, what have I offended in saying, that "Christ's priesthood cannot pass from him to another?" And as for the Greek words, παράβατον and διάδοχον signify any manner of succession, whether it be by inheritance, adoption, election, purchase, or any other means. And he that is instituted and inducted into a benefice after another, is called his successor. And Erasmus calleth ἀπαράβατον "*quod in alium transire non potest.*" And so doth ἀδιάδοχον signify "*quod successione caret;*" that is to say, "a thing that hath no succession, nor passeth to none other." And because Christ is a perpetual and everlasting priest, that by one oblation made a full sacrifice of sin for ever, therefore his priesthood neither needeth nor can pass to any other: wherefore the ministers of Christ's church be not now appointed priests to make a new sacrifice for sin, as though Christ had not done that at once sufficiently for ever, but to preach abroad Christ's sacrifice, and to be ministers of his words and sacraments. And where but a little before you had truly taught, that "the only immolation of Christ by himself upon the altar of the cross is the very satisfactory sacrifice for our reconciliation to God;" now in the end, like a cow that casteth down her milk with her own feet, you overthrow all again in few words, saying that "priests make daily the self-same sacrifice that Christ made:" which is so foul an error and blasphemy, that, as I said in mine other book, "if the priests daily make the self-same sacrifice that Christ did himself, and the sacrifice that he made was his death and the effusion of his most precious blood upon the cross, then followeth of necessity, that every day the priests slay Christ and shed his blood, and be worse than the Jews, that did it but once."

Heb. vii.

Now followeth in your confutation thus.

WINCHESTER.

And where the author would avoid all the testimony of the fathers, by pretence it should be but a manner of speech, the canon of the council of Nice before rehearsed, and the words of it, where mysteries be spoken of in proper terms for doctrine, avoideth all that shift; and it hath no absurdity to confess, that Christ in his supper did institute, for a remembrance of

364   THE FIFTH BOOK.

*Christ is of- the only sacrifice, the presence of the same most precious substance[1] to be (as the canon of the
fered really,
not his sacri- council in proper teacheth) sacrificed by the priests, to be the pure sacrifice of the church
fice remem-
bered or re- there offered for the effect of increase of life in us, as it was offered on the cross to achieve
presented
only. life unto us. And St Cyril, who for his doctrine was in great authority with the council
[Epistola ad
Nestor. Orig. Ephesine, writeth "the very body and blood of Christ to be the lively and unbloody sacrifice
ed. Winch.]
391. of the church;" as likewise in the old church other commonly termed the same, and among
other Chrysostom, whom the author would now have seem to use it but for a manner of
[xvii. Hom. speech, which in deed Chrysostom doth not, but doth truly open the understanding of that is
ad Heb. Orig.
ed. Winch.] done in the church, wherein by this sacrifice, done after the order of Melchisedech, Christ's
death is not iterate, but a memory daily renewed of that death, so as Christ's offering on the
cross once done and consummate to finish all sacrifices after the order of Aaron, is now only
remembered according to Christ's institution, but in such wise as the same body is offered daily
on the altar, that was once offered on the altar of the cross; but the same manner of offering is
not daily that was on the altar of the cross, for the daily offering is without bloodshed, and
is termed so to signify that bloodshedding once done to be sufficient. And as Chrysostom
openeth it by declaration of what manner our sacrifice is, that is to say, this daily offering
to be a remembrance of the other manner of sacrifice once done, and therefore saith rather
we make a remembrance of it; this saying of Chrysostom doth not impair his former words,
where he saith, "the host is the same offered on the cross and on the altar;" and therefore
by him the body of Christ that died but once is daily present in deed, and, as the council of
Nice saith, "sacrificed not after the manner of other sacrifices;" and, as Chrysostom saith,
"offered, but the death of that precious body only daily remembered, and not again iterate."

                                CANTERBURY.

The effect of   For answer hereto, read the thirteenth chapter of my fifth book[2], and that which
Christ's sacri-
fice is both to I have written here a little before of Nicene council[3]. And where you say, that "the
give life and
to continue effect of the sacrifice of Christ's body, made by the priests, is to increase life in us,
the same. as the effect of the sacrifice of the same body made by himself upon the cross is to
give life unto us;" this is not only an absurdity, but also an intolerable blasphemy
against Christ. For the sacrifice made upon the cross doth both give us life, and
also increase and continue the same: and the priest's oblation doth neither of both.
For our redemption and eternal salvation standeth not only in giving us life, but in
John x. continuing the same for ever; as Christ said, that "he came not only to give us
life, but also to make us increase and abound therein:" and St Paul said: "The life
Gal. ii. which I now live in flesh, I live by the faith of the Son of God, who loved me, and
gave himself for me." And therefore, if we have the one by the oblation of Christ,
and the other by the oblation of the priest, then divide we our salvation between Christ
and the priest. And because it is no less gift to continue life for ever, than to give
it us, by this your mad and furious blasphemy we have our salvation and redemption
as much by the sacrifice made by the priest, as we have by sacrifice made by Christ
himself. And thus you make Christ to be like an unkind and unnatural mother,
who, when she hath brought forth her child, putteth it to another to nurse, and maketh
herself but half the mother of it. And thus you teach christian people to halt on
both sides, partly worshipping God, and partly Baal; partly attributing our salvation
to Christ, the true, perfect, eternal priest, and partly to antichrist and his priests.
Cyril* in   And concerning Cyril, he speaketh not of a sacrifice propitiatory in that place, as
Ephesine
council. † I have more plainly declared in mine answer to Doctor Smith's prologue.
What is, and   And whereas you call the daily sacrifice of the church an "unbloody sacrifice," here
wherein
standeth the it were necessary, if you would not deceive simple people, but teach them such doctrine
sacrifice of
the church. as they may understand, that you should in plain terms set forth and declare what
392. the daily offering of the priest without blood-shedding is, in what words, deeds, crosses,
signs, or gestures it standeth, and whether it be made before the consecration or after,
and before the distribution of the sacrament or after, and wherein chiefly resteth the
very pith and substance of it. And when you have thus done, I will say you mean

---

[1 The presence of the most precious substance,   [2 Vide supra, p. 351.]
Orig. ed. Winch.]   [3 Vide supra, p. 356.]

WINCHESTER.

And where the author saith the old fathers, calling the supper of our Lord a sacrifice, meant a sacrifice of laud and thanksgiving; Hippinus of Hamburgh, no papist, in his book dedicate to the king's majesty that now is, saith otherwise, and noteth how the old fathers called it a sacrifice propitiatory, "for the very presence of Christ's most precious body there:" thus saith he; which presence all christian men must say requireth on our part lauds and thanksgiving, which may be, and is, called in scripture by the name of sacrifice; but that sacrifice of our lauds and thanks cannot be a sacrifice giving life, as it is noted by Cyril the sacrifice of the church to do, when he saith it is vivificum, *which can be only said of the very body and blood of Christ. Nor our sacrifice of lauds and thanksgiving cannot be said a pure and clean sacrifice, whereby to fulfil the prophecy of Malachi; and therefore the same prophecy was in the beginning of the church understood to be spoken of the daily offering of the body and blood of Christ for the memory of Christ's death, according to Christ's ordinance in his supper, as may at more length be opened and declared. Thinking to the effect of this book sufficient to have encountered the chief points of the author's doctrine, with such contradiction to them as the catholic doctrine doth of necessity require; the more particular confutation of that is untrue on the adversary part, and confirmation of that is true in the catholic doctrine, requiring more time and leisure than I have now, and therefore offering myself ready by mouth or writing to say further in this matter as shall be required; I shall here end for this time, with prayer to Almighty God, to grant his truth to be acknowledged and confessed, and uniformly to be preached and believed of all, so as, all contention for understanding of religion avoided, which hindereth charity, we may give such light abroad as men may see our good works, and glorify our Father who is in heaven, with the Son and Holy Ghost in one unity of Godhead reigning without end. Amen.*

* The sacrifice of the church giveth life. [Mal. iii. Orig. ed. Winch.]

CANTERBURY.

Æpinus saith, that "the old fathers called the supper of our Lord a sacrifice:" but that the old fathers should call it a sacrifice propitiatory, I will not believe that Æpinus so said, until you appoint me both the book and place where he so saith. For the effect of his book is clean contrary, which he wrote to reprove the propitiatory sacrifice, which the papists feign to be in the mass. Thus indeed Æpinus writeth in one place: *Veteres eucharistiam propter corporis et sanguinis Christi præsentiam primo vocaverunt sacrificium, deinde propter oblationes et munera quæ in ipsa eucharistia Deo consecrabantur, et conferebantur ad sacra ministeria et ad necessitatem credentium*[4]. In which words Æpinus declareth, that "the old fathers called the supper of our Lord a sacrifice, for two considerations: one was for the presence of Christ's flesh and blood, the other was for the offerings which the people gave there of their devotion to the holy ministration and relief of the poor." But Æpinus speaketh here not one word of corporal presence, nor of propitiatory sacrifice, but generally of presence and sacrifice, which maketh nothing for your purpose, nor against me, that grant both a presence and a sacrifice. But when you shall shew me the place where Æpinus saith, that "the old

---

[4 Vide supra, p. 20. Æpinus de purgatorio, &c. of which Strype gives the following account:— "I add another book in quarto, of a foreigner, dedicated this year* to the king, in a long epistle dated from Hamburgh. The author was Johannes Æpinus. The subjects of his book were, *De Purgatorio, Satisfactionibus, Remissione Culparum et Pœnæ, &c.* This Æpinus was chief minister of the Church of Hamburgh, and was sent twelve years before, as envoy from Hamburgh into England to king Henry, upon matters of religion."—Strype, Memorials, Vol. II. p. 229. Ed. Oxford, 1822.]

* Anno 1548.

fathers called the Lord's supper a propitiatory sacrifice," I shall trust you the better, and him the worse.

Cyril. And as for Cyril, if you will say of his head, that "the sacrifice of the church giveth life;" how agreeth this with your late saying, that "the sacrifice of the church increaseth life, as the sacrifice on the cross giveth life?" And if the sacrifice, made by the priest, both give life and increase life, then is the priest both the mother and nurse, and Christ hath nothing to do with us at all, but as a stranger.

Mal. i. And the sacrifice that Malachi speaketh of is the sacrifice of laud and thanks, which all devout christian people give unto God, whether it be in the Lord's supper, in their private prayers, or in any work they do at any time or place to the glory of God; all which sacrifices, not of the priests only, but of all faithful people, be accepted of God through the sacrifice of Christ, by whose blood all their filth and unpureness is clean sponged away.

Inconstancy. But in this last book, it seemeth you were so astonied and amazed, that you were at your wit's end, and wist not where to become. For now the priest maketh a sacrifice propitiatory, now he doth not: now he giveth life, now he giveth none: now is Christ the full Saviour and satisfaction, now the priest hath half part with him: now the priest doth all. And thus you are so inconstant in yourself, as one that had been nettled, and could rest in no place; or rather as one that had received such a stroke upon his head, that he staggered withal, and reeled here and there, and could not tell where to become.

And your doctrine hath such ambiguities, such perplexities, such absurdities, and such impieties in it, and is so uncertain, so uncomfortable, so contrary to God's word and the old catholic church, so contrary to itself, that it declareth from whose spirit it cometh, which can be none other but antichrist himself.

Whereas, on the other side, the very true doctrine of Christ and his pure church from the beginning is plain, certain, without wrinkles, without any inconvenience or absurdity, so cheerful and comfortable to all christian people, that it must needs come from the Spirit of God, the Spirit of truth and all consolation. For what ought to be more certain and known to all christian people, than that Christ died once, and but once, for the redemption of the world? And what can be more true, than that his only death is our life? And what can be more comfortable to a penitent sinner, that is sorry for his sin, and returneth to God in his heart and whole mind, than to know that Christ dischargeth him of the heavy load of his sin, and taketh the burden upon his own back? And if we shall join the priest herein to Christ in any part, and give a portion hereof to his sacrifice, as you in your doctrine give to the priest the one half at the least, what a discourage is this to the penitent sinner, that he may not hang wholly upon Christ! what perplexities and doubts rise hereof in the sinner's conscience!

394. And what an obscuring and darkening is this of the benefit of Christ! Yea, what injury and contumely is it to him!

And furthermore, when we hear Christ speak unto us with his own mouth, and shew himself to be seen with our eyes, in such sort as is convenient for him of us in this mortal life to be heard and seen; what comfort can we have more? The minister of the church speaketh unto us God's own words, which we must take as spoken from God's own mouth, because that from his mouth it came, and his word it is, and not the minister's. Likewise, when he ministereth to our sights Christ's holy sacraments, we must think Christ crucified and presented before our eyes, because the sacraments so represent him, and be his sacraments, and not the priest's: as in baptism we must think, that as the priest putteth his hand to the child outwardly, and washeth him with water, so must we think that God putteth to his hand inwardly, and washeth the infant with his holy Spirit; and moreover, that Christ himself cometh down upon the child, and apparelleth him with his own self: and as at the Lord's holy table the priest distributeth wine and bread to feed the body, so we must think that inwardly by faith we see Christ feeding both body and soul to eternal life. What comfort can be devised any more in this world for a christian man? And on the other side, what discomfort is in your papistical doctrine, what doubts, what perplexities, what absurdities, what iniquities! What availeth it us that there is no bread nor wine? or that Christ is really under the forms and figures of bread and wine, and not in us? or if he be in us, yet he is but in the lips or the stomach, and tarrieth not with us. Or what benefit is it to a wicked man to eat Christ, and to receive death by him that is life? From this your obscure, perplex, uncertain, uncomfortable, devilish, and papistical doctrine, Christ defend all his; and grant that we may come often and worthily to Christ's holy table, to comfort our feeble and weak faith by remembrance of his death, who only is the satisfaction and propitiation of our sins, and our meat, drink, and food of everlasting life. Amen.

☙ Here endeth the answer of the most reverend father in God, Thomas, Archbishop of Canterbury, &c., unto the crafty and sophistical cavillation of doctor Stephen Gardiner, devised by him to obscure the true, sincere, and godly doctrine of the most holy sacrament of the body and blood of our Saviour CHRIST.

THE ANSWER

OF

THOMAS, ARCHBISHOP OF CANTERBURY, &c.,

AGAINST THE

FALSE CALUMNIATIONS OF DOCTOR RICHARD SMITH, WHO HATH
TAKEN UPON HIM TO CONFUTE THE DEFENCE OF THE TRUE
AND CATHOLIC DOCTRINE OF THE BODY AND
BLOOD OF OUR SAVIOUR CHRIST.

---

395. I HAVE now obtained, gentle reader, that thing which I have much desired, which was, that if all men would not embrace the truth lately set forth by me, concerning the sacrament of the body and blood of our Saviour Christ, at the least some man would vouchsafe to take pen in hand and write against my book, because that thereby the truth might both better be searched out, and also more certainly known to the world. And herein I heartily thank the late bishop of Winchester, and doctor Smith, who partly have satisfied my long desire; saving that I would have wished adversaries more substantially learned in holy scriptures, more exercised in the old ancient ecclesiastical authors, and having a more godly zeal to the trial out of the truth, than are these two, both being crafty sophisters, the one by art, and the other by nature; both also being drowned in the dregs of papistry, brought up and confirmed in the same; the one by Duns and Dorbell, and such like sophisters; the other by the popish canon law, whereof by his degree, taken in the university, he is a professor. And as concerning the late bishop of Winchester, I will declare his crafty sophistications in mine answer unto his book.

But doctor Smith, as it appeareth by the title of his preface, hath craftily devised an easy way to obtain his purpose, that the people, being barred from the searching of the truth, might be still kept in blindness and error, as well in this as in all other matters, wherein they have been in times past deceived.

Falsehood feareth the light, but light desireth to be tried.

He seeth full well that the more diligently matters be searched out and discussed, the more clearly the craft and falsehood of the subtile papists will appear. And therefore in the preface to the reader he exhorteth all men to leave disputing and reasoning of the same by learning, and to give firm credit unto the church, as the title of the said preface declareth manifestly: as who should say, the truth of any matter that is in question might be tried out, without debating and reasoning by the word of God, whereby, as by the true touchstone, all men's doctrines are to be tried and examined. But the truth is not ashamed to come to the light, and to be tried to the uttermost. For as pure gold, the more it is tried the more pure it appeareth, so is all manner of truth: whereas, on the other side, all maskers, counterfeiters, and false deceivers abhor the light, and refuse the trial. If all men, without right or reason, would give credit unto this papist and his Romish church, against the most certain word of God and the old holy and catholic church of Christ, the matter should be soon at an end, and out of all controversy. But forasmuch as the pure word of God and the first church of

396. Christ from the beginning taught the true catholic faith, and Smith with his church of Rome do now teach the clean contrary, the chaff cannot be tried out from the pure corn (that is to say, the untruth discerned from the very truth) without threshing, windowing, and fanning, searching, debating, and reasoning.

Faith ought to be grounded upon God's word, but the papists ground their faith upon themselves.

As for me, I ground my belief upon God's word, wherein can be no error, having also the consent of the primitive church, requiring no man to believe me further than I have God's word for me. But these papists speak at their pleasure what they list, and would be believed without God's word, because they bear men in hand that they be the church. The church of Christ is not founded upon itself, but upon Christ and his word: but the papists build their church upon themselves, devising new articles of the faith from time to time, without any scripture, and founding the same upon the pope and his clergy, monks and friars; and by that means they be both the makers and judges of their faith themselves. Wherefore this papist, like a politic man, doth right wisely provide for himself and his church in the first entry of his book, that all men should leave searching for the truth, and stick hard and fast to the church, meaning himself and the church of Rome. For from the true catholic church the Romish church, which he accounteth catholic, hath varied and dissented many years past, as the blindest that this day do live may well see and perceive, if they will not purposely wink and shut up their eyes. This I have written to answer the title of his preface.

Now in the beginning of the very preface itself, when this great doctor should recite the words of Ephesine council[1], he translateth them so unlearnedly, that if a young boy, that had gone to the grammar school but three years, had done no better, he should scant have escaped some schoolmaster's hands with six jerks. And beside that, he doth it so craftily to serve his purpose, that he cannot be excused of wilful depravation of the words, calling "celebration" an "offering," and referring the participle "made" to Christ, which should be referred to the word "partakers," and leaving out those words that should declare that the said council spake of no propitiatory sacrifice in the mass, but of a sacrifice of laud and thanks, which christian people give unto God at the holy communion by remembrance of the death, resurrection, and ascension of his Son Jesus Christ, and by confessing and setting forth of the same. *Ephesine council. Cyril the author of the words in the council.*

Here by the ungodly handling of this godly council at his first beginning, it may appear to every man how sincerely this papist intendeth to proceed in the rest of this matter.

And with like sincerity he untruly belieth the said council, saying that it doth plainly set forth the holy sacrifice of the mass, which doth not so much as once name the mass, but speaketh of the sacrifice of the church, which the said council declareth to be the profession of christian people in setting forth the benefit of Christ, who only made the true sacrifice propitiatory for remission of sin. And whosoever else taketh upon him to make any such sacrifice, maketh himself antichrist. *Smith belieth the council.*

And then he belieth me in two things, as he useth commonly throughout his whole book. The one is, that I deny the sacrifice of the mass, which in my book have most plainly set out the sacrifice of christian people in the holy communion or mass, (if Doctor Smith will needs so term it;) and yet I have denied that it is a sacrifice propitiatory for sin, or that the priest alone maketh any sacrifice there. For it is the sacrifice of all christian people to remember Christ's death, to laud and thank him for it, and to publish it and shew it abroad unto other, to his honour and glory. *Smith belieth me twice in one place. The first lie. 397.*

The controversy is not, whether in the holy communion be made a sacrifice or not, (for herein both Doctor Smith and I agree with the foresaid council at Ephesus;) but whether it be a propitiatory sacrifice or not, and whether only the priest make the said sacrifice, these be the points wherein we vary. And I say so far as the council saith, that there is a sacrifice; but that the same is propitiatory for remission of sin, or that the priest alone doth offer it, neither I nor the council do so say, but Doctor Smith hath added that of his own vain head.

The other thing wherein Doctor Smith belieth me is this: he saith, that I "deny that we receive in the sacrament that flesh which is adjoined to God's own Son." I *The second lie.*

[¹ Concilium Ephesinum, A. D. 431. Καταγγέλλοντες τὸν κατὰ σάρκα θάνατον τοῦ μονογενοῦς υἱοῦ τοῦ Θεοῦ, τουτέστιν Ἰησοῦ Χριστοῦ, τήν τε ἐκ νεκρῶν ἀναβίωσιν καὶ τὴν εἰς οὐρανοὺς ἀνάληψιν ὁμολογοῦντες, τὴν ἀναίμακτον ἐν ταῖς ἐκκλησίαις τελοῦμεν θυσίαν· πρόσιμέν τε οὕτω ταῖς μυστικαῖς εὐλογίαις, καὶ ἁγιαζόμεθα, μέτοχοι γενόμενοι τῆς τε ἁγίας σαρκὸς, καὶ τοῦ τιμίου αἵματος τοῦ πάντων ἡμῶν σωτῆρος Χριστοῦ· καὶ οὐχ ὡς σάρκα κοινὴν δεχόμενοι· μὴ γένοιτο· οὔτε μὴν ὡς ἀνδρὸς ἡγιασμένου, καὶ συναφθέντος τῷ λόγῳ κατὰ τὴν ἑνότητα τῆς ἀξίας, ἤγουν ὡς θείαν ἐνοίκησιν ἐσχηκότος· ἀλλ' ὡς ζωοποιὸν ἀληθῶς, καὶ ἰδίαν αὐτοῦ τοῦ λόγου.—Epist. Cyrilli, et Synodi Alexandr. ad Nestorium, § vii. Tom. V. p. 399. Conc. Ed. Paris. 1644.]

marvel not a little what eyes Doctor Smith had, when he read over my book. It is like that he had some privy spectacles within his head, wherewith whensoever he looketh, he seeth but what he list. For in my book I have written in more than an hundred places, that we receive the self-same body of Christ that was born of the virgin Mary, that was crucified and buried, that rose again, ascended into heaven, and sitteth at the right hand of God the Father Almighty: and the contention is only in the manner and form how we receive it.

For I say (as all the old holy fathers and martyrs used to say), that we receive Christ spiritually by faith with our minds, eating his flesh and drinking his blood: so that we receive Christ's own very natural body, but not naturally nor corporally. But this lying papist saith, that we eat his natural body corporally with our mouths; which neither the council Ephesine, nor any other ancient council or doctor ever said or thought.

And the controversy in the council Ephesine was not of the uniting of Christ's flesh to the forms of bread and wine in the sacrament, but of the uniting of his flesh to his divinity at his incarnation in unity of person. Which thing Nestorius the heretic denied, confessing that Christ was a godly man as other were, but not that he was very God in nature; which heresy that holy council confuting, affirmeth that the flesh of Christ was so joined in person to the divine nature, that it was made the proper flesh of the Son of God, and flesh that gave life: but that the said flesh was present in the sacrament corporally, and eaten with our mouths, no mention is made thereof in that council.

And here I require Doctor Smith, as proctor for the papists, either to bring forth some ancient council or doctor, that saith as he saith, that Christ's own natural body is eaten corporally with our mouths, understanding the very body in deed, (and not the signs of the body, as Chrysostom doth,) or else let him confess that my saying is true, and recant his false doctrine the third time, as he hath done twice already[1].

Smith saith, that Christ called not bread his body.
398.
Luke xxii.

1 Cor. x.

THEN forth goeth this papist with his preface, and saith, that these words, "This is my body that shall be given to death for you," no man can truly understand of bread. And his proof thereof is this, because that bread was not crucified for us. First, here he maketh a lie of Christ. For Christ said not, as this papist allegeth, "This is my body, which shall be given to death for you;" but only he saith, "This is my body which is given for you;" which words some understand not of the giving of the body of Christ to death, but of the breaking and giving of bread to his apostles, as St Paul said: "The bread which we break," &c.

But let it be that he spake of the giving of his body to death, and said of the bread, "This is my body, which shall be given to death for you:" by what reason can you gather hereof, that the bread was crucified for us?

If I look upon the image of king David, and say, "This is he that killed Goliath;" doth this speech mean, that the image of king David killed Goliath? Or if I hold in my hand my book of St John's gospel, and say, "This is the gospel that St John wrote at Pathmos," (which fashion of speech is commonly used,) doth it follow hereof that my book was written at Pathmos? or that St John wrote my book, which was but newly printed at Paris, by Robert Stephanus? Or if I say of my book of St Paul's epistles, "This is Paul that was the great persecutor of Christ;" doth this manner of speech signify, that my book doth persecute Christ? Or if I shew a book of the new testament, saying, "This is the new testament, which brought life unto the world;" by what form of argument can you induce hereof, that my book that I bought but yesterday, brought life unto the world? No man that useth thus to speak doth mean of the books, but of the very things themselves that in the books be taught and contained. And after the same wise, if Christ called bread his body, saying, "This is my body, which shall be given to death for you;" yet

---

[¹ Vide Strype's Memorials of Cranmer, Vol. I. p. 243, and Vol. II. p. 795. Appendix. Num. xxxix. Ed. Oxford. 1840; also, Strype's Ecclesiastical Memorials, Vol. II. p. 61. cap. vi. Ed. Oxford. 1822.]

he meant not, that the bread should be given to death for us, but his body, which by the bread was signified.

If this excellent clerk and doctor understand not these manner of speeches, that be so plain, then hath he both lost his senses, and forgotten his grammar, which teacheth to refer the relative to the next antecedent. But of these figurative speeches I have spoken at large in my third book: first in the eighth chapter[2], proving by authority of the oldest authors in Christ's church, "that he called bread his body, and wine his blood;" and again in the ninth[3], tenth[4], eleventh[5], and twelfth chapters[6], I have so fully entreated of such figurative speeches, that it should be but a superfluous labour here to speak of any more: but I refer the reader to those places.

And if Master Doctor require a further answer herein, let him look upon the late bishop of Winchester's book, called "The Detection of the Devil's Sophistry," where he writeth plainly, that when Christ spake these words, "This is my body," he made demonstration of the bread.

THEN further in this prologue this papist is not ashamed to say, that I set the cart before the horses, putting reason first, and faith after: which lie is so manifest, that it needeth no further proof but only to look upon my book, wherein it shall evidently appear, that in all my five books I ground my foundation upon God's word. And lest the papists should say, that I make the expositions of the scripture myself, as they commonly use to do, I have fortified my foundation by the authority of all the best learned and most holy authors and martyrs, that were in the beginning of the church and many years after, until the antichrist of Rome rose up and corrupted altogether. *Setting of the cart before the horses.*

399.

And as for natural reason, I make no mention thereof in all my five books, but in one place only, which is in my second book, speaking of transubstantiation. And in that place I set not reason before faith, but, as an hand-maiden, have appointed her to do service unto faith, and to wait upon her. And in that place she hath done such service that D. Smith durst not once look her in the face, nor find any fault with her service, but hath slyly and craftily stolen away by her, as though he saw her not.

But in his own book he hath so impudently set the cart before the horses in Christ's own words, putting the words behind that go before, and the words before that go behind, that, except a shameless papist, no man durst be so bold to attempt any such thing of his own head. For where the evangelist and St Paul rehearse Christ's words thus, "Take, eat, this is my body;" he in the confutation of my second book turneth the order upside down, and saith: "This is my body, take and eat." *Matt. xxvi. 1 Cor. xi.*

After this, in his preface, he rehearseth a great number of the wonderful works of God, as that God made all the world of nought, that he made Adam of the earth, and Eve of his side, the bush to flame with fire and burn not, and many other like; which be most manifestly expressed in holy scripture. And upon these he concludeth most vainly and untruly that thing which in the scripture is neither expressed nor understood, that Christ is corporally in heaven and in earth, and in every place where the sacrament is. *Of the wonderful works of God.*

And yet D. Smith saith, that God's word doth teach this as plainly as the other: using herein such a kind of sophistical argument as all logicians do reprehend, which is called *petitio principii*, when a man taketh that thing for a supposition and an approved truth, which is in controversy. And so doth he in this place, when he saith: "Doth not God's word teach it thee as plainly as the other?" Here by this interrogatory he required that thing to be granted him as a truth, which he ought to prove, and whereupon dependeth the whole matter that is in question; that is to say, whether it be as plainly set out in the scripture, that Christ's body is corporally in every place where the sacrament is, as that God created all things of nothing,

---

[2 Vide supra, pp. 104, 5.]
[3 p. 110.]
[4 pp. 110, 111, 113, 114—116.]
[5 pp. 118, 119, 121—132.]
[6 pp. 135—137.]

Adam of the earth, and Eve of Adam's side, &c. This is it that I deny, and that he should prove. But he taketh it for a supposition, saying by interrogation, "Doth not the word of God teach this as plainly as the other?"—which I affirm to be utterly false, as I have shewed in my third book, the eleventh[1] and twelfth[2] chapters, where I have most manifestly proved, as well by God's word as by ancient authors, that these words of Christ, "This is my body," and "This is my blood," be no plain speeches, but figurative.

THEN forth goeth this papist unto the sixth chapter of St John, saying, Christ promised his disciples to give them such bread as should be his own very natural flesh, which he would give to death for the life of the world. "Can this his promise," saith Master Smith, "be verified of common bread? Was that given upon the cross for the life of the world?"

400. Whereto I answer by his own reason: Can this his promise be verified of sacramental bread? was that given upon the cross for the life of the world? I marvel here not a little of Master Smith's either dulness or maliciousness, that cannot or will not see, that Christ in this chapter of St John spake not of sacramental bread, but of heavenly bread; nor of his flesh only, but also of his blood and of his Godhead, calling them heavenly bread that giveth everlasting life. So that he spake of himself wholly, saying: "I am the bread of life. He that cometh to me shall not hunger: and he that believeth in me shall not thirst for ever." And neither spake he of common bread, nor yet of sacramental bread: for neither of them was given upon the cross for the life of the world.

And there can be nothing more manifest than that, in this sixth chapter of John, Christ spake not of the sacrament of his flesh, but of his very flesh; and that, as well for that the sacrament was not then instituted, as also that Christ said not in the future tense, "The bread which I will give shall be my flesh," but in the present tense, "The bread which I will give is my flesh;" which sacramental bread was neither then his flesh, nor was then instituted for a sacrament, nor was after given to death for the life of the world.

John iv. But as Christ, when he said unto the woman of Samaria, "The water which I will give shall spring into everlasting life," he meant neither of material water, nor of the accidents of water, but of the Holy Ghost, which is the heavenly fountain, *John vi.* that springeth unto eternal life; so likewise when he said, "The bread which I will give is my flesh, which I will give for the life of the world," he meant neither of the material bread, neither of the accidents of bread, but of his own flesh. Which although of itself it availeth nothing, yet (being in unity of person joined unto his divinity) it is the same heavenly bread that he gave to death upon the cross for the life of the world.

But here Master Smith asketh a question of the time, saying thus: "When gave Christ that bread, which was his very flesh that he gave for us to death, if he did it not at his last supper, when he said, 'This is my body, that shall be given for you'?"

I answer, according to Cyril's mind[3] upon the same place, that Christ alone suffered for us all, and by his wounds were we healed, he bearing our sins in his body upon a tree, and being crucified for us, that by his death we might live.

But what need I, Master Smith, to labour in answering to your question of the time, when your question in itself containeth the answer, and appointeth the time of Christ giving himself for the life of the world, when you say, that he gave himself for us to death; which, as you confess scant three lines before, was not at his supper, but upon the cross?

And if you will have none other giving of Christ for us, but at his supper, (as your reason pretendeth, or else it is utterly nought,) then surely Christ is much bound unto you, that have delivered him from all his mocking, whipping, scourging, crucifying, and all other pains of death, which he suffered for us upon the cross, and bring

---

[1 Vide supra, pp. 118, 119, 121—32.]
[2 pp. 135—137.]

[3 Cyril. in Joan. Lib. IV. cap. 12.]

to pass that he was given only at his supper, without blood or pain, for the life of the world. But then is all the world little beholding unto you, that by delivering of Christ from death, will suffer all the world to remain in death, which can have no life but by his death.

AFTER the gospel of St John, M. Smith allegeth for his purpose St Paul to the Corinthians, who biddeth every man to examine himself, before he receive this sacrament. "For he that eateth and drinketh it unworthily, is guilty of the body and blood of Christ, eating and drinking his own damnation, because he discerneth not our Lord's body."

<small>401. The place of St Paul. 1 Cor. xi.</small>

Here by the way it is to be noted, that D. Smith, in reciting the words of St Paul, doth alter them purposely, commonly putting this word "sacrament" in the stead of these words, "bread and wine," (which words he seemeth so much to abhor, as if they were toads or serpents, because they make against his transubstantiation,) whereas St Paul ever useth those words, and never nameth this word "sacrament."

But to the matter: "What need we to examine ourselves," saith D. Smith, "when we shall eat but common bread and drink wine of the grape? Is a man guilty of the body and blood of Christ, which eateth and drinketh nothing else, but only bare bread made of corn, and mere wine of the grape?" Who saith so, good sir? Do I say in my book, that those which come to the Lord's table do "eat nothing else but bare bread made of corn, nor drink nothing but mere wine made of grapes?" How often do I teach and repeat again and again, that as corporally with our mouths we eat and drink the sacramental bread and wine, so spiritually with our hearts, by faith, do we eat Christ's very flesh, and drink his very blood, and do both feed and live spiritually by him, although corporally he be absent from us, and sitteth in heaven at his Father's right hand! And as in baptism we come not unto the water as we come to other common waters, when we wash our hands, or bathe our bodies, but we know that it is a mystical water, admonishing us of the great and manifold mercies of God towards us, of the league and promise made between him and us, and of his wonderful working and operation in us; wherefore we come to that water with such fear, reverence, and humility, as we would come to the presence of the Father, the Son, and the Holy Ghost, and of Jesus Christ himself, both God and man, although he be not corporally in the water, but in heaven above; and whosoever cometh to that water, being of the age of discretion, must examine himself duly, lest if he come unworthily, none otherwise than he would come unto other common waters, he be not renewed in Christ, but instead of salvation receive his damnation: even so it is of the bread and wine in the Lord's holy supper. Wherefore "every man," as St Paul saith, "must examine himself," when he shall approach to that holy table, and not come to God's board as he would do to common feasts and banquets; but must consider that it is a mystical table, where the bread is mystical, and the wine also mystical, wherein we be taught that we spiritually feed upon Christ, eating him and drinking him, and as it were sucking out of his side the blood of our redemption and food of eternal salvation, although he be in heaven at his Father's right hand. And whosoever cometh unto this heavenly table, not having regard to Christ's flesh and blood, who should be there our spiritual food, but cometh thereto without faith, fear, humility, and reverence, as it were but to carnal feeding, he doth not there feed upon Christ, but the devil doth feed upon him, and devoureth him, as he did Judas.

And now may every man perceive how fondly and falsely M. Smith concludeth of these words of St Paul, "that our Saviour Christ's body and blood is really and corporally in the sacrament."

<small>402.</small>

AFTER this he falleth to railing, lying, and slandering of M. Peter Martyr, a man of that excellent learning and godly living, that he passeth D. Smith as far as the sun in his clear light passeth the moon being in the eclipse.

<small>Master Peter Martyr.</small>

"Peter Martyr," saith he, "at his first coming to Oxford, when he was but a Lutherian in this matter, taught as D. Smith now doth. But when he came once to the court, and saw that doctrine misliked them that might do him hurt in his living, he anon after turned his tippet, and sang another song."

Of M. Peter Martyr's opinion and judgment in this matter, no man can better testify than I; forasmuch as he lodged within my house long before he came to Oxford, and I had with him many conferences in that matter, and know that he was then of the same mind that he is now, and as he defended after openly in Oxford, and hath written in his book. And if D. Smith understood him otherwise in his lectures at the beginning, it was for lack of knowledge, for that then D. Smith understood not the matter, nor yet doth not, as it appeareth by this foolish and unlearned book, which he hath now set out: no more than he understood my book of the catechism, and therefore reporteth untruly of me, that I in that book did set forth the real presence of Christ's body in the sacrament. Unto which false report I have answered in my fourth book, the eighth chapter[1].

But this I confess of myself, that not long before I wrote the said catechism, I was in that error of the real presence, as I was many years past in divers other errors: as of transubstantiation, of the sacrifice propitiatory of the priests in the mass, of pilgrimages, purgatory, pardons, and many other superstitions and errors that came from Rome; being brought up from youth in them, and nousled therein for lack of good instruction from my youth, the outrageous floods of papistical errors at that time overflowing the world. For the which, and other mine offences in youth, I do daily pray unto God for mercy and pardon, saying: *Delicta juventutis meæ et ignorantias meas ne memineris, Domine.* "Good Lord, remember not mine ignorances and offences of my youth."

But after it had pleased God to shew unto me, by his holy word, a more perfect knowledge of his Son Jesus Christ, from time to time as I grew in knowledge of him, by little and little I put away my former ignorance. And as God of his mercy gave me light, so through his grace I opened mine eyes to receive it, and did not wilfully repugn unto God and remain in darkness. And I trust in God's mercy and pardon for my former errors, because I erred but of frailness and ignorance. And now I may say of myself, as St Paul said: "When I was like a babe or child in the knowledge of Christ, I spake like a child, and understood like a child: but now that I come to man's estate and growing in Christ, through his grace and mercy, I have put away that childishness."

1 Cor. xiii.

Now after that Doctor Smith hath thus untruly belied both me and M. Peter Martyr, he falleth into his exclamations, saying: "O Lord, what man is so mad to believe such mutable teachers, which change their doctrine at men's pleasure, as they see advantage and profit? They turn, and will turn, as the wind turneth."

403.

Do you not remember, M. Smith, the fable, how the old crab rebuked her young, that they went not straight forth; and the common experience, that those that look asquint sometimes find fault with them that look right? You have turned twice and retracted your errors, and the third time promised, and breaking your promise, ran away[2]. And find you fault with me and M. Peter Martyr, as though we "for men's pleasures turn like the wind, as we see advantage?" Shall the weathercock of Paul's, that turneth about with every wind, lay the fault in the church, and say that it turneth?

I will not here answer for myself, but leave the judgment to God, who seeth the bottom of all men's hearts, and at whose only judgment I shall stand or fall; saving that this I will say before God, who is every where present, and knoweth all things that be done, that as for seeking to please men in this matter, I think my conscience clear, that I never sought herein but only the pleasure and glory of God. And yet will I not judge myself herein, nor take D. Smith for my judge, but will refer the judgment to him that is the rightful judge of all men. But as for Doctor Peter Martyr, hath he sought to please men for advantage? who, having a great yearly revenue in his own country, forsook all for Christ's sake, and for the truth and glory of God came into strange countries, where he had neither land nor friends, but as

[1 Vide supra, pp. 225, 6.]   [2 Vide Strype's Cranmer, Vol. I. pp. 244, 289.]

God of his goodness, who never forsaketh them that put their trust in him, provided for him?

But after his exclamation, this papist returneth to the matter, saying: "Tell me, why may not Christ's body be as well in the sacrament and in heaven both at once, as that his body was in one proper place with the body of the stone that lay still upon his grave when he rose from death to life, and as his body was in one proper place at once with the body of the door or gate, when, the same being shut, he entered into the house where the apostles were?" The argument of the door and sepulchre.

Make you these two things to be all one, M. Smith, "divers bodies to be in one place, and one body to be in divers places?" If Christ's body had been in one place with the substance of the stone or door, and at the same time, then you might well have proved thereby, that his body may as well be in one place with the substance of bread and wine. But what availeth this to prove, that his body may be in divers places at one time? which is nothing like to the other, but rather clean contrary. Marry, when Christ arose out of the sepulchre, or came into the house when the doors were shut, if you can prove that at the same time he was in heaven, then were that to some purpose to prove that his body may be corporally in heaven and earth both at one time.

And yet the controversy here in this matter is, not what may be, but what is. "God can do many things, which he neither doth nor will do." And to us his will, in things that appear not to our senses, is not known but by his word. Christ's body may be as well in the bread and wine, as in the door and stone; and yet it may be also in the door and stone, and not in the bread and wine.

But if we will stretch out our faith no further than God's word doth lead us, neither is Christ's body corporally present in one proper place with the bread and wine, nor was also with the stone or door. For the scripture saith in no place, that the body of Christ was in the door, or in the stone that covered the sepulchre; but it saith plainly that "an angel came down from heaven, and removed away the stone from the sepulchre; and the women that came to see the sepulchre found the stone removed away." And although the gospel say, that "Christ came into the house when the door was shut," yet it saith not that "Christ's body was within the door, so that the door and it occupied both but one place." 404.
Matt. xxviii.
Mark xvi.
John xx.

But peradventure M. Smith will ask me this question: "How could Christ come into the house, the door being shut, except he came through the door, and that his body must be in the door?" To your wise question, M. Smith, I will answer by another question: Could not Christ come as well into the house, when the door was shut, as the apostles could go out of prison, the door being shut? Could not God work this thing, except the apostles must go through the door, and occupy the same place that the door did? Or could not Christ do so much for his own self, as he did for his apostles? Acts v.

But M. Smith is so blind in his own phantasies, that he seeth not how much his own examples make against himself. For if it be like in the sacrament as it was in the stone and door, and Christ's body was in one proper place with the body and substance of the stone and door, then must Christ's body in the sacrament be in one proper place with the body and substance of bread and wine. And so he must then confess that there is no transubstantiation.

Then from the door and sepulchre, D. Smith cometh to the revelations of Peter and Paul, which saw Christ (as he saith) bodily upon earth after his ascension: which declareth, that "although Christ departed hence at the time of his ascension into heaven, and there sitteth at the right hand of his Father, yet he may be also here in the blessed sacrament of the altar." I am not so ignorant but I know that Christ appeared to St Paul, and said to him, "Saul, Saul, why dost thou persecute me?" But St Augustine saith that "Christ at his ascension spake the last words that ever he spake upon earth. And yet we find that Christ speaketh," saith he, "but in heaven and from heaven, and not upon earth. For he spake to Paul from above, The appearing of Christ in his ascension.

Acts ix.
St Augustine.

saying: 'Saul, Saul, why dost thou persecute me?' The head was in heaven, and yet he said, 'Why dost thou persecute me?' because he persecuted his members upon earth[1]."

And if this please not Master Smith, let him blame St Augustine and not me, for I feign not this myself, but only allege St Augustine.

Matt. iii. & xvii. Acts vii.

And as the Father spake from heaven, when he said, "This is my beloved Son, in whom I am pleased;" and also St Stephen "saw Christ sitting in heaven at his Father's right hand:" even so meant St Augustine, that St Paul and all other that have seen and heard Christ speak since his ascension, have seen and heard him from heaven.

The church.

Now, when this papist, going forward with his works, seeth his building so feeble and weak that it is not able to stand, he returneth to his chief foundation, the church and councils general, willing all men to stay thereupon, and to leave disputing and reasoning. And chiefly he shoareth up his house with the council Lateranense, "whereat," saith he, "were thirteen hundred fathers and fifteen." But he telleth not that eight hundred of them were monks, friars, and canons, the bishop of Rome's own dear dearlings and chief champions, called together in his name, and not in Christ's. From which brood of vipers and serpents what thing can be thought to come, but that did proceed from the spirit of their most holy father that first begat them, that is to say, from the spirit of antichrist?

And yet I know this to be true, that Christ is present with his holy church, which is his holy elected people, and shall be with them to the world's end, leading and governing them with his holy Spirit, and teaching them all truth necessary for their salvation. And whensoever any such be gathered together in his name, there is he among them, and he shall not suffer the gates of hell to prevail against them. For although he may suffer them by their own frailness for a time to err, fall, and to die, yet finally neither Satan, hell, sin, nor eternal death, shall prevail against them.

But it is not so of the church and see of Rome, which accounteth itself to be the holy catholic church, and the bishop thereof to be most holy of all other. For many years ago Satan hath so prevailed against that stinking whore of Babylon, that her abominations be known to the whole world, the name of God is by her blasphemed, and of the cup of her drunkenness and poison have all nations tasted.

The true faith was in the church from the beginning, and was not taught first by Berengarius.

AFTER this cometh Smith to Berengarius, Almericus, Carolostadius, Œcolampadius, and Zuinglius, affirming that the church ever sithens Christ's time, a thousand five hundred years and more, hath believed that Christ is bodily in the sacrament, and never taught otherwise until Berengarius came, about a thousand years after Christ, whom the other followed.

But in my book I have proved by God's word and the old ancient authors, that Christ is not in the sacrament corporally, but is bodily and corporally ascended into heaven, and there shall remain unto the world's end.

And so the true church of Christ ever believed from the beginning without repugnance, until Satan was let loose, and antichrist came with his papists, which feigned a new and false doctrine, contrary to God's word and the true catholic doctrine.

And this true faith God preserveth in his holy church still, and will do unto the world's end, maugre the wicked antichrist and all the gates of hell. And Almighty God from time to time hath strengthened many holy martyrs, for this faith to suffer death by antichrist and the great harlot of Babylon, who hath embrued her hands, and is made drunken with the blood of martyrs. Whose blood God will revenge

---

[[1] Adscensurus enim dixit verba novissima, post ipsa verba non est locutus in terra. Adscensurum caput in cœlum, commendavit membra in terra; et discessit. Jam non invenis loqui Christum in terra: invenis illum loqui, sed de cœlo. Et de ipso cœlo quare? quia membra calcabantur in terra. Persecutori enim Saulo dixit desuper, Saule, Saule, quid me persequeris?—August. Op. Par. 1679-1700. In Epist. Johan. cap. v. Tractat. x. 9. Tom. III. Pars ii. col. 899.]

at length, although in the mean time he suffer the patience and faith of his holy saints to be tried.

ALL the rest of his preface containeth nothing else but the authority of the church, which, Smith saith, "cannot wholly err:" and he so setteth forth and extolleth the same, that he preferreth it above God's word, affirming not only that it is the pillar of truth, and no less to be believed than holy scripture, but also that we should not believe holy scripture but for it. So that he maketh the word of men equal, or above the word of God.

What church it is that cannot err.

And truth it is indeed that the church doth never wholly err; for ever in most darkness God shineth unto his elect, and in the midst of all iniquity he governeth them so with his holy word and Spirit, that the gates of hell prevail not against them. And these be known to him, although the world many times know them not, but hath them in derision and hatred, as it had Christ and his apostles. Nevertheless at the last day they shall be known to all the whole world, when the wicked shall wonder at their felicity, and say: "These be they whom we sometime had in derision and mocked. We fools thought their lives very madness, and their end to be without honour. But now, lo, how they be accounted among the children of God, and their portion is among the saints. Therefore we have erred from the way of truth, the light of righteousness hath not shined unto us, we have wearied ourselves in the way of wickedness and destruction."

406.

Wisd. v.

But this holy church is so unknown to the world, that no man can discern it, but God alone, who only searcheth the hearts of all men, and knoweth his true children from other that be but bastards.

Psal. vii.
2 Tim. ii.

This church is "the pillar of truth," because it resteth upon God's word, which is the true and sure foundation, and will not suffer it to err and fall. But as for the open known church, and the outward face thereof, it is not the pillar of truth, otherwise than that it is, as it were, a register or treasury to keep the books of God's holy will and testament, and to rest only thereupon, as St Augustine and Tertullian mean in the place by M. Smith alleged.

1 Tim. iii.

And as the register keepeth all men's wills, and yet hath none authority to add, change, or take away anything, nor yet to expound the wills further than the very words of the will extend unto, (so that he hath no power over the will, but by the will;) even so hath the church no further power over the holy scripture, which containeth the will and testament of God, but only to keep it, and to see it observed and kept. For if the church proceed further to make any new articles of the faith, besides the scripture, or contrary to the scripture, or direct not the form of life according to the same; then it is not the pillar of truth, nor the church of Christ, but the synagogue of Satan, and the temple of antichrist, which both erreth itself, and bringeth into error as many as do follow it.

And the holy church of Christ is but a small herd or flock, in comparison to the great multitude of them that follow Satan and antichrist; as Christ himself saith, and the word of God, and the course of the world from the beginning until this day hath declared.

Luke xii.

For, from the creation of the world until Noe's flood, what was then the open face of the church? How many godly men were in those thousand and six hundred years and more? Did not iniquity begin at Cain to rule the world, and so increased more and more, that at the length God could no longer suffer, but drowned all the world for sin, except eight persons, which only were left upon the whole earth?

Gen. vii.

And after the world was purged by the flood, fell it not by and by to the former iniquity again? so that within few years after, Abraham could find no place where he might be suffered to worship the true living God, but that God appointed him a strange country, almost clearly desolate and unhabited, where he and a few other, contrary to the usage of the world, honoured one God.

Gen. xii.

And after the great benefits of God shewed unto his people of Israel, and the law also given unto them, whereby they were taught to know him, and honour him, yet how many times did they fall from him! Did they not, from time to time, make them new Gods, and worship them? Was not the open face of the church so miserably deformed, not only in the wilderness, and in the time of the Judges, but also in time of the Kings, that after the division of the kingdom, amongst all the kings of Judah there was but only three in whose times the true religion was restored, and among all the kings of Israel not so much as one? Were not all that time the true priests of God a few in number? Did not all the rest maintain idolatry and all abominations in groves and mountains, worshipping Baal and other false Gods? And did they not murder and slay all the true prophets that taught them to worship the true God? Insomuch that Elias the prophet, knowing no more of all the whole people that followed the right trade, but himself alone, made his complaint unto Almighty God, saying: "O Lord, they have slain thy prophets, and overthrown thine altars, and there is no more left but I alone, and yet they lie in wait to slay me also." So that although Almighty God suffered them in their captivity at Babylon no more but seventy years, yet he suffered them in their idolatry, following their own ways and inventions, many hundred years, the mercy of God being so great, that their punishment was short and small, in respect of their long and grievous offences. And at the time of Christ's coming, the high priests came to offices by such fraud, simony, murder, and poisoning, that the like hath not been often read nor heard of, except only at Rome.

And when Christ was come, what godly religion found he? what Annases and Caiphases! what hypocrisy, superstition, and abomination before God, although to men's eyes things appeared holy and godly! Was not then Christ alone and his apostles, with other that believed his doctrine, the holy and true church? Although they were not so taken, but for heretics, seditious persons, and blasphemers of God, and were extremely persecuted and put to villanous death, by such as accounted themselves and were taken for the church, which fulfilled the measure of their fathers that persecuted the prophets: upon whom came all the righteous blood that was shed upon the earth, from the blood of just Abel, unto the blood of Zachary, the son of Barachi, whom they slew between the temple and the altar.

And how many persons remained constantly in the true lively faith, at the time of Christ's passion? I think, Master Smith will say, but a very few, seeing that Peter denied Christ his master three times, and all his apostles fled away, and one for haste without his clothes.

What wonder is it then, that the open church is now of late years fallen into many errors and corruption, and the holy church of Christ is secret and unknown? seeing that Satan, these five hundred years, hath been let loose, and antichrist reigneth, spoiling and devouring the simple flock of Christ. But as Almighty God said unto Elias, "I have reserved and kept for mine own self seven thousand, which never bowed their knee to Baal;" so it is at this present. For although Almighty God hath suffered these four or five hundred years the open face of his church to be ugly deformed, and shamefully defiled by the sects of the papists, (which is so manifest that now all the world knoweth it,) yet hath God of his manifold mercy ever preserved a good number, secret to himself, in his true religion, although antichrist hath bathed himself in the blood of no small number of them.

And although the papists have led innumerable people out of the right way, yet the church is to be followed: but the church of Christ, not of antichrist; the church that concerning the faith containeth itself within God's word, not that deviseth daily new articles contrary to God's word; the church, that by the true interpretation of scripture and good example gathereth people unto Christ, not that by wrasting of the scripture and evil example of corrupt living draweth them away from Christ. And now, forasmuch as the wicked church of Rome, counterfeiting the church of our Saviour Christ, hath in this matter of the sacrament of the blessed body and blood of our Saviour Christ varied from the pure and holy church in the apostles' time, and many hundred years after, (as in my book I have plainly declared and manifestly proved,) it is an easy matter to discern, which church is to be followed. And I cannot but marvel that Smith allegeth for him *Vincentius Lirenensis*, who, contrary to Doctor

Smith, teacheth plainly that "the canon of the bible is perfect and sufficient of itself for the truth of the catholic faith;" and that "the whole church cannot make one article of the faith, although it may be taken as a necessary witness for the receiving and establishing of the same, with these three conditions, that the thing which we would establish thereby hath been believed in all places, ever, and of all men[1]." Which the papistical doctrine in this matter hath not been, but came from Rome since Berengarius' time by Nicolas the second, Innocentius the third, and other of their sort: whereas the doctrine, which I have set forth, came from Christ and his apostles, and was of all men every where with one consent taught and believed, as my book sheweth plainly, until the papists did transform and transubstantiate the chief articles of our christian faith.

Thus is an answer made unto the false calumniations of Smith in the preface of his book, or rather unto his whole book, which is so full of bragging, boasting, slandering, misreporting, wrangling, wrasting, false construing, and lying, that, those taken out of the book, there is nothing worthy in the whole book to be answered. Nevertheless in answering to the late bishop of Winchester's book, I shall fully answer also D. Smith in all points that require answer. And so with one answer shall I despatch them both. And in some places where one of them varieth from another, as they do in many great matters, and in the chief and principal points, I shall set them together *Bithum cum Bacchio, et Esernium cum Pacidiano*[2], to try which of them is more stout and valiant to overthrow the other.

⁋ Here endeth the answer unto the Preface of Master Smith's book, which he wrote against the defence of the true and catholic doctrine of the Sacrament of the body and blood of our Saviour CHRIST.

[[1] Cum sit perfectus scripturarum canon, sibique ad omnia satis superque sufficiat, quid opus est ut ei ecclesiasticæ intelligentiæ jungatur auctoritas?—Vincent. Lirin. Commonit. I. cap. ii. Bibl. Vet. Patr. Colon. 1618. Tom. V. Pars ii. p. 238.]

In ipsa item catholica ecclesia magnopere curandum est, ut id teneamus, quod ubique, quod semper, quod ab omnibus creditum est.—Ibid. cap. iii.]

Plerumque propter intelligentiæ lucem, non novum fidei sensum novæ appellationis proprietate signando.—Ibid. cap. xxxii. p. 246.]

[[2] Two pairs of gladiators, equally matched.—Horace, Sat. I. vii. 20. Cicero, Tusc. Qu. IV. 21.]

MATTERS WHEREIN THE BISHOP OF WINCHESTER VARIED FROM OTHER PAPISTS[1].

OTHER say, that the body of Christ is made of bread. He saith, that the body of Christ is not made of bread, nor was never so taught, but is made present of bread, p. 72, line 14, and p. 178, line 10.

He saith that Christ made the demonstration of the bread, and called it his body, when he said, "This is my body," p. 257, line 27. And in the Devil's Sophistry, fol. 27. Other say contrary. And Smith, fol. 53.

He saith, that "this is my body," is as much to say as, "this is made my body." And so he taketh *est* for *fit*, p. 295, line 35. Other say, that *est* is taken there *substantive*, that is to say, only for "is," and not for "is made." Marcus Antonius, fol. 171, facie 2, consideratione 6.

He saith, that Christ is present in the sacrament after the same manner that he is in heaven, p. 141, line 6. Other say contrary, that he is in heaven after the manner of quantity, and that he is not so in the sacrament.

He saith, that where the body of Christ is, there is whole Christ, God and man; and that when we speak of Christ's body, we must understand a true body, which hath both form and quantity, p. 71, line 37. Smith saith, that Christ's body in the sacrament hath not his proper form and quantity, fol. 106.

He saith, we believe simply, that Christ's body is naturally and corporally in the sacrament, without drawing away his accidences or adding, p. 353, line 1. Smith saith, we say that Christ's body is in the sacrament against nature with all his qualities and accidents, fol. 105.

He saith, that God's works be all seemliness without confusion, although he cannot locally distinct Christ's head from his foot, nor his legs from his arms, p. 70, line 27[2]. Other say, that Christ's head and foot and other parts be not indeed locally distinct in the sacrament, but be so confounded, that wheresoever one is, there be all the rest.

They teach that the body of Christ is made of bread: he saith, it was never so taught, p. 79, line 6, &c.

He saith, that Christ's body is in the sacrament sensibly, naturally, carnally, and corporally, p. 159, line 9, &c. Other say contrary, Smith, fol. 39.

Other say, that Christ's feet in the sacrament be there, where his head is: he saith, that whosoever say so may be called mad, p. 61, line 34.

He saith, that Christ's body is in the sacrament naturally and carnally, p. 156, line 6.

Other say, that corporally Christ goeth into the mouth or stomach, and no further. He saith contrary, p. 52, line 36.

He saith, that Christ dwelleth corporally in him that receiveth the sacrament worthily, so long as he remaineth a member of Christ, p. 53, line 1, p. 56, line 31, &c. Other say contrary, but that Christ flieth up into heaven so soon as the bread is chawed in the mouth or changed in the stomach, Smith, fol. 64, p. 65, line 2, and 25.

He saith, that no creature can eat the body of Christ, but only man, p. 66, line 30. Other say clean contrary.

He saith, that an unrepentant sinner receiving the sacrament hath not Christ's body nor spirit within him, p. 225, line 36. Smith saith, that he hath Christ's body and spirit within him, fol. 136.

[1 This table of matters, &c. is only appended to the 1580 ed. As the paging of that edition has been carefully noted in the margin of this re-print, it has been thought advisable to give it as it stands in the original copy. The reader will find no difficulty in referring to the passages according to the direction of archbishop Cranmer.]

[2 Thus in ed. 1580. It is, however, a misprint, and should be p. 61, line 30.]

He saith, that of the figure it may not be said, "Adore it, worship it," and that is not to be adored, which the bodily eye seeth, p. 178, line 40, p. 239, line 32. Marcus Antonius, fol. 176, fac. 2. Smith saith contrary, fol. 145, fac. 2.

He saith, that reason will agree with the doctrine of transubstantiation well enough, p. 264, line 47. Smith saith, that transubstantiation is against reason and natural operation, fol. 60.

Other say, that worms in the sacrament be gendered of accidences. He saith, that they be wrong borne in hand to say so, p. 355, line 3.

He saith, that the accidences of bread and wine do mould, sour, and wax vinegar, p. 265, line 11, and 355, line 8. And Marcus, fol. 168, fac. 1. Smith saith thus: "I say that the consecrated wine turneth not into vinegar, nor the consecrated bread mouldeth nor engendereth worms, nor is burned, nor receiveth into it any poison, as long as Christ's body and blood are under the forms of them which do abide there, so long as the natural qualities and properties of bread and wine tarry there in their natural disposition and condition, that the bread and wine might be naturally there, if they had not been changed into Christ's body and blood; and also as long as the host and consecrated wine are apt to be received of man, and no longer; but go and depart thence by God's power, as it pleaseth him. And then a new substance is made of God, which turneth into vinegar, engendereth worms, mouldeth, is burned, feedeth men and mice, receiveth poison," &c. fol. 64 and 105.

He saith, "Every yea containeth a nay in it naturally, so as whosoever saith, This is bread, saith it is no wine. For in the rule of common reason, the grant of one substance is the denial of another: and therefore reason hath these conclusions throughly, whatsoever is bread is no wine, whatsoever is wine is no milk, &c. So Christ saying, 'This is my body,' saith it [is] no bread," p. 256, line 38, and p. 265, line 5. Smith saith, a boy "which hath only learned the sophistry," will not dispute so fondly, fol. 77.

Other say, that the mass is a sacrifice satisfactory by devotion of the priest, and not by the thing that is offered. He saith otherwise, p. 80, line 43.

He saith, that the only immolation of Christ in himself upon the altar of the cross is the very satisfactory sacrifice for the reconciliation of mankind to the favour of God, p. 437, line 1, 2, and 31. Smith saith, "What is it to offer Christ's body and blood at mass, to purchase thereby everlasting life, if it be not the mass to be a sacrifice to pacify God's wrath for sin, and to obtain his mercy?" Smith, fol. 24, 148, 164. Priests do offer for our salvation to get heaven and to avoid hell, fol. eodem.

MATTERS WHEREIN THE BISHOP VARIED FROM HIMSELF.

"The body of Christ in the sacrament is not made of bread, but is made present of bread," p. 79, line 6, &c., and p. 202, line 40, &c.

"Of bread is made the body of Christ," p. 344, line 8.

"The catholic faith hath from the beginning confessed truly Christ's intent to make bread his body," p. 26, line 40. "Christ gave that he made of bread," p. 257, line 50. "And of many breads is made one body of Christ," p. 144, line 23. "And faith sheweth me that bread is the body of Christ, that is to say, made the body of Christ," p. 295, line 30.

"Christ spake plainly, 'This is my body,' making demonstration of the bread, when he said, 'This is my body,'" in the Devil's Sophistry, fol. 27. "I will pass over the phantasies of them who wrote the principal chief text, 'This is my body,' from consecration of the sacrament, to the demonstration of Christ's body, &c." in the devilish Devil's Sophistry, fol. 70.

"The demonstration 'this,' may be referred to the invisible substance," p. 106, line 42. "The 'is,' was of his body and blood, and not of the bread and wine," p. 251, line 8.

Illis verbis, "*Hoc est corpus meum,*" *substantia corporis significatur, nec de pane quicquam intelligitur, quum corpus de substantia sua, non aliena prædicetur, fol.* 24, *fac.* 2. *Mar. Ant. Constant.*

"When Christ said 'This is my body,' the truth of the literal sense hath an absurdity in carnal reason," p. 138, line 19.

"What can be more evidently spoken of the presence of Christ's natural body and blood in the most blessed sacrament of the altar, than is in these words, 'This is my body'?" in the Devil's Sophistry, fol. 5.

"Where the body of Christ is, there is whole Christ, God and man. And when we speak of Christ's body, we must understand a true body, which hath both form and quantity," p. 71, line 47. "And he is present in the sacrament as he is in heaven," p. 141, line 6, &c.

"We believe simply the substance of Christ's body to be in the sacrament without drawing away of accidents, or adding," p. 353, line 1.

"Christ is not present in the sacrament after the manner of quantity, but under the form and quantity of bread and wine," p. 71, line 50, p. 90, line 43.

"In such as receive the sacrament worthily Christ dwelleth in them corporally, and naturally, and carnally," p. 166, line 19, and p. 173, line 54, and p. 191, line 47.

"The manner of Christ's being in the sacrament is not corporal, not carnal, not natural, not sensible, not perceptible, but only spiritual," p. 159, line 17, and p. 197, line 32.

"We receive Christ in the sacrament of his flesh and blood, if we receive him worthily," p. 167, line 9, and p. 174, line 1.

"When an unrepentant sinner receiveth the sacrament, he hath not Christ's body within him," p. 225, line 43.

"He that eateth verily the flesh of Christ, is by nature in Christ, and Christ is naturally in him," p. 17, line 38, &c.

"An evil man in the sacrament receiveth indeed Christ's very body," p. eadem, line 7.

"Evil men eat verily the flesh of Christ," p. 225, line 47.

"Christ giveth us to be eaten the same flesh that he took of the virgin," p. 241, line 27.

"We receive not in the sacrament Christ's body that was crucified," p. 243, line 16.

"Saint Augustine's rule, *De Doctrina Christiana*, pertaineth not to Christ's supper," p. 117, line 21.

"The sixth of John speaketh not of any promise made to the eating of a token of Christ's flesh," p. 4, line 40.

"St Augustine meaneth of the sacrament," p. 119, line 24.

"The sixth of John must needs be understand of corporal and sacramental eating," p. 17, line 48.

"Reason in place of service (as being inferior to faith) will agree with the doctrine of transubstantiation well enough," p. 265, line 1. "And as reason, received into faith's service, doth not strive with transubstantiation, but agreeth well with it; so man's senses be no such direct adversaries to transubstantiation, as a matter whereof they can no skill, for the senses can no skill of substances," p. 271, line 24, &c.

"Thine eyes say, there is but bread and wine: thy taste saith the same. Thy feeling and smelling agree fully with them." "Hereunto is added the carnal man's understanding, which because it taketh the beginning of the senses, proceedeth in reasoning sensually," in the Devil's Sophistry, fol. 6. "The church hath not forborne to preach the truth, to the confusion of man's senses and understanding," fol. 15.

"It is called bread because of the outward visible matter," p. [257.]

"When it is called bread, it is meant Christ the spiritual bread," p. 284, line 25.

"The fraction is in the outward sign, and not in the body of Christ," p. 144, line 39, and p. 348, line 21. And in the Devil's Sophistry, fol. 17.

"That which broken is the body of Christ," p. 348, line 18.

"The inward nature of the bread is the substance," p. 286, line 23.

"Substance signifieth the outward nature," p. 359, line 22.

"The substances of bread and wine be visible creatures," p. 285, line 48, and p. 286, line 44.

"Accidents be the visible natures and visible elements," p. 363, line 39.

"Christ is our satisfaction wholly and fully, and hath paid our whole debt to God the Father, for the appeasing of his wrath against us," p. 81, line 39.

"The act of the priest done according to God's commandment must needs be propitiatory, and ought to be trusted on to have a propitiatory effect," p. 437, line 13[1].

"The demonstration 'this,' may be referred to the invisible substance," p. 106, line 44. "The 'is,' was of his body and blood, and not of the bread and wine," p. 251, line 8. Contrary in this, Devil's Sophistry, 27, 70. Contrary in the Devil's Sophistry, 5.

"When Christ said, 'This is my body,' the truth of the literal sense hath an absurdity in carnal reason," p. 138, line 19. "And it is a singular miracle of Christ understanded as the plain words signify in their proper sense," ibidem, line 21.

"The sacrifice of our Saviour Christ was never reiterate," p. 368, line 46.

"Priests do sacrifice Christ," p. 381, line 42, &c. "And the catholic doctrine teacheth the daily sacrifice to be the same in essence that was offered on the cross," p. 436, line 11. 413.

"The Nestorians granted both the Godhead and manhood always to be in Christ continually," p. 309, line 18.

"The Nestorians denied Christ conceived God or born God, but that he was afterward God, as a man that is not born a bishop is after made a bishop. So the Nestorians said, that the Godhead was an accession after by merit, and that he was conceived only man," p. 309, line 12.

"Christ useth us as familiarly as he did his apostles," p. 83, line 54.

"Christ is not to be said conversant in earth," p. 101, line 16.

CONCESSA.

"On what part thou, reader, seest craft, sleight, shift, obliquity, or in any one point an open manifest lie, there thou mayest consider, whatsoever pretence be made of truth, yet the victory of truth not to be there intended," p. 12, line 19.

"When Christ had taught of the eating of himself, being the bread descended from heaven, declaring that eating to signify believing, then he entered to speak of the giving of his flesh to be eaten," p. 27, line 7.

"Christ must be spiritually in a man before he receive the sacrament, or he cannot receive the sacrament worthily," p. 48, line 46, and p. 140, line ultima, and p. 172, line 28, and 181, line 28.

"How Christ is present," p. 61, line 10, and p. 71, line 41, and p. 90, line 44, p. 57, line 17, and p. 197, line 30.

"By faith we know only the being present of Christ's most precious body, not the manner thereof," p. 61, line 43.

"What we speak of Christ's body, we must understand a true body, which hath both form and quantity," p. 71, line 34.

"Although Christ's body have all those truths of form and quantity, yet it is not present after the manner of quantity," p. 71, line 37.

"For the worthy receiving of Christ we must come endued with Christ, and clothed with him seemly in that garment," p. 92, line 31.

"Really, that is to say, verily, truly, and in deed, not in phantasy or imagination," p. 140, line 21.

"All the old prayers and ceremonies sound as the people did communicate with the priest," p. 145, line 9[2].

"'Really' and 'sensibly' the old authors in syllables used not, for so much as I have read; but 'corporally' and 'naturally' they used, speaking of this sacrament," p. 155, line 13.

"Christ may be called sensibly present," p. 155, line 26, and p. 159, line 10.

"By faith Christ dwelleth in us spiritually," p. 158, line 16.

"Our perfect unity with Christ is to have his flesh in us, and to have Christ Falsa.

[[1] Thus in ed. 1580. It should be p. 387, line 13.]   [[2] Ibid. It should be line 13.]

bodily and naturally dwelling in us by his manhood," p. 166, line 30, &c., and p. 17, line 34.

"Evil men eat the body of Christ, but sacramentally, and not spiritually," p. 222, line 47.

414.

"Christ's flesh in the sacrament is given us to eat spiritually, and therefore there may be no such imaginations to eat Christ's body carnally, after the manner he walked here, nor drink his blood as it was shed upon the cross; but spiritually understood it giveth life," p. 241, line 18.

"To eat only in faith is specially to remember Christ's flesh as it was visibly crucified," p. 243, line 28.

"We eat not Christ as he sitteth in heaven reigning," p. 243, line 32.

Falsum. "The word 'transubstantiation' was first spoken of by public authority in a general council, where the bishop of Rome was present," p. 250, line 28.

"The word 'nature' signifieth both the substance and also property of the nature," p. 291, line 27.

Falsum. "The sensible thing after the capacity of common understanding is called 'substance,' but the inward nature in learning is properly called 'substance,'" p. 338, line 31.

Falsum. "In common bread the substance is not broken at all," p. 257, line 32.

"The catholic doctrine teacheth not the daily sacrifice of Christ's most precious body and blood to be an iteration of the once perfected sacrifice on the cross, but a sacrifice that representeth the sacrifice, and sheweth it also before the faithful eyes," p. 386, line 20.

"The effect of the offering on the cross is given and dispensed in the sacrament of baptism," p. 386, line 30.

"By virtue of the same offering on the cross, such as fall be relieved in the sacrament of penance," p. eadem, line 16.

"The daily sacrifice of the church is also propitiatory, but not in that degree of propitiation, as for redemption, regeneration, or remission of deadly sin, (which was once purchased, and by force thereof is in the sacraments ministered,) but for the increase of God's favour, the mitigation of God's displeasure provoked by our infirmities, the subduing of temptations, and the perfection of virtue in us," p. 387, line 15, &c.

"All good works, good thoughts, and good meditations, may be called sacrifices, and sacrifices propitiatory also, forasmuch as in their degree God accepteth and taketh them through the effect and strength of the very sacrifice of Christ's death," p. eadem, line 19, &c.

"To call the daily offering a sacrifice satisfactory, must have an understanding that signifieth not the action of the priest, but the presence of Christ's most precious body and blood, the very sacrifice of the world once perfectly offered being propitiatory and satisfactory for all the world," p. eadem, line 43[1], &c.

"Or else the word 'satisfactory' must have a signification and meaning that declareth the acception of the thing done, and not the proper countervail of the action. For otherwise the daily sacrifice in respect of the action of the priest cannot be called satisfactory, and it is a word indeed that soundeth not well so placed, although it might be saved by a signification," p. eadem, line 46[2], &c.

"I think this speech to be frequented, that the only immolation of Christ in himself upon the altar of the cross is the very satisfactory sacrifice for the reconciliation of mankind to the favour of God," p. eadem, line 50[3].

"I have not read the daily sacrifice of Christ's most precious body to be called a 'sacrifice satisfactory,'" p. eadem, line 52[4].

"But this speech hath indeed been used, 'that the priest should sing satisfactory,' which they understood of the satisfaction of the priest's duty to attend the prayer he was required to make," ibid. line 53[5].

"In the sacrifice of the church Christ's death is not iterated, but a memory daily renewed of that death, so as Christ's offering on the cross once done and consummate is now only remembered," p. 391, line 5.

"The same body is offered daily on the altar that was once offered upon the cross,

[[1] It should be line 32.]   [[2] line 35.]   [[3] line 43.]   [[4] line 47.]   [[5] line 48.]

but the same manner of offering is not daily that was on the altar of the cross. For the daily offering is without blood-shedding, and is termed so, to signify that blood-shedding once done to be sufficient," p. eadem, line 8, &c.

MATTERS WHEREIN THE BISHOP VARIETH FROM THE TRUTH AND FROM THE OLD AUTHORS OF THE CHURCH.

"If we eat not the flesh of the Son of man, we have not life in us, because Christ hath ordered the sacrament," &c. p. 17, line 12.

"When Christ said, 'Take eat, this is my body,' he fulfilled that which he promised in the sixth of John, that he would give his flesh for the life of the world," p. 27, line 28. Mar. Ant. fol. 168. _{Nota.}

"When Christ said, 'the flesh profiteth nothing,' he spake not of his flesh as it is united unto his divinity," p. 27, line 53, and p. 329, line 24.

"God in baptism giveth only the Spirit of Christ, and in the sacrament of the altar the very body and blood of Christ," p. 34, line 44.

"Unworthy receivers of the sacrament receive Christ's body with mouth only, the worthy receivers both with mouth and heart," p. 54, line 47, &c. *Concessum.*

"We must believe Christ's words to be most perfectly true according to the truth of the letter, where no absurdity in scripture driveth us from it, howsoever it seem repugnant to reason," p. 62, line 20. *Concessum.*

"The fathers did eat Christ's body, and drink his blood in truth of promise, not in truth of presence," p. 74, line 23, &c. *Concessum.*

"The fathers did eat Christ spiritually, but they did not eat his body present spiritually and sacramentally," p. eadem, line 26. *Sacramenta in signis fuerunt diversa, si in re paria.*

"Their sacraments were figures of the things, but ours contain the very things," ibid., line 27.

"Albeit in a sense to the learned men it may be verified, that the fathers did eat the body of Christ and drink his blood, yet there is no such form of words in scripture. And it is more agreeable to the simplicity of scripture to say, the fathers before Christ's nativity did not eat the body and drink the blood of Christ," p. 78, line 28.

"And although St Paul in the tenth to the Corinthians be so understood of some, that the fathers should eat and drink the spiritual meat, and drink that we do, yet to that understanding all do not agree," ibid., line 34, &c.

"Their sacraments contained the promise of that which in our sacraments is given," ibid., line 36.

"And although that willing obedience was ended and perfected upon the cross, (to the which it continued from the beginning,) yet as in the sacrifice of Abraham the earnest will and offering was accompted for the offering in deed, so the declaration of Christ's will in his last supper was an offering of himself to God the Father," p. 82, line 2, &c.

"In that mystery he declared his body and blood to be the very sacrifice of the world, by the same will that he said his body should be betrayed for us," ibid., line 12. _{416.}

"As Christ offered himself upon the cross in the execution of his will, so he offered himself in his supper in declaration of his will," p. 82, line 13, &c.

"Christ's body in the supper or communion is represented unto us as a sacrifice propitiatory for all the sins of the world, and it is the only sacrifice of the church, and the pure and clean sacrifice whereof Malachi spake," p. 84, line 4; p. 88, line ultima, &c.

"As Christ declareth in the supper himself an offering and sacrifice for our sin, offering himself to his Father as our mediator; so the church at the same supper, in their offering of lauds and thanks, join themselves with their head Christ, representing and offering him," p. 89, line 10.

"The sun-beams be of the same substance with the sun," p. 92, line 5.

"We have in earth the substantial presence of the Son," ibid., line 7.

"When Christ said, 'This is my body,' this word 'This,' may be referred to the invisible substance," p. 106, line 44.

"To eat Christ's flesh and drink his blood is of itself a proper speech," p. 112, line 35; "carnally," ibid., line 50; "with teeth and mouth," p. 112, line 8, and p. 34, line 38.

"To eat Christ's body carnally may have a good signification," p. 113, line 4.

"Origen doth not mean to destroy the truth of the letter in these words of Christ, 'Except you eat the flesh of the Son of man,'" &c. p. 114, line 40.

"St Augustine taketh the same for a figurative speech, because it seemeth to command in the letter, carnally understood, an heinous and wicked thing, to eat the flesh of a man," p. 116, line 40.

"The said words of Christ, 'Except you eat,' &c. is to the unfaithful a figure, but to the faithful they be no figure, but spirit and life," ibid. line 48.

"The fathers called it a figure, by the name of a figure reverently to cover so great a secresy, apt only to be understand of men believing," p. 117, line 3.

"That is spiritual understanding, to do as is commanded," ibid. line 13.

"This word 'represent' in St Hierome and Tertullian signifieth a true real exhibition," p. 120, line 27, and p. 128, line 11.

Nota.   "The word *eucharistia* cannot well be Englished," p. 161.

"In God's word, and in baptism, we be made participant of Christ's passion by his Spirit, but in the Lord's supper we be made participant of his Godhead by his humanity exhibited to us for food. So as in this mystery we receive him as man and God, and in the other by mean of his Godhead we be participant of the effect of his passion suffered in his manhood. In this sacrament we receive a pledge of the regeneration of our flesh to be in the general resurrection spiritual with our soul: in baptism we have been made spiritual by regeneration of the soul," p. 158, line 45, &c.

417. Concessum etiam.   "In baptism Christ's humanity is not really present, though the virtue and effect of his most precious blood be there," p. 159, line 4.

"The manner of Christ's being in the sacrament is only spiritual," ibid., line 16.

"To understand Christ's words spiritually is to understand them as the Spirit of God hath taught the church," ibid., line 34.

"Our perfect unity with Christ is to have his flesh in us, and to have Christ bodily and naturally dwelling in us by his manhood," p. 166, line 32.

Concessum.   "By Christ's flesh in the sacrament we be naturally in him, and he is naturally in us," ibid., lin. 45, &c.

Concessum.   "Christ dwelleth naturally in us, and we be corporally in him," ibid., line 35.

Concessum etiam.   "Christ's flesh is very spiritual and in a spiritual manner delivered unto us," p. 167, line 12, and p. 243, line 11, and p. 243, line 28, and p. 295, line 33.

Concessum.   "Christ dwelleth in us naturally for the natural communication of our body and his," p. 167, line 19.

"When Christ united himself unto us as man, (which he doth giving his body in the sacrament to such as worthily receive it,) then he dwelleth in them corporally," p. 172, line 27.

"In baptism man's soul is regenerate in the virtue and effect of Christ's passion and blood, Christ's Godhead present there without the real presence of his humanity," p. 181, line 16, &c.

"In baptism our unity with Christ is wrought without the real presence of Christ's humanity, only in the virtue and effect of Christ's blood," p. 181, lines 2 and 16.

"In baptism our soul is regenerate and made spiritual, but not our body in deed, but in hope only," p. 181, line 6.

"In baptism we be united to Christ's manhood by his divinity, but in the Lord's supper we be in nature united to Christ as man, and by his glorified flesh made partakers also of his divinity," p. 181, line 8.

Concessum.   "Christ's body and flesh is a spiritual body and flesh, and is present in the sacrament after a spiritual manner, and is spiritually received," p. eadem, 26, [p.] 351, line 19.

"In this sacrament Christ's humanity and Godhead is really present, and in baptism his Godhead with the effectual virtue of his blood (in which we be washed), not requiring any real presence thereof," p. 191, line 35.

"Spirit and life may fall upon naughty men, although for their malice it tarrieth not," p. 211, line 17.

"Christ's words were not figurative, but true and proper, when he said, 'This is my body'," p. 9, line 1, p. 257, line 1 and 14. Marcus Antonius, fol. 24, fa. 1.

"All the naming of bread by Christ and St Paul and all other must be understand before sanctification, and not after," p. 258, line 15.

"When St Paul said, 'We be partakers of one bread,' he speaketh not of material bread," p. 258, line 7.

"No man knoweth the difference between the substance of bread, cheese, and ale," p. 271, line 39; p. 272, line 23; p. 339, line 33.

"The accidents of bread may be called the visible part of bread, the outward kind and form of bread, the appearance of bread, a true sensible part of bread, bread, the nature of bread, the matter of bread, the visible matter of bread, not that it is properly bread, but after the common speech and capacity of men," p. 272, line 16, and p. 273, line 25, p. 283, line 11, and p. 289, line 31, and 290, line 7, and 292, line 16, and p. 396, line 43, &c., and p. 305, line 44, &c., and p. 243, line 45, p. 359, line 22.

"The accidents of bread do corrupt, putrify, and nourish," p. 273, line 30, p. 290, line 7, and p. 296, line 48, and p. 358, line 28.

"The glorified body of Christ is of the own nature neither visible nor palpable," p. 273, line 40.

"In baptism the whole man is not regenerated, but the soul," p. 286, line 10.

"The soul only of man is the substance of man," ibidem.

"The soul only is made the Son of God," p. 286, line 23.

"It is called meat because of the outward visible matter," p. 290, line 9.

"As really and as truly as the soul of man is present in the body, so really and so truly is the body of Christ present in the sacrament," p. 296, line 5, and p. 396, line 15.

"The sacrifice of the church is perfected before the perception," p. 396, line 32.

"In the sacrament, being a mystery ordered to feed us, is the truth of the presence of the natures earthly and celestial. The visible matter of the earthly creature in his property and nature for the use of signification is necessarily required," p. 310, lines 44, 48.

"This saying of Gelasius, 'The substance or nature of bread and wine cease not to be there still,' may be verified in the last, and nature he taketh for the propriety," p. 310, line 50.

"Theodorete's saying, that 'the substance of bread remaineth,' seemeth to speak of substance after the common capacity, and not as it is truly in learning understanded, an inward, invisible, and not palpable nature," p. 321, line 2.

"Christ in his supper fulfilled this promise, *Panis quem ego dabo*," &c., p. 329, line 25.

"Accidents in common understanding be called substances," p. 339, line 31.

"In common bread the substance is not broken at all," ibidem, line 39.

"Accidents be broken without substance," p. 339, line 6, &c.

"All alteration is in accidents and the corruption of accidents in the generation of new accidents," p. 355, line 4.

"Substance in Theodorete signifieth the outward visible nature, that is to say, accidents," p. 359, line 20.

"One thing is but one substance, saving only in the person of Christ," p. 359, line 41.

"Baptism is not[1] wondered at, how the Holy Ghost is there; but the wonder in this sacrament is specially directed to the work of God in the visible creatures, how

---

[[1] This word "not" is not found in the passage referred to.]

they be changed into the body and blood of Christ, which is wrought before we receive the sacrament," p. 366, line 45.

419. "Priests do offer daily Christ's flesh and blood," p. 384, line 26.

"Christ offered himself in his supper," p. eadem, line 27.

"Otherwise than Christ did cannot be now done," p. 384, line 28.

"The daily offering by the priest is daily offered for sin, because we daily fall," p. eadem, line 30.

"That is done in the altar is a sacrifice, and the same that is offered once, and daily to be the same," [ibid.]

"Visible priests, ministers to our invisible priest, offer the daily sacrifice in Christ's church," p. 392[1], line 46.

"The body and blood of Christ is properly sacrificed by the priests, and is there offered for the effect of increase of life in us, as it was offered upon the cross to achieve life unto us," p. 390, line 46, &c.

"The same body is offered daily upon the altar that was once offered upon the cross, but the same manner of offering is not daily that was on the altar of the cross; for the daily offering is without bloodshedding, and is termed so to signify that bloodshedding once done to be sufficient," p. 391, line 7, &c.

"The sacrifice of the church is propitiatory," p. 391, line 8.

"The sacrifice of the church is a sacrifice giving life," ibidem, line 8.

"Our sacrifice of laud and thanksgiving cannot be said a pure and clean sacrifice to fulfil the prophecy of Malachi," ibidem, line 10.

[1 Thus in the original text; the paging being by mistake printed 392 instead of 389.]

DISPUTATIONS

AT

OXFORD.

¶ HOW THOMAS CRANMER, ARCHBISHOP, BISHOP RIDLEY, AND M. LATIMER, WERE SENT DOWN TO OXFORD TO DISPUTE, WITH THE ORDER AND MANNER, AND ALL OTHER CIRCUMSTANCES, UNTO THE SAID DISPUTATION, AND ALSO TO THEIR CONDEMNATION, APPERTAINING.

[This Disputation is found in Foxe's Acts and Monuments, and is extracted from Ed. 1583, p. 1428, et sqq.]

About the tenth of April, Cranmer archbishop of Canterbury, Ridley bishop of London, and Hugh Latimer bishop also sometime of Worcester, were conveyed as prisoners from the Tower to Windsor; and after, from thence to the university of Oxford, there to dispute with the divines and learned men of both the universities, Oxford and Cambridge, about the presence, substance, and sacrifice of the sacrament. The names of the university doctors and graduates appointed to dispute against them were these: of Oxford, Doctor Weston, prolocutor, Doctor Tresham, Doctor Cole, Doctor Oglethorpe, Doctor Pie, Master Harpsfield, Master Fecknam: of Cambridge, Doctor Yong, vice-chancellor, Doctor Glin, Doctor Seaton, Doctor Watson, Doctor Sedgewicke, Doctor Atkinson, &c. The articles or questions whereupon they should dispute were these: *[marginal: Foxe, Acts, &c. Ed. 1583. p. 1428. April 10. D. Cranmer, D. Ridley, and M. Latimer sent down to Oxford to dispute. The university doctors appointed to dispute against the archbishop and his fellows.]*

I. Whether the natural body of Christ be really in the sacrament after the words spoken by the priest, or no?

II. Whether in the sacrament, after the words of consecration, any other substance do remain, than the substance of the body and blood of Christ?

III. Whether in the mass be a sacrifice propitiatory for the sins of the quick and the dead?

* * * * * * *

On Saturday, being the 14th of April, at eight of the clock, the aforesaid vice-chancellor of Cambridge, with the other doctors of the same university, repaired to Lincoln college again, and found the prolocutor above in a chapel, with the company of the house, singing Requiem mass, and tarried there until the end. Then they, consulting all together in the master's lodging, about nine of the clock came all to the university church called St Mary's; and there, after a short consultation in a chapel, the vice-chancellor, the prolocutor, &c. of Oxford, caused the vice-chancellor of Cambridge, and the rest of the doctors of that university, to send for their scarlet robes, brought from Cambridge; save that doctors Seton and Watson borrowed of the Oxford men. And in this time, the regents in the congregation-house had granted all the Cambridge doctors their graces, to be incorporate there; and so they went up, and were admitted immediately. Doctor Oglethorpe presenting them, and the proctor reading the statute, and giving them their oaths. *[marginal: The doctors in their scarlet robes.]*

That done, they came all into the quire, and there held the convocation of the university. They had mass of the Holy Ghost solemnly sung in prick-song by the quire-men of Christ's church. But first, the cause of the convocation was opened in English, partly by the vice-chancellor, and partly by the prolocutor, declaring that they were sent by the queen, and wherefore they were sent; and caused master Say, the register, openly to read the commission. That done, the vice-chancellor read Cambridge letters openly, and then concluded, that three notaries, master Say for the convocation, a beadle of Cambridge for that university, and one master White for Oxford, should testify of their doing; and then willed the said notaries to provide parchment, that the whole *[marginal: Mass in pike-sauce—prick-song, I would say. The causes of their assembly declared. Cambridge letters read. Three notaries assigned.]*

Subscribing to the articles.	assembly might subscribe to the articles, save those that had subscribed before in the convocation-house at London and Cambridge. And so the vice-chancellor began first; after him the rest of the Oxford men, as many as could in the mass-time.
Procession in Oxford. The array of the solemn procession.	The mass being done, they went in procession: first, the quire in their surplices followed the cross; then the first-year regents and proctors; then the doctors of law, and their beadle before them; then the doctors of divinity of both universities intermingled, the divinity and art beadles going before them, the vice-chancellor and prolocutor going together: after them bachelors of divinity, *regentes, et non regentes,* in their array; and last of all, the bachelors of law and art; after whom followed a great company of scholars and students not graduate. And thus they proceeded through the street to Christ's church; and there the quire sang a psalm, and after that a collect was read. This done, departed the commissioners, doctors, and many others to Lincoln college, where they dined with the mayor of the town, one alderman, four beadles, master Say, and the Cambridge notary. After dinner they went all again to St Mary's
Another consultation of the doctors and priests.	church; and there, after a short consultation in a chapel, all the commissioners came into the quire, and sat all on seats before the altar, to the number of thirty-three persons; and first they sent to the mayor, that he should bring in doctor Cranmer, which within a while was brought to them with a great number of rusty-bill-men.
Archbishop Cranmer brought before the doctors and high priests, at St Mary's church. The reverend humility and behaviour of the archbishop before them.	Thus the reverend archbishop, when he was brought before the commissioners, reverenced them with much humility, and stood with his staff in his hand, who, notwithstanding having a stool offered him, refused to sit. Then the prolocutor, sitting in the midst in a scarlet gown, began with a short preface or oration in praise of unity, and especially in the church of Christ; declaring withal his bringing up, and taking degrees in Cambridge, and also how he was promoted by king Henry, and had been his councillor, and a catholic man, one of the same unity, and a member thereof in times past; but of late years did separate and cut off himself from it, by teaching and setting forth of erroneous doctrine, making every year a new faith: and therefore it pleased the queen's grace to send them of the convocation, and other learned men, to bring him to this unity again, if it might be. Then shewed he him, how they of the convocation-house had agreed upon certain articles, whereunto they willed him to subscribe.
The answer of the archbishop to D. Weston.	The archbishop answered to the preface very wittily, modestly, and learnedly, shewing that he was very glad of an unity, forasmuch as it was *conservatrix omnium rerum publicarum, tam ethnicorum quam Christianorum;* i.e., "the preserver of all commonwealths, as well of the heathen as of the Christians:" and so he dilated the matter with one or two stories of the Romans' commonwealth. Which thing when he had done, he said that he was very glad to come to an unity, so that it were in Christ, and agreeable to his holy word.
	When he had thus spoken his full mind, the prolocutor caused the articles[1] to be read unto him, and asked if he would grant and subscribe unto them. Then the bishop of Canterbury did read them over three or four times, and touching the first article, he asked what they meant by these terms, *Verum et naturale;* i.e. "true and natural." "Do you not mean," saith he, "*corpus organicum;* i.e. a sensible body?" Some answered, *Idem quod natum est ex virgine;* i.e. "the same that was born of the virgin;" and so confusedly some said one thing, some another. Then the bishop of
The articles denied by the archbishop.	Canterbury denied it utterly: and when he had looked upon the other two, he said they were all false, and against God's holy word; and therefore he would not agree, he said, in that unity with them. Which done, the prolocutor, first willing him to write his
Scarborough warning given to Cranmer to dispute.	mind of them that night, said moreover, that he should dispute in them, and caused a copy of the articles to be delivered him, assigning him to answer thereunto on Monday next; and so charged the mayor with him again, to be had to Bocardo, where he was

[1 The following are the articles:

1. In sacramento altaris, virtute verbi Domini a sacerdote prolati, præsens est realiter sub speciebus panis et vini naturale corpus Christi conceptum de virgine Maria: item, naturalis ejusdem sanguis.

2. Post consecrationem non remanet substantia panis et vini, neque alia ulla substantia, nisi substantia Christi, Dei et hominis.

3. In missa est vivificum ecclesiæ sacrificium pro peccatis tam vivorum quam mortuorum propitiabile. Harl. MSS. 3642.]

kept before; offering moreover unto him to name what books he would occupy, and should have them brought unto him. The archbishop was greatly commended of every body for his modesty; insomuch that some masters of art were seen to weep for him, which in judgment were contrary to him.

* * * * * * *

On Sunday after Master Harpsfield preached at St Mary's, the university church, at nine of the clock, where were divers of the doctors of the university in their robes, and placed accordingly. After the sermon they went all to dinner to Magdalene college, and there had a great dinner. They supped at Lincoln college with the prolocutor, whither Doctor Cranmer sent answer of his mind upon the articles in writing.

On Monday, being the 16th of April, Master Say and Master White, notaries, went about in the morning to the colleges, to get subscriptions to the articles. And about eight of the clock the prolocutor with all the doctors and the vice-chancellor met together at Exeter college, and so they went into the schools; and when the vice-chancellor, the prolocutor, and doctors were placed, and four appointed to be *exceptores argumentorum* set at a table in the midst, and four notaries sitting with them, D. Cranmer came to the answerer's place, the mayor and aldermen sitting by him: and so the Disputation began to be set a-work by the prolocutor with a short *præludium*. Doctor Chedsey began to argue first, and ere he left, the prolocutor divers times, Doctors Tresham, Oglethorpe, Marshall, vice-chancellor, Pie, Cole, and Harpsfield did interrupt and press him with their arguments; so that every man said somewhat, as the prolocutor would suffer, disorderly, sometime in Latin, sometime in English; so that three hours of the time was spent ere the vice-chancellor of Cambridge began, who also was interrupted as before. He began with three or four questions subtilly. Here the beadles had provided drink, and offered the answerer; but he refused with thanks.

April 16. Subscription.

Four Exceptores argumentorum. Cranmer set in the respondent's place. D. Cranmer closed in by the mayor and aldermen for running away. Disputers against the archbishop.

The archbishop offered drink.

* * * * * *

Thus the Disputation continued until almost two of the clock, with this applausion *audientium*, 'Vicit veritas.' Then were all the arguments, written by the four appointed, delivered into the hand of Master Say, register. And as for the prisoner, he was had away by the mayor; and the doctors dined together at the University college.

D. Cranmer after disputation returned again to Bocardo.

And thus much concerning the general order and manner of these Disputations, with such circumstances as there happened, and things there done, as well before the Disputation, and in the preparation thereof, as also in the time of their disputing. Now followeth to infer and declare the orations, arguments, and answers, used and brought forth in the said Disputations on both parts.

THE ARGUMENTS, REASONS, AND ALLEGATIONS USED IN THIS DISPUTATION.

On Monday, Doctor Weston, with all the residue of the visitors, censors, and opponents, repairing to the Divinity school, each one installed themselves in their places. Doctor Cranmer with a rout of rusty bills was brought thither also, and set in the answerer's place, with the mayor and aldermen sitting by him: where Doctor Weston, prolocutor, apparelled in a scarlet gown, after the custom of the university, began the Disputation with this oration. His words in Latin, as he spake them, were these:

April 16.

Convenistis hodie, fratres, profligaturi detestandam illam hæresin de veritate corporis Christi in sacramento, &c.: that is, "Ye are assembled hither, brethren, this day, to confound the detestable heresy of the verity of the body of Christ in the sacrament," &c. At which words, thus pronounced of the prolocutor unawares, divers of the learned men there present, considering and well weighing the words by him uttered, burst out into a great laughter, as though even in the entrance of the disputations he had bewrayed himself and his religion, that termed the opinion of the verity of Christ's body in the sacrament a "detestable heresy." The rest of his oration tended all to

D. Weston speaketh truer than he wist.

this effect, that it was not lawful by God's word to call these questions into controversy: for such as doubted of the words of Christ, might well be thought to doubt both of the truth and power of God. Whereunto Doctor Cranmer, desiring licence, answered in this wise.

D. Cranmer's answer to the preface.

"We are assembled," saith he, "to discuss these doubtful controversies, and to lay them open before the eyes of the world; whereof ye think it unlawful to dispute. It is indeed no reason," saith he, "that we should dispute of that which is determined upon before the truth be tried. But if these questions be not called into controversy, surely mine answer is looked for in vain." This was the sum and effect of his answer; and this done he prepared himself to disputations.

D. Chedsey.

Then Chedsey, the first opponent, began in this wise to dispute.

"Reverend Master Doctor, these three conclusions are put forth unto us at this present to dispute upon:

Articles.

1. In the sacrament of the altar is the natural body of Christ conceived of the virgin Mary, and also his blood, present really under the forms of bread and wine, by virtue of God's word pronounced by the priest.

2. There remaineth no substance of bread and wine after the consecration, nor any other substance but the substance of [Christ,][1] God and man.

3. The lively sacrifice of the church is in the mass, propitiatory as well for the quick as the dead.

These be the conclusions propounded, whereupon this our present controversy doth rest. Now, to the end we might not doubt how you take the same, you have already given up unto us your opinion thereof. I term it your opinion, in that it disagreeth from the catholic. Wherefore thus I argue:

Argument.

Your opinion differeth from the scripture:

Ergo, You are deceived.

Cranmer:—I deny the antecedent.

Chedsey:—Christ, when he instituted his last supper, spake to his disciples, "Take, eat; this is my body which shall be given for you:"

But his true body was given for us:

Ergo, His true body is in the sacrament.

The right form of this argument is thus to be framed.

Da- The same which was given for us, is in the sacrament:
ri- But his true body was given for us:
i. *Ergo,* His true body is in the sacrament.

Answer.

How Christ's body is present in the sacrament.

Cranmer:—His true body is truly present to them that truly receive him; but spiritually. And so is it taken after a spiritual sort. For when he said, "This is my body," it is all one as if he had said, This is the breaking of my body; this is the shedding of my blood: as oft as you shall do this, it shall put you in remembrance of the breaking of my body, and the shedding of my blood; that as truly as you receive this sacrament, so truly shall you receive the benefit promised by receiving the same worthily.

Argument of the authority of the church.

Chedsey:—Your opinion differeth from the church, which saith, that the true body is in the sacrament:

Ergo, Your opinion therein is false.

Answer.

Cranmer:—I say and agree with the church, that the body of Christ is in the sacrament effectually, because the passion of Christ is effectual.

Chedsey:—Christ, when he spake these words, "This is my body," spake of the substance, but not of the effect.

Christ's body effectually, not substantially, in the sacrament.

Cranmer:—I grant he spake of the substance, and not of the effect, after a sort: and yet it is most true, that the body of Christ is effectually in the sacrament. But I deny that he is there truly present in bread, or that under the bread in his organical body. And because it should be too tedious, he said, to make discourse of the whole, he delivered up there his opinion thereof to D. Weston, written at large, with answers to every one of their three propositions; which he desired D. Weston,

---

[¹ See the article in Latin, p. 382, note 2.]

sitting there on high, to read openly to the people; which he promised to do. But it was not the first promise that such papists have broken.

Papists false of promise.

The copy of this writing, although it were not there read, yet the contents thereof here we have drawn out as followeth.

AN EXPLICATION OF CRANMER UPON THE AFORESAID CONCLUSIONS, EXHIBITED IN WRITING[2].

Cranmer:—In the assertions of the church and of religion, trifling and new-fangled novelties of words, so much as may be, are to be eschewed, whereof riseth nothing but contention and brawling about words; and we must follow, so much as we may, the manner of speaking of the scripture.

The contents of Cranmer's explication given up in writing.

In the first conclusion, if ye understand by this word "really," *re ipsa*, i. e. "in very deed and effectually," so Christ, by the grace and efficacy of his passion, is in deed and truly present to all his true and holy members.

How Christ is really present.

But if ye understand by this word "really," *corporaliter*, i. e. "corporally," so that by the body of Christ is understood a natural body and organical; so the first proposition doth vary, not only from usual speech and phrase of scripture, but also is clean contrary to the holy word of God and christian profession: when as both the scripture doth testify by these words, and also the catholic church hath professed from the beginning, Christ to have left the world, and to sit at the right hand of the Father till he come unto judgment.

Organical is called that which is a perfect body, having all the members and parts complete belonging unto the same.

And likewise I answer to the second question; that is, that it swerveth from the accustomed manner and speech of scripture.

Answer to the second conclusion.

The third conclusion, as it is intricate and wrapped in all doubtful and ambiguous words, and differing also much from the true speech of the scripture, so, as the words thereof seem to import in open sense, it is most contumelious against our only Lord and Saviour Christ Jesus, and a violating of his precious blood, which upon the altar of the cross is the only sacrifice and oblation for the sins of all mankind.

Answer to the third conclusion.

The third conclusion contumelious against Christ.

Chedsey:—By this your interpretation which you have made upon the first conclusion, this I understand; the body of Christ to be in the sacrament only by the way of participation, insomuch as we communicating thereof, do participate the grace of Christ; so that you mean hereby only the effect thereof. But our conclusion standeth upon the substance, and not the efficacy only, which shall appear by the testimony both of scriptures and of all the fathers a thousand years after Christ.

And first, to begin with the scripture, let us consider what is written in Matt. xxvi. Mark xiv. Luke xxii. and 1 Cor. xi. Matthew saith, "As they sat at supper, Jesus took bread," &c. In Mark there is the same sense, although not the same words; who also for one part of the sacrament speaketh more plainly, "Jesus taking bread," &c. After the same sense also writeth Luke xxii. "And when Jesus had taken bread," &c. "In the mouth of two or three witnesses," saith the scripture,

Matt. xxvi.

Mark xiv.

Luke xxii.

[2 *Doctor Cranmerus*:—"In ecclesiasticis dogmatibus immanes vocum novitates (quoad licet) fugiendæ sunt, (ex quibus oriuntur contentiones et pugnæ verborum,) et scripturæ loquendi modus maxime imitandus est.

In prima conclusione, si per verbum 'realiter' intelligatur 'reipsa et effectualiter,' sic Christus cum passionis suæ gratia et effectu adest omnibus vere piis et sanctis illius membris. Sin per 'realiter' intelligatur 'corporaliter,' et per 'Christi corpus' intelligatur 'corpus naturale et organicum;' prima propositio non tantum a more loquendi sacræ scripturæ aliena est, sed etiam sancto Dei verbo et professioni Christianæ plane contraria, quum Christum hoc modo mundum reliquisse ac ad dexteram Patris usque ad judicium sedere, et testantur scripturæ et ab initio professa est ecclesia catholica.

Ad secundam conclusionem similiter respondeo.

Tertia quoque conclusio prorsus aliena est et a scripturæ locutione et veritate.

Quarta demum conclusio, ut ambiguis vocibus obvoluta est et a scripturæ loquendi phrasi ac veritate longe diversa, ita, ut verba ipsa proprium sensum habent, in Servatorem nostrum unicum Jesum Christum summe contumeliosa est, et sanguinis illius pretiosissimi conculcatio; cujus effusio in sanctissima ara crucis unicum est totius mundi sacrificium et oblatio pro omnibus omnium hominum peccatis."—Harl. MSS. 3642. The Latin originals in this note and the following are supplied from Dr Jenkyns's edition.]

"standeth all truth." Here we have three witnesses together, that Christ said that to be his body, which was given for many; and that to be his blood, which should be shed for many; whereby is declared the substance, and not only the efficacy of his body. *Ergo*, it is not true that you say there to be, not the substance of his body, but the efficacy alone thereof.

Substance and efficacy both granted in the sacrament.

Cranmer:—Thus you gather upon mine answer, as though I did mean of the efficacy, and not of the substance of the body; but I mean of them both, as well of the efficacy as of the substance. And forsomuch as all things come not readily to memory, to a man that shall speak extempore, therefore, for the more ample and fuller answer in this matter, this writing here I do exhibit.

AN EXPLICATION EXHIBITED BY CRANMER[1].

Another explication for answer, exhibited in writing by the Archbishop.

Our Lord and Saviour Jesus Christ, at the time of his maundy, preparing himself to die for our cause, that he might redeem us from eternal death, to forgive us all our sins, and to cancel out the handwriting that was against us; that we through ungrateful oblivion should not forget his death, therefore at the time of his

---

[1 *Responsio domini Cranmeri ad articulos supra recitatos, in scriptis exhibita et per eum subscripta.*

1. Dominus et Servator noster Jesus Christus in sancta Parasceue, nostra causa obiturus, ut nos a morte redimeret æterna, condonaret omnia delicta, ac chirographum quod contra nos erat deleret, ne mortis suæ ingrati unquam obliviscerimur, perpetuam illius memoriam apud Christianos in pane et vino celebrandam pridie passionis in sacratissima sua instituebat cœna; juxta illud: "Hoc facite in mei memoriam:" et, "Quotienscunque manducabitis panem hunc et calicem bibetis, mortem Domini annunciabitis donec veniat." Atque hanc passionis suæ, id est, cæsi corporis et fusi sanguinis in pane et vino memoriam sive sacramentum omnes Christianos jussit sumere, juxta illud: "Accipite, et manducate, et bibite ex hoc omnes." Quicunque igitur propter traditionem humanam laicis sanguinis poculum denegant, palam Christo repugnant, prohibentes fieri quod Christus fieri jussit, et similes sunt Scribis illis ac Pharisæis, de quibus Dominus dicebat, "Irritum fecistis mandatum Dei propter traditionem vestram. Hypocritæ, bene prophetavit de vobis Esaias, dicens, Populus hic labiis me honorat; cor autem eorum longe est a me. Sine causa autem colunt me, docentes doctrinas mandata hominum." Panis ille sacramentalis seu mysticus, fractus et distributus juxta Christi institutionem, et vinum mysticum eodem modo haustum et acceptum, non tantum sacramenta sunt vulneratæ pro nobis carnis Christi et fusi cruoris, sed certissima sunt nobis sacramenta et quasi signacula divinarum promissionum ac donorum; ut, communionis nostræ cum Christo ac omnibus membris ejus; cœlestis nutritionis, qua alimur ad vitam æternam, æstuantisque conscientiæ sitis restinguitur; ineffabilis lætitiæ, qua fidelium corda perfunduntur, et ad omnia pietatis officia roborantur. "Unus panis," inquit Paulus, "et unum corpus multi sumus, omnes qui de uno pane et de uno calice participamus." Et, "Manducate," inquit Christus, "hoc est corpus meum; bibite, hic est sanguis meus." Et, "Ego sum panis vivus qui de cœlo descendi. Qui manducat me, et ipse vivet propter me." Manent igitur in eucharistia, donec a fidelibus consumantur, verus panis verumque vinum: ut quasi signacula divinis promissionibus affixa divinorum donorum nos efficiant certiores.

Manet et Christus in illis, et illi in Christo, qui illius carnem edunt et sanguinem bibunt, sicut Christus promisit: "Qui manducat meam carnem, et bibit meum sanguinem, in me manet, et ego in eo." Manet denique et Christus in illis, qui digne externum sacramentum suscipiunt, et non discedit statim consumpto sacramento; sed continuo manet, nos pascens et nutriens, quamdiu nos illius capitis corpora manemus et membra. Nullum agnosco corpus Christi naturale, quod solum spirituale sit, intellectuale, et insensibile, quod nullis membris aut partibus sit distinctum: sed illud tantum corpus agnosco ac veneror, quod ex virgine natum est, quod pro nobis passum est, quod visibile, palpabile, ac omnibus humani ac organici corporis formis in partibus absolutum est.

2. Christus non de substantia aliqua incerta, sed de substantia certa panis, quem et manibus tenebat, et discipulorum oculis demonstrabat, dixit: "Comedite, hoc est corpus meum." Et similiter de vero vino dixit: "Hic est sanguis meus." Nimirum de pane, qui est creatura hujus conditionis quæ est secundum nos, qui ex fructibus terræ acceptus est, de multorum granorum adunitione congestus, qui ab hominibus fit, et per manus hominum ad illam visibilem speciem perducitur, qui rotundæ est figuræ sensusque omnis expers, qui corpus nutrit et confortat cor hominis; de tali, inquam, pane, non de substantia aliqua incerta et vaga, aiunt veteres Christum dixisse: "Comedite, hoc est corpus meum." Perinde ac de vino, quod est creatura vitis, fructus vitis, de botris atque acinis plurimis expressa, et lætificat cor hominis, dicebat Christus: "Bibite, hic est sanguis meus." Adeoque Christi locutionem vocant veteres figuratam, tropicam, anagogicam, allegoricam; quod ita interpretati sunt, ut quamvis panis vinique substantia maneat, et a fidelibus sumatur, Christus tamen ideo appellationem mutavit, et panem quidem carnis, vinum vero sanguinis nomine appellavit, non rei veritate, sed significante mysterio: ut non quid sint, sed quæ ostendant, consideraremus, non carnaliter, sed spiritualiter sacramenta intelligeremus, non ad visibilem sacramentorum naturam attenderemus, non humiliter ad panem et poculum intenti essemus, non putaremus nos nihil quam oculis panem et vinum videre, sed exaltatis mentibus Christi corpus et sanguinem aspiceremus fide, mente contingeremus, atque inte-

holy supper did institute a perpetual memory of this his death, to be celebrated among Christians in bread and wine; according as it is said, "Do this in remembrance of me:" and, "So often as you shall eat this bread, and drink this cup, you shall shew forth the Lord's death till he come." And this remembrance or sacrament of his holy passion, that is, of his body slain, and blood shed, he would all Christians to frequent and celebrate in bread and wine; according as he said, "Take, eat, and drink ye all of this." Therefore whosoever for man's tradition denieth the cup of Christ's blood to laymen, they manifestly repugn against Christ, forbidding that which Christ commandeth to be done, and be like to those scribes and Pharisees of whom the Lord spake, "Ye hypocrites, ye have rejected the commandments of God for your traditions. Well did Esay prophesy of you, saying, This people honoureth me with their lips, but their heart is far from me. Without cause do they worship me, teaching the doctrines and precepts of men." The sacrament and mystical bread being broken and distributed after the institution of Christ, and the mystical wine likewise being taken and received, be not only sacraments of the flesh of Christ wounded for us, and of his bloodshedding, but also be most certain sacraments to us, and, as a man would say, seals of God's promises and gifts, and also of that holy fellowship which we have with Christ and all his members. Moreover, they be to us memorials of that heavenly food and nourishment, wherewith we are nourished unto eternal life, and the thirst of our boiling conscience quenched, and, finally,

[Side notes: The final cause why the supper was ordained. Matt. xv. Luke vii. Sacraments seals of God's promise.]

---

riore homine hauriremus; ut aquilæ in hac vita facti ad ipsum cœlum sursum cordibus evolemus, ubi ad dexteram Patris resident Agnus ille, qui tollit peccata mundi, cujus amore sanamur, cujus passione in hac mensa satiamur, cujus sanguinem e divino illius latere haurientes æternum vivimus, Christique hospites effecti, ipsum in nobis veræ naturæ gratia virtuteque ac totius passionis efficacia habitantem habemus : nec minus certi efficimur, Christi carne crucifixa et fuso cruore, necessario animorum pabulo, nos spiritualiter pasci ad vitam æternam, quam cibo et potu in hac vita corpora pascuntur. Atque hujus rei μνημόσυνον, pignus, symbolum, sacramentum, signaculum nobis sunt mysticus in Christi mensa panis mysticumque vinum juxta Christi institutionem administrata et accepta. Hinc est quod Christus non dixit, "Hoc est corpus meum, edite:" sed ubi jussisset edere, postea addidit, "Hoc est corpus meum, quod pro vobis tradetur." Quod perinde est, ac si dixisset, "In edendo hoc pane, considerate illum non communem esse, sed mysticum; non aspicite quod corporeis oculis vestris proponitur, sed quid intus vos pascat. Considerate corpus meum pro vobis cruci affixum, hoc animis vestris devorate, satiemini morte mea. Hic verus est cibus, hic inebrians potus, quo vere saturati et inebriati æternum vivetis. Quæ ob oculos vobis proponuntur, panis et vinum, mei duntaxat symbola sunt; ego vero ipse æternus pastus sum. Proinde cum in mensa mea sacramenta aspicietis, non tam ad illa respicite, quam quid per ea vobis pollicear, nempe meipsum pabulum vitæ æternæ."

3. Christi unica oblatio, qua seipsum Deo Patri obtulit in mortem semel in ara crucis pro nostra redemptione, tantæ fuit efficaciæ, ut nullo alio sacrificio opus sit pro totius mundi redemptione. Sed omnia veteris legis sacrificia sustulit, id re vera præstans quod illa figurabant et promittebant. Quisquis igitur salutis suæ spem in ullo alio constituerit sacrificio, is a Christi excidit gratia, et contumeliosus est in sanctum Christi sanguinem. "Ipse enim vulneratus est propter iniquitates nostras, attritus est propter scelera nostra." "Omnes nos quasi oves erravimus, unusquisque in viam suam declinavit; et posuit Dominus in eo iniquitates omnium nostrum." "Ille enim non per sanguinem hircorum aut vitulorum, sed per proprium sanguinem introivit semel in sancta, æterna redemptione inventa." Et "in ipsum cœlum intravit, ut appareret nunc vultui Dei pro nobis, non ut sæpe offerat seipsum : alioqui oportebat eum frequenter pati : nunc autem semel ad destructionem peccati per hostiam suam apparuit. Et quemadmodum constitutum est hominibus semel mori, sic et Christus semel oblatus est." "Ille unam offerens pro peccatis hostiam in sempiternum sedet in dextra Dei." "Una enim oblatione consummavit in sempiternum sanctificatos. Ubi enim peccatorum remissio est, jam non est amplius oblatio pro peccato." Propter* hoc Christi sacrificium quisquis aliud quæsierit pro peccatis sacrificium propitians, invalidum et inefficax efficit Christi sacrificium. Si enim hoc ad remittenda peccata sufficiens est, alio non est opus; alterius enim necessitas hujus arguit infirmitatem ac insufficientiam. Faxit Deus Omnipotens ut uni Christi sacrificio vere innitamur, ac illi rursus rependamus sacrificia nostra, gratiarum actiones, laudis, confessionis nominis sui, veræ resipiscentiæ ac pœnitentiæ, beneficentiæ in proximos, aliorumque omnium pietatis officiorum. Talibus enim sacrificiis exhibebimus nos nec in Deum ingratos, nec Christi sacrificio indignos.

Ecce habetis, ex sacrarum scripturarum et veterum ecclesiæ doctorum sententia, verum et sincerum dominicæ cœnæ usum, ac veri sacrificii Christi fructum. Quæ quisquis tortis interpretationibus aut humanis traditionibus aliter quam Christus ordinavit mutare aut transubstantiare voluerit, ipse respondebit Christo in novissimo die, quando intelliget, sed sero nimis, nihil sibi cum Christi corpore esse et sanguine, sed ex æternæ vitæ cœna se æternam damnationem manducasse ac bibisse.

Thomas Cranmer.

Vide official report in the British Museum, Collier. Vol. II. No. 71. MSS. C.C.C.C. 340, p. 266, under the title "Præfatio et Protestatio Thomæ Cranmeri scripta et tradita propria manu in schola publica." Harl. MSS. 422. f. 44.]

---

* Præter, MS. C. C. C. C.

whereby the hearts of the faithful be replenished with unspeakable joy, and be corroborated and strengthened unto all works of godliness. "We are many," saith St Paul, "one bread, and one body, all we which do participate of one bread and one cup." And Christ saith, "Eat ye; this is my body:" and, "Drink ye; this is my blood:" and, "I am the living bread which came down from heaven. He that eateth me shall also live for me. Not as your fathers did eat manna in the desert, and are dead. He that eateth me shall also live for me." Thus therefore true bread and true wine remain still in the eucharist, until they be consumed of the faithful, to be signs, and as seals unto us, annexed unto God's promises, making us certain of God's gifts towards us. Also Christ remaineth in them, and they in Christ, which eat his flesh, and drink his blood, as Christ himself hath promised: "They that eat my flesh, and drink my blood, abide in me, and I in them." Moreover, he abideth also in them which worthily receiveth the outward sacrament; neither doth he depart so soon as the sacrament[1] is consumed, but continually abideth, feeding and nourishing us so long as we remain bodies of that head, and members of the same. I acknowledge not here the natural body of Christ, which is only spiritual, intelligible, and unsensible, having no distinction of members and parts in it: but that body only I acknowledge and worship, which was born of the virgin, which suffered for us, which is visible, palpable, and hath all the form and shape and parts of the true natural body of man.

2. Christ spake not these words of any uncertain substance, but of the certain substance of bread, which he then held in his hands, and shewed his disciples, when he said, "Eat ye; this is my body:" and likewise of the cup, when he said, "Drink ye; this is my blood:" meaning verily of that bread, which by nature is usual and common with us, which is taken of the fruit of the ground, compacted by the uniting of many grains together, made by man, and by man's hand brought to that visible shape, being of a round compass, and without all sense or life, which nourisheth the body, and strengtheneth the heart of man: of this same bread, I say, and not of any uncertain and wandering substance, the old fathers say that Christ spake these words, "Eat ye; this is my body." And likewise also of the wine, which is the creature and fruit of the vine, pressed out of many clusters of grapes, and maketh man's heart merry: of the very same wine, I say, Christ spake, "Drink ye; this is my blood." And so the old doctors do call this speaking of Christ tropical, figurative, anagogical, allegorical; which they do interpret after this sort, that although the substance of bread and wine do remain, and be received of the faithful, yet notwithstanding, Christ changed the appellation thereof, and called the bread by the name of his flesh, and the wine by the name of his blood, *non rei veritate, sed significante mysterio;* i. e. "not that it is so in very deed, but signified in a mystery:" so that we should consider, not what they be in their own nature, but what they import to us and signify; and should understand the sacrament, not carnally, but spiritually; and should attend, not to the visible nature of the sacraments, neither have respect only to the outward bread and cup, thinking to see there with our eyes no other things but only bread and wine; but that, lifting up our minds, we should look up to the blood of Christ with our faith, should touch him with our mind, and receive him with our inward man; and that, being like eagles in this life, we should fly up into heaven in our hearts, where that Lamb is resident at the right hand of his Father, which taketh away the sins of the world; by whose stripes we are made whole; by whose passion we are filled at his table; and whose blood we receiving out of his holy side, do live for ever; being made the guests of Christ, having him dwelling in us through the grace of his true nature, and through the virtue and efficacy of his whole passion; being no less assured and certified that we are fed spiritually unto eternal life by Christ's flesh crucified, and by his blood shed, the true food of our minds, than that our bodies be fed with meat and drink in this life: and hereof this said mystical bread on the table of Christ, and the mystical wine, being administered and received after the institution of Christ, be to us a memorial, a pledge, a token,

---

[¹ Sacraments, Ibid.]

a sacrament, and a seal. And thereof is it that Christ saith not thus, "This is my body; eat ye:" but after he had bidden them eat, then he said, "This is my body, which shall be given for you." Which is to mean, as though he should say, 'In eating of this bread, consider you that this bread is no common thing, but a mystical matter; neither do you attend that which is set before your bodily eyes, but what feedeth you within. Consider and behold my body crucified for you; that eat and digest in your minds. Chaw you upon my passion, be fed with my death. This is the true meat, this is the drink that moisteneth, wherewith you being truly fed and inebriate shall live for ever. The bread and the wine which be set before your[2] eyes are only declarations of me, but I myself am the eternal food. Wherefore, whensoever at this my table you shall behold the sacraments, have not regard so much to them, as consider ye what I promise to you by them, which is myself, to be meat for you of eternal life.' *What is meant by eating the mystical bread. What the crucified body of Christ doth to our souls.*

3. The only oblation of Christ (wherewith he offered himself to God the Father once to death upon the altar of the cross for our redemption) was of such efficacy, that there is no more need of any sacrifice for the redemption of the whole world; but all the sacrifice of the old law he took away, performing that in very deed, which they did signify and promise. Whosoever therefore shall fix the hope of his salvation in any other sacrifice, he falleth from the grace of Christ, and is contumelious against the blood of Christ. For "he was wounded for our transgressions, and was broken for our iniquities. All we like sheep have wandered astray; every man hath turned after his own way; and the Lord hath laid all our iniquities upon him." "For he hath entered once for all into the holy place, by the blood, not of goats or calves, but by his own blood, finding eternal redemption;" and "hath entered into heaven, to appear now in the sight of God for us; not to offer himself oftentimes, (for so should he have suffered many times:) but now hath he appeared once to put away sin through his own oblation. And as it is appointed to all men once to die, so also Christ once was offered:" "who offering up one oblation for sins, sitteth now for ever on the right hand of God. For by one oblation hath he made perfect for ever those that be sanctified." For "where is remission of sins, there is now no more oblation for sin," but this only sacrifice of Christ. Whosoever shall seek any other sacrifice propitiatory for sin, maketh the sacrifice of Christ of no validity, force, or efficacy. For if it be sufficient to remit sins, what need is there of any other? for the necessity of another argueth and declareth this to be insufficient. Almighty God grant that we may truly lean to one sacrifice of Christ, and that we to him again may repay our sacrifices of thanksgiving, of praise, of confessing his name, of true amendment, of repentance, of mercifulness towards our neighbours, and of all other good works of charity! For by such sacrifices we shall declare ourselves neither ungrateful to God, nor altogether unworthy of this holy sacrifice of Christ. *The sacrifice of Christ's body once, sufficient for all. Isai. liii. Heb. ix. Heb. ix. Heb. x. No sacrifice now for sin but one. Christ sacrificed once for sin; we sacrifice daily by thanksgiving and thankful works of charity.*

And thus you have, out of the testimonies of holy scripture and of the ancient doctors of the church, the true and sincere use of the Lord's holy supper, and the fruit of the true sacrifice of Christ: which whosoever, through captious or wrested interpretations, or by men's traditions, shall go about, otherwise than Christ ordained them, to alter or transubstantiate, he shall answer to Christ in the latter day, when he shall understand, (but then too late,) that he hath no participation with the body and blood of Christ, but that out of the supper of eternal life he hath eaten and drunken eternal damnation to himself.

Weston :—Because we will not consume and spend the time in waste, this your writing which you exhibit hereafter shall be read in his place. In the mean season let us now fall to the arguments.

Chedsey :—The scriptures in divers places do affirm, that Christ gave his natural body, Matt. xxvi. Mark xiv. Luke xxii.: *Argument.*

Ergo, I do conclude that the natural body is in the sacrament.

Cranmer :—To your argument I answer, If you understand by the body natural, *Answer.*

[2 Foxe, ed. 1583, has *our*, which is undoubtedly a misprint.]

organicum, that is, having such proportion and members as he had living here, then I answer negatively.

Furthermore, concerning the evangelists, thus I say and grant, that Christ took bread, and called it his body.

Chedsey:—The text of the scripture maketh against you; for the circumstance thereto annexed doth teach us, not only there to be the body, but also teacheth what manner of body it is, and saith, "The same body which shall be given."

<small>Argument.</small>

 Ba- That thing is here contained that is given for us:
 ro- But the substance of bread is not given for us:
 co. *Ergo,* The substance of bread is not here contained.

<small>Answer. This word "contained" distinguished. The body of Christ contained not really, but sacramentally. Christ saith not, "This is my body which is here contained;" but, "This is my body which shall be given for you."</small>

Cranmer:—I understand not yet what you mean by this word "contained:" if ye mean really, then I deny your major.

Chedsey:—The major is the text of scripture. He that denieth the major, denieth the scripture: for the scripture saith, "This is my body which shall be given for you."

Cranmer:—I grant he said it was his body that should be given; but he said it was not his body which is here contained, but "the body," saith he, "that shall be given for you." As though he should say, "This bread is the breaking of my body, and this cup is the shedding of my blood." What will ye say then? Is the bread the breaking [of his body,]¹ and the cup the shedding of the blood, really? If you so say, I deny it.

Chedsey:—If you ask what is the thing therein contained; because his apostles should not doubt what body it was that should be given, he saith, "This is my body which shall be given for you," and "my blood which shall be shed for many." *Ergo,* here is the same substance of the body, which the day after was given, and the same blood which was shed. And here I urge the scripture, which teacheth that it was no phantastical, no feigned, no spiritual body, nor body in faith, but the substance of the body.

Cranmer:—You must prove that it is contained; but Christ said not, "which is contained." He gave bread, and called that his body. I stick not in the words of the scripture, but in your word, which is feigned and imagined of yourself.

Chedsey:—When Christ took bread and brake it, what gave he?

Cranmer:—He gave bread: the bread sacramentally, and his body spiritually; and the bread there he called his body.

Chedsey:—This answer is against the scripture, which saith, that he gave his body.

Cranmer:—It did signify that which they did eat.

Chedsey:—They did not eat the body as the Capernaites did understand it, but the selfsame body which was given for the sins of the world. *Ergo,* It was his body which should be given, and his blood which should be shed.

¶ In some other copies I find this argument to be made by Chedsey:

<small>Argument.</small>

 Ba- The same body is in the sacrament, which was given for us on the cross:
 ro- But bread was not given on the cross for us:
 co. *Ergo,* Bread is not given in the sacrament.

<small>Answer.</small>

Cranmer:—I deny the major, which is, that the same natural body is given in the sacrament, which was given on the cross; except you understand it spiritually.

And after, he denied also the argument as utterly naught, as he well might do, the major in the second figure being not universal.

When M. Chedsey had put forth this argument, and prosecuted the same, and doctor Cranmer answered as before is shewed, doctor Oglethorpe, one of those doctors which the prolocutor called *Censores,* (belike to be arbiters, to order the disputations,) said on this wise.

<small>D. Oglethorpe breaketh Priscian's head, and speaketh false Latin.</small>

D. Oglethorpe:—You come in still with one evasion or starting-hole to flee to. He urgeth the scriptures, saying that Christ gave his very body. You say that he gave his body in bread. *Quomodo prædicatur corpus? qualis est corpus? qualis est prædicatio? panis est corpus.*

<small>Cranmer answereth to Oglethorpe.</small>

Cranmer:—You should say, *Quale corpus.* I answer to the question; it is the

---

[¹ These words are not in Foxe, ed. 1583.]

same body which was born of the virgin, was crucified, ascended; but tropically, and by a figure. And so I say, *Panis est corpus* is a figurative speech, speaking sacramentally; for it is a sacrament of his body.

Oglethorpe:—This word "body," being *prædicatum*, doth signify "substance:"
But *substantia* is not predicated denominatively:
Ergo, It is an essential predication; and so it is his true body, and not the figure of his body.

Dr Cranmer might have found fault with this argument, as well as with his Latin, being made in no mode or figure.

Cranmer:—*Substantia* may be predicated denominatively in an allegory, or in a metaphor, or in a figurative locution.

Oglethorpe:—It is not a likely thing that Christ hath less care for his spouse, the church, than a wise householder hath for his family in making his will or testament.

Cranmer:—Your reason is drawn out of the affairs of men, and not taken out of the holy scriptures.

Oglethorpe:—But no householder maketh his testament after that sort.

Cranmer:—Yes, there are many that so do. For what matter is it, so it be understood and perceived? I say, Christ did use figurative speech in no place more than in his sacraments, and specially in this his supper.

Tropes may be used in men's testaments. Why not?

Oglethorpe:—No man of purpose doth use tropes in his testament; for if he do, he deceiveth them that he comprehendeth in his testament: therefore Christ useth none here.

Cranmer:—Yes, he may use them well enough. You know not what tropes are.

Oglethorpe:—The good man of the house hath a respect, that his heirs after his departure may live in quiet, and without brabbling:
But they cannot be in quiet, if he do use tropes:
Therefore, I say, he useth no tropes.

Cranmer:—I deny your minor.

Weston:—Augustine, in his book entitled *De Unitate Ecclesiæ*[2], the tenth chapter, hath these words following:

Quid hoc est, rogo? Cum verba novissima hominis morientis audiantur ituri ad inferos, nemo eum dicit esse mentitum; et illius non judicatur hæres, qui forte ea contempserit. Quomodo ergo effugiemus iram Dei, si vel non credentes, vel contemnentes, expulerimus verba novissima, et unici Filii Dei et Domini nostri Salvatoris, et ituri in cœlum, et inde prospecturi, quis ea negligat, quis non observet, et inde venturi ut de omnibus judicet?[3]

A place of Augustine recited by the prolocutor. De Unitate Ecclesiæ.

That is to say:

"What a thing is this, I pray you? When the last words of one lying upon his death-bed are heard, which is ready to go to his grave, no man saith that he hath made a lie; and he is not accounted his heir which regardeth not those words. How shall we then escape God's wrath, if either not believing, or not regarding, we shall reject the last words both of the only Son of God and also of our Lord and Saviour, both ascending into heaven, and beholding from thence who despiseth, and who observeth them not; and shall come from thence to judge all men?"

The argument is thus formed:

Bar- Whosoever saith that the testator did lie, is a wicked heir:
ba- But whosoever saith that Christ spake by figures, saith that he did lie:
ra. *Ergo*, Whosoever saith that Christ here spake by figures, is a wicked heir.

Argument.

Cranmer:—I deny the minor: as who say it is necessary that he which useth to speak by tropes and figures should lie in so doing?

Answer.

Oglethorpe:—Your judgment is disagreeing with all churches.

[2 This authority is stated in the Cambridge manuscript to have been alleged by Oglethorpe: vide Jenkyns's Cranmer, Vol. IV. p. 24.]

[3 The passage will be found in cap. xi, (and not x, as quoted by Weston,) of the letter de Unitate Ecclesiæ, (i.e. contra Donatistas Epistola, in the Benedictine arrangement,) Tom. VII. p. 148. Ed. Paris. 1635.]

Cranmer:—Nay, I disagree with the papistical church.

Oglethorpe:—This you do through the ignorance of logic.

Cranmer:—Nay, this you say through the ignorance of the doctors.

Weston:—I will go plainly to work by scriptures. What took he?

Cranmer:—Bread.

Weston:—What gave he?

Cranmer:—Bread.

Weston:—What brake he?

Cranmer:—Bread.

Weston:—What did they eat?

Cranmer:—Bread.

Weston:—He gave bread; therefore he gave not his body. He gave not his body; therefore it is not his body verily, in deed and in truth.

Cranmer:—I deny the argument[1].

Cole:—This argument holdeth *a disparatis*. It is bread; *ergo*, it is not the body: and it is such an argument or reason as cannot be dissolved.

Cranmer:—The like argument may be made: he is a rock; *ergo*, he is not Christ.

Cole:—It is not like.

Weston:—He gave not his body indeed; *ergo*, it was not his body indeed.

Cranmer:—He gave his death, his passion, and the sacrament of his passion. And in very deed, setting the figure aside, formally it is not his body.

Weston:—Why? then the scripture is false.

Cranmer:—Nay, the scripture is most true.

Weston:—This saith Chrysostom, Homil. LXI. ad Populum Antiochenum. *Necessarium est, dilectissimi, mysteriorum dicere miraculum, quid tandem sit, et quare sit datum, et quæ rei utilitas*[2], &c.

That is to say:

"Needful it is, dear friends, to tell you what the miracle of the mysteries is, and wherefore it is given, and what profit there is of the thing. We are one body, and members of his flesh and of his bones. We that be in the mystery, let us follow that thing which was spoken. Wherefore, that we may become this thing, not only by love, but also that we may become one with that flesh indeed, that is brought to pass by this food which he gave unto us, minding to shew his great good-will

---

[1 "According to the Cambridge manuscript, the Disputation up to this point was conducted in Latin. Cole first spoke English, and the dialogue appears to have been carried on in that language till Chedsey resumed the Latin." Jenkyns.]

[2 Διὸ καὶ ἀναγκαῖον μαθεῖν τὸ θαῦμα τῶν μυστηρίων, τί ποτέ ἐστι, καὶ διατί ἐδόθη, καὶ τίς ἡ ὠφέλεια τοῦ πράγματος. ἓν σῶμα γινόμεθα μέλη, φησίν, ἐκ τοῦ σαρκὸς αὐτοῦ, καὶ ἐκ τῶν ὀστέων αὐτοῦ. οἱ δὲ μεμυημένοι παρακολουθείτωσαν τοῖς λεγομένοις.

"Ἵν᾽ οὖν μὴ μόνον κατὰ τὴν ἀγάπην γενώμεθα, ἀλλὰ καὶ κατ᾽ αὐτὸ τὸ πρᾶγμα, εἰς ἐκείνην ἀνακερασθῶμεν τὴν σάρκα. διὰ τῆς τροφῆς γὰρ τοῦτο γίνεται ἧς ἐχαρίσατο, βουλόμενος ἡμῖν δεῖξαι τὸν πόθον ὃν ἔχει περὶ ἡμᾶς· διὰ τοῦτο ἀνέμιξεν ἑαυτὸν ἡμῖν, καὶ ἀνέφυρε τὸ σῶμα αὐτοῦ εἰς ἡμᾶς, ἵνα ἕν τι ὑπάρξωμεν, καθάπερ σῶμα κεφαλῇ συνημμένον. τῶν γὰρ σφόδρα ποθούντων ἐστὶ τοῦτο δεῖγμα. τοῦτο γοῦν καὶ ὁ Ἰὼβ αἰνιττόμενος ἔλεγε περὶ τῶν ἑαυτοῦ οἰκετῶν, οἷς ἦν οὕτω μεθ᾽ ὑπερβολῆς ποθεινός, ὡς προσφῦναι ταῖς σαρξὶν αὐτοῦ ἐπιθυμεῖν. ἐκεῖνοι γὰρ τὸν πολὺν αὐτῶν ἐνδεικνύμενοι πόθον ὃν εἶχον· τίς ἂν δῴη ἡμῖν τῶν σαρκῶν αὐτοῦ, ἔλεγον, ἐμπλησθῆναι; διὸ δὴ καὶ ὁ Χριστὸς αὐτὸ πεποίηκεν, εἰς φιλίαν ἡμᾶς ἐνάγων μείζονα, καὶ τὸν αὐτοῦ πόθον ἐπιδεικνὺς τὸν περὶ ἡμᾶς, οὐκ ἰδεῖν αὐτὸν μόνον παρέσχε τοῖς ἐπιθυμοῦσι· ἀλλὰ καὶ ἅψασθαι, καὶ φαγεῖν, καὶ ἐμπῆξαι τοὺς ὀδόντας τῇ σαρκὶ, καὶ συμπλακῆναι, καὶ τὸν πόθον ἐμπλῆσαι πάντα. ὡς λέοντες τοίνυν πῦρ πνέοντες, οὕτως ἀπὸ τῆς τραπέζης ἀναχωρῶμεν ἐκείνης, φοβεροὶ τῷ διαβόλῳ γινόμενοι, καὶ τὴν κεφαλὴν τὴν ἡμετέραν ἐννοοῦντες, καὶ τὴν ἀγάπην ἣν περὶ ἡμᾶς ἐπεδείξατο. οἱ μὲν οὖν γεννήσαντες πολλάκις ἑτέροις τρέφειν διδόασι τὰ τεχθέντα· ἐγὼ δὲ οὐχ οὕτω, φησίν, ἀλλὰ ταῖς σαρξὶ τρέφω ταῖς ἐμαῖς· ἐμαυτὸν ὑμῖν παρατίθημι, πάντας ὑμᾶς εὐγενεῖς εἶναι βουλόμενος, καὶ χρηστὰς ὑμῖν περὶ τῶν μελλόντων ὑποτείνων ἐλπίδας. ὁ γὰρ ἐνταῦθα ὑμῖν ἐκδοὺς ἑαυτὸν πολλῷ μᾶλλον ἐν τῷ μέλλοντι. ἀδελφὸς ἠθέλησα ὑμέτερος γίνεσθαι· ἐκοινώνησα σαρκὸς καὶ αἵματος δι᾽ ὑμᾶς· πάλιν αὐτὴν ὑμῖν τὴν σάρκα καὶ τὸ αἷμα, δι᾽ ὧν συγγενὴς ἐγενόμην, ἐκδίδωμι.—Chrysost. in Joan. Hom. xlvi. (al. 45.) Tom. VIII. p. 272. Ed. Bened. Paris. 1728. It must be remembered however, that Weston did not quote from this homily on St John, but from the Hom. LXI. ad Pop. Antioch. in the Latin edition, parts of which certainly are composed of the Greek homily on John.]

that he hath toward us: and therefore he mixed himself with us, and united his own body with us, that we should be made all as one thing together, as a body joined and annexed to the head; for this is a token of most ardent and perfect love. And the same thing Job also insinuating, said of his servants, of whom he was desired above measure; insomuch that they, shewing their great desire toward him, said, 'Who shall give unto us to be filled with his flesh?' Therefore also Christ did the same, who, to induce us into a greater love toward him, and to declare his desire toward us, did not only give himself to be seen of them that would, but also to be handled and eaten, and suffered us to fasten our teeth in his flesh, and to be united together, and so to fill all our desire. Like lions therefore, as breathing fire, let us go from that table, being made terrible to the devil, remembering our Head in our mind, and his charity which he shewed unto us. For parents many times give their children to other to be fed; but I do not so, saith he, but feed you with mine own flesh, and set myself before you, desiring to make you all jolly people, and pretending to you great hope and expectation to look for things to come, who here give myself to you, but much more in the world to come. I am become your brother; I took flesh and blood for you. Again, my flesh and blood, by the which I am made your kinsman, I deliver unto you."

Thus much out of Chrysostom. Out of which words I make this argument:

The same flesh, whereby Christ is made our brother and kinsman, is given of Christ to us to be eaten: *D. Weston's argument without true form or figure.*

Christ is made our brother and kinsman by his true, natural, and organical flesh:

Ergo, His true, natural, and organical flesh is given to us to be eaten.

Cranmer:—I grant the consequence and the consequent.

Weston:—Therefore we eat it with our mouth.

Cranmer:—I deny it. We eat it through faith.

Weston:—He gave us that same flesh to eat, whereby he became our brother and kinsman: *D. Weston's argument denied: We eat the true body of Christ: Ergo, We eat it with our mouth. A figureless argument.*

But he became our brother and kinsman by his true, natural, and organical flesh:

Therefore he gave his true, natural, and organical flesh to be eaten.

Cranmer:—I grant he took and gave the same true, natural, and organical flesh wherein he suffered; and yet he feedeth spiritually, and that flesh is received spiritually.

Weston:—He gave us the same flesh which he took of the virgin: *Fallacia a dicto secundum quid ad simpliciter.*

But he took not his true flesh of the virgin spiritually, or in a figure:

Ergo, He gave his true natural flesh, not spiritually.

Cranmer:—Christ gave to us his own natural flesh, the same wherein he suffered, but feedeth us spiritually.

Weston:—Chrysostom is against you, Hom. LXXXIII. in cap. xxvi. Matt., where he saith: *Veniat tibi in mentem quo sis honore honoratus, qua mensa fruaris. Ea namque re nos alimur, quam angeli*[3], &c.   *Answer. Chrysostom alleged by Doctor Weston. Hom. lxxxiii. in 26 cap. Matt.*

That is:

"Let it come into thy remembrance, with what honour thou art honoured, and what table thou sittest at: for with the same thing we are nourished, which the

---

[3 The whole passage, as quoted in the text in several divisions, runs thus in Chrysostom: Οὐδὲ γὰρ ἤρκεσεν αὐτῷ τὸ γενέσθαι ἄνθρωπον, οὐδὲ τὸ ῥαπισθῆναι καὶ σφαγῆναι, ἀλλὰ καὶ ἀναφύρει ἑαυτὸν ἡμῖν, καὶ οὐ τῇ πίστει μόνον, ἀλλὰ καὶ αὐτῷ τῷ πράγματι σῶμα ἡμᾶς αὐτοῦ κατασκευάζει. τίνος οὖν οὐκ ἔδει καθαρώτερον εἶναι τὸν ταύτης ἀπολαύοντα τῆς θυσίας; ποίας ἡλιακῆς ἀκτῖνος τὴν χεῖρα τὴν ταύτην διατέμνουσαν τὴν σάρκα, τὸ στόμα τὸ πληρούμενον πυρὸς πνευματικοῦ, τὴν γλῶσσαν τὴν φοινισσομένην αἵματι φρικωδεστάτῳ; ἐννόησον ποίαν ἐτιμήθης τιμήν, ποίας ἀπολαύεις τραπέζης. ὅπερ οἱ ἄγγελοι βλέποντες φρίττουσι, καὶ οὐδὲ ἀντιβλέψαι τολμῶσιν ἀδεῶς διὰ τὴν ἐκεῖθεν ἐκφερομένην ἀστραπὴν, τούτῳ ἡμεῖς τρεφόμεθα, τούτῳ ἀναφυρόμεθα, καὶ γεγόναμεν ἡμεῖς Χριστοῦ σῶμα ἓν καὶ σὰρξ μία. Τίς λαλήσει τὰς δυναστείας τοῦ Κυρίου, ἀκουστὰς ποιήσει πάσας τὰς αἰνέσεις αὐτοῦ; τίς ποιμὴν τοῖς οἰκείοις μέλεσι τρέφει τὰ πρόβατα; καὶ τί λέγω, ποιμήν; μητέρες πολλάκις εἰσὶν, αἳ μετὰ τὰς ὠδῖνας ἑτέραις ἐκδιδόασι τροφοῖς τὰ παιδία· αὐτὸς δὲ τοῦτ' οὐκ ἠνέσχετο, ἀλλ' αὐτὸς ἡμᾶς τρέφει οἰκείῳ αἵματι, καὶ διὰ πάντων ἡμᾶς ἑαυτῷ συμπλέκει.—Chrysost. in Matt. cap. xxvi. Hom. lxxxii. (al. 83.) Tom. VII. p. 788.]   Psal. cv.

angels do behold and tremble at; neither are they able to behold it without great fear, for the brightness which cometh thereof: and we be brought and compact into one heap or mass with him, being together one body of Christ and one flesh with him. Who shall speak the powers of the Lord, and shall declare forth all his praises? What pastor hath ever nourished his sheep with his own members? Many mothers have put forth their infants after their birth to other nurses; which he would not do, but feedeth us with his own body, and conjoineth and uniteth us to himself."

Whereupon I gather this argument:

<small>Another false argument, where in the third figure the minor is a negative.</small>

Like as mothers nurse their children with milk, so Christ nourisheth us with his body:

But mothers do not nourish their infants spiritually with their milk:

Therefore Christ doth not nourish those that be his spiritually with his blood.

<small>Answer.</small>

Cranmer:—He gave us the wine for his blood.

<small>Argument.</small>

Weston:—If he gave the wine for his blood, as you say, then he gave less than mothers do give:

But Chrysostom affirmeth, that he gave more than mothers give:

Therefore he gave not the wine for his blood.

<small>Christ nourisheth us both with bread and with his body: with bread our bodies, with his body our souls.</small>

Cranmer:—You pervert mine answer. He gave wine, yet the blood is considered therein. As for example: when he giveth baptism, we consider not the water, but the Holy Ghost, and remission of sins. We receive with the mouth the sacrament; but the thing and the matter of the sacrament we receive by faith.

Weston:—When Christ said, "Eat ye," whether meant he, by the mouth or by faith?

Cranmer:—He meant that we should receive the body by faith, the bread by the mouth.

<small>A gross saying.</small>

Weston:—Nay, the body by the mouth.

Cranmer:—That I deny.

<small>Chrysostom alleged by D. Weston. Chrysost. in Psal. l. Item Hom. 83. in 26 cap. Matt.</small>

Weston:—I prove it out of Chrysostom, writing upon the fiftieth Psalm:

Erubescit fieri nutrix, quæ facta est mater. Christus autem non ita: ipse nutritor est noster: ideo pro cibo carne propria nos pascit, et pro potu suum sanguinem nobis propinavit. Item, in 26 cap. Matthæi, Homil. LXXXIII.: *Non enim sufficit ipsi hominem fieri, flagellis interim cædi; sed nos secum in unam, ut ita dicam, massam reducit, neque id fide solum, sed re ipsa nos corpus suum efficit."*

That is:

"She that is a mother shameth sometime to play the nurse. But Christ, our nurse, doth not so play with us. Therefore, instead of meat, he feedeth us with his own flesh; and, instead of drink, he feedeth us with his own blood[1]." Likewise, upon the twenty-sixth chapter of Matthew, the eighty-third Homily, he saith: "For it shall not be enough for him to become man, and in the meanwhile to be whipped; but he doth bring us into one mass or lump with himself, as I may so call it, and maketh us his body, not by faith alone, but also in very deed[2]."

Cranmer:—I grant we make one nature with Christ: but that to be done with mouth we deny.

<small>Chrysostom alleged by D. Weston. Hom. 29. in epist. 2. Cor. cap. 13.</small>

Weston:—Chrysost. 2 Cor. cap. xiii. Hom. XXIX. hath these words: "*Non vulgarem honorem consequutum est os nostrum, accipiens corpus Dominicum;*" i.e. "No little honour is given to our mouth, receiving the body of the Lord[3]."

<small>The words of Chrysostom expounded.</small>

Cranmer:—This I say, that Christ entereth into us both by our ears and by our eyes. With our mouth we receive the body of Christ, and tear it with our teeth; that is to say, the sacrament of the body of Christ. Wherefore I say and

---

[¹ Chrysost. in Psal. l. Tom. V. p. 578. Τίκτει ἡ μήτηρ, καὶ οὐ γίνεται τροφός· αἰσχύνεται γὰρ γενέσθαι τροφὸς ἡ γενομένη μήτηρ· ὁ δὲ Χριστὸς οὐχ οὕτως· ἐγέννησε γὰρ ἡμᾶς, καὶ αὐτὸς τροφεὺς ἡμῶν ἐγένετο. διὰ τοῦτο καὶ ἀντὶ βρωμάτων τὴν ἰδίαν σάρκα ἡμᾶς ἔθρεψε, καὶ ἀντὶ πόματος τὸ ἴδιον αὐτοῦ αἷμα ἡμᾶς ἐπότισεν.—The genuineness of this homily is doubted by Sir H. Saville, and by Fronto Ducæus and Montfaucon it is rejected as spurious.]

[² See the note on the preceding page.]

[³ Οὐχ ὡς ἔτυχε τὸ στόμα ἡμῶν τετίμηται, δεχόμενον τὸ σῶμα τὸ δεσποτικόν.—Chrysost. in Epist. II. ad Cor. Hom. XXX. Tom. X. p. 650.]

affirm, that the virtue of the sacrament is much: and therefore Chrysostom many times speaketh of sacraments no otherwise than of Christ himself, as I could prove, if I might have liberty to speak, by many places of Chrysostom, where he speaketh of the sacrament of the body of Christ.

With the which word, "of the sacrament of the body," &c., doctor Cole being highly offended, denied it to be the sacrament of the body of Christ, save only of the mystical body, which is the church.

D. Cole denieth the sacrament to be a sacrament of the body of Christ, but only a sacrament of the congregation, that is, of the mystical body of Christ.

Cranmer:—And why should we doubt to call it the sacrament of the body of Christ, offered upon the cross, seeing both Christ and the ancient fathers do so call it?

Cole:—How gather you that of Chrysostom?

Cranmer:—Chrysostom declareth himself, Lib. III. De Sacerdotio, cap. iii. *O miraculum! O Dei in nos benevolentia! qui sursum sedet ad dexteram Patris, sacrificii tamen tempore hominum manibus continetur, traditurque lambere cupientibus eum. Fit autem id nullis præstigiis, sed apertis et circumspicientibus circumstantium omnium oculis.*

Chrysostom alleged by D. Cranmer. Lib. III. de Sacerdotio, cap. iii.

That is:

"O miracle! O the good-will of God towards us! which sitteth above at the right hand of the Father, and is holden in men's hands at the sacrifice-time, and is given to feed upon, to them that are desirous of him. And that is brought to pass by no subtlety or craft, but with the open and beholding eyes of all the standers-by[4]."

Thus you hear Christ is seen here in earth every day, is touched, is torn with the teeth, that our tongue is red with his blood; which no man having any judgment will say or think to be spoken without trope or figure.

Weston:—What miracle is it, if it be not his body, and he spake only of the sacrament, as though it were his body?

But hearken what Chrysostom saith[5]: *Quod summo honore dignum est, id tibi in terra ostendo. Nam quemadmodum in regiis non parietes, non lectus aureus, sed regium corpus in throno sedens omnium præstantissimum est; ita quoque in cœlis regium corpus, quod nunc in terra proponitur. Non angelos, non archangelos, non cœlos cœlorum, sed ipsum horum omnium Dominum tibi ostendo. Animadvertis, quonam pacto quod omnium maximum est atque præcipuum in terra, non conspicaris tantum, sed tangis, neque solum tangis, sed comedis, atque eo accepto domum redis. Absterge igitur ab omni sorde animam tuam.*

Chrysostom alleged by D. Weston, Hom. xxxiv.

That is:

"I shew forth that thing on the earth unto thee, which is worthy the greatest honour. For like as in the palace of kings, neither the walls, nor the sumptuous bed, but the body of kings sitting under the cloth of estate, and royal seat of majesty, is of all things else the most excellent; so is in like manner the king's body in heaven, which is now set before us on earth. I shew thee neither angels nor archangels, nor the heaven of heavens, but the very Lord and Master of all these things. Thou perceivest after what sort thou dost not only behold, but touchest, and not only touchest, but eatest, that which on the earth is the greatest and chiefest thing of all other; and when thou hast received the same, thou goest home: wherefore cleanse thy soul from all uncleanness[6]."

[4 Ὦ τῆς τοῦ Θεοῦ φιλανθρωπίας· ὁ μετὰ τοῦ πατρὸς ἄνω καθήμενος, κατὰ τὴν ὥραν ἐκείνην τῶν ἁπάντων κατέχεται χερσί, καὶ δίδωσιν αὐτὸν τοῖς βουλομένοις περιπτύξασθαι καὶ περιλαβεῖν. ποιοῦσι δὲ τοῦτο πάντες διὰ τῶν ὀφθαλμῶν τῆς πίστεως.—Chrysost. de Sacerdotio, Lib. III. Tom. I. p. 382.]

[5 What follows is said by a scholar of Oxford, who was present, to have been "the strongest argument which was thought to blank him."—Foxe, Acts, 1st edit. p. 933. See Jenkyns.]

[6 Τὸ γὰρ πάντων ἐκεῖ τιμιώτερον τοῦτό σοι ἐπὶ τῆς γῆς δείξω κείμενον. ὥσπερ γὰρ ἐν τοῖς βασιλείοις τὸ πάντων σεμνότερον οὐ τοῖχοι, οὐκ ὄροφος χρυσοῦς, ἀλλὰ τὸ βασιλικὸν σῶμα τὸ καθήμενον ἐπὶ τοῦ θρόνου· οὕτω καὶ ἐν τοῖς οὐρανοῖς τὸ τοῦ βασιλέως σῶμα. ἀλλὰ τοῦτό σοι νῦν ἔξεστιν ἐπὶ γῆς ἰδεῖν. οὐ γὰρ ἀγγέλους, οὐδὲ ἀρχαγγέλους, οὐδὲ οὐρανοὺς καὶ οὐρανῶν οὐρανῶν, ἀλλ' αὐτόν τὸν τούτων σοι δείκνυμι δεσπότην. εἶδες πῶς τὸ πάντων τιμιώτερον ὁρᾷς ἐπὶ γῆς; καὶ οὐχ ὁρᾷς μόνον, ἀλλὰ καὶ ἅπτῃ; καὶ οὐχ ἅπτῃ μόνον, ἀλλὰ καὶ ἐσθίεις; καὶ λαβὼν οἴκαδε ἀναχωρεῖς; ἀπόσμηχε τοίνυν τὴν ψυχήν.—Hom. xxiv. (al. 34.) Tom. X. p. 218.]

*Upon this I conclude that the body of Christ is shewed us upon the earth.

Cranmer:—What! upon the earth? No man seeth Christ upon the earth: he is seen with the eyes of our mind, with faith and spirit.

Weston:—I pray you, what is it that seemeth worthy highest honour on the earth? It is the sacrament, or else the body of Christ?

Cranmer:—Chrysostom speaketh of the sacrament, and the body of Christ is shewed forth in the sacrament.

Weston:—*Ergo*, Then the sacrament is worthy greatest honour.

Cranmer:—I deny the argument.

Weston:—That thing is shewed forth and is now in the earth, *ostenditur et est*, which is worthy highest honour:

But only the body of Christ is worthy highest honour:

Ergo, The body of Christ is now on the earth.

Cranmer:—I answer, the body of Christ to be on the earth, but so as in a sacrament, and as the Holy Ghost is in the water of baptism.

Weston:—Chrysostom saith, *ostendo*, "I shew forth;" which noteth a substance to be present.

Cranmer:—That is to be understood sacramentally.

Weston:—He saith, *ostendo in terra*, "I shew forth on the earth;" declaring also the place where.

Cranmer:—That is to be understand figuratively.

Weston:—He is shewed forth and is now on the earth, &c. as before.

Cranmer:—Your major and conclusion are all one.

Weston:—But the major is true. *Ergo*, the conclusion also is true.

That thing is on the earth, which is worthy of most high honour:

But no figure is worthy of highest honour:

Ergo, That which is on the earth is no figure.

Cranmer:—I answer, that is true sacramentally.

Here Weston crieth to him that he should answer to one part, bidding him repeat his words. Which when he went about to do, such was the noise and crying out in the school, that his mild voice could not be heard. For when he went about to declare to the people how the prolocutor did not well English the words of Chrysostom, using for *ostenditur in terra*, "he is shewed forth on the earth," *est in terra*, "he is on the earth;" whereas Chrysostom hath not *est*, nor any such word of being on the earth, but only of shewing, as the grace of the Holy Ghost *in baptismo ostenditur*, i. e. "is shewed forth in baptism;" and oftentimes did inculcate this word, *ostenditur*: then the prolocutor, stretching forth his hand, set on the rude people to cry out at him, filling all the school with hissing, clapping of hands, and noise; calling him *indoctum, imperitum, impudentem;* i. e. "unlearned, unskilful, impudent:" which impudent and reproachful words this reverend man most patiently and meekly did abide, as one that had been inured with the suffering of such like reproaches. And when the prolocutor, not yet satisfied with this rude and unseemly demeanour, did urge and call upon him to answer the argument, then he bade the notary repeat his words again.

Notary:—That which is worthy most high honour, here I shew forth to thee in earth:

The body of Christ is worthy highest honour:

Ergo, He sheweth forth the body of Christ here in earth.

Cranmer:—That is shewed forth here on the earth which may be seen, which may be touched, and which may be eaten; but these things be not true of the body.

Cole:—Why should not these things be true of the body of Christ?

Cranmer:—The major out of Chrysostom is true, meaning of the sacrament: for in the sacrament the true body of Christ, and not the figurative body, is set forth.

Weston:—Shew me somewhat in earth worthy greatest honour.

Cranmer:—I cannot, but in the sacrament only.

Weston :—Ergo, The sacrament is worthy greatest honour.

*Cranmer :—*So it is.

*Judges :—*Let it be written.

*Cranmer :—*I pray you, let my answer be written likewise. I affirm, that the body of Christ is shewed forth unto us. It is our faith that seeth Christ.

Weston :—Ostendo tibi, i. e. "I shew it to thee," saith Chrysostom, not to thy faith.

*Cranmer :—*He speaketh sacramentally.

Weston :—Ergo, Chrysostom lieth. For he, speaking of shewing, saith, *Ego Chrysostomus ostendo;* i. e. "I Chrysostom do shew." But he can shew nothing sacramentally.

*Chedsey :—*By force of argument we are brought to this point, that the body of Christ is proved to be on earth, not only sacramentally, but in very deed also, by this reason, that it is worthy highest honour. The reason is indissoluble.

*Cranmer :—*I never heard a more vain argument, and it is most vain: also it hath mine answer unto it.

*Chedsey :—*Will you affirm, that it is absurd which Chrysostom saith, that the body of Christ is touched?

I touch the body of Christ in the sacrament, as Thomas touched Christ:

Thomas touched Christ, and said, *Dominus meus, Deus meus;* "My Lord, my God:"

Ergo, That which he touched was the Lord God.

¶ This argument, as I received it out of the Notary's book, is not formal; but rather he should conclude in the third figure thus:

Da-   As Thomas touched the body of Christ, so we touch it in the sacrament:
ti-   Thomas touched the body of Christ corporally:
si.   *Ergo*, We touch the body of Christ corporally in the sacrament.

*Cranmer :—*I deny your argument. He touched not God, but him which was God. Neither is it sound doctrine to affirm, that God is touched.

*Chedsey :—*This is because of the union: so that God is said to be touched, when Christ, which is both God and man, is touched.

Tertullian, *De Carnis Resurrectione*, saith: *Videamus de propria christiani hominis forma, quanta huic substantiæ frivolæ et sordidæ apud Deum prærogativa sit. Etsi sufficeret illi quod nulla omnino anima salutem posset adipisci, nisi dum est in carne crediderit: adeo caro salutis cardo est, de qua cum anima Deo alligatur, ipsa est quæ efficit ut anima alligari possit; sed et caro abluitur, ut anima emaculetur; caro inungitur, ut anima consecretur; signatur, ut anima muniatur; caro manus impositione adumbratur, ut anima Spiritu illuminetur; caro corpore et sanguine Christi vescitur, ut anima de Deo saginetur*[1].

That is to say:

"Let us consider, as concerning the proper form of the christian man, what great prerogative this vain and foul substance of ours hath with God. Although it were sufficient to it, that no soul could ever get salvation, unless it believe while it is in the flesh: so much the flesh availeth to salvation, by the which flesh it cometh, that whereas the soul so is linked unto God, it is the said flesh that causeth the soul to be linked: yet the flesh moreover is washed, that the soul may be cleansed; the flesh is anointed, that the soul may be consecrated; the flesh is signed, that the soul may be defended; the flesh is shadowed by the imposition of hands, that the soul may be illuminated with the Spirit; the flesh doth eat the body and blood of Christ, that the soul may be fed of God."

Whereupon I gather this argument:

The flesh eateth the body of Christ:

Ergo, The body of Christ is eaten with the mouth.

[1 Tertullian. De Resurrectione Carnis, cap. viii. p. 330. Ed. Paris. 1664.]

Photius, 1 Cor. xi.

Item Phocëus, 1 ad Cor. cap. xi. upon these words: *Reus erit corporis et sanguinis*[1], &c.

Photius alleged by Chedsey.

Ὁ ἔνοχος τοῦ σώματος καὶ τοῦ αἵματος, τοῦτο δηλοῖ, ὅτι καθάπερ παρέδωκε μὲν αὐτὸν ὁ Ἰούδας, παρῴνησαν εἰς αὐτὸν οἱ Ἰουδαῖοι, οὕτως ἀτιμάζουσιν [αὐτὸν οἱ τὸ πανάγιον αὐτοῦ σῶμα χερσὶν][2] ἀκαθάρτοις δεχόμενοι, ὡς Ἰουδαῖοι κρατοῦντες αὐτὸν τότε, καὶ καταράτῳ προσφέροντες στόματι· διὰ δὲ τὸ εἰπεῖν πολλάκις, τοῦ σώματος καὶ τοῦ αἵματος τοῦ Κυρίου, δηλοῖ, ὅτι [οὐκ] ἄνθρωπος ψιλὸς ὁ θυόμενος, ἀλλ' αὐτὸς ὁ Κύριος ὁ ποιητὴς πάντων, ὡς δῆθεν διὰ τούτων ἐκφοβῶν αὐτούς: i. e. Quod ait, 'Reus corporis et sanguinis,' istud declarat, quod sicuti Judas ipsum quidem tradidit, Judæi contumeliose in ipsum insaniebant; sic ipsum inhonorant qui sanctissimum ipsius corpus impuris manibus suscipiunt, [et] tanquam Judæi ipsi tenent et execrabili ore recipiunt. Quod crebro mentionem facit corporis et sanguinis Domini, manifestat, quod non sit simplex homo qui sacrificatur, sed ipse Dominus omnium factor, tanquam per hæc quidem ipsos perterrefaciens.

That is to say:

"Whereas he saith, 'Is guilty of the body and blood,' this he declareth, that like as Judas betrayed him, and the Jews were fierce and spiteful against him; so do they dishonour him, which receive his holy body with their impure hands, and as the Jews did hold him then, do now receive him with unpure mouths. And whereas he often maketh mention of the body and blood of the Lord, he declareth that it is not simply man that is sacrificed, but even the Lord himself, being the Maker of all things; hereby, as it were, making them afraid."

Ergo, (as it is hereby gathered,) the body of Christ is touched with the hands.

Cranmer:—You vouch two authors against me upon sundry things. First, I must answer Tertullian, and then the other.

Chedsey:—They tend both to one meaning.

Answer to Tertullianus.

Cranmer:—Unto Tertullian I answer, (because our disputation is wandering and uncertain,) that he calleth that the flesh which is the sacrament. For although God work all things in us invisibly, beyond man's reach, yet they are so manifest, that they may be seen and perceived of every sense. Therefore he setteth forth baptism, unction, and last of all the supper of the Lord unto us, which he gave to signify his operation in us. The flesh liveth by the bread, but the soul is inwardly fed by Christ.

D. Weston urgeth him with the words of Tertullian.

Weston:—Stick to those words of Tertullian, *Corpus vescitur, ut anima saginetur*; i. e. "The body eateth, that the soul may be fed."

Chedsey:—The flesh eateth the body of Christ, that the soul may be fed therewith.

Weston:—Here you see two kinds of food, of the soul and of the body.

Chedsey:—He saith, that not only the soul, but the flesh is also fed.

Cranmer:—The soul is fed with the body of Christ, the body with the sacrament.

Chedsey:—Is the soul fed with the body of Christ, and not with the sacrament?

Inwardly we eat the body, outwardly the sacrament.

Cranmer:—Read that which followeth, and you shall perceive, that by things external an operation internal is understand. Inwardly we eat Christ's body, and outwardly we eat the sacrament. So one thing is done outwardly, another inwardly: like as in baptism the external element, whereby the body is washed, is one; so the internal thing, whereby the soul is cleansed, is another.

Chedsey:—The soul is fed by that which the body eateth:

But the soul is fed by the flesh of Christ:

Ergo, The body eateth the flesh of Christ.

Cranmer:—We eat not one thing outwardly and inwardly: inwardly we eat Christ's body; outwardly we eat the sacrament.

Chedsey:—I will repeat the argument.

The form of this argument which he repeateth, stood better before: for the form of

The flesh eateth Christ's body, that the soul may be fed therewith:

The soul is not fed with the sacrament, but with Christ's body:

Ergo, The flesh eateth the body of Christ.

[1 Photius apud Œcumen. Tom. I. p. 532. Paris. 1631.]
[2 Not in Foxe, Ed. 1583.]

Cranmer:—The sacrament is one thing; the matter of the sacrament is another. Outwardly we receive the sacrament; inwardly we eat the body of Christ. this connexion answereth to none of the three figures of syllogisms.

Chedsey:—I prove that we receive that outwardly wherewith the soul is fed.
The soul is fed with the body of Christ:
Ergo, We eat the body of Christ outwardly. Consequence.
The flesh eateth Christ his body: Consequence.
Ergo, The soul is fed therewith.

Cranmer:—The flesh, I say, eateth the sacrament; it eateth not Christ's body. For Tertullian speaketh of the sacrament; and the place hath not *inde,* "thereof," but *de Deo,* "of God." Answer.

Chedsey:—What say ye to Photius' saying? "They which receive the body with impure hands are guilty of the Lord's blood, as Judas was."

Weston:—That which followeth in Tertullian doth take away your shift, where as he saith, *Non possunt ergo separari in mercede, quos opera conjungit;* i. e. "They cannot be separated in reward, whom one work joineth together."

But manducation is the work or labour: *Ergo,* &c.

The form of this argument may be thus collected:

Da- One work or labour joineth body and soul together:
ri- Manducation is a work or labour:
i. *Ergo,* One manducation joineth together both body and soul.

☞ To the major of which argument thus it may be answered, expounding the saying of Tertullian, *Una opera conjungit, sed non idem operandi modus.* Again, *opera* here in Tertullian may be taken for temptations and afflictions. As the body and soul are joined in the work of baptism, so are they joined in the communion of the Lord's supper. For as the flesh is washed with water, that the soul may be purged spiritually; so our body eateth the outward sacrament, that the soul may be fed of God.

Cranmer:—Your authority, I suppose, is taken out of the book *De Resurrectione Carnis,* i. e. "Of the Resurrection of the Flesh." And the meaning thereof is this: Tertullian goeth about there to prove, that the flesh shall rise again, because it is joined together in one work with the soul. Through baptism in this world the body is washed, and the soul is washed: the body outwardly, the soul inwardly; the work is one. In this work they are joined. And he speaketh of signs. Answer to Tertullian, De Resurrect.

Weston:—He speaketh of eating in a sign:
Ergo, The reward is in a sign.

Cranmer:—They are coupled in one work, namely, in the sacrament.

Weston:—There are two works:
Ergo, There are two rewards.
If the work be in a figure;
Ergo, The reward is in a figure.

Cranmer:—He speaketh not of two works. Two works are but one work. And yet he saith not, *Quos una opera conjungit,* i.e. "Whom one work joineth together;" but *opera,* i. e. "a work:" as in baptism the soul and the body are joined in understanding.

Weston:—The flesh and soul shall have one and the selfsame reward, because they have one work.

Cranmer:—Because they be joined together in one work.

Tresham:—Forasmuch as the reverend doctors here have impugned and overthrown your assertion and your answers sufficiently, I will fall to another matter, not altogether impertinent to the purpose, and that in a few words, against a certain sequel of your opinion. The sequel is this: that between us and Christ there is no further conjunction, whiles we receive the eucharist, than a conjunction of the mind, or a spiritual conjunction, whereby we are united and knit unto Christ through faith and love. As for the presence of Christ, concerning the substance, that you utterly deny. Whereupon in very deed you leave but a spiritual union and joining together of mind. Howbeit you would seem to think otherwise by your subtle answers. But I will declare by manifest testimonies of the fathers, that this your sequel, which you account so sure, is far wide from the truth. And I will begin D. Tresham disputeth.

with St Hilary, who is both an ancient and a learned author. For disputing against the Arians, *octavo De Trinitate*, he saith, that this was their opinion, that the Father and the Son are conjoined only through unity of will. Whereupon Arius himself, when scripture was alleged against him, did (as you do now) elude the right meaning of it by his false interpretations. But the catholic church hath always believed, and ever maintained, that Christ is one with the Father in nature, and not by consent of will only. To the proof whereof when the catholics vouched this testimony of John, *Pater et ego unum sumus*, i.e. "The Father and I are one;" the Arians answered, that *unum sumus* was to be understand by the assent of their wills and agreement of their minds, not by unity of their natures. Thus it happeneth now-a-days, where men do doubt of the sacrament. But Hilary going on, and proving the natural conjunction between the Father and the Son *a fortiori*, questioneth with his adversaries after this manner: "I demand of them now, which will needs have the unity of will only between the Father and the Son, whether Christ be now in us truly by nature, or only by the agreement of wills? If," saith he, "the Word be incarnate in very deed, and we receive at the Lord's table the Word made flesh, how then is he to be thought not to dwell in us naturally, who, being born man, hath both taken the nature of our flesh upon him, that is now inseparable, and hath also mingled the nature of his own flesh unto the nature of eternity under the sacrament of his flesh to be communicated unto us[1]?" Thus much hath Hilary. Whereupon I ask of you this question: How Christ dwelleth now in us? according to faith, or according to nature?

Cranmer:—I say that Christ dwelleth verily in us carnally and naturally, for that he hath taken of the virgin our flesh upon him, and because he hath communicated his nature unto us.

Tresham:—Bucer, *Contra Abrincensem*, referreth these words only to the eucharist, saying, "Christ doth exhibit all this unto us in his holy supper;" and according to the holy fathers, saith he, "Christ liveth thereby in us, not only by faith and love, as absent, but naturally, corporally, and carnally[2]." Wherefore he is not absent, neither are we joined to Christ only by a spiritual union, as you suppose, but also by a corporal and carnal union.

Cranmer:—I know that Master Bucer was a learned man: but your faith is in good case, which leaneth upon Bucer.

Tresham:—I do not bring Bucer as a patron of our faith, but because he is a man of your sort, and yet bringeth this place of Hilary for that union which we have by the sacrament, and confesseth that by it we are carnally united to Christ, whereas you think that we are joined by it only through faith and love.

Cranmer:—I say that Christ was communicated unto us, not only by faith, but in very deed also, when he was born of the virgin. We have fellowship with Christ, when we are united in the unity of the church, when we are made flesh of his flesh, and bones of his bones; and so we are united in the communion, in baptism, and in faith.

Tresham:—I pray you, what fellowship have we with Christ, in that he is made man? Are not the Turks and Jews therein joined with him? for they are men as we are, and are joined with him in man's nature, in that he was born of a woman. I speak now of a more near unity: we are made one with Christ by the communion in a perfect unity.

[1 Eos nunc qui inter Patrem et Filium voluntatis ingerunt unitatem, interrogo utrumne per naturæ veritatem hodie Christus in nobis sit, an per concordiam voluntatis? Si enim vere Verbum caro factum est, et nos vere Verbum carnem cibo dominico sumimus, quomodo non naturaliter manere in nobis existimandus est, qui et naturam carnis nostræ jam inseparabilem sibi homo natus assumpsit, et naturam carnis suæ ad naturam æternitatis sub sacramento nobis communicandæ carnis admiscuit?—Hilar. de Trinitate, Lib. VIII. p. 133. Ed. Basil. 1535.]

[2 Bucer. Script. Angl. p. 616. Ex quo loco et iis quæ Dominus in Joan. VI. de manducatione carnis suæ disseruit, sancti patres Hilarius, Chrysostomus, Cyrillus, et ceteri affirmarunt Dominum Jesum in nobis habitare et vivere non jam per fidem solum et dilectionem, ceu absens, sed etiam naturaliter, carnaliter, et corporaliter, quia suam naturam et carnem nobis communicat, suaque nos membra esse efficit, idque omne nobis in sacra eucharistia exhibet.]

Cranmer:—We are made so, I grant: but we are made so also by baptism; and the unity in baptism is perfect.

Tresham:—We are not made one by baptism in a perfect unity, as Hilary there speaketh, but by the communion, by which we are carnally made one, but not likewise by baptism: wherefore you understand not Hilary. You shall hear his words, which are these: "He had now declared afore the sacrament of his perfect union, saying, 'As the living Father sent me, so do I also live by the Father;' and, 'He that eateth my flesh, shall also live through me.'" And a little after that he writeth thus: "This truly is the cause of our life, that we have Christ dwelling by his flesh in us that are fleshly, which also by him shall live in such sort as he liveth by his Father[3]." Wherefore of these words it is manifest, that we obtain this perfect unity by means of the sacrament, and that Christ by it is carnally united unto us.

Cranmer:—Nay, Hilary in that same place doth teach, that it is done by baptism: and that doctrine is not to be suffered in the church, which teacheth, that we are not joined to Christ by baptism.

Weston:—Repeat the argument.

Cranmer:—You must first make an argument.

Tresham:—It is made already, but it shall be made again in this form:

Da- As Christ liveth by his Father, so they that eat Christ's flesh live by the same flesh:

ti- But Christ liveth by the Father, not only by faith and love, but naturally:

si. *Ergo*, We live, not through the eating of Christ's flesh by faith and love only, but naturally.

Cranmer:—We live by Christ, not only by faith and love, but eternally indeed.

Tresham:—Nay, naturally. I prove it thus:

As Christ liveth by the Father, so live we by his flesh eaten of us;

But Christ liveth not by his Father only by faith and love, but naturally:

Therefore we do not live by eating of Christ's flesh only by faith and love, as you suppose, but naturally.

Cranmer:—The minor is not true.

Tresham:—This is the opinion of Arius, that Christ is united to his Father by conjunction of mind, and not naturally.

Cranmer:—I say not so yet, neither do I think so. But I will tell you what I like not in your minor. You say, that Christ doth not live by his Father only by faith and love: but I say, that Christ liveth not at all by his faith.

Weston:—Mark and consider well this word "by faith," lest any occasion of cavilling be given.

Tresham:—Let that word "by faith" be omitted. Neither did I mean, that Christ liveth by his Father through faith. Yet the strength of the argument remaineth in force. For else Hilary doth not confute the Arians, except there be a greater conjunction between us and Christ, when he is eaten of us, than only a spiritual conjunction. You do only grant an union. As for a carnal or natural union of the substance of flesh, by which we are joined more than spiritually, you do not grant. But our Lord Jesus give you a better mind, and shew you the light of his truth, that you may return into the way of righteousness!

Weston:—We came hither to dispute, and not to pray.

Tresham:—Is it not lawful to pray for them that err?

Weston:—It is not lawful yet. But proceed.

Tresham:—Again I reason thus: As Christ liveth by his Father, after the same manner do we live by the eating of his flesh:

But Christ liveth not by his Father only in unity of will, but naturally:

[3 Perfectæ autem hujus unitatis sacramentum superius jam docuerat, dicens: "Sicut me misit vivens Pater, et ego vivo per Patrem, et qui manducat meam carnem, et ipse vivet per me."......Hæc ergo vitæ nostræ causa est, quod in nobis carnalibus manentem per carnem Christum habemus; victuris nobis per eum ea conditione qua vivit ille per Patrem.—Hilar. de Trinitate, Lib. VIII. p. 134.]

Ergo, We do not live, when we eat the flesh of Christ, only by faith and unity of will, but naturally.

Cranmer:—This is my faith, and it agreeth with the scripture: Christ liveth by his Father naturally, and maketh us to live by himself in deed naturally, and that not only in the sacrament of the eucharist, but also in baptism. For infants, when they are baptized, do eat the flesh of Christ.

Weston:—Answer either to the whole argument, or to the parts thereof. For this argument is strong, and cannot be dissolved.

Cranmer:—This is the argument:

As Christ liveth by his Father, after the same manner do we live by his flesh, being eaten of us:

But Christ liveth not by his Father only in unity of will, but naturally:

Ergo, We eating his flesh do not live only by faith and love, but naturally.

But the major is false; namely, that by the same manner we live by Christ, as he liveth by his Father.

Weston:—Hilary saith, "After the same manner;" these be his words: "He that eateth my flesh shall live by me:" *Ergo*, Christ liveth by his Father; and as he liveth by his Father, after the same manner we shall live by his flesh. Here you see that Hilary saith, "After the same manner."

Cranmer:—"After the same manner" doth not signify, "like in all things," but "in deed and eternally:" for so do we live by Christ, and Christ liveth by his Father. For in other respects Christ liveth otherwise by his Father, than we live by Christ.

Weston:—He liveth by his Father naturally and eternally:

Ergo, We live by Christ naturally and eternally.

Cranmer:—We do not live naturally, but by grace, if you take "naturally" for the manner of nature. As Christ hath eternal life of his Father, so have we of him.

Weston:—I stick to this word "naturally."

Cranmer:—I mean it touching the truth of nature: for Christ liveth otherwise by his Father, than we live by Christ.

Weston: — Hilary, in his eighth book *De Trinitate*, denieth it, when he saith, "He liveth therefore by his Father; and as he liveth by his Father, after the same manner we shall live by his flesh."

Cranmer:—We shall live after the same manner, as concerning the nature of the flesh of Christ: for as he hath of his Father the nature of eternity, so shall we have of him.

Weston:—Answer unto the parts of the argument:

As Christ liveth by his Father, after the same manner shall we live by his flesh:

But Christ doth not live by his Father only in unity of will, but naturally:

Ergo, We, eating his flesh, do not live only by faith and love, but naturally.

Cranmer:—I grant, as I said, we live by Christ naturally; but I never heard that Christ liveth with his Father in unity of will.

Weston: — Because it seemeth a marvel unto you, hear what Hilary saith: "These things are recited of us to this end; because the heretics, feigning an unity of will only between the Father and the Son, did use the example of our unity with God; as though that we being united to the Son, and by the Son to the Father, only by obedience and will of religion, had no propriety of the natural communion by the sacrament of the body and blood[1]."

But answer to the argument. Christ liveth by his Father naturally and eternally: therefore do we live by Christ naturally and eternally.

Cranmer:—Cyril and Hilary do say, that Christ is united to us, not only by will, but also by nature: he doth communicate to us his own nature, and so is Christ

---

Answer.
The archbishop repeateth the argument. Christ, not after his manhood, but after his divine nature, liveth naturally by his Father; which divine nature of his worketh also in his manhood an immortality: so our spirit and soul, receiving the natural body of Christ in the mysteries, by faith do receive also the nature of his body, that is, his pureness, justification, and life; the operation whereof, redounding likewise unto our bodies, doth make the same also capable of the same glory and immortality. And thus it is true, that as Christ liveth naturally by his Father, so we live naturally by the body of Christ eaten in the mysteries, having respect both to the manhood of him and of us. For as the flesh of Christ, in respect of bare flesh, liveth not naturally by the Father, but for that it is joined to his divinity; so our flesh liveth not naturally by Christ's body eaten in the sacrament, (for then every wicked man eating the sacrament should live naturally by him,) but for that our flesh is joined to the spirit and soul, which truly eateth the body of Christ by faith: and so only the bodies of the faithful do live by eating the body of Christ naturally, in participating the natural properties of the body of Christ. "Naturally" expounded. The argument the third time repeated.

[1 Hæc autem idcirco a nobis commemorata sunt, quia voluntatis tantum inter Patrem et Filium unitatem hæretici mentientes unitatis nostræ ad Deum utebantur exemplo, tanquam nobis ad Filium et per Filium ad Patrem obsequio tantum ac voluntate religionis unitis, nulla per sacramentum carnis et sanguinis naturalis communionis proprietas indulgeretur.— Hilar. de Trinitate. Lib. VIII. p. 135.]

made one with us carnally and corporally, because he took our nature of the virgin Mary. And Hilary doth not say only that Christ is naturally in us, but that we also are naturally in him and in the Father; that is, that we are partakers of their nature, which is eternity, or everlastingness. For as the Word, receiving our nature, did join it unto himself in unity of person, and did communicate unto that our nature the nature of his eternity; that like as he, being the everlasting Word of the Father, had everlasting life of the Father, even so he gave the same nature to his flesh: likewise also did he communicate with us the same nature of eternity, which he and the Father have, and that we should be one with them, not only in will and love, but that we should be also partakers of the nature of everlasting life.

Ex exemplari manu Cranmeri descripto. "Naturally" expounded; that is, our bodies do participate the nature and properties of Christ's holy and immortal body.

Weston:—Hilary, where he saith, "Christ communicated to us his nature," meaneth that, not by his nativity, but by the sacrament.

Cranmer:—He hath communicated to us his flesh by his nativity.

Weston:—We have communicated to him our flesh when he was born.

Cranmer:—Nay, he communicated to us his flesh when he was born, and that I will shew you out of Cyril upon this place, *Et homo factus est*.

Then had Christ a sinful flesh.

Weston:—*Ergo*, Christ, being born, gave us his flesh.

Cranmer:—In his nativity he made us partakers of his flesh.

Weston:—Write, sirs[2].

Cranmer:—Yea, write.

That is, made us partakers of the properties, life, innocency, and resurrection of his body.

Chedsey:—This place of Hilary is so dark, that you were compelled to falsify it in your book, because you could not draw it to confirm your purpose:

"If Christ have taken verily the flesh of our body, and the man that was verily born of the virgin Mary is Christ, and also we do receive under the true mystery the flesh of his body, by means whereof we shall be one, (for the Father is in Christ, and Christ in us,) how shall that be called the unity of will? when the natural property, brought to pass by the sacrament, is the sacrament of unity. We must not speak in the sense of man, or of the world, in matters concerning God; neither must we perversely wrest any strange or wicked sense out of the wholesome meaning of the holy scripture, through impudent and violent contention. Let us read those things that are written, and let us understand those things that we read, and then we shall perform the duty of perfect faith. For as touching that natural and true being of Christ in us, except we learn of him, we speak foolishly and ungodly that thing that we do speak. For he saith, 'My flesh is meat indeed, and my blood is drink indeed. He that eateth my flesh, and drinketh my blood, abideth in me, and I in him.' As touching the verity of his flesh and blood, there is left no place of doubt: for now, both by the testimony of the Lord, and also by our faith, it is verily flesh, and verily blood[3]."

D. Chedsey again disputeth. Hilar. 8. De Trinitate.

Here you have falsified Hilary; for you have set *vero sub mysterio* for *vere sub mysterio*, "we receive truly under a mystery." Hilary thrice reporteth *vere sub mysterio*, and you interpret it twice *vere sub mysterio*, but the third time you have *vero* for *vere*.

Thus far was their talk in English.

Cranmer:—Assuredly I am not guilty of any deceit herein. It may be that the copy which I followed had *sub vero mysterio*, i.e. "under a true mystery;" although touching the sense it differeth little. God I call to witness, I have alway hated falsifying; and if you had leisure and lust to hear false citations, I could recite unto you six hundred.

Seeing Master Cranmer had twice "vere," and but once "vero," they had no cause to be grieved, but that they were disposed to find a knot in a rush.

[2 A direction to the notaries.]

[3 Si vere igitur carnem corporis nostri Christus assumpsit, et vere homo ille qui ex Mariâ natus fuit Christus est, nosque *vere sub mysterio* carnem corporis sui sumimus, et per hoc unum erimus, quia Pater in eo est, et ille in nobis; quomodo voluntatis unitas asseritur, cum naturalis per sacramentum proprietas perfectæ sacramentum sit unitatis? Non est humano aut seculi sensu in Dei rebus loquendum, neque per violentam atque impudentem prædicationem cœlestium dictorum sanitati alienæ atque impiæ intelligentiæ extorquenda perversitas est. Quæ scripta sunt legamus, et quæ legerimus intelligamus, et tunc perfectæ fidei officio fungemur. De naturali enim in nobis Christi veritate quæ dicimus, nisi ab eo discimus, stulte atque impie dicimus. Ipse enim ait: " Caro mea vere est esca, et sanguis meus vere est potus. Qui edit carnem meam, et bibit sanguinem meum, in me manet et ego in eo." De veritate carnis et sanguinis non relictus est ambigendi locus; nunc enim et ipsius Domini professione et fide nostra vere caro est, et vere sanguis est.—Hilar. de Trinitate, Lib. VIII. pp. 133, 34.]

Weston:—Here shall be shewed you two copies of Hilary, the one printed at Basil, the other at Paris.

Cranmer:—I suppose that Doctor Smith's books hath *vero*.

Weston:—Here is Doctor Smith; let him answer for himself.

M. Smith, M. Doctor, what say you for yourself? Speak, if you know it.

Here Doctor Smith, either for the truth in his book alleged, or else astonied with Doctor Weston's hasty calling, staid to answer: for he only put off his cap, and kept silence.

Weston:—But your own book, printed by Wolfe your own printer, hath *vere*[1].

Cranmer:—That book is taken from me, which easily might have ended this controversy. I am sure the book of Decrees hath *vero*.

<small>Here D. Cole beginneth to carp.</small>

Cole:—Now you admit the book of Decrees, when it maketh for you.

Cranmer:—Touching the sense of the matter there is little difference. The change of one letter for another is but a small matter.

Weston:—No is? *Pastor*, as you know, signifieth a "bishop," and *pistor* signifieth a "baker." But *pastor* shall be *pistor*, a bishop shall be a baker, by this your change of one letter, if *vere* and *vero* do nothing change the sense.

Cranmer:—Let it be so, that in *pistor* and *pastor* one letter maketh some difference; yet let *pistor* be either a baker or maker of bread, ye see here the change of a letter, and yet no great difference to be in the sense[2].

<small>D. Yong cometh in with his socratical interrogations.</small>

Yong:—This disputation is taken in hand, that the truth might appear. I perceive that I must go another way to work than I had thought. It is a common saying, Against him that denieth principles we must not dispute. Therefore, that we may agree of the principles, I demand, whether there be any other body of Christ than his instrumental body?

Cranmer:—There is no natural body of Christ but his organical body.

Yong:—Again I demand, whether sense and reason ought to give place to faith?

Cranmer:—They ought.

Yong:—Thirdly, whether Christ be true in all his words?

Cranmer:—Yea, he is most true, and truth itself.

Yong:—Fourthly, whether Christ at his supper minded to do that which he spake, or no?

Cranmer:—*Dicendo dixit, non fecit dicendo; sed fecit discipulis sacramentum;* i.e. In saying he spake, but in saying he made not; but made the sacrament to his disciples.

<small>D. Yong's sophistical interrogatories.</small>

Yong:—Answer according to the truth. Whether did Christ that, as God and man, which he spake, when he said, "This is my body"?

Cranmer:—This is a sophistical cavillation. Go plainly to work. There is some deceit in these questions. You seek subtleness. Leave your crafty fetches.

Yong:—I demand, whether Christ by these words wrought any thing or no?

Cranmer:—He did institute the sacrament.

Yong:—But answer, whether did he work any thing?

Cranmer:—He did work in instituting the sacrament.

Yong:—Now I have you; for before you said it was a figurative speech: But a figure worketh nothing:

<small>This syllogism, speaking of a figure, hath no perfect form nor figure.</small>

Ergo, It is not a figurative speech. A liar ought to have a good memory.

[1 Several editions of Foxe, 1570, 1576, 1583, 1641, 1684, read here *vero*, but that of 1563 has *vere*. As to Cranmer's "own book printed by Wolfe," the "Defence" printed by him in 1550 does not contain the original passage of Hilary, but it stands in the translation "under the true mystery," which of course assumes *vero* to be in the original. In Cranmer's "Reply to Gardiner," printed by Wolfe in 1551, the original passage is not cited by Cranmer, but is inserted in Cranmer's work as quoted by Gardiner, and there read correctly *vere*. (See p. 161. of this volume.) The same reading appears also in the Latin edition of the "Defence" published in 1553. It will be seen from the above reference, that Gardiner had first quoted *vero* from his "first copy," as he calls it, which he afterwards corrected to *vere* (see p. 162.); but what that "first copy" was, or how the wrong reading got into it, it is not now easy to ascertain. In five editions of Gratian which have been examined, viz. Paris 1517 and 1528, Antwerp 1573, and Lugd. 1525 and 1624, the reading is uniformly *vere*.—See further the extracts from Foxe printed below, p. 428.]

[2 This answer of Cranmer is not found in the first edition of Foxe.]

Cranmer:—I understood your sophistry before. You by working understand converting into the body of Christ: but Christ wrought the sacrament, not in converting, but in instituting.

Yong:—Woe to them that make Christ a deceiver! Did he work any other thing than he spake, or the selfsame thing?

Cranmer:—He wrought the sacrament, and by these words he signified the effect.

Fes- *Yong:*—A figurative speech is no working thing:
ti-   But the speech of Christ is working:
no.   *Ergo*, It is not figurative.

Cranmer:—It worketh by instituting, not by converting.

Yong:—The thing signified in the sacrament, is it not in that sacrament?

Cranmer:—It is. For the thing is ministered in a sign. He followeth the letter, that taketh the thing for the sign. Augustine separateth the sacrament from the thing[3]. "The sacrament," saith he, "is one, and the thing of the sacrament another." Answer to D. Yong by St Austin.

Weston:—Stick to this argument.
It is a figurative speech:
Ergo, It worketh nothing.

Yong:—But the speech of Christ is a working thing:
Ergo, It is not figurative.

Cranmer:—Oh, how many crafts are in this argument! They are mere fallacies. I said not, that the words of Christ do work, but Christ himself; and he worketh by a figurative speech.

Weston:—If a figure work, it maketh of bread the body of Christ.

Cranmer:—A figurative speech worketh not.

Weston:—A figurative speech, by your own confession, worketh nothing:
But the speech of Christ in the supper, as you grant, wrought somewhat:
Ergo, the speech of Christ in the supper was not figurative.

Cranmer:—I answer, these are mere sophisms: the speech doth not work, but Christ by the speech doth work the sacrament. The figurative speech worketh not, but Christ by the figurative speech worketh the sacrament.

I look for scriptures at your hands; for they are the foundation of disputations[4].

Yong:—Are not these words of scripture, "This is my body;" "The word of Christ is of strength;" and "By the Lord's words the heavens were made"? He said, "This is my body:"
Ergo, He made it.

Cranmer:—He made the sacrament; and I deny your argument.

Yong:—If he wrought nothing, nothing is left there. He said, "This is my body." You say, contrary to the scriptures, it is not the body of Christ; and fall from the faith.

Cranmer:—You interpret the scriptures contrary to all the old writers, and feign a strange sense.

Yong:—Ambrosius, De iis qui initiantur Sacris, cap. ix., saith: *De totius mundi operibus legisti, quia " Ipse dixit, et facta sunt; ipse mandavit, et creata sunt." Sermo Christi, qui potuit ex nihilo facere quod non erat, non potest ea quæ sunt in id mutare quæ non erant? Non enim minus est novas res dare, quam mutare naturas. Sed quid argumentis utimur? Suis utamur exemplis, incarnationisque exemplo adstruamus mysterii veritatem. Numquid naturæ usus præcessit, cum Dominus Jesus ex Maria nasceretur? Si ordinem quærimus, viro mixta fœmina generare consuevit. Liquet igitur, quod præter naturæ ordinem virgo generavit; et hoc quod conficimus corpus ex virgine est. Quid hic quæris naturæ ordinem in Christi corpore, cum præter naturam sit ipse Dominus Jesus partus ex virgine? Vera utique caro Christi, quæ crucifixa est, quæ sepulta est: vere ergo illius sacramentum est. Clamat Dominus Jesus, "Hoc est corpus meum." Ante benedictionem verborum cœlestium (alia[5]) species nominatur; post consecrationem corpus significatur. Ipse dicit sanguinem suum.* Ambros. de iis qui initiantur, &c. cap. 9.

[3 Decret. Gratian. in Corpus Juris Canon. De Consecr. Dist. ii. "Hoc est." Tom. I. col. 1936. Ed. Lugd. 1618.]

[4 Affers doctores, expecto scripturas.—Cambr. MS. Kk. 5. 14. Jenkyns's Cranmer, Vol. IV. p. 51.]

[5 Not in original text.]

Ante consecrationem aliud dicitur: post consecrationem sanguis nuncupatur. Et tu dicis, 'Amen,' hoc est, 'Verum est.' Quod os loquitur, mens interna fateatur: quod sermo sonat, affectus sentiat[1].

That is to say:

<small>As Christ Jesus was conceived against the order of nature, so in the instituting of this sacrament the order of nature is not to be sought.</small>

"Thou hast read of the works of all the world, that 'He spake the word, and they were made; he commanded, and they were created.' Cannot the word of Christ, which made of nothing that which was not, change those things that are into that they were not? For it is no less matter to give new things than to change natures. But what use we arguments? Let us use his own examples, and let us confirm the verity of the mystery by example of his incarnation. Did the use of nature go before, when the Lord Jesus was born of Mary? If you seek the order of nature, conception is wont to be made by a woman joined to a man. It is manifest therefore, that contrary to the order of nature a virgin did conceive; and this that we make is the body of[2] the virgin. What seekest thou here the order of nature in the body of Christ, when against the order of nature the Lord Jesus was conceived of a virgin? It was the true flesh of Christ which was crucified, and which was buried: therefore it is truly the sacrament of him. The Lord Jesus himself crieth, 'This is my body.' Before the blessing of the heavenly words it is named another kind; but after the consecration the body of Christ is signified. He calleth it his blood. Before consecration it is called another thing: after consecration it is called blood. And thou sayest, 'Amen;' that is, 'It is true.' That the mouth speaketh, let the inward mind confess; that the word soundeth, let the heart perceive."

<small>Ambrosius, Lib. de sacramentis. cap. 4.</small>

The same Ambrose, in his fourth book of Sacraments, the fourth chapter, saith thus: *Panis iste panis est ante verba sacramentorum; ubi accesserit consecratio, de pane fit caro Christi. Hoc igitur adstruamus. Quomodo potest, qui panis est, corpus esse Christi? consecratione. Consecratio igitur quibus verbis est, et cujus sermonibus? Domini Jesu. Nam (ad*[3]*) reliqua omnia quæ dicuntur, laus Deo defertur, oratione petitur*[4] *pro populo, pro regibus, pro ceteris. Ubi venitur ut conficiatur venerabile sacramentum, jam non suis sermonibus sacerdos utitur, sed sermonibus Christi*[5]. *Ergo sermo Christi hoc conficit sacramentum. Quis sermo? Nempe is quo facta sunt omnia. Jussit Dominus, et factum est cœlum; jussit Dominus, et facta est terra; jussit Dominus, et facta sunt maria, &c. Vides ergo quam operatorius sit sermo Christi. Si ergo tanta vis est in sermone Domini, ut inciperent esse quæ non erant, quanto magis operatorius est, ut (sint*[3]*) quæ erant, et in aliud commutentur*[6]?

That is to say:

<small>The words of Ambrose in English.</small>

"This bread is bread before the words of the sacraments; when the consecration cometh to it, of bread it is made the flesh of Christ. Let us confirm this therefore. How can that which is bread, by consecration be the body of Christ? By what words then is the consecration made, and by whose words? By the words of our Lord Jesus. For touching all other things that are said, praise is given to God, prayer is made for the people, for kings, and for the rest. When it cometh that the reverend sacrament must be made, then the priest useth not his own words, but the words of Christ: therefore the word of Christ maketh this sacrament. What word? That

<small>But the Lord Jesus here used not such words of commanding in the sacrament as in creation; for we read not 'fiat hoc corpus meum,' as we read 'fiat lux,' &c.</small>

word by which all things were made. The Lord commanded, and heaven was made; the Lord commanded, and the earth was made; the Lord commanded, and the seas were made; the Lord commanded, and all creatures were made. Dost thou not see then, how strong in working the word of Christ is? If therefore so great strength be in the Lord's word, that those things should begin to be, which were not before; how much the rather is it of strength to work, that these things which were, should be changed into another thing?"

Ambrose saith, that the words are of strength to work.

[1 Ambros. de Initiandis. Tom. IV. p. 166. Ed. Colon. 1616. Vide supra, p. 210.]

[2 Of, i. e. from.]

[3 Not in the original text.]

[4 Laudem Deo deferunt: oratio præmittitur pro populo. Orig. text.]

[5 Jam non suis sermonibus sacerdos, sed utitur sermonibus Christi. Ibid.]

[6 Ambros. de Sacramentis. Lib. IV. cap. iv. Tom. IV. p. 173. Vide supra, p. 210.]

Weston: — You omit those words which follow, which maketh the sense of Ambrose plain. Read them.

Yong: —*Cœlum non erat, mare non erat, terra non erat. Sed audi dicentem:* "*Ipse dixit, et facta sunt; ipse mandavit, et creata sunt.*" *Ergo tibi ut respondeam, non erat corpus Christi ante consecrationem, sed post consecrationem. Dico tibi quod jam corpus Christi est*[7]. That is: "Heaven was not, the sea was not, the earth was not. But hear him that said, 'He spake the word, and they were made; he commanded, and they were created.' Therefore, to answer thee, it was not the body of Christ before consecration, but after the consecration. I say to thee, that now it is the body of Christ." Ambros. de Sacram. cap. 5. Alloiosis rerum et symbolorum.

Cranmer: — All these things are common. I say, that God doth chiefly work in the sacraments.

Yong: —How doth he work?

Cranmer: —By his power, as he doth in baptism.

Yong: —Nay, by the word he changeth the bread into his body. This is the truth: acknowledge the truth, give place to the truth.

Cranmer: —O glorious words! you are too full of words.

Yong: —Nay, O glorious truth! you make no change at all.

Cranmer: —Not so, but I make a great change: as in them that are baptized is there not a great change, when the child of the bond-slave of the devil is made the son of God? So it is also in the sacrament of the supper, when he receiveth us into his protection and favour.

Yong: —If he work in the sacraments, he worketh in this sacrament.

Cranmer: —God worketh in his faithful, not in the sacraments.

Weston: —In the supper the words are directed to the bread; in baptism, to the Spirit. He said not, The water is the Spirit; but of the bread he said, "This is my body."

Cranmer: —He called the Spirit a dove, when the Spirit descended in likeness of a dove. As the dove is called the Spirit, so the bread is called the body.

Weston[8]*:* —He doth not call the Spirit a dove; but he saith, that "he descended as a dove:" "he was seen in the likeness of a dove." As in baptism the words are directed to him that is baptized, so in the supper the words are directed unto the bread.

Cranmer: — Nay, it is written, "Upon whomsoever thou shalt see the Spirit descending." He calleth that which descended "the Holy Spirit." And Augustine calleth the dove the Spirit. Hear what Augustine saith in John i.: *Quid voluit per columbam, id est, per Spiritum Sanctum? Docere, qui miserat eum*[9]. That is, "What meant he by the dove, that is, by the Holy Ghost? Forsooth, to teach who sent him." John i. August. in Joan. cap. 1.

Yong: — He understandeth of the Spirit descending as a dove: the Spirit is invisible. If you mind to have the truth heard, let us proceed. Hear what Ambrose saith: *Vides quam operatorius sit sermo Christi. Si ergo tanta vis in sermone Domini, &c. ut supra.* That is, "You see what a working power the word of Christ hath. Therefore, if there be so great power in the Lord's word, that those things which were not begin to be; how much more of strength is it to work, that those things that were should be changed into another thing?" Ambrose again repeated. De Sacram. cap. 4.

And in the fifth chapter: *Antequam consecretur, panis est: ubi autem verba Christi accesserint, corpus est Christi*[10]: i. e. "Before it is consecrated, it is bread; but when the words of Christ come to it, it is the body of Christ."

But hear what he saith more: *Accipite, edite…hoc est corpus meum:* "Take ye, eat ye; this is my body." *Ante verba Christi calix est vini et aquæ plenus.*

[7 Ibid. cap. v.]
[8 "The MS. in the Public Library at Cambridge attributes this explanation to Cole, and the following argument from Ambrose to Weston." Vide Jenkyns's Cranmer, Vol. IV. p. 55.]

[9 In Joann. Evang. cap. i. Tractat. v. 9. Tom. III. Pars ii. col. 324. August. Op. Par. 1679-1700.]
[10 Ambros. de Sacramentis, Lib. IV. cap. v. Tom. IV. p. 173.]

Ubi verba Christi operata fuerint, ibi sanguis (Christi¹) efficitur, qui redemit plebem²: i. e. "Before the words of Christ, the cup is full of wine and water; when the words of Christ have wrought, there is made the blood of Christ which redeemed the people." What can be more plain?

Cranmer:—Nay, what can be less to the purpose? The words are of strength to work in this sacrament, as they are in baptism.

Pie:—The words of Christ, as Ambrose saith, are of strength to work. What do they work? Ambrose saith, they make the blood which redeemed the people:

Ergo, The natural blood is made.

Cranmer:—The sacrament of his blood is made. The words make the blood to them that receive it: not that the blood is in the cup, but in the receiver.

Pie:—"There is made the blood which redeemed the people."

Cranmer:—The blood is made, that is, the sacrament of the blood, by which he redeemed the people. *Fit*, "it is made;" that is to say, *ostenditur*, "it is shewed forth there³." And Ambrose saith, we receive in a similitude: "As thou hast received the similitude of his death, so also thou drinkest the similitude of his precious blood⁴."

Weston:—He saith, "in a similitude," because it is ministered under another likeness. And this is the argument:

There is made the blood which redeemed the people:

But the natural blood redeemed the people:

Ergo, There is the natural blood of Christ.

You answer, that words make it blood to them that receive it; not that blood is in the cup, but because it is made blood to them that receive it. That all men may see how falsely you would avoid the fathers, hear what Ambrose saith in the sixth book and first chapter:

Forte dicas,...quomodo vera? Qui similitudinem video, non video sanguinis veritatem. Primo omnium dixi tibi de sermone Christi, qui operatur, ut possit mutare et convertere genera instituta naturæ⁵. Deinde ubi non tulerunt sermonem Christi discipuli ejus, audientes quod carnem suam daret manducari⁶, et sanguinem suum daret bibendum, recedebant: solus tamen Petrus dixit, "Verba vitæ æternæ habes, et ego a te quo recedam?" Ne igitur plures hoc dicerent, veluti quidam esset horror cruoris, sed maneret gratia redemptionis, ideo in similitudinem⁷ quidem accipis sacramentum, sed vere naturæ gratiam virtutemque consequeris⁸.

That is to say:

"Peradventure thou wilt say, how be they true? I which see the similitude, do not see the truth of the blood. First of all I told thee of the word of Christ, which so worketh, that it can change and turn kinds ordained of nature. Afterward, when the disciples could not abide the words of Christ, but hearing that he gave his flesh to eat, and his blood to drink, they departed: only Peter said, *Thou hast the words of eternal life; whither should I go from thee?* Lest therefore mo should say this thing, as though there should be a certain horror of blood, and yet the grace of redemption should remain; therefore in a similitude thou receivest the sacrament, but indeed thou obtainest the grace and power of his nature."

Cranmer:—These words of themselves are plain enough. (And he read this place again:) "Thou receivest the sacrament for a similitude." But what is that he saith, "Thou receivest for a similitude?" I think he understandeth the sacrament to be the similitude of his blood⁹.

Chedsey:—That you may understand, that truth dissenteth not from truth, to

---

[¹ Not in original text.]
[² Qui plebem redemit. Orig. text.]
[³ *Cant.* "Fit sanguis, id est, ostenditur sanguis. Ex hoc responso orta sunt sibila." MS. Public Library, Cambridge. Vide Jenkyns's Cranmer, Vol. IV. p. 57.]
[⁴ See the quotation on the following page.]
[⁵ Convertere in aliud instituta naturæ. Orig. text.]

[⁶ Manducandum. Ibid.]
[⁷ Similitudine. Ibid.]
[⁸ Ambros. de Sacramentis. Lib. vi. Cap. i. Tom. IV. p. 176. Ed. Colon. 1616.]
[⁹ Here is added in the manuscript in the Public Library at Cambridge,
  Weston:—Are ye not weary?
  Cranmer:—No, Sir.]

overthrow that which you say of that similitude, hear what Ambrose saith, Lib. IV. cap. 4. *De Sacrament.*

Si operatus est sermo cœlestis in aliis rebus, non operatur in sacramentis cœlestibus[10]? Ergo didicisti quod e pane corpus fiat Christi, et quod vinum et aqua in calicem mittitur, sed fit sanguis consecratione verbi cœlestis. Sed forte dices[11], Speciem sanguinis non video. Sed habet similitudinem. Sicut enim mortis similitudinem sumpsisti, ita etiam similitudinem pretiosi sanguinis bibis; ut nullus horror cruoris sit, et pretium tamen operetur redemptionis. Didicisti ergo, quia quod accipis corpus est Christi[12].

Ambros. de Sacram. Lib. iv.

That is to say:

"If the heavenly word did work in other things, doth it not work in the heavenly sacraments? Therefore thou hast learned, that of bread is made the body of Christ, and that wine and water is put into that cup, but by consecration of the heavenly word it is made blood. But thou wilt say peradventure, that the likeness of blood is not seen. But it hath a similitude. For as thou hast received the similitude of his death, so also thou drinkest the similitude of his precious blood; so that there is no horror of blood, and yet it worketh the price of redemption. Therefore thou hast learned, that that which thou receivest is the body of Christ."

Note, that Ambrose saith, We drink a similitude of Christ's blood.

Cranmer:—He speaketh of sacraments sacramentally. He calleth the sacraments by the names of the things; for he useth the signs for the things signified: and therefore the bread is not called bread, but his body, for the excellency and dignity of the thing signified by it. So doth Ambrose interpret himself, when he saith, *In cujus typum nos calicem mysticum sanguinis ad tuitionem corporis et animæ nostræ percepimus.* 1 Cor. xi.[13]

Answer to the place of Ambrose. Sacraments be called by the name of the things. Ambrose. 1 Cor. cap. xi.

That is to say:

"For a type or figure whereof we receive the mystical cup of his blood, for the safeguard of our bodies and souls."

Chedsey:—A type! he calleth not the blood of Christ a type or sign; but the blood of bulls and goats in that respect was a type or sign.

Cranmer:—This is new learning; you shall never read this among the fathers.

Chedsey:—But Ambrose saith so.

Cranmer:—He calleth the bread and the cup a type or sign of the blood of Christ and of his benefit.

Weston:—Ambrose understandeth it for a type of his benefit, that is, of redemption; not of the blood of Christ, but of his passion. The cup is the type or sign of his death, seeing it is his blood.

Cranmer:—He saith most plainly, that the cup is the type of Christ's blood.

Chedsey:—As Christ is truly and really incarnate, so is he truly and really in the sacrament:

Ambrose alleged against Ambrose. Argument.

But Christ is really and truly incarnate:

Ergo, The body of Christ is truly and really in the sacrament.

Cranmer:—I deny the major.

Chedsey:—I prove the major out of Justine, in his second apology: Ὃν τρόπον διὰ λόγου Θεοῦ σαρκοποιηθεὶς Ἰησοῦς Χριστὸς ὁ σωτὴρ ἡμῶν, καὶ σάρκα καὶ αἷμα ὑπὲρ σωτηρίας ἡμῶν ἔσχεν, οὕτω καὶ τὴν δι' εὐχῆς λόγου τοῦ παρ' αὐτοῦ εὐχαριστηθεῖσαν τροφήν, ἐξ ἧς αἷμα καὶ σάρκες κατὰ μεταβολὴν τρέφονται ἡμῶν, ἐκείνου τοῦ σαρκοποιηθέντος Ἰησοῦ καὶ σάρκα καὶ αἷμα ἐδιδάχθημεν εἶναι[14].

Justin.

Cranmer:—This place hath been falsified by Marcus Constantius[15]. Justin

---

[10 In cœlestibus sacramentis. Orig. text.]
[11 Dicis. Ibid.]
[12 Ambros. de Sacramentis. Lib. IV. Cap. iv. Tom. IV. p. 173. Ed. Colon. 1616.]
[13 Ambros. in Epist. I. ad Cor. Cap. xi. Tom. II. p. 184. Ed. Colon. 1616. But these commentaries are certainly spurious.]
[14 Justin Martyr. Apologia I. (Vulg. II.) p. 83, Ed. Bened. Paris. 1742.]
[15 "Marcus Constantius was the fictitious name under which Gardiner published his Confutatio Cavillationum, &c. The following is his translation: 'Cibum illum, ex quo sanguis et carnes nostræ per mutationem nutriuntur, postquam per verbum precationis fuerit ab eodem benedictus, edocti sumus esse carnem et sanguinem illius Jesu,

Answer to the place of Justinus. meant nothing else, but that the bread which nourisheth us is called the body of Christ.

Chedsey:—To the argument. As Christ is truly and naturally incarnate, &c. *ut supra.*

Cranmer:—I deny your major.

Chedsey:—The words of Justin are thus to be interpreted word for word:

Mutationem. *Quemadmodum per verbum Dei caro factus Jesus Christus Salvator noster carnem habuit et sanguinem pro salute nostra; sic et cibum illum consecratum per sermonem precationis ab ipso institutæ, quo sanguis carnesque nostræ per communionem nutriuntur, ejusdem Jesu, qui caro factus est, carnem et sanguinem esse accepimus.*

That is to say:

Mutation.
Of thanksgiving. "As by the word of God Jesus Christ our Saviour being made flesh had both flesh and blood for our salvation; so we are taught, that the meat consecrated by the word of prayer instituted of him, whereby our blood and flesh are nourished by communion, is the flesh and blood of the same Jesus which was made flesh."

Answer. *Cranmer:*—You have translated it well; but I deny your major. This is the sense of Justin; that that bread is called the body of Christ, and yet of that sanctified meat our bodies are nourished.

Chedsey:—Nay, he saith, of that sanctified meat both our bodies and souls are nourished.

Αἷμα καὶ σάρκες, i. e. "blood and flesh." *Cranmer:*—He saith not so; but he saith that it nourisheth our flesh and blood: and how can that nourish the soul, that nourisheth the flesh and blood?

Cole:—It feedeth the body by the soul.

Cranmer:—Speak uprightly. Can that which is received by the soul and the spirit, be called the meat of the body?

Irenæus. *Weston:*—Hear then what Irenæus saith: *Eum calicem qui est creatura, suum corpus confirmavit, ex quo nostra auget corpora. Quando et mixtus calix, et fractus panis percipit verbum Dei, fit eucharistia sanguinis et corporis Christi; ex quibus augetur et consistit carnis nostræ substantia*[1]. "This, the same cup which is a creature, he confirmed to be his body, by which be increaseth our bodies. When both the cup mixed, and the bread broken, hath joined to it the word of God, it is made the sacrament of the body and blood of Christ, of which the substance of our flesh is increased and consisteth."

Argument. The substance of our flesh is increased by the body and blood of Christ:

Ergo, Our body is nourished by the body and blood of Christ."

Irenæus answered by Tertullian. *Cranmer:*—I deny your argument. He calleth it the flesh and blood for the sacrament of the body and blood, as Tertullian also saith: *Nutritur corpus pane symbolico, anima corpore Christi:* that is, "Our flesh is nourished with symbolical or sacramental bread, but our soul is nourished with the body of Christ."

Weston:—Look what he saith more: *Quomodo carnem negant capacem esse donationis Dei quæ est vita æterna, quæ sanguine et corpore Christi nutritur*[2]? Lib. v. post duo fol. a principio. That is, "How do they say, that the flesh cannot receive the gift of God, that is, eternal life, which is nourished with the blood and body of Christ?" That is in the fifth book, two leaves from the beginning.

Cranmer:—The body is nourished both with the sacrament and with the body

---

qui pro nobis fuit incarnatus.' Peter Martyr's complaint against it is, that the clause 'ex quo—nutriuntur' is transposed, for the purpose of avoiding the inference which may be drawn from the original expressions of Justin, that the bread and wine *after* consecration, as well as *before,* nourish our bodies by the ordinary process of digestion.—Gardiner, Confutat. Object. 151; P. Martyr, De Eucharist. p. 311." Jenkyns, Cranmer, Vol. IV. p. 60.]

[1 Τὸ ἀπὸ τῆς κτίσεως ποτήριον αἷμα ἴδιον ὡμολόγησε, ἐξ οὗ τὸ ἡμέτερον δεύει αἷμα, καὶ τὸν ἀπὸ τῆς κτίσεως ἄρτον ἴδιον σῶμα διεβεβαιώσατο, ἀφ' οὗ τὰ ἡμέτερα αὔξει σώματα. Ὁπότε οὖν καὶ τὸ κεκραμένον ποτήριον καὶ ὁ γεγονὼς ἄρτος ἐπιδέχεται τὸν λόγον τοῦ Θεοῦ, καὶ γίνεται ἡ εὐχαριστία σῶμα Χριστοῦ, ἐκ τούτων δὲ αὔξει καὶ συνίσταται ἡ τῆς σαρκὸς ἡμῶν ὑπόστασις.—Irenæus adversus Hæreses. Valent. Lib. V. Cap. 2. p. 294. Ed. Bened. Par. 1710.]

[2 Πῶς δεκτικὴν μὴ εἶναι λέγουσι τὴν σάρκα τῆς δωρεᾶς τοῦ Θεοῦ, ἥτις ἐστὶ ζωὴ αἰώνιος, τὴν ἀπὸ τοῦ σώματος καὶ αἵματος τοῦ Κυρίου τρεφομένην, καὶ μέλος αὐτοῦ ὑπάρχουσαν;—Irenæus. Ibid.]

of Christ: with the sacrament to a temporal life; with the body of Christ to eternal life.

Chedsey:—I cannot but be sorry when I see such a manifest lie in your writings. For where you translate Justin on this fashion, "that the bread, water, and wine are not so to be taken in this sacrament, as common meats and drinks are wont to be taken of us; but are meats chosen out peculiarly for this, namely, for the giving of thanks; and therefore be called of the Greeks *eucharistia*, that is, 'thanksgiving:' they are called moreover the blood and body of Christ;" (so have you translated it:) the words of Justin are thus: "We are taught, that the meat consecrated by the word of prayer, by the which our flesh and blood is nourished by communion, is the body and blood of the same Jesus which was made flesh."

Cranmer:—I did not translate it word for word, but only I gave the meaning; and I go nothing from his meaning.

Harpsfield:—You remember, touching Justin, to whom this apology was written, namely, to an heathen man. The heathen thought that the Christians came to the church to worship bread. Justin answereth, that we come not to common bread, but as to, &c. as is said before. Weigh the place well; it is right worthy to be noted. Our flesh is nourished according to mutation.

Cranmer:—We ought not to consider the bare bread; but whosoever cometh to the sacrament, eateth the true body of Christ.

Weston:—You have corrupted[4] Emissenus; for instead of *cibis satiandus*, that is, "to be filled with meat," you have set *cibis satiandus spiritualibus*, that is, "to be filled with spiritual meats."

Cranmer:—I have not corrupted it; for it is so in the Decrees[3].

Weston:—You have corrupted another place of Emissenus; for you have omitted these words: *Mirare, cum reverendum altare cibis spiritualibus satiandus ascendis: sacrum Dei tui corpus et sanguinem fide respice; honorem mirare; merito continge*, &c. that is, "Marvel thou, when thou comest up to the reverend altar to be filled with spiritual meats: look in faith to the holy body and blood of thy God; marvel at his honour; worthily touch him."

Cranmer:—This book hath not that.

Weston:—Also, you have falsified this place by evil translating: *Honora corpus Dei tui*, i. e. "Honour the body of thy God." You have translated it, *Honora eum qui est Deus tuus*, i. e. "Honour him which is thy God:" whereas Emissenus hath not "honour him," but "honour the body of thy God[4]."

Cranmer:—I have so translated him; and yet no less truly, than not without a weighty cause: else it should not have been without danger, if I had translated it thus, "Honour the body of thy God;" because of certain that, according to the error of the Anthropomorphites, dreamed that God had a body.

Weston:—Nay, you most of all have brought the people into that error, which so long have taught that he sitteth at the right hand of God the Father, and counted me for an heretic, because I preached, that God had no right hand. Then I will oppose you in the very articles of your faith.

Christ sitteth at the right hand of God the Father:
But God the Father hath no right hand:
Ergo, Where is Christ now?

Cranmer:—I am not so ignorant a novice in the articles of my faith, but that I understand, that to sit at the right hand of God doth signify, to be equal in the glory of the Father.

Weston:—Now then take this argument:
Wheresoever God's authority is, there is Christ's body:
But God's authority is in every place:
Ergo, What letteth the body of Christ to be in every place?
Moreover, you have also corrupted Duns.

[3 Vide supra, p. 268.]   [4 Supra, p. 269.]

Cranmer:—That is a great offence, I promise you.

Weston:—For you have omitted *secundum apparentiam*, i.e. "as it appeareth;" where his words are these: *Et si quæras, quare voluit ecclesia eligere istum intellectum ita difficilem hujus articuli, cum verba scripturæ possent salvari secundum intellectum facilem et veriorem, secundum apparentiam, de hoc articulo*[1], &c. That is, "If you demand why the church did choose this so hard an understanding of this article, whereas the words of scripture may be salved after an easy and true understanding, as appeareth, of this article," &c.

Cranmer:—It is not so.

<small>D. Cranmer challenged for setting forth the Catechism in the name of the convocation.</small>

Weston:—Also, you have set forth a Catechism in the name of the synod of London, and yet there be fifty which, witnessing that they were of the number of that convocation, never heard one word of this Catechism.

<small>D. Cranmer purgeth himself concerning the Catechism.</small>

Cranmer:—I was ignorant of the setting to of that title; and as soon as I had knowledge thereof, I did not like it: therefore, when I complained thereof to the council, it was answered me by them, that the book was so entitled, because it was set forth in the time of the convocation[2].

<small>D. Cranmer Charged with mistranslating Tho. Aquinas.</small>

Weston:—Moreover, you have in Duns translated *In Romana ecclesia, pro ecclesia catholica;* "In the church of Rome," for "the catholic church."

Cranmer:—Yea, but he meant the Romish church.

Weston:—Moreover, you have depraved St Thomas[3]; namely, where he hath these words: *In quantum vero est sacrificium, habet vim satisfactivam: sed in satisfactione attenditur magis affectio offerentis, quam quantitas oblationis. Unde Dominus dicit apud Lucam de vidua quæ obtulit duo æra, quod plus omnibus misit. Quamvis ergo hæc oblatio ex sui quantitate sufficiat ad satisfaciendum pro omni pœna; tamen fit satisfactoria illis pro quibus offertur, vel etiam offerentibus, secundum quantitatem suæ devotionis, et non pro tota pœna.* That is, "Inasmuch as it is a sacrifice, it hath the power of satisfaction: but in satisfaction the affection of the offerer is more to be weighed than the quantity of the oblation. Wherefore the Lord said in Luke's gospel of the widow which offered two mites, that 'she cast in more than they all'." Therefore although this oblation of the quantity of itself will suffice to satisfy for all pain, yet it is made satisfactory to them for whom it is offered, or to the offerers, according to the quantity of their devotion, and not for all the pain."

You have thus turned it: *Quod sacrificium sacerdotis habet vim satisfactivam*, &c. that is, "That the sacrifice of the priest hath power of satisfaction," &c. And therefore in this place you have chopped in this word, *sacerdotis*, "of the priest;" whereas in the translation of all the New Testament you have not set it, but where Christ was

---

[1 Vide supra, p. 302.]

[2 Dr Jenkyns, in his edition of Cranmer's works, (Vol. IV. p. 65) has given the following note on this passage:

"A different explanation of this title was given by Philpot; who in the convocation of the preceding October, 'stood up, and spake concerning the catechism, that he thought they were deceived in the title of the catechism, in that it beareth the title of the Synod of London last before this, although many of them which were then present, were never made privy thereof in setting it forth; for that this house had granted the authority to make ecclesiastical laws unto certain persons to be appointed by the king's majesty; and whatsoever ecclesiastical laws they, or the most part of them, did set forth, according to a statute in that behalf provided, it might well be said to be done in the Synod of London, although such as be of this house now had no notice thereof before the promulgation.' Foxe, Vol. III. p. 20. See also Lamb, Hist. of the XXXIX. Articles, p. 8. It is a question who was the author of this Catechism. By the Oxford disputants it was attributed, on the assertion, as they pretended, of Cranmer, to Ridley: but Ridley himself, though he admitted that he noted many things for it and consented to it, denied that he was its author. It has been ascribed also to Ponet, bishop of Winchester, and to Alex. Nowell. Ward, one of the English divines sent to the Synod of Dort, believed it to be Nowell's; and Strype, in his later publications, expresses the same opinion. But it must be confessed that his reasons are not convincing. See Burn. Ref. Vol. III. p. 410. Strype, Cranm. p. 294; Memor. Vol. II. p. 368; Annals, Vol. I. p. 353. Preface to Cranmer's Catechism, Oxford, 1829."

It may be added, that the idea that bishop Ponet was the author of this Catechism seems to be the most correct. It is strengthened by the following passage in a letter, obtained from Zurich by the Parker Society, written by Sir John Cheke to Bullinger, dated June 7, 1553: "Nuper etiam J. Wintoniensis Episcopi [Ponet] Catechismum auctoritate sua scholis commendavit, et articulos synodi Londinensis promulgavit, quos tu si cum Tridentina compares, intelliges spiritus spiritui quid præstet."]

[3 Vide supra, p. 84.]

put to death. And again, where St Thomas hath *pro omni pœna,* "for all pain," your book omitteth many things there[4].

Thus you see, brethren, the truth stedfast and invincible: you see also the craft and deceit of heretics: the truth may be pressed, but it cannot be oppressed. Therefore cry all together, *Vincit veritas;* i.e. "The truth overcometh[5]."

Weston triumpheth before the victory.

This disordered disputation, sometime in Latin, sometime in English, continued almost till two of the clock. Which being finished, and the arguments written, and delivered to the hands of Master Say, the prisoner was had away by the mayor, and the doctors dined together at the University college.

HARPSFIELD DISPUTETH TO BE MADE DOCTOR.

It followed furthermore, after disputation of these three days being ended, that Mr Harpsfield, the next day after, which was the nineteenth of April, should dispute for his form, to be made doctor. To the which disputation the archbishop of Canterbury was brought forth, and permitted, among the rest, to utter an argument or two in defence of his cause, as in sequel hereof may appear.

[Foxe, Acts and Monuments, pp. 1459, et sqq. ed. 1583.]

DISPUTATION OF MASTER HARPSFIELD, BACHELOR OF DIVINITY, ANSWERING FOR HIS FORM TO BE MADE DOCTOR[6].

[Weston argued for some time against Harpsfield, who concluded with reference to a passage from Fulgentius.]

After these words, not waiting Harpsfield's answer, he offered M. Cranmer to dispute; who began in this wise[7]:

Cranmer :—I have heard you right learnedly and eloquently entreat of the dignity of the scriptures, which I do both commend and have marvelled thereat within myself. But whereas you refer the true sense and judgment of the scriptures to the catholic church, as judge thereof, you are much deceived; specially, for that under the name of the church you appoint such judges as have corruptly judged, and contrary to the sense of the scriptures. I wonder likewise why you attribute so little to the diligent reading of the scriptures, and conferring of places; seeing the scriptures do so much commend the same, as well in divers other places, as also in those which you yourself have already alleged. And as touching your opinion of these questions, it seemeth to me neither to have any ground of the word of God, nor of the primitive church. And to say the truth, the schoolmen have spoken diversely of them, and do not agree therein among themselves. Wherefore, minding here briefly to shew my judgment also, I must desire you first to answer me to a few questions, which I shall demand of you. Which being done, we shall the better proceed in our disputation. Moreover, I must desire you to bear also with my rudeness in the Latin tongue, which, through long disuse, is not now so prompt and ready with me as it hath been. And now, all other things set apart, I mind chiefly to have regard to the

The opinion of M. Harpsfield reproved, referring the sense of the scripture rather to the judgment of the church, than to the diligent reading and conferring of places.

[4 "*Cranmer :*—Because I would not write all that long treatise. MS. Public Library."]

[5 Vide MS. in which it seems Cranmer, having responded, now required that he should become the opponent.

"*Cranmer :*—Oppono : vos respondete scripturis.

Weston :—Habebis alium diem ad opponendum.

This day was the following Thursday, April 19 ; Tuesday and Wednesday having been occupied by the disputations with Ridley and Latimer." Vide Jenkyns's Cranmer, Vol. IV. p. 66.]

[6 "The title of this disputation in the manuscript in the Public Library, Cambridge :

"Disputationes habitæ Oxoniæ de vera præsentia naturalis et organici corporis Christi in sacramento altaris.

"Defendit D. Harpsfield veritatem, respondentis agens partes.

"Opponit primum D. Weston disputandi gratia, deinde D. Cranmerus ex suæ opinionis fide." Jenkyns's Cranmer, p. 67.]

[7 "An Oxford scholar, who was present at this disputation, relates, that Cranmer 'passed all men's expectation in doing the same. I myself, which did ever think that he was better learned than many reported he was, yet would I have thought he could not have done so well, nor would not have believed it, if I had not heard him myself.' Foxe, Acts, &c. 1st edit. p. 935." Ibid.]

truth. My first question is this: How Christ's body is in the sacrament, according to your mind or determination?

Christ present in the sacrament in substance, but not after the manner of substance.

Then answered a doctor, He is there as touching his substance, but not after the manner of his substance.

Harpsfield:—He is there in such sort and manner as he may be eaten.

Cranmer:—My next question is, Whether he hath his quantity and qualities, form, figure, and such like properties?

Harpsfield:—Are these your questions? said Master Harpsfield. I may likewise ask you, When Christ passed through the virgin's womb, *an ruperit necne?*

When they had thus a while contended, there were divers opinions in this matter.

The rabbins could not agree among themselves.

All the doctors fell in a buzzing, uncertain what to answer: some thought one way, some another; and thus master doctors could not agree[1].

Then Master Cranmer said thus: You put off questions with questions, and not with answers; I ask one thing of you, and you answer another. Once again I ask, Whether he have those properties which he had on the earth?

Christ's body without his properties in the sacrament.

Tresham:—No, he hath not all the quantities and qualities belonging to a body.

Smith:—Stay you, Master Tresham. I will answer you, Master Doctor, with the words of Damascene: *Transformatur panis,* &c.; "The bread is transformed," &c. But if thou wilt inquire how, *Modus impossibilis;* "The manner is impossible."

The doctors in a doubt.

Then two or three others added their answers to this question, somewhat doubtfully. A great hurly-burly was among them, some affirming one thing, and some another.

Cranmer:—Do you appoint me a body, and cannot tell what manner of body? Either he hath not his quantity, or else you are ignorant how to answer it.

Harpsfield:—These are vain questions, and it is not meet to spend the time on them.

Lanfrancus contra Berengarium.

Weston:—Hear me awhile: Lanfrancus, sometime bishop of Canterbury, doth answer in this wise unto Berengarius, upon such like questions: *Salubriter credi possunt, fideliter quæri non possunt;* i.e. "They may be well believed, but never faithfully asked[2]."

Cranmer:—If ye think good to answer it, some of you declare it.

Harpsfield:—He is there as pleaseth him to be there.

Cranmer:—I would be best contented with that answer, if that your appointing of a carnal presence had not driven me of necessity to have inquired, for disputation's sake, how you place him there, since you will have a natural body.

The papists would have Christ's body in the sacrament, but they cannot tell how.

When again he was answered of divers at one time; some denying it to be a *quantum*, some saying it to be *quantitativum;* some affirming it to have *modum quanti*, some denying it; some one thing, some another: up starts D. Weston, and doughtily decided, as he thought, all the matter, saying, "It is *corpus quantum, sed non per modum quanti;*" i.e. "It is a body," saith he, "having quantity," but not "according to the manner of quantity."

M. Ward in the misty clouds of Duns his quiddities.

Whereunto Master Ward, a great sophister[3], thinking the matter not fully answered, did largely declare and discourse his sentence: how learnedly and truly I cannot tell, nor I think he himself neither, ne yet the best learned there. For it was said since, that far better learned than he laid as good ear to him as they could, and yet could by no means perceive to what end all his talk tended. Indeed he told a formal tale to clout up the matter. He was full of *quantum* and *quantitativum*. This that follows was, as it is thought, the effect; yet others think no. Howbeit we will rehearse the sum of his words, as it is thought he spake them.

Ward:—We must consider, saith he, that there are *duæ positiones*, "two positions." The one standeth by the order of parts, with respect of the whole; the other in respect

---

[1 "According to the account of the Oxford scholar, 'they were mad with him for asking, whether there were in the natural body of Christ a proportion, space, or distance betwixt member and member.' Foxe, Acts, &c. 1st edit. p. 935." Jenkyns's Cranmer, Vol. IV. p. 68.]

[2 Si quæris modum quo id fieri possit, breviter ad præsens respondeo: Mysterium fidei credi salubriter potest, vestigari utiliter non potest.—Lanfranc. de Corp. et Sang. Domini, cap. x. fin. p. 175, Venet. 1745.]

[3 "In the first edition of Foxe, 'philosopher' is read in the place of 'sophister,' p. 938." Jenkyns's Cranmer, Vol. IV. p. 70.]

of that which containeth. Christ is in the sacrament in respect of the whole. This proposition is, in one of Aristotle's Predicaments, called *situs*. I remember I did entreat these matters very largely, when I did rule and moderate the philosophical disputations in the public schools. This position is *sine modo quantitativo*, as, by an ensample, you can never bring heaven to a quantity. So I conclude that he is in the sacrament *quantum, sine modo quantitativo*. Aristotle must help to tell us how Christ is in the sacrament. Christ "sine modo quantitativo" in the sacrament.

These words he amplified very largely; and so high he climbed into the heavens with Duns' ladder, and not with the scriptures, that it is to be marvelled how he could come down again without falling. To whom M. Cranmer said, "Then thus do I make mine argument."

Cranmer:—In heaven his body had quantity; in earth it hath none, by your saying: D. Cranmer's argument.

Ergo, He hath two bodies; the one in heaven, the other in earth.

Here some would have answered him, that he had quantity in both, and so put off the antecedent; but thus said M. Harpsfield:

Harpsfield:—I deny your argument: (though some would not have had him say so.)

Cranmer:—The argument is good: it standeth upon contradictories, which is the most surest hold.

Harpsfield:—I deny that there are contradictions.

Cranmer:—I thus prove it: *Habere modum quantitativum et non habere, sunt contradictoria*:

Sed Christus in cœlis, ut dicitis, habet modum quantitativum, in terra non habet:

Ergo, Duo sunt corpora ejus, in quæ cadunt hæc contradictoria: nam in idem cadere non possunt.

Weston:—I deny the minor. Aristotle 4, Metaph. "Impossibile est idem simul esse et non esse."

Harpsfield:—I answer, that the major is not true: for *habere quantum, et non habere, non sunt contradictoria, nisi considerentur ejusdem ad idem, eodem modo et simpliciter*.

Weston:—I confirm the same: for one body may have *modum quantitativum*, and not have; and *idem corpus* was passible and impassible; one body may have wounds, and not wounds.

Cranmer:—This cannot be at one time.

Weston:—The ensample of the potter doth prove that which I say; who, of that which is clay now, maketh a pot or cup forthwith.

Cranmer:—But I say again, that it is so, but at divers times; as one piece of meat to be raw and sodden cannot be at one time together. But you would have it otherwise, that Christ should be here and in heaven at one time, and should have *modum quantitativum*, and not have: which cannot be, by such argument as I have shewed you.

Weston:—But I say, Christ's body was passible and not passible at one instant.

Seaton:—You may ask as well other questions, How he is in heaven? Whether he sit or stand? and, Whether he be there as he lived here? Passible and impassible cannot stand together in one subject, "simul et ejusdem respectu et eodem tempore, propter rerum pugnantiam." Christ's body to be passible, and not impassible, at the supper, it appeareth by these words, "That shall be given for you." That remaineth yet unproved. Harpsfield seemed a little before to note the contrary, where he said, that the

Cranmer:—You yourself, by putting a natural presence, do force me to question how he is there. Therefore next I do ask this question, Whether good and evil men do eat the body in the sacrament?

Harpsfield:—Yea, they do so, even as the sun doth shine upon kings' palaces and on dung-heaps.

Cranmer:—Then do I inquire, How long Christ tarrieth in the eater?

Harpsfield:—These are curious questions, unmeet to be asked.

Cranmer:—I have taken them out of your schools and school-men, which you yourselves do most use: and there also do I learn to ask, How far he goeth into the body?

Harpsfield:—We know that the body of Christ is received to nourish the whole man, concerning both body and soul: *Eo usque progreditur corpus quousque species*.

Cranmer:—How long doth he abide in the body?

Seaton:—St Augustine saith, our flesh goeth into his flesh. But after he is once received into the stomach, it maketh no matter for us to know how far he doth pierce, or whither he is conveyed.

Here Master Tresham and one Master London answered, that Christ being given there under such form and quantity as pleased him, it was not to be inquired of his tarrying, or of his descending into the body.

Harpsfield:—You were wont to lay to our charge, that we added to the scripture; saying always, that we should fetch the truth out of the scripture: and now you yourself bring questions out of the school-men, which you have disallowed in us.

Cranmer:—I say, as I have said alway, that I am constrained to ask these questions, because of this carnal presence which you imagine; and yet I know right well that these questions be answered out of the scriptures. As to my last question, How long he abideth in the body, &c., the scripture answereth plainly, that Christ doth so long dwell in his people, as they are his members. Whereupon I make this argument:

Ba- They which eat the flesh of Christ, do dwell in him, and he in them:
ro- But the wicked do not remain in him, nor he in them:
co. *Ergo*, The wicked do not eat his flesh, nor drink his blood.

Harpsfield:—I will answer unto you, as St Augustine saith; not that howsoever a man doth eat, he eateth the body; but he that eateth after a certain manner.

Cranmer:—I cannot tell what manner ye appoint, but I am sure that evil men do not eat the flesh and drink the blood of Christ, as Christ speaketh in the sixth of John.

Harpsfield:—In the sixth of John some things are to be referred to the godly, and some to the ungodly.

Cranmer:—Whatsoever he doth entreat there of eating, doth pertain unto good men.

Harpsfield:—If you do mean only of the word of eating, it is true; if concerning the thing, it is not so: and if your meaning be of that which is contained under the word of eating, it may be so taken, I grant.

Cranmer:—Now to the argument: "He that eateth my flesh, and drinketh my blood, dwelleth in me, and I in him." Doth not this prove sufficiently, that evil men do not eat that the good do?

Tresham:—You must add, *Qui manducat digne*, "He that eateth worthily."

Cranmer:—I speak of the same manner of eating that Christ speaketh of.

Weston:—Augustinus *Ad fratres in Eremo*[1], Sermon. XXVIII. *Est quidam manducandi modus;* that is, "There is a certain manner of eating." Augustine speaketh of two manners of eating; the one of them that eat worthily, the other that eat unworthily.

Harpsfield:—All things in the sixth of John are not to be referred to the sacrament, but to the receiving of Christ by faith. The fathers do agree, that there is not entreaty made of the supper of the Lord before they come unto, *Panis quem dabo vobis, caro mea est,* &c.

Cranmer:—There is entreating of manna both before and after.

Harpsfield:—I will apply another answer. This argument hath a kind of poison in it, which must be thus bitten away; that manna and this sacrament be not both one. Manna hath not his efficacy of himself, but of God.

Cranmer:—[2]But they that did take manna worthily, had fruit thereby; and so,

---

[1 These sermons are not considered to be Augustine's. See edit. Bened. Tom. VI. James' Corruption of Scripture, &c. p. 61. Ed. Lond. 1843.]

[2 "*Cranmer:*—Sacramentum hoc est figura:
Ergo, Non est verum corpus Christi in eo.
Harpsfield:—Negatur antecedens.
Cranmer:—Probatur: Sacramentum hoc non plus valet quam figura:
Ergo, Est figura.
Harpsfield:—Negatur antecedens.
Cranmer:—Probatur: Sacramentum hoc non plus valet quam manna in veteri testamento valebat:
Sed manna fuit figura tantum:
Ergo, Sacramentum hoc non plus valet quam figura.
Harpsfield:—

by your assertion, he that doth eat the flesh of Christ worthily, hath his fruit by that.

Therefore the like doth follow of them both, and so there should be no difference between manna and this sacrament, by your reason.

Harpsfield:—When it is said, that they which did eat manna are dead, it is to be understand that they did want the virtue of manna.

Cranmer:—They then which do eat either of them worthily, do live.

Harpsfield:—They do live, which do eat manna worthily, not by manna, but by the power of God given by it. The other, which do eat this sacrament, do live by the same.

Cranmer:—Christ did not entreat of the cause, but the effect which followed: he doth not speak of the cause whereof the effect proceedeth.

Harpsfield:—I do say the effects are divers, life and death, which do follow the worthy and the unworthy eating thereof.

Cranmer:—Sithens you will needs have an addition to it, we must use both in manna and in the sacrament indifferently, either worthily or unworthily.

Christ spake absolutely of manna and of the supper; so that, after that absolute speaking of the supper, wicked men can in no wise eat the flesh of Christ, and drink his blood.

Further, Augustine upon John, Tractat. xxvi. upon these words, *Qui manducat*, &c. saith: "There is no such respect in common meats as in the Lord's body. For who that eateth other meats hath still hunger, and needeth to be satisfied daily: but he that doth eat the flesh of Christ, and drinketh his blood, doth live for ever[3]." But you know wicked men not to do so:

Ergo, Wicked men do not receive.

Harpsfield:—St Augustine meaneth, that he who eateth Christ's flesh, &c., after a certain manner, should live for ever. Wicked men do eat, but not after that manner.

Cranmer:—Only they which participate Christ, be of the mystical body:

But the evil men are not of the mystical body:

Therefore they do not participate Christ.

Weston:—Your wonderful gentle behaviour and modesty, good Master D. Cranmer, is worthy much commendation: and that I may not deprive you of your right and just deserving, I give you most hearty thanks in mine own name, and in the name of all my brethren.

At which saying, all the doctors gently put off their caps[4].

Marginal notes: If M. Harpsfield do mean of bodily life, they which eat the sacrament do die, as well as they which did eat the manna. If he mean of spiritual life, neither be they all damned that did eat manna, nor all saved that do eat the sacrament. Wherefore the truth is, that neither the eating of manna bringeth death, nor the eating of the sacrament bringeth salvation; but only the spiritual believing upon Christ's bodily passion, which only justifieth both them and us. And therefore, as the effect is spiritual, which Christ speaketh of in this chapter, so is the cause of that effect spiritual whereof he meaneth; which is our spiritual believing in him, and not our bodily eating of him.

August. in Joan. Tract. 26.

D. Cranmer commended for his modesty.

Harpsfield:—Negatur major.
Cranmer:—Probatur: Qui manna habuerunt, habuerunt vitam æternam:
Sed qui hoc sacramentum digne sumunt, non plus habent:
Ergo, Hoc sacramentum non plus valet quam manna in veteri testamento valebat.
Harpsfield:—Non habuerunt Israelitæ vitam æternam ex manna per se, aut ex ipso cibo, sed de gratia Dei propter fidem recipientium: nos autem ex corpore Christi habemus; quia, ut dixit Cyrillus, vivificam salutem ex ipso corpore Christi habemus: ideo fit, ut plus valeat hoc quam manna.
Cranmer:—Nihil interest quoad effectum:
Ergo, Non plus hoc valet quam alterum."—MS. Public Library, Cambridge. Vide Jenkyns's Cranmer, Tom. IV. p. 74.]

[3 Non ita est in hac esca, quam sustentandæ hujus temporalis vitæ causa sumimus. Nam qui eam non sumserit, non vivet: nec tamen qui eam sumserit vivet....In hoc vero cibo et potu, id est, corpore et sanguine Domini, non ita est: nam et qui eam non sumit, non habet vitam; et qui eam sumit, habet vitam, et hanc utique æternam...Cum enim cibo et potu id appetant homines, ut neque esuriant neque sitiant; hoc veraciter non præstat nisi iste cibus et potus, qui eos a quibus sumitur immortales et incorruptibiles facit.—August. in Joannem. Tractat. xxvi. de cap. vi. Tom. IX. p. 94. Ed. Paris. 1635.]

[4 For the remainder of this Disputation, which was wholly between Weston and Harpsfield, see Foxe, *Acts*, &c. p. 1462. Ed. 1583.]

A NOTE CONCERNING DR CRANMER IN HIS DISPUTATION.

[Foxe, Acts, &c., 1684, Vol. III. p. 839.—See before, p. 414.]

THAT day wherein Doctor Cranmer, late bishop of Canterbury, answered in the divinity school at Oxford, there was alleged unto him by Doctor Weston, that he the said Cranmer, in his book of the Sacrament, falsely falsified the saying of the doctors, and specially the saying of Saint Hilary in these words, *vero* for *vere*, shewing a print or two thereof, to have defaced his doings therein: but Doctor Cranmer with a grave and fatherly sobriety answered, that the print of S. Hilary's works, whereout he took his notes, was *verbatim* according to his book, and that could his books testify if they were there to be seen: saying further, that he supposed D. Smith in that order rehearsed it in his book of the Sacrament; to the which D. Smith there present (though he were demanded the answer thereof) stood in silence, as *canis mutus non valens latrare*. But by and by D. Weston without shame, to shadow D. Smith's silence, spitely said to Cranmer, "Belike you took your learning out of Master D. Smith's book."

All this already is testified before.

It chanced at that present to be in the school one William Holcot, gentleman, then a sojourner in the University college: he hearing the same untruth, and remembering that he had amongst his books in his study the said book of Doctor Smith, at his return to his said study, desirous to see the truth therein, found it agreeable to the writing and affirmation of Doctor Cranmer. And the said Holcot, then and there better remembering himself, found amongst his books the book of Stephen Gardiner, intituled "The Devil's Sophistry:" in which book was the said saying of Hilary alleged by the said Stephen *verbatim*, both in Latin and English, according to Doctor Cranmer's confirmation. Then the said William Holcot, intending (for the manifest opening and trial of the truth therein) to have delivered the said Gardiner's book to Doctor Cranmer, brought it to Bocardo, the prison in Oxford, where Doctor Cranmer then remained; but there in the delivery thereof he was apprehended by the bailiffs, and by them brought before Doctor Weston and his colleagues (then at dinner at Corpus Christi college), who straightways laid treason to the charge of the said William Holcot for the maintenance of Cranmer in his naughtiness, as they called it.

A DECLARATION[1]

OF THE

REVEREND FATHER IN CHRIST

THOMAS ARCHBISHOP OF CANTERBURY,

CONCERNING

THE UNTRUE REPORT AND SLANDER OF SOME, WHICH REPORTED, THAT HE SHOULD SET UP AGAIN THE MASS IN CANTERBURY[2].

As the devil, Christ's ancient adversary, is a liar and the father of lying, even so he hath ever stirred up his servants and members to persecute Christ and his true word

[1 This Declaration is here published from the MS. in the Library of Emmanuel College, Cambridge, 2. 2.15., which has been carefully collated for this edition. Dr Jenkyns, whose copy differs considerably from this, and agrees more nearly with the C.C.C.C. MS., states that he printed from the Emm. Coll. MS. but refers also to MSS. C.C.C.C. cv. p. 321. Harl. Collect. 417. Coverdale, Letters of the Martyrs. Foxe, Acts, &c. vol. iii. p. 94. Cranmer's Answer, &c. edit. 1580. Strype, Cranmer, p. 305. Acta Disputationis Londinensis, &c., edita a Valerando Pollano, 1554. Burn. Ref. App. vol. ii. B. ii. No. 8.]

[2 There can be no doubt that this Declaration was the "seditious bill" referred to in the following minute from the council book. On the 8th of

DECLARATION CONCERNING THE MASS.

and religion, which lying he feareth not to do most earnestly at this present. For whereas a prince of famous memory, king Henry the Eighth, seeing the great abuses of the Latin mass, reformed some things therein in time; and after, our late sovereign lord Edward the Sixth took the same wholly away for the manifold errors and abuses thereof, and restored in the place thereof Christ's holy supper according to Christ's institution, and as the apostles in the primitive church used the same in the beginning: now goeth the devil about by lying to overthrow the Lord's holy supper again, and to restore his Latin satisfactory mass, a thing of his own invention and device. And to bring the same the more easily to pass, some of his inventors have abused the name of me, Thomas archbishop of Canterbury, bruiting abroad that I have set up the mass again in Canterbury, and that I offered myself to say mass at the burial of our late sovereign prince king Edward the Sixth, and also that I offered myself to say mass before the queen's highness at Paul's church in London, and I wot not where. And although I have been well exercised these xx years in suffering and bearing evil bruits, reports, and lies, and have not been much grieved thereat, but have borne all things quietly; yet when untrue reports and lies turn to the hinderance of God's truth, then are they in no wise tolerate or to be suffered. Wherefore this is to signify to the world, that it was not I that did set up the mass in Canterbury, but it was a false, flattering, and lying monk[3], with a dozen of his blind adherents, which caused the mass to be set up there, and that without mine advice or counsel. *Reddat illi Dominus in die illo.*

And as for offering myself to say mass before the queen's highness at Paul's, or in any other place, I never did it, as her grace well knoweth. But if her grace will give me leave, I will and by the might of God shall be ready at all times to prove against all that would say the contrary, that all that is said in the holy communion, set forth by the most innocent and godly prince, king Edward the Sixth, in his court of parliament, is conformable to that order that our Saviour Christ did both observe and command to be observed; which also his apostles and primitive church used many years: whereas the mass in many things not only hath no foundation of Christ's apostles nor the primitive church, but also is manifestly contrary to the same, and containeth in it many horrible abuses. Whereabout though that many do maliciously report of Mr Peter Martyr, that he is a man of no learning[4], and therefore not to be credited; yet, if the queen's highness will grant it, I with the said Mr Peter, and other four or five which I will choose, will by God's grace take upon us to defend, that not only the common prayers of the church, the ministration of the sacraments, and other rites and ceremonies, but also that all the doctrine and religion set forth by our sovereign lord king Edward the Sixth is more pure and according to God's word, than any other that hath been used in England these thousand years: so that God's word may be the judge, and that the reasons and proofs upon both parties may be set out in writing; to the intent that all the world may judge therein, and that no man shall start back from their writings. And where they boast of the faith of the church in the olden time these xv hundred years, we will join with them in this point, that that doctrine and usage is to be followed, which was in the church fifteen hundred years past. And we shall prove, that the order of the church set out in this realm by our said sovereign lord king Edward the Sixth, by act of parliament, is the same that was used fifteen hundred years past. And so shall they never be able to prove theirs.

September, 1553, "Thomas archbishop of Canterbury appeared before the lords, as he was the day before appointed. After long and serious debating of his offence by the whole board, it was thought convenient that as well for the treason committed by him against the queen's majesty, as for the aggravating of the same his offence, by spreading about seditious bills moving tumults to the disquietness of the present state, he should be committed to the tower, there to remain and be referred to justice, or further ordered as shall stand with the queen's pleasure."—Extracts from the Proceedings of the Privy Council, printed in *Archæologia*, vol. xviii. p. 175. According to Foxe, the Declaration was circulated in London on the 7th of September; according to Burnet's Latin copy, it was "lecta publice in vico mercatorum ab amico qui clam autographum surripuerat, 5 Septemb. anno Dom. 1553." Jenkyns.]

[3 "Whom the archbishop afterward named to be Thornton." Foxe, *Acts*, &c. 1st edit. p. 1478.]

[4 This report had been circulated, and contradicted by Cranmer two years before. See Answer to Gardiner, p. 195, and Answer to Smith, p. 373, of this volume.]

[Many copies of the foregoing Declaration were hastily written out and dispersed abroad. Foxe states that every scrivener's shop almost was occupied in writing and copying it out (see p. xxi. of the present volume); which accounts for numerous small variations. Strype (p. 436) states that it was sent by Grindal to Foxe, and gives it more nearly to the form in which it appears in the *Acts and Monuments,* and which is here subjoined from p. 1395, of the edition of 1576.]

A PURGATION OF
THOMAS ARCHBISHOP OF CANTERBURY,
AGAYNST CERTAINE SCLAUNDERS FALSELY RAYSED UPON HYM.

As the devil, Christ's ancient adversary, is a liar and the father of lies, even so hath he stirred up his servants and members to persecute Christ and his true word and religion with lying; which he ceaseth not to do most earnestly at this present time. For whereas the prince of famous memory, king Henry the eight, seeing the great abuses of the Latin mass, reformed some things therein in his lifetime; and after our late sovereign lord king Edward VI. took the same whole away for the manifold and great errors and abuses of the same, and restored in the place thereof Christ's holy supper according to Christ's own institution, and as the apostles used the same in the primitive church: the devil goeth about now by lying to overthrow the Lord's holy supper again, and to restore his Latin satisfactory mass, a thing of his own invention and devise. And to bring the same more easily to pass, some have abused the name of me, Thomas archbishop of Canterbury, bruiting abroad that I have set up the mass again at Canterbury, and that I offered to say mass at the burial of our late sovereign prince king Edward the VI., and that I offered also to say mass before the queen's highness, and at Paul's church, and I wot not where. And although I have been well exercised these xx years to suffer and bear evil reports and lies, and have not been much grieved thereat, but have borne all things quietly; yet when untrue reports and lies turn to the hinderance of God's truth, they are in no wise to be suffered. Wherefore these be to signify unto the world, that it was not I that did set up the mass at Canterbury, but it was a false flattering, lying, and dissembling monk, which caused mass to be set up there without mine advice or counsel. *Reddat illi Dominus in die illo.*

And as for offering myself to say mass before the queen's highness, or in any other place, I never did it, as her grace well knoweth. But if her grace will give me leave, I shall be ready to prove against all that will say the contrary, that all that is contained in the holy communion set out by the most innocent and godly prince king Edward the VI., in his high court of parliament, is conformable to that order which our Saviour Christ did both observe and command to be observed, and which his apostles and primitive church used many years: whereas the mass in many things not only hath no foundation of Christ, his apostles, nor the primitive church, but is manifestly contrary to the same, and containeth many horrible abuses in it. And although many, either unlearned or malicious, do report, that M. Peter Martyr is unlearned, yet, if the queen's highness will grant thereunto, I with the said M. Peter Martyr, and other four or five which I shall choose, will by God's grace take upon us to defend, not only the common prayers of the church, the ministration of the sacraments, and other rites and ceremonies, but also all the doctrine and religion set out by our said sovereign lord king Edward the VI., to be more pure and according to God's word, than any other that hath been used in England these 1000 years: so that God's word may be judge, and that the reasons and proofs of both parties may be set out in writing; to the intent, as well that all the world may examine and judge thereon, as that no man shall start back from his writing. And where they boast of the faith that hath been in the church these 1500 years, we will join with them in this point, and that the same doctrine and usage is to be followed, which was in the church 1500 years past. And we shall prove, that the order of the church set out at this present in this realm by act of parliament, is the same that was used in the church 1500 years past, and so shall they be never able to prove theirs.

INDEX.

(The asterisks denote the paging of the Latin Version of the Defence.)

ABSURDITIES, Gardiner rejects conclusions from, 333.

Accidents, of the bread and wine in the sacrament remain; but, the papists say, they hang alone in air, 45, 256, 328; no philosopher ever said that they might stand without any substance, 254, 6; Gardiner's joke upon them, 256; cannot be the nature of substances, and the very substances themselves, 260, 1, 7, 73, 4, 84, 301, 23; substances cannot be without them, 326; cannot be broken, eaten, &c., 324.

Adam, his creation out of clay; Gardiner's argument from, 266.

Adminicles, helps, supports, 37.

Adnihilation of the sacramental bread, 305, 6; can only be wrought by the power of God, 306.

Adoration in the sacrament, 228, 9, 34, 5.

Æpinus, or Hippinus, quoted by Gardiner as supporting the real presence, although an enemy of the Church of Rome, 20, 159; says that *eucharistia* is called a sacrifice, because it is a remembrance of the true sacrifice which was offered upon the cross, and that in it is dispensed the very body and blood, yea, the very death of Christ, 160; Gardiner alleges that he considered the Lord's supper a sacrifice propitiatory, 365; Cranmer asserts that he wrote to reprove the papists for feigning the mass to be propitiatory, *ibid.*

Agrippa, Cornelius, agrees with Cranmer about the king's divorce, xi.

Ἀληθής and ἀληθῶς, (John vi.) 24.

Algerus on the sacrament, commended by Erasmus, 20.

Aliud and *aliud*, diversity of nature, 290, 4.

Alius and *alius*, diversity of person, 290, 4.

Altar, the calling it reverend does not prove the real presence of Christ there, 228.

Ambrose, his words upon the eating of Christ's body to be understood figuratively, 55; says that we must not seek Christ upon earth, nor in earth, but in heaven, 96, *49; that before the consecration, in the sacrament, another kind is named, but after the consecration the body of Christ is signified; and again he writes, 'thou dost receive the sacrament for a similitude of the flesh and blood of Christ, but thou dost obtain the grace and virtue of his true nature,' 122, 178, 9, *59; other passages from his writings upon this similitude, *ibid.*; says that the bread is bread before the consecration, but after the words of the consecration it is the body of Christ, 177, 8, *72; affirms that the body of Christ is a spiritual meat, and spiritually eaten, 179; speaks figuratively of the bread after consecration, 179; Erasmus judges that the books *de sacramentis, et de mysteriis*, ascribed to Ambrose, were none of his, and Melancthon suspected the same thing, 180; says, Jesus is the bread that is the meat of saints, and he that taketh this bread dies not a sinner's death, 210, *81; that this bread of life which came down from heaven doth minister everlasting life, and is the body of Christ; and how it differs from manna, *ibid.*; his words upon the worshipping of God's footstool, 236, 7; says that if the word of God can make things of nought, much more can it change things that were before into other things, 276, *31; his words *de initiandis*, upon which the papists rely to support their transubstantiation, 318, *41; it is doubtful whether the book *de initiandis* is his, 319; but it only says that the nature of the bread and wine, not the substance, is changed, *ibid.*; tells how the sacramental bread is changed, by adding to it the grace of Christ's body, 320; says the forms of bread and wine are changed, the papists say they remain, 323.

Angels cannot be at one time in two places, 97.

Anthropomorphites, their heresy, 172, 3, 91.

Apollinaris, a heretic, 262, 77; maintained that the Godhead and manhood in Christ were so mixed and confounded together that they both made but one nature, 286, 338.

Aquinas, Thomas, speaks of the body of Christ going no farther than the stomach, 56; says that the whole of Christ's body is in every part of the bread and wine, 64; asserts that, if a mouse or dog eat the sacramental bread, it is the body of Christ, 68; says that the sacrifice of the priest is satisfactory in proportion to his devotion, 84.

Argument, a good one, but nothing to the purpose, (Gardiner) 316.

Arians denied Christ to be of the same substance with his Father, 63, 7, 273, 339.

Aristotle cited by Gardiner on transubstantiation, 251; his philosophy referred to, 331.

Arselacton, Nottinghamshire, the birth-place of Cranmer, vii.

Artemon, held that Christ was very man, and not God, 278.

Athanasius, speaking of the eating of Christ's flesh, and drinking of his blood, says, for this cause he made mention of his ascension into heaven, to pluck them from corporal phantasy, 209, *80.

Augustine, cited by Gardiner, 22, 26, 59; his interpretation of Christ's words in the sacrament, 24; speaks the same words as St Cyprian, and as Christ himself, 27; declares the eating of Christ's flesh to be only a figurative speech, in the mind, not with the mouth, *ibid.*; cited by Gardiner as saying that we receive in the sacrament the body of Christ with our mouth, 55; his words about eating the body of Christ to be understood figuratively, *ibid.*; says that the Lord's supper was the same to Peter and to Judas, but that the effect differed in them, 57; that the ways of evil men do not obstruct the sacraments of God, but that the sacraments hinder the ways of evil men, 58; declared it to be figuratively only that Christ carried himself in his own hands, 61; says that the sacraments worthily used bring reward, unworthily, judgment, 68, 9; proves that Christ is gone hence, as concerning his manhood, 73; marks this difference, that the sacraments of the fathers of the old testament contained the promise of that which in our sacrament is given, 74, 7; says that both we and the prophets received one thing in the diversity of sacraments, 75; his exposition of St Paul, 1 Cor. x., and Psalm lxxvii., 76; thinks those mad who see diversity of things because of diversity of signs in the old and new testament, *ibid.*; says the memorial of the true sacrifice made upon the cross is called by the name of a sacrifice, 87; says that we may not think Christ everywhere in his man's nature, but that he is everywhere as God, 94, 5, 6, *48; observes that, as a body must needs be in some place, if it is not within the compas of a place, it is nowhere; and if it be nowhere, then it is not, 97, 101, *50; says that we call that the body and blood of Christ which is taken of the fruit of the earth, and consecrated by mystical prayer; and also that Jesus called meat his body, and drink his blood, 105, *54; his rules to discern a proper speech from a figurative one, 115, 137; says that to keep in our minds that Christ was crucified and shed his blood for us, is to eat his flesh and drink his blood, 115, *57; says, 'prepare not your mouth, or jaws, but your heart; believe, and thou hast eaten,' 118, 208; meant that Christ's flesh is not to be eaten carnally, but spiritually, at the Lord's supper as well as at all other times, *ibid.*; his reply to Boniface, who asked him how parents and friends could answer for an infant in baptism, 124, *59; says that a thing which signifies is wont to be called by the name of the thing which it signifies, 125, 351; writes, that in the sacraments we must not consider what they be, but what they signify, 126, 221; says that he serves under a sign, who worketh or worshippeth any sign, not knowing what it signifieth, and that every man, when he receives the sacraments of baptism and the Lord's supper, knows that we may not worship with a carnal bondage their visible signs, 134; says Christ reigns not carnally in heaven, 139; declares that our resurrection, although it shall be of true flesh, yet it shall not be carnally, (Gardiner) *ibid.*; says that Christ's body is circumscribed and contained in one place, 140; declares that the gospel is to be received or heard with no less fear and reverence than the body of Christ, 146; says, contrary to Chrysostom, that we touch not Christ with our hands, 153; did not reprove the Messalians, 173; gives as a rule, that we must foresee that we do not so affirm the divinity of him that is man, that we should thereby take away the truth of his body, 186; says that Christ is everywhere in that he is God, but in heaven in that he is man, *ibid.*; speaks of the visible and invisible sacrament, 201, 4; declares that to eat Christ's body, and to drink his blood, is to have life, 203; says, the wicked neither eat Christ's flesh nor drink his blood, although every day they eat the sacrament thereof, to the condemnation of their presumption, 205; declares the words of Christ to be spirit and life, though not to him that carnally understands them, 206; declares that he that agreeth not with Christ, doth neither eat his body nor drink his blood, 210, *81; that neither heretics, nor hypocritical professors have either a true faith, or are to be counted among the members of Christ, 211, *81; that a man may eat and drink the bread and wine, and nevertheless die; but the very body and blood of Christ no man eateth but that hath everlasting life, 212, *82; says that the sacrament is taken in the Lord's table, of some men to life, and of some men to death, but the thing itself (whereof it is a sacrament) is taken of all men to life, and of no man to death, 212; that this is to eat that meat, and drink that drink, to dwell in Christ, and have Christ dwelling in him; and this is a token or knowledge that a man hath eaten and drunken, if he dwell in Christ, and have Christ dwelling in him, *ibid.*; declares that to eat Christ's flesh and to drink his blood is a figurative speech, signifying the participation of his passion, *ibid.*; says that the eating is to be refreshed, and the drinking is but to live, *ibid.*; that when the apostles did eat bread, that was the Lord, Judas did but eat the bread of the Lord, and not the bread that was the Lord, 213, 224; says that evil men receive the sacrament of Christ's body, although it availeth them not, 216; his words *contra Cresconium*, 221, *85; his words on baptism against the Donatists, 221, 2; his words on the text "who eateth my flesh and drinketh my blood, dwelleth in me, and I in him," cited by Gardiner, 222; says that, after a certain manner, the sacrament of Christ's body is Christ's body, 225; when he says, no man doth eat the flesh of Christ, unless he first worship him, speaks of worshipping in heaven, 230; declares that although the sacrament be visibly ministered, yet it must be invisibly understood, 230, 1, *87; his words that Christ has given us a sacrament of the eating of his body, to be understood invisibly and spiritually, 231; declares plainly, in many places, that Christ body is not corporally present, nor corporally eaten in the sacrament, 232; says that to eat Christ's flesh is fruitfully to remember that the same flesh was crucified for us, 232; his exposition of Psalm xcviii., where it is commanded to worship the earth, God's footstool, by which may be understood the flesh of Christ, 236; says that sometimes, in scripture, a thing is told after that was done before, 248; writes, with other old authors, that St Paul (1 Cor. x.) spake of such bread as is made of a great multitude of grains of corn united into one material loaf, as the spiritual members of Christ be joined together into one mystical body of Christ, 249; says that that which you see in the altar is the bread and the cup, which also your eyes do shew you; but faith sheweth further, that the bread is the body of Christ, and the cup his blood, 277, *31; declares the sacrifice of the church consists of two things, of the visible kind of the element, and of the invisible flesh and blood of our Lord, *ibid.*, 282; proves, that as the heavenly bread, which is Christ's flesh, after a manner is called the body of Christ, so is the sacrament of faith, which is baptism, faith, 282; says that Nestorius taught that Christ was man only, and that Eutyches denied Christ's manhood, 293; writes that that which men call a sacrifice is a sign or representation of the true sacrifice, 351, *95.

Baldus, 194.

Baptism: the washing outwardly teacheth the washing God worketh inwardly, 17; injury to from popish doctrines, 25, 34, 45; in every part of the water in baptism is whole Christ and the Holy Spirit sacramentally, 64; the Holy Ghost doth not only come to us in baptism, and Christ there clothe us, but they do so long as we dwell in Christ, 71; Christ given in the sacrament of, as in the sacrament of his flesh and blood, 76; Christ present as well in baptism as in the Lord's supper, 92, 228, 342, 356, 366; how parents and friends can answer for an infant in, 124; Christ not only in them that duly receive the sacrament of the Lord's supper, but in them that duly receive the sacrament of baptism, and in all other true christian people at other times, 140; Christ and the Holy Ghost not in the water of, 148; how water called *aqua regenerans* and *aqua sanctificans* in, yet it doth not regenerate indeed, 150; because it is the sacrament of regeneration and sanctification, *ibid.*, 153; Christ manifested and exhibited in, spiritually, 156; how we are made new therein, 176; regenerated as well in baptism as in the sacrament of the body and blood of Christ, *ibid.*; the water is changed in nature therein, 180, 308; those that come feignedly, and those that come unfeignedly, both be washed with the holy water, but both be not washed with the Holy Ghost, 221; sacramentally, 254, 322; there is none without water, as well as the Holy Ghost, spiritually regenerating, 304; Nazianzen, Emissen, Chrysostom, Ambrose, and all the ancient authors, speak of the change in this sacrament, 311; Gardiner's statement respecting the effect of Christ's sacrifice on the cross dispensed in, 360.

Barrett, Dr, rejected by Cranmer at Cambridge, viii.

Basil, proves that the Holy Ghost is God by being in several persons at one time, 97, *50; says we eat Christ's flesh and drink his blood, being made, by his incarnation and sensible life, partakers of his word and wisdom, 209; a passage from him about a separation of the accidents to discover the substance by itself alone, 324, 6.

Basilides, a heretic, 277.

Batholus, 194.

Berengarius, his recantation, 13; was constrained by Nicholas II. to recant, 14, 46, 196, 203; his confession that the body of Christ was torn in pieces by the teeth of the faithful, 46 *n.*, 48, 113 *n*; Smith's exposition of his meaning, 48, 9.

Bernardus, *de cœna Domini*, 41 *n*; says as Christ gave his life for us, so he gave his flesh, the one to redeem, the other to feed us, 63.

Bertram, cited by Gardiner, 13; only wrote of the sacrament at the request of King Charles [the bald], 14; his doctrine of the old and new sacraments, 78; did not write secretly but openly what the doctrine of the church then was, 173; was never charged with error but by Gardiner, 196.

Biel, *see Gabriel.*

Bishops do not lose their original names upon their consecration, and in like manner the sacramental bread remains bread still, though called the Lord's body, 275.

Bocardo, the prison at Oxford, Cranmer confined therein, xxii. xxiii., 392.

Body of Christ, present spiritually, not corporally, in those that receive the sacrament, 3; not really given by the priest, 182.

Bonaventure speaks of the body of Christ going no further than the stomach, 56.

Bread, wine, and water, not holy, but holy tokens; not bare tokens, 11; miscalled for the figures of them, 53, 4, 323; bread is not Christ's body, 110, 179; bread and wine not holy before the consecration, 180; the divinity may be said to be poured sacramentally into the bread, as the Spirit of God is said to be in the water of baptism, 181; bread may have another use than to feed the body, *ibid.*; whether Christ's body be made of the matter of bread, 194; Smith's doctrine of the corruption in the sacramental bread and wine, 381.

Bucer, cited by Gardiner, as professing the faith of the real and substantial presence, 19; his words upon the similitude of the sun and Christ's presence in the sacrament, 90; says faith must relieve the default of our senses, *ibid.*; his exposition of St Augustine's words upon the sacrament of the body of Christ, 126; denies that Christ is really and substantially present in the bread of the sacrament, but in the ministration, 225; dissents in nothing from Œcolampadius and Zuinglius, *ibid.*

Butts, Dr, the king's physician, informs the king of the shameful treatment of Cranmer by the council, xviii.

Calling, whether it means making, 106, 7, 181, 323.

Canon-law, purposely corrupts the truth of God's word, 33.

Canons of the apostles respecting priests at the communion, disregarded by the papists, 353, *96.

Capharnaites murmured at eating man's flesh, 116, 231, 249; cannot understand any action taken spiritually, 185.

Carnally and corporally, how these terms are used, 139, 40.

Cart, putting it before the horses, 371.

Cassiodorus, 195, *75.

Catechism, of Germany, translated by Cranmer, 188, 90; says that with our bodily mouths we receive the body and blood of Christ, 226; Gardiner refers to a picture contained in it, to prove what it taught, 227; it was not put there by Cranmer, but by some idle painter, *ibid.*

Catherine, queen, Cranmer consulted by Henry VIII. about her divorce, ix.

Catholic faith, Gardiner's and Cranmer's definition of it, 12, 31, 51, 2; Gardiner's doctrine of it not true by his own definition, 13; papists the cause of its hinderance of late, 14; church of Rome not its true mother, 18; the papistical faith wrongly called catholic, 113; has taught from the beginning that as in the sacrament there are two diverse natures, bread and wine; so in the person of Christ remain two natures, his divinity and his humanity, 297; the true catholic faith upon the sacrament, 337; the true faith was in the church from the beginning, and not first taught by Berengarius, 376.

Cautels, cautions, chicaneries, 337, 48.

Cerdon, a heretic, 277.

Chantries, dissolution of, during the king's nonage, resisted by Cranmer, xii.

Christ, his real presence should prove no transubstantiation of the bread and wine, 4; why he came into the world, and how the benefits of his coming are perverted and obscured by the papists, 5; how he is present in his sacraments, 11; is spiritually present, though corporally in heaven, 12, 46, 7, 54, 74, 87, 127, 203; offering of, every day by the priest, not in scripture, nor any ancient author, 13; his doctrine and St John Baptist's no worse because they were put to death for it, 15; did not give his body, but the figure of it, to be eaten, *ibid.*; does not make his body corporally to be in many places at one time, 16; the real and substantial presence of his body and blood in the sacrament is truly the faith of the papists, 21, 46; the eating of his body and blood, quoted from John vi., 24, *15; distinction between the giving his flesh on the cross, and in the last supper, 24; received whole, body and soul, manhood and godhead, in baptism as well as in the holy communion, 25; did not speak of corporal eating in John vi., *ibid.*; there is no will of his set forth in scripture, that he is really, carnally, corporally, and naturally, under the forms of bread and wine, 34, 61; cannot be eaten again now, nor could his body have been crucified on the morrow, if it had been so eaten up, as the papists say, in the last supper, 35; if he fulfilled his promise of life at his last supper, as the papists say he did, he needed not to die for us afterwards, *ibid.*; his ambiguous speeches not always expounded by the evangelists, 36; told his disciples of another kind of eating and drinking than that which belongs only to the preservation of temporal life, 39; there is no kind of meat that is comfortable to the soul but the death of Christ's blessed body, nor drink that can quench her thirst, but only the blood-shedding of our Saviour Christ, 40; far excels all corporal meats and drinks, *ibid.*; unity of his mystical body, 42; does not feed Jews, Turks, and infidels, if they receive the sacrament, 45; his daily sacrifice an error of the papists, 47; is not in the sacramental bread and wine, but in them that worthily eat and drink it, 52, 3; is present corporally in heaven only, and spiritually in them that worthily take the bread and wine, 54, 5, 93; is received in the heart, and not in the mouth, as the papists say, 57, 373; remains in the man that worthily receives the bread, as long as he remains a member of Christ, 59; whether a beast or a bird eat his body, 67; whether evil men eat his body, 69; whether the fathers and prophets of the old testament ate Christ's flesh and drank his blood, 75; whether his body is every day many times made, and of bread and wine; or never but once, and then of the substance of his blessed mother, 79, 194; his declaration of his willingness to die was not a sacrifice propitiatory for sin, or else his death was in vain, 85, 6; not his body, but the crucifying of it, and the effusion of his blood unto death, was the very sacrifice for our sins, 88; did not declare in his supper that he was then a sacrifice, but that a sacrifice should be made of his body, which was done the day after, *ibid.*;

434   INDEX.

whether he is corporally in many places at one time, or only, like the sun, in heaven, and nowhere else, 89, &c. 186, 371; is corporally in heaven, and there shall continue until the last judgment, 93; his presence in this world, in his divinity, 94; is in heaven as concerning his manhood, and everywhere as concerning his godhead, 94, 5, 6, 7; how it may be true that he is with us, and yet gone from us, 102; interpretation of his words, "this is my body," 103, 261; whether he called bread his body, 103, 9, 10, 370; eating his body horrible to be heard of any Christian, 110, 12; "to eat his body and drink his blood," and "to call bread his body, and wine his blood," are figurative speeches, 110, 11, 12, 13, 14, 15, 18, 132, 145, 181, 232; why Christ's body is not always to be taken as a figure, 120; his humanity not changed from the very nature of man after his resurrection, 129; all passages which declare Christ to be here on earth, and to be eaten and drunken of christian people, are to be understood either of his divine nature, or else figuratively, or spiritually, 138, 40, 185; is present in the sacrament as he is in heaven (Gardiner), 140; whether he is in heaven only after a spiritual manner, 141; his unity with us, 162, 3, 4, 5; no man can eat his flesh and drink his blood but spiritually, 203; spirit and life not in evil men because they hear Christ's words, 206; the godly only eat Christ, 207; is not eaten with the teeth, but with faith, 208; the eating his flesh gives everlasting life, 213; when an unrepentant sinner receives the sacrament, whether he have Christ's body within him or no, 216, 17, 18; his body, in the sacrament, is the same, however described, the diversity is in the eating thereof, no man eating it carnally; but the good eating it both sacramentally and spiritually, and the evil only sacramentally, that is, figuratively, 224; what kind of body he has in the sacrament, 228; of the manner and form of worshipping him in the sacrament, ibid.; although continually in heaven, yet he is worshipped here also, at all times, and in all places, 230; at his transfiguration, and after his resurrection, remained like a man in all proportions and members, 233; his humiliation, his incarnation and conversation with us here on earth, 235; whole Christ, God and man, ought to be honoured with one entire and godly honour, 236; whether by the earth, God's footstool, was meant the flesh of Christ to be worshipped, 236, 7; is not in any wise to be worshipped as being corporally in the bread in the sacrament, 238; his body must have been burnt, if the papist's doctrines are true, as in the old church they burned all the sacramental bread that remained uneaten, 250; retained his divine nature after his incarnation, 278; two examples given by the old catholic writers of his two-fold nature —one the body and soul, in man,—and the other the bread and wine, and the body and blood of Christ, in the sacrament, ibid., 284; how bread is his body, 281; his divine nature rests in his body, 228; he is the spiritual pasture and food of our souls, as meat and drink is of our bodies, 304; his body is whole in every part of the bread divided sacramentally, as it is in the whole undivided, 327; it is not necessary that his manhood should be where his divinity is, 340; we may now look for no other priest, nor sacrifice, than him, to take away our sins, 347; his priesthood cannot pass to another, 363; no ancient council or doctor says that his very body is eaten in the sacrament, 370; it was upon the cross that he gave his flesh for us, not at his supper, 372; is present with his holy church, 376.

Christians in the latter days so dazzled by the Romish antichrist as to believe whatever he prescribed to them, 46.

Chrysostom and other old authors do not speak as Berengarius does about Christ's flesh, 49; his words upon the eating of Christ's body to be understood figuratively, 55; says with the other Greek writers, that Christ's calling bread his body means making (Gardiner), 106; affirms, that, if any man understand the words of Christ carnally, he shall surely profit nothing thereby, 114; says that Christ ordained the table of his holy supper for this purpose, that in that sacrament he should daily shew unto us bread and wine for a similitude of his body and blood, 122; not only says that Christ is in our hands, but also that we see him with our eyes, touch him, feel him, and grope him, fix our teeth in his flesh, taste it, break it, eat it, and digest it; make red our tongues, and dye them with his blood, &c.; which things cannot be understood of the body and blood of Christ, but by a figurative speech, 153, 226; his writings are full of tropes and figures, 182; says, speaking of the Lord's supper, When you come to these mysteries, do not think that you receive by a man the body of God, meaning of Christ, 182; affirms that it is not man which makes the bread and wine, being consecrated, the body and blood of Christ; but it is Christ himself that makes himself to be there present, by which he means present in such sort as he is in heaven only, 183; makes no difference between receiving Christ in the holy communion and in baptism, ibid.; says we ascend into heaven, and do eat Christ sitting there above, meaning by the marvellous working of God in the hearts of them that receive the sacraments, ibid.; where he speaks of the great miracle of Christ, that "he sitteth above with his Father, and is the same hour here with us in our hands," it is true that he sits above in his natural body, and yet is in our hands sacramentally and in our hearts by grace and spiritual nourishment, 186; says that the true worshippers of Christ ascend up and feed upon him where he sitteth in his high throne of glory with his Father, 235; writes, against those who use only water in the sacrament, that Christ, minding to pluck up that heresy by the roots, used wine as well before his resurrection, when he gave the mysteries, as after at his table without mysteries, 274; says that the bread, when it is sanctified by means of the priest, is delivered from the name of bread, and is exalted to the name of the Lord's body, although the nature of the bread still remains, ibid.; his epistle ad Cæsarium Monachum, ibid. n.; proves the unity of the two natures of Christ, 286; Cranmer translated his words from a copy at Florence not in print, 287; his words cited to prove transubstantiation by the papists, 312; but he adds, 'do not think that you receive by a man the body of God,' &c. ibid., 313, 14, 15; was much addicted to the use of negatives by comparison, 314; his admonition to withdraw our minds at the Lord's table from sensible to heavenly and godly things, 315; says that Christ is both gone up into heaven, and yet is here received of us; for he is gone up to heaven carnally, but is here received spiritually, 341; after speaking of the sacrifice of Christ, says, that which we do is done for a remembrance of that which was done by Christ, for Christ says, "do this in remembrance of me," 352; speaking of christian people ever offering one sacrifice of christ, corrects himself by saying, "but rather we make a remembrance of Christ's sacrifice," ibid.

Church of Rome, not the true mother of the catholic faith, 18.

Church, God preserves the true faith in his holy church, 376; never wholly errs, 377; no man can discern it, but God alone, ibid.; cannot make new articles of faith, ibid.; compared to a registry for keeping men's wills, ibid.; the holy church but a small flock in comparison with the followers of antichrist, ibid.; Christ and his apostles were in their time the only true church, 378; the open church has been for four or five hundred years defiled by the papists, *ibid.*; the church of Christ, not antichrist, is to be followed, *ibid.*

Clement, Saint, alleged to say that if any portion of the host remain it must be consumed by the clerks, with fear and trembling, and that they must fast for some hours afterwards, lest the residue should mix with other common meats digested by the belly, 141; his epistles were feigned before the papists had run so far into errors as now, 144; his epistles not mentioned by Eusebius, St Jerome, nor Gennadius, 144; Peter could not have made him his successor, as said in his epistles, *ibid.*

Cockle among clean corn, 360.

Cole, Dr, ordered to prepare a sermon for Cranmer's execution-day, and visits him in prison, xxii.

Common Prayer, book of, alleged by Gardiner to teach the doctrine of the real presence, 51, 5, 62, 3, 79, 83, 92, 229, 325; Cranmer denies that it so teaches, 53, 6, 64, 327; we do not there pray that the bread and wine be made the body and blood of Christ, but that unto us, in that holy mystery, they may be so, 79, 271.

Communion, holy, a short instruction thereto, 354.

Consecration defined, 177, 8, 80.

Constantius, Marcus, (Gardiner's assumed name), 67 *n.*, 419.

Council, Ephesine, cited by Gardiner, 23; Cyril and this council decreed truly that Christ's flesh, when eaten, must be joined to his divinity, or it could not give everlasting life, 27; words of perverted by Smith, 369; the controversy therein was not of uniting Christ's flesh to the forms of the bread and wine, but to his divinity in his incarnation, 370; of Lateran, the fourth, transubstantiation first named there, A.D. 1215, 239, 40, 376; of Nice, its decree respecting priests at the communion, disregarded by the papists, 353, *96; its doctrine on the sacrifice of Christ set forth by Gardiner, 355; speaks of a sacrifice of lauds and thanksgivings, and not of propitiation, 356; does not say that Christ is corporally in the bread and wine, but intimates that he is gone up to heaven, *ibid.*

Cranmer, his life, vii.; born at Arselacton, Nottinghamshire, *ibid.*; chosen fellow of Jesus College, Cambridge, *ibid.*; married and became reader in Buckingham College, *ibid.*; slanderous report of his being hosteler of the Dolphin inn, at Cambridge, viii.; rechosen into Jesus College upon the death of his wife, and made reader of divinity there, and public examiner in the University, *ibid.*; refuses Wolsey's fellowship, *ibid.*; confers with Drs Gardiner and Foxe, at Waltham, upon Queen Catherine's divorce, *ibid.*; is sent for by the king upon the subject, and tells him that the pope cannot dispense with the word of God, *ibid.*; is assigned by the king to consider the question of his divorce, and is sent ambassador to Rome upon the subject, x.; made penitentiary to the pope, *ibid.*; goes ambassador to the emperor, and confers with Cornelius Agrippa, upon the subject of the divorce, xi.; is made archbishop of Canterbury, *ibid.*; his qualifications for the office, studies, and habits, *ibid.*; opposes Gardiner on the Six Articles, xii.; Cromwell and the lords sent to dine and console with him under his disappointment thereon, *ibid.*; resists the dissolving of chantries during the king's non-age, *ibid.*; his character for patience, xiii.; releases from the Fleet a priest who had been sent there for calling him an hosteler, xiv.; his liberality and justice in paying his debts before his attainder, xv.; relieves the sick poor returned from the wars at Boulogne, xvi.; opposes the king's wishes about the Six Articles, and, at length, wins him to his side, xvii.; Gardiner and others urge the king to commit him to the Tower for exciting heresy, *ibid.*; the king consents, but tells Cranmer to appeal to him by his signet, xviii.; is treated with great indignity by the council, but the king rebukes them for their malice, and they are glad to make friends with him again, xix.; was always defended by the king, Henry VIII. *ibid.*; advances in the royal favour under Edward VI. *ibid.*; confers with bishop Ridley upon the holy sacrament, and sets forth the true doctrine thereof in five books, xx.; is answered by Gardiner, in his "Explication," to which he replies, *ibid.*; some of his other works, *ibid.*; is condemned for high treason under Queen Mary, but is pardoned of this, and accused of heresy, xxi.; is taken from the Tower to dispute with the divines at Oxford, *ibid.*; is condemned as a heretic, and thrown into gaol, xxii.; is induced to recant, but the queen orders Dr Cole to prepare a sermon for his execution-day, *ibid.*; is visited in prison by Cole and a Spanish friar, and prevailed upon to write his recantation in his own hand, but also writes secretly a contrary address to the people, xxiii.; is taken to St Mary's church and placed upon a stage to hear Cole's sermon, *ibid.*; the substance of the sermon, xxiv.; is exhorted to die patiently, and promised *diriges* and masses for his soul, xxv.; his prayer and last exhortation to the people at his death, xxvi.; he renounces his recantation, and is led to the stake, xxviii.; his appearance at the place of execution, *ibid.*; the Spanish friars try to bring him back to their faith, and one Ely, a priest, chides the people for shaking hands with him, *ibid.*; his behaviour in the flames, xxix.; a list of his writings, xxx.; his motives for writing against the errors of popery, 6; his answer to Gardiner's "Explication," 9; his catechism mistaken by ignorant men, 14, 374; asserts that Gardiner concludes his book with blasphemous words against both sacraments, 45; says Gardiner changed the order of his books to avoid coming first to transubstantiation, because of its having so much less appearance of truth than the doctrine of the real presence, 50, 185; asserts that the true catholic faith is not that Christ is in the bread and wine, which is Luther's doctrine, but that his body and blood is present under the form of bread and wine, 51; acknowledges his former ignorance, and says it is good at all times to turn from error to truth, 64; compares Gardiner's doctrines to a third part in a voluntary descant out of tune, 92; taunts him with being an ignorant lawyer, 157, 185, 235, 7, 48, 301, 68; ridicules Gardiner's absurdities by a play upon "lies" and adverbs in "ly," 157; affirms that his doctrine is not new, but was the public faith of the Catholic church till the time of Nicholas II., 196; says, that in writing his book, he foresaw all the objections that Gardiner could make to it, 220; repels Gardiner's insinuation that he was prompted by some "man" or "friend," 221; declares he writes in English, which all men know, in order that the truth may no longer lie hid under a bushel, 224, 357; confesses that formerly he was in darkness, and defended the error of transubstantiation, 241, 374; denies that his second book, against transubstantiation, was written when he intended to maintain Luther's opinion only, 285; charges Gardiner with being more full of words than learning, 301; his answer to Smith's preface, 368; congratulates himself that Gardiner and Smith have taken up their pens against him, but wishes it had been persons more learned, *ibid.*; Smith perverts the words of the Ephesine council against him, 369; agrees with Smith and the council that the mass is a sacrifice, but denies that it is propitiatory, *ibid.*; asserts that he admits that the same body of Christ, born of the virgin Mary, is received in the sacrament, but contends only about the manner of receiving it, 370; acknowledges his former errors and details his conversion, 374; disclaims worldly motives for the change, and asserts that he sought only the glory of God, *ibid.*; his disputation at Oxford, before Dr Weston and the vice-chancellor of Cambridge, with other members of both universities, 391; three notaries are appointed, and the articles of belief are subscribed to, *ibid.*; after a procession and dinner, Cranmer is brought from Bocardo, the gaol, before the commissioners in St Mary's church, 392; his reply to Weston's exhortation to unity, *ibid.*; the articles are read to him, and utterly denying their truth, he refuses to subscribe to them, *ibid.*; has a copy of the articles given to write his mind upon them, and is remanded to Bocardo, *ibid.*; the modesty of his demeanour before the assembly, 393; sends his answer the next day, *ibid.*; on the third day Cranmer is brought to answer the articles, closed in by the mayor and aldermen for security, *ibid.*; Dr Chedsey, the first opponent, begins, and is followed by several others, whom Cranmer answers amid much interruption and disorder, *ibid.*; he refuses the drink offered him, and at the conclusion is taken back to Bocardo, *ibid.*; sketch of the arguments, and Weston's mistake at the beginning, *ibid.*; Cranmer's answer to him on the folly of disputing that which was determined before the truth was tried, 394; his argument with Chedsey upon the presence of Christ's body in the sacrament, *ibid.*; his explication, in writing, upon the conclusions, 395; Chedsey controverts his explication, *ibid.*; Cranmer replies to him, and puts in a further explication upon the ordinance of the Lord's supper, 396; the disputation resumed by Chedsey, 399; Cranmer denies that Christ's organic body is in the sacrament, *ibid.*; grants that Christ said his body should be given, but denies that it was contained in the bread, 400; Oglethorpe charges Cranmer with evasion; Cranmer corrects Oglethorpe's Latin, *ibid.*; Weston takes up the argument with a passage from Augustine, 401; Cranmer refutes him, *ibid.*; Weston cites St Chrysostom, 402; Cranmer answers him, 403; Weston quotes other passages from Chrysostom, and Cranmer replies, *ibid.*; Cranmer is interrupted by clamour excited by Weston, 406; Chedsey interposes, 407; Cranmer denies his argument, *ibid.*; Chedsey quotes Tertullian and Photius, *ibid.*; Cranmer answers him on Tertullian, 408; Weston interposes, *ibid.*; Cranmer replies to both, *ibid.*; Tresham starts another argument, 409; Cranmer answers him, 410; Tresham refers to Bucer, *contra Abrincensem*, *ibid.*; Cranmer retorts upon his relying on Bucer, *ibid.*; Tresham admonishes Cranmer, but Weston tells him to dispute, and not to pray, 411; Cranmer refutes them by Cyril and Hilary, 412; Chedsey again takes up the argument, and charges Cranmer with falsifying Hilary, 413; Weston calls on Smith to speak to the point, but Smith keeps silence, 414; Yong demands whether there is any body of Christ but his instrumental body, *ibid.*; Cranmer answers him, and he puts other sophistical questions, *ibid.*; Cranmer charges him with perverting the scriptures, 415; Yong quotes from Ambrose, *ibid.*; Cranmer replies to him, 417; argument upon the Holy Ghost in the likeness of a dove, *ibid.*; Yong again cites Ambrose, *ibid.*; Chedsey quotes Justin Martyr, 419; Cranmer asserts that the passage has been falsified by Marcus Constantius, *ibid.*; Weston quotes Irenæus, 420; Cranmer denies his argument, *ibid.*; Chedsey charges Cranmer with a lie in translating Justin, 421; Cranmer replies he gave the meaning, not the words, *ibid.*; Weston charges him with corrupting Emissenus, *ibid.*; Cranmer says it was as in the Decrees, *ibid.*; Weston charges him with other falsifications, from which he clears himself, *ibid.*; Weston reproaches him with bringing the people into error, and calling him (Weston) a heretic, for teaching that God had no right hand, *ibid.*; charges him with falsely putting a catechism in the name of the synod of London, 422; Cranmer declares that he was ignorant of that title, and had complained against it, *ibid.*; Weston charges him with several falsifications, *ibid.*; Harpsfield disputes with Cranmer for his doctor's degree, 423; Cranmer addresses him upon leaving the interpretation of scripture to the church, and apologises for his rudeness in the Latin tongue, *ibid.*; puts questions to Harpsfield, 424; complains of being answered with questions, *ibid.*; Smith and Weston take up the argument, *ibid.*; several of the doctors argue at once against Cranmer; Ward interposes with Aristotle and Duns, *ibid.*; Cranmer contends with him and several others, 425; Weston commends Cranmer's gentle behaviour and modesty, upon which the doctors take off their caps, 427; the Declaration of Cranmer against the false report that he had again set up the mass at Canterbury, 428.

Creed, christian, as it so expressly mentions Christ's ascension, would also have noticed his tarrying with us still on earth, if it had been so, 93.

Cressey, Mr, of Waltham abbey, Drs Gardiner and Foxe confer with Cranmer, at his house, about Queen Catherine's divorce, ix.

Curtius, 194.

Cuttle-fish, simile of, 24, 237, 84, 93.

Cyprian, says that our dwelling in Christ is the eating of him, 27; that Christ called such bread as is made of many corns his body, and such wine he named his blood, as is pressed out of many grapes, 33, 104, *54; that Christ offered the same thing which Melchisedech offered, bread and wine, that is, his body and blood, 86, 158; speaks of bread by God's omnipotency being made flesh (Gardiner), 1CG; says that Christ's blood is shewn in the wine, and the people in the water mixed with it, so that the mixture signifies the spiritual commixtion and joining of us unto Christ, 121, *58; that Christ in the cross gave his very body to be wounded with the hands of the soldiers, that the apostles might declare to the world how and in what manner bread and wine may be his flesh and blood, *ibid.*; his words upon receiving the mysteries of the Lord's supper, 208, *79; on the eating and drinking of Christ, 209; writing against those that ministered the sacrament with water only, says, 'forasmuch as Christ said, I am a true vine, therefore the blood of Christ is not water, but wine; nor can it be thought that his blood is in the cup, when wine is not in the cup, whereby the blood of Christ is shewed,' 267; and that, 'by the words of Christ we perceive that the cup which the Lord offered was not only water, but also wine, and that it was wine that Christ called his blood; whereby it is clear that Christ's blood is not offered if there is no wine in the chalice,' *ibid.*; says further, 'how shall we drink with Christ new wine of the creature of the vine, if in the sacrifice we do not offer wine?' 267, *30; shews that sacramentally the divinity is poured into the bread and wine, the same bread and wine still remaining, 308, *37; speaks of the eating and not of the keeping the bread in the previous citation, 311; speaks of the wonderful nourishment in the bread and wine as the ineffable work of God, 341.

Cyril and Nestorius, 22; agreed in the substance, but differed as to the manner of the eating of Christ's flesh, 25; Cyril and the Ephesine council, *see Council*; comparison between Cyril and Nestorius, 290, 5; quoted by Gardiner, as asserting Christ to have given his very body in the last supper, 31; cited again by him, 59; by Cranmer, 60; agrees with Augustine in saying, that although Christ took away from hence the presence of his body, yet in majesty of his Godhead he is ever here; and that although Christ be absent from us, as concerning his body, yet by his power he governeth us in all things, 96, *49; says, that if the nature of the Godhead were a body, it must needs be in a place, and have quantity, greatness, and circumscription, 97, *50; commenting upon St John, says, Christ gave to his disciples pieces of bread, saying, Take, eat, this is my body, 105, *54; denies that we have no conjunction in our flesh with Christ, 165, 6, 7, *71; says that those which did eat manna died, because they received thereby no strength to live for ever, but they that receive the bread of life shall be made immortal, 213, *83; affirms that, forasmuch as the flesh of Christ doth naturally give life, therefore it maketh them to live that be partakers of it, *ibid.*; concludes that as two waxes, molten together, do run every part into other, so he that receiveth Christ's flesh and blood must needs be so joined with him that Christ must be in him and he in Christ, *ibid.*; declares that Christ fulfilled his promise of giving his flesh for the life of the world, upon the cross, and not in his supper, 307.

Damascenus, varies from the ancient authors, 196, *75; was the pope's right hand to set up idolatry, *ibid.*; loss and restitution of his hand, 197; sum of his doctrine, *ibid.*; the natural presence of Christ's body in the bread and wine not to be gathered from his writings; nor the adoration of the visible sacrament, 198, 9; wrote of the faith of the sacrament as it was in his time (Gardiner), 200.

Daring (frightening) of larks, 107.
Delaying hot wine, diluting it, 312.
Detection of the Devil's Sophistry, Gardiner's book so called, 107, 8, 94, 241, 56, 307, 8, 71.
Diamond and sapphire, argument from their difference in substance, 257, 60.
Didymus proves that the Holy Ghost is very God, because he is in many places at one time, 97, *96.
Dionysius, 42 *n.*, *21, 255 *n.*, *29; never said that the flesh and blood of Christ were in the bread and wine corporally, but calls them signs, &c. 151, *67; declares the high mystery to be in the marvellous and secret working of God in his reasonable creatures, and not in the bread and wine, 153; calls the bread holy bread, and the cup a holy cup, 177, *73.
Diriges and masses promised to Cranmer at his execution, xxv.
Donatists, 58, 69.
Dorbell, a sophist, 368.
Duns Scotus, a chief pillar of the papists, 64; says that Christ is whole in every part of the bread and wine, *ibid.*; that his quantity is in heaven and not in the sacrament, 73; shews why the school-authors took up the doctrine of transubstantiation, 302, *34, *35; Cranmer refers Gardiner to him upon satisfactory masses, 362.
Durandus acknowledged that but for the church of Rome he should not have believed in transubstantiation, 305.

Eating, signifies believing, 35.
Ebion, a heretic, 301.
Emissenus, Eusebius, cited by Gardiner, 83; does not speak of a corporal conversion, nor taking, but of a sacramental conversion of the bread and wine, and of a spiritual eating and drinking, 174, *72; shews how we are made new in baptism, 175, 6; speaks of looking on the body and blood of Christ and touching him; but these are spiritual things, and require no corporal presence, 226, 7, 8, *86; speaks of only receiving with our hearts, 228; his calling the altar reverend does not prove the real presence of Christ in it, 228; says that the conversion of the bread and wine is like our conversion in baptism, where outwardly nothing is changed, but all the alteration is inwardly and spiritually, 254, 68; speaks of looking upon Christ with our faith, of touching him with our minds, and the hands of our hearts, &c., 317.

English papists speak more grossly upon transubstantiation than the pope himself, 302.
Epiphanius says that Christ, speaking of a loaf which is round in fashion, and can neither see, hear, nor feel, said of it, "this is my body," 33, 104, *54; did not reprove the Messalians, 173; says that the bread is meat, but the virtue that is in it is it that giveth life, 273, *31; speaking of the bread in the Lord's supper, and of the water in baptism, says, that they have no power nor strength of themselves, but by Christ, 273.
Erasmus, cited by Gardiner as commending authors that assert the real presence, although he condemned the abuses of the church, and was taken for no papist, 20; his observation upon the saying that Christ prayed alone, although some of his disciples were with him, 200; his application of St Paul's words "to be guilty of Christ's body" to the Jews, 219; his interpretation of St Paul on Christ's priesthood, Heb. vii., 363.
Error, danger, in opposing one error, of being suspected of another contrary to it, 299.
Eucharistia, meaning of this word, 149, 151, 263, 4.
Eusebius Emissenus. *See Emissenus.*
Euthemius, 24 *n.*
Eutyches, his heresy, 277, 80; said Christ was very God, but not man, exactly contrary to Nestorius, 289, 93, &c.; says that Christ's humanity is absorbed up by his divinity, 297, 338, 40.
Evangelists, whether they told the history of the Lord's supper out of order, 248.

Faith, not to be given without asking "how," or "why," 255; Gardiner denies, by the authority of faith, that there is substance in the matters of the sacrament because they nourish, 333; ought to be grounded on God's word, 368.
Fathers, ancient, their words about the eating of Christ's body to be understood figuratively, 55; whether by the word figure they meant a mystery, 116, 17, 18; taught, that both the sacrament and the thing represented thereby remain in their proper substance, 285; Gardiner appeals to their doings, independent of their words, to shew their faith in the real presence, 337; their true meaning upon the eating of Christ's flesh, 339; argued that the bread and wine were not extinguished, but continue with all their natural properties, 340; Gardiner argues as to their faith from their expressions of wonder and marvelling, 340; the wonderful working of God which they speak of is in the receivers, not in the outward signs, 341; their declaration of figures, relied on by Gardiner, 342; and their writing upon the adoration of the sacrament, *ibid.*; teach that Christ is to be honoured of him that is baptized as well as of him that receives the holy communion, *ibid.*
Figure, how this word is used by the fathers, 116.
Figures, signs and figures have the names of the things they signify, 122, 5, 172, 3, 225; two in these words, "this cup is a new testament in my blood," 136; do not require the presence of the thing that is signified, 288; change their names, and why, 335.
Figurative speeches, how discernible from plain ones, 115; often reputed to be plain speeches, 137; taken literally have often an absurdity in reason, 181, 8; examples of, 181, 2.
Fisher, bishop of Rochester, his book against Œcolampadius, 46, 173, 90, 228, 344.
Form, use of this word by the papists in their arguments for transubstantiation, 251, 3, 4.
Fulgentius, his words upon the distinction between Christ's Godhead and his humanity, 98, *51.

INDEX.

Gabriel Biel says, that the doctrine of transubstantiation was received because it is written, *de hæreticis, ad abolendam,* that all men must hold as the holy church of Rome does, 302, *34.

Gardiner, Stephen, bishop of Winchester, his attempts against Cranmer opposed by Henry VIII. vii.; his six articles opposed by Cranmer, xii.; urges the king to commit Cranmer to the Tower for heresy, xvii.; answers Cranmer's book upon the holy sacrament, xx.; was bishop of Winchester then, but not when Cranmer answered him, 3; how his doctrine varies from that of other papists, and from the principles of philosophy, 4; his " Explication" misnamed, and has little learning in it, 9; his book was written before he was summoned to appear before the Commissioners, 10; his sermon on St Peter's day, *ibid.*; only suppressed Cranmer's name in his "Explication," that he might revile him the more freely, *ibid.*; his account of Cranmer's book, 11; denies that any of the fathers have Cranmer's doctrine in plain terms, 13; objects that Cranmer's doctrines have been maintained before by others who have recanted, and that Cranmer himself is condemned by his former writings, 13; asserts that there is no text in scripture to alter the popish sense of Christ's words, " this is my body," 15; that there is no miracle at all in the Lord's supper by Cranmer's understanding of it, *ibid.*; his doctrine of tokens, 16; says that if the very body of Christ be not delivered in the Lord's supper, the eating has no special promise, but only a commandment for remembrance, *ibid.*; derides the reformed doctrines as new tenets, 17; argues by the judgment of Solomon that the truth will be discovered upon the side that is free from craft and sleight, 18; denies that the faith of the real and substantial presence is the mere doctrine of the papists; for that Luther, and many others who abhorred everything popish, maintained the same opinion, 19; asserts that we receive the real body and blood of Christ in the Lord's supper, to continue and preserve life, as we receive his spirit in baptism to renew life, 22; quotes the evangelists and St Paul against Cranmer, on the real presence, 30; says that neither St Paul nor the evangelists add anything to shew that Christ did not give his very body and blood to be eaten and drunken in the last supper, 32; varies from Smith upon the sacrament, *ibid.*; teaches that the catholic faith is, that Christ feeds such as be regenerate in him, not only by his body and blood, but also with his body and blood delivered by him in deed to us, 37; variation between his printed book and the written copies, 48; says that Cranmer is contrary to himself in his Catechism, in which he wills that children be taught that they receive with their bodily mouth the body and blood of Christ, which is the most true catholic doctrine of the substance of the sacrament, 55; his absurdity in talking of a body's going into a soul, 57; says we must understand the words of Christ in the institution of his sacraments without figure in the substance, 59; that the catholic church denies all that reason without faith devises in the mystery of the sacrament, and that all christian men believe simply Christ's words, and trouble not their heads with such consequences as seem to strive with reason, 62; denies that a dog or a cat may eat the body of Christ, and asserts that man alone may eat it, 67; affirms that there are three ways of eating Christ's body and blood, spiritually, spiritually and sacramentally, and sacramentally only, 70; says that the fathers and prophets of the old testament ate Christ spiritually, but not sacramentally and spiritually, as we do, 74; his doctrine of the presence of Christ's body in the sacraments, 89, 155; his book of the 'Detection of the Devil's Sophistry,' 107, 8, 94, 241, 56, 307, 8; charges Cranmer with using terms meeter to express how dogs devour paunches, 111; declares that to understand Christ's words spiritually, is to understand them as the Spirit of God hath taught the church, although the manner exceedeth our capacities, 156; stole all his authorities from copies furnished him by Smith, 163; was fated to light upon false books, *ibid.*; affirms that only six learned men have, since the time of Christ, maintained Cranmer's doctrine—Bertram, Berengarius, Wickliff, Œcolampadius, Zuinglius, and Joachimus Vadianus, 195; charges Cranmer with being a mere translator of Peter Martyr, *ibid.*; his doctrine of the eating and drinking of Christ's body and blood, 201; insinuates that Cranmer was prompted by some 'man or friend,' 222, 3; charges him with wittingly corrupting the words of Justin, 264; his doctrine makes for the heresies of Eutyches and Nestorius, 294; describes Cranmer's doctrines as a new catholic faith, 309; said by Cranmer to fancy himself, and brag of his being still bishop of Winchester, after his deprivation, 324; list of his inconsistencies upon various points, 381; list of matters wherein he varies from the truth and from the old authors of the church, 385; assumed the name of Marcus Constantius in his *Confutatio Cavillationum,* 419 n.

Gelasius, says that the nature and substance of bread and wine cease not to be in the sacrament, 261, 289, 93, *33; proves, against Eutyches and Nestorius, that Christ is both God and man, 289, 93, 4, 5; was bishop of Rome A.D. 492, *ibid.*; Gardiner disputes his meaning, 289, 90, 1, 2, 3; says, that by the sacrament of Christ's body and blood we be associate unto the divine nature, and yet ceases not the substance, or nature, of bread and wine to be, 296; declares that the image and similitude of the body and blood of Christ is celebrate in the action of the mystery; and that, by the sacrament, we be made partakers of the godly nature, *ibid.*

Generation and nutrition, spiritual, knowledge of obscure, and to be attained only by faith, 41.

God, his will, not his power, a subject of dispute, 15; his will and pleasure as set forth in the scripture to be submitted to in all matters of christian faith, we believing him to be omnipotent, 34; his promises under condition, 206.

Gold and certain precious stones asserted by Gardiner to be known to give nurture to another substance, without diminution of their own substance, 333; virtues of, *ibid.*

Greek church has only one common mass in a day, 354.

Gregory, says that Christ is not here by the presence of his flesh, yet he is absent nowhere by the presence of his majesty, 96, *50; that he shewed his glorified body to St Thomas palpable, to declare that it was of the same nature that it was of before his resurrection, 262; that the lack of faith in Thomas profited more to our faith than did the faith of the disciples that believed, *ibid.*

Gregory Nazianzen, says although Christ shall come in the last day to judge, so as he shall be seen, yet there is in him no grossness, 139; meant that Christ should not come in a corruptible and mortal flesh, such as he had before his resurrection, but yet absolute and perfect in all parts and members of a man's body, 141.

Heath and Skippe, bishops, desert Cranmer on the articles, xvii.

Henry VIII. supports Cranmer against Gardiner, vii.; sends for him about queen Catherine's divorce, ix.; makes him one of his ambassadors to Rome, and afterwards to the emperor, x. xi.; is urged to commit Cranmer to the Tower for heresy, but gives him privately his signet that he may appeal to him, xviii.; rebukes the council for ill-treating Cranmer, xix.

Heretics, some who said that Christ was no man, although he appeared in the form of man, 256, 77; some who denied his being God, 278; some who confessed him both God and man, but not both at one time, *ibid.*; Eutyches and Nestorius, an account of their heresies, 289, 93, &c.

Hesychius cited by Gardiner, 59; says that none of the sacramental materials ought to be reserved, but that the remains should be burned, 60.

Hilary, his words upon the question, "if the Word were made very flesh, and we verily receive the Word being flesh, in our Lord's meat, how shall not Christ be thought to dwell naturally in us?" 160, 1, *68; concludes against Arius, that Christ is one with his Father, not in purpose and will only, but also in very nature, 161; says that in the true ministration of the sacrament is both a figure and a truth; the figure outwardly, and the truth inwardly, 247, 72, *31; Cranmer charged with falsifying him, 413.

Hippinus, *see Æpinus.*

Holy Ghost is God, because in many places at one time, 97, 102; is not made a dove because of the words of St John, 306.

Honorius III. ordained that the people should be taught to worship the host when it was lifted up by the priest, and carried unto sick folks, 238.

Host, leavings of to be consumed reverently by the clerks, who are to fast thereafter, lest they should mix with the common meats digested by the belly, 141, 2, 3, 6; each piece is Christ's whole body (Gardiner), 143, 6; was hanged up in England by the priests, contrary to the usage of other countries, 143, 6; idolatrous worship of, 229; Smith's doctrine on the corruption thereof, 381.

Hugo de S. Vict. 41 *n*, 42 *n*, 56 *n*.

Hunger and thirst of the soul, 38; not easily perceived in the carnal man; his mind is in the kitchen and buttery, 39.

Idolatry at the elevation of the host, 229.

Ignatius takes *eucharistia* to be the flesh of our Saviour, the same that suffered and that rose again (Gardiner), 149; means that *eucharistia* is the sacrament or mystery of Christ's flesh, 151.

Impanation of Christ's body, 251, 3, 80; as Christ's body is joined only sacramentally to the bread there is no impanation, 305.

Inaquation and invination, 305, 6.

Incarnation, what it means, 288; Gardiner makes the sacramental bread incarnate, 306.

Individuum vagum, or *individuum in genere*, what some say Christ meant when he said 'this' is my body, 106, 8.

Infundo, dispute about the English word for, 309, 10.

Innocent III. (pope) says, as well as Hugo, that the body of Christ remains no longer than the sacrament is in the eating, and may be felt, seen, and tasted in the mouth, 56, *24; taught that Christ's body was made of bread, 194; ordained that the host should be diligently kept under lock and key, 238; was the father of transubstantiation, 240, *88.

Irenæus says Christ confessed bread to be his body and the cup his blood, 33, 104, *54; his argument against those heretics who denied the resurrection of our bodies, 150; his words on the *eucharistia*, 265, 6, *30; says that St Paul meant not a spiritual body, when he said, "we be members of Christ's body, and of his flesh, and his bones," 285; proved the resurrection of our bodies to eternal life, because they are nourished with the everlasting food of Christ's body, 338.

Jacob worshipped Christ before he was born, 235.

Jerome, his interpretation of Christ's words in the sacrament, 24; says (writing *ad Hedibiam*) that Christ called the bread which he brake his body, 33, 104, *54; says that Christ took bread which comforteth man's heart, that he might represent thereby his very body and blood, 122, *59; whether the word 'represent' in the last passage means 'real exhibition,' 123; his comparison of the *panes propositionis* and the body of Christ, 192, 342, *75; says, all that love pleasure more than God eat not the flesh of Jesu, nor drink his blood, 210, *80; declares that heretics do not eat and drink the body and blood of the Lord, and that heretics eat not the flesh of Jesu, whose flesh is the meat of faithful men, *ibid.*, 225; says, if the sacraments be violated, then is he violated whose sacraments they be, 228; his words on the two ways of understanding the flesh and blood of Christ, 232, 3.

Joan of Kent, her heresy, 74, 8.

John vi., interpretation thereof, 24, 5, 6, 7; speaks of spiritual bread, 307, 72.

Jonas, Justus, his catechism, 19; teaches that Christ's calling bread his body means making, 106.

Judas, whether he received the body and blood of the Lord, 221, 2, 3, 4, 5.

Judgment of Solomon used as a lesson, 18, 92.

Juniper-berries sold for pepper, 262.

Justin Martyr, says nothing of a reservation of the host for sick persons, as Gardiner reports, 146; says that the bread, water, and wine, are meats ordained purposely to give thanks to God, and are therefore called *eucharistia*, and are called also the body and blood of Christ; and yet the same meat and drink is changed into our flesh and blood, and nourishes our bodies, 263, *30; dispute about the real words of this passage, 263, 4, 5.

Lactantius teaches, with other old writers, that figures be vain and serve to no purpose, when the things by them signified be present, 288, 97.

Lambeth, audience of Gardiner at, 182.

Last supper, what figurative speeches were used at it, 136.

Latimer, Hugh, sent with Cranmer and Ridley from the Tower to dispute at Oxford, 391.

Latin English, the using of, 309, 10.

Leo, 94 *n.*, *48, 195, *75.

Lies and adverbs in "ly," Cranmer's play upon, 157.

Linehood, or Lindwood, his provincial constitutions, 143.

Lirinensis, Vincentius, teaches that the bible is sufficient for the truth of the catholic faith, and that the church cannot make one article of it, 379.

Livy, his account of a supper of many dishes all made of hog's flesh, cited by Gardiner, 257.

Lombardus, Petrus, much quoted by the school-authors, 351, *94; says that that which is offered and consecrated of the priest is called a sacrifice and oblation because it is a memory and representation of the true sacrifice and holy oblation made in the altar of the cross, *ibid.*; cited at length by Gardiner, upon the same point, 357; confirms Cranmer's doctrine, 358, 9. *See Master of the Sentences.*

Lord's table, we ought not to approach it unreverently and unadvisedly, 142, 6, 7, 373; Christ is present thereat with Spirit and grace, 219; what is to be considered by those who come worthily to it, *ibid.*; to those who eat unworthily it is the devil's table, 220, 373; is to be considered as a mystical table, 373.

Luther, Martin, cited by Gardiner as condemning the reformed doctrines in Germany, 13; asserted by Gardiner to have defended the presence of Christ's body in the sacrament, 19; Gardiner insinuates that Cranmer's second book was written to maintain Luther's opinion against transubstantiation only, 281, 5.

Manes, his heresy, 277.

Manichees, their heresy, 277, 89.

Manna eaten by the good and bad; none eat Christ but they have everlasting life, 207, 220.

Marcellus, his heresy, 278.

Marcion, his heresy, 177, 215, 262; said that Simon Cyrenæus was crucified instead of Christ, 256; that Christ was very God, but not very man, though he appeared to be so, 277, 85; says that only the appearance of Christ's humanity remains in accidents, and not the substance itself, 297.

Marcus Constantius says that heathen, perhaps, eat only the same as brutes in the sacrament, 68 *n*.

Martyr, Peter, cited by Gardiner as shewing that the doctrine of the real presence was maintained by others as well as the papists, 20; vindicated from Gardiner's charge of his want of learning, 195, 6; Gardiner intimates that he did not wish his writings to appear in English, 222, 4; refers to his translation of Chrysostom, 287; is defended by Cranmer against Smith's charge of mercenary motives, 374; lodged with Cranmer before he went to Oxford, *ibid.*; abandoned a great income in his own country, and went into strange countries to promote the truth and glory of God, *ibid.*

Mass, whether it is a sacrifice satisfactory for sin by the devotion of the priest, 81, *et seq.*; popish priests make it a sacrifice propitiatory to remit the sins as well of themselves as others, both quick and dead, 345; the offering of the priest cannot deserve the remission of sins, and it is an abominable blasphemy to give that dignity to a priest that pertains only to Christ, 348; to put the oblation of the priest instead of the oblation of Christ, is detestable idolatry, 349, 50; St Paul saying that every high priest is ordained to offer gifts and sacrifices for sins, spoke not of priests of the new testaments, but of the old, which offered calves and goats, and could not take away sins, 351; the prophet Malachi spoke nothing of any offering propitiatory to be made by the priests when he said that everywhere should be offered unto God a pure sacrifice and oblation, *ibid.*; is neither a sacrifice propitiatory nor of laud and praise, 352; there were no papistical masses in the primitive church, *ibid.*; private masses chiefly sprang from lucre and gain, 353; how they entered into the church, *ibid.*; the abuses of them by the papists, *ibid.*, 354; satisfactory masses, their absurdity, 362; devised by the devil, 422.

Master of the Sentences, 67, 279, 80, 328, 51. *See* Lombardus.

Melancthon cited by Gardiner, as professing the belief of the real presence, and proving it to have been the old faith by the early fathers, 20; upon figurative speeches, 137; says St Ambrose would never have travailed to accumulate so many miracles as he did, had he not thought the nature of bread to be changed in the mystery of the Lord's supper, 178; meant a sacramental change in the last passage, 179.

Menander, a heretic, 262, 77.

Messalians, or Euchites, their heresy, 172, 3.

Miracle, of the Lord's supper, consists in the eating of Christ's flesh and drinking his blood, and how by flesh and blood we have everlasting life, 186; papists make the excellency of the sacrament to depend upon a multitude of miracles, 255; miracles not to be assumed without necessity, *ibid.*

Momus' quarrelling with Venus' slipper when he could find no fault with her, 294.

Mowes and mowing, mouths and mouthing, or mocking, 226, 7.

Mysteries, of God, Gardiner deprecates search and inquiry into, 334.

Names, change of, makes no alteration in the substance, or transubstantiation, 249; does not deliver from the old name, 275.

Nature, operation of, arguments upon transubstantiation from, 250, 1, 2, 3, 4.

Negatives by comparison, examples of, 313, 14, 15.

Nestorius, 22; imagined a carnal eating of Christ's flesh, like the papists, and that Christ was a pure man, and not God by nature, 25, 278, 80, 9, 93, &c.; divided Christ's flesh from the deity (Gardiner), 172, 338.

Nicholas II. (pope) forced Berengarius to recant, 14, 46; was the first to condemn the true doctrine of the sacrament, 14; taught that Christ's body was torn with the teeth of the faithful, 113, 203.

Nicodemus, he and the Capernaites understand not Christ, nor any spiritual act, 185.

Nicolaites, their heresy that all things ought to be common, including wives, 145.

"Not," Cranmer charged with omitting it, 299; denied, 301.

Œcolampadius, Melancthon's epistle to him, 20; defended against the charge of corrupting the text of Cyril, 171, 2; his doctrine on the sacrifice of Christ set forth by Gardiner, 355.

Œcumenius, 202, 206.

Oglethorpe's disputation with Cranmer, 400.

Origen, his interpretation of Christ's words in the sacrament, 24; his argument upon Christ's presence in this world, 94, *47; says that if we follow the letter of the words, "except ye eat my flesh, and drink my blood," the letter kills us, 113, *56; is noted for drawing his text to allegory (Gardiner), *ibid.* Although he says that manna signified Christ to come, who is now come indeed, and is manifested to us in the sacrament of his word, in the sacrament of regeneration, and of bread and wine, yet he meant not that Christ is corporally either in his word, in the water of baptism, or in the bread and wine, &c., 154, *68; says that to understand the words of Christ spiritually, is to understand them otherwise than the words sound; for he that understands them after the letter understands them carnally, and that understanding hurts and destroys, 158; writes that the word was made flesh and very meat, which whoso eateth shall surely live for ever, which no evil man can eat, 208, *80; says that the matter of bread availeth nothing; but as regarding the material part thereof, it goeth down into the belly, and is avoided downward, 261; the word of God spoken upon the bread is it that availeth, 266, *30.

Panes propositionis, 193, 4, 342.

Papists, the state of religion brought in by them, 5; were the cause of the failure of former attempts at reform, 14; their doctrines no older than the bishop of Rome's usurped supremacy, 18; were the first authors and inventors of the faith of the real presence, 21, 173; their four principal errors, 44, 5, 6, 7, 8; they vary among themselves about the presence of Christ in the sacrament, 46; say that evil and ungodly men, in the sacrament, receive the very body and blood of Christ, 47; have set up a new faith within these four or five hundred years, that Christ did not go up into heaven, but remains still in this world, and in a hundred thousand places at one time, 52; say, that when any man eateth the bread and drinketh the cup, Christ goeth into his mouth or stomach, but no further, 55, 6, 60; some of them say the body of Christ remains so long as the form and fashion of bread remains, although it be in a dog, mouse, or in the jakes, 56; make the devil and Christ both enter Judas at once, 58; say, that Christ is in the sacramental bread a whole year, or so long as the form of bread remains; but after the receiving thereof he flies up into heaven, as soon as it is chewed, or changed in the stomach, 58, 61; that in every part of the bread and wine, all the corporal members of Christ's body are mixed together, without distinction, 62, 4, 5, 6; their doctrine not the doctrine of the church, 65, 354; say, that a dog or a cat may eat the body of Christ, 67, 8; teach that the oblation of the priest is satisfactory by devotion of the priest, 84; craftily inculcate that Christ's passion was not the only and sufficient sacrifice for remission of our sins, 85; invented a new faith, that Christ is here still on earth, shut up in a box, 93; make Christ's body to be God, by affirming that it is in many places at one time, and so confound the two natures of Christ, 97; have made another new faith, that Christ's natural body is here in earth, and at the right hand of God in heaven, 100; their argument for transubstantiation, 103; talk of eating Christ's body, as dogs do paunches, 112; teach that Christ's body is torn with the teeth of the faithful, 113; make and unmake new articles of faith, from time to time, at their pleasure, without any scripture, 132, 369; and enforce them with fire and fagot, *ibid*.; their authorities and arguments answered, 138; their manner of administering the sacrament, 143; their doctrines have increased in errors and corruptions, more and more, from time to time, 144; the terms "really," and "sensibly," which they use in speaking of the body of Christ, are not found in any old author, 152, 4; delight in darkness, 185; subvert the natural order of things to conceal the falsehood of their arguments, 185, 6; live by indulgences, pardons, and other remissions of sin coming from the pope, 194; teach that Christ's body is made of the matter of bread, *ibid*.; their gross error is the carnal eating and drinking of Christ's flesh and blood with our mouths, 207; affirm that the substance of the sacrament is all one, by God's ordinance, and that, therefore, evil men receive the same therein that good men do, 214, 19; make God and the devil dwell together in one man, 217; delude people to worship things visible, and made with their own hands, as their Creator, 228, 9; are the false prophets and seducers of the people of whom we are warned by Christ beforehand, 238; were the authors of transubstantiation, 240; their variations from each other as to the conversion of the bread and wine by consecration, 249; make Christ to have two bodies, or else that the self-same body was made of two divers matters, and at divers times, *ibid*.; ground their doctrine of transubstantiation upon Christ's words, "this is my body," 302; make every day a new Christ, not born of the virgin Mary, nor that was crucified by the Jews, 303; would bring the worship of Christian people from Christ, born of the virgin Mary, to that of a new Christ, made of bread and wine, through the consecration of popish priests, 303; make bread to be joined to Christ's body in greater unity than his humanity is to his godhead, 306; wrest the meaning of authors from the truth to support their doctrines, 308; the three principal authorities upon which they rely for transubstantiation answered, *ibid*.; say, nothing is broken, eaten, drunken, &c. in the sacrament, but the "accidents," 324, 6, 7; bind people, under peril of damnation, to believe things that they cannot understand, 327; seek nothing but the advancement of their pope, with whom they say no one can find fault, *ibid*.; say that the accidents of bread and wine hang alone in the air, 328; that the substance of Christ's body is in the sacrament really, corporally, and naturally, without any accident of the same, 329; make accidents to be without substances, and substances without accidents, *ibid*.; that the place where the accidents of bread and wine be, hath no substance to fill it, and so they must grant a *vacuum*, 330; that substance is made of accidents, as when the bread moulds, or is turned into worms, or the wine sours, *ibid*.;

that substance is nourished without substance, by accidents only, if by chance any cat, dog, or mouse, eat the sacramental bread, 332; bring christian people from the true honouring of Christ to idolatry, 333; after vainly and arrogantly prying into the secrets of God's majesty and wisdom, command others to keep silence about his mysteries, 335; take those for heretics who teach according to God's word, *ibid*.; teach us to honour and reverence the forms and accidents of the bread and wine, if they be vomited up, after the body and blood of Christ be gone away, and say, that the ashes into which they are to be burned must be kept with great reverence, 343; their priests, under the pretence of holiness, take upon themselves to be Christ's successors, 345; say they make no new sacrifice, but the self-same sacrifice which Christ himself made, which is to slay Christ and shed his blood every day, 348; the abuses and superstitions promoted by their masses, 353, 4; inconsistencies of their doctrine, 366; pretend that they are the church, and would be believed without God's word, 368.

Parkhurst, his Latin verses on Cranmer's answer to Gardiner, 8.

Paschal Lamb, a token and figure of the shedding of Christ's blood then to come, 135, 6.

Paul, St, his words in the eleventh of Corinthians discussed, 205, 17, 18, 19, 20; means unworthy eating of the bread, and not of the body of Christ, 220; always uses the words 'bread and wine,' and never 'sacrament,' 373.

Penance, relief by, 360.

Peryn, Dr, master of the Blackfriars in Smithfield, 68.

Petitio principii, 333, 71.

Phenomena, natural, arguments from divers examples of, 259.

Philosophers, some have made themselves laughing-stocks, 254.

Philosophy, Gardiner argues it should not move the faith of a Christian, 252; of Aristotle, Plato, and Pliny, referred to by Cranmer, 331; conclusions from, 333; teaches that every corporal thing has two substances, the matter and the form, 337.

Photinus, a heretic, 278.

Photius, 408, 9.

Physicians, surgeons, and alchemists use strange languages to hide their sciences from others, 311.

Pighius, Albertus, followed by Gardiner, 127.

Plato, his philosophy referred to, 331.

Plautus, his Amphitryo cited, 262.

Pliny, his philosophy, 331.

Poison, divers popes have been poisoned with the sacramental wine, and have poisoned others with it, 250, 5.

Ponet, bishop, author of a Catechism set forth by Cranmer, 422.

Pope, has no authority to dispense with the word of God, x.

Popish priests take upon themselves to make both God and man, 303.

Presence of Christ, God, or the Holy Ghost, in scripture, always means spiritually, 3; present 'spiritually,' and 'after a spiritual manner,' discussion upon, 91, 2; wherever Christ is in his divine nature by power or grace, he is there really, whether we speak of heaven or earth (Gardiner), 139.

Priest, can apply the benefit of Christ's passion to no man, 353.

Prophets and fathers of the old testament, whether they ate Christ's flesh, and drank his blood, 75; ate and drank them before he was born, 76.

Purgatory, trusting to have remission of our sins by the sacrifice of the priest in the mass, and thereby also to obtain release from the pains in purgatory, is doing injury to Christ, and committing detestable idolatry, 349; a device of the papists, 353.

Rabanus *de instit. clericorum*, 41 n., *21.
Reason and natural operation, although they do not prevail against God's word, yet when they join with it are of great moment to confirm any truth, 250, 2; conclusions from, 251, 2, 3, 4; Christ appealed to them to prove his resurrection, 252; reason the handmaid of faith, 371.
Reformers, early, quoted in support of the papists on some points, although accounted vile and filthy heretics by them, 21.
Resurrection, scripture declares that we shall have diversity of members, and a due proportion of men's natural bodies at the last day, 141, 150, 177; our bodies and souls not to be all spiritual thereat, 177.
Ridley, bishop, sent with Cranmer and Latimer to dispute at Oxford, 391.

Sabellius, his doctrine, 63, 7, 278.
Sacrament, meanings given to this word by Cranmer, 3; true doctrine of, never condemned by any council before the time of pope Nicholas II., 14; comparison of the words of the evangelists and St Paul thereon, 28; evil men eat it, but not the body of Christ, 29; things spoken and done by Christ, and written by the evangelists and St Paul, ought to suffice the faith of Christian people upon it, 30; was ordained to move all men to friendship, love, and concord; but, through the enemies of Christ, nothing raises so much contention, *ibid.*, 42, 3, 4; God's miraculous working therein, not in the bread, but in them that duly eat it, and drink the drink, 34; the effect of eating it is the communication of Christ's body and blood only to the faithful receiver, and not to the dumb creatures of bread and wine; to the wicked eater the effect is damnation and woe, 36; the bread and wine an apt figure and similitude to admonish how we are fed invisibly and spiritually by the flesh and blood of Christ, 37; why ordained in bread and wine, 41; the spiritual eating is with the heart, not with the teeth, 43, 373; evil men do not spiritually eat Christ's flesh in the sacrament, but their own damnation, 47; what Augustine, Ambrose, Chrysostom, and others, say of eating the body of Christ, is to be taken figuratively, 55, 282; how long Christ tarries with the receiver of it, 59; what is to be wondered at in it, 66; true eating of it, 71; whether Christ be really eaten without it, *ibid.*; whether Christ's body has his proper form and quantity in it, 73; the bread and wine are similitudes, mysteries, and representations, significations, sacraments, figures, and signs of Christ's body and blood, 122; the priests ought not to receive it alone, 142, 3; the people received it with the priests in the old time, 147, 8; though the sacramental tokens be only tokens and significations and figures, yet doth Almighty God effectually work, in them that duly receive his sacraments, those divine and celestial operations which he has promised, and by the sacraments be signified, 148; why bread is called Christ's body and wine his blood, 150; the corporal receiving without the spiritual hurts much, as in Judas and Simon Magus, 173; the bread and wine must be received reverently with the mouth, because of the things thereby represented, 174; double use of the word "sacrament," by Gardiner, 203; Christ is present spiritually, and is spiritually eaten in the true ministration of it, 203; visible and invisible sacraments, 204; only good men eat and drink the body and blood of Christ spiritually, *ibid.*; only two manner of eatings of Christ, 205; St Paul spoke not of eating the body and blood of Christ, but only of the bread and wine, in 1 Cor. xi., *ibid.*; all men, good and evil, may with their mouths visibly and sensibly eat the sacrament, but the very body and blood themselves be not eaten but spiritually, 213; the bread and wine remain after the consecration, 241, 2, 3, 80; they are sensible signs and sacraments, to teach us outwardly what feeds us inwardly, 247; the real presence of Christ therein not necessary for our salvation nor comfort, but his spiritual presence is essential for both, 283; the conversion of the bread and wine is spiritual, 304; Christ is no more in the bread and wine than the Holy Ghost is in the water of baptism, 306; the bread is changed in nature therein, not in shape nor substance, 308; the marvellous alteration to a higher estate is chiefly in the persons, and only in signification in the sacramental signs, 323; the true gospel doctrine of the first catholic christian faith therein, 328, 32; two parts therein, the earthly and the heavenly, 337; every man ought to receive it himself, and the priest or another man ought not to receive it for him, 350; the only difference between the priest and the layman is in the ministration, *ibid.* See *Christ*.
Sacraments, Christ is present in them, 11; were ordained to confirm our faith, and to enable us to perceive Christ with all our senses, 41; of the old and new testament, their diversity, 75; do most assuredly certify us that we be partakers of Christ's godly nature, having given unto us by him immortality and life everlasting, 161; baptism and the Lord's supper compared, 221; why their signs change their names, 335; how to be contemplated, 366.
Sacrifices, all the works that christian people do to the glory of God, are sacrifices of the church, 88, 346; Gardiner agrees that the sacrifice of Christ was full and perfect, and needed not to be done more than once, but to be often remembered, 344; alleges that the body and blood of Christ is the only sacrifice propitiatory for all the sins of the world, *ibid.*, 345; the doctrine is untrue and feigned by the papists as concerning the real presence in the bread and wine, *ibid.*; the death of Christ upon the cross was the true sacrifice propitiatory that purchased the remission of sin, 345, 6; was of such force that there was no need to renew it every year, 346; there are two kinds of sacrifices, the sacrifice of Christ, and the sacrifice of the church, *ibid.*; of the old law could not take away our sins, but signified beforehand the sacrifice of Christ to come, 347; were partly used as ceremonies whereby those who had offended against the law were declared to be absolved, *ibid.*; we must under the new law offer spiritual oblations in place of calves, sheep, goats, and doves, 349; the lay people make a sacrifice as well as the priest, by thanksgiving and humble submission to the will of God, 352; so meant the ancient fathers when they called the mass a sacrifice, 353; Gardiner denies that the daily sacrifice of Christ's body and blood is an iteration of the sacrifice on the cross, 360; the effect of the offering on the cross is dispensed in baptism, *ibid.*; Gardiner asserts that the mass, as well as all good works, is propitiatory, *ibid.*; distinction between sacrifices propitiatory and gratificatory, 361; the effect of Christ's sacrifice is both to give and to continue life, 364; what the daily offering of the priest without blood-shedding may mean, not explained, *ibid.*
Sacring, lifting up the consecrated bread by the papists for the people to worship, 229.
Samosatenus, Paulus, a heretic, 278.
Savours, nourishment from, 333.
School-authors, study of, discountenanced by Cranmer, viii.; what made them take up the doctrine of transubstantiation, 302; had no devotion but to the pope, the god that made them, 327.
Scory, bishop of Rochester, disseminates Cranmer's Declaration against the mass, xx.
Scriptures, knowledge of, encouraged by Cranmer in opposition to the study of school-authors, viii.; Cranmer maintains that the pope cannot dispense

with them, x.; their proper sense restored under Henry VIII. and Edward VI., 6.

Sedulius, 195.

Senses, papistical doctrines contrary to our, 245, 6, 62, 3; articles of faith may be above, but not contrary to our senses, *ibid.*; if we may not trust them, the sensible sacrament is but an illusion and a piece of jugglery, 256.

Shalm: shawm, a sort of musical pipe, or hautboy, 259.

Shew-bread of the law but a dark shadow of Christ to come, but the sacrament of Christ's body a clear testimony that he is already come, 193.

Signs are called by the names of the things signified, 125, 335; the visible signs of the sacraments are not to be worshipped, 134; difference between sacramental signs and vain outward shews, 322; may change their names, and why, 335; may be called by their real names without offence, 336.

Similitudes, whether God's mysteries can be thoroughly expressed by them, 89; argument upon the use of, 124, 7; Christ himself often used them, but chiefly when he spoke of the sacraments, 135; not to be pressed in all points, to purposes for which they are not used, 283, 4.

Simon, his heresy, said that Christ was very God, but not very man, although he appeared so, 277.

Sin, whether the devotion of the priest offering the mass be a satisfaction for it, or whether the only host and satisfaction for all the sins of the world, is the death of Christ and the oblation of his body upon the cross, 81, *et seq.*

Smith, Dr, his "Confutation," answered by Cranmer, 9, 45; varies from Gardiner upon the sacrament, 32; his absurdities, 33, 71; denies the charge made against the papists about the body of Christ being in the sacrament as it was born of the virgin, and being torn in pieces with our teeth, 47, 56 *n.*; more candid than Gardiner, 53, 73, 8, 101; his distinction between Christ's presence visibly, naturally, and by circumscription, and above nature, invisibly, and without circumscription, 101; says that Christ called his body bread, 108, 9; jests of Cranmer's taking the sacramental tokens, as baker's bread, and wine drunk in a tavern, 150; condemns Gardiner for saying that Christ's body is in the sacrament naturally, or carnally, 153; furnished Gardiner with his authorities, 163; both he and Gardiner wrote against Cranmer, but agreed very ill together, 173; reference to his preface, 307; he and Gardiner differ from other papists about Christ's body in the sacrament, 329; says that, when the host moulds and engenders worms, another substance succeeds it of which such things are made, 331; Cranmer refers Gardiner to his book on the sacrifice of the mass, 362; his preface answered by Cranmer, 368; he exhorts men to leave disputing and reasoning, and to give credit to the church, 368; argues for Christ's real presence from his resurrection and re-appearance on earth, 375; is appealed to by Weston in the disputation at Oxford, 414; disputes against Cranmer there, 424.

Stercoranists, a sect so called, 55.

Substance, Gardiner's disquisition on, 256, 7, 324; answered by Cranmer, 259, 60, 98; many examples alleged from scripture of miraculous changes where the substances remained the same, 319, 22; cannot be without accidents, 326.

Sun, used as a similitude in the sacrament, 89, 90, 1.

Supper of the Lord, abuse of, 23.

Swink: sweat, labour, 293.

Synagogue of the devil, the church of Rome, 302; of antichrist, 332.

Temple of God, whether one man can be both the temple of God and the temple of the devil, 216, 17, 18.

Terminus a quo and *terminus ad quem*, 331.

Tertullian says, in many places, Christ called bread his body, 33, 104, *54; cited by Gardiner as saying, that Christ "made" bread his body, 106, 154; what he meant by a figure of Christ's body, 119, 120, 1, *58; says that bread and wine were figures in the old testament, and so taken in the prophets, and now be figures again in the new testament, and so used of Christ himself in his last supper, 120; is alleged to affirm that in the sacrament of the altar we eat the body and drink the blood of our Saviour Jesus Christ, 153, 4, *67; proves that Christ had a very body on earth, 194.

Theodorete says, that when Christ gave the holy mysteries, he called the bread his body, and the cup mixed with wine and water he called his blood, 33, 105, *54; holds that the bread and wine are sacraments of Christ's body and blood, and not of his divinity, 72; shews how the names of things are changed in scripture, 127; his dialogues on the changing of names in scripture, 128, 225, *61; his dialogue upon Christ's coming again in the same form as that in which his disciples saw him go to heaven, 129; papists falsely say he was infected with the error of Nestorius, 130; the five things principally to be noted in his writings on the sacrament, *ibid.*; dispute about the translation of his words upon the sacramental signs, 132, 3, 4; says, with Chrysostom, that the bread remains after consecration, although we call it by a more excellent name of dignity, that is to say, by the name of Christ's body, 249, *74; asserts that Christ called bread and wine his body and blood, and yet changed not their natures, 261; that after consecration they lose not their proper nature, but keep their former substance, form, and figure, 261; says, he that called his natural body wheat and bread, and also called himself a vine, the self-same called bread and wine his body and blood, and yet changed not their natures, 299, *34; confirms this in another passage, *ibid.*; shews that when Christ called the bread his body, it was to cause the receivers to lift their minds from earth to heaven, 336.

Theodorus, a heretic, held that Christ was very man, and not God, 278.

Theophilus Alexandrinus, a saying of Theophylact falsely attributed to him by the papists, to give it greater antiquity, 187, 90.

Theophylact, although he speaks of the eating of the very body of Christ, and the drinking of his very blood, means a celestial and spiritual eating, and a sacramental conversion of the bread and wine, 187, *75; Œcolampadius translated his works into Latin (Gardiner), 188; his words on the eating of Christ's flesh, cited by Gardiner, 188; mistranslated by Gardiner, 192.

Thomas, St, arguments from his incredulity, 255, 8, 61, 2.

Tokens, scriptural, their nature, 16; bread in the Lord's supper, not a vain and bare token, *ibid.*; are not the more holy in themselves, notwithstanding any holiness or godliness wrought in the receivers of them, 153.

Translation, ought to be literal where the sense is ambiguous, 190.

Transubstantiation, the real root of the corruption of Christianity, 6; maintained by no scripture, 12; not contained in scripture, nor any ancient author, 13; to be deemed a popish faith, unless proved to have been received and believed universally before the bishops of Rome defined it, 22; not to be believed on account of God's omnipotency, unless it can be proved from scripture, 34; subverts our faith in Christ, 43; defined, 45; was first spoken of by public authority at the fourth general council of Lateran, at which Innocent III. was present, 239, 40; the articles supporting it were passed in England while popish darkness and ignorance still remained, 240; not proved by real presence, 241; is contrary to God's word, *ibid.*, 95, 304; the papists teach to play with syllables in a high mystery, by teaching that the conversion does not take place till the last syllable of *hoc est corpus meum* is pronounced, 246; St Paul's words prove that the bread remains bread after the sanctification, 250; argument against it from nature's abhorrence of a *vacuum*, 250, 1, 2; from the operation of natural causes upon the sacramental meats, *ibid.*; papistical doctrine of it passes the fondness of all the philosophers, 254; is contrary to the evidence of our senses, 255, 304; is contrary to the faith of the old authors of Christ's church, 263; if the nature and substance of bread and wine remain in the sacrament after consecration, the doctrine must be given up, or else the error of the Nestorians must be followed, 299, 301; what moved the school-authors to take up the doctrine against all reason, 302; Christ is every day made anew by it, 303; is plainly a papistical doctrine, 305; simple and plain people cannot understand, nor the papists defend it, 328; scripture constrains no man to believe in it, although Christ were really present in the sacrament, 329; answers to six of the principal absurdities therein, 332; encourages the heresies of the Valentinians, Arians, and others, 339, 40.

Trinity, various similitudes have been used to express it, yet it cannot be thoroughly set forth (Gardiner), 89.

Truth is not afraid of the light, 368.

Ulpian, argument from, upon the change of wine into vinegar, 251, 4, 330, 2.

Vacuum, nature's abhorrence of, argument against transubstantiation from, 250, 1, 2, 330.

Variations between Gardiner and other papists, list of, 380.

Vadianus, Joachimus, 195.

Valentines, (Valentinians,) heretics who denied the resurrection, 150, 7, 177, 215, 258, 262; said that Christ was not crucified, but that Simon Cyrenæus was for him, 256; that Christ was very God, but not very man, 277, 85, 339.

Vere and *vero* confounded, 414.

Vigilius, concerning the nature of Christ's manhood, 73; his argument upon both the natures of Christ, his humanity and his divinity, 98, 9, 100, *51; Gardiner quotes his account of the heresies of Eutyches and Nestorius, 289.

Vincentius. *See Lirinensis.*

Warham, archbishop of Canterbury, succeeded by Cranmer, vii., xi.

Weston, Dr, prolocutor of the commissioners appointed to examine Cranmer at Oxford, 391.

Whet-stone, simile of, which sharpens and has no sharpness in it, 179.

Wicked steward, parable of, not to be used to justify fraud in servants, 283.

Wickliff, cited by Gardiner, 13; set forth the truth of the gospel, 14; condemned for a heretic, 195, 6.

Wolsey, Cardinal, offers a fellowship to Cranmer, viii.

Zuinglius, 195, 225, 73; cited by Gardiner as supporting transubstantiation, 239, 41, 4, 5, 279, 335.

The Editor thinks it desirable to add, that his notice of Dr Jenkyns's valuable work in the prefatory remarks (page iv.) is meant to express that he has taken nothing from it *upon trust*, but, as he there stated, he has examined the early editions and references for himself. Direct references to Dr Jenkyns's edition are also made, where it has facilitated his own labours.

DEFENSIO

VERÆ ET CATHOLICÆ DOCTRINÆ

DE SACRAMENTO.

Defensio
veræ et Catholi-
cæ Doctrinæ de Sacra-
mento corporis et sanguinis Christi Servatoris nostri, et quorundam in hac causa errorum confutatio, verbo sanctissimo Domini
nixa atque fundata, et consensu antiquissimorum Ecclesiæ scriptorum firmata,
a Reverendiss. in Christo Patre ac
Domino D. Thoma Cran-
mero Archiepiscopo Cantuariensi, Primate totius
Angliæ et Metropolitano, scripta.

Jesus Christus.
Joannis 6.
Spiritus est qui vivificat, caro
non prodest quicquam.

M.D.LIII.

[This translation is supposed to have been made by Sir John Cheke, tutor to Edward VI. and the first Greek Professor in the University of Cambridge. It is attributed however by Strype (Mem. Cran. Vol. I. p. 365) to John Yong, who afterwards complied with the old religion in the reign of queen Mary.]

DEFENSIO

VERÆ ET CATHOLICÆ DOctrinæ de Sacramento corporis & sanguinis CHRISTI Seruatoris nostri, & quorundam in hac causa errorum confutatio, verbo sanctissimo Domini nixa atque fundata, & consensu antiquissimorum Ecclesiæ scriptorum firmata, à Reuerendiss. in Christo Patre ac Domino D.

THOMA CRANMERO
Martyre, Archiepiscopo Cantuariensi, Primate totius Angliæ, & Metropolitano,
scripta,
ab autore in vinculis recognita & aucta.

IESVS CHRITTVS
Ioannis. 6.
Spiritus est qui viuificat, caro non prodest quicquam.

Vsquequo Domine, qui es sanctus & verax, non iudicas, ac vindicas sanguinem nostrum de his, qui habitant in terra? Apoc. 6. c.

Embdæ, apud Gellium Ctematium.
M. D. LVII.

HOC VOLUMEN IN QUINQUE LIBROS DIVIDITUR.

LIB. I.

Primus, de Vera et Catholica Doctrina et usu Sacramenti Corporis et Sanguinis Domini tractat.

LIB. II.

Alter, de Transubstantiationis Errore.

LIB. III.

Tertius, quomodo Christus in sanctissima Cœna præsens sit.

LIB. IV.

Quartus, de Perceptione Corporis et Sanguinis Christi.

LIB. V.

Quintus, de Oblatione et Sacrificio Servatoris Christi.

PIO LECTORI S[1].

Quemadmodum muliercula illa evangelica, amissa drachma, omnes adeo domus suæ angulos everrit, et diligenter conquirit, donec eam inveniat, ac ea inventa, ipsa non veluti in sinu sola gaudet, sed convocatas amicas et vicinas, ut sibi congratulentur, monet: eodem modo neque nos potuimus, pie lector, quin reperto hujus libelli thesauro (quem libellum sanctissimus Christi martyr et reverendissimus pater, D. Thomas Cranmerus Cantuariensis archiepiscopus, non minus docte quam pie de Cœna Domini conscripsit) gaudium nostrum tibi quoque contestatum faceremus. Indignum enim judicavimus, si hunc libellum, non parvo nostro sumptu typis excusum, ecclesiæ Dei invideremus, ac non potius eam ecclesiam, quæ tam insigni membro, tam electo Dei organo (auctorem libri loquor) orbata sit, ad publicam etiam gratulationem hujus operis editione vocaremus. Ut autem hoc ipsum gaudium pio etiam dolore temperes, amice lector, constitui hac quidem dedicatoria epistola calamitosum reipublicæ christianæ per Angliam statum tibi ob oculos ponere, ut hujus rei occasione iram Dei in illud regnum immodice, imo horribiliter effusam, (promerentibus ita peccatis nostris,) nobiscum depreceris, si forte piorum omnium precibus vel tandem motus cœlestis Pater nostri misereatur. Quam enim plausibili successu sancta et vere apostolica religio sub Edvardo sexto, Angliæ Rege, nunquam satis laudato, annis superioribus floruit, tam nunc omnia ibi (propter summam gentis nostræ ingratitudinem cum nimia securitate animi conjunctam) deformata sunt, ut superioris illius ecclesiæ vestigium vix ullum amplius ibi appareat. Etenim, cum illustrissimis Regis Angliæ Henrici octavi (qui Edvardi sexti pater erat) temporibus, omnes totius regni proceres, archiepiscopi, episcopi, reliquique ordinis ecclesiastici viri, ad hæc duces quoque omnes, comites, barones, equites, et tam legum municipalium, quam juris ecclesiastici, ut vocant, administri et judices, deinde civitatum quoque, urbium, pagorum, et municipiorum omnium rectores, præfecti, omneque genus magistratus, denique cujuscumque conditionis, status, aut ordinis viri (qui modo decimum sextum ætatis suæ annum excesserant), juramento verbis conceptis præstito, sancte fidem dedissent, se quidem nunquam consensuros, ut vel ipse Romanus pontifex, vel ullus alius civili potestate præditus homo, supra regiam in regno Angliæ potestatem evectus, supremum regni caput agnosceretur; prodierunt tum quidem in medium nonnulli primi nominis apud Anglos viri, qui libris publice editis, et habitis super ea re frequentibus concionibus, pro confirmatione ejusdem juramenti, et idoli illius Romani ejectione fortiter laborantes dimicarent. In quorum numero facile primos fuisse accipio (ut plerosque alios taceam melioris notæ atque nominis homines) Stephanum illum Gardinerum Wintoniensis episcopum, Cutbertum Tonstallum Dunelmensis, et Edmundum Bonerum Londonensis episcopos; qui tamen postea (mutatis cum rege animis) ex Paulo facti sunt Sauli.

Ab hoc publico totius regni decreto, consensu omnium inito, cum in suscepta religione animi popularium magis atque magis confirmarentur, et patri optimo rebus humanis exempto Edvardus filius, optimæ et indolis et spei juvenis (qui religionis causam præ multis aliis non tenebat modo, sed ardebat etiam) succederet, factum est, ut omnia altaria Baalitica, omnis superstitiosus cultus, omnes adulterini ritus, et idola, summo omnium quoque ordinum consensu abrogati tollerentur; cœnæ quoque dominicæ usus, ad præscriptum ipsius Christi et primitivæ ecclesiæ formam revocatus, (habita tamen super ea re in Parlamento (quod vocant) publico et multa et libera disputatione,) restitueretur. Verum enimvero, cum jam annos aliquot, sub ejusdem Edvardi regis auspiciis, bono loco stetisset reformata religionis causa, evenit (proh dolor!) ut e medio sublato, atque in beatorum numerum ex generatione hac prava et adultera recepto pientissimo rege, (quemadmodum et in Israelitico regno, extincto pio Josia rege, olim

[1 Not in ed. 1553.]

factitatum legimus,) totius ecclesiæ simul et regni facies mutaretur in pejus. Ibi enim statim, non sine magno grassantium in bonos omnes impetu, et regni antea bene constituti turbatione, Baalitica (quæ diximus) altaria, omnis adulterinus cultus, omnia idola, et superstitiosi (qui jam exoleverant) ritus et ceremoniæ in pristinam abominationem restituebantur, non sine magno piorum omnium dolore.

Quid quod ibi tum translato ad alium successorem Angliæ imperio, omnes omnium ordinum homines (posthabita prorsus juramenti antea in contrarium præstiti religione, de nunquam amplius admittenda papisticæ abominationis impietate) antichristo Romano nomen dare (non sine perjurii crimine) nihil quicquam erubuerunt? Adeo verum est, quod ille ait, *Mobile nam vulgus mentem cum principe mutat.*

Quæ autem calamitas ex hac regni in deterius mutatione publice orta sit, pronum est videre in antichristi satellitibus et diaboli mancipiis, qui deinde in eos, qui Christum profiterentur, aut evangelion pure docerent, gravissime cœperunt animadvertere; quorum alios securi percutiunt, alios flammis perdunt, alios vero aut fame enecant, aut exilio damnant, ita ut neque ætati, neque sexui, neque generis dignitati ibi parcatur. Quicunque enim vel religionis amore, vel juramenti ratione, vel pietatis christianæ zelo moti, ab eorum fœdis, perjuris et impiis constitutiunculis, humanitus inventis decretis, et ipsorum placitis vel abstinent, vel non subscribunt (etiamsi nihil turbarum dent, et latere potius ament, quam ut eorum impietati, anathemati et damnationi scientes volentesque semet involvant,) ii nisi sponte sua exulent, aut tempestive illorum manus effugiant, vel perpetuis carceribus includantur, vel extremum statim supplicium ferant, oportet.

Nam ut multorum ego martyrum, tam virginum quam epheborum, supplicia taceam, non possum quin eorum saltem nomina percurram, qui in hac martyrum corona primores fuisse, egregiumque fidei suæ specimen constantissime dedisse, comperiuntur. Quales sunt, Hugo Latimerus, octogenarius senex, ad hæc episcopus Vigorniensis, Nicolaus Ridleus Londonensis, Joannes Hoperus Glocestriensis, Robertus Ferrarius Menevensis, omnes episcopi: quos proxime subsequuntur Joannes Rogerus, Laurentius Sanderus, Rolandus Taylerus, Ricardus Cardmakerus, Joannes Bradfordus, Joannes Philpotus, Robertus Gloverus, Joannes Blandius, et Thomas Heyodus; qui viri egregie docti, cum essent et concionatores publici, omnes tamen (post diuturnam captivitatem, et varia tormentorum genera) ignibus concremati sunt, propterea quod antichristo Romano nomen dare noluerunt.

Quid autem D. Thomam Cantuariensem archiepiscopum, virum et pietate et eruditione insignem et annis gravem, dicam, qui cum primas regni apud Anglos esset, et dignitate omnibus aliis præstaret, post olentissimi carceris (unde non semel causam dixit) diuturna simul et arctiora vincula in constantissima fidei suæ confessione ignibus tandem concrematus est, idque Oxoniæ, claro Angliæ oppido et veteris Academiæ nomine insignito? Hic ille est gregis dominici vere apostolicus pastor et episcopus, qui et inimicis suis exemplo Christi benefacere, et quam innocentissime vivere, et universam sophistarum cohortem eruditione sua pudefacere semper studuit, ut non semel eam pudefecit. Quod si licebit leonem veluti ab unguibus æstimare, hic certe libellus Edvardi sexti temporibus hoc auctore primum scriptus, deinde evulgatus, sed in carcere postea ab ipso recognitus, et nunc demum magno Dei beneficio veluti e flamma servatus, talis est, qui suum auctorem, etiamsi nos taceamus, affatim commendet. Nam cœnæ dominicæ controversiam ea hic dexteritate tractat, ut plerosque omnes, qui in hoc scripti genere ingenii sui nervos extenderant, multis emunctæ naris viris a tergo reliquisse videatur.

Ne quis autem putet, hunc sanctum Dei martyrem, ad asserendam hanc de cœna dominica explicationem (quæ multis fortasse sciolis pro paradoxo quodam habeatur) vel temere vel factiose descendisse, neutiquam id te latere velim, pie lector, hunc virum, post multam scripturarum pervestigationem, ex unius beati martyris Ridlei episcopi Londonensis institutione, sero tandem (nimirum anno 46) in eam, quam hic tuetur, sententiam adductum esse. Non mirum igitur cuiquam videri debet, si vir ille post multam cum doctissimis quibusque viris habitam concertationem, post diligentem scripturarum omnium collationem, et veterum scriptorum excussam sententiam, hunc libellum primo conscriptum evulgavit, deinde et in carcere recognovit, et sanguinis etiam sui profusione ad postremum confirmare voluit. Ut ne autem de hujus libelli vel fide vel auctore dubites, amice lector, autographon ejus in nostra apud Æmdanos ecclesia pro thesauro quodam et clarissimi viri sanctique Christi martyris mnemosyno servamus. In hoc autem illud omnibus piis hac libelli publicatione communicari voluimus, ne talentum hoc qualecunque nostræ fidei concreditum pressisse, atque adeo humi defodisse videamur.

Diximus, quæ calamitas ceremoniis ecclesiasticis et reipublicæ christianæ statui apud Anglos ex mutatione regni illius acciderit: nunc audiat pius lector, quam calamitosa mutatio et sacerdotum ordini postea allata sit. Postquam enim, rerum potiunte Edvardo sexto, sæpe ac multum in communi ecclesiæ Anglicanæ concilio disputatum tractatumque fuisset de tollendo sacerdotum cœlibatu, obtinuit ea sententia, quæ (ut omnium ordinum suffragiis approbata erat) præceptum illud Romani antichristi de non ducendis uxoribus, tanquam a spiritu erroris profectum, sacerdotibus abrogavit: quippe quod non modo verbo Dei et apostolorum doctrinæ repugnaret, sed etiam tam veteris legis quam primitivæ ecclesiæ exemplis adversaretur. Ceterum cum multi, hac ipsa totius regni constitutione freti, uxores duxissent, et legitime procreatis inde liberis benedictionem propagationis consequuti essent, coacti fuere (eodem Edvardo sexto e vivis sublato) cum uxoribus suis divortium facere, et liberos etiam suos abdicare. Hic certe, aut nusquam alibi, miserrimam rerum faciem videre licebat; dum alii ex sacrificorum ordine hypocritæ, repudiatis uxoribus et ejectis e sua familia liberis, ad execratum papismi vomitum redirent, alii vero retentis uxoribus, et facultatibus suis exuti, et munere ecclesiastico exauctorati, exulare cogerentur.

In propheticis literis scriptum legimus, "Labia sacerdotum custodire scientiam, et legem requiri ex ore eorum." Atqui in regno Angliæ, quos ex professo conveniebat religionis antistites esse, et velut oves in medio luporum agere, ii nunc in lupos conversi, primi in ovile Christi (proh dolor!) irruunt, et mactare tantum ac deglubere oves, non pascere, sibi studio habent. Quid vulgus sacerdotum autem? Ii Arcadicis asinis rudiores cum sint, nihil minus quam populo scelera sua nuntiare curant: quin potius omne genus libidini frena laxantes, cum fœde scortentur, strenue quoque crapulentur domi, foris tamen pro sanctulis haberi gestiunt, ita ut nullus ibi amplius virtuti locus sit, aut honos deferatur. Etenim si vel fidem Abrahæ habeas, si dotibus vere pontificiis præditus sis, si quam innocentissime vivas, nisi coronatam illam bestiam adores, nihil egeris, quo minus, ne sacerdotio fungaris, ab istis scortationis patronis abjiciaris, et bene tecum actum erit, si non etiam ad mortis supplicium rapiaris. O sacerdotum collegium antichristo dignum! quod cum omne genus sceleribus inquinatos sacrificulos benigne habeat, laute foveat, et ad pulpita ecclesiastica etiam provehat, solos maritos sacerdotes ferre nequit; cum apostolus tamen perhibeat, melius esse matrimonium contrahere, quam ferventi libidine æstuari. O gravissimam Dei iram, in regnum Angliæ horribiliter adeo effusam! A quanta dignitate, Deique benedictione, in quantam vastitatem, Deique indignationem regnum illud antea florentissimum decidisse videmus! O duram piorum sortem in eo regno, ubi non modo negatum est Christum salutaremque evangelii doctrinam profiteri, sed piaculare etiam habetur antichristum non adorasse, cœnæ dominicæ profanationem non probasse, ad elevationem panis mystici non procubuisse, neque pectoribus iteratis ictibus tutudisse! imo nisi ibi ad omnes Sathanæ operationes in superstitiosis divorum ceremoniis conniveas, nisi statuas ibi ad cultum erectas, et exorcizatas creaturas, panem, cereos, oleum, et ramos, religiose habeas et colas, denique nisi, contemptim habito Jesu Christi sanguine, peccatorum condonationem ab episcopi Romani diplomatis expectare te fatearis, dicet, actum est, peristi; et veluti ter hæreticus, aut sane regni proditor (is enim titulus illorum sanguinariæ tyrannidi prætexitur), ad mortis supplicium raperis.

Hæc cum ita habeant, lector optime, quis non bene factum prædicet, quod bona piorum hominum pars (dum effugiendi illinc copia datur) relicta patria, relictis bonis et amicis, eo se recipiant, ubi salva conscientia Deo militare queant, potius quam ut ibi antichristum Romanum tantum non adorent? Equidem non possum non laudare eorum consilium, qui ex Christi Jesu mandato solum vertere, quam sub tali animarum tyrannide in patria vivere malunt: ut certe, præter multas concionatorum, nobilium, mercatorum, opificum, et plebeiorum hominum in dispersione Germaniæ passim nunc degentium) chiliades, multi clarissimi viri tam tragicam regni ac religionis mutationem in tempore evaserunt; quamobrem et facultatum suarum direptionem patiebantur. In quorum numero mihi primi omnium sunt habendi, Joannes Poynetus Winton., Guliel. Barlous Bathonen., Jo. Scoreus Cicestrien., Milo Coverdalus Exon., et Jo. Balus Osrien. episcopi; ut Katarinam Suffolciæ ducem, cum Joanna Wilkensona vidua (fœminas æterna memoria dignas), et multos alios concionatores in suo catalogo postea memorandos, prætereram; qui omnes ignominiam crucis exulando ferre, quam in patria magni haberi cum animæ suæ periculo, præoptarunt.

Verum enimvero, quoniam non desunt, qui nos omnia mala hæc, tam domi quam foris, ea propter perpeti calumniantur, quod de re sacramentaria (ex pituoso illorum judicio) parum religiose parumque reverentur et loquamur et sentiamus; ideo hunc libellum, et scripturæ sanctæ consentanea dogmata complectentem, et auctoris sanguine confirmatum (qui quidem auctor ecclesiæ nostræ Anglicæ primarius antistes fuit), in lucem dedimus, ut ubi positis affectibus illum legeris, amice lector, et ad veram fidei scripturæque sanctæ normam expenderis, ipse videas, nos quidem patria extorres factos non mala causa niti, neque quicquam perperam de cœnæ dominicæ usu tum sentire, tum loqui ac docere.

Ut autem expeditior hujus libri lectio fiat, nonnullis locis manus indicem parenthesi inclusimus, ut ibi intelligas aliquid esse, quod priori hujus libelli editioni ipse auctor (etiamdum in carcere agens) additum voluit. Deinde in ejusdem libri margine annotatum passim invenias objectum numerum asterisco insignitum, qui numerus ea loca ostendit, quæ sub personati Marci cujusdam Antonii nomine Stephanus ille Gardinerus sycophanta impudentissimus (auxilio cujusdam Watsoni et Smithi sophistarum) scripto convellere frustra tentavit.

Hæc ea sunt, pie lector, quæ te scire volui. Quod superest, enixe Deum precor, ut in Christo Domino, vero animarum nostrarum Pastore, Sacerdote, et Episcopo, quam optime valeas, et hanc doctrinæ evangelicæ veritatem, qua decet fide, amplecten salvus fias. Amen.

CATALOGUS[1]

ILLORUM EPISCOPORUM PRÆLATORUM ET PRÆCIPUORUM CONCIONATORUM, QUI EX ORDINE ECCLESIASTICO BENE CONSTITUTO, PROPTER FIDEI SUÆ CONSTANTEM CONFESSIONEM, SUA PATRIA IN CHRISTO EXULARE, QUAM PALINODIAM IMPIE CANERE, MALUERUNT.

EPISCOPI.

Jo. Poynet, Winto. Guliel. Barlo, Bathon. et Vellen. Jo. Scory, Cicest. Milo Coverdale, Exon. Jo. Bale, Osrien.

DECANI.

Doct. Jo. Cox, Edoar. Regis in eleemosynis elargiendis dispensator, Westmo. D. Jaco. Haddon, Exon. D. Rober. Horne, Dunel. D. Guliel. Turner, Vellen. Tho. Sampson, Cicestr.

ARCHIDIACONI.

Edmundus Cranmer, Cantuar. hujus martyris frater. D. Jo. Ælmer, Stoven. D. Bullin, Lincol. Tho. Yonge, præcentor Meneven.

DOCTORES THEOLO.

Edmundus Grindal, Rober. Kinge, Sandes, Renoldes, Pilkinton, Jo. Joseph.

CONCIONATORES.

David Whitheed, Jo. Alvei, Jo. Pedder, Jo. Biddill, Tho. Becon, Rob. et Ric. Turneri, Edmundus Allein, Leveri fratres tres, Jo. Pekins, Tho. Cottesford, Tho. Donel, Alex. Nowel, cum fratre, Bartho. Traheron, alius Pilkinton, Jo. Wolloc, Jo. Olde, Jo. Medwel, Jo. Rough, Jo. Knokes, Jo. Appelbie, Jo. Perkehurst, Edoa. Large, Galfri. Jones, Rob. Crowley, Ro. Wysdome, Ro. Watson, Guil. Goodman, Anto. Gilbie, Whittingham, Macbrey, Henri. Renold, Jac. Perse, Jugge, Edmundes, Cole, Mounteyn, duo Fischeri, Da. Simson, Jo. Bendel, etc.

[1 Not in ed. 1553.]

ILLUSTRISSIMO AC NOBILISSIMO

PRINCIPI EDVARDO SEXTO,

ANGLIÆ, FRANCIÆ, ET HIBERNIÆ REGI, FIDEI DEFENSORI, ET IN
TERRIS SECUNDUM CHRISTUM ECCLESIÆ ANGLICANÆ
ET HIBERNICÆ CAPITI SUPREMO, THOMAS
CANTUARIENSIS ARCHIEPISCOPUS.

Pro cura dominici gregis mihi commissa, in quo salutari pastu verbi divini erudiendo omnem curam cogitationemque meam collocare debeo, illustrissime princeps, cœnam Domini (quæ multis et magnis superstitionibus violata est, et ad quæstum translata) renovandam ad Servatoris Christi instituta et redintegrandam putavi; et de vero ejus usu ex verbi divini et veteris ac sanctæ ecclesiæ auctoritate commonefaciendos esse omnes judicavi, quorum cura et instructio ad officii mei auctoritatem aliqua ex parte pertinet.

Itaque ante triennium missæ papisticæ abusus præcipuos (quibus non modo ecclesia Anglica, sed etiam totus pene orbis fœdatus atque infectus fuerat) libello quodam Anglo confutavi, et verum atque christianum ejus usum restituendum docui. Quo libro ita multi sunt ad sanam de ea re opinionem adducti, ut veritatis vim, quanta esset, sentirem, et gratiæ Servatoris Christi beneficia intelligerem, ut ad veritatis lucem patefactam occæcati homines splendorem lucis acciperent, et (ut Paulus prædicante Anania) oculorum aciem perciperent. Hoc ita ægre Stephanus Gardinerus Wintoniensis tum episcopus tulerat, ut nihil sibi prius faciendum putarit, quam ut librum tam utilem et plausibilem confutaret, ratus nisi opera sua aliqua impedimenta objicerentur, nullos deploratæ jam et derelictæ pene sententiæ adjutores fore. Itaque eadem ipse lingua librum iisdem de rebus conscribit, et firmatam jam de vero cœnæ usu sententiam evertere conatur, et papisticam opinionem, superstitionibus undique diffluentem, revocare conatur. Post hunc prodiit M. Antonius Constantius, Stephano Gardinero ita affinis et germanus, ut idem ipse esse videatur; tanta est ingeniorum subtilitas, scripturæ sophisticæ similitudo. Sed uterque idem tractat, alio tamen modo.

Constantius enim libro Latine scripto ita argumenta mea persequitur, ut sibi optimum videtur; et ut causam juvet, sæpe truncata, sæpe inversa, sæpe disjecta, sic introducit, ut non magis a me agnosci potuerint, quam Medeæ liberi in multa membra disjecti et deformati. Neque enim de hujusmodi corporis forma, neque de ulla re recte judicare possumus, ubi tota species ante oculos proposita non est, in quam intueri, quasi in Phidiæ Minervam, debemus, et non particulam aliquam, sicuti Momus crepidam Veneris, lacessere. Itaque ut melius mea de hac controversa opinione sententia teneretur, librum meum de Anglico in Latinum convertendum curavi, ut omnes intelligerent, nos neque obscuram nostram sententiam neque abditam esse velle, quam cum multis bonis et doctis viris communem habemus, et cum verbo Dei, et verbi defensatrice vera ecclesia, consentientem.

Nemo est autem ex omnibus dignior, in cujus nomine libellus hic appareat quam in tuo. Es enim non modo papistarum opinione fidei defensor (qui hoc non a seipsis protulerant, sed Deo per illos ad ipsorum perniciem præmonente), sed etiam bonorum omnium auctoritate dignus, in quem tantum ecclesiæ munus conferatur. Es hujus ecclesiæ Anglicæ et Hibernicæ supremus in terris moderator, sub quo, quasi sub Moyse, partem spiritus et magnam multorum curam atque administrationem commissam habeo. Es etiam non modo legibus nostris tanti regni rex, sed etiam natura, quæ majestatem tuam ita ad omnem excellentiam formavit, ut quæ singula in aliis exquisita sunt, ea in majestate tua perfecta emineant. Video in regibus mediocre aliquid esse non posse, et auctoritate veteris proverbii in eo confirmor; et gaudeo hanc excellentiam non modo ad meliorem partem, sed etiam ad optimam esse translatam. Hæc non laudandæ majestatis tuæ gratia, sed cohortandæ potius dico, ut res in hac ætate tam illustres uberrimos posthac et excellentissimos tantæ dignitatis splendores in constanti ætate ferant. Quanta enim ornamenta ingenii et doctrinæ vel ab optima natura vel bonis præceptoribus tribui poterant, eadem in te omnia excellentia sunt; et quod in primis laudabilissimum est, timor Dei et veræ religionis studium, in quibus majestas tua ea cum laude versatur, qua seipsum rex et propheta commendavit quum dixerat, "senibus se intelligentiorem esse, quia mandata Dei inquirebat."

His aliisque gravibus de causis commoveor, ut hunc librum jam Latinum factum nomini tuo offeram. Spero autem rei ipsi satisfactum hoc libro esse, qui non modo summam veræ doctrinæ continet, sed omnia adversariorum argumenta (quæ quidem recitatu digna sunt) refutat. Sed quia nimis curiosi quidam sunt, et nulla ne diligenti quidem et plena rerum explicatione contenti, et eandem materiam argumentorum (ne nihil dicere videantur) in alias formas transmutant, et ordinem naturæ pro licentia ingeniorum confundunt; ideo nostram ad Stephani Gardineri librum responsionem, Latinam factam, brevi in lucem educemus, ut nullus (ne sophistis quidem) ad contradicendum locus relictus sit: qua ratione putabo non modo uni, sed Gardinero etiam et Constantio quoque esse satisfactum; et quod de comœdiis ille dixit, hoc de personatis istis dicendum, "Unum cognoris, ambos noris." Quod si quædam uno in libro pertractata sunt, quæ in altero prætermissa fuerint, iisdem ego responsionem meam adjungam, ut adversarii, si qui relicti sint, vel non habeant quod objiciant, vel si objecerint, videant quid responderi ad illa possit. Hæ sunt causæ, rex nobilissime, quæ me ad emittendum hunc librum impulerunt, eumque sub majestatis tuæ auctoritate divulgandum. Te spero ita hoc meum studium accepturum, quemadmodum et causæ æquitas fert, et officium meum postulat, et clementia tua in aliis honestis causis solet facere. Dominus Jesus majestatem tuam servet. Lambethæ, Idibus

Martiis. M.D.LIII.

PROŒMIUM AD LECTOREM.

<small>Eximium in nos Christi beneficium.</small>

CHRISTUS Servator noster, pro sempiterni Patris sui voluntate (cum statutum ad id tempus expletum esset), suscepta in se natura nostra, e cœlestis Patris altissimo solio in hunc mundum descendit, ut nobis miseris peccatoribus fausta ac felicia nuntiaret; ut ægrotis sanitatem, cæcis visum, surdis auditum, mutis sermonem, vinctis libertatem, hominibus in tenebris et mortis umbra versantibus lucem tribueret; ut tempus gratiæ et misericordiæ jam adesse demonstraret, ut electis omnibus veniam et plenam peccatorum omnium remissionem daret et promulgaret. Quod ut præstaret, hostiam sui corporis immolavit in cruce, et sacrificium ejusmodi fecit, ut plena atque integra redemptio, satisfactio, et propitiatio pro peccatis universi mundi eo contineretur. Atque ut hoc sacrificium omnibus fidelibus commendaret, et spem ac fiduciam æternæ salutis in eo collocandam confirmaret, perpetuum hujus sacrificii monumentum instituit, in ecclesia sua assidue celebrandum, ad æternam divini nominis laudem et gloriam, et singulare nostrorum omnium solatium et commodum. Sacrosanctæ enim cœnæ celebratio ita nobis a Christo proposita est, ut in ea se suaque omnia libenter libereque donasse testaretur his, qui rite secundum præscriptum ab illo modum ad eam accederent.

<small>Error papistarum obscurans Christi beneficium.</small>

Sed antichristus Romanus, ut hoc ingens Christi beneficium imminueret et labefactaret, hoc sacrificium in cruce factum haud satis idoneum ad hæc quæ diximus esse docet, nisi aliud adhibeatur sacrificium ab ipso excogitatum, et a sacerdotibus ejus factum; aut indulgentiæ, preculæ ligneæ, peregrinationes, atque aliæ ejusmodi quisquiliæ seu σκύβαλα proponantur, ad inchoatum Christi beneficium explendum atque absolvendum. Deinde Christianos amplissimæ mortis Christi beneficium aut accommodare sibi non posse, sed illud episcopi Romani arbitrio relinqui distribuendum; aut per Christum plenam remissionem non habere, sed peccatis solum liberari, pœnam autem illis debitam in purgatorio restare luendam, nisi per antichristum Romanum et ejus administros, post hujus vitæ confectum iter, remittatur: qua in re sibi hoc pro sceleribus nostris efficere arroganter præsumunt, quod Christus vel noluit vel non potuit efficere.

<small>2 Thess. ii.</small>

O dira maledicta, et injuriam in Christum execrandam! O impium in templo Dei nefas! O superbiam antichristi intolerandam, et certissimum filii perditionis argumentum, supra Deum se extollentis, et Luciferi in modum sedem suam et potentiam supra majestatem Dei collocantis! Nam qui hoc sibi assumit perficiendum, quod in Christo rude adhuc et inchoatum judicat, se Christo meliorem et præstantiorem facit, atque adeo antichristus existit. Quid enim est, si hoc non est, Christo repugnare, atque illum in contemptum deducere, qui vel caritatis quadam inopia nollet, aut imbecillitate quadam magnitudinis et potentiæ non posset, ne cum acerbissima quidem morte et sanguinis profusione, fideles suos omnino liberare, atque illis plenam peccatorum omnium remissionem condonare, nisi harum rerum plena quædam et absoluta confectio ab antichristo Romano ejusque administris requiratur? Quis (quæso) hæc intelligens, et cupidus gloriæ Christi, siccis oculis hanc injuriam Christo illatam, et religionis statum a papistis inductum, intueri poterit? cum verum divini verbi sensum, falsis humanorum commentorum interpretationibus obscurari videat, veram Christi religionem in simulatas quasdam et superstitiosas sectas degenerare, plebem in templis et ore precari, et auribus accipere quæ non intelligat, et ita rudem atque professionis suæ et disciplinæ christianæ ignaram, ut hypocrisim et superstitionem a vera et sincera religione nequeant internoscere? Hæc fuit nuper in Anglia deformata religionis facies, quæ in plerisque adhuc regionibus fœdata et horrida permanet. Sed immortales nobis gratiæ agendæ sunt Deo Patri, per Dominum nostrum Jesum Christum, quod nobilissimi et clarissimi regis nostri auctoritate et sententia superstitiosorum sacerdotum factiones (quemadmodum illustrissimi Henrici octavi memoria omnes in hoc regno fraterculorum et monachorum hæreses) sublatæ et deletæ sunt, scriptura ad verum et proprium sensum restituta est, populus quotidie legere et audire cœleste Dei verbum poterit, et sua ipsorum lingua intelligenter orare, atque adeo lingua atque animo consentienter congruere, neque ex eorum numero esse, de quibus Christus queritur, " Populus hic labiis me colit, cor autem eorum longe a me abest." Multæ (de quibus magnas merito gratias agere Deo possumus) perniciosæ herbæ radicitus extractæ atque evulsæ sunt, quæ gregem Christi non modo contagione inficere, sed etiam messis dominicæ incrementum retardare solent. Sed quid refert globulos precatorios, indulgentias, peregrinationes, reliquumque papismum tollere, quamdiu quatuor perniciosissimæ radices infixæ inhærent, neque adhuc fibræ illarum vel motæ loco vel labefactatæ sunt? quæ quamdiu permanent, priora tum messis dominicæ impedimenta, tum gregis exitia, ex eis repullulare et amplificare necesse est. Quæ hactenus sublatæ sunt superstitiones veluti frondes et folia sunt, quarum amputatio frondationi similis est, aut noxiarum herbarum truncationi, trunco relicto, aut radicibus in terra inhærentibus. Truncus autem ipse, vel potius radices in terra defixæ, sunt papistica illa et perniciosa dogmata de transubstantiatione, de corporis et sanguinis Christi reali præsentia in sacramento (ut vocant) altaris, de manducatione Christi a sceleratis diaboli membris, et de sacrificio et oblatione Christi per sacerdotem facta pro viventium et mortuorum salute. Hæ radices si in vinea Domini crescere permittantur, universam iterum terram nefariis superstitionibus et inveteratis erroribus opplebunt.

<small>Matt. xv.</small>

<small>Quatuor præcipuæ errorum papisticorum radices.</small>

Hæ in Christum injuriæ ita graves et intolerabiles sunt, ut lubenter ista tolerare nemo Christianus vivus et videns possit. Itaque cum multi manus admoverint, et omnia ingenii ac industriæ arma exacuerint, ad nefarias has herbas sarriendas, et universum errorum truncum exscindendum, ego (cum scirem me alia ratione meipsum excusare non posse, cum severus paterfamilias rationem factorum a servis suis requiret) hoc in libro operam meam et industriam obtuli, et securim etiam cum reliquis adhibui ad truncum hunc protinus exscindendum, et omnes stirpium ac radicum fibras penitus elidendas, quas cœlestis Pater nunquam sevit, sed ab adversario diabolo et ministro ejus antichristo satæ fuerunt. Dabit (spero) Dominus, ut hic labor, quem in vinea ejus excipio, inanis non sit, sed bene procedat, et bonos fructus ad honorem gloriamque suam ferat. Nam cum vineam ejus video spinis, tribulis, et permultis aliis noxiis herbis obsitam, intelligo execrationem sempiternam mihi impendere, si tacitus ista silentio præteream, neque manus et linguam ad laborem in vinea Domini suscipiendum admoveam. Testificor autem Deum, qui abdita et intima penitus scrutatur, me hunc laborem nulla alia de causa capere, quam ad divini nominis gloriam, et officii mei functionem, et animi studium atque ardorem (quo erga gregem dominicum afficior) ostendendum. Haud ignoro quo in gradu me Deus, et ad quem finem collocavit, ut (quantum in me situm est) verbum ejus sincere propagetur, et sine ulla vel rerum vel personarum ratione in illum solum actiones meæ intueantur. Scio quam me oportet rationem illo tempore reddere, cum unusquisque pro se munereque suo dicet, et bonum vel malum pro factis suis percepturus est. Scio antichristum veram Dei gloriam et puritatem verbi ejus obscurasse, errorum atque ignorantiæ tenebris offusis, et anilibus ac deliris interpretationum commentis adhibitis. Doloris enim acerbitatem mihi non mediocrem injicit, cum videam simplicem et famescentem Christi gregem in pascua pestilentia abduci, et occæcatum in omnes errores abripi, et pro salutari cibo venenatis rebus pasci. Non parum igitur officii mei locique munere excitatus (in quo benignus Deus electione sua me locavit) omnes auctoritate Christi moneo, qui Christi nomen professi sunt, ut longe a Babylone fugiant (siquidem animas suas salvas volunt) et meretricem illam magnam, sedem nempe Romanam, vitent, ne suavi illos potione ad ebrietatem deducat. Nolite fidem blandis ejus promissis adhibere, nolite cum illa epulari: nam vini loco amaras fæces porrigit, et pro cibo mortiferum venenum apponit. Ad Servatorem autem et Redemptorem Christum accedite, qui omnes advenientes ad se refocillat, etiam in acerbissimis et gravissimis perturbationibus. Illi fidem adjungite, cujus in ore nihil doli, nihil falsi repertum est. Ille vos ab omni ægritudine levabit, ille vobis plenam a pœna et culpa remissionem tribuet. Ille omnes

<small>Quid auctorem ad scribendum impulerit.</small>

<small>*Deformata religionis facies, a papistis inducta.</small>

<small>Admonitio auctoris ad omnes Christianos. Hier. li.</small>

<small>Apoc. xiv. xvii. xviii.</small>

<small>Matt. xi.</small>

<small>Esa. liii. 1 Pet. ii.</small>

<small>Esa. liii.</small>

[1 The asterisk prefixed denotes that the passage is not found in ed. 1553.]

Joan. iv. suos carne sua, quæ in cruce pependerat, perpetuo pascit. Ille omnibus poculum ministrat sanguinis de latere ejus profluentis, et dimanare facit in illos aquam scaturientem ad vitam æternam. Neque aures neque animos falsis incantationibus, suavibus susurris, vaferrimis præstigiis papistarum advertite, quibus multos jam annos deceperunt, occæcarunt, et fascinarunt mundum; sed Christum audite, in illius verba et disciplinam vos tradite, quæ recta vos ad æternam vitam ducent, cum Christo regni cœlestis hæreditate perpetuo fruituros. Amen.

Joan. 6.
Caro mea revera est cibus, et sanguis meus revera est potus.

D. Augustinus.
Hanc escam manducare, et illum bibere potum, est in Christo manere, et Christum manentem in se habere.
etc.

DE
VERA ET CATHOLICA DOCTRINA,

ET USU CORPORIS ET SANGUINIS CHRISTI SERVATORIS NOSTRI.

CAPUT PRIMUM.

Cœna Domini, quæ sacra synaxis, vel sacramentum corporis et sanguinis Christi Servatoris nostri appellatur, variis est rationibus et a multis hominibus male tractata, præcipue autem his quadringentis aut quingentis annis. A quibusdam pro sacrificio propitiante et peccatum expiante est habita, et aliis superstitionibus profanata, longe a primi auctoris Christi mente, ad magnam sanctissimæ mortis ejus injuriam et contumeliam. Quibusdam autem res levis et nugatoria visa est, et quasi nullius auctoritatis aut momenti esset, spreta et contempta jacuit. Ita utrinque magnæ dimicationes ortæ, et diversis in locis diversorum hominum opiniones in varias sententias distractæ sunt. Itaque ne hoc sacramentum posthac vel his in contemptum vel illis in abusum veniat, aut utrisque ad aliam rationem traducatur, quam Christus, primus auctor atque inventor ejus, constituit; atque adeo contentiones utrinque susceptæ sedari et tranquillari possint; certissima et expeditissima via est sanctis scripturis adhærere; in quibus quicquid invenitur, pro certissimo fundamento et firmissima veritate habendum est. Quod autem ad fidem nostram pertinet, quicquid ex scripturis probari non potest, humanum inventum, commutabile atque incertum est. Ideo hic ipsa scripturæ verba referemus, quæ tam Christus ipse quam ejus apostolus Paulus, tum de edenda carne et bibendo sanguine, tum de edendis et bibendis carnis et sanguinis sacramentis, locuti sunt.

Abusus dominicæ cœnæ.

CAPUT II.

DE MANDUCATIONE ET POTATIONE CORPORIS ET SANGUINIS CHRISTI.

De corpore Christi vere edendo et sanguine ejus bibendo, Christus ipse, in sexto Joannis, ad hunc modum loquitur: "Amen amen dico vobis, nisi ederitis carnem Filii hominis, et biberitis ejus sanguinem, non habetis vitam in vobis. Qui edit meam carnem et bibit sanguinem meum, habet vitam æternam: et ego excitabo illum in extremo die. Caro enim mea revera est cibus, et sanguis meus revera est potus. Qui edit carnem meam, et bibit sanguinem meum, in me manet, et ego in illo. Quemadmodum misit me vivens Pater, et ego vivo propter Patrem; et qui edit me, etiam ille vivet propter me. Hic est panis qui de cœlo descendit: non quemadmodum ederunt patres manna, et mortui sunt: qui edit hunc panem, vivet in æternum."

Joan. vi.

Ex hisce Christi verbis clarum efficitur, perceptionem carnis et sanguinis ejus minime similem esse ceterorum ciborum potionumque perceptioni. Quamvis enim sine cibo et potione vivi non potest, non tamen efficitur, ut qui edit et bibit perpetuo vivat. Quod vero ad corporis et sanguinis Christi perceptionem attinet, verum est, quod et qui illa edit et bibit habet vitam æternam, et qui non edit nec bibit non habet vitam æternam. Hanc enim escam manducare, et illum bibere potum, est in Christo manere, et Christum manentem in se habere. Qui igitur in Christo non manet, et in quo Christus non manet, non se dicat aut existimet manducare corpus Christi, aut bibere sanguinem ejus. Quid sit igitur revera corpus Christi manducare, et sanguinem ejus bibere, audivistis.

August. in Joan. Tract. xxvi.

Eodem Tract.

August. de Civit. Lib. xxi. cap. 25.

CAPUT III.

DE MANDUCATIONE ET POTATIONE SACRAMENTI CORPORIS ET SANGUINIS CHRISTI.

SACRAMENTA eorundem Servator noster Christus pridie mortis ejus extrema in cœna, quam cum apostolis suis habuit, in pane et vino instituit.

Matt. xxvi. Quo tempore (sicuti Matthæus refert) vescentibus illis, "Jesus panem accipiens, et gratiis actis, fregit, et dedit discipulis, et dixit: Capite, edite, hoc est corpus meum. Et accepto poculo, gratiisque actis, dedit illis dicens: Bibite ex hoc omnes. Hic enim est sanguis meus novi testamenti, qui pro multis effunditur in remissionem peccatorum. Dico autem vobis, me non deinceps ex hoc fructu vitis bibiturum, usque ad eum diem, cum illum bibam vobiscum novum in Patris mei regno."

Marc. xiv. Hoc idem Marcus his verbis repetit: "Vescentibus illis, Jesus acceptum panem, ubi gratias egisset, fregit, et dedit illis, et dixit: Accipite, edite: hoc est corpus meum. Atque ut accepisset poculum, et gratias egisset, dedit illis; et biberunt ex eo omnes. Et dixit illis, Hic est sanguis meus novi testamenti, qui pro multis effunditur. Amen dico vobis, non bibam posthac e fructu vitis, usque ad eum diem, quo illud novum bibam in regno Dei."

Luc. xxii. Lucas rem ad hunc modum exponit: "Cum autem tempus adesset, accubuit, et duodecim apostoli cum illo. Et dixit illis, Magna cupiditate teneor edendi vobiscum hoc pascha, priusquam patiar. Dico enim vobis, me deinceps ex eo non comesturum, usque dum in regno Dei compleatur. Et accepto poculo gratias egit, et dixit: Capite hoc, et inter vos dividite. Dico enim vobis, me non bibiturum ex fructu vitis, usque dum regnum Dei venerit. Et acceptum panem, gratiis jam actis, fregit, et dedit illis, dicens: Hoc est corpus meum, quod pro vobis datur: hoc facite ad recordationem mei. Similiter et poculum (cœna jam finita), dicens: Hoc poculum novum est testamentum in sanguine meo, qui pro vobis effunditur."

Hucusque Christi facta et dicta audistis, quibus illum in extrema cœna usum evangelistæ commemorant, in synaxi celebranda, et sacramento corporis et sanguinis ejus instituendo.

1 Cor. x. Nunc quid de eadem re D. Paulus in decimo prioris ad Corinthios capite commemorat, exponendum est: "Poculum benedictionis, cui benedicimus, nonne communio sanguis Christi est? Panis quem frangimus, nonne communio corporis Christi est? Unus panis, unum corpus multi sumus: omnes enim de uno pane participamus."

1 Cor. xi. Et in undecimo capite, in eadem epistola, ad hunc modum: "Ego enim accepi a Domino, quod et tradidi vobis: Dominum Jesum, eadem nocte qua prodebatur, cepisse panem; et gratiis actis, fregisse et dixisse: Hoc est corpus meum, quod pro vobis frangitur: hoc facite ad recordationem mei. Pari modo, ut cœnasset, cepisse poculum etiam, et dixisse: Hoc poculum novum testamentum est in meo sanguine: hoc facite, quotiescunque biberitis, ad mei recordationem. Quoties enim cunque ederitis panem hunc, et poculum hoc biberitis, mortem Domini nuntiate, usque dum veniat. Itaque qui panem hunc ederit, aut biberit poculum Domini indigne, reus erit corporis et sanguinis Domini. Exquirat autem seipsum homo, et sic de pane hoc edat, et de poculo bibat. Qui enim ederit et biberit indigne, judicium sibi edit et bibit, non discernens corpus Domini. Propterea multi in vobis languentes atque infirmi sunt, et complures dormiunt.

Ex his Christi verbis, quæ evangelistæ commemorant, et hac doctrina Pauli, quam se fatetur a Christo accepisse, duo in primis observanda sunt.

CAPUT IV.
CHRISTUS PANEM VOCAVIT CORPUS SUUM.

Primum, Christum Servatorem nostrum panem, quem confregerat, corpus suum, et vinum, fructum vitis, sanguinem suum appellavisse. Neque vero hoc ita Christus dixit, ut ex granis confectum panem verum ejus corpus esse quisquam putaret; aut contra, Corpus ejus esse panem ex granis confectum, neque vinum ex uvis expressum esse verum ejus sanguinem; aut contra, verum ejus sanguinem esse vinum ex uvis expressum: sed ut id significaret nobis, quod Paulus dixit, Poculum esse communionem vel consortionem sanguinis Christi pro nobis effusi, et panem esse societatem vel communionem carnis ejus pro nobis cruci affixæ. Itaque quamvis naturæ illius humanæ substantia in cœlo sit, et ad dexteram Dei Patris sedeat, quicunque tamen de hoc pane Marc. ult. in cœna dominica, secundum Christi institutionem, edit, Christi ipsius promissis et testamento certior factus est, se membrum esse corporis Christi, et participem beneficiorum mortis ejus, quam pro nobis in cruce perpessus est. Pari modo, qui ex hoc sanctissimo poculo in cœna dominica, secundum Christi institutionem, biberit, is legatione et testamento Christi certior factus est, se sanguinis Christi participem esse, quem pro nobis profudit. Hoc enim nobis significavit Paulus his verbis, "Poculum benedic- 1 Cor x. tionis, cui benedicimus, nonne communio sanguinis Christi est?" Ex quo fit, ut hanc sacrosanctam communionem nemo contemnere aut parvo æstimare poterit, nisi Christi corpus et sanguinem quoque contemnat, et non multum sua interesse putet, utrum particeps illorum fuerit, an non. Hos Paulus ait suam ipsorum condemnationem edere 1 Cor. xi. et bibere, quia Christi corpus non discernunt.

CAPUT V.
MALI EDUNT SACRAMENTUM, NON VERUM CORPUS CHRISTI.

Alterum, quod ex verbis Christi et apostoli intelligitur, est, Quod quamvis nemo verum corpus Christi edat, et verum ejus sanguinem bibat, quin idem vitam æternam habeat (quemadmodum ex his liquet, quæ apud Joannem commemorantur), boni tamen quoque et mali panem et vinum, quæ sacramenta corporis et sanguinis sunt, edant et bibant: sed præter sacramenta boni æternam vitam, mali sempiternam mortem comedunt. Itaque Paulus dicit, "Qui panem hunc ederit, et poculum Domini biberit indigne, reus erit corporis et sanguinis Domini." Hic Paulus, non qui panem illum ederit, aut poculum sacramenti biberit indigne, dicit corpus Christi et sanguinem ejus edere et bibere, sed reum esse corporis et sanguinis Domini. Quid autem edat et bibat, Paulus aperte exponit his verbis: "Qui edit et bibit indigne, judicium sibi edit et bibit."

Jam paucissimis declaratum est, quæ sit summa eorum omnium, quæ de Christi corpore et sanguine, et de sacramento eorundem percipiendo, scriptura docet.

CAPUT VI.
QUÆ AD CHRISTIANORUM DE HOC SACRAMENTO FIDEM SATIS SUNT.

Et quemadmodum certissima hæc et verissima sunt, quæ a Christo ipso, omnis veritatis auctore, et ab apostolo ejus Paulo, quemadmodum a Christo accepit, traduntur; sic omnes doctrinæ, quæ huic repugnant, falsæ et commentitiæ sunt, et ab omnibus Christianis (quia verbo Dei adversantur) repudiandæ. Quæ autem aliquid amplius istis de rebus continent, quod verbo Dei non nitatur, illæ nihil necessarium in se habent; neque vel ingenia hominum ejusmodi rebus non necessariis exerceri, vel conscientiæ perturbari debent. Itaque dicta et facta Christi, et Pauli atque evangelistarum scripta, quod ad hanc de cœna Domini et sanctissima synaxi sive sacramento corporis et sanguinis Christi doctrinam spectat, fidei Christianorum satisfacere debent.

Hæc si bene considerata et pertractata fuerint, satis erunt ad omnes controversias et dissensiones pacificandas, tum eorum qui antehac ista contempserunt et non magno æstimarunt, tum eorum qui vel ignorantia, vel alia quavis de causa nefarie profanarunt, atque ad alienos usus traduxerunt.

CAPUT VII.

SACRAMENTUM AMORIS ET CONCORDIÆ AD DISSENSIONUM ET RIXARUM OCCASIONEM ARRIPITUR.

Christus hoc sacramentum instituit, ut ex inimicis amicos faceret, et omnes discordiarum varietates tolleret, et omnes Christianos ad amoris et caritatis stabilitatem inter se devinciendam duceret. Sed diabolus, Christi ipsius et omnium Christi membrorum adversarius, tam versute præstigiis quibusdam et captionibus lusit, ut ex hoc sacramento, quod ad omnes contentiones sedandas institutum est, maximæ dissensiones et dissidia excitentur. Faxit Deus, ut omnibus dissensionibus abjectis, ad hanc sacrosanctam communionem omnes vera in Christum fide, et ardenti erga Christi membra amore, accedamus: ut quemadmodum carnaliter ore sacramentalem panem comedimus et vinum bibimus, sic spiritualiter animo verum Christi corpus et sanguinem percipiamus, in cœlo jam existentis, et ad dexteram Dei Patris sedentis: denique ut illius opera, regni et gloriæ cœlestis participes cum illo ad omnem ævi æternitatem efficiamur.

CAPUT VIII.

AUCTORIS QUODNAM SIT HIS IN LIBRIS PROPOSITUM.

Quanquam in prima hujus operis parte satis de sacramento corporis et sanguinis Domini tractatum sit, tum quod ad institutionem pertinet, tum quod ad evangelistarum et Pauli verba spectat intelligenda; minime tamen alienum fuerit fusius illa ad sacræ scripturæ et sanctorum patrum sententiam exponere, idque ita plane et perspicue, omissis controversiarum ambiguitatibus et inanibus quæstionibus, ut rudes etiam atque imperiti ista facile addiscant, et fructum inde percipiant.

Hoc enim (Deo juvante) mihi in hoc opere efficiendum proposui, ut grex Christi, in hoc regno dispersus (cujus ego pastor designatus sum), hujus divinæ et cœlestis cognitionis fructu non careat: quo enim clarius ista cernuntur, eo majorem atque uberiorem suavitatem, fructum, consolationem, ædificationem adferunt his, qui ista pie percipiunt. Ad meliorem autem horum intelligentiam, quædam diligenter nobis consideranda sunt.

CAPUT IX.

QUÆNAM SIT SPIRITUALIS FAMES ET SITIS ANIMÆ.

[I.]
Eph. ii.
Rom. iii.

Primum, omnes homines natura sua peccatores esse, et propter peccata in Dei iram offensionemque incurrere, longe ab illo exules atque ejectos, inferni et sempiternæ damnationis convictos esse, neminemque (Christum solum excipio) prorsus innocentem esse, statuendum est. Qua de causa mentes hominum, a Deo inspiratæ, valde expetunt, ut a peccato et inferno liberentur, et apud clementem Deum misericordiam, favorem, justitiam, et sempiternam salutem adipiscantur.

Psal. xli.

Atque hæc ardens et vehemens cupiditas vocatur in scripturis fames et sitis animi: quo genere famis cum David laborasset, dicit, "Quemadmodum affectat cervus fontes aquarum, ita anima mea te, O Deus, expetit. Sitivit anima mea Deum fontem vivum."

Psal. lxii.

Et, "Anima mea sitivit te, caro mea te exoptabat."

Rom. iv.
Rom. vii.
Rom. viii.

In hanc famem afflicta et peccatis oppressa mens legis vi impellitur, quæ tetrum peccati horrorem et turpitudinem, atrocem divinæ indignationis terrorem, mortis et sempiternæ condemnationis acerbissimum supplicium proponit.

Ubi enim dura et severa legis accusatione nihil nisi æternam mortem sibi imminere videt, eamque sibi ante oculos semper objectam habet, ibi tum magnitudine dolorum oppressa mens atque exæstuans aliquam hujus miseriæ et ærumnarum levationem quærit. Atque hic condemnationis suæ quasi sensus, et magna eripiendæ miseriæ et remedii inveniendi cupiditas, spiritualis animi fames dicitur. Quicunque autem hac divina fame affecti sunt, felices apud Deum reputantur, et cibo ac potione explebuntur. Sic enim Christus ait: "Beati qui esuriunt et sitiunt justitiam, quia satiabuntur." Contra Matt. v. autem, qui impium et damnabilem statum suum non vident, sed seipsos satis pios, satis Deo placentes, satis bono in loco et gradu justitiæ esse putant, quemadmodum spiritualem nullam habent famem, ita nullo spirituali pastu a Deo satiabuntur. Quemadmodum Luc. i. enim Pater cœlestis esurientes pascit, ita eos qui nullo famis sensu tanguntur, inanes ablegat.

Hæc autem fames et sitis minime potest a carnali percipi. Ubi enim cibi ac potionis mentionem audit factam, statim animus in patinis et in culina ac promptuario jactatur, et de palato ac ventre cogitat. Sed scriptura, variis in locis, disertis quibusdam ac peculiaribus verbis et sententiis utitur, ut crassas et concretas mentes a crassis ventribus et a rebus corporeis et sub sensum cadentibus ad cœlestem et spiritualem cogitationem traduceret. Apostoli enim et discipuli Christi, cum adhuc carnales essent, quid hujus sitis et famis notione intelligeretur, non adverterunt: qua de causa, cum eum ad edendum Joan. iv. invitassent, ut illos a corporali cibo abduceret, alium se dixit cibum habere, quem illi ignorarent. Cur autem ignorabant? Quia mentes illorum crassæ adhuc et stupentes erant, neque plenitudinem spiritus adhuc perceperant. Itaque Servator Christus illos a corporis ad animi pastum cogitans transferre, aliud illis cibi genus memorabat, quam quod illi cogitatione comprehendebant: et quasi accusabat, quod minime intelligerent, esse aliud genus cibi et potionis, præter id quod ore et gula percipiebatur.

Itemque cum Samaritanæ dicebat, "Quicunque ex hac aqua biberit, quam ego dabo, Joan. iv. non sitiet unquam;" qui hæc auditione acceperant, satis intelligere poterant, aliud esse bibendi genus, quam quod ore et gula hauriretur. Nullum enim ejusmodi genus potionis est, quod semel acceptum universam hominis sitim delere perpetuo possit. His itaque verbis, "Non sitiet unquam," cogitationes illorum a potione ea, quæ ore percipitur, ad aliud potandi genus traducebat, quod tectum illis atque abditum fuit, et ad aliud sitis genus, quod minus adhuc familiare illis erat. Ubi etiam a Servatore nostro dictum est, "Qui venit ad me, non esuriet iterum, et qui credit in me, haud unquam postea sitiet;" Joan. vi. evidens testimonium dederat, longe aliud genus cibi et potionis esse, quam quo illos ultra mare pascebat, et aliud esuriendi et sitiendi genus, quam esuries et sitis corporis est.

Ex his omnibus datur intelligi, aliud edendi et bibendi, esuriendi et sitiendi genus propositum populo fuisse, quam quod ad vitam hanc fluxam et caducam alendam et sustentandam pertineret. Quemadmodum igitur, quod corpus alit, cibus et potio dicitur; ita quod mentem pascit, cibi et potionis nominibus in sacris literis appellatur.

CAPUT X.

SPIRITUALIS ANIMI PASTUS QUINAM SIT.

Superiori in loco, quæ esuries et sitis animi esset, exposuimus: nunc quidnam cibus, II. potio et pastus animi sit, dicendum videtur. Cibus, potio, et pastus animorum nostrorum Christus est. Sic enim Servator de se ait: "Venite ad me omnes qui laboratis et Matt. xi. onerati estis, et ego reficiam vos." Et alio loco: "Si quis (inquit) sitiat, veniat ad me, Joan. vii. et bibat. Qui credit in me, flumina e ventre ejus manabunt aquæ vivæ." Et, "Ego sum Joan. vi. panis vitæ," inquit Christus: "qui accedit ad me, non esuriet: qui credit in me, nunquam sitiet." Quemadmodum enim cibus et potio famelicum corpus sustentant et fovent, ita corporis Christi mors et sanguinis effusio animam levant et pascunt, cum suo modo esurit et sitit. Quid est quod miserum et exhaustum corpus reficit? Cibus et potio. Quibus igitur nominibus appellabimus carnem et sanguinem Christi, quæ reficiunt et sustentant mentem, nisi cibi et potionis? Atque hæc similitudo Christum Servatorem induxit, ut diceret: "Caro mea est revera cibus, et sanguis meus est revera potus." Joan. vi. Nullum enim cibi genus jucundum animo esse potest, nisi mors Christi: neque ullum potionis genus æstuantis animi sitim restinguere queat, nisi sanguis Christi, pro peccatis in cruce profusus.

Quemadmodum enim carnalis quidam ortus est, et carnalis pastus, et carnale nutrimentum, sic spiritualis ortus et spirituale quoque nutrimentum est atque nutritio.

Et quemadmodum carnali ortu ex patre et matre carnaliter nascimur ad hanc caducam vitam, sic quivis pius Christianus spiritualiter ex Deo per Christum nascitur ad æternam vitam.

Et quemadmodum quivis carnaliter pascitur et nutritur cibo et potione, sic quivis pius Christianus spiritualiter pascitur et nutritur carne et sanguine Servatoris Christi: *Joan. vi.* sicuti Christus ipse in vi. Joannis docuit, his verbis: "Amen amen dico vobis, nisi ederitis carnem Filii hominis, et biberitis ejus sanguinem, non habetis vitam in vobis. Qui edit meam carnem, et bibit meum sanguinem, habet æternam vitam: et ego illum in extremo die excitabo. Caro enim mea revera est cibus, et sanguis meus revera est potus. Qui edit meam carnem, et bibit meum sanguinem, in me manet et ego in illo. Quemadmodum vivens Pater misit me, et ego vivo propter Patrem; sic qui edit me, *Gal. ii.* vivet propter me." Hoc ipsum Paulus de se confessus est: "Quod nunc vivo in carne, per fidem vivo Filii Dei; et nunc non ego vivo, sed vivit in me Christus."

CAPUT XI.

CHRISTUS OMNEM CORPORALEM PASTUM SUPERAT.

III. Quamvis Servator Christus carnem et sanguinem suum cibo et potioni comparet, longe tamen longeque plurimum omni cibo et potioni præstat. Quanquam enim cibus et potus hanc præsentem vitam nutriunt et conservant, principia tamen vitæ nostræ non sunt. Principium enim vitæ nostræ parentum est satus; et ubi semel procreati sumus, cibus et potus nutriunt nos, et vitam nostram ad tempus continent. Christus autem non modo procreator noster est, qui nos primum Deo Patri regenerat, sed etiam vitalis pastus, vitale nutrimentum est.

His accedit, quod cibus et potus corpora nostra tantum alunt; Christus autem verum et sempiternum nutrimentum est, tum corporis, tum animi. Insuper corporalis pastus vitam ad tempus conservat; Christus autem ita perfectus et spiritualis pastus est, ut corpus et animam ad perpetuitatem conservet. Quemadmodum ille ipse Mar*Joan. xi.* thæ dixerat: "Ego sum resurrectio et vita: qui credit in me, etiam si moriatur, vivet: et quicunque vivit et credit in me, non morietur in æternum."

CAPUT XII.

SACRAMENTA AD CONFIRMANDAM FIDEM INSTITUTA SUNT.

IV. Vera harum rerum cognitio vera est Christi cognitio: et hæc docere, sincere et recte Christum docere est: et harum rerum fiducia et sensus est vere in Christum credere, et illum in cordibus nostris sentire. Quantoque clarius ista videmus, intelligimus et credimus, tanto clarius Christum videmus et intelligimus, et pleniorem fiduciam et consolationem in illo habemus.

Quanquam autem carnalis ortus et carnalis pastus noster omnibus quotidiana experientia et communi hominum sensu cognoscatur: spiritualis tamen ortus et pastus adeo obscurus abditusque est, ut ad veram perfectamque ejus cognitionem sensumque ejus, nisi fide, verbo Dei sacramentisque nitente, pervenire nequeamus.

Hac de causa Servator Christus non solum ista a nobis in verbo suo auribus accipienda proposuit, sed etiam visibilia sacramenta (unum, spiritualis regenerationis in aqua, alterum, spiritualis pastus in pane et vino) instituit; ut quoad fieri posset, ipsum oculis, ore, naribus, tactu, sensibus denique omnibus percipiamus. Quemadmodum enim verbum Dei, cum prædicatur, Christum in aures infundit; sic hæc aquæ, panis, et vini elementa, verbo Dei adjuncto, sacramentali modo Christum in oculis, auribus, manibus, atque adeo omnibus sensibus defigunt.

Qua de causa Christus baptismum in aqua instituit: ut quemadmodum propalam aquam corporibus nostris videmus, tangimus, tractamus, et ea abluimur, sic baptizati certo credamus Christum vere nobiscum præsentem, per illum nos spiritualiter regeneratos, omnibus peccatis elutos, in corporis Christi stirpem insitos, et illo vestitos tectosque ita esse, ut quemadmodum diabolus nullam in illum potestatem habet, sic quamdiu in hac stirpe insiti et hoc vestitu tecti sumus, nullam in nos auctoritatem aut dominatum gerat. Ita fit, ut aqua baptismi lavari nihil sit aliud, quam Christum ante oculos ponere, ac illum quasi manibus tangendum, palpandum, et pertractandum, ad nostram in illum fidem confirmandam, adhibere.

Pari modo Christus corporis et sanguinis sui sacramentum in pane et vino, ad nos commonefaciendos atque instruendos, instituit, ut quemadmodum corpora nostra cibo et potione pascuntur, nutriuntur, et conservantur, sic quod ad spiritualem vitam nostram erga Deum pertinet, corpore et sanguine Christi Servatoris nostri pascimur, nutrimur et conservamur; atque ita conservamur, ut neque diabolus, infernus, nec mors æterna, nec peccatum ipsum, quicquam contra nos valere possint, quamdiu hoc cibo et potione nutriamur. Qua de causa Christus in pane et vino (quæ ad quotidianum pastum et præcipuum nutrimentum adhibemus) hoc sacramentum instituit, ut æque ac panem et vinum oculis, ore, ceterisque sensibus percipimus, Christum spiritualem animorum pastum credamus, et non magis dubitemus animos pasci et vivere Christo, quam corpora cibo et potione vivant. Itaque Christus, sciens nos in hoc mundo quasi pueros et infirmos fide versari, signa quædam et notas instituit, quæ in sensus nostros incurrerent, et nos ad majorem firmitatem et constantiorem in Christum fidem pertraherent. Ita fit, ut hæc sacramentalis panis et vini perceptio sit quædam Christi ante oculos nostros collocatio, et illius non modo in ceteros sensus defixio, sed etiam perpetua comestura, concoctio et pastus, ad plenam spiritualem firmitatem et perfectionem. *Hugo de Sacramentis, Tract. vi. cap. 3.*

CAPUT XIII.

QUARE HOC SACRAMENTUM IN PANE ET VINO INSTITUTUM EST.

Quamvis multa ciborum potionumque genera sunt, quibus corpus alitur, hoc tamen sacramentum spiritualis pastus Christus in pane et vino, potius quam in ceteris cibis instituit, quia illa nobis spiritualem omnium fidelium cum Christo et inter se conjunctionem plane exprimunt. Quemadmodum enim ex magna vi granorum tritici molita, subacta, pista, unus panis conficitur; et magnus uvarum numerus in vasculum unum depressus vinum facit; sic universa Christianorum multitudo primo Christo, deinde inter se, una fide, uno baptismo, uno spiritu, uno nexu et vinculo amoris consociantur. V. *Hugo de Sacramentis, Tract. vi. cap. 3. Rabanus de Instit. Clericorum. Lib. i. cap. 31. Bernardus de Cœna Dom.*

CAPUT XIV.

MYSTICI CORPORIS CHRISTI UNITAS.

Quemadmodum panis et vinum, quæ percipimus, in carnem et sanguinem nostrum convertuntur, atque ita carni et sanguini admiscentur, ut unum corpus integrum efficiant: ita omnes fideles Christiani spiritualiter in corpus Christi convertuntur, atque adeo tum Christo, tum ipsi inter se ita junguntur, ut unum Christi corpus mysticum efficiant. Quemadmodum Paulus ait: "Unus panis et unum corpus sumus, quotquot unius panis et poculi participes sumus." VI. *1 Cor. x.*

Et quemadmodum unus panis multis ita dividitur, ut singuli ejusdem panis participes sint; et pari modo unum poculum multis ita distribuitur, ut singuli idem quoque poculum participent: ita Servator noster Christus (cujus caro et sanguis mystico pane et vino in cœna Domini repræsentantur) seipsum omnibus ejus membris tradit, ut spiritualiter illos pascat, nutriat, et perpetuam veramque vitam illis subministret. Et quemadmodum arborum rami aut corporis membra, si vel emortua fuerint vel avulsa, neque vivunt, neque ex corpore aut stirpe aliquem pastum aut nutrimentum capiunt; ita impii ac nefarii homines, qui e corpore Christi mystico exscinduntur, aut mortua ejusdem corporis membra sunt, neque spiritualiter Christi corpore et sanguine pascuntur, neque vitam, robur, aut conservationem aliquam inde consequuntur. *Dionys. Eccle. Hier. cap. 3.*

CAPUT XV.

SACRAMENTUM HOC OMNES AD AMOREM ET CARITATEM EXCITAT.

VII. Cum nihil in hac vita sit gratius Deo, aut acceptius hominibus, quam ut Christiani inter se quiete, cum caritate, pace et consensione animorum vivant, hoc sacramentum nos ad id aptissime et efficacissime movet. Quid enim potius, cum unius sacræ mensæ participes effecti sumus, cogitandum est, quam unius corporis spiritualis (cujus caput Christus est) membra nos esse, ita Christo conjunctos, quemadmodum magnus granorum numerus unum in panem confertur? Duros homines et præfractos necesse est esse, qui istis rebus non commoventur; et bestiis ipsis magis efferatos et crudeles, qui adduci non possunt, ut christianos fratres et pervicinos benevolentia atque officiis prosequantur, cum hoc sacramento admoneantur, Christum Filium Dei non modo amorem suum, verum etiam sanguinem et vitam pro inimicis suis profudisse. Usus enim vitæ communis nos perpetuo edocet, consuetudinem cibi et potionis una capiendi non modo progignere, sed etiam adaugere amicitias: quanto magis hoc de mensa Domini nobis judicandum censendumque est? Feræ etiam ipsæ adhibendo cibo et potione cicurantur: cur igitur Christiani, cœlestis hujus cibi et potionis perceptione commonefacti, non mitescerent? Ad hoc ipsum in hac sacra cœna excitamur, tum pane et vino, tum sacræ scripturæ verbis, quæ tunc citantur.

Si quis igitur sit, cujus animum hujus cœnæ dominicæ perceptio ad proximos amore complectendos non exsuscitat, et invidiam omnem, odium, nequitiam ex illius animo non ejicit, atque amicitiam, conjunctionem, et consociationem non inserit, is sibi imponit, si Spiritum Christi in se inhabitantem habere se putet.

Doctrina transubstantiationis fiduciam nostram in Christum eripit.

Sed prædictas omnes adhortationes, commonitiones, consolationes, papistæ (quantum in ipsis est) transubstantiatione sua tollunt, et Christianis omnibus eripiunt.

Si enim neque panem neque vinum sacra illa communione percipimus, omnia monita et solatia, quæ percipiendo pane et vino cepissemus, exciderunt, levisque ista opinio occasionem præbet universæ in Christum fidei evertendæ. Cum enim sacramentum hoc in pane et vino institutum est, ad spiritualem pastum nobis in Christo demonstrandum; si corporalis hic noster panis et vini pastus opinatus tantum sit et imaginarius, neque panis ibi aut vinum revera sit, (quamvis externa ejus species in sensus nostros cadat,) efficitur ex eo, ut neque spiritualis in Christo pastus noster solidus aut verus sit, sed opinatus tantum; imo revera nullus sit. Hæc doctrina ita impia atque injuriosa in Christum est, ut a nullo alio, nisi a diabolo aut ejus primario administro antichristo, proficisci possit.

CAPUT XVI.

SPIRITUALIS PASTUS CORDE NON DENTIBUS FIT.

VIII. Hic spiritualis corporis et sanguinis pastus neque ore percipitur, neque ventre conficitur, (quemadmodum ceteri cibi et potiones, qui corporibus accipiuntur,) sed puro animo et sincera fide assumitur. Atque hic verus est corporis et sanguinis Christi pastus, ubi constanti veraque fide credimus, Christum corpus suum pro nobis objecisse in crucem, et sanguinem effudisse, atque adeo conjunxisse et concorporasse nos sibi, ut ille nostrum caput, nos illius membra, et caro de carne ejus, et os de ossibus ejus essemus, et ille in nobis maneret et nos in illo. Atque hic universa vis et efficientia sacramenti versatur. Hanc fidem Deus intus in cordibus nostris Spiritu sancto suo efficit, et eandem partim auribus nostris verbi ejus auditione, partim ceteris sensibus panis et vini perceptione, in sacra synaxi confirmat.

Quid igitur majorem nobis afferre consolationem potest, quam ejusmodi cibo et potione uti, quo Christus nos certiores reddit, nos vere et spiritualiter ab illo pasci, et nos in illo, et illum in nobis habitare? Potestne hoc clarius nobis exponi, quam suis ipsius verbis? Dicit enim, "Qui edit me, is vivet propter me."

Joan. vi.

Quicunque igitur vitæ æternæ impius contemptor non est, quomodo non maximo æstimabit hoc sacramentum? quomodo non illud (quasi certissimum æternæ salutis pignus) omni mente ac voluntate complectetur? et cum pios videat religiose ad hoc sacramentum accedere, quomodo ipse non frequenter et multo studio accedet? Nemo certe est, quin si hæc recte intelligat, et diligenter consideret, ardenti studio flagret ad hanc sanctissimam Domini cœnam frequentandam.

Omnes hoc expetunt, ut aliqua in gratia apud Deum sint: et cum contra intelligunt, se in aliqua offensione apud illum esse, et ab illius benevolentia abesse plurimum, quæ res levationem illorum mentibus adferre potest? quibus, quæso, perturbationibus vexantur? quantis cruciatibus conscientiæ torquentur? Omnia a Deo creata illis adversari, illis minari, illis terrorem injicere videntur, utpote quæ divinæ ultionis in illos et vindictæ administri sint: neque consolationem aut requietem ullam, vel domi vel foris, inveniunt: atque adeo Deum et diabolum simili fere odio prosequuntur; Deum quasi severum et crudelem judicem, diabolum quasi dirum et immanem tortorem.

Sed in his gravissimis perturbationibus accedit scriptura et docet, Patrem cœlestem nullo modo redire in gratiam nobiscum aut placari velle, nisi unigeniti Filii sacrificio et morte, quo Deus perpetuam amicitiam et pacem nobiscum confirmat, offensas eorum qui in Christum credunt, remittit, eosdem in filios adoptat, et primogenitum suum Christum illis donat, ut illi incorporentur, per ipsum serventur, ac hæredes regni cœlestis efficiantur. Et in hujus sanctissimæ cœnæ perceptione mortis Christi et mysterii redemptionis nostræ admonemur; ubi etiam testamenti illius, et nostræ cum Christo communionis, et remissionis peccatorum, per illius sacrificium in cruce propositum, mentio fit.

Quocirca in hoc sacramento, si vera fide et recte percipiatur, de peccatorum remissione certiores reddimur, et fœdus pacis et testamentum Dei nobiscum confirmatur. Itaque qui vera fide Christi corpus et sanguinem percipit, vitam æternam per Christum habet, quod ubi animis in sacra cœna celebranda repetimus, nihil lætius, nihil jucundius, nihil consolationis plenius esse potest.

Hæc omnia esse verissima, ex Christi ipsius verbis apertissime liquet, quæ habuit, cum pridie mortis ejus sanctissimam cœnam institueret, sicuti tum evangelistarum, tum Pauli ipsius verba declarant: "Hoc facite, quotiescunque biberitis, ad recordationem mei." "Quotiescunque ederitis panem hunc, et poculum Domini biberitis, mortem Domini nunciate, usque dum veniat." Atque iterum: "Hoc poculum est novum testamentum meo factum sanguine, qui pro multis profunditur ad remissionem peccatorum." *Luc. xxii. 1 Cor. xi. Matt. xxvi. Marc. xiv. Luc. xxii.*

Hæc doctrina hic a nobis commemorata satis esse potest moderatis et piis viris, et nihil otiosum aut supervacaneum quærentibus, sed tantum necessaria atque utilia sequentibus; atque adeo illis hic finis esse potest. Contentiosis autem papistis et idololatris nihil satis esse potest, quamvis expletum id perfectumque sit, et ad salutis nostræ summam complectendam satis instructum. Atqui ut minus gloriari vel de subtili acumine, vel de doctrina, reipsa detestabili, sed illorum opinione gloriosa, queant, quasi nemo illorum sententiam refutare posset; precabor a lectoribus, ut aliquod tempus patiantur me leviter consumere in illorum levissima vanitate confutanda. Quamquam haud arbitror me temere hoc tempus consumpturum, cum ex eo manifeste cernetur, quid lux sit, quid tenebræ, quid verum, quid fucatum, quid certissimum verbum Dei, et quæ vana hominum somnia.

CAPUT XVII.

QUATUOR PRÆCIPUI PAPISTARUM ERRORES.

SED hæc manifeste apparere lectori non possunt, nisi præcipua capita proponantur, in quibus papistæ a veritate verbi Dei dissentiunt: hæc autem quatuor sunt.

Primum aiunt in cœna Domini post verba consecrationis (sic enim appellant) nullam aliam substantiam remanere præter substantiam carnis et sanguinis Christi, atque adeo neque panem neque vinum percipiendum a nobis esse reliquum. Et quamquam panis et vini color, sapor, odor, magnitudo, forma, reliquaque omnia acci- *Primus error, de transubstantiatione.*

dentia, sive qualitates sive quantitates, adsint, panem tamen et vinum ibi esse negant, sed in substantiam corporis et sanguinis Christi converti affirmant; et hanc conversionem transubstantiationem nominant, hoc est, unius substantiæ in aliam conversionem: quamvis autem accidentia panis et vini remaneant, ea tamen in nulla re subjecta hærere dicunt, sed in aëre pendula esse, nullo sustentata fulcro. In corpore enim et sanguine Christi hæc accidentia inesse posse negant. Imo vero neque in aëre. Neque enim caro et sanguis Christi, neque aër eadem magnitudine, sapore, colore, forma, qua panis et vinum sunt. Neque in pane et vino aiunt hæc accidentia inesse posse; omnis enim illorum substantia prorsus abiit. Ita fit ut candor maneat, sed nihil sit album: colores maneant, sed nihil sit coloratum: rotunditas maneat, sed nihil sit rotundum: magnitudo maneat, sed nihil sit magnum: suavitas adsit, sed nihil suave sit: mollities sine aliquo molli: fractio sine re fracta: divisio, et nihil dividatur: reliquæque qualitates et quantitates absque ullo omnino subjecto per se subsistent. Atque hæc doctrina necessarium apud illos fidei nostræ caput est, quæ tamen doctrina Christi non est, sed subtile quoddam antichristi inventum, primum ab Innocentio tertio decretum, deinde fusius a scholasticis explicatum, quorum omne studium atque opera ponebatur in Romanorum episcoporum decretis confirmandis et stabiliendis. Et diabolus per ministrum suum antichristum ita omnium fere Christianorum oculos his ultimis temporibus perstrinxit, ut fidem suam non ex clarissima divini verbi luce, sed ab antichristo Romano peterent, et omnibus illius decretis, quanquam rationi et sensibus et verbo divino adversarentur, omnem fidem et obedientiam quoque adhiberent. Antichristus enim esse non potuisset, nisi Christo ita ex adverso seipsum objecisset, ut ejus doctrina cum Christo ex diametro repugnaret. Docet enim nos Christus panem et vinum in cœna, quasi sui sacramenta, percipere, hisque admoneri et certiores reddi, ut quemadmodum corporaliter pane et vino pascimur, sic Spiritu nos carne et sanguine Servatoris Christi ali. Qua ratione etiam in baptismo aquam admotam habemus, quæ declaret nobis, ut quemadmodum aquæ elementum corpus abluit, sic intus per Spiritum sanctum mentes nostras mundari.

Alterum, in quo papistæ se a veritate verbi disjunxerunt, hoc est, nempe verum et naturale corpus Christi, (quod pro nobis acerbissimam mortem in cruce perpessum est, quod ad dexteram Dei Patris in cœlo considet,) realiter, substantialiter, corporaliter et naturaliter in accidentibus sacramentalis panis et vini, quas illi species panis et vini nominant, inesse. Atque in varias sententias homines acuti distrahuntur. Quidam enim illorum contendunt, verum et naturale corpus Christi ibi adesse, sed non naturaliter aut sensibiliter. Alii contra naturaliter et sensibiliter adesse dicunt, idque eadem magnitudine et forma, qua ex Maria virgine nascebatur, et qua jam in cœlo est, et nostris illum dentibus teri et comminui. Hoc partim scholasticorum scriptis, partim Berengarii confessione, ad quam illum Nicolaus secundus adegit, facile apparet. Cogebatur enim Berengarius profiteri, se in ea sententia de sacramento corporis et sanguinis Domini permansurum, in qua Nicolaus tunc reliquique ejusdem farinæ homines fuerant, non modo sacramenta panis et vini, sed veram quoque carnem et sanguinem Domini nostri Jesu Christi, sensualiter a sacerdote in altari tractari, frangi, et fidelium dentibus atteri. Sed vera et catholica fides (quæ constantissimæ divini verbi veritati nititur) docet nos, Servatorem Christum (quod ad humanam naturam et corporis præsentiam attinet) in cœlum conscendisse, ad dexteram Dei Patris sedere, atque ibi ad mundi usque finem permansurum esse; tunc autem reversurum, et vivos ac mortuos judicaturum, quemadmodum multis scripturis ipse de se testatus est. "Relinquo mundum (inquit) atque ad Patrem abeo." Atque alibi: "Pauperes semper apud vos habebitis, me vero non semper." Et iterum: "Multi venient et dicent, Ecce hic est Christus, aut illic; sed non credatis." Petrus in Actis Apostolorum ait, "oportere cœlum eousque capere Christum, dum omnium rerum redintegratio futura sit." Paulus ad Colossenses: "Superna quærite, ubi Christus ad dexteram Patris sedet." Et de sacramento ipso mentionem faciens: "Quotiescunque ederitis (inquit) panem hunc, et poculum Domini biberitis, mortem Domini annuntiate dum veniat;" significans illum non esse corpore præsentem. Quis enim hic esset loquendi modus, aut qui sermo hominum, de eo qui corpore præsens est, dicere, "dum veniat," cum hoc ipsum "dum veniat" significet illum nondum venisse? Hæc fides catholica est, quam ab ineunte ætate in fidei symbolo discimus, quam Christus docuit, apostoli sequuti sunt, martyres sanguine suo confirmarunt.

Et quamquam Christus cum humana natura substantialiter, realiter, corporaliter, naturaliter, sensibiliter, (sic enim cum crassis crasse loquendum est,) cum Patre suo in cœlis est, sacramentaliter tamen et spiritu adesse dicitur, in aqua quidem, pane et vino, quasi in signis et sacramentis, sed revera in fidelibus Christianis, qui vel vero baptismo lavantur, vel idonee sanctam communionem percipiunt, vel sincere fiduciam suam in illum collocarunt.

Jam accepistis duo insignia capita, in quibus papistæ a veritate verbi et catholica fide desciverunt.

Tertium vero ejusmodi est, quod affirment impios verum Christi corpus et sanguinem in hoc sacramento percipere, et iisdem rebus vesci, quibus integri et pii solent. Huic autem verbi divini veritas adversatur. Omnes enim qui pia membra Christi sunt, quemadmodum corporibus edunt panem et bibunt vinum, ita mentibus percipiunt veram carnem et sanguinem Christi: impia autem membra diaboli edunt panem et bibunt vinum sacramento tenus, sed spiritu neque carnem Christi neque sanguinem ejus percipiunt. *Tertius error, quod mali manducant Christum.*

Quartum, in quo sacerdotes papistici ab apertissimo verbo divino dissentiunt, est, quod dicant se Christum quotidie pro remissione peccatorum nostrorum offerre, et mortis Christi merita per missas suas distribuere et applicare. At prophetæ, apostoli et evangelistæ prædicant, Christum ipsum suo ipsius corpore sacrificium pro nobis in *Quartus error, de quotidiano ecclesiæ sacrificio.*
    cruce fecisse, cujus vulneribus ægritudines omnes sanarentur, et peccata re-
        mitterentur: hoc nullus unquam sacerdos, nec homo, nec creatura
           ulla fecerat, præter Christum solum, nec is quidem sæpius
              quam semel. Hujus etiam oblationis beneficium aliis
                  distribuere nemo mortalis potest, sed fide
                      cuique sua (quemadmodum pro-
                        pheta ait) a Christo
                          accipiendum
                            est.

FINIS LIBRI PRIMI.

LIBER SECUNDUS.

CONTRA TRANSUBSTANTIATIONEM.

CAPUT I.

Hactenus accepistis quatuor eximia capita, in quibus potissimum papistica doctrina a veritate verbi divini et a christiana veterum catholicorum fide, in hac cœnæ dominicæ tractatione, discedat. Nunc, favente Deo, tum errorum papisticorum refutationem, tum catholicæ fidei defensionem non modo ex certissimo Dei verbo, sed etiam antiquissimorum auctorum et martyrum, qui in ecclesia Dei floruerunt, auctoritate susceptam, audietis: ne quis arbitretur, hanc meam contra transubstantiationem sententiam esse nuper e cerebro meo excogitatam.

CAPUT II.

PAPISTICA DOCTRINA DE TRANSUBSTANTIATIONE VERBO DEI ADVERSATUR.

Principio, panem et vinum post verba consecrationis remanere, et in cœna dominica etiam percipi, ex Christi ipsius verbis apertissime et certissime colligitur. Nam cum cœnam discipulis suis daret, Christus acceptum panem fregit, et dedit discipulis suis, et dixit: "Accipite, edite: hoc est corpus meum."

_{Matt. xxvi.}
_{Marc. xiv.}
_{Luc. xxii.}

Hic papistæ triumphum canunt propter hæc Christi verba, "Hoc est corpus meum," quæ verba consecrationis appellant: his enim verbis prolatis, aiunt, neque panem ullum reliquum esse, neque ullam aliam substantiam præter subtantiam corporis Christi. Atque dicunt, cum Christus dixisset "Hoc," panem mansisse: cum "est," panem etiam mansisse: cum "corpus," eodem modo: confecta autem tota sententia, "hoc est corpus meum," panem discessisse aiunt, et præter substantiam corporis Christi nihil aliud mansisse contendunt: quasi sacramentum cum re significata consistere non posset. Ceterum hoc adserere, nullum remanere panem, illorum inventum est, quod ex non scriptis veritatibus (has enim maximo religionis cultu prosequuntur) eliciunt. Deus bone! quantum gloriarentur, si Christus dixisset, Hoc non est panis? Sed Christus non dixit, Hoc panis non est: sed affirmative dixit, "Hoc est corpus meum;" non panem tollendo, sed corporis sui comesturam affirmando: illud nobis intelligendum, et judicii veritate complectendum dans, ita corpus ejus spiritu accipi, quemadmodum panis ore et corpore percipitur. Itaque hunc fuisse sensum Christi, ex Paulo liquet. Sic enim ait: "Panis quem frangimus, nonne communio corporis Christi est?" Quis sensum Christi melius Paulo intellexit? cui Christus maxime abdita et recondita patefecit. Hic ad meliorem et clariorem intelligentiam (ne forte verbis Christi in aliam sententiam abuteremur) ita illa explicavit, ut minus obscura aut depravata nobis esse possent. Ubi enim Christus panem accepit ac fregit, et dixit, "Hoc est corpus meum;" Paulus explicuit his verbis: "Panis quem frangimus, nonne communio corporis Christi est?" Quod Christus dixit corpus suum, Paulus communionem appellat corporis, non varietate verborum a Christi mente dissentiens, sed spiritu intelligentiæ Christum exponens: nimirum eos qui panem digne edunt, participes esse corporis Christi; itaque Christus panem corpus suum appellat (quemadmodum veteres declarant) quia corpus ejus repræsentat et significat; illos qui panem

_{*Ob. 126.}

_{1 Cor. x.}

hunc secundum instituta Christi edunt, spiritu edere corpus, et spiritu pasci ac nutriri; pane nihilominus, quasi sacramento ad illud idem declarandum, remanente. Sed de verbis consecrationis fusius posthac disputabitur.

Ut igitur ad propositum revertamur: ex Christi verbis, quæ ante consecrationem dixit, perspicuum est panem remanere, et in hoc sacramento percipi. Christus enim panem accepit, fregit, dedit, jussit accipere, edere: hæc omnia ante verba consecrationis posita sunt. Ita fit, ut necessario de pane intelligantur; Christum videlicet cepisse panem, fregisse panem, distribuisse panem discipulis, et præcepisse ut panem caperent, et panem ederent. De vino autem, hoc planius et illustrius est (non ex verbis modo, quæ consecrationem præcedunt, sed ex his etiam quæ sequuntur), vinum remanere, et in cœna Domini ab omnibus hauriri. Nam ante verba consecrationis Christus poculum vini accepit, et discipulis suis dedit, et dixit: "Bibite ex hoc omnes." Post verba vero consecrationis sequitur: "Et biberunt ex eo omnes." *Ob. 19. Matt. xxvi. *Ob. 24. Matt. xxvi Marc. xiv.

Nunc autem quæro a papistis, quid sit, quod Christus apostolis bibere præceperit, cum dixit, "Bibite ex hoc omnes?" Sanguis Christi minime adhuc (quemadmodum illi ipsi asseverant) adfuit: nam verba hæc ante consecrationem dicebantur. Itaque nihil aliud nisi vinum esse potuit, quod illis bibere præceperat.

Tum a papistis iterum quæro, Vinum necne biberint apostoli? Si fateantur, errorem suum revocent, nempe nullum jam vinum post consecrationem remanere. Sin negant, contumaciæ condemnant apostolos, qui illud non biberant, quod Christus præceperat. Imo vero Christum præstigiarum potius accusant, qui apostolis ut vinum biberent præceperat, et cum id facere parati essent, ipse, ne facerent, vinum e medio sustulerat. Deinde priusquam poculum vini discipulis tradidisset, dixerat illis, "Dividite hoc inter vos." *Ob. 26. Luc. xxii.

Hic iterum a papistis quæro, quidnam id fuerit quod Christus apostolis inter se dividere præceperat? Poculum ipsum credo illos nolle dicere, nisi velint semet omnibus deridendos proponere. Nec respondebunt (ut opinor) fuisse sanguinem, tum quia verba illa ante consecrationem pronunciabantur; tum quia sanguis Christi non dividitur, sed integer in sacramento spiritualiter sumitur. Ita efficitur, ut nulla alia de re, nisi de vino, quod illis divideretur, quod ab illis biberetur, intelligi ista possint. Jam communione finita, Christus apostolis dixerat: "Amen dico vobis, non bibam posthac de fructu vitis, donec bibero novum in regno Patris mei." Ex quibus perspicuum est, verum fuisse vinum, quod apostoli in cœna Domini biberant. Neque enim sanguis Christi, neque accidentia vini, fructus vitis sunt: imo præter vinum fructus vitis alius nullus est. *Ob. 27. Matt. xxvi. Marc. xiv.

Et quomodo potuisset Christus clarius mentem suam de permansione panis et vini exponere, quam panem accipiendo, panem frangendo, panem discipulis tribuendo, panem ut ederent imperando? et poculum similiter accipiendo, poculum discipulis porrigendo, ut poculum inter se dividerent et biberent præcipiendo, et poculum fructum vitis vocando? Hæc ita illustria testimonia sunt, ut si angelus e cœlo contra ista diceret, fides illi minime adhibenda esset. Multo igitur minus deliris papistis, inania commenta hæc fingentibus, credendum est. *Ob. 18.

Si Christus nos huic de discessione panis et vini opinioni ita fidem habere voluisset, ut necessarium fidei caput contineat, hocne modo loqueretur, ut clarissimis uteretur verbis, quibus significaretur panem et vinum ibi permanere? Cujusmodi tandem doctorem volunt Christum esse, quem aliud dixisse, aliud sensisse contendunt? Quis hanc de Christo contumeliam æquo animo ferat?

At quam callidi et versuti doctores sunt papistæ! qui ex suis ipsorum cerebris hujusmodi deliria confingunt, quæ maxime christianæ religioni adversantur, et tamen Christianis omnibus firmissime credenda pro Christi ipsius doctrina proponunt. Haud ita Paulus hac in re fecerat, qui formam loquendi a Christo usitatam sequutus, panem et vinum suis nominibus appellavit. "Panis," inquit, "quem frangimus, an non communio corporis Christi est?" *Ob. 30. 1 Cor. x.

Hic iterum a papistis quæro, utrum de pane consecrato vel non consecrato verba fecerat? At de pane non consecrato loqui non potuit, quia (quemadmodum illi ipsi judicant) communio corporis Christi non est. Sin de consecrato pane loquutus sit, fateantur necesse est, ejusmodi panem post consecrationem permanere, ut frangi possit,

1 Cor. x. qui nisi verus et materialis panis, nullus esse potest. Et statim addidit, nos unius panis participes esse. Et in proximo capite fusius de eadem re loquens, quater panem et poculum nominavit, neque ullius unquam transubstantiationis, aut accidentium sine substantia permansionis, mentionem fecit: quod in primis frequenti oratione usurpasset, si discessio substantiæ panis et vini necessarium aliquod caput religionis fuisset. Ita perspicuum est ex ipsis scripturæ verbis, panem et vinum post consecrationem manere, et papisticam hanc de transubstantiatione doctrinam verbo Dei aperte repugnare.

CAPUT III.

PAPISTICA DOCTRINA RATIONI EST CONTRARIA.

*Ista retractantur infra, cap. 14.

CONSIDERANDUM etiam nobis diligenti animi attentione est, quomodo huic tam confirmatæ illorum sententiæ adversetur naturalis tum ratio tum operatio: quæ quanquam contra verbum Dei minime valent, ubi tamen annexæ verbo Dei sunt, magnum adferunt ad veritatis confirmationem momentum.

*Ob. 70.

Naturalis ratio a vacuo abhorret, et sustinere non potest, locus aliquis ut sit, qui corpore non compleatur. Atqui detracto pane et vino, locus in quo ante erant, et ubi nunc etiam accidentia existunt, contra universum naturæ ordinem, nulla substantia repletur, sed vacuus existit.

*Ob. 73.

Videmus etiam vinum, quamvis consecratum sit, si diutius servetur, in acetum converti, et panem mucidum fieri, quæ nihil aliud tum sunt, quam vinum acidum et panis mucidus. Quod utique non fieret, si nullum ibi vinum aut panis esset, quod acescere aut mucescere posset.

*Ob. 69.

Atque si sacramentum combureretur, (quemadmodum reliquiæ, a communicantibus non perceptæ, antiquitus comburi solebant,) dicant quid comburatur: vel panem esse, vel corpus Christi, necesse est. Panem nullum esse aiunt, corpus igitur Christi necessario comburunt; (et merito Christi ipsius combustores appellentur, sicut antehac multa ipsius membra concremarunt;) nisi, contra naturæ totius ordinem, accidentia comburi dicant, omni substantia prius detracta.

*Ob. 66.

Mysticus deinde panis et vinum nutrire corpus solent, quæ quidem nutritio e substantia, non ex accidentibus proficiscitur.

*Ob. 68.

Vinum etiam, veneno adhibito, necare solet, (quemadmodum ex episcopis Romanis complures testificari possunt, qui partim alios veneno sustulerunt, partim ipsi veneno sublati sunt;) quod veneficium salutari Christi sanguini assignari non potest, sed venenato tantum vino.

*Ob. 106.

Quid, quod maxime contra naturam accidentium est, in nulla re subjecta consistere, cum definitionis illorum hæc sit ratio, in subjecto aliquo hærere? Ita fit, ut si sint, in aliquo hærere illa necesse sit; si vero nulli rei insint, neque ipsa accidentia sint.

Sexcenta alia sunt, quæ papistæ hac transubstantiationis defensione contra naturæ ordinem et rationis defendere coguntur. Hujus generis sunt: Duo corpora uno in loco esse: Unum corpus multis in locis simul esse: Substantias ex accidentibus gigni: Accidentia in substantias converti: Accidentia sine substantia locum explere: Corpus in loco esse, et locum non explere: Rei alicujus generationem esse sine cujusquam corruptione, et corruptionem sine ullius generatione: aut ex nihilo aliquid fieri, et in nihilum aliquid mutari; et multa his similia, quæ tum naturæ, tum rationi adversantur.

CAPUT IV.

SENSUUM JUDICIO DOCTRINA PAPISTICA ADVERSATUR.

*Ob. 63.

SENSIBUS etiam nostris hæc papistarum doctrina contraria esse videtur. Oculi enim, si testes citarentur, panem et vinum se videre dicerent, nares odorari, ora gustare, manus tractare panem se et vinum asseverarent. Et quamquam fidei nostræ capita longe sensuum nostrorum captum anteeant, (ita ut multa variaque credamus, quæ sub sensus cadere non possunt,) haud ita tamen sensibus repugnant, ut in his, quæ perpetuo sensibus nostris subjecta sunt, fidem nullam sensibus habere debeamus, sed in contrariam partem fide nitamur.

Fides jubet credere, quæ non videntur: at his, quæ in conspectum quotidianum cadunt, quæ auditione accipimus, quæ manibus tenemus, fidem derogare non jubet. Quanquam enim fidei altitudinem sensus non attingant, in his tamen, quæ quotidie sensibus comprehenduntur, fides sensibus non adversatur, sed sensus potius fidei stabilitatem confirmant. Nam quid Thomæ ad Christi resurrectionem confirmandam profuit, lateri Christi manum admovisse, aut vulnera pertractasse, si nulla sensibus fides habenda esset? *Ob. 61.
*Ob. 123. Joan. xx.

Quanta autem Valentiniano et Marcioni (qui Christum cruci affixum fuisse negant, sed Symonem Cyrenæum illius loco supplicia perpessum affirmant,) ad opinionum suarum commenta confirmanda fenestra aperitur! Quanta aliis hæreticis, qui Christum verum fuisse hominem inficiabantur, quanquam in oculis omnium homo esse, formam sibi humanam assumpsisse, esurire, sitire, fatigari, lacrymari, dormire, edere, bibere, et mori etiam videretur? Si enim semel concesserimus, nullam fidem sensibus tribuendam esse, quantus aditus et quanta occasio sit infinitis opinionum erroribus! *Ob. 121 et 122. Le. Augus. in Psal. xxix. Præfa. Enarrationis 2. et Hilarium de Trin. Lib. iii. et contra Constantium Augustum vi. in Bocardo, fol. 70 et 71.

Sin in hoc sacramentario negotio nulla fides tribuenda sensibus sit, cur tam obstinate a papistis affirmatur, accidentia post consecrationem permanere? quod nisi sensibus judicari non potest. Nihil enim scriptura de accidentibus panis et vini, sed de ipso pane et vino diserte loquitur; et contra naturam et definitionem accidentium est, ut, nulla re sibi subjecta, sola consistant. Si nulla igitur sensibus fides adhibenda est, (in hoc præsertim Eucharistiæ negotio,) cur, si substantia panis et vini discessit, non etiam discessisse accidentia putabimus? Quod si sensibus necessario credendum sit, dum judicant accidentia manere, cur non idem potius de substantia statuendum est; cum post consecrationem scriptura nullibi dicat, substantiam panis et vini abesse, sed iis nominibus perpetuo appellet, quæ substantiam, non accidentia significent? *Ob. 106.

Denique si sensus nostri hac in re quotidie decipiantur, tum hoc sacramentum nihil aliud nisi sensuum nostrorum ludificatio est: quo nihil magis facere pro illorum sententia potest, qui Christum vaferrimum præstigiatorem appellarunt, qui ita oculos mortalium perstrinxerit, ut viderentur esse, quæ non erant. *Ob. 123.

Sed ut in pauca conferam: ostendant (si possint) papistæ ullum fidei caput ita plane cum sensuum judicio pugnans, ut quod sensus universi quotidiana experientia nobis demonstrant, illud fides contendat non esse.

CAPUT V.

PAPISTICAM DOCTRINAM ANTIQUORUM PATRUM SENTENTIIS REPUGNARE.

Cum igitur satis ostensum sit, quemadmodum hæc papistica de transubstantiatione opinio plane verbo Dei, naturæ rerum, rationis judicio, sensuum comprehensioni adversetur, nunc pari ratione demonstrabimus, quemadmodum fidei et doctrinæ antiquissimorum scriptorum repugnet, qui ut Christi et apostolorum ætate viciniores erant, ita facile, quid verissimum esset, tenere poterant.

Ignatius ad Philadelphenses: "Una est caro Domini Jesu, et unus ejus sanguis qui pro nobis fusus est: unus etiam panis pro omnibus confractus, et unus calix totius ecclesiæ."

Clemens in Pædagogo, Lib. ii. cap. 2. "Ipse quoque vino usus est, nam ipse quoque homo, et vinum benedixit, cum dixit: Accipite, bibite, hoc est sanguis meus. Sanguis vitis, verbum, quod pro multis effunditur in remissionem peccatorum, sanctum lætitiæ fluentum allegorice significat." Et mox: "Quod autem vinum esset, quod benedictum est, ostendit rursum, dicens discipulis, Non bibam ex fructu vitis hujus, donec bibero ipsum vobiscum in regno Patris mei." "Pontifex opertum panem et indivisum aperit, in frusta concidens," &c.

Ac primo Justinus prodeat, gravis vir et eruditus martyr, antiquissimus omnium, qui de sacramentis tractasse cognoscuntur, qui ad centum plus minus annos post ascensionem Christi floruit. *Dion. Eccl. Hier. cap. 3. Huc pertinent quæ citavi infra, iii. cap. 8. Idem, Lib. v.

<small>Justinus in 2. Apologia pro Christianis.
*Ob. 151.
Justini verba habentur infra, Lib. iii. cap. 8.</small>

Is in secunda apologia sua ita scripsit: "Panem, aquam, et vinum in hoc sacramento non ita percipi debere, quemadmodum alii cibi et potus, quibus quotidie utimur, sed tanquam epulæ ad hoc destinatæ, ut gratiæ Deo agerentur, atque nunc Eucharistiam, nunc corpus et sanguinem Christi nominare: neque fas esse, ut quis illa percipiat, nisi qui Christum professus sit, et convenienter professioni suæ vivat." Hunc tamen cibum et potionem ille in carnem et sanguinem nostrum converti, et corpora nostra nutriri affirmat.

Hinc efficitur, Justinum putasse panem et vinum in sacramento permanere: aliter enim sic in carnem et sanguinem nostrum converti non possent, ut ex illis nutriremur.

<small>Irenæus adversus Hæreses, Lib. iv. cap. 34.</small>

Hunc sequutus est Irenæus, centum et quinquaginta annos post Christum, qui in necessariis fidei nostræ capitibus decipi non potuit: fuerat enim Polycarpi discipulus, qui Johannis evangelistæ auditor fuit. Irenæus autem in hoc negotio sensum Justini et verba etiam imitatus, "Panis (ait) in quo gratiæ actæ sunt, qui est a terra, per-

<small>*Ob. 152.
*Ob. 153.</small>

cipiens vocationem Dei, jam non communis panis est, sed Eucharistia, ex duabus rebus constans, terrena et cœlesti." Cœleste hoc quidnam, quæso, est? Dominus Jesus. Terrestre autem quid? Panis de quo supra mentionem fecit, quod ex terra esset, quemque corpora nostra pascere ait, quemadmodum reliqui panes, qui ad usum vitæ adhibentur.

<small>*Huc pertinent quæ citavi infra, Lib. iii. cap. 8.</small>

Et idem Irenæus, Lib. v. "Quando mixtus calix et fractus panis percipit verbum Dei, fit Eucharistia corporis et sanguinis Christi, ex quibus augetur et consistit carnis nostræ substantia." Et in eodem: "Cum membra ejus simus, et per creaturam nutrimur, eum calicem, qui est creatura, suum corpus confirmavit, ex quo nostra auget corpora."

<small>*Idem, Lib. iv. cap. 34.</small>

Idem Lib iv. cap. 38. "Quomodo constabit eum panem, in quo gratiæ actæ sunt, corpus esse Domini sui, et calicem sanguinis ejus, si non ipsum fabricatoris mundi Filium esse dicant?"

<small>Origenes in Matt. cap. xv.</small>

Paulo post Irenæum Origenes fuit, ducentos annos post Christi ascensionem. Hic panem ait sanctificatum, "juxta id quod habet materiale, in ventrem abire, et in secessum

<small>*Ob. 166 et 167.</small>

ejici; nec materiam panis, sed sermonem qui super illum dictus est, prodesse non indigne Domino comedenti illum." Idem contra Celsum, Lib. iv. "Ubi pro collatis in nos beneficiis gratias diximus, oblatis panibus vescimur."

Post Origenem Cyprianus sanctus martyr fuerat anno Domini ducentesimo quinquagesimo. Hic contra illos, qui sacramentum aqua sola sine vino ministrabant, ad hunc modum verba fecit. "Cum dicat Christus (inquit), Ego sum vitis vera; sanguis

<small>*Ob. 166.</small>

Christi non aqua est utique, sed vinum. Nec potest videri sanguis ejus, quo redempti et vivificati sumus, esse in calice, quando vinum desit calici, quo Christi sanguis ostenditur."

Quid planius pro vini subsistentia dici potest, quam si nullum ibi vinum sit, nullum esse sanguinem Christi?

<small>Matt. xxvi.</small>

Et paulo post in eadem epistola. "Christus (inquit) accipiens calicem benedixit, et dedit discipulis suis, dicens: Bibite ex hoc omnes. Hoc est enim sanguis novi testamenti, qui pro multis effundetur in remissionem peccatorum. Dico vobis, non bibam a modo ex ista creatura vitis usque in diem illum, quo vobiscum bibam novum vinum in regno Patris mei. Qua in parte invenimus calicem mixtum fuisse, quem Dominus obtulit, et vinum fuisse, quod sanguinem suum dixit. Unde apparet, Christi sanguinem non offerri, si desit vinum calici." Et mox: "Quomodo de creatura vitis novum vinum cum Christo in regno Patris bibemus, si in sacrificio Dei Patris et Christi vinum non offerimus?"

Ex his divi Cypriani verbis manifestissime liquet, non solum in hoc sacramento vinum offerri, ex uvis expressum, ex vite ortum, sed etiam nos idem bibere. Quod tum si digne bibamus, admonemur nos spiritualiter bibere verum sanguinem Christi, pro peccatis nostris effusum.

<small>*Idem Serm. de Laps.
Idem de Cœn. Dom.</small>

Idem in sermone de Lapsis: "Sanctificatus in Domini sanguinem potus de pollutis visceribus erupit." Et de Cœna Domini: "Sceleratum os panis sanctificatus intravit." Et in eodem: "Ante verba consecrationis panis ille communis, &c." infra cap. 2. præsentis libri.

<small>Eusebius Emissenus.</small>

Eusebius Emissenus, homo singulari quadam doctrinæ excellentia, trecentos annos post Christi ascensionem, paucissimis universam rem ita complexus est, tum quomodo panis et vinum in corpus et sanguinem Christi convertuntur, et a pristino naturæ statu non discedunt; tum quomodo, præter externam panis et vini perceptionem, Christus interna fide recipiatur in corda, ut nihil amplius requiri in hac causa possit. Atque ut universa res melius ante oculos constituatur, conversionem visibilium creaturarum in corpus et sanguinem Christi similem esse ait mutationi nostræ in baptismo, ubi foris nihil mutatur, sed idem per omnia remanet, intus autem et spiritualiter universa commutatio et conversio existit.

"Si cupias scire," inquit, "quomodo novum tibi et impossibile esse non debeat, quod in Christi substantiam terrena et mortalia convertuntur, teipsum, qui in Christo es regeneratus, interroga. Dudum alienus a vita, peregrinus a misericordia et a salutis via, intrinsecus mortuus exulabas: subito initiatus Christi legibus, et salutaribus mysteriis innovatus, in corpus ecclesiæ non videndo, sed credendo transisti, et de filio perditionis adoptivus Dei filius fieri occulta puritate meruisti. In mensura visibili permanens, major factus es te ipso invisibiliter, sine quantitatis augmento. Cum idem ipse esses, multo alter fieri fidei processibus meruisti. In exteriori nihil additum est, et totum in interiori mutatum est. Ac sic homo Christi filius effectus, Christusque hominis in mente formatus est. Sicut ergo sine sensu corporali, præterita vilitate deposita, subito novam indutus es dignitatem; et sicut hæc, quod Deus læsa in te curavit, infecta diluit, maculata detersit, non oculis sed sensibus sunt credita; ita et cum reverendum altare cibis spiritualibus satiandus ascendis, sacrum Dei tui corpus et sanguinem fide respice, honore mirare, mente continge, cordis manu suscipe, et maxime haustu interioris hominis assume."

Hucusque Eusebius, cujus verba ita plana sunt, ut nihil planius esse possit, neque nostræ sententiæ convenientius, panis et vini conversionem in corpus et sanguinem Christi spiritualem esse, et nihil foris mutari: sed quemadmodum externus homo panem et vinum ore, sic internus homo per fidem, spiritu, veram carnem et sanguinem Christi percipit.

Hilarius paucis eadem complexus est. "Corpus Christi (inquit), quod sumitur de altari, figura est, dum panis et vinum extra videtur: veritas autem, dum corpus et sanguis Christi in veritate interius creditur." Hic trecentos quinquaginta annos post Christum floruit. Hilarius, dist. 2. "Corpus."

Epiphanius hunc paulo post consequens: "Cibum quidem (ait) esse panem, virtutem in ipso ad vivificationem esse." Quod si nullus panis esset, quomodo cibus esset? Epiphanius contra Hæreses, Lib. iii. Tom. ii.

Eadem ætate Chrysostomus, qui ad annos quadringentos post Christum fuit, scribit ad hunc modum: "Christus quando hoc mysterium tradidit, vinum tradidit: etiam post resurrectionem in nuda mysterii mensa vino usus est, ex genimine autem (ait) vitis, quæ vinum, non aquam producit." Et in Anacephalæosi. Chrysostomus in Matt. cap. xxvi.

Hæc verba Chrysostomi clarissime exponunt, Christum in sanctissima mensa bibisse vinum, et aliis bibendum dedisse: quod certe verum esse non possit, si nullum vinum post consecrationem (quemadmodum papistæ fingunt) remaneret.

Alio autem loco Chrysostomus hoc planius declarat his verbis: "Antequam sanctificetur panis, panem nominamus: divina autem illum sanctificante gratia, mediante sacerdote, liberatus quidem est ab appellatione panis, dignus autem est habitus dominici corporis appellatione, etiamsi natura panis in ipso permansit." *Ob. 201. Ad Cæsarium Monachum.

At si natura panis maneat, quomodo tandem gloriantur papistæ, sua de transubstantiatione, et substantiæ fuga, et accidentium permansione commenta defensantes?

Hoc sæculo vixit Ambrosius, qui conversionem panis et vini in corpus et sanguinem Christi minime ejusmodi esse ostendit, ut natura et substantia panis et vini recedant, sed gratia spiritualem conversionem per Dei omnipotentiam esse, ita ut qui digne hunc panem edit, spiritu Christum edat, et in Christo habitet, et Christus in eo. Nam de hac conversione panis in corpus Christi Ambrosius sic loquitur: Ambrosius.

"Si tanta vis in sermone Domini, ut incipiant esse, quæ non erant, quanto magis operatorius est ut sint quæ erant, et in aliud convertantur!" *Ob. 191. De his qui Mysteriis initiantur, cap. ult. Et de Sacra. Lib. iv. cap. 4.

Ad hanc rem confirmandam exemplum adfert nostræ in baptismo mutationis, cujus exempli etiam Eusebius meminit; ubi ita mutatur homo, ut nova creatura sit, ita nova creatura est, ut substantia tamen prior maneat.

Eadem etiam ætate Augustinus ad hunc modum scripsit: "Quod vidistis, panis August. in Sermone ad Infantes.

est et calix, quod vobis etiam oculi vestri renuntiant: quod autem fides postulat instruenda, panis est corpus Christi, calix est sanguis."

Et mox: "Panis non fit ex uno grano, sed ex multis." Et mox: "Illas nubes et ignes quæ fecerint vel assumpserint angeli, ad significandum quod annuntiabant, quis novit hominum, sicut infantes non norunt," &c. Et mox: "Infantes non norunt quod in altari ponitur, et peracta pietatis celebratione consumitur, unde vel quomodo conficiatur, unde in usum religionis assumatur. Et si nunquam discant experimento, vel suo vel aliorum, et nunquam istam speciem rerum videant, nisi inter celebrationes sacramentorum cum offertur et datur, dicaturque illis auctoritate gravissima, cujus corpus et sanguis sit, nihil aliud credent nisi omnino in illa specie Dominum oculis apparuisse mortalium, et de latere tali percusso liquorem illum omnino fluxisse." Et ante, cap. 4. "Panis et vinum non sanctificantur, ut sint tam magnum sacramentum, nisi per invisibilem operationem Spiritus sancti."

Idem Aug. de Trin. Lib. iii. cap. 10., loquens de novem modis, quibus Deus aliquid nobis annuntiat, nonum modum dicit esse "in re quæ sit quidem eadem specie, sed peracto mysterio transitura aliquando (inquit) ad hoc fit eadem species, vel aliquantulum mansura (sicut potuit serpens ille æneus exaltatus in eremo, sicut possunt literæ,) vel peracto transitura, sicut panis ad hoc factus in accipiendo sacramento consumitur. Sed quia hæc hominibus nota sunt (sed quia per homines fiunt,) honorem tanquam religiosa possunt habere, stuporem tanquam mira non possunt."

Idem in Joan. Homil. xxvi. "Dominus noster Jesus Christus corpus et sanguinem suum in iis rebus commendavit, quæ ad unum aliquid ex multis rediguntur. Aliud enim ex multis granis conficitur, aliud ex multis racemis confluit." Et mox: "Securus accede, panis est, non venenum."

_{In Lib. Sen. Prosperi.}

Hoc idem etiam alio loco apertissime exponit his verbis: "Sacrificium ecclesiæ in duobus consistit, visibili elementorum specie et invisibili Domini nostri Jesu Christi carne et sanguine, et sacramento et re sacramenti; sicut Christi persona constat ex Deo et homine, quum ipse Christus verus sit Deus et verus sit homo: quia omnis res illarum rerum naturam et veritatem in se continet, ex quibus conficitur. Conficitur autem sacrificium ecclesiæ duobus, sacramento et re sacramenti, id est, corpore Christi. Est igitur sacramentum, et res sacramenti corpus Christi."

Hesychius in Levit. Lib. ii. cap. 8. "Simul panis et caro est." Gregorius in Registro: "Tam azymum quam fermentatum dum sumimus, unum corpus Domini Salvatoris efficimur." Rabanus dicit, "Sacramentum in alimentum corporis redigi."

Quid contra papistarum errorem planius dici potest, qui nec panem nec vinum remanere in sacramento contendunt?

Quemadmodum enim persona Christi constat et conficitur ex Deo et homine, atque adeo utraque natura in Christo manet, ita (inquit Augustinus) sacramentum ex duabus rebus conficitur, elementis panis et vini, et Christi corpore et sanguine: qua de causa hæc duo in sacramento manere necesse est.

Sed ad meliorem harum rerum intelligentiam animadvertendum est, quosdam fuisse hæreticos, Simonem, Menandrum, Marcionem, Valentinum, Basilidem, Cerdonem, Manem, Eutychen, Manichæum, Apollinarem, et ejus generis permultos, qui Christum verum Deum fuisse fatebantur, sed verum hominem fuisse negabant; quamvis edendo, bibendo, dormiendo, ceterisque actionibus, opinionem afferret se esse hominem.

Alii contra, in quibus Artemon, Theodorus, Sabellius, Paulus Samosatenus, Marcellus, Photinus, Nestorius, multique ex eadem hæresi, hominem Christum confitebantur, Deum esse negabant; quamvis dando visu cæcis, sermone mutis, auditu surdis, sanandis confestim verbo morbis, excitandis mortuis, ceterisque divinis actionibus, speciem quandam Dei præ se ferret.

Erant etiam qui cum scripturas utraque in re apertas et certas viderent, tum Deum, tum hominem, Christum asseverabant, sed uno atque eodem tempore negabant. Nam ante incarnationem, inquiunt, Deus fuit et non homo: post incarnationem vero desiit esse Deus, et homo jam effectus est, idque ad resurrectionis aut ascensionis tempus: quo tempore relicta iterum humanitate, quemadmodum ante incarnationem, ita etiam post, Deus tantum fuerit, et non homo.

Sed adversus hæresum harum levitatem fides catholica, expresso Dei verbo nixa, tenet et credit, Christum post incarnationem suam divinam naturam non deseruisse, sed uno eodemque tempore (sicuti nunc est) perfectum Deum hominemque fuisse.

Quod ut planius intelligatur, antiqui scriptores hujus rei duo tradiderunt exempla: unum hominis, qui duabus ex partibus efficitur, anima et corpore, quarum utraque simul in homine eodemque tempore manent. Itaque ubi anima Dei omnipotentis efficientia in corpus infunditur, neutra pars alterius corruptrix est, sed perfectus ex his partibus homo efficitur, et perfectum corpus perfectam animam simul habet. Alterum, quod antiqui ad hanc causam citant, de eucharistia est, quam aiunt quoque duabus ex partibus effici, sacramento, vel visibilis panis et vini elemento, et Christi Servatoris corpore et sanguine. Et quemadmodum panis et vini natura non discedit, sed ab his qui digne sacramentum sumunt, ita corpore percipitur, quemadmodum corpus et sanguis Christi spiritu percipiuntur, sic divina Christi natura cum humana perpetuo conjungitur.

Eant nunc papistæ, et opinionem suam de transubstantiatione venditent, et nullam panis aut vini substantiam remanere contendant, si impias simul hæreses de Christo defendere velint, et illum aut Deum solum, aut hominem solum, et non utrumque simul esse existiment. Atque hanc fuisse veterum sententiam, tum ex Augustino (quem citavimus), tum ex aliis etiam compluribus, intelligitur.

Chrysostomus adversus perniciosum Apollinaris errorem de divinæ et humanæ naturæ in Christo ita confusa mistione, ut una tantum ex his natura efficeretur, ad Cæsarium monachum sic scripsit: "Deum quando dicis, agnovisti id quod simplex est natura, quod incompositum, quod inconvertibile, quod invisibile, quod immortale, quod incircumscriptibile, quod incomprehensibile, et his similia. Hominem autem dicens, significasti id quod natura est infirmum, esuritionem, sitim, lacrymas, metum, sudoris ejectionem, et his similia, passum, quibus id quod divinum est obnoxium non est. Christum autem quando dicis, conjunxisti utrumque. Unde et passibilis dicitur idem ipse et impassibilis: passibilis quidem carne, impassibilis autem deitate." *Chrysost. ad Cæsarium monachum.*

Et paulo post sic concludit: "Propter quod et Deus et homo est Christus: Deus propter impassibilitatem, homo propter passionem: unus Filius, unus Dominus, idem ipse proculdubio unitarum naturarum unam dominationem, unam potestatem possidens (etiamsi non consubstantiales existunt), et unaquæque incommixtam proprietatis conservat agnitionem propter hoc, quod inconfusa sunt duo. Sicut enim antequam sanctificetur panis, panem nominamus, divina autem illud sanctificante gratia, mediante sacerdote, liberatus est quidem ab appellatione panis, dignus autem habitus est dominici corporis appellatione, etiamsi natura panis in ipso permansit, et non duo corpora, sed unum Filii corpus prædicatur: sic et hic divina ἐνιδρυσάσης, id est, inundante corporis natura, unum Filium, unam personam, utraque hæc fecerunt."

Hæc Chrysostomi sententia non obscure sed expresse declarat, post consecrationem naturam panis remanere, quamvis sublimius longe et excelsius nomen consequatur: et corpus Christi adeo appellatur, ut qui religiose hujus sacramenti participes sunt, intelligant se spiritu supernaturalem panem corporis Christi, spiritu præsentis, edere, et illum in his et hos in illo habitare, quamvis corpore ad dexteram Dei Patris in cœlo assideat.

Gelasius item, adversus Eutychen et Nestorium scribens, (e quibus hic Christum perfectum hominem et non Deum, ille vero contra, Deum et non hominem esse asseverabat,) apertissimis scripturæ testimoniis probat, Christum verum Deum et verum hominem fuisse, et post incarnationem ejus naturam etiam divinitatis remansisse, ita ut cum duas naturas et naturales quoque utriusque proprietates haberet, unus tamen Christus esset. *Gelasius contra Eutychen et Nestorium.*

Hæc ut explicatiora essent, duo adfert exempla: unum hominis, qui cum unus sit, ex duabus naturis, iisque diversis, corpore et animo, et tamen consistentibus atque omnem vim suam conditionemque naturarum retinentibus, conficitur: alterum sacramenti corporis et sanguinis Domini, quam divinam rem esse ait, dicens: "Sacramenta quæ sumimus corporis et sanguinis Christi, divina res est propter quod et per eadem divinæ efficimur consortes naturæ, et tamen esse non desinit substantia vel natura panis et vini. Et certe imago et similitudo corporis et sanguinis Christi in actione mysteriorum celebrantur. Satis ergo nobis evidenter ostenditur, hoc nobis in ipso Christo Domino sentiendum, quod in ejus imagine profitemur, celebramus et sumus: ut sicut in hanc, scilicet divinam, transeunt (Spiritu sancto perficiente) substantiam, permanent tamen in suæ proprietate naturæ; sic illud ipsum mysterium principale (cujus nobis efficientiam virtutemque veraciter repræsentant), his ex quibus constat proprie permanentibus, unum Christum (quia integrum verumque) permanere demonstrant."

Advertant hic nostri temporis papistæ, Gelasium (qui ante mille annos episcopus Romanus fuerat) de hoc sacramento ita loquutum fuisse, ut panem et vinum dicat minime seipsa deserere, quemadmodum neque Christus per incarnationem divinitatem deseruit, sed perfectus Deus, sicut antea, permansit.

*Leo.

Et Leo, ut habetur de Consecra. dist. ii. "Incarnationis quoque exemplo astruamus mysterii veritatem." Idem habet Ambrosius, "de iis qui initiantur mysteriis. ca. ult."

Theodoretus.
Primo dialogo.
*Ob. 245.

Theodoretus etiam in eadem sententia est, ut ex primo et secundo ejus dialogo liquet. In primo enim ad hunc modum scribit: "Qui naturale corpus suum frumentum et panem vocavit, atque item seipsum vitem nominavit, idem ipse etiam panem et vinum corporis et sanguinis sui appellatione honoravit; non equidem naturam ipsam transmutans, sed adjiciens gratiam naturæ."

In 2. dialogo.

In secundo autem eadem expressius loquitur. "Sicut," inquit, "panis et vinum post sanctificationem propria natura sua non egrediuntur, sed manent in priore sua substantia, forma et figura; sic et corpus dominicum post assumptionem in divinam est substantiam transmutatum."

Eligant nunc papistæ, utrum ex his duobus largiri velint (alterutrum enim necesse est), vel naturam et substantiam panis et vini in sacramento post consecrationem remanere, (et tum revocanda est sua de transubstantiatione opinio;) vel se in eodem errore cum Nestorio et ceteris fateantur, qui naturam divinitatis in Christo nullam post incarnationem esse contendebant. Hoc est enim communi antiquorum assensione firmatum, ut quemadmodum in uno est, ita etiam in altero sit.

CAPUT VI.

TRANSUBSTANTIATIO E ROMA PRIMUM PROFECTA EST.

*Ob. 127.

NUNC quoniam satis expositum est, tum ex scriptura, tum ex naturali operatione, ratione, sensibus, antiquissimis et doctissimis auctoribus, et sanctis martyribus ecclesiæ Christi, substantiam panis et vini remanere, et a fidelibus in coena percipi, operæ pretium est videre, quid scholasticos recentiores commoverit ad contrariam opinionem defendendam, non modo a sensuum comprobatione et rationis judicio disjunctam, sed etiam cum antiqua Christi ecclesia et sanctissimo Dei verbo pugnantem. Certe nihil æque illos commovit, ac vana illa et inutilis fiducia quam in ecclesia et sede Romana collocarant.

Jo. Scotus
super 4.
Sent. di. 11.

Scotus enim, scholasticorum omnium subtilissimus, in transubstantiationis causa tractanda, hujus rei rationem affert. Ait enim: "Ad hanc sententiam principaliter videtur movere, quod de sacramentis tenendum est, sicut tenet sancta Romana ecclesia. Ipsa autem tenet panem transubstantiari in corpus, et vinum in sanguinem: ut patet *De summa trinitate et fide catholica*, Firmiter credimus."

Gabriel. in
Can. Missæ
lect. 40.

Gabriel etiam, qui præ ceteris omnibus de canone missæ fusissime scripsit, in eadem fuit (ut videtur) sententia. His enim verbis usus est: "Notandum, quod quamvis expresse tradatur in scriptura, quod corpus Christi veraciter sub speciebus panis continetur, et a fidelibus sumitur, tamen quomodo ibi sit corpus Christi, an per conversionem alicujus in ipsum, aut sine conversione incipiat esse corpus Christi cum pane, manentibus substantia et accidentibus panis, non invenitur expressum in canone bibliæ. Quia tamen de sacramentis tenendum est, sicut tenet sancta Romana ecclesia, ut habetur *De hæreticis*, Ad abolendam; nunc autem ipsa tenet et determinavit, panem transubstantiari in corpus Christi, et vinum in sanguinem; ideo ab omnibus catholicis acceptatur hæc opinio, quod substantia panis non manet, sed realiter et veraciter in substantiam corporis Christi convertitur, transubstantiatur seu commutatur."

CAPUT VII.

PAPISTARUM ANGLICORUM ARGUMENTA CONFUTANTUR.

Ex his intelligitur, hanc de transubstantiatione opinionem a compluribus defensam et propugnatam esse, quia ecclesia Romana ita constituit; quamvis contrariam sententiam etiam papistæ ipsi fateantur faciliorem videri, veriorem, et scripturis convenientiorem. "Quoniam autem ecclesia Romana transubstantiationem esse declaravit, ideo *Scotus. eligitur hic intellectus" (ut inquit Scotus) "ita difficilis, cum verba scripturæ possent salvari secundum intellectum facilem, et veriorem secundum apparentiam."

Sed quia nostrates papistæ (qui crassius de hac re, quam papa ipse, et sentiunt et loquuntur, affirmantes naturale corpus et sanguinem Christi naturaliter in pane et vino contineri) neque possunt neque audent fidem de transubstantiatione suam in ecclesia Romana fundare, (quæ quamvis sanctissima appellari postulet, revera tamen impurissima omnis impietatis sentina est, Satanæ synagoga, quam quicunque sequitur, non potest non labi, et in errorum barathrum ruere,) confugiunt ad ficulnea folia, id est, ad inania et levia argumenta, suo ipsorum cerebro fabricata, et ad veterum testimonia a mente et sententia auctorum longe detorta, quibus probrosos et ignominiosos suos errores velare et tegere moliuntur. Itaque placuit in eo paululum laboris sumere, ut iis ficulneis foliis (quibus tecti sunt) sublatis, illorum impudentes errores ante oculos omnium constituantur.

CAPUT VIII.

PRIMA RATIO, QUA PAPISTÆ TRANSUBSTANTIATIONEM CONFIRMANT.

Gravissima illorum ratio, quam maximi momenti esse putant, et in qua tantum auctoritatis pondus inesse judicant, ut (quemadmodum præ se ferunt) ne universum quidem orbem dissolvere posse illam existiment, hæc est: "Servator noster Christus acceptum panem fregit, et dedit discipulis suis dicens: Hoc est corpus meum. Hæc Matt. xxvi. verba, inquiunt, ubi Christus semel pronuntiasset, panis statim mutatus, et substantia Marc. iv. Luc. xxii. ejus in substantiam corporis Christi conversa est."

Quæ autem Christianæ aures hanc doctrinam patienter ferant, quod Christus quo- Hujus rationis confutatidie de integro fiat, aut quod ex alia substantia fiat, quam ex qua in utero virginis tio. effectus est? Ubi enim incarnationis tempore ex natura et substantia beatæ virginis *Roffen. contra Œcofactus est, nunc hac papistarum sententia quotidie ex natura panis et vini efficitur, lamp. Lib. ii. cap. 20. quæ, sicuti prædicant, in substantiam corporis et sanguinis ejus convertuntur. O admirabilem μεταμόρφωσιν! O horrendam hæresim, dicere Christum quotidie recens et recenti ex natura factum! Ex quo necessario efficitur illos nobis quotidie novos cudere et effingere Christos, ab illo diversos qui e virgine Maria nascebatur, quique in crucem suffixus fuit. Quemadmodum clarissime comprobabitur his subsequentibus argumentis.

Primum enim, si Christi corpus, quod cruci affixum fuit, nequaquam ex pane effec- *Ob. 111. Si corpus tum fuit, corpus autem quod in cœna edebatur, ex pane factum fuit, (sicuti papistæ Christi in sacramento ex contendunt,) fit, ut corpus quod in cœna manducatum est, non idem fuerit quod pane fiat, non est idem cruci affigebatur. pus quod

Deinde, si Christi corpus quod cruci affixum est, ex pane et vino factum non est, natum est et Christi corpus quod cruci affixum est, idem sit quod etiam in cœna edebatur, tum et passum. *Ob. 112. Christi corpus, quod edebatur, minime ex pane effectum est.

Tum, si Christi corpus quod in cœna edebatur, idem sit quod crucifixum est, et *Ob. 113. Christi corpus quod in cœna edebatur, ex pane factum sit, (sicuti papistæ venditant,) fit ut Christi corpus quod cruci affixum fuit, ex pane factum fuerit.

Ad hæc, si corpus Christi in sacramento ex substantia panis et vini efficiatur, idem- *Ob. 114. que corpus in utero virginis conceptum sit, tum corpus Christi in utero virginis ex pane et vino effectum est.

Vel, si mavis, ad hunc modum. Corpus Christi in utero virginis minime ex pane *Ob. 115. et vino effectum fuit. Corpus autem Christi in sacramento ex pane et vino factum est. Ita concluditur, hoc Christi corpus non esse id quod conceptum est in virginis utero.

Ob. 116. Præterea Christus qui de utero virginis natus est, quantum ad corpus attinet, nulla ex alia quam ex sanctæ virginis substantia factus est. Christus autem in sacramento ex alia substantia factus est: Christus igitur alius ille est.

Antichristus itaque Romanus, omnis impii cultus auctor, Christianos et fideles a vero Christi cultu, qui ex sanctissima virgine sancti Spiritus opera factus natusque est, nostraque causa in crucem actus, ad alterius Christi cultum abducere contendit, ex pane et vino facti papisticorum sacerdotum consecratione, qui se Dei effectores *Ob. 110.* faciunt: verbis enim consecrationis aiunt illud effici, quod in cœna percipitur. Hoc autem Christum ipsum Deum et hominem esse contendunt: ita efficitur, ut tum Dei tum hominis effectores sint.

At qui veræ pietatis studiosi sunt, unum Deum colant, et unum Christum, semel corporaliter factum ex Mariæ solius substantia, semel pro nobis mortuum, semel exsuscitatum, semel in cœlum sublatum, ibique perpetuo ad dexteram Patris sedentem, quamvis Spiritu quotidie nobiscum sit, et in medio illorum sit, qui in nomine ejus congregantur. Ille animorum (quemadmodum cibus corporum) pastus est; quod nobis institutione sacramenti in pane et vino demonstravit, significans, quemadmodum panis et vinum corpora nostra corporaliter pascunt et recreant, ita etiam illum carne et sanguine suo spiritualiter consolari et pascere mentem.

Hoc modo facillime dissolvitur papistarum (quod tantopere venditant) argumentum. Quantumcunque enim insolenter ostentent et maxime crepent suam panis et vini conversionem in corpus et sanguinem Christi, conversio tamen hæc spiritualis est, neque corporalem materiati panis et vini præsentiam tollit. Et quoniam sanctissimum est spiritualis pastus sacramentum, quem ex corpore et sanguine Servatoris nostri percipimus, necessario consistit elementum, quod sub sensus cadit, sine quo nullum consistit sacramentum. Quemadmodum enim in regeneratione nostra baptismi sacramentum nullum esse potest, si aqua absit; sic neque corporis et sanguinis Domini sacramentum ullum esse potest, si panis et vinum dimoveantur. Baptismus enim perfectum sacramentum spiritualis regenerationis non est, nisi elementum aquæ adsit, quod foris abluat, quemadmodum Spiritus sanctus interne spiritualiter regenerat baptizatum, quod aqua significatur: et cœna Domini perfectum spiritualis pastus sacramentum esse non potest, nisi tam panis et vinum adsint, quæ corpora nutriant, quam corpus et sanguis Christi, quæ spiritum pascant, quod pane et vino significatur. Quomodo autem cunque corpus et sanguis Christi adsint, æque cum substantia panis et vini ac cum accidentibus adesse possunt, sicut scholastici ipsi fatentur, et facillime (si adversarii id negare auderent) comprobari possit. Itaque facillime intelligitur, quemadmodum firmissima illorum ratio et præcipuum fundamentum (quo nituntur, et unde sibi hanc transubstantiationem architectati sunt) funditus everti ac deleri possit.

CAPUT IX.

ALTERA PAPISTARUM RATIO, QUA TRANSUBSTANTIATIONEM CONFIRMANT.

ALTERA illorum ratio est, parem undique dignitatem et auctoritatem habens. "Si panis," inquiunt, "remaneret, multa et magna absurda sequerentur: illudque in primis, quod quemadmodum Christus naturam hominis assumpsit, et sibi adjunxit, ita etiam naturam panis assumeret, et sibi adjungeret. Ex quo fieret, ut quemadmodum Deum pro redemptione nostra incarnatum habemus, ita etiam impanatum haberemus."

Hujus rationis confutatio. Hic facillime cernitur, quam leves reliquæ rationes sint, cum hæ gravissimæ et firmissimæ habeantur. Certum autem est, Christum omnino impanatum fuisse debere, si sibi panem unitate personæ adjunxisset; hoc est, si naturam panis ita cum natura sua copulasset, ut ex utraque natura una persona effecta fuisset. Sed quoniam sacramentaliter tantum pani adjunctus est, non magis ex eo impanatus Christus est, quam Spiritus sanctus inaquatus, cum sacramentaliter aquæ in baptismo adjungatur; aut columba effectus est, cum columbæ formam indueret, ut significaret illum, quem Joannes baptizabat, verum Christum fuisse. Imo vero (quemadmodum error errorem elicere solet) hæc ipsa quæ illi absurda objiciunt, ex illorum ipsorum sententia sequerentur; nempe Christum impanatum et invinatum (ut ita loquar) fuisse. Si enim Christus ita pane utitur, ut illum non ad nihilum redigat (sicuti illi prædicant), sed ex eo corpus suum efficiat; tum panis corpori Christi majore adunatione conjungitur, quam humanitas divinitati. Divinitas enim humanitati unitate personæ, non naturæ, adjungitur. Sed Servator Christus verbo suo efficit (sicuti ferunt) ut panis corpori, non modo unitate personæ, sed etiam naturæ jungeretur. Ex quo fit, ut panis et corpus Christi unum sint, tum natura tum persona, et quod major intercedat unitas corpori Christi cum pane, quam humanitati cum divinitate, aut corpori cum animo. Hoc modo papistarum argumenta in ipsos rectissime reflectuntur.

*Ob. 120.

CAPUT X.

TERTIA PAPISTARUM RATIO, QUA TRANSUBSTANTIATIONEM CONFIRMANT.

Tertiam adhuc habent, quam ex sexto Joannis colligunt, ubi Christus ait: "Ego sum panis vivus, qui de cœlo descendi: si quis edat ex hoc pane, vivet in æternum. Et panis quem ego dabo, caro mea est, quam ego dabo pro mundi vita."

Sic illi ex hoc loco disputant: "Si panis quem Christus dat, caro ejus sit, non potest etiam materiatus panis esse; atque adeo sequi necesse est, ut materiatus panis discedat, neque substantia ulla remaneat præter carnem Christi solam."

Hic facilis est responsio: Christum hoc in loco Joannis minime de materiato et sacramentali pane loquutum, neque de sacramentali perceptione (biennium enim ante aut triennium hic sermo habitus est, quam sacramentum institutum fuit), sed de spirituali pane, (unde sæpius repetit se panem vivum esse, qui de cœlo descendit,) et de spirituali per fidem perceptione, qua eodem illo tempore ab omnibus qui in illum credebant, manducabatur, quando cœna nondum facta aut sacramentum adhuc institutum fuerat. Itaque dixit, "Patres vestri ederunt manna in deserto, et mortui sunt: qui autem hunc panem edit, vivet perpetuo." Hic igitur Joannis locus de sacramentato pane intelligi non potest, qui neque de cœlo descendit, neque vitam hominibus tribuit. Neque tum temporis poterat Christus de sacramentali pane verba facere, et carnem suam appellare; nisi forte dicant, Christum tam longo ante spatio cœnam suam sacravisse.

Hujus rationis dissolutio.

Joan. vi.

CAPUT XI.

AUCTORES QUOS PAPISTÆ AD STABILIENDUM TRANSUBSTANTIATIONIS ERROREM DETORQUENT.

Nunc cum plene et perfecte levibus illorum et anilibus rationibus atque argutiis responderim, restat ut eodem modo sophisticis et nugatoriis auctorum allegationibus respondeam, quos ad sua commenta confirmanda depravarunt. Tria sunt loca præcipua, quæ speciem magnam præ se ferunt hujus erroris confirmandi: sed ea si quis studiose excutiat, et attentius aliquanto consideret, videbit nihil ea ad hujusmodi propositum facere.

Primus locus Cypriani est, in sermone de Cœna Domini. "Panis," inquit, "quem Dominus discipulis porrigebat, non effigie sed natura mutatus, omnipotentia verbi factus est caro."

*Mar. An. fo. 192. Cyprianus de Cœna Domini.

Huic sententiæ papistæ mordicus inhærent, et his verbis, "natura mutatus," maxime nituntur. Natura igitur panis, aiunt, mutatur. Hæc diabolicæ sophistices non minima pars est, qua diabolus in citandis scripturis uti solet, ut aliquid addat aut detrahat, aut sensum commutet. Sic hoc loco ea verba a papistis prætermitti solent, quæ universam causam planam facerent. Illis enim hæc quæ sequuntur adjungi debebant:

Responsio.

"Sicut in persona Christi humanitas videbatur, et latebat divinitas, ita sacramento visibili ineffabiliter se divina infudit essentia: ut esset religioni circa sacramenta devotio, et ad veritatem, cujus corpus sacramenta sunt, sincerior pateret accessus, usque ad participationem Spiritus, non usque ad consubstantialitatem Christi, sed usque ad societatem germanissimam ejus hæc unitas perveniret." Et ibidem: "Ex consueto rerum effectu fidei nostræ adjuta infirmitas sensibili argumento edocta est, visibilibus sacramentis inesse vitæ æternæ effectum; non tam corporali quam spirituali transitione Christo nos uniri." Et mox: "Nostra vero et ipsius conjunctio nec miscet personas, nec unit substantias; sed affectus consociat, et confœderat voluntates."

Hæc Cypriani verba aperte demonstrant, quod sacramentum simul cum divinitate adjuncta permaneat, et sacramentaliter divinitatem in panem et vinum infundi, ipsis pane et vino etiamnum remanentibus, quemadmodum divinitas humanitatem Christi sibi conjunxit, et simul cum illa habitavit.

Et tamen panis non effigie nec substantia, sed natura (quemadmodum Cyprianus verissime dicit) mutatur. Neque enim hoc sentiebat, naturalem panis substantiam protinus discessisse, sed verbo Dei altiorem ei vim, naturam, conditionemque adjectam, quæ longe longeque plurimum vim et naturam communis panis superaret. Mysticus enim panis hoc demonstrat (sicuti idem Cyprianus ait), nos Spiritus divini participes effectos, arctissime Christo conjungi, et spiritualiter illius carne et sanguine pasci: ita ut hic sacramentatus panis sit non modo corporale corporis nutrimentum, sed etiam spiritualis pastus animi.

Eodem modo in baptismo aquæ natura communis mutatur: ad communem enim naturam aquæ, quæ in abluendo et extergendo corpore versatur, accedit etiam, quod sit ablutionis nostræ et expiationis per Spiritum sanctum certissimum testimonium.

Augustinus in Joan. tract. lxxx. "'Jam vos mundi estis, propter verbum quod loquutus sum vobis.' Quare non ait, Mundi estis propter baptismum quo loti estis, sed ait, propter verbum quod loquutus sum vobis; nisi quia et in aqua verbum mundat? Detrahe verbum: quid est aqua nisi aqua? Accedit verbum ad elementum, et fit sacramentum: etiam ipsum tanquam visibile verbum." Et mox: "Unde ista tanta virtus aquæ, ut corpus tangat, et cor abluat, nisi faciente verbo? Non quia dicitur, sed quia creditur. Nam et in ipso verbo aliud est sonus transiens, aliud virtus remanens. Hoc est verbum fidei quod prædicamus."

Itaque præcipuum doctorum testimonium (quod illi firmissimum erroris sui præsidium existimant) facile intelligitur, quam parum pro illis faciat. Sed ad meliorem sententiæ Cypriani explicationem, haud inutile fuerit locum illius, supra capite quinto citatum, animadvertere.

CAPUT XII.

CHRYSOSTOMI SENTENTIA A PAPISTIS AD TRANSUBSTANTIATIONEM DEPRAVATA.

Chrysostomi sententiam adferunt, quam indissolubilem esse putant. Ille enim in quadam de eucharistia homilia sic scribit: "Num panem, num vinum vides? num in secessum ut reliqui cibi abeunt? absit. Non sic cogitandum est: quemadmodum enim si cera igni adhibita assimilatur illi, nihil substantiæ remanet, nihil redundat; ita et hic puta mysteria consumi corporis substantia."

*Marcus Antonius, fo. 294.

Hic se papistæ magnifice efferunt, et quasi victoria parta triumphant. Ecce, inquiunt, an non gravissimus et eruditissimus vir apertissimis verbis dicit, nos neque panem, neque vinum videre, illa prorsum, quasi ceram igni adhibitam, ad nihilum consumi, nullam præterea substantiam remanere?

At si ea verba, quæ proxime in Chrysostomo sequuntur, recitassent (quæ astute de industria prætermiserant), quodnam Chrysostomi judicium et quis sensus esset, facillime patefieret, et in ruborem (nisi valde impudentes fuerint) conjicerentur.

Chrysostomus enim statim subjungit: "Propterea accedentes, ne putetis vos divinum corpus ex homine accipere, sed ex ipsis seraphin forcipe ignem. Reputate salutarem sanguinem quasi e divino et impolluto latere effluere, et ita approximantes labiis puris accipite. Quocirca, fratres, oro vos et obsecro, ne absimus ab ecclesiis, neque in aliis colloquiis occupati simus: stemus trementes et timidi, demissis oculis, renata autem anima, gementes sine voce, jubilantes corde."

Cum igitur hæc verba continenter ea subsequantur, quæ a papistis commemorata sunt, siquidem hi concludere ex verbis ab se citatis volunt, neque panem neque vinum in sacramento esse, mihi eodem modo concludere licebit, neque sacerdotem ibi neque Christi corpus esse.

Quemadmodum enim in priori sententia Chrysostomus præcipit, ut ne cogitemus nos panem aut vinum videre, ita in altera mandat, ut ne existimemus nos Christi corpus a sacerdotis manu capere. Quocirca, si ex altera sententia (quemadmodum papistæ ipsi prædicant) vere colligi non potest, in sacra communione minime Christi corpus a sacerdote nobis tribui; fateantur etiam necesse est, neque necessario nec vere ex prima sententia concludi, nullum ibi panem aut vinum adesse.

Atqui hæc omnia in sacrosancta cœna pariter existunt. Christus ipse spiritualiter perceptus et fideles pascens, panis et vinum id nobis demonstrantia sacramento, et sacerdos horum minister. Itaque Chrysostomus præcise non negat panem et vinum, corpus Christi et sacerdotem adesse; sed figura quadam loquendi, non simplici negatione utitur, sed comparata.

Hic loquendi modus non modo a scriptura est usurpatus, sed etiam omnium scriptorum et linguarum communis est. Cum enim duo inter se conferuntur, in præstantiori re extollenda, et humiliori deprimenda, negationibus comparatis utimur, quæ simpliciter aliquid non negant, sed comparate. Cum populus (verbi causa), rejecto Samuele propheta, regem expeterent, Deus Samueli dixit: "Non te, sed me rejecerunt." Haud hic simpliciter intelligitur, Samuelem non rejectum, cujus in loco regem collocari cupiebant; sed in negatione comparata duæ affirmationes intelliguntur, una rejectum esse Samuelem, altera Deum etiam, et in primis, rejectum esse. *Negationes per comparationem.* *1 Reg. viii.*

Eodem modo, cum David in persona Christi se vermem dixerat, et non hominem; nequaquam hac negatione, Christum esse hominem, tollit, sed ut magnitudine orationis Christum ad infimam conditionem abjiceret, significavit Christum non modo ad humanæ imbecillitatis conditionem demissum, sed etiam in tantam humilitatem et obscuritatem depressum, ut potius vermis quam homo appellandus esset. *Psal. xxi.*

Quæ forma loquendi Paulo familiaris admodum erat. "Non ego hæc efficio," inquit, "sed peccatum in me habitans." Et alio loco: "Non misit me Christus ut baptizem, sed ut evangelizem." Atque iterum: "Sermo meus et prædicatio mea non in probabilibus humanæ sapientiæ sermonibus, sed in spiritus et potestatis demonstratione." Et rursus: "Neque qui plantat est aliquid, neque qui rigat, sed qui incrementum dat Deus." Et porro: "Non ego, sed Christus in me vivit." Et, "Mihi absit ut glorier, nisi in cruce Domini nostri Jesu Christi." Tum, "Non est nobis luctatio adversus carnem et sanguinem, sed adversus spiritus tenebrarum." *Rom. vii.* *1 Cor. i.* *1 Cor. ii.* *1 Cor. iii.* *Gal. iv.* *Gal. vi.* *Eph. vi.*

In his sententiis et permultis aliis ejus generis, quanquam negationes insint, non tamen cogitavit Paulus prorsus inficiari, se hoc malum patrasse, de quo loquebatur, aut penitus asseverare, se non missum ut baptizaret, (qui aliquando baptizabat, et ad omnia salutis nostræ munera obeunda missus erat,) aut in verbo evangelii illustrando ingeniosis et acutis persuasionibus non uti, (quibus certe peropportune usus est,) aut satorem et irrigatorem nihil esse, (qui Dei creaturæ sunt, ad similitudinem ejus factæ, sine quorum opera neque sementis fit neque messis,) aut negare se vivere, (qui et vixit, et omnes regiones lustravit, ad Dei gloriam amplificandam,) aut plane confirmare, se nulla alia in re gloriari, nisi in Christi cruce, (qui lætabatur cum lætantibus omnibus, et angebatur cum anxiis,) aut omnino negare cum carne et sanguine nos decertare, qui nunquam luctationem et perpetuum cum mundo, carne, et diabolo bellum intermittimus. His in sententiis omnibus Paulus (sicuti dixi) non omnino cogitavit absolute illa negare, quæ sine ulla dubitatione erant verissima: sed voluit præ majoribus illis hæc leviora minoris æstimanda esse, et maximam majorum rerum rationem habendam esse: nempe ut peccatum, naturæ infirmitate admissum, originali potius peccato et naturæ corruptæ (quæ intus inclusa delitescit) quam voluntati illius et assensioni assignetur; et quanquam ad omnes sacramento baptismi tingendos missus esset, præcipue tamen ad verbum Dei prædicandum constitutus a Deo fuerat; et quamvis argumentis usus sit prudentiæ plenis, rerum tamen felix eventus atque exitus divina potentia et sancti Spiritus *1 Cor. i.* *Rom. xv.* *2 Cor. xi.*

efficientia proficiscebatur. Pari modo, quamvis sator et irrigator aliquid sunt, et multum in munere suo obeundo faciunt, Deus tamen præcipue amplificationem affert. Vixerat quoque Paulus in hoc mundo, sed præcipua illius vita in Christo fuit, quem apud se viventem gerebat. Multis in rebus gloriabatur, etiam in infirmitatibus; maxima tamen ejus gloriatio in Christi cruce fuerat. Quotidiana est nobis cum carne lucta, sed gravissima et acerrima dimicatio est adversus hostes spirituales et subtiles spiritus malos et diabolos.

Gal. ii.
2 Cor. xi. et xii.
Gal. vi.
Eph. vi.

Hac loquendi forma etiam Petrus in prima epistola usus est, præcipiens fœminarum ornatum ut ne externus sit, vel crinium calamistro, vel auri adjectione, vel vestium amictu; sed internus cordis homo sit, cum integritate mitis ac tranquilli spiritus, quæ res coram Deo magni pretii est.

1 Pet. iii.

Hic non omnino compositos capillos, aurum, sumptuosas vestes vetuit, (unumquemque enim is apparatus decet, qui est ordini suo convenientissimus;) sed superbiam nimiamque ornamentorum externorum cupiditatem detrahere cogitavit, et fœminas omnes hortari, ut mentes studeant intus omnibus virtutum luminibus illustrare, neque de externo corporum apparatu et sumptuoso vestitu sollicite laborare.

Servator etiam Christus istius sermonis plenus fuit. "Ne," inquit, "vobis thesaurum in terris cumuletis:" inde admonens, ut potius mentes nostras ad durabilem et perpetuum thesaurum transferamus, quam in terreno hoc, qui variis modis corrumpitur et nobis eripitur, hæreamus. Externa enim hæc et mundana, pro locis, temporibus et personis, ab hominibus possideri possunt.

Matt. vi.

Item alio loco: "Ubi deducti," inquit, "ad reges fueritis et principes, ne cogitetis, quid aut quomodo respondendum sit." Hac ille negatione minime voluit nos negligenter et inconsiderate, quicquid in mentem venerit, respondere, sed ut cœlesti Patri toti niteremur, sperantes nos sancto illius Spiritu satis idonee instruendos potius, quam responsis nostro ipsorum ingenio et studio excogitandis fideremus.

Matt. x.

Quid illud, "Non vos estis qui loquimini, sed Spiritus Dei, qui in vobis loquitur?" An non similem omnino rationem in se habet? Spiritus enim Dei salutaria et divina verba in ora nostra infundit, nos tamen illo suggerente atque incitante loquimur.

Matt. x.

Denique in his quæ sequuntur omnibus: "Ne vobis patrem in terris quenquem appelletis;" "Nemo vos domini aut magistri nomine appellet;" "Ne timeatis illos qui occidunt corpus;" "Non veni, ut pacem in terram mitterem;" "In mea potestate situm non est, ad dexteram vos aut lævam collocare;" "Non adorabitis Patrem, neque hoc in monte, neque Hierosolymis;" "Testimonium ab hominibus non accipio;" "Doctrina mea non est mea;" "Non quæro gloriam meam:" in negationibus his omnibus Servator Christus non ita restricte locutus est, ut prorsus hæc omnia removeret, sed ut istis alia anteponeret; ut Patrem videlicet cœlestem et Dominum terreno; timorem ejus ullius creaturæ timori; verbum ejus et evangelium universæ mundanæ paci; et internum ac spiritualem Dei cultum, ex puro corde atque anima profectum, externo honori, corporibus aut locis definito, præponeremus: quemadmodum Christus Patris gloriam suæ ipsius anteposuit.

Matt. xxiii.
Matt. x.
Matt. x.
Joan. iv.
Joan. v.
Joan. vii.
Joan. viii.

Nunc quoniam copiose negationum harum naturam et vim exposui (quæ simplices negationes non sunt, sed comparatæ), perfacile est Chrysostomo respondere, qui istiusmodi formarum loquendi plenus fuit, et præ ceteris in hoc genere excelluit. Neque enim in ea concione cogitavit unquam, in cœnæ dominicæ administratione panem, vinum, sacerdotem, corpus Christi adesse negare, (quod papistas etiam fateri necesse est;) sed propositum ejus fuerat, mentes nostras a terrenis rebus ad cœlestia traducere, ut non tam panem, vinum, sacerdotem et Christi corpus consideraremus, quam divinam ejus naturam et sanctum Spiritum, nobis ad æternam salutem datum.

Responsio ad Chrysost. in Homilia de Cœna Domini.

Itaque persæpe eodem in loco his verbis usus est, "Cogita, ne cogites, ne putes, aut existimes;" ut ne mentes et cogitationes nostras in panem, vinum, sacerdotem, corpus Christi, defigeremus, sed longe altius ad Spiritum et divinam ejus naturam attolleremus, sine quibus (ut de his ipse testatur) caro nihil prodest: "Spiritus (inquiens) est qui vivificat, caro non prodest quicquam."

Et quemadmodum Chrysostomus multis in locis nos hortatur, ut ne in aquam in baptismo, sed in Spiritum sanctum in baptismo perceptum, et aqua repræsentatum intueamur: ita in hac de cœna Domini homilia impellit nos, ut mentes nostras a rebus corporatis et sub sensum cadentibus, ad res spirituales et minime sub aspectum subjectas, transferamus.

Chrysostomus in 1 Cor. ii. "Infidelis cum baptismatis lavacrum audit, simpliciter aquam esse sibi persuadet. Ego vero non simpliciter video quod video, sed animæ per Spiritum purgationem, nec non sepulturam, resurrectionem, justitiam, adoptionem, hæreditatem, regnum cœlorum, Spiritus societatem considero. Non enim aspectu judico quæ videntur, sed mentis oculis." Hac loquendi forma usus est Chrysostomus, cum non solum de eucharistia, sed de baptismo quoque dicit, "nihil sensibile traditum nobis a Christo."

Et quamquam Christus semel tantum in crucem actus sit, studuit tamen Chrysostomus, ut illud nobis propositum haberemus, nos quotidie illum videre flagris vexatum atque afflictum, corpus ejus in cruce dependens, hastam lateri ejus transfixam, sanctissimum sanguinem de latere ejus in ora nostra profluentem. Quo in genere locutionis Paulus ad Galatas scripsit, "Christum depictum et cruci affixum in illorum conspectu." Gal. iii.

Itaque in eadem homilia, paulo ante hunc locum citatum, Chrysostomus his verbis usus est: "Quid facis, homo? Non promisisti sacerdoti, qui dixit, 'Sursum mentem et corda?' et dixisti, 'Habemus ad Dominum?' Non revereris et erubescis? Et illa ipsa hora mendax inveniris? Papæ, mensa mysteriis instructa est, et Agnus Dei pro te immolatur: sacerdos pro te angitur, ignis spiritualis ex sacra mensa refluit: seraphin astant sex alis faciem tegentia, omnes incorporeæ virtutes pro te cum sacerdote intercedunt; ignis spiritualis e cœlo descendit; sanguis in crateram, in tuam purificationem, ex immaculato latere haustus est: et non erubescis? revereris? et confunderis? neque Deum tibi propitium facis? Non conscientia tua judicat te, O homo? Centum sexaginta octo horas habente hebdomada, unam et solam horam sibi ipsi segregavit Deus; et hanc in opera secularia, et in ridicula, et in conventicula insumis? Cum qua postea fiducia ad mysteria accedes? O quam polluta conscientia!" *Chrysostomus.

Hucusque Chrysostomi verba recitavi, quæ declarant, quibus rebus mentes nostræ in hac cœna Domini attentæ esse debent, nempe ab ea rerum, quæ sub sensus cadunt, cogitatione traductæ ad divinarum rerum et cœlestium perspicientiam. Sic igitur concludo, satis plane et aperte responsum esse huic loco Chrysostomi, quem papistæ inexplicabilem et indissolubilem esse putant. Atque ut hæc Chrysostomi sententia melius intelligatur, non abs re fuerit locum illius superius citatum capite quinto legere.

CAPUT XIII.

AMBROSII LOCUS EXPLICATUS, QUEM PAPISTÆ PRO SE ADDUCUNT.

Adhuc Ambrosii locus restat, quem papistæ multum pro se facere judicant; quem si diligentius et attentius paulo intueamur, animadvertemus, quantum in eo decipiantur. Locus est in libro de iis qui initiantur mysteriis: "Quantis igitur utimur exemplis, ut probemus non hoc esse quod natura formavit, sed quod benedictio consecravit; majoremque vim esse benedictionis, quam naturæ, quia benedictione etiam natura ipsa mutatur! Virgam tenebat Moses, projecit eam, et facta est serpens: rursus apprehendit caudam serpentis, et in virgæ naturam revertitur. Vides igitur prophetica gratia bis mutatam esse naturam, et serpentis et virgæ. Currebant Ægypti flumina puro aquarum meatu: subito de fontium venis sanguis cœpit erumpere. Non erat potus in fluviis: rursus ad prophetæ preces cruor cessavit fluminum, aquarum natura remeavit. Circumclusus undique erat populus Hebræorum, hinc Ægyptiis vallatus, inde mari clausus: virgam levavit Moses, separavit se aqua, et in murorum speciem congelavit, atque inter undas via pedestris apparuit. Jordanis retrorsum conversus contra naturam in sui fontis revertitur exordium. Nonne claret naturam vel maritimorum fluctuum vel fluvialis cursus esse mutatum? Sitiebat populus, tetigit Moses petram, et aqua de petra fluxit. Numquid non præter naturam operata est gratia, ut aquam vomeret petra, quam non habebat natura? Marath fluvius amarissimus erat, ut sitiens populus bibere non posset: misit Moses lignum in aquam, et amaritudinem suam aquarum natura deposuit, quam infusa subito gratia temperavit. Sub Eliseo

Ambrosius de iis qui mysteriis initiantur.

Exod. vii.
Exod. vii.
Exod. xiv.
Jos. iii.
Exod. xvii.

propheta uni ex filiis prophetarum excussum est ferrum de securi, et statim mersum est: rogavit Elisæum qui amiserat ferrum; misit etiam Elisæus lignum in aquam, et ferrum natavit. Utique et hoc præter naturam factum esse cognoscimus: gravior est enim ferri species quam aquarum liquor. Advertimus igitur majoris esse virtutis gratiam quam naturam; et adhuc tamen propheticæ benedictionis numeramus gratiam. Quod si tantum valuit humana benedictio, ut naturam converteret, quid dicimus de ipsa consecratione divina, ubi verba ipsa Domini Salvatoris operantur? Nam sacramentum id quod accipis, Christi sermone conficitur. Quod si tantum valuit sermo Eliæ, ut ignem de cœlo deponeret, non valebit Christi sermo, ut species mutet elementorum? De totius mundi operibus legisti, quia 'ipse dixit, et facta sunt, ipse mandavit et creata sunt.' Sermo autem Christi, qui potuit ex nihilo facere quod non erat, non potest ea quæ sunt in id mutare quod non erant? Non enim minus est, novas rebus dare, quam mutare naturas. Vera utique caro Christi, quæ crucifixa est, quæ sepulta est; veræ ergo carnis illius sacramentum est. Ipse clamat Dominus Jesus, 'Hoc est corpus meum.' Ante benedictionem verborum cœlestium alia species nominatur: post consecrationem corpus Christi significatur."

Psal. cxlviii.

Hucusque Ambrosius, siquidem hic liber ejus sit, quod[1] a gravissimis et doctissimis viris minime existimatur. E quibus verbis papistæ colligunt, in cœna Domini post verba (quæ vocant) consecrationis neque panem remanere neque vinum; quia Ambrosius hoc loco ait, naturam panis et vini mutari.

Atqui ut illis satisfiat, qui alias contentiosi esse non desinunt, hoc in gratiam illorum donemus, Ambrosii librum hunc esse; nihil tamen facit ad illorum sententiam promovendam, sed eam potius oppugnat. Neque enim ait, substantiam panis et vini discedere, sed naturam mutari. Quod perinde est, ac si diceret: In cœna Domini minime capiendus panis et vinum est, quemadmodum ceteri vulgares cibi et potiones capiuntur, sed ut res in altiorem longe naturam et vim mutatæ, et pro sancto pastu percipiendæ, ubi spirituali, et naturam longo intervallo superante, cibo et potione complemur, et cœlitus alimur carne Christi et sanguine, omnipotentia Dei, et admirabili Spiritus sancti efficientia. Hæc ita cum panis et vini substantia permanente conveniunt, ut si e medio tolleretur, et non consisteret, hic spiritualis pastus minime nobis per illam significaretur.

Itaque in quam plurimis exemplis, ab Ambrosio pro admirabili naturarum mutatione adductis, substantiæ illarum permanebant, postquam natura et vis illarum mutata esset. Ut cum aqua Jordanis contra naturam quasi murus consisteret, aut contra decurrentis alvei cursum ad fontem reverteretur, aquæ tamen substantia eadem remansit, quæ ante fuit. Et saxum illud, quod præter naturam aquam profuderat, idem saxum remansit quod ante fuerat. Fluvius Marath, qui virus illud amaritudinis mutavit, nullam substantiæ partem mutavit. Nec ferrum, quod contra naturam in summa aqua natabat, ullam substantiæ partem amisit. Quocirca, quemadmodum in his naturarum conversionibus substantiæ nihilominus eædem remanebant, quæ ante conversionem fuerant; eodem modo panis et vini substantiæ in cœna Domini remanent, et naturaliter percipiuntur, et in ventriculo concoquuntur, quamvis sacramentalis mutatio in Christi corpus et sanguinem fiat. Atque hæc sacramentalis mutatio hunc supernaturalem et spiritualem et inexplicabilem pastum, nutrimentum, concoctionem corporis et sanguinis Domini omnibus illis declarat, qui pie et religiose panem sacramentalem et vinum percipiunt.

Quod vero Ambrosius de substantia panis et vini permansione ad hunc modum judicarit, ex tribus aliis eadem de re, in eodem capite comprehensis, exemplis satis perspicuum est. Primum, ex his qui regenerantur, in quibus post regenerationem prior substantia eadem manet: alterum, de incarnatione Servatoris Christi, ubi nulla omnino discessit substantia, sed æque divinitatis ac humanitatis (quam de virgine accepit) substantia remanet: tertium de aqua baptismi est, ubi aqua etiam aqua esse non desinit, quanquam Spiritus sanctus in aquam se infundat, vel potius in eum cui aqua affunditur.

Lib. iv. de Sacram. cap. 4.

Quanquam autem Ambrosius alio in libro, qui inscribitur "de sacramentis," dicat, "Panis iste panis est ante verba sacramentorum; ubi accesserit consecratio, de pane

[1 Old editions, *quas.*]

fit caro Christi:" eodem tamen in libro et capite narrat, quibus modis et rationibus id efficiant verba Christi: "Non sublata panis substantia, sed adjecta pani corporis Christi gratia, atque adeo imposito illi corporis Christi nomine."

Hujus rei quatuor ponit exempla: primum de hominis regeneratione, alterum de aqua maris rubri stante, tertium de amara Marath aqua, quartum de ferro quod aquæ supernatavit. Quibus in exemplis perspicuum est, quamvis quædam naturæ sit commutatio, priorem tamen substantiam perpetuo eandem permanere. Ita universam causam his verbis concludit: "Si ergo tanta vis est in sermone Domini Jesu, ut inciperent esse quæ non erant, quanto magis operatorius est, ut sint quæ erant, et in aliud commutentur?" Ex quibus manifestum est, quamvis hæc admirabilis sacramentalis et spiritualis panis conversio fiat in corpus Christi, eadem tamen substantia panis maneat, quæ fuit.

Ad hunc modum satis responsum est tribus præcipuis patrum auctoritatibus, Cypriani, Chrysostomi et Ambrosii, quibus papistæ præcipue abutuntur ad transubstantiationis errorem confirmandum. Alias rationes et auctoritates habent, quas eandem ad rem afferunt: sed quia perexiguum et leve pondus habent, et refutatu faciles sunt, prætermitto; neque lectorem hoc tempore perturbare volo, sed judicio ejus æstimandas relinquere.

CAPUT XIV.

ABSURDA QUÆ TRANSUBSTANTIATIONEM SEQUANTUR.

NUNC doctrinarum monstra et portenta recensebo, quæ hunc transubstantiationis errorem necessario consequuntur, quum nihil omnino hujusmodi veram et orthodoxam fidem, verboque Dei innixam, consequatur. *Ista tractantur supra, cap. 3.*

Ac primum, si a papistis interrogetur, quid frangatur, edatur, bibatur, labiis, ore, dentibus in hoc sacramento teratur, nihil habent præter accidentia, quod respondeant. Panem enim et vinum aiunt visibile elementum in hoc sacramento non esse, sed accidentia sola. Atque ita fateri coguntur, accidentia frangi, edi, bibi, teri, deglutiri, sine ulla prorsus substantia: quæ res non modo rationi, verum etiam antiquorum patrum doctrinæ repugnat.

Deinde, (quod omni generi disciplinarum est contrarium,) transubstantiatores hi affirmant, panis et vini accidentia in aëre sola, absque ulla cui nitantur substantia, pendere. Quo quid absurdius dici possit?

Tertio, substantiam corporis Christi ibi reipsa, corporate et naturaliter, sine ullis accidentibus adesse. Itaque substantiam sine accidentibus, et accidentia sine substantia, papistæ constituunt. *Ob. 74.*

Quarto, locum ubi panis et vini accidentia sunt, nullam habere ad se explendum substantiam, atque adeo vacuum, a quo natura maxime abhorret, necessario confitentur.

Quinto, minime verentur asseverare, ubi panis mucidus est, aut in vermes conversus, aut ubi vinum acescit, substantiam ex accidentibus effici.

Sexto, substantiam solis accidentibus sine ulla substantia nutriri, si quando felem, murem, canem, aut aliud quodvis animal, sacramentalem panem devorare contingat.

Hæ atque aliæ ejus generis infinitæ ineptiæ atque absurditates necessario consequuntur hanc transubstantiationem papisticam, quibus (quemadmodum illi ipsi confitentur) nunquam poterint respondere.

Et admirabile certe est, quomodo inter se dissentiant, dum objecta dissolvere cupiunt.

Doctrina vero scripturæ, et antiquæ et catholicæ (non istius recens corruptæ Romanæ) ecclesiæ, non modo ad intelligendum aperta est, verum etiam ad objecta refutanda satis expedita, et ab omnibus his absurdis erroribus et ineptiis vacua, et cum verbo Dei, cum antiqua ecclesia, cum ratione humana, cum philosophia consentiens.

Nam quod ad primum attinet, quid frangitur, quid editur, quid bibitur, quid dentibus hoc sacramento teritur, facile respondetur: Panis et vinum. Ita enim Paulus: "Panis quem frangimus." *1 Cor. x.*

De secundo et tertio tenendum est, neque substantiam corporis Christi sine suis accidentibus esse, neque panis et vini accidentia a substantia disjuncta in aëre sola pendere; sed juxta omnem et rationem et rerum experientiam, substantiam cum panis et vini, tum corporis Christi, sua sibi accidentia retinere, et accidentia quoque suis ipsorum substantiis niti.

Ad quartum dicitur, nullum locum post consecrationem omni substantia vacuum relictum esse (quemadmodum papistæ somniant), sed panem et vinum sua ipsorum loca, quemadmodum antea, explere.

In quinto et sexto quid aliud affirmandum est, quam vermes, mucorem, acetum, cursu quodam naturæ (quemadmodum usus communis et disciplinæ omnium recte de rebus sentientium docent) ex substantia panis et vini, nimis diu asservata, gigni, et non ex accidentibus solis (sicuti papistæ leviter existimarunt); et substantiam panis et vini, non accidentia sola, alere et sustentare corpora edentium eam?

His in responsionibus nihil absurdum aut ineptum est, nihil dictum vel contra sacram scripturam, vel naturalem rationem, vel philosophiæ studium, vel usum communem rerum, vel aliquem ex antiquis patribus, vel primam illam et catholicam ecclesiam, sed tantum contra impiam et irreligiosam Romanæ et papisticæ ecclesiæ disciplinam. Execranda autem hæc antichristi synagoga multa et varia in hac causa adversus Christi doctrinam, adversus antiquam et catholicam ecclesiam, adversus sanctos patres et martyres, adversus naturam, philosophiam, atque omnem denique disciplinam pronunciavit, statuit, et pro fidei legibus decrevit, ut nos a vera fide averteret.

Quis enim alius hujus antichristianæ disciplinæ finis esse potest, quam subdola quadam astutia Christianos a vero Christi cultu ad gravissimam et perniciosissimam omnium idololatriam, quæ unquam antehac excogitatæ fuerant, abducere? Quod in consequenti oratione mea planius demonstrabo.

FINIS LIBRI SECUNDI.

LIBER TERTIUS.

QUEMADMODUM CHRISTUS IN SACRAMENTO PRÆSENS SIT.

CAPUT PRIMUM.

Hac jam de transubstantiatione causa satis pertractata (quæ prima pars est, in qua papistica doctrina a catholica veritate dissentit), sequitur ut de modo præsentiæ corporis et sanguinis Christi in sacramento ejus disseramus, quæ secunda pars est, et non minorem opinionum dissensionem quam prima continet.

Ad cujus rei planiorem explicationem illud intelligendum est, quod Christianis omnibus satis est cognitum, Christum Servatorem, perfectum Deum, et in omnibus æqualem et coæternum Patri, nostra causa perfectum hominem effectum esse, carne et sanguine de beata virgine sumptis, et in ceteris (peccatum tantum excipio) nostri similem, perfecta anima et perfecto corpore ad divinam naturam adjunctis. Hujus anima vita, sensu, voluntate, ratione, prudentia, memoria, ceterisque ad humanam animam aliqua ex parte pertinentibus, prædita est. Corpus autem ex vera carne et ossibus constabat, non modo humani corporis membrorum justam conformationem et ordinem continens, sed etiam fame, siti, labore, sudore, defatigatione, frigore, calore, ceterisque infirmitatibus et perturbationibus humanis affectum, et morte etiam ipsa, eaque in cruce vilissima et ærumnosissima. Post mortem eodem cum corpore, tum visibili, tum contrectabili surrexit, et in conspectum suorum venit, et apostolis illud ostendit, et in primis Thomæ, cui jusserat ut manus lateri admoveret, et vulnera ejus contrectaret. Tum eodem ipso cum corpore in cœlum conscendit, apostolis illud videntibus, et dum ascenderet intuentibus; ibique ad dexteram Dei Patris sedet, ad extremum usque diem permansurus, quo tempore ad judicium de vivis et mortuis ferendum rediturus est.

Hæc vera est et catholica fides, quam scriptura docet, et universa Christi ecclesia a suo jam inde ortu usque ad hæc fere tempora credidit, nisi quod quadringentis aut quingentis ab hinc annis episcopus Romanus, cum papistarum quorundam assensu, novam quandam et recens excogitatam fidem exstruxerat; et hoc nobis deinceps credendum proposuerat: nempe quod hoc idem corpus reipsa, corporate, et sensibiliter, in hoc mundo remanserit, et sexcentis simul in locis sit, et in omnibus arculis, pixidibus, et panibus consecratis, inclusum delitescat.

CAPUT II.

DE DIFFERENTIA INTER VERAM ET PAPISTICAM DE PRÆSENTIA CHRISTI DOCTRINAM.

Quanquam Christum ita fatemur esse in omnibus, qui in illum credunt, ut carne et sanguine suo spiritualiter pascat et sustentet eos, et vitam largiatur æternam, ejusque rei certiores illos reddat, tum promissione verbi, tum sacramentali in cœna pane et vino, quæ eandem ob causam ante mortem suam instituerat; non parum tamen a gravissimis papistarum erroribus dissentimus.

1. Illi enim docent, Christum in pane et vino, ("id est, sub speciebus panis et vini") esse. Nos vero (quemadmodum veritas ipsa fert) Christum in illis esse docemus, qui digne panem hunc et vinum percipiunt.

2. Illi contendunt, ubi quis hæc elementa perceperit, Christum in os, fortasse etiam in ventriculum, sed non ulterius, ingredi. Nos vero dicimus Christum in toto homine

esse, tum in corpore, tum animo ejus, qui digne hæc elementa percipit, nedum in ventre aut ore.

3. Illi, Christum ore percipi, et cum pane ac vino intrare: nos, mente tantum ac animo percipi, et per fidem intrare, asseveramus.

4. Illi, Christum in sacramentali pane, etiam integrum annum asservato, vel quamdiu forma panis manet, reipsa inesse; sed post perceptionem sacramenti, ubi panis ore teritur, aut in ventre mutatur, in cœlum avolare disputant: sed nos Christum in homine, digne panem percipiente, remanere dicimus, quamdiu homo membrum Christi maneat.

5. Illi, in sacramento corporata Christi membra minime locis inter se disclusa esse, sed ubicunque caput sit, ibi pedes; et ubicunque brachia fuerint, ibi tibias; ita ut in singulis panis et vini frustulis integrum caput, integros pedes, carnem, sanguinem, cor, pulmonem, pectus, latera, omniaque confusa atque admixta, sine ulla partium vel distinctione vel differentia esse dicunt. O quam stolida hæc atque anilis excogitatio est, sanctissimum et perfectissimum Christi corpus in tam perturbatum et monstrosum corpus convertere! Et tamen nihil tam ineptum et nugatorium invenire papistæ possunt, quod non ab omnibus, quasi certissimum Dei oraculum et expressum fidei articulum, sine ulla dubitatione suscipi jubeant.

6. Hoc præterea papistæ asserunt, canem vel catum corpus Christi edere, si forte sacramentalem panem edant: nos vero dicimus, præter hominem, nullam terrenam creaturam percipere carnem aut sanguinem ejus posse.

7. Illi dicunt, tum bonos tum malos quosque corpus Christi edere: nos vero, utrosque sacramentalem panem et vinum percipere, sed neminem verum Christi corpus et sanguinem percipere, nisi qui vivum corporis ejus membrum fuerit.

8. Illi dicunt, bonos corpus et sanguinem Christi solummodo tum percipere, cum sacramentum percipiunt: nos dicimus, illos tam diu vesci, bibere, ali Christo, quamdiu membra corporis illius sunt.

9. Illi dicunt, corpus Christi in sacramento suam propriam formam et quantitatem habere: nos dicimus, Christum ibi sacramentaliter et spiritualiter adesse, sine ulla vel forma vel quantitate.

10. Illi dicunt, patres et prophetas veteris testamenti non percepisse corpus et sanguinem Christi: nos dicimus, illos corpus et sanguinem ejus percepisse, quamvis nondum natus aut incarnatus fuerit.

11. Illi dicunt, corpus Christi quotidie toties effici, quoties missatur, et ex pane ac vino tum effici: nos dicimus, Christi corpus semel tantum effectum, idque non ex panis et vini, sed beatæ virginis substantia.

12. Illi dicunt, missam sacrificium esse peccata expians, non rei oblatæ præstantia, sed offerentis sacerdotis religione: nos dicimus, hanc illorum sententiam insigne mendacium et fœdissimum errorem ad Christi gloriam evertendam esse. Nostra enim pro peccatis satisfactio neque religio neque oblatio sacerdotis est; sed unica pro universi mundi peccatis hostia et satisfactio est mors Christi, et corporis ejus in cruce oblatio, quam ipsemet semel tantum in cruce, et præter ipsum nemo unquam obtulit. Illæ itaque oblationes, quas sacrifici quotidie papisticis in missis offerunt, non possunt esse pro aliorum peccatis ministri religione satisfactio, sed vanissimum commentum et dolus malus diaboli sunt, quo antichristus multos jam annos elusit atque occæcavit mundum.

13. Illi dicunt, Christum corporate multis in locis uno atque eodem tempore simul esse, asseverantes ibi Christum revera et corporate præsentem, ubicunque panes consecrati fuerint: nos dicimus, quemadmodum sol corporate in cœlo et non alibi est, virtute tamen atque efficientia in terris est, cujus vi atque influxu mundana hæc gignuntur, aluntur, et ad naturæ perfectionem accedunt, ita Servator Christus corporate in cœlo est, ad dexteram Patris sedet, quamvis Spiritu promiserit se nobis in terris usque ad mundi interitum affuturum. Et quotiescunque duo aut tres in nomine ejus congregantur, in medio illorum est, cujus cœlesti gratia omnes pii per illum primo spiritualiter regenerantur, deinde augentur et crescunt ad spiritualem in Christo perfectionem, spiritualiter per fidem corpore et sanguine illius percipiendo, quanquam idem in cœlo corporate et longe ab oculorum nostrorum acie disclusus maneat.

CAPUT III.

SENTENTIÆ NOSTRÆ EX FIDEI SYMBOLO CONFIRMATIO.

Nunc vero, ut ad præcipuum sententiæ nostræ caput revertamur, ne hoc novum commentum videri posset, recens a nobis excogitatum, Christum, quod ad humanam naturam pertinet, in cœlo et non in terris esse, planum faciemus (volente Deo) non hoc fictitium aut nuperum esse, sed veterem et antiquam semper hanc fidem ecclesiæ catholicæ fuisse, usque dum papistæ multa novassent, et recens hoc de corporata Christi naturali et in sensum cadente permansione, et in capsula aut intra panis et vini ambitum inclusione, commentum invexissent. Hoc non aliam confirmationem postulat, quam generalem in fidei articulis omnium Christianorum professionem, ubi de humana Christi natura fide hoc constanter tenendum docemur: conceptum e Spiritu sancto Christum, natum ex Maria virgine, Pontio Pilato præside passum, in crucem actum, mortuum, sepultum, descendisse ad inferos, tertio die resurrexisse, in cœlum ascendisse ad dexteram Patris omnipotentis sedere, inde venturum ad vivos et mortuos judicandos.

Hæc semper fuerat Christianorum fides catholica, Christum (quod ad corpus et humanam naturam pertineret) in cœlo esse, et ibi permansurum, usque dum ad extremum judicium veniret.

Et quoniam in hac summa fidei nostræ de discessu ejus a terra et ascensu ejus ad cœlos expressa mentio facta est; siquidem fidem nostram ulla ratione attingeret, Christi corpus simul etiam in terris esse, hoc certe loco tanta necessitas illius commemorandi objecta fuit, ut illud haud dubie silentio præteritum non fuisset. Christus enim, si (quod ad humanam naturam spectat) tum sit hic, tum hinc discesserit, et horum utrumque fide nostra contineri debet; in publica fidei professione, ubi unius mentio facta est, debebat etiam alterius mentio fieri, ne dum hoc profiteremur, ab illa longe discederemus, cum tantum inter se dissentiant.

CAPUT IV.

EJUSDEM SENTENTIÆ EX SCRIPTURIS CONFIRMATIO.

Cum hoc fidei capite universa scriptura et antiqui ecclesiæ Christianæ patres consentiunt. Christus enim ipse ait: "Relinquo mundum, et abeo ad Patrem." Et alio loco: "Pauperes semper habebitis vobiscum, me autem non semper habebitis." Hujus ille nos erroris admonuit, his verbis: "Veniet tempus, cum multi impostores in mundo futuri sunt, et dicent, Ecce hic est Christus, et illic est Christus: sed ne credatis," inquit Christus. Et Marcus scribit, "Dominum Jesum in cœlum sublatum, et ad dexteram Patris sedere." Paulus hortatur omnes ut cœlestia quærant, "ubi Christus," inquit, "ad dexteram Dei Patris sedet." Et alibi: "Ejusmodi pontificem habemus, qui in cœlo sedet ad dexteram solii amplitudinis." Et, "Unica hostia pro peccatis oblata, ad dexteram Dei perpetuo sedet, de cetero expectans, usque dum hostes ejus scabellum sub pedes ejus subjiciantur." "Quem oportet cœlum suscipere usque ad tempus restitutionis omnium."

*Ob. 3.
Joan. xvi.
Matt. xxvi.
*Ob. 2.
Matt. xxiv.

Marc. xvi.
Col. iii.
Heb. x.

Heb. x.

Act. iii.

CAPUT V.

EJUSDEM SENTENTIÆ EX ANTIQUIS PATRIBUS CONFIRMATIO.

Atque hæc est perpetua veterum omnium ecclesiæ scriptorum de hac re sententia. Ac primo Origenes in Matthæum hanc causam disputat, quomodo Christus peregrinus appellari possit, qui in aliam regionem discesserit, cum nobiscum ipse sit usque ad mundi interitum, et adsit his omnibus, qui in nomine ejus congregantur. Ad hunc itaque modum loquitur: "Primum quæramus de peregrinatione ipsius, maxime quia peregrinationi ejus videtur esse contrarium, quod ipse de se discipulis suis promittit, dicens: 'Ubi fuerint duo vel tres congregati in nomine meo, ibi sum in medio eorum.' Item illud: 'Ecce ego vobiscum sum omnibus diebus, usque ad consummationem seculi.' Et quod Baptista dicit de eo, ubique cum esse demonstrans, ita: 'In medio autem vestrum

Origenes in Matt. cap. 25. hom. xxxiii.

stat, quem vos nescitis, ipse est qui post me venit.' Propterea dicet[1] aliquis, Si in medio etiam nescientium se stat; si ubicunque duo vel tres congregati fuerint in nomine ejus, inter eos habetur; si per omnes dies vitæ discipulorum cum eis est, usque ad consummationem seculi; quomodo in ista parabola proponitur peregrinans? Tractantes autem assumere debemus et illud quod Paulus ait de se: 'Ego autem absens corpore, præsens spiritu, jam judicavi ut præsens, congregatis vobis et meo spiritu cum virtute Domini Jesu, eum qui talis est tradere Sathanæ in interitum carnis, ut spiritus ejus salvus sit in die Domini nostri Jesu Christi.' Si enim virtus Jesu congregatur cum his qui congregantur in nomine ejus, non peregrinatur a suis, sed semper præsto est eis. Quod si semper omnibus suis est præsens, quomodo introducunt eum parabolæ ejus peregrinantem? Vide ut possumus solvere hoc modo quod quæritur. Qui enim dicit discipulis suis, 'Ecce ego vobiscum sum, usque ad consummationem seculi;' et item, 'Ubi fuerint duo vel tres congregati in nomine meo, ibi sum in medio eorum,' &c.; et qui in medio etiam nescientium se consistit, unigenitus Dei est, Deus Verbum, et Sapientia, et Justitia, et Veritas, qui non est corporeo ambitu circumclusus. Secundum hanc divinitatis suæ naturam non peregrinatur, sed peregrinatur secundum dispensationem corporis quod suscepit; secundum quod et turbatus est, et tristis factus est, dicens, 'Nunc anima mea turbatur:' et iterum, 'Tristis est anima mea usque ad mortem.' Hæc autem dicentes non solvimus suscepti corporis hominem (cum scriptum apud Joannem, 'Omnis spiritus qui solvit Jesum non est ex Deo,') sed unicuique substantiæ proprietatem reservamus."

His verbis Origenes aperte sententiam suam exposuit, Christi corpus nequaquam simul nobiscum præsens et absens esse. Id enim esset ex uno corpore duas naturas efficere, et corpus Christi dividere, cum fieri non posset, ut una eademque natura simul nobiscum sit, et longe a nobis absit. Docet itaque Origenes, ut præsentia ejus de divina natura, absentia autem de humana intelligatur.

Augustinus ad Dardanum epist. lvii.

In hanc quoque sententiam Augustinus in epistola ad Dardanum: "Noli itaque dubitare, ibi esse nunc hominem Christum Jesum, unde venturus est; memoriterque recole et fideliter tene Christianam confessionem, quoniam resurrexit a mortuis, ascendit in cœlum, sedet ad dexteram Patris, nec aliunde quam inde venturus est ad vivos mortuosque judicandos. Et sic venturus est (illa angelica voce testante) quemadmodum ire visus est in cœlum, id est, in eadem carnis forma atque substantia, cui profecto immortalitatem dedit, naturam non abstulit. Secundum hanc formam putandus non est ubique diffusus. Cavendum est enim, ne ita divinitatem astruamus hominis, ut veritatem corporis auferamus."

Hunc locum citat Leo, epistola ultima, ad probandum in Christo veram formam humanam. Et in tota epistola forma accipitur pro substantia.

Hæc Augustini verba aperta sunt: et statim adjicit: "Dominus Jesus est ubique per id quod Deus est; in cœlo autem per id quod homo." Et tandem sic concludit: "Dominum Jesum Christum ubique præsentem esse non dubites, tanquam Deum, et in eodem templo Dei esse tanquam inhabitantem Deum, et in loco aliquo cœli propter veri corporis modum."

*In Joan. Tract. xxx. * Ob. 230.*

Et rursus Augustinus in Joannem. "Dominus (inquit) Jesus sursum est, sed etiam hic est veritas Dominus. Corpus enim Domini in quo resurrexit, in uno loco esse opertet, veritas ejus ubique diffusa est."

Et alio ejusdem libri loco, in his Christi verbis explicandis, 'Pauperes semper habebitis vobiscum, me autem non semper habebitis,' Christum ait, "de corporis sui præsentia hæc locutum. Nam secundum majestatem suam (inquit Augustinus), secundum providentiam, secundum ineffabilem et invisibilem gratiam, impletur quod ab eo dictum est, 'Ecce ego vobiscum sum usque ad consummationem seculi:' secundum carnem vero (quam Verbum assumpsit), secundum id quod de virgine natus est, secundum id quod a Judæis compræhensus est, quod ligno crucifixus, quod de cruce depositus, quod linteis involutus, quod in sepulchro conditus, quod in resurrectione manifestatus, non semper habebitis me vobiscum. Quare cum conversatus est secundum corporis præsentiam quadraginta diebus cum discipulis suis, et eis deducentibus, videndo ac sequendo, ascendit in cœlum, et non est hic, (ibi enim sedat ad dexteram Dei Patris,) et est hic, non enim recessit præsentia majestatis. Aliter secundum præsentiam majestatis semper habemus Christum; secundum præsentiam carnis recte dictum est discipulis, 'Me autem

---

[1 Dicit, ed. 1553.]

non semper habebitis.' Habuit enim illum ecclesia, secundum præsentiam carnis, paucis diebus: modo fide tenet, oculis non videt. Ergo si ita dictum est, 'Me autem non semper habebitis,' quæstio, sicut arbitror, jam nulla est, quæ duobus modis soluta est." Hucusque Augustinus.

In alio autem libro, qui Augustino inscribitur, hæc verba insunt: "Dei Filium secundum substantiam divinitatis suæ invisibilem, incorporeum, immortalem et incircumscriptum, nos credere et confiteri oportet: juxta humanitatem vero visibilem, corporeum, localem, atque omnia membra humana veraciter habentem, credere convenit et confiteri." *De Essentia Divinitatis.*

Augustinus de Verbis Domini, Sermone 53. "In cœlis Christus erat et persecutori dicebat, 'Quid me persequeris?' Ubi Dominus expressit sic, et hic se esse in nobis. Sic totus crescit, quia quemadmodum ille in nobis hic, sic et nos ibi in illo sumus." Idem in Joan. tract. 50. "Quomodo tenebo absentem? Quomodo in cœlum manum mittam, ut ibi sedentem teneam? Fidem mitte, et tenuisti: parentes tui tenuerunt carne; tu tene corde, quoniam Christus absens etiam præsens est. Nisi præsens esset, a nobis teneri non posset: sed quoniam verum est quod ait, 'Ecce ego vobiscum sum,' &c. et abiit et hic est, et rediit et nos deseruit. Corpus suum intulit cœlo, majestatem non abstulit mundo." Et mox: "'Me autem non semper habebitis.' Quid est enim 'non semper?' Si bonus es, si ad corpus Christi pertines (quod significat Petrus), habes Christum et in præsenti, et in futuro: in presenti per fidem, in præsenti per signum, in præsenti per baptismi sacramentum, in præsenti per altaris cibum et potum." Idem in Joan. tract. 102. super illis verbis, 'Relinquo mundum,' &c. "Reliquit mundum corporali discessione; perrexit ad Patrem hominis ascensione; nec mundum deseruit præsentiæ gubernatione."

Idem de Symbolo ad Catechumenos, Lib. ii. "Quis est iste sponsus absens et præsens? Quis est iste sponsus præsens et latens; quem sponsa ecclesia fide tantum concipit, et sine ullo amplexu membra ejus quotidie parit?" Et mox: "Ipsa est virtus omnipotentiæ tuæ, ut plus possis in ipsis fidelibus, quando absens ab eis in homine illo suscepto sentiris: ceterum præsentia tuæ majestatis de cordibus fidelium tuorum nunquam discedis." Et mox: "Accepit Petrus ut moreretur pro absente, quem desperando negaverat præsentem."

Ex his Augustini dictis perspicuum est, hanc catholicæ fidei professionem esse, Christum juxta corpoream hominis naturam in cœlo esse, et minime nobiscum in terris præsentem esse. Hæc enim est propria veri corporis natura, ut unius loci spatio contineatur, non autem vel ubique sit, vel multis simul locis diffundatur. Quanquam autem Christi corpus post resurrectionem immortale factum sit, hæc tamen corporis natura minime ablata est: tum enim (sicuti Augustinus ait) verum corpus non esset. Viam præterea et rationem, qua Christus hic nobiscum præsens in terris, et absens sit, Augustinus demonstrat: ait enim illum divina natura, majestate, providentia et gratia præsentem esse; humana natura et corporea absentem ad hoc mundo, et præsentem in cœlo esse.

Cyrillus in evangelium Joannis cum hac Augustini sententia convenit, ita loquens:

"Etsi Christus corporis sui præsentiam hinc subduxit, majestate tamen divinitatis semper adest, sicut ipse a discipulis abiturus pollicetur: 'Ecce ego vobiscum sum omnibus diebus usque ad consummationem seculi'." *Cyrillus in Joannem, Lib. vi. cap. 14.*

Rursus alio loco sic scribit:

"Credere oportet fideles, quamvis a nobis corpore absit, virtute tamen sua omnia et nos gubernari, adesseque semper ipsum omnibus qui eum diligunt. Propterea dicebat: 'Amen amen dico vobis, ubicunque sunt duo vel tres congregati in nomine meo, ibi sum in medio eorum.' Nam quemadmodum, quando ut homo in terra conversabatur, tunc etiam cœlos implebat, et angelorum consortia non relinquebat; eodem nunc modo, quum sit in cœlis cum carne, terram tamen replet, et cum eis est qui eum diligunt. Observandum autem est, quia quamvis secundum carnem solummodo abiturus erat (adest enim semper virtute Deitatis, ut diximus), modico tamen tempore cum discipulis se futurum dicebat." Hæc Cyrillus. *Lib. ix. cap. 21.*

Eodem modo Ambrosius ait, "Christum nec supra terram, nec in terra quærendum esse, sed in cœlo, ubi sedet ad dexteram Patris." *Ambros. in Luc. Lib. x. cap. 14.*

[CRANMER.]

Gregorius in Hom. Paschali.

Quid Gregorius? annon eodem spiritu ductus, conspirasse videbatur cum ceteris, quum ita scribit? "Christus," inquit, "non est hic per præsentiam carnis, qui tamen nusquam deest per præsentiam majestatis." Beda in homilia Paschali quadam super illis verbis, 'Ecce ego vobiscum sum:' "Ipse Deus et homo assumptus est humanitate, quam de terra susceperat; manet cum sanctis in terra divinitate, qua terram pariter implet et cœlum." Idem super illis verbis, 'Modicum jam, et non videbitis me:' "Ac si aperte diceret: Propterea me suscitatum a mortuis modico tempore videbitis quia non semper in terra corporaliter mansurus, sed per humilitatem quam assumpsi jam sum ascensurus in cœlum." Idem in homilia in vigilia pentecostes: "Ille post resurrectionem ascendens in cœlum, eos corporaliter deseruit, quibus tamen divinæ præsentia majestatis nunquam defuit: ideo recte de hoc paracleto subjunxit, 'Ut maneat vobiscum in æternum'."

Quas hic subtilitates (quæso) papistæ reperire poterunt ad hunc perniciosum errorem defendendum, Christum in humana natura corporate in consecratis pane et vino inesse, cum universa Christi catholica et antiqua ecclesia longe diversum senserit, et antiqui patres longe diversum scripserint?

Omnes enim affirmarunt et crediderunt Christum unam tantum personam, duas naturas et substantias habere, divinam et humanam. Aiunt præterea Christum hinc in cœlum abiisse, atque etiam nobiscum in terris esse, sed non humanitus, quemadmodum papistæ contendunt. Nam quod ad eam naturam spectat, in cœlo esse dicunt; hic tamen atque illic et ubique divinitus esse. Quamvis enim divina illius natura infinita, immensa, interminata sit, nullis locorum, regionum, aut temporum finibus circumscripta, sed ubique sit, et universa compleat; ea est tamen naturæ suæ humanæ conditio, ut mensura, spatio, loco, tempore terminetur: ita ut cum hic in terris versaretur, in cœlo non fuerit; et nunc, cum in cœlum ascenderit, quod ad eam naturam spectat, terram reliquerit, et in cœlo tantum existat.

CAPUT VI.

UNUM CORPUS EODEM TEMPORE DIVERSIS IN LOCIS ESSE NON POTEST.

*Ob. 11.

Ejus autem naturæ, quæ locorum spatio definitur, hoc proprium est, ut diversis in locis uno atque eodem tempore esse non possit. Atque hæc antiquæ ecclesiæ catholicæ fides fuit, quemadmodum non modo ex superius citatis auctoribus, verum etiam ex sequentibus facile liquebit.

Aug. ad Dardanum, epistola lvii.
*Ob. 234.
Cyrill. De Trin. Lib. ii.

Augustinus, probaturus necessario corpus quodam loco contineri, "Spatia," inquit, "locorum tolle corporibus, nusquam erunt: et quia nusquam erunt, nec erunt."

Et Cyrillus, veri corporis propriam naturam considerans, dixit: "Si divina natura corpus esset, et in loco omnino et in magnitudine et quantitate esset, nec effugeret circumscriptionem."

Quod si divina natura corpus esset, necessario circumscriberetur: multo magis humana natura Christi circumscribetur, et certis locorum finibus terminabitur.

Didymus de Spiritu Sanc. Lib. i. cap. 1.
*Ob. 182.

Didymus in libro de Spiritu sancto, Spiritum sanctum probat esse Deum, quia multis in locis simul existit: quod cadere in creaturam nullam potest. "Ipse Spiritus sanctus," inquit, "si unus de creaturis esset, saltem circumscriptam haberet substantiam, sicut universa quæ facta sunt. Nam etsi non circumscribantur loco et finibus invisibiles creaturæ, tamen proprietate substantiæ finiuntur. Spiritus autem sanctus cum in pluribus sit, non habet substantiam circumscriptam."

*Ob. ead.
Basilius de Spiritu Sanc. cap. 22.

Idem etiam affirmat Basilius. "Angelus," inquit, "qui astitit Cornelio, non erat in eodem loco etiam apud Philippum: neque qui ab altari Zachariam alloquebatur, eodem tempore etiam in cœlo propriam sedem ac stationem implebat. At vero Spiritus simul in Abacuc, et in Daniele in Babylonia operari creditus est, et in cataracta cum Hieremia esse dictus est, et cum Ezechiele in Chobar." Quo argumento probat Spiritum sanctum esse Deum.

Quamobrem papistæ (qui corpus Christi uno atque eodem tempore infinitis pene locis constituunt) corpus illius Deum faciunt, atque adeo duas in Christo naturas confundunt, humanæ illud naturæ tribuentes, quod est divinæ proprium: qua re nihil perniciosius aut nefarium magis esse potest.

Contra quos Fulgentius, de duarum in Christo naturarum distinctione loquens, sic disputat: Fulgentius ad Trasimundum Regem, Lib. ii. *Ob. 249.

"Christus unus idemque homo localis ex homine, qui est Deus immensus ex Patre, unus idemque secundum humanam substantiam absens cœlo, cum esset in terra, et derelinquens terram cum ascendisset in cœlum; secundum divinam vero immensamque substantiam nec cœlum dimittens, cum de cœlo descendit, nec terram deserens, cum ad cœlum ascendit. Quod ipsius Domini certissimo potest cognosci sermone, qui ut localem ostenderet humanitatem suam, dicit discipulis suis: 'Ascendo ad Patrem meum, et Patrem vestrum; Deum meum, et Deum vestrum.' De Lazaro quoque cum dixisset, 'Lazarus mortuus est,' adjunxit, dicens: 'Et gaudeo propter vos, ut credatis, quoniam non eram ibi.' Immensitatem vero suæ divinitatis ostendens discipulis dicit: 'Ecce ego vobiscum sum omnibus diebus usque ad consummationem seculi.' Quomodo autem ascendit in cœlum, nisi quia localis et verus est homo? Aut quomodo adest fidelibus suis, nisi quia idem immensus et verus est Deus?" Joan. xvi.
Joan. xi.
Matt. xxviii.

Et Lib. iii. "Idem atque inseparabilis Christus secundum solam carnem de sepulchro surrexit: secundum totum hominem quem accepit, terram localiter deserens, ad cœlum ascendit, et in dextris Dei sedet: secundum eundem totum hominem venturus est ad judicandum vivos et mortuos."

Ex his Fulgentii verbis apertissime cernitur, Christum nisi divinitus nobiscum in terris esse non posse, humanitus autem in cœlo tantum esse, et a nobis absentem esse.

Quod si istis aliquid clarius et luculentius dici possit, a Vigilio episcopo et martyre hæc clarius dicuntur. Etenim adversus Eutychen hæreticum (qui Christi humanitatem sustulit, et solum Deum, non etiam hominem, fuisse sensit) disputans, in illius errore confutando probat Christi duas naturas, humanam et divinam, unius personæ conjunctione contineri, his verbis: Vigilius contra Eutychen, Lib. i.

"Dixit Christus discipulis suis, 'Si diligeretis me, gauderetis, quia vado ad Patrem: quia Pater major me est.' Et iterum, 'Expedit vobis ut ego eam. Si enim ego non abiero, Paracletus ad vos non veniet.' Et certe Verbum Dei, Virtus Dei, Sapientia Dei, semper ad Patrem et in Patre fuit, etiam quando in nobis nobiscum fuit. Neque enim cum terrena misericorditer incoluit, de cœlesti habitatione recessit: cum Patre enim ubique est totus pari divinitate, quem nullus continet locus. Plena sunt quippe omnia Filio, nec est aliquis locus divinitatis ejus præsentia vacuus. Unde ergo et quo se iturum dicit; aut quomodo se ad Patrem perrecturum adserat, a quo sine dubio nunquam recessit? Sed hoc erat ire ad Patrem et recedere a nobis, auferre de hoc mundo naturam, quam susceperat ex nobis. Vides ergo eidem naturæ proprium fuisse, ut auferretur et abiret a nobis, quæ in fine temporum reddenda est nobis, secundum attestantium vocem angelorum: 'Hic Jesus qui receptus est a vobis, sic veniet, quemadmodum vidistis eum euntem in cœlum.' Nam vide miraculum: vide utriusque proprietatis mysterium. Dei Filius secundum humanitatem suam recessit a nobis; secundum divinitatem suam ait nobis, 'Ecce ego vobiscum sum omnibus diebus usque ad consummationem seculi'." Joan. xiv.
Joan. xvi.
Act. i.
*Ob. 251.
Matt. ult.

Hucusque Vigilius: et paulo post concludit hoc modo. "Et nobiscum est, et non est nobiscum: quia quos reliquit, et a quibus discessit humanitate sua, non reliquit nec deseruit divinitate sua. Per formam enim servi, quam abstulit a nobis in cœlum, absens est a nobis: per formam Dei, quæ non recedit a nobis, in terris præsens est nobis; tamen et præsens et absens ipse unus idemque est nobis." Hoc modo Vigilium audistis loquentem, Christum, quod ad corporis sui præsentiam et humanam naturam attinet, discessisse a nobis, sublatum a nobis, in cœlum ascendisse, non esse nobiscum, reliquisse nos, deseruisse nos; divinitus autem nobiscum perpetuo esse; atque adeo nobiscum esse, et non nobiscum; nobiscum divinitus, humanitus autem non nobiscum.

Quod ipsum alio etiam loco planissime Vigilius declarat his verbis: Contra Eutychen, Lib. iv.

"Si Verbi et carnis una natura est, quomodo cum Verbum ubique sit, non ubique inveniatur et caro? namque quando in terra fuit, non erat utique in cœlo: et nunc quia in cœlo est, non est utique in terra. Et in tantum non est, ut secundum ipsam

Christum spectemus venturum de cœlo, quem secundum Verbum nebiscum esse credimus in terra. Igitur secundum vos, aut Verbum cum carne sua loco continetur, aut caro cum verbo ubique est, quoniam una natura contrarium quid et diversum non recipit in se ipsa. Diversum est autem et longe dissimile, circumscribi loco, et ubique esse. Et quia Verbum ubique est, caro autem ejus ubique non est, apparet unum eundemque Christum utriusque esse naturæ, et esse quidem ubique secundum naturam divinitatis suæ, et loco contineri secundum naturam humanitatis suæ: creatum esse, et initium non habere: morti subjacere, et mori non posse: quod unum illi est ex natura Verbi, qua Deus est, aliud ex natura carnis, quia idem Deus homo est. Igitur unus Dei Filius, idemque hominis factus filius, habet initium ex natura carnis suæ, et non habet initium ex natura divinitatis suæ: creatus est per naturam carnis suæ, et non est creatus per naturam divinitatis suæ: circumscribitur loco per naturam carnis suæ, et loco non capitur per naturam divinitatis suæ: minor est etiam angelis per naturam carnis suæ, et æqualis est Patri secundum naturam divinitatis suæ: mortuus est natura carnis suæ, et non est mortuus natura divinitatis suæ. Hæc est fides et confessio catholica, quam apostoli tradiderunt, martyres roboraverunt, et fideles nunc usque custodiunt."

Hæc Vigilius, qui prædictorum scriptorum auctoritatem et sententiam sequutus, ex apostolorum, martyrum, omniumque ea ætate Christianorum fide et catholica confessione confirmat, Christum humanitus, cum in terris versaretur, in cœlo non fuisse; et nunc, cum in cœlo sit, in terris non esse. Nulla enim creaturæ cujusque natura contineri simul loco in cœlo potest, et in terris eodem tempore esse. Quoniam autem Christus nobiscum in terris est, atque etiam locum in cœlo terminatum habet, ex eo efficit, Christum duas in se naturas habere, humanam qua discessit a nobis et in cœlum ascendit, et divinam qua nobiscum in terris degit: itaque minime eandem esse naturam, quæ abiit a nobis, et quæ hic permanet, aut quæ loco definita conscendit in cœlum, et quæ nobiscum in terris commoratur.

Quocirca papistæ, qui recentem nuper fidei articulum confinxerunt, (Christi videlicet naturale corpus revera et naturaliter tum hic in terris nobiscum versari, tum in cœlo ad dexteram Patris sedere,) duas gravissimas in hæreses prolabuntur:

Duæ papistarum hæreses. Unam, quod duas naturas, divinitatem et humanitatem, confundunt; illud humanitati tribuentes, quod divinitatis solius est proprium, ut in cœlo et terra multisque in locis simul sit.

Alteram, quod corpus seu humanam naturam ejus in duas partes dividunt, et ex una natura duas fingunt; unam in cœlo aspectabilem, tractabilem, omnes artus, partes, et universam formam veri et perfecti hominis (ut natura postulat) complexam; alteram, quam ferunt hic in terris sub omni pane et vino consecrato occultari, nulla membrorum forma aut ordine aut distinctione præditam. Quæ cum pugnantia atque adversa sibi inter se sint, una natura (sicuti sanctissimus martyr Vigilius docet) contineri non possunt.

CAPUT VII.

RESPONDETUR PAPISTIS VERBA CHRISTI, HOC EST CORPUS MEUM, PRO SE OBJICIENTIBUS.

Jam vero, cum non modo scripturæ auctoritas et veterum patrum sententiæ aperte et plane doceant, Christum Servatorem nostrum humanitus in cœlum ascendisse, et in terris non esse, atque hæc vera et catholica fuerit ab ascensu Christi fides; considerandum nobis est diligenti attentione, quibus rationibus inducti papistæ novam sibi doctrinam gignebant, et quas scripturas ad opinionis suæ defensionem adducunt. Quid illos commoverit nescio, nisi forte quod poeta dixit, "Mala mens, malus animus;" aut etiam sedis Romanæ (quam illi sanctissimam judicant) quædam jamdiu insita depravatio, quæ ex aliis omnibus maxime est Christo infesta, atque adeo dignissima quæ antichristi sedes appelletur. E scriptura nihil præterquam unum, et illud male intellectum, afferunt: quod (ut pro illis facere possit) ita contorquent, ut a ceteris omnibus scripturis ad idem pertinentibus planissime discrepet.

"Christus acceptum panem (inquiunt) benedixit et fregit, et dedit discipulis, dicens: Hoc est corpus meum." Hæc verba assidue repetunt atque inculcant, "Hoc est corpus meum." Hæc sacra illorum anchora est, qua tum realem (sicut ipsi loquuntur) et naturalem Christi præsentiam in sacramento, tum fictitiam suam transubstantiationem, propugnant. Hæc verba Christi (aiunt) certissima et planissima sunt: quoniam igitur ipse dixit, "Hoc est corpus meum," necessario concluditur, hoc quod sacrifici manibus continetur esse corpus Christi: quæ cum ita sint, panis esse non potest. Itaque efficiunt, Christi corpus ibi re ipsa præsens esse, panem autem non adesse. Argumentum papistarum.
Mar. An. fol. 169.

Sed quoniam universa illorum confirmatio his Christi verbis nititur, "Hoc est corpus meum," verus et germanus horum verborum sensus exquirendus est. Sed quid (inquiunt) indagatione hic ulla aut inquisitione opus est? Quid his verbis magis apertum aut perspicuum esse potest, "Hoc est corpus meum?"

Negari sane non potest, hæc verba apertissime dici, sed sensum illorum non ita planum esse his qui accurate considerant contextus illius circumstantias, manifestum est. Nam cum Christus panem discipulis suis dederat, et dixerat, "Hoc est corpus meum," nemo est qui mediocrem rerum intelligentiam et cognitionem habeat, quin ex verborum ipsorum serie intelligat, Christum hæc de pane loquutum, atque illum corpus suum vocavisse: quemadmodum permulti ex antiquis patribus (reclamantibus ei rei papistis) affirmant. Quocirca alium subesse verbis sensum necesse est, quam præ se ferunt, et aliquam occultari figuram, quæ in verba ipsa leviter intuentibus non apparet. Nam si hæc propria loquendi forma esset, et non figurata, necessario relinqueretur panem esse Christi corpus, et Christi corpus esse panem: a qua re christianæ aures longissime abhorrent. In his igitur verbis aliud quærendum est, quam verba ipsa præ se ferunt. Responsio.
Christi locutio figurata fuit.

Hilarius de Trin. Lib. iv. "Intelligentia dictorum ex causis est assumenda dicendi; quia non sermoni res, sed rei est sermo subjectus." Et Lib. ix. "Dictorum intelligentia aut ex præpositis aut ex sequentibus est expectanda."

CAPUT VIII.

CHRISTUS PANEM CORPUS SUUM ET VINUM SANGUINEM SUUM VOCAVIT.

Et quanquam verus horum verborum sensus, ubi de transubstantiatione agebatur, satis explicatus sit; ut res tamen planior atque evidentior fiat, et nulla difficultas aut ambiguitas remaneat, plenius hic (quoniam ita se occasio offert) eandem rem tractabimus. Series autem ipsa et contextus orationis satis planum faciet, hæc verba Christi, "Hoc est corpus meum," et, "Hic est sanguis meus," figurata esse. Et quanquam ex ipso evangelio satis liquet, et satis multum probatum sit in eo loco, in quo de transubstantiatione agebatur, Christum hæc verba, "Hoc est corpus meum," de pane, et, "Hic est sanguis meus," de vino loquutum; ne tamen papistæ cavillentur, nostra hæc commenta esse, domi nostræ orta, et non ex antiquorum fontibus hausta, veterum sententias ponemus in medium, et hanc veram atque antiquam catholicæ ecclesiæ fidem esse demonstrabimus: cum neque scholastici neque papistæ auctorem vel unum quidem ex antiquis habeant, quem adversus ista proferre possint. Ac primum Clemens in Pædago. Lib. i. cap. 6. "Dominus dixit: 'Comedite carnes meas et bibite sanguinem meum;' evidenter fidei et promissionis quod est esculentum et poculentum dicens allegorice, per quæ ecclesia tanquam homo ex multis constans membris irrigatur et augetur." Clemens ut supra, Lib. ii. cap. 5.

Justinus in Apolo. II. "Hoc alimentum apud nos eucharistia dicitur, cujus participem esse nemini licet, nisi qui crediderit vera esse, quæ a nobis docentur, et lavacro regenerationis in remissionem peccatorum lotus fuerit, et ad eum modum quem Christus tradidit vitam instituerit. Non enim ut communem panem, aut communem potum, hæc accipimus; sed quemadmodum Jesus Christus Servator noster, per verbum Dei factus caro, et carnem et sanguinem nostræ salutis causa habuit, sic etiam cibum illum, postquam per precationem verbi illius fuerit benedictus, ex quo sanguis et carnes nostræ per mutationem nutriuntur, edocti sumus esse carnem et sanguinem illius Jesu, qui pro nobis fuit incarnatus. Apostoli enim in commentariis ab eis factis (quæ dicuntur evangelia) sic tradiderunt præcepisse illis Jesum: cum accepisset panem, gratias agentem dixisse, Justinus.

'Hoc facite in mei commemorationem,' 'Hoc est corpus meum,' 'Hic est sanguis meus,' et solis ipsis impartisse."

Irenæus.

Deinde Irenæus in quarto adversus Valentinianos libro, cap. 32, ait: "Christus suis discipulis dans consilium, primitias Deo offerre de suis creaturis (non quasi indigenti, sed ut ipsi nec infructuosi nec ingrati sint), eum qui ex creatura panis est accepit, et gratias egit dicens: 'Hoc est corpus meum.' Et calicem similiter, qui est ex ea creatura quæ est secundum nos, suum sanguinem confessus est, et novi testamenti novam docuit oblationem." Et cap. 34: "Panis in quo gratiæ actæ sunt, qui est a terra, percipiens vocationem Dei, jam non communis panis est, sed eucharistia, ex duabus rebus constans, terrena et cœlesti." Atque etiam eodem in libro ad hunc modum: "Christus, hujus conditionis quæ est secundum nos accipiens panem, suum corpus confitebatur; et temperamentum calicis, suum sanguinem confirmavit."

Ob. 156.

Ob. 157. Cap. 34.

Ob. 154.

Cap. 57. Lib. v.

In quinto autem sic scribit: "De calice, qui est sanguis ejus, homo nutritur, et de pane, qui est corpus ejus, augetur." Et ibidem: "Quando mixtus calix et fractus panis percipit verbum Dei, fit eucharistia corporis et sanguinis Christi, ex quibus augetur et consistit carnis nostræ substantia."

Hæc Irenæi verba apertissima sunt, Christum verum et materiatum panem, Dei creaturam, et eundem cum nostro vulgari ac communi pane, accepisse, et corpus suum appellasse, cum diceret, "Hoc est corpus meum:" similiter etiam vinum, quo corpora nostra aluntur ac recreantur, sanguinem suum vocavisse.

Tertul. adversus Judæos.
Ob. 159.
Ob. 161.

Quid Tertullianus? annon in libro adversus Judæos scribit, "Christum panem vocavisse corpus suum?" Et adversus Marcionem, hæc eadem verba sæpius repetit.

Quære postea, cap. xi.

Cyprianus ad Magnum, Lib. i. Epis. 6.
Ob. 170.

Cyprianus autem in primo epistolarum libro hoc idem affert: "Dominus corpus suum panem vocat, de multorum granorum adunatione congestum: et sanguinem suum vinum appellat, de botris atque acinis plurimis expressum, atque in vinum coactum."

Lib. ii. Epistola 3.

Et in secundo libro hæc ait: "Sanguis Christi non aqua est utique, sed vinum." Rursus in eadem epistola ait, "Vinum fuisse, quod sanguinem suum Christus dixit; et quod de creatura vitis novum vinum cum Christo in regno Patris non bibemus, si in sacrificio Dei Patris et Christi vinum non offerimus." Et in eadem epistola scribit: "Corpus Domini non potest esse forma sola, aut aqua sola, nisi utrumque adunatum fuerit et copulatum, et panis unius compage solidatum."

Ob. 177.

Ob. 186. Epiphanius in Ancorato.

Huic consentit Epiphanius, dicens: "Christus de eo quod rotundæ est figuræ, et insensibile quantum ad potentiam, voluit per gratiam dicere, 'Hoc est corpus'."

Ob. 26. Hieronymus ad Hedibiam.

Hieronymus item, scribens ad Hedibiam, hæc habet verba: "Nos audiamus, panem, quem fregit Dominus, deditque discipulis suis, esse corpus Domini Salvatoris, ipso dicente ad eos, 'Accipite et comedite; hoc est corpus meum:' et calicem illum esse de quo item loquutus est, 'Bibite ex hoc omnes: hic est sanguis meus novi testamenti, qui pro multis effundetur,' &c. Iste est calix de quo in propheta legimus, 'Calicem salutaris accipiam;' et alibi, 'Calix tuus inebrians quam præclarus est'."

Ob. 240. Augustinus de Tri. Lib. iii. cap. 4.

Augustinus item dicit, quod "etsi licet Dominum Jesum Christum prædicare per linguam, per epistolam, et per sacramentum corporis et sanguinis ejus, tamen nec linguam, nec membranas, nec atramentum, nec significantes sonos lingua editos, nec signa literarum conscripta pelliculis, corpus Christi et sanguinem dicimus, sed illud tantum, quod ex fructibus terræ acceptum, et prece mystica consecratum, rite sumimus ad salutem spiritualem, in memoriam pro nobis dominicæ passionis." Idem alio loco dicit: "Dominus Jesus corpus dixit escam, sanguinem potum."

Ob. 237. De verbis Apostoli, Serm. 2.

Cyrillus, Lib. xii. cap. 58. "Fractum panem distribuebat, dicens: 'Hoc est corpus meum'."

Ob. 217. Cyrill. in Joan. Lib. iv. cap. 14.

His suffragatur Cyrillus, sic scribens: "Christus discipulis fragmenta panis dedit, dicens: 'Accipite et manducate: hoc est corpus meum'."

Ob. 246. Theodoretus, Dial. i.

Similiter Theodoretus ait: "In ipsa mysteriorum traditione Christus corpus panem vocavit, et sanguinem poculum mixtum."

Rabanus.

Rabanus, Lib. i. cap. 31. "Quia panis corporalis cor confirmat, ideo ille corpus Christi congruenter nuncupatur. Vinum autem, quia sanguinem operatur in carne, ideo ad sanguinem Christi refertur."

Ex his et permultis aliis clarissimorum patrum testimoniis facile intelligitur, Christum

Servatorem, cum panem dedisset discipulis, dicens, "Accipite et edite; hoc est corpus meum;" et cum poculum porrexisset, jubens ut inter se dividerent, et ex eo omnes biberent, illud sanguinis nomine appellans, panem materiatum corpus suum, et vinum ex uvis expressum sanguinem suum nominasse: panem videlicet illum, qui terrena apud nos creatura est, qui ex terra funditur, ex multis tritici granis conficitur, in farinam molitur, aquæ admixtus pinsitur, et panis efficitur, sensus et rationis est expers, et qui corpora nostra alit et sustentat, illum (inquam) panem Christus corpus suum appellavit his verbis: "Hoc est corpus meum." Et illud vinum quod ex multis acinis collectum, et ex uvis expressum, liquorem habet corpora nostra rigantem et nutrientem, Christus sanguinem suum appellavit.

Hæc vera est Christi doctrina, tum sacræ scripturæ, tum antiquorum patrum (partim Græcorum, partim Latinorum) auctoritate confirmata, Christum videlicet cum panem et vinum distribuisset discipulis, et hæc verba dixisset, "Hoc est corpus meum," et "Hic est sanguis meus," panem et vinum permansisse, et corporis ac sanguinis nomine appellata esse.

Nunc vero auctoritatem aliquam afferant papistæ, vel ex scripturis, vel ex sanctis patribus, ad opinionis suæ defensionem corroborandam: neque ceteros cogant hæc suarum opinionum commenta sequi, hoc tantum nomine quia sic ipsi dicunt, et nihil præterea solidum aut firmum præter suam ipsorum assertionem afferunt. Talis enim fides verbo Dei tantum, non humano, adhibenda est.

Quotquot ex illis ego legi (Wintoniensem solum excipio), dicunt Christum, cum diceret, "Hoc est corpus meum," et "Hic est sanguis meus," neque panem corpus, neque vinum sanguinem suum appellasse: et in his tamen explicandis hærent, et magna opinionum dissensione sunt, quod incertæ illorum doctrinæ certum est testimonium.

Quidam enim ex illis dicunt, in pronomine demonstrativo 'hoc' Christum intellexisse, non panem aut vinum, sed corpus et sanguinem suum. *Ob. 15.

Alii autem sentiunt in pronomine 'hoc' Christum neque panem aut vinum, neque corpus aut sanguinem intellexisse, sed indefinitum aliquid et incertum, quod illi individuum vagum, aut individuum in genere nominant; aliquid mathematicum arbitror, aut aliud quid, quod ne illi quidem ipsi comprehendere animo et intelligentia possunt.

Sed conferant se in unum omnes papistæ, et ostendant (si possunt) vel scripturæ vel alicujus Græci aut Latini scriptoris auctoritate, qui quidem antiquus et probatus est, Christum neque panem, neque vinum, sed individuum aliquod vagum, corpus suum appellasse; et ego, quod ad me attinet, illis cedam, et fatebor illos vera sentire.

Quod si nihil antiquum habent, quod pro se afferant, sed ipsi sibi ipsis suæ fidei et doctrinæ auctores sunt, æquum et par est, ut veritati scripturarum et patrum sententiis confirmatæ cedant, et fateantur, Christum panem materiatum corpus suum appellasse, et vinum ex uvis confectum sanguinem suum nominasse.

CAPUT IX.

PANEM ESSE CORPUS CHRISTI, ET VINUM SANGUINEM, SIMILITER EDERE CHRISTI CORPUS, ET BIBERE ILLIUS SANGUINEM, SUNT FORMÆ LOQUENDI FIGURATÆ.

His ita constitutis, necessario efficitur, hanc loquendi formam esse figuratam. Si enim proprie et simpliciter loquamur, minime verum est, panem esse Christi corpus, et vinum sanguinem. Christi enim corpus anima, vita, sensu et ratione est præditum; at panis animæ, vitæ, sensus, rationis est expers.

Eodem modo, si proprie loquamur, verum non est, nos Christi corpus edere et sanguinem ejus bibere. Edere enim et bibere (si proprie significant) est lingua, dentibus, labiis arripere, mandere, comminuere, deglutire; quod Christi carni et sanguini facere, horroris plenum est.

Hæ igitur formæ dicendi, Christi corpus edere, et sanguinem ejus bibere, et panem corpus, et vinum sanguinem ejus dicere, figuratæ dicendi formæ sunt; altera a propria corporearum rerum significatione ad spiritualem intelligentiam traducta, in altera signis rerum significatarum nomine appellatis. Quod genus nec novum nec infrequens esse solet, sed commune, et sermone quotidiano passim usurpatum.

CAPUT X.

QUOD EDERE CORPUS CHRISTI ET BIBERE ILLIUS SANGUINEM FIGURATÆ SUNT LOCUTIONES, COMPROBATIO.

ATQUE ut ne hoc nobis vitii assignetur, nostra hæc commenta esse, nosque (ut papistæ solent) ista sine aliorum auctoritate affingere, ad hæc probanda cum scripturæ auctoritatem, tum veterum sententias ascribemus.

Joan. vi.   Primum, ubi Servator Christus apud Joannem dixit, se panem vitæ esse; qui ex eo pane ederit, non moriturum, sed vitam sempiternam acturum; et panem quem ille daturus esset, carnem esse suam; itaque quicunque carnem ejus ederit et sanguinem ejus biberit, vitam æternam habiturum; qui autem carnem ejus non ederit, nec sanguinem ejus biberit, vitam æternam non habiturum: ubi Christus hæc et permulta alia de carnis et sanguinis sui manducatione et potatione disputasset, tum Judæi, tum permulti alii ex discipulis ejus offendebantur, et dixerant, Dura hæc oratio est; quis enim dare nobis carnem suam edendam poterit? Tum Christus murmurantes illos intelligens, quoniam aliam carnis manducationem animo complecti non poterant, quam quæ in mandendo cibo et deglutiendo fit, ut animos illorum a tam crassa et carnali cogitatione abduceret, et ad veram manducationis intelligentiam transferret, "Quid (inquit) si videretis Filium hominis ascendentem, ubi fuit prius? Spiritus est qui vivificat, caro nihil prodest. Hæc quæ loquor spiritus et vita sunt."

Hanc orationem Servator Christus habuit ad mentes illorum a terra ad cœlum, a rebus carneis ad spirituales excitandas, ut nullo modo cogitarent se dentibus illum præsentem in terris percepturos. Caro enim ejus (ut ipse ait) ita percepta nihil prodesset. Et ne cogitarent, quod hoc modo illum ederent, corpus suum ab illis in cœlum se sublaturum dixit, atque ibi fide et non dentibus, spiritu non carne, illum ad dexteram Patris sedentem ederent. Quocirca dixit, "Verba quæ ego loquor spiritus et vita sunt." Quasi diceret: Hæc quæ apud vos disserui, minime ita accipienda sunt, quasi me dentibus crasse et carnaliter arriperetis; sed ut spiritu, mente, fide carnem absentem, et in cœlo versantem, perciperetis: quemadmodum Abrahamus reliquique patres illum, multos antequam incarnatus esset annos, comedebant. Sic *1 Cor. x.* enim Paulus ait, eundem illos spiritualem cibum, quem nos, edisse, et eundem spiritualem potum, id est, Christum, hausisse. Illi enim spiritualiter et fide Christi corpore et sanguine sustentabantur, et æterna per illum (antequam nasceretur) vita fruebantur, quemadmodum et nos nunc fruimur, qui post ejus ascensum nati sumus.

Itaque satis, ut arbitror, Christo et Paulo explicantibus, intelligitur carnis et sanguinis Christi esum et potum non ita crasse accipi debere, ut rem præsentem ore, dentibus, gutture hauriamus, sed vitali cordis et mentis fide rem absentem percipiamus et concoquamus, vel in cœlo post ascensum versantem, vel nondum in terris editam.

Origenes in Levit. Hom. vii. cap. 10.   Origenes, hanc carnis et sanguinis perceptionem non simpliciter sed figurate capiendam demonstrans, in hæc verba Christi, 'Nisi ederitis carnem meam, et sanguinem meum biberitis, non habebitis vitam in vobis,' sic scribit: "Nisi manducaveritis carnem meam, et biberitis meum sanguinem, non habebitis vitam in vobis. Agnoscite quia figuræ sunt, quæ in divinis voluminibus scriptæ sunt, et ideo tanquam spirituales, et non tanquam carnales, examinate et intelligite quæ dicuntur. Si enim quasi carnales ista suscipitis, lædunt vos et non alunt. Est enim et in evangeliis *Ob. 164.* litera quæ occidit. Non solum in veteri testamento occidens litera deprehenditur: est et in novo testamento litera quæ occidat eum, qui non spiritualiter, quæ dicuntur, advertit. Si enim secundum literam sequaris hoc ipsum quod dictum est, 'Nisi manducaveritis carnem meam, et biberitis meum sanguinem,' occidet hæc litera."

Quis apertius demonstrare potest, hæc verba a communi et propria significatione removenda esse debere, quam Origenes hoc loco facit?

Chrysost. in Joan. Homil. xlvi.   Annon hoc idem quoque Chrysostomus? "Si carnaliter verba Christi quis acceperit, nihil sane lucraretur. Quid igitur? Caro non prodest quicquam? Non de ipsa carne dicit, (absit!) sed de iis qui carnaliter accipiunt quæ dicuntur. Quid autem est carnaliter intelligere? Simpliciter ut res dicuntur, neque aliud quippiam excogitare. Non enim ita judicanda sunt quæ videntur, sed mysteria omnia interioribus oculis consideranda, hoc est, spiritualiter."

Hæc verba plane indicant, Christi verba nequaquam crasse et proprie sumenda, sed spiritualiter et figurate.

Omnium vero clarissime Augustinus in libro de Doctrina Christiana, quo loco Christianos instruit, quemadmodum difficillima scripturæ loca intelligenda sunt. "Rarissime (inquit) et difficillime inveniri potest ambiguitas in propriis verbis (quantum ad libros divinarum scripturarum spectat), quam non aut circumstantia ipsa sermonis (qua cognoscitur scriptorum intentio), aut interpretum collatio, aut præcedentis linguæ solvat inspectio." Cap. 5. "Sed verborum translatorum ambiguitates (de quibus deinceps loquendum est) non mediocrem curam industriamque desiderant. Nam in principio cavendum est, ne figuratam loquutionem ad literam accipias. Et ad hoc etiam pertinet quod ait apostolus: 'Litera occidit, Spiritus autem vivificat.' Cum enim figurate dictum sic accipitur, tanquam proprie dictum sit, carnaliter sapitur. Neque ulla mors animæ congruentius appellatur, quam cum id etiam, quod in ea bestiis antecellit (hoc est intelligentia), carni subjicitur sequendo literam. Qui enim sequitur literam, translata verba sicut propria tenet," &c. Et mox: "Ea demum est miserabilis animæ servitus, signa pro rebus accipere, et supra creaturam corpoream oculum mentis ad hauriendum æternum lumen levare non posse." Cap. 10. "Neque contra, propriam quasi figuratam velis accipere. Demonstrandus est igitur (inquit Augustinus) modus inveniendæ locutionis, propriane an figurata sit." Cap. 15. "Servabitur autem in loquutionibus figuratis regula hujusmodi, ut tamdiu versetur diligenti consideratione quod legitur, donec ad regnum caritatis interpretatio perducatur. Si autem hoc jam proprie sonat, nulla putetur figurata loquutio." Cap. 16. "Si præceptiva loquutio est, aut flagitium aut, facinus vetans, aut utilitatem aut beneficentiam jubens, non est figurata. Si autem flagitium aut facinus videtur jubere, aut utilitatem aut beneficentiam vetare, figurata est. 'Nisi manducaveritis (inquit) carnem Filii hominis et sanguinem biberitis, non habebitis vitam in vobis,' facinus vel flagitium videtur jubere. Figura est ergo, præcipiens passioni Domini esse communicandum, suaviter atque utiliter recondendum in memoria, quod pro nobis caro ejus crucifixa et vulnerata sit."

Hæc ejus est, in eo quem citavi libro, breviter commemorata sententia.

Hanc eandem habet in libro de Catechizandis Rudibus, et contra Adversarium Legis et Prophetarum, et permultis aliis in locis, quos brevitatis causa prætereo. Nam si omnia afferam, quæ ex Augustino aliisque dici in hanc sententiam possent, lectorem multitudine rerum facile opprimerem.

Aug. de Catechizandis Rudibus, cap. 26. "De sacramento quod accepit, cum ei bene commendatum fuerit, signacula quidem rerum divinarum esse visibilia, sed res ipsas invisibiles in eis honorari, nec sic habendam esse speciem illam benedictione sanctificatam, quemadmodum habetur in usu quolibet. Dicendum etiam quid significet, et sermo ille quem audivit, quid in illo condatur, cujus illa res similitudinem gerit. Deinde monendus est (catechizandus), ut si quid in scripturis audiat quod carnaliter sonat, etiam si non intelligit, credat tamen spirituale aliquid significari, quod ad sanctos mores futuramque vitam pertineat. Hoc autem breviter discet, ut quicquid audierit ex libris canonicis, quod ad dilectionem æternitatis, et veritatis, et sanctitatis, et ad dilectionem proximi referre non possit, figurate dictum vel gestum esse credat, atque ita conetur intelligere, ut ad illam geminam referat dilectionem." Idem contra Adversarium Legis et Prophetarum, Lib. ii. cap. 9. "Mediatorem Dei et hominum, hominem Christum Jesum, carnem suam nobis manducandam, bibendumque sanguinem dantem, fideli corde atque ore suscipimus, quamvis horribilius videatur humanam carnem manducare quam perimere, et humanum sanguinem potare quam fundere. Atqui in omnibus sanctis scripturis, secundum sanæ fidei regulam, figurate dictum vel factum si quid exponitur, de quibuslibet rebus vel verbis, quæ sacris paginis continentur, expositio illa ducatur, non aspernanter sed sapienter audiamus."

Justinus in secunda Apologia ad Gentes: "Deinde profertur illi qui fratribus præest, panis et poculum aqua et vino mixtum; quæ cum is acceperit, laudem et gloriam ei, qui Pater est omnium, per nomen Filii et Spiritus sancti destinat, et gratiarum actionem, quod ab illo dignus his sit habitus, prolixe facit. Quibus rite peractis precibus cum gratiarum actione, populus omnis qui adest benedicit, dicens, Amen. Illud autem *amen* Hebraica lingua significat, *fiat*. Cum autem is qui præest gratias egerit, et totus populus benedixerit, hi qui apud nos vocantur diaconi distribuunt unicuique præsentium, ut participent de pane, in quo gratiæ actæ sunt, et de vino et aqua, et his qui non sunt præsentes deferunt. Atque hoc alimentum vocatur apud nos eucharistia," &c. ut supra, cap. viii.

Bonaventura.

Bonaventura, Lib. iv. Di. 9. "Manducatio primo et proprie in corporalibus invenitur, et ab illis ad spiritualia est translata. Et ideo si volumus accipere rectam illam manducationem spiritualem, necesse habemus a propria acceptione vocabuli nos transferre."

Itaque omnibus his, qui nihil animo præjudicatum habent, hæc satis esse possunt ad probandum, Christi corporis et sanguinis manducationem et potationem minime simpliciter et communiter accipiendam, ut crasse significet nos ore et dentibus ea percipere, sed figurate potius et spiritualiter intelligi debere, quod scilicet altius in animis nostris defigendum sit, et fructuose cordibus nostris credendum, illius carnem pro nobis in crucem actam, et sanguinem ejus pro nostri redemptione profusum. Atque hæc nostra in illum fides est carne illius vesci, et sanguinem ejus bibere, quamvis nobiscum præsens non sit, sed in cœlum ascenderit. Quemadmodum majores nostri ante Christi adventum similiter carnem ejus ederunt et sanguinem biberunt, quamvis tam longe ab illis abfuerit, ut nondum Christus natus, nondum carne nostra quasi vestitus fuerit.

CAPUT XI.

HOC EST CORPUS MEUM, ET HIC EST SANGUIS MEUS, FIGURATAS DICENDI FORMAS ESSE COMPROBATIO.

Hæc est quoque consentiens et vera sanctorum patrum sententia, Christum, cum panem corpus suum, et vinum sanguinem suum nominasset, nequaquam proprie loquutum: sed quemadmodum sacramenta omnia figuræ aliarum rerum sunt, nomina tamen earum rerum habent, quarum significantia sunt; sic Christus pretiosissimi corporis et sanguinis sui sacramentum instituens, figurate loquutus est, et panem corporis nomine appellavit, quod corpus ejus significaret, et vinum sanguinem, quia sanguinem ejus repræsentaret.

*Ob. 1. 60.
Tertullianus contra Marcionem, Lib. i. Lib. iv.
*Ob. 161.
Cyprianus, Lib. ii. Epist. 3.

Tertullianus adversus Marcionem scribens ait, "Christum non reprobavisse panem, quo ipsum corpus suum repræsentat." Atque iterum in Lib. iv. sic scribit: "Jesus acceptum panem, et distributum discipulis, corpus suum illum fecit, 'Hoc est corpus meum,' dicendo, id est, (inquit Tertullianus) figura corporis mei. Atque hac de causa (inquit Tertullianus) Christus panem vocavit corpus suum, et vinum sanguinem, quia in veteri testamento panis et vinum corporis et sanguinis ejus figuræ fuerant."

Cyprianus.
*Ob. 178.

Cyprianus quoque sanctissimus martyr in hac causa sic loquitur: "Videmus in aqua populum intelligi, in vino ostendi sanguinem Christi: quando autem in calice vino aqua miscetur, Christo populus adunatur, et credentium plebs ei in quem credidit copulatur et jungitur."

Qua similitudine Cyprianus usus, minime cogitavit sanguinem Christi vinum esse, aut aquam populum: sed quemadmodum aqua significat et repræsentat populum, sic vinum significat et repræsentat Christi sanguinem; et aquæ cum vino conjunctio significat Christianorum cum Christo ipso conjunctionem.

Cyprianus de Unctione Chrismatis.

Atque alio loco eadem de re scribens, in hac est sententia: "Dedit Dominus in mensa, in qua ultimum cum apostolis participavit convivium, propriis manibus panem et vinum, in cruce vero manibus militum corpus tradidit vulnerandum, ut in apostolis secretius impressa sincera veritas et vera sinceritas exponeret gentibus, quomodo

*Ob. 174.

vinum et panis caro esset et sanguis, et quibus rationibus causæ effectibus convenirent, et diversa nomina vel species ad unam reducerentur essentiam, et significantia et significata eisdem vocabulis censerentur."

Hic Cypriani auctoritate certissimum est, quamobrem et qua ratione panis Christi caro, et vinum Christi sanguis appelletur; quia significantia et repræsentantia rerum significatarum nominibus appellantur.

Itaque Chrysostomus ait: "Ista mensa agnoscitur altaris Dei consecratio; et quia istam mensam præparavit, ut quotidie in similitudinem corporis et sanguinis Christi panem et vinum secundum ordinem Melchisedek nobis ostenderet in sacramento." Chrys. in Psal. xxii. *Ob. 200.

Hieronymus similiter in evangelium Matthæi scribit: "Postquam typicum pascha fuerat impletum, et agni carnes cum apostolis comederat, assumit panem qui confortat cor hominis, et ad verum paschæ transgreditur sacramentum; ut quomodo in præfiguratione ejus Melchisedek summi Dei sacerdos fecerat, ipse quoque veritatem sui corporis repræsentaret." Hieron. in Matt. xxvi. *Ob. 210.

Ambrosius item (siquidem Ambrosii liber sit, qui "De his qui mysteriis initiantur" inscribitur) ad hunc modum scribit: "Ante benedictionem verborum cœlestium alia species nominatur; post consecrationem corpus Christi significatur. Ipse dicit sanguinem suum. Ante consecrationem aliud dicitur, post consecrationem sanguis nuncupatur." Ambrosius de his qui mysteriis initiantur, cap. ult. *Ob. 192.

Et in libro de Sacramentis (si Ambrosius auctor sit) sic scribit: "In similitudinem quidem accipis sacramentum, sed veræ naturæ gratiam virtutemque consequeris. Et tu, quia accipis panem, divinæ ejus substantiæ in illo participaris alimento." Ambros. de Sacramentis, Lib. vi. cap. 1.

Et libro iv. hæc dicit: "Sicut in baptismo mortis similitudinem sumpsisti, ita etiam in eucharistia similitudinem pretiosi sanguinis bibis; ut nullus horror cruoris sit, et pretium tamen operetur redemptionis." Rursus in eodem libro sic scribit: "Dicit sacerdos, Fac nobis hanc oblationem ascriptam, rationabilem, acceptabilem, quod est figura corporis et sanguinis nostri Domini Jesu Christi." Lib. iv. cap. 4.
Lib. iv. cap. 5.

Idem interpretans epistolam Pauli ad Corinthios ait, quod "in edendo et potando panem et vinum, carnem et sanguinem (quæ pro nobis oblata sunt) significamus. Et testamentum (inquit) vetus sanguine constitutum est, quia beneficii divini sanguis testis est: in cujus typum nos calicem mysticum sanguinis ad tuitionem corporis et animæ nostræ percipimus." 1 Cor. xi. *Ob. 188.
*Ob. 189.

Ex his Chrysostomi, Hieronymi, et Ambrosii locis perspicuum est, in sacramentali pane et vino non esse revera et corporate veram et naturalem substantiam carnis et sanguinis Christi, sed panem et vinum, similitudines, mysteria, repræsentationes, sacramenta, figuras, et signa corporis et sanguinis ejus, atque adeo nomine veri corporis et sanguis ejus appellari.

Planius adhuc et plenius his omnibus Augustinus, idque potissimum in epistola ad Bonifacium, ubi ait: "Sæpe ita loquimur ut pascha appropinquante dicamus, crastinam vel perendinam esse Domini passionem, cum ille ante tam multos annos passus sit, nec omnino nisi semel illa passio facta sit. Nempe ipso die dominico dicimus, Hodie Dominus resurrexit, cum ex quo resurrexit, tot anni transierunt. Cur nemo tam ineptus est, ut nos ita loquentes arguat esse mentitos, nisi quia istos dies secundum illorum, quibus hæc gesta sunt, similitudinem nuncupamus, ut dicatur ipse dies, qui non est ipse, sed revolutione temporis similis ejus, et dicatur illo die fieri propter sacramenti celebrationem, quod non illo die, sed jam olim factum est? Nonne semel immolatus est Christus in seipso? et tamen in sacramento non solum per omnes paschæ solennitates, sed omni die populis immolatur: nec utique mentitur, qui interrogatus, eum responderit immolari. Si enim sacramenta quandam similitudinem earum rerum, quarum sacramenta sunt, non haberent, omnino sacramenta non essent. Ex hac autem similitudine plerumque etiam ipsarum rerum nomina accipiunt. Sicut ergo secundum quendam modum sacramentum corporis Christi corpus Christi est, sacramentum sanguinis Christi sanguis Christi est: ita et sacramentum fidei fides est. Nihil est autem aliud credere, quam fidem habere. Ac per hoc cum respondetur parvulus credere, qui fidei nondum habet effectum, respondetur fidem habere propter fidei sacramentum, et convertere se ad Deum propter conversionis sacramentum, quia et ipsa responsio ad celebrationem pertinet sacramenti. Sicut de ipso baptismo apostolus, 'Consepulti,' inquit, 'sumus Christo per baptismum in mortem.' Non ait, sepulturam significamus, sed prorsus Aug. ad Bonifac. Epist. 23.

*Ob. 227.

ait, 'Consepulti sumus.' Sacramentum ergo tantæ rei non nisi ejusdem rei vocabulo nuncupavit."

Hucusque Augustinus erudito cuidam episcopo Bonifacio respondens, quærenti quomodo parentes et amici pro infante in baptismo respondeant, et in illius persona dicant se credere et ad Deum converti, cum infans neque agat neque cogitet tale aliquid.

Cui ita ab Augustino responsum est: Quoniam baptismus sacramentum professionis nostræ fidei est, et nostræ ad Deum conversionis, par est ita pro infantibus ad id accedentibus respondere, quemadmodum tanto sacramento conveniens est, etiam si revera pueri harum rerum notitiam non habeant.

Et in responsis nostris minime, quasi vani aut mendaces, reprehendendi sumus, cum in sermone pene quotidiano sacramentis et figuris rerum significatarum nomina tribuamus, quamvis eadem revera non sint. Ita singulos Parasceves dies (annis versantibus) diem passionis Christi, et pascha diem resurrectionis vocamus: et singulis diebus dicimus Christum offerri: et sacramentum corporis corpus ejus vocamus, et sacramentum sanguinis sanguinem appellamus: et baptismum nostrum Paulus sepulturam cum Christo nominat; cum tamen revera Christus semel tantum passus sit, semel resurrexit, semel tantum oblatus sit: et baptismus sepultura non sit: nec sacramentum corporis corpus ejus sit; nec sacramentum sanguinis sanguis ejus sit; sed sic appellentur, quia figuræ sacramenta et repræsentationes rerum sint, quas significant, quarumque nominibus notantur.

Sic Augustinus in hac epistola clarissime rem explicat.

De hac etiam forma loquendi, ubi signa rerum significatarum nominibus appellantur, copiose Augustinus in quæstionibus in Leviticum, et contra Adimantum, declarans quomodo sanguis in scriptura anima nominetur. "Solet (inquit) res quæ significat, ejus rei nomine quam sinificat nuncupari, sicut scriptum est: 'Septem spicæ septem anni sunt.' Non dicit, septem annos significant. Et 'septem boves septem anni sunt': et multa hujusmodi. Hinc est quod dictum est: 'Petra erat Christus.' Non enim dixit, petra significat Christum, sed tanquam hoc esset: quod utique per substantiam non hoc erat, sed per significationem. Sic et sanguis, quoniam propter vitalem quandam corpulentiam animam significat, in sacramentis anima dictus est."

Aug. super cap. 17. Lev. quest 67. Gen. iv. 1 Cor. x.

Contra Adimantum, cap. 12.

His affinia sunt, quæ contra Adimantum scribens dicit: "Sic est sanguis anima, quomodo petra erat Christus. Nec tamen apostolus ait, petra significabat Christum, sed ait, 'Petra erat Christus.' Et paulo ante hoc dictum, 'Sanguis est anima,' possum interpretari in signo esse positum. Non enim Dominus dubitavit dicere, 'Hoc est corpus meum,' cum signum daret corporis sui."

Ob. 225.

Hic Augustinus multas loquutiones figuratas repetens, cum una res alterius rei nomine vocata, non eadem substantia, sed significatione sit; ut sanguis est anima, septem vaccæ sunt septem anni, septem spicæ sunt septem anni, petra erat Christus; in his loquendi generibus ea repetit, quæ Christus ultima in cœna fecit, 'Hoc est corpus meum.' Ex qua Augustini sententia evidenter colligitur, Christum hæc verba figurate loquutum, minime sentientem, panem corpus esse suum substantia, sed significatione.

Matt. xxvi.

Ob. 236. Aug. contra Maximinum, Lib. iii. cap. 22.

Itaque Augustinus contra Maximinum. "In sacramentis (ait) minime considerandum, quid sint, sed quid significent. Signa enim rerum sunt, aliud existentia, aliud significantia." Atque hæc potissimum de hoc sacramento loquitur. "Cœlestis (inquit) panis, qui Christi caro est, suo modo vocatur corpus Christi, cum revera sit sacramentum corporis Christi; vocaturque ipsa immolatio carnis, quæ sacerdotis manibus fit, Christi passio, mors, crucifixio, non rei veritate, sed significante mysterio." Gloss. ibidem. "Cœlestis panis, id est, cœleste sacramentum, quod vere repræsentat Christi carnem, dicitur corpus Christi, sed improprie: unde dicitur suo modo, sed non rei veritate, sed significante mysterio. Ut sit sensus, vocatur Christi corpus, id est significatur."

In Lib. Sententiarum Prosp. De consecratione dist. 2. "Hoc est."

August. in Psal. iii. "Dominus Judam adhibuit in convivium, in quo corporis et sanguinis sui figuram discipulis commendavit et tradidit." Idem contra Faustum, Lib. xx. cap. 21. "Nostri sacrificii caro et sanguis ante adventum Christi per victimas similitudinum promittebatur, in passione Christi per ipsam veritatem reddebatur, post ascensum Christi per sacramentum memoriæ celebratur."

Quid utilius autem, aut quid jucundius esse potest, quam dialogos Theodoreti in hanc sententiam scribentis legere, ubi fuse et copiose disputat, nomina rerum in scripturis mutari rebus ipsis in sua substantia permanentibus? Verbi gratia, probat Christi carnem interdum velum vel tegumentum, interdum vestem, interdum stolam; et sanguinem uvæ Christi vocari sanguinem. Theodoretus in Dialogis.

Tum panis ac vini, et carnis ac sanguinis Christi, sic mutari nomina, ut interdum corpus suum granum aut panem, interdum contra panem vocet corpus suum; pari modo, sanguinem suum interdum vinum vocet, interdum contra vinum sanguinem appellet.

Atque ut ista melius intelligantur, haud abs re fuerit ea hic ponere, quæ de hac causa clarissimus vir in dialogis suis conscripserat. Personæ sunt, Orthodoxus, recta sentiens de religione Christi, et socius ejus Eranistes, veræ fidei minus intelligens.

Orthodoxus sic socium appellat: "Nostin' quod panem Deus proprium corpus suum vocavit?" ERAN. "Novi." Dialog. 1.

ORTH. "Atque alias rursum carnem suam frumentum appellavit?"

ERAN. "Novi et hoc. Audivi enim illum dicentem: 'Venit hora ut glorificetur Filius hominis.' Et, 'Nisi granum frumenti dejectum in terram mortuum fuerit, ipsum solum manet: si vero mortuum fuerit, multum profert fructum.'" Joan. xii.

ORTH. "In ipsa nimirum mysteriorum traditione corpus panem vocavit, et sanguinem poculum mixtum." *Ob. 246. Matt. xxvi. Marc. xiv. Luc. xxii.

ERAN. "Sic sane nominavit."

ORTH. "Sed et secundum naturam corpus, corpus utique suum et sanguis vocari potuerit?"

ERAN. "Confessum est."

ORTH. "Imo vero ipse Servator noster commutavit nomina, et corpori quidem symboli nomen dedit, symbolo vero corporis nomen. Ad eundem item modum, cum seipsum vitem esse dixisset, sanguinem ipsum symbolum appellavit." Joan. xv.

ERAN. "Id quidem vere dixisti; vellem autem causam discere mutationis nominum."

ORTH. "Manifestus est scopus iis, qui sunt initiati sacris: voluit enim eos qui divina mysteria percipiunt, ne ad eorum, quæ videntur, naturam attendant, sed per nominum mutationem credant illi, quæ ex gratia facta est, transmutationi. Qui enim naturale corpus suum frumentum et panem vocavit, atque item seipsum vitem nominavit, idem ipse etiam quæ videntur symbola corporis et sanguinis sui appellatione honoravit, non equidem naturam ipsam transmutans, sed adjiciens gratiam naturæ." Joan. xii. Matt. xxvi. Joan. xv. *Ob. 246.

ERAN. "Sane mystice dicta sunt mystica, et clare sunt manifestata, quæ non sunt omnibus nota."

ORTH. "Quandoquidem igitur profitetur et stolam et vestem a patriarcha dominicum vocari corpus, nosque in sermonem de divinis mysteriis ingressi sumus, dic revera, cujusnam symbolum ac typum esse putas sanctissimam illam escam? ipsiusne divinitatis Christi Domini, an vero corporis et sanguinis ipsius?" Gen. xlix.

ERAN. "Sane eorum quorum appellationes receperant."

ORTH. "Corporis et sanguinis dicis?"

ERAN. "Sic dico."

ORTH. "Vere dixisti. Etenim Dominus sumpto symbolo non ait, Hoc est divinitas mea, sed, 'Hoc est corpus meum.' Ac rursum, 'Hic est sanguis meus;' et alias, 'Panis autem quem ego dabo, caro mea est, quam ego dabo pro mundi vita.'" Joan. vi.

ERAN. "Vera equidem hæc omnia: divina enim verba sunt."

ORTH. "Porro si sunt vera, corpus utique habebat Dominus."

ERAN. "Et ego incorporeum illum esse dico."

ORTH. "Sed fateris illum habuisse corpus."

Omnia hæc in primo dialogo Theodoretus scribit.

In secundo in eandem sententiam multa scribit, et quædam etiam planius, adversus eos hæreticos, qui humanam Christi naturam, posteaquam semel in cœlum ascendisset, in divinam naturam esse mutatam prædicabant, contra quos sic ille: Dialog. 2.

ORTH. "Corruptionem ergo, interitum, et mortem, accidentia et non substantias nominare convenit: eveniunt enim et recedunt."

Eran. "Convenit."

Orth. "Ergo etiam hominum corpora surgentia quidem a corruptione et interitu et mortalitate liberantur, sed tamen propriam naturam non amittunt."

Eran. "Verum."

Orth. "Igitur corpus Domini, cum surrexit quidem a corruptione et interitu alienum, et impatibile, et immortale, et divina gloria glorificatum, et a coelestibus adoratur potestatibus, corpus tamen est, et habet quam prius habuit circumscriptionem."

Eran. "In his videris dicere verisimilia et rationi consentanea. Sed postquam in coelos assumptus est, non existimo te dicturum, eum non fuisse conversum in naturam divinitatis."

Orth. "Ego quidem non dixerim, humanis rationibus persuasus, nec sum usque adeo audax et temerarius, ut dicam aliquid, quod sacra scriptura silentio praeteriit: sed tamen audivi divum Paulum clamantem, 'Statuit Deus diem, in quo judicaturus est terrarum orbem in justitia, in viro quem praefiniit, fidem praebens omnibus, suscitans e mortuis ipsum.' Didici etiam a sanctis angelis, quod 'veniet eo modo, quo viderunt ipsum discipuli euntem in coelum.' Viderunt autem naturam circumscriptam, non eam quae circumscribi non potest. Audivi autem etiam Dominum dicentem: 'Videbitis Filium hominis venientem in nubibus coeli.' Scio vere esse circumscriptum, quod videtur ab hominibus: videri enim non potest natura, quae non potest circumscribi. Dominum quoque dicentem audivi: 'Videbitis Filium hominis venientem in nubibus coeli.' Porro autem et sedere in throno gloriae, et statuere quidem agnos a dextris, haedos vero a sinistris, id quod circumscriptum est significat."

Hactenus Theodoreti verba recensui. Et paulo post Eranistes sic loquitur:

Eran. "Oportet omnem movere lapidem, (ut est in proverbio,) ut verum inveniatur, sed vel maxime cum divina decreta proponuntur."

Orth. "Dic ergo mystica symbola, quae Deo a Dei sacerdotibus offeruntur: quorumnam dicis esse symbola?"

Eran. "Corporis et sanguinis Domini."

Orth. "Corporis quod vere est, vel vere non est?"

Eran. "Quod vere est."

Orth. "Optime; oportet enim imaginis esse exemplar archetypum. Etenim pictores imitantur naturam, et eorum quae videntur depingunt imagines."

Eran. "Verum."

Orth. "Si ergo divina mysteria corpus quod vere est repraesentant, ergo corpus etiam nunc Domini quoque corpus est, non in naturam divinitatis mutatum, sed impletum divina gloria."

Eran. "Opportune accidit, ut verba faceres de divinis mysteriis. Jam vel ex eo ipso tibi ostendam, corpus Domini in aliam mutari naturam. Responde ergo ad mea interrogata."

Orth. "Respondebo."

Eran. "Quid appellas donum, quod offertur ante invocationem sacerdotis?"

Orth. "Non oportet aperte dicere: est enim verisimile adesse aliquos mysteriis non initiatos."

Eran. "Respondeatur aenigmatice."

Orth. "Id quod fit ex hujusmodi seminibus nutrimentum."

Eran. "Aliud autem signum quomodo nominamus?"

Orth. "Commune etiam hoc nomen, quod potus speciem significat."

Eran. "Post sanctificationem autem quomodo ea appellas?"

Orth. "Corpus Christi, et sanguinem Christi."

Eran. "Et credis te fieri participem Christi corporis et sanguinis?"

Orth. "Ita credo."

Eran. "Sicut ergo symbola Domini corporis et sanguinis alia quidem sunt ante invocationem sacerdotis, sed post invocationem mutantur et alia fiunt: ita etiam corpus Domini post assumptionem mutatur in divinam substantiam."

Orth. "Quae ipse texuisti, retibus captus es. Neque enim signa mystica post sanctificationem recedunt a sua natura: manent enim in priori substantia et figura et forma, et videri et tangi possunt, sicut et prius: intelliguntur autem ea esse quæ facta sunt, et creduntur et adorantur, ut quæ illa sint quæ creduntur. Confer ergo imaginem cum exemplari, et videbis similitudinem. Oportet enim figuram esse veritati similem. Illud enim corpus habet priorem quidem formam, et figuram, et circumscriptionem, et (ut semel dicam) corporis substantiam. Immortale autem post resurrectionem factum est, et potentius quam ut ulla in ipsum cadat corruptio et interitus, sessioneque a dextra dignatum est, et ab omni creatura adoratur, ut quod appelletur corpus naturæ Domini."

ERAN. "Atqui symbolum mysticum priorem mutat appellationem, neque enim amplius nominatur quod prius vocabatur, sed corpus appellatur. Oportet ergo etiam veritatem Deum, et non corpus, vocari."

ORTH. "Ignarus mihi esse videris; non enim corpus solum, sed etiam panis vitæ nominatur: ita Dominus ipse appellavit. Porro autem ipsum corpus divinum corpus nominamus, et vivificum, et dominicum, docentes non esse commune alicujus hominis, sed Domini nostri Jesu Christi, qui est Deus et homo. Jesus enim Christus heri et hodie, ille ipse et in æternum."

Hæc eruditissimus ille et sanctissimus episcopus Theodoretus, quem nonnulli e papistis, intelligentes tam manifeste contra se facere, gravi oratione lacessunt, et Nestoriano illum infici errore dicunt.

Hic papistæ antiquam illam et inveteratam in re manifesta calumniandi consuetudinem suam declarant, et malunt potius cum impudentia mentiri, quam veritati cedere, et errorem suum agnoscere. Et quanquam illius adversarii ejusmodi de illo (etiamnum vivente) rumorem divulgarunt, ante mille tamen et centum annos ab hac infamia per universum Chalcedonense concilium liberatus est. Quem Leo primus epistola 61. carissimum fratrem appellat.

Atque etiam in libro quem adversus hæreses conscripsit, nominatim Nestorium condemnat. Tum dialogorum libros tres præcipue adversus Nestorium scripsit: neque hac labe infamiæ hos mille annos a quoquam est aspersus; sed semper eruditus vir, gravis auctor, et sanctus episcopus est habitus, usque dum hoc tempore, ubi papistæ nihil habent quo se defendant, incipiunt lacessendo illo sese excusare.

Hæc ego pro Theodoreto dixi, quem talem virum judico, ut cupiam omnes sæpe et deliberate, et diligenti animi attentione, hæc quæ citavi legere. Continent enim brevem et perspicuam christiani hominis institutionem in ea causa, quam nunc tractandam suscepimus.

Quinque enim res sunt, quæ diligenter in eo loco evolvendo consideranda nobis sunt: Quinque præcipua in Theodoreto notanda.

Primum, Christum Servatorem in extrema cœna, cum panem et vinum apostolis dedisset dicens, 'Hoc est corpus meum,' et, 'Hic est sanguis meus,' panem ipsum et vinum ipsum nominibus corporis et sanguinis sui vocasse, ita ut nomina panis et vini (quæ mysteria, sacramenta, figuræ, signa et symbola Christi carnis et sanguinis fuerant) commutarit, et rerum significatarum ac repræsentatarum nominibus notavit, atque adeo panem carnis et vinum sanguinis nomine appellarit.

Deinde, quanquam panis et vini nomina post sanctificationem mutabantur, res tamen eædem immutatæ manent, quæ ante sanctificationem fuerant; eandemque naturam, substantiam, formam, figuram panis et vinum retinent.

Tertio, cum substantia panis et vinum non mutatur, docet cur mutantur nomina, et panis corpus, vinum autem sanguis dicitur. Causam hujus hanc Theodoretus offert: nequaquam nobis tantam panis et vini rationem habendam (quæ occulis atque ore accipimus), quantam Christi ipsius, in quem corde credimus, quem fide gustamus, cujus carne et sanguine credimus nos illius benignitate ali et sustentari.

Hæc repetenda nobis, atque altius in animis nostris defigenda sunt, ut corda a pane et vino ad Christum in cœlis sedentem transferamus: hoc ut diligenter et assidue fieret, post consecrationem non jam panis et vinum, sed corpus et sanguis Christi appellantur.

Quarto, quemadmodum in ipso Christi corpore, ita in his quoque sacramentis fit. Corpus enim Christi ante et post resurrectionem una atque eadem natura, substantia, magnitudine, forma et figura est; non tamen (quasi commune aliquod et vulgare corpus) simpliciter corpus appellatur, sed propter exaltationis dignitatem cum adjectione, cœleste, divinum, immortale et Domini corpus appellatur. Ita panis ante et post consecrationem idem manet natura, substantia, magnitudine, forma, et figura; neque tamen communis panis appellationem habet, sed propter dignitatem ejus ad quod assumitur, cum adjectione cœlestis panis, panis vitæ, panis eucharistiæ.

Quinto, neminem sibi tantum arrogare atque assumere debere, ut aliquid pro certo in religione affirmet, cujus rei nulla in sacris scripturis mentio fiat. Atque hoc ad convincendos et condemnandos papistas apertissime dicitur, qui quotidie novas religionis leges et sanciunt et abrogant, nullis scripturarum testimoniis freti, imo vero contra scripturas hoc apertissime facientes. Et tamen in pericula Geennæ et perpetui incendii conjecturos se minitantur, qui hæc commenta non fuerit universa fidei et intelligentia complexus. Itaque ad sequentes errores credendos fasciculis et incendio homines impulerunt:

Primum, post verba consecrationis neque panem neque vinum remanere, sed Christi carnem et sanguinem ex his effici.

Deinde, Christi corpus reipsa corporate, substantiate, sensibiliter et naturaliter in pane et vino esse.

Tertio, impios veram Christi carnem et sanguinem edere ac bibere.

Quarto, sacerdotes Christum quotidie offerentes, ex ipso novum sacrificium expiatorium efficere.

Sed ut brevior hac in causa sim, cum quæ dicta sunt satis plana sint, (has formas loquendi, edere Christum et bibere sanguinem ejus, et, 'Hoc est corpus meum,' et, 'Hic est sanguis meus,' figuratas esse,) vel citandi amplius Theodoreti, vel aliorum antiquorum commemorandorum, finem faciam.

CAPUT XII.

FIGURATAS LOQUENDI FORMAS NEQUE NOVAS NEQUE ADMIRABILES VIDERI DEBERE.

Neque mirandum est Christum eo tempore, cum sacramentum hoc institueret, figurate fuisse loquutum, cum sacramentorum natura sit figuras continere. Et quanquam plena ubique figurarum scriptura sit, tum earum quæ $\sigma\chi\acute{\eta}\mu\alpha\tau\alpha$ tum quæ $\tau\rho\acute{o}\pi o\iota$ appellantur, nullibi tamen refertior est quam ubi de sacramentis tractat. Cum arca, quæ divinam majestatem repræsentarat, in Israelitarum castra venisset, Palestini dixerunt, Deum in castra venisse: et Deus ipse per prophetam Nathanum memorat se, ex quo tempore Israelitas ex Ægypto eduxisset, nequaquam in ædibus, sed in tentoriis et tabernaculis habitasse. Minime autem existimandum est, Deum ipsum ita devectum et transportatum esse; sed quia arca (quæ Dei figura erat) ita de loco in locum deferebatur, de seipso loquebatur, quod de arca intelligebatur. Christus ipse figuris, similitudinibus, parabolis, persæpe utebatur; et agrum mundum, inimicum diabolum, semen verbum Dei, Joannem Eliam, se vitem, apostolos palmites, se panem vitæ esse dixit. Atque etiam abundantius istorum usu delectatus, quasi ad communem hominum intelligentiam satis pertinerent, his præterea vocibus est usus: "Pater meus agricola est," "ventilabrum in manu ejus est," "expurgabit aream suam," "triticum in horreum suum congregabit, paleam autem in ignem inextinguibilem conjiciet." "Cibum habeo edendum, quem vos ignoratis:" "ne accuretis cibum qui perit, sed qui ad sempiternam vitam durat:" "ego sum pastor bonus:" "Filius hominis oves ad dexteram suam collocabit, et hædos ad sinistram." "Ego sum ostium." "Unus ex vobis diabolus est." "Quicunque facit quod Pater meus vult, hic frater et soror et mater est:" atque illa etiam quæ matri et Joanni dixit, "Ecce filium tuum: ecce matrem tuam."

Hæc atque alia ejus generis permulta Christus in parabolis, translationibus, et figuris loquutus est. At ubi de sacramentis verba fecit, frequentius illis usus est.

Ubi enim de baptismo disputaverat, dixit nos baptizari Spiritu sancto debere: et spiritualem ibi baptismum intellexerat. Ita Joannes Baptista de Christo: "Hic, inquit, baptizabit vos Spiritu sancto et igni." Et Christus "vel vos denuo nasci debere" dixit, "vel videre regnum cœleste non posse."

Atque iterum: "Qui eam aquam, quam ego dabo, biberit, haud unquam iterum sitiet: sed aqua, quam ego dabo, fiet illi fons manans in vitam sempiternam." Joan. iv.

Paulus in baptismo vestiri nos Christo ait, et cum Christo sepeliri. In his locis baptismus, ablutio, nova et igne et Spiritu sancto generatio, aqua in homine emanans et profluens in vitam sempiternam, Christi indumentum et consepultura, non potest de ulla naturali aqua, ablutione, ortu, indumento et sepultura intelligi, sed per metaphoram et translationem a spectabilibus rebus, in res sub aspectum non cadentes, spiritualiter et figurate intelligenda sunt. Rom. vi. Gal. iii.

Ad hunc modum nostræ redemptionis mysterium, et passio in cruce Servatoris Christi, tum in novo tum veteri testamento multis figuratis loquendi formis exponitur.

Ut agnus paschalis integer et purus Christum significat, agnini sanguinis effusio sanguinis Christi effusionem significat: filiorum Israel ab interitu corporis per agninum sanguinem liberatio salutem nostram et æternæ mortis per Christi sanguinem depulsionem significat: ut quemadmodum omnipotens Ægyptum peragrans omnes Ægyptiorum primogenitos singulis in ædibus interfecit, neque vivum ex illis ullum reliquit, ædes vero filiorum Israel (ubi ostia agnino sanguine aspersa viderat) transiens, neminem ex illis attigit, sed sparsi agnini cruoris causa servavit; ita in postremo mundi judicio nemo salvus prætermittetur, nisi qui purissimi atque integerrimi agni Jesu Christi sanguine imbutus fuerit. Agnus paschalis.

Et quemadmodum agnini sanguinis effusio signum et figura sanguinis Christi pro nobis profundendi fuerat, omniaque sacramenta et figuræ veteris testamenti cessabant, et finem in Christo habebant; ne nos ingrati homines tanti et tam late patentis beneficii immemores essemus, ideo Christus in extrema cœna, ubi ex hoc mundo discessurus valedixit apostolis, novum declaravit testamentum, ubi nobis peccatorum remissionem et sempiternæ vitæ hæreditatem legavit, illudque postridie sanguine et morte sua confirmavit. Cœna Domini.

Atque ne oblivione obrueretur hoc beneficium, sed nostris firmius animis hæreret, non solennem et annuam aliquam memoriam, cujusmodi agni paschalis epulæ fuerant, instruxit, sed quotidianum ejus, in pane et vino ad hoc consecrato, monumentum tradidit, atque hoc elogium adjecit, "Hoc est corpus meum;" "Hic calix est sanguis meus, qui ad peccatorum vestrorum remissionem funditur; hoc ad mei recordationem facite." His ille (ut melius animis nostris tam insigne beneficium commendaret), cum testamentum faceret, et jam ex hoc mundo in cœlum proficisceretur, nos admonuit, ut quandocunque in cœna illa panem et vinum perciperemus, quantum esset Christi beneficium (qui se ad mortem pro nobis offerebat) cogitaremus. Itaque Paulus, "Quotiescunque," inquit, "ex hoc pane ederitis, aut ex hoc poculo biberitis, mortem Domini annuntiabitis, donec veniat." Matt. xxvi. Marc. xiv. 1 Cor. xi.

Et quoniam hic sacer panis fractus, et vinum divisum, passi pro nobis Christi mortem repræsentat (quemadmodum agni paschalis occisio eandem futuram repræsentabat), idcirco Servator Christus eandem loquendi formam de pane et vino adhibuit, qua Deus ante de agno paschali usus est.

Quemadmodum enim in veteri testamento Deus dixit, "Hoc pascha Domini est," ita in novo testamento dixit Christus, "Hoc est corpus meum:" "Hic est sanguis meus." Sed ut in antiquo mysterio et sacramento agnus pascha Domini non fuerat, sed figura quæ pascha Domini repræsentavit; ita in novo testamento panis et vinum non sunt ipsum Christi corpus et sanguis, sed figuræ sunt, quæ piis participibus sacramenta, signa, et repræsentationes sunt veri corporis et sanguinis ejus: et fidem instruunt, ut quemadmodum panis et vinum mortalem hanc et caducam vitam sustentant, ita vera Christi caro et sanguis spiritualiter illos pascit, et vitam sempiternam donat. Exod. xi. Matt. xxvi.

Cur autem novum aut peregrinum putaret quis, figuras hoc loco admittere, cum tota ejus noctis collocutio figuris abundet, quemadmodum papistæ fatentur? Apostoli enim figurate loquebantur, Christum rogantes, ubinam paschate vesci vellet. Christus etiam eadem est figura usus, dicens: "Magno teneor desiderio hujus paschatis vobiscum edendi." Imo vero neque ipsimet papistæ proprie dici putabunt hæc, edere corpus Christi et sanguinem ejus bibere, ut sic ea, quemadmodum ceteros cibos, edant et bibant. Quibus tropis usus sit Christus in cœna. Matt. xxvi. Marc. xiv. Luc. xxii.

Quid hæc verba Christi, "Hoc poculum est novum testamentum in meo sanguine?"

Annon duas figuras continent? unam in hoc verbo, "poculo," quod non poculum, sed rem quæ continetur significat; alteram in "testamento," quia neque poculum, neque vinum poculo infusum, Christi testamentum est, sed signum et figura vinum est, quo nobis testamentum ejus sanguine confirmatum repræsentatur.

Quod si papistæ (ut solent) contendant, poculo nec poculum ipsum nec vinum poculo contentum intelligi, sed sanguinem Christi in poculo, adhuc tamen figuram in illis verbis inesse fateantur necesse est. Christi enim sanguis (si proprie loqui volumus) novum testamentum non est, sed id quod novum testamentum confirmavit. Sed hac nova et inaudita explicatione papistæ longe peregriniorem et mirabiliorem dicendi formam invehunt, quam ulla figura sit. Hunc enim sensum afferunt, 'Hic sanguis est novum testamentum in meo sanguine;' quæ sententia ita absurda et inepta est, ut ea cujusmodi sit, facile cuivis appareat.

CAPUT XIII.

RESPONDETUR ARGUMENTIS ET TESTIMONIIS, QUÆ PAPISTÆ PRO SE ADDUCUNT.

Nunc cum satis aperte probatum est, Christum vocasse panem corpus suum, et vinum sanguinem, et has dicendi formas figuratas esse, Christum humanitus et corporis sui præsentia cum universa carne et sanguine in cœlum abiisse, neque in terris versari, substantiam panis et vini manere et in sacramento percipi, et quanquam maneant, nomina tamen nova habere, et panem Christi corpus, vinum sanguinem vocari; et mutatorum nominum hanc causam esse, ut mentes nostræ a rebus aspectabilibus sublatæ ad res cœlestes et in fidem cadentes protinus ferrentur:

His rebus bene et diligenter pertractatis, omnes papistarum auctoritates, et argumenta omnia, quæ illi ad propositum suum undique corrogarunt, facillime non modo elevantur, sed etiam solvuntur.

CAPUT XIV.

BREVIS AD OMNIA PAPISTARUM ARGUMENTA RESPONSIO.

Sive enim auctor quicunque ab eis citatus dicat, nos Christi carnem edere et sanguinem ejus bibere, aut panem et vinum converti in substantiam carnis ejus et sanguinis, aut nos in illius carnem converti, aut in cœna Domini verum corpus et sanguinem ejus nos percipere, aut in pane et vino id nos percipere, quod in cruce pendebat, aut Christum carnem suam nobiscum reliquisse, aut Christum in nobis et nos in illo, aut illum totum hic et totum in cœlo, aut idem in poculo esse, quod ex latere ejus defluxerat, aut idem ore percipi, quod fide creditur, aut panem et vinum post consecrationem esse corpus et sanguinem Christi, aut nos corpore et sanguine Christi nutriri, aut Christum hinc discessisse, et hic quoque esse, aut Christum in ultima cœna seipsum in manibus suis gestasse; minime ista accipi debent quasi simpliciter et proprie dicta, quemadmodum popularis intelligentia primo aspectu exponit.

Ita enim neque carnem Christi edimus, neque saguinem bibimus, nec panis et vinum in carnem et sanguinem ejus convertuntur, nec nos in illum commutamur, nec panis et vinum post consecrationem caro ejus aut sanguis efficitur, neque ita caro et sanguis ejus hic integra sunt, aut dentibus nostris interuntur, neque ita Christus manibus suis ferebatur.

Sed hæ atque aliæ ejus generis sententiæ (quæ Christum in terris esse ostendunt, et a Christianis in cibo et potione percipi) vel de divina ejus natura intelligendæ sunt (qua ubique est), vel figurate aut spiritualiter accipiendæ sunt. Figurate enim in pane et vino est, spiritualiter in his qui panem et vinum digne percipiunt; sed reipsa, et corpore ac carne tenus, in cœlo tantum est, unde ad judicium de vivis et mortuis ferendum venturus est.

Hæc brevis responsio, si apte et loco suo accommodetur, satis esse poterit ad ea omnia, quæ papistæ pro se adducunt, dissolvenda. Atque ut hoc magis pateat ad hujusmodi loca, quæ papistæ pro se inducunt, et arbitrantur pro se maxime facere, hoc responsum adhibebo, ut ex certa ad quædam loca responsione facilior aditus pateat ad reliqua solvenda.

Clementem inducunt, cujus verba (sicuti illi prædicant) hæc sunt: "Tribus gradibus commissa sunt sacramenta divinorum secretorum, id est, presbytero, diacono et ministro, qui cum timore et tremore clericorum reliquias corporis dominici debent custodire fragmentorum, ne putredo in sacrario inveniatur; ut cum negligenter agitur, portioni corporis Domini gravis inferatur injuria." Et continuo hæc subjungit: "Tanta in altari certe holocausta offerantur, quanta populo sufficere debeant. Quod si remanserint, in crastinum non reserventur, sed cum timore et tremore clericorum et diligentia consumantur. Qui autem residua corporis Domini, quæ in sacrario relicta sunt, consumunt, non statim ad accipiendos communes cibos conveniant, ne putent sanctæ portioni miscere cibum, qui per aqualiculos digestus in secessum diffunditur. Si ergo mane dominica portio editur, usque ad sextam jejunent ministri, qui eam consumpserint: et si tertia vel quarta hora acceperint, jejunent usque ad vesperam." *(Responsio ad ea quæ citantur ex Clemente, Epist. 2.)*

Hucusque Clemens, siquidem hæc Clementis epistola esset, quemadmodum revera non est; sed ad fictitios errores stabiliendos permulta aliorum nominibus ficta et supposititia proferunt: sed cujuscunque tandem hæc epistola sit, si accuratius exquiratur, magis contra papistas, quam pro illis, facere videbitur. Nam ex eadem epistola tria sunt, quæ papistarum errores evidenter tollunt. *(Mar. An. fol. 188. Tria contra papistas docet Clemens.)*

1. Primum est, panem in sacramento vocari corpus Christi, et confracti panis partes vocari corporis dominici portiones: quæ nisi figurate intelligi non possunt.

2. Alterum est, panem conservari et suspendi non debere, quemadmodum ubique papistæ faciunt.

3. Tertium est, ministros solos non debere sacramentum percipere, (ut papistæ solent facere,) atque illud populo nundinari, sed communicari sacram cœnam cum populo oportere.

Atque hic circumspecte providendum est, ut ne temere aut irreligiose ad mensam dominicam accedamus, quemadmodum ad quotidianas epulas, sed magno cum timore et tremore, ne ad epulas tam sacrosanctas indigne accedamus, ubi non solum repræsentatur nobis, verum etiam spiritualiter exhibetur, Christus.

Itaque (sicuti par et conveniens officio nostro est) accedere cum omni reverentia, fide, amore, et caritate, timore et tremore debemus.

Atque hic Ignatium et Irenæum prætereo, qui pro papistarum sententia nihil faciunt, sed in sacræ synaxewς laudatione versantur, et in assidua omnium exhortatione, ut pie et frequenter eam percipiant. Nemo autem pro dignitate prædicare aut extollere potest tantam rem et tam utilem, si pie et ad auctoris Christi mentem ea utamur. *(Ad Ignatium in epistola ad Ephesin. et Irenæum, Lib. v. contra Hæreses.)*

Dionysius etiam, cujus auctoritatem papistæ usurpant, et illum prædicant mirabili laude hoc sacramentum efferre, (quemadmodum certe negari non potest, sacramentum excellentis cujusdam dignitatis et perfectionis esse, cum nobis perfectam et spiritualem conjunctionem cum Christo, perpetuum pastum, nutritionem, consolationem et spiritualem in illo vitam repræsentet,) nunquam dicebat carnem et sanguinem Christi in pane et vino reipsa, corporate, sensibiliter, naturaliter esse (sicut papistæ vehementer contendere solent); sed panem et vinum signa, arrhabones et symbola vocat, et fidelibus qui pie et religiose percipiunt, ostendit illos Christum spiritualiter percipere, et spiritualiter illius carnem edere, et sanguinem bibere. Quanquam autem panis et vinum figuræ, signa et symbola sunt carnis et sanguinis Christi (quemadmodum illa Dionysius, tum ante, tum post consecrationem appellat), Græca tamen in eundem scholia dicunt res ipsas in cœlestibus locis esse. *(Ad Dionysium Eccle. Hierar. cap. 3.)*

Atque ut Dionysius nihil pro papistarum opinione facit, quod ad Christi realem et corporalem præsentiam attinet, ita permultis aliis in rebus illorum sententiis adversatur, idque potissimum in his tribus, transubstantiatione, sacramenti repositione, et perceptione sacramenti a ministro solo. *(Tria contra papistas docet Dionysius.)*

Tertullianum præterea citant, et illum constanter affirmare dicunt, nos in sacramento corpus et sanguinem Christi edere et bibere. Quibus hoc libenter damus, carnem nostram pane vesci et vinum bibere, quæ corporis et sanguinis nomine appellantur, quia (ut Tertullianus ait) corpus et sanguinem ejus repræsentant, quamvis reipsa corpus et sanguis ejus non sunt. Damus etiam, mentes nostras per fidem verum corpus ejus manducare, et sanguinem ejus bibere, sed id spiritualiter, atque inde haurire vitam æternam. Sed negamus prorsus ad hunc spiritualem pastum realem aut corporalem præsentiam aliqua ex parte requiri.

Ad Tertullianum de Resurrectione Carnis.
Mar. An. fol. 190.

Itaque nihil adversus catholicæ doctrinæ veritatem disserit Tertullianus, sed apertissime multa in nostram sententiam loquitur, et potissimum tria. Primum ait, Christum vocare panem corpus suum: deinde, Christum sic eum vocasse, quod corpus ejus repræsentaret: tum, quod hæc verba Christi, "Hoc est corpus meum," hunc habent sensum, Hæc est figura corporis mei.

Tria contra papistas docet Tertullianus.

Origenem etiam pro se inducunt, quia videri volunt multos ex antiquis scriptoribus erroris sui patronos habere; cum tamen nemo manifestius illis adversetur. Quamvis enim scribat (sicuti illi ipsi afferunt), quod quæ prius in ænigmate designabantur, nunc in specie et veritate compleantur; et in hujus rei confirmationem tria adferat exempla, primum de petra unde emanavit aqua, alterum de mari et nube, tertium de manna (quod in veteri testamento significabat Christum venturum, qui jam in hunc mundum revera venit, et quasi facie ad faciem et sensibiliter nobis manifestatus et exhibitus est, tum in verbo tum in sacramento regenerationis, tum sacramento panis et vini); nequaquam tamen sentiebat Origenes, Christum corpore tenus vel in verbo, vel in aqua baptismi, vel in pane et vino consecratis inesse, vel nos carnaliter et corporaliter regenerari et renasci, aut carnem et sanguinem Christi percipere. Nostra enim in Christo regeneratio spiritualis est, et pastus noster spiritualis quoque est, quæ res non realem aut corporalem Christi præsentiam requirit, sed spiritualem solam, cum gratia et efficientia operante.

Ad Origenem in Num. Hom. vii.

Mar. An. fol. 119.

Hanc autem esse ipsam Origenis sententiam (Christi carnem et sanguinem spiritualem esse pastum, neque carnis et sanguinis ejus perceptionem ad literam, sed spiritualiter intelligendam esse), satis patet ex septima in Leviticum homilia ejus, ubi aperte ostendit hæc verba figurate intelligenda, et eum (inquit) qui secundum literam intelligit, occidit hæc litera.

Origenes in Levit. Hom. vii.

In hac quoque sententia Cyprianus est, quem adversarii veritatis de vera præsentia corporis et sanguinis Christi pro se afferunt.

Cyprianus, Lib. ii. epist. 3.

Cyprianus enim de crassa et carnali oris perceptione non loquitur, sed de interna et pura cordis atque animi perceptione: quæ tota in hoc est sita, ut firma fide teneamus, Christi carnem pro nobis in cruce dilaniatam, et sanguinem ejus pro nostra redemptione fusum, eandemque carnem nunc ad dexteram Patris sedere, et perpetuas ibi pro nobis precationes adhibere. Et hoc beneficium in animis nostris insitum impressumque habere, et universam salutis et æternitatis fiduciam in illo collocare, et nos ipsos ad colendum et serviendum illi totos tradere omne vitæ nostræ tempus, hæc est vera, sincera et spiritualis carnis et sanguinis ejus perceptio.

Mar. An. fol. 191.

Illud autem Christi sacrificium in cruce ea est oblatio, quæ (ut Cyprianus ait) antequam fieret, vino Noe, pane et vino Melchisedeci, et multis aliis figuris, quæ Cyprianus ibi commemorat, significabatur.

Gen. ix.
Gen. xiv.

Nunc autem, cum Christus advenerit, et hoc sacrificium complevit, hoc idem nobis figuratur, significatur, et repræsentatur eo pane et vino, quæ fideles quotidie in sacramento percipiunt: ubi quemadmodum ore carnaliter panem et vinum capiunt, ita fide spiritualiter veram carnem et sanguinem Christi percipiunt. Ex quo liquet, Cyprianum constanter hanc doctrinam affirmare, quam nos quoque verissimam esse profitemur.

Contra papistas autem aperte docet, sacram communionem ab omnibus sub utraque specie sumi debere: Christum panem corpus suum vocasse et vinum sanguinem: nullam esse transubstantiationem, sed panem ibi manere ad Christi corpus repræsentandum, et vinum ad Christi sanguinem pari modo repræsentandum: atque eos qui viva Christi membra non sunt, panem quidem et vinum percipere, illisque ali, sed veram carnem et sanguinem Christi minime percipere. Atque hæc Cypriani sententia est.

Quatuor contra papistas docet Cyprianus.

At Hilarius illis unus ex omnibus esse videtur, qui auctoritate sua illorum sententiam propugnare possit. Atque hæc verba ejus afferunt:

"Si vere Verbum caro factum est, et nos vere verbum carnem factum cibo dominico sumimus, quomodo non naturaliter in nobis manere existimandus est? qui et naturam carnis nostræ jam inseparabilem sibi homo natus assumpsit, et naturam carnis suæ ad naturam æternitatis sub sacramento nobis communicandæ carnis admiscuit. Ita enim omnes unum sumus, quia et in Christo Pater est, et Christus in nobis est. Quisquis ergo naturaliter Patrem in Christo negabit, neget prius naturaliter vel se in Christo, vel Christum sibi inesse. Quia in Christo Pater, et Christus in nobis, unum in his esse nos faciunt. Si vere igitur carnem corporis nostri Christus assumpsit, et vere homo ille, qui ex Maria natus fuit, Christus est, nosque vere sub mysterio carnem corporis sui sumimus, et per hoc unum erimus, (quia Pater in eo est, et ille in nobis,) quomodo voluntatis unitas asseritur, cum naturalis per sacramentum proprietas perfectæ sacramenti sit unitatis?"

Ad Hilarium de Trin. Lib. viii.

Hoc modo papistæ, et veritatis divinæ hostes, vel consulto auctoritatem Hilarii depravant illius verbis ad suum propositum flectendis, vel vero non intelligunt, quid gravissimus scriptor in hac causa senserit.

Quamvis enim dicat, Christum naturaliter in nobis esse, dicit etiam nos naturaliter in Christo esse. Hæc ille cum dixerat, nequaquam de naturali et corporali præsentia substantiæ corporis Christi aut nostri corporis cogitavit. Sicut enim ad eum modum corpora nostra in illius corpore non sunt, ita neque illius corpus eo modo in corporibus nostris inest. At ille senserat Christum, incarnatione sua mortali nostra natura vestitum, divinæ illam naturæ adunasse, itaque nos naturaliter in illo esse.

Et sacramenta baptismi et cœnæ (si recte illis utamur) certiores nos sine ulla dubitatione reddunt, nos divinæ ejus naturæ esse participes, immortalitate nobis et æternitate per illum donata, et eo modo Christus naturaliter in nobis est. Atque ita unum cum Christo sumus, et Christus nobiscum, non modo mente ac voluntate, sed etiam naturali proprietate.

Sic igitur adversus Arium concludit Hilarius, Christum cum Patre unum, non modo proposito ac voluntate, sed etiam natura.

Quemadmodum autem hæc junctio unitatis inter Christum et nos in baptismo spiritualis est, nec realem aut corporalem præsentiam requirit; ita nostra cum Christo communio in cœna spiritualis est, nec realem aut corporalem præsentiam desiderat.

Quocirca hoc loco de utroque sacramento Hilarius loquens, nullam adhibuit differentiam inter communionem nostram cum Christo in baptismo, et communionem nostram cum illo in cœna. Addit etiam, quod ut Christus in nobis est, sic nos in illo; quod papistæ corporaliter et realiter intelligere non possunt, nisi contendere velint omnia nostra corpora in Christi corpore corporaliter esse inclusa. Atque hæc ad recte intelligendum Hilarium sint satis.

Idem Hilarius de Trin. Lib. viii. "Quorum anima una et cor unum omnium erat, quæro utrum per fidem Dei unum erat? utique per fidem. Et interrogo, utrum fides una anne altera sit? una certe. Si ergo per fidem, id est, per unius fidei naturam, utique unum omnes erant: quomodo non naturalem in his intelligis unitatem, qui per naturam unius fidei unum sunt? Omnes enim renati erant ad innocentiam, ad immortalitatem, &c. Sin vero regenerati in unius vitæ atque æternitatis naturam sunt (per quod anima eorum et cor unum est), cessat in his assensus unitas, qui unum sunt in ejusdem regeneratione naturæ, &c. Docet apostolus ex natura sacramentorum esse hanc fidelium Dei unitatem, ad Galathas scribens: 'Quotquot enim in Christo baptizati estis Christum induistis,' &c. Quod unum sunt in tanta gentium, conditionum, gentium diversitate, nunquid ex assensu voluntatis est, aut ex sacramenti unitate, quia his et baptisma sit unum, et unum Christum induti omnes sunt? Quid ergo hic animorum concordia facit, cum per id unum sint, quod uno Christo per naturam unius baptismi induantur? &c. Itaque qui per rem eandem unum sunt, natura etiam unum sunt, non tantum voluntate, &c. Dominus Patrem orat, ut qui in se credituri sint, unum sint, et sicut ipse in Patre est, et Pater in eo est, ita omnes in his unum sint, &c. Primum precatio est, ut omnes unum sint, tum deinde unitatis profectus exemplo unitatis ostenditur, cum ait: 'Sicut tu, Pater, in me, et ego in te, ut et ipsi unum sint in nobis:' ut sicut Pater in Filio et Filius in Patre est, ita per hujus unitatis formam in Patre et Filio unum omnes essent, &c. Per id ergo mundus

Act. iv.

Joan. xvii.

crediturus est Filium a Patre missum esse, quod omnes qui credituri in eum sunt, unum in Patre et Filio erunt; et quomodo erunt, mox docemur: 'Et ego honorem quem dedisti mihi dedi eis.' Et nunc interrogo, utrum id ipsum sit honor quod voluntas (cum voluntas motus mentis sit), an vero honor naturæ, aut species, aut dignitas? Honorem ergo acceptum a Patre Filius omnibus qui in se credituri sunt dedit, non utique voluntatem, &c. Et cum per honorem datum Filio, et a Filio præstitum credentibus, omnes unum sunt; quæro, quomodo Filius diversi honoris a Patre sit? Cum credentes omnes honor Filii ad unitatem paterni honoris assumat, &c. Fidem teneo, atque causam unitatis accipio; sed nondum apprehendo rationem, quomodo datus honor unum omnes esse perficiat. Sed Dominus, nihil conscientiæ fidelium incertum relinquens, ipsum illum naturalis efficientiæ docuit effectum, dicens: 'Ut sint unum, sicut et nos unum sumus: ego in his, et tu in me, ut sint perfecti in unum.' Eos nunc qui inter Patrem et Filium voluntatis ingerunt unitatem, interrogo, utrumne per naturæ veritatem hodie Christus in nobis sit, an per concordiam voluntatis?

"De naturali in nobis Christi veritate ipse ait: 'Caro mea vere est esca, et sanguis meus vere est potus. Qui edit carnem meam, et bibit sanguinem meum, in me manet, et ego in eo.' De veritate carnis et sanguinis non relictus est ambigendi locus: nunc enim et ipsius Domini professione et fide nostra vere caro est, et vere sanguis est. Et hæc accepta atque hausta id efficiunt, ut et nos in Christo, et Christus in nobis sit." Et mox: "Est ergo in nobis ipse per carnem, et sumus in eo, dum secum hoc, quod nos sumus, in Deo est. Quod autem in eo per communicationem sacramenti carnis et sanguinis simus, ipse testatur dicens: 'Et hic mundus jam me non videt, vos autem me videbitis: quoniam ego vivo, et vos vivetis, quoniam ego in Patre meo, et vos in me, et ego in vobis.' Si voluntatis tantum unitatem intelligi vellet, cur gradum quendam atque ordinem consummandæ unitatis exposuit, nisi ut cum ille in Patre per naturam divinitatis esset, nos contra in eo per corporalem ejus nativitatem, et ille rursum in nobis per sacramentorum inesse mysterium crederetur, ac sic perfecta per mediatorem unitas doceretur? cum nobis in se manentibus ipse maneret in Patre, et in Patre manens ipse maneret in nobis, et ita ad unitatem Patris proficeremus, cum qui in eo naturaliter secundum nativitatem inest, nos quoque in eo naturaliter inessemus, ipso in nobis naturaliter permanente. Quod autem in nobis naturalis hæc unitas sit, ipse ita testatus est, 'Qui edit carnem meam et bibit sanguinem meum, in me manet, et ego in eo.' Non enim quis in eo erit, nisi in quo ipse fuerit; ejus tantum in se assumptam habens carnem, qui suam sumpserit. Perfectæ autem hujus unitatis sacramentum superius jam docuerat, dicens: 'Sicut me misit vivens Pater, et ego vivo per Patrem, et qui manducat meam carnem, et ipse vivet per me.' Vivet ergo per Patrem, et quomodo per Patrem vivit, eodem modo nos per carnem ejus vivemus. Omnis enim comparatio ad intelligentiæ formam præsumitur, ut id de quo agitur secundum propositum exemplum assequamur. Hæc vero vitæ nostræ causa est, quod in nobis carnalibus manentem per carnem Christum habemus, victuris nobis per eum, ea conditione qua vivet ille per Patrem. Si ergo nos naturaliter secundum carnem per eum vivimus, id est, naturam carnis suæ adepti, quomodo non naturaliter secundum Spiritum in se Patrem habeat, cum vivat ipse per Patrem?" Et mox: "Hæc autem idcirco a nobis commemorata sunt, quia voluntatis tantum inter Patrem et Filium unitatem hæretici mentientes, unitatis nostræ ad Deum utebantur exemplo, tanquam nobis ad Filium, et per Filium ad Patrem, obsequio tantum ac voluntate religionis unitis, nulla per sacramentum carnis et sanguinis naturalis communionis proprietas indulgeretur, cum et per honorem nobis datum Dei Filii, et per manentem in nobis carnaliter Filium, et in eo nobis corporaliter et inseparabiliter unitis, mysterium veræ ac naturalis unitatis sit prædicandum."

Idem lib. eodem: "'Hoc est opus Dei, ut credatis ei quem misit ipse.' Sacramentum et concorporationis et divinitatis suæ Dominus exponit, fidei quoque nostræ et spei doctrinam locutus est, ut escam non pereuntem, sed permanentem in vitam æternam operemur, ut hanc æternitatis escam dari nobis a Filio hominis meminissemus, ut Filium hominis signatum a Deo Patre sciremus, ut hoc esse opus Dei nosceremus, credere in eum quem misisset. Et quis est quem Pater misit? Nempe, quem signavit Deus. Et quis est quem signavit Deus? Filius utique hominis, escam scilicet præbens vitæ æternæ. Qui tandem sunt quibus præbet eam? Illi namque qui operabuntur escam non intereuntem. Atque ita, quæ operatio escæ est, eadem operatio Dei est, in eum scilicet credidissse quem misit."

Idem Lib. ix. "'Videte ne quis vos decipiat per philosophiam, &c. et non secundum Jesum Christum, quia in ipso inhabitat omnis plenitudo divinitatis corporaliter, et estis in illo completi,' &c. Exposita itaque habitantis corporaliter divinitatis in eo plenitudine, sacramentum assumptionis nostræ continuo subjecit, dicens: 'Et estis in eo repleti.' Ut enim in eo divinitatis est plenitudo, ita in eo et nos sumus repleti. Neque sane ait, Estis repleti, sed, In eo estis repleti; quia per fidei spem in vitam æternam regenerati et regenerandi omnes nunc in Christi corpore manent, replendis postea ipsis, non jam in eo, sed in ipsis, secundum tempus illud de quo apostolus ait: 'Qui transfigurabit corpus humilitatis nostræ, conforme corpori claritatis suæ,' &c. Demonstrato autem et naturæ suæ et assumptionis nostræ sacramento, cum in eo plenitudine divinitatis manente nos in eo, per id quod homo natus est, repleamur, reliquam dispensationem humanæ salutis exequitur, dicens: 'In quo et circumcisi estis circumcisione non manu facta in despoliatione corporis carnis, sed in circumcisione Christi, consepulti ei in baptismate, in quo et consurrexistis per fidem operationis Dei, qui excitavit eum a mortuis,' &c. Regeneratio baptismi resurrectionis est virtus, &c. In eo enim resurgimus per ejus Dei fidem, qui eum suscitavit a mortuis." Col. ii.

Phil. iii.

Idem Lib. ii. "Virgo, partus, et corpus, postque crux, mors, inferi, salus nostra est. Humani enim generis causa Dei Filius natus ex virgine est Spiritu sancto, ipso sibi in hac operatione famulante, et sua videlicet Dei inumbrante virtute, corporis sibi initia consevit, et exordia carnis instituit; ut homo factus ex virgine naturam in se carnis acciperet, perque hujus admixtionis societatem sanctificatum in eo universi generis humani corpus existeret; ut quemadmodum omnes in se, per id quod corporeum se esse voluit, conderentur, ita rursum in omnes ipse, per id quod ejus est invisibile, referretur." Et mox: "Non ille eguit homo effici, per quem homo factus est; sed nos eguimus ut Deus caro fieret, et habitaret in nobis, id est, assumptione carnis unius membra universæ carnis incoleret. Humilitas ejus nostra nobilitas est, contumelia ejus honor noster est: quod ille est Deus in carne consistens, hoc nos vicissim in Deum ex carne renovat."

Hæc etiam responsio rectissime adhiberi potest ad ea quæ ex Cyrillo proferuntur, quem aiunt ut Hilarium esse loquutum, Christum in nobis naturaliter esse. Adversus hæreticum Cyrillus inquit: "Non negamus, recta nos fide caritateque sincera Christo spiritualiter conjungi; sed nullam nobis conjunctionis rationem secundum carnem cum illo esse, id profecto pernegamus, idque a divinis scripturis omnino alienum dicimus. Quis enim dubitavit, Christum etiam sic vitem esse, nos vero palmites, qui vitam inde nobis acquirimus? Audi Paulum dicentem: 'Quia omnes unum corpus sumus in Christo: quia etsi multi sumus, unum tamen in eo sumus: omnes enim uno pane participamus.' An fortassis putat ignotam nobis mysticæ benedictionis virtutem esse? Quæ cum in nobis fiat, nonne corporaliter quoque facit, communicatione carnis Christi, Christum in nobis habitare? Cur enim membra fidelium membra Christi sunt? 'Nescitis (inquit) quia membra vestra membra sunt Christi? Membra igitur Christi meretricis faciam membra? absit.' Salvator etiam: 'Qui manducat carnem meam, ait, et bibit sanguinem meum, in me manet, et ego in eo'." Ad Cyrillum in Joan. Lib. xx. cap. 13.

1 Cor. vi.
Joan. vi.

Quanquam his verbis Cyrillus dicat Christum in nobis corporaliter habitare, mysticam benedictionem percipientibus, non tamen dicit, Christum in pane corporaliter habitare, neque illum in nobis corporaliter habitare eo tantum tempore, quo sacramentum percipimus, neque illum in nobis habitare, et non nos in illo; sed perinde ait, nos in illo, ac illum in nobis habitare. Hæc habitatio neque corpore neque loco definita aut terminata est, sed cœlestis, spiritualis, et naturæ vim longe superans; quo fit, ut quamdiu in illo habitamus, et ille in nobis, vitam habeamus per illum æternam. Itaque Cyrillus eodem in loco dicit, Christum vitem esse, et nos palmites, quia per illum vitam habemus. Quemadmodum enim palmites vitam hauriunt et nutrimentum e vite ipsa ex qua oriuntur, sic nos per illum naturalem corporis sui Mar. An. fol. 196.

Joan. xv.

proprietatem, hoc est, vitam et immortalitatem, quo fit ut, membra illius cum simus, vivamus et spiritualiter nutriamur.

Hoc modo verbo 'corporaliter' usus est Cyrillus, cum Christum corporaliter in nobis habitare dixerat. Hoc modo etiam verbo 'naturaliter' Hilarius est usus, cum Christum in nobis naturaliter inesse scribebat. Et quemadmodum Paulus ipse, cum omnem abundantiam divinitatis corporaliter in Christo habitare dixerat, non senserat divinam naturam esse corpus, atque adeo illam in Christo corporaliter habitare, sed divinam naturam in Christo non tenuiter, leviter, atque adumbrate esse, sed solide, substantialiter, et perfecte, (ut Christus non modo homo mortalis ad oppetendam pro nobis mortem, sed etiam Deus ad redimendam universam Adami progeniem, fuerit;) sic Cyrillus, cum Christum in nobis corporaliter inesse dicebat, hoc voluit, nos illum habere non leviter, inaniter, aut supervacanee, sed insignite, substantialiter, efficienter, ita ut per illum redemptione et æternitate potiamur.

In Joan. Lib. iv. cap. 17.

Neque hæc mei est ingenii excogitatio: a Cyrillo hoc didici; his enim ille verbis utitur: "Parvula benedictio totum hominem in seipsum attrahit, et sua gratia replet, et hoc modo in nobis Christus manet, et nos in Christo."

Quod autem ad corporalem oris perceptionem et ventris concoctionem pertinet, Cyrillus certe nunquam cogitaverat, eo modo Christum in nobis manere. Ait enim:

Anathematismo, 11.

"Sacramentum nostrum hominis manducationem non asserit, mentes credentium ad crassas cogitationes irreligiose introtrudens, et humanis cogitationibus subjicere enitens ea, quæ sola et pura et inexquisita fide capiuntur."

In Joan. Lib. cap. 17.

"Sed quemadmodum (inquit) si quis liquefactæ ceræ aliam ceram infuderit, alteram cum altera per totum commisceat: necesse est, si quis carnem et sanguinem Domini recipit, cum ipso ita conjungatur, ut Christus in ipso, et ipse in Christo uniatur."

Mar. An. fol. 198.

Cum pateat igitur quæ fuerit Cyrilli mens, constat, nequaquam crasse et imperite debere nos de Christo ore percipiendo cogitare, sed hoc esse firmiter tenendum, fide illum accipi et teneri; qua perceptione fit, ut quanquam corpore absens sit, et in vita ac gloria sempiterna cum Patre sit, nos tamen illius naturæ participes simus, et immortali ac nunquam interitura vita et gloria cum illo fruamur.

Atque isto modo nobis Cyrilli atque Hilarii sententia exposita sit.

Ad Basilium, Nyssenum et Nazianzenum.

Nunc autem Basilium, Gregorios Nazianzenum et Nyssenum, dimittamus, quod parum admodum de hac causa loquuntur, tum quod ea quæ superius et sæpius a nobis commemorata sunt, satis idoneam intelligentiam illorum dabunt. Illud enim observandum in primis est, figuram ejus nomen sibi sumere, cujus figura est, atque quod de re ipsa dicitur, illud ad figuram accommodari solere.

Spiritualem illi per fidem corporis Christi manducationem scriptis suis prodiderunt, carnalem autem comestionem, et eam quæ ore et dentibus fit masticationem, non item.

Ad Emissenum, Mar. An. fol. 201.

Ad Eusebium quoque Emissenum facilis responsio est. Neque enim de ulla reali aut corporali panis et vini conversione in corpus et sanguinem Domini verba facit, neque de ulla corporali aut reali ejusdem perceptione, sed de sacramentali conversione et spirituali perceptione disseruit, quomodo etiam in baptismo, quemadmodum in cœna est, ut idem eodem in loco aperte commemorat. Hoc autem non carnaliter et corporaliter, sed fide et spiritualiter fit. Sed ad hujus auctoris explicationem, ubi de transubstantiatione agebatur, multo plura.

Mar. An. fol. 203. Ad Ambros. De Sacra. Lib. iv. cap. 4.

Nunc ad Ambrosium veniamus, qui semper in illorum ore est: "Panis iste panis est ante verba sacramentorum; ubi accesserit consecratio, de pane fit caro Christi."

Ut isti loco respondeamus, primo intelligendum est, quid sit consecratio.

Consecratio quid sit.

Consecratio est cujusvis rei a profano et mundano usu ad spiritualem et divinum traductio.

Cum igitur usitata et communis aqua ab omni alio usu detrahitur, atque ad usum baptismi in nomine Patris et Filii et Spiritus sancti confertur, tum aqua rite consecrata dicitur, et sancto usui dicata.

Pari modo, ubi panis et vinum a communi vitæ usu segregantur, atque ad sanctæ communionis usum transferuntur, ea panis et vini portio, quanquam communem cum ceteris substantiam habeat, a quibus separatur, nunc tamen consecratus et sanctus panis et vinum dicitur.

Non quod panis et vinum ullam in se sanctitatem habeant, sed quia in sacrum usum transferuntur, et sanctas res atque divinas repræsentant. Itaque Dionysius panem hunc sanctum panem nominat, et poculum hoc sanctum poculum appellat, statim ut ad sacræ communionis usum mensæ admoventur. Eccl. Hierar. cap. 3.

Præcipue autem tum sancta et consecrata appellari possunt, ubi Christi verbis eum ad usum separantur, quæ Christus ea de causa protulit, "Hoc est corpus meum," de pane loquens, et de vino, "Hic est sanguis meus." Matt. xxvi. Marc. xiv. Luc. xxii.

Unde plerique auctores, antequam hæc verba fiant, panem et vinum pro usitatis et communibus pane et vino accipiunt; postquam autem hic sermo de illis est habitus, tum panem et vinum consecrata esse judicant.

Neque hic ita crassus quisquam esse debet, ut ullius sanctitatis aut divinitatis participia esse panem et vinum putet, aut posse corpus et sanguinem Christi esse; sed repræsentare verum corpus et sanguinem Christi, et verum animorum atque vitalem pastum, quo per illum abundamus. Itaque corporis et sanguinis nominibus ita appellantur, quemadmodum signa, figuræ, symbola, ejus rei nominibus vocantur, quam significant.

Sicut autem in illis Ambrosii verbis (quæ adversarii citant) dicitur, ante consecrationem esse panem, post consecrationem vero corpus Christi; ita aliis in locis explicatius posuit, quæ sensit, his verbis usus: "Ante benedictionem verborum cœlestium alia species nominatur, post consecrationem corpus Christi significatur." Similiter: "Ante consecrationem aliud dicitur, post consecrationem sanguis nuncupatur." Rursus ait: "Cum de sacramentis tractarem, dixi vobis, quod ante verba Christi quod offertur panis dicatur; ubi Christi verba deprompta fuerint, jam non panis dicitur, sed corpus appellatur." Ambrosius de iis qui mysteriis initiantur, cap. ult. Mar. An. fol. 203. De Sacra. Lib. v. cap. 4.

Ex his efficitur, panem quidem nomine corporis Christi vocari post consecrationem, et quanquam panis substantia eadem permaneat, ejus rei nomine, quam repræsentat, illustratur: quemadmodum copiose a nobis antea (ubi de transubstantiatione egimus) explicatum est, atque ibi potissimum ubi Theodoreti verba posuimus.

Et sicut panis corporis est cibus, et corpore editur, sic (inquit Ambrosius) corpus Christi spiritus est cibus, et spiritu editur, ad quod præsentia Christi corporea non est opus. De Sacra. Lib. vi. cap. 1.

Nunc Chrysostomum excutiamus, qui leviter illius sententiam pertractanti speciem præ se fert propugnandi hujus erroris papistici: sed quibus Chrysostomus familiariter est cognitus, nempe quod allusionibus, tropis, schematibus et figuris abundet, hi facile intelligent, quam longe Chrysostomus ab hujus sententiæ defensione absit. Hoc melius patebit, si duo ea loca diligenti inquisitione scrutemur, quæ papistæ pro se potissimum allegant, e quibus unus est in sermone de Eucharistia in Encæniis, alter vero de Proditione Judæ. Ad Chrysostomum.

At nemo sane apertius contra illos loqui potest, quam Chrysostomus in priori loco scripsit. Quocirca mirari jure possumus, cur illum pro se citarent, nisi si ita suis ipsorum erroribus occæcati sint, ut neque videre neque dijudicare possint, quid pro illis et quid contra illos faciat. Hæc enim in eo loco verba ejus sunt:

"Ad hæc mysteria accedentes, ne putetis quod accipiatis divinum corpus ex homine." Hæc Chrysostomus. In ser. de Euchari. in Encæniis.

Si igitur corpus Christi a nullius hominis manibus accipimus, necessario efficitur, corpus Christi nec realiter, nec corporaliter, nec naturaliter in sacramento esse, neque nobis a ministro porrigi, atque adeo papistas insignes mendaciorum architectos esse, qui fingunt contraria.

Sed hic locus Chrysostomi fusius tractatur, ubi de transubstantiatione antea mentionem fecimus.

Nunc igitur ad secundum locum respondebimus: quem ex Chrysostomo citant in hæc verba: "Nunc ille præsto est Christus, qui illam ornavit mensam, ipse istam quoque consecrat. Non enim homo est, qui proposita de consecratione mensæ Domini corpus Christi facit et sanguinem, sed ille qui crucifixus pro nobis est, Christus. Sacerdotis ore verba proferuntur, et Dei virtute consecrantur et gratia: "Hoc est," ait, "corpus meum." Hoc verbo proposita consecrantur. Et sicut illa vox quæ dicit, "Crescite et multiplicamini et replete terram," semel quidem dicta est, sed omni tempore sentit effectum ad De proditione Judæ. Gen. i.

generationem, operante natura; ita et vox illa Christi, "Hoc est corpus meum," semel quidem dicta est, sed per omnes mensas ecclesiæ, usque ad hodiernam diem, et usque ad ejus adventum, præstat sacrificio firmitatem."

> Matt. xxvi.
> Marc. xiv.
> Luc. xxii.

Hæc papistæ ex Chrysostomo, quæ quanquam illorum sententiam magnopere adjuvare videntur, si plenius tamen et diligentius inspiciantur, et cum universa illius sententia (quæ multis et dispersis in locis patet) conferantur, clare liquebit, illum nihil minus cogitasse, quam Christi corpus naturaliter et corporaliter in pane et vino præsto esse; sed ea ratione in cœlo solum esse, animosque nostros fide in cœlum migrare, atque illic tam salutari cibo pasci, quanquam sacramentaliter in pane et vino quasi in signo et figura sit, sicuti etiam in aqua baptismi est. In his autem qui rite panem et vinum percipiunt, multo plenius fructuosiusque inest, quam si corporaliter adesset, quod nihil prodesset. Spiritualiter enim et divinitus inest, et vitæ æternitatem illis largitur.

> Mar. An. fol. 210.

Et quemadmodum in primo mundi ortu omnes res a Deo creatæ vitæ participes Dei verbo effectæ sunt, (ubi enim aliquid verbo Deus fieri mandasset, illud statim, ut par fuit, effectum erat,) et post rerum omnium ortum hæc verba fecit, "Crescite et multiplicate," atque horum vi verborum omnia ex eo tempore et producta in lucem et aucta sunt: ita postquam Christus semel dixisset, "Edite, hoc est corpus meum," "Bibite, hic est sanguis meus," "Hoc facite ad recordationem mei;" horum verborum vi, et non humana aliqua potentia, factum est, ut panis et vinum consecrentur, eamque sibi naturam adsciscant, ut quisquis illa viva fide percipiat, spiritualiter alatur et sustentetur, Christo ad dextram Patris considente in cœlo. Atque hic Chrysostomi animus in hac causa est.

> Gen. i.

> Matt. xxvi.
> Marc. xiv.
> Luc. xxii.

Quoties enim inculcat, nos Christum etiam in baptismo percipere; et ubi de perceptione ejus in sacra cœna loquutus est, continuo etiam de perceptione ejus in baptismo mentionem facit, sine ulla differentiæ aut varietatis adjectione, quomodo in cœna, et quomodo in baptismo Christus sit.

Idemque multis in locis habet, nos in cœlum ascendere, et Christum ibi sedentem edere.

> Ad popul. Antiochenum, Hom. lxi. Et in Joan. Hom. xlv.

Ubi autem Chrysostomus et ceteri scriptores de admirabili Dei in sacramentis suis efficientia (omnes hominum sensus, rationem, ingenium superante) loquuntur, non de aliqua effectione Dei in aqua, pane, et vino sentiunt, sed de inexplicabili Dei effectione in percipientium cordibus, qua tacite, spiritualiter, intrinsecus transformat, renovat, pascit, consolatur, nutrit illos per Spiritum sanctum ea carne et sanguine, quæ in cœlo solum permanet, quo et nos spiritu et fide conscendimus.

Hæc ad Chrysostomum satis, cum plura hac de re scripserimus, ubi Chrysostomi sententiam de transubstantiatione tractabamus.

> Theophylact. in Marc. xiv.

Habent adhuc Theophilum Alexandrinum: ex eo hæc verba pro se citant: "'Christus gratias agens, fregit,' quod et nos facimus, orationes superaddentes: 'et dedit eis |dicens, Sumite, hoc est corpus meum;' hoc scilicet quod nunc do, et quod nunc sumitis. Non autem panis figura tantum corporis Christi est, sed in proprium Christi corpus transmutatur. Nam Dominus ait: 'Panis quem ego dabo caro mea est.' Sed tamen caro Christi non videtur propter nostram infirmitatem. Panis et vinum de nostra consuetudine est; si vero carnem et sanguinem cerneremus, sumere non sustineremus: propter hoc Dominus nostræ infirmitati condescendens, species panis et vini conservat, sed panem et vinum in veritatem convertit carnis et sanguinis."

> Joan. vi.

Hæc papistæ ex Theophilo in evangelium Marci adducunt. Unde facile intelligitur, vel quam negligentes papistæ sint in exquirendis et eruendis veterum scriptorum sententiis, quas ad opinionis suæ confirmationem afferunt, aut quam dolosi et falsarii sint, qui prudentes et scientes uno eodemque in loco duas ingentes fraudes commenti sunt.

Una est, ut majorem auctoritatem his verbis afferrent (quemadmodum falsi pharmacopolæ, quid pro quo vendentes), auctoris nomen adulterant, et Theophylacti Bulgariensis recentioris scriptoris verba THEOPHILO ALEXANDRINO, antiquo sane et pervetusto scriptori, ascribunt. Sed hæc communis et pervagata illorum fraus est, ut antiquitatis personam illorum somniis et anilibus ineptiis imponant.

Altera est, auctoris verba et sensum depravant, et doctrinæ veritatem ab illo positam corrumpunt. Ubi enim Theophylactus (veterum ecclesiasticorum scriptorum in hoc disciplinam sequutus) omnipotentem Deum ait, "infirmitatis nostræ ratione habita, speciem panis et vini reservasse, et ea tamen in δύναμιν, id est, virtutem corporis et sanguinis Christi convertisse;" illi citant illum formas et figuras exteriores panis et vini reservasse, et convertisse in "veritatem" carnis et sanguinis sui: ita species in figuras, et virtutem in veritatem, transmutantes, ut ex virtute carnis et sanguinis veritatem carnis et sanguinis efficiant. Atque hoc modo corruperunt et depravarunt auctoris tum nomen tum verba, et veritatem in perspicuam et apertam falsitatem converterunt.

Sed ut Theophylacti sensus plane ante oculos constituatur: Quemadmodum candens et concalefactum ferrum ferrum esse non desinit, vim tamen ignis in se continet; et quemadmodum caro Christi hanc carnis substantiam non deserit, et vitam etiam (ut caro Dei) tribuit; ita sacramentalis panis et vinum, quod ante fuerant, etiamnum sunt, his tamen qui ea digne percipiunt, non in corporalem præsentiam, sed in vim carnis et sanguinis Christi convertuntur. Mar. An. fol. 217.

Quanquam autem Theophylactus de vera corporis et sanguinis Christi perceptione, et non solum de figuris illorum, loquutus est, et de conversione quoque panis et vini in corpus et sanguinem Christi verba fecit, minime tamen de crassa, carnali, corporali et sub sensum cadente conversione, nec de hujusmodi carnis manducatione disseruit, (ita enim non modo ventriculus horreret, et cor contremisceret ad ejusmodi epulum, verum etiam inutile nobis et supervacuum esset;) sed de spirituali et cœlesti perceptione Christi et sacramentali panis conversione loquebatur, panem non modo figuram, verum etiam corpus Christi vocans. Ex quo datur intelligi, non modo nos in sacramento corporaliter panem edere (qui sacramentum et figura corporis Christi est), sed spiritualiter etiam verum corpus et sanguinem ejus percipere. Atque hæc Theophylacti sententia vera, pia, et consolationis plena est.

Post hæc omnia ab adversariis Hieronymus in epistolam ad Titum profertur, ubi hæc scribit: "Tantum interest inter propositionis panes et corpus Christi, quantum inter umbram et corpora, inter imaginem et veritatem, inter exemplaria futurorum, et ea ipsa quæ per exemplaria præfigurabantur." Ad Hieronymum in epistolam ad Titum.

Hæc Hieronymi verba recte intellecta nihil afferunt, in quo se papistæ venditare possint. Ille enim panes propositionis voluit obscuram quandam umbram Christi venturi fuisse, sed sacramentum corporis Christi evidens testimonium esse, Christum jam advenisse, promissa fecisse, et quanquam corpore in cœlum migravit, spirituali tamen corporis et sanguinis sui pastu nos alere.

Hæc eadem responderi possunt, si quis ex Augustino, Sedulio, Leone, Fulgentio, Cassiodoro, Gregorio et ceteris, quod papisticum videatur, de Christi in sacramento manducatione objiciat. Augustinus, Sedulius, Leo, Fulgentius, Cassiodorus, Gregorius.

Neque enim plane, neque ad simplicem verborum sensum ista capienda sunt, sed figurate et spiritualiter, sicuti abunde antea comprobatum est, et in quarto etiam libro plenius tractabitur.

Sed dum ceteros transimus, cavendum est nobis, ne Joannes Damascenus dimittatur, quem fortissimum et acerrimum propugnatorem naturalis et corporalis præsentiæ adversarii inducunt, quemque solum universam causam defendere posse judicant. Ad Damascenum de Fide Orthodoxa, Lib. iv. cap. 14.

Sed neque auctoritas Damasceni tanta est, ut ea nos opprimere debeat, neque dicta tam perspicua, ut de illo se potissimum jactare possint. Recens enim scriptor est præ illis, quos pro nostra parte adduximus. Et multis in locis ab antiquorum scriptorum auctoritate dissentit, si hæc sit illius mens, quam papistæ ei attribuunt: ut cum ait, panem et vinum figuras non esse, quæ antiqui scriptores figuras appellant; et panem ac vinum minime consumi, nec ex alvo ejici, contra quam Origenes et Augustinus affirmant; vel quod exemplaria corporis Christi post consecrationem non appellentur, in quo manifeste contradicit liturgiæ illi quæ Basilio ascribitur.

Quid, quod adversus ætatis suæ principes, qui imperatorium tum tenebant gradum, acerrimus episcopi Romani defensor fuerat, et ad scriptis propagandam de simulacrorum cultu nefandam impietatem et idolatriam deliciæ illius et quasi dextra fuerat? Quo minus mirum est, si justo et divino judicio dexteram amiserit, quicquid de ea restituta alii fabulentur. Quicquid autem, et quale id cunque sit, quod aliis in locis scribat, hoc certe loco, quem adversarii afferunt, pie et erudite scribit, etiamsi papistæ vel ignorantia quadam non recte illius dicta accipiant, vel consulto contra illius sententiam alienum in sensum depravent.

Summa ejus doctrinæ hæc est. Quemadmodum Christus Deus et homo duas in se habet naturas, ita duplicem nativitatem habuit; unam æternam, alteram tempori subjectam. Sic et nos, quasi singuli duo homines essemus, vel potius duos in nobis homines contineremus, (novum et veterem, spiritualem et carnalem,) duplicem quoque ortum habemus, unum carnalem ex parente nostro Adamo, (per quem ad nos, quasi hæreditario jure, maledictio et sempiterna condemnatio veniunt,) alterum spiritualem ex cœlesti Adamo, Christo nempe, per quem cœlestis benedictionis et æternæ atque immortalis gloriæ hæreditatem adimus.

Quoniam autem hic Adamus spiritualis est, necesse est non modo ortum nostrum, verum etiam pastum quoque spiritualem esse. Ac ortus quidem is in baptismo, pastus vero in cœna, quasi oculis subjicitur. Quia enim nostrorum oculorum acies ad spiritualis aquæ aspectum, qua abluimur, valde hebescit, et tanta est spiritualis quoque pastus subtilitas, ut fugiat aciem; ideo ad hanc nostram imbecillitatem juvandam (ut clarius pura integraque fide ista cernamus), Servator ista signis perspicuis et sub sensum cadentibus, et ad quotidianum usum cultumque vitæ pertinentibus, ante oculos nostros collocavit.

Cum autem consuescant homines, ubi se abluunt, aquam adhibere, ideo hic sive spiritualis ortus, sive ablutio in illius sanguine, nobis in baptismo per aquam proponitur. Spiritualis item pastus noster per panem et vinum ob oculos nobis ponitur, quia in assiduum et quotidianum victus subsidium veniunt, ut quemadmodum illa corpus, sic Christi caro et sanguis animum, pascant.

Hac de causa panis et vinum exemplaria carnis et sanguinis Christi dicuntur, atque etiam caro et sanguis Christi appellantur, ut nos admoneant et ad cogitationem beneficii Christi excitent, et evidenti ratione concludant, sic nos ad æternam vitam Christi carne et sanguine spiritualiter sustentari, quemadmodum pane et vino corpus nostrum alitur et recreatur.

Atque ut omnipotens Deus magnitudine verbi, sancto Spiritu, et immensa potentia omnes res creatas initio produxit, et ex eo tempore perpetuo conservavit; ita eodem ille verbo et eadem potentia hunc spiritualem in nobis ortum continenter efficit, et spiritualem similiter pastum adhibet, quæ omnia a Deo solo efficiuntur, et a nobis fide sola percipiuntur et tenentur.

Itemque ut panis et vinum facultate naturæ in humanum corpus mutantur, corpus tamen idem est quod ante fuit, et non mutatur; ita quanquam panis et vinum sacramentaliter in Christi corpus et sanguinem convertantur, corpus tamen Christi, mutationis omnis expers, eodem loco quo antea continetur, et cœli certo spatio definitur.

Neque vero panis et vinum sic in Christi corpus mutantur, ut in unam naturam cum eo conveniant; sed naturam sejunctam et diversam habent, sic ut neque panis in se corpus Christi sit, nec vinum sanguis, sed his qui digne ea percipiunt caro et sanguis Christi fiunt, hoc est, a rebus naturalibus et usitatis ad res naturæ dignitatem longe superantes extolluntur. Sacramentatus enim panis et vinum non nuda sunt atque inania signa, sed ita actuosa et efficacia, ut quicunque digne perceperit, spiritualiter Christi carnem et sanguinem percipiat, atque adeo vitam nactus sit æternam.

Quicunque igitur ad hanc mensam accedit, par atque æquum est, ut omni cum animi subjectione, timore, reverentia, integritate vitæ veniat, quasi non modo panem et vinum, verum etiam Servatorem Christum, Deum atque hominem, et omnia ejus beneficia, ad magnam lenitionem et recreationem tum animi tum corporis, percepturus.

Hoc fuit Damasceni de hac causa judicium.

Qui igitur ex illo colligunt, vet naturalem corporis Christi in sacramentis panis et vini præsentiam, vel externi et aspectabilis sacramenti venerationem, vel substantiæ panis et vini post consecrationem discessum, et substantiæ solius corporis Christi permansionem, vel Damascenum non intelligunt, vel obstinata quadam contumacia intelligere nolunt, quod mihi sane verisimilius videtur propter ejusmodi conclusiunculas, quas iniqui homines ex illius dictis colligunt et decerpunt.

Quamvis enim dicat, Christum spiritualem pastum esse, intelligendum est tamen, quemadmodum in baptismo Spiritus sanctus in aqua non est, sed in illo qui non simulate baptizatur, ita noluisse Damascenum, Christum esse in pane, sed in eo qui digne percipit panem.

Et quanquam panem Christi corpus et vinum sanguinem vocet, non sensit tamen panem per se, aut vinum nondum perceptum, carnem et sanguinem ejus esse, sed his qui non ficta fide digne panem et vinum percipiunt, vocari a Damasceno ea corpus et sanguinem Christi, quod ejusmodi homines efficientia Spiritus sancti ita conjunguntur, et spiritualiter cum Christi carne et sanguine et divina quoque ejus natura cohærescunt, ut illis ad æternitatem et immortalitatem pascantur.

Neque vero Damascenus sacramentum venerandum aut adorandum dicit, (sicut papistæ loquuntur, quæ res aperta idololatria est,) sed Christum Deum et hominem venerandum prædicat; neque tamen illum in pane et vino colendum, sed ad dexteram Patris sedentem, et Spiritu in nobis existentem. Mar. An. fol. 220.

Neque ille dicit, nec panem nec vinum permanere, nec ullam aliam substantiam præter substantiam corporis et sanguinis Christi; sed aperte fatetur, quemadmodum candens carbo non solum lignum est, sed ignis et lignum simul juncta, sic panis eucharistiæ non solum panis est, sed panis divinæ naturæ junctus. Qui vero contendunt nullam substantiam permanere, nisi substantiam corporis et sanguinis Christi, non modo negant panis et vini, sed etiam divinæ naturæ et animæ humanæ Christi, præsentiam. Si enim caro et sanguis, anima, et divina natura Christi, quatuor substantiæ sunt, et in sacramento duæ tantum ex illis (caro et sanguis) insunt, ubi tandem erit anima et divina ejus natura? Ita fit, ut Jesum dividant, et humanam naturam a divina segregent: de quibus Joannes dicit ad hunc modum, "Quicunque dividit Jesum, non ex Deo est, sed antichristus est." Error papistarum. 1 Joan. iv.

Neque vero hoc solum faciunt, sed Christum a membris suis omnibus in sacramento discludunt, ita ut nullum ibi prorsus corpus humanum relinquant. Recte enim Damascenus distinctionem membrorum ita ad naturam humani corporis asserit pertinere, ut ubi nulla ejusmodi distinctio sit, ibi perfectum corpus esse non possit. In libr. de duabus in Christo voluntatibus.

At papistæ docent, nullam hujusmodi membrorum in sacramento distinctionem esse: vel enim caput, oculos, os, aures, brachia, manus, tibias, pedes, plane in sacramento esse negant; vel totum caput, totum oculos, totum aures, os, brachia, manus, tibias, pedes, esse dicunt; atque adeo ex Christi corpore nullum plane corpus faciunt.

Jam vero cum papistarum errores tum de transubstantiatione, tum de reali,
    corporali, et naturali præsentia Christi in sacramento, satis (ut arbitror)
        confutati sint, (quæ duo ex præcipuis erant, quæ nobis in hoc
            opere proposuimus;) tempus esse videtur, ut de tertio
                errore papistarum, qui de vera manduca-
                    tione et potatione est corporis et
                        sanguinis Christi, verba
                            faciamus.

FINIS LIBRI TERTII.

LIBER QUARTUS.

DE PERCEPTIONE CORPORIS ET SANGUINIS CHRISTI IN SACRAMENTO.

CAPUT PRIMUM.

CRASSUS hic papistarum et absurdus error est, quem habent de carne et sanguine Christi ore percipiendo.

Tantum pii manducant Christum.

Aiunt enim eos, qui panem et vinum percipiunt, veram carnem et sanguinem Christi ore percipere, quantumvis sceleratam vitam atque impuram degant. At Christus ipse longe aliud docuit, nos nequaquam ore carnaliter, sed fide spiritualiter, carnem suam manducare. Ait enim: "Hoc etiam atque etiam affirmo vobis, Qui credit in me, vitam æternam habet. Ego sum panis vitæ. Patres vestri vescebantur manna in deserto, et mortui sunt: hic est panis qui descendit de cœlo: qui ex hoc pane ederit, non morietur. Ego sum panis vivus, qui de cœlo descendi: si quis hunc panem ederit, vivet ad æternitatem. Panis autem quem ego dabo, caro mea est, quam daturus sum pro mundi vita."

Joan. vi.

Ob. 101.
Joan. vi.

Hæc certissima est et constantissima Servatoris Christi doctrina, omnes, quicunque illum edunt, vitam æternam habituros. His statim adjungitur: "Hoc etiam atque etiam affirmo vobis, Nisi ederitis carnem Filii hominis, et sanguinem ejus biberitis, non habebitis vitam in vobis. Qui meam carnem edit, habet vitam æternam: et ego exsuscitabo illum in supremo die. Caro mea revera est cibus, et sanguis meus vere est potus. Qui edit meam carnem et bibit meum sanguinem, in me manet, et ego in illo. Quemadmodum misit me vivens Pater, et ego vivo propter Patrem; qui edit me, vivet etiam ille propter me. Hic est panis, qui de cœlo descendit: non quemadmodum ederant patres vestri manna, et mortui sunt. Qui manducat hunc panem, vivet in æternum."

Hæc Servator Christus tum Judæos tum discipulos suos in Capernaum docuit, perceptionem corporis et sanguinis sui non esse perceptioni mannæ similem. Boni enim et mali manna vescebantur; qui autem carnem ejus et sanguinem percipit, vitam æternam habet. Quemadmodum enim Pater in illo habitat, et ille in Patre, atque adeo vivit propter Patrem; sic qui carnem et sanguinem ejus percipit, in Christo habitat, et Christus in illo, et per Christum vitam æternam habet.

Aliisne testibus hac in causa opus est? cum Christus ipse tam aperte testificetur, quicunque ederit ejus carnem aut biberit ejus sanguinem, habiturum vitam æternam, et veram perceptionem carnis et sanguinis ejus esse fidem in Christum, et omnem, qui fidem suam in illum collocarit, habiturum vitam æternam. Ex quo necessario efficitur, impios (cum membra diaboli sint) nec carnem ejus manducare, nec sanguinem ejus bibere: nisi forte papistæ dicturi sint, illos vitam æternam habere.

Ob. 95.

Sed quemadmodum diabolus impiorum hominum pastus est, quos in omni scelerum genere alit et fovet ad supplicium æternum, ita Christus verus est omnium illorum pastus, qui corporis sui membra sunt: illos alit, sustentat, educat, atque ad vitam æternam pascit.

August. in Joan. Hom. xxvi.

Aug. in Joan. Homil. xxvi. super hunc locum, 'Patres vestri manducaverunt manna in deserto, et mortui sunt:' "Quantum," inquit, "pertinet ad mortem istam visibilem et corporalem, nunquid nos non morimur, qui manducamus panem de cœlo descendentem?" Et mox: "Quantum autem pertinet ad illam mortem de qua terret Dominus, quia mortui sunt patres istorum, manducavit manna et Moses, manducavit et Aaron, manducavit manna et Phinees, manducaverunt ibi multi, qui Domino placuerunt, et mortui non sunt. Quare? Quia visibilem cibum spiritualiter intellexerunt, spiritualiter esurierunt, spiritualiter gustaverunt, ut spiritualiter satiarentur. Nam et nos hodie accepimus visibilem cibum; sed aliud est sacramentum, aliud virtus sacramenti. Quam multi de altari accipiunt et moriuntur, et accipiendo moriuntur! Unde dicit Apostolus: 'Judicium sibi manducat et bibit.' Nonne buccella dominica venenum fuit Judæ? Et tamen accepit, et cum accepit, in eum inimicus intravit, non quia malum accepit, sed quia bonum malus male accepit. Videte ergo, fratres, panem cœlestem spiritualiter manducate." Et mox: "Patres vestri manna manducaverunt, et mortui sunt, non quia malum erat manna, sed quia male manducarunt: hic est panis qui de cœlo descendit; hunc panem significavit manna, hunc panem significavit altare Dei. Sacramenta illa fuerunt, in signis diversa sunt, sed in re quæ significatur paria sunt," &c. *1 Cor. xi.* *Joan. xiii.*

Et mox: "Ut si quis manducaverit ex ipso, non moriatur in æternum: sed quod pertinet ad virtutem sacramenti, non quod pertinet ad visibile sacramentum. Qui manducat intus, non foris, qui manducat in corde, non qui premit dente."

CAPUT II.

QUIDNAM SIT CARNEM CHRISTI COMEDERE SANGUINEMQUE EJUS BIBERE.

Quisque bonus ac fidelis Christianus apud se sentit, quomodo edat Christi carnem, et sanguinem ejus bibat, ipsoque nutriatur. Universam enim spem ac fiduciam redemptionis et salutis suæ collocat in unico illo sacrificio, quod Christus in cruce fecerat, corpore illius transfixo, et sanguine pro nobis fuso, ad remissionem peccatorum. Hoc tantum et tam memorabile beneficium Christi fidelis quisque diligenter animo pertractat, mandit, ac ruminat, et cordis quasi ventriculo digerit, spiritualiter in se universum Christum recipiens, ac se rursum Christo totum tradens. *Ob. 93.

Atque hæc est carnis et sanguinis Christi manducatio et potatio. Quod hominem in se sentire, est corporis et sanguinis Christi nutritionem sentire: quod nemo malus aut membrum diaboli facere poterit.

CAPUT III.

CHRISTUS NON DENTIBUS SED FIDE EDITUR.

Quemadmodum Christus spiritualis cibus est, sic spirituali parte nostri spiritualiter editur et digeritur, et spiritualem atque æternam vitam subministrat; non autem ore, lingua, gula, ventre, vel editur, vel deglutitur, vel digeritur. *Ob. 89.

Itaque Cyprianus ait: "Hanc Dei gratiam recolens qui de sacro calice bibit, amplius sitit, et ad Deum vivum erigens desiderium, ita singulari fame illo uno appetitu tenetur, ut deinceps fellea peccatorum horreat pocula, et omnis sapor delectamentorum carnalium fit ei quasi rancidum radensque palatum, acutæ mordacitatis acetum. Ad hæc, inter sacra mysteria ad gratiarum actiones convertitur, et inclinato capite, munditia cordis adepta, se intelligens consummatum, restitutus peccator sanctificatam Deo animam, quasi depositum custoditum, fideliter reddit, et deinceps cum Paulo gloriatur et lætatur dicens: 'Vivo jam non ego, vivit vero in me Christus.' Hæc in Christi commemoratione retractantur a fidelibus: et defæcatis animis carnis ejus edulium non est horrori, sed honori, potuque sancti et sanctificantis sanguinis spiritus delectatur. Hæc quoties agimus, non dentes ad mordendum acuimus, sed fide sincera panem sanctum frangimus et partimur." Hæc Cyprianus. *Cyprianus de Cœna Domini.* *Ob. 173.

His similia Augustinus: "Noli parare fauces, sed cor." Et alio in loco (quemadmodum de eo commemoratur) sic scribit: "Ut quid paras dentes et ventrem? crede, et manducasti." Sed de hac re satis multa dicta sunt, ubi confirmabatur has de carne et sanguine Christi edendo et bibendo voces figuratas esse. *Aug. de verbis Domini, Sermo. 33.* *Ob. 244. *In Joan. Tract. 25.*

Aug. in Joan. Tract. xxvi. "Credere in eum, hoc est manducare panem vivum. Qui credit in eum, manducat, invisibiliter saginatur, quia et invisibiliter renascitur. Infans intus est, novus intus est; ubi novellatur, ibi satiatur." Idem Psal. xxi. in expositione prima: "Sacramenta corporis et sanguinis mei reddam coram timentibus eum. Edent pauperes et saturabuntur, edent humiles et contemptores seculi, et imi- *August.*

tabuntur. Ita enim nec copiam hujus seculi concupiscent, nec timebunt inopiam. Et laudabunt Dominum, qui requirunt eum: nam laus Domini est eructatio saturitatis illius. Vivunt corda eorum in seculum seculi, nam cibus ille cordis est."

Clemens. Clemens Alexandrinus in Pædagogo, Lib. ii. cap. 2. "Hoc est bibere Jesu sanguinem, esse participem incorruptionis Domini."

De Consecra. Dist. 2. "Utrum. Quia Christum fas vorari dentibus non est," &c.

CAPUT IV.

BONOS TANTUM CHRISTUM EDERE.

Atque ut ad propositum nostrum revertamur, tantum vera et vitalia Christi membra carnem et sanguinem ejus edere et bibere, ex permultis antiquorum locis, minime adhuc citatis, comprobabo. Origenes aperte de ea re scribit hoc modo: "Verbum factum est caro, verusque cibus, quem qui comederit, omnino vivet in æternum; quem nullus malus potest edere. Etenim si fieri possit, ut qui malus adhuc perseveret, edat Verbum factum carnem, quum sit Verbum et panis vivus, nequaquam scriptum fuisset, 'Quisquis ederit panem hunc, vivet in æternum'." Hæc ita perspicua sunt, ut longioris explicationis non egeant. Itaque quomodo cum hoc conveniat Cyprianus, videamus.

*Orig. in Matt. cap. xv. *Ob. 169.*

Is in sermone de Cœna Domini (qui illi ascribitur) sic ait: "Dixerat sane hujus traditionis magister, quod nisi manducaremus et biberemus ejus sanguinem, non haberemus vitam in nobis; spirituali nos instruens documento, et aperiens ad rem adeo abditam intellectum, ut sciremus quod mansio nostra in ipso sit manducatio, et potus quasi quædam incorporatio, subjectis obsequiis, voluntatibus junctis, affectibus unitis. Esus igitur carnis hujus quædam aviditas est, et quoddam desiderium manendi in ipso, per quod sic imprimimus et eliquamus in nos dulcedinem caritatis ut hæreat."

Cyprian. in Serm. de Cœna Domini.

Hæc Cyprianus de esu et potu corporis et sanguinis Domini. Et paulo post ait: "Nullus huic agno communicat, quem Israelitici nominis generositas non commendat."

Athanasius autem de carnis et sanguinis Christi perceptione refert, "ideo Christum ascensus sui in cœlum meminisse, ut illos a corporali cogitatione avelleret; et posthac discant, carnem dictam cibum cœlestem, superne venientem, et spiritualem alimoniam, quam ipse det. Nam 'quæ locutus sum vobis, inquit, spiritus sunt et vita.' Quod idem est perinde ac dicat, Quod quidem ostenditur, occiditur, pro mundi dabitur alimonia, ut spiritualiter in unoquoque distribuatur, ac fiat omnibus conservatorium in resurrectionem vitæ æternæ."

*Athanas. de Peccato in Spiritum sanctum. *Ob. 180.*

Joan. vi.

Hic Athanasius causam ostendit, cur Christus suæ in cœlum ascensionis mentionem fecerit, cum de esu et potu carnis et sanguinis sui loqueretur. Causa autem hæc fuit, ut auditores de nulla carnali Christi perceptione ore adhibenda cogitarent, (cum quod ad corporis præsentiam pertineret, ab illis tollendus et in cœlum subvehendus esset,) sed intelligerent illum spiritualem cibum esse, spiritualiter percipiendum, et hoc pastu vitam æternam nobis donandam, quod nullis nisi vitalibus membris suis facit.

De hac perceptione similiter Basilius: "Edimus (inquit) Christi carnem, et bibimus ipsius sanguinem, per incarnationem participes fientes et sensibilis vitæ, verbi et sapientiæ. Carnem enim et sanguinem totam suam mysticam conversationem in carne nominat, et doctrinam ex activa et naturali ac theologica constantem indicavit, per quam nutritur anima, et interim ad veritatis speculationem præparatur."

*Basilius, Epist. 141. *Ob. 184.*

Hic nos docet Basilius, quomodo carnem et sanguinem Christi percipiamus, quod ad vera et fidelia Christi membra pertinet.

Hieronymus autem hæc habet: "Omnes voluptatis magis amatores quam Dei non comedunt carnem Jesu, neque bibunt sanguinem ejus, de quo ipse loquitur: 'Qui comedit carnem meam et bibit meum sanguinem, habet vitam æternam'."

*Hieron. in Esai. cap. lxvi. *Ob. 207.*

Ob. 208.

Atque alio loco Hieronymus: "Hæretici non comedunt nec bibunt corpus et sanguinem Domini."

Addit præterea: "Hæretici non comedunt carnem Jesu, cujus caro cibus credentium est." *Ob. 209. In Hiere. cap. xxii.

Itaque Hieronymus cum superioribus in hoc consentit, hæreticos ceterosque, qui carnis suæ libidines sequuntur, carnem et sanguinem Christi non percipere; Christus enim ait, "Qui edit meam carnem et bibit meum sanguinem, vitam æternam habet."

Ambrosius autem "Jesum ait esse panem qui est esca sanctorum, quem qui accipit non moritur peccatoris morte, quia panis hic remissio peccatorum est." Et alibi quodam in libro, qui illi ascribitur, sic loquitur: "Iste panis vivus qui descendit de cœlo, vitæ æternæ substantiam subministrat. Et quicumque hunc panem manducaverit, non morietur in æternum, et corpus est Christi." In alio autem libro (qui sub nomine illius prodit) his verbis usus est: "Manna qui manducavit, mortuus est: qui manducaverit hoc corpus, fiet ei remissio peccatorum, et non morietur in æternum." Et alio loco: "Quotiescunque bibis, remissionem accipis peccatorum." *Ob. 194. Ambros. de Benedictio. Patriarch. cap. 9. *Ob. 195. De his qui mysteriis initiantur,cap.6. De Sacramentis, Lib. iv. cap. 5. *Ob. 193. Lib. v. cap. 3.

Hæ Ambrosii sententiæ ita perspicuæ sunt, ut repetitionis tantum, non etiam explicationis, egeant.

Augustinus permultis in locis hanc dubitationem explicuit. Itaque quodam in loco sic ait: "Qui discordat a Christo, nec panem ejus manducat nec sanguinem bibit, etiamsi tantæ rei sacramentum ad judicium suæ præsumptionis quotidie indifferenter accipiat." Aug. in Sententiis Prospe. decerptis, cap. 339. *Ob. 233.

Sed planissime Augustinus in libro de Civitate Dei hac de re sententiam suam pronuntiavit: ubi adversus duo hæreticorum genera disputat, quorum hi omnibus baptismo lotis, et sacramento corporis et sanguinis Christi pastis, vitam æternam promittebant, qualescunque tandem fides aut mores eorum essent, quia Christus dixit: "Hic est panis qui de cœlo descendit. Si quis ex ipso manducaverit, non morietur. Ego sum panis vivus, qui de cœlo descendi. Si quis manducaverit ex hoc pane, vivet in æternum." Ex hoc Christi dicto colligebant, omnes hujus sacramenti participes ab æterna morte liberandos, et tandem ad æternam vitam perducendos. De Civit. Dei, Lib. xxi. cap. 25. Joan. vi.

Alii vero dicebant, quod hæretici et schismatici, etsi sacramentum corporis Christi comederent, verum tamen corpus Christi percipere non possent, quia membra corporis ejus non sunt. Ideoque non omnibus, baptismo et sacramento corporis Christi initiatis, vitam æternam pollicebantur, sed illis qui fidem veram præ se ferrent, etsi mores impii essent: affirmabant enim tales, non tantum in sacramento, sed etiam reipsa corpus Christi manducare, quia membra sint corporis Christi.

At Augustinus utrosque confutans ait, neque hæreticos, neque eos quorum vita a fidei professione dissideat, aut veram habere fidem, (quæ per caritatem efficax est, et malum non operatur,) aut in membris Christi consendos esse: non enim possunt simul esse et membra Christi et membra diaboli. "Qui ergo est," inquit, "in corporis Christi unitate, id est, in christianorum compage membrorum, (cujus corporis sacramentum fideles communicantes de altari sumere consueverunt,) ipse vere dicendus est manducare corpus Christi et bibere sanguinem Christi. Ac per hoc hæretici et schismatici, ab hujus unitate corporis separati, possunt idem percipere sacramentum, sed non sibi utile, imo vero etiam noxium." Et mox: "Recte intelligunt, non dicendum eum manducare corpus Christi, qui in corpore non est Christi." Et mox: "Nec isti ergo dicendi sunt manducare corpus Christi, quoniam nec in membris computandi sunt Christi. Ut enim alia taceam, non possunt simul esse et membra Christi et membra meretricis. Denique ipse dicens, 'Qui manducat carnem meam et bibit meum sanguinem, in me manet et ego in eo,' ostendit quid sit, non sacramento tenus, sed revera corpus Christi manducare, et ejus sanguinem bibere; hoc est enim in Christo manere, ut in illo maneat et Christus. Sic enim hoc dixit, tanquam diceret, Qui non in me manet, et in quo ego non maneo, non se dicat aut existimet manducare corpus meum, aut bibere sanguinem meum." *Ob. 224.

His verbis Augustinus apertissime asseverat, illos qui vitam impiam et sceleratam degunt, quanquam Christi corpus edere videantur, quia sacramentum corporis ejus percipiunt, revera tamen neque membra corporis sui esse, neque corpore illius vesci.

In Evangelium autem Joannis hæc scribit: "Qui non manducat ejus carnem, nec bibit ejus sanguinem, non habet in se vitam. Et qui manducat ejus carnem, et In Joan. Tract. 26.

bibit ejus sanguinem, habet vitam æternam. Ad utrumque autem respondit, quod dixit æternam. Non ita est in hac esca, quam sustentandæ hujus corporis vitæ causa sumimus: nam qui eam non sumpserit, non vivet, nec tamen qui eam sumpserit, vivet. Fieri enim potest, ut senio, ut morbo, vel aliquo casu, plurimi et qui eam sumpserint, moriantur. In hoc vero cibo et potu, id est, corpore et sanguine Domini, non ita est: nam et qui eam non sumit, non habet vitam, et qui eam sumit, habet vitam, et hanc utique æternam." Et mox: "Hunc itaque cibum et potum societatem vult intelligi corporis et membrorum suorum, quod est sancta ecclesia in prædestinatis, et vocatis, et justificatis, et glorificatis, sanctis et fidelibus ejus." Et mox: "Hujus rei sacramentum, id est, unitatis corporis et sanguinis Christi, alicubi quotidie, alicubi certis intervallis dierum, in dominica mensa præparatur, et de mensa dominica sumitur, quibusdam ad vitam, quibusdam ad exitium. Res vero ipsa, cujus et sacramentum est, omni homini ad vitam, nulli ad exitium, quicunque ejus particeps fuerit." Deinde his ista subjungit: "Hoc est manducare illam escam, et illum bibere potum, in Christo manere, et illum manentem in se habere." Ac per hoc, "qui non manet in Christo, et in quo non manet Christus, proculdubio nec manducat spiritualiter carnem ejus, nec bibit ejus sanguinem, licet carnaliter et visibiliter premat dentibus sacramentum corporis et sanguinis Christi, sed magis tantæ rei sacramentum ad judicium sibi manducat."

Hæc Augustini verba diligenter ponderanda sunt: panem et vinum ceterosque cibos et potiones, quibus corpus sustentatur, ab hominibus posse percipi, nihilominus morituris; verum autem corpus et sanguinem Christi neminem posse percipere, nisi qui sempiternam vitam habeat: atque adeo impios illa percipere non posse; ex eo enim futurum, ut vitam æternam haberent.

In Joan. Tract. 27.

Hæc ille xxvi. homilia in Joannem. In homilia autem sequenti hæc habet: "Hodierna die sermo est de corpore Domini, quod dicebat se dare manducandum propter æternam vitam. Exposuit autem modum attributionis hujus et doni sui, quomodo daret carnem suam manducare, dicens: 'Qui manducat carnem meam et bibit sanguinem meum, in me manet et ego in illo.' Signum quia manducavit et bibit hoc est, si manet et manetur, si habitat et inhabitat, si hæret ut non deseratur. Hoc ergo nos docuit et admonuit mysticis verbis, ut simus in ejus corpore, sub ipso capite, in membris ejus, edentes carnem ejus, non relinquentes unitatem ejus."

Ob. 226. De Doctr. Christiana, Lib. iii. cap. 14.

Et in libro de Doctrina Christiana tertio scribit, quod "manducare carnem Christi et bibere ejus sanguinem est figura, præcipiens passioni Domini esse communicandum, atque utiliter recondendum in memoria, quod pro nobis caro ejus crucifixa et vulnerata sit."

*De Verbis Apostoli, Serm. 2. *Ob. 236.*

In alio autem sermone de Verbis Apostoli, quæ sit corporis et sanguinis Christi perceptio, docet his verbis: "Illud manducare refici est, sed sic reficeris, ut non deficiat unde reficeris. Illud bibere quid est, nisi vivere? Manduca vitam, bibe vitam, habebis vitam, et integra est vita. Tunc autem hoc erit, id est, vita unicuique erit corpus et sanguis Christi, si quod in sacramento visibile sumitur, in ipsa veritate spiritualiter manducetur, spiritualiter bibatur."

Ex his omnibus Augustini sententiis intelligitur, omnes tum bonos tum malos posse ore visibiliter et sensibiliter corporis et sanguinis Christi sacramentum edere, ipsum autem corpus et sanguinem nisi spiritualiter percipi non posse, idque a spiritualibus Christi membris, qui in Christo habitant, et Christum in se habitantem habent, per quem reficiuntur, et sempiterna vita fruuntur.

*In Joan. Tract. 59. *Ob. 235.*

Qua de causa Augustinus ait, quod "cum ceteri apostoli manducabant panem Dominum, Judas panem Domini, non panem Dominum, comedebat. Ceteri itaque apostoli cum sacramentali pane Christum etiam ipsum ederant, quem Judas non ederat." Permulta sunt ejusmodi apud Augustinum, quæ ego fastidii vitandi gratia hoc tempore prætermitto, et ad Cyrillum me confero.

Psal. xxii.

Augustinus in Psal. xxi. in expositione 2. 'Vota mea reddam coram timentibus eum.' "Quæ sunt vota sua? Sacrificium quod obtulit Deo. Nostis quale sacrificium? Norunt fideles vota quæ reddit coram timentibus eum. Nam sequitur: 'Edent pauperes et saturabuntur.' Beati pauperes, quia ideo edunt, ut saturentur. Edunt enim pauperes; qui autem divites sunt, non satiantur, quia non esuriunt. Comedent pauperes: inde erat piscator ille Petrus, inde erat alius piscator Joannes et Jacobus frater ipsius, inde erat etiam publicanus Matthæus de pauperibus. Ipsi erant qui comederunt et saturati sunt, talia passi, qualia manducaverunt. Cœnam suam dedit, passionem suam dedit. Ille saturatur qui imitatur. Imitati sunt pauperes, ipsi enim sic passi sunt, ut Christi vestigia sequerentur," &c. Et mox: "Sacrificium pacis, sacrificium caritatis, sacrificium corporis sui norunt fideles; disputari inde modo non potest. 'Vota mea reddam coram timentibus eum.' Edant publicani, edant piscatores, manducent, imitentur Dominum, patiantur, saturentur."

Idem de Verbis Domini, sermone liii. "Quicunque in corpore ejus et membrorum ejus esse voluerit, non miretur quia odit eum mundus. Corporis autem ejus sacramentum multi accipiunt, sed non omnes qui accipiunt sacramentum, habituri sunt apud eum etiam locum promissum membris ejus. Pene quidem sacramentum omnes corpus ejus dicunt, quia omnes in pascuis ejus simul pascunt; sed venturus est qui dividat, et alios ponat ad dexteram, alios ad sinistram."

Beda in Homilia quadam Paschali: "Aderit nobis Christus in fractione panis, cum sacramenta corporis ejus, videlicet panis et vini, casta et simplici conscientia sumimus."

Cyrillus in Evangelium Joannis hæc habet: "Majores qui manna comedebant, naturæ tamen concesserunt; non enim vivificabat, sed famem solummodo corporalem removebat: sed qui panem vitæ suscipiunt, immortalitatem consequentur, et omnia interitus mala effugient, cum Christo æternaliter viventes." Et alio loco ait: "Quia Verbum humanitati conjunctum totam in seipsum ita reduxit, ut indigentia vitæ possit vivificare, sic interitum a natura humana expulit, et mortem quæ peccato plurimum poterat, destruxit. Quare qui carnem Christi manducat, vitam habet æternam." *Ob. 212. Cyrillus in Evangelium Joannis, Lib. iv. cap. 10. Cap. 15. *Ob. 214.

Et alio loco paucis in hunc modum concludit: "Quando carnem Christi comedimus, tunc vitam habemus in nobis. Quod si solo tactu suo corrupta redintegrantur, quomodo non vivemus, qui carnem illam et gustamus et manducamus?" Et præterea dicit: "Quemadmodum si quis liquefactæ ceræ aliam ceram infuderit, alteram cum altera per totum commisceat necesse est: siquis carnem et sanguinem Domini recipit, cum ipso ita conjungatur, ut Christus in ipso, et ipse in Christo inveniatur." In Joan. cap. 14. *Ob. 215. Cap. 17. *Ob. 216.

Hic Cyrillus carnis Christi dignitatem, inseparabiliter divinitati adjunctam, vim hanc et naturam habere dicit, ut vitam æternam afferat; et quamcunque vel mortis occasionem, vel vitæ æternæ impedimentum reperit, illud protinus tollit, atque ex his expellit, qui hunc vel cibum capiunt, vel medicinam percipiunt. Ceteræ medicinæ cum admoventur, interdum sanant, interdum non sanant. Hæc medicina autem ejusmodi vim habet, ut omnem vel putrescentem vel emortuam carnem exedat, omnia vulnera ulceraque, quibus admovetur, ad perfectam sanitatem integritatemque deducat.

Hæc carnis et sanguinis Christi cum divinitate ejus conjuncti dignitas est et excellentia, qua papistæ, infensissimi hostes Christi, illum spoliant, cum affirmant illum hominem carnem ejus percipere, et ejusmodi medicamento uti, qui æger adhuc infirmitate valetudinis languet, neque quicquam inde ad sanitatem adipiscendam juvatur.

CAPUT V.

Ad corroborandam autem Cyrilli sententiam, libenter a papistis quærerem, utrum nulla peccator pœnitentia ductus, et sacramentum percipiens, Christi corpus in se habeat, necne? Num peccator impœnitens Christum in se habeat. *Ob. 96.

Si negant, satis dant, malos, etiamsi sacramentum corporis Christi percipiant, verum ejus corpus minime tamen percipere. Sin affirmant, libenter illos etiam rogarem, utrum Christi Spiritum in se habeant, necne? Hoc si negant, Christi corpus a Spiritu, humanitatem a divinitate ejus, separant, et quasi antichristi ipsi, Christum dividentes, a scriptura condemnantur.

Sin affirmaverint, impium in se Spiritum Christi habere, etiam hic scriptura illos condemnat, his verbis: "Qui non habet Spiritum Dei, hic non est ejus." In quo autem Rom. viii.

Christus est, vivit propter justificationem: "Quod si spiritus ejus, qui exsuscitavit Jesum ex mortuis, habitat in vobis, qui exsuscitavit Jesum ex mortuis, vita afficiet mortalia corpora vestra, propter illius Spiritum in vobis inhabitantem."

Ita undique scriptura verbi divini adversarios condemnat.

Hæc autem papistarum impietas monstrosa est, dicere Christi carnem, sanguinem, animam, Spiritum et Deitatem, in homine esse sub peccatum subjecto, et membrum jam diaboli effecto.

*Ob. 97.

Admirabiles sunt hi præstigiatores et exorcistæ, qui, verbulis quibusdam adhibitis, Deum faciunt et diabolum simul eodem in homine habitare, et templum simul Dei ac diaboli esse. Itaque videtur illos sic occæcatos esse, ut lucem a tenebris, Belial a Christo, mensam Domini a mensa diabolorum, nequeant discernere. Sic ergo a nobis hoc tempore papistarum immanis atque intolerabilis error refutatur, qui eos, qui membra diaboli sunt, edere verum corpus Christi, et ejus sanguinem bibere affirmant, longe contra sententiam et auctoritatem Christi, cujus hæc verba sunt: "Qui edit meam carnem et bibit meum sanguinem, vitam æternam habet."

CAPUT VI.

RESPONDETUR QUIBUSDAM PAPISTARUM OBJECTIONIBUS.

1 Cor. xi.

Ne autem videantur papistæ tam misero in loco esse, ut nihil habeant, quod pro se afferre queant, Paulum in undecimo ad Corinthios citant: ait enim, "Qui bibit et edit indigne, judicium sibi edit et bibit, non dijudicans corpus Domini."

Paulus autem hoc loco de panis et vini perceptione, et non de perceptione corporis et sanguinis Domini, loquitur, sicuti satis constat singulis verba Pauli recte considerantibus. Hæc enim Paulus: "Exquirat seipsum homo, atque adeo de pane illo edat, et de poculo bibat. Qui enim edit et bibit indigne, judicium sibi edit et bibit, non dijudicans corpus Domini."

Paulus hoc loco hanc habet sententiam, quoniam in cœna Domini panis et vinum verum corpus et sanguinem Christi Servatoris repræsentant, quemadmodum ille ipse instituit et decrevit, ideo quamvis in cœlo ad dexteram Patris Christus consideat, ad hæc tamen mysteria panis et vini tanta fide, reverentia, puritate, timore, accedere debemus, ac si Christum ipsum sensibus nostris objectum reciperemus. Ita enim Christus fidelibus in cœna adest magnitudine Spiritus et gratiæ suæ, et fructuosius ab illis percipitur, quam si corporaliter illum præsentem perciperent. Qui igitur digne ad cœnam hanc accedunt, post diligentem ac debitam sui ipsorum inquisitionem, debent accurate considerare, quis hanc cœnam instituit, quem cibum et potionem percepturi sint, et quemandmodum seipsos gerere in hoc munere debeant. Qui cœnam instituit, Christus ipse est; cibus autem et potio (quibus convivas suos digne et accommodate accedentes pascit) caro et sanguis ejus sunt. Accedentes autem hoc diligenti et attenta animi consideratione tenere debent, quod corpus ejus pro illis cruci affixum, et sanguis pro illorum redemptione profusus sit. Itaque ad has sublimes et cœlestes epulas summissis et religiosis animis ita accedere debent, ac si Christus ipse in illis propositus esset. Qui aliter huc accedunt, indigne huc accedunt, nec corpus et sanguinem Christi, sed suam ipsorum condemnationem, percipiunt; quia non satis officiose ac convenienter intuentur in verum Christi corpus et sanguinem (quæ nobis spiritualiter ad cibum offeruntur), sed, despecta Christi cœna, quasi ad communem et vulgarem pastum accedunt, nulla corporis Christi (qui spiritualis hujus mensæ cibus est) ratione habita.

CAPUT VII.

RESPONDETUR SCRIPTORIBUS ILLIS QUOS PAPISTÆ PRO SE CITANT.

Neque vero hic transeundi hi loci sunt, quos ex antiquis scriptoribus papistæ pro se inducunt, qui primo aspectu videntur pro illis facere, qui malos corpus et sanguinem Domini percipere dicunt. Quod si diligenter hi loci perpendantur, inveniemus ne unum quidem ex illis hunc errorem ulla ex parte defendere.

Primus locus ex Augustino contra Cresconium grammaticum est: verba hæc sunt: *Aug. contra Cresconium, Lib. ii. cap. 25.* "Quamvis ipse Dominus dicat, 'Nisi quis manducaverit carnem meam et biberit sanguinem meum, non habebit in se vitam;' tamen nonne apostolus docet, hoc perniciosum male utentibus fieri? Ait enim, 'Quicunque manducaverit panem et biberit sanguinem Domini indigne, reus erit corporis et sanguinis Domini'."

Ex quibus Augustinus efficere videtur, tum bonos tum malos corpus et sanguinem Christi percipere, quamvis mali nullum inde beneficium, sed incommodum habeant.

Sed paulo altius in hunc locum intueamur, et videbimus eum non de perceptione corporis Christi, sed sacramenti ejus verba fecisse. Hoc enim Augustini propositum *Mar. An. fol. 214.* est, bona nihil prodesse male utentibus, et quædam per se et quibusdam bona, aliis bona non esse. Lumen integris oculis bonum est, laborantes autem oculos lædit: cibus aliis salubris, aliis noxius habetur: eadem medicina alios sanos, alios languentes efficit. Eadem arma aliis usui, aliis impedimento sunt: et eadem vestis satis laxa uni, et nimis astricta alteri. Denique, post multa exempla producta, Augustinus eadem demonstrat in sacramentis baptismi et corporis Domini vera esse, quæ illis tamen prodesse ait, qui ea digne percipiunt.

Pauli verba, quæ Augustinus citat, de sacramentali pane et poculo, non autem de corpore et sanguine Domini, mentionem faciunt. Hic tamen Augustinus panem et poculum corpus et sanguinem Domini vocat, non quod illa sint, sed quod illa signifi- *Contra Maximi. Lib. iii. cap. 22.* cent: quemadmodum alio in loco contra Maximinum disputat. "In sacramentis," inquit, "non quid sint, sed quid ostendant semper attenditur, quoniam signa sunt rerum aliud existentia, et aliud significantia."

Itaque quemadmodum in baptismo, qui ficte accedunt, et qui sincere, ambo sacramentali aqua abluuntur, sed ambo Spiritu sancto non tinguntur, nec Christo vestiuntur; sic in cœna Domini ambo sacramentalem panem et scyphum percipiunt, sed ambo Christo non vescuntur, nec carne et sanguine ejus pascuntur, sed hi soli, qui digne sacramentum percipiunt. Atque hoc responsum alio etiam loco adversus Donatistas *De Baptismo, contra Donatist. Lib. v. cap. 8.* satisfacere potest, ubi "Judam," ait, "corpus et sanguinem Domini percepisse." Quemadmodum enim Augustinus eo in loco de sacramenti baptismi loquitur, ita etiam *Mar. An. fol. 215.* de sacramento corporis et sanguinis Domini verba facit: quod tamen corpus et sanguinem ejus vocat, quia nobis verum corpus, carnem, et sanguinem Christi repræsentat.

CAPUT VIII.

FIGURÆ ILLARUM RERUM NOMINIBUS APPELLANTUR QUAS SIGNIFICANT.

Figura (quemadmodum superius multis a me explicatum est) nomen ejus rei habet quam significat. Sic hominis, leonis, avis, arboris, stirpis simulacrum, homo, leo, avis, arbor, stirps, nominatur. Ita dici solitum est, "Diva Maria Walsinghamica," "Guipsiaca," "Maria gratiæ," "Maria miserationis," "divus Petrus Mediolanensis," "divus Joannes Ambianus," atque hujus generis nonnulla; quibus tamen res ipsas non intelleximus, sed simulacra ipsa nominibus rerum quas repræsentabant appellabamus. Itemque sermone omnium usitatum hoc et contritum est, "Magnus Christophorus Eboracensis, Lincolniensis," "beata virgo ridet," "agitat in cunis infantem," "peregrinando visamus Petrum Romæ, Jacobum Compostellæ;" et sexcenta alia sunt hujusmodi, quæ non de rebus ipsis, sed de simulacris rerum intelligi solent.

Quæ res Chrysostomum etiam adduxit, ut diceret nos Christum oculis intueri, tangere, tractare et palpare manibus, in carne ejus dentes nostros defigere, eam degustare, interere, comedere, concoquere, sanguine ejus linguas nostras colorare atque inficere, eum haurire atque ebibere.

Hæc verba et his similia nonnulla (quæ ex Chrysostomo citavi) minime de vera carne et sanguine Christi Servatoris intelligenda sunt, quæ re vera neque in tactum neque in aspectum nostrum cadunt, sed ea quæ erga panem et vinum geruntur: figurate erga carnem et sanguinem Christi geri dicuntur, quia vera signa, figuræ, monumenta a Christo instituta sunt, ad carnem ejus et sanguinem nobis repræsentandum. Quemadmodum autem corporis oculis, manibus, et ore panem et vinum (quæ signa et sacramenta corporis et sanguinis Christi sunt) corporaliter videmus, tractamus, gustamus, percipimus; ita spiritualibus oculis, manibus, ore, spiritualiter veram ejus carnem et sanguinem videmus, tractamus, gustamus, et percipimus.

<small>Eusebius Emiss. in Sermo. de Eucharist.</small>

Sic Eusebius Emissenus: "Cum reverendum altare cibis spiritualibus satiandus ascendis, sacrum Dei tui corpus et sanguinem fide respice, honore mirare, mente continge, cordis manu suscipe, et maximo haustu interioris hominis assume. Hæcque spiritualia nullam Christi ipsius corporalem præsentiam requirunt, perpetuo ad dexteram Dei Patris in cœlo considentis."

Et quemadmodum hæc, quæ dicimus, verissima sunt, ita plenam et justam continent ad ea omnia responsionem, quæ cum ulla probabilitate papistæ pro se afferre queant.

CAPUT IX.

DE VENERATIONE SACRAMENTI.

Jam vero necessarium in primis est, aliquid de veneratione Christi explicare, ne qui sacramentum percipiunt, loco Christi sacramentum ipsum venerentur. Quemadmodum enim humanitas ejus cum divinitate conjuncta, et ad dexteram Patris in cœlum sublata, ab omnibus creaturis cœlestibus, terrenis, et subterraneis veneranda est; ita si pro Christo signa et sacramenta cultu ac veneratione prosequamur, in maximam et teterrimam idololatriam incurrimus, et horribilissimum ac nefandissimum coram Deo scelus admittimus.

<small>*Ob. 39. Rudi populo a papistis imponitur.</small>

Antichristi hi tamen, infensissimi et callidissimi Christi hostes, magna ingeniorum subtilitate et scholasticis commentis, quibus abundant, multos simplices ac modestos deceperunt, et ad tam immanem idololatriam abduxerunt, ut res sub aspectum cadentes, atque ipsorum manibus formatas, adorarent, et creaturas pro creatore et opifice Deo Optimo Maximo colerent.

Quid enim alioqui transversos illos in insaniam agebat, ut ab altaribus ad altaria, et ab uno sacrificio ad alium, dum elevabatur hostia, currerent, et fixis, intentis, atque hiantibus quasi oculis lustrarent, quod sacerdotis manibus elevabatur, nisi ut quod oculis atque aspectu capiebant, illud omni mente atque animo colerent? Quid sacerdotes ipsos commovit, ut sacramentum tam alte supra caput tollerent? aut quid plebem concitavit, ut levanti sacerdoti acclamarent, "Tolle altius, tolle altius?" Aut quid illos promovit qui longius ab elevante sacrifico distabant, ut eos qui propius adstabant se inclinare rogarent, ne erecti aspectum impedirent? Aut quid sibi volunt hæ vulgi voces, Hodie Servatorem aut Creatorem meum vidi? aut, Quo die Servatorem meum non videro, quieto et sedato animo esse non possum? Cur tum sacerdos tum plebs ipsa tam reverenter genu terram tangerent, pectora duris et frequentibus ictibus pulsarent? Quæ horum omnium causa, nisi quod aspectabile illud, quod oculis intuebantur, adorarent, et pro Deo etiam haberent? Si enim Christum solummodo spiritu venerabantur, ad dexteram Patris in cœlo sedentem, quid opus esset seipsos suis sedibus movere? quid oculos in rem visam defigere, perinde ac apostoli fecerant, cum Christum in cœlum subvectum intuerentur? Si nihil aspectabile venerantur, cur ad aspiciendum surgunt? Simplex sine dubio populus, quod videbat, colebat, et in eo venerationis ac cultus sui summam collocavit.

Neque me latet, quod tegere hoc et dissimulare papistæ vellent, dicentes, se hoc quod oculis complectuntur sacramentum non venerari, sed illud quod fide credunt reipsa et corporaliter sacramento inesse. Cur ergo de loco in locum vagantur ad ea ipsa tam avide oculis haurienda, quæ nullo religioso cultu et honore prosequuntur? Certe hoc suo exemplo ignaris hominibus atque imperitis magnam occasionem præbent earum rerum colendarum, quas sub aspectum subjectas habent. Cur non quiete se suis sedibus continent, et populum ad hanc moderationem revocant; et Deum (sicuti debent) spiritu et veritate colunt; potius quam ita cursitent ad ea videnda, quæ illi ipsi fatentur nulla veneratione colenda esse?

Atque dum hoc absurdum devitant, quod de veneratione objicitur, in aliud æque vanum incidunt, ut nihil omnino colant. Illud enim se venerari dicunt, quod reipsa et corporaliter, non aspectabiliter, sub specie panis et vini subjicitur; quod sane (uti ante docuimus) nihil est. Itaque imperitis et crassis hominibus occasionem afferunt panis et vini adorandi, cum illi ipsi nihil ibi prorsus adorent.

Sed papistæ, ut ad suum ipsorum lucrum populum etiamnum in idololatria contineant, quendam locum Augustini in Psalmos citant, ubi scribitur: "Nemo carnem Christi manducat, nisi prius adoraverit. Et non solum non peccamus adorando, sed peccamus non adorando."

Ac sane verum est, quod eo in loco Augustinus habet. Quotus enim quisque est, qui Christum profitetur, et spiritualiter illius carne et sanguine pascitur, quin illum ad dexteram Dei Patris sedentem omni religionis veneratione afficiat, illique toto (ut dicitur) pectore laudationes et gratiarum actiones pro immensa ejus et clementissima redemptione attribuat?

Et ut negari non potest, verissimum esse quod ex Augustino depromitur, sic contra falsissimum est, quod illorum verborum auctoritate, de panis et vini aut alicujus aspectabilis rei in sacramento veneratione, probare contendunt. Tantum enim Augustini sententia ab ejusmodi cogitatione abfuit, ut prorsus vetet carnem Christi et sanguinem solum adorare, nisi quatenus divinitate ejus colligantur et connectuntur. Quanto igitur minus vel sentire vel approbare potuit, ullum pani aut vino, aut alicui externo et aspectabili sacramento, cultum adhiberi? quæ umbræ duntaxat, figuræ, et repræsentationes veræ carnis et sanguinis Christi sunt.

Ac verebatur sane Augustinus, ne vero Christi corpore adorando offenderemus; ideoque præcipit, ut dum illum veneramur, nequaquam defixis animis in carne ejus (quæ sola nihil juvat) hæreamus, sed animos nostros a carne in spiritum tollamus, qui vitam et salutem tribuit. Et tamen audent papistæ, quibus possunt astutiis, eo nos inducere, ut eas res religiosissime colamus, quæ corporis Christi signa et sacramenta sunt.

Sed quid non audent impudentes papistæ pro se afferre, cum non erubescant his Augustini verbis venerationem sacramenti stabilire? ubi de sacramenti adoratione nullum omnino verbum facit, de Christi autem adoratione expresse loquitur.

Quanquam autem dicat, Christum carnem suam nobis edendam dedisse, nequaquam tamen id voluit Christi carnem vel corporaliter hic adesse, vel corporaliter edi, sed spiritualiter tantum. Hæc ex sequentibus eodem in loco verbis planissime colliguntur, ubi Augustinus, in persona quasi Christi loquens, sic ait: Mar. An. fol. 212.

"Spiritus est qui vivificat, caro autem non prodest. Verba quæ loquutus sum vobis, spiritus sunt et vita: spiritualiter intelligite quod loquutus sum. Non hoc corpus quod videtis, manducaturi estis, et bibituri illum sanguinem, quem fusuri sunt qui me crucifigent: sacramentum aliquod vobis commendavi; spiritualiter intellectum vivificabit vos. Et si necesse est illud visibiliter celebrari, oportet tamen invisibiliter intelligi."

Hæc atque illa superius commemorata planissime indicant Augustinum sensisse, Christum nulla alia ratione edi, nisi spirituali, quæ corporalem præsentiam nulla ex parte requirit; neque illum cogitasse, ullam vel sub aspectum cadentium sacramentorum, vel alterius cujusquam corporalis rei sub illis contentæ, venerationem profiteri. Sine ulla enim dubitatione verum est, nihil revera aut corporaliter pane aut vino contentum venerandum esse, quamvis papistæ ferant, Christum in quovis pane consecrato esse.

Horum nos olim Christus admonuit, falsos ejusmodi Christianos et doctores venturos, et illos vitari præcipit: "Si quis," inquit, "vobis dicat, Ecce hic est Christus, aut ecce illic, nolite credere: surgent enim falsi Christi et falsi prophetæ, multaque signa et portenta edent, ita ut (si fieri posset) in errorem etiam ducantur electi. Cavete, hæc prædixi vobis." *Ob. 9. Matt. xxiv. Marc. xiii. Luc. xvii.

Ita amantissimus Pastor et Servator animarum nostrarum Christus horum periculorum et discriminum imminentium admonuit et præcepit, ut ab istiusmodi doctoribus caveremus, qui suaderent panem veneratione prosequendum, flexis genibus colendum, crebris pectorum ictibus adorandum, humi reptando, supplicationibus solennibus sectando, manus expansas erigendo, munera offerendo, cereos accendendo, in cistula aut capsula includendo, omni honore et cultu prosequendo, majorem venerationem quam Deo ipsi exhibendo, hanc idolatriæ suæ excusationem afferendo, "Ecce hic est Christus." Sed Servator Christus illos falsos prophetas vocat, dicens: "Cavete, prædico vobis." Ne fidem illis adhibeatis. "Si vobis dixerint, Christus foris est, aut in solitudine est, ne exeatis: sin in locis inclusis atque abditis dicant esse, ne credatis."

CAPUT X.

PAPISTÆ HIS ERRORIBUS DECEPERUNT POPULUM.

Quod si quæras, quinam hi falsi prophetæ et seductores sint, facilis est et expedita responsio: antichristi Romani et illorum sectarii, qui omnis erroris, ignorantiæ, cæcitatis, superstitionis, hypocriseos et idololatriæ extiterunt auctores.

Innocentius tertius. Innocentius tertius, unus omnium perniciosissimus, qui hanc sacerrimam sedem occuparunt, hostiam instituit diligenter sub seræ et clavis custodia asservari.

Ob. 40. Honorius tertius. Honorius autem tertius non solum idem confirmarat, sed præceperat etiam, ut sacrifici diligenter singulis quibusque temporibus docerent, ut, sublata in altum hostia, populus reverenter et demisse se flecteret, neque tum solum, sed etiam cum sacerdos sacramentum ægrotis defert. Hæc illa episcoporum Romanorum decreta et statuta sunt, quibus simulatione sanctitatis plebem in omnem errorem et idololatriam abducerent, non illos per panem ad Christum, sed a Christo ad panem transferentes.

CAPUT XI.

EXHORTATIO AD VERAM CHRISTI IN SACRAMENTO VENERATIONEM.

Omnes itaque admoneo, qui Christum amant, et qui sincera fide illi nituntur, ut avertant animos ab hac cogitatione de corporata Christi in pane præsentia, sed sublatis in cœlum animis illum ad dexteram Patris sedentem colant: Christum in seipsis adorent, (cujus templa sunt, in quibus habitat et vivit spiritualiter,) et a cultu Christi in pane quam longissime absint. Neque enim spiritualiter in pane (quemadmodum in homine) nec corporaliter in pane (quemadmodum in cœlo) est, sed sacramentaliter solum, quemadmodum res in figura esse dicitur, per quam significatur.

Satis itaque hoc loco tertius ex præcipuis papistarum erroribus de cœna Domini convictus et damnatus est, quo docent, impios veram carnem et sanguinem Christi percipere.

LIBRI QUARTI FINIS.

LIBER QUINTUS.

DE OBLATIONE ET SACRIFICIO SERVATORIS CHRISTI.

CAPUT PRIMUM.

GRAVISSIMA contumelia et injuria quæ inferri Christo potest, et per omne regnum papisticum latissime patet, ea est, quod sacerdotes missam hostiam propitiantem esse asseverant, ad remittenda non modo peccata sua, verum etiam aliorum, tum viventium, tum mortuorum, quibus illam voluerint applicare. Ita simulatione pietatis papistici sacerdotes hoc sibi sumpserunt, ut Christi successores essent, et ejusmodi sacrificium facerent, quale nullum unquam a quoquam, præterquam a Christo ipso, factum est, idque eo solum tempore, cum morte sua pœnas peccatorum nostrorum in cruce lueret.

CAPUT II.

DIFFERENTIA INTER SACRIFICIUM CHRISTI ET SACRIFICIA SACERDOTUM VETERIS LEGIS.

PAULUS ad Hebræos testatur, quanquam sacerdotes veteris legis sæpe offerebant, Heb. ix. (ad minimum autem semel quotannis,) "Christum tamen non sæpe seipsum obtulisse; alioqui sæpius mortem obiisset. Nunc autem semel seipsum obtulit, ut hac hostia peccata nostra deleret: et quemadmodum hominibus constitutum est, ut semel moriantur, ita Christus semel oblatus est, ut multorum peccata tolleret."

Accedunt eodem, quæ sequuntur in Paulo, sacrificia veteris legis, quanquam con- Heb. x. tinenter offerebantur, "nunquam potuisse vel peccata tollere, vel homines perfectos reddere. Si enim semel pacare conscientias hominum potuissent, peccatis tollendis, haud iterum ea sacrificia facienda fuisse: Christum autem unico hoc sacrificio sanctificatos, perfectos, perpetuo effecisse, peccatis nostris ex animo delendis, et perpetua quasi oblivione obruendis. Ubi enim peccatorum remissio est, ibi nullum pro peccatis sacrificium reliquum est."

Atque alio loco de veteri testamento ait, "abrogatum illud et deletum fuisse, quod Heb. vii. imbecillum atque inutile esset, (nihil enim ad perfectionem deduxerat,) et plures illius legis sacerdotes fuisse, quia diutius in vita manere non poterant, atque adeo ab uno ad alium deferebatur sacerdotium: Christum autem, quia ad æternitatem in vita maneret, transitionis omnis vacuum sacerdotium habere. Itaque prorsus servare poterit eos, qui per illum ad Deum accedunt, sempiternam vitam agens, ut pro nobis intercedat. Par enim est ejusmodi nobis sacerdotem esse, qui sanctus, simplex, incorruptus, a peccatoribus sejunctus, altior cœlis esset; cui minime necesse esset quotidie (quemadmodum summis sacerdotibus) prius pro suis, deinde pro peccatis populi, victimas offerre; hoc enim semel fecerat seipso offerendo." Hac in epistola Paulus plene et plane descripsit nobis differentiam inter sacerdotium et sacerdotes veteris testamenti, et longe præstantissimum atque excellentissimum Christi sacerdotium, et perfectissimum illud et summe necessarium sacrificium et beneficium, quod nobis inde dimanat.

Neque enim Christus sanguinem vitulorum, ovium, aut hircorum obtulit, (quemadmodum veteris testamenti sacerdotes facere consueverunt,) sed sanguinem suum in cruce offerebat: neque in sacrarium aliquod ingressus est hominum opera fabricatum, (sicuti Aharon fecerat,) sed in cœlum ascendit, ubi æternus Pater habitat, et apud illum continuatam precationem pro peccatis totius mundi adhibet, corpus suum pro nobis laniatum, et sanguinem quem infinita bonitate sua pro nobis in cruce profudit, ante oculos Patris constituens.

Atque hoc sacrificium eam vim habet, ut minime necesse sit illud quasi solenne quotannis renovare, quemadmodum antistites veteris testamenti faciebant: quorum sacrificia, etiam sæpius facta, nullius momenti aut utilitatis erant, (quia tum sacerdotes ipsi qui offerebant, peccatores fuerant, tum sanguinem animantium rationis expertium, et non suum offerebant;) cum Christi sacrificium semel factum ad omnem æternitatem valeat.

CAPUT III.
DUO ESSE GENERA SACRIFICIORUM.

ATQUE ut omnes melius hoc sacrificium Christi intelligant, quo summum Christianorum beneficium continetur, pernecessarium est sacrificiorum distinctionem et varietatem exponere.

Sacrificiorum duo sunt genera; unum, quod expians vel propitians dicitur, hoc est, quod Dei iram et offensionem placat, veniam ac remissionem omnium peccatorum impetrat, et ab æterna condemnatione nobis debita liberat.

Sacrificium Christi. Quanquam autem in veteri testamento quædam sacrificia hoc nomine notabantur, unum tamen revera hujusmodi sacrificium est, quo peccata nostra relaxantur, et misericordia ac benevolentia Dei impetratur; eaque mors Domini nostri Jesu Christi est, qua excepta, nullum unquam sacrificium expians fuit.

Hic honor, hæc gloria summi nostri Pontificis est, quod unica sui oblatione pro peccatis omnium Patri satisfecit, illorum culpas præstitit, et universum genus humanum illi reconciliavit. Qui autem illi hunc honorem eripiunt, et sibi ipsis assumunt, ipsissimi antichristi sunt, et impurissimis ac superbiæ plenissimis contumeliis Deum Patrem et Filium ejus Dominum Jesum Christum lacessunt.

Sacrificium ecclesiæ. Alterum genus sacrificii est, quod nos Deo minime reconciliat, sed ab his fit qui per Christum reconciliantur, ad nostram in Deum pietatem testificandam, et gratos nos atque obedientes Deo præstandos. Hæc autem sacrificia laudis et gratiarum actiones vocantur.

Ac primum quidem sacrificii genus Christus pro nobis Deo obtulit, alterum autem nos Deo per Christum offerimus.

Per primum sacrificium Christus nos Deo Patri obtulit, per alterum autem nos ipsos omniaque nostra Christo et Patri offerimus.

Hocque sacrificium generaliter universam obedientiam nostram continet, quæ versatur in legibus et præceptis Dei servandis. Hoc de sacrificio David his verbis usus est, Psal. l. "Sacrificium Deo cor contritum:" et D. Petrus omnes Christianos esse ait "sacerdotium 1 Pet. ii. sanctum ad sacrificia spiritualia facienda, accepta Deo per Jesum Christum." Et D. Heb. xiii. Paulus: "Nos (inquit) semper offerimus Deo sacrificium laudis per Jesum Christum."

CAPUT IV.
SACRIFICIUM CHRISTI PLENIUS EXPONITUR.

NUNC autem, ut de sacrificio et sacerdotio Christi plenius atque uberius pertractemus, intelligendum est, ejusmodi pontificem Christum esse, ut semel seipsum offerendo satis Heb. vii. valuerit ad omnia peccata suo sanguine abluenda. Ita perfectus sacerdos fuit, ut una oblatione sui infinitum peccatorum acervum expurgarit atque expiarit, facilemque nobis et parabilem peccatoribus medicinam reliquit, ut omnibus mortalibus (qui se in-1 Joan. ii. dignos hoc beneficio nolunt reddere) sacrificium hoc perpetuo sufficeret. Neque vero in se recepit illorum tantum peccata, qui multos ante annos ex hac vita excesserunt, sed illorum quoque, qui usque ad reditum ejus certam et confirmatam fidem evangelio illius habituri essent. Itaque nunc nullum alium nec sacerdotem nec sacrificium ad peccata nostra tollenda expectare oportet, nisi eum solum, et hoc eximium sacrificium ab illo factum. Et quemadmodum semel moriens pro omnibus immolatus est, ita, quantum in se fuit, peccata omnium in se recepit. Ita fit ut nunc nullæ pro peccatis hostiæ reliquæ fiant, sed severum extremo in die judicium restet. Tunc autem in conspectu omnium iterum rediturus est, non quasi nocens aliquis ad perferendum supplicium, aut ut victima pro peccatis nostris immoletur (quemadmodum ante immolatus est), sed cum gloria magna venturus est, omnis peccati vacans, ad magnam lætitiam et consolationem illorum, qui illius morte abluti et expiati sunt, et in pia ac integra vivendi ratione versantur, atque ad magnum terrorem et cruciatum illorum, qui in impia et scelerata vita permanent. Heb. ix. et x.

Matt. xxv.

Hac igitur ratione nos scriptura docet, Christum, si sæpius hostiam se pro peccatis immolasset, sæpius fuisse moriturum, cum nulla pro peccatis hostia possit esse præter illius mortem. Nunc autem nulla est alia pro peccatis hostia, cum per illum peccata remittantur, et conscientiæ placentur. Heb. ix.

CAPUT V.

DE SACRIFICIIS VETERIS LEGIS.

Quanquam in veteri testamento certa quædam sacrificia fuerant, quæ sacrificia pro peccato nominabantur, non tamen ejus generis fuerant, ut peccata coram Deo tollerent; sed cæremoniæ quædam erant ad hoc institutæ, ut umbræ quædam et figuræ essent ad excellens Christi sacrificium præmonstrandum, quod verum et perfectum pro totius mundi peccatis sacrificium futurum erat. Hoc nomine igitur sacrificia propitiatoria et sacrificia pro peccatis dicebantur, non quod revera peccata nostra delerent, sed quia imagines, umbræ, figuræ erant, quibus pii de vero Chritsi futuro sacrificio admonerentur, quod peccatum et sempiternam damnationem funditus tolleret. Heb. x.

Clarissime autem in epistola ad Hebræos Paulus exposuit, non potuisse illa sacrificia, quæ a sacerdotibus veteris legis fiebant, veniam peccatorum vel impetrare vel promereri. Fieri non potest (inquit) ut peccata nostra sanguine taurorum vel hircorum tollantur. Heb. x.

Quanquam igitur pii omnes his sacrificiis a Deo præscriptis utebantur, non tamen ita magno æstimanda illa putabant, ut inde remissionem coram Deo se consequi posse putarent; sed partim pro figuris et signis a Deo institutis capiebant, (quibus certiores illos reddidit, se illud Semen esse missurum, quod verum pro peccatis sacrificium futurum promisit, atque adeo velle se eos, qui hujus promissi fiducia niterentur, recipere, et propter futurum sacrificium illis peccata condonare,) partim vero pro cæremoniis habebant, quibus hi qui adversus legem Mosis aliquid admiserant, et ex cœtu Israelitico ejecti erant, in gregem illorum iterum recipiebantur, et absoluti esse nuntiabantur.

Hisque iisdem de causis in ecclesia Christi sacramentis per illum institutis utimur. Et hæc externa e populo dominico ejectio et revocatio secundum legem et hominum judicium facta fuit: vera autem cum Deo reconciliatio et peccatorum remissio nec veteris testamenti patribus conferebantur, nec nobis confertur, nisi per Christi sacrificium in monte Calvariæ factum. Ac veteris sane legis sacrificia ita præsagia quædam et notæ istius sacrificii venturi fuerant, quemadmodum sacramenta nostra ejusdem sacrificii præteriti figuræ et testimonia existunt.

CAPUT VI.

MISSAM NON ESSE SACRIFICIUM PROPITIATORIUM.

Ex his datur intelligi, sacrificium sacerdotis in missa, vel muneris sui viventibus et mortuis pro libidine sua applicationem, neque sibi ipsi neque aliis promereri aut nancisci peccatorum remissionem posse; sed hanc doctrinam papisticam doctrinæ Christi repugnantem, et sacrificio Christi injuriosam esse. Si enim sola mors Christi oblatio, sacrificium, et pretium remissionis peccatorum nostrorum est, tum munus hoc et administratio sacerdotis idem efficere et præstare non potest. Itaque insignis est et horribilis contumelia, vel hoc officium et munus sacerdoti tribuere, quod ad solum Christum pertineat, vel existimare ecclesiam tali egere sacrificio; quasi si quis diceret, Christi sacrificium ad nostrorum peccatorum remissionem satis non esse, vel Christi sacrificium ex oblatione sacerdotis pendere.

Sed hi sacerdotes, qui sese successores Christi esse prædicant et illum sacrificare, tetri et odiosi hostes religionis sunt. Nemo enim Christum, præter Christum ipsum, sacrificio obtulit. Qua de causa Paulus ait, "Christi sacerdotium ab illo ad alterum transire non posse." Quid enim sacrificiis aliis opus est, si quidem Christi sacrificium perfectum et seipso contentum sit? Et quemadmodum a Paulo dictum est, Si sacrificia et munus Aharonicum, ceterorumque illius ætatis sacerdotum, nullius rei eguissent, sed consummata fuissent, non ita admodum Christi sacrificio fuisset opus, (temerarium enim atque inane fuisset ei rei aliquid adjicere, quæ res per seipsam integra et perfecta est;) ita si Christi sacrificium plenum atque omnibus numeris perfectum sit, quid opus est illis quotidianis et repetitis sacrificiis? Papistici igitur hi sacerdotes (qui Christi corpus quotidie sacrificandum sibi sumunt) vel Christi sacrificium inchoatum, leve, et irritum pene faciunt suis addendis, vel sua ipsorum vana, temeraria, et supervacanea judicant, Christi sacrificio sua adjungentes, cum illud per se perfectum et seipso contentum sit.

Admirabile est autem videre, quos dolos et quas astutias antichristi papistici excogitant ad impios suos errores simulatione pietatis tegendos. Et quemadmodum catenæ partes aliæ aliis nexæ sunt, ita vitia et errores quodam quasi vinculo junguntur, ut unus alterum post se semper trahat. Id quod etiam hoc loco fit.

CAPUT VII.

CAVILLATIONIS PAPISTICÆ CONFUTATIO.

Papistæ ad seipsos excusandos hoc afferunt, se nullum neque novum sacrificium instituere, neque aliud quam Christus ipse fecit facere, (neque enim tam cæcos esse, quin viderent se tum aliud sacrificium sacrificio Christi addere, atque adeo sacrificium Christi imperfectum facere;) sed hoc idem sacrificium, quod Christus ipse fecerat, contendunt se pro peccatis facere.

Atque hic præcipites in gravissimum et perniciosissimum omnium errorem ruunt. Si enim idem sacrificium pro peccatis quotidie faciunt, quod antea Christus ipse fecerat, atque ea mors ejus fuerat et pretiosissimi sanguinis ejus pro peccatorum nostrorum redemptione profusio; necessario efficitur, illos quotidie trucidare Christum, et ejus sanguinem effundere, atque adeo Judæis et Pharisæis ipsis deteriores esse, qui semel tantum illum neci addixerunt, et sanguinem atque vitam ejus exhauserunt.

CAPUT VIII.

VERUM OMNIUM CHRISTIANORUM SACRIFICIUM.

Deus Omnipotens, Pater omnis lucis et veritatis, omnes errorum tenebras et ignorantiæ caliginem, et harum rerum auctores et principes, vel ex ecclesia sua expellat atque ejiciat; vel corda illorum ad se convertat, et lumen fidei omnibus tribuat, ut fiduciam certam de remissione peccatorum habeant, et ab æterna morte et horrendis cruciatibus inferni liberentur, per singulare unius mortis et sanguinis Christi meritum; et ut sua quisque fide ad se hoc beneficium applicet, neque illud arbitrio ac meritis papistarum sacerdotum accipiat.

Si (quod nomine profitemur) revera Christiani sumus, nulli hunc ascribere honorem, sed soli Christo assignare debemus. Itaque universam tam immensi beneficii laudem illi tribuamus; ad illum quasi ad perfugium et portum omnium ærumnarum nostrarum fugiamus: illi adhærescamus, illi innitamur, illi nos totos tradamus, et quia seipsum morti nostra causa objecit, ut hostia Deo Patri pro nobis esset, nosmetipsos rursum illi dedamus, et victimam illi offeramus, non hircorum, taurorum, aut aliorum animantium rationis expertium, (quemadmodum ante Christi tempora fieri est solitum,) sed hostiam ratione præditam (hoc est, nosipsos), non corporibus nostris mactandis, sed efferatis et immanibus animi perturbationibus domandis, et morte afficiendis, quæ imperium in nobis et dominatum crudelissimum, nisi coercerentur, exercerent. Rom. xii

Quamdiu legis auctoritas viguit, permisit Deus muta et rationis expertia sibi offerri: nunc autem spirituales cum simus, brutorum animantium loco spiritualia a nobis requirit, nempe ut intolerabilem superbiam, immanem iram, insatiabilem pecuniæ cupiditatem, turpe lucrum, sordidam et inquinatam carnis libidinem, exitiale odium, vulpinas fraudes, lupina spolia, et omnes alios animi impetus et commotiones, Spiritui repugnantes, jugulemus. Quicunque Christi sunt, hi cruci et neci dare, Christi causa, hæc omnia debent, quemadmodum Christus illorum causa seipsum morti addixit. Gal. v.

Hæc sacrificia Christianorum sunt, hæ hostiæ et victimæ gratæ Christo. Et quemadmodum Christus seipsum pro nobis obtulit, ita nos vicissim debemus nos ipsos Christo offerre. Ita fiet ut non tantum nomine Christiani simus, sed quod verbis et vultu profitemur, hoc reipsa et vita profitebimur, et omnes animi motus ad illius normam dirigemus. Ita fiet, ut foris et intus omnino illius simus, et ab omni hypocriseos simulatione vacui et liberati erimus. Quod si hoc modo affectibus nostris in crucem agendis, et nobismetipsis totis illi tradendis, offerre nos Deo recusaverimus, ingrati prorsus et inhumani erimus, superstitiosi hypocritæ, vel potius brutæ pecudes, aut brutis ipsis deteriores, digni qui ab omni beneficio oblationis Christi excludamur.

CAPUT IX.

MISSA PAPISTICA EST DETESTANDA IDOLOLATRIA, ET EX OMNI CHRISTIANORUM CŒTU PRORSUS EJICIENDA.

Quod si oblationem sacerdotis loco oblationis Christi ponamus, et perceptionem sacramenti corporis et sanguinis, quemadmodum ille ipse instituit, repudiemus, et remissionem peccatorum e sacrificio sacerdotis petamus, indeque relaxationem aliquam cruciatuum, qui in purgatorio sunt, venemur; non solum injuriam Christo facimus, sed etiam horribile idololatriæ scelus admittimus. Hæc enim doctrina falsa est, impudenter ab impiis papistis, superstitiosis monachis et fraterculis conficta, qui quæstus gratia depravarunt et corruperunt sanctissimam cœnam Domini, et in manifestam idololatriam traduxerunt. Qua de causa hi omnes debent omnibus opibus ac viribus elaborare, ut ejusmodi in Dei Filium contumelia profligetur.

Et quoniam in ejusmodi missis aperta impietas et idololatria est, in quibus sacerdos solus sacrificium propitians offert, illudque viventibus et mortuis pro sua libidine accommodat, omnes ejusmodi missæ papisticæ radicitus Christianorum cœtibus evellendæ atque ejiciendæ sunt, et verus cœnæ usus restituendus, ut congregatus in unam frequentiam populus pro se quisque sacramentum percipiat, et testificetur hoc facto, se membrum corporis Christi esse, et carnis ac sanguinis ejus perceptione spiritualiter sustentari.

CAPUT X.

QUISQUE PRO SE SACRAMENTUM PERCIPERE DEBET, ET NON UNUS PRO ALIO.

Sacramenta a Christo nequaquam ad hoc instituta sunt, ut unus pro alio, aut sacerdos pro omni populo, sacramenta perciperet, sed ut pro se quisque hoc faceret, et fidem suam ac sempiternam salutem confirmaret et stabiliret. Et quemadmodum si unus pro alio salutari baptismi fonte tingatur, nihil illi hic baptismus prodesse poterit, sic nemo sacram cœnam pro alio percipere debet. Si enim esurie quis aut siti afficiatur, cupiditas ejus nullo modo vel extinguitur vel levatur, si quis pro illo cibum aut potionem caperet; aut si qua illuvie sordescat, non multum juvatur, si quis pro illo mundetur: ita nihil valere homini potest, pro quo ab aliis vel baptismus vel cœna percipitur. Quocirca Petrus dicebat: "Baptizetur quisque in nomine Christi." Et Servator Christus multitudini inquit, "Capite, edite:" adjecit præterea, "Bibite ex hoc omnes." Qui igitur spiritualiter renasci in Christo vult, baptizari illum pro se oportet: et qui per se vivere in Christo voluerit, per se carnem ejus et sanguinem percipere debet.

<small>Act. ii.
Matt. xxvi.</small>

Atque ut paucis absolvamus, qui ad Christi regnum ipse pervenire cogitat, debet et ipse ad sacramenta ejus accedere, ipse mandata ejus servare, ipse omnia, quæ ad christiani hominis munus et vocationem pertinent, facere: ne si hæc omnia aliis pro se agenda relinquat, aliis etiam hæreditatem regni cœlestis pro se adeundam dimittat.

CAPUT XI.

QUÆ SIT INTER SACERDOTEM RELIQUUMQUE POPULUM DIFFERENTIA.

CHRISTUS nullam hujusmodi differentiam inter sacerdotem et populum docuit, ut sacerdos pro populo sacrificium de Christo faceret, solus cœnam pro aliis perciperet, eamque pro libidine sua, quibus et quomodo vellet, distribueret. Sed hæc vera est inter illos differentia, quod sacerdos publicus ecclesiæ administer sit, et cœnam Domini ceteris distribuat, illi autem de sacerdotis manu accipiant. Cœna autem ipsa a Christo instituta, et toti ecclesiæ concessa fuit, non ut a ministro et sacerdote pro aliis offeratur et percipiatur, sed ut per sacerdotem omnibus justa ratione petentibus tribuatur.

Quemadmodum in aula regia ceterorumque principum virorum ædibus ministri mensas instruunt, ceteri autem peræque epulantur; sic sacerdotes et ministri cœnam Domini parant, evangelium legunt, verba Christi recitant, sed universus populus illis respondet, Amen. Omnes memoriam mortis Christi celebrant, omnes Deo gratias agunt, omnes ad pœnitentiam et mutationem vitæ feruntur, omnes se quasi sacrificium Deo offerunt, omnes illum pro Deo et Servatore habent, omnes illum spiritualiter epulantur, cujus rei certissimum argumentum, perceptionem panis et vini in cœna, faciunt.

Atque hæc res auctoritatem et dignitatem sacerdotii, reliquorumque ecclesiæ ministrorum non detrahit, sed auget potius atque amplificat. Si enim benevolentia et honore prosequendi sunt, qui prætores, judices, quæstores, et rerum externarum administri regii sunt, quanto majore cultu ac veneratione prosequendi sunt, qui verbi et sacramentorum Christi administri sunt, et ad excludendos atque admittendos homines evangelii administratione claves sibi regni cœlestis concreditas et commissas habent!

CAPUT XII.

PAPISTIS ET EORUM OBJECTIONIBUS RESPONDETUR.

QUONIAM igitur satis (ut spero) expositum vobis est, quidnam sacrificium propitians sit, (ut qui ullam notionem Christi habent, intelligentiam ex eo et consolationem capiant,) et gravem immanitatem atque idololatriam missæ papisticæ declaravimus, in qua sacerdotes sibi sumpserunt officium Christi, ut sacrificium propitians pro peccatis populi facerent; pernecessarium judico, ut papistarum subtilitatibus et inanitati sophisticæ respondeam, quibus et eruditos et simplices quoque, sed non satis circumspectos, deceperunt.

<small>Heb. v.</small>

Locus Pauli ad Hebræos, quem pro se citant, adversari illis maxime videtur. Ubi enim Paulus unumquemque pontificem ait a Deo constitutum, ad dona et sacrificia Deo pro peccatis offerenda, de veteris testamenti, et non de novi, sacerdotibus loquitur:

qui (sicuti ipse commemorat) vitulos et hircos offerebant, non tamen ejusmodi fuerant, ut illorum oblationibus et sacrificiis populi peccata tollerent, sed umbræ et figuræ Christi fuerant, qui solus agnus Dei est, mundi peccata tollens. Itaque papistici sacerdotes, qui hunc textum sibi applicant, longe contra Pauli sententiam faciunt, ad gravissimam injuriam et offensionem Christi, per quem solum Paulus ait hostiam et sacrificium pro peccatis totius mundi expletum et absolutum fuisse.

Atque autem ille locus Malachiæ prophetæ adversari illorum sententiæ videtur, ubique offerendum Deo purum sacrificium et oblationem. Propheta enim hoc loco nullum verbum de missa aut sacrificio propitiante, a sacerdotibus offerendo, fecerat, sed de oblatione fidelium omnium (ubicunque terrarum fuerint) meminit, qui Deo puris cordibus atque animis sacrificia laudis et gratiarum actionis offerunt; vocationem gentium prædicens, et Dei misericordiam in omnes dilatandam monstrans, et illum declarans futurum Deum non Judæorum modo, sed omnium nationum ab ortu ad occasum usque, qui sincera fide illum invocant, et nomen ejus gloria afficiunt.

_{Mal. i.}

CAPUT XIII.

RESPONDETUR PATRUM QUORUNDAM AUCTORITATIBUS.

ADVERSARII Christi magnum numerum locorum ex antiquis scriptoribus congerunt, qui (ut ipsi ferunt) missam vel sacram cœnam sacrificium vocant. Sed illis omnibus una responsio satis esse potest, quod non ita sacrificium vocent, ut peccata tollat, quæ sola morte Christi delentur; sed quia institutum a Christo fuerat, ut nos in memoriam sacrificii ab illo in cruce facti revocet. Atque hac de causa sacrificii nomine notatur, quemadmodum Augustinus in epistola ad Bonifacium (a me superius citata) et in libro de Fide ad Petrum diaconum (antea quoque a me inducto) indicat. In libro autem de Civitate Dei hæc verba habet: "Sacrificium visibile invisibilis sacrificii sacramentum, id est, sacrum signum est."

August. ad Bonifacium. Et de Fide ad Petrum Diac. De Civitate Dei, Lib. xx. cap. 5.

Idem in Psal. xxi. in præfatione expositionis secundæ: "Passio Domini (sicut scimus) semel facta est; semel enim Christus mortuus est, justus pro injustis. Et scimus, et certum habemus, et fide immobili retinemus, quia 'Christus resurgens a mortuis jam non moritur, et mors ei ultra non dominabitur.' Verba ista apostoli sunt: tamen ne obliviscamur quod factum est semel, in memoria nostra semel omni anno sit. Quoties pascha celebratur, numquid toties Christus moritur? Sed tum anniversaria recordatio quasi repræsentat quod olim factum est, et sic nos facit moneri, tanquam videamus in cruce pendentem Dominum."

In Psal. xxi. Præfa. Expo. ii.

Lombardus autem (e cujus scriptis, tanquam ex equo Trojano, omnis scholasticorum turba profluxit) vere hac in causa judicasse videtur. Dicit enim: "Illud quod offertur et consecratur a sacerdote, vocatur sacrificium et oblatio, quia memoria est et repræsentatio veri sacrificii et sanctæ immolationis factæ in ara crucis."

Lomb. Lib. iv. Distin. 12.

Et Chrysostomus, postquam Christum sacerdotem nostrum dixisset hostiam nos mundantem obtulisse, nuncque nos eandem offerre; ne quis hoc sermonis genere falleretur, sensum suum planius exponit, dicens: "Hoc autem quod facimus, in commemorationem quidem fit ejus quod factum est. 'Hoc enim facite,' inquit, 'in meam commemorationem.'" Et cum Chrysostomus fusius exposuisset, quod sacerdotes in veteri lege semper novas offerebant hostias, easque per singulos dies mutabant, quodque a Christianis hoc non fit (qui unum semper sacrificium offerunt); ne quis ex his verbis offendiculi occasionem acciperet, continuo seipsum quasi corrigit, dicens: "Magis autem recordationem sacrificii operamur;" quasi diceret, Quanquam quadam loquendi formula dicere possemus, nos Christum quotidie sacrificare, revera tamen (si proprie loqui volumus) nullum sacrificium facimus, sed monumentum quoddam et recordationem illius sacrificii celebramus, quod ille solus, et præter illum nemo, fecerat. Neque vero hunc honorem Christus ulli creaturæ attribuit, ut quisquam illum sacrificaret; neque sanctissimæ cœnæ sacramentum instituit, ut vel populus iterum Christum sacrificaret, vel sacerdotes illum pro populo offerrent: sed sanctissima ejus cœna ad hoc instituta est, ut quisque eam percipiens mortis Christi memoriam repeteret, et

Chrysost. ad Heb. Hom. xvii.

fiduciam sui in illum excitaret, et beneficiorum Christi recordatione se ipse solaretur, atque adeo magnis et frequentibus Deo gratiis agendis seipsum totum illi addiceret.

Itaque hæc Christi institutio persequenda nobis est, ut sacramentum sacerdos populo administret, et illi ad consolationem suam eo utantur. Hæc cœnæ celebratio et perceptio minime a nobis vel efficitur vel putatur esse hostia pro peccatorum remissione propitians.

CAPUT XIV.

POPULUS ÆQUE AC SACERDOS SACRIFICAT.

Humilis et seria pœnitentis et fracti cordis confessio, beneficiorum Christi agnitio, perpetua illi et debita gratiarum actio, fiducia et solatium in Christo susceptum, demissa atque abjecta sui ipsius prostratio, et obedientia ad illius voluntatem et præcepta servanda, a quocunque tandem christiano et pio proficiscatur, sacrificium laudis et prædicationis est, non minus Deo gratum quam sacrificium sacerdotis. Omnipotens enim et justus Deus, sine iniqua personarum approbatione, sacerdotis et populi, regis et subjecti, heri et servi, viri et fœminæ, minoris et majoris natu, Angli, Galli, Scoti, Græci et Latini, Judæi aut alterius gentis barbaræ, sacrificia atque hostias ex æquo respicit, idque pro fiducia et obedientia animi, quam quisque in illum habet, per Jesu Christi Servatoris nostri propitians sacrificium.

CAPUT XV.

PAPISTICA MISSA NEQUE SACRIFICIUM PROPITIANS EST NEQUE GRATIARUM ACTIONIS.

Missa, sicuti a sacerdote celebrari solet, neque sacrificium propitians est, neque laudis aut gratiarum actionis, neque Deo accepta aut probata; sed horribilis et detestabilis res, de qua Servatoris illud verissime dici poterit, "Quod celsum est coram hominibus, id abominandum est coram Deo."

Luc. xvi.

Qui igitur hoc ex antiquis scriptoribus colligunt, missam sacrificium pro peccatis esse, et a sacerdote quibus ipse velit accommodari et applicari posse, intolerabilem injuriam sanctis patribus afferunt, et falso ac maligne illos calumniantur.

CAPUT XVI.

PAPISTICÆ MISSÆ IN PRIMITIVA ECCLESIA NULLÆ FUERUNT.

Portentosa hæc monstra in prima et veteri ecclesia nulla fuerant, nec in una ecclesia multæ tum quotidie missæ fuerant; sed certis quibusdam diebus mensa Domini proposita est, quam frequentans populus sacram synaxin percipiebat. Nullæ tamen privatæ missæ et quotidianæ fuerant, ubi sacramentum sacerdos solus percipiebat; quemadmodum etiam ad hodiernum usque diem in Græcorum ecclesiis observatur, ut una tantum uno die missa celebretur.

Sancti patres autem tam impios et diros abusus cœnæ dominicæ suis temporibus non tolerassent.

Privatarum missarum origo nuper in ecclesia germinavit, partim rudium atque imperitorum monachorum et fraterculorum ignorantia ac superstitione, (qui cum ignorarent quid sacrificium esset, missam, ut sacrificium propitians esset, et peccata ac pœnas peccatis debitas relaxaret, effinxerunt,) præcipue autem quæstu, quem sacerdotes vendendis missis invenerant; ex quo tanta vis missarum in ecclesiam invecta est, ut quotidie infinitæ pene dicerentur, et nullus sacerdos de alterius sacerdotis manu sacramentum perciperet, neglecto interim saluberrimo et sanctissimo concilio Niceno (ubi statuebatur, quo loco sacerdotes, et quo diaconi in synaxi collocarentur), et apostolorum etiam canonibus, ubi præcipitur, ut in synaxi celebranda sacerdotes omnes ad eam percipiendam conveniant, vel anathema sint. Adeo a veteribus improbatum est, ut sacramentum quis solus percipiat.

Nicenum Concilium, cap. 14. Canon Apostolorum, cap. 8.

Cum igitur sancti patres cœnam Domini sacrificium appellabant, sacrificium laudis et gratiarum actionis esse intelligebant; qua ratione non minus populus quam sacerdos sacrificium faciebat: vel etiam monumentum quoddam veri et propitiantis sacrificii Christi esse voluerunt; sed longissime ab eo aberant, ut id pro peccatis sacrificium facerent, et yiventibus ac mortuis, sacerdotis arbitrio, applicabile putarent.

Sacerdos verba Christi et sacramenta omnibus administrare tum bonis tum malis poterit; sed beneficium Christi ulli applicare provectæ ætatis et sapientiæ non poterit, sed pii omnes sibi ipsis sua ipsorum fide hoc applicant. Quivis enim rationis judicio præditus, aut vera et vitali fide, (quæ per caritatem efficiens est,) Christi beneficium assequitur, aut impietate et simulata fide illud abjicit.

Atque hæc scripturarum doctrina impia papistarum inventa, extremis hisce temporibus ab illis excogitata, prorsus damnat, qui purgatorium ad animas post mortem excarnificandas comminiscebantur, et missarum oblationes per sacerdotes habitas ad omnes hos cruciatus minuendos et tollendos affinxerunt, aliaque hujus generis lethalia venena rudi et imperitæ multitudini pro veris et salutaribus medicinis vendiderunt.

CAPUT XVII.

CAUSÆ ET RATIONES QUIBUS PAPISTICÆ MISSÆ IN ECCLESIAM DEI SE INSINUARUNT.

Cum natura humana semper ad idololatriam inclinata fuerit, et papistæ omnibus opibus et viribus elaborarunt, ut non modo ad suam utilitatem missam defenderent, verum etiam omni laudatione eveherent; et populus superstitioso quodam animi ardore in missam, quasi in omnium malorum præsens remedium, ferretur; et magna pars principum (papisticæ doctrinæ auctoritate occæcata, quietis amans, scripturæ non intelligens, et papisticorum sacerdotum populique superstitiosi offensionem declinans) antichristo Romano subjecta fuerit; minime admirandum est, rerum statu hoc loco posito, si magni abusus in ecclesia non modo adoleverint, verum etiam ad immensitatem quandam excreverint, inani superstitione et idololatria pro sanctitate et pietate habita, et multis odiosis in ecclesiam sine auctoritate Christi inductis.

Nam purgatorium, oblationem et sacrificium Christi per sacerdotem solum factum, definitam ejusdem pro arbitrio sacerdotis applicationem, non modo ad quoscunque vel superstites vel vita defunctos, verum etiam ad abusus permultos, ad quosdam e purgatorio liberandos, quosdam ex inferno eripiendos (nisi certa et constituta Dei sententia supplicio perpetuo addicti essent), ad cœlum vel serenum vel pluvium efficiendum, ad pestes et alias ægrotationes ab hominibus et feris depellendas, ad sanctitate et salute afficiendos illos, qui Hierosolymam, qui Romam, qui Compostellam et cetera loca superstitionis causa adeunt, ad tempestates et tonitrua propulsanda, ad pericula et discrimina maris imminentia, ad pecudum contagia, ad animi angores, ad omnia afflictionum et perturbationum genera minuenda, invexerunt. Missarum papisticarum abusus.

Missam denique ipsam longe supra mortem Christi extollunt, multa nobis per illam pollicentes, quæ morte Christi nobis non promittebantur. Hujus generis hæc exempla sunt: quo quis die missam audit, victus et pastus satis eo die suppeditabitur, nullis necessariis rebus egebit, nullam itineris moram aut impedimentum accipiet, oculorum aciem non amittet, repentina morte non occumbet, nullo senio missæ tempore conficietur, nulli mali spiritus illi infesti esse possunt, quantumvis sceleratus fuerit, quamdiu in sacramentum oculos defixos habuerit. Has deliras atque impias superstitiones papistæ callidissimo artificio recens excogitarunt, quæ primæ ac florenti ecclesiæ nunquam cognitæ fuerant.

CAPUT XVIII.

QUÆ SIT NOBIS ECCLESIA SEQUENDA.

Adversus evangelii professores pleno ore exclamant et vociferantur, illos ab ecclesia dissentire; cupientes omni studio, ut ecclesiæ suæ exemplum sequantur. Quod illi lubenter (scio) facerent, si papistæ primam et apostolicam ecclesiam sequerentur, quæ purissima atque incorruptissima omnium fuit. Sed papistæ ab usu et exemplo primæ ecclesiæ longissime desciverunt, et nova commenta architectati sunt: et cum ipsi primam ecclesiam ducem sequi nolint, alios tamen vellent suam ecclesiam sequi, inventa sua constitutionibus apostolorum longe præferentes.

Nunc autem Deo Patri gratiæ nobis etiam atque etiam agendæ sunt, quod ea sacræ cœnæ ratio, quæ hoc in regno Christianis omnibus proposita est, cum institutione Christi, cum Pauli, et primæ ac apostolicæ ecclesiæ auctoritate, cum recta fiducia de sacrificio Christi, in cruce pro redemptione nostra facto, cum vera doctrina salutis, justificationis, et remissionis omnium peccatorum nostrorum, per unicum illud sacrificium exhibitæ, consentiat.

OPERIS CONCLUSIO.

Quid restat aliud, nisi ut omnes hæc æquis animis accipiant, ea omni studio complectantur, mœstis animis pristinam ignorantiam defleant, scelerum ac malefactorum suorum pœnitentia ducantur, ad meliorem vitæ modum se convertant, sese totos Deo tradant, omne vitæ tempus in obedientia et custodia mandatorum ejus transmittant, et sanctissimam cœnam, quam Dominus et Servator Christus apparavit, frequentent? Qua in cœna, quemadmodum corpore verum panem et vinum percipimus, ita spiritu vero corpore et sanguine Servatoris et Redemptoris nostri Jesu Christi alimur, memoria mortis ejus colenda, gratiis de beneficentia tam illustri agendis, nullo pro peccatis sacrificio a sacerdotibus requirendo, fiducia in solo Christi sacrificio collocanda. Christus enim non modo summus Pontifex, verum etiam Agnus Dei ad peccata mundi tollenda, ante mundum conditum præparatus, seipsum semel obtulit, ut perpetuum esset apud Patrem sacrificium ad odorem suavitatis, atque mundi universi redemptionem per illud exsolveret. Hic ante nos cœlos penetravit, ad dexteram Patris patronus, defensor, et intercessor pro nobis sedet: ibi loca et sedes pro omnibus vitalibus corporis sui membris præparavit, ut in gloria Patris cœlestis ad omnem ævi æternitatem regnent. Cui cum Patre et Spiritu sancto sit omnis honos, gloria, laudatio, ad omnem seculorum infinitatem.
Amen.

CATALOGUS SCRIPTORUM

QUI IN HOC LIBRO CITANTUR.

Ambrosius 31, 34, 41, 42, 49, 59, 72, 73, 81
Athanasius 80
Augustinus 15, 29, 31, 32, 33, 38, 48, 49,
     50, 54, 57, 59, 60, 75, 78,
     79, 81, 82, 83, 85, 87, 95

Basilius 50, 80
Beda 50, 83
Bernardus 21
Bonaventura 58

Canones Apostolorum 96
Cassiodorus 75
Chrysostomus 31, 33, 38, 40, 41,
     56, 59, 73, 95
Clemens [Alexandrinus] 29, 53, 67, 80
Concilium Nicenum 96
Cyprianus 30, 37, 54, 58, 68, 79, 80
Cyrillus [Alexandrinus] ... 49, 50, 54, 71, 72, 83

Damascenus 75
Didymus 50
Dionysius [Areopagita] 21, 29, 67, 73

Epiphanius 31, 54
Eusebius Emissenus 30, 72, 86

Fulgentius 51, 75

Gabriel [Biel] 34
Gelasius 33
Gratianus 24

Gregorius 32, 50
Gregorius Nazianzenus 72
Gregorius Nyssenus 72

Hesychius 32
Hieronymus 54, 59, 75, 80
Hilarius .... 29, 31, 53, 68—71
Honorius 88
Hugo 21

Ignatius 29, 67
Innocentius Tertius 24, 88
Irenæus 30, 54

Justinus 29, 30, 53, 57

Leo 34, 48, 75
Lombardus 95

Origenes 30, 47, 56, 68, 80

Rabanus 21, 32, 54

Scotus 34, 35
Sedulius 75

Tertullianus 54, 58, 67, 68
Theodoretus .... 34, 54, 61—63
[Theophilus Alexandrinus .... 74]
Theophylactus 74, 75

Vigilius 51

www.ingramcontent.com/pod-product-compliance
Lightning Source LLC
Chambersburg PA
CBHW080719300426
44114CB00019B/2426